Special Edition Using HTML 4

Planning Web Sites

Perhaps the most overlooked aspect of Web development is the planning process. This might be because most people need or want their Web sites yesterday, so a mad dash to get the site up ensues. The optimistic world of Web development is akin to a fast-moving train: It arrives on time but can leave a sloppy mess in its path!

Web developers need to slow down, take a deep breath, and apply planning and production techniques to their site development goals. At the end of the day, they are sure to be more gratified knowing that they've done the job well—and they don't have to go back and redo something because it was a rush job.

There is simply no reason that developers cannot draw from existing methodologies to create a framework upon which to build their sites. Two areas of strength already exist: media production techniques and software application development guidelines. By combining these methodologies, developers can significantly strengthen their work (Figure 1).

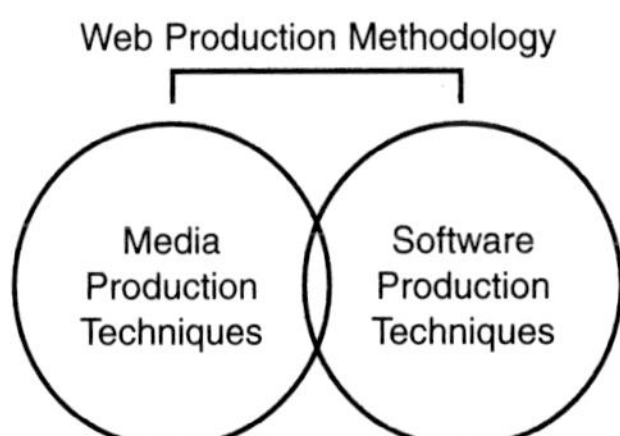

Figure 1
A combination of media production and software development methods is a natural for Web site design.

Three Essentials for Site Success

The following highlights will help you incorporate methods into a sensible system you can use to effectively produce Web sites in a rapid and effective fashion:

- **Define site intent and goals.** Ensure that your site's reason for being is absolutely clear to site visitors, and plan for growth and change.
- **Understand audience needs.** Be certain that you're designing for your audience. This means deciding who they are *before* designing a site.
- **Have a specific site development process.** Knowing the steps you're going to take to get from planning to publishing will help keep you on track, on time, and reduce stress—which no one needs!

Defining Site Intent and Goals

Have you ever loaded a Web page and spent the next minute or so trying to figure out what its purpose was? I have, and for me, a site that doesn't immediately tell me something about what it is, what it does, and why it's there is a site where I don't stay! The only exception to this rule is with artistic or highly visual site designs—and even then, the images must be so compelling as to draw me in deeper.

The Web is a fast medium. It's been said that people wait somewhere between 9 and 11 seconds to determine whether the site is somewhere they want to be. If you don't capture their attention or assure them that the site is in fact for them, they're going to head on down the virtual road.

The first step in creating a Web site is clearly defining its intent and goals. This means determining why the site exists and ensuring that you justify the site to visitors.

Let's say you have a small business site where you are selling handmade wedding dresses. The site's intent is to sell wedding dresses, and the goal is to encourage site visitors to buy the dresses—you'll want to say this clearly (Figure 2). Or, perhaps you're creating a home page where you want to simply express yourself. The site's intent must be made clear. Putting icons, links to other pages, and images on your site without a clear definition doesn't achieve anything (Figure 3). An honest effort to create a personal home page fails when there is no clear purpose in evidence. Identify yourself, your goals, and your intent! This helps site visitors stick around.

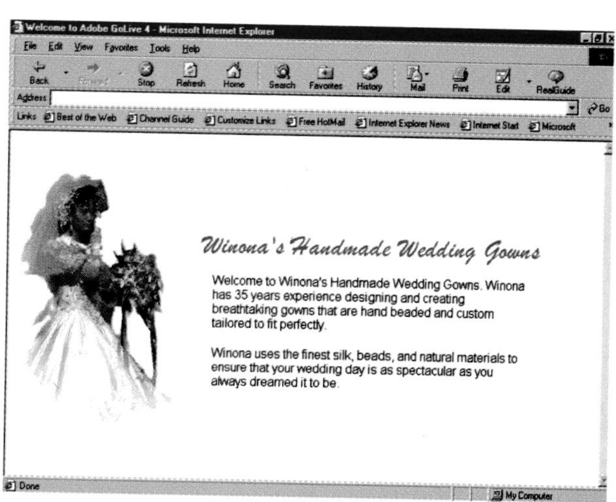

Figure 2

Using an image and introductory paragraph that conveys the goal of the site helps to clearly define the site's purpose to visitors.

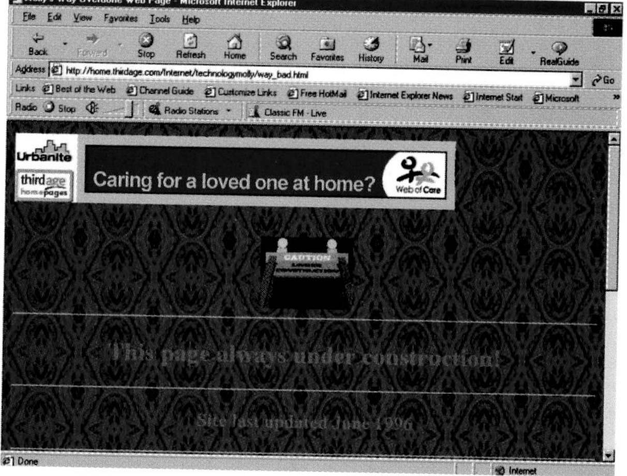

Figure 3

A site like this might fail to attract visitors because they have no idea as to the site's reason for being.

Knowing Your Audience

Audience is the reason most Web sites are designed. Whether you're attracting visitors to a business or personal page, or you're working on a corporate intranet site, the bottom line is that the site should somehow serve the people who access it.

- **Create focus groups.** If you have a product but no precise audience, it is in your best interest to organize a group that can provide you with feedback about your product Figure 4. The people to whom the product most appeals will likely fit certain demographic features: economic status, gender, cultural background, and age. Use this information to shape your site's development.

Figure 4
Focus groups can help you determine how to shape your site.

- **Gather statistics.** If you already have a Web site and have kept a statistical log of who is visiting the site, use this information to help position or reposition your project.
- **Get feedback!** There's no one more knowledgeable or able to give you information regarding your content than the people who use it. Check with friends and family to see what they would enjoy seeing on your site. Professional developers can offer surveys and feedback forms to site visitors, helping to keep the site's design on track.

Because Web sites are constantly evolving and changing, it's important to stay current with your audience. You might find yourself having to adjust the site or move certain products or information to the forefront to make them happy—and achieve your goals!

Designing for the Audience

After you have a good idea of who your audience is and what they want, designing a new site or redesigning an existing site should reflect their needs. All too often, developers fall into the trap of designing for themselves or their bosses. Follow these design tips for specific audience types:

- **Young products with a young audience benefit from energetic designs.** Use bright colors, active typefaces, upbeat language, and multimedia to bring a fresh look that will appeal to this audience (Figure 5).
- **Conservative corporations and products should be presented with subtle design.** Typically, deep blues, black, and white will appeal to more traditional thinkers. Avoiding wild background designs, neon colors, and highly decorative typefaces will aid you in creating a calm, dignified site (Figure 6).
- **If you're designing a site for high-ticket items such as luxury cars and clothing, elegance is the name of the game.** Black, silver, gold, or copper tones can set an elegant mood (Figure 7).

Figure 5
Younger, active audiences enjoy bright colors and dynamic shapes.

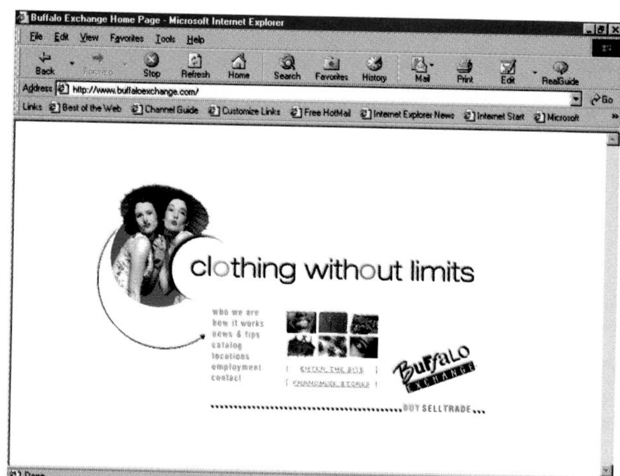

Figure 6
Corporate identity is best when appealing to the more subtle and traditional audience.

Figure 7
Luxury is personified with silver and black.

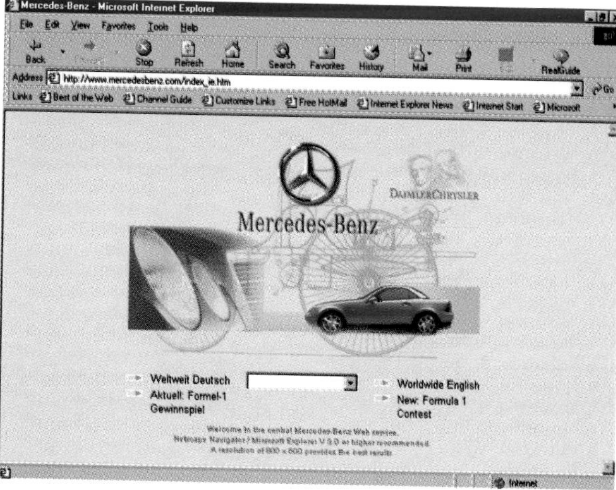

Defining a Development Process

With clear intent, goals, and strong knowledge of the audience, your work is already more clearly defined. However, you'll want to have a production process in place to apply the foundational principles of intent and audience to an actual task-oriented methodology. A step-by-step Web Production Methodology can be designed from the methods set forth by media production and software application development techniques.

Pre-Production

This first crucial step involves some of what you've already done: defining your goals and audience. But before you can sit down to do the work, you'll need to focus on several other concerns that will help firm up the foundation of your design.

- **Gather and generate content.** Sitting down with clients and determining what information will be on the site is fundamental to the way the site will be constructed. Depending on the type and scope of the site, this organizational step might be as simple as gathering the content for a few pages and as complex as managing content for thousands of pages.
- **Construct the site map.** Mapping the site, also known as *storyboarding*, defines all of the content within a specific structure. This structure will be used to determine not only the location of various site components and information, but also how the navigation will work.
- **Develop and approve a look and feel.** Using your knowledge of site intent, audience, and content, you'll apply design techniques to come up with an appropriate visual design and navigation scheme. Sometimes this will take several tries or minor adjustments before the client is satisfied (Figures 8 and 9).
- **Determine technological needs.** Will your site require search capabilities, shopping carts, complex databases? Perhaps you're developing on a closed intranet and have security concerns. Now is the time to map out your technology needs and determine what is needed and what solutions you'll choose to meet those needs.

The first mockup wasn't approved by the site's client, who felt they wanted stronger colors.

Figure 8

Figure 9

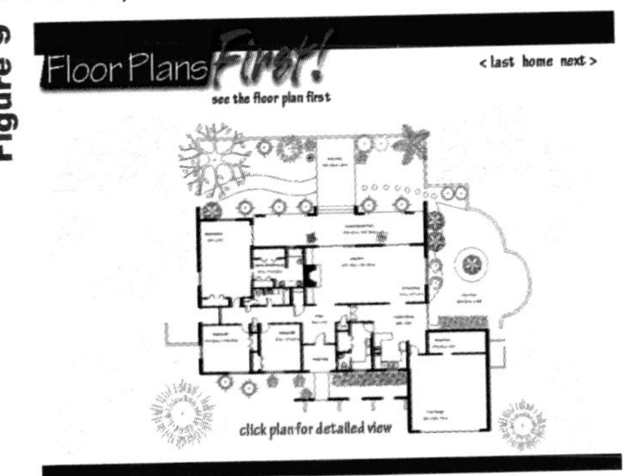

The second mockup with bolder blue was a success.

Production

Production is the heart of Web development. In professional, team-based development, a Web Project Manager is often in the lead role, acting as a liaison between different specialists. Even if you're wearing the only hat in the shop, following these production techniques will help you get your project done quickly and effectively.

- **Schedule milestone goals.** When managing a site, it's good to break up the project into digestible portions and set milestone goals for each.
- **Coordinate efforts between teams.** Take the time to ensure that everyone's concerns and work are appropriately addressed and acknowledged...you won't be sorry!
- **Perform quality testing whenever possible.** During the early stages of your site, take advantage of feedback from your focus groups, friends or anyone you trust to evaluate your site. It will help you to identify any problem areas.
- **Reposition where appropriate.** Whenever you see the need to revise something from the original plan, do it now rather than later if it is critical to the operations of the site.

Certainly, there are many other details that go into managing the production phase including preparing the site for publication with META tags, testing pages for cross-browser/cross-platform compatibility, checking links, and copyediting the site. But it's amazing how just knowing some simple techniques such as those shared here can dramatically improve your work methods.

Publication

Publication is the act of transferring the finished site to the live server and testing it completely. Here are some steps to take in the Publication portion of the design process:

- **Test all pages for cross platform compatibility.** Yes, you did this when the site was offline or on a staging server, but now you're live—do it again! This critical step ensures that your site will be usable for all the platforms coming to visit. The only instance in which this step might not be necessary is if you're developing for a closed intranet.
- **Use a variety of browsers to see if the pages are readable.** For public Web sites, test with a variety of browsers. Ideally, you've performed this step pre-publication, but you want to do it yet again now that the site is live.
- **Is your code neat? Are all your META tags in place?** Look at your code. Does it look neat and professional? Are all the META tags properly coded and in place? If not, now is a good time to repair any problems.
- **Check all links to be sure they are working properly.** While you've checked links offline, you might find link problems now that you're live on the server.
- **Look for spelling problems and poor grammar.** It's easy to miss copyediting problems no matter what the site's status. But after you're set up for the entire world to see, it becomes crucial that your site is clean and free of these troublesome problems.
- **Have people outside of your organization try to break the site.** Can they find problems related to navigation, linking, browser, or platform compatibility? Have them test forms. You might be too close to the information, so it's always good to get a fresh set of eyes.

Post-Production

After the site is live, there are a number of concerns that you will want to address.

- **Maintenance and updates.** The upkeep of a site is important. Links get out of date, content needs to be modified, and new content should be made available at regular intervals. Plan and schedule site maintenance tasks now.
- **Promotions.** The site will need to be registered with search engines and indexed. If it's a business site, you also might want to consider online advertising such as banner ads, and ample offline marketing including radio, TV, and newspapers, as well as less obvious or traditional methods.
- **Redesigns and mergers.** There are natural points in a site's (and company's) evolution that will cause a redesign or site merger to occur. While redesigns and other major changes are difficult to prepare for, you can be sure that if you manage the site effectively, there will be fewer traumas as major changes are undertaken.

Six Tips for Effective Site Management

The following six tips will help you manage the production of your Web site more effectively.

1. **Prepare a site style guide.** Keep your code, language, and style elements on track by pre-determining a style guide for each project you work on. The guide should include code conventions, page weight maximums, color palettes, and editorial guidelines for content.
2. **Keep all original sketches and mockups.** Always keep your original design materials. This way, if you need to reference something, change a color or design direction, or redesign a site, you can quickly access all the original elements and reuse them wherever possible.
3. **Use version control.** Keep tabs on which version of a graphic, coded page, or other Web element is in use. You can do this in your filename, or use a comment within the document. Some development tools, such as Visual Source Safe, track and control versions of code. This way, you (or someone helping you) can always be sure to choose the correct file when sitting down to work.
4. **Use comment tags.** Comment tag your pages with information including version, author, and date. Also, use comment tags to clearly denote sections of code and content. This allows anyone else stepping in to work with the code to quickly grasp what you're doing.
5. **Archive every version of a site.** Backup those files! There's nothing so heartbreaking as losing hard work. Create an archival system and make use of it.
6. **Document the process.** Tape or take minutes at meetings, make notes as you go. Keep a paper trail of all emails, relevant changes, contracts, and printed materials related to the site.

WHAT'S NEW IN THIS EDITION

Special Edition Using HTML 4, Sixth Edition takes all the strengths of the previous edition and places them into a more contemporary perspective. The original goal of the book: To provide solid learning about HTML 4 within the context of real-world use, remains its greatest strength.

The Sixth Edition has been revised in terms of structure and updated content. Unlike prior editions, the book can be used in a linear fashion, allowing readers to progress sequentially through chapters and build upon prior learning. However, the book can still be used as a non-linear reference. Care has been taken to include cross-references in every chapter, pointing you to other chapters and appendices where you'll find additional information regarding the techniques at hand.

The challenge is to help you create professional, sophisticated Web sites using contemporary technologies and tools with ease. To do this most effectively, I've added and improved various aspects of the previous edition, including

- **Updated software and operating system version coverage**—Browsers and software applications for the Web are evolving! New versions of operating systems have come to the forefront. I've used the latest available platforms and browsers during the writing of this book to give you the most current information possible. I've also included updated information on all software products discussed in the book, and used the most recent versions of software available at the time of writing.
- **Improvement of Forms, JavaScript, and DHTML Information**—*Special Edition Using HTML 4.0, Sixth Edition* contains improved information on Forms, a wider and more stable selection of JavaScript, and an updated DHTML chapter that can help you gain perspective on the state of DHTML in current browsers.
- **Addition of Accessibility Concerns in HTML 4.0**—One important aspect of HTML 4.0 is its concern with accessibility. The unfortunate reality is that browsers are still lagging far behind where they should be in terms of compliance in this regard. I've provided a detailed chapter in which you learn to use those accessibility elements that are currently supported, as well as learn how to use them even where they are not supported. This ideally prepares professional HTML coders for eventual compatibility in a wide range of browsers and also for compliance in the United States with various laws and judgement decisions regarding access to Web sites.
- **Internationalization**—Web sites are truly becoming worldwide. Learn how to make your pages more flexible in the context of multi-lingual circumstances.

- **Emerging Technologies Coverage**—The influence of the Extensible Markup Language (XML) on the current state of HTML technologies is impressive. New languages, including the Synchronized Multimedia Integration Language (SMIL) and Extensible HTML (XHTML), are discussed, with ample information to prepare HTML professionals to deal with the many changes they'll face within the next year.
- **Addition of Case Studies and Project Pages**—Each chapter contains either a case study or project. In case studies, you will visit a real-world work situation, Web site, or individual. Case studies provide perspective directly related to the subject matter at hand. Project Pages are used to step you through more intensive or specialized techniques, giving you valuable hands-on experience with plenty of associated tips and guidelines.

Naturally, I've kept the real-world, day-to-day content intact, refining it in areas and reorganizing it where appropriate. The book provides a strong understanding of the available tools, methods, and HTML topics necessary for any professional developer or active hobbyist. Within *Special Edition Using HTML 4, Sixth Edition* you'll find the following:

- A comprehensive approach to HTML applications for personal and professional HTML development and design
- An emphasis on hand-coding techniques
- Methods to go beyond ho-hum HTML: layout, design, use of browser space, and management of data
- Information on the production and publication of individual HTML documents and complete Web sites

Of course, you'll need plenty of visual design information as well as the technical edge. Learn about

- The conceptual as well as technical applications of Web color
- How the computer screen significantly impacts your design
- The growing wealth of professional-quality Web graphic and production tools
- How to create sensible yet sophisticated Web graphics
- How graphic designers approach typography on the Web

You'll also enjoy a look into the life of Web site planning, production, and design via the new tear booklet and within the chapters themselves. A comprehensive look at the concepts and techniques used in creating such Web sites as home pages, small business and e-commerce sites, corporate intranets and extranets, and online communities provides perspective on the state of the industry and community that is today's Web.

Special Edition Using HTML 4

Sixth Edition

Molly E. Holzschlag

A Division of Macmillan USA
201 W. 103rd Street
Indianapolis, Indiana 46290

Contents at a Glance

Special Edition Using HTML 4, Sixth Edition

International Standard Book Number: 0-7897-2267-4

Library of Congress Catalog Card Number: 99-66452

Printed in the United States of America

First Printing: December 1999

00 4

Trademarks

All terms mentioned in this book that are known to be trademarks or service marks have been appropriately capitalized. Que cannot attest to the accuracy of this information. Use of a term in this book should not be regarded as affecting the validity of any trademark or service mark.

Warning and Disclaimer

Every effort has been made to make this book as complete and as accurate as possible, but no warranty or fitness is implied. The information provided is on an "as is" basis. The authors and the publisher shall have neither liability or responsibility to any person or entity with respect to any loss or damages arising from the information contained in this book or from the use of the CD or programs accompanying it.

Executive Editor
John Pierce

Acquisitions Editor
John Pierce

Development Editor
Laura Norman

Managing Editor
Thomas F. Hayes

Project Editor
Leah Kirkpatrick

Copy Editors
Julie McNamee
Sossity Smith
Kay Hoskin

Indexer
Chris Barrick

Proofreader
Tricia Sterling

Technical Editor
Bob Correll

Software Development Specialist
Jay Payne

Interior Designer
Ruth Harvey

Cover Designer
Dan Armstrong

Layout Technician
Darin Crone

Contents

V Web Graphic Design 503

About the Author

A writer, instructor, and designer, **Molly E. Holzschlag** brings her irrepressible enthusiasm to books, magazines, classrooms, and Web sites. Honored as one of the Top 25 Most Influential Women on the Web, Molly has spent an almost unprecedented decade working in the online world. She has written and contributed to more than 10 books about Internet and Web technologies, and writes regular articles for Builder.Com and developerWorks.

Molly's column, *Integrated Design*, appears regularly in Web Techniques Magazine. Molly enjoys public events and speaks regularly at such conferences as Web Design and Development. She currently offers public and on-site training in HTML, Web Design, Internet Technologies, and Media Studies. Visit her Web site at—where else? `http://www.molly.com/`.

Dedication

To the loving memory of Jack Schwanke, whose life was art and whose art gave life. Thanks Jack, for teaching me how to see.

Acknowledgments

My most sincere thanks to the team at Macmillan Computer Publishing. I'd specifically like to thank John Pierce for his kindness and support, Laura Norman for being the most awesome developmental editor I've ever had, and Bob Correll, whose technical edits and contributed wisdom are simply the best. Bob Correll also wrote the fantastic HTML 4.0 reference found in Appendix A of this book.

From Waterside Productions: I have no finer ally in my professional life than my agent, David Fugate. A special thanks to Maureen Maloney for managing contracts and details with finesse.

For keeping my professional focus on course, and for being a good friend and true mentor, author Harley Hahn. A special thought to Lynda Weinman, for her loving energy and deep knowledge. As always, I thank my dear friend Matt Straznitskas, who continues to astonish me with his accomplishments and talent. Wil Gerken is a great technologist to whom I owe much of my technical education.

For their contributions, support, and friendship: Eric Agardy, Julie Ciamporcero, Jane Caton, Vito Ciavarelli, Bob Correll, David and Rhonda Crowder, Chris Hawkins, Julie and David Katsel, Greg and Jennifer Kettell, Robert McDaniel, Jody McFadden, Eleanor Mitchell, Kelly Murdock, and Steven Romaniello.

Patty Sundberg, you are my harmony. Ro Logrippo, for your vivaciousness and loving heart. Michelle Armitage, sister in soul. To my wonderful family: Dr. Phillipa Kafka, Ole Kenen, Morris Kafka-Holzschlag, and Linus Holzschlag-Kafka.

I thank Candice Courcy, Jeff Rogers, Patricia Hursh, Ph.D., and Andrea Morken for keeping me in body and spirit.

To all the readers of my books: thank you for your letters, gifts, and ongoing encouragement and support. You make any of the harder days worthwhile.

Tell Us What You Think!

As the reader of this book, *you* are our most important critic and commentator. We value your opinion and want to know what we're doing right, what we could do better, what areas you'd like to see us publish in, and any other words of wisdom you're willing to pass our way.

As Publisher for Que, I welcome your comments. You can fax, email, or write me directly to let me know what you did or didn't like about this book—as well as what we can do to make our books stronger.

Please note that I cannot help you with technical problems related to the topic of this book, and that due to the high volume of mail I receive, I might not be able to reply to every message.

When you write, please be sure to include this book's title and author as well as your name and phone or fax number. I will carefully review your comments and share them with the author and editors who worked on the book.

Fax: 317.581.4666

Email: `que.programming@macmillanusa.com`

Mail: Publisher
Macmillan USA
201 West 103rd Street
Indianapolis, IN 46290 USA

INTRODUCTION

In this chapter

Who Should Buy This Book

Each chapter in this book is written to standalone but work in tandem with other chapters in the book. The best way to read the book will be determined by you! You can start at the beginning and work your way through; this is an especially good way for intermediate readers to build and refine skills.

If you want to know about a specific topic, you can jump right to that topic by using the Table of Contents as your guide or checking the Index for topic references. Let's say you are interested in Dynamic HTML. You can go right to Chapter 21, "Working with Dynamic HTML (DHTML)," and get the information you need. Within that chapter, and all chapters in this book, I've taken every opportunity to include cross-references with related materials, so you can follow your needs and preferences to the next topic of interest.

The bookshelves are toppling over with HTML and Web-design books. New software products are shipped every day, proclaiming to be the best way to get a Web site up and running. Colleges are scrambling to add Web development courses to their Computer Science and Graphic Design curricula.

The demand for technical skills and knowledge surrounding the Internet, and especially the Web, has never been greater. Even the pros have to keep their skills well-honed and their eyes on tomorrow's technological prize to stay neck and neck with the pack—much less get ahead.

Whether you, as a reader, are after clear-cut, up-to-date information on HTML and related technologies for professional advancement or you are an enthusiast interested in taking your skills to the next level, this book provides you with both a close-up and a broad-spectrum view of the Web development industry as it is today. Using HTML 4.0 as the foundation, you will quickly find what you need and, more importantly, how to get started using it, right away.

How This Book Is Organized

Special Edition Using HTML 4.0, Sixth Edition, has been reorganized from the Fifth Edition to better serve your needs. The new edition includes 10 parts with a total of 44 chapters, four helpful appendixes, an index, and a CD-ROM with code samples and software.

Part 1: What You Need to Know

The chapters in this section give you a good look at the foundations of HTML 4.0. Intermediate and advanced readers will review HTML's history as well as present concerns facing the HTML programmer in today's fast-paced Web environment. A comprehensive look at available tools helps you make good decisions as to where to put your effort and money in terms of development software. The part finishes up with information on how to manage HTML documents—helping you to avoid common pitfalls and learn to power code HTML 4.0 with speed and accuracy.

Part 2: HTML Basics

While many readers already know the basics, I've included them here both for your review and for the purposes of helping coders refine their practices and position the basics in the context of the HTML 4.0 standard. I cover the syntax of HTML and discuss how to properly structure HTML documents, format text, add lists, link pages, work with images, manage `BODY` attributes and use `FONT` tags in transitional HTML 4.0.

Part 3: HTML Layout and Design Fundamentals

In this section, chapters focus on HTML as it relates to layout and design. You'll work with Cascading Style Sheets (CSS), style sheet typography, table layouts, frames, and build feedback forms.

Part 4: HTML Technologies

With strong foundations in HTML, it's time to have some fun and use advanced HTML 4.0 and related techniques. In this section, you'll work with JavaScript to add function and beauty to your sites. Element positioning and style sheet scripting are both covered in this section, helping you to gain experience with these excellent if not-quite-ready-for-prime-time methods. You'll work with Dynamic HTML and also become familiar with HTML 4.0's approach to making Web sites accessible to people with special needs and international language concerns. The section wraps up with a look at the future of HTML and related languages including XHTML, XML, and emerging technologies.

Part 5: Web Graphic Design

This part looks at a variety of Web graphic issues, from the simple to the complex. You'll learn about color and how to work with the constraints of the computer screen. A comprehensive look at design tools helps to debunk myths about what is professional, what is not, and how you can get the best mileage out of whatever design tools are available to you. You'll learn about standard Web graphic formats, as well as up-and-coming technology. The part finishes up with several chapters geared toward sophisticated design: creating professional graphics, working with graphic type, and designing specialty graphics such as imagemaps, animations, and advertising banners.

Part 6: Multimedia and Embedded Objects

How to get your site interactive is the focus here: audio, video, streaming media, multimedia, Java applets, virtual reality, and the creation of active content are the focus in this part.

Part 7: Server-Side and Backend Applications

If you're looking for more functionality, the chapters in this section will be very helpful. CGI scripting and preprocessing, Active Server Pages (ASP), and database information are covered.

Part 8: Putting Your Skills to Work

In this part, a look at how Web sites are made helps put planning, design, and deployment concerns into perspective. You'll examine a home page, business and e-commerce sites, learn how to design corporate intranets and extranets, and discover why the online community has become so popular.

Part 9: Publishing, Maintaining, and Promoting Web Sites

So you've got a Web site. How do you get it ready for its life on the Internet? This section looks at preparing your sites for online publishing, how to get your sites up and running on the Internet, and how to market your Web site so it's not lost in a traffic jam on one of the Web's busy information intersections.

Part 10: Appendixes

There are four appendixes in *Special Edition Using HTML 4.0, Sixth Edition*:

- Appendix A "HTML 4.0 Element and Tag Reference" An exhaustive HTML 4.0 reference, including tags, attributes, values, and related information.
- Appendix B "HTML Special Character Set" This section examines the special characters and entities within HTML 4.0.
- Appendix C "CSS Reference" A comprehensive overview of Cascading Style Sheets 1.0 and 2.0.
- Appendix D "HTML and Design Resources" A hand-picked selection of Web sites, books, organizations, and educational opportunities for Web designers.

Conventions Used in This Book

Special conventions are used to help you get the most from this book and from Office 2000.

Text Conventions

Various typefaces in this book identify terms and other special objects. These special typefaces include the following:

Type	Meaning
Italic	New terms or phrases when initially defined. An italic term followed by a page number indicates the page where that term is first defined.
Underline	Menu and dialog box options with letters that appear underlined onscreen indicate shortcut keys (hotkeys).
`Monospace`	Information that you type, Web addresses, or onscreen messages.
Initial Caps	Menus, dialog box names, dialog box elements, and commands are capitalized.

Key combinations are represented with a plus sign. For example, if the text calls for you to enter Ctrl+S, you would press the Ctrl key and the S key at the same time.

DESIGNING IN THE REAL WORLD

Each chapter of this book contains a project page or case study at the end of the chapter. Use these to enhance your skills with professional applications, examples, tips, and wisdom.

SPECIAL ELEMENTS

Throughout this book, you'll find Signature Tips, Notes, Cautions, Troubleshooting Notes, Cross References, and Sidebars. These elements provide a variety of information ranging from warnings you shouldn't miss to ancillary information that will enrich your HTML 4.0 experience.

MOLLY'S "SIGNATURE" TIPS

Tip from

Tips are designed to help you facilitate your workflow, avoid problems, and learn new ways to solve old concerns. Look for tips with my signature throughout the book.

NOTES

Note

Notes provide extra information on a topic that is related and relevant to the topic, but not specific to the given task at hand.

CAUTIONS

Caution

Watch your step! Avoid pitfalls by keeping an eye on the cautions available in many of this book's lessons.

TROUBLESHOOTING NOTES

These elements call attention to common issues. When you see a Troubleshooting Note, you can flip to the Troubleshooting section at the end of the chapter to learn how to solve or avoid a problem.

CROSS REFERENCES

Cross references are designed to point you to other locations in this book (or other books in the Que family) that will provide supplemental or supporting information. Cross references appear as follows:

→ To learn more about adding video to your page, **see** "Adding Video," **p. 671**

SIDEBARS

Want to Know More?
Sidebars are designed to provide information that is ancillary to the topic being discussed. Read these if you want to learn more about an application or task.

PART I

What You Need to Know

CHAPTER 1

UNDERSTANDING HTML 4.0

In this chapter

THE MORE THINGS CHANGE

I'm sure you've heard the saying "The more things change, the more they stay the same." Well, whoever said that could not have anticipated the changes in HTML and the interrelated changes caused by HTML to the World Wide Web.

This couldn't be better demonstrated than by what's happening in the world of HTML standards these days. New rules, language versions, and actual languages are growing out of the needs that HTML leaves unfulfilled. Organizational structures are undergoing shifts to improve the definition of HTML, making it a more sophisticated, precise language despite its renegade past. But at the same time, aspects of the language remain intransigent.

In its earliest incarnation, HTML was a formatting language. Its entire responsibility was to manage the basic formatting of hypertext documents. Format controls were limited to items such as headers, paragraphs, and limited text formatting such as bold and italics.

From these modest roots, a dynamic language has emerged. HTML 4.0 adds a new range of powerful options to the original language, shifting it from a limited, formatting language to a full-fledged layout tool. The first change came when hypertext could be viewed with a graphical user interface (GUI, or "gooey"), instead of only within a text-based browser. This happened in 1993, when the Mosaic browser was born. In the years since then, and with each standard version of HTML, the changes have moved farther away from static information and more toward movement, advanced design, and multiple forms of media.

HTML 4.0 ushers in an entirely new level of control for the HTML author, and it is a hallmark point in the evolution of HTML. The reason for this memorable advancement lies mostly in the addition of style sheets and related technologies (see Chapter 13, "Cascading Style Sheet Techniques") to the standard. In earlier versions of HTML, browsers were more technologically diverse than the stricter standards, and HTML authors were constantly frustrated by the lack of the standards committee to quickly bridge any gaps by rushing to publication with a new standard.

Not so with HTML 4.0. This standard, unlike those before it, is much more complex and advanced than Web browsers in current use. This puts HTML designers in another type of frustrating position—having to eschew the standard in favor of more time-honored techniques that they can rely upon in terms of cross-platform, cross-browser design (see Chapter 2, "Using HTML 4.0 in the Real World").

Before I jump headlong into the meat-and-potatoes of HTML 4.0, I want to give you some background on the language, its history, and its features to date.

WHAT IS HTML?

The Internet's early roots began taking hold as early as 1961. Since that time, a variety of languages and protocols were developed and have evolved within the Internet's growing structure.

It's important to remember that the Web is only one part of the Internet! Many people think of the Web and the Internet as being the same thing, but this is far from the truth.

The variety of Internet protocols facilitate a broad range of Internet-based applications, including the familiar sending of electronic mail and popular newsgroups.

The World Wide Web is only one of these protocols, and Hypertext Markup Language, HTML, is only one of the many languages used to deliver information via the Internet.

HTML is a markup language. This means that it isn't a high-level language such as C or Visual Basic. Instead of being compiled and executed, HTML is read, or interpreted, by a user agent. This user agent is known to you as a Web browser.

HTML's primary use is to create Web pages. It is inseparable from the concept and entity referred to as the World Wide Web. The framework for its inception and the event of its creation historically is attributed to Tim Berners-Lee, a programmer at the European Center for Particle Physics (CERN). Berners-Lee developed HTML to

- Provide a medium that enables scientists to publish, resource, and retrieve 24 hours a day.
- Create a computer coding international language that facilitates universal access independent of platform, network, or terminal.

From the standpoint of providing an application-specific solution for the scientific community, HTML originally provided access for a text-based environment and facilitated the exchange of research information.

Note

It's interesting that the switch to a graphic environment has put so much of a dent in some of HTML's original goals that it has inspired the creation of accessibility and internationalization initiatives.

→ For further information about HTML and accessibility and internationalization, **see** "Accessibility and Internationalization", **p. 474**

HTML's origin is as an application-specific coding language based on the Standard Generalized Markup Language (SGML) model. SGML is a system that has been in use for many years by documentation specialists as a means of marking up technical documents. As a formatting language, HTML uses SGML declarations and the document type definition (DTD).

In terms of universality, HTML, along with the Hypertext Transfer Protocol (HTTP), is a language that solved a need for one computer document type to interface with another—perhaps of a different type—and expedite the exchange of information. The problem that HTML specifically addresses is one of different networks speaking different languages.

Note

HTML solves translation problems between computers and computer networks, making a variety of documents broadly accessible.

HTML is the language that enables this process from the client, or end-user, side. Serving up HTML is HTTP, which is the protocol that channels, or piggybacks, the code from the server to the client.

> **Note**
>
> HTTP enables the cross-platform, cross-enterprise multimedia exchange of information. HTTP has evolved to become a powerful distributed object system–not just the vehicle for the download of graphics or Web pages. Since 1991, the World Wide Web Consortium has allowed the standardization of this protocol to include more expressive, more extensible, and faster versions of HTTP. Currently, the Consortium, which manages standards related to the World Wide Web, is working with HTTP/1.1.

HTML as a language of access is effective. So why such radical changes, expansion, and fragmentation? The drive, like so many of the changes seen in the Internet itself, has grown out of the popularization of the medium. The Internet, shortly after HTML's entrance onto the scene, exploded into the widely sought-after, public entity that is the Web today.

Suddenly, the Internet is on desktops not only in the offices of academics, but in the home of everyday folks. This turned an information structure into what is essentially a product. The innovation of hypertext—and most specific to this book, its use on the World Wide Web—has radically altered the landscape of the Internet.

THE EVOLUTION OF HTML

Here's how it happened. Looking at HTML's output, a natural question arose: If text could be linked, why not graphics? The Web had already been used as a source for graphic files—the difference was that in the text environment, you had to download them locally and view them with a separate piece of software. So the challenge then became how to include graphics *inline*, right in the browser.

To accommodate this need, the original formatting concept of HTML had to be modified. This modification has allowed for the technological emergence of the browser as a primary interface to not just the Web, but to the entire Internet! If you add to the influx of a visual environment the complexity of backend programming available for today's Web applications, you can see how in just a few short years what was a simple and intelligent, albeit limited, formatting language, has become the infrastructure for a mass medium.

These rapid and dramatic changes have continued throughout HTML's short life span and have matured with the publication of HTML 4.0.

HTML INFRASTRUCTURE

You might have heard that the hypertext and hypermedia environment of the Web is considered to be *non-linear*. What this means is that instead of following information in a linear, page-by-page fashion, the infrastructure of the Web enables visitors to Web sites to click a link and jump off to ancillary information and related sites.

This also means that HTML authors need to have some sense of the environment and how to create effective architecture within its framework. Because most people are taught to think in linear terms and are accustomed to reading in one direction, one page at a time, the sudden wildness of the Web can be both exhilarating and overwhelming. It's up to the architect of Web pages to make sense of the Web for visitors.

In many cases, this means providing a linear, page-by-page structure within Web sites, or creating sites based on familiar, hierarchical structures. This controls the environment and gives people a sense of security, so when they are using hypertext and hypermedia as a nonlinear jumping-off place, there is much less confusion.

An easy way to think of this rather cerebral concept is to remember your last visit to a Web page that had multiple links, navigation, and advertising banners. A good example of this is the type of site that's been coined a *portal*. Portals (see Figure 1.1) are doorways to the rest of the Web. They organize information, and often allow you to customize the kind of information that you see.

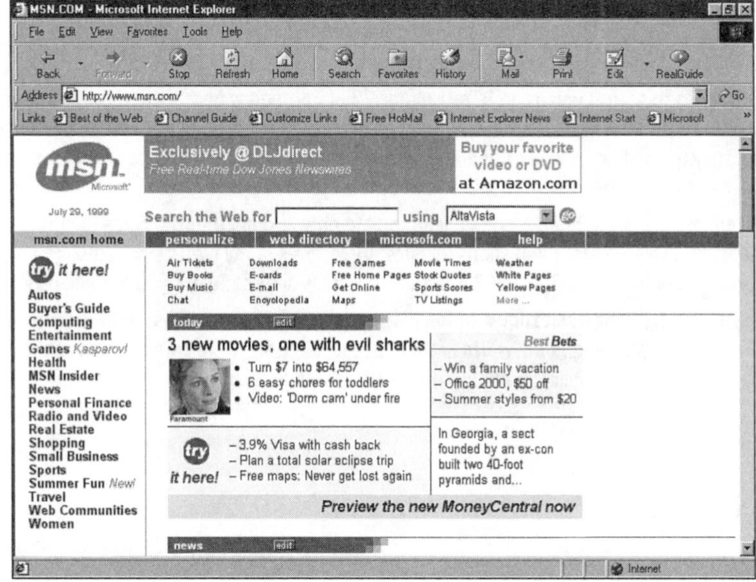

Figure 1.1
The MSN portal provides numerous links as well as news, weather, and personalized stock reports.

Do you read all the material first and then choose a link from the navigation menu? If you do this, which link do you choose? Perhaps you'll decide to proceed through the site in a linear fashion, first reading the content, moving to the link at the topmost or left side of the page, and so forth. Or, maybe you'll be adventuresome and click randomly on a navigational link.

Either way, these options clearly show how the Web is an environment of opportunity—and confusion!

A Philosophical Approach

What I find particularly interesting about this non-linear environment is that ancillary to its primary function of data exchange, the environment can facilitate humankind to challenge both the left and right side of the brain.

How is this possible, and why is it even important? Well, HTML, and the structure of the Web, are astonishingly similar in construct to human memory. The way we store and retrieve information can be described as a linked mechanism.

It's possible to speculate that the similarities between hypermedia and memory are more than coincidental. We can also visit the idea that working both sides of our brain, and operating in an environment more like our thought patterns than the limited linear pathway, provides an opportunity to strengthen our thinking and open ourselves up to opportunities that might not have come our way before.

If you'll allow me to wax philosophical for a moment, I believe that this speaks to not only the potential of individuals to become more well rounded as individuals, but also to the forging of global communities. In my own life, the use of the Web has made me a better scientist as well as a more creative person. Moreover, because I have the *awareness* of this, I'm motivated to strengthen the aspects of my knowledge that are weaker.

That this self-examination is taking place within the context of a global community provides an awe-inspiring sense that if we embrace this technology for educational purposes, as well as commercial ones, we provide each other the opportunity to grow.

Like the telegraph, railroad, and globally connected air travel routes, the whole world is getting even smaller and now fits in a small space on our desktops.

How does this affect you as an HTML author? That question is best answered by your own experience with HTML. When I've suggested these philosophical ideas in a technological environment, I'm occasionally met with resistance. I had one student put it very succinctly most recently, when he said, "I just want the meat." He wanted to know the how of HTML, and not the why.

As an instructor, I've often seen that learning the how and not the why limits the potential of the student. As a designer, I've seen these limitations manifest themselves in my own work. Although most of this book will teach you *how* to use HTML 4.0, I will also stop occasionally and ask you to think *why* you're doing something.

Innovation has long been known to facilitate awareness, and awareness has the potential to lead toward greater understanding of the world around us. I believe that this awareness can directly influence your skills, and ultimately your ability to author innovative as well as technologically proficient sites.

Standards Versus Conventions

Now that we've explored some of the foundational issues of HTML, let's move toward the beefy stuff—the "meat" of the matter.

The challenge in this chapter is to help you achieve an understanding of HTML, and particularly the HTML 4.0 standard. To help you gain that understanding, it's good to look at what a standard is, how it comes about, and how it might look different from what is done on a day-to-day basis by HTML designers.

Standards are formal rules that must pass rigorous examination by committee. In the case of HTML, that committee is referred to as The World Wide Web Consortium (W3C).

This group, discussed in greater detail in just a moment, is the governing body of combined academic, professional, and industrial experts who study, argue, and ultimately determine what is to be published as a standard.

Standards are important because they are the guidelines by which browsers, as well as HTML authors, determine how they work. However, there is an odd shift occurring with HTML—where once standards couldn't keep up with the changes, they've now far exceeded them. This means HTML authors, using HTML for cross-platform, cross-browser design, must work around some of the standard issues and use conventional methods to effectively create their sites. However, just as an artist might choose to eschew a rule, he or she *should know the rule* before breaking it.

Conventions unlike standards, aren't rules. A convention is simply a *commonplace* way of doing a particular task. Unlike a standard, which formalizes the rules and expected behavior of a community, a convention reflects the real-world practices of that community.

Think about a hobby, profession, or pastime you have, and try to determine if there are standards and conventions applied to that activity. One example would be photography. At the professional level, complex standards exist when working with photographic technologies. Does that mean great pictures can't be taken outside of those standards? Of course not; in fact, even the professionals don't always follow the rules.

I first learned how to cook from my mother and father. Many of the dishes they prepared were derived from Old World Hungarian, Polish, and traditional Jewish recipes. A measuring spoon or cup *was never a factor* in the process! It was always a pinch of this, a dab of that, to taste. In fact, I doubt there are any true recipes (standardized methods of preparing food) that reflect the kinds of dishes my parents taught me how to make.

When I was in college, I worked for a time in a bakery, assisting the baker. Baking, as I quickly learned, is very standardized. Without those standards, cakes will fall, crumble, or be rendered inedible! Measure by measure, standards were applied to baking to ensure consistent taste from cake to cake.

Working as an HTML author requires a sense of compromise. You have to know both the conventional trends *as well as* the standard process to make effective decisions at every turn.

Furthermore, your conventional actions have a direct affect on the adoption of standards. A prime example of this is the `<CENTER>` element. Originally introduced by Netscape to argue for the centering of text or objects on a page, the tag worked effectively, but it didn't match any known structural aspect of HTML. What's happened since? Well, although the `<CENTER>` element is still in wide use and highly supported, it's been set to the side in HTML 4.0 in favor of other alignment tags, attributes, and styles because it didn't fit the logical structure of the language.

Note

Flexibility is the active issue here. You'll need to remain aware of conventions, but equally aware of standards.

THE WORLD WIDE WEB CONSORTIUM (W3C)

The organization that can help give you the flexibility you'll need as an HTML author is the World Wide Web Consortium (see Figure 1.2). The Consortium was formalized on December 14, 1994. It's an independent, international organization made up of people from across the Internet and Web development community—from individuals to representatives from major corporations such as Microsoft, IBM, Sun Microsystems, and Netscape.

The job of the Consortium is to oversee the standardization of HTML, as well as the various protocols and languages related to the Web, including XML, CSS, SMIL, HTTP, URL, FTP, NNTP, and SGML. I'll be discussing these languages and protocols in greater detail throughout this book.

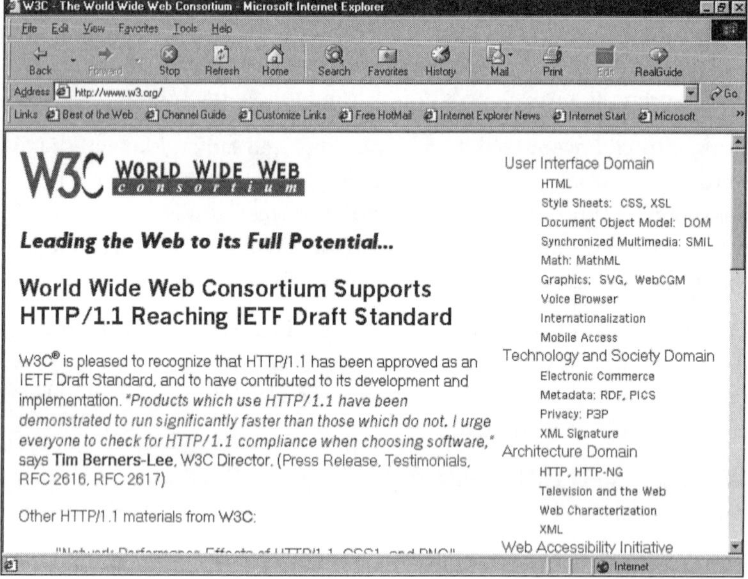

Figure 1.2
The World Wide Web Consortium site provides detailed information on current HTML and related technology standards.

Although the W3C has been the leader in providing Internet information systems, the Web has been overcome, as described earlier, by the popularity of the format and the demands of developers and audiences alike. Some concerns of the Consortium have been set aside to accommodate more pressing needs to appease Web enthusiasts and developers itching for more flexibility.

Some of the proposed changes include protocol enhancements. HTTP, the facilitator of HTML, is undergoing major changes. The new proposed changes speak to the technologies that will enhance Web site design and functionality.

Anyone interested in the history, evolution, use, and future of HTML should visit the W3C at regular intervals.

Note

To keep up with what's happening with current standards, visit the site at `http://www.w3.org/`.

THE 4.0 STANDARD

Now its time to get down to the present day nitty gritty. Set aside history, philosophy, and method. I'm going to give you a glimpse of some of the primary reasons HTML 4.0 is different from prior standards.

Let me begin by describing the conceptual breakdown of HTML 4.0, which falls within one of three types:

- **Strict HTML 4.0**—This is the most pure of HTML 4.0. Anything deprecated or obsolete is not used—ever. It's also the most optimistic version of HTML 4.0 because many of its rules are ahead of the stability user agents, or browsers, offer.
- **Transitional, or "loose" HTML 4.0**—By combining aspects of HTML 3.2 with elements from the strict HTML 4.0 standard, a more realistic, usable version of the language emerges.
- **Frameset HTML 4.0**—This includes all the information within the transitional version combined with the newly adopted frame-based elements such as `FRAME`, `FRAMESET`, `NOFRAMES`, and `IFRAME`.

Which type do you choose? Much of this book is dedicated to helping you find a good method and sticking to it. As I mentioned earlier—it's good to know the rules before you break them. So knowing the HTML 4.0 standard is critical. This knowledge will determine how you use the language day-to-day.

GOALS OF HTML 4.0

Let's examine the three primary things that HTML 4.0 attempts to encourage authors to do to ameliorate problems and concerns with the language's current use:

- **Separate document structure from presentation and style**—Much of HTML 4.0 is focused on taking any element from prior language versions used for presentation or style of information and setting it aside. In its favor, style sheets for presentation and design are typically recommended.
- **Think carefully about access**—Because HTML was originally built for all people to access documents, including those on a variety of platforms, using different user agents, and with a special concern for those having physical impairments, the standard asks that we use forethought when authoring code.
- **Make documents load more quickly via careful table design**—HTML 4.0 has several element additions that help tables render incrementally.

→ For more information on presentation and style, **see** "Cascading Style Sheet Techniques," **p. 253**, "Designing Type with CSS," **p. 283**, and "Element Positioning and Style Sheet Scripting," **p. 429**

→ For accessibility concerns, **see** "Accessibility and Internationalization," **p. 474**

→ To find table increment details, **see** "Table Fundamentals", **p. 304**

Along with the aforementioned principles, three categories describe the status of HTML elements:

- **New elements**—These are new additions to the standard. Those of you familiar with HTML will see certain tags in this list and think "Hey! That's not new—I've been using it for two years." Well, that's a perfect example of convention versus standard.
- **Deprecated elements**—A deprecated element is one that claims that the element is *outdated*. What's humorous about this is that while the *idea* is to say this is outdated because we have this other, much more effective technology available, the *reality* is that an element's new or deprecated status is irrelevant in the context of browser support.
- **Obsolete elements**—These elements are those that are no longer in use and are, in essence, stricken from the HTML record. Usually, there's nothing disconcerting about this, because most obsolete elements are tags that even seasoned HTML authors such as myself have *never* used.

For the purposes of brevity, I'm going to only discuss the major changes and impact of these changes on the HTML author in this chapter. However, as you work your way through the many chapters in this book, I'll frequently point out elements that fall into the new, deprecated, or obsolete categories in HTML 4.0.

→ For a comprehensive look at the current availability of elements, attributes, and other HTML syntactical options, **see** "HTML 4.0 Element and Tag Reference," **p. 926**

New Elements

Here's a taste of some of the new elements available as part of the HTML 4.0 Standard. You'll note that most of the ones I've selected here have been added to the standard to accommodate frames, scripts, and cascading style sheets, and are elements that HTML authors use with frequency.

- **FRAME**—This tag has actually been in use since frame-compliant browsers were developed—quite a few years now! Finally, the FRAME tag has been formally entered into the standard.
- **FRAMESET**—This tag is also used by Microsoft Internet Explorer and Netscape's browser for frames. It's been conventionally used with no problems for as long as the FRAME tag.
- **IFRAME**—Introduced by Microsoft for Internet Explorer, this interesting tag allows for a "frame within a frame." Netscape never adopted it, despite the fact that it is extremely powerful. Now that it's a standard, however, it will require support from any browser worth its salt.
- **NOFRAMES**—A very helpful tag, this makes framed sites accessible to text-based readers. It's been in conventional use as long as the FRAME and FRAMESET tags.
- **NOSCRIPT**—Much like the NOFRAMES tag, NOSCRIPT allows you to code information in a script-dominated document for those individuals and browsers unable to manage the script.

- **OBJECT**—Used by Microsoft IE for some time, this tag really isn't new. It is being recommended over the APPLET tag, which Netscape still uses and IE understands, too.
- **SPAN**—This is a very helpful tag, most useful when working with cascading style sheets (CSS).

→ For more information on frames, **see** "Working with Frames," **p. 355**
→ For more on how to use the OBJECT tag, **see** "Using Java Applets and ActiveX Components," **p. 704**
→ For style sheet techniques, **see** "Cascading Style Sheet Techniques," **p. 253**

DEPRECATED ELEMENTS

The following elements are examples of deprecated tags—tags considered to be outdated. Tags that have been deprecated usually have a component tag or application to replace their loss.

- **APPLET**—The deprecation of APPLET is a good thing, because it forces Netscape to adopt the OBJECT tag, which will ultimately provide better, more stable management of embedded objects in a Web page.
- **BASEFONT**—This tag had its uses, but they were limited. The idea was to try and create a way of making a single font as a default for an entire page, but it never seemed to work consistently.
- **CENTER**—The infamous center tag has been set aside for other alignment methods, especially within cascading style sheets. Another tag for alignment is the <DIV> tag along with the align attribute.
- **FONT**—Ouch. This one is a bit painful, but the reality is that as cascading style sheets become a real-world option for HTML authors, we'll all be glad it's gone. For now, however, the use of the FONT tag remains the only way to gain some control over HTML-based font attributes.

OBSOLETE ELEMENTS

Three elements have been rendered obsolete: LISTING, PLAINTEXT, and XMP. I cannot honestly say that I've ever used a single one of these elements. What I have done is use the tag that is recommended to take their place—the <PRE>, or preformatted text element.

SUMMING UP THE CHANGES

There are, of course, many other changes to HTML 4.0. However, they follow a few generalized ideas. Here's a rundown of the major areas where HTML 4.0 has been extended to incorporate a variety of new information:

- Style sheets
- Scripting

- Frames support
- Embedded objects
- Improved support for text alignment and handling
- Richer tables (usually with offerings that enhance accessibility)
- Forms enhancements (also offering a variety of information for accessibility purposes)

Keep this list handy as you read this book. It will help you anchor a given method firmly into the fundamentals of the HTML 4.0 Standard.

TROUBLESHOOTING

DECISION-MAKING FOR HTML AUTHORS

How does an HTML author effectively apply the standard but embrace conventional or progressive options, too?

Although HTML authors must strive to understand and incorporate the important contributions of the Consortium, in reality the organization has no official enforcement status. It exists only as an advisory and consultative organization. It can recommend the adoption of formalized standards to facilitate an efficient and effective transfer of information.

Therefore, as HTML authors, the approach to the problem of accessibility versus progress lies in our hands. It is our responsibility to adopt and administer the standard to the best of our abilities and circumstances. We are personally entrusted with the task of making implementation decisions within the framework and structure of a given site's individual HTML needs.

DESIGNING FOR THE REAL WORLD

HTML AND WEB DEVELOPERS: REAL WORLD CONCERNS

At a recent Web Design and Development conference in San Francisco, I presented a large class about HTML 4.0. I wanted to gain a sense of the general skill level of attendees, so I asked several questions.

The first question was "*How many people here code HTML by hand?*" I was surprised to find that of approximately 400 attendees, nearly *all* of them were hand coders. Impressive!

My next question was "*How many people have been coding HTML for longer than two years?*" Again, the response was overwhelming. At least 3/4 of the attendees were seasoned HTML coders.

Then, I asked, "*How many people here feel somewhat familiar with the HTML 4.0 specification?*" I expected maybe half of the attendees to respond positively. In fact, maybe 10 of the nearly 400 students in that room expressed any confidence that they had a fundamental understanding of the HTML 4.0 specification.

I found this very intriguing. Naturally, one of the reasons these individuals were in the class in the first place was to gain a better understanding of the specification. But for that many skilled, professional developers to not feel confident with the HTML 4.0 specification indicates some communication problem.

The first thing that comes to mind as to this lack of confidence is that HTML coders are a busy lot. They might know *where* the information is, but getting there means taking time out from the demands of the day. The other issue that comes to mind is that, despite the W3C's excellent work, the material is very detailed and often difficult to decipher. Certainly, many popular columns and books exist to help offset the button-down, white paper details.

My goal with this book is to offer up HTML and related technologies in a palatable way. I believe it is imperative that anyone coding in today's world needs to have some understanding of the current status of the languages with which they work.

Even if the choice is ultimately made to *not* follow the rules—a professional understands that he or she is purposely breaking those rules for a specific reason that, through experience and education, is understood to be a real world concern.

CHAPTER 2

Using HTML 4.0 in the Real World

In this chapter

Seeking Control in a World of Chaos

Okay, so I'm a control freak, I admit it! I want to have as much say in how my HTML code behaves as possible. An unruly child at its best, HTML requires a firm hand to effectively socialize it well.

If you look at the history of HTML, you'll see that it was never meant to be a language of design. Its purpose was to format documents, plain and simple. In just a few short years it went from the most basic aspects of page structure control to becoming the primary layout tool used by graphic designers on the Web.

This radical shift in use has led to loopholes in the capability of HTML to express itself consistently and accurately in the day-to-day world of the Internet. This is one reason there's been such a push for standards, as I examined in Chapter 1, "Understanding HTML 4.0." But, as I also describe within that chapter, the real use of HTML relies much less on the standard as it is today and much more on the conventional wisdom born of understanding various cross-platform, cross-browser concerns.

To gain this wisdom, individuals often go through a frustrating process of having to learn by their mistakes. No matter where you are in the process of learning and using HTML, you are likely to be challenged by these intricacies—I've been actively using the language since its birth and I still rely heavily on references when coding complicated sites.

Newcomers to HTML are challenged by the inadequacies of software as well as the overwhelming and oft-times conflicting information available. Programmers used to syntactical rule sets often get quite a laugh out of some of the less precise aspects of HTML, and are frustrated by its every-rule-has-an-exception environment. Graphic designers are perhaps most harried by the HTML experience. Used to precise, point-by-point, pixel-by-pixel control of space, shape, and color—the layout methods available via HTML are maddeningly inefficient.

Does this mean that we should throw up our hands in utter disgust and try to find a better way? That's one road, of course, and several alternatives have been suggested. But HTML is still the Web's dominant language, so seeking the right relationship with it is imperative.

Which brings me back to the idea of control. If you endeavor to create Web sites that are going to be as stable as possible between platforms, browsers, and the variety of hardware available, you must begin with an understanding of what variables exist within the application of HTML. This chapter gets you started with just those issues, and this book as a whole takes you well beyond them. You will venture into the sophisticated use of HTML 4.0 by systematically learning its quirks and eccentricities, and empower yourself by tethering its rebellious nature and exploiting its most powerful aspects.

Computer Platforms

The first variable with which we must contend is that of the computer platform. The challenge in terms of control is to create HTML code and designs that will be managed with relative stability across the variety of platforms that exist. This process is referred to as cross-platform design.

The definition of the phrase *computer platform* is often misunderstood. We tend to use it casually, without really understanding what it means. When most people think of a computer platform, they are probably thinking of a *type of computer*, as in hardware. Although that's not entirely incorrect, a more accurate description of platform relates to the type of user interface the computer uses. User interfaces are not necessarily hardware-dependent, but they always rely on *software*, or programming, as the framework for the interface.

There are a number of user interfaces, also referred to as operating systems (OSs for short) that must be carefully considered when thinking about compatible, real-world HTML design. Because of the different programming interfaces used by these systems, the software designed to work with them can be very different.

Tip from molly

When I discuss cross-platform considerations, what I'm after is the method to make a Web site run comparably from platform to platform.

For the purposes of this chapter, and this book, computer platform should first be thought of as the user interface. Now, as I said in the last paragraph, user interfaces are not *always* hardware dependent. Where it gets confusing is that for the two dominant platforms existing on personal desktop computers, there is a hardware dependency.

The Macintosh runs a proprietary interface, and most personal computer platforms outside the realm of the Macintosh Operating System (Mac OS) are running some version of Microsoft DOS or Windows. Another platform of concern to the Internet world is UNIX. Furthermore, there are distinctions within these groups that break down considerations even more.

Tip from molly

It's important to realize that although most people visiting Web sites are probably on a Macintosh or Windows, there may be variations in the software versions being used. Furthermore, there are many people visiting and working on Web sites that are using other platforms, such as UNIX, Linux, and Virtual Memory System (VMS).

What this means is that while the *hardware* for these platforms does in fact have differences, the challenge the HTML coder faces is managing the code between the software interfaces of these platforms.

Let's take a comparative look at common platforms and some of the specific software issues involved.

- **DOS and Windows**—DOS is a line-based operating system still in use worldwide, particularly on older computers. Typically, people using DOS machines for the Web are also operating some kind of graphical interface environment, such as Windows 3.1. Windows 3.1 is an environment as opposed to an operating system—a distinction that becomes important because of the *integrative* aspects of browsers and graphical operating systems. For example, Windows 95 is well integrated with browsers, and Windows 98 (see Figure 2.1) is so well integrated with Internet technologies that there have been questions regarding Microsoft's fair trade practices because of this OS-to-Web relationship.

Figure 2.1
The Windows 98 graphic user interface.

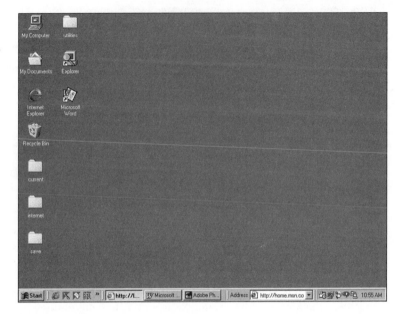

- **Windows NT**—Another operating systems that falls under the Windows selection is Windows NT—the networking operating system from Microsoft that is used not only by certain Web visitors but many Web host Internet infrastructure machines.
- **Windows 2000**—Advancing the technology of both Windows 98 and Windows NT, Windows 2000 will soon be in use by individuals with desktop PCs, as well as networks running NT technology.
- **Macintosh**—Developed by Apple, the Macintosh uses a different type of microprocessor and different file formats than those found supporting Windows operating systems. The operating system in a Macintosh is always the proprietary Mac OS (see Figure 2.2), although the Power PC enables a version of Windows to be run on the machine simultaneously. With the release of the appealing iMac and iBook personal computers, a renewed interest in the Mac platform has come about.
- **UNIX**—Unlike Windows operating systems and Macintosh OSs, UNIX was never dependent on a specific piece of hardware such as a microprocessor. It was, in fact, built specifically to be as portable and adaptable as possible, with the special capability to function in a multi-user environment. Until recently, UNIX had the distinction of being the leading operating system for workstations. The Internet's infrastructure demands the kind of power UNIX offers, and it is thought that many of its Web servers as well as computer users use this platform daily.

Figure 2.2
Macintoshes are popular computers for the public as well as the desktop publishing and graphic design industry, and therefore carry a lot of weight in the Web design world.

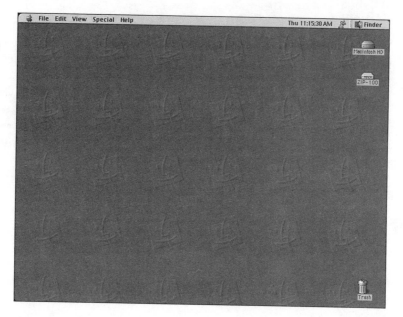

- **VMS**—The Virtual Memory System runs on DEC's VAX minicomputers and workstations, and is found with some frequency as Internet servers.
- **Sun Microsystems and SGI (Silicon Graphics Incorporated)**—These platforms are less frequent but specialized toward graphics and therefore exist as an interface to the Internet.
- **Linux**—A takeoff of UNIX that is freely distributed and runs on a number of hardware platforms. Linux has a *very* enthusiastic user base that has grown significantly in the past several years.

Note

UNIX and Linux users can choose graphical interfaces for the OS, making the environment more similar to Windows or Macintosh.

There are other, less common platforms as well as variations within these platforms. All of these listed platforms are supported by Microsoft Internet Explorer and Netscape Navigator browsers. However, browser software differs in terms of functionality as well as look-and-feel, fully exemplifying the difficult but very real relationship between operating systems and Web-based software.

Note

A strong interest in specialty browsers for Palm products, cell phones, digital pagers, and other handheld technologies has come to the forefront in recent months. Another area under scrutiny is WebTV. While still carrying less than 1% of the browser market, this may conceivably change.

Resources on the Web

These sites will help you understand more about computer platforms.

PC Webopaeida–This site is a virtual storehouse of any and all information about personal as well general computer information. It's located at `http://www.pcwebopaedia.com/`.

Microsoft–This corporate giant has one of the most jam-packed Web sites on the Net. Check it out at `http://www.microsoft.com/`.

Apple–To learn more about the Macintosh, visit Apple's site at `http://www.apple.com/`.

Digital Equipment Corporation–An extremely interesting site for DEC computers, on which many UNIX and VAX machines run. It's found at `http://www.dec.com/`.

Web Browsers

The developmental history of Web browsers is both disturbing and fascinating. Anyone interested in HTML will benefit from an understanding of that history. Ultimately, you will be better prepared to work with the limitations of browsers and the complicated issues they create when combined with cross-platform concerns.

As the user interface to the Web, the development of Web browsers has been accelerated and confounding. Any person using HTML who wants to make a site broadly available, stable, and also tout the newer technologies allowed by HTML 4.0 and related applications, is challenged by this unstable environment.

Do all developers have to design for browsers that accommodate HTML 4.0? See, "Audience Is Paramount" in the Troubleshooting section at the end of this chapter to find out.

I like to compare browser development to the process of evolution. When an environment is unstable, newly introduced evolutionary attributes can gain foothold in a species very rapidly. The biological process of natural selection seeks to keep those aspects that work, and will not only allow for, but also enhance survival.

Carry this comparison over to the rapid-fire pace of Web technologies, and it's apparent that many of the attributes picked up during this unstable time are in fact strong, although others fail because of their inherent weakness and inability to thrive.

In the corporate world, contrary to the natural order of things, the fittest doesn't always mean the best. The issue is further complicated by industry politics and positioning. In the case of Web browsers vying for market dominance, it becomes difficult to determine if one is a better browser because of more effective HTML 4.0 and broad-based technological support, or if the strategies used by the corporations behind the browsers have simply been more effective.

As most readers are well aware, the two browser developers that have made it to the top of the heap, Netscape Communications Corporation and Microsoft Corporation, are continually engaged in this positioning and politicking, using market strategies as well as technological advances in attempts to survive the environmental upheaval of the Web environment. Both browsers seek to dominate, and neither has the full spectrum of attributes required for that survival.

Browser Help

Keep up with browser information by visiting these great sites:

Statmarket–This site uses its statistics analysis programs to determine which browsers and versions are in mass-market use, **http://www.statmarket.com/**.

Microsoft's Internet Explorer–News, product downloads, and general information, found at **http://www.microsoft.com/ie/**.

Netscape Navigator–Product information, version downloads, and white papers at **http://home.netscape.com/**.

Mecklermedia's BrowserWatch–All the latest about browsers, including statistical information, found at **http://www.browserwatch.com/**.

C|Net's Browser.Com–Keep up-to-date with browser downloads, and download any browser or related software you need from this comprehensive site at **http://www.browsers.com/**.

For an HTML designer to address cross-browser concerns, he or she has to step far back from trend and follow conventions (see Chapter 1) that might not apply to the latest and greatest in Web technology. Most importantly, designers must find clever ways to bridge the gaps.

➔ For more information on current conventions, **see** "Understanding HTML 4.0", **p. 15**

To gain insight into the historical basis of Web browsers, the next section provides you with a short history, and then takes a look at some of the statistical issues that are current to the concerns of HTML coders today.

WHERE IT ALL BEGAN

The Web began as a hypertext-based environment viewable only by line browsers such as Lynx (see Figure 2.3). But in 1993, Marc Andreessen (who co-founded Netscape Communications in 1994, and is now Chief Technology Officer and Senior Vice President, America Online, Inc.) and Eric Bina developed a graphic user interface (GUI) at the National Center for Supercomputing Applications (NCSA). Figure 2.4 shows the Mosaic home page, where you can download the browser, which hasn't been in development for over two years. However, the Mosaic browser can be cited as the single most important factor in the shift of the Internet to widespread, commercial use. Its interface was easy to use, and the fact that it could display graphics was an attractive feature.

The advent of Mosaic literally created the opportunity for the growth of a new evolutionary attribute—the Web as a graphic medium. From this grew the enormous and popular industry with which we are familiar today.

After Mosaic entered the scene, it seemed only mere moments before a medley of Web browsers began to pop eventually, Netscape Navigator—a cousin to Mosaic. Netscape released its first version of Navigator in 1994, only one short year after Mosaic had entered the scene.

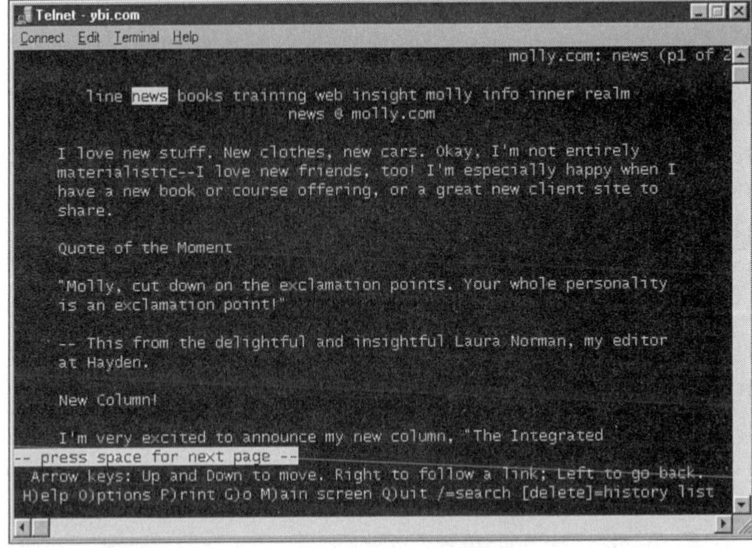

Figure 2.3
Lynx, one of the original line-based browsers, is no longer being developed but is still in wide use and available on most Unix or Linux servers.

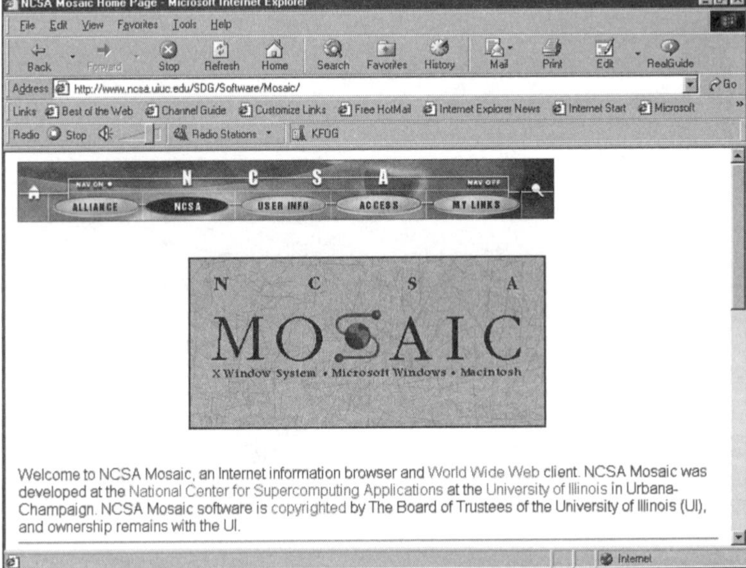

Figure 2.4
The Mosaic home page archives old versions of the browser and stands as an historical reminder of where browser technology began.

Netscape moved quickly to the forefront of browsers because of its constantly growing features and cross-platform interoperability. Essentially, Netscape used Mosaic's gift of visual—and therefore commercially inviting—Web browsing potential and took (and continues to take) it to the next available level.

Features such as background colors and graphics, plug-in technologies for video and audio, and the foundations for new software language development such as JavaScript (via LiveScript) and the Virtual Reality Modeling Language (VRML), moved the browser from its role as an interface to the window on, and perpetrator of, a thriving, worldwide community.

Never willing to take a back seat to anyone, Microsoft decided to jump into the fray. Already interested with the Internet as a medium, and looking to create integrated software applications, Microsoft was a natural contender in the browser game. With plenty of money, a huge technical support infrastructure in place, and developmental resources unequalled anywhere, Microsoft began its penetration of the browser market. But, it did so somewhat quietly.

By obtaining the early code of Spry Mosaic, evaluating Netscape conventions, and adding technological features and interface appeal of its own, Microsoft's Internet Explorer browser was born. Microsoft then added aggressive, functional support including inline video, support for background sound, scrolling marquees, and a whole range of new HTML tags and technologies.

The crowning market decision, which ultimately has been productive in bringing the Microsoft browser into a better position to compete with Netscape, was to make the browser available to everyone for *free*. Eventually, Netscape had to follow suit.

At this point, the strategic lines were drawn. Both Netscape and Microsoft continue to aggressively compete, each one attempting to out-do the other in terms of functionality, cross-platform interoperability, and new technologies. And, of course, the ultimate goal is dominating market share.

Note

How is money made by browsers when both Internet Explorer and Netscape are now free products? Money spent by third-party developers and purchasers of operating systems, computer hardware manufacturers and other necessary equipment to *run* the browsers can be expensive–particularly for large businesses. Consumers also pay for upgrades as well as a variety of products that are made by browser manufacturers and associate companies.

So where do things stand today? At the time of this writing, Internet Explorer 5.0 (see Figure 2.5) is in widespread use, and the Netscape Communicator package, containing the Navigator browser (see Figure 2.6), is in its 4.61 version, with the 5.0 version in development but not yet ready for prime time. Netscape made its source code completely available several years ago, and this has become known as "The Mozilla Project"—an open source movement allowing developers to create a wide range of browsers. What this means for HTML 4.0 is that support for its strict adherence is getting closer to reality—at least in terms of mainstream browsers such as Netscape and IE.

→ For details on strict HTML 4.0 and its requirements, **see** "Understanding HTML 4.0," **p. 17**

But here's the rub: Just because the latest and greatest browser is available *doesn't mean that it is being used* by individuals. Understanding HTML 4.0 in its complete sense and coupling that with practical, real-world experience, will empower you in the long run. Without an awareness of cross-browser design, you are in a potentially dangerous, vulnerable position—leaving your Web site open to the interpretation (or misinterpretation!) of the code you write.

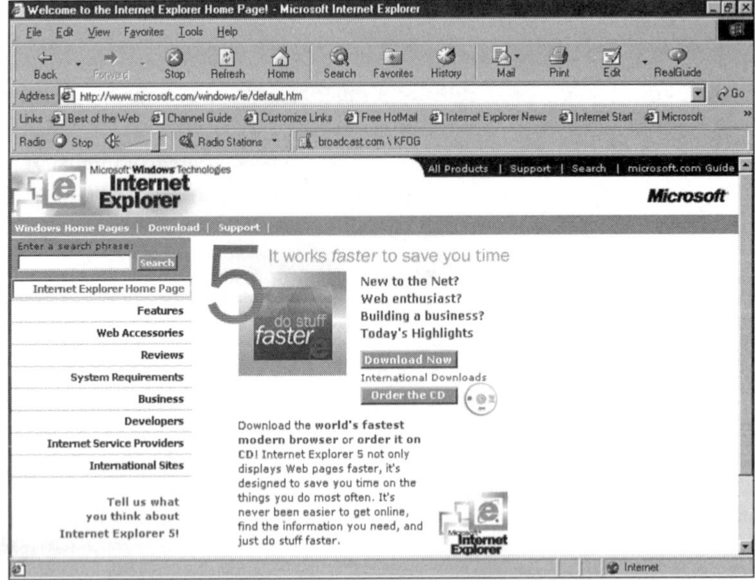

Figure 2.5
Internet Explorer 5.0. offers advanced support for style sheets and streaming media.

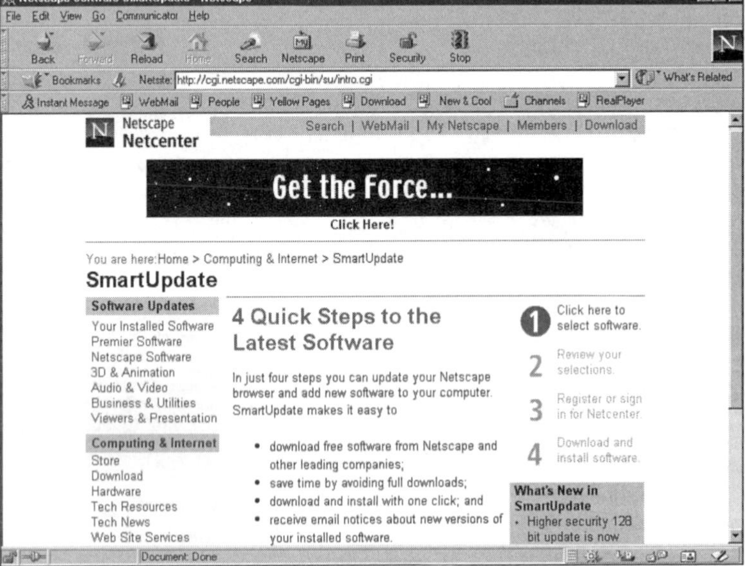

Figure 2.6
Netscape Navigator 4.61 is an interim release of the browser, but the 5.0 version will have more stable style sheet and other HTML 4.0-specific support.

Tip from molly

If there is any single piece of wisdom that I can provide you with in this chapter, it's that real world HTML means accommodating the fact that using strict HTML 4.0 is not always a realistic way of approaching all HTML design.

WEB BROWSER STATISTICS

Let's take a look at some of the information currently being reported by various sources. Bear in mind that there simply are no cut-and-dry, get-your-hands-around it statistics that truly represent what is going on with Web browsers. This information just gives us a ballpark idea of what browsers are being used in certain environments.

Having trouble finding out how to get statistics for your Web site? See, "Tracking Statistics" in the Troubleshooting section at the end of this chapter.

This first statistic is derived from information available at StatMarket (see Figure 2.7). The statistics demonstrate an appended breakdown of browser visits to StatMarket sites on the day I visited.

Figure 2.7 StatMarket.com provides daily statistics about browsers and Web technologies.

> **Note**
>
> The remainder of these statistics is given to other non-standard browser versions as well as UNIX, which I didn't include in the statistics for the sake of brevity.

General Use on August 25, 1999:

Microsoft Internet Explorer: 73.82% of visitors.

Netscape Navigator: 24.71% of visitors.

General Use one year ago (approximate):

Netscape Navigator: 44.2% of visitors.

Microsoft Internet Explorer: 38.0% of visitors.

When you take a look at some of the individual browsers and corresponding versions you'll notice that the percentages, without the complete information, are best used to get an idea of the role browsers play in site visitations—not in the specific market share that they take up.

For Microsoft IE:

Version	Percent of Visitors
5.x	25.99%
4.x	45.53%
3.x	3.38%

For Netscape:

Version	Percent of Visitors
5.x	00.36%
4.x	22.56%
3.x	3.03%

These general statistics do reflect a significant change in the way people are browsing Web sites. Generally speaking, the majority of individuals are visiting at the 4.0 browser level. This is encouraging to those of us interested in using HTML 4.0 to its highest and best.

I personally believe that the Netscape/Microsoft competition is very healthy. It forces both browser developers to work toward a stronger, more diverse product, as well as coming up with cutting-edge ideas that could work themselves into future standards. Undeniably, it's frustrating as all get out to have to actually design for this unstable environment—but I like to think of that as part of the challenge!

For the record, I don't personally have a favorite browser. When working within the Windows environment, I have a tendency to favor Microsoft's Internet Explorer, because I think it handles design issues and HTML 4.0 compliance such as Cascading Style Sheets more elegantly. Netscape, on the other hand, is more stable in terms of JavaScript. On the Macintosh, I prefer Netscape for a number of reasons, and interestingly, I prefer Netscape 3.0 for the Macintosh over the more recent 4.0 version. So in the end, my feelings about these two competitors are pretty neutral. Mostly, I'm just happy to have a choice.

Tip from molly

Despite the fact that you may have a browser that is your personal favorite, if you are developing Web sites for a broad-based audience, setting aside that bias and designing your sites to look great in all major browsers is imperative.

HARDWARE ISSUES

Now that platforms and browser issues have been covered, it's time to revisit the hardware concerns that the platform section hinted at but didn't detail.

Hardware issues influence HTML design in several ways. First, there's how HTML color is displayed. In HTML 4.0, this is especially significant because of Cascading Style Sheets (CSS), which hand the HTML coder a lot of power over the way color is applied to portions of a page, as well as text and links.

Of course, there's always the issue of speed. Hardware will affect the way your pages load—if your computer is less-than-surf ready, pages exploiting many general HTML as well as advanced HTML 4.0 technologies might cause an end user serious woes.

Following is a short list of hardware issues that will affect your decision when coding HTML 4.0 for your particular audience:

- **Monitors, Video Cards, and Video RAM**—These three hardware components function together to create visual output. If a site visitor's hardware is sub-standard, he or she is not going to be able to best view your site.
- **Audio, Video, and Multimedia Support**—With the growing interest in Web-based multimedia, the concern for HTML designers is that the end user has hardware capable of managing audio, video, and a variety of multimedia.
- **Memory (RAM) and Hard Drive Space**—RAM is essential for speeding up browsers and maximizing their productivity. Browsers also rely on *cache*, which is a method of storing graphical and other information on the visitor's hard drive. This process also helps speed up the display of HTML-based information on the computer screen.
- **Bandwidth Access**—Although a growing number of Web fans are connected to the Internet via screaming fast, advanced bandwidth technologies such as *Digital Subscriber Line* (DSL) and cable modems, most people on the homefront are using modems ranging from 14.4Kbps to 56Kbps speeds. Bandwidth is a paramount concern when designing sites, and dictates all cross-browser, cross-platform decisions.

Some of these hardware issues are also modified by software. For example, many people have computers with monitors that support higher resolutions and color options—but they keep the settings at factory default because they don't know any better. This is one reason why the 640×480 resolution can be a limitation for today's HTML designer.

Furthermore, audio, video, and multimedia can be facilitated on the right machines with appropriate plug-in software. If you are coding a site that has this kind of advanced media, be sure that your visitors have access to the companion software.

TROUBLESHOOTING

AUDIENCE IS PARAMOUNT

I'm working on an intranet site and all the browsers used by individuals on the network are the most recent versions. Do I still have to subscribe to the HTML standard?

If you know the exact nature of your audience, you are free to make decisions about the kinds of technology you want to use. For example, if you are using a style-sheet compliant browser across the network, you can freely use style sheets without having to include transitional information for other browsers. However, subscribing to the standard is, generally speaking, considered best practice.

TRACKING STATISTICS

I want to track statistics for my Web site. How do I do this?

The first place to look is to your ISP or network administrator to see if a statistical analysis program is available on the server. All Web servers log data, but often don't break it down into specific, usable chunks. Software programs on the server-side can do this comprehensively. If software of this nature is not available, see if you can encourage your ISP or administrator to add such software to the server.

If server statistics are simply not available to you, you can get statistical analysis services for no or low cost. Hitbox and Hitometer are two popular products that can give you comprehensive information about your site.

Note

To find information on Hitbox, visit **http://www.hitbox.com/**. Hitometer is offered by Netscape, and is available at **http://hitometer.netscape.com/**.

DESIGNING FOR THE REAL WORLD

BROWSER STATISTICS AND THE DESIGN OF MOLLY.COM

The site I use to promote my books, seminars, and activities, Molly.Com, uses statistical analysis tools that give me daily, weekly, and monthly information that I can use to make decisions about what I offer my site visitors.

In 1998 it was clear that with the predominance of Netscape 3.0 browsers, style sheets were not going to be an option to control presentation. But studying the statistics in recent months has shown trends similar to StatMarket in that more and more of my site visitors are using compliant browsers.

Here's a look at the statistics from August 25, 1999 regarding browsers:

Microsoft IE:

Version	Percent of Visitors
5.x	23.00%
4.x	41.9%

Netscape:

Version	Percent of Visitors
4.x	32.3%
3.x	1.4%
Other Browsers (unspecified)	1.4%

Of 291 total visitors for the day, the above statistics break down to the following number of actual visitors:

Microsoft IE:

Version	Number of Visitors
5.x	67
4.x	122

Netscape:

Version	Number of Visitors
4.x	94
3.x	4
Unknown browsers	4

Based on this information, I decided that I could begin to use style sheets and some dynamic HTML *as long as* I also accommodated browsers that did not support these technologies. This meant understanding HTML 4.0 clearly enough to understand how to do just that.

Chapter 1 "Understanding HTML 4.0," gave some basic information about transitional HTML 4.0. Using this interpretation, the Molly.Com site was re-designed to incorporate technologies that appeal to the majority of its current users, and still be accessible and enjoyable for those visitors that do not have the supportive technology.

CHAPTER 3

HTML Tools

In this chapter

APPROACHES TO CODING

How many times have you tried to use a screwdriver because you couldn't find a hammer, a knife when scissors would have been better, or tried a cheap corkscrew on a stubborn cork? If you're like me, you have suffered sore thumbs, painful nicks and cuts, and ended up drinking cork along with your wine!

Hard-won experience teaches us all that using the right tool for the job is going to make that job easier and will help to avoid painful or unfortunate results. To generate HTML, using the right tool is imperative. Yet there are so many tools available, it's hard to decide which one is appropriate to your circumstances.

Whether you are a hobbyist, newcomer, or professional, selecting the appropriate tool for HTML is going to make an enormous difference. This chapter will help you understand the tools that are available, the advantages and disadvantages that come with specific types of tools, and how you can maximize your work experience and minimize risk.

Your first task is to put aside everything you've heard about HTML applications: that coding HTML is easy or hard, or that the best coders only code by hand. All of these attitudes are just that—attitudes. From experience, I can confidently tell you that no one tool is the catchall answer for every situation. Just as you want to choose a hammer when a hammer is required, and a knife when you need a knife, so you must choose the best HTML tool for the circumstance in which you work.

There are several approaches to coding HTML that are popular. These include text-based, or "hand" coding; using HTML editing environments; working with HTML conversion programs; and employing What-You-See-Is-What-You-Get (WYSIWYG) applications.

HAND CODING

Some time ago, I attended a figure drawing class. I found it challenging because I knew precious little about the actual mechanics of drawing. As I became more acquainted with techniques—such as visualizing a grid and breaking down areas into small sections—my skills improved. Without the mechanical knowledge, however, I could be creative and expressive, but I was not accurate, adept, or confident in my approach.

If you want total control over your code and your design, you must know the mechanics of HTML. This book focuses on giving you the opportunity to control your HTML documents and Web design issues. The most powerful and effective way of gaining that control and relying on the underlying mechanics of HTML is coding HTML in a text-based environment.

HTML information is saved in plain text format. Many of you are already familiar with this concept—plain text is text that has no formatting codes added by a program such as a word processor. Text is the natural format for HTML, therefore coding in text is a natural approach. Historically speaking, it was the first approach.

But coding in a text editor means having to *know the code*. There are no cheat sheets available in this environment. Yes, you'll want to keep a copy of this book around for reference purposes while coding in this fashion, but text editing means relying on your own knowledge with no added power tools.

The advantages? There are many. The most important one is that knowing the code is incredibly empowering—especially for professionals. Text editing forces you to know your HTML, and this in turn frees you from the constraints of a software interface. If something doesn't work, you'll have the skills to troubleshoot, debug, and eventually repair the problem.

Relying on your own skills also allows you to be creative. The better you know the language, the more creatively you can use it. This creativity is the precursor to progress in the industry. By knowing the rules, using them creatively, or even breaking them, new opportunities are born.

As you'll soon read in the WYSIWYG section of this chapter, software applications are limited by software update issues. For example, if a new code standard is adopted, a text-coder can begin to use that code immediately. The software application may not support it until the next update, however, and could possibly cause endless frustration as you attempt to work with that new code standard.

Finally, if you know your code and are comfortable coding in a text environment, you can take that anywhere you go, to any company, onto any computer platform. What's more, text editors are native to all operating systems, and that means you'll spend *no money* on HTML software!

Are there disadvantages to hand-coding? You bet. One of the most pervasive is the time it takes to become proficient with HTML. The language and its supporting technologies have become very sophisticated, and it takes time, not only to learn the individual aspects of the language, but also to integrate that knowledge into your working world.

Along the same lines, even a proficient and fast coder will require extra time during the coding process without power tools. To provide you with a down-to-earth example, I've been coding HTML since 1994, and although I'm knowledgeable and experienced, I still have to rely on reference materials to do more advanced or obscure processes.

This extra time is costing someone precious money. That's a definite disadvantage, and one that you'll want to weigh seriously when analyzing your personal needs and coming up with a good coding approach.

TEXT EDITORS FOR WINDOWS

Most text editors are native or freely available within any given operating system.

In Windows, the choice is Notepad, shown in Figure 3.1, is an extremely popular HTML tool. It is available in the 3.1, 95, 98, 2000 versions of Windows and 3.51 and 4.0 Windows NT.

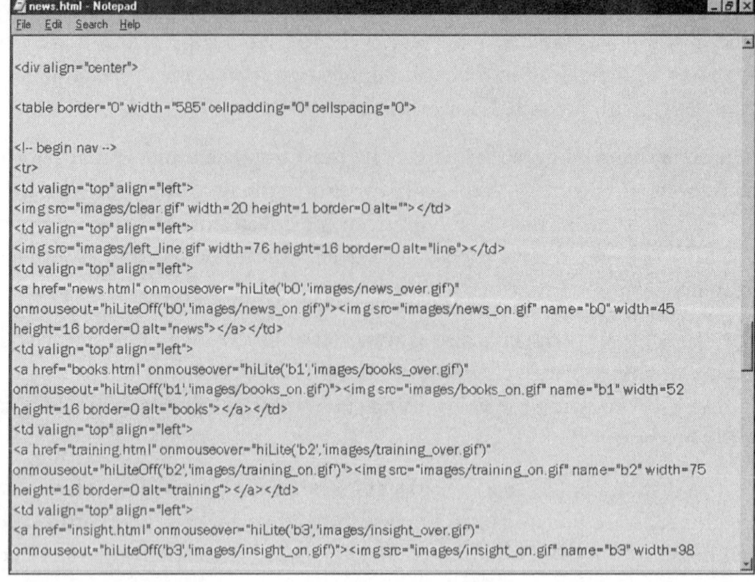

Figure 3.1
Windows Notepad requires the coder to enter every tag manually and provides no special features for color-coding or other special helps.

TEXT EDITORS FOR MACINTOSH AND UNIX

In contrast, Macintosh fans use SimpleText as their editorlike SimpleText because it allows you to color-code your text editing, giving you reference points for your tags, as shown in Figure 3.2.

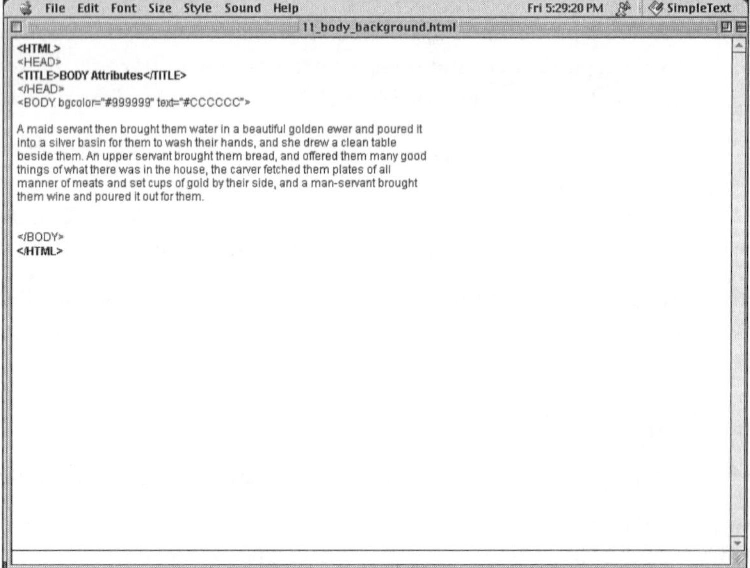

Figure 3.2
Macintosh's SimpleText provides the color coding capabilities, which can help make coding more efficient and debugging a little quicker.

Many coders are working on UNIX servers and require easy access to line-based HTML editors. Three such editors that are recommended by coders include

- **vi**—This UNIX and Linux text editor is extremely popular among hard-core coders from the "old school" of HTML coding.
- **Pico**—This basic, no-frills text editor can be used for generating HTML.
- **Emacs**—Another popular editor used on the UNIX platform (it's also prevalent among VMS users). It's more complicated than vi or Pico, so much so that it comes with an online psychologist "Meta-X-Doctor" to help you endure the psychological problems you will face while using it. It is considered to be very powerful, and many programmers prefer it to other options.

Although you must weigh all the advantages and disadvantages of HTML coding approaches and make decisions based on your needs, there simply *is* no substitute for knowing HTML well. If you are running a professional design company, or have sophisticated HTML requirements, having someone on your staff who is proficient with code—no matter what approach you ultimately select for your needs—is going to be a very valuable resource.

Looking to improve the spelling of your HTML documents? See "Spell Checking Documents" in the Troubleshooting section at the end of this chapter.

HTML Editing Environments

An HTML editing environment is the middle ground between the hard-core text editor and the WYSIWYG application. All the advantages that come with text editing are available to those of you who choose editing environments, and the disadvantages are addressed.

Editing environments typically use a graphical user interface (GUI), so there are a lot of intuitive, familiar options available on the toolbar as well as numerous power tools. It's good to think of the editing environment as a text editor with enhancements.

I personally rely on HTML editing environments when doing the bulk of my code work. The reason is that it affords me all the control and creativity of a text editor, but speeds up the process by providing tools such as online help, quick tag interfaces, and spell-checking.

If your HTML skills are strong, and you're looking for an application that will help you work more effectively, an HTML editing environment might suit you well. To help determine if this is true, consider some of the features of this popular coding approach.

Advantages of HTML Editing Environments

The HTML editing environment of my choice offers templates, toolbars that automatically insert specific tags, and an image wizard that automatically inserts the size of my images as well as providing me with a full range of alternative text options. This places value-added services right at my fingers—whether by mouse click or keyboard shortcut, I get what I need done, and done fast.

→ For more information on adding images to HTML documents, **see** "Working with Images," **p. 195**

A common problem on the Web is that people forget that spell-checking is a critical part of the site development process. Well written, properly spelled language is extremely important if you want to maximize site success. Spell-checking is available in most HTML editing environments, and I know you'll appreciate this option as much as I do.

Another advantage is that most editing environments come with a syntax checker. This helpful tool examines your code, helping you troubleshoot problems, and fixes any unsightly errors.

Although the SimpleText editor on the Macintosh allows you to color code your work, text options for DOS, Windows, and UNIX do not. This problem is solved with the HTML editing environment. Tag colorization is very effective in terms of making tags quickly identifiable. You can color all your image tags yellow, for example, and your table tags blue. This will help you find information quickly, particularly within very complex pages of code.

By far, my favorite tool in the HTML editing environment is the multi-file search and replace. This feature allows you to search documents for specific code strings and replace them with a new string. You can update hundreds of pages with this feature. Imagine having to use a text editor to do this task—it could take you days, even weeks! The editing environment addresses this need quickly and efficiently.

In terms of the pocketbook, HTML editing environments are affordable, running between $50.00 to $200.00 each.

HTML EDITING ENVIRONMENT APPLICATIONS

Users of Windows are in luck—there are several excellent HTML editing environments available.

My favorite is Allaire HomeSite. It has all the features I've mentioned, and its interface can be customized to your tastes (see Figures 3.3 and 3.4).

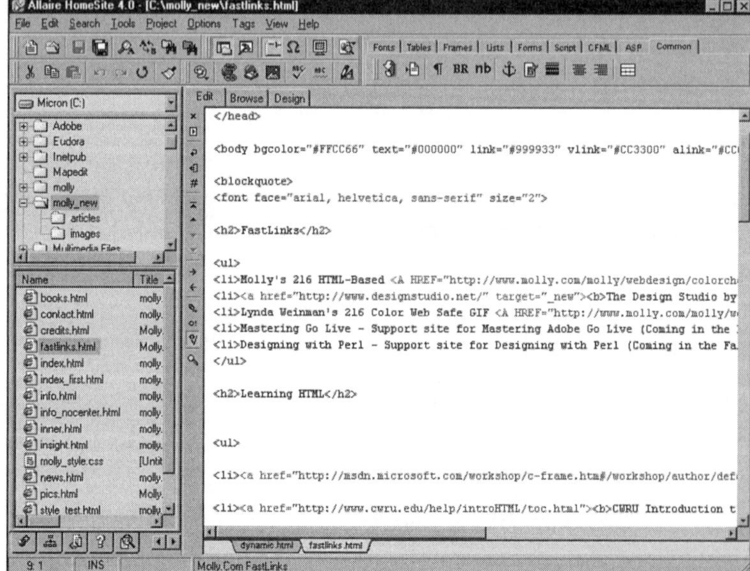

Figure 3.3
Allaire's HomeSite standard view offers the hand coder with many useful features including access to all available toolbars and a powerful file management system.

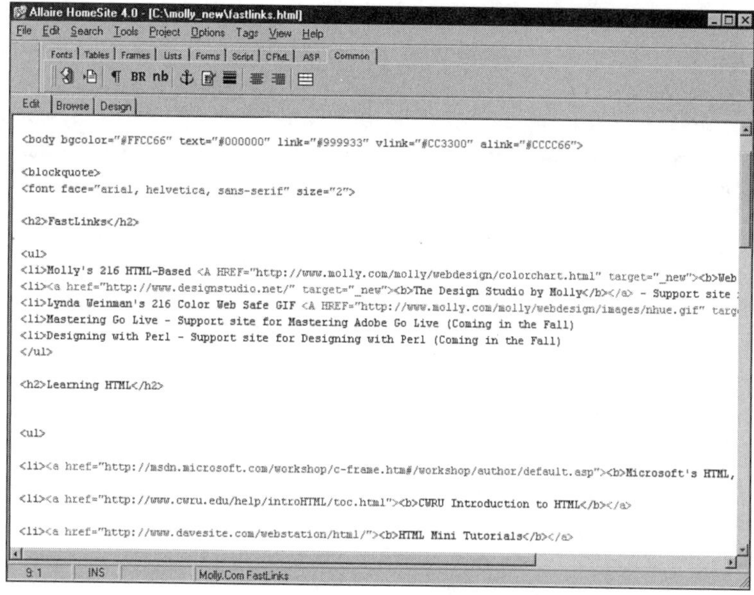

Figure 3.4 Allaire's HomeSite, pared down into my preferred custom view, provides immediate access to the tools and options that I want at my fingertips.

I sometimes use HotDog Pro from Sausage software (see Figure 3.5). The interface isn't as user-friendly as HomeSite's, still, I highly recommend this editor. I encourage you to download it and try it for yourself.

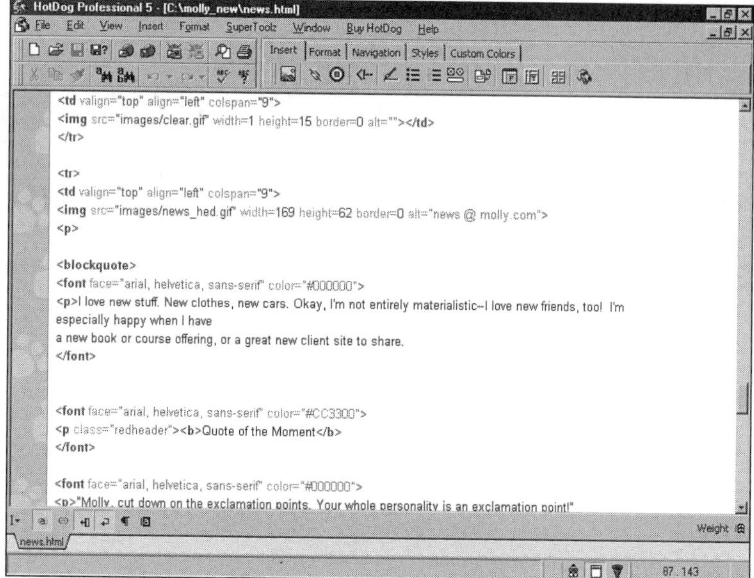

Figure 3.5 Coding with HotDog Pro provides the hand coder with many useful tools to get the job done.

Although there are many Macintosh editing environments, I only have three favorites. BBEdit (see Figure 3.6) from Bare Bones Software is probably the more popular of my recommendations. It is really a plain text editor with some extensions added to bump it up into the editing environment class. Web Weaver (see Figure 3.7) is a fine editing environment, and I use it as an editing environment example when I teach web design on the Macintosh platform. Another favorite is PageSpinner, which has quite the cult following (see Figure 3.8).

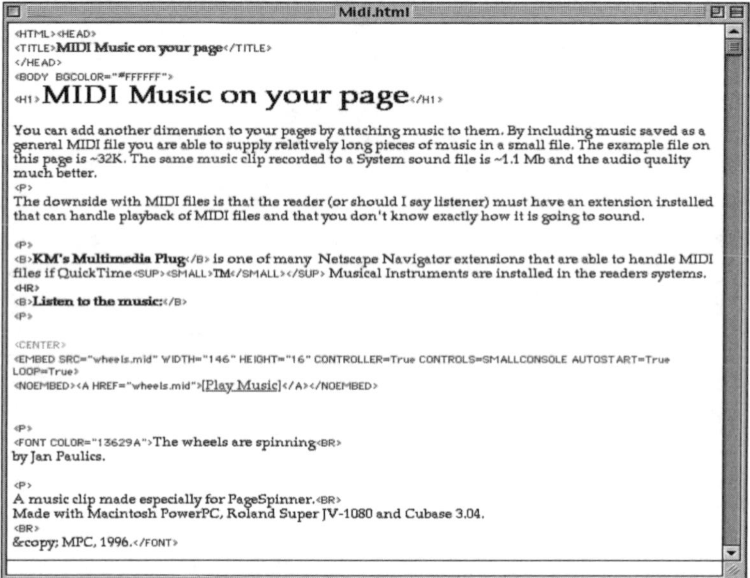

Figure 3.6
Editing an HTML page in BBEdit.

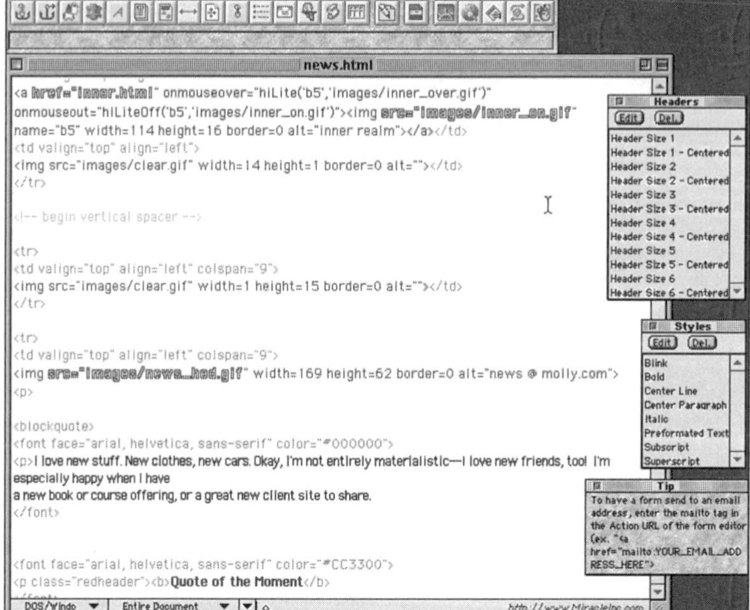

Figure 3.7
Working with Web Weaver. Note the floating palettes, which provide easy access to headers and styles, as well as tips to help you through the coding process.

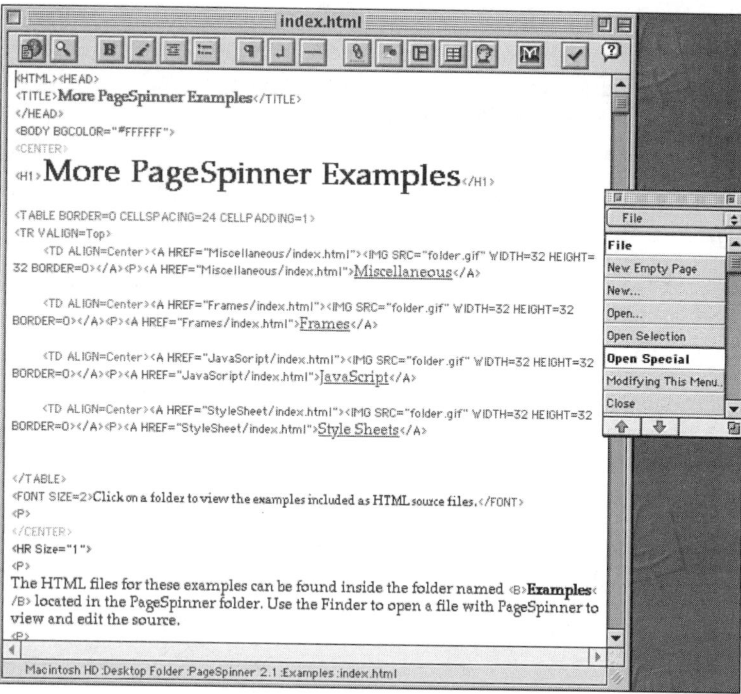

Figure 3.8
Spinning pages with PageSpinner. The simple interface makes this an extremely popular editor for Macintosh fans.

Where to Find HTML Editing Environments

Download demos of software previously mentioned from these Web sites:

Allaire's HomeSite: `http://www.allaire.com/products/homesite/`

HotDog Pro: `http://www.sausage.com/`

HTML Assistant Pro: `http://www.brooknorth.com/`

BBEdit: `http://www.barebones.com/products/products.html`

WebWeaver: `http://www.miracleinc.com/`

PageSpinner: `http://www.optima-system.com/pagespinner/`

Emacs Add-In: `http://www.tnt.uni-hannover.de/~muenkel/software/own/hm--html-menus/overview.html`

For those of you out there using UNIX or Linux, there is one popular editing environment option available. Emacs, described earlier, has an add-on package that provides an HTML mode to the editor. This emulates an editing environment by providing you with a variety of power tools.

HTML Conversion Utilities

If you have a lot of documents to process, and aren't highly concerned about the consistency and quality of your HTML code, an HTML conversion utility might be in order.

HTML conversion utilities are software applications that stand alone or are integrated within another application. For example, a word processor might offer a Save As option for HTML. When you invoke this option, the document you've created will be converted to and saved as an HTML document.

The advantages to this process are obvious. You don't need to learn HTML to have a document processed as HTML, and it's the utility—not you—that has to take the time and code the page.

Sadly, however, what you trim off of the HTML learning curve and coding time issues, you pay for heavily in the type of code that is generated. Typically, conversion utilities create what I call "fat code."

Fat code is filled with unnecessary tags and information. Fat code also tends to be illogical and messy. Let's take a comparative look at a short passage of code generated by an HTML conversion utility, and the same code as I would create it.

Listing 3.1 shows the code from the conversion utility. The one I used is Word 97's integrated application, and I converted a selection from this chapter.

LISTING 3.1 CODE PREPARED BY A CONVERSION UTILITY

```
<HTML>
<HEAD>
<META HTTP-EQUIV="Content-Type" CONTENT="text/html; charset=windows-1252">
<META NAME="Generator" CONTENT="Microsoft Word 97">
<TITLE>Fat Code</TITLE>
</HEAD>
<BODY>

<P>Fat code is filled with unnecessary tags and information. Fat code also tends
to be illogical and messy. Let's take a comparative look at a short passage of
code generated by an HTML conversion utility, and the same code as I would
create it. </P>

<P>Here's the code from the conversion utility. The one I used is Word 8.0's
integrated application:</P>

<B><I><P>***List 3.1***</P>
<P>Code Prepared by a Conversion Utility</P>

<P>***End List***</P>
</I>
</B><P>And here's the same code as I would create it by hand. Note the
cleanliness, and take a look at how "slim," or free of extraneous tags,
my code is:</P>

<OL START=3 TYPE="a">

<B><LI>Summary</LI></OL>

</B><P> </P>
<P> </P></FONT></BODY>
</HTML>
```

Listing 3.2 shows the same code as I would create it by hand. Note the cleanliness, simplicity, and take a look at how "slim," or free of extraneous tags, my code is.

LISTING 3.2 THE SAME CODE DONE BY HAND

```
<HTML>
<HEAD>
<TITLE>Fat Code</TITLE>
</HEAD>
<BODY>

<P>Fat code is filled with unnecessary tags and information. Fat code also tends
to
be illogical and messy. Let's take a comparative look at a short passage of code
generated by an HTML conversion utility, and the same code as I would create it.

<P>Here's the code from the conversion utility. The one I used is Word 97's
integrated application:

<P><B><I>***List 3.1***
<P>Code Prepared by a Conversion Utility
<BR>
<BR>

***End List***</b></i>
<P>And here's the same code as I would create it by hand. Note the cleanliness,
and take a look at how "slim," or free of extraneous tags, my code is:

<P><b><OL><LI>Summary</OL></b>

<BODY>
</HTML>
```

Now, compare the following two screen shots of the output in Figures 3.9 and 3.10. Notice that there *is no visual difference* in the results, but there sure is a difference in the way the code is written.

Why Should You Care?

So if the output of HTML looks the same, why should you care about the way the code looks? There are several important reasons including:

- Superfluous code can translate to extra page weight.
- If you want to open the code and add something, or change it, finding your way around may be difficult.
- Conversion utilities typically write very poor code, potentially rendering HTML pages useless in certain browsers.
- Professionals should aim to adhere to some conventions, if not the standards themselves. This is an issue of quality control: conversion utilities cannot replace a savvy coder's ability to ensure that the code is compliant, neat, and human-readable.

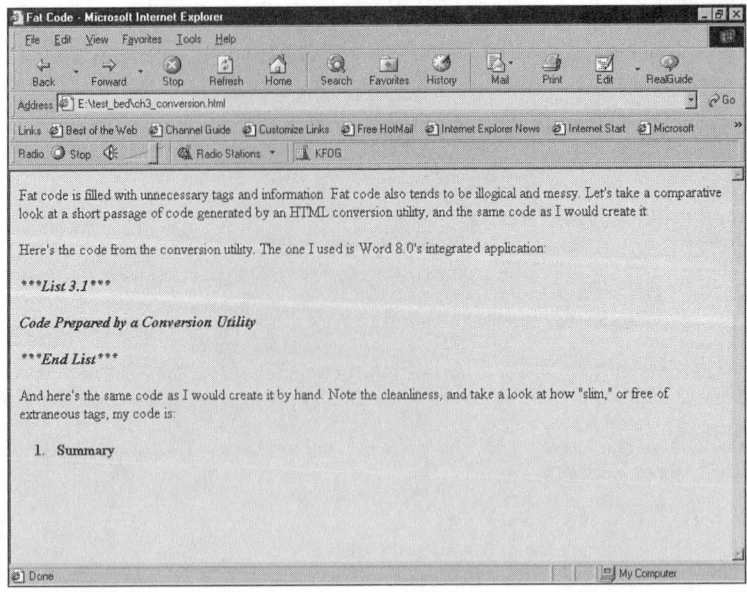

Figure 3.9
Screen shot of HTML converted from a Word 97 document as seen in Internet Explorer 5.0.

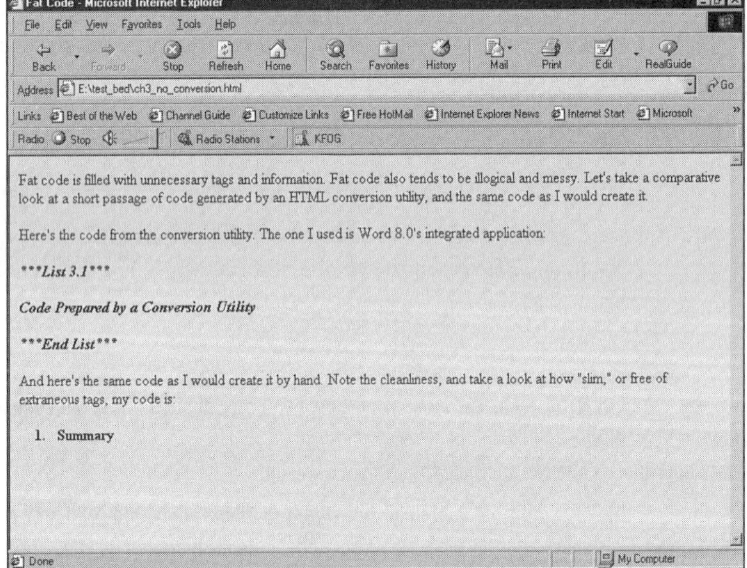

Figure 3.10
Screen shot of hand-coded HTML.

Another problem with conversion utilities is that they usually cannot properly manage graphics, multimedia applications, or specialty coding such as JavaScript or other programming-oriented functions. These utilities are best for text documents or documents created from their primary applications, such as Microsoft Word or Excel.

Because of their speed, conversion utilities are certainly good resources to have on hand. However, if you're working in a professional situation, you're going to have to ask your HTML expert to sweep up some of the code mess conversion utilities create and add your graphics and code by hand anyway. Otherwise, you risk having your documents be text-based, technically problematic, and unprofessional in appearance.

Note

It's important to point out that many of the editing environments mentioned in this chapter have HTML conversion utilities integrated into the interface. The level of sophistication in some of these utilities is a bit better in less HTML-specific programs. Check to see if your editing environment offers this option. And, if you like the code it generates, you've found an excellent method of quickly converting text documents to HTML.

Popular Conversion Applications

Windows-based conversion was originally available via Microsoft's Internet Assistant. This utility integrated word processing, Web browsing, and Web document creation. Its understanding of HTML was very limited and development stopped in 1995, being replaced in concept by Microsoft's popular WYSIWYG application, FrontPage.

Internet Assistant conversion capabilities, however, are still included within Microsoft applications. The conversion software now exists in all major products within the Microsoft Office 2000 suite. I've known some savvy Web developers who have tapped into the power of macros and created extensive, customized add-ins to the utility, cleaning up code problems and automating conversion processes.

The same conversion utilities are available for Microsoft applications on the Macintosh platform.

A set of HTML conversion utilities for Word documents, called The Ant, is used enthusiastically by some coders. The Ant is available in both Windows and Macintosh flavors. The Ant provides support for tables and a utility for forms, and it can also manage batch processing.

Interleaf is a code conversion program that supports a variety of word processing and publication applications. Included in that list are Microsoft Word, WordPerfect, and FrameMaker.

Tip from

Use these Web addresses to check out some popular conversion utilities:

Microsoft Internet Assistant: `http://support.microsoft.com/support/kb/articles/Q153/8/60.asp`

The Ant: `http://telacommunications.com/ant/`

Interleaf: `http://www.interleaf.com/`

WHAT-YOU-SEE-IS-WHAT-YOU-GET (WYSIWYG) APPLICATIONS

Relying on a graphical interface to effectively relate with users, WYSIWYG is popular not only because of its low learning curve, but because of its easy portability from user to user. This is especially important for companies who have a lot of individuals working on HTML code—a WYSIWYG application will help keep coding styles consistent.

Another advantage is that WYSIWYG applications allow you to design a Web page without *ever* learning HTML. In the graphical interface, a user will place the graphics and text he or she requires, and then manipulate them until he or she finds the most satisfying look. The software, then, is responsible for generating the code.

Certain WYSIWYGs, such as Microsoft's FrontPage, are very powerful beyond the scope of design: they have extensions that allow for project management and specialty applications, such as search and forms support. These features make the WYSIWYG option attractive for many people.

Although I totally understand the reasons why WYSIWYG software is such a popular choice, I also find most WYSIWYGs to be extremely problematic, for a number of reasons.

The first of those reasons has to do with control. HTML allows authors precious little control, and certainly, while the 4.0 standard offers technologies that solve many of these control issues, the real-world employment of these technologies is still limited. This means that a coder relies on the relationship of HTML to his or her entire design. It is an integrated process—one that is best determined by experience, which a software application simply cannot match.

Whether it's choosing percentages over pixels in a given instance, or wanting to adjust a selection of code to your own tastes, WYSIWYGs typically do not give you that option, or if they do give you that option, you may be unaware of why you should be making a specific choice.

Note

Many WYSIWYG programs—especially older versions of FrontPage—change or modify code that you write in the HTML interfaces of the program in question.

You've already been introduced to the concept of fat code, and WYSIWYGs are equally a culprit in this problem. Although you have more control over customizing WYSIWYGs to suit your tastes, the application does the coding—not you. This means, ultimately, that the code is going to reflect the style of the application and not the coder. Listing 3.3 shows code generated by the WYSIWYG application, Adobe GoLive. Listing 3.4 shows code I generated with HTML.

LISTING 3.3 CODE FROM GOLIVE

```
<HTML>

<HEAD>
<META http-equiv="content-type" content="text/html;charset=iso-8859-1">
<META name="generator" content="Adobe GoLive 4">
```

```
<TITLE>Home Page</TITLE>
</HEAD>

<BODY>
        <TABLE cool width="586" height="586" border="0" cellpadding="0"
cellspacing="0" gridx="16" showgridx usegridx gridy="16" showgridy usegridy>
<TR height="1" cntrlrow>
<TD width="1" height="1"></TD>
<TD width="585" height="1"><SPACER type="block" width="585" height="1"></TD>
</TR>
<TR height="585">
<TD width="1" height="585"><SPACER type="block" width="1" height="585"></TD>
<TD width="585" height="585" colspan="1" rowspan="1" valign="top" align="left"
xpos="0" content csheight="176">Whether it's choosing percentages over pixels in a
given instance, or wanting to adjust a selection of code to your own tastes,
WYSIWYGs typically do not give you that option. sure, you can go in and change the
information and save the file, but open it again and your code will have been
altered by the application! <P>You've already been introduced to the concept of
&quot;Fat Code,&quot; and WYSIWYGs are equally a culprit in this problem. while
you have more control over customizing WYSIWYGs to suit your tastes, the
application does the coding, not you. this means that ultimately, the code is
going to reflect the style of the application, and not the coder.
</TD>
</TR>
</TABLE>
</BODY>

</HTML>
```


LISTING 3.4 CODE AS I'VE CODED IT

```
<HTML>

<HEAD>

<TITLE>Home Page</TITLE>

</HEAD>
<BODY>

<P>Whether it's choosing percentages over pixels in a given instance, or wanting
to adjust a selection of code to your own tastes, WYSIWYGs typically do not give
you that option. sure, you can go in and change the information and save the
file, but open it again and your code will have been altered by the application!

<P>You've already been introduced to the concept of "Fat Code," and WYSIWYGs are
equally a culprit in this problem. while you have more control over customizing
WYSIWYGs to suit your tastes, the application does the coding, not you. this
means that ultimately, the code is going to reflect the style of the application,
and not the coder.

</BODY>
</HTML>
```

You'll note that I used no tables, I just used simple HTML. Furthermore, I used no extra graphics, such as a spacer graphic to achieve the end result. This demonstrates how a coder who *knows the code* can make much more sophisticated decisions about how to work with a given page.

In Figure 3.11, you see the results of the WYSIWYG's code. Notice the unsightly horizontal scrollbar. Certainly, a skilled designer would fix this problem, but what of the novice who isn't familiar with HTML? He or she is going to have output that lacks professional appeal.

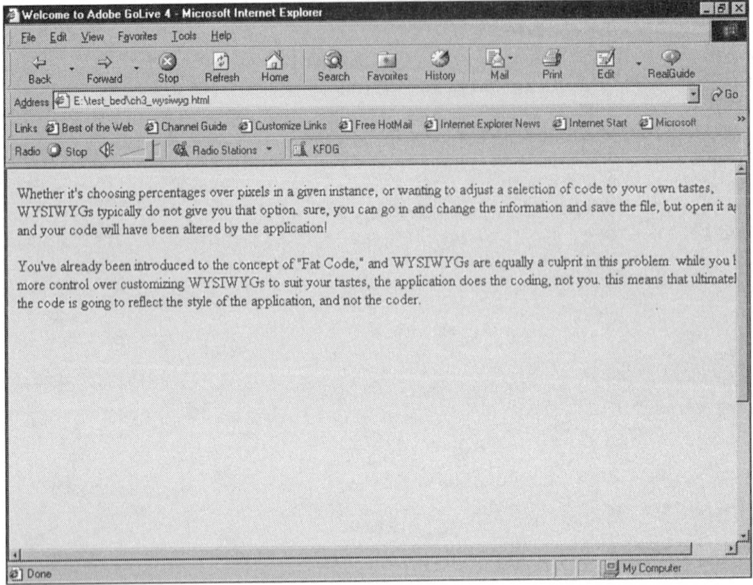

Figure 3.11
Viewing the WYSIWYG code results as created using GoLive.

Figure 3.12 shows the results of my code. Not only do I have very similar results, but I've also avoided the annoying scrollbar problem. I've been able to do this because I *know the code*, but what's more—I've done it using significantly less and supremely more logical code.

Note

The code problems demonstrated here reflect my bias toward clean code with maximum control for the HTML coder and Web designer. This example should serve to help you understand the issues that arise when working with WYSIWYGs, not to dissuade you from their use. Adobe GoLive, and other similar WYSIWYG products, have tremendous advantageous including great layout environments, a variety of preset styles, built-in graphic optimization, and an array of other power features that make them all worthy of consideration.

Another problem with WYSIWYG applications is that they are limited by release dates. HTML is a growing, dynamic language, as I established in Chapter 1, "Understanding HTML 4.0." Software applications can logically only produce software updates at certain intervals, usually determined by fiscal concerns rather than customer demand.

Figure 3.12
The hand-created code results produce the same output but with cleaner code.

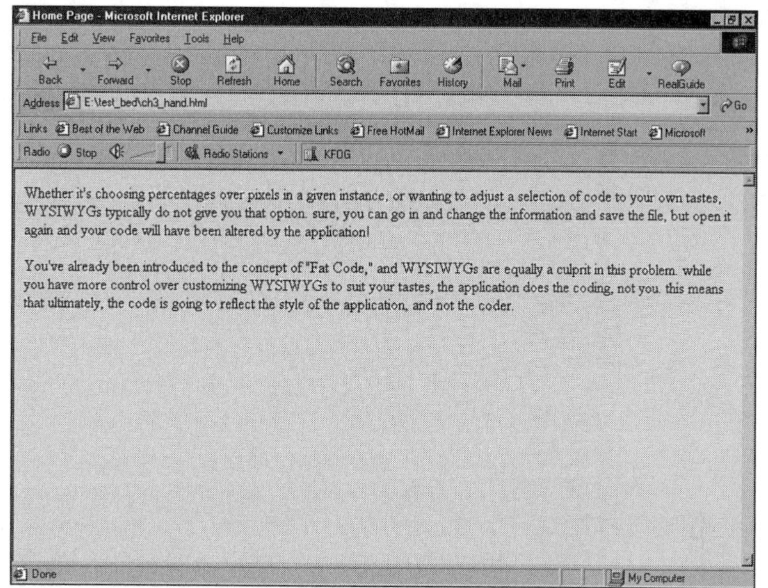

So, certain tags or updated techniques that you might like to use might not be available until an upcoming software version. Try to add the tag or technique anyway, and your current software version might override code it doesn't recognize, removing it from your work. This makes it difficult to update, alter, or effectively troubleshoot problems in the WYSIWYG environment.

To be fair, many companies accommodate this issue by offering patches and updates via the Web, but the bottom line is that the software package you bought last year is probably not going to have the sophistication you may require today—a serious disadvantage that you need to consider before investing in a software application that might not suit your needs.

POPULAR WYSIWYGS

Despite the problems with WYSIWYGs, the needs of individuals and companies interested in a quick, portable solution for HTML generation are undeniably met by WYSIWYGs.

Some of the more popular WYSIWYG applications include Microsoft's FrontPage (see Figure 3.13), which is available on both the Windows and Macintosh platforms. This prevalent program is used by hobbyists and professionals alike, and, as I've mentioned, there are many extended features that make the product well worth a serious test-drive. Improvements to the software in the 2000 version including the fact that it does not rewrite a coder's HTML to its own specifications, and an improved interface have greatly facilitates the software's usability, and I can confidently say that many individuals use the product with a great deal of satisfaction.

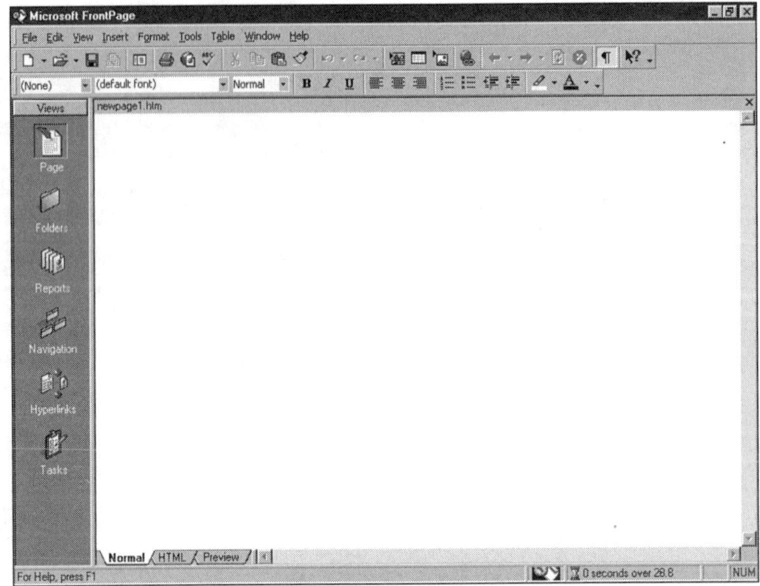

Figure 3.13
Microsoft's FrontPage WYSIWYG in the current 2000 version does offer many powerful features that help extend your Web site functionality.

Adobe fans might lean toward Adobe's WYSIWYG software, GoLive (see Figure 3.14), now available for the Windows 98 and Mac platforms. GoLive has the advantage of being integrated into the Adobe suite of design software, making it a strong contender in the design marketplace.

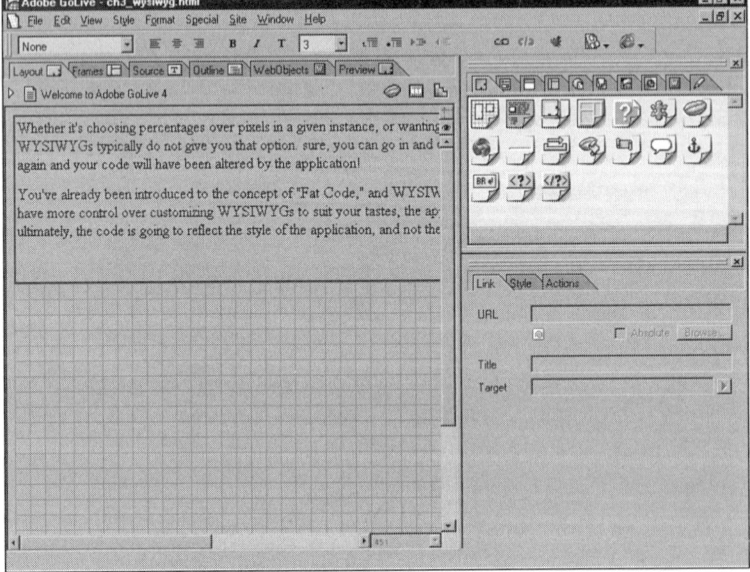

Figure 3.14
Adobe GoLive is growing in popularity among Web designers looking for a good WYSIWYG alternative.

Macromedia's DreamWeaver (see Figure 3.15) is an especially impressive product. Of all the WYSIWYG programs, Macromedia's code tends to be the cleanest. This product was created with the designer in mind—not only is the user interface sensible, the WYSIWYG editor comes packaged with an editing environment so that you can make adjustments as you see fit.

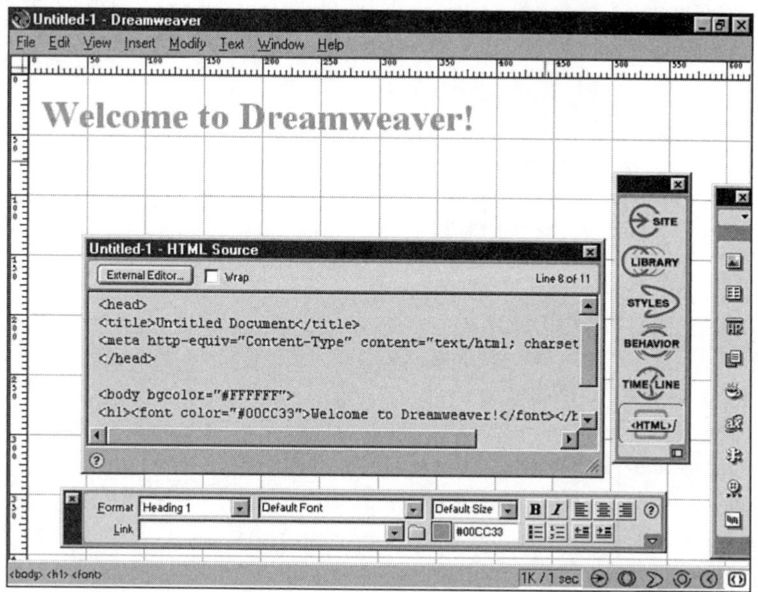

Figure 3.15 Macromedia's DreamWeaver uses panels and inspectors to provide the Web designer with a wide variety of tools and options.

Macromedia offers BBEdit as the companion editing environment for the Mac, and for Windows, Allaire's HomeSite is the environment of choice. This approach is extremely considerate because the HTML coder is given *options*. Furthermore, after a file that you have altered is reloaded into the WYSIWYG, no alterations to the code are made.

A variety of other WYSIWYG editors, such as NetObjects Fusion and Softquad's HotMetal Pro are also used across platforms by a portion of dedicated professionals.

If you want a fast solution for HTML concerns, see "Need Your Site Yesterday?" in the Troubleshooting section at the end of this chapter.

UNIX users have many choices, as quite a few of the previously mentioned applications have been made available for the UNIX platform. Quadralay's WebWorks Publisher is a specific program that you can combine with FrameMaker for a full HTML WYSIWYG package for UNIX.

Available WYSIWYG Software Applications

Microsoft FrontPage: `http://www.microsoft.com/frontpage/`

NetObjects Fusion: `http://www.netobjects.com/`

Softquad HotMetal Pro: `http://www.sq.com/`

Qudralay's WebWorks: `http://www.quadralay.com/`

AdobeGoLive: `http://www.adobe.com/prodindex/golive/main.html`

Macromedia DreamWeaver: `http://www.macromedia.com/software/dreamweaver.html`

One thing that becomes obvious when working with these software applications is that what you see is decidedly *not* always what you get. The ultimate decision is to weigh the pros and cons, test them against your personal needs, and see what pans out. An easy decision? No. But an important one that will help you save time, money, and countless hours of frustration.

TROUBLESHOOTING

SPELL CHECKING DOCUMENTS

I am very happy coding my HTML in an ASCII or plain text editor. But, I want to be able to spell check documents. How can I do it?

One way to check the spelling in your documents is to view the page in a browser, and then copy and paste the text into a Word processor that has spell checking. This is a bit of an awkward and time consuming process, but it works. You might also consider using an HTML editor with built-in spell checking. This way, you get the best of the ASCII world with the best HTML tools available. And, you can customize most HTML editors so that no extraneous windows or menus are showing—just the tools you want to use as you code.

NEED YOUR SITE YESTERDAY?

I'm just beginning to dig seriously into HTML and I want to learn to code by hand, but also need to be developing sites today. What's the best way to go?

Any WYSIWYG editor worth its salt has an HTML editing environment available alongside the graphic layout workspace. This is true of major players such as Adobe GoLive, Macromedia Dreamweaver, and Microsoft FrontPage 2000. You can use the HTML editors in any of these programs to work on HTML yourself, and the graphic interfaces to generate the pages you need right now.

Do be cautious, however. Some older versions of HTML WYSIWYG programs will alter your HTML code to their own methods after you've made a change. This used to be the case in FrontPage, but the 2000 version offers hands-off coding, allowing you to tinker without any tinkering back! Dreamweaver should be applauded for stepping into the fray and ensuring hands-off coding for its users. Adobe GoLive will leave code that you add to a page alone, but you'll notice a lot of odd, proprietary tags that GoLive uses as a mechanism to create its own layout grids.

DESIGNING FOR THE REAL WORLD

CREATING TEMPLATES FOR SPEED AND ACCURACY

An advanced concern for professionals is how to work with the variety of HTML editors and maximize the speed, accuracy, and consistency between documents. In this section, you'll create a basic template that will help set you up for future HTML exercises. You can also use this template as a starting point for all your HTML pages. I'm also including some helpful information in your quest for solid solutions, including creation of company guidelines and the development of proprietary applications where necessary.

To build the template, follow these steps:

1. Begin by opening your text, HTML, or WYSIWYG editor in HTML mode.
2. Type the template code directly into your editor (as shown in Listing 3.5).

LISTING 3.5 SIMPLE PAGE TEMPLATE

```
<!-- site design by: Molly E. Holzschlag molly@molly.com -->
<!-- http://www.molly.com/ -->
<!-- page last updates: *add date here* -->

<HTML>

<!-- Begin Head Information -->

<HEAD>

<TITLE>place_title_here</TITLE>
</HEAD>

<!-- Begin Body (add <p> after each individual paragraph -->
<BODY>


<!-- Begin Footer Information (copyright, mailto, etc) -->


</BODY>
</HTML>
```

3. Modify the code to match your own custom needs. For example, add your own name in place of mine, and your URL and contact information.
4. Save the file as template.html to a directory or folder where you keep frequently used files.

Templates can be of great assistance to you and your co-workers. Naturally, they will become more complex as your sites evolve. Sometimes I create a template for an individual site, and use it for only that site. Another approach would be to set up templates for different types of sites: framed sites, left-margin table sites, standard pages, and so on.

These templates can then act as guidelines for the company standards you want to remain consistent no matter the type of site being constructed.

COMPANY GUIDELINES AND CHECKLISTS

Help new members of your company become accustomed to your style by first defining what that style is and then developing a style guide and companion checklist. Hobbyists or individuals will appreciate such a guide too because it will help keep them on track when a style question arises.

Let's say I want all the HTML in my company to use the single `<p>` paragraph style, as opposed to the open/close style. I would put this in my guide, along with an example of its use. I could also create a checklist that employees can use to make sure they've followed the guidelines effectively.

PROPRIETARY APPLICATIONS

In many advanced environments, the requirements of the day-to-day management of Web sites becomes very complex. Think about a daily newspaper, for example. That's a lot of content to prepare effectively and continuously if you're working by hand. It becomes obvious that although you'll require knowledge of HTML hand-coding to troubleshoot and solve problems, the task of publishing that much content on a daily basis screams "automate!"

In these cases, it's wise to investigate available software that might exist in your specialty niche. If you're having trouble finding such software, or you are not satisfied with what's available, you might consider working with a qualified analyst and programmer who can help create a proprietary management tool for your needs. This approach is often the best, most professional solution for today's aggressive and varied site needs.

Tip from molly

Looking for a qualified programmer to help you determine your software needs? There are many online databases that can help employers find the qualified individuals they need. Visit `http://www.jobengine.com/` and `http://www.jobs-online.net/`. There are plenty of other databases, so a visit to your favorite search engine for a list of high-tech resumes online will help expand your options.

No matter the toolkit you ultimately end up with, understanding the pros and cons of the available types of tools will help you customize that toolkit to your personal needs. Whether your desire is to use this book to learn HTML, or to have a comprehensive, desktop reference for available tools and materials, you end up ahead by knowing how to approach the job at hand.

CHAPTER 4

Managing HTML Documents Locally

In this chapter

THE IMPORTANCE OF FILE MANAGEMENT

While this subject may seem quite basic to the intermediate reader, the reality is that significant problems arise when files are named improperly. The reason this is such a common occurrence is that many computer professionals are accustomed to working on one primary platform. For example, the designers among you will likely be most familiar with Macintosh computers, die-hard programmers and system administrators with Unix and Linux, and IT professionals with Windows NT and Windows-related software. Hobbyists will also typically fall into the Mac or Windows camps.

Files are managed differently on each platform. However, in order for files to be correctly rendered in a browser or located properly on a Web server, those files—and the directories in which they reside—must adhere to specific rules in order to be readable across all platforms. This chapter will review some file basics, and provide you with tips that will help reduce problems arising from cross-platform naming differences.

There are a wide variety of file types, but only a few are of immediate concern to people working with HTML. Most of these files relate either to the HTML information itself, graphic files, specialty programming, or multimedia files. I won't go over all the extensions here, but I've provided several notes with Web addresses that will enable you to explore this issue at greater length.

One of the difficulties I see time and again is that students of HTML run into problems because of faulty file management. This chapter is intended to provide you with some simple and effective guidelines for managing your local files. I'll step away from discussion of standards or specific HTML 4.0 issues—the information in this chapter will help you no matter what level of HTML you're working with. Topics covered include how to name your files, structure your file directories, save files, and address troubleshooting concerns.

NAMING CONVENTIONS

This is by far the biggest stumbling block for HTML students. One of the main culprits is that people who come from a UNIX or Macintosh background, or who started using home computers with the release of Windows 95, are accustomed to using long filenames. These naming structures allow you to call a file just about anything you want—with no specific concern as to length, logic, or consistent relationship between a prefix and suffix (also referred to as *extension*).

The primary problems with naming are

- **Improperly formed filenames**—To allow for global access, filenames must adhere to specific naming formats.
- **Unclear filenames**—Filenames get confusing if you don't create a system that clearly identifies, at least to you, what each file contains.
- **Names that are too long**—There's already enough length to many URLs—don't add to the problem by naming your file with an unreasonably long filename.

- **Names with no or improper prefixes and suffixes**—If you don't use the proper prefix and suffix locally, how will it work on the Internet itself? Get used to the available suffixes and use them.

Unable to bring your site up once you've posted it to the Web? You may have incorrectly named your default file, see "Setting the Default Page" in the Troubleshooting section at the end of this chapter.

IMPROPERLY FORMED FILENAMES

To avoid problems with badly formed names, follow these simple rules:

- **Don't use spaces**—Even if you're used to doing this on your Mac, you'll have trouble testing your files locally and running them on the Internet if you have a space in the name. In place of spaces, you can use underscores or dashes.
- **Don't use any extraneous characters**—Stick to letters, numbers, underscores, and dashes. Especially troublesome characters include apostrophes (as in "molly'swebsite"), dollar signs, percent signs, pound signs, parenthesis, and so on.
- **Put the period in the right place**—Similarly, you must avoid using a period, or "dot" in any position other than between the prefix and suffix of a filename.
- **Name your files in all lowercase**—Even though at this point you're working locally and this won't trouble your individual computer, it's a good practice to get into early. Many Unix servers still perceive filenames by case, meaning that index.html, INDEX.html, and IndEX.html are three different files! You'll avoid many a future headache by following this simple guideline.

UNCLEAR FILENAMES

One of the best ways to stay organized is to give your files understandable names. This becomes especially important when you begin managing many HTML files in a single project.

You can always assign a project a two or three-letter code, and then give the filename a logical identifier. This is something I've gotten in the habit of doing on larger sites. For smaller sites, I stick to simple names.

The following is a series of filenames from my personal Web site:

index.html
new.html
books.html
bio.html
resume.html
contact.html

If I were going to have many, many files on that site, I might consider giving it a code, such as mh, for Molly Holzschlag. Then I would follow this up with a logical name and perhaps a numeric value to indicate a date or portion of a series.

index.html
mh_new.html
mh_books.html
mh_bio.html
mh_resume.html
mh_contact.html
mh_article1.html
mh_article2.html
mh_daily_1100.html

The important issue, as is so often the case in coding, is to *be consistent*. Pick a style that works for you and stick to it. You'll be happy that you did!

FILENAME LENGTH

Have you ever come across a URL so long that you couldn't copy it to send to a friend—even though the information at that location was really something to write about?

Avoid adding to the often lengthy naming process on the Web by working with shorter filenames locally. This sets you up for a longer-term consistency rate with file-naming conventions.

I like to use the old DOS-naming convention as a guide. DOS allows for a maximum of eight characters in the prefix. I recommend not exceeding the eight-character rule too much, or you start getting into filenames that are going to be too long.

Of course, DOS limits the suffix to three characters, which doesn't carry conceptually over to the Internet structure itself. A bit more about this later when I discuss suffixes.

A good rule of thumb with filename length is to make the name sensible and logical without exceeding much more than eight characters in the prefix. Ten characters would be perfectly acceptable, twenty characters would not.

Caution

Mac users need to understand the filename and length structure as much, if not more, than any computer user. The reason is that filenames exceeding these guidelines risk getting truncated, rendering the file unreadable by a browser.

CORRECT PREFIX AND SUFFIX NAMES

The only time a prefix name is going to matter is when a file goes live on the Internet. Locally, you can start with any name. However, plan ahead and find out what prefix your server will allow you to use for the first default page. Name that file accordingly, and you'll be prepared when the time comes to upload your pages.

The following are a few possible prefix choices:

index.html

default.html

welcome.html

Once again, certain operating systems have contributed to bad filenaming habits. On the Macintosh, you're not required to put a suffix onto a filename. Will your file run? Not when you're trying to link to it—even local, poorly managed files will choke.

For standard HTML files, two primary options exist for the suffix: .html and .htm.

To find out which one you should use, do a bit of study regarding where you will ultimately place your work on the Internet. If your server requires .html as a suffix, that's what you should use. The .htm suffix is a carry-over from the three-letter suffix convention, and is found on Windows-based servers.

In most cases, you can use either one. As always, follow the consistency rule and choose one when the option is available. Never mix the two within a site—that spells trouble.

You'll run into a few other HTML-related extensions, but that won't affect you when working locally. Most of these extensions are related to server-sided includes or backend processes such as CGI and Perl, as well as Active Server Pages (ASP). They include variants such as:

.htmlx

.shtml

.pl

.asp

.cgi

Graphic files must be named properly at all times. For GIFs, always use the .gif extension, and for JPEGs, the .jpg (NOT .jpeg) extension.

➔ Unfamiliar with CGI? **See** "CGI and Perl Fundamentals," **p. 736**

A variety of other file types can be incorporated into your HTML structure. Their suffixes vary depending upon the file type. When in doubt, consult the documentation for the suffix information, or check with the system administrator who manages the server on which your local documents will eventually be placed.

Note

> Looking for filename information? Here are a few sites to help you out.
>
> A great resource is available at **`http://www.whatis.com/`**. Follow the link to "Every File Format in the World" and, sure enough, you'll have every file format with its proper extension available to you, on demand.

continues

continued

Another Web resource that's helpful with filename extensions can be found at `http://www2.crosswinds.net/san-marino/~jom/filex/extensio.htm`.

One of the most complete lists of extensions and corresponding applications I've ever found can be viewed at `http://www-f.rrz.uni-koeln.de/themen/Graphik/ImageProcessing/fileext.html`.

FILE DIRECTORY STRUCTURE

As you already have noticed, working locally but thinking for the long term is a natural way to avoid problems. In terms of directory structure, it's good to set up a system that you can use consistently, whether you are managing your documents locally or on a server.

Tip from molly

Think of directories as folders, and vice-versa. Depending on what operating system you're using, they are conceptually one and the same. Use the guidelines set out earlier for filenames for naming directories, helping you to avoid problems with naming that arise across platforms.

You can legally place all the files for a site into one directory. This is fine if you have only a few pages and graphics files. But when you start working with larger sites containing numerous HTML files, countless graphics, and other media, it becomes near to impossible to manage one directory of files.

A conventional bit of wisdom is shared by many HTML designers when managing files. I'm going to follow this wisdom and ask you to follow along as I set up a series of folders to help you manage your data.

1. Create a new folder on your hard drive.
2. Give this folder an identifying name related to the site, such as `webdesign`.
3. Within that folder, create a subfolder.
4. Name that folder images.
5. Place any HTML files in the webdesign folder. This folder is considered your "root."
6. Place any images into the image subfolder.

Figure 4.1 shows the directory structure I just created.

Note

The topmost directory in any given structure is referred to as the *root directory*. Any directory within the root is referred to as a *subdirectory*. A *parent* directory is the directory immediately above any given subdirectory.

Did you know that once your site is "live" on the Web, if you should happen to lose files from your hard drive you can still retrieve them? See, "Lost Files" in the Troubleshooting section at the end of this chapter.

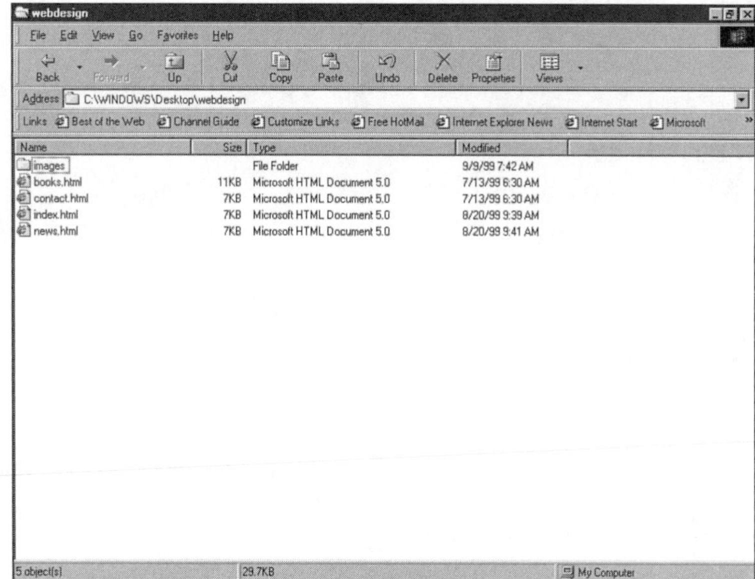

Figure 4.1
A simple but effective directory structure.

You can expand on this idea even further, if necessary. Let's say I want to have a number of subtopics within my primary topic of webdesign. I can break the information up into several subfolders, placing the HTML and other files within the appropriate, corresponding folder. If I want to have an articles subfolder, a scripts subfolder, and a media subfolder, I simply create those folders within the main folder (see Figure 4.2).

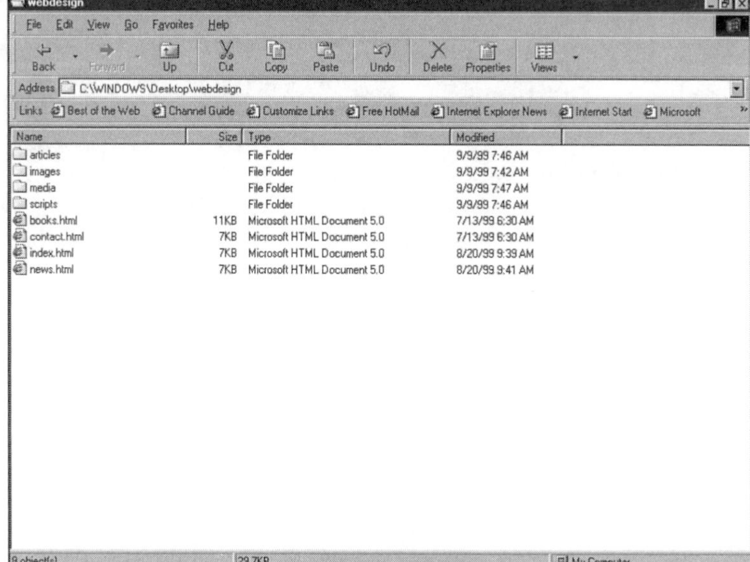

Figure 4.2
Multiple subfolders make large data management easy.

➔ You'll need to follow the appropriate coding method when managing files in subdirectories. For information on how to do this, **see** "Linking Pages," **p. 174**

Saving Files

File management is easy, but it's also dangerous. It's possible to overwrite files, lose data, and save files to the wrong area of your computer. You also can run the risk of saving files improperly.

Follow these tips for general saving and file management:

- **Save your work regularly**—Whenever I begin a new file, I immediately name it properly and save it to the correct location on my drive.
- **Back up your work!**—Whether you make a copy of the file to floppy disk, zip disk, or tape drive is no matter—just make sure you keep a copy! I can't express how many times I've worked for an hour just to lose all of my sweat equity by making a critical mistake when saving the file.
- **Create your directory structure first, and save files to that area**—This way you'll know where your files are, setting up a logical structure upon which to form the linking of pages and page elements to a given HTML document.

If you've got the directory structure and file-naming issues handled, but are working with a team and having trouble knowing who is doing what because files are getting overwritten when different team members make changes, see "Version Control" in the Troubleshooting section at the end of this chapter.

Tip from

Many software programs automatically save (auto-save) data on a regular basis. I have this feature in my HTML editor. If you have such an option, be sure to set it to save files frequently. I usually do an auto-save about every five minutes. This means if I have a crash, I reduce data loss.

Another problem I see quite often has to do with saving files to the wrong format. Let's say you're in Photoshop, and you want to save a file as a JPEG, but you mistakenly select PCX. If you give the file the wrong suffix name, you'll have a corrupt file that's impossible to use.

This problem holds true when saving HTML files and related documents. It's important to remember that HTML is saved in ASCII format. If you save it as a binary file, or you transfer it as a binary file, the file will be corrupt. The same is true with binary formats—you can't try to save or transfer them in ASCII, for example, because you will destroy the file's integrity.

TROUBLESHOOTING

SETTING THE DEFAULT PAGE

I created a Web page, but it doesn't appear when I type in the domain name. What could be the problem?

You may have created your file with a name that is not recognized as a default by your Web server. If you named the file index.html, for example, try renaming it as default.htm. Alternatively, contact your Web service provider and ask for the default naming convention required by their servers.

LOST FILES

My hard disk crashed, and the local copy of the site I was working on is lost. I didn't make a backup. Can I recover lost files?

If your site is already live on the Web, you can recover the files from the server. Simply use your favorite FTP application to download the files. Be sure to preserve the directory structure so you don't wind up with broken links to repair. And be sure to create a backup in the future!

VERSION CONTROL

I am making revisions on a page, but now I want to revert to an earlier version of the page. How can I keep versions without renaming multiple files and constantly updating links?

Version control software will help manage your files. If you work on a development team, this software enables you to lock the other members of the team out of a particular file while you're working on it. You can also easily track revisions and revert to previous versions of a file. Version control software ranges from expensive enterprise-level applications, such as Microsoft Visual SourceSafe, to home-developer applications, such as QVCS, a shareware package available on the Internet.

DESIGNING FOR THE REAL WORLD

SITE MAPPING

If you've been surfing the Web for some time, you've surely come across sites that contain a site map or index to help you navigate the site. Site maps not only help the end user, however. They are also a great planning exercise for your site. Working from a site map ensures that you have considered the future growth of the site and allows you to predetermine the subdirectories and filenames you want to use.

You can create a site map in several ways. The low-tech method is to simply use a blank sheet of paper and a pencil to draw boxes and lines. This process can quickly become cumbersome as you make changes and add to your site. Before you know it, the page gets so filled with lines and erasures that it's a jumbled mess.

A better solution is to design your site map right on the computer. If you have Microsoft Office, you can use the Organization Chart applet to create a hierarchical map of your site. This is useful in setting up a navigation structure for your site. Each of the major navigational headings can then become a subdirectory to organize your files.

If your site is more complex, with pages accessible from multiple links, a diagramming program such as Visio or SmartDraw better fits the bill. In these packages, you use stencils of boxes and other shapes to signify your pages and images and add lines and arrows to show the links between files. If you are only designing one site, this type of package may be overkill, but if you are involved in multiple projects, the software pays for itself in time saved.

The site mapping tools you need may also already be on hand, depending on your development environment. Microsoft FrontPage and Adobe GoLive (see Figure 4.3) have site mapping tools within their applications. These packages automatically track your links to both pages and images.

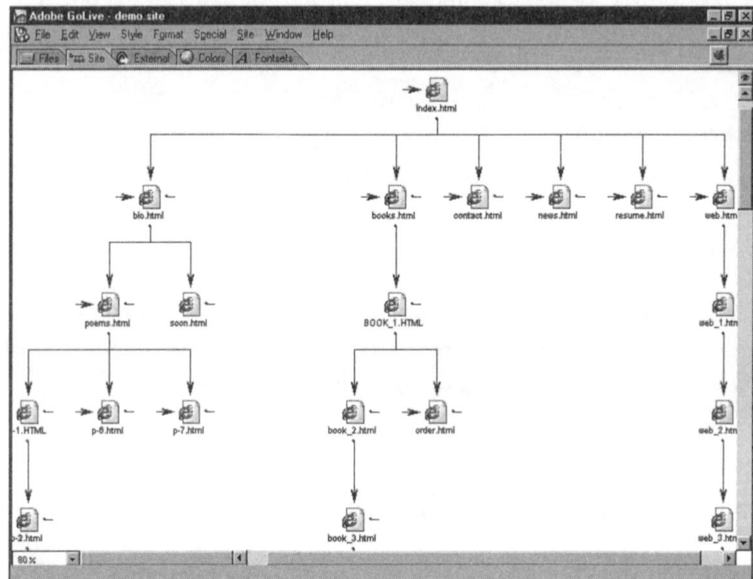

Figure 4.3
A site map in Adobe GoLive.

PART II

HTML BASICS

CHAPTER 5

Defining HTML Syntax

In this chapter

SYNTAX AND STRUCTURE

To build a strong understanding of HTML, we look to the structure of the language itself. You might remember the painful task of diagramming sentences in grammar school. You may already know that working with HTML, although similar, isn't quite as painful. However, it does follow certain rules of order.

HTML is really quite logical, unlike the English language (and many other languages, for that matter). Certainly, there are exceptions to rules, and there are modifications or interpretations of those rules. However, after a sense of the basic structure is intact, it's easy to see that HTML is simply a set of logical pieces that make up a fairly sensible language.

Although change is the natural state of HTML, these changes usually do *not* affect the basic rules. As aspects of the language become obsolete, and new components are added to the language, the *syntax*, or correct structure, rarely, if ever, changes.

→ For more about the nature of HTML as a changing language, **see** "Understanding HTML 4.0," **p. 10**

To understand the concept of syntax, think of a sentence. You have to have a subject and a verb. Adjectives and adverbs are added to provide color and quality, making that sentence more descriptive.

HTML is, at its heart, no different than a simple sentence. In fact, the components of HTML follow the same concept as subject, verb, and descriptor.

For the purposes of this chapter, I will introduce, or, for those of you who are more advanced in your HTML studies, revisit the three foundational components of HTML, and one subsidiary component known as "special characters." Other portions of the HTML 4.0 standard, such as style sheets, use other syntactical methods, but they will be introduced later. For now, let's focus on the cornerstones of HTML components, and get our foundation firmly laid.

TAGS, ATTRIBUTES, AND VALUES

The central pillar of all HTML commands is the *tag* (sometimes referred to as an *element*). A tag is the identity of HTML, it says "do this." But tags become powerful with modification, and that modification begins with an *attribute* (also referred to as an *argument*).

Attributes are like verbs in that they promote activity—with them, the HTML tag can suddenly come to life and not only do something, but do it in a certain way.

Attributes must be modified by *values*. A value defines the way an attribute will act. Think of an adjective or adverb modifying an action—How did John run? John ran quickly! Values add concepts such as "quickly," telling the tag, and the attribute, not only what and how, but to what specific degree.

Metaphorically, the sentence "John ran quickly" equals the basic syntactical structure of HTML. "John" is equivalent of an HTML tag, "ran" is much like an HTML attribute, and "quickly" is the value ascribed to that attribute and ultimately describes the way in which the tag will act.

TAGS

There are specific as well as general rules about HTML tags. The first rule is that all standard tags are contained within a less-than and greater-than symbol, as follows:

```
<HTML>
```

Note that there are no spaces between the symbols and the tag, and no spaces between the letters that denote the tag.

The next rule is a little less consistent. It states that tags have an opening and closing component. The closing component uses the same less-than and greater-than symbols to contain the tag, but adds a forward slash (/) before the tag to denote the tag's closure:

```
</HTML>
```

This means that with most standard tags, what you open, you must close at the appropriate place within your code. This rule gets a bit muddy when there are many tags that do not behave according to the rules. Some tags *can* stand alone, like the `<P>` for paragraph tag—this tag can be used legally both in a singular `<P>` or open/close `<P>...</P>` format. Other tags *must* stand without a closing tag, like the `<IMG>` tag, which never takes a closing tag. In other words, there is no such thing as `</IMG>`.

→ For a list of all the tags, attributes, and values in HTML 4.0, **see** "HTML 4.0 Element and Tag Reference," **p. 926**

General rules include selecting a case for your tagging and sticking to it. My personal preference is lowercase, I think it looks neater in the code environment, and, as any veteran of the online world knows, uppercase is the virtual equivalent of shouting.

I like calm surroundings, and I certainly don't want my code shouting at me, so I code in lowercase (see Figure 5.1). You might have a different point of view—perhaps you like uppercase because it's easier on your eyes. In fact, for this book, I chose to use a different convention from my normal code habits: to put the tags in uppercase, and all attributes and values in *lower*case.

Note

An upcoming code methodology known as *XHTML* (extensible HTML) insists on all tags being in lowercase. This is a good reason to use lower-case tags now, so as changes come along, you'll be prepared.

→ For more information about XHTML, **see** Chapter 23, "Understanding XHTML, XML, and Emerging Languages" **p. 492**

```
<IMG src="my.gif">
```

This is a common method that allows coders to find their tags quickly. It also makes identifying areas of the code easier when printed out—which is one of the reasons this convention was chosen for this book.

Tip from

No matter the case style you choose, *be consistent*! This will keep your code looking professional and clean.

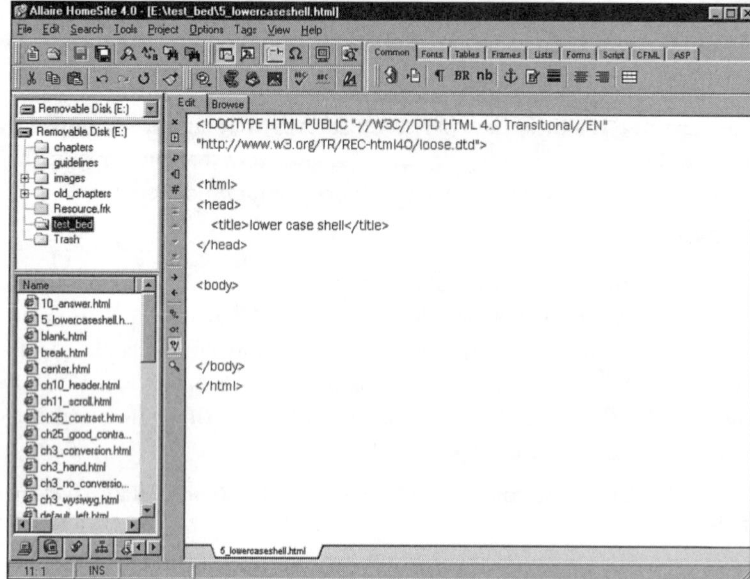

Figure 5.1
An HTML shell coded in lowercase. The results are visually consistent and conform with upcoming XHTML guidelines.

Another important thing to be aware of is spacing—sometimes you must have spaces between certain points in an HTML "sentence," and sometimes one extra space will confuse a browser so completely that no information displays.

There's also a phenomenon I call "horizontal symmetry." This is the logical process of keeping tags in appropriate order—something that many coders and sadly, most WYSIWYG applications pay little attention to. More about this toward the latter part of this chapter in a section naturally named "Horizontal Symmetry."

ATTRIBUTES

Attributes, as mentioned, modify the action of a tag. Many tags can act perfectly fine alone, but there are a variety of tags that *must* have attributes to function.

The `<HTML>` tag and its companion closing tag, `</HTML>` denote that an HTML document is about to begin or end. This tag takes no attributes whatsoever. The `<BODY>` tag, and its companion `</BODY>` closing tag denote the area of an HTML document that will be viewed within a browser. Although this tag can conceptually stand alone, nothing happens to it until an attribute, such as `bgcolor` for "background color," or `text` to indicate the text color, are applied.

Caution

Attributes, when applied to a tag, *only exist in the opening tag*. Never, ever put an attribute into a closing tag. For example, `<BODY bgcolor="#FFFFFF">` is a correct syntactical string, and will be closed simply with `</BODY>`. I've seen many student coders try to close a tag with the attribute, coding the closing tag as `</BODY bgcolor="#FFFFFF">`. This is completely illegal, and you should be vigilant in making sure that you never do it.

Attributes are often whole words, and sometimes they are partial words. Some whole word attributes include `align`, `color`, `link`, and `face`. Partial word examples include `src` for "source," and `vlink` for "visited link."

Note

When attributes are added to a tag, and values are added to attributes, the term used to define the resulting HTML sentence is *string*.

Where do attributes go in a syntactical string? They follow the tag and one space:

```
<BODY bgcolor…
```

and are then modified by a value before the tag is closed.

A tag can have more than one attribute, and, in fact, some tags take on many attributes at the same time. In this case, the syntax follows the same concept: first the tag, a space, and then an attribute. The attribute will receive a value, and then a space is once again introduced *before* the next attribute:

```
<BODY bgcolor="#FFFFFF" text="#000000">
```

and so forth, until all the attributes and companion values are included.

➔ For more information on the `<BODY>` tag and its attributes, **see** "Using Text and Background Color," **p. 216**

VALUES

Values are the defining aspect of attributes and ultimately modify the tag. Their responsibility is to determine the way a particular activity is to take place by quantifying or qualifying it in some way.

Values, like attributes, can be made up of a whole word. If I'm using the `<DIV>`, or division, tag, and I want to align all the information in that division, I can select from several values that will modify the `align` attribute. Such values include `left`, `right`, `center`, and `justify`.

A resulting string would be

```
<DIV align="right">
```

and, because I know that the `<DIV>` tag does in fact require a closing tag, I would be sure to end my division with

```
</DIV>
```

Now, all the information in that division will be aligned to the right, because I've first used the `<DIV>` tag to identify the start of the division, modified that tag with the `align` attribute, and further modified the attribute with the *value* of `right`. This action will continue until I've appropriately closed the division, `</DIV>`.

Some values are numeric, referring to pixels or percentages, browser-defined sizes, or hexadecimal numbers to define HTML color. A pixel value example is well described by the `width` attribute. If I'm coding a table, I might define that table's width as being 595 pixels wide. The syntax for this would be

```
<TABLE width="585">
```

and, of course, the table would be closed using the `</TABLE>` tag in the appropriate place.

Similarly, I can use a percentage value in the same instance. The code would then be

```
<TABLE width="100%">
```

and in this case, the table would flex to 100% the available space.

→ For more information on the `<TABLE>` tag, including its attributes and values, **see** "Table Fundamentals," **p. 308**

Browser-defined sizes are those sizes that the browser selects. In other words, you cannot predetermine the exact size, such as with pixels, but you can approximate the size. The best example of this is with the `<FONT>` tag attribute `size`. The `size` attribute can opt to take a value ranging from 1–7, 1 being the smallest, 7 the largest:

```
<FONT size="5">
```

Any text between this and the closing `</FONT>` tag takes on the browser's interpretation of a size `5`. Figure 5.2 shows a paragraph of size `5` text as viewed through Netscape Navigator for Windows. The same page is shown in Figure 5.3, but in Internet Explorer. On close examination, you'll see that there is a visual difference in the respective interpretation of the numeric value.

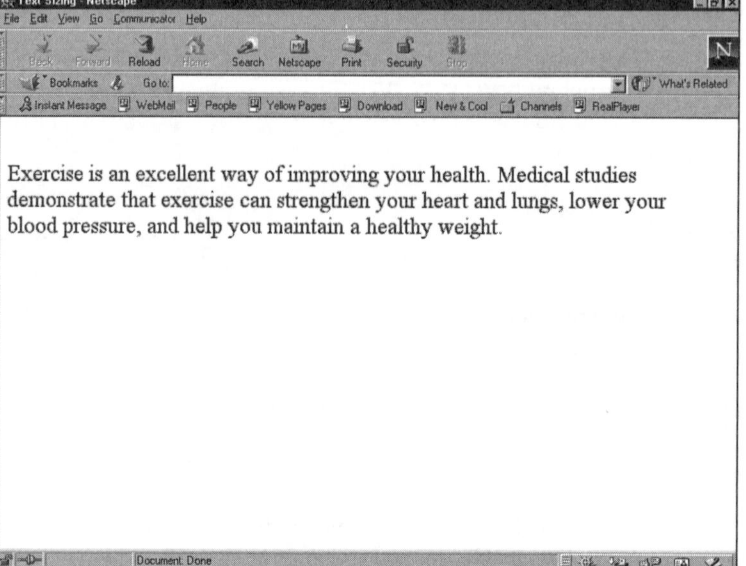

Figure 5.2
Text sizing in Netscape. I've set the size to `5`.

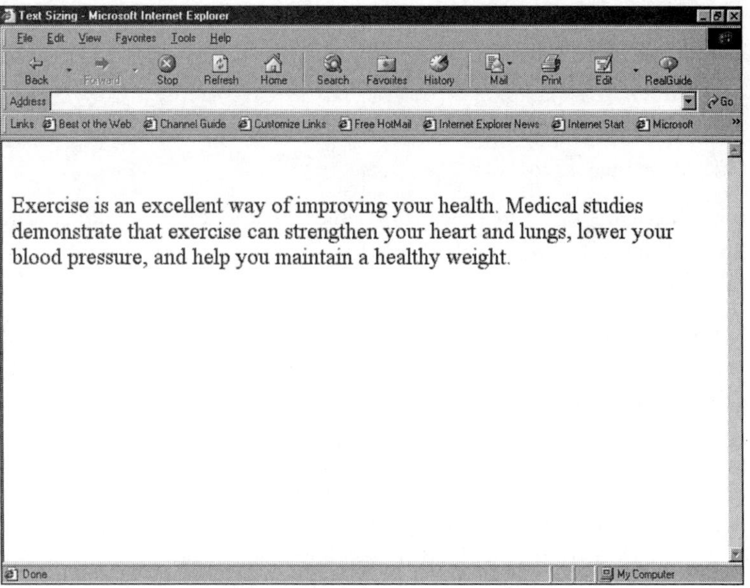

Figure 5.3
The same information in Internet Explorer. Compare this with Figure 5.2, and you'll find a minor difference in the size and a more significant difference in the placement of the text on the page.

Caution

Because different browsers and platforms interpret and display browser-defined sizes differently, you will have to test your pages by using as many variations as possible to ensure that you are getting results that are satisfactory.

➔ For more information on the <FONT> tag and its attributes, **see** "Working with Fonts," **p. 239**

Another numeric type of value is known as *hexadecimal* code. This is the base-16 alphanumeric code that defines the range of available HTML colors. You've already seen an example of a hexadecimal color earlier, when I demonstrated the `bgcolor` and `text` attributes:

```
<BODY bgcolor="#FFFFFF" text="#000000">
```

The `FFFFFF` code translates into a background color of white, with the text value of `000000` as black.

➔ To learn more about hex codes, **see** "Color Concepts," **p. 537**

Tip from molly

Always include the pound (#) sign in each of your hexadecimal values.

There are other types of values of which to be aware. One such value is a relative or absolute link, meaning that a directory, series of directories, filename, or complete Web address can be included in certain attributes to fulfill a value:

```
<A href="http://www.molly.com/">Go to My Home Page</A>
```

This string will create a link that, when clicked, goes to my home page. The `A` tag, or anchor tag, creates a link; the attribute is `href`, or hypertext transfer protocol reference; and the value is the URL, **`http://www.molly.com/`**.

Similarly, I can point to a directory and an image:

```
<IMG src="images/molly.gif">
```

In this case, the tag is `IMG`, or image (which, by the way, takes no closing tag), the attribute is `src` ("source"), and the value is a combination of the images directory and the specific file, `molly.gif`.

Another interesting value example is the companion value to the `alt` attribute. This attribute appears in image or object tags and offers a descriptive definition of the image or object for those individuals who cannot or do not want to see the image or object:

```
<IMG src="molly.gif" alt="picture of Molly">
```

In this situation, you see that the value ascribed to the `alt` attribute is actually a self-defined series of words used to describe the picture. You can also see in this example how a tag can have multiple attributes with corresponding values.

→ To locate information on the anchor tag and its attributes, **see** "Linking Pages," **p. 174**

→ If you want to examine image syntax in detail, **see** "Working with Images," **p. 196**

By now, you probably have noticed that all values are preceded by an = symbol (the equal sign), and the value is within quotation marks. With the exception of hexadecimal values, which add a # (pound sign) to the alphanumeric value, this is a proper and consistent way of coding and identifying values within an HTML string.

Tip from

Always use quotations marks. While not all values *require* quotation marks, and, in fact, many coders and software applications leave them out, this can lead to troublesome code.

SPECIAL CHARACTERS

There is a subset of information in HTML that is referred to as the "special character set." This is HTML syntax that creates punctuation and symbols necessary to content formatting.

Interestingly, many WYSIWYG programs *always* use special characters to invoke punctuation marks such as parenthesis, quotations, or brackets. However, many hand coders simply type the punctuation and rarely is there any problem with a browser interpreting the ASCII, or text-based, character.

The best use for special characters is to create symbols or to clearly differentiate ASCII from HTML.

Special characters look nothing like a standard HTML tag. A perfect example is the copyright symbol, which can be coded as:

```
&copy;
```

The & symbol is the denotation for a special character's beginning, and the ; semi-colon closes the character. This way, the browser knows not to display the literal word "copy," but interprets the entire piece as the actual © copyright symbol, as shown in Figure 5.4.

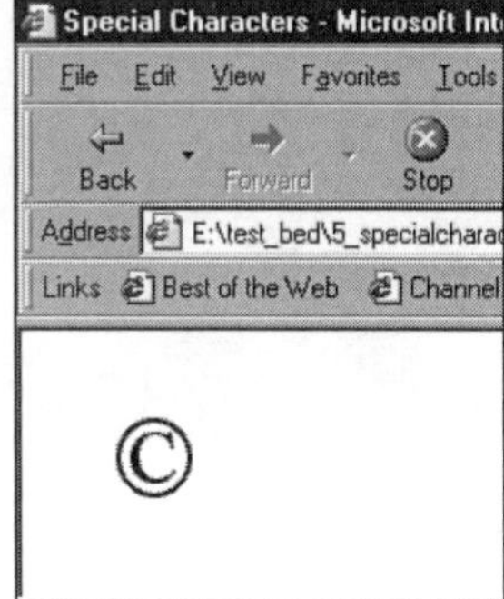

Figure 5.4
You can create the copyright symbol using a special character in HTML.

Sometimes, I want to show HTML code examples on an HTML page. Special characters allow me to do this—because otherwise the HTML would be interpreted literally. If I type in `<IMG src="dude.gif">`, the browser isn't going to display that literal text information, but rather interpret the HTML tag and go out looking for the image named `dude.gif`.

To make my syntax visually available to you, I would simply code the less-than and greater-than symbols as special characters, and then the literal string will be displayed rather than the HTML:

```
&lt;IMG src="dude.gif"&gt;
```

Figures 5.5 and 5.6 clearly show why special characters are so handy.

The special character set is vast, sometimes with several codes representing the same character.

→ For a complete reference of special characters, **see** "Special Characters," **p. 1010**

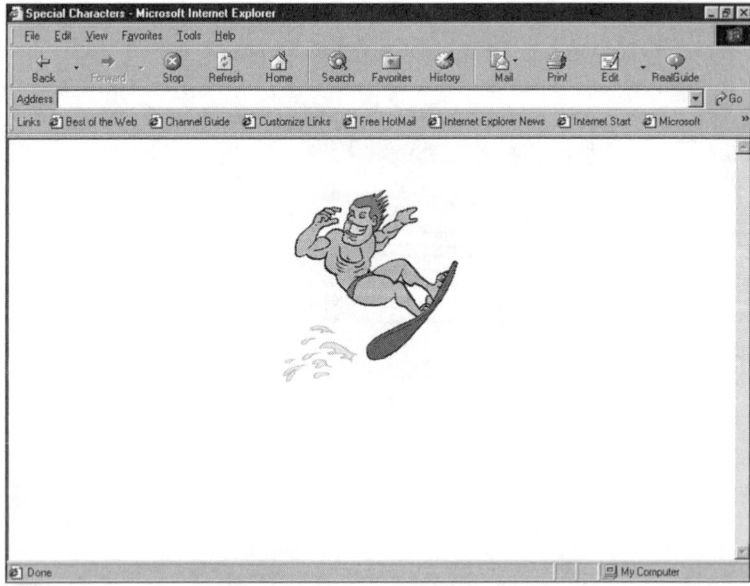

Figure 5.5
Without special characters, the browser interprets the information as HTML and displays the image.

Figure 5.6
With special characters, I can display an example of HTML within an HTML page.

WELL-FORMED CODE

As you've already noticed, the exceptions and variations on these basic HTML fundamentals sometimes run into vague areas. This especially becomes problematic when using software applications that don't take the rules of HTML into account and throw out syntactical rules. Someone studying the output of a WYSIWYG application will often learn *bad code*.

Does this mean browsers won't properly interpret bad code? Not at all. Browsers tend to be forgiving of lousy code. Just as you and I tend to understand vernacular speech, a browser recognizes most sloppy code.

Wondering if there are really any hard and fast rules to the issue of structure and symmetry in coding pages? In some cases there are, but in most instances it is more a matter of ease of coding and speed of debugging, see "Line Length" in the Troubleshooting section at the end of this chapter.

However, every so often there's going to be one piece of bad code that will choke a browser completely. Imagine speaking with someone from a different part of the country from you. Although you might readily recognize what a person means when he or she says "Let's go have a pop," instead of "Let's go have a soda," you may not understand when they say "Hey, home, let's go chill." As the vernacular becomes more particular to a given person, or to follow the metaphor, a particular software program, the code gets harder and harder to make logical sense of.

You can avoid this problem by putting HTML rules to work. What's more, you can look to both XML and XHTML for some practices that will ensure what is referred to as *well-formed* code. This way, when you see something broken, you'll know it—and when you're searching for the reasons why nothing is displaying on a browser despite all the code you've created, you'll know how to go about troubleshooting the problem.

→ For detail on changing syntax rules, **see** "Understanding XHTML, XML, and Emerging Languages," **p. 493** (chapter 23)

A few specific troubles spots exist. I've identified them here, and gone into some guidelines and methods that will help you create clean, precise code that makes logical sense and helps you avoid trouble.

Case Sensitivity

I discussed the issue of case earlier, when describing HTML tags. I'll repeat the general rule: tags and attributes can, in HTML 4.0, be in upper- or lowercase, depending upon your personal tastes and needs. This is reflected in the way that code in this book is formatted. You'll see tags in uppercase, whereas attributes and values are in lowercase. However, where an issue arises that causes some concern is in any value that reflects case sensitivity.

XHTML—the proposed reorganization of HTML-related languages—adopts stricter syntax rules for case. The reason is because in languages related to HTML, including SGML and XML, case sensitivity is alive and well. In other words, a lowercase tag such as `<li>` might be different than a tag in uppercase, `<LI>`. Typically, if you stick to lowercase you will be in adherence with the rules of XHTML and avoid document problems. However, when using HTML 4.0, you may still use combinations, particularly if they are consistent ones.

Quotation Marks

I will personally demonstrate all HTML values in this book as being encased in quotation marks. However, if you were to sneak a look at any of my own code, you'll see quotation mark inconsistency. Why is this? Well, the absolute necessity of quotation marks around values isn't a rule in HTML 4.0.

Moreover, the use of quotations in HTML is inconsistent. Although I can confidently leave the quotations out from around a `width="x"` or `align="center"` attribute and value, making the `width=x` and `align=center`, there are many cases in which removing the quotations means trouble.

One such instance is around hexadecimal values. In a `BODY` tag, for example, I can potentially render my HTML code unreadable by missing a quotation around those values. The same is true of any time I use a URL or directory/filename value for an anchor or image tag.

So, to help you keep track of when or when not to quote, I always defer to keeping the quotation marks. The reason is simple: It is never wrong to quote a value. It is sometimes wrong to *not* quote a value. Therefore, if you always quote, you'll never go wrong. A good piece of advice that will keep you trouble-free.

Furthermore, inconsistency looks unprofessional—and yes, I'm the first coder that has to raise her hand and say "guilty" to that small act against my own prescription.

For that bit of human frailty, I'll leave you with an old saying: "Do as I say, not as I do!"

→ Well-formed code in XHTML insists on quotes around values, for details **see** "Understanding XHTML, XML, and Emerging Languages," **p. 494**

SPACES

Spaces can also cause browser chokes. They are absolutely necessary in certain instances, absolutely disallowed in some instances, and positively ignored in other instances.

Spaces are absolutely necessary between a tag and an attribute, and an attribute and another attribute. `<BODY bgcolor="#FFFFFF">` *cannot* be coded as `<BODYbgcolor="#FFFFFF">`. A browser won't know what to do with this information, because it can't separate the tag from the attribute. It will think that you're trying to use a tag it doesn't understand, `BODYbgcolor`, which of course doesn't exist.

Tip from molly

My good friend and long-time colleague Wil Gerken of WeeklyWire insists that browsers are "stupid." His advice is to *never* let a browser think for itself. This means that you must always be careful to use proper syntax, eliminating any possibility that a browser will misinterpret your intentions.

Similarly, spaces are required between strings of attributes and values. `<BODY bgcolor="#FFFFFF" text="#000000">` *cannot* be coded as `<BODY bgcolor="#FFFFFF"text="#000000">`. The spaces are absolutely required to avoid browser code parsing problems.

Spaces are absolutely *disallowed* between an attribute and a value. `<BODY bgcolor="#FFFFFF">` *cannot* be coded as `<BODY bgcolor = "#FFFFFF">`. This will also confuse a browser, which will be unable to identify the attribute and value as a unit that works together.

Additional spaces are completely ignored after the first logical space in body text. For example, if I have four spaces between the word "My" and the words "red balloon" in code, the browser will ignore the additional three spaces completely:

```
My    red balloon was swept out of my hands and into the sky.
```

In Figure 5.7, I've taken a snapshot of the way this code looks in Netscape. Look, Ma, only one space! The browser ignores everything beyond the logical space.

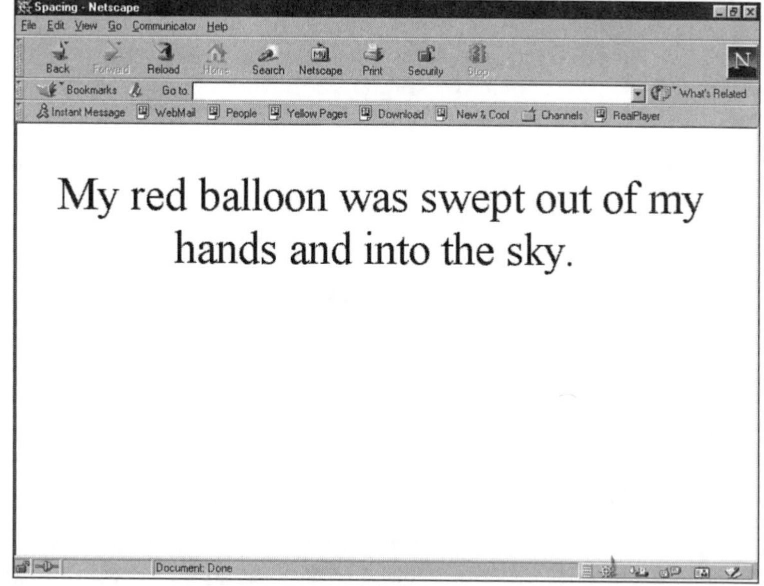

Figure 5.7
Despite the fact that I've entered four spaces in the code, the browser displays only one.

Another place spaces cause concern is between tags and content. In the following example, I hit my spacebar once within the bold tags for the first sentence. In the second sentence, I waited to tap my space bar until after I coded the closing bold tag:

```
<B>This sentence </B>has a space
<BR>

<B>This sentence</B> has a space in the same place.
```

In Figure 5.8, you'll see both sentences appear the same in the context of the browser. However, the spaces I placed into the code is different.

Tip from molly

How do you avoid inconsistencies with this? My recommendation is to leave your spaces *outside* the code, as shown in the second coded sentence. It's not wrong to do it within the code, but it is confusing. And although there is no noticeable difference in the output when using the <B> or <I> tags, you will notice a big difference when using the <U> tag. It's best to be consistent and keep your tags close to the text.

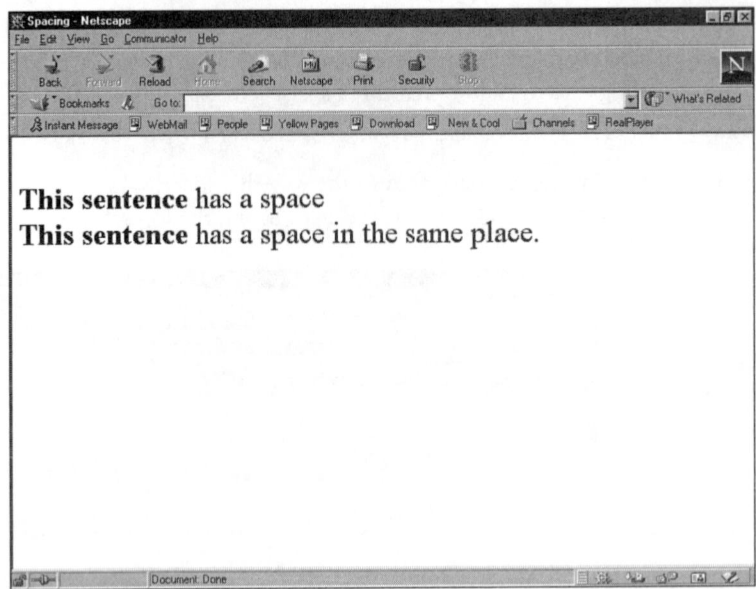

Figure 5.8
There's no visible difference here, until you look at the underlying code.

Spaces are a source of endless frustration for newcomers to HTML coding. I've had students stare at a page searching for the problem with their code and not be able to see that it's simply one missing space, or one additional space, where spacing rules must be put into place (okay, I'll admit it, it used to happen to me a lot, too)!

Take the hard-won advice of my many students and keep spaces *after* tags. After finding a space problem and seeing their work finally appear in the browser the way they *thought* it would, they now follow these guidelines. They're sure to keep you out of trouble.

And remember, it's often the browser, and not *you*, who has the problem. Put blame where it's due. Just keep your eyes peeled when trying to debug a site, it may be a space issue contributing to the code problem.

→ **See** chapter 42, "Preparing Your Site for Publication" to learn more about checking your code for trouble spots, **p. 887**

Really need that space in there but just can't get it to work? Check out "Adding Spaces" in the Troubleshooting section at the end of this chapter for help.

Horizontal Symmetry

Another area where browsers are forgiving, and coders are sloppy, is in following a logical sequence of code. Because code can run in a single sentence or from the top to bottom of a page, I separate the two into the horizontal and vertical. This is really just a method and not a rule, but I have found it to be invaluable in helping keep HTML syntax in proper form.

→ In this chapter, horizontal symmetry takes the stage. For more information on vertical symmetry, **see** "Building HTML Documents," **p. 105** (chapter 6) which looks into the same method from a different perspective.

Let's say I wanted to add two tags to modify a bit of text, bold <B>...</B> and italic, <I>...</I>, rendering that text both bold and italic.

Symmetry means opening and closing the tags in the proper order. First let me bold the text selection:

```
<B>My red balloon was swept out of my hands and into the sky.</B>
```

and now I'll add italics:

```
<I><B>My red balloon was swept out of my hands and into the sky.</B></I>
```

Because I approached the code methodically, I didn't run into a problem. I could have started with italics:

```
<I>My red balloon was swept out of my hands and into the sky.</I>
```

and then added the bold:

```
<B><I>My red balloon was swept out of my hands and into the sky.</I></B>.
```

Either example is correct—it doesn't matter which begins first, the bold or the italic, as long as the tags resolve in *order*! What I *cannot* have is the following:

```
<B><I>My red balloon was swept out of my hands and into the sky.</B></I>
```

or

```
<I><B>My red balloon was swept out of my hands and into the sky.</I></B>.
```

These are syntactically incorrect, causing a disturbance in HTML logic and horizontal symmetry.

THE CONTAINER METHOD

To help keep code free of symmetry problems, I've developed an approach known as "The Container Method." This method requires the coder to always code both the opening and closing tags required before adding another set.

In other words, if I code <B> and immediately follow it with a </B>, then I've created a container in which to put my text. I can create another container, either within that container or outside of that container, to accommodate another type of code. What I *cannot* do is overlap.

Figure 5.9 shows the container method at work, and I've drawn lines along the horizon, pointing out the container elements. This is symmetrical syntax because no overlapping occurs.

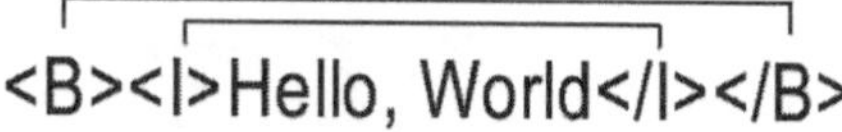

Figure 5.9
Horizontal symmetry requires that the tags follow in a logical, symmetrical sequence.

But look what happens in Figure 5.10. Overlap! This is the container method test: If your lines intersect at any point, you've got a symmetry problem.

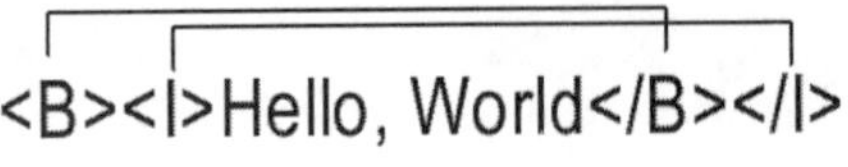

Figure 5.10
Intersecting lines means a symmetry disturbance.

Will browsers forgive you? They might. I don't take my chances, because there are just too many variables—again, this speaks to the issue of *control*. Don't let that browser do the thinking for you—tell it exactly what you want, when, and how, and your code will be stable, neat, and professional because of your precise approach.

Learning proper HTML syntax is no different than understanding the rules of language. Most English speakers know that saying "I ain't going to the store" is slang, and, although it's understandable, it isn't correct.

Although I might say "I ain't" in a casual or joking moment, I know that when I want to be formal and professional, I must say, "I'm not going to the store," because this is the correct, sophisticated use of the language.

Similarly, although browsers might forgive you your syntactical slang, those that are more discerning will not. To avoid adding to the load of browser headaches that already exist, stick to the guidelines.

HTML syntax is fairly simplistic. Although it has twists and turns, if you are educated enough in the English language to be reading and understanding this book, you've accommodated a much more complex syntactical system than HTML. Rely on logic, and use the techniques in this chapter as a strong foundation for all your HTML code. You can rest assured that the results will be sophisticated, correct, and professional.

TROUBLESHOOTING

LINE LENGTH

Is there a limit to the number of characters on one line of code?

No. You can actually put the code for an entire page on one line. The browser knows how to parse the tags so the page appears as you've coded it. Just because you can do this, however, does not mean that you should. It is difficult to edit an HTML file without any line breaks, and also leaves you open to coding errors.

ADDING SPACES

If using the spacebar doesn't insert additional spaces within text, how can I add them?

One of the special characters in HTML is a non-breaking space. It is coded as ` ` and you can string as many of these in sequence as necessary.

DESIGNING FOR THE REAL WORLD

WHAT A DIFFERENCE A KILOBYTE MAKES

We all know how frustrating it can be to wait for a page to load when we're surfing the Internet. In this age of fast food and 65 mph speed limits, we want sites that load quickly.

When you think about streamlining your code, your first thought may be squeaking an extra kilobyte out of your image files. What you may not think to do is take a hard look at the HTML code itself. If you look closely, you're sure to find an extra space here and there, an extraneous tag, even an extra period at the end of a sentence. You may have put several carriage returns between sections of your code while you composed your content, but no longer need after the content is in place. Every character in the file adds to the size of the file, which translates to download time on the Web. One of the most common space wasters is empty `<B>…</B>`, and `<I>…</I>` tags.

The biggest benefit to looking at your code so closely is that you're bound to catch other mistakes before they become glaring errors. When you're coding by hand, it's easy to put a closing tag in the wrong syntactical order (`<B/>` instead of `</B>`) or using the , instead of the < when you're typing quickly. In a large block of text, however, you might not notice the typo right away.

Don't expect any major gains (or, more accurately, losses) in file size when you streamline your code. If you use whitespace to divide sections of your code, don't worry about eliminating every extraneous carriage return. The end result is likely to be rather unsubstantial. But you might just be able to shave off enough to make someone's browsing experience just a little bit faster and improve your coding skills at the same time.

CHAPTER 6

Building HTML Documents

In this chapter

UNDERSTANDING DOCUMENT STRUCTURE

Just as a human being is structured in a logical way, so is an HTML document. If you study the shape of your spouse or child, you are likely to notice that they all have a similar structure—even if the *features* of their individual compositions are different.

When I look at myself in the mirror, I see my face, my hair, my eyes, my mouth—my head. And below my head is my body, with its particular physical attributes. My body can conceivably be divided into parts, too—upper body and lower body. Although my face and hair are different than yours, as is the shape of my upper and lower body, the *organization* of our physical beings is essentially the same.

HTML documents mimic this arrangement. There is a head and a body. The head of an HTML document contains features that are more mental than physical—occurring "behind the scenes" to accomplish or direct complex activities. I think of the HTML body as being the domain of physical attributes—everything within the HTML body is what is viewed, literally seen on the visible page.

Just as it would be an anomaly for an aspect of my head to manifest within the context of my body, or vice-versa, so it is not logical to place the aspects of HTML that function in the HEAD into the BODY, and so forth.

This distinction is an important one, and is further broken down into parts within the HEAD and BODY. There are divisions within the BODY, and there are special markers to help us label, or indicate, where certain features are to go.

Even for the more advanced coders among you, this basic concept is important. By keeping the document tags structured, you will avoid errors and enable yourself to power-code documents with efficiency and speed.

DOCUMENT TAGS

The following tags are used to describe document formatting in this chapter:

- **<HTML>…</HTML>**—The HTML tag.
- **<HEAD>…</HEAD>**—The head tag denotes the head portion of an HTML document.
- **<TITLE>…</TITLE>**—The title tag. Information placed within this tag appears in the browser's title bar.
- **<BODY>…</BODY>**—This is the body of the HTML document, where all information that is to be visible on the screen is placed.
- **<!--…-->**—The comment tag is used for assisting coders with code navigation.

THE HTML SHELL

I like to begin all of my HTML by first building the shell of a document, giving myself the structural basis for all HTML pages. The shell is simply the combined tags that make up the head and body aspects of a page, with some specific tags that add to your page's basic functionality.

The shell defines the HEAD and the BODY, as well as the skeletal system of the head and body. I consider the shell a combination of HTML "must-haves." Without these tags in place, your HTML document is not a formal, proper document.

Listing 6.1 shows an HTML shell as I code it.

LISTING 6.1 THE HTML SHELL (TRANSITIONAL)

```
<!DOCTYPE HTML PUBLIC "-//W3C//DTD HTML 4.0 Transitional//EN"
"http://www.w3.org/TR/REC-html40/loose.dtd">
<HTML>
<HEAD>
<TITLE>    </TITLE>
</HEAD>
<BODY>
</BODY>
</HTML>
```

You'll notice that the shell consists of a few tags, all with opening and closing tags in place with some empty space between certain tags.

Tip from molly

To ensure adherence to the HTML 4.0 standard, include the appropriate HTML version information.

Defining Version and Interpretation

To define a document as being a strict HTML 4.0 document, use this version information before the opening <HTML> tag:

```
<!DOCTYPE HTML PUBLIC "-//W3C//DTD HTML 4.0//EN"
"http://www.w3.org/TR/REC-html40/strict.dtd">
```

A transitional version will contain this code:

```
<!DOCTYPE HTML PUBLIC "-//W3C//DTD HTML 4.0 Transitional//EN"
"http://www.w3.org/TR/REC-html40/loose.dtd">
```

Any frameset following HTML 4.0 standard rules will contain this version information:

```
<!DOCTYPE HTML PUBLIC "-//W3C//DTD HTML 4.0 Frameset//EN"
"http://www.w3.org/TR/REC-html40/frameset.dtd">
```


The first tag you see after the version information is the <HTML> tag, and the last tag on the page is its closing companion, </HTML>. I consider this the skeletal aspects of the document. The <HTML> tag says "Hey, browser! I'm an HTML page, and I'm about to speak to you in HTML, so you need to get ready to interpret." Similarly, the closing </HTML> tag tells the browser, "I'm done with the HTML, now."

Always begin and end a page with the proper <HTML> tag. Within this skeletal structure, you can then divide the document into HEAD and BODY. This simple shell can be saved as a master template that you always open when beginning to code.

The following section examines the individual tags within the HTML shell.

HEAD STRUCTURE

Look closely at the shell and you'll see that following the <HTML> tag there's a <HEAD> tag, which is closed a few lines down. This is the HEAD of your document. The information that goes into the head of a document includes the following:

- **Page title**—The <TITLE> and corresponding </TITLE> tag allow you to select a page title. This title does not appear in the body of an HTML page—in other words, when the document is viewed with a browser, this information will not be seen in the main viewing screen. Where it *will* appear is within the title bar of the browser's interface. Note that you cannot add any other HTML tags into a TITLE element. However, you can use special characters.
- **Scripting**—Any script that will be performed on a page, such as JavaScript, is embedded into the head of a document. Remember, I said that much of the HEAD is used for *mental* processes rather than visual ones. A script is a perfect example of this, as it is itself an invisible process, although its results will shape the action and behavior of a page.
- **Style**—For those coders interested in adding control and style to their pages with HTML 4.0, Cascading Style Sheets can be embedded into or linked to from a Web page. This information will appear within the HEAD of an HTML document.
- **META information**—The META tag is a diverse and powerful tag that allows for a variety of mental rather than visual processes such as document author, search words, and special action items.

→ Read about special characters, **see** Appendix B: "HTML Special Character Set," **p. 1010**
→ JavaScript is covered fully later, **see** "Using JavaScript," **p. 404**
→ For more information about Cascading Style Sheets, **see** "Cascading Style Sheet Techniques," **p. 254** and "Element Positioning and Style Sheet Scripting," **p. 430**

For the purposes of my simple shell, I've only included the <TITLE> tag from this list of HEAD possibilities. The reason is that many pages will not require scripting, style, or META information. But all pages require titling. Therefore, I consider the <TITLE> tag a "must" for the HTML shell.

Within the <TITLE> tag, you should place the name of your page. Get in the practice of working with a good description for your page title, keeping it simple but clear. Let's say I was making a home page for myself. I would title the page, simply, "Molly's Home Page."

```
<TITLE>Molly's Home Page</TITLE>
```

This information then appears in the browser's title bar. In Figure 6.1, I created a sample page with "Titling Information" within the TITLE tags. Note how "Titling Information" appears in the title bar? This is where your well-written title page description goes to work.

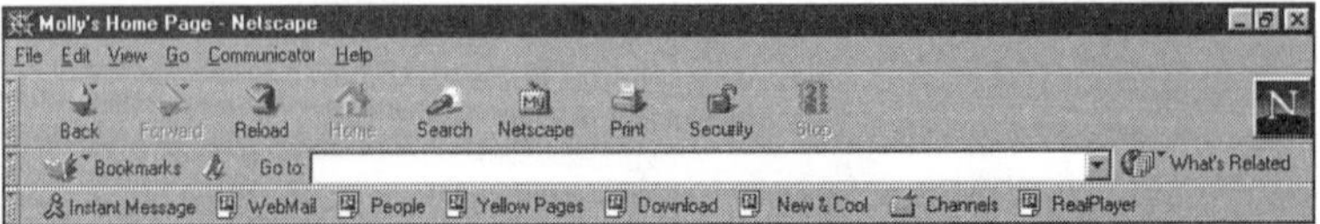

Figure 6.1
The title bar with Titling Information can be seen along the top of the window in Netscape.

BODY STRUCTURE

The body of an HTML document will include all the content information that you will be visually offering your audience. As you can tell from the shell, the BODY is left empty at this point, demonstrating only the available *space* for this information. One of your first jobs after creating the shell is to add BODY information such as the following:

- **Text**—The textual content of your site is placed in the BODY, using appropriate formatting to be readable and visually accessible for those who visit your page.
- **Images**—Whether using a header graphic to define a site's purpose, a photograph to enhance the text content, or a set of navigation buttons, images are an important part of what goes into the BODY of a document.
- **Links**—The heart and soul of the Web, links allow people to navigate your site as well as leave your site for Web destinations beyond. Links always go in the BODY of a page.
- **Multimedia and special programmed events**—Shockwave, Flash, Java Applets, even inline video is managed by code placed in the BODY of an HTML document.

Of course, there are many other elements that can be added within the BODY. We'll be taking a closer look at items such as lists, tables, and forms throughout the book.

→ For more information about textual content, **see** "Formatting and Aligning Text," **p. 110**

The BODY of an HTML document, like our bodies, ends up being larger and more physically varied than our heads. We accommodate this by preparing the shell with some space in which to work. Obviously, as we add information (see Figure 6.2), the BODY can become quite long.

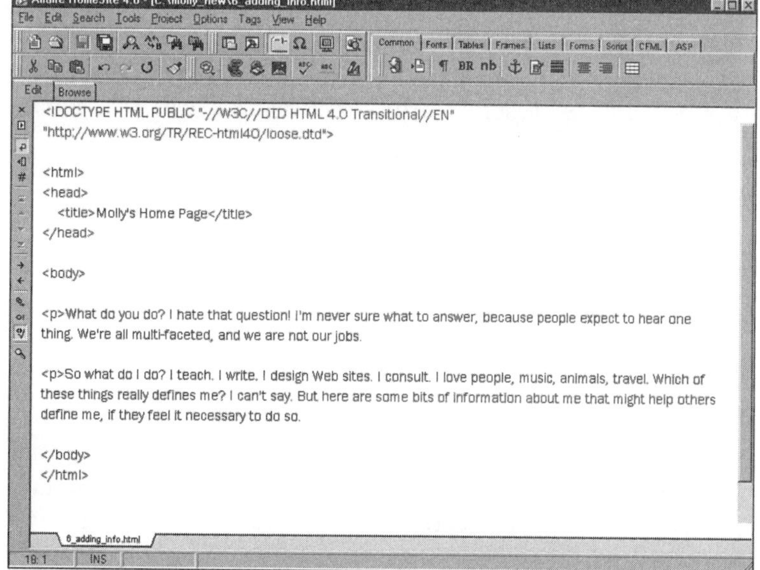

Figure 6.2
Adding information to the BODY section as seen in HomeSite.

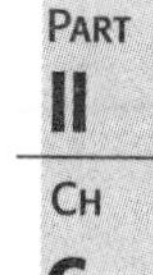

BUILDING AN HTML SHELL

I'm going to step with you through the building of a simple HTML document. The method I use, known as "container method," is something I developed to help coders avoid missing tags. And, as you'll see a bit later in the chapter, in the section, "Special Concerns," this method keeps your code symmetry intact.

→ The container method and proper tag symmetry was introduced previously, **see** "Defining HTML Syntax," **p. 74**

As you step through the process, you'll be coding in "containers:"

1. Open the ASCII editor or editing environment of your choice (I'm using HomeSite).
2. Open a new file—it should be completely blank.
3. Enter the appropriate document version. I've chosen strict HTML 4.0 for this exercise.
4. Add the opening and closing `HTML` tags with 10 carriage returns in between. This creates your first container.

```
<!DOCTYPE HTML PUBLIC "-//W3C//DTD HTML 4.0//EN"
"http://www.w3.org/TR/REC-html40/strict.dtd">

<HTML>










</HTML>
```

5. Now add the head container directly beneath the opening `HTML` tag, consisting of the opening and closing `HEAD` tags, with three carriage returns in between:

```
<!DOCTYPE HTML PUBLIC "-//W3C//DTD HTML 4.0//EN"
"http://www.w3.org/TR/REC-html40/strict.dtd">

<HTML>
<HEAD>



</HEAD>






</HTML>
```

6. Next, introduce the `TITLE` tag into the header tag by using both the open and closing tag. My personal preference is to keep these on the horizontal, as follows:

```
<!DOCTYPE HTML PUBLIC "-//W3C//DTD HTML 4.0//EN"
"http://www.w3.org/TR/REC-html40/strict.dtd">
<HTML>
<HEAD>

<TITLE>          </TITLE>
</HEAD>






</HTML>
```

7. Go ahead and add the title to your page:

```
<!DOCTYPE HTML PUBLIC "-//W3C//DTD HTML 4.0//EN"
"http://www.w3.org/TR/REC-html40/strict.dtd">

<HTML>
<HEAD>

<TITLE>Shell Exercise</TITLE>
</HEAD>






</HTML>
```

8. And finally, add the BODY tags directly below the closing HEAD tag. Add some additional carriage returns to anticipate body information:

```
<!DOCTYPE HTML PUBLIC "-//W3C//DTD HTML 4.0//EN"
"http://www.w3.org/TR/REC-html40/strict.dtd">

<HTML>
<HEAD>

<TITLE>Shell Exercise</TITLE>
</HEAD>

<BODY>





</BODY>

</HTML>
```

Figure 6.3 shows the shell within my editor. Check your code against this; you should be right on track.

Tip from

Save the file to a work folder, naming the file **`html_shell.html`**. You'll want to keep this safe and separate because you'll be modifying it later in the chapter—and you can use it as you wish for any future pages that you develop.

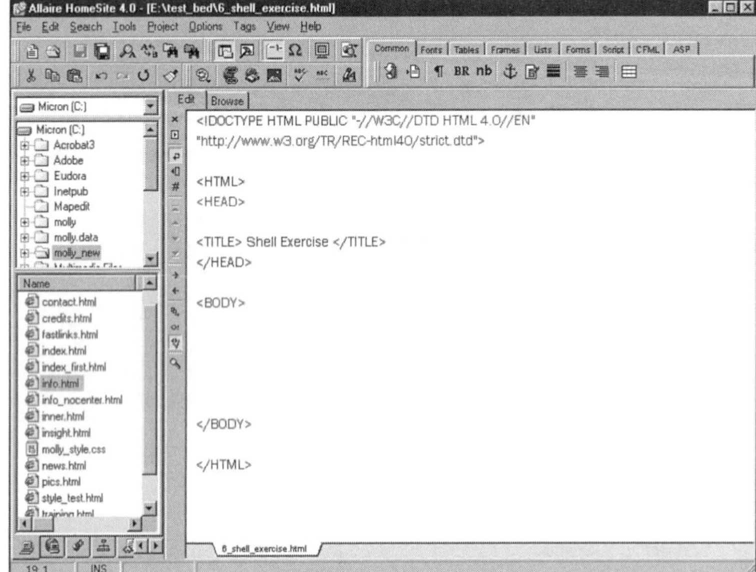

Figure 6.3
The HTML within the HomeSite editor shows how clean and easy to read your code is when you use the container method to create a shell.

Is that all there is to an HTML document? The simple answer is: Yes! By understanding that there is a `HEAD` and a `BODY` within the `<HTML>` opening and `</HTML>` closing tags, you've got the basic concept of document formatting down.

Of course, there are many other concerns that go beyond the apparently easy structure of an HTML page. Included in this list is how to denote divisions and maneuver through complex document information, how to format documents for clarity and ease of use, and how to work with vertical symmetry.

Commenting Sections in an HTML Document

Although there are no formal methods of dividing the body into custom sections by using standard tags, there is a conventional way of helping yourself manage such areas within a `BODY`, and, in fact, within the entirety of an HTML document.

This is done using a specialty tag known as a *comment* tag. The comment tag is unlike any other tag in HTML in that it follows none of the predetermined rules I described in Chapter 5, "Defining HTML Syntax." Still, the comment tag is an extraordinarily powerful tag that helps you, as well as those who work on your pages, maneuver through the code. This becomes especially helpful when your pages become extremely long and complex.

→ For information on the comment tag, **see** "HTML Tools," **p. 40**

Here's a look at a comment tag in its simplest form:

```
<!-- -->
```

The tag is familiar in that it begins with a less-than sign, and ends with a greater-than sign. The exclamation point is a marker that tells the browser to ignore the following information—as if it doesn't exist.

Placing a comment within this tag allows you to divide up your HTML document. Here's a comment tag with a literal comment:

```
<!-- begin copyright information -->
```

This comment tells me, or anyone viewing or working with my source code, that the copyright information will appear after the tag. Comment tags are *never* displayed on an HTML page, even if they appear within the BODY tag.

Comment tags can be used anywhere it makes logical sense to break up and mark an HTML document. You can also use comment tags as a means of adding pertinent information to a page, such as the author's name, contact information, and update information. Comment tags can span multiple lines, with the opening tag on one line and the closing tag on any other line you wish.

Tip from molly

Comment tags should serve to assist, not confuse, you and your assistants. Don't overuse them, but do use them where it seems necessary and important, particularly when dividing up the physical HTML document.

I'm going to now revisit the simple shell I demonstrated earlier, this time adding comment tags to my needs and tastes (see Listing 6.2).

Listing 6.2 Adding Comment Tags to the Code

```
<!-- page design by: Molly E. Holzschlag -->
<!-- email molly@molly.com or visit http://www.molly.com/ -->
<!-- materials contributed by Molly.com, Inc. -->
<!-- page last updated December 4th, 1999 -->
<!DOCTYPE HTML PUBLIC "-//W3C//DTD HTML 4.0 Transitional//EN"
"http://www.w3.org/TR/REC-html40/loose.dtd">
<HTML>
<HEAD>
<TITLE>MainStay Communications, Inc.: About the Company </TITLE>
</HEAD>

<!-- begin body information -->

<BODY>

<!-- begin content: note to content providers - please use <P> style
paragraphs -->
```

continues

LISTING 6.2 CONTINUED

```
<!--  begin page copyright -->

<!-- begin mailto: -->

</BODY>
</HTML>
```

If you study the previous code carefully, you'll see that I've included a variety of HTML information within the code. In the second comment tag, I place an email address and a URL:

```
<!-- email molly@molly.com or visit http://www.molly.com/ -->
```

and in a later comment tag, I make a note to others regarding a style preference. I actually typed in the literal tag, `<P>`:

```
<!-- begin content: note to content providers - please use <P> style paragraphs -->
```

but the browser *will not see this* as HTML code. Why? Because it is safely contained within a comment tag.

Note

Because browsers do not pay attention to what's within a comment tag, you can use these powerful, handy tags far beyond just describing a document's division. In fact, if you have a large section of text, an image, an object, or any combination thereof that you want to hide from the browser, placing that information within a comment tag will do the trick. This is useful when you cycle content on a page and don't want to keep multiple copies of a particular page.

Follow these steps to learn how to add some comment codes to your standard shell template:

1. Begin by opening the `html_shell.html` file in your HTML editor.
2. At the top, add a comment tag, as follows:

```
<!-- -->
<!DOCTYPE HTML PUBLIC "-//W3C//DTD HTML 4.0 Transitional//EN"
"http://www.w3.org/TR/REC-html40/loose.dtd">
<HTML>
<HEAD>

<TITLE>Shell Exercise</TITLE>
</HEAD>

<BODY>




</BODY>

</HTML>
```

3. Now add a literal comment, such as identifying yourself as the author of the document:

```
<!-- page authored by B. A. Coder -->
<!DOCTYPE HTML PUBLIC "-//W3C//DTD HTML 4.0 Transitional//EN"
"http://www.w3.org/TR/REC-html40/loose.dtd">


<HTML>
<HEAD>

<TITLE>Shell Exercise</TITLE>
</HEAD>

<BODY>





</BODY>

</HTML>
```

4. Now add another comment tag denoting the beginning of the BODY area:

```
<!-- page authored by B. A. Coder -->
<!DOCTYPE HTML PUBLIC "-//W3C//DTD HTML 4.0 Transitional//EN"
"http://www.w3.org/TR/REC-html40/loose.dtd">


<HTML>
<HEAD>

<TITLE>Shell Exercise</TITLE>
</HEAD>

<!-- begin body -->
<BODY>





</BODY>

</HTML>
```

5. And add a comment tag showing where you plan to add your email and copyright information:

```
<!-- page authored by B. A. Coder -->
<!DOCTYPE HTML PUBLIC "-//W3C//DTD HTML 4.0 Transitional//EN"
"http://www.w3.org/TR/REC-html40/loose.dtd">


<HTML>
<HEAD>

<TITLE>Shell Exercise</TITLE>
```

```
</HEAD>

<!-- begin body -->
<BODY>




<!-- begin copyright and email information -->

</BODY>

</HTML>
```

6. Compare your code to that shown in Figure 6.4.
7. If the code is correct, save the file as `html_comment.html`.

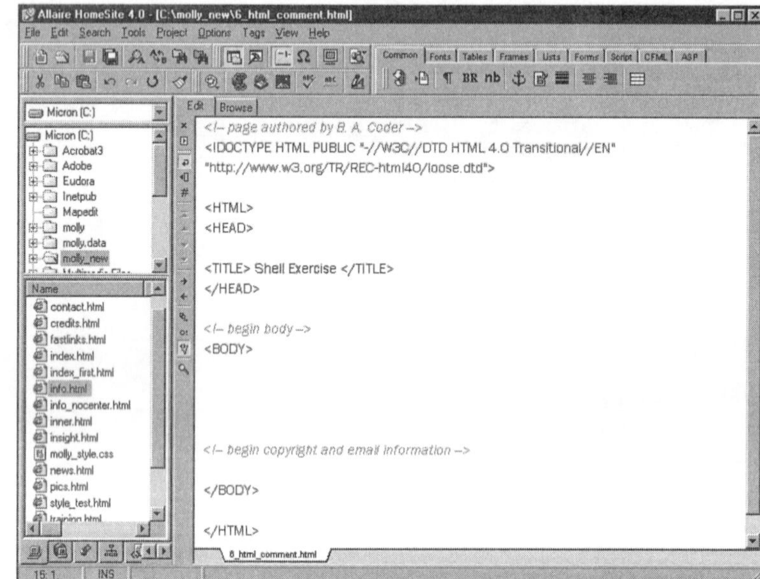

Figure 6.4
Adding comment tags to the shell allows you, and those working on a project with you, to denote page sections, keep track of changes to a page, or make remarks on who made them.

WRITING DOCUMENTS FOR CLARITY AND EASE-OF-USE

Another issue when writing HTML documents is to be sure that you add plenty of visual space. This solves problems when navigating code because you can always *find* what you're looking for.

Different coders rely on different methods for cueing themselves with regard to clarity. I'll show you a few approaches here and point out which I prefer. You'll find out which methods you prefer as you work more with the language. Either way, the point is to make the process of coding easier on you, and ultimately, more fun.

Some of the methods of writing documents for ease-of-use include the following:

- **Flushing primary tags left**—This is putting all of your main tags to the absolute left of the page. This helps keep you oriented on a page of code because the left is a natural place for our eyes to go—as readers of English, we are accustomed to moving our eyes to the left for visually oriented language clues.
- **Placing carriage returns between tags and content**—Adding visual space (also referred to as "whitespace") between tags and content, as well as between tags and other tags, helps cushion, rest, and guide your eye to the next tag.
- **Indenting certain tags**—Some coders feel that indenting specific types of tags, such as TABLE tags or table cell tags, helps them to navigate code more efficiently. This is not a personal favorite of mine; however, I've seen many coders use it effectively, and it just may suit your needs.
- **Color coding tags**—Certain editors, editing environments, and HTML software applications allow you to color code tags. I love this feature; it is extremely helpful. Figure 6.5 shows the dialog box in HomeSite where I can set my own colors for specific tags. This way, if I'm looking for an image, I know to be on the lookout for a yellow tag. This is a great method of staying oriented within a page of code.

→ For more about editors and editing environments, **see** "HTML Tools," **p. 43**

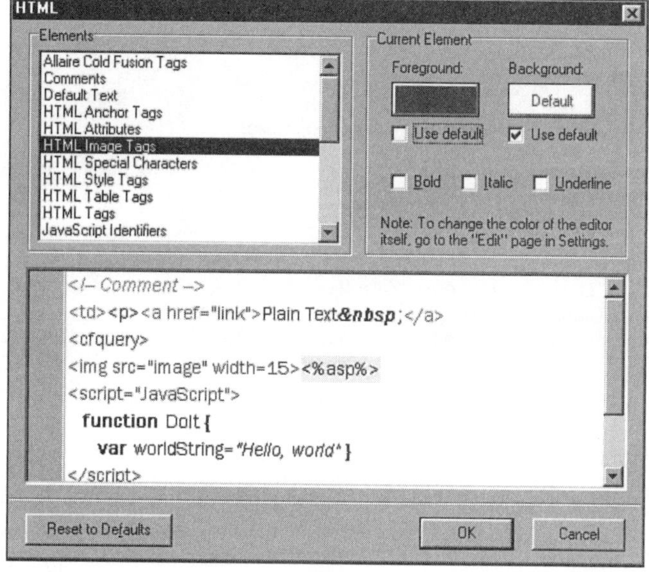

Figure 6.5
Setting up color coding in HomeSite allows the coder to easily create and edit code and stay oriented to the page without hunting around for certain tags.

To get a good feel of how cluttered code can frustrate the coder, I'm going to give you an example of code I saved using Microsoft FrontPage. Notice that the code and text in Listing 6.3 are all jammed together: no whitespace, no flushing. This makes it hard to find anything.

LISTING 6.3 CLUTTERED CODE FROM FRONTPAGE

```
<P><font face="century schoolbook,garamond,times,serif"><img src="images/molly-
h5.jpg" width="145" height="200" hspace="10" vspace="10" border="0" align="right"
alt="picture of molly"> You're at a party, you don't know too many people. Someone
starts a conversation with you. Maybe they ask your name. Invariably, they ask
this question: <I>&quot;What do you do?&quot;</I> Maybe you have an easy answer.
Maybe you choke on your beer, wondering why people seek to define one another by
what they <I>do.</I> Perhaps you struggle to explain what it is you <I>really</I>
spend your time doing. </P>

<P>I spend a lot of time choking, as I haven't found a catchall word for my
activities. I suppose one could say that I'm a Renaissance Woman, but that would
sound terribly arrogant, don't you think? Of course sputtering and hacking and
spitting beer on a fellow partygoer is almost as unattractive as arrogance. If you
have a better idea of what I might say in such a situation, or have a funny answer
that you use, feel free to <A href="mailto:molly@molly.com">email</A> me your
thoughts. I'm compiling a list of reader's ideas, so be sure to send in your vote
today! </P>

<P>If I'm going to define myself professionally, I'd have to say I'm an author, an
instructor, and a designer. Most of my books are about HTML and Web design,
although I have published literary works as well. I write feature articles and
columns on a number of subjects including the Internet, Music, Music on the
Internet, Health, and Backgammon. I    also write <A href="poems.html">poetry</A>
and have created several <A ref="soon.html">multimedia poems</A>
online.</P></FONT>
```

Now let's take a look at the same code (see Listing 6.4) as I've hand-coded it.

LISTING 6.4 NEATER, CLEANER CODE

```
<FONT face="century schoolbook,garamond,times,serif">

<IMG src="images/molly-h5.jpg" width=145 height=200 hspace=10 vspace=10 border=0
align="right" alt="picture of molly">

<P>You're at a party, you don't know too many people. Someone starts a
conversation with you. Maybe they ask your name. Invariably, they ask this
question: <I>"What do you do?"</I> Maybe you have an easy answer. Maybe you choke
on your beer, wondering why people seek to define one another by what they
<I>do.</I> Perhaps you struggle to explain what it is you <I>really</I> spend your
time doing.

<P>I spend a lot of time choking, as I haven't found a catchall word for my
activities. I suppose one could say that I'm a Renaissance Woman, but that would
sound terribly arrogant, don't you think? Of course sputtering and hacking and
spitting beer on a fellow partygoer is almost as unattractive as arrogance. If you
have a better idea of what I might say in such a situation, or have a funny answer
that you use, feel free to <A href="mailto:molly@molly.com">email</A> me your
thoughts. I'm compiling a list of reader's ideas, so be sure to send in your vote
today!

<P>If I'm going to define myself professionally, I'd have to say I'm an author, an
instructor, and a designer. Most of my books are about HTML and Web design,
although I have published literary works as well. I write feature articles and
columns on a number of subjects including the Internet, Music, Music on the
Internet, Health, and Backgammon.
```

```
<P>I also write <A href="poems.html">poetry</A> and have created several <A
href="soon.html">multimedia poems</A> online.
</FONT>
```

My code flushes tags left, separates certain code from content, and adds carriage returns to create whitespace to help soothe and guide my eye as I work on the code. I'm personally much happier with this kind of environment—I feel less constrained, less tense, and more capable of getting to the code I need to change, update, or remove.

Concerned about how to manage existing, unruly code? See "Using Different Tools" in the "Troubleshooting" section at the end of this chapter.

Note

Some coders are concerned about adding space, because they think that carriage returns will reflect on their visual page via the browser. This is simply not the case. You can have as many carriage returns between lines of code as you want, and the browser will ignore them–it's waiting for code, not space, to tell it what to do. Another concern is that carriage returns will add weight to the resulting file. This is actually true. If you jam all your code together, you're going to end up with smaller file sizes. The end result will not be *that much smaller, however*! Use space wisely, and it won't add noticeable weight to your file, but it will make the coding experience a much easier, more pleasurable one.

VERTICAL SYMMETRY

Symmetry is the logical order of code. I have already demonstrated symmetry along the horizon line. Now that we are working with a full HTML document, I want to show you how symmetry works along the vertical.

→ Horizontal symmetry of code was introduced previously, **see** "Defining HTML Syntax," **p. 86** (chapter 5)

Re-examine the HTML shell in simple format. See Listing 6.5.

LISTING 6.5 THE SIMPLE HTML SHELL RE-EXAMINED

```
<!DOCTYPE HTML PUBLIC "-//W3C//DTD HTML 4.0 Transitional//EN"
"http://www.w3.org/TR/REC-html40/loose.dtd">

<HTML>
<HEAD>

<TITLE>     </TITLE>
</HEAD>

<BODY>



</BODY>
</HTML>
```

Vertical symmetry relates to the logical open/close relationship between tags on the vertical axis. For example, my HTML tags encase my HEAD tags and so forth. There is no overlap. Listing 6.6 is an example of asymmetrical, illegal code.

LISTING 6.6 ASYMMETRICAL, ILLEGAL CODE

```
<HTML>
<HEAD>

<TITLE>    </TITLE>
</HEAD>

<BODY>

</HTML>
</BODY>
```

See how my closing </HTML> tag comes, in this case, *before* my closing </BODY> tag? This is a major no-no. Will a browser forgive you? It might, but you are definitely taking your chances.

If you learn to think in containers, you avoid problems with symmetry. This becomes even more important when we get to one of the problem children of HTML, the FONT tag. This tag, although deprecated in the HTML 4.0 standard, is in such wide conventional use—due to browser compatibility issues—that we must address it and its problems. Putting it aside for a more elegant approach such as style sheets is part of HTML 4.0's wisdom, but, until we have widespread compliance, we have to be very, very careful of how we approach the idiosyncrasies of this tag. Learning symmetry well is one of the ways that you can avoid problems with FONT, as well as other HTML tags.

Figure 6.6 shows how symmetry works. Note that in this figure there are *no* intersecting lines. Each container is appropriately configured. However, when I have a piece of asymmetrical code and draw my lines, they intersect (see Figure 6.7). This method is always a test, and proof, of symmetry.

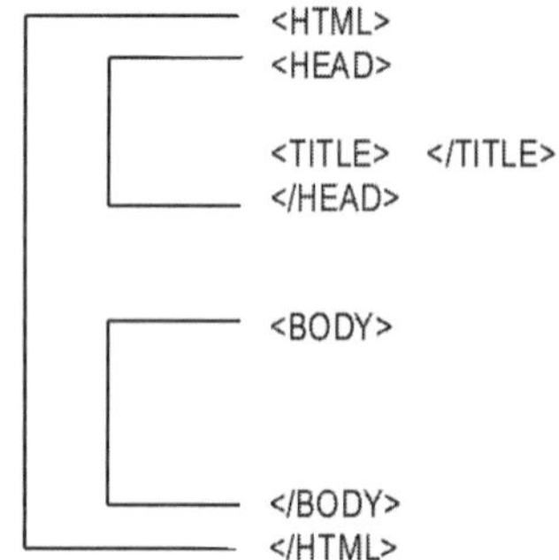
<HTML>
<HEAD>
<TITLE> </TITLE>
</HEAD>
<BODY>
</BODY>
</HTML>

Figure 6.6
Symmetrical code follows along logically in an easily recognizable manner.

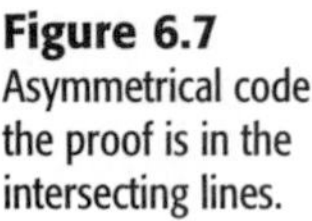

Figure 6.7
Asymmetrical code: the proof is in the intersecting lines.

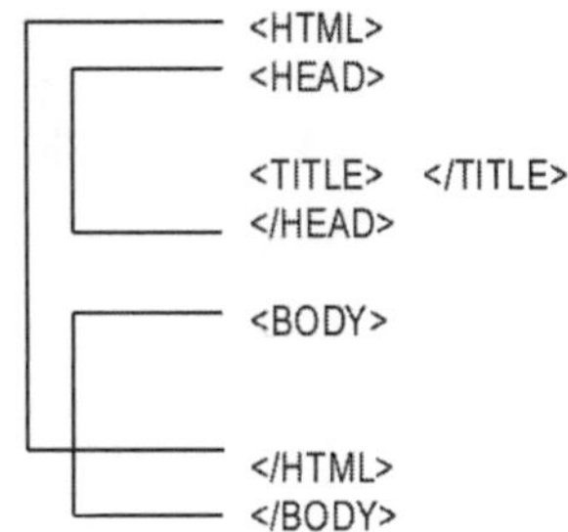
<HTML>
<HEAD>
<TITLE> </TITLE>
</HEAD>
<BODY>
</HTML>
</BODY>

Troubleshooting

Using Different Tools

If someone takes over a project that's been originated in FrontPage, is it worth taking the time to re-format the code?

The first thing to consider before taking on such a large task is where the work is going to remain. If a project entails moving back and forth from FrontPage, it's not worth re-formatting the code because this will become a constant task. If the project will remain in a Notepad—or HomeSite—type environment henceforth, it is definitely worth the effort. You will find that it's easier to make sense of the code and eliminate extraneous tags after it's in a workable format.

Designing for the Real World

A Study in Coding Styles

You can learn a lot about HTML coding by studying the code of others. That is, a lot about what to do and a lot more about what not to do. Even the most successful sites approach their code in different ways. How do I know this? By studying their code!

Whenever you see a site that appeals to you on some level—whether it be its simplicity or complexity—all you need to do is right-click the page and choose View Source. You'll instantly get an inside look into how the Web developer approaches his work.

For example, go to the Yahoo! site and view the source of their main page. You'll notice that the code is lumped together. There are no comments in the source. There are also some instances of overlapping tags, particularly `<FONT>` tags.

A visit to Excite yields slightly better code, from a readability standpoint. There are no carriage returns between blocks of code, but the tags are all flush left, making it much easier to analyze and tear apart. The Go Network site is similarly coded, with flush left tags. Watch out for those overlapping tags, however!

Finally, look at Lycos and Netcenter. Both are tagged flush left, and they've even separated blocks of code with carriage returns. Netcenter has also included comments to help the coders keep track of what goes where. Isn't it easier to make sense of the code on these sites?

As you navigate the Web, you'll find no shortage of examples to study. Just make sure those examples are good ones.

Note

Visit these pages for a look under the hood of the biggest sites on the Net.

Yahoo!—**`http://www.yahoo.com/`**

Excite—**`http://www.excite.com/`**

Lycos—**`http://www.lycos.com/`**

Go Network—**`http://www.go.com/`**

Netscape Netcenter—**`http://www.netcenter.com/`**

Ebay—**`http://www.ebay.com/`**

Microsoft—**`http://www.microsoft.com/`**

CHAPTER 7

Formatting and Aligning Text

In this chapter

Formatting Elements

Text formatting is where HTML is its most simplistic—and most powerful. After all, the HTML was developed to format text-based documents and make them available on the Internet, with the major enhancement being the capability to hyperlink documents.

Most of the concepts in text formatting are straightforward, from standard headers, breaks, paragraphs, and text styles such as bold, italic, and underlined text.

The following tags can be used to format text:

- `<H1>…</H1>-<H6>…</H6>`—The range of header tags used to denote paragraph and content headings and subheadings.
- `<BR>`—The break tag, which is equivalent to one carriage return.
- `<P>`—The paragraph tag, used to denote a paragraph.
- `<P>…</P>`—The open/close approach to paragraph denotation.
- `<PRE>…</PRE>`—The preformatted text tag.
- `<NOBR>…</NOBR>`—When you want to force a line without a natural break, use the no break tag. This tag is not an official part of HTML 4.0, but it is widely supported and frequently used.
- `<B>…</B>`—The bold tag, for bolding text.
- `<I>…</I>`—The italics tag, for italicizing text.
- `<U>…</U>` —The underline tag, used for underlining text.

We will also examine several associated tags and special formatting tags, in addition to these standard text-formatting tags.

Exploring Text Concepts

When approaching text content for a Web page, you should follow a number of helpful guidelines.

Just as you would prepare any professional text document, all Web-based text should be free of grammatical or spelling errors, appropriately written with the audience in mind, and follow a clear, concise pattern of development. A good structure to follow is to begin with an introduction, have several paragraphs that detail the content, and follow this with a conclusion, restating the intent of the communication.

The Web has certain visual constraints. It's important to keep in mind that extremely long pages of text are tiring on the eyes. Furthermore, keeping paragraphs short can be helpful in getting information across to HTML document visitors, who tend not to stay on individual Web pages for very long periods of time.

→ For more information about the Web's visual environment, **see** Chapter 26, "Resolution, Gamma, and the Visual Environment," **p. 546**

Following a logical arrangement of text is wise. For example, if you've structured your text well, you can highlight certain areas by using headers or text emphasis. There is a logical order for headers, beginning with the largest size and then moving into smaller sizes where necessary. When emphasizing text with bold, italic, or underlined styles, the important thing to remember is that a light touch is wise. Be consistent and logical, never deviating from the clean and precise output that is so necessary for effective Web communication.

WORKING WITH HEADERS

HTML headers help you announce specific areas of a document by titling that individual area. The header tag is an alphanumeric combination of an "H" plus a numeric value ranging from 1–6, 1 being the largest, and 6 being the smallest. As many seasoned coders already know, you can use headers to represent distinct layers of information within the natural progress of text. My title, for example, would be a large header, the first sub-section would be titled by using a header size one size smaller than the chapter head, and so forth.

Caution

Header tags seemingly work "backwards," with the lowest value, "1," creating the largest visual header. Remember that this is a convention born of document formatting, where a larger header denotes the dominant level of concept, and so forth. In HTML, this applies only to header tags, and does not follow through with other HTML size conventions, such as with the `FONT` tag, where sizing runs from small numbers to denote small text, to larger numbers for larger text.

Header tags work simply by surrounding the text you want to use for titling with the appropriately sized tag:

```
<H1>Health Benefits of Exercise</H1>
```

```
This information will appear on an HTML page as being the largest header size (see
Figure 7.1).
```

Simply change the numeric value to get a different size:

```
<H5>Other Benefits of Exercise</H5>
```

Figure 7.2 shows the smaller header size.

Note

Headers maintain consistency in general size and appearance across browsers and platforms. However, when viewed at different resolutions, the appearance of the header size will naturally change.

→ To read more about these concepts in detail, **see** "Resolution, Gamma, and the Visual Environment," **p. 546**

Tip from molly

Use headers sparingly, and where absolutely necessary. Keeping to header sizes 1–3 is safest, because at smaller sizes, headers are hard to read.

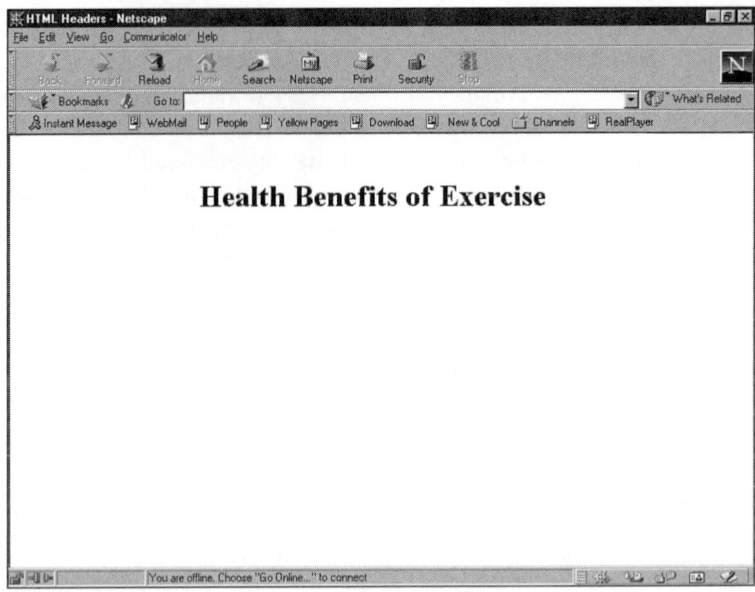

Figure 7.1
Headers of size 1 are used most commonly when formatting the primary heading of a page.

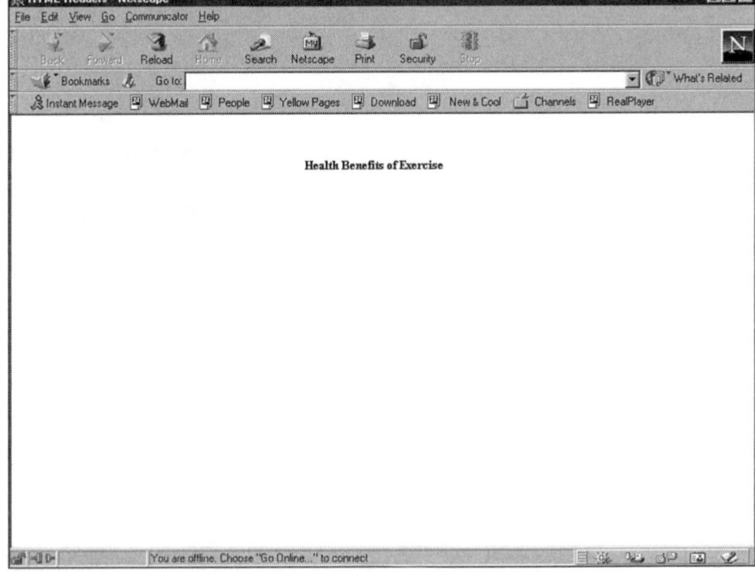

Figure 7.2
A Header, size 5. This size header will appear quite small on all browsers.

Let's add a header to a paragraph of text:

1. Open one of your HTML shell templates in a favorite editor:

```
<HTML>
<HEAD>
```

```
<TITLE>          </TITLE>
</HEAD>

<BODY>


</BODY>

</HTML>
```

2. Add a paragraph of text within the body area:

```
<HTML>
<HEAD>

<TITLE>          </TITLE>
</HEAD>

<BODY>

Exercise is an excellent way of improving your health. Medical studies
demonstrate that exercise can strengthen your heart and lungs, lower
your blood pressure, and help you maintain a healthy weight.

</BODY>

</HTML>
```

3. Add a header:

```
<HTML>
<HEAD>

<TITLE>          </TITLE>
</HEAD>

<BODY>


<H1>Health Benefits of Exercise</H1>
Exercise is an excellent way of improving your health. Medical studies
demonstrate that exercise can strengthen your heart and lungs, lower
your blood pressure, and help you maintain a healthy weight.

</BODY>

</HTML>
```

4. Title your page:

```
<HTML>
<HEAD>

<TITLE>Benefits of Exercise</TITLE>
</HEAD>

<BODY>
```

```
<H1>Health Benefits of Exercise</H1>
Exercise is an excellent way of improving your health. Medical studies
demonstrate that exercise can strengthen your heart and lungs, lower
your blood pressure, and help you maintain a healthy weight.

</BPDY>

</HTML>
```

5. Save your file.
6. View in your browser and check the results with Figure 7.3.
7. If they are similar, save your file.

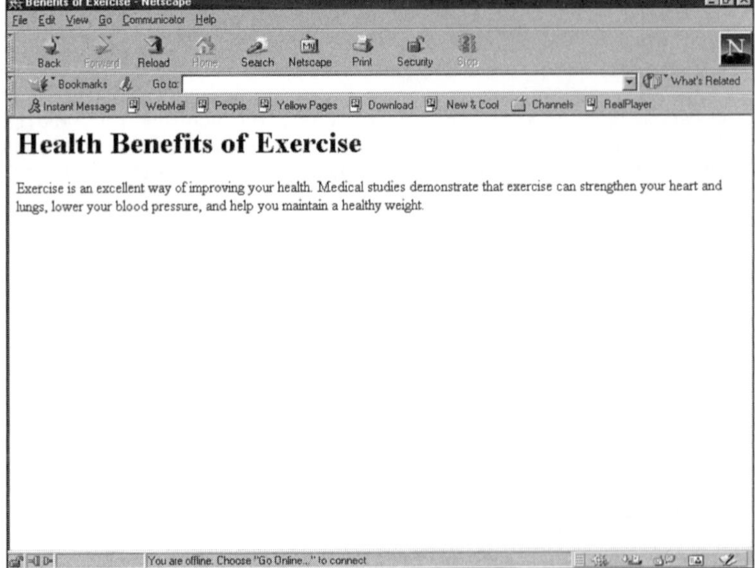

Figure 7.3
Header, size 1, in relation to a paragraph of text, which is a default size (size 3).

Headers are automatically left-aligned on a page, so if you want to center them, or align them to the right, the best way to do this is use an alignment method, which you can find later in this chapter.

INSERTING PARAGRAPHS AND BREAKS

By using paragraph element options, you can separate your paragraphs into discrete, visible blocks. The paragraph tag formats these blocks by invoking two carriage returns where you determine the end of your paragraph to be.

UNDERSTANDING THE PARAGRAPH TAG APPROACH

There are two common paragraph-tagging styles. The first is to simply use the `<P>` tag before the natural beginning of a paragraph as shown in Listing 7.1.

LISTING 7.1 SINGLE <P> TAG BEFORE PARAGRAPH

```
<HTML>
<HEAD>

<TITLE>Benefits of Exercise</TITLE>
</HEAD>

<BODY>

<H1>Health Benefits of Exercise</H1>
<P>Exercise is an excellent way of improving your health. Medical
studies demonstrate that exercise can strengthen your heart and
lungs, lower your blood pressure, and help you maintain a healthy
weight.

<P>Exercise can also assist with improving your mood. In fact, people who
exercise have demonstrated better self-esteem, stronger decision
making, and a generally more positive outlook on life.

</BODY>

</HTML> Tag After Paragraph (listing 7.1)> Tag After Paragraph>
```

This style is neat and clean, and I, as well as many hand-coders, prefer it. However, the alternative style, which uses an opening <P> and closing </P> at the beginning and end of a given paragraph, has the added advantage of allowing attributes to be applied to that paragraph.

Caution

Whichever style you choose, be sure to be consistent. You should never combine the styles, because this will potentially cause disturbances in your text formatting.

The open/close technique becomes especially handy when you want to align text, or you want to add styles using a style sheet.

→ To learn how to work with style sheets, **see** "Cascading Style Sheet Techniques", **p. 254**

Listing 7.2 shows the same code example, this time using the open/close paragraph style.

LISTING 7.2 THE OPEN AND CLOSE PARAGRAPH APPROACH

```
<HTML>
<HEAD>

<TITLE>Benefits of Exercise</TITLE>
</HEAD>

<BODY>

<H1>Health Benefits of Exercise</H1>
<P>
```

PART II CH 7

continues

LISTING 7.2 CONTINUED

```
Exercise is an excellent way of improving your health. Medical studies
demonstrate that exercise can strengthen your heart and lungs, lower
your blood pressure, and help you maintain a healthy weight.
</P>

<P>
Exercise can also assist with improving your mood. In fact, people who
exercise have demonstrated better self-esteem, stronger decision making,
and a generally more positive outlook on life.
</P>

</BODY>

</HTML>
```

WORKING WITH THE BREAK TAG

Sometimes you'll want to force a carriage return, and this can be done using the `<BR>` tag. A great example of where you might do this is when coding an address:

```
Natural Health Products<BR>
1 Happy Trails Way<BR>
Anytown, USA, 000000<BR>
```

The break tag in each instance forces a carriage return to the next available line, with no extra lines in between (see Figure 7.4).

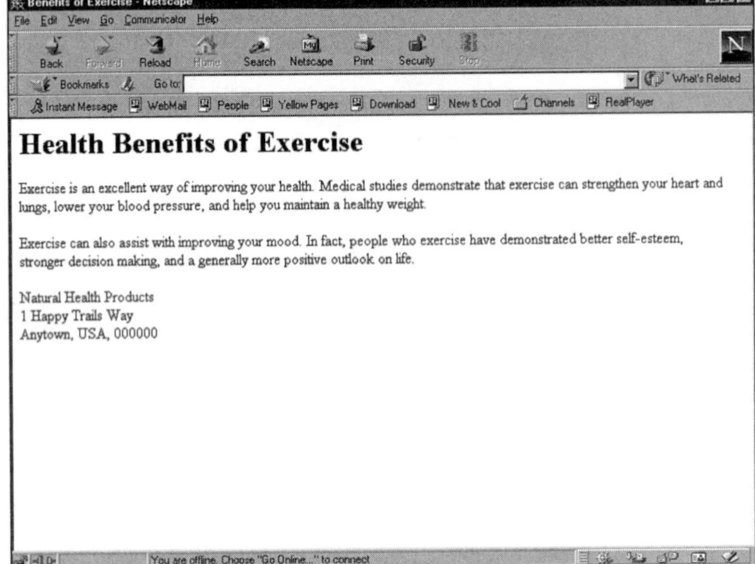

Figure 7.4
Using the break tag gives you added control over text placement and spacing on your Web page.

An ancillary tag that you can use once in a while is the <NOBR>, or "no break" tag:

```
<HTML>
<HEAD>

<TITLE>nobreak test</TITLE>
</HEAD>

<BODY>
<NOBR>
If I have a very long line of text and I do not want it to break at
all, I can use the nobreak tag to accomplish that. This entire line
will display without ever breaking.
</NOBR>

</BODY>
</HTML>
```

This tag ensures that no natural break occurs—the line continues until you tell the browser otherwise (see Figure 7.5).

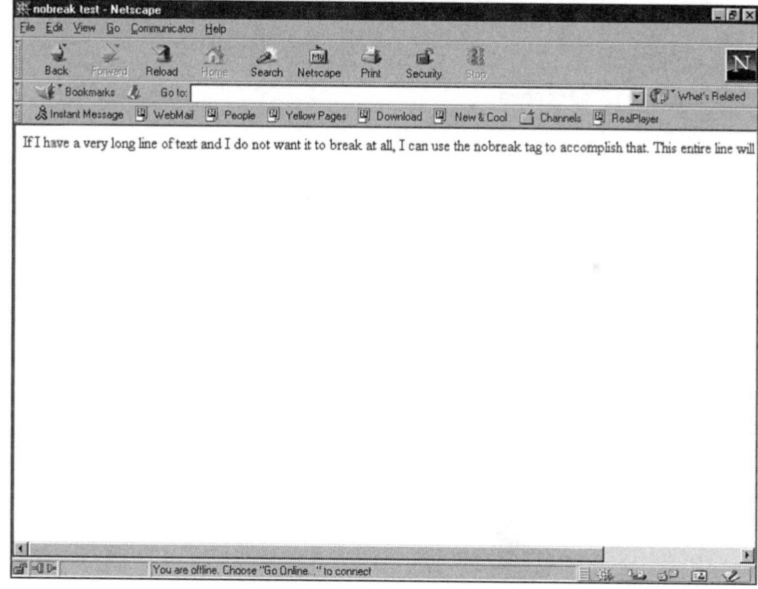

Figure 7.5
When using the nobreak tag, note that your reader will need to scroll horizontally to see the entire line of text.

However, this tag is not used very much, because it can cause horizontal scrolls (not good!) and can cause you to lose, rather than gain, control of the page's formatting.

CREATING SPACE WITH PARAGRAPHS AND BREAKS

Many people seek to use paragraphs and breaks to create whitespace between paragraphs, and even images or objects. Although not illegal, it's important to understand a bit about how browsers deal with paragraphs and breaks to avoid problems.

When using a paragraph tag to gain space, it's important to use only the single <P> method. An individual <P>, as mentioned, generates *two* carriage returns—one from the last available line (just as a break tag would), and one more line beyond that. So any time you want one free line of space, you can use a <P> tag to achieve it. A paragraph tag follows this equation:

```
1 <P> = 2 <BR>
```

In Figure 7.6, I coded an image followed by a <P> tag, followed by some text to show you the space that results.

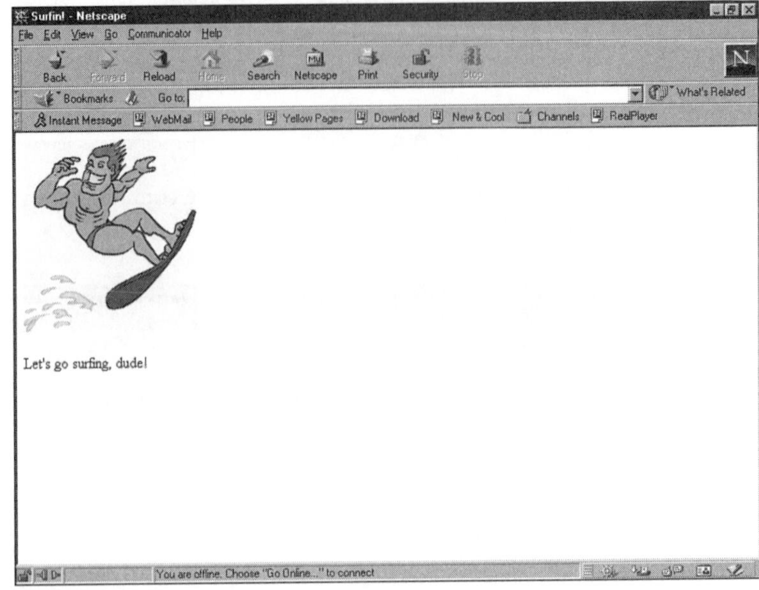

Figure 7.6
An image followed by one paragraph tag adds two lines of space between the image and the text below.

Many people think that they can get more space by stacking paragraph tags. This is *not true*! Browsers almost always ignore any other paragraph tag, so you cannot do the following to get three spaces:

```
<P>
<P>
<P>
```

Instead, you only end up with the same amount of space shown earlier in Figure 7.6.

However, you *can* add breaks to one paragraph. Remember the equation that states one paragraph is equivalent to two breaks? Simply add the amount of breaks you want after the first paragraph to gain space:

```
<P>
<BR>
<BR>
<BR>
```

Figure 7.7 is the same image followed by this set of one paragraph and three breaks.

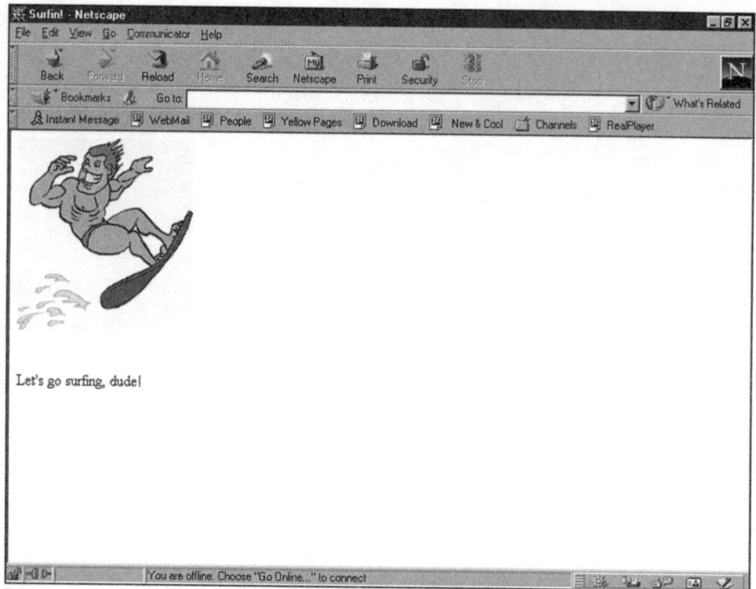

Figure 7.7
An image followed by one paragraph tag and three breaks.

Generally, it's not wise to try and add more than three breaks after a paragraph tag. There are other methods to gain space, such as using the <PRE>, or preformatted text, tag; using tables for greater spatial control; employing the `vspace` attribute; and using Cascading Style Sheets for positioning.

→ For information on how to use the `vspace` attribute, **see** "Working With Images", **p. 203**

→ To find out how to use style sheets for positioning, **see** "Element Positioning and Style Sheet Scripting", **p. 430**

WORKING WITH THE PREFORMATTED TEXT TAG

The preformatted text tag, <PRE>, and its companion closing tag </PRE> were originally developed as a method of allowing columnar data in an HTML page. This was done before the advent of tables, and it was not an effective way of controlling data.

The way the tag works is by including all the formatting you place within the tags—including carriage returns, spaces, and text—*without* the use of tags. In other words, you don't need a <P> tag to get a paragraph break, all you need to do is manually enter the paragraph tags, and so forth:

```
<PRE>
This sentence is broken
Not by a break tag, but
By the preformatted carriage
Returns I've placed within
This section of code.
</PRE>
```

Figure 7.8 shows how this code appears, complete with breaks.

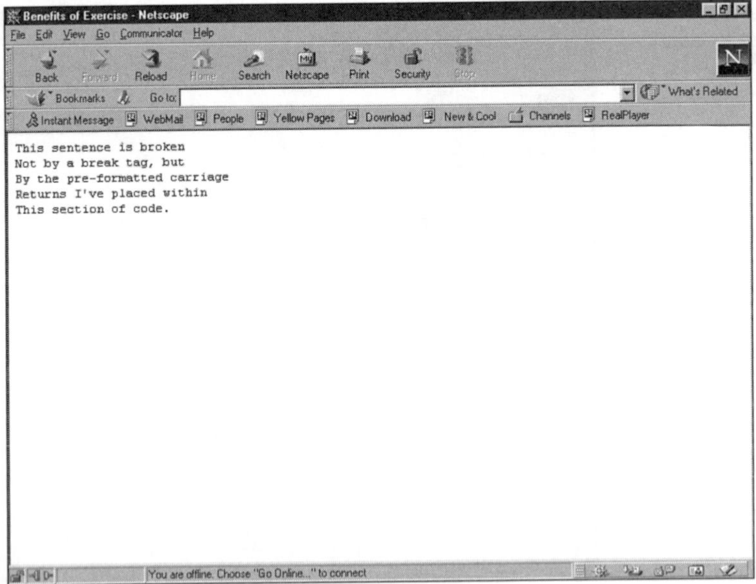

Figure 7.8
Using the preformatted text tag means that any text formatting options, such as the line breaks shown here, that are used when typing the text, will remain part of the text with no other tags necessary to invoke the formatting.

If you're very observant, you'll probably have noticed that the preformatted text tag does something else: it forces a fixed-width, or monospaced, font. This is different from the default font, and can be unattractive when the two are combined without forethought.

Tables have solved the irregularity problems caused when trying to arrange columnar material with the PRE tag, and font tags and style sheets allow you to have infinitely more control over your fonts. The PRE tag is still used from time to time to add space, however, and you can choose this option over or in addition to paragraphs and breaks when you want more space between elements on a page.

I've taken the same image from our earlier examples, and followed it up with the PRE tag, using 10 carriage returns before the subsequent text. Figure 7.9 shows the space created using this method.

The preformatted text tag is still supported by all contemporary browsers, and can be confidently used for any of the tag's legal applications. However, choosing tables or sticking with paragraph and break tags is usually a more consistent choice than using the preformatted text tag.

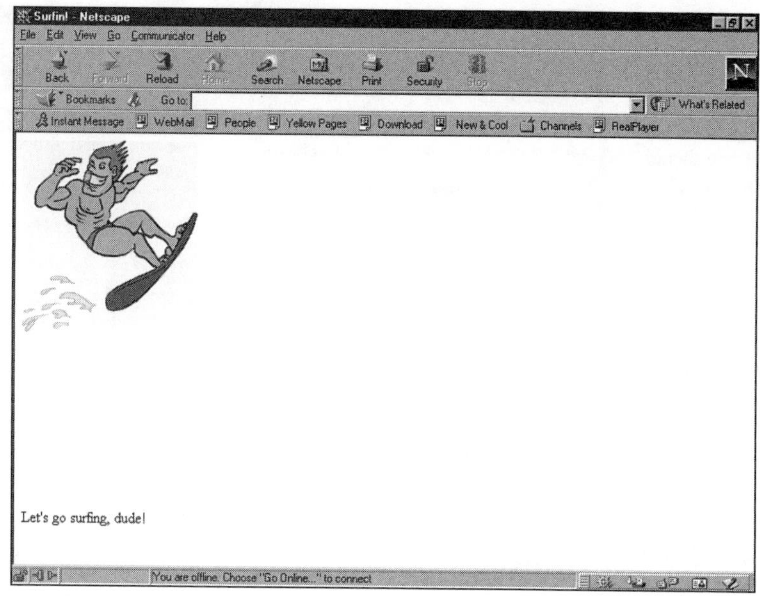

Figure 7.9
Using the preformatted text tag, you can create whitespace on your page without inserting any break tags or paragraph tags.

USING TEXT STYLES

Writers and designers often want to draw attention to specific information within a text document. There are also conventional methods of formatting text information, such as creating bibliographic references.

Three main text styles can be used in HTML to accommodate these text formatting concerns: the bold, italic, and underline styles.

The bold tag, or `<B>` (and its companion tag, `</B>`) is simply placed around a set of text that you want to render in bold:

```
Sally Forth sallies forth to <B>boldly</B> go where no one has gone before.
```

The same is true of italic tags, which use the `<I>` and closing `</I>` to achieve emphasis:

```
Janet did a <I>terrific</I> job organizing this year's conference.
```

The underline tags, with `<U>` and companion `</U>`, are no different:

```
The novel I'm currently reading, <U>Fugitive Pieces</U>, is a poetic look at
the life of a Holocaust survivor.
```

In Figure 7.10, I've put each of these sentences together into an HTML document and displayed them in my browser.

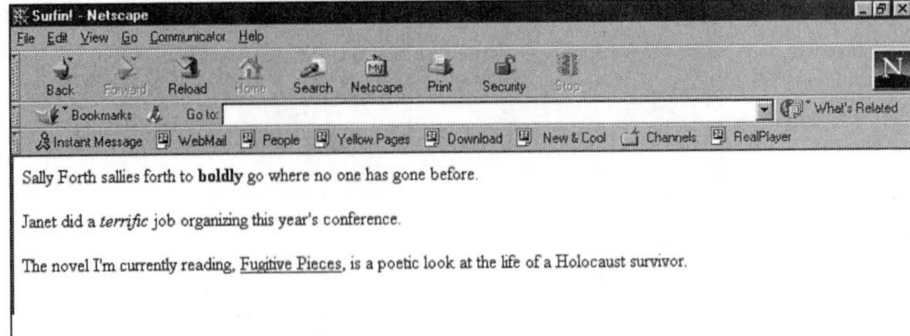

Figure 7.10
Bold, italic, and underlined text are all text formatting options, as seen here. However, you should use them for emphasis, and only where appropriate.

Caution

The use of underlined text should be approached with care. The reason for this is because links tend to be underlined, and people might mistake your underlined text for a link. Does this mean you should avoid underlining? I personally don't think so, but I do believe that it should be used only when necessary.

There are also tags related to bold and emphasis that will accomplish the same results. They are the `<STRONG>…</STRONG>` and `<EM>…</EM>` tags respectively. These tags are often used by WYSIWYGs, but are rarely used by professional hand-coders.

Listing 7.3 shows a sample paragraph using standard bold and italics as well as the strong and emphasis options.

LISTING 7.3 USING THE `Strong` AND `Emphasis` ATTRIBUTES

```
<HTML>
<HEAD>

<TITLE>Strong and Emphasis</TITLE>
</HEAD>

<BODY>
<P>People who <EM>want</EM> to be professional chefs usually learn by
apprenticing <STRONG>accomplished</STRONG> chefs, or by
attending an accredited culinary institute.


<P>For those individuals <I>simply</I> interested in improving their
cooking skills, many <B>local</B> adult education and recreation
programs offer gourmet cooking classes.


</BODY>

</HTML>
```

Figure 7.11 shows this code in the browser. You'll see that there is no visible difference between the two types of codes.

Note

It's interesting to point out that text formatting elements such as emphasis and italics are not dictated as appearing in italics by the standard. It's the browsers that make the decision to render the elements as you are seeing in Figure 7.11.

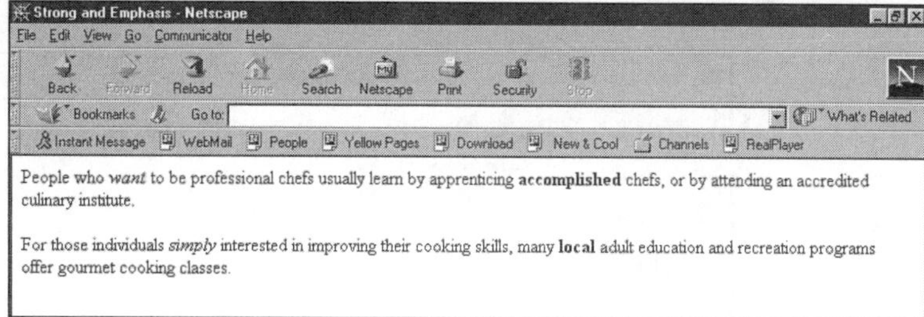

Figure 7.11 Strong and emphasis are not visibly different from bold and italic.

Caution

Use text styles sparingly. The point is to emphasize a few words or ideas on a page. More than this results in losing the impact that emphasis intends, so tread lightly. Furthermore, don't use italics, bold, or underline for long sections of body text–they are all more difficult to read for most people than standard weight text.

CREATING SPECIAL TEXT FORMATTING

Other, special types of text formatting are not as widely used, but do come in handy for certain kinds of text management.

If you want to make a section of text appear smaller than the surrounding body text, you can use the <SMALL> tag:

```
This text is normal, <SMALL>whereas this text is smaller.
</SMALL> This text is again normal.
```

You can do the reverse by using the <BIG> tag:

```
This text is normal, <BIG>whereas this text is bigger.</BIG>
This text is again normal.
```

If you want to use superscript, which places the affected text slightly above the horizon line, you can use the <SUP> element:

```
This text is normal, <SUP>whereas this text is superscripted.</SUP> This
text is again normal.
```

Subscript text, which appears below the horizon line, uses the <SUB> tag:

```
This text is normal, <SUB>whereas this text is subscripted.</SUB> This
text is again normal.
```

And the editing convention known as strikethrough, can be achieved using the <STRIKE> tag:

```
This text is normal, <STRIKE>whereas this text uses strikethrough.
</STRIKE> This text is again normal.
```

Figure 7.12 shows a screen shot of all these tags in action. You'll see that these really are specialty formats—most people rarely, if ever, have cause to use them.

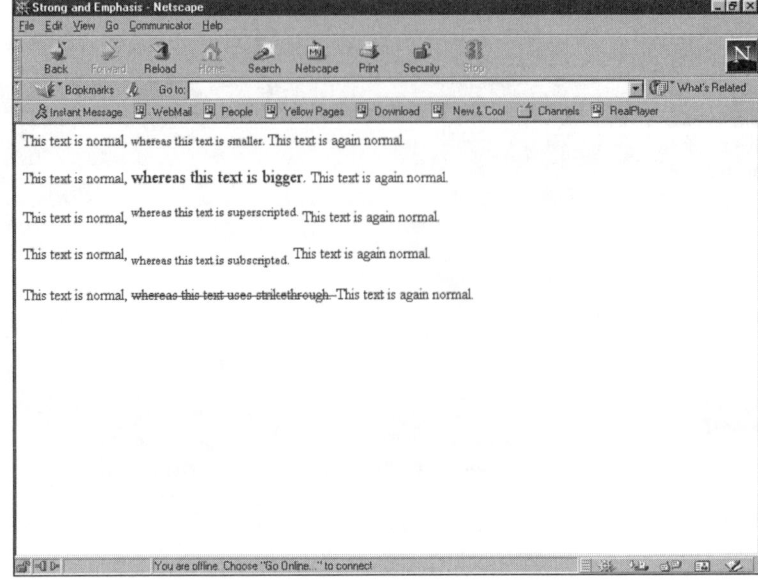

Figure 7.12
Specialty formatting tags provide another element of control over the formatting and presentation of text on your Web page.

Wondering what other specialty formatting tags you might use? See, "Other Formatting Elements" in the Troubleshooting section at the end of this chapter.

FORMATTING A COMPLETE TEXT DOCUMENT

If you've never coded a document by hand before, or if you just want a warm-up refresher, the next exercises will walk you through the creation of a complete document, start to finish.

First, let's add paragraphs with some text formatting to a standard shell:

1. Open up a simple shell template in a favorite editor:

```
<HTML>
<HEAD>

<TITLE> </TITLE>
</HEAD>

<BODY>



</BODY>
</HTML>
```

2. Add three paragraphs of text:

```
<HTML>
<HEAD>

<TITLE> </TITLE>
</HEAD>

<BODY>

A maid servant then brought them water in a beautiful golden ewer
and poured it into a silver basin for them to wash their hands, and
she drew a clean table beside them.

An upper servant brought them bread, and offered them many good things
of what there was in the house, the carver fetched them plates of all
manner of meats and set cups of gold by their side, and a man-servant
brought them wine and poured it out for them.

Then the suitors came in and took their places on the benches and
seats. Forthwith men servants poured water over their hands, maids
went round with the bread-baskets, pages filled the mixing-bowls
with wine and water, and they laid their hands upon the good things
that were before them.

</BODY>
</HTML>
```

3. Add paragraphs in the open/close style and title the page:

```
<HTML>
<HEAD>

<TITLE> Excerpt from Homer's Odyssey </TITLE>
</HEAD>

<BODY>

<P>A maid servant then brought them water in a beautiful golden ewer
and poured it into a silver basin for them to wash their hands, and
she drew a clean table beside them.</P>

<P>An upper servant brought them bread, and offered them many good things
of what there was in the house, the carver fetched them plates of all
manner of meats and set cups of gold by their side, and a man-servant
brought them wine and poured it out for them.</P>

<P>Then the suitors came in and took their places on the benches and
seats. Forthwith men servants poured water over their hands, maids
went round with the bread-baskets, pages filled the mixing-bowls
with wine and water, and they laid their hands upon the good things
that were before them.</P>

</BODY>
</HTML>
```

4. Add bold to several words:

```
<HTML>
<HEAD>

<TITLE> Excerpt from Homer's Odyssey </TITLE>
</HEAD>

<BODY>

<P>A maid servant then brought them water in a beautiful golden ewer
and poured it into a <B>silver basin</B> for them to wash their
hands, and she drew a clean table beside them.</P>

<P>An upper servant brought them bread, and offered them many good things
of what there was in the house, the carver fetched them plates of all
manner of meats and set <B>cups of gold</B> by their side, and a
man-servant brought them wine and poured it out for them.</P>

<P>Then the suitors came in and took their places on the benches and
seats. Forthwith men servants poured water over their hands, maids
went round with the bread-baskets, pages filled the mixing-bowls
with <B>wine and water</B>, and they laid their hands upon the good
things that were before them. </P>

</BODY>

</HTML>
```

5. Add italics to several words:

```
<HTNL>
<HEAD>

<TITLE> Excerpt from Homer's Odyssey </TITLE>
</HEAD>

<BODY>

<P>A maid servant then brought them water in a <I>beautiful</I> golden
ewer and poured it into a <B>silver basin</B> for them to wash their
hands, and she drew a clean table beside them.</P>

<P>An upper servant brought them bread, and offered them <I>many</I>
good things of what there was in the house, the carver fetched them
plates of all manner of meats and set <B>cups of gold</B> by their
side, and a man-servant brought them wine and poured it out for them.</P>

<P>Then the suitors came in and took their places on the benches and
seats. Forthwith men servants poured water over their hands, maids
went round with the bread-baskets, pages filled the mixing-bowls with
<B>wine and water</B>, and they <I>laid their hands</I> upon the
good things that were before them.</P>

</BODY>
</HMTL>
```

6. Add underlining to one selection of words:

```
<HTML>
<HEAD>

<TITLE> Excerpt from Homer's Odyssey </TITLE>
</HEAD>

<BODY>

<P>A maid servant then brought them water in a <I>beautiful</I> golden
ewer and poured it into a <B>silver basin</B> for them to wash their
hands, and she <U>drew a clean table beside them</U>.</P>

<P>An upper servant brought them bread, and offered them <I>many</I>
good things of what there was in the house, the carver fetched them
plates of all manner of meats and set <B>cups of gold</B> by their
side, and a man-servant brought them wine and poured it out for them.</P>

<P>Then the suitors came in and took their places on the benches and
seats. Forthwith men servants poured water over their hands, maids
went round with the bread-baskets, pages filled the mixing-bowls with
<B>wine and water</B>, and they <I>laid their hands</I> upon the
good things that were before them.</P>

</BODY>
</HTML>
```

7. Save your file.
8. View the file in a browser.
9. If you get the proper results (similar to Figure 7.13), save the file as `text_sample_1.html`.

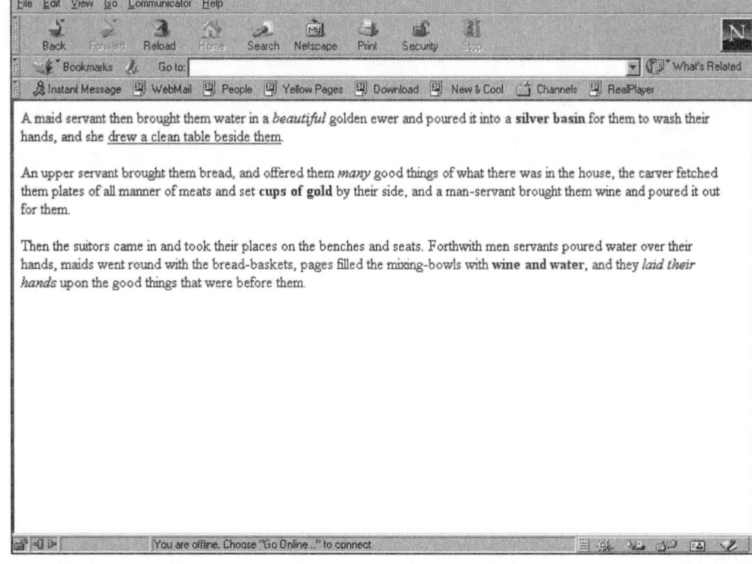

Figure 7.13
Adding paragraphs and text formatting.

This time do the same thing, only replace the open/close style with the single <P> option:

1. Open up your shell template.
2. Change the paragraph style to reflect the single rather than open/close style:

```
<HTML>
<HEAD>

<TITLE> Excerpt from Homer's Odyssey </TITLE>
</HEAD>

<BODY>

<P>A maid servant then brought them water in a <I>beautiful</I> golden
ewer and poured it into a <B>silver basin</B> for them to wash their
hands, and she <U>drew a clean table beside them</U>.

<P>An upper servant brought them bread, and offered them <I>many</I>
good things of what there was in the house, the carver fetched them
plates of all manner of meats and set <B>cups of gold</B> by their
side, and a man-servant brought them wine and poured it out for them.

<P>Then the suitors came in and took their places on the benches and
seats. Forthwith men servants poured water over their hands, maids
went round with the bread-baskets, pages filled the mixing-bowls with
<B>wine and water</B>, and they <I>laid their hands</I> upon the
good things that were before them.

</BODY>
</HTML>
```

3. Check your work for syntactical errors.
4. Save the file as `text_sample_2.html`.
5. View the results in your browser.

In this exercise, you'll add an address using the break <BR> tag:

1. Open up `text_sample_2.html`.

```
<HTML>
<HEAD>

<TITLE> Excerpt from Homer's Odyssey </TITLE>
</HEAD>

<BODY>


<P>A maid servant then brought them water in a <I>beautiful</I> golden
ewer and poured it into a <B>silver basin</B> for them to wash their
hands, and she <U>drew a clean table beside them</U>.

<P>An upper servant brought them bread, and offered them <I>many</I>
good things of what there was in the house, the carver fetched them
```

```
plates of all manner of meats and set <B>cups of gold</B> by their
side, and a man-servant brought them wine and poured it out for them.

<P>Then the suitors came in and took their places on the benches and
seats. Forthwith men servants poured water over their hands, maids
went round with the bread-baskets, pages filled the mixing-bowls with
<B>wine and water</B>, and they <I>laid their hands</I> upon the
good things that were before them.

</BODY>
</HTML>
```

2. Add an address somewhere logical in the document:

```
<HTML>
<HEAD>

<TITLE> Excerpt from Homer's Odyssey </TITLE>
</HEAD>

<BODY>

<P>A maid servant then brought them water in a <I>beautiful</I> golden
ewer and poured it into a <B>silver basin</B> for them to wash their
hands, and she <U>drew a clean table beside them</U>.
<P>An upper servant brought them bread, and offered them <I>many</I>
good things of what there was in the house, the carver fetched them
plates of all manner of meats and set <B>cups of gold</B> by their
side, and a man-servant brought them wine and poured it out for them.

<P>Then the suitors came in and took their places on the benches and
seats. Forthwith men servants poured water over their hands, maids
went round with the bread-baskets, pages filled the mixing-bowls with
<B>wine and water</B>, and they <I>laid their hands</I> upon the
good things that were before them.

<P>Did you enjoy reading this excerpt? You can find the entire text of
the Odyssey in the University Bookstore,

<P>University Bookstore
1111 Central Gate Drive
University City, USA

</BODY>
</HTML>
```

3. Use the `<br>` tag to format the address:

```
University Bookstore<BR>
1111 Central Gate Drive<BR>
University City, USA
```

4. Check your work against Figure 7.14.
5. Save the file as `text_sample_3.html`.

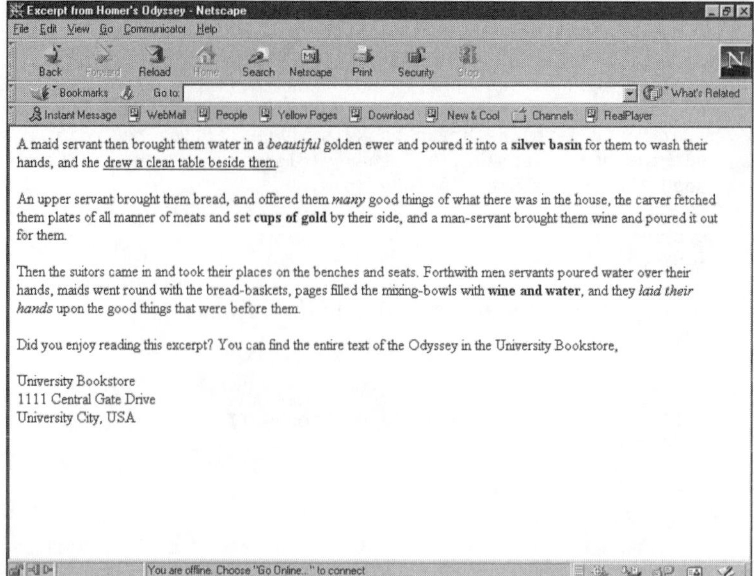

Figure 7.14
Adding the break tag to the document. The results are a single break, evenly spaced between each lines.

Now, try some preformatting for space:

1. In your favorite editor, open up `text_sample_3.html`, the file you just saved in the last task.
2. Add the `<PRE>` tags using the container method, with four carriage returns between the sentence and before the address:

```
<HTML>
<HEAD>

<TITLE> Excerpt from Homer's Odyssey </TITLE>
</HEAD>

<BODY>

<P>A maid servant then brought them water in a <I>beautiful</I> golden
ewer and poured it into a <B>silver basin</B> for them to wash their
hands, and she <U>drew a clean table beside them</U>.
<P>An upper servant brought them bread, and offered them <I
>many</I>
good things of what there was in the house, the carver fetched them
plates of all manner of meats and set <B>cups of gold</B> by their
side, and a man-servant brought them wine and poured it out for them.

<P>Then the suitors came in and took their places on the benches and
seats. Forthwith men servants poured water over their hands, maids
went round with the bread-baskets, pages filled the mixing-bowls with
<B>wine and water</B>, and they <I>laid their hands</I> upon the
good things that were before them.
```

```
<P>Did you enjoy reading this excerpt? You can find the entire text of
the Odyssey in the University Bookstore,
<PRE>



</PRE>
University Bookstore<BR>
1111 Central Gate Drive<BR>
University City, USA<BR>

</BODY>
</HTML>
```

3. Check your work against Figure 7.15.
4. Save the file as `text_sample_4.html`.

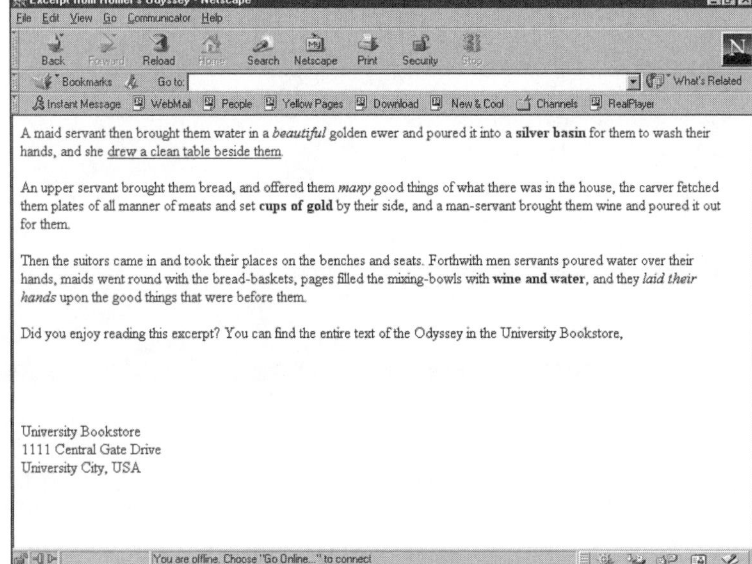

Figure 7.15
Using preformatted text within your document is another way to control the spacing of paragraphs of text.

Although you might never need to use special text formatting, let's have some fun and play with `big`, `small`, and other special format codes in the following exercise.

1. Open `text_sample_4.html`, which you just saved.
2. Add your choice of special character formats:

```
<HTML>
<HEAD>

<TITLE> Excerpt from Homer's Odyssey </TITLE>
</HEAD>

<BODY>
```

```
<P>A maid servant then brought them water in a <I>beautiful</I> golden
ewer and poured it into a <B>silver basin</B> for them to <SUB>
wash their hands</SUB>, and she <U>drew a clean table beside them</U>.

<P>An upper servant brought them bread, and offered them <I>many</I>
good things of what there was in the house, the carver fetched them
plates of all manner of meats and set <B>cups of gold</B> by their
side, and a man-servant brought them wine and poured it out for them.

<P>Then the suitors came in and <STRIKE>took their places</STRIKE> on
the benches and seats. Forthwith men servants poured water over their
hands, maids went round with the bread-baskets, pages filled the
mixing-bowls with <B>wine and water</B>, and they <I>laid their hands
</I> upon the good things that were before them.

<P>Did you enjoy reading <BIG>this</BIG> excerpt? You can find the entire
text of <STRONG>The Odyssey</STRONG> in the University Bookstore,
<PRE>



</PRE>
University Bookstore<BR>
1111 Central Gate Drive<BR>
University City, USA<BR>

</BODY>
</HTML>
```

3. Check your work, and save it as `text_sample_5.html`. You can view my version of the file in Figure 7.16.

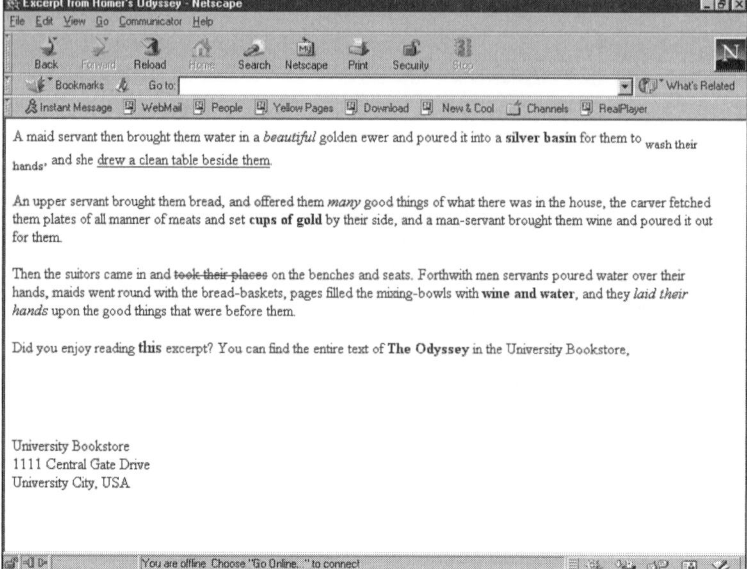

Figure 7.16
For fun, I added special formatting as an example of another way you might add emphasis to your text.

Aligning Text

The way text appears on a page is important to both readability and esthetics. *Alignment*—also known as *justification*—describes how the text is positioned both in relation to itself, and in relation to other objects on a page. Alignment plays a large role in the way text looks, determining where and how that text is placed.

Typically, text is justified to the left (at least with most Western languages). This means it begins at the flush-left margin of the page. Along the right side, the text is uneven. This is referred to as *ragged right*.

However, there are other alignment options that you'll want to use. For shorter sections of text, you can right-align or center the text. This can add emphasis to the text in question, as well as break up the space to provide a bit of visual respite from the standard justification.

Note

You can use several methods to control text alignment. There are common HTML tags, attributes, and values of which you should be aware. It's important to remember that because alignment is really a layout rather than formatting process, style sheet alignment is recommended in the HTML 4.0 standard over the common HTML.

➔ To learn how to align text using style sheets, **see** "Designing Type with CSS," **p. 284**

Before getting to the actual tags, take a look at what values or types of alignment are available:

- Default—When no alignment is specified for text, browsers cause it to default to the standard flush left, ragged right (see Figure 7.17).
- Left—This is the same as browser default. However, you can use left as a fixed value with alignment. This is especially helpful when you're using another kind of alignment on the page and want to secure anything that you want to appear as left-justified.
- Right—Right alignment is the flushing of text to the right margin leaving a ragged left margin, as shown in Figure 7.18. Right alignment is an interesting special effect, but generally should be used as enhancement, not standard body text.
- Center—The centering of text, like right justification, creates a visual effect (see Figure 7.19). It's important not to overuse centering. Many novice designers will use a lot of centered text. What they're really after is whitespace and visual texture, because centering creates a more interesting look. However, it is difficult to read for any length of time.
- Justify—Justification is the spacing of text so that each margin is flush rather than ragged. Compare Figure 7.20 to the left, or default, justification in Figure 7.17 to get an idea of the difference.

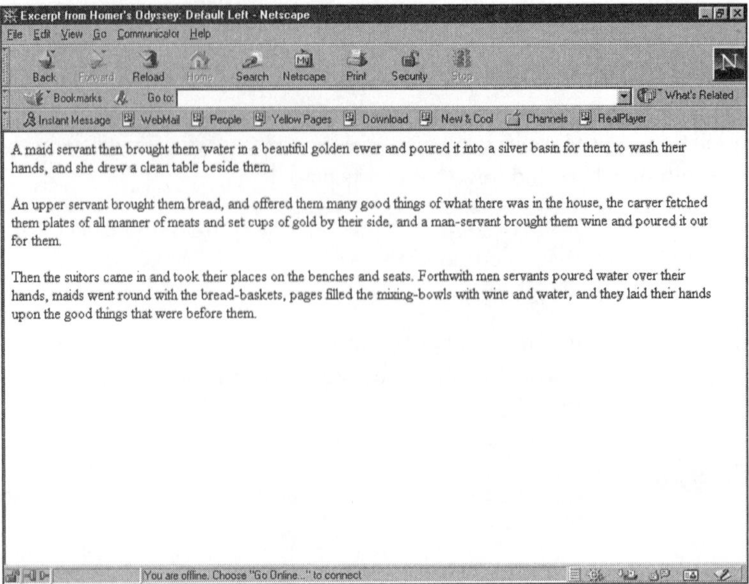

Figure 7.17
Default or flush-left alignment.

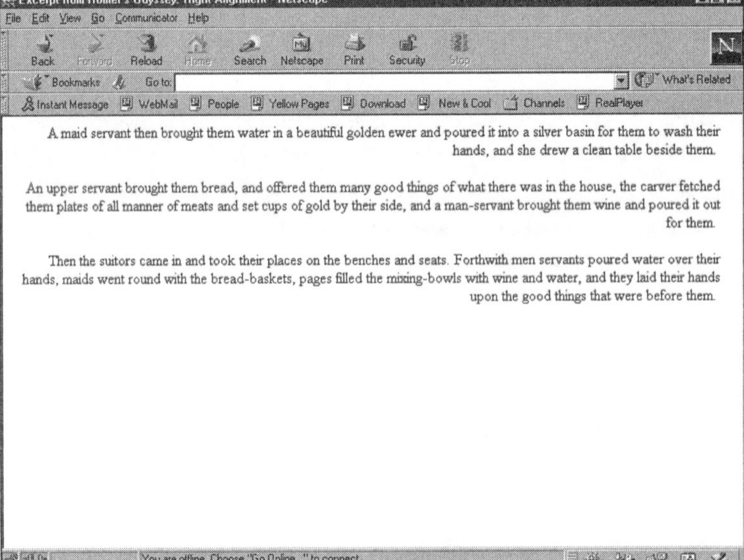

Figure 7.18
Right alignment. Note ragged left margin.

Caution

The `justify` attribute is only available for Internet Explorer and Netscape 4.0 and later. If you choose to use it, your alignment reverts to the default left in browsers that cannot read it.

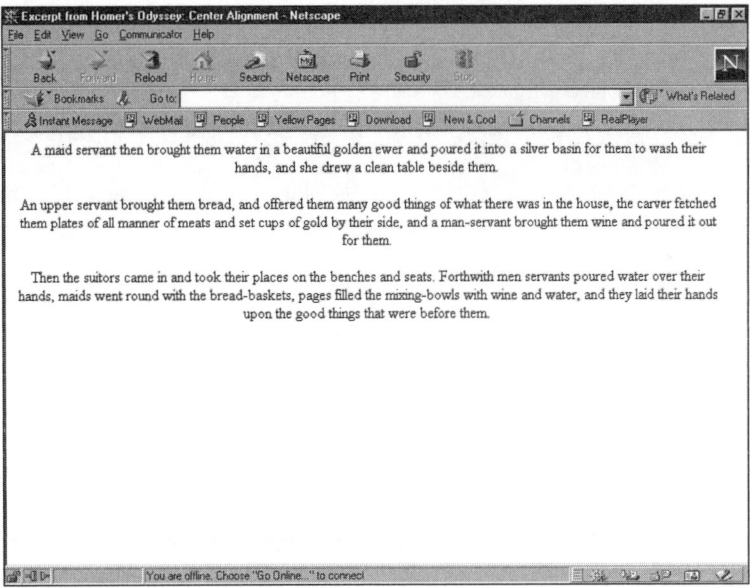

Figure 7.19
Centered text. Centering should be used for emphasis, not for body text.

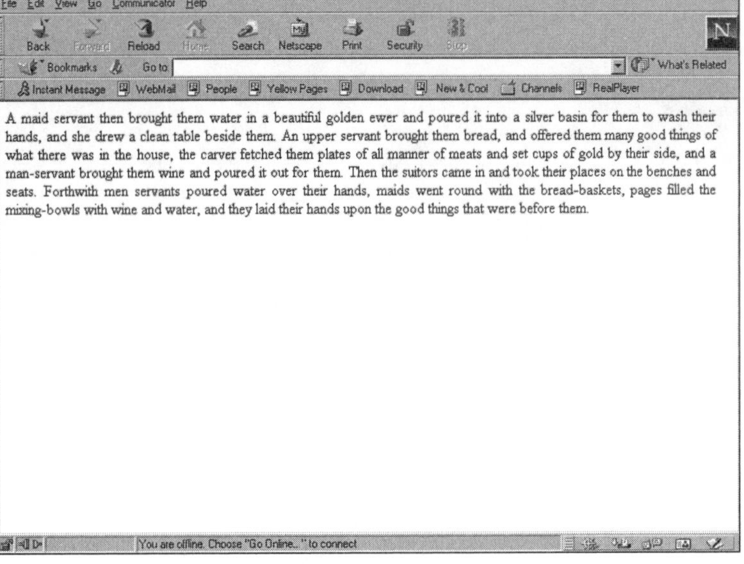

Figure 7.20
Justified text has flush left and right margins. I've removed the paragraphs so that you can see clearly how each line is flush left and right.

Alignment with Style

Style sheets are the preferred method in strict HTML 4.0 for many layout concerns. Text alignment can be controlled with style sheets.

The appropriate syntax for aligning text with style sheets is as follows:

```
text-align: value
```

Your `value` can equal `left`, `center`, `right`, or `justify`—just as with standard HTML tagging.

For more information about applying style sheets, be sure to visit Chapter 13, "Cascading Style Sheet Techniques."

USING THE DIV ELEMENT

The `DIV` element is a powerful tool for a number of reasons. Not only can it be used to divide sections of an HTML document and align information within that section, it is one of the pillars of Cascading Style Sheets.

→ To find out how to use Cascading Style Sheets to control formatting options, **see** "Cascading Style Sheet Techniques," **p. 263**

Using `DIV` tags, whether for simple HTML formatting or for more advanced applications, has become one of the primary methods of controlling documents in HTML 4.0.

To align text by using the `DIV` element, you'll need to select one of the alignment attributes discussed in the previous section.

Note

You'll see that I've added the `BLOCKQUOTE` element to many of the examples in this chapter. Although this element has lost emphasis in the HTML 4.0 standard in favor of style sheet positioning, it's a simple and effective way to block sections of text attractively within a page that isn't using style sheets. It's important to realize that `BLOCKQUOTE` was never intended for this purpose, but it's become a conventional method of gaining margins and attractive spacing of text.

If you have a section of text that you want to center, you apply the `DIV` tags in a step-by-step fashion to the document, adding formatting along the way:

1. Begin with a standard HTML shell:

```
<HTML>
<HEAD>
<TITLE>Alignment Exercise</TITLE>
</HEAD>
<BODY>

</BODY>
</HTML>
```

2. Add the text for the page:

```
<HTML>
<HEAD>
```

```
<TITLE>Alignment Exercise</TITLE>
</HEAD>
<BODY>
The Odyssey, by Homer
Book XXIII
"My good nurse," answered Penelope, "you must be mad. The gods sometimes send
some very sensible people out of their minds, and make foolish people become
sensible. This is what they must have been doing to you; for you always used
to be a reasonable person.

Why should you thus mock me when I have trouble enough already-talking such
nonsense, and waking me up out of a sweet sleep that had taken possession of
my eyes and closed them? I have never slept so soundly from the day my poor
husband went to that city with the ill-omened name.

Go back again into the women's room; if it had been any one else, who had woke
me up to bring me such absurd news I should have sent her away with a severe
scolding. As it is, your age shall protect you."

"My dear child," answered Euryclea, "I am not mocking you. It is quite true as
I tell you that Ulysses is come home again. He was the stranger whom they all
kept on treating so badly in the cloister. Telemachus knew all the time that
he was come back, but kept his father's secret that he might have his revenge
on all these wicked people.

Then Penelope sprang up from her couch, threw her arms round Euryclea, and
wept for joy. "But my dear nurse," said she, "explain this to me; if he has
really come home as you say, how did he manage to overcome the wicked suitors
single handed, seeing what a number of them there always were?"
</BODY>
</HTML>
```

3. Format the text to your needs:

```
<HTML>
<HEAD>
<TITLE>Alignment Exercise</TITLE>
</HEAD>
<BODY>
<BLOCKQUOTE>
<H2>The Odyssey, by Homer</H2>
<B>Book XXIII</B>
<P>"My good nurse," answered Penelope, "you must be mad. The gods sometimes
send some very sensible people out of their minds, and make foolish people
become sensible. This is what they must have been doing to you; for you always
used to be a reasonable person.

<P>Why should you thus mock me when I have trouble enough already-talking such
nonsense, and waking me up out of a sweet sleep that had taken possession of
my eyes and closed them? I have never slept so soundly from the day my poor
husband went to that city with the ill-omened name.
```

```
<P>Go back again into the women's room; if it had been any one else, who had
woke me up to bring me such absurd news I should have sent her away with a
severe scolding. As it is, your age shall protect you."

<P>"My dear child," answered Euryclea, "I am not mocking you. It is quite true
as I tell you that Ulysses is come home again. He was the stranger whom they
all kept on treating so badly in the cloister. Telemachus knew all the time
that he was come back, but kept his father's secret that he might have his
revenge on all these wicked people.

<P>Then Penelope sprang up from her couch, threw her arms round Euryclea, and
wept for joy. "But my dear nurse," said she, "explain this to me; if he has
really come home as you say, how did he manage to overcome the wicked suitors
single handed, seeing what a number of them there always were?"

</BLOCKQUOTE>
</BODY>
</HTML>
```

4. Now add the opening and closing DIV tags around the text you want to align:

```
<HTML>
<HEAD>
<TITLE>Alignment Exercise</TITLE>
</HEAD>
<BODY>
<BLOCKQUOTE>
<DIV>
<H2>The Odyssey, by Homer</H2>
<B>Book XXIII</B>
</DIV>

<P>"My good nurse," answered Penelope, "you must be mad. The gods sometimes
send some very sensible people out of their minds, and make foolish people
becomesensible. This is what they must have been doing to you; for you always
used to be a reasonable person.

<P>Why should you thus mock me when I have trouble enough already-talking such
nonsense, and waking me up out of a sweet sleep that had taken possession of
my eyes and closed them? I have never slept so soundly from the day my poor
husband went to that city with the ill-omened name.

<P>Go back again into the women's room; if it had been any one else, who had
woke me up to bring me such absurd news I should have sent her away with a
severe scolding. As it is, your age shall protect you."

<P>"My dear child," answered Euryclea, "I am not mocking you. It is quite true
as I tell you that Ulysses is come home again. He was the stranger whom they
all kept on treating so badly in the cloister. Telemachus knew all the time
that he was come back, but kept his father's secret that he might have his
revenge on all these wicked people.
```

```
<P>Then Penelope sprang up from her couch, threw her arms round Euryclea, and
wept for joy. "But my dear nurse," said she, "explain this to me; if he has
really come home as you say, how did he manage to overcome the wicked suitors
single handed, seeing what a number of them there always were?"

</BLOCKQUOTE>
</BODY>
</HTML>
```

5. Type the attribute and center value into the opening DIV tag:

```
<HTML>
<HEAD>
<TITLE>Alignment Exercise</TITLE>
</HEAD>
<BODY>
<BLOCKQUOTE>

<DIV align="center">
<H2>The Odyssey, by Homer</H2>
<B>Book XXIII</B>
</DIV>

<P>"My good nurse," answered Penelope, "you must be mad. The gods sometimes
send some very sensible people out of their minds, and make foolish people
become sensible. This is what they must have been doing to you; for you always
used to be a reasonable person.

<P>Why should you thus mock me when I have trouble enough already-talking such
nonsense, and waking me up out of a sweet sleep that had taken possession of
my eyes and closed them? I have never slept so soundly from the day my poor
husband went to that city with the ill-omened name.

<P>Go back again into the women's room; if it had been any one else, who had
woke me up to bring me such absurd news I should have sent her away with a
severe scolding. As it is, your age shall protect you."

<P>"My dear child," answered Euryclea, "I am not mocking you. It is quite true
as I tell you that Ulysses is come home again. He was the stranger whom they
all kept on treating so badly in the cloister. Telemachus knew all the time
that he was come back, but kept his father's secret that he might have his
revenge on all these wicked people.

<P>Then Penelope sprang up from her couch, threw her arms round Euryclea, and
wept for joy. "But my dear nurse," said she, "explain this to me; if he has
really come home as you say, how did he manage to overcome the wicked suitors
single handed, seeing what a number of them there always were?"

</BLOCKQUOTE>
</BODY>
</HTML>
```

6. Save your document as `div_center.html`.
7. View the page in your browser.

The text header should now be center-aligned and the body text default left, as in my example shown in Figure 7.21.

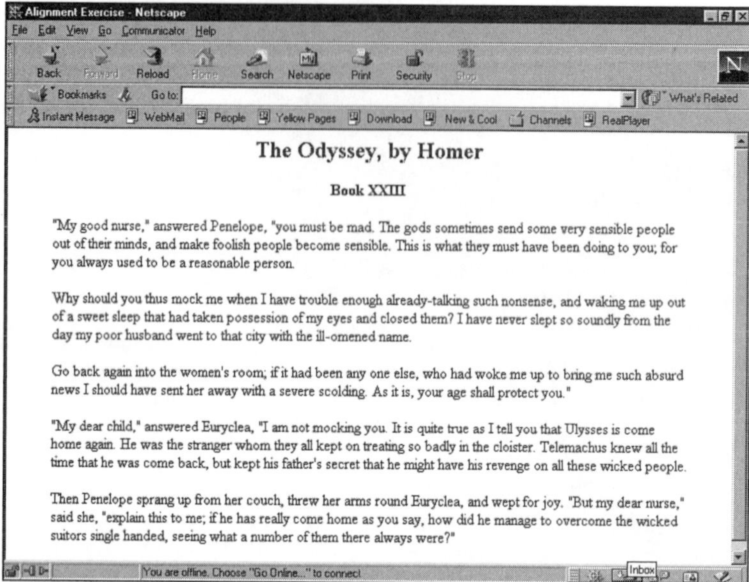

Figure 7.21
Using the `DIV` tag to center the alignment of the header enables me to leave the rest of the page defaults at the original left alignment.

> **Note**
>
> Many HTML authors use the `CENTER` element to center text. This element has been deprecated in the HTML 4.0 standard. Although it is still considered part of the transitional interpretation, it was deprecated primarily due to its lack of flexibility: No attributes or values can be added to it. Choosing the `DIV` element or other elements discussed in this chapter for centering text is a more sophisticated choice. The centering of text with the `DIV` tag renders the same visual results to the text or images in question as the `CENTER` element did.

If you want to alter your selection of text and make it align to the right, change the code to reflect the `right` value (see Listing 7.4).

LISTING 7.4 ALIGNING TO THE RIGHT

```
<HTML>
<HEAD>
<TITLE>Alignment Exercise</TITLE>
</HEAD>
```

```
<BODY>
<BLOCKQUOTE>
<DIV align="right">
<H2>The Odyssey, by Homer</H2>
<B>Book XXIII</B>
</DIV>
<P>"My good nurse," answered Penelope, "you must be mad. The gods sometimes send
some very sensible people out of their minds, and make foolish people become
sensible. This is what they must have been doing to you; for you always used to be
a reasonable person.
<P>Why should you thus mock me when I have trouble enough already-talking such
nonsense, and waking me up out of a sweet sleep that had taken possession of my
eyes and closed them? I have never slept so soundly from the day my poor husband
went to that city with the ill-omened name.
<P>Go back again into the women's room; if it had been any one else, who had woke
me up to bring me such absurd news I should have sent her away with a severe
scolding. As it is, your age shall protect you."
<P>"My dear child," answered Euryclea, "I am not mocking you. It is quite true as
I tell you that Ulysses is come home again. He was the stranger whom they all kept
on treating so badly in the cloister. Telemachus knew all the time that he was
come back, but kept his father's secret that he might have his revenge on all
these wicked people.
<P>Then Penelope sprang up from her couch, threw her arms round Euryclea, and wept
for joy. "But my dear nurse," said she, "explain this to me; if he has really come
home as you say, how did he manage to overcome the wicked suitors single handed,
seeing what a number of them there always were?"
</BLOCKQUOTE>
</BODY>
</HTML>
```

Figure 7.22 shows the header with right alignment as formatted with the DIV element. The remaining text defaults to the left.

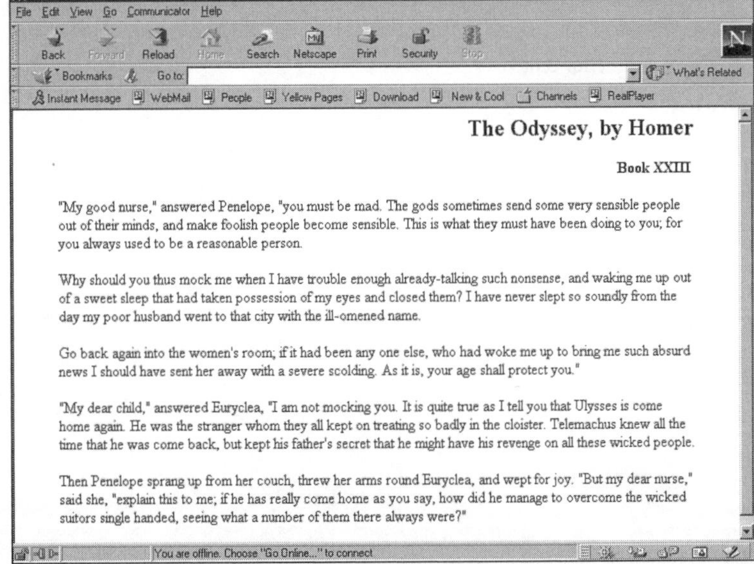

Figure 7.22
Using the DIV element here results in right alignment of the header with all text outside of the element defaulting to the left.

Similarly, by changing the value to `justify`, you can use the `DIV` element to justify the text. In the code sample shown in Listing 7.5, I've justified the entire page of text, making the entire page a single division.

LISTING 7.5 JUSTIFYING TEXT

```
<HTML>
<HEAD>
<TITLE>Alignment Exercise</TITLE>
</HEAD>
<BODY>
<BLOCKQUOTE>
<DIV align="justify">
<H2>The Odyssey, by Homer</H2>
<B>Book XXIII</B>

<P>"My good nurse," answered Penelope, "you must be mad. The gods sometimes send
some very sensible people out of their minds, and make foolish people become
sensible. This is what they must have been doing to you; for you always used to be
a reasonable person.
<P>Why should you thus mock me when I have trouble enough already-talking such
nonsense, and waking me up out of a sweet sleep that had taken possession of my
eyes and closed them? I have never slept so soundly from the day my poor husband
went to that city with the ill-omened name.
<P>Go back again into the women's room; if it had been any one else, who had woke
me up to bring me such absurd news I should have sent her away with a severe
scolding. As it is, your age shall protect you."
<P>"My dear child," answered Euryclea, "I am not mocking you. It is quite true as
I tell you that Ulysses is come home again. He was the stranger whom they all kept
on treating so badly in the cloister. Telemachus knew all the time that he was
come back, but kept his father's secret that he might have his revenge on all
these wicked people.
<P>Then Penelope sprang up from her couch, threw her arms round Euryclea, and wept
for joy. "But my dear nurse," said she, "explain this to me; if he has really come
home as you say, how did he manage to overcome the wicked suitors single handed,
seeing what a number of them there always were?"
</DIV>
</BLOCKQUOTE>
</BODY>
</HTML>
```

Figure 7.23 demonstrates the attractive, tight look of justified text.

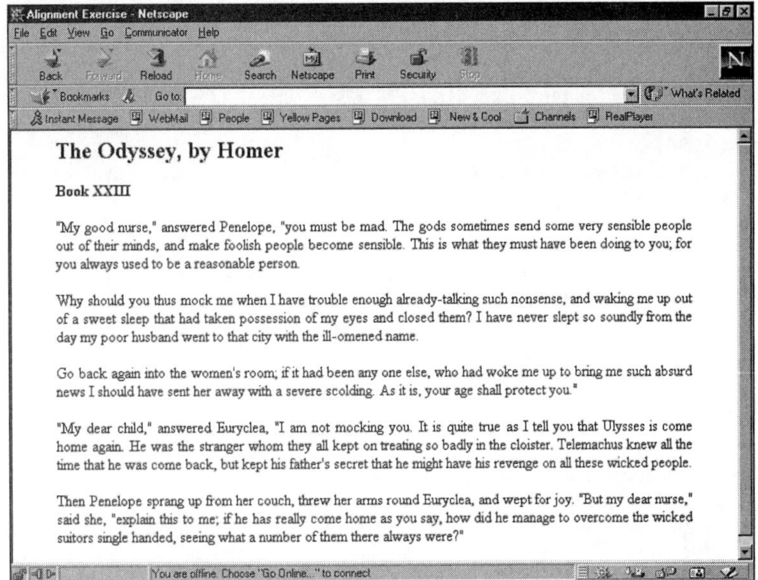

Figure 7.23
Justified text is clean and attractive, which enhances the readability of the text for your site visitors and attracts their attention more readily than uneven edges or long blocks of centered text.

USING THE PARAGRAPH ELEMENT TO ALIGN TEXT

You can also use the starting and ending paragraph tags, combined with the same attributes as found within the <DIV> tag, to create the exact same type of alignment.

Once again, left is the standard default for paragraphs, so you will rarely, if ever, use this attribute with a paragraph tag.

Paragraph alignment requires an opening and closing tag at each section of data that requires alignment. For this reason, we'll use the open/close paragraph style (covered earlier in this chapter) in the paragraph examples that follow.

In the following stepped example, you'll align text to the center using the open/close paragraph tags.

1. Begin with a standard HTML shell:

```
<HTML>
<HEAD>
<TITLE>Alignment Exercise</TITLE>
</HEAD>
<BODY>

</BODY>
</HTML>
```

2. Add your text selection:

```
<HTML>
<HEAD>
<TITLE>Alignment Exercise</TITLE>
</HEAD>
<BODY>
The Odyssey, by Homer
Book XXIV

"Happy Ulysses, son of Laertes," replied the ghost of Agamemnon, "you are
indeed blessed in the possession of a wife endowed with such rare excellence
of understanding, and so faithful to her wedded lord as Penelope the daughter
of Icarius. The fame, therefore, of her virtue shall never die, and the
immortals shall compose a song that shall be welcome to all mankind in honour
of the constancy of Penelope.

How far otherwise was the wickedness of the daughter of Tyndareus who killed
her lawful husband; her song shall be hateful among men, for she has brought
disgrace on all womankind even on the good ones."

Thus did they converse in the house of Hades deep down within the bowels of
the earth. Meanwhile Ulysses and the others passed out of the town and soon
reached the fair and well-tilled farm of Laertes, which he had reclaimed with
infinite labour. Here was his house, with a lean-to running all round it,
where the slaves who worked for him slept and sat and ate, while inside the
house there was an old Sicel woman, who looked after him in this his country-
farm. When Ulysses got there, he said to his son and to the other two:

"Go to the house, and kill the best pig that you can find for dinner.
Meanwhile I want to see whether my father will know me, or fail to recognize
me after so long an absence."
</BODY>
</HTML>
```

3. Format the text with paragraphs and other formatting you want to use:

```
<HTML>
<HEAD>
<TITLE>Alignment Exercise</TITLE>
</HEAD>
<BODY>
<H2>The Odyssey, by Homer</H2>
<B>Book XXIV</B>
<BLOCKQUOTE>

<P>"Happy Ulysses, son of Laertes," replied the ghost of Agamemnon, "you are
indeed blessed in the possession of a wife endowed with such rare excellence
of understanding, and so faithful to her wedded lord as Penelope the daughter
of Icarius. The fame, therefore, of her virtue shall never die, and the
immortals shall compose a song that shall be welcome to all mankind in honour
of the constancy of Penelope.</P>
```

```
<P>How far otherwise was the wickedness of the daughter of Tyndareus who
killed her lawful husband; her song shall be hateful among men, for she has
brought disgrace on all womankind even on the good ones."</P>

<P>Thus did they converse in the house of Hades deep down within the bowels of
the earth. Meanwhile Ulysses and the others passed out of the town and soon
reached the fair and well-tilled farm of Laertes, which he had reclaimed with
infinite labour. Here was his house, with a lean-to running all round it,
where the slaves who worked for him slept and sat and ate, while inside the
house there was an old Sicel woman, who looked after him in this his country-
farm. When Ulysses got there, he said to his son and to the other two:</P>

<P>"Go to the house, and kill the best pig that you can find for dinner.
Meanwhile I want to see whether my father will know me, or fail to recognize
me after so long an absence."</P>

<BLOCKQUOTE>
</BODY>
</HTML>
```

4. Now, add the `center` align value to the section you want to center:

```
<HTML>
<HEAD>
<TITLE>Alignment Exercise</TITLE>
</HEAD>
<BODY>
<H2>The Odyssey, by Homer</H2>
<B>Book XXIV</B>

<P>"Happy Ulysses, son of Laertes," replied the ghost of Agamemnon, "you are
indeed blessed in the possession of a wife endowed with such rare excellence
of understanding, and so faithful to her wedded lord as Penelope the daughter
of Icarius. The fame, therefore, of her virtue shall never die, and the
immortals shall compose a song that shall be welcome to all mankind in honour
of the constancy of Penelope.</P>

<P align="center">How far otherwise was the wickedness of the daughter of
Tyndareus who killed her lawful husband; her song shall be hateful among men,
for she has brought disgrace on all womankind even on the good ones."</P>

<P>Thus did they converse in the house of Hades deep down within the bowels of
the earth. Meanwhile Ulysses and the others passed out of the town and soon
reached the fair and well-tilled farm of Laertes, which he had reclaimed with
infinite labour. Here was his house, with a lean-to running all round it,
where the slaves who worked for him slept and sat and ate, while inside the
house there was an old Sicel woman, who looked after him in this his country
farm. When Ulysses got there, he said to his son and to the other two:</P>
```

```
<P>"Go to the house, and kill the best pig that you can find for dinner.
Meanwhile I want to see whether my father will know me, or fail to recognize
me after so long an absence."</P>

</BODY>
</HTML>
```

5. Save the file as `p_align.html`.
6. Compare your file to the example I've captured in Figure 7.24. Your alignment may appear slightly different than mine if you've set your font size or resolution differently than I have, but the type of alignment you see should be the same.

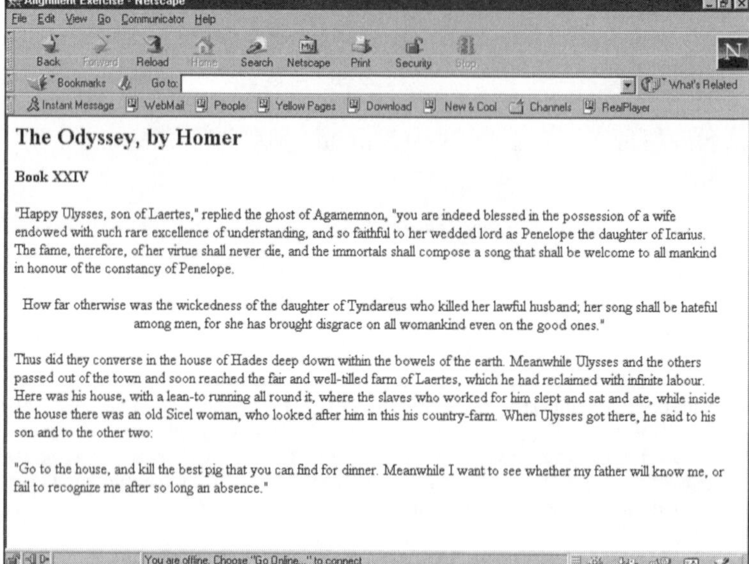

Figure 7.24
Center alignment with the paragraph element. The `P` element controls only what is immediately within the scope of the paragraph, whereas the `DIV` element can control the alignment of multiple paragraphs.

As with the `DIV` element, you can simply change the value to create another alignment style (see Listing 7.6).

LISTING 7.6 USING THE <P> ELEMENT FOR ALIGNMENT

```
<HTML>
<HEAD>
<TITLE>Alignment Exercise</TITLE>
</HEAD>
<BODY>
<H2>The Odyssey, by Homer</H2>
<B>Book XXIV</B>

<P>"Happy Ulysses, son of Laertes," replied the ghost of Agamemnon, "you are
indeed blessed in the possession of a wife endowed with such rare excellence of
understanding, and so faithful to her wedded lord as Penelope the daughter of
Icarius. The fame, therefore, of her virtue shall never die, and the immortals
```

```
shall compose a song that shall be welcome to all mankind in honour of the
constancy of Penelope.</P>
<P align="right">How far otherwise was the wickedness of the daughter of Tyndareus
who killed her lawful husband; her song shall be hateful among men, for she has
brought disgrace on all womankind even on the good ones."</P>
<P>Thus did they converse in the house of Hades deep down within the bowels of the
earth. Meanwhile Ulysses and the others passed out of the town and soon reached
the fair and well-tilled farm of Laertes, which he had reclaimed with infinite
labour. Here was his house, with a lean-to running all round it, where the slaves
who worked for him slept and sat and ate, while inside the house there was an old
Sicel woman, who looked after him in this his country-farm. When Ulysses got
there, he said to his son and to the other two:</P>
<P>"Go to the house, and kill the best pig that you can find for dinner. Meanwhile
I want to see whether my father will know me, or fail to recognize me after so
long an absence."</P>
</BODY>
</HTML>
```

As you can see in Figure 7.25, the paragraph where I've added the right value to the align attribute is right-aligned as expected.

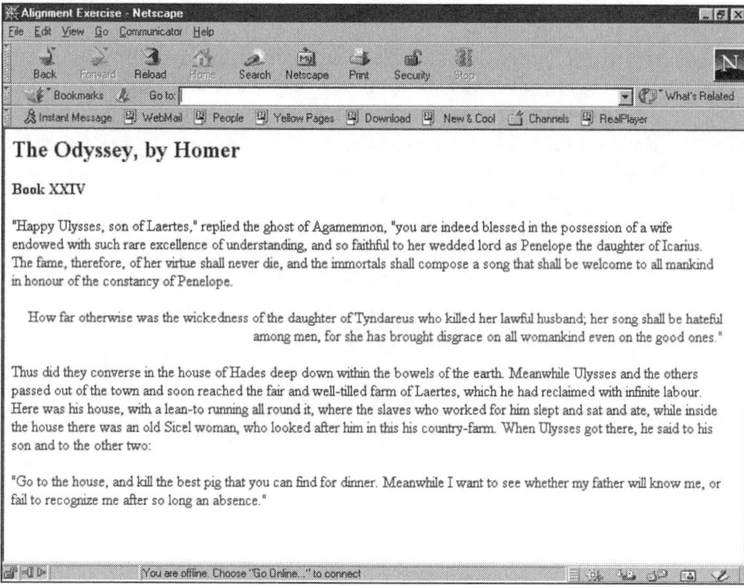

Figure 7.25
Right alignment using the paragraph element. Use this approach sparingly, as the resulting ragged left can be difficult to read.

However, because the paragraph element only influences individual paragraphs, you would have to add the value to *every* opening paragraph tag to format an entire page to that value (see Listing 7.7).

LISTING 7.7 ALIGNING A FULL PAGE OF TEXT WITH THE PARAGRAPH ELEMENT, INCLUDING THE ALIGNMENT IN EACH OPENING PARAGRAPH TAG

```
<HTML>
<HEAD>
<TITLE>Alignment Exercise</TITLE>
</HEAD>
<BODY>
<H2>The Odyssey, by Homer</H2>
<B>Book XXIV</B>

<P align="right">"Happy Ulysses, son of Laertes," replied the ghost of Agamemnon,
"you are indeed blessed in the possession of a wife endowed with such rare
excellence of understanding, and so faithful to her wedded lord as Penelope the
daughter of Icarius. The fame, therefore, of her virtue shall never die, and the
immortals shall compose a song that shall be welcome to all mankind in honour of
the constancy of Penelope.</P>

<P align="right">How far otherwise was the wickedness of the daughter of Tyndareus
who killed her lawful husband; her song shall be hateful among men, for she has
brought disgrace on all womankind even on the good ones."</P>

<P align="right">Thus did they converse in the house of Hades deep down within the
bowels of the earth. Meanwhile Ulysses and the others passed out of the town and
soon reached the fair and well-tilled farm of Laertes, which he had reclaimed with
infinite labour. Here was his house, with a lean-to running all round it, where
the slaves who worked for him slept and sat and ate, while inside the house there
was an old Sicel woman, who looked after him in this his country-farm. When
Ulysses got there, he said to his son and to the other two:</P>

<P align="right">"Go to the house, and kill the best pig that you can find for
dinner. Meanwhile I want to see whether my father will know me, or fail to
recognize me after so long an absence." </P>

</BODY>
</HTML>
```

While this technique works and is perfectly legal code, it is somewhat cumbersome. In a case such as this, I would choose using the `DIV` element to manage the page's alignment. I would re-code the page as shown in Listing 7.8.

LISTING 7.8 USING THE DIV ELEMENT—A MORE ELEGANT SOLUTION FOR LONGER SECTIONS OF TEXT

```
<HTML>
<HEAD>
<TITLE>Alignment Exercise</TITLE>
</HEAD>
<BODY>
<H2>The Odyssey, by Homer</H2>
<B>Book XXIV</B>
<DIV align="right">

<P>"Happy Ulysses, son of Laertes," replied the ghost of Agamemnon, "you are
indeed blessed in the possession of a wife endowed with such rare excellence of
understanding, and so faithful to her wedded lord as Penelope the daughter of
Icarius. The fame, therefore, of her virtue shall never die, and the immortals
shall compose a song that shall be welcome to all mankind in honour of the
constancy of Penelope.

<P>How far otherwise was the wickedness of the daughter of Tyndareus who killed
her lawful husband; her song shall be hateful among men, for she has brought
```

```
disgrace on all womankind even on the good ones."
<P>Thus did they converse in the house of Hades deep down within the bowels of the
earth. Meanwhile Ulysses and the others passed out of the town and soon reached
the fair and well-tilled farm of Laertes, which he had reclaimed with infinite
labour. Here was his house, with a lean-to running all round it, where the slaves
who worked for him slept and sat and ate, while inside the house there was an old
Sicel woman, who looked after him in this his country-farm. When Ulysses got
there, he said to his son and to the other two:
<P>"Go to the house, and kill the best pig that you can find for dinner. Meanwhile
I want to see whether my father will know me, or fail to recognize me after so
long an absence."
</DIV>
</BODY>
</HTML>
```

Figure 7.26 shows the results.

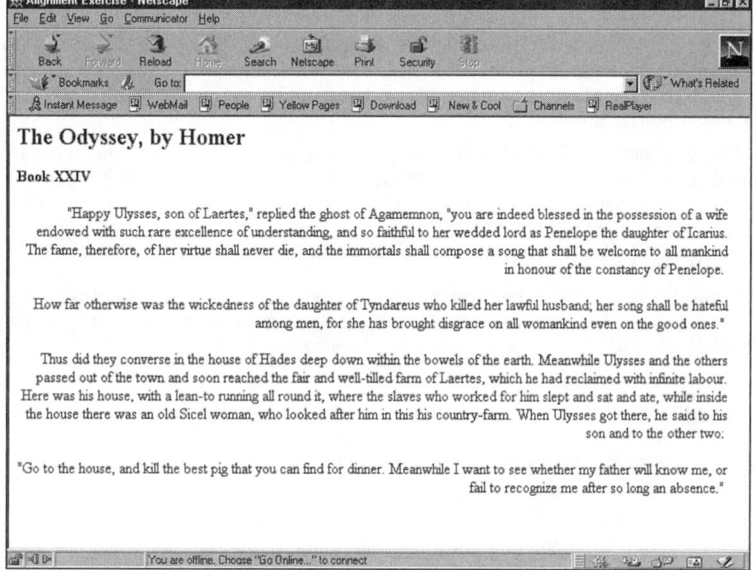

Figure 7.26
All-over alignment with the DIV element streamlines the code across longer sections of text.

NESTING THE DIV ELEMENT

The DIV element can be nested. This is a convenient way to apply alignment—and style—to divisions within divisions of a document.

Remember those nested boxes, where you would open one, then another, and finally another smaller one inside of that one? This is the concept of nesting. As with nesting lists, the nesting of divisions can help you gain a lot of control over the format of your HTML document with ease.

In Listing 7.9, I have first applied right alignment to the entire page; in other words, I've placed an opening DIV tag at the top of the text, and a closing DIV tag at the end of the text. This formats the entire page align-right.

Because I wanted to center a section, I simply added the DIV tags with the `align="center"` attribute and value around that individual section. The alignment is applied *only* to that section, but the browser understands that this is a nested element, and reverts back to the original right-alignment after the centered section is closed.

Trying to decide if the DIV *tag is right for you? See, "Backward Compatibility" in the Troubleshooting section at the end of this chapter.*

LISTING 7.9 NESTING THE DIV ELEMENT

```
<HTML>
<HEAD>
<TITLE>Alignment Exercise</TITLE>
</HEAD>
<BODY>
<BLOCKQUOTE>
<DIV align="right">
<H2>The Odyssey, by Homer</H2>
<B>Book XXIII</B>
<P>"My good nurse," answered Penelope, "you must be mad. The gods sometimes send
some very sensible people out of their minds, and make foolish people become
sensible. This is what they must have been doing to you; for you always used to be
a reasonable person.
<P>Why should you thus mock me when I have trouble enough already-talking such
nonsense, and waking me up out of a sweet sleep that had taken possession of my
eyes and closed them? I have never slept so soundly from the day my poor husband
went to that city with the ill-omened name.
<P><DIV align="center">
Go back again into the women's room; if it had been any one else, who had woke me
up to bring me such absurd news I should have sent her away with a severe
scolding. As it is, your age shall protect you."
</DIV>
<P>"My dear child," answered Euryclea, "I am not mocking you. It is quite true as
I tell you that Ulysses is come home again. He was the stranger whom they all kept
on treating so badly in the cloister. Telemachus knew all the time that he was
come back, but kept his father's secret that he might have his revenge on all
these wicked people.
<P>Then Penelope sprang up from her couch, threw her arms round Euryclea, and wept
for joy. "But my dear nurse," said she, "explain this to me; if he has really come
home as you say, how did he manage to overcome the wicked suitors single handed,
seeing what a number of them there always were?"
</DIV>
</BLOCKQUOTE>
</BODY>
</HTML>
```

In Figure 7.27 you'll see the influence of the `<DIV align="center">` tag. I've highlighted it so you can see the difference in formatting with ease.

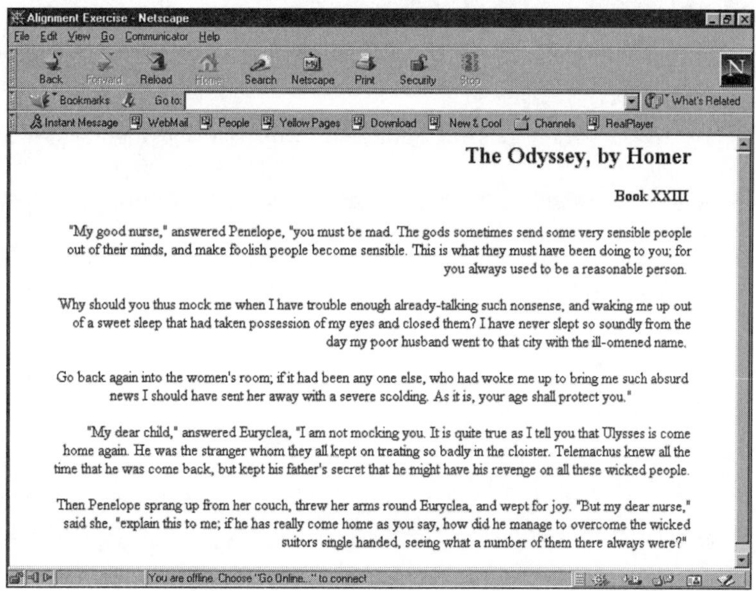

Figure 7.27
Right justification and a centered division on the same page.

→ Alignment styles for images and objects will be covered in Chapter 10, "Working with Images."

TROUBLESHOOTING

OTHER FORMATTING ELEMENTS

I've occasionally seen the `<TT>` element in use. What does this do?

The `<TT>` element forces any text within its opening and closing tags to appear in a "typewriter" (monospaced) font. This can be used much as the deprecated `<code>` element—formatting sections of text such as code listings in the monospace style. In both instances, style sheets are favored over the formatting options in HTML 4.0.

BACKWARD COMPATIBILITY

I want to use the `DIV align="center"` option to center text. Won't older browsers have trouble interpreting this?

The simple answer is yes, older browsers will ignore the `DIV` method of alignment. However, most browsers in use today can manage it. If it's imperative to have a section of text centered in as many browsers as possible, you can opt for using the `<P align="center">` option, or use the rather clumsy but effective combination of either `P` or `DIV` and the deprecated `center` tags.

DESIGNING FOR THE REAL WORLD

ALL TOGETHER, NOW

Figure 7.28 shows a page using numerous formatting and alignment methods.

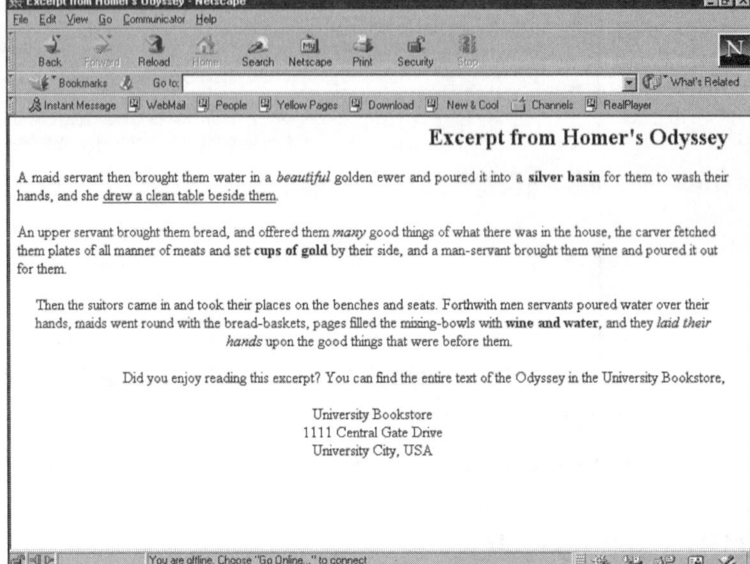

Figure 7.28
Match this layout using the formatting and alignment techniques discussed in this chapter.

Using this as a guide, create the code for the page. You can compare your results to the correct code, found in the code section of the CD-ROM that accompanies this book. The filename is `7_all.html`.

CHAPTER 8

Adding Lists

In this chapter

USING LISTS

Lists are HTML's way of helping to separate information into a logical series of items. Built on text formatting styles, HTML lists tend to be stable because they've been supported by browsers from early on in the history of the language.

Although HTML 4.0, in its strict interpretation, deprecates some aspects of attributes related to lists, the actual tags are going strong. In this chapter, you'll get a chance to look at why lists are so valuable, learn how to use them, and to prepare for some of the special concerns to be aware of when using them.

COMMON LIST TAGS

The following tags are explored in this chapter:

- `<UL>...</UL>`—The unordered, or *bulleted* list.
- `<OL>...</OL>`—The ordered, or *numbered* list.
- `<LI>`—The list item tag. Note that this tag requires no closing tag.
- `<DL>...</DL>`—Definition list tag.
- `<DT>...</DT>`—Definition term, which is part of a definition list.
- `<DD>...</DD>`—The definition within a definition term.

THE VALUE OF LISTS

Why are lists so valuable? There are several important reasons, and as you work with HTML both as a strict language and in the context of Web design, you'll see that, time and again, lists play an important role in the formatting of text documents.

Many times in this book I discuss the importance of being clear and concise when presenting information onscreen. Lists help you do just that by clarifying important items, people are drawn directly to the information they must see, rather than having to wade through a lot of heavy text to find it.

Lists not only help to clarify, but they logically order information, allowing you to guide your readers from one precise item to the next at a predetermined pace. This allows you to prepare your document content in such a way as to get people to the main ideas within that content quickly, and in the exact order you see fit.

Another powerful aspect of lists is that because they indent information, they create whitespace. This guides the eye toward important information, but also allows for a subtle but important design element to emerge: the flow, rather than constraint, of space. Visual real estate is so precious on a computer screen that too much constrained information is detrimental to keeping people involved with the material.

Lists, then, strengthen a document logically, organizationally, and visually. This powerful combination can help every HTML coder create pages with maximum impact.

→ For more information on how to maximize the visual impact of onscreen data, **see** "Resolution, Gamma, and the Visual Environment," **p. 546**

BULLETED (UNORDERED) LISTS

The bulleted list is probably the most commonly used to achieve logical organization within the text of an HTML document. Bulleted lists place symbols rather than numeric values next to each list item. The default symbol of a standard, un-nested bulleted list is a disk.

→ For more information about list variations, **see** "List Attributes," **p. 170**

Unordered lists begin and end with the <UL> and </UL> tags. As always, I like to apply the container method when working with code, avoiding problems with symmetry.

```
<UL>

</UL>
```

Now you need to put information between the tags. The most common information to use at this point is some unordered items, preceded by the list item <LI> tag, as follows:

```
<UL>

<LI>A pen
<LI>A glass of water
<LI>A small, yellow pad

</UL>
```

This information appears as single line items preceded by a round bullet, as shown in Figure 8.1.

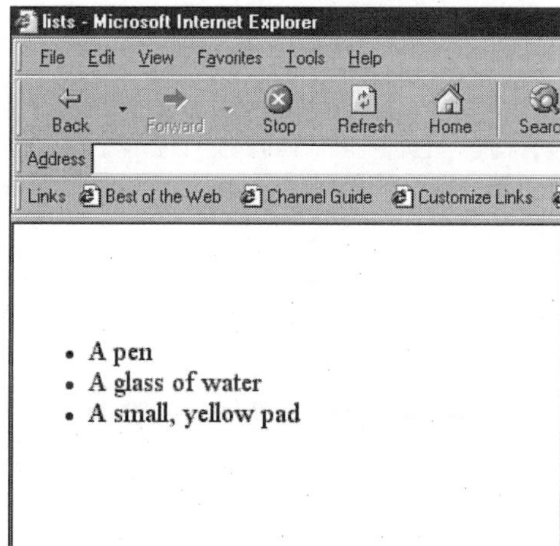

Figure 8.1 A bulleted, or unordered list is commonly used to present small bits of information in a clean, orderly manner.

You'll notice that the browser naturally added a carriage return after each listed item. If you want more space between individual list items, you'll need to add that with paragraph or break tags:

```
<UL>

<LI><P>A pen</P>


<LI><P>A glass of water</P>


<LI><P>A small, yellow pad</P>

</UL>
```

Figure 8.2 shows the additional space.

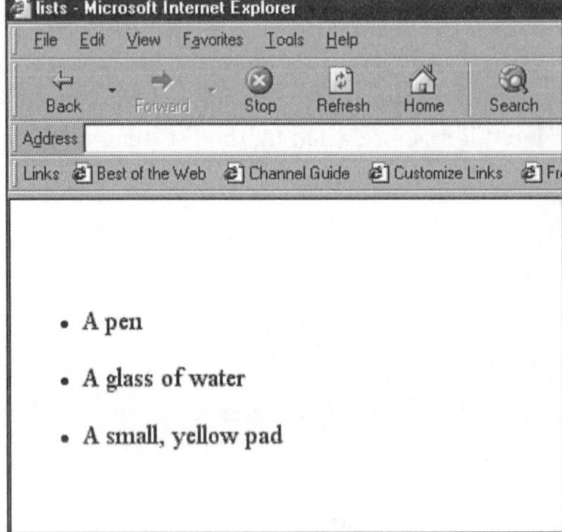

Figure 8.2
Additional space between line items can increase the readability of your list by providing additional whitespace—particularly if you are working with a smaller typeface.

Caution

Different browsers interpret the amount of space between each line item differently. Therefore, if you choose to add a paragraph tag or other method of adding space between code, you'll need to check your work in a variety of environments.

Some coders use an indentation style to help them navigate code. Lists are one place where this can be done, as in the following:

→ For an explanation of indentation style and other coding styles, **see** "Defining HTML Syntax," **p. 74**

```
<UL>

        <LI>A pen
        <LI>A glass of water
        <LI>A small, yellow pad
```

```
</UL>
```

This indentation is a personal call—if you like the style and feel and it will help you with speed and accuracy in your work, then go ahead and use it. My only concern is that you remain consistent in the style that you choose.

Numbered (Ordered) Lists

Ordered lists work exactly like bulleted lists, with the one exception being that instead of a round bullet being displayed by the line item tag, sequential numeric values are shown.

Begin with the container:

```
<OL>

</OL>
```

Use ordered lists wherever numeric ordering makes more sense than simple bullet points, as in the following:

```
<P>To get to Maple Drive follow these directions:
<OL>

<LI>Go to the first light on Main and take a left.
<LI>Drive 3 miles and turn right on High Street.
<LI>Follow High Street until you pass the Maple Elementary on your right. Maple
Drive is the first right after the school.

</OL>
```

The numeric results are demonstrated in Figure 8.3. Note that standard numerals are displayed.

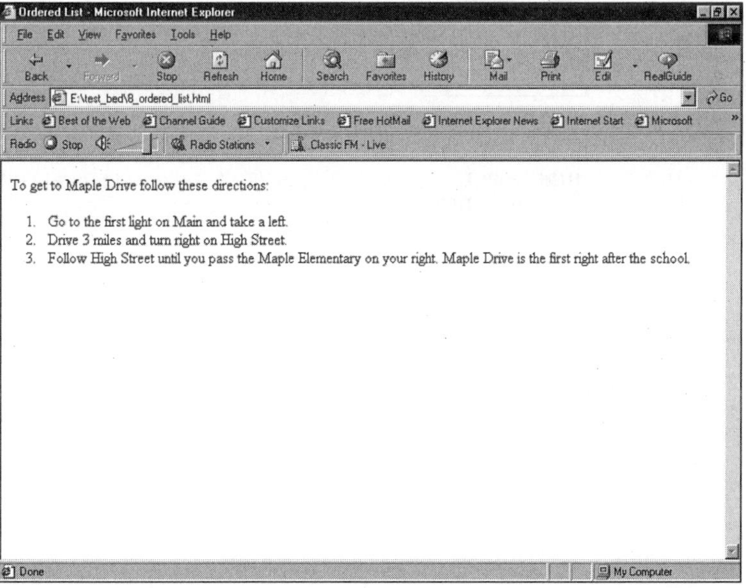

Figure 8.3
An Ordered List presents information in a sequential manner.

As with numbered lists, you can add extra space between each line item using paragraph or break tags. However, the same caution as to testing applies here, too.

Want to use Roman numerals instead of standard numbers? See the Troubleshooting section for information on how to do just that.

Note

You can list as many items as you want to on a page, but you cannot stop a list and start another one and have it pick up at the numeric value where you left off. To set values on lists, you can use the *value* attribute, discussed in the "List Attributes" section toward the end of this chapter.

Are you needing to use letters or Roman numerals for your lists rather than Arabic numbers? See, "Alphabetical Lists" in the Troubleshooting section at the end of this chapter.

Building a Page with Lists

In this task, you'll build a page with both an ordered and unordered list.

1. Begin with an HTML shell and title it `lists`.

```
<!DOCTYPE HTML PUBLIC "-//W3C//DTD HTML 4.0 Transitional//EN"
"http://www.w3.org/TR/REC-html40/loose.dtd">

<HTML>
<HEAD>

<TITLE>lists</TITLE>
</HEAD>

<BODY>



</BODY>
</HTML>
```

2. Now add an unordered container:

```
<!DOCTYPE HTML PUBLIC "-//W3C//DTD HTML 4.0 Transitional//EN"
"http://www.w3.org/TR/REC-html40/loose.dtd">

<HTML>
<HEAD>

<TITLE>lists</TITLE>
</HEAD>

<BODY>

<UL>

</UL>

</BODY>
</HTML>
```

3. Add several list items with a description and appropriate formatting:

```
<!DOCTYPE HTML PUBLIC "-//W3C//DTD HTML 4.0 Transitional//EN"
"http://www.w3.org/TR/REC-html40/loose.dtd">

<HTML>
<HEAD>

<TITLE>lists</TITLE>
</HEAD>

<BODY>

What's on my desk:
<P>

<UL>

<LI>A reading lamp
<LI>A telephone
<LI>A clock
<LI>A computer
<LI>Stacks of paper
<LI>Books

</UL>

</BODY>
</HTML>
```

4. Now separate the ordered list with a paragraph and add a new description:

```
<!DOCTYPE HTML PUBLIC "-//W3C//DTD HTML 4.0 Transitional//EN"
"http://www.w3.org/TR/REC-html40/loose.dtd">

<HTML>
<HEAD>

<TITLE>lists</TITLE>
</HEAD>

<BODY>

What's on my desk:
<P>

<UL>

<LI>A reading lamp
<LI>A telephone
<LI>A clock
<LI>A computer
<LI>Stacks of paper
<LI>Books

</UL>
<P>

What's in my purse:
```

```
<P>

</BODY>
</HTML>
```

5. Add the ordered list container:

```
<!DOCTYPE HTML PUBLIC "-//W3C//DTD HTML 4.0 Transitional//EN"
"http://www.w3.org/TR/REC-html40/loose.dtd">

<HTML>
<HEAD>

<TITLE>lists</TITLE>
</HEAD>

<BODY>

What's on my desk:
<P>

<UL>

<LI>A reading lamp
<LI>A telephone
<LI>A clock
<LI>A computer
<LI>Stacks of paper
<LI>Books

</UL>
<P>

What's in my purse:
<P>

<OL>

</OL>
</BODY>
</HTML>
```

6. And the list items:

```
<!DOCTYPE HTML PUBLIC "-//W3C//DTD HTML 4.0 Transitional//EN"
"http://www.w3.org/TR/REC-html40/loose.dtd">

<HTML>
<HEAD>

<TITLE>lists</TITLE>
</HEAD>

<BODY>

What's on my desk:
<P>

<UL>
```

```
<LI>A reading lamp
<LI>A telephone
<LI>A clock
<LI>A computer
<LI>Stacks of paper
<LI>Books

</UL>
<P>

How to find my wallet:
<P>

<OL>
<LI>Go up the stairs.
<LI> Open the door to my office.
<LI>Climb over the mess.
<LI>Move all the papers off my desk.
<LI>My wallet will be at the bottom of the pile.

</OL>
</BODY>
</HTML>
```

7. Save the file as `lists.html` and compare it to Figure 8.4.

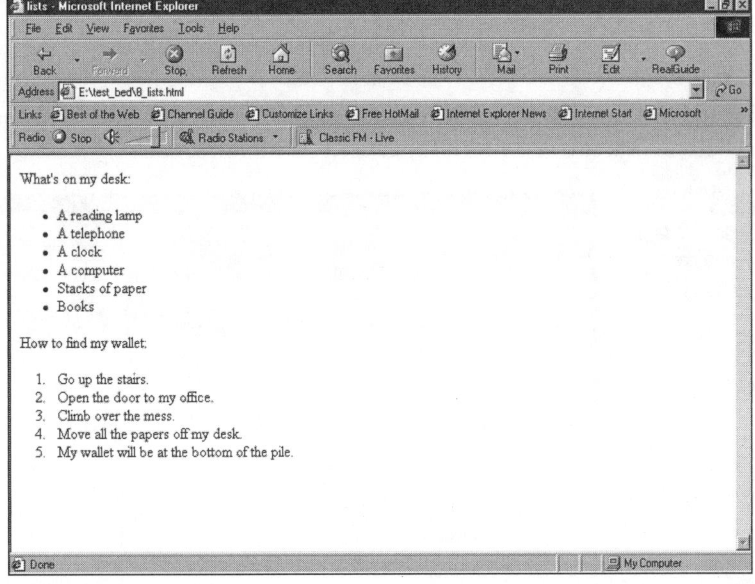

Figure 8.4
An unordered and ordered list on the same page. The unordered list is a random list of items; the ordered list describes a sequence of actions.

Want to know how to have lists with more than just plain round bullets? See "Alternate Bullets" in the Troubleshooting section at the end of this chapter for details.

DEFINITION LISTS

Definition lists come in handy when you want to offset information in dictionary-like style. These lists were created to manage such information as glossaries. The syntax for definition lists are a bit odd compared to the straightforward nature of ordered and unordered lists. Although the primary definition list tag, <DL>, and its required companion </DL> are standard, there are two unique internal tags that you can use, <DD> and <DT>.

Begin with the <DL> container:

```
<DL>


</DL>
```

Then, you add a definition term:

```
<DL>

<DT>Tag

</DL>
```

and then, the definition itself:

```
<DL>

<DT>Tag
<DD>A tag, also referred to as an element, can be considered the "command
center" of HTML document formatting.

</DL>
```

Figure 8.5 shows these tags in action. As with ordered and unordered lists, the tags used in definition lists also assume breaks between the information.

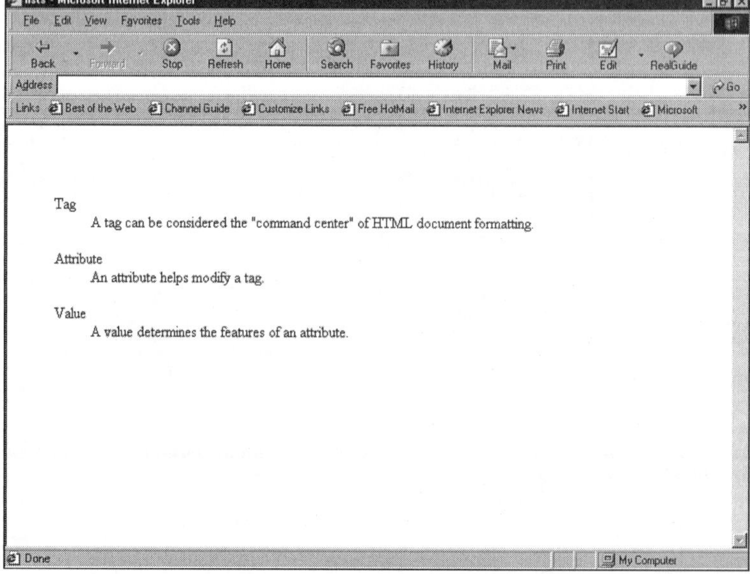

Figure 8.5
The definition list tags enable you to create a glossary type list on your site.

Note

Definition term tags (<DT>) and definitions (<DD>) do not require closing tags. Although they are optional, most people never use them.

Several complications and additional issues must be addressed when working with lists. These include nesting lists, using lists for other purposes than their original intent, and working with list attributes.

ADVANCED LIST TECHNIQUES

There are several techniques that you can use to manipulate list and list attributes more effectively. They include nesting lists, using lists for indentation, and altering list attributes.

NESTING LISTS

Nesting is the act of putting one container within another. Do you remember those magical Chinese boxes from childhood, where you would open one only to find another, identical but smaller, one inside the first? This concept is akin to the process of nesting.

Lists can be nested, creating an outline style of information. When nesting lists, it's important to remember horizontal symmetry rules, or you can run into problems.

Let's build an unordered list with one level of nesting.

1. Open a basic HTML shell in your favorite editor and title it `nested lists`.

```
<!DOCTYPE HTML PUBLIC "-//W3C//DTD HTML 4.0 Transitional//EN"
"http://www.w3.org/TR/REC-html40/loose.dtd">

<HTML>
<HEAD>

<TITLE>Nested Lists</TITLE>
</HEAD>

<BODY>



</BODY>
</HTML>
```

2. Add the unordered list tags using the container method:

```
<!DOCTYPE HTML PUBLIC "-//W3C//DTD HTML 4.0 Transitional//EN"
"http://www.w3.org/TR/REC-html40/loose.dtd">

<HTML>
<HEAD>

<TITLE>Nested Lists</TITLE>
</HEAD>

<BODY>
```

```
<UL>

</UL>

</BODY>
</HTML>
```

3. Add several list items:

```
<!DOCTYPE HTML PUBLIC "-//W3C//DTD HTML 4.0 Transitional//EN"
"http://www.w3.org/TR/REC-html40/loose.dtd">

<HTML>
<HEAD>

<TITLE>Nested Lists</TITLE>
</HEAD>

<BODY>

<UL>

<LI>Chocolate
<LI>Coffee
<LI>Sugar

</UL>

</BODY>
</HTML>
```

4. Now, add another unordered list container *beneath* a list item (I've indented this one for the sake of clarity):

```
<!DOCTYPE HTML PUBLIC "-//W3C//DTD HTML 4.0 Transitional//EN"
"http://www.w3.org/TR/REC-html40/loose.dtd">

<HTML>
<HEAD>

<TITLE>Nested Lists</TITLE>
</HEAD>

<BODY>

<UL>

<LI>Chocolate

    <UL>


    </UL>

<LI>Coffee
<LI>Sugar

</UL>

</BODY>
</HTML>
```

5. Place several list items within that container:

```
<!DOCTYPE HTML PUBLIC "-//W3C//DTD HTML 4.0 Transitional//EN"
"http://www.w3.org/TR/REC-html40/loose.dtd">

<HTML>
<HEAD>

<TITLE>Nested Lists</TITLE>
</HEAD>

<BODY>

<UL>

<LI>Chocolate

    <UL>
        <LI>unsweetened
        <LI>semi-sweet
        <LI>dark
    </UL>

<LI>Coffee
<LI>Sugar

</UL>

</BODY>
</HTML>
```

6. View the file and check it against Figure 8.6.
7. Save the file as `nested_list.html`.

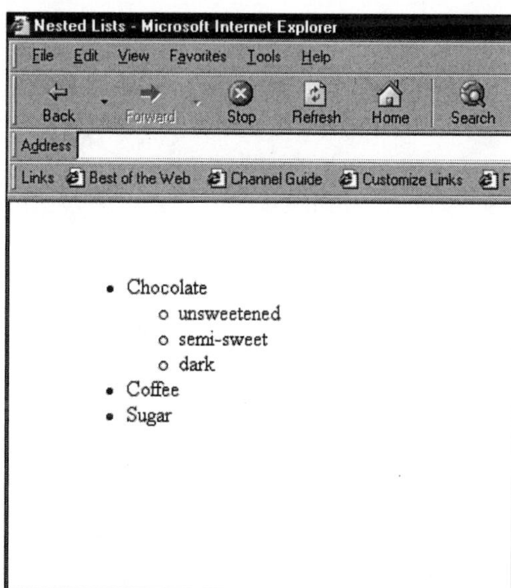

Figure 8.6
You'll notice that your nested list has a different kind of bullet than the primary level list. This is the browser's way of helping you and your page visitors distinguish between lists and sub-lists.

If you want to do the same thing with an ordered list, simply change the unordered tags to ordered tags, as shown in Listing 8.1.

LISTING 8.1 NESTED LISTS

```
<!DOCTYPE HTML PUBLIC "-//W3C//DTD HTML 4.0 Transitional//EN"
"http://www.w3.org/TR/REC-html40/loose.dtd">

<HTML>
<HEAD>

<TITLE>Nested Lists</TITLE>
</HEAD>

<BODY>
<P>The three most important food groups in order of importance:
<OL>

<LI>Chocolate

    <OL>
        <LI>Buy the chocolate.
        <LI>Unwrap it quickly.
        <LI>eEat it immediately!
    </OL>

<LI>Coffee
<LI>Sugar

</OL>

</BODY>
</HTML>
```

If you view this code in a browser, as I did (see Figure 8.7), you'll notice that the nested numeric list is *not* differentiated with another numeric system. The listing simply starts over, but indented under the primary reference.

You can combine list types, too. Listing 8.2 shows the same list, but with the primary level as unordered, and the secondary level as ordered.

LISTING 8.2 MIXING NESTED LISTS

```
<!DOCTYPE HTML PUBLIC "-//W3C//DTD HTML 4.0 Transitional//EN"
"http://www.w3.org/TR/REC-html40/loose.dtd">

<HTML>
<HEAD>

<TITLE>Nested Lists: Mixed Lists</TITLE>
</HEAD>

<BODY>
```

```
<UL>

<LI>Chocolate
<OL><LI>Buy the chocolate.
        <LI>Unwrap it quickly.
        <LI>Eat it immediately!
</OL>


<LI>Coffee
<LI>Sugar

</UL>

</BODY>
</HTML>
```


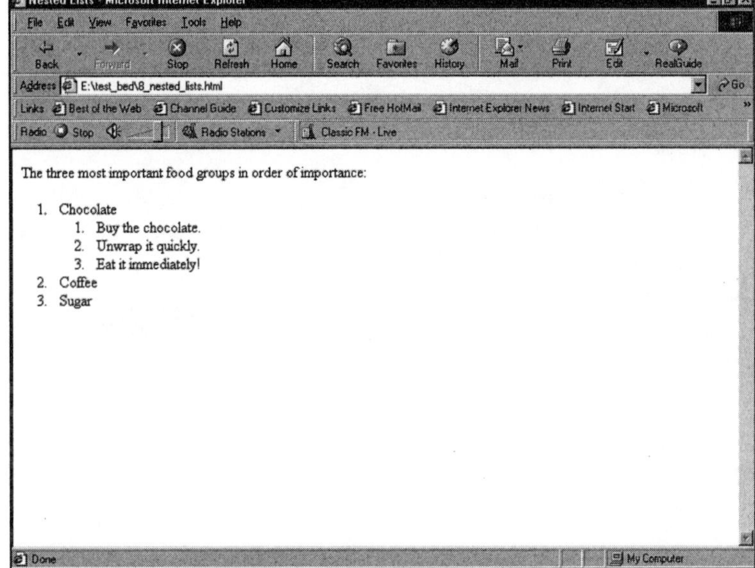

Figure 8.7
A nested, ordered list is displayed with the same formatting but with numbers rather than bullets.

In this case, the bullets appear in the primary list, and the numerals in the secondary.

Try one more exercise, this time adding a third nested list to the original, unordered nested example:

1. Open `nested_list.html` in your editor.
2. Add a third level unordered list container:

```
<!DOCTYPE HTML PUBLIC "-//W3C//DTD HTML 4.0 Transitional//EN"
"http://www.w3.org/TR/REC-html40/loose.dtd">

<HTML>
<HEAD>
```

```
<TITLE>Nested Lists: Three Deep</TITLE>
</HEAD>

<BODY>

<UL>

<LI>Chocolate

    <UL>
        <LI>unsweetened
               <UL>

               </UL>
        <LI>semi-sweet
        <LI>dark
   </UL>

<LI>Coffee
<LI>Sugar

</UL>

</BODY>
</HTML>
```

3. Add the list items:

```
<!DOCTYPE HTML PUBLIC "-//W3C//DTD HTML 4.0 Transitional//EN"
"http://www.w3.org/TR/REC-html40/loose.dtd">

<HTML>
<HEAD>

<TITLE>Nested Lists: Three Deep</TITLE>
</HEAD>

<BODY>

<UL>

<LI>Chocolate

    <UL>
        <LI>unsweetened
               <UL>
               <LI>Hershey's
                <LI>Cadbury's
                       <LI>Toblerone
      </UL>
        <LI>semi-sweet
        <LI>dark
    </UL>

<LI>Coffee
<LI>Sugar

</UL>
```

```
</BODY>
</HTML>
```

4. Compare the file to Figure 8.8.
5. Save the file as `3nested_lists.html`.

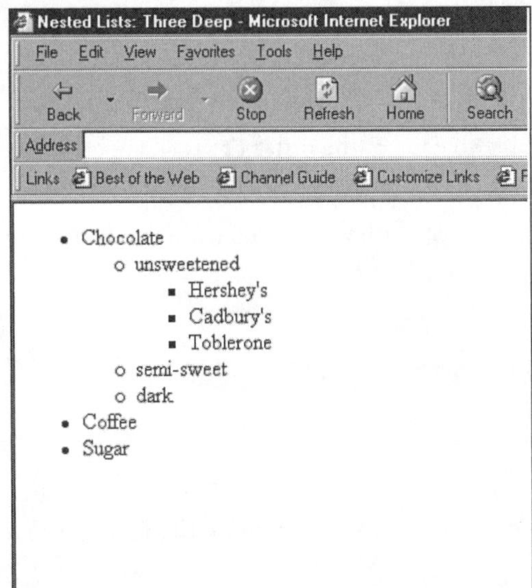

Figure 8.8
Nested List with three sections.

You'll see that your third list now has a square, rather than round, symbol, to help differentiate the levels of information. If you were to do this example with an ordered list, the same results for double lists would apply: The third list will take on numeric values, beginning from 1, but with no differentiation in type.

Using Lists for Indenting Items

Frustrated by lack of control, particularly in the early days of HTML, coders got clever and saw that they could exploit certain aspects of tags to get results that were never intended by that tag.

A prime example of this is lists. You may have noticed that all lists naturally create indentations to achieve the logical placement of specific items. So some coders, and some software applications, exploit lists to achieve indentation.

Look at this little snippet of code I took from a WYSIWYG editor.

```
<P><UL>
</UL>
<P>
```

What on earth is this, you might be thinking? Well, it's an empty list within a paragraph—]a poor attempt at adding an indent, exploiting list properties.

The problems with this are twofold. First, there's the fact that you're using a tag for which it was never intended setting yourself up for possible problems with certain browsers. Second, there are much more stable and appreciable ways of indenting information with HTML 4.0.

→ To find other methods of indenting content, **see** "Table Fundamentals," **p. 307** and "Element Positioning and Style Sheet Scripting," **p. 430**

LIST ATTRIBUTES

Some people want to be able to control the order or visual appearance of list elements. This can be done by using several list attributes, including VALUE and TYPE.

If I want to pick up where I left off with an ordered list, I can add a numeric value to the list item:

```
<OL>

<LI value="30">This is item 30
<LI>this is 31
<LI>and so forth

</OL>
```

I can change the visual appearance of my bullets using the `type` attribute in the list item, as follows:

```
<UL>

<LI type="disc">This bullet appears as a disc
<LI type="circle">This appears as a circle
<LI type="square">and this bullet appears as a square

</UL>
```

Figure 8.9 shows these attributes at work.

Although some people do use the `type` attribute with list items, and it is supported by contemporary browsers, it's not a recommended use. In fact, the `type` attribute has been deprecated.

→ For more about the deprecation of attributes, **see** "Understanding HTML 4.0," **p. 19**

In the strict interpretation of the HTML 4.0 Standard, the recommendation is to rely on style sheets to gain visual control over bullets and numerals rather than this attribute.

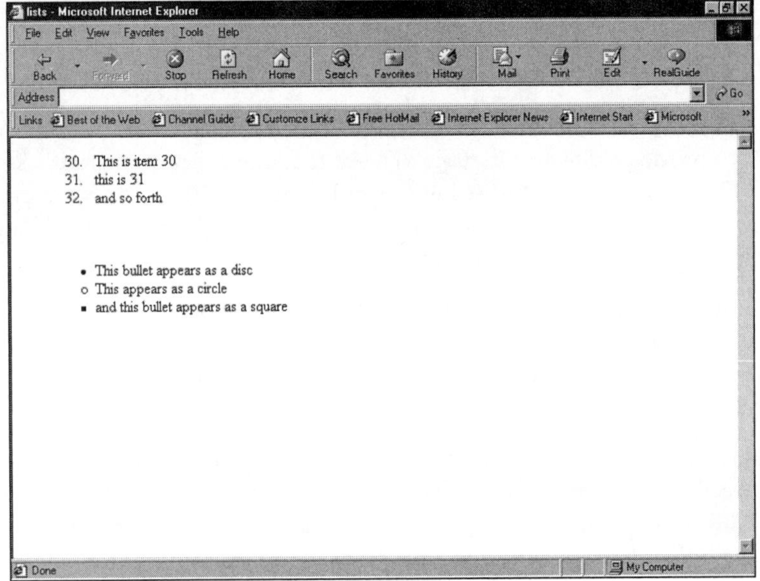

Figure 8.9
Adding value and type to lists can help to differentiate your list items especially when nesting one or more lists.

TROUBLESHOOTING

ALPHABETICAL LISTS

How do you create a list in alphabetical, rather than numerical, order?

You can use the type attribute within your ordered list element to specify alphabetical order or even Roman numeration, but this is a deprecated attribute. The best method is to use style sheets to define classes for lists. These classes can specify alphabetical or Roman numerical order, as well as other formatting information.

→ To learn more about style sheets and Web typography, **see** "Designing Type with CSS," **p. 284**

ALTERNATE BULLETS

What about all the lists on the Web that use fancy bullets?

There are several different ways to break content into a list. Many of these methods do not use the <OL> or <UL> tags, however, and instead use tables or images to give the appearance of a bulleted list format.

→ To find more information on creating tables, **see** "Table Fundamentals," **p. 304** and "Advanced Table Layouts," **p. 334**

→ To learn how to prepare images, **see** "Creating Professional Web Graphics," **p. 598**

DESIGNING FOR THE REAL WORLD

USING LISTS: DINOSAURIA AND PUBLISHER'S WEEKLY

As mentioned throughout this chapter, lists help create a flow to your Web pages. They also provide built-in whitespace to make the page easier on the eyes. As with all things HTML, lists need to be used in proper balance with the rest of your content. If you break your content down into too many bullet items, you risk losing depth in your subject matter as everything becomes a "sound bite."

Lists don't necessarily have to be used as a series of one-liners, however. The Dinosauria uses lists to divide larger chunks of information. The bullets allow your eyes to easily jump from topic to topic, while each item provides a complete explanation of a particular dinosaur myth.

Lists also make great jumping-off points. The Publishers Weekly Bestsellers site makes excellent use of HTML lists. The list items are nested in a table, creating a two-column list. This opens up even more whitespace than a standard, one-column list. Also, each item on the list is a link to another area on the site. The main page is left uncluttered and easy to navigate, while the real meat of the site's content is left to internal pages.

Note

The Dinosauria—**`http://www.ucmp.berkeley.edu/diapsids/dinosaur.html`**

Publishers Weekly Bestsellers—**`http://www.publishersweekly.com/bestsellersindex.asp`**

CHAPTER 9

Linking Pages

In this chapter

THE WEB'S VERY ESSENCE

I have a friend Joe who lives in Tucson, Arizona. I have another friend, Jo, who lives in Southeast Asia. Before the advent of the Internet, the two would probably have had little opportunity to meet—to *link* together and form a relationship.

Linking—it's the essence of the Web. Without it, the concept would be reduced to the publication of text documents on the Internet. Linking is what takes you beyond the framework of not only a single document to other, related documents—but farther beyond and into the human potential of relating ideas as well as people.

Originally referred to as *hyperlinking*, the technical method to offer linking opportunities to documents has also expanded to include more than just text links. In fact, today's Web uses a variety of media and objects that are active links. Another term, *hypermedia*, has been added to include this aspect.

If you attempt to picture this vast network of linked information—from text documents to entertainment Web sites, to personal home pages to people—you can begin to see what a complex Web is woven by this seemingly simple act of linking.

And, although the HTML syntax for linking is fairly straightforward, there are some details you must become familiar with to harness the Web's potential and facilitate the opportunities that linking allows.

Such issues include working with the anchor tag, using relative and absolute links, and managing specialty links such as those used to link from one point on a page to another or to email.

THE ANCHOR TAG

If the essence of the Web can be defined as linking, the essence of linking can most certainly be exemplified by the HTML tag at its core—the anchor, or `A` tag.

This tag is what allows one HTML document to attach, or anchor itself, to another. That other document can be nearby, or it can be far away—much like my friends Joe and Jo. If each had a Web site located in their native areas, those sites could be attached, or anchored, to each other using the anchor tag.

Caution

You can always link to another's site if you know the proper address. Most people are happy if you link to their sites; however, some sites want to know who is linking to them and why. Out of consideration for others, get in touch before linking to them without express permission.

This tag takes the following start and finish tag: `<A>…</A>`.

To function properly, the anchor tag must have attributes and values. Typically, and at the most basic, the common attribute is `href`, or *hypertext reference*. This is followed by a value, most often consisting of a URL.

> **Note**
>
> URL, or Uniform Resource Locator, is a Web site's address. It consists of the prefix `http://`, which stands for hypertext transfer protocol, the language used by Web servers to exchange Web-based information. A URL also has a "www" prefix (but not always) before the domain name, as in: **`http://www.molly.com/`**. URL can be pronounced by its individual letters, U-R-L, or spoken like the name "Earl."

In this case, I'm going to use the URL of Macmillan Computer Publishing's Web site:

```
<a href="http://www.mcp.com/">
```

Between this string of tag, attribute, and value, and the closing tag, *any text or object* that is placed there will be considered "hot." This means it is a clickable link that takes you from the page you're on to the page to which the anchor refers:

```
<A href="http://www.mcp.com/">Click on this to go Macmillan Computer Book
Publishing's Home Page</A>
```

This link (see Figure 9.1) will then take you to the Macmillan Web site (see Figure 9.2).

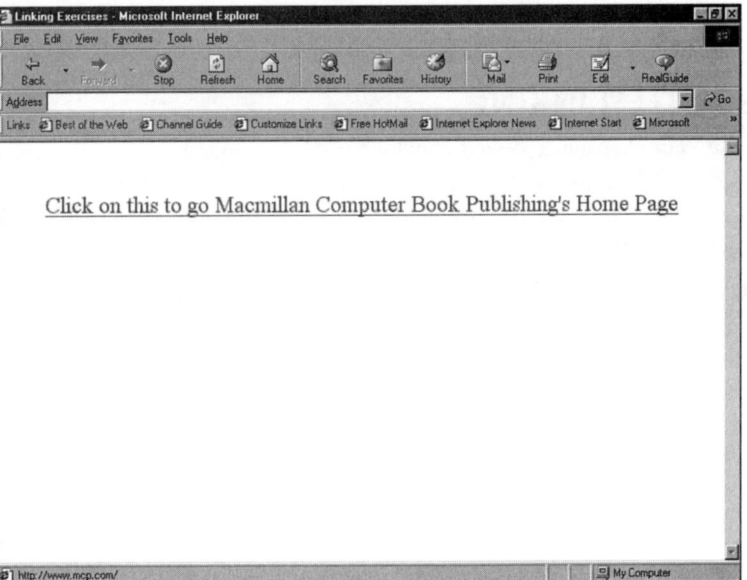

Figure 9.1
The hyperlink to Macmillan's Page.

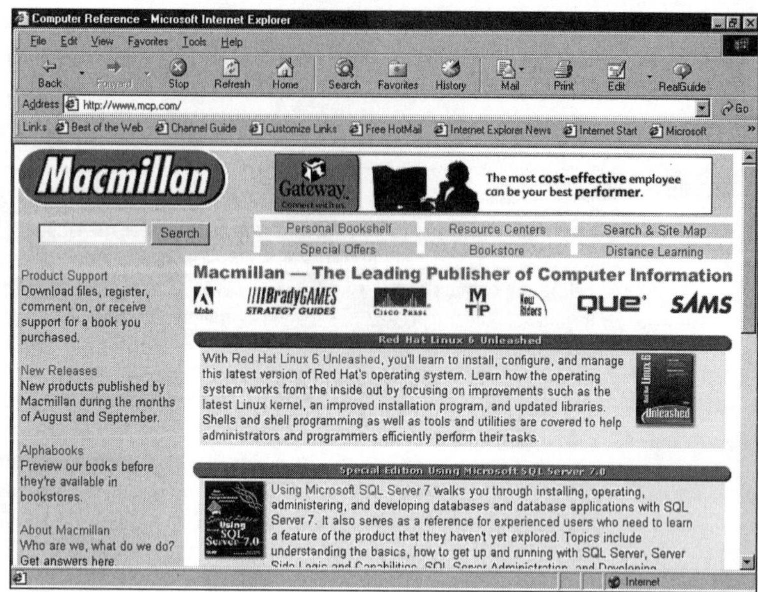

Figure 9.2
Click the link, and the referred page loads.

Anchor tags create links, and there are two kinds of links of note, *absolute* and *relative*. Many of you are familiar with these linking techniques already, but for those of you who want clarification, I'll go over them in the following sections.

Absolute Linking

The example we just looked at, which used a complete URL as its value, is referred to as an *absolute* link. This means that you use *absolutely the entire* Web address—not just a part of it. You must include the beginning `http:` information, as well as the domain. This will then take you to that Web site's default home page.

Concerned about linking to other people's pages? How about having other people link to yours? See, "Reciprocal Link Refusal" in the Troubleshooting section at the end of the chapter for more information.

Absolute linking is important when addressing anchors to sites other than your own—in other words, sites that reside on other servers. The use of the absolute address allows your browser to query the correct server and actually go to a specific file on that server if you code your anchor to do so. Joe, and his site in Arizona, will require an absolute link to Jo's site in Southeast Asia.

Tip from

Linking off of your site is what the Web is all about. Still, you should be sure to place your offsite links wisely. Creating a special links page or linking within the text can be effective. What you want to avoid is linking within the first paragraph of any page's text–you could lose your site visitors and never see them again!

→ For a detailed look at structuring Web sites, **see** "Effective Page Design," **p. 509**

If you want to refer to a particular section within a Web site, you will have to include relevant directories. In this example, I want to send you to the resource area of the Macmillan Web site, so I use the following URL as my value:

```
<A href="http://www.mcp.com/resources/">MCP Resources</A>
```

This URL takes you to the default page set up for searching MCP's catalogs. Now if there's a specific page within an area on a Web site, you can code the reference with a specific page's filename:

```
<A href="http://www.mcp.com/resources/webdesign/dhtml_frame.html">Learn about
Dynamic HTML</A>
```

This link takes you directly to the Dynamic HTML Guru resource of the Macmillan Computer Publishing Web site (see Figure 9.3).

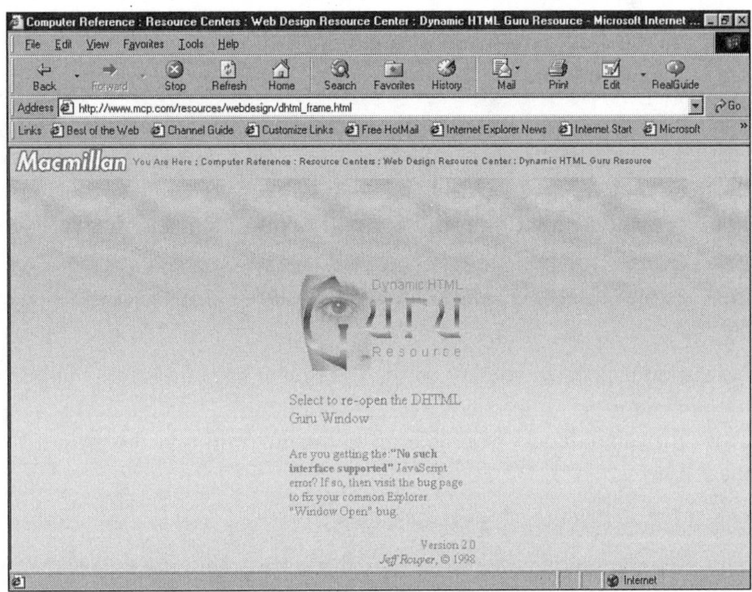

Figure 9.3
Following my specific page link, I end up on the Dynamic HTML Guru page as indicated in my link code.

Caution

Although current versions of browsers allow you to eliminate the `http://` and simply type in **`www.mcp.com`** to access a site, this by no means suggests that you can drop the `http://` code from an absolute URL in the HTML code. In fact, if you do so, you'll wind up with an ineffective link.

RELATIVE LINKING

Now let's say that Joe and Jo are going to set up housekeeping in the same house. However, Joe is in the study, and Jo is in the living room. We want to link them up, but do we need to specify a direct address—an absolute link—as we did when they were half a world away from one another? No! After all, they're already at the same address.

Relative linking allows you to link to files residing at the same address, on the same server. The files can be in the same directory as one another, or they might be in another directory. In either case, there are methods of linking *relatively* (in relation to) rather than absolutely to these files.

If you are linking from one page to another page within a site, and both files reside in the same directory, all you need to do is state the *hypertext reference* value as the filename:

```
<A href="jo.html">Jo's Home Page</A>
```

Where things get a bit more complex is when you want to link to a document in another directory on that server. Let's say I had my HTML page in my main folder, but I had a subfolder called "Jo" where I've placed the file, jo.html. I then have to place the path to that file into the hypertext reference, as follows:

```
<A href="jo/jo.html">Jo's Home Page</A>
```

Now the browser knows to look under the jo directory, rather than in the same directory as the original document.

You will always have to refer to the exact path to the file from your initial page. If I had a subfolder in the jo directory called "stories," and I wanted to link from my first document in the main folder, I have to include the entire path to the file I want to have the browser load. In this instance, I want to load the file "travels1.html." The syntax would then look like the following:

```
<A href="jo/stories/travels1.html">Read About Jo's Adventures in Southeast
Asia</A>
```

Now what happens if you are on the Jo's Home Page (jo.html), but you want to link back up to the main page? In relative linking, you use the `..` (double dot) to take you to the folder above the subfolder. So from jo.html to the index.html in the main folder, I'll have to code the following:

```
<A href="../index.html">Go Back Home</A>
```

This now takes me to the top, or *root*, directory, where my `index.html` file exists.

Follow these steps to create a relative link:

1. On your computer, create a folder and name it `root`.
2. Open root and create a subfolder, named `articles`.
3. Create an HTML page as follows:

```
<HTML>
<HEAD>

<TITLE>Relative Link Example</TITLE>

</HEAD>
<BODY>
```

```
<P>This page will appear in the root directory. If I want to link it to
an article in the "articles" directory, I would use relative linking.

</BODY>
</HTML>
```

4. Save this file in the root folder as `index.html`.

Now you have an index page within the root directory. You have to have something to link to for relative linking to work.

1. Open your HTML editor and code the following page:

```
<HTML>
<HEAD>

<TITLE>Sample Article I</TITLE>

</HEAD>
<BODY>

<P>This page will appear in the article directory.

</BODY>
</HTML>
```

2. Save this page as `article1.html` *in the article directory* (see Figure 9.4).

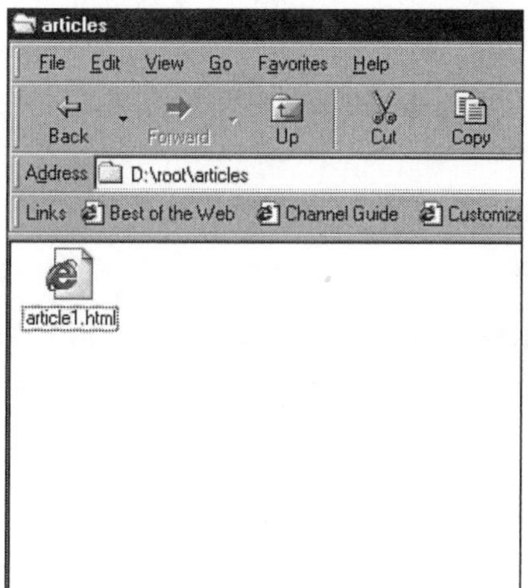

Figure 9.4
article1.html is saved to the article directory and ready to be used on your site by a relative link.

Follow these steps to add the link to the original document:

1. Open `index.html` in your editor and add the following syntax:

```
<HTML>
<HEAD>

<TITLE>Relative Link Example</TITLE>
```

```
</HEAD>
<BODY>

<P>This page will appear in the root directory. If I want to link it to an
article in the "articles" directory, I would use relative linking.

<P>If you <A href="articles/article1.html">Click This Link</A> the
articles1.html page will load. This is a relative link example!

</BODY>
</HTML>
```

2. Save the file.
3. Check your link. It should load `articles1.html`, as shown in Figure 9.5.

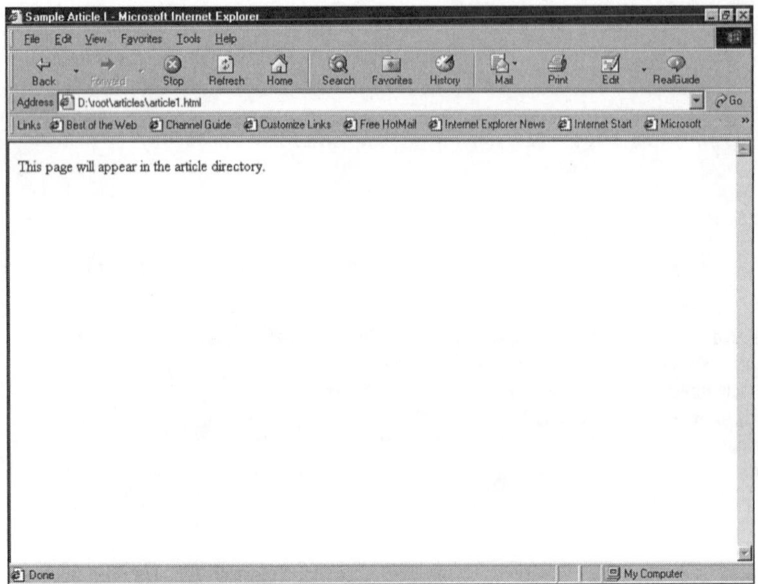

Figure 9.5
Clicking my first relative link loads the sample article page.

If you want to link back to the index, follow these steps:

1. Open the artciles1.html file in your editor and add the following relative link:

```
<HTML>
<HEAD>

<TITLE>Sample Article I</TITLE>

</HEAD>
<BODY>

<P>This page will appear in the article directory.
```

```
<P>If you <A href="../index.html">Click Right Here</A> you'll return to the
index page. This link is also a relative link!

</BODY>
</HTML>
```

2. Save the file, and test the link. I just did, and the index.html file loaded into my browser (see Figure 9.6).

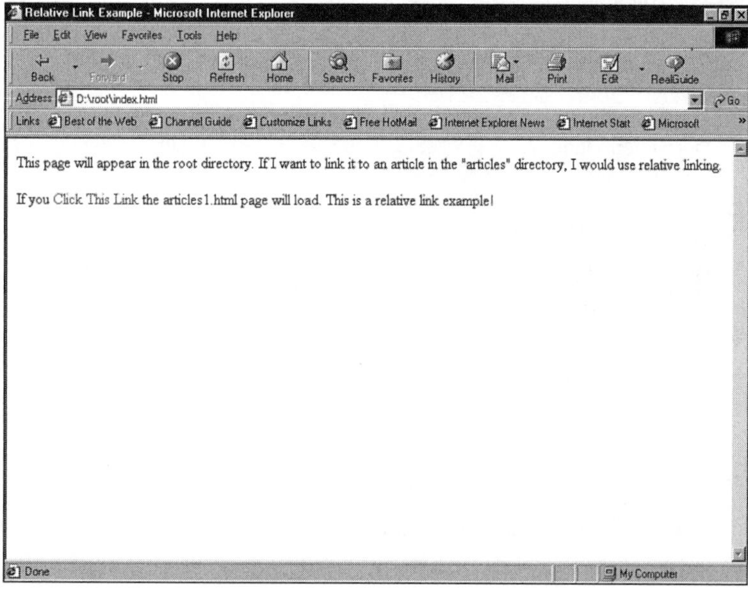

Figure 9.6
When I click the link, it loads the referring file. The link returns me to the home page, located in the root directory.

Relative linking is simple, and powerful. You will use this form of linking every time you are working locally or on the same server, unless you choose to link out to the Internet at large.

Want to troubleshoot links? See the Troubleshooting section at the end of this chapter.

In Listing 9.1, I show our sample article page with an external, absolute link added.

LISTING 9.1 RELATIVE LINKING

```
<HTML>
<HEAD>

<TITLE>Sample Article I</TITLE>

</HEAD>
<BODY>

<P>This page will appear in the article directory.
```

continues

LISTING 9.1 CONTINUED

```
<P>If you <A href="../index.html">Click Right Here</A> you'll return to the index
page. This link is also a relative link!

<P>If you decide to visit the Macmillan Computer Publishing site, you can do so by
<A href="http://www.mcp.com/">Clicking Right Here!</A>

</BODY>
</HTML>
```

When two sites each contain a link to the other, the term used to define this is *reciprocal linking*. The concept of *reciprocity* is an important one—because it can promote the flow of traffic between Web sites, a helpful aspect in marketing sites.

→ For more information about marketing Web sites, **see** "Web Site Marketing and Promotion," **p. 906**

LINKING IMAGES

So far, the examples used in this chapter show hypertext links. In other words, it's *text* that is active. However, as mentioned earlier, a variety of media—particularly images—can be made "hyper," or linkable.

Using images as links is easy to do, too. All that is necessary is to place the image *within* the context of the anchor tag, and that image will become hyper—anchored to the relative or absolute link that you've designated.

```
<A href="computers.html"><img src="computer_image.gif"></A>
```

In Figure 9.7, you'll see the computer image. If I click the image, it will take me to the `computers.html` page.

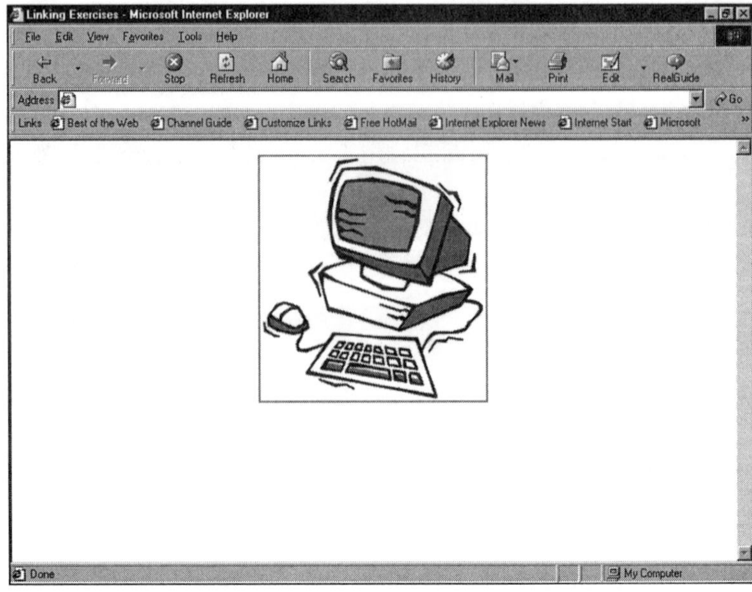

Figure 9.7
A linked image automatically appears with a border around it to indicate that the image is acting as a link.

Tip from molly

A border surrounding images is not always esthetically pleasing. To remove the border, you can add the `border="0"` attribute and value to the IMG code.

→ For more about images and borders, **see** "Working with Images," **p. 199**

Here's the modified code:

```
<a href="computers.html"><img src="computer_image.gif" border="0"></a>
```

The link now has no border (see Figure 9.8).

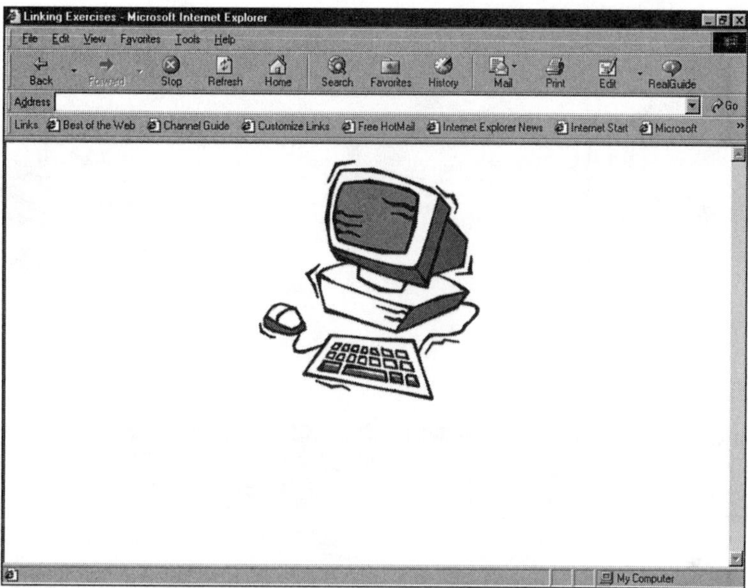

Figure 9.8
The same linked image without the border is much more appealing to the eye and won't disturb the visual quality of the overall design of the page the way links with borders tend to do.

INTRA-PAGE LINKING

A helpful method of navigating within a page is to use a process called intra-page linking. Figure 9.9 shows a site for the Ramada Inn in Tucson, Arizona. You can see that there are three links to the left of the photo, each pointing to a specific topic that appears not on *another* page, but rather on the same page as those links.

If I click the Amenities link, I'm taken to the Amenities page, which contains a range of information regarding the hotel. What happens if I want a quick route back to the top of the page? Well, the little "up" arrow (see Figure 9.10) provides just that—an intra-page link that takes me back to the offerings on that page.

Intra-page linking is convenient for visitors, and helps coders organize pages in a succinct, sensible fashion. Here's a look at the link that takes us from the top of the page to the directions:

```
<A href="#direct">Directions</A>
```

As you can see, it looks like a regular, relative link. The only difference is that instead of a filename, there's a pound sign followed by a single word.

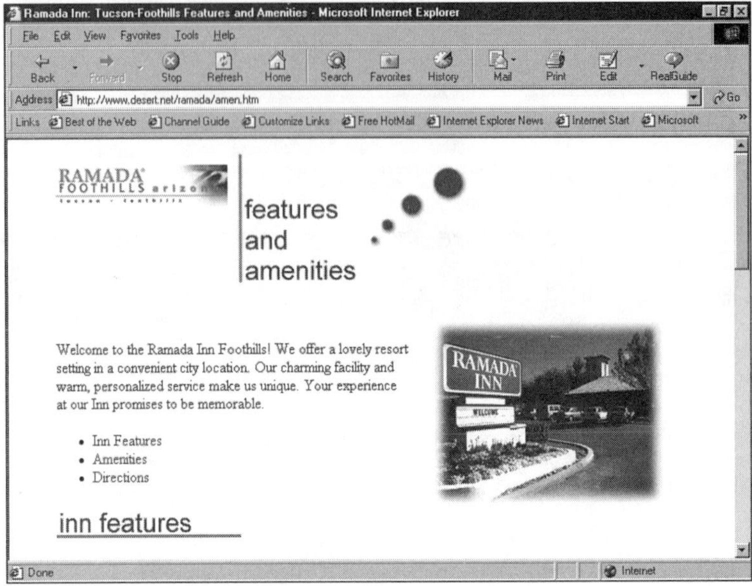

Figure 9.9 Ramada Inn intra-page links enable their site visitors to quickly get to the information they want without scrolling up and down the page to locate it.

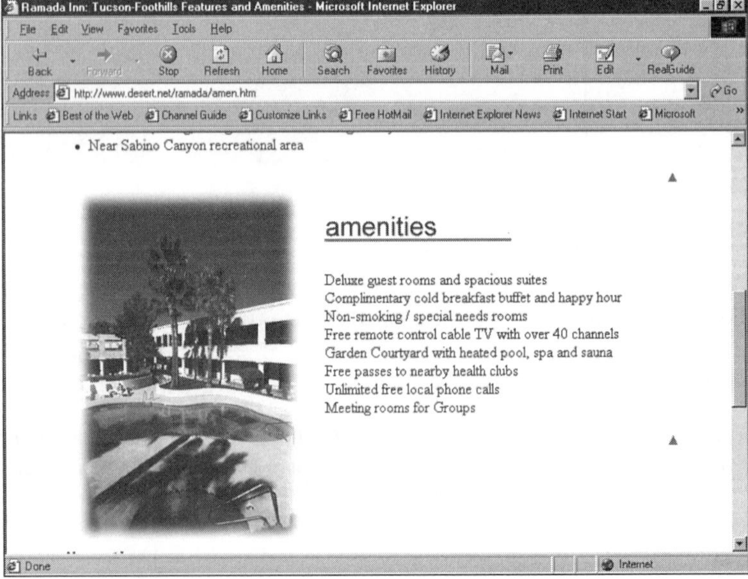

Figure 9.10 The up arrow link offers a quick return to the top of the Web page.

Because we have no file to link to, we have to create somewhere for this link to go. This is called a *named target*. It looks like the following:

```
<A name="direct"><img src="direct.gif" alt="amenities" width="200" height="42"
border="0"></A>
```

In this case, the anchor tag names a point on the page for the initial link to the *named target*. The anchor can be text or, as shown in this example, a graphic. So, when I click the initial link, Directions, I'm taken to the target anchor.

To help you understand this method here is an exercise for intra-page linking:

1. In your HTML editor, build a simple shell:

```
<HTML>
<HEAD>

<TITLE>Intra-Page Link Example</TITLE>

</HEAD>
<BODY>

</BODY>
</HTML>
```

2. To the shell, add several link items:

```
<HTML>
<HEAD>

<TITLE>Intra-Page Link Example</TITLE>

</HEAD>
<BODY>

<P>Gentle Ben's Gem Shop Offers Amethyst, Aquamarine, and Rose Quartz.


</BODY>
</HTML>
```

3. Now add text that will make a natural target for those items:

```
<HTML>
<HEAD>

<TITLE>Intra-Page Link Example</TITLE>

</HEAD>
<BODY>

<P>Gentle Ben's Gem Shop Offers Amethyst, Aquamarine, and Rose Quartz.


<H1> Amethyst</H1>
<P>Amethyst is a beautiful gem, with clear as well as purple coloration that
ranges in depth and intensity. The depth of the purple color relates to the
age of the gem. The older the gem, the deeper the color can get.
```

```
<H1>Aquamarine</H1>
<P>It's almost as if the depths of the ocean are reflected in this gem. From
clear crystal to the purest aqua, this is a breathtaking gemstone.
<H1>Rose Quartz</H1>
<P>Rosy pink and smooth, Rose quartz is favored by many gem collectors for use
in making jewelry as well as figurines.
It is thought to have powerful healing properties where the heart is
concerned.
Some say that keeping a piece of Rose Quartz near you will help bring a
perfect love into your life.


</BODY>
</HTML>
```

4. Now let's name the first target amethyst:

   ```
   <A name="amethyst"><H1>Amethyst</H1></A>
   ```

5. When you're finished, move back up to the top list, and link the word *amethyst* to the target you just created:

   ```
   Gentle Ben's Gem Shop Offers <A href="#amethyst">Amethyst</A>, Aquamarine, and
   Rose Quartz.
   ```

6. Save your file as `intra_link.html` and check the link in your browser.

Now that you've stepped through the first natural intra-page link instance in our example, you can go ahead and finish the page. Listing 9.2 shows the final code.

LISTING 9.2 INTRA-PAGE LINKING

```
<HTML>
<HEAD>

<TITLE>Intra-Page Link Example</TITLE>

</HEAD>
<BODY>

<P>Gentle Ben's Gem Shop Offers <A href="#amethyst">Amethyst</A>,
<A href="#Aquamarine">Aquamarine</A>, and <A href="#rose">Rose Quartz</A>.
<A name="Amethyst"><h1> Amethyst</h1></A>
<P>Amethyst is a beautiful gem, with clear as well as purple coloration that
ranges in depth and intensity. The depth of the purple color relates to the age of
the gem. The older the gem, the deeper the color can get.
<A name="Aquamarine"><h1>Aquamarine</h1></A>
<P>It's almost as if the depths of the ocean are reflected in this gem. From clear
crystal to the purest aqua, this is a breathtaking gemstone.
```

```
<A name="rose"><h1>Rose Quartz</h1></A>
<P>Rosy pink and smooth, Rose quartz is favored by many gem collectors for use in
making jewelry as well as figurines.
It is thought to have powerful healing properties where the heart is concerned.
Some say that keeping a piece of Rose Quartz near you will help bring a perfect
love into your life.


</BODY>
</HTML>
```


You can compare your page to mine, as shown in Figure 9.11.

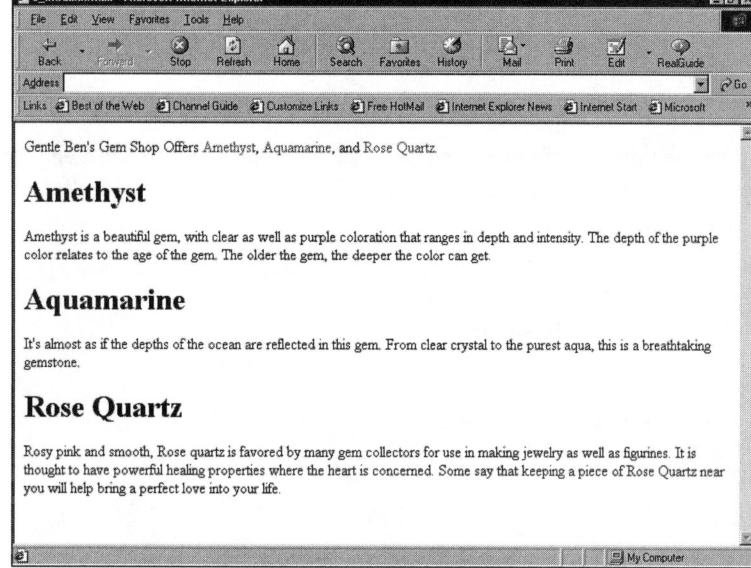

Figure 9.11
Intra-page linking exercise.

And what of the little "back to top" image? It works exactly the same way. Here's the named target at the top of the page:

```
<A name="top">Welcome</A>
```

And here's the code for the linked arrow:

```
<A href="#top"><img src="uparrow.gif" alt="click here and go to top" width="20"
height="12" border="0" align="right"></A>
```

Many people rely heavily on this method to organize their sites. It can be a powerful, easy way to set up intra-page navigation, and offers the site visitor easy methods of moving around a page.

Caution

Although intra-page linking can be an HTML coder's best helper in organizing material within a page, it's important to keep the length of pages to a reasonable size. You will see pages on the Internet that scroll for many screens–even with intra-page linking this is not an ideal situation. Keep to no more than five or six total screens per page, with three screens being best. This way, your users don't have to scroll forever to find information.

MAIL LINKS

A convenient way of enabling Web site visitors to reach you via your Web page is to provide a link to your mail address. This can be managed using the anchor tag and a reference known as `mailto:`.

The following is an example:

```
<A href="mailto:molly@molly.com">Send an e-mail to Molly</A>
```

Click the link, and your browser calls up a mail program that automatically lets you type in an email to the designated account.

Tip from molly

Mail links can be used around images, too. Simply use the `mailto:` code and addressing as shown in this section, and place an image rather than text between the open anchor tag and closing tag.

Figure 9.12 shows how doing this in Internet Explorer pulls up my default mail reader, Eudora.

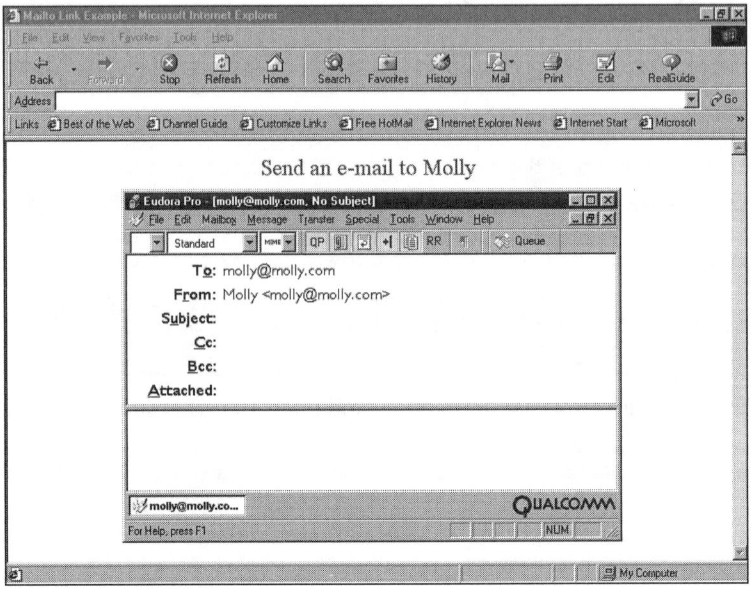

Figure 9.12
With `mailto:`, the browser launches a default mail reader.

Tip from molly

Using forms is another popular way to offer mail links to site visitors, and there are other methods to choose from as well.

➔ For more about creating and managing forms, **see** "Building Forms," **p. 386**

Because mail links are such an effective method of getting people to contact you, many individuals like to put a `mailto:` link on every page of their site. This can be done discreetly in the footer information. In Figure 9.13, the footer information for the Ramada Inn site shown earlier in this chapter reflects this convenience.

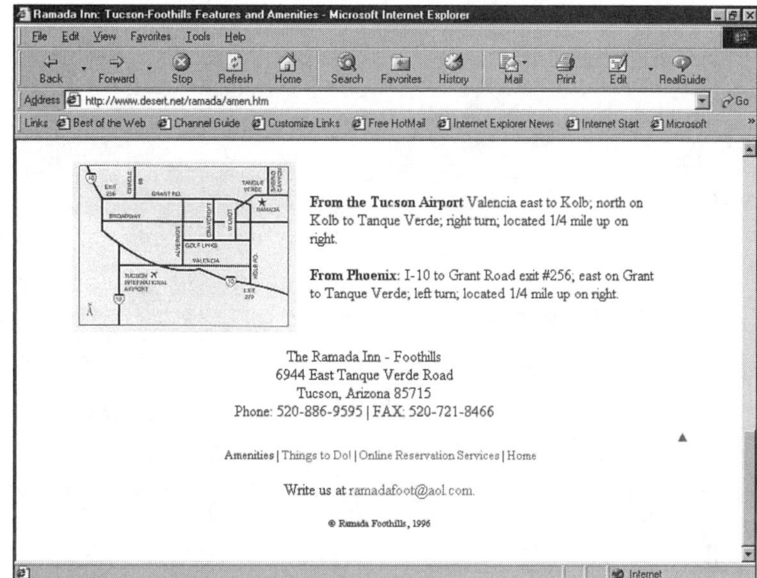

Figure 9.13
`mailto:` is often used on every page to make it more convenient for the site visitor to contact the site owner.

USING MULTIPLE LINKS ON A PAGE

Pages can have multiple link styles. There's no limitation to how many links or the type of links you can have on a single page. It is wise to balance your links throughout a page so that they make sense.

Follow these steps to create a page that uses every kind of link covered in this chapter: absolute, relative, intra-page, and `mailto:`.

1. In your HTML editor, create a shell:

```
<HTML>
<HEAD>
<TITLE>Link Mania</TITLE>
</HEAD>

<BODY>
```

```
</BODY>
</HTML>
```

2. Now set up some text for a variety of link styles:

```
<HTML>
<HEAD>
<TITLE>Link Mania</TITLE>
</HEAD>

<BODY>

<P>Select from these options:


<OL>
<LI>See a mailto: link
<LI>Shoot to a named anchor
<LI>How about a relative link?
<LI>Check out an absolute link
</OL>

<P>Since my first online experience, I've been enraptured with the Internet.
When the World Wide Web came along, I thought "this is so cool!"

<P>One of the reasons I really, really like the Web is because you can link to
the rest of the world in a variety of ways. For example, if you wanted to have
a page that let people send me email, all I'd have to do is set up an email
link, like this one.

<P>Or, if I want to link to another document in the same site, I can have a
relative link.

<P>Absolute links are particularly cool, because they take you away from one
site to another site of interest. In fact, if you click here, you can go visit
one of my favorite sites!

</BODY>
</HTML>
```

3. Add the relative, absolute, and `mailto:` links:

```
<HTML>
<HEAD>
<TITLE>Link Mania</TITLE>
</HEAD>

<BODY>

<P>Select from these options:

<OL>
<LI>See a mailto: link
<LI>Shoot to a named anchor
<LI>How about a relative link?
<LI>Check out an absolute link
</OL>
```

```
<P>Since my first online experience, I've been enraptured with the Internet.
When the World Wide Web came along, I thought "this is so cool!"

<P>One of the reasons I really, really like the Web is because you can link to
the rest of the world in a variety of ways. For example, if you wanted to have
a page that let people send me email, all I'd have to do is set up an email
link, <A href="mailto:molly@molly.com">like this one</A>.

<P>Or, if I want to link to another document in the same site, I can have a <A
href="new_page.html">relative</A> link.

<P>Absolute links are particularly cool, because they take you away from one
site
to another site of interest. In fact, if you click here, you can go visit one
of my <A href="http://www.filmvault.com/filmvault/">favorite sites!</A>

</BODY>
</HTML>
```


4. Now set up your named targets:

```
<HTML>
<HEAD>
<TITLE>Link Mania</TITLE>
</HEAD>

<BODY>

<P>Select from these options:

<OL>
<LI>See a mailto: link
<LI>Shoot to a named anchor
<LI>How about a relative link?
<LI>Check out an absolute link
</OL>

<P>Since my first online experience, I've been enraptured with the Internet.
When the <A name="namedanchor">World Wide Web</A> came along, I thought "this
is so cool!"

<P>One of the reasons I really, really like the Web is because you can link to
the rest of the world in a variety of ways. For example, if you wanted to have
a page that let people send me email, all I'd have to do is set up an email
link,
<A name="mailto"><a href="mailto:molly@molly.com">like this one</A>.</A>

<P>Or, if I want to link to another document in the same site, I can have a <A
name="relative"><A href="new_page.html">relative</A> link.</A>

<P>Absolute links are particularly cool, because they take you away from one
site to another site of interest. In fact, if you click here, you can go visit
one of my <A name="absolute"><A
href="http://www.filmvault.com/filmvault/">favorite sites!</A></A>

</BODY>
</HTML>
```

5. Finally, add your intra-page links:

```
<HTML>
<HEAD>
<TITLE>Link Mania</TITLE>
</HEAD>

<BODY>

<P>Select from these options:

<OL>
<LI><A href="#mailto">See a mailto: link</A>
<LI><A href="#namedanchor">Shoot to a named anchor</A>
<LI><A href="#relative">How about a relative link?</A>
<LI><A href="#absolute">Check out an absolute link</A>
</OL>

<P>Since my first online experience, I've been enraptured with the Internet.
When the <A name="namedanchor">World Wide Web</A> came along, I thought "this
is so cool!"

<P>One of the reasons I really, really like the Web is because you can link to
the rest of the world in a variety of ways. For example, if you wanted to have
a page that let people send me email, all I'd have to do is set up an email
link, <A name="mailto"><A href="mailto:molly@molly.com">like this one</A>.</A>

<P>Or, if I want to link to another document in the same site, I can have a <A
name="relative"><A href="new_page.html">relative</A> link.</A>

<P>Absolute links are particularly cool, because they take you away from one
site to another site of interest. In fact, if you click here, you can go visit
one of my <A name="absolute"><A
href="http://www.filmvault.com/filmvault/">favorite sites!</A></A>

</BODY>
</HTML>
```

6. Save your file as `linkmania.html` and test in your browser. Click each link and watch it work.

You can compare your page to mine, shown in Figure 9.14.

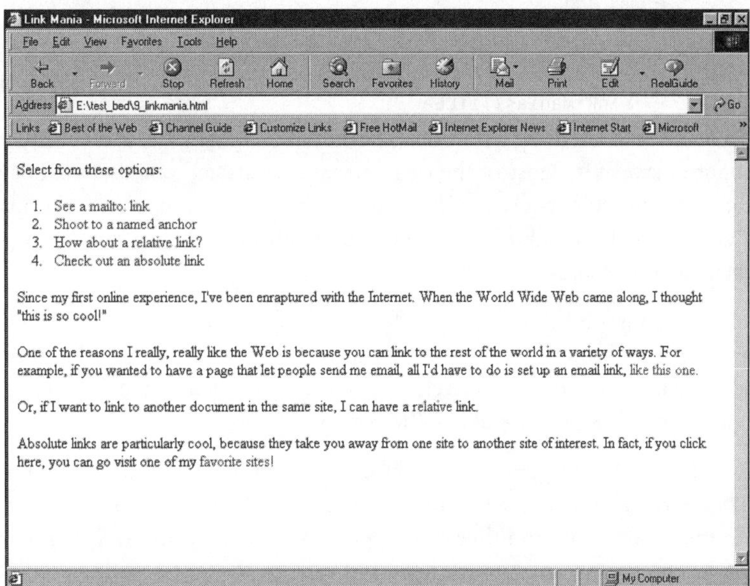

Figure 9.14
The Link Mania page. Save this exercise as it will be a good reference should you run into questions about how to properly code links.

TROUBLESHOOTING

LINKING TO FILES IN DIFFERENT FOLDERS

What is the syntax for linking from a page in one subdirectory to a page in a different subdirectory?

If you are linking from, say molly_books.html within the books subdirectory to molly_music.html within the music subdirectory, the link would look as follows:

```
<A href="../music/molly_music.html">Molly's Music</A>
```

Notice that you have told the browser to go back to the root (the `../`) and then look in the music subdirectory. For more on this refer back to the section on relative links.

RECIPROCAL LINK REFUSAL

Why would someone turn down an opportunity for their site to gain more exposure through a link on another site?

In most cases, Web developers are honored when you choose to link to their site. There are some instances when this is not the case. Some Web-hosting services charge based on the number of server hits per month. If the site that adds the link is extremely popular, this can result in extra fees for the linked site because of the extra hits. In some cases, the extra hits are enough to cause the server to crash if it is not able to handle such a high usage load.

DESIGNING FOR THE REAL WORLD

ABOUT ABOUT.COM

If you've read anything about the Internet in the past year, you've surely read something about portal sites. Most of the large portal sites started out as search engines and expanded their offering to encourage visitors to stay on the site longer. Yahoo! and Excite have added clubs and user communities that enable members to chat or post on message boards about their favorite topics.

About.com has taken a slightly different approach. About has created communities, called guide sites, within which visitors can search for sites of interest. Each About community serves almost as a custom search engine for a particular topic. The links within each community are chosen by a guide—the community leader.

A look at an About guide site shows examples of just about every type of linking imaginable. There are, of course, relative links to and from the various pages within the guide site. There are also links to other related guide sites. Note, however, that even though the other guide sites are part of About, they have a unique URL, requiring absolute links to be used. The sites also have links to other About services, requiring more absolute links, and links to the various recommended sites elsewhere on the Web.

Each guide site also contains a link to email the guide, using a `mailto:` link. Finally, there is a `mailto:` form, which enables you to send information about the site to a friend just by filling in their email address.

Note

About.com—`http://www.about.com`

Yahoo!—`http://www.yahoo.com`

Excite—`http://www.excite.com`

CHAPTER 10

Working with Images

In this chapter

MOVING TOWARD DESIGN

Adding images to a Web page is the first step in moving away from simple document formatting and into the world of design. Images add identity, color, shape, and presence. They are a powerful and important aspect of the Web, yet one that eludes many Webmasters.

In this chapter, you'll learn how to add images to your pages by using HTML. As I've said in many places throughout this book, you're going to learn how to do some things that are conventional rather than standard.

In the case of images, this is particularly true when it comes to positioning. There are several ways to position an image on a page. You can use conventional HTML tags that are transitioning out in favor of style sheets, you can use tables, and you can choose to use HTML 4.0's style sheet positioning.

In this chapter, the focus is on conventional HTML tags. Although more advanced methods are exciting and troublesome in turn, the designer can always rely on conventional HTML wisdom to manage images. That's the focus here—making sure that your foundation skills are in place *before* sending you off into the less stable and more complex methods of image control.

→ You can learn about other methods of placing images in related chapters. To learn how you can use tables to control the position and appearance of images on a page, **see** "Advanced Table Layouts," **p. 334**

→ For a discussion on how to accomplish similar results with style sheets, **see** "Element Positioning and Style Sheet Scripting," **p. 435**

THE IMG TAG

You'll use the `<IMG>` tag to place images on a page. This tag is truly a tag—it has no closing companion:

```
<IMG>
```

The `<IMG>` tag requires a source that is called with the `src=` attribute. The source directs the HTML to get the image in question:

```
<IMG src="guitar.gif">
```

This string alone is sufficient to add an image to your page, provided the image resides in the same location as the HTML document.

Typically, HTML developers place images in a specific directory below the root HTML directory. This directory is aptly named *images* or *graphics*, depending on your preference. If your image resides in such a subdirectory and your HTML page is in the root directory, you'll need to address the source appropriately, by using relative linking:

```
<IMG src="images/guitar.gif">
```

→ For a discussion on the management of files, **see** "Managing HTML Documents Locally," **p. 62**

→ To get insight into how to manage relative links, **see** "Linking Pages," **p. 177**

Caution

Some people will link to an image that resides off their site by using an absolute URL to reach the location of an image. This is not a recommended practice for several reasons. One consideration is that you risk a bad connection and the image might never load any time you go off your own server. Another concern is ownership: If that graphic element isn't yours and you link to it without the owner's express permission, you could be in violation of copyright.

Images always go within the BODY section of an HTML document. Listing 10.1 shows a simple HTML page with a graphic.

LISTING 10.1 ADDING AN IMAGE TO AN HTML PAGE

```
<HTML>
<HEAD>
<TITLE>Adding an Image to an HTML Page</TITLE>
</HEAD>
<BODY>
<IMG src="images/guitar.gif">
</BODY>
</HTML>
```


Figure 10.1 shows the results. You'll notice that the image appears on the left of the page.It has no special position, other than that determined according to the browser's default settings.

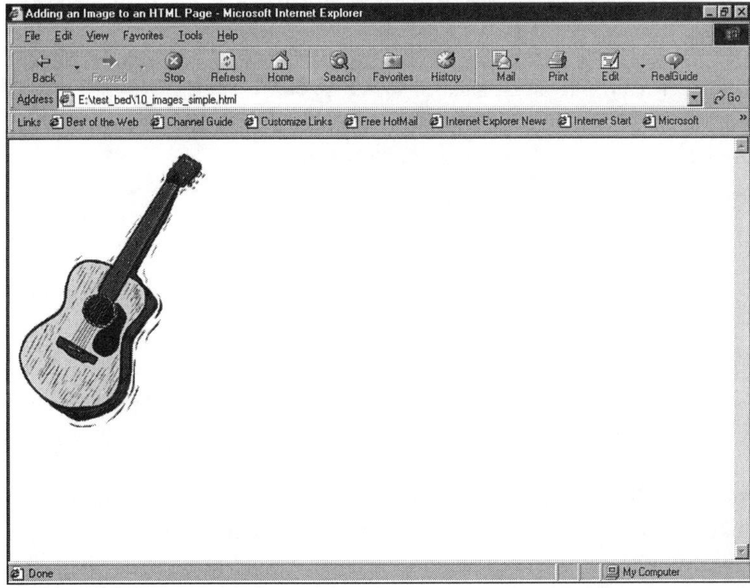

Figure 10.1
Using the <IMG> tag with no other attributes, this image is positioned on the page to the default left position within the browser.

The `IMG` tag allows you to add attributes that will control the action and the appearance of an image on a page.

IMAGE TAG ATTRIBUTES

A variety of attributes can be added to an `IMG` tag to control the way a browser manages the image. These attributes include the following:

- **`src="x"`**—This is the source attribute, and is used with either an absolute or relative URL that points to the location of the image.
- **`width="x"`**—This allows a browser to predetermine the width, in pixels, that your image requires.
- **`height="x"`**—Along with the `width` attribute, the browser can prepare the necessary space for your image in advance. This controls the way your images are loaded on a page.
- **`border="x"`**—To add or remove a border, use this attribute, where `"x"` is a numeric value.
- **`align="x"`**—You can align an image horizontally and vertically on a page by using this attribute.
- **`alt="description of image"`**—The powerful `alt` attribute allows you to describe the image to text-only browsers, tagging the image before it loads onto a page, and allow a ToolTip to appear with the description as a mouse passes over the image.
- **`hspace="x"`**—*Horizontal space* is used to add space, with a numeric value, around the horizontal axis of the image.
- **`vspace="x"`**—*Vertical space* controls the spacing of the image along the vertical axis.

→ For information on the `ismap` and `usemap` attributes that are used in imagemapping, **see** "Imagemaps, Animation, and Special Graphic Techniques," **p. 648**

The sections to follow take a more in-depth look at these attributes and how they work.

`width` AND `height`

The best advice I can give you regarding these attributes is twofold:

- Always, always include `width` and `height` in your `IMG` tag. This helps the browser manage the image data throughout the page.
- Never, never use inaccurate `width` and `height` values for any image except for single pixel GIFs. Standard image values must *always* be exact, or you'll cause your browser to abnormally stretch or minimize an image.

You might be thinking: "But Molly, I've seen people create thumbnails of large images by making the `width` and `height` values smaller. I thought that was a clever idea!" It's clever, and it's very problematic.

This is because your large image *still* has to download to the browser. Let's say you have five images of 50KB each, and you resize them on your page by using the `width` and `height` attributes. You haven't resized the image by doing this—only the *appearance* of the image. Your browser must retrieve all 200KB of those images even though it will display them as being smaller than their actual dimension. The weight remains the same—and your site visitors may not remain on your site waiting for the downloads.

Following the rules, this code shows my guitar image with the proper width and height:

```
<IMG src="images/guitar.gif" width="200" height="284">
```

To find the exact `width` and `height` of your image, look at it in your imaging program. The image size is available there (see Figure 10.2).

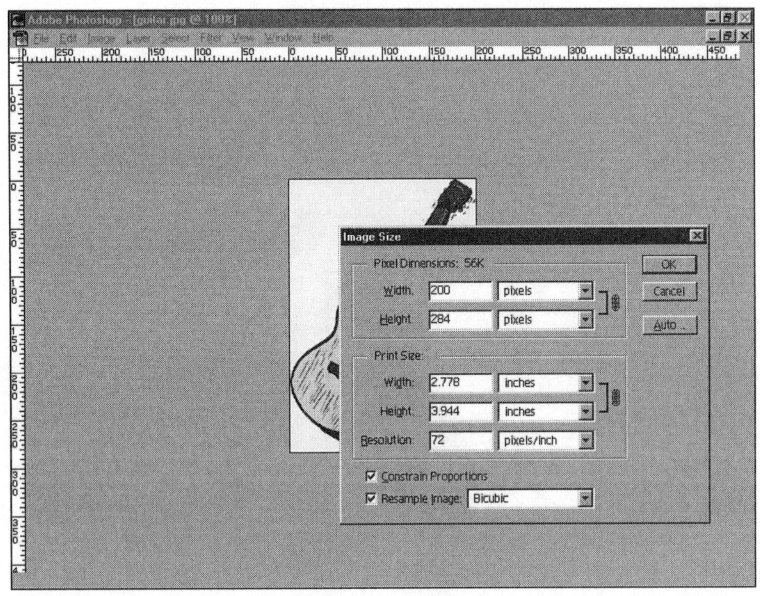

Figure 10.2
Image `width` and `height` information can be found by checking the image in a graphics software program, such as what is seen here in Adobe Photoshop.

Tip from molly

Another way to determine the `width` and `height` of your image is to open the graphic in Netscape. The image's dimensions are noted along the top bar of the interface.

→ For information on various imaging programs, **see** "Web Graphic Formats and Professional Tools," **p. 566**

→ When you design your graphics, you should size them appropriately for the Web. To learn how to do this properly, **see** "Creating Professional Web Graphics," **p. 603**

IMAGE BORDERS

Borders around images were once the default of most Web browsers, particularly if the image was linked. The default now is to have no border. This isn't an accident—borders around images constrain the image.

→ To learn why borders around images are problematic, **see** "Resolution, Gamma, and the Visual Environment," **p. 546**

To ensure that your graphics always appear without borders, it's wise to include a value of "0" with the border attribute:

```
<IMG src="images/guitar.gif" width="200" height="284" border="0">
```

This string protects your image from appearing with borders in older browsers or browsers that still use a border as its default if no border information is included in the IMG string.

If you really want a border around an image, you can set it by setting a numeric value in the border attribute:

```
<IMG src="images/guitar.gif" width="200" height="284" border="4">
```

Figure 10.3 shows the image with the border.

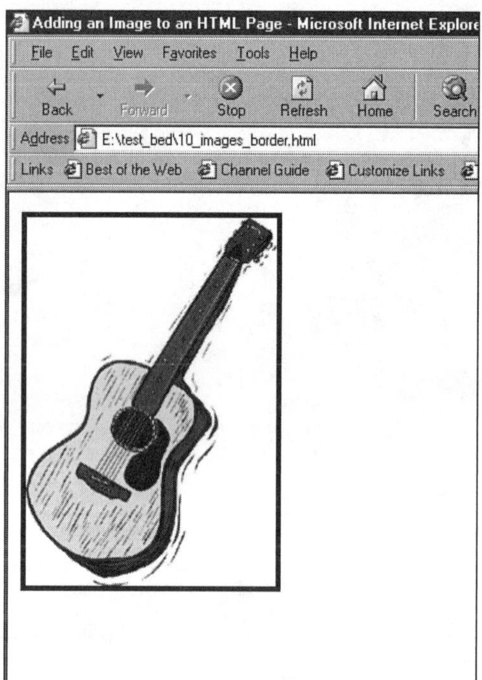

Figure 10.3
This figure shows the guitar image with a border value of "4".

Borders pick up the color of your text if they are not linked. If they are linked, borders appear in either the browser defaults of blue for an unvisited link, purple for a visited link, the user's custom colors, or the link and vlink colors that you personally specify within the BODY tag.

→ For more information on setting colors in the BODY tag, **see** "Working with the BODY Element," **p. 217**

ALIGNMENT

There are a number of ways to align your image. On the horizon line, the default is left for a solitary object. You can also set the alignment to a value of `left` (this is important when wrapping text, discussed in the "Floating Images" section later in this chapter) or a value of `right`.

```
<IMG src="images/guitar.gif" width="200" height="284" border="0" align="right">
```

In Figure 10.4, you can see that this alignment value has caused the image to appear along the right of the browser.

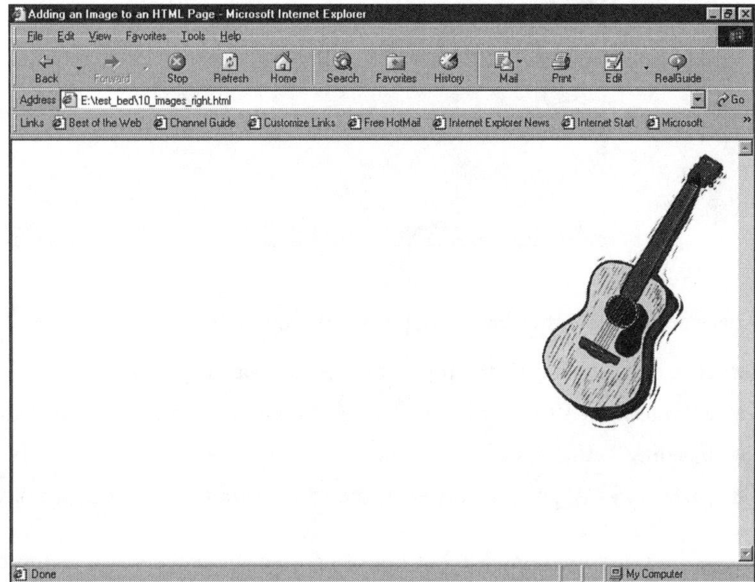

Figure 10.4
Using the `align` attribute with a value of `right`, I've successfully aligned this image to the right rather than default left of the browser.

→ To center images, you must use another method such as the `DIV` tag; for information on how to manage centering of text and media, **see** "Formatting and Aligning Text," **p. 136**

Although the horizontal alignment values of `left` and `right` are likely to be used most frequently, you can also use the `align` attribute to align an image vertically:

```
<IMG src="little_guitar.gif" align="top">
```

Standard, cross-browser values for this include the following:

- **`top`**—This puts the image along the topmost part of the horizon line.
- **`middle`**—The image is aligned with the middle or baseline of the horizon.
- **`bottom`**—With this value, the image is aligned with the bottom of the horizon line.

I've set up an example of each of these, which you can see in Figure 10.5.

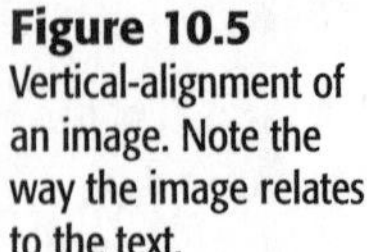

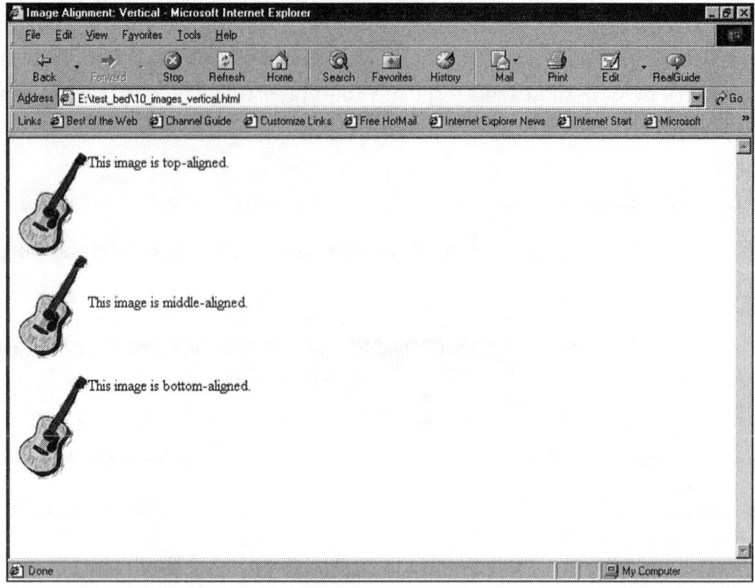

Figure 10.5
Vertical-alignment of an image. Note the way the image relates to the text.

There are several other browser-specific alignment values, including

- **textop**—Aligns with the top of highest text or image on that line.
- **absmiddle**—Aligns with the *absolute* middle of the highest surrounding text or image.
- **baseline**—Aligns to the bottom.
- **`absbottom`**—Aligns the bottom of the image with the lowest image or text along the line.

These are sometimes helpful, but not often used. In fact, vertical alignment of images by using the `align` attribute is reserved for instances when the need for precise alignment is desired. In HTML 4.0, such alignment is better handled with tables and, most especially, style sheets.

→ To learn more about CSS, **see** "Cascading Style Sheet Techniques," **p. 254** and "Designing Type with CSS," **p. 284**

THE `alt` ATTRIBUTE

This important attribute allows you to write out a description of the image. For example, because my guitar image is actually a drawing rather than a photo, I could describe the image as a "drawing of a guitar" as follows:

```
<IMG src="images/guitar.gif" width="200" height="284" border="0"
alt="drawing of a guitar">
```

For those individuals without graphics—whether using text browsers due to blindness, limited Internet resources, or for those individuals who surf the Web with graphics turned off—the `alt` attribute provides a great way to describe the visual nature of what's going on (see Figure 10.6).

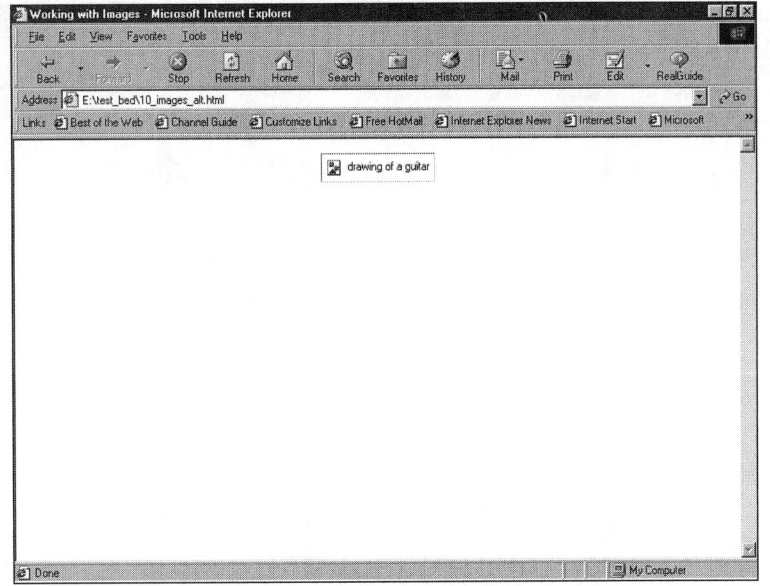

Figure 10.6
The `alt` description appears when image loading is turned off.

➔ For detailed information about providing accessible Web sites, **see** "Accessibility and Internationalization," **p. 475**

The `alt` description appears in two other instances. One is as a page is loading graphics. The description shows up before the associated graphic is loaded. This is a helpful way of keeping visitors interested in what's coming. Descriptions defined with this attribute also appear when a mouse passes over a given image (see Figure 10.7). Also thought to be helpful, I and others *sometimes* find the extra visual information annoying. It's a compromise—one I'm willing to make at this point to provide people with the most extensible support possible.

You should use this attribute with one exception: when an image is a single-pixel graphic used for fixing graphic placement. In this case, the `alt` attribute can be left out or left blank. Many developers prefer to leave the attribute in, but place no value within the quotes:

```
<IMG src="images/spacer.gif" width="20" height="1" border="0 alt="">
```

Tip from

Why add an `alt` attribute with quotes and no value? Well, when you do this, there will be *no demarcation* of the image in a text-based environment. If you don't use this clever technique, `[inline]` appears where the graphic should be.

HORIZONTAL AND VERTICAL SPACE

Values for `hspace` and `vspace` are numeric. For demonstration purposes, I'm going to use values that are a bit exaggerated for these attributes:

```
<IMG src="images/guitar.gif" width="200" height="284" border="1" align="right"
alt="drawing of a guitar" hspace="100">
```

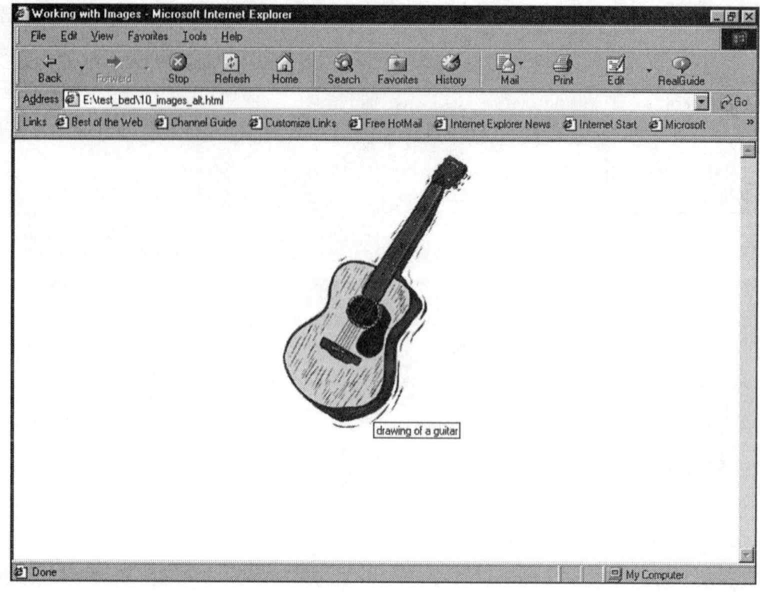

Figure 10.7
The `alt` description also appears when a mouse passes over the image.

Compare Figure 10.8 and Figure 10.9. In Figure 10.8, I use no horizontal spacing; but in Figure 10.9, I use the horizontal spacing value of `"100"`. I've added a border of `"1"` to the image so that you can easily see how this puts space between the text and the image.

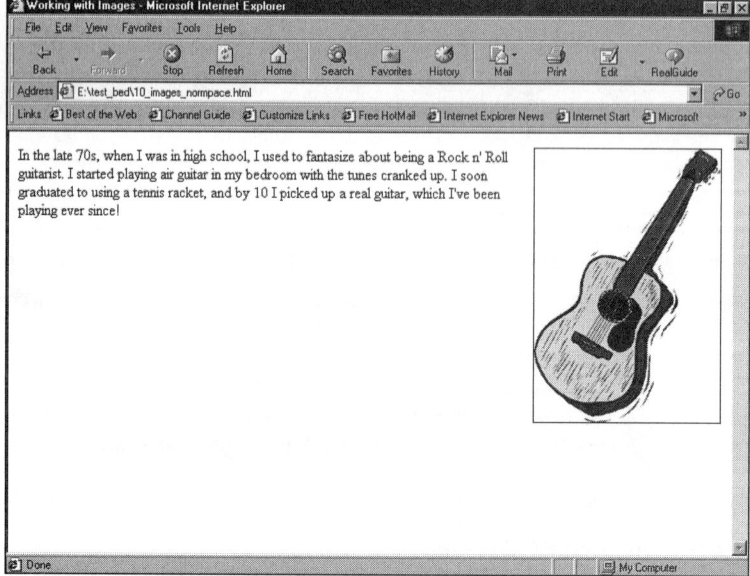

Figure 10.8
Normal spacing between text and image.

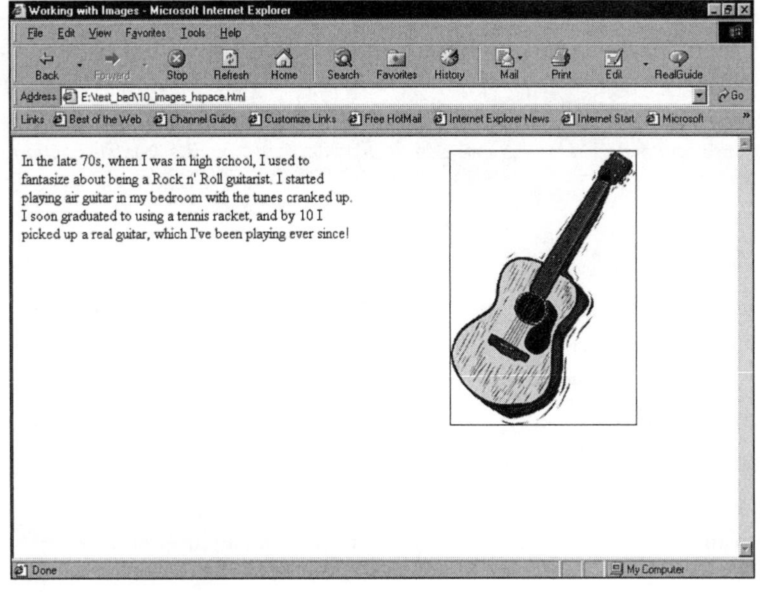

Figure 10.9
Horizontal space added between text and image.

Now compare Figure 10.8 and Figure 10.10, where I've used a vertical spacing of `"40"`. Here's the code:

```
<IMG src="images/guitar.gif" width="200" height="284" border="0" align="right"
alt="drawing of a guitar" vspace="40">
```

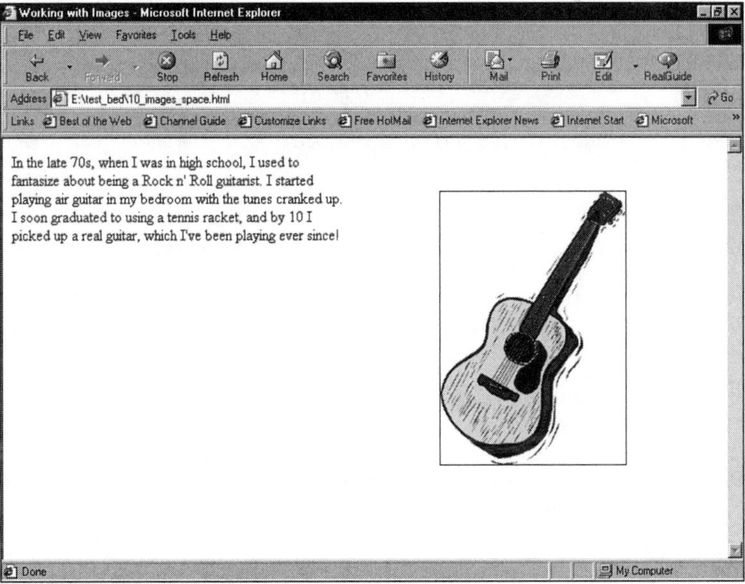

Figure 10.10
In this case, vertical space appears between text and image, providing necessary white space in between. Without that space, the text and image would be too close together, making the text difficult to read and diminishing the unique importance of the image.

Using the hspace and vspace attributes is particularly helpful when wrapping text around images. This is called *dynamic* text wrapping, or *floating* images. More about this technique in the next section.

What if you want to use a horizontal line to help create space between text or images, but don't want to use an image file for the line? See, "Horizontal Rules," in the Troubleshooting section at the end of this chapter.

FLOATING IMAGES

Using a combination of attributes within the IMG tag, you can achieve attractive, dynamic layout of graphics and text. Although tables and style sheets are perhaps more sophisticated ways of addressing this matter, you're likely to have plenty of need for this technique.

To float images, you first must align the image. Even if you want to place your image to the left, which is typically the default position, you must use the align attribute to achieve this technique.

Listing 10.2 shows an HTML page with text and a left-aligned image.

LISTING 10.2 FLOATING IMAGE AND DYNAMIC TEXT

```
<HTML>

<HEAD>

<TITLE>Floating Image and Dynamic Text: Left</TITLE>

</HEAD>


<BODY>


<IMG src="images/little_guitar.gif" width="75" height="107" border="0"
align="left"

alt="drawing of a guitar">

In my other life, I'm a guitar player and vocalist. I've been singing since I was
a child, and was formally trained as a vocalist. I spent many years singing
soprano in a variety of school choirs and other music organizations.  My first
instrument was the piano, which I like but never had the discipline to achieve any
level worthy of impressing anyone!  In the late 70s, when I was in high school, I
used to fantasize about being a Rock n' Roll guitarist. I started playing air
guitar in my bedroom with the tunes cranked up.  I soon graduated to using a
tennis racket, and by 10 I picked up a real guitar, which I've been playing ever
since! I've been playing in a duo named Courage Sisters, with my music partner,
Patti Sundberg, for the last several years. We play a variety of original,
acoustic music typically comprised of two guitars and two voices. We're especially
known for complex harmonies.

</BODY>

</HTML>
```

Figure 10.11 shows the left-aligned image and the text that wraps *dynamically* around the graphic.

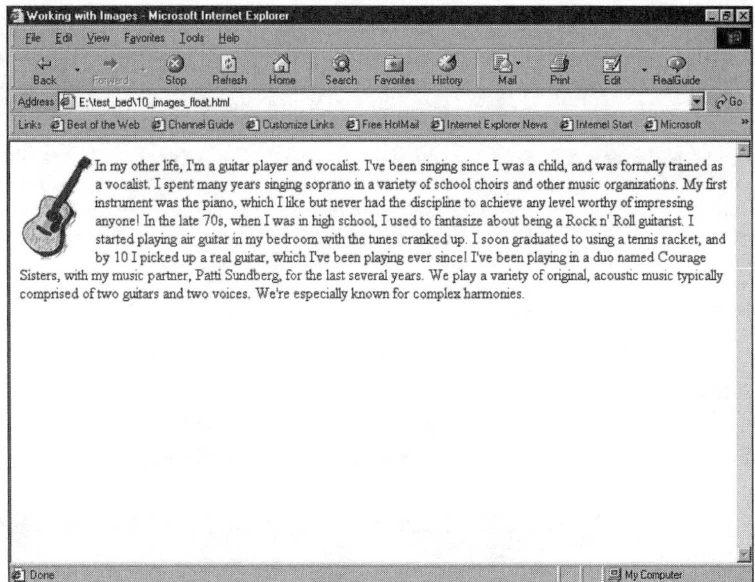

Figure 10.11
A left-aligned image with text wrapping. This dynamic approach to relating text and visual objects creates a natural flow that is both visually appealing and easy on the eyes.

Note

The word *dynamic* is used frequently but often improperly in the Web design field. In the case of text wrapping, dynamic refers to the fact that the text naturally finds its way around the image, taking up whatever available space exists. Let's say I viewed the page in Figure 10.11 at 1,024×768 resolution. The text will move into the extra space, continuing to wrap around the image. With style sheets or tables, the positioning is *absolute*. This means that the text and image would be fixed, regardless of the viewing circumstance.

I can also have my image aligned to the right. Listing 10.3 is the same image and text, but the alignment is now right, with the text wrapping around the image from the left.

LISTING 10.3 RIGHT-ALIGNED FLOATING IMAGE AND DYNAMIC TEXT

```
<HTML>

<HEAD>

<TITLE>Floating Image and Dynamic Text: Right</TITLE>

</HEAD>


<BODY>
```

continues

LISTING 10.3 CONTINUED

```
<IMG src="images/little_guitar.gif" width="75" height="107" border="0"
align="right" alt="drawing of a guitar">

In my other life, I'm a guitar player and vocalist. I've been singing since I was
a child, and was formally trained as a vocalist. I spent many years singing
soprano in a variety of school choirs and other music organizations.  My first
instrument was the piano, which I like but never had the discipline to achieve any
level worthy of impressing anyone!  In the late 70s, when I was in high school, I
used to fantasize about being a Rock n' Roll guitarist. I started playing air
guitar in my bedroom with the tunes cranked up.  I soon graduated to using a
tennis racket, and by 10 I picked up a real guitar, which I've been playing ever
since! I've been playing in a duo named Courage Sisters, with my music partner,
Patti Sundberg, for the last several years. We play a variety of original,
acoustic music typically comprised of two guitars and two voices. We're especially
known for complex harmonies.

</BODY>

</HTML>
```

Figure 10.12 shows the right-aligned image and floating text.

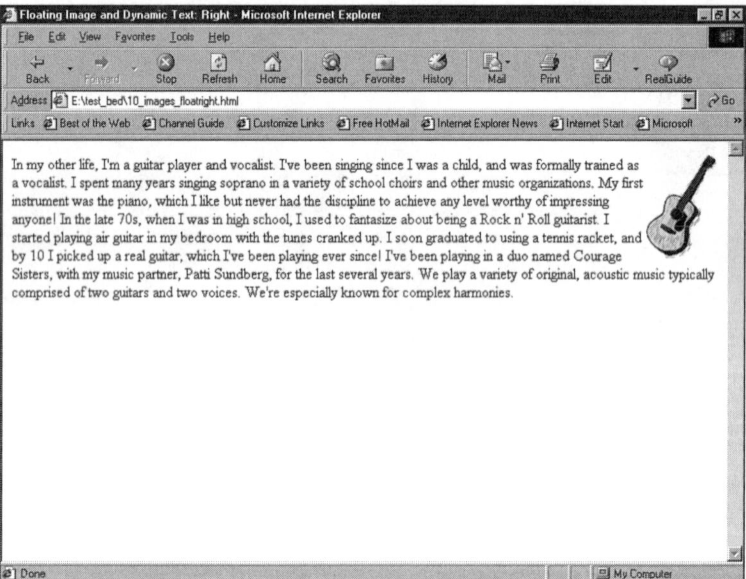

Figure 10.12
Right alignment and text wrap. If you're using a square image with no padding or with a distinct border, be sure to add `hspace` and `vspace`.

You might notice that the text bumps into the edges of the image a bit. It's slightly less noticeable in this particular instance, because my image is angled and has some whitespace around it. However, if you're using a regular photograph, square image, or image with a border, alignment and text wrapping without the use of `hspace` and `vspace` can make a page looked cramped and cluttered (see Figure 10.13).

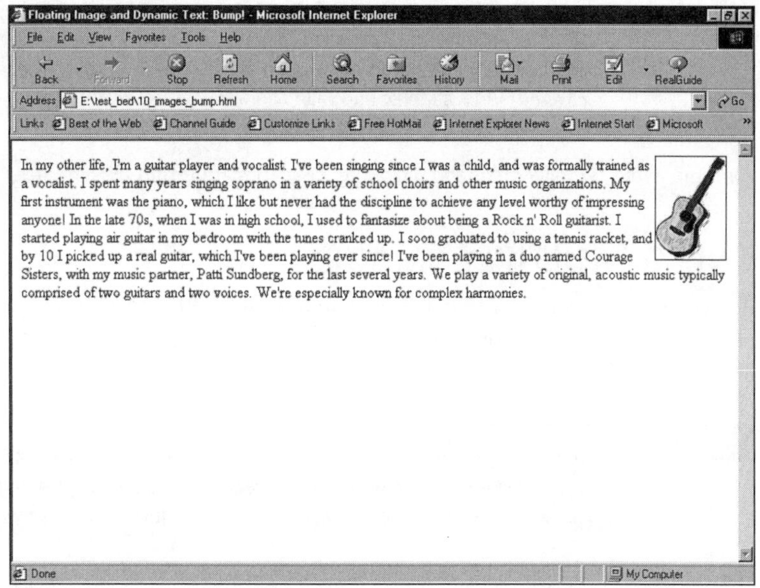

Figure 10.13 Bordered image and text are too close, cramping the page's style.

To avoid this problem, add a numeric value of about 5–15 to each of the spacing attributes:

```
<IMG src="images/little_guitar.gif" width="75" height="107" border="0"
➥align="right"
alt="drawing of a guitar" hspace="15" vspace="10">
```

This adds a nice amount of whitespace (see Figure 10.14), and makes the image and text relationship more harmonious and readable!

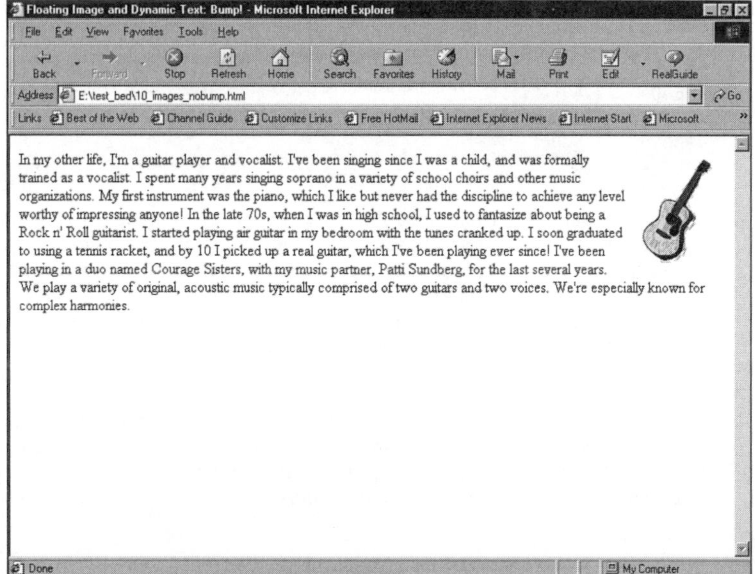

Figure 10.14 More whitespace makes the text readable.

Tip from

Want to put some distance between an aligned graphic and another element, such as another image or text? To break out of the dynamic wrapping, use a <BR> tag with the `clear="all"` attribute and value.

→ For more about text alignment and wrapping, **see** "Formatting and Aligning Text," **p. 133**

ALIGNING MULTIPLE IMAGES

As Web pages become more complex, you'll want to effectively place images so they look balanced and in proportion to other elements on the page. Let's walk through a page that has a graphic header, an image, and dynamic text.

Note

You'll see that I'm using BLOCKQUOTE to achieve margins. HTML 4.0 purists reject this use of the element, but it has been in conventional practice for years in this context. If you already know style sheets or tables, you can use them to achieve your margins instead.

→ To learn more about style sheet margins, **see** "Designing Type with CSS," **p. 284**

→ For information on using tables for layout, **see** "Advanced Table Layout," **p. 334**

1. Begin in your HTML editor with a standard shell:

```
<HTML>
<HEAD>
<TITLE>An Excerpt from Homer's Odyssey</TITLE>
<BODY>


</BODY>
</HTML>
```

2. Add the text and page formatting (in this case, <P> and <BLOCKQUOTE>):

```
<HTML>
<HEAD>
<TITLE>An Excerpt from Homer's Odyssey</TITLE>
<BODY>
<BLOCKQUOTE>

<P>A maid servant then brought them water in a beautiful golden ewer and
poured it into a silver basin for them to wash their hands, and she drew a
clean table beside them. An upper servant brought them bread, and offered them
many good things of what there was in the house, the carver fetched them
plates of all manner of meats and set cups of gold by their side, and a man-
servant brought them wine and poured it out for them.


<P>Then the suitors came in and took their places on the benches and seats.
Forthwith men servants poured water over their hands, maids went round with
the bread-baskets, pages filled the mixing-bowls with wine and water, and they
laid their hands upon the good things that were before them.
```

```
<P>As soon as they had had enough to eat and drink they wanted music and
dancing, which are the crowning embellishments of a banquet, so a servant
brought a lyre to Phemius, whom they compelled perforce to sing to them. As
soon as he touched his lyre and began to sing Telemachus spoke low to Minerva,
with his head close to hers that no man might hear.

</BLOCKQUOTE>
</BODY>
</HTML>
```

3. Add the header image, aligned right, with all the appropriate attributes. I used the `<BR clear="all">` trick to break out of the right alignment:

```
<HTML>
<HEAD>

<TITLE>Excerpt from Homer's Odyssey</TITLE>
</HEAD>

<BODY>

<BLOCKQUOTE>

<IMG src="images/odyssey_hed.gif" width="350" height="50" border="0"
align="right" alt="an excerpt from homer's odyssey">
<BR clear="all">

<P>A maid servant then brought them water in a beautiful golden ewer and
poured it into a silver basin for them to wash their hands, and she drew a
clean table beside them. An upper servant brought them bread, and offered them
many good things of what there was in the house, the carver fetched them
plates of all manner of meats and set cups of gold by their side, and a man-
servant brought them wine and poured it out for them.

<P>Then the suitors came in and took their places on the benches and seats.
Forthwith men servants poured water over their hands, maids went round with
the bread-baskets, pages filled the mixing-bowls with wine and water, and they
laid their hands upon the good things that were before them.

<P>As soon as they had had enough to eat and drink they wanted music and
dancing, which are the crowning embellishments of a banquet, so a servant
brought a lyre to Phemius, whom they compelled perforce to sing to them. As
soon as he touched his lyre and began to sing Telemachus spoke low to Minerva,
with his head close to hers that no man might hear.

</BLOCKQUOTE>
</BODY>
</HTML>
```

4. Add the image you intend to float with all the necessary attributes, including `<BR clear="all">`, which forces anything that's to come after the image to the next available line:

```
<HTML>
<HEAD>

<TITLE>Excerpt from Homer's Odyssey</TITLE>
</HEAD>

<BODY>

<BLOCKQUOTE>

<IMG src="images/odyssey_hed.gif" width="350" height="50" border="0"
align="right" alt="an excerpt from homer's odyssey">
<BR clear="all">

<P>A maid servant then brought them water in a beautiful golden ewer and
poured it into a silver basin for them to wash their hands, and she drew a
clean table beside them. An upper servant brought them bread, and offered them
many good things of what there was in the house, the carver fetched them
plates of all manner of meats and set cups of gold by their side, and a man-
servant brought them wine and poured it out for them.

<P><img src="images/schooner2.jpg" width="270" height="140" border="0"
align="right" hspace="5" vspace="5" alt="image of schooner">

<P>Then the suitors came in and took their places on the benches and seats.
Forthwith men servants poured water over their hands, maids went round with
the bread-baskets, pages filled the mixing-bowls with wine and water, and they
laid their hands upon the good things that were before them.

<P>As soon as they had had enough to eat and drink they wanted music and
dancing, which are the crowning embellishments of a banquet, so a servant
brought a lyre to Phemius, whom they compelled perforce to sing to them. As
soon as he touched his lyre and began to sing Telemachus spoke low to Minerva,
with his head close to hers that no man might hear.

</BLOCKQUOTE>
</BODY>
</HTML>
```

Figure 10.15 shows the page. Notice how there's plenty of whitespace, balance between the graphics and the text, and the text and images flow naturally along the page.

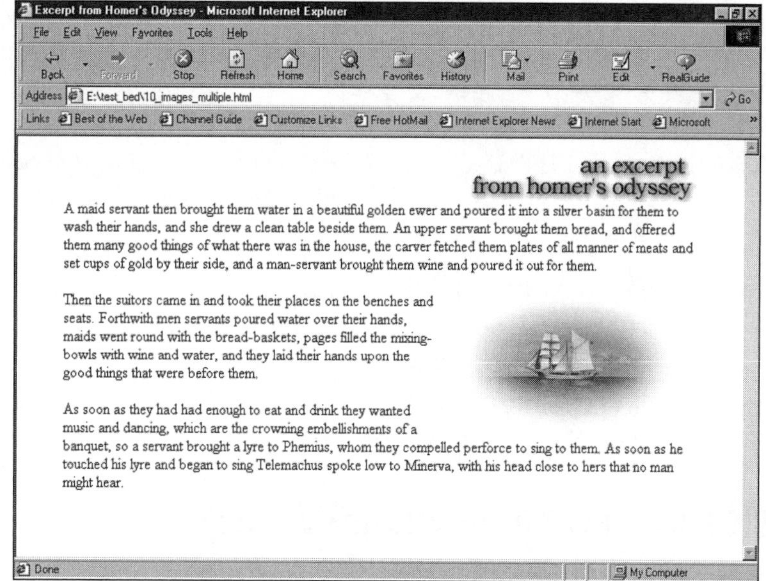

Figure 10.15
Images and text define the two most critical elements of visual design.

This technique demonstrates not only the appeal images add to a Web page, but the strong relationship that exists between text and images.

What do you do if you want more control over laying out multiple images than this method provides? See, "Working with Many Images," in the Troubleshooting section at the end of this chapter.

LINKING IMAGES

Images, like text, can be linked. Making an image "hot" is a common practice and a foundational part of navigation.

Linking images is easy. All you need to do is surround the code for the image with the standard linking element, the `<A>`, or *anchor* element.

→ For more about links, **see** "Linking Pages," **p. 174**

The following is a sample linked image:

```
<A href="index.html"><IMG src="images/home_button.gif" width="50" height="100"
border="0" alt="click to go home"></A>
```

Tip from molly

If you want an image to clearly be noted as a link, you can set the border to a numeric value to show the link border. With the border set to `off ("0")`, this image will appear seamless with the rest of the page. A smoother, more consistent design is achieved by leaving borders off—my preferred method.

→ Another method of linking images is with imagemapping. To read more about this method, **see** "Imagemaps, Animation, and Special Graphic Techniques," **p. 648**

PART II

CH 10

TROUBLESHOOTING

HORIZONTAL RULES

How do you add a horizontal rule to a page?

There is a standard HTML element for generic horizontal rules, the <HR> tag. For graphical horizontal rules, however, you use the standard image tags to insert the graphic, as explained in this chapter.

WORKING WITH MANY IMAGES

What happens when I have numerous images that I'd like to lay out with greater control? How can I do that more effectively than with these simplistic techniques?

You have two options. The first, and most realistic in the current browser environment, is the use of tables. You can also use style sheet positioning to achieve more complex layouts.

DESIGNING FOR THE REAL WORLD

EXHIBITING YOUR WORK

Now that you know how to use images on your Web pages, you can use those skills to create a gallery on your site. Although your photos or images may or may not be of the same quality as Christopher Burkett's, you can share your visions with the world.

Christopher Burkett is a renowned photographer. His Web site displays some of his best work (don't miss a look at Summer Heather Garden). The site is simple and easy to navigate, letting the power of Burkett's photographs send the message of the site. Each thumbnail image links to a larger image of the same work. This enables visitors to see several images at once and choose the specific works they want to see in more detail. The thumbnails also load quickly, because they are very small in size. By clicking a thumbnail, the visitor is accepting the longer download time of a larger image.

You can do the same for your galleries. Simply create two versions of your images, one at a very small scale and lower quality, the other on a larger scale and high quality. Add the small images to your page. Then link each of those images to the higher quality version. Some Web designers choose to set the larger image against the same background and navigational elements as the rest of the site to maintain a consistent look. Others simply link to the image, which then displays against a plain background without any navigational elements. Personally, I would recommend adding at least a "back" link to help visitors navigate easily.

Note

Visit Christopher Burkett's Web site, `http://www.christopherburkett.com/`.

Artistic images on the Web add culture and visual appeal to the slick, information-rich and often commercial focus of today's Web site. Using the Web to display art is a wonderful opportunity to balance the way we use the Web—and to share and promote your artistic works.

CHAPTER 11

WORKING WITH THE BODY ELEMENT

In this chapter

The BODY Element: Global Control

The BODY element is one of the most powerful in HTML. It controls much of the visual foundation of your Web page design. Its attributes help you control background color, background design, text color, link colors—all of this just within the opening <BODY> tag!

In fact, this tag is where the look-and-feel of your site begins. Certainly, images add appeal and important visual features, but your primary color control is found right in the <BODY> tag.

How do these attributes compare to advanced style methods such as Cascading Style Sheets? Even there, the BODY selector is where many foundations for the page's features are set.

→ For details on how the BODY selector is used with CSS, **see** "Cascading Style Sheet Techniques," **p. 263**

The <BODY> tag is responsible for what I call *browser-based* design. This means that before any image is added to a page, you can create colorful, interesting pages just by working from a color palette and applying the various attributes contained within the BODY. The browser, except where background images are concerned, never has to query the server for this information once the HTML page is loaded—if you code your background, text, and link attributes properly, all the information is translated right in the browser. This adds speed *and* design to the page without any additional download time.

In this chapter, you'll learn to use the BODY element and its attributes for effective, fast loading pages that move you from standard pages into the realm of colorful design.

The BODY element is a document formatting element, meaning that it is, before attributes are added to it, responsible for demarcating the area of the Web browser that contains the body of your work: text, images, and media.

→ For more information about document formatting, **see** "Building HTML Documents," **p. 92**

The element has an opening and closing tag, and appears below the HEAD container. Along with the HTML element and the TITLE element, it makes up the standard HTML shell shown in Listing 11.1.

Listing 11.1 The BODY Element Is Part of HTML Document Formatting

```
<HTML>
<HEAD>
<TITLE>The HTML Shell</TITLE>
</HEAD>
<BODY>

</BODY>
</HTML>
```

While the opening <BODY> tag requires no attributes, it's the addition of those attributes that adds power to the BODY's punch in conventional HTML.

Note

I always thought that the term "body tag" was a bit gruesome. This is how I remember that you never want more than one. I've seen HTML students try to put two or more opening and closing `<BODY>` tags within a page–this is illegal. One opening and companion closing `<BODY>` tag is all that's required.

It's time to tap into the power of the tag by examining its primary attributes.

MANAGING COLOR FOR BACKGROUNDS, TEXT, AND LINKS

There are a number of specific attributes that should be added to the `<BODY>` tag to assist the browser in managing backgrounds, text, and link colors. Values for these attributes are either color names or hexadecimal codes, as described after the following attribute list:

- `text="x"`—This attribute tells the browser what color your default body text will be.
- `link="x"`—Without this attribute, browsers will usually use blue as a default link color, unless the user has configured another default link color into his or her browser. To maintain the integrity of your design, you should always use this attribute and set it to a value in step with your site palette—even if the color is blue.
- `vlink="x"`—This is the *visited* link. As with the link attribute, if you don't set this with a value, the browser will look for a default (usually purple), or a user-defined setting. For the same reasons as mentioned for using the `link="x"`, you should include an appropriate visited link color in your `BODY` string.
- `alink="x"`—Active link. This is a color that appears when the link is made active—when a mouse clicks it or passes over the link, depending on the browser you're using.
- `bgcolor="x"`—This sets the color that will fill your background. Browsers used to default to a very ugly gray, but now they usually default to white. Users can set this, too, so you always want to define it—even if you choose to use a background graphic (more on this in a bit).
- `background="url"`—Only use this attribute when you want to include a background graphic on your page.

The following sections will look at these attributes and how they work.

TEXT AND LINK COLORS

Understanding color theory and how color works on a computer screen and within a browser is very significant when it comes to selecting your text and link colors.

→ For a detailed explanation of color theory, **see** "Color Concepts," **p. 528**

The reason is two-fold:

- Esthetic—The quality of your page's design is always increased when you use color in a sophisticated fashion. It is important to learn how to make an individual palette that unifies your theme and sends a specific, visual message with each page you create.
- Functional—If you use colors that don't have enough contrast, your site visitors will have trouble reading your pages. You must choose colors that make visual as well as artistic sense.

Are you unsure of how to get your link colors and JPEG background colors to work together? See "Matching Colors" in the Troubleshooting section at the end of this chapter.

Predefined Color Names

There are 136 predefined browser color names. Selecting from these colors, this exercise will step through setting up text and link colors on a page.

Note

For a color chart that defines these colors by name, be sure to look for `136_colors.html` on the CD-ROM. You can also visit this page online at **`http://www.molly.com/molly/webdesign/136_colors.html`**.

1. Begin with the HTML shell:

```
<HTML>
<HEAD>
<TITLE>Adding BODY attributes</TITLE>
</HEAD>
<BODY>

</BODY>
</HTML>
```

2. Add the `text` attribute and the color `"black"`:

```
<HTML>
<HEAD>
<TITLE>Adding BODY Attributes</TITLE>
</HEAD>
<BODY text="black">
</BODY>
</HTML>
```

3. For the link color, select `"cyan"`:

```
<HTML>
<HEAD>
<TITLE>Adding BODY Attributes</TITLE>
</HEAD>
<BODY text="black" link="cyan">
</BODY>
</HTML>
```

4. The visited link color is "dark cyan":

```
<HTML>
<HEAD>
<TITLE>Adding BODY Attributes</TITLE>
</HEAD>
<BODY text="black" link="cyan" vlink="dark cyan">
</BODY>
</HTML>
```

5. Finally, the active link color is "dark goldenrod":

```
<HTML>
<HEAD>
<TITLE>Adding BODY Attributes</TITLE>
</HEAD>
<BODY text="black" link="cyan" vlink="dark cyan" alink="dark goldenrod">
</BODY>
</HTML>
```

6. Add text and several links:

```
<HTML>
<HEAD>
<TITLE>Adding BODY Attributes</TITLE>
</HEAD>
<BODY text="black" link="cyan" vlink="dark cyan" alink="dark goldenrod">

<P>These are a few of my favorite links:

<P>The <A href="http://www.weeklywire.com/">Weekly Wire</A>, a collection of
alternative, online newsweeklies.<P>I enjoy visiting <A
href="http://www.mrshowbiz.com/">Mr. Showbiz</A> because I
like the content and the design!
<P>My friend the <A href="http://www.dumpsterdive.com/">Internet Baglady</A>
always has something fun (and free!) to download.
</BODY>
</HTML>
```

7. Save the file and view it in your browser. You should see a white or gray body (browser default), black text, and cyan links. When you click a link, you should see the goldenrod appear and, once the link has been visited, the link will turn dark cyan.

Now that you know how to do this, I'm going to tell you not to do it! It's a helpful method for quickly coding mockups, but there's a problem with this technique. First off, many older browsers don't support the naming convention, and those that do, don't necessarily recognize the colors in this palette as being safe. This means your colors run the risk of dithering and causing all kinds of unstable results.

➔ For information on dithering and other color issues, **see** "Color Concepts," **p. 528**

Worried about how your link colors might affect the overall design or content of your page? See "Link Colors" in the Troubleshooting section at the end of this chapter.

WORKING WITH WEB-SAFE COLORS

So what do you do? Well, most professionals work from the 216-color Web-safe palette to achieve visual stability when adding colors to links.

Note

This palette is viewable on the CD-ROM as `colorchart.html`, or you can view it live at **`http://www.molly.com/molly/webdesign/colorchart.html`**.

Step through the process again, this time selecting from Web-safe colors. I'm going to use shades of gray so I can effectively show you the results using a figure.

1. Begin with the HTML shell:

```
<HTML>
<HEAD>
<TITLE>Adding BODY Attributes</TITLE>
</HEAD>
<BODY>

</BODY>
</HTML>
```

2. Add the `text` attribute and the color `"#000000"`:

```
<HTML>
<HEAD>
<TITLE>Adding BODY Attributes</TITLE>
</HEAD>
<BODY text="#000000">


</BODY>
</HTML>
```

3. For the link color, select `"#CCCCCC"`:

```
<HTML>
<HEAD>
<TITLE>Adding BODY Attributes</TITLE>
</HEAD>
<BODY text="#000000" link="#CCCCCC">


</BODY>
</HTML>
```

4. The visited link color is `"#999999"`:

```
<HTML>
<HEAD>
<TITLE>Adding BODY Attributes</TITLE>
</HEAD>
<BODY text="#000000" link="#CCCCCC" vlink="#999999">


</BODY>
</HTML>
```

5. The active link color is `"#FFFFFF"`:

```
<HTML>
<HEAD>
<TITLE>Adding BODY Attributes</TITLE>
</HEAD>
```

```
<BODY text="#000000" link="#CCCCCC" vlink="#999999" alink="#FFFFFF">


</BODY>
</HTML>
```

6. Add text and several links:

```
<HTML>
<HEAD>
<TITLE>Adding BODY Attributes</TITLE>
</HEAD>
<BODY text="#000000" link="#CCCCCC" vlink="#999999" alink="#FFFFFF">

<P>These are a few of my favorite links:

<P>The <A href="http://www.weeklywire.com/">Weekly Wire</A>, a collection of
alternative, online newsweeklies.<P>I enjoy visiting
<A href="http://www.mrshowbiz.com/">Mr. Showbiz</A> because I
like the content and the design!

<P>My friend the <A href="http://www.dumpsterdive.com/">Internet Baglady</A>
always
has something fun (and free!) to download.

</BODY>
</HTML>
```

7. Save the file and view it in your browser. You should see a white or gray body (browser default), black text, and a light gray for your links. When you click a link, you'll see the text disappear (if your background is white).

Tip from molly

Matching your active link color to the body's background color is a fun affect that makes the text seem to disappear. Once you click the link and return to the page, the link turns dark gray.

Figure 11.1 shows the page with links.

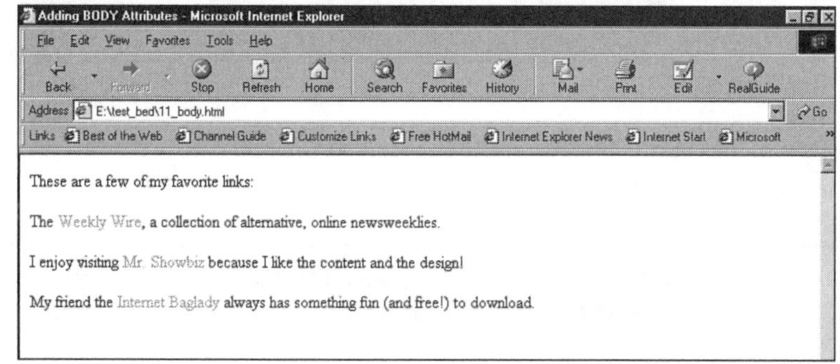

Figure 11.1
An HTML page with text, link, active link, and visited link attributes. When you try this on your own, you'll begin to see how setting these attributes will add more color and visual interest to your page.

BACKGROUND COLOR

It's important to remember the issue of *contrast* when working with background color. In the example used in Figure 11.1, there's a white background with black text. This is a very effective contrast.

However, if I used the dark gray as a background color and the light gray for text, the contrast is reduced and readability is affected—particularly if you have to read at this contrast level for any length of time. Listing 11.2 shows an example of this:

LISTING 11.2 BACKGROUND COLOR AND POOR TEXT COLOR CONTRAST

```
<HTML>
<HEAD>
<TITLE>BODY Attributes</TITLE>
</HEAD>
<BODY bgcolor="#999999" text="#CCCCCC">
A maid servant then brought them water in a beautiful golden ewer and poured it
into a silver basin for them to wash their hands, and she drew a clean table
beside them. An upper servant brought them bread, and offered them many good
things of what there was in the house, the carver fetched them plates of all
manner of meats and set cups of gold by their side, and a man-servant brought them
wine and poured it out for them.
</BODY>
</HTML>
```

Figure 11.2 shows a low contrast example.

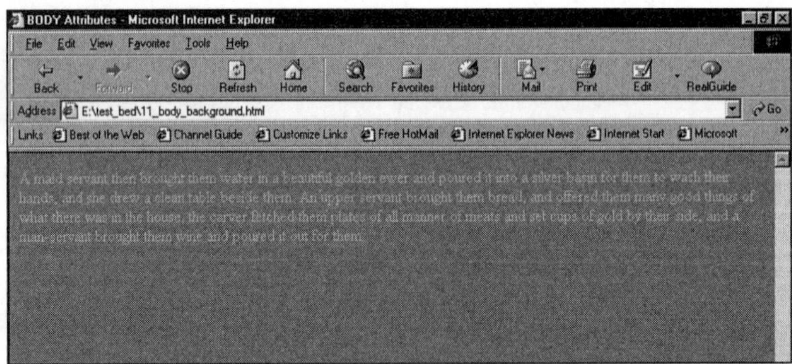

Figure 11.2 Low contrast is not conducive to readability, particularly for long periods of time.

To avoid this problem, you must choose background colors that are well contrasted with the text and link attributes.

Tip from molly

To achieve high contrast, use a light background with dark text and links, or a dark background with light text and links (referred to as *reverse text*).

Listing 11.3 is a sample of high contrast: white text on a black background with gray and white links.

LISTING 11.3 HIGH CONTRAST BACKGROUND AND TEXT

```
<HTML>
<HEAD>
<TITLE>BODY Attributes</TITLE>
</HEAD>
<BODY bgcolor="#000000" text="#FFFFFF" link="#CCCCCC" vlink="#FFFFFF" alink=
"#000000">

<P>These are a few of my favorite links:


<P>The <A href="http://www.weeklywire.com/">Weekly Wire</A>, a collection of
alternative, online newsweeklies.


<P>I enjoy visiting <A href="http://www.mrshowbiz.com/">Mr. Showbiz</A> because I
like the content and the design!


<P>My friend the <A href="http://www.dumpsterdive.com/">Internet Baglady</A>
always
has something fun (and free!) to download.

</BODY>
```


Figure 11.3 shows the higher contrast results.

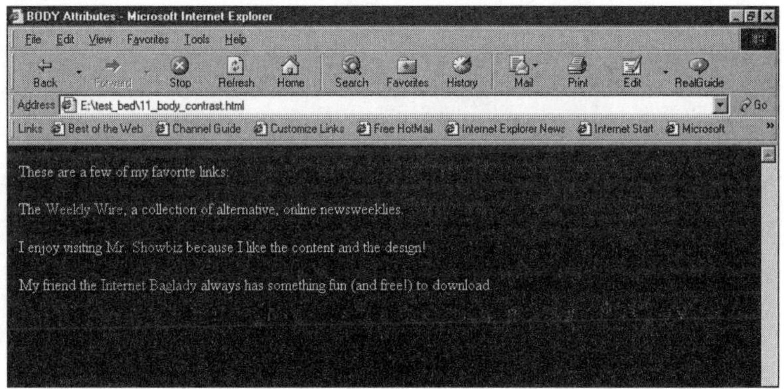

Figure 11.3
Higher contrast is easier to read. Ideally, you would use colors other than the grays I've used here. I'm limited by grayscale because of this book's design.

ADDING A BACKGROUND GRAPHIC

Now that you have the basic color palette going, you can choose to add a background graphic. This, of course, is optional and will depend upon your design goals.

The general syntax for adding a background graphic is to use the `background` attribute combined with the path to your graphic:

```
<BODY background="images/gray_paper.gif">
```

As I mentioned earlier, it's always a good idea to have a background color described whenever you also use a background graphic. There are two very strong reasons for this:

- Your background graphic will take longer to reach your visitor's browser because it has to be delivered by the server. The background color will load first, giving the visitor a taste of the design to come.
- If for some reason your background graphic does *not* load, you still maintain a certain amount of design integrity.

Tip from molly

When using a background color behind a background graphic, always try to match the background color to the most prevalent area of color or design that will fall behind the body text.

→ To read more about background graphics, **see** "Creating Professional Web Graphics, "**p. 603**

Listing 11.4 uses a tiled background graphic. It's a very light gray speckled tile that creates a look of recycled paper.

LISTING 11.4 A BACKGROUND IMAGE IS ADDED TO THE DESIGN

```
<HTML>
<HEAD>
<TITLE>BODY Attributes</TITLE>
</HEAD>
<BODY bgcolor="#FFFFFF" text="#000000" link="#999999" vlink="#999999"
alink="#FFFFFF" background="images/gray_paper.gif">

<P>These are a few of my favorite links:


<P>The <A href="http://www.weeklywire.com/">Weekly Wire</A>, a collection of
alternative, online newsweeklies.


<P>I enjoy visiting <A href="http://www.mrshowbiz.com/">Mr. Showbiz</A> because I
like the content and the design!


<P>My friend the <A href="http://www.dumpsterdive.com/">Internet Baglady</A>
always
has something fun (and free!) to download.

</BODY>
</HTML>
```

Figure 11.4 shows the result. You'll note that I modified the link colors in this case for the purposes of the screen shot, which appears in grayscale. You can use any colors you like, bearing in mind that you need to accommodate readability concerns.

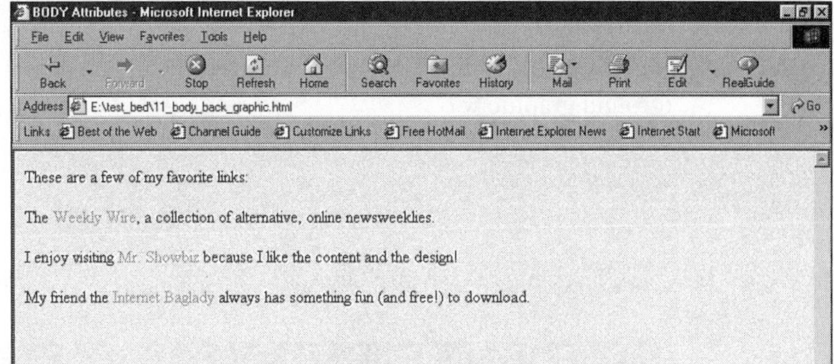

Figure 11.4
A background image added to the HTML page.

BROWSER-SPECIFIC BODY FEATURES

There are several useful attributes affecting body layout that are available only in Internet Explorer. They include the following:

- `bottommargin`—Set the bottom margin for the entire page. The value is in pixels: `bottommargin="10"`.
- `topmargin`—This allows you to set the top margin for the page in pixels; `topmargin="0"` will flush your information to the top of the available viewing space.
- `leftmargin`—Fix the left margin in pixels: `leftmargin="100"`.
- `rightmargin`—As with `leftmargin`, you can set the right margin in pixels: `rightmargin="100"`.

Listing 11.5 demonstrates the use of fixed margins. I made the margin values a bit dramatic to clearly show you how this works. You'll want to use values that are more appropriate for your design, of course.

LISTING 11.5 FIXED MARGINS IN INTERNET EXPLORER

```
<HTML>
<HEAD>
<TITLE>BODY Attributes</TITLE>
</HEAD>
<BODY bgcolor="#FFFFFF" text="#000000" link="#CCCCCC" vlink="#999999"
alink="#FFFFFF" background="images/gray_paper.gif" bottmmargin="100"
topmargin="100" leftmargin="100" rightmargin="100">

<P>These are a few of my favorite links:

<P>The <A href="http://www.weeklywire.com/">Weekly Wire</A>, a collection of
alternative, online newsweeklies.


<P>I enjoy visiting <A href="http://www.mrshowbiz.com/">Mr. Showbiz</A> because I
like the content and the design!
```

continues

LISTING 11.5 CONTINUED

```
<P>My friend the <A href="http://www.dumpsterdive.com/">Internet Baglady</A>
always
has something fun (and free!) to download.

</BODY>
</HTML>
```

In Figure 11.5, you'll see how these attributes affect my page.

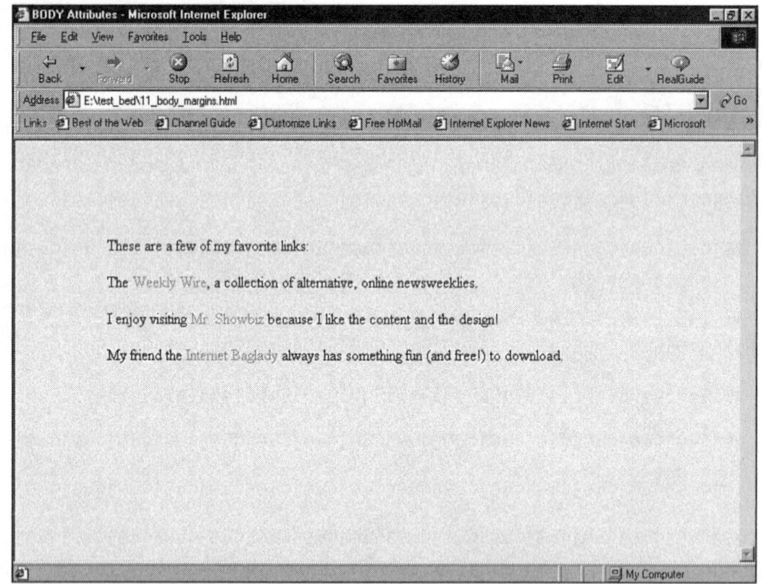

Figure 11.5
Body-based margins in Internet Explorer. This effective method of adding margins is unfortunately browser-specific and unsupported by Netscape and other, non-Microsoft browsers.

Note

For more information on additional BODY element attributes specific to IE, visit the Microsoft Developer Network at **`http://msdn.microsoft.com/`**.

TROUBLESHOOTING

LINK COLORS

Does the visited link color always have to be different from the link color?

Changing visited links to a different color helps visitors keep track of where they've already clicked and what's left to explore. For design or content purposes, it may be preferable to have visited links retain the same color as unvisited links. In these cases, just give the vlink the same color value as the link.

MATCHING COLORS

How can you match a color in a JPEG background to choose a text or link color?

Because of the compression methods used in JPEGs, it is almost impossible to find an exact color match between a JPEG and a Web-safe color. Try to find complimentary text and link colors, and simply do the best you can. Unless it is absolutely necessary for your background to be a JPEG, also try to use GIF backgrounds as much as possible.

DESIGNING FOR THE REAL WORLD

BEYOND BLACK AND WHITE

Choosing a palette for your Web site goes beyond choosing colors that work well together. Your color choices also work in conjunction with your images to create a tone for the site. If you're developing a site for "Sunny Days Farms," using blacks and grays would be incongruous with the name of the farm and the image it is likely to want to project.

A better example of how background and text colors can set a tone is `funschool.com`, a site with activities and games for children. In keeping with the name of the site and its target audience, the colors are bright and fun. There are more colors on the screen than I generally recommend, but they are used to good effect. When you enter, you immediately know that you are on a family site.

Although the site is brightly colored, `funschool.com` does not sacrifice readability. The contrast between the yellow background and blue text works well. The site also has the color convention of using black text on notes for parents and blue text to describe the child-oriented games and activities. The black connotes a more serious, adult tone, while the blue is playful.

Note funschool.com—**`http://www.funschool.com`**

CHAPTER 12

Working with Fonts

In this chapter

TYPOGRAPHIC CONCEPTS

Designing with impact. It's what every Web designer is seeking. What gives design for the Web impact? It's quite a delicate mix of technology and visual design.

Working with type is an area where we fully see the demand for designers who can achieve this delicate balance. Type on the Web is as challenging as HTML-based design gets.

Many graphic artists fully understand how important type is, but may not know how to separate out the complexities of HTML 4.0 to put type to work.

Conversely, many technologists may be more adept at the code rationale behind HTML-based type, but have little familiarity with typographic concepts.

This chapter will help balance the type challenges inherent in HTML 4.0 code, as well as teach some basic typography. It's important to remember that Typography is a major element of quality design, and all Web designers seeking designs with impact should work to understand both the artistic as well as technical ends of the typographic spectrum.

UNDERSTANDING TYPE CONCEPTS

This chapter begins by demonstrating why type is such a profound feature in design, providing a strong conceptual basis for those of you who feel the need to strengthen your basic typographic skills. After you have those concepts down, you'll tackle the code issues, looking specifically at the `FONT` element, and how to use it well within transitional HTML 4.0. This chapter also provides a conceptual foundation for using Cascading Style Sheets for type design.

→ For details on Transitional HTML 4.0, **see** "Understanding HTML 4.0," **p. 17**

→ For information on methods to design type using style sheets, **see** "Designing Type with CSS," **p. 284**

TYPE CATEGORIES, FAMILIES, AND FACES

There are so many different kinds of type that they've been grouped into sensible containers so that we can keep track of them.

The following are the three main typographic groupings:

- **Category**—A type category is the *master* group or family. You can think of this as a font's ethnic heritage. For example, I'm of Slavic descent. All typefaces have a heritage, too.
- **Family**—Within my ethnic group, I am identified by a *specific* family. This identifier is found in my last name, Holzschlag. The family to which a font belongs is the family name of that font.

- **Face**—Carrying the metaphor into the personal realm: My face, although similar in feature to both my ethnic background and certain members of my specific family, is also unique. A font *face* is the unique look of a specific font within a category and family group.

Note

The word *font* is actually a carry-over from the days of the printing press. On the Web, it is often used interchangeably with *typeface*, but they are in fact different. A font is the technical term used to describe the physical component of type design, whereas typeface refers to the face, or visual features, of the type.

TYPE CATEGORIES

The master families, or *categories*, of type include the following:

- **Serif**—This is a standard, familiar group that is identified by strokes on the individual letters.
- **Sans-Serif**—A common group to Web design is the "sans" (meaning *without*) serif category. These families tend to be rounded and have no strokes.
- **Monospaced**—In this group, each letter within a face takes up the same space as another. This is often referred to as a *typewriter* font, because it resembles the monospaced type used by those old-fashioned type contraptions.
- **Script**—This category includes all families that resemble handwriting.
- **Decorative**—(sometimes referred to as *Fantasy*) This group is identified as having special decorative features such as dots, strokes, and other designs applied to the families and faces.

Table 12.1 shows some of the individual families within a given category.

TABLE 12.1 TYPE FAMILIES

Category	Familiar Families
Serif	Times, Century Schoolbook, Garamond
Sans-Serif	Helvetica, Arial, Verdana
Monospaced	Courier, Courier New,
Script	Nuptial Script, Boulevard, Signature
Decorative	Whimsy, Arriba!, Bergell

Figure 12.1 shows an example of each.

Category	Familiar Families
Serif	Times, Century Schoolbook, Garamond
Sans-Serif	Helvetica, Arial, Verdana
Monospaced	Courier, Courier New
Script	Nuptial Script, Boulevard, Signature
Decorative	Whimsy, Arriba!, Bergell

Figure 12.1
This list of familiar font and families gives you a look at some of the most commonly used type.

In Table 12.2 I'm taking an example of a familiar family, and defining the face for you.

TABLE 12.2 TYPEFACES

Family	Face
Times	Roman, Italic
Arial	Regular, Bold Italic
Courier	Regular, Oblique
Whimsy	Regular, Bold

Figure 12.2 shows the same table using the fonts from Table 12.2.

Family	Face
Times	Roman, *Italic*
Arial	Regular, ***Bold Italic***
Courier	Regular, *Oblique*
Whimsy	Regular, **Bold**

Figure 12.2
Within each font family there may be multiple faces, such as the Roman and Italic seen in the Times family.

Tip from

Many designers spend their entire lives learning how to design with and create type. This demonstrates how powerful a design element it is. Choose the right type, and your work will have the impact you're after. Choose a clashing or inappropriate typeface, and your work will be unattractive or worse, boring.

TYPE FORM

Very often, how our bodies look and act comes from our familial background. How light or heavy, wide or narrow, stooped or straight we are depends largely upon our nature and nurture.

Type is no different. As you've seen in Table 12.2, typefaces have specific attributes, referred to as *form*.

Form includes weight, width, and posture. Form specifically relates to the shape and direction in which a given typeface is presented.

TYPE WEIGHT

Some typefaces are dark and heavy, others, light and slender. Still others are of "average" build, appearing to have an overall average weight and appearance. Type weight influences the way a given face appears.

- **Regular**—This is the average weight class, simplistic and unadorned.
- **Bold**—Bold emphasizes text. It is heavier and slightly wider than the regular weight.
- **Light**—Slender, lighter typefaces carry less obvious impact than regular or bold forms, but they can be perfect when a subtle, simple look is required.

Figure 12.3 shows examples of these type forms.

Figure 12.3
Regular, bold, and light type forms have obvious differences but are still part of the same font family.

Tekton Regular
Tekton Bold
Tekton Light

TYPE WIDTH

Typefaces can have a variety of widths, which refers to the actual space the face takes up along the horizontal axis. The two that are most common are

- **Condensed**—A condensed, or *compressed* form is one where the width of the letterforms is tighter than in a standard, or regular, form.
- **Expanded**—Some designers refer to expanded type as being *extended*. Unlike the condensed form, the expanded face is wider.

In Figure 12.4, you can see the difference between a condensed and expanded form.

Figure 12.4
Condensed and expanded type give two different looks from the same typeface.

Minima Expanded
Minima Condensed

TYPE POSTURE

The voice of my mother saying, "Stand up straight, honey" still rings through my ears. She hated the way I slouched. Of course, I thought I was being cool.

Posture in type is the angle at which the type is set.

- **Italic**—Like bold, italic emphasizes text. This is done by slanting the text to the right.
- **Oblique**—This is strictly an electronic type form. Obliques are more rigid than italics.

Check out Figure 12.5 for examples of italic and oblique type.

Courier Oblique
Courier New Italic

Figure 12.5
Italic and oblique: Despite appearing very similar, there are subtle differences between the flowing lines of italic and the more rigid lines of the oblique type.

Caution

Remember studying handwriting in school? I always wanted to slant my letters to the left, rather than to the right. I liked the look, but my teacher most assuredly did not. This is called backslanting, and, although it may look cool, it's best to avoid backslanted type due to the fact that it's difficult to read.

Type Size and Proportion

Another consideration when working with typefaces is their size and proportion to one another—and to other elements on a page.

Type is measured in a variety of ways, including points or pixels. Point measurement is based on print measurement, whereas pixel measurement uses a computer's pixel-based technology to interpret point size.

Generally speaking, you'll use the point system when setting graphic type. However, HTML based-type has limitations concerning size, which you'll read about a bit later in the chapter.

12-point type, which is roughly what is displayed as a default by most Web browsers, is thought to be the easiest to read and is suitable for body text.

The *proportions* of a given typeface with regard to another is important. Size can help indicate what role the typeface is laying on the page—larger type is used for headers, medium-sizes for body text, small sizes for notes, `mailto:`, and less-emphasized information such as copyright notices (see Figure 12.6).

Orientation

The direction in which your typeface runs will have a significant impact on how the type is perceived. Direction in type is referred to as *orientation*. Standard type runs along the horizon line, but type can also be vertical, reversed, placed upside-down, or rendered in a shape (see Figure 12.7).

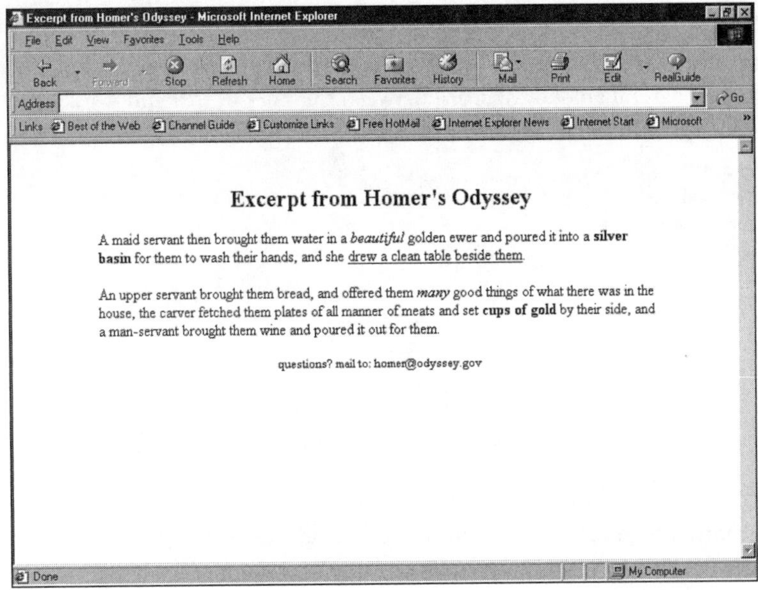

Figure 12.6
Headers and footers should be larger and smaller than body text.

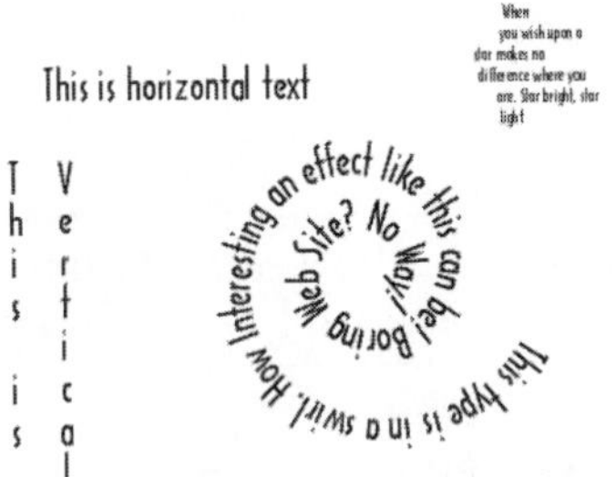

Figure 12.7
This figure shows some of the fun ways you can work with type orientation.

Horizontal type is more stable, less full of motion. That's why it's used as body text. When designing for impact, however, you should think about other orientation options when designing your site. Type orientation can provide a sense of movement and intrigue.

Note

Although you can't achieve any other orientation than horizontal using standard HTML, Cascading Style Sheets as well as DHTML *do* address typographic orientation.

→ For examples of how to use DHTML to control type orientation, **see** "Working with Dynamic HTML (DHTML)," **p. 454**

LEADING

Typography also concerns itself with the space between lines, which is called *leading* (pronounced led-ing). In style sheets, you'll see this referred to as *line height*.

→ For more information about controlling leading, **see** "Designing Type with CSS," **p. 296**

How close or how far a line is from another line influences readability tremendously.

In Figure 12.8, I've set 18-point type with a leading of 18 points. You'll see that this appears to be a natural amount of space between the lines of text and is easy to read.

Figure 12.8
18-point type with 18-point leading is natural and easy to read.

This is 18 point type with
18 point leading. Natural.
Easy to read.

The face, by the way,
is Book Antiqua. It is
a Serif typeface.

Tip from molly

As a general rule, leading set close to the type's own point size will be suitable for body text.

Now I'm going to reduce the leading to 10 points, but keep the size of the type steady at 18 points. The text becomes impossible to read (see Figure 12.9).

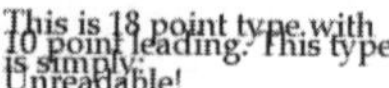

Figure 12.9
18-point type and 10-point leading make this type impossible to read.

If I set the leading, or line-height, at too great a distance, readability would also be affected.

Tip from molly

Using unusual leading for impact is effective in short sections of text such as headers or sidebars. However, avoid leading that is too far from the normal range for body text.

Caution

Use special-effect leading sparingly! Anything outside the norm can strain the eyes.

KERNING AND SPACING

Kerning is the space between individual letters within a font. In normal setting, you'll notice that letters touch one another and this can sometimes interfere with readability. This occurs frequently with serif fonts, although it can effect any font.

Kerning allows a typesetter to adjust this space. Doing so requires accessing information contained within the font. This information is contained in what is referred to as a kerning table. Kerning tables contain mathematical information related to the units of each letterform within the font.

Spacing is the horizontal space between letters outside the font. In other words, you don't have to access the kerning table to set a letter farther from or closer to another over the entire word.

Spacing, however, affects the entire word or phrase you are setting, rather than the individual letters.

The problem? Kerning and spacing cannot be achieved with HTML.CSS2 does offer some letter spacing control, and of course you can always set type using an imaging program such as Adobe Illustrator or Photoshop, which have options for letter spacing.

➔ To learn more about how to use kerning and spacing, **see** "Graphic Type for the Web," **p. 623**

ADDING COLOR TO FONTS

Adding color to fonts can help give a page distinction. As with size and face, a light touch is important—you don't want to overwhelm your site visitors with too many different color choices on a page.

In fact, sticking to two static colors—one for headers and auxiliary text, and one for body text—is a safe way to get a bit of color into your design.

However, color is important to type design because the use of different colors influences the way a word is perceived in relation to others.

Contrast is the name of the game when it comes to color design and type. According to most designers, color contrast can bring attention to certain words, while detracting emphasis from others.

On the Web, you can use color for text, text-based headers, links, visited links, and active links. This gives you a lot of opportunity to apply color to text, but again, subtlety must rule the day.

But even when you are limited to black, white, and gray, you can use contrast to gain a sense of color. As mentioned earlier in the discussion of type forms, bold, italic, and oblique can be used to create emphasis within a page. Light type is softer and warmer than bold type, which has a more profound presence on the screen.

Caution

Because bold type carries more weight (if you'll pardon a typographic pun) on a page, many individuals want to bold *all* their body text, thinking that it carries more impact. Actually, this is ill advised, because bold forms tend to blur the individual letters somewhat. It's best to stick with the conventional method of using bold type to emphasize a specific section of text, rather than trying to emphasize all your text.

When designing type for a full Web page, many designers will use a darker color for primary headers, and then lighten the color (or change it) as the headers descend. Figure 12.10 shows a Web page with black text and two headers, each in a lighter gray.

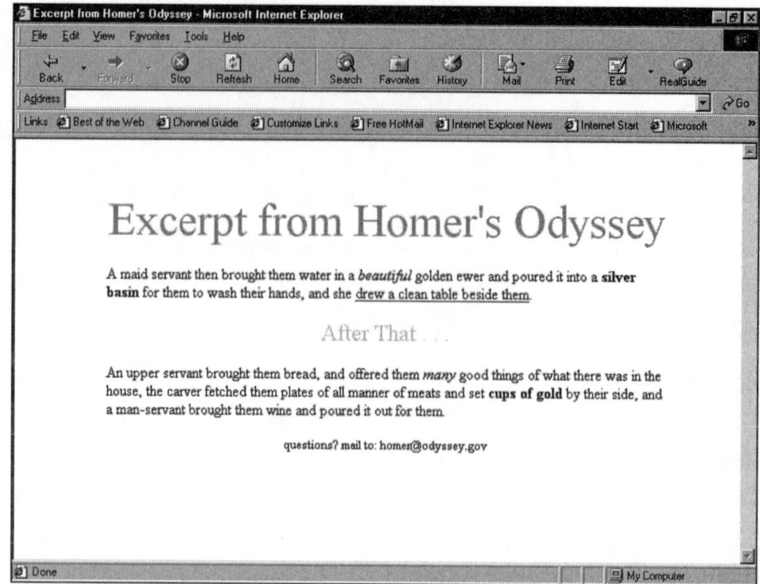

Figure 12.10
Lightening headers in descending order is an effective use of type color.

Tip from molly

Using the darker-to-lighter header technique creates visual texture, as well as demonstrating the emphasis of each individual section: The bolder the header, the more dominant a position the information associated with it commands.

THE FONT ELEMENT

With some strong typographic design information providing a conceptual foundation for the practical application of HTML-based type, we now turn to the `FONT` element.

You might be thinking: But wait! I read in Chapter 1, "Understanding HTML 4.0" that the `FONT` element has been deprecated. And so it has.

Remember also the discussion about Transitional HTML 4.0. This is the current state of affairs with HTML-based design because, quite simply, your audience and the standards committee aren't using the same technologies. So, to create pages that are high in impact but *stable across browsers*, you must understand how the `FONT` element works.

This gives you the most control available in HTML typography, which, as mentioned in the introduction to this chapter, is an area of great instability. With the `FONT` element, you can write your code to work with browsers that do not favor HTML 4.0 standards. You can also add style sheets to control typographic design.

→ For more information on how to control type with CSS, **see** "Designing Type with CSS," **p. 286**

Note

There is probably no more effective example of Transitional HTML 4.0 in use by professional coders today than just this issue: the deprecated FONT element used in combination with the favored CSS.

The FONT element uses the standard opening <FONT> and closing </FONT> tags, as shown in Listing 12.1.

LISTING 12.1 USING THE FONT TAG

```
<FONT>
As soon as they had had enough to eat and drink they wanted music and dancing,
which are the crowning embellishments of a banquet, so a servant brought a lyre to
Phemius, whom they compelled perforce to sing to them. As soon as he touched his
lyre and began to sing Telemachus spoke low to Minerva, with his head close to
hers that no man might hear.
</FONT>
```

Of course, if you were to load this into a browser, nothing would happen. There are a variety of attributes you'll need to use to grab hold of the design-oriented issues discussed in the typographic section of this chapter.

FONT ELEMENT ATTRIBUTES

The following list defines the available attributes for the FONT element.

- **size**—This attribute helps determine the font's size.
- **color**—Using this attribute, combined with a color, adds that color to the selection of text.
- **face**—This attribute allows HTML designers to write out the name of the type they want.

THE size ATTRIBUTE

Font sizing in HTML is fairly rudimentary, with whole-number values determining the size of the font. The default standard size is 3. Obviously, anything higher is going to be bigger and anything lower will be smaller.

Setting a Base Font

Some designers use the BASEFONT tag to apply a default font face, size, and color to an entire page. The concept is to override a browser's default but allow for additional FONT tags to be used throughout the document.

To do this, add the tag to the top of the page (under the opening BODY tag) and set your attributes and values.

```
<BASEFONT face="arial" size="2" color="#FFFFFF">
```

Note that there is *no* closing tag. Also, it's important to remember that the BASEFONT tag is not supported by many browsers. Furthermore, the tag has been deprecated in the 4.0 standard, making it increasingly less important to Web typography.

The following is an example of a paragraph of text using font size:

```
<FONT size="5">
As soon as they had had enough to eat and drink they wanted music and dancing,
which are the crowning embellishments of a banquet, so a servant brought a lyre
to Phemius, whom they compelled perforce to sing to them. As soon as he touched
his lyre and began to sing Telemachus spoke low to Minerva, with his head close
to hers that no man might hear.
</FONT>
```

Figure 12.11 shows the results.

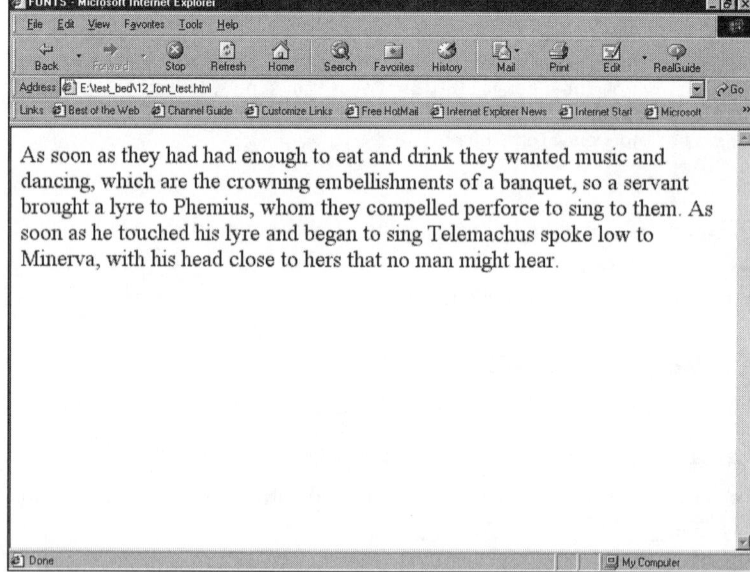

Figure 12.11
Here the font size is set to 5.

Anything much bigger than a size 5 is ungainly. Smaller sizes, such as 2, allow you to put more body text on a page, but you run the risk of making it difficult for people to read.

You can also use the minus and plus sign in front of a numeric value. The way this works is by adding the numeric size to the default (see Figure 12.12), as in the following:

```
<FONT size="-1">
As soon as they had had enough to eat and drink they wanted music and dancing,
which are the crowning embellishments of a banquet, so a servant brought a lyre
to Phemius, whom they compelled perforce to sing to them. As soon as he touched
his lyre and began to sing Telemachus spoke low to Minerva, with his head close
to hers that no man might hear.
</FONT>
```

The `size` attribute is essentially rudimentary because there's no standardization across browsers and platforms. This means that any size font will look different from one browser to another.

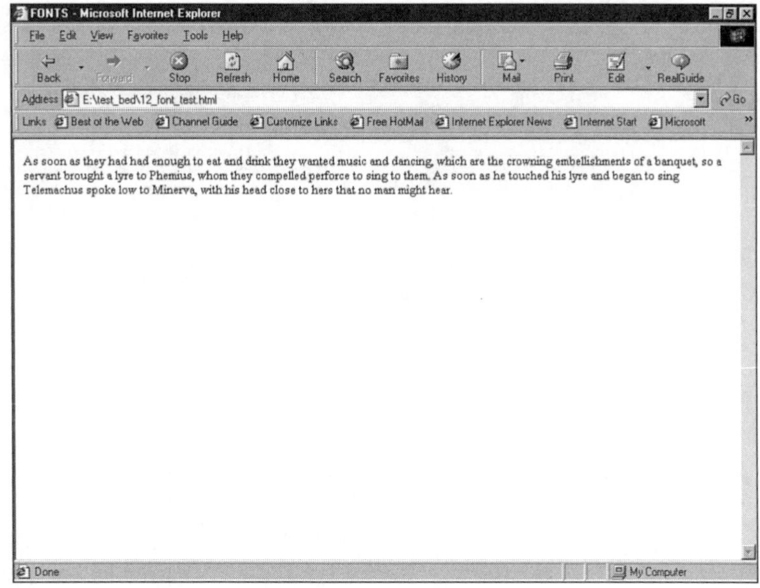

Figure 12.12 Subtract 1 from a standard default and you end up with a point size of 2.

In Figure 12.13, I show text in the Netscape browser. This selection uses the standard, default size, with a header set at size 5. I show the same code in Internet Explorer in Figure 12.14. If you compare the two, you'll see that there's a slight difference in the sizing.

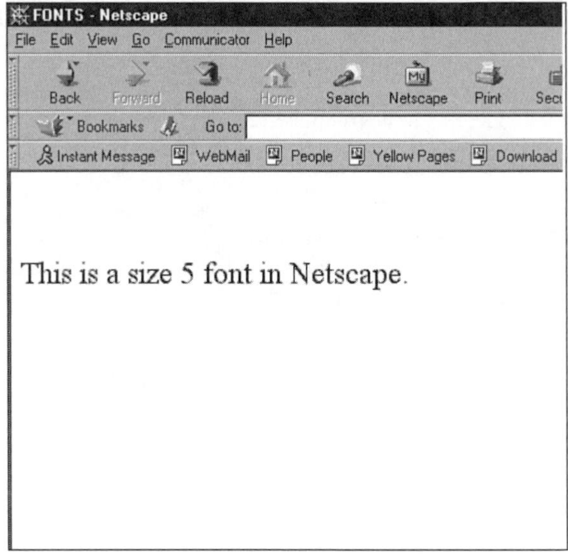

Figure 12.13 Font size "5" as seen in Netscape Navigator.

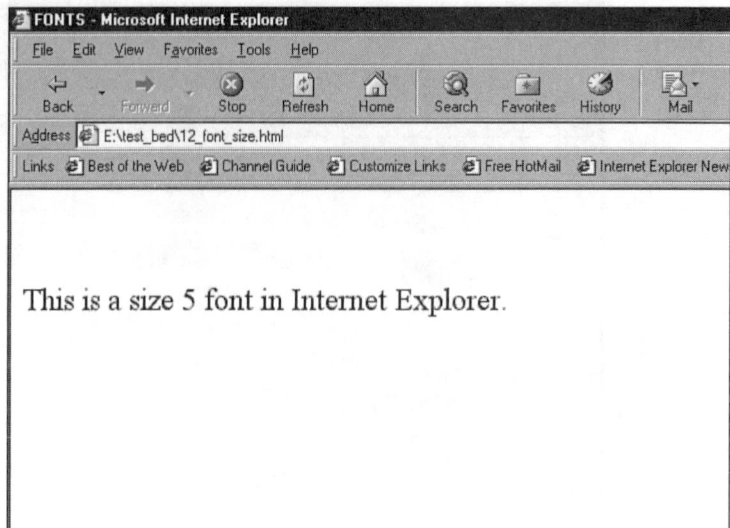

Figure 12.14
Font size "5" in Internet Explorer is slightly larger than in Figure 12.13.

The Color Attribute

An example of the `FONT` tag with the `color` attribute added looks like the following:

```
<FONT size="2" color="#99999">
As soon as they had had enough to eat and drink they wanted music and dancing,
which are the crowning embellishments of a banquet, so a servant brought a lyre
to Phemius, whom they compelled perforce to sing to them. As soon as he touched
his lyre and began to sing Telemachus spoke low to Minerva, with his head close
to hers that no man might hear.
</FONT>
```

By using Hexadecimal code, the base 16 equivalent of RGB (Red, Green, Blue) values, I've selected a gray color for my text.

Note

You can also use the literal name of standard colors, such as blue, green, red, and the like. I'm not too fond of this technique–it's limiting because it doesn't allow for all 216 colors of the Web-safe palette to be expressed.

→ For more about the Web-safe color palette, **see** "Color Concepts," **p. 539**

Note

For a good hexadecimal color chart visit **`http://sdc.htrigg.smu.edu/HTMLPages/RGBchart.html`** or download the nhue.gif file from **`http://www.lynda.com/files/`**. These charts put color selection and hexadecimal values right at your fingertips.

The Face Attribute

If you want to add a font face to a selection of text, you can do so by using the `face` attribute and then defining the category, or *master family* name.

Note

You can use specific face names, too. However, master families are going to be more stable in most instances.

The following is an example of font code with the `face` attribute included:

```
<FONT face="arial">
As soon as they had had enough to eat and drink they wanted music and dancing,
which are the crowning embellishments of a banquet, so a servant brought a lyre
to Phemius, whom they compelled perforce to sing to them. As soon as he touched
his lyre and began to sing Telemachus spoke low to Minerva, with his head close
to hers that no man might hear.
</FONT>
```

Figure 12.15 shows the selection, and, indeed, the face that appears is Arial regular.

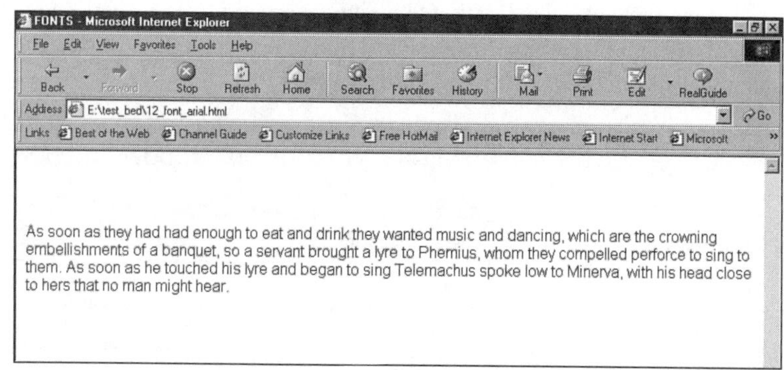

Figure 12.15
The Arial typeface is in the sans-serif family.

Sounds easy enough—and it is. The caveat is that if the font isn't resident on your visitor's machine, he or she isn't going to see the font face that you're coding unless you provide some options.

Arial is a font native to Windows machines, but rarely, if ever, is it found on a Macintosh. Without that font being resident on the Macintosh, the browser will simply display the default font, which is normally set to Times. It's easy to see how quickly this can degrade any design you might have set out to create.

Wondering if you really need to worry about whether a font is installed on your site visitor's machine? See "Using Other Fonts," in the Troubleshooting section at the end of this chapter.

Fortunately, the `face` attribute allows you to stack fonts into the value. The browser looks for the first font, and, if it doesn't find it, moves on to the next named font, and so on.

This stacking method gives you better control than just letting the browser do the thinking for you. You can put as many font names as appropriate and reasonable into the stack. This way, the browser will look for your preferred font and then for a similar font. In the case of the Macintosh, Helvetica is a sans-serif font that is similar to Arial.

```
<FONT face="arial, helvetica">
```

With this in the string, the browser looks for Helvetica if it cannot find Arial.

There's another option that you can add to the string as well. It's supported only by later browser versions, such as 4.0 and later. This allows you to put the generic family name into the string, as follows:

```
<FONT face="arial, helvetica, sans-serif">
```

Now the browser, if it cannot find Arial or Helvetica, will seek out the first sans-serif font that it can find on the resident machine and use that.

Need to be sure that your corporate identity isn't lost by substituted fonts in your headers and other design elements? See "Need a Specific Font" in the Troubleshooting section at the end of this chapter.

This technique demonstrates clearly why it's so important to have an understanding of basic typography. You end up with ever so much more control.

Another important consideration is making sure you have a good understanding of what fonts are generally resident on standard machines. Table 12.3 shows the standard fonts that come loaded on Macintosh and Windows machines.

TABLE 12.3 COMPARISON OF RESIDENT FONTS ON WINDOWS AND MACINTOSH PLATFORMS

Windows	Macintosh
Arial	Chicago
Arial Black	Courier
Arial Narrow	Geneva
Arial Rounded MT Bold	Helvetica
Book Antiqua	Monaco
Bookman Old Style	New York
Century Gothic	Palatino
Century Schoolbook	Times
Courier	
Courier New	
Garamond	
MS Dialog	
MS Dialog Light	
MS LineDraw	
MS Sans Serif	
MS SystemX	
Times New Roman	
Verdana	

It's a little daunting to think that the *only two fonts* that are completely cross-platform compatible are Times and Courier!

However, if you combine typographic knowledge with an understanding of the cross-platform limitations of fonts, you can gain some control over standard HTML documents.

Even if you want to use a fancy, decorative font (see Figure 12.16) that isn't available on an end-user's machine, you can stack alternatives so the user still gets a stylish page:

```
<FONT face="whimsy ICG, garamond, times, serif">
It's time for a refill on my coffee!
</FONT>
```

Figure 12.17 shows the results.

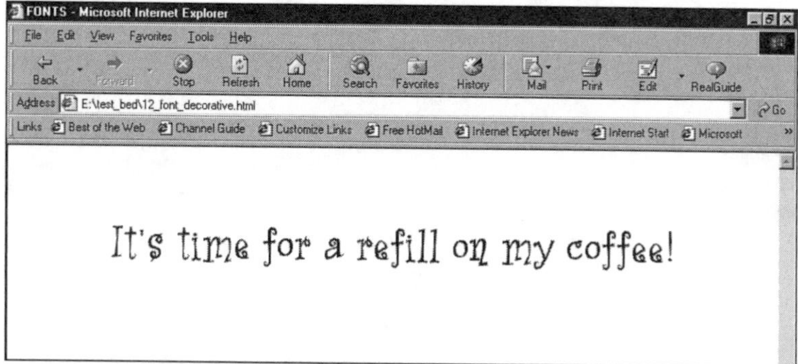

Figure 12.16
An example of a decorative font (set to size 7) via HTML.

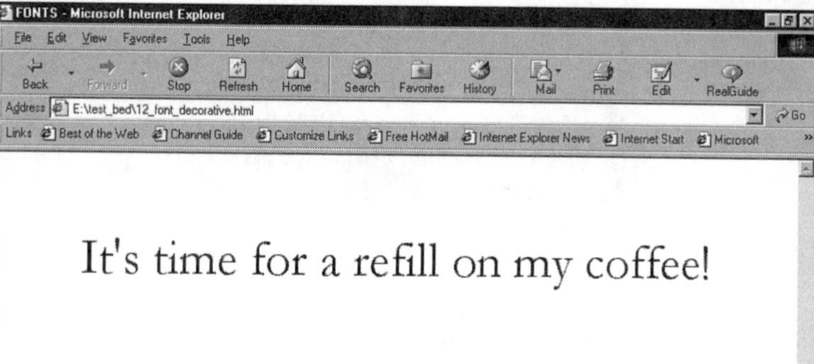

Figure 12.17
The look of the page on a machine without the specialty font installed isn't as dramatic as the chosen font, but with another serif typeface being displayed is still probably better than what the default type might result in.

Caution

You *must* remember that if a font face isn't available on a given machine, the default face will appear. Default is almost always a Serif font such as Times, unless the user has selected another font for his or her default.

Now you can put the FONT face, color, and size attributes together to come up with a singular style:

```
<FONT size="4" color="#999999" face="century schoolbook, times, serif">
As soon as they had had enough to eat and drink they wanted music and dancing,
which are the crowning embellishments of a banquet, so a servant brought a lyre
to Phemius, whom they compelled perforce to sing to them. As soon as he touched
his lyre and began to sing Telemachus spoke low to Minerva, with his head close
to hers that no man might hear.
</FONT>
```

Figure 12.18 shows the results: a size "4" gray type in the Century Schoolbook typeface.

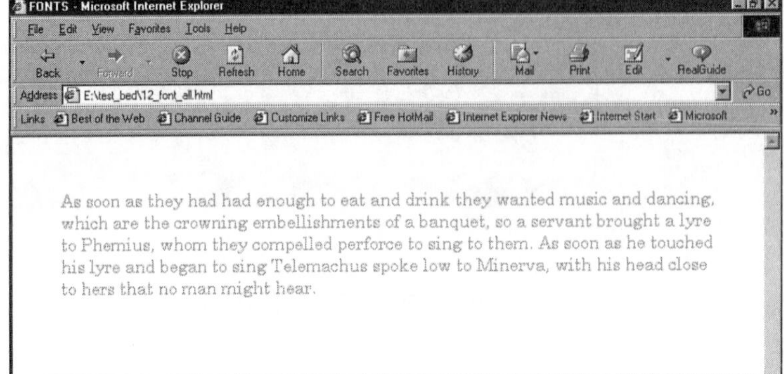

Figure 12.18
The FONT tag with all attributes in action gives you a lot of control over the look of your type as you design your pages without having to employ anything more than HTML.

Note

If Web typography interests you, here are some resources to get you started:

DesktopPublishing.Com: A truly amazing place as it contains thousands of resources, **http://www.desktoppublishing.com/**.

Microsoft's Typography on the Web: Excellent resource for all that's happening in Web typography, located at **http://www.microsoft.com/typography/web/default.htm**.

TYPE CONSIDERATIONS

There are several considerations that are important to mention when working with fonts. They include the following:

- Anti-aliasing and font smoothing
- Embedded fonts
- Fonts and tables

These specialty techniques are available only in certain instances, with the exception of the way fonts work within tables.

Anti-Aliasing and Font Smoothing

Anti-aliasing is also known as font smoothing in the computer world. Without anti-aliasing, type can appear jagged. Figure 12.19 shows large HTML-defined type. The jagged edges can be smoothed in two ways. You could choose to use a graphic for this text instead and select an anti-aliasing option when preparing the type for the graphic.

Figure 12.19
The jagged appearance of aliased, unsmoothed fonts is not very appealing.

Jagged Fonts

Another option is controlling aliasing, as Microsoft has done with its font smoother, which is downloadable for PCs running Windows 95 and 98.

Note

Microsoft's font smoother is available at `http://www.microsoft.com/typography/grayscal/smoother.htm`.

Figure 12.20 shows a header as viewed with the font smoothing turned on.

Figure 12.20
Font smoothing makes the font more readable—and attractive.

Smooooooth!

Unfortunately, you run into a Windows platform centricity with font smoothing. It's only available on the Windows platform—and not only that, it only smoothes TrueType fonts.

Embedding Fonts

Embedded fonts are an interesting concept that allows for the font you want to use to be embedded within a page and downloaded to the end user. The user will then have the information to properly display the page as you've set it up.

Both Netscape and Internet Explorer have methods by which to offer embedded fonts. In Netscape, font embedding is dealt with by using a technology developed by Bitstream known as TrueDoc. Font embedding is delivered via a font format known as OpenType in Internet Explorer. It's interesting to note that OpenType is also backed by Adobe, which gives the format a lot of respectability and punch for future font issues on the Web.

Although there is a lot of general interest in the idea of font embedding, I've rarely seen it used.

Note

For Bitstream's TrueDoc, check out **http://www.bitstream.com/products/developer/truedoc/td_embed.html**.

Microsoft covers the OpenType format at **http://www.microsoft.com/truetype/**.

FONTS AND TABLES

A major concern with the FONT tag is that it does not span table cells. In other words, you have to open and close your font information not only every time you want to change a font face, color, or size, but every time you create a new table cell.

Here's a simple table:

```
<TABLE border="0" width="100%">
<TR>
<TD>
This is my first cell
</TD>
<TD>
This is my second cell
</TD>
</TR>
</TABLE>
```

Now let's say you want to add a single font style to the text within the table. To achieve this, you must do the following:

```
<TABLE border="0" width="100%">
<TR>
<TD>
<FONT face="arial, helvetica, sans-serif" size="4">
This is my first cell
</FONT>
</TD>
<TD>
<FONT face="arial, helvetica, sans-serif" size="4">
This is my second cell
</FONT>
</TD>
</TR>
</TABLE>
```

Note that each cell contains the same font information applied to just that cell. Anything else, and you'll lose the integrity of the font formatting. In Figure 12.21, you can see that all the text is formatted in Arial, size 4.

However, if you code this improperly, as follows:

```
<TABLE border="0" width="100%">
<TR>
<TD>
<FONT face="arial, helvetica, sans-serif" size="4">
This is my first cell
</TD>
<TD>
This is my second cell
```

```
</FONT>
</TD>
</TR>
</TABLE>
```

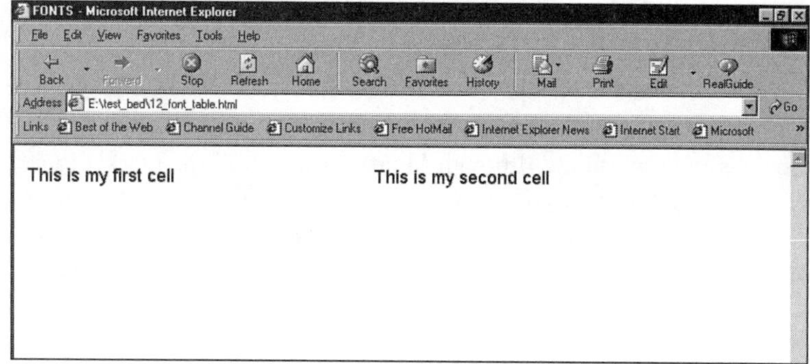

Figure 12.21
A stable table contains font information for each cell. It's more work, but in transitional HTML 4.0, it aids in ensuring that your fonts are as consistent throughout the layout as possible.

The font integrity will vanish in the second cell (see Figure 12.22).

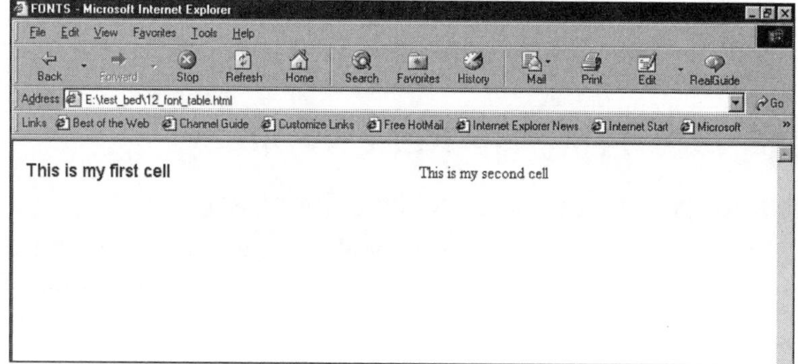

Figure 12.22
Font integrity degrades between cells with careless coding.

PART II CH 12

TYPOGRAPHY IN HTML 4.0

But what of all the fancy typographic elements we discussed earlier, such as orientation and leading? This kind of control simply cannot be attained with the deprecated FONT tag. However, graphic type and style sheets are the answer.

→ For more about graphic type, **see** "Graphic Type for the Web," **p. 624**

In fact, it's because of the control that style sheets offer that the W3C deprecated the FONT tag in the first place. The hope was to push browsers to quickly adopt this excellent method of controlling type. And what control! In terms of those issues we've covered with the FONT element in this chapter, you can actually describe size in points, pixels, percentages—even centimeters.

But even when you begin to employ style sheets, you're going to have to use the methods described here as well to remain fully compatible with non-conforming browsers. Again, this is Transitional HTML 4.0 at its most realistic—where deprecated elements must still be employed to allow for graceful degradation from bionic to more simplistic browsers.

TROUBLESHOOTING

USING OTHER FONTS

Can't you assume that most computers are using Microsoft Word and, therefore, have certain other fonts installed?

Don't assume anything. Although Microsoft may lead the market in certain applications, there are still thousands of people using alternate packages. Also, not everyone installs the additional fonts that come with Microsoft or any other company's applications. The only fonts you can rely upon are those that come installed on the computer.

NEED A SPECIFIC FONT

If you need to use a specific font for headers to match a corporate identity, how can you ensure another font will not be substituted?

The only way to ensure that visitors will see your headers exactly as you intend is to create your headers in a graphics package and insert them as images into your HTML page. Even then, keep in mind that some visitors will be browsing without graphics, and will then only see the alternate text you code into your images, formatted in the default font.

DESIGNING FOR THE REAL WORLD

COMBINING HTML AND GRAPHIC TYPE SUCCESSFULLY

It can be tempting to create all your headers and font changes as graphic images, relying on HTML text only for the body of your content. Don't underestimate the potential of using HTML, however. You can use the `color`, `size`, and `face` attributes of the `FONT` tag to create a clean, readable Web site that meshes well with your images.

CareerBuilder is such a site. CareerBuilder helps visitors polish their resume and interview skills and search thousands of listings to find a job. Content certainly takes precedence over bells and whistles on this site. If you look at the design, however, you will see that Career-Builder has made good use of HTML typography to generate a basic but compelling site.

The color choices are simple. A white background provides easy readability, complemented with orange, black, and blue text. Although the main headers on the site are images, the sub-headers and text are all coded in HTML. The use of orange headlines in the right column draws your eye to those features without detracting from the rest of the site. The consistency of font face usage gives the whole site a cohesive look and feel.

Note

You can check out the CareerBuilder site at **`http://www.careerbuilder.com/`**.

PART III

HTML Layout and Design Fundamentals

CHAPTER 13

Cascading Style Sheet Techniques

In this chapter

STYLE SHEETS: AN OVERVIEW

Cascading Style Sheets (*CSS*) is the broad term used to refer to several methods of applying style elements to HTML pages. In this case, think of a style as any kind of design element: including typeface, background, text, link colors, margin controls, and placement of objects on a page.

Why should you use style sheets if HTML can do at least some of this work by itself? The developers of HTML originally intended for it to be only a formatting language, responsible for the basic layout of a page, including body, headers, paragraphs, and a few specific items such as bulleted lists. Web designers and browser developers are the ones who have pushed and pulled at HTML to make it accommodate aspects of style.

To gain some separation between HTML's original function as a formatting tool but still offer a powerful addition to the designer's toolbox in terms of style Cascading Style Sheets were developed. In fact, as of the HTML 4.0 standard, many of the style-oriented tags (such as the font tag) were deprecated (made obsolete) in favor of CSS.

Caution

Web browsers don't fully support CSS. Although Internet Explorer introduced CSS in the Windows 95 3.0 browser version, it had some bugs with the implementation. Netscape, in a rush to meet the competition, built Navigator 4.0 to be CSS compliant. But the compliance is very inconsistent at best. Add to this the fact that many Web visitors do not keep up-to-date with the latest and greatest browsers, and the reality of following HTML 4.0's strict standard is still to be carefully considered by most commercial and hobbyist designs. Of course, transitional HTML 4.0 allows you to combine methods.

Until Cascading Style Sheets entered the picture, however, HTML was missing an important element. Although some control of style with headers and font tags is possible, these techniques are limited because of the limitations of HTML. In many ways, style sheets provide a long-awaited solution for many of HTML's restrictions. The results are better font control, color management, margin control, and even the addition of special effects such as text shadowing. Another powerful benefit is the ability to control multiple pages within a site from a single sheet, and use multiple types of style sheets in a sequence for very precise control.

Note

You can find a significant source for information on style sheets at the World Wide Web Consortium's site at `http://www.w3.org/Style/`.

The logic and power of style sheets outweigh the current problems with browser support, and for this reason, designers clearly must learn the concepts and techniques and be at the ready to employ them where necessary.

Types of Style Sheets

Style sheets can be delivered to an HTML document by a variety of methods.

You can use these three types of style sheets:

- **Inline**—This method allows you to take any HTML tag and add a style to it. Using the inline method gives you maximum control over any aspect of a Web page. Say you want to control the look and feel of a specific paragraph. You could simply add a `style="x"` attribute to the paragraph tag, and the browser would display that paragraph using the style values you added to the code.
- **Embedded**—Embedding allows for control of a full page of HTML. Using the `<STYLE>` tag, which you place within the `<HEAD>` section of an HTML page, you can insert detailed style attributes to be applied to the entire page.
- **Linked**—Also referred to as an "external" style sheet, a linked style sheet provides a powerful way for you to create master styles that you can apply to an entire site. You create a main style sheet document using the .css extension. This document contains the styles you want a single page or even thousands of pages to adopt. Any page that links to this document takes on the styles called for in that document.

In the following examples, you'll see a variety of syntaxes that will look unfamiliar if you are new to style sheets. Bear with me through these examples. You first need to understand the methods used to apply style. Then I'll provide a closer look at style sheet syntax itself. Finally, you'll have a chance to go through some exercises that will help you put both the method and the syntax to work.

Inline Style

You can add inline style to any HTML tag that makes sense. Such tags include paragraphs, headers, horizontal rules, anchors, and table cells. Each is a logical candidate for inline style. The following example uses the paragraph tag along with the `style` attribute to achieve inline style:

```
<P>The text in this paragraph will display as 13 point text using the
default font.</P>

<P style="font: 13pt verdana">The text in this paragraph will display as 13 point
text using the
verdana font.</P>
```

Part III Ch 13

Figure 13.1 shows two paragraphs, one with the standard default typeface for a Windows machine (Times) and one with the Verdana type face applied.

Two elements can help you apply inline style to sections of a page. These elements are particularly useful not only for style sheets, but also later when you combine style sheets with dynamic events through DHTML. They are the division, or `DIV` element, and the `SPAN` element.

→ To read more about the `DIV` element, **see** "Formatting and Aligning Text," **p. 136**

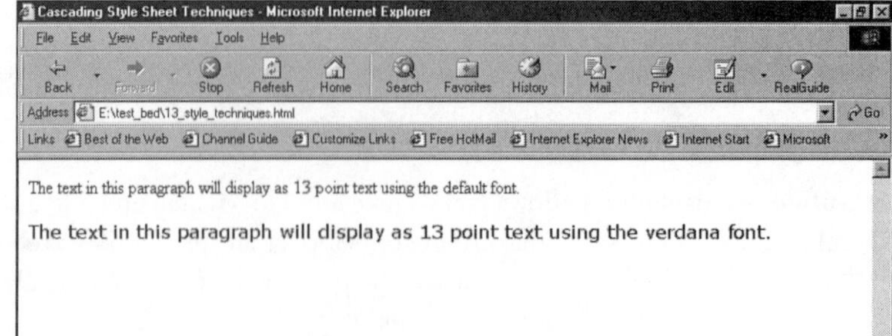

Figure 13.1
Using inline style, I applied the Verdana font to the second paragraph.

DIV and SPAN specify a defined range of text, so everything in between them adopts the style you want to use. The primary difference between DIV and SPAN is that DIV is a block level element, meaning it can contain all other HTML elements, whereas SPAN can only be used inline. For example you can align a table with DIV, but you couldn't do the same with SPAN. Another major difference is that DIV forces a line break after the division, whereas SPAN does not. For this reason, SPAN is especially useful within sentences or paragraphs, and DIV is most powerful when used to define larger sections of text, including paragraphs, headings, lists, and nested elements.

Tip from molly

Use SPAN to modify the style of any portion of text shorter than a paragraph.

The following is an example of the division element at work:

```
<DIV style="font-family: garamond; font-size: 14pt;">All of the text within this
section is 14 point Garamond.
</DIV>
```

This example shows the <SPAN> tag:

```
<SPAN style="color: #999999">This text appears in the color gray, with no line
break after the closing span tag </SPAN> and the rest of the text.
```

Figure 13.2 shows the combined results of the DIV and SPAN elements with style attributes applied.

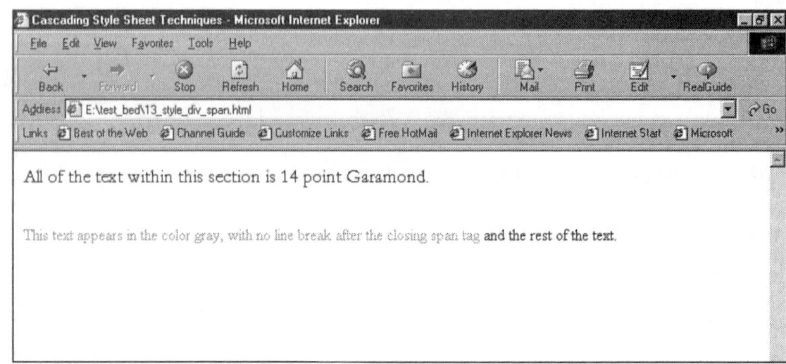

Figure 13.2
Adding inline style to a paragraph with the DIV and SPAN tags gives you precise control over fonts and colors as seen in this example.

Embedded Style

Embedded styles use the STYLE element, which you place within the HEAD section of an HTML document, as shown in Listing 13.1.

Listing 13.1 Using the STYLE Element

```
<HTML>
<HEAD>
<TITLE>Embedded Style Sheet Example I</TITLE>

<STYLE>

<!--

BODY {
background: #FFFFFF;
color: #000000;
}
H1 {
font: 14pt verdana; color: #CCCCCC;
}
P {
font: 13pt times;
}
A {
color: #FF0000; text-decoration: none;
}

-->

</STYLE>
</HEAD>
<BODY>

<H1>A Midsummer Night's Dream: Act I Scene I</H1>

Either to die the death or to abjure <BR>
For ever the society of men. <BR>
Therefore, fair <A href="hermia.html">Hermia</A>, question your desires; <BR>
Know of your youth, examine well your blood, <BR>
Whether, if you yield not to your father's choice, <BR>
You can endure the livery of a nun, <BR>
For aye to be in shady cloister mew'd, <BR>
To live a barren sister all your life, <BR>
Chanting faint hymns to the cold fruitless moon. <BR>
Thrice-blessed they that master so their blood, <BR>
To undergo such maiden <A HREF="pilgrim.html">pilgrimage</A>; <BR>
But earthlier happy is the rose distill'd, <BR>
Than that which withering on the virgin thorn <BR>
Grows, lives and dies in single blessedness.

</BODY>
</HTML>
```

As you can tell from the preceding example, an HTML document using a style sheet begins to look quite a bit different from older HTML standards, but following the logic is not difficult. In this case, the page's body calls for a background color, a text color, an H1 font style, a paragraph style, and a link style.

Figure 13.3 shows the results of the embedded style sheet in Listing 13.1.

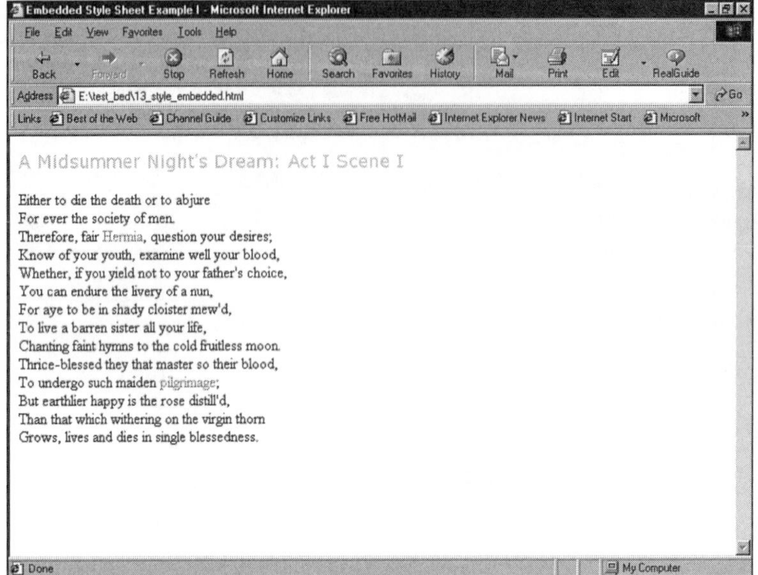

Embedded Style Sheet Example I - Microsoft Internet Explorer
File Edit View Favorites Tools Help
Back Forward Stop Refresh Home Search Favorites History Mail Print Edit RealGuide
Address E:\test_bed\13_style_embedded.html
Go
Links Best of the Web Channel Guide Customize Links Free HotMail Internet Explorer News Internet Start Microsoft
A Midsummer Night's Dream: Act I Scene I
Either to die the death or to abjure
For ever the society of men.
Therefore, fair Hermia, question your desires;
Know of your youth, examine well your blood,
Whether, if you yield not to your father's choice,
You can endure the livery of a nun,
For aye to be in shady cloister mew'd,
To live a barren sister all your life,
Chanting faint hymns to the cold fruitless moon.
Thrice-blessed they that master so their blood,
To undergo such maiden pilgrimage;
But earthlier happy is the rose distill'd,
Than that which withering on the virgin thorn
Grows, lives and dies in single blessedness.
Done
My Computer

Figure 13.3
In this case, I used embedded style to add color and type styles to the page.

Notice how the level one heading, H1, calls for a font using the font's name as well as a literal point size. This figure is a prime example of one reason why Cascading Style Sheets are so powerful: Not only can you choose to control sizing in points, but you also can use pixels (px), percentages (75%), and centimeters (cm).

→ To read more about the way style sheets influence type, **see** "Designing Type Using Style Sheets," **p. 284**

Another interesting aspect of this style sheet includes the difference in fonts as defined by the header and paragraph style; they're different in color and face. With HTML 4.0 and style sheets, the days of having an HTML page littered with font tags are limited. Style is handled in a nice, compact fashion.

Tip from molly

To ensure that your embedded style sheet is hidden from older browsers, you can place comment tags such as <!-- style sheet goes here --> around the sheet. Begin the comment tag underneath the <STYLE> tag and end the comment immediately before the </STYLE> tag.

The <A> (anchor) tag in the style sheet shows yet another handy piece of syntax. The `text-decoration: none` string forces underlining to be removed from links, allowing for clean, attractive results. More details on how to control syntax within a style sheet are discussed in the next chapter. A complete style reference is available in the Appendix at the end of this book.

→ For more CSS syntax details, **see** "Designing Type with CSS," **p. 286**

→ For a comprehensive style sheet reference, **see** "CSS Reference," **p. 1016**

Linked Style

Linked style sheets, also called *external* style sheets, extend the form of embedded style. Using the same code contained within the STYLE element as you saw in the embedded sample, you can place this information in a separate document. You then can save the document with the file extension .css. You should be sure that this document is either in the root directory with the HTML files that you intend to have it affect or that you code the link properly when linking to the sheet.

→ To read more about directory structure and linking, **see** "Managing HTML Documents Locally," **p. 66** and "Linking Pages," **p. 174**

The power of linked style is that you can link all the pages in a site that you want to have influenced by the style to this single sheet. Whether you link one page or one thousand makes no difference.

Listing 13.2 shows the syntax for a linked, or external, style sheet.

Listing 13.2 A Linked Style Sheet

```
BODY {
background: #000000;
color: #FFFFCC;
}
H1 {
font: 14pt Garamond; color: #CCCCCC;
}
P {
font: 13pt arial;
}
A {
color: #FF0000; text-decoration: none;
}
```


Now, you can take this style sheet and step through the process of making it into an actively linked external sheet:

1. Make sure that you have a standard HTML page that has been coded and saved to a directory. Here's my page, saved to a directory as linked_style1.html:

```
<HTML>
<HEAD>
<TITLE>Linked Style Sheet Example</TITLE>
```

```
</HEAD>
<BODY>

<H1>A Midsummer Night's Dream: Act I Scene I</H1>

Either to die the death or to abjure <BR>
For ever the society of men. <BR>
Therefore, fair <A href="hermia.html">Hermia</A>, question your desires; <BR>
Know of your youth, examine well your blood, <BR>
Whether, if you yield not to your father's choice, <BR>
You can endure the livery of a nun, <BR>
For aye to be in shady cloister mew'd, <BR>
To live a barren sister all your life, <BR>
Chanting faint hymns to the cold fruitless moon. <BR>
Thrice-blessed they that master so their blood, <BR>
To undergo such maiden <A HREF="pilgrim.html">pilgrimage</A>; <BR>
But earthlier happy is the rose distill'd, <BR>
Than that which withering on the virgin thorn <BR>
Grows, lives and dies in single blessedness.

</BODY>
</HTML>
```

2. Open your text or HTML editor, and type the code shown in Listing 13.2.
3. Save the file as `mystyle_1.css`.
4. Place this file in the directory where the `linked_style1.html` file resides.
5. Reopen `linked_style1.html`.
6. Add the following link in the `HEAD` section of the HTML document:

```
<HTML>
<HEAD>
<TITLE>Linked Style Sheet Example</TITLE>
<link rel=stylesheet href="mystyle_1.css" type="text/css">

</HEAD>
<BODY>

<H1>A Midsummer Night's Dream: Act I Scene I</H1>

Either to die the death or to abjure <BR>
For ever the society of men. <BR>
Therefore, fair <A href="hermia.html">Hermia</A>, question your desires; <BR>
Know of your youth, examine well your blood, <BR>
Whether, if you yield not to your father's choice, <BR>
You can endure the livery of a nun, <BR>
For aye to be in shady cloister mew'd, <BR>
To live a barren sister all your life, <BR>
Chanting faint hymns to the cold fruitless moon. <BR>
Thrice-blessed they that master so their blood, <BR>
To undergo such maiden <A HREF="pilgrim.html">pilgrimage</A>; <BR>
But earthlier happy is the rose distill'd, <BR>
Than that which withering on the virgin thorn <BR>
Grows, lives and dies in single blessedness.

</BODY>
</HTML>
```

7. Save the file.
8. View the file in a style-sheet–compliant browser. It should match the results shown in Figure 13.4.

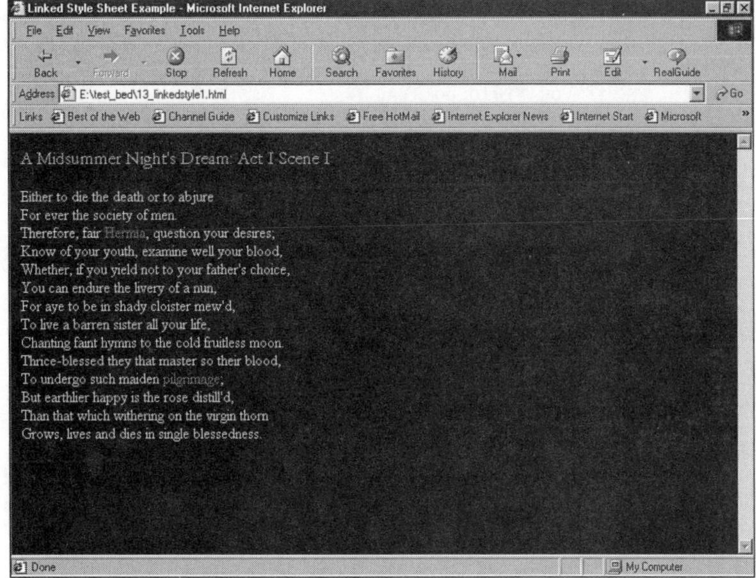

Linked Style Sheet Example - Microsoft Internet Explorer
File Edit View Favorites Tools Help
Back Forward Stop Refresh Home Search Favorites History Mail Print Edit RealGuide
Address E:\test_bed\13_linkedstyle1.html
Go
Links Best of the Web Channel Guide Customize Links Free HotMail Internet Explorer News Internet Start Microsoft
A Midsummer Night's Dream: Act I Scene I
Either to die the death or to abjure
For ever the society of men.
Therefore, fair Hermia, question your desires;
Know of your youth, examine well your blood,
Whether, if you yield not to your father's choice,
You can endure the livery of a nun,
For aye to be in shady cloister mew'd,
To live a barren sister all your life,
Chanting faint hymns to the cold fruitless moon.
Thrice-blessed they that master so their blood,
To undergo such maiden pilgrimage;
But earthlier happy is the rose distill'd,
Than that which withering on the virgin thorn
Grows, lives and dies in single blessedness.
Done
My Computer

Figure 13.4
Any page containing this link adopts the styles defined in mystyle_1.css.

If you want to have 1,000 HTML pages globally affected by this one style sheet, you can do so by linking them to this page. Then, if you want to make style adjustments to those 1,000 pages, you simply have to change the *one* file—mystyle_1.css.

THE CASCADE: COMBINING LINKED, EMBEDDED, AND INLINE STYLE

One of the powers of style sheets is that you can combine all these methods, or any number of individual types of style sheets for maximum control. Say you have a large site that you're controlling with a single style sheet. However, you have a page on which you want to alter some of the styles. No problem! You can simply place the modified style as an embedded sheet within the individual page. The browser will first look for the embedded style and apply that information. Whatever isn't covered in the embedded sheet the browser will seek out in the linked sheet.

You also can override both styles by adding an inline style. When all three forms are in place, the style-sheet–compliant browser looks for that style first, then the embedded style, and then the linked sheet; it reads the information in that order.

I've created a page with a link, an embedded sheet, and some inline styles, as you can see in Listing 13.3.

Listing 13.3 Linked, Embedded, and Inline Styles Applied to the Same Page

```
<HTML>
<HEAD>
<TITLE>Combination Style Sheet Example</TITLE>

<LINK rel=stylesheet href="mystyle_1.css" type="text/css">

<STYLE>

<!--

P {
font: 13pt verdana;
}

-->

</STYLE>
</HEAD>

<BODY>

<H1 style="font-family: garamond; font-size: 22pt;">
A Midsummer Night's Dream: Act I Scene I</H1>

<P>Either to die the death or to abjure <BR>
For ever the society of men. <BR>
Therefore, fair <A href="hermia.html">Hermia</A>,
question your desires; <BR>
Know of your youth, examine well your blood, <BR>
Whether, if you yield not to your father's choice, <BR>
You can endure the livery of a nun, <BR>
For aye to be in shady cloister mew'd, <BR>
To live a barren sister all your life, <BR>
Chanting faint hymns to the cold fruitless moon. <BR>
Thrice-blessed they that master so their blood, <BR>
To undergo such maiden <A HREF="pilgrim.html">pilgrimage</A>; <BR>
But earthlier happy is the rose distill'd, <BR>
Than that which withering on the virgin thorn <BR>
Grows, lives and dies in single blessedness.
</P>

<BODY>
</HTML>
```

In Figure 13.5, you can see the cascade in action—with the inline style overpowering the embedded style, and so forth. In a sense, the linked sheet becomes the default.

Tip from

Whenever possible, streamline the style sheets in a cascade. If you can accomplish the same results using a single linked sheet or an embedded sheet, do so. Use the cascade concept whenever you need to override a linked sheet at specific points in the style relationship, such as linked to embedded to inline, or linked to inline, or embedded to inline and so forth.

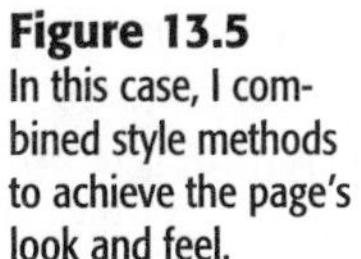

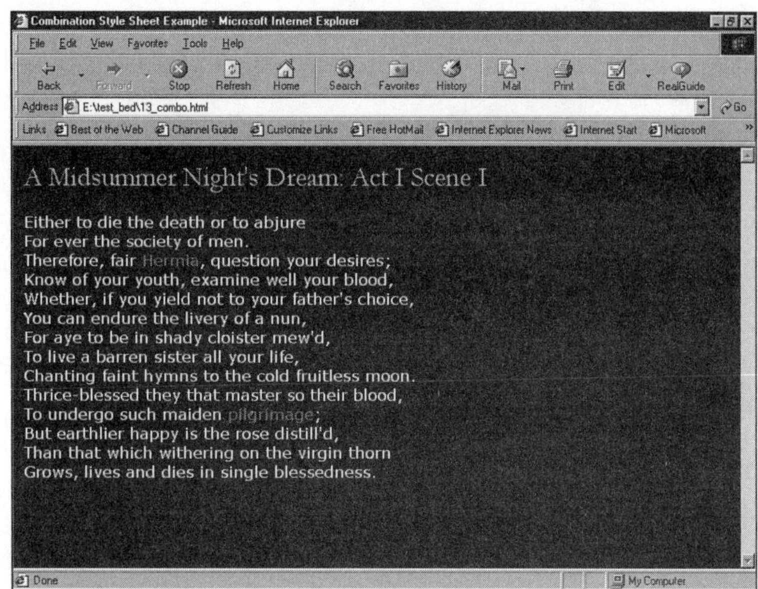

Figure 13.5
In this case, I combined style methods to achieve the page's look and feel.

Style Sheet Syntax

If you recall the discussion about HTML syntax, sentences require specific elements, as do mathematical equations. Style sheets are similar to both in that if they do not follow a specified order, or syntax, they might not function properly.

→ For a refresher on HTML syntax, **see** "Defining HTML Syntax," **p. 74**

Whatever method you choose to deliver your style to HTML documents, the syntax is going to be similar in all cases. Style sheets, like sentences, are made up of very specific parts. These parts include the following:

- **Selector**—This element receives the properties and values you assign. Selectors are usually standard HTML elements, such as a header, `H1`, or a paragraph, `P`. Style sheets allow for modified selectors, including classes, which are discussed later in the chapter.
- **Property**—A property defines a selector. For example, if you have a paragraph, `P`, as a selector, properties you include will define that selector. Margins, fonts, and backgrounds are some property concepts. Style sheets contain many properties, and you can use a variety of properties to define a selector.
- **Value**—Values define properties. Say you have a level one header, `H1`, as your selector, and you've included a type family, `type-family`, as a property. The face that you actually define is the value of that property.

Properties and values combined make up a *declaration*. A selector and a declaration make up a *rule*, as shown here:

```
H1 {
type-family: garamond, times, serif;
}
```

Note that the curly brackets are used to contain the declaration. This syntax is only true for embedded or linked styles. Whenever using inline style, you use quotations to contain your declaration. Selectors aren't defined in this case, as the application of the declaration is inherent to the tag to which the style is being applied:

```
<H1 style="type-family: garamond, times, serif;">This text will
be defined by the declaration</H1>
```

Any time you have multiple declarations, you'll end each individual declaration with a semicolon (;). In the case of a single declaration, it's not necessary to use the semicolon.

Tip from molly

Even though a semicolon is unnecessary when ending a single style declaration, many working developers, WYSIWYG programs, and HTML editors use the semicolon anyway. This can reduce errors and I use the final semicolon myself when coding style sheets.

EXPLORING PROPERTIES AND VALUES FOR TEXT AND SPACE

The numerous style sheet properties cover text, space, color, fonts, and positioning. They pose many more issues than can easily be taught in one chapter. However, to get you off to a working start, I've included some useful style sheet properties and values here.

➔ For a valuable listing of style sheet properties and values, **see** "CSS Reference," **p. 1016**

Many design elements of controlling page layout, margins, indents, and text alignment can help bring a sophisticated look to your pages.

➔ One of the most relevant uses of Cascading Style Sheets for designers lies in the area of typography and positioning. For more information on style-sheet–based typography, **see** "Designing Type With CSS," **p. 284**

➔ Style sheet positioning is also covered in more detail, **see** "Element Positioning and Style Sheet Scripting," **p. 430**

Properties and values can be very helpful when you're designing with style sheets. I've included some of the most commonly used in Table 13.1.

TABLE 13.1 STYLE SHEET PROPERTIES AND VALUES

Property and Value	Results
`margin-left`	To set a left margin, use a distance in points, inches, centimeters, or pixels. The following sets a left margin to three-fourths of an inch: `{margin-left: .75in;}`.
`margin-right`	For a right margin, select from the same measurement options as provided for the `margin-left` attribute. Here's an example: `{margin-right: 50px;}`.
`margin-top`	You can set top margins using the same measurement values as for other margin attributes. Consider this example: `{margin-top: 20pt;}`.

Property and Value	Results
`text-indent`	Again, points, inches, centimeters, or pixel values can be assigned to this attribute, which serves to indent any type of text. Consider this example: `{text-indent: 0.5in;}`.
`text-align`	This long-awaited feature allows for justification of text. Values include `left`, `center`, and `right`, as shown in this example: `{text-align: right;}`

Text alignment is a powerful layout tool, and designers will enjoy being able to place text in a variety of alignments without having to rely on tables, divisions, or other, less graceful, HTML workarounds that existed in the past.

Caution

Cascading Style Sheets allow for negative values for margin properties. These values allow the designer to overlap areas of a page's design, which is a powerful capability with no existing relative in standard HTML. However, browser support is still sketchy regarding negative values, so they should be used with care.

→ For a complete look at HTML alignment as well as examples of style sheets, **see** "Formatting and Aligning Text," **p. 133**

Applying Margins with Style

In the following exercise, you can get started using margins with style:

1. Open your HTML editor.
2. Create a standard shell:

```
<HTML>
<HEAD>
<TITLE>Style Sheet Exercise</TITLE>

</HEAD>
<BODY>


</BODY>
</HTML>
```

3. Add a selection of text:

```
<HTML>
<HEAD>
<TITLE>Style Sheet Exercise</TITLE>

</HEAD>
<BODY>

"The most beautiful thing we can experience is the mysterious; It is the
source of all true art and science"
<BR>
-- Albert Einstein
```

```
</BODY>
</HTML>
```

4. Add the STYLE elements into the HEAD of the document:

```
<HTML>
<HEAD>
<TITLE>Style Sheet Exercise</TITLE>

<STYLE>

<!--


-->

</STYLE>

</HEAD>
<BODY>

"The most beautiful thing we can experience is the mysterious; It is the
source
of all true art and science"
<BR>
-- Albert Einstein


</BODY>
</HTML>
```

5. Add the following margin syntax alongside the BODY selector within the STYLE section:

```
BODY {
margin-left: 2.75in;
margin-right: 2.75in;
margin-top: 2.75in;
margin-bottom: 2.75in;
}
```

6. Save the file as `style_margin.html`.
7. View the file in your browser. It should be similar to my example in Figure 13.6.

Note

Although I added the margin values to the entire page with the BODY attribute in Figure 13.6, you can add margins to *any* HTML tag you want. For example, if you want to control the headers with different margins, place the margin values in the string next to the header of your choice. Similarly, you can adjust margins on individual paragraphs by adding the margin values you seek to the P string.

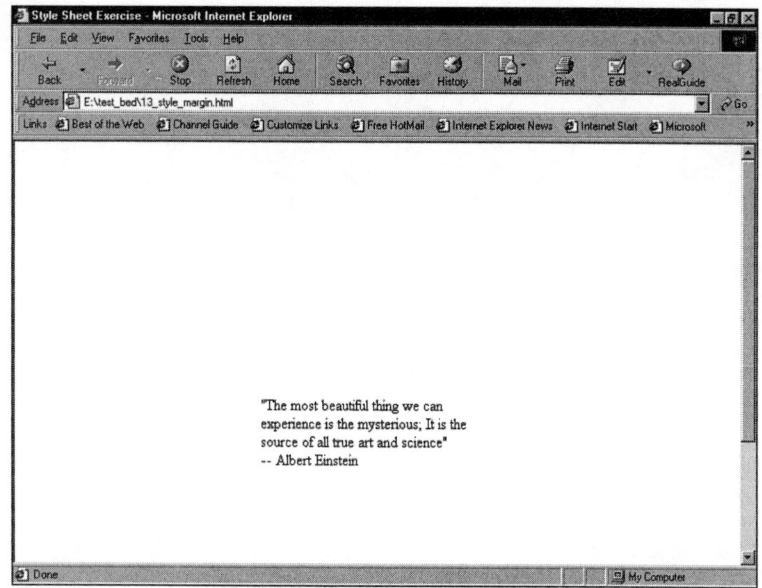

Figure 13.6
Here, I applied a margin of 2.75 inches to the left, right, top, and bottom of the quote. Note that a scrollbar has appeared in order to accommodate the overlap the bottom margin causes. Try a number of measurements on your own!

In Listing 13.4, I've created an embedded style sheet that includes margins, text alignment, and indents.

Listing 13.4 Margins, Alignment, and Indentation

```
<HTML>
<HEAD>
<TITLE>Margins, Alignment, Indents</TITLE>

<STYLE>

<!--

BODY {
margin-left: 1.00in;
margin-right: 1.00in;
margin-top: 1.00in;
margin-bottom: 1.00in;
}

H2 {
text-align: center;
}

P {
text-align: justify;
text-indent: .50in;
}

-->
```

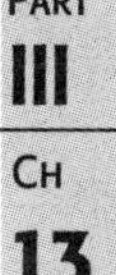

continues

LISTING 13.4 CONTINUED

```
</STYLE>

</HEAD>
<BODY>

<H2>A Midsummer Night's Dream</H2>

<P>Either to die the death or to abjure
For ever the society of men.</P>

<P>Therefore, fair <A href="hermia.html">Hermia</A>, question your desires;
Know of your youth, examine well your blood,
Whether, if you yield not to your father's choice,
You can endure the livery of a nun,
For aye to be in shady cloister mew'd,
To live a barren sister all your life,
Chanting faint hymns to the cold fruitless moon.</P>

<P>Thrice-blessed they that master so their blood,
To undergo such maiden <A HREF="pilgrim.html">pilgrimage</A>;
But earthlier happy is the rose distill'd,
Than that which withering on the virgin thorn
Grows, lives and dies in single blessedness.</P>

</BODY>
</HTML>
```

You can see the style results in Figure 13.7.

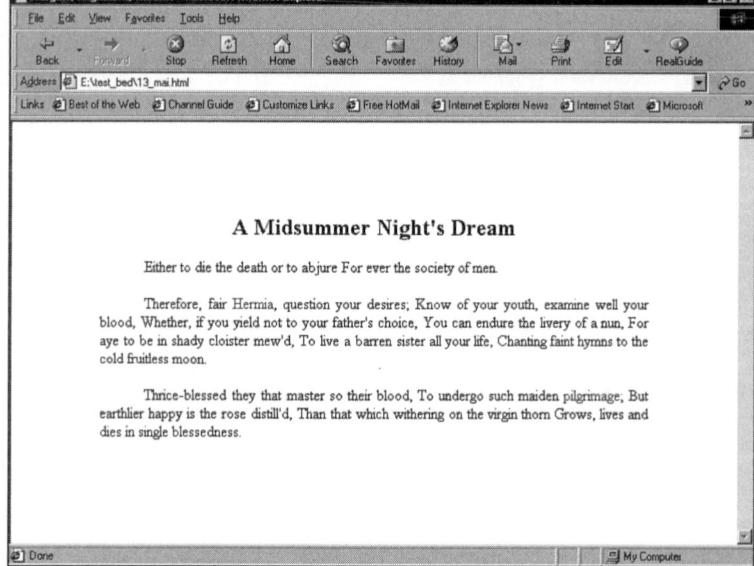

Figure 13.7
On this page, I used style sheets to control margins, alignment, and indentation.

You can create more detailed layouts if you study style sheets further; for example, you can add and control whitespace and also the placement and alignment of elements, overlays, and special effects.

Understanding Cascade and Inheritance

The term *cascading* refers primarily to the fact that not only can you use multiple styles in an individual HTML page, but also that the style-sheet–compliant browser will follow an order—a cascade—to interpret style information. You therefore can use all three style types, and the browser will interpret the linked styles first; embedded, second; and inline, last. Even though you might have master styles applied to an entire site, you can control aspects of individual pages with embedded styles and individual areas within those pages with inline styles.

Problems with your cascade? See "Cascade Woes," in the Troubleshooting section at the end of this chapter.

Another aspect of cascading is *inheritance*. This concept claims that unless you command otherwise, a particular style will be inherited by other influenced aspects of the HTML page. For example, if you command for a specific text color in a paragraph tag, all tags within that paragraph will inherit that color unless you state otherwise.

Created your style sheets and still aren't seeing the results as you thought you would? See "Troublesome Browsers," in the Troubleshooting section at the end of this chapter.

Exploring Class and Grouping

Two other interesting aspects of style sheets include class and grouping. *Class* refers to ways of breaking down your style rules into very precise pieces. Whenever you want some of the text on your pages to look different from the other text, you can create what amounts to a custom-built HTML tag. Each type of specially formatted text you define is called a *style class*.

For example, suppose you want two different kinds of `H1` headings in your documents. You can create a style class for each one by putting the following text in the style sheet:

```
<style>

<!--

H1.serif {
font: 24pt Century Schoolbook
}
H1.sans {
font: 18pt Arial
}

-->

</style>
```

You then assign the class `serif` or `sans` inline to achieve the results.

Grouping is achieved when style properties and values are condensed, resulting in tighter rules. Consider the following class example:

```
P.1 {
font: arial;
font-size: 13pt;
line-height: 14pt
}
```

In this example, all paragraphs with the class of 1 will show up as a 13-point Arial font with a line height of 14 points. If you apply grouping to this class, you end up with the following results:

```
P.1 {font: 13pt/14pt arial}
```

The design will be the same, either way. Notice, however, that you place the font size first, the line height after the forward slash, and then the name of the font.

Caution

Grouping requires a specific syntactical order to work properly. With type, the font size comes first, the line height comes second, and then the font name is included.

WORKING WITH CLASS

To get the most variation in style, assign classes to individual HTML tags. You do so very simply by adding a named extension to any HTML tag.

If you have two headers and two paragraph styles that you want to add attributes to, you can name each one and assign styles to the individual paragraphs. You then can call on the name within the specific HTML tag in the body of the document, as shown here:

```
<STYLE>

<!--

H1.left {
font: arial 14pt;
color: #FF0033;
text-align: left
}

H2.right {
font: arial 13pt;
color: #FF6633;
text-align: right
}

-->

</STYLE>
```

In the HTML, you place the class name:

```
<h1 class="left">This is my Left Heading</h2>
```

All the H1 headers that you name class="left" will have the H1.left class attributes. Similarly, the H2.right headers named class="right" will have the attributes defined for that class.

In Listing 13.5, I show an HTML page with the embedded style sheet and class combination used to achieve the page style.

Listing 13.5 Working with Classes

```
<HTML>
<HEAD>

<TITLE>style sheet sample: class</TITLE>
<STYLE>

<!--

P.center {
font-family: garamond, times, serif;
font-size: 14pt;
text-align: center;
}

P.right {
font-family: verdana, helvetica, sans-serif;
font-size: 13pt;
text-align: right;
}

P.name {
font-family: garamond, times, serif;
font-size: 10pt;
text-align: center;
text-weight: bold;
text-style: italic;
}

-->

</STYLE>

</HEAD>

<BODY>

<P class="center">
Brain researchers estimate that your unconscious data base outweighs the
conscious on an order exceeding ten million to one. This data base is the
source of your hidden, natural genius. In other words, a part of you is much
smarter than you are. The wise people regularly consult that smarter part.
</P>
```

continues

LISTING 13.5 CONTINUED

```
<P class="right">
Crazy people who are productive are geniuses. Crazy people who are rich are
eccentric. Crazy people who are neither productive nor rich are just plain
crazy. Geniuses and crazy people are both out in the middle of a deep ocean;
geniuses swim, crazy people drown. Most of us are sitting safely on the shore.
Take a chance and get your feet wet.
</P>

<P class="name">
-- Michael J. Gelb
</P>
</BODY>
</HTML>
```

Figure 13.8 shows class in action.

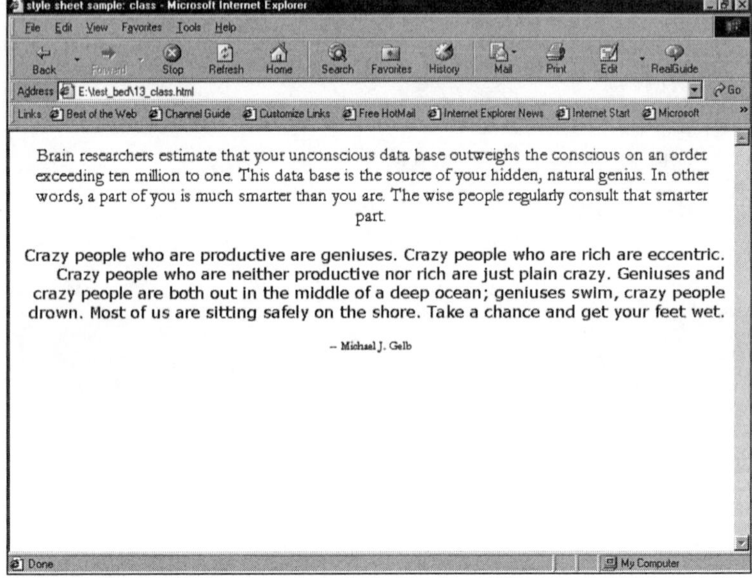

Figure 13.8
Using class, I varied the paragraph alignment and text appearance on this page.

If you'd like to create a custom class, you can do so by simply naming the class—it doesn't have to be attached to a familiar HTML selector. For example, let's say I'd like to have the style assigned to "right" in the previous example be globally useful to *any* HTML tag rather than just a paragraph tag. In this case, you'd write the style code as follows:

```
.right {
font-family: verdana, helvetica, sans-serif;
font-size: 13pt;
text-align: right;
}
```

Then, you'd add the style to any tag you like using the custom class. The information contained within that tag will pick up the style information described using the `right` custom class.

USING GROUPING

To group style sheets, you can do the following:

- Group multiple selectors
- Group properties and values

Say you want to assign the same properties to a number of header styles. One reason you might do so is to force all headers to update to a single style after attached to the sheet.

Without grouping, the code would look like this:

```
<STYLE>

<!--

H1 {
font-family: arial;
font-size 14pt;
color: #000000;
}

H2 {
font-family: arial;
font-size 14pt;
color: #000000;
}

H3 {
font-family: arial;
font-size 14pt;
color: #000000;
}

-->

</STYLE>
```


Here's the same example grouped:

```
H1, H2, H3 {
font-family: arial;
font-size 14pt;
color: #000000;
}
```

The processes of grouping properties and grouping values are similar in concept. Without grouping, an example of properties and values within the `BODY` would look like this:

```
BODY {
font-family: arial, san-serif;
font-size: 13pt;
```

```
line-height: 14pt;
font-weight: bold;
font- style: normal;
}
```

With grouping, you can simply name the attribute `font:` and then stack the arguments like this:

```
BODY {
font: bold normal 13pt/14pt arial, san-serif;
}
```

Note

When grouping properties and values, you must remember that order is significant. Font weight and style must come before other font properties, the size of the font must come before the leading, and then you can add additional information to the string.

To exemplify how order in grouping works, you can group margins using the `margin:` property. However, you must follow the property with the top, right, left, and bottom margin values in that order. Be sure to specify all these values when grouping; otherwise, you'll end up with the same value applied to all:

```
BODY {
margin: .10in .75in .75in .10in;
}
```

Note that no commas appear between the values. However, the declaration can end with a semicolon.

Listing 13.6 describes a style sheet using class and grouping.

LISTING 13.6 CLASS AND GROUPING

```
<HTML>
<HEAD>
<TITLE>Class and Grouping</TITLE>

<STYLE>

<!--

BODY {
margin: 0.10in 0.50in 0.50in;
}

H1.left {
font: 16pt ZapfChancery;
text-align: left;
}

H2.right {
font: 14pt ZapfChancery;
text-align: right;
color: #FF0033;
}
```

```
P.left {
font: 13pt/11pt garamond;
text-align: left;
}

P.right {
font: 13pt arial;
text-align: right;
margin: 0in .75in .50in;
}

A {
text-decoration: none;
font-weight: bold;
}

-->
</STYLE>

</HEAD>
<BODY>

<H1 class="left">A Midsummer Night's Dream</H1>

<P class="left">
Either to die the death or to abjure
For ever the society of men.
</P>

<P class="right">
Therefore, fair <A href="hermia.html">Hermia</A>,
question your desires;
Know of your youth, examine well your blood,
Whether, if you yield not to your father's choice,
You can endure the livery of a nun,
For aye to be in shady cloister mew'd,
To live a barren sister all your life,
Chanting faint hymns to the cold fruitless moon.
</P>

<P class="left">
Thrice-blessed they that master so their blood,
To undergo such maiden <A HREF="pilgrim.html">pilgrimage</A>;
But earthlier happy is the rose distill'd,
Than that which withering on the virgin thorn
Grows, lives and dies in single blessedness.
</P>

<H2 class="right">From Act I, Scene I</H2>

</BODY>
</HTML>
```

Figure 13.9 shows the combination of class and grouping.

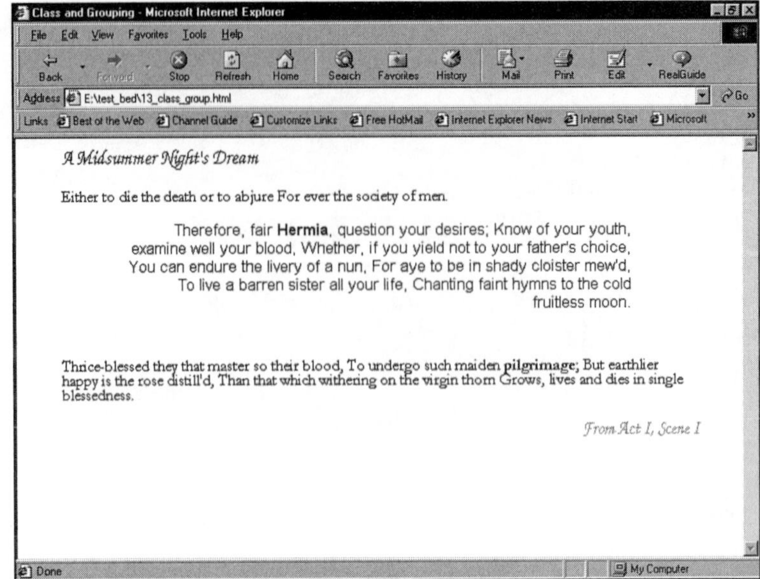

Figure 13.9
By combining class and grouping, you can achieve concise code and varied style.

More Style Resources

You will definitely require more information about style sheets if you find that you are using them regularly in your design work. Up-to-date style sheet resources are available on the Web, and many books address working with styles.

A primary online resource for style sheet information is the World Wide Web Consortium's style sheet section at **`http://www.w3c.org/Style/`**. In this area, you can find the complete specification and latest information on HTML style sheets.

Because Microsoft's Internet Explorer pioneered popular browser support of style sheets, Microsoft has accumulated some excellent references on its developer site at **`http://www.microsoft.com/sitebuilder/`**.

Another powerful style reference is the Web Review Style Sheets Reference Guide at **`http://style.webreview.com/`**. This page contains general information, and links to Eric Meyer's excellent style compatibility browser charts.

TROUBLESHOOTING

TROUBLESOME BROWSERS

I've put together a style sheet and checked the syntax. The style is picked up by IE, but not Netscape 4.0. What's the problem?

Netscape 4.0 is much less style-sheet-compliant than Microsoft IE 5.0 and earlier. Netscape 5.0 remedies much of these support concerns, but the version difference can be frustrating! The best recommendation I have is to not rely on style sheets if you want the best consistency for a wide range of even compliant browsers.

CASCADE WOES

I've got a linked style sheet, an embedded style sheet, and an inline style set to cascade. Something isn't working right. How can I fix it?

The best way to troubleshoot problems in a cascade is to comment out any embedded and inline style, and unlink from the linked style sheet. Test the page without any style. Are there any errors? If not, go ahead and add the inline style back in and test. Does it work? If so, add the embedded style sheet. Does the linked style override the embedded style that it's supposed to? If not, look carefully at your code for any errors. If so, go ahead and look at the page with the linked style only. If you are error free at this point, with no problems in either the HTML or CSS code, it's likely there is a compatibility or non-compliance issue with the browser you're using.

DESIGNING FOR THE REAL WORLD

CREATING BACKWARD COMPATIBLE STYLE

If you'd like to create an HTML 4.0 document that uses style sheets and provides backward compatibility for non-compliant browsers, the way to go is to use HTML 4.0 transitional.

1. To do this, first design a page that sets up the design in a more conventional HTML 3.2 fashion:

```
<HTML>
<HEAD>
    <TITLE>molly.com: info</TITLE>

</HEAD>

<BODY BGCOLOR="#FFCC66" TEXT="#000000" LINK="#999933" VLINK="#CC3300"
➥ALINK="#CCCC66">

<FONT FACE="arial, helvetica, sans-serif" COLOR="#CC3300" SIZE="4">
<H1>Molly Info</H1>
</FONT>

<FONT FACE="arial, helvetica, sans-serif" COLOR="#000000">
<P>What do you do? I hate that question! I'm never sure what to answer,
because people expect to hear one thing. We're all multi-faceted, and we are
not our jobs.

<P>So what do I do? I teach. I write. I design Web sites. I consult. I love
people, music, animals, travel. Which of these things really defines me? I
can't say. But here are some bits of information about me that might help
others define me, if they feel it necessary to do so.
</FONT>

<FONT FACE="arial, helvetica, sans-serif" COLOR="#CC3300">
<P><B>Molly's Current Bio</B>
</FONT>

<FONT FACE="arial, helvetica, sans-serif" COLOR="#000000">
```

```
<P>An author, instructor, and designer, Molly E. Holzschlag brings her
irrepressible enthusiasm to books, classrooms, and Web sites. Honored as one
of the Top 25 Most Influential Women on the Web, Molly has spent an almost
unprecedented decade working in the online world. She has written and
contributed to more than ten books about the Internet and, in particular, the
Web. She holds a B.A. in communications and writing, and a M.A. in media
studies from the New School for Social Research.
</FONT>

<FONT FACE="arial, helvetica, sans-serif" COLOR="#CC3300">
<P><B>Photos</B>
</FONT>

<FONT FACE="arial, helvetica, sans-serif" COLOR="#000000">
<P>A few <A HREF="pics.html"><B>pics</B></A> for you to enjoy.
</FONT>

<DIV ALIGN="right">
<FONT FACE="arial, helvetica, sans-serif" SIZE="2" COLOR="#999933">
<P><A HREF="contact.html"><B>get in touch</B></A><BR>
&copy; copyright 1999, molly e. holzschlag<BR>
<A HREF="credits.html">click for credits & service mark info</A></FONT>
</DIV>

</BODY>
</HTML>
```

2. Test the page and see if you like the results (see Figure 13.10).

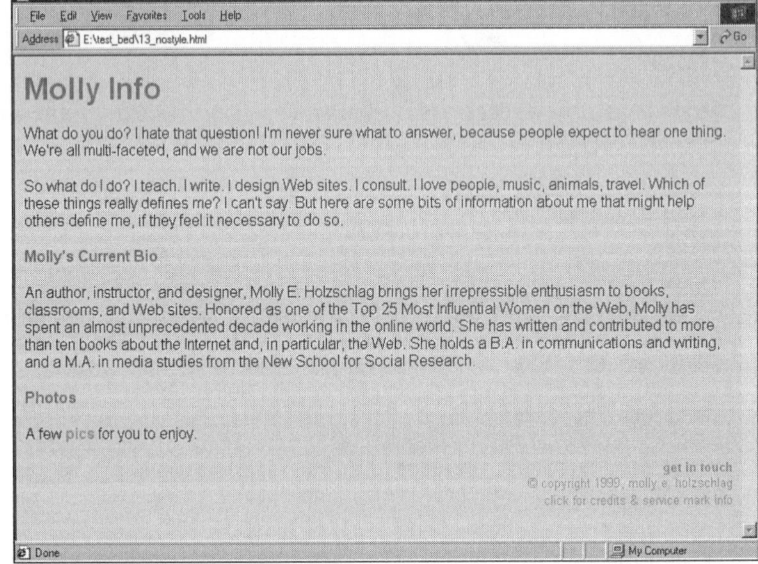

Figure 13.10
An HTML 3.2 document provides the basis for the transitional 4.0 document with style.

3. Create a style sheet that manages the style elements of the page. You can create this sheet as either embedded or linked:

```
<HTML>
<HEAD>
    <TITLE>molly.com: info</TITLE>


<!-- begin style -->

<STYLE>

BODY  {
    color : #FFCC66;
}

P  {
    font-size : 11pt;
    font-family : arial, helvetica, sans-serif;
    color : #000000;
    line-height : 12pt;
}

H1 {
    font-size : 14pt;
    font-family : arial, helvetica, sans-serif;
    color: #CC3300;
}

A  {
    color : #999933;
    font-weight: bold;
}

A:Visited  {
    color : #CC3300;

}

A:Active  {
    color : #CCCC66;
}

A:Hover  {
    color : #FFFFFF;
}

.redheader  {
    font-size : 11pt;
    font-family : arial, helvetica, sans-serif;
    color: #CC3300;
    font-weight : bold;
}

.address  {
    font-size : 8pt;
    color: #999933;
    font-family : arial, helvetica, sans-serif;
}
```

```
</STYLE>

</HEAD>

<BODY BGCOLOR="#FFCC66" TEXT="#000000" LINK="#999933" VLINK="#CC3300"
➥ALINK="#CCCC66">

<FONT FACE="arial, helvetica, sans-serif" COLOR="#CC3300" SIZE="4">
<H1>Molly Info</H1>
</FONT>

<FONT FACE="arial, helvetica, sans-serif" COLOR="#000000">

<P>What do you do? I hate that question! I'm never sure what to answer,
because people expect to hear one thing. We're all multi-faceted, and we are
not our jobs.
<P>So what do I do? I teach. I write. I design Web sites. I consult. I love
people, music, animals, travel. Which of these things really defines me? I
can't say. But here are some bits of information about me that might help
others define me, if they feel it necessary to do so.
</FONT>

<FONT FACE="arial, helvetica, sans-serif" COLOR="#CC3300">
<P CLASS="redheader"><B>Molly's Current Bio</B>
</FONT>

<FONT FACE="arial, helvetica, sans-serif" COLOR="#000000">
<P>An author, instructor, and designer, Molly E. Holzschlag brings her
irrepressible enthusiasm to books, classrooms, and Web sites. Honored as one
of the Top 25 Most Influential Women on the Web, Molly has spent an almost
unprecedented decade working in the online world. She has written and
contributed to more than ten books about the Internet and, in particular, the
Web. She holds a B.A. in communications and writing, and a M.A. in media
studies from the New School for Social Research.
</FONT>

<FONT FACE="arial, helvetica, sans-serif" COLOR="#CC3300">
<P CLASS="redheader"><B>Photos</B>
</FONT>

<FONT FACE="arial, helvetica, sans-serif" COLOR="#000000">
<P>A few <A HREF="pics.html"><B>pics</B></A> for you to enjoy.
</FONT>

<DIV ALIGN="right">
<FONT FACE="arial, helvetica, sans-serif" SIZE="2" COLOR="#999933">
<SPAN CLASS="address">
<P><A HREF="contact.html"><B>get in touch</B></A><BR>
&copy; copyright 1999, molly e. holzschlag<BR>
<A HREF="credits.html">click for credits & service mark info</A></SPAN></FONT>
</DIV>

</BODY>
</HTML>
```

4. Test your page in a style-sheet–compliant browser.

Your audiences without style-sheet–compliant browsers will get an acceptably presented page, and those with style sheet support will gain the refined presentation that style sheets afford (see Figure 13.11).

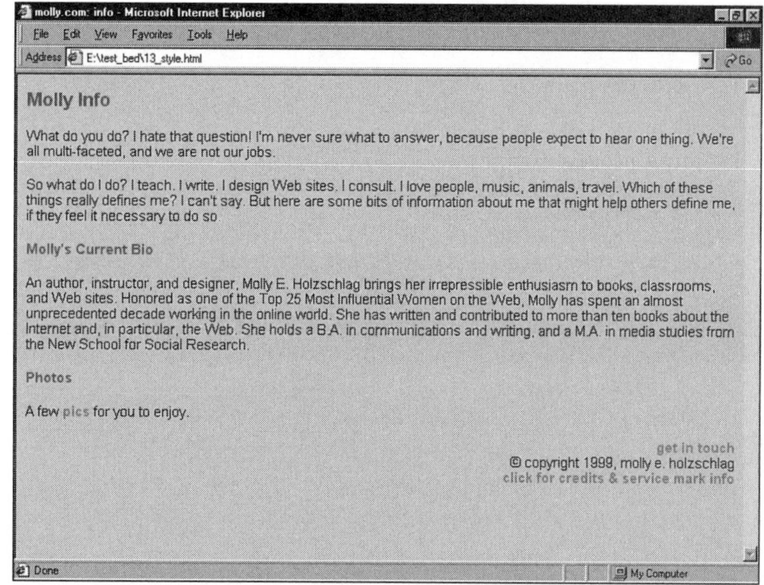

Figure 13.11
Add style, and you get a refined look. In this case, the colors, type size, and type style are all affected in ways that are not approachable without style sheets.

Note

To make this page a strict HTML 4.0 page, remove all HTML 3.2 presentation elements, such as the FONT tags, and the BODY attributes, ultimately relying on *only* the style sheet for the page's style.

CHAPTER 14

DESIGNING TYPE WITH CSS

In this chapter

DESIGNING TYPE IN HTML 4.0

Setting type using style sheets is one of the most exciting design aspects of HTML 4.0. Not only do you have the ability to call for many type styles to appear on a page or a site, but you also have the control that only the methods of style allow.

→ Test the integrity of your style sheet fundamentals, **see** "Cascading Style Sheet Techniques," **p. 254**

This control becomes especially important when you're creating large sites. Instead of having to work with multiple, worrisome `<FONT>` tags and attributes, with HTML 4.0 you can create a single style sheet that defines all the styles required for the entire site, including a variety of links, specialty links, anchors, and lists.

Instead of the `<FONT>` tag, you now can use the style sheet property `font-family`. You can then add a variety of values along with it, or you can use classes and grouping to fully flex the power of type through the use of style sheets. What's more, you can add a wide variety of typographic conventions to type that extend far above and beyond the `FONT` element, providing you with extended options and more refined design results.

The Trouble with Fonts

The reality of font support in style sheets is much the same as those issues encountered by the designer when employing the `<FONT>` tag and its attributes. The specific typeface must be available on the computer viewing your page. And, as with the `<FONT>` tag, style sheets do allow you to stack any number of typefaces so that you can maximize the chances that your browser will pick up a typeface that you want your audience to see.

If the people viewing your pages don't have Arial, for example, they'll probably have Helvetica, and so forth. Although these typefaces have some minor differences, they are similar enough to be considered workable in the context of style sheet design.

STYLE SHEET FONT FAMILIES

Style sheets recognize five font families, attempting to address the major family groups available in typography.

Note

In HTML 4.0, font categories, or master families, are simply referred to as *families*. This terminology is one of the confusing differences found between the technology of the Web and the older, venerable typographic standards.

For style sheets, five font categories, or master families, are defined, as shown in Table 14.1.

Table 14.1 Font Categories

Font Category	Description
Serif	Serif faces are those faces with strokes. These strokes are said to aid in readability; therefore, serif typefaces are often very popular for printed body text. Some examples of serif faces include Times, Garamond, and Century Schoolbook.
Sans Serif	These typefaces tend to be rounded and have no strokes. Common sans-serif faces include Helvetica, Arial, Avant Garde, and Verdana.
Script	A script face is one that looks similar to cursive writing or handwriting. Common script typefaces include Park Avenue and Lucida Handwriting.
Monospace	These faces look like typewriter fonts. They are called monospace fonts because each letter within the face takes up the same width as another. For example, the letter *w*, which is wider in most faces than an *i*, is actually the same width in a monospace font. Courier is the common monospace font found on both the Windows and Macintosh platforms.
Fantasy	Referred to by most typographers as *decorative*, the fonts available in this category are best used for headers and artistic text rather than body text. Decorative fonts include Whimsy and Party.

→ For advanced details regarding type conventions, **see** "Graphic Type for the Web," **p. 624**

To apply a family inline, you follow a stacking convention such as is found with the <FONT> tag. You do so in all cases of style, whether using the inline, embedded, or linked methods.

Here's an inline example:

```
<p style="font-family: arial, helvetica, sans-serif">
In this selection, the browser will search the user's computer for the Arial
font. If it's found, it will be displayed. If it isn't found, it will look for
Helvetica. If neither is found, the browser will display the first sans-serif
typeface available.
</p>
```

In Listing 14.1, I've taken this paragraph and added it to an HTML page with other text that has no style or font information added.

Listing 14.1 Style Applied to a Single Paragraph

```
<HTML>
<HEAD>

<TITLE>style sheet sample</TITLE>
</HEAD>

<BODY>
<P>
This paragraph has no style or font information added to it. Therefore, it
relies on the browser's own defaults for a typeface. You'll see this paragraph
appear in Times
</P>
```


continues

LISTING 14.1 CONTINUED

```
<P style="font-family: arial, helvetica, sans-serif">
In this selection, the browser will search the user's computer for the Arial
font. If it's found, it will be displayed. If it isn't found, it will look for
Helvetica. If neither is found, the browser will display the first sans-serif
typeface available.
</P>
</BODY>
</HTML>
```

Figure 14.1 shows the difference between the first paragraph, with only the browser's defaults to figure out what typeface to include, and the second paragraph, where the typeface is controlled by style.

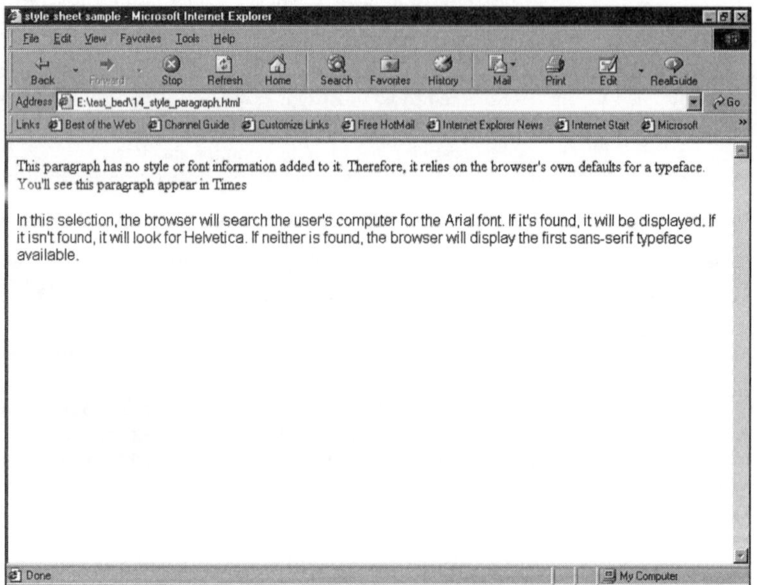

Figure 14.1
The default font compared to the Arial font created with style sheets.

Caution

You are always in some danger that you'll lose control with typefaces, particularly those within the Fantasy family. The Fantasy fonts tend to be the ones that are installed by individuals rather than shipped with the computer in question.

➔ For a complete list of Windows and Macintosh system fonts, **see** "Working with Fonts," **p. 244**

TYPE PROPERTIES AND VALUES

You can apply a range of properties to typefaces using style sheets, and you can apply an admirable selection of values to those properties. I'll focus on the most immediate and familiar here so that you can get started quickly using them in your designs.

As with standard HTML fonts, properties are available to control size and color. With style sheets, unlike HTML fonts, you can also control the weight and style of a typeface, as well as line height, also known as *leading*, which is the measurement between individual lines of set type.

Furthermore, the available methods to control font size are very specific, and far exceed anything that HTML prior to the 4.0 standard has to offer.

Setting Type Size

You can accomplish sizing by using the `font-size` property or using grouped properties.

→ To find out more about grouping properties, **see** "Cascading Style Sheet Techniques," **p. 269**

Type size in style sheets can be defined using points, pixels, inches, centimeters, millimeters, and picas. For Web designers, points or pixels are going to be the most natural choice, although this choice ultimately depends on your preferences.

Want to develop sites using style exclusively? Find out when you can in "The Advantage of Intranet Design" in the Troubleshooting section at the end of this chapter.

I prefer to stick with points, because this is the measurement I use when setting graphical type for the Web. This way, a streamlined, consistent effect is achieved.

Caution

Although having so many size options is undeniably exciting, using measurements other than points can create some serious problems. One of these problems is the no-print phenomenon found when pixels are used as a measurement rather than points. Although the type will appear in style sheet browsers, such as Internet Explorer 3.0 and higher and Netscape 4.0 and higher, type defined in pixels may not print. For the sake of stability and consistency, I recommend using points as a preferred measurement when you're setting type using style sheets.

The following is an example of inline style setting the size of the typeface in points:

```
<p style="font-family: century schoolbook, times, serif; font-size: 24pt;">

"The most beautiful thing we can experience is the mysterious; It is the source
of all true art and science"
<BR>
-- Albert Einstein

</p>
```

Figure 14.2 shows how the font face and size are applied to this quote.

In this instance, I've set up a style sheet that can be embedded into a single page or linked to from a page. The style then affects any standard paragraphs on that page:

```
<STYLE>

<!--

P{
```

```
font-family: arial, helvetica, sans-serif;
font-size: 14pt;

     }

-->

</STYLE>
```

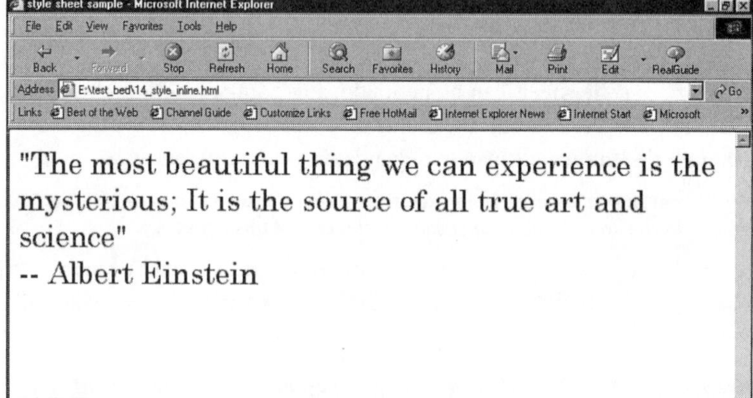

Figure 14.2
Using inline style, I applied the Century Schoolbook font at 24 points.

In Figure 14.3, you can see the embedded style sheet in action. The text is now made up of 14-point Arial text.

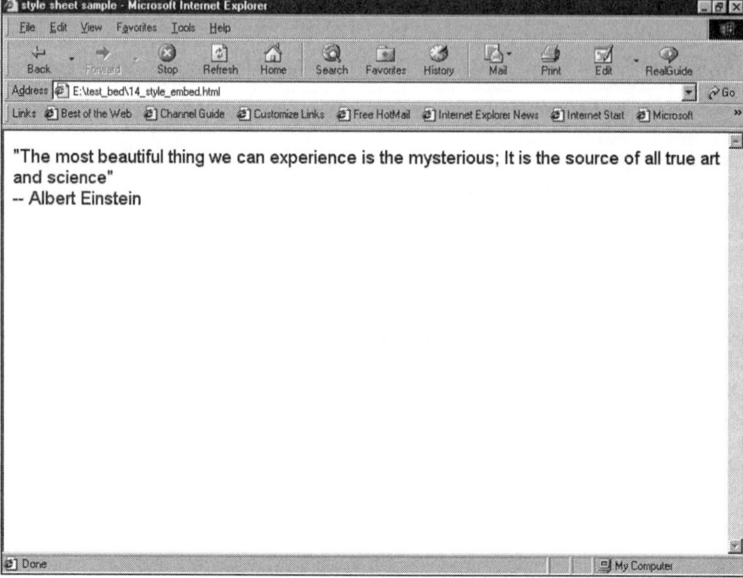

Figure 14.3
Here, an embedded style sheet set the text to 14-point Helvetica.

Note

In Chapter 12, "Working with Fonts," I discussed the issue of *font smoothing*. This method, used in Windows 95 and higher, smoothes out the often jagged edges that appear when fonts render on a computer screen. Even with font smoothing installed, it does not influence any kind of font that is not a TrueType font. PostScript fonts, such as the Helvetica that I am using, may appear with jagged edges despite the smoothing option.

Tip from molly

To ensure that people with Windows font smoothing turned on see smooth fonts, call for TrueType fonts first, and then any other kind of fonts you want to put in the set. For example, if you're creating a conventional sans-serif set, use Arial before Helvetica. Windows machines will receive the sans-serif, smooth font, and Mac visitors will see Helvetica.

Adding Color

Style sheets rely on standard browser color techniques. In other words, you'll use hexadecimal—and preferably browser-safe—colors for the best results.

Note

You can use RGB (Red, Green, Blue) values in style sheets, too. Most hand coders stick with hex, whereas some WYSIWYG programs use the RGB values instead.

→ To learn about hexadecimal color, **see** "Color Concepts," **p. 537**

You can add color, like all style properties, to any reasonable HTML tag using inline, embedded, or linked sheet methods, with the `color` property.

To add a typeface, type size, and color to an HTML page, follow these steps:

1. Begin with an HTML shell:

```
<HTML>
<HEAD>

<TITLE>style sheet sample</TITLE>
</HEAD>

<BODY>


</BODY>
</HTML>
```

2. Add a paragraph of text:

```
<HTML>
<HEAD>

<TITLE>style sheet sample</TITLE>
</HEAD>

<BODY>
```

```
A human being is a part of the whole called by us universe, a part limited in
time and space. He experiences himself, his thoughts and feeling as something
separated from the rest, a kind of optical delusion of his consciousness. This
delusion is a kind of prison for us, restricting us to our personal desires
and to affection for a few persons nearest to us. Our task must be to free
ourselves from this prison by widening our circle of compassion to enhance all
living creatures and the whole of nature in its beauty -- Albert Einstein


</BODY>
</HTML>
```

3. Add the paragraph tags, using both an open and closing tag (open/close method):

```
<HTML>
<HEAD>

<TITLE>style sheet sample</TITLE>
</HEAD>

<BODY>

<P>
A human being is a part of the whole called by us universe, a part limited in
time and space. He experiences himself, his thoughts and feeling as something
separated from the rest, a kind of optical delusion of his consciousness. This
delusion is a kind of prison for us, restricting us to our personal desires
and to affection for a few persons nearest to us. Our task must be to free
ourselves from this prison by widening our circle of compassion to enhance all
living creatures and the whole of nature in its beauty -- Albert Einstein
</P>

</BODY>
</HTML>
```

4. To the opening paragraph tag, add the `font-family` property and its associated values:

```
<HTML>
<HEAD>

<TITLE>style sheet sample</TITLE>
</HEAD>

<BODY>

<P style="font-family: courier new, courier, monospace;">
A human being is a part of the whole called by us universe, a part limited in
time and space. He experiences himself, his thoughts and feeling as something
separated from the rest, a kind of optical delusion of his consciousness. This
delusion is a kind of prison for us, restricting us to our personal desires
and to affection for a few persons nearest to us. Our task must be to free
ourselves from this prison by widening our circle of compassion to enhance all
living creatures and the whole of nature in its beauty -- Albert Einstein
</P>

</BODY>
</HTML>
```

5. Add the point size:

```
<HTML>
<HEAD>

<TITLE>style sheet sample</TITLE>
</HEAD>

<BODY>

<P style="font-family: courier new, courier, monospace; font-size: 12pt;">
A human being is a part of the whole called by us universe, a part limited in
time and space. He experiences himself, his thoughts and feeling as something
separated from the rest, a kind of optical delusion of his consciousness. This
delusion is a kind of prison for us, restricting us to our personal desires
and to affection for a few persons nearest to us. Our task must be to free
ourselves from this prison by widening our circle of compassion to enhance all
living creatures and the whole of nature in its beauty -- Albert Einstein
</P>

</BODY>
</HTML>
```

6. Choose a hexadecimal color, and add the color property and value to the string:

```
<HTML>
<HEAD>

<TITLE>style sheet sample</TITLE>
</HEAD>
<BODY>

<P style="font-family: courier new, courier, monospace; font-size: 12pt;
color: #999999";>

A human being is a part of the whole called by us universe, a part limited in
time and space. He experiences himself, his thoughts and feeling as something
separated from the rest, a kind of optical delusion of his consciousness. This
delusion is a kind of prison for us, restricting us to our personal desires
and to affection for a few persons nearest to us. Our task must be to free
ourselves from this prison by widening our circle of compassion to enhance all
living creatures and the whole of nature in its beauty -- Albert Einstein
</P>

</BODY>
</HTML>
```

7. Save the file as `style_color.html`.
8. View the file in your browser.

Your paragraph should appear in gray. Compare your results with mine, shown in Figure 14.4.

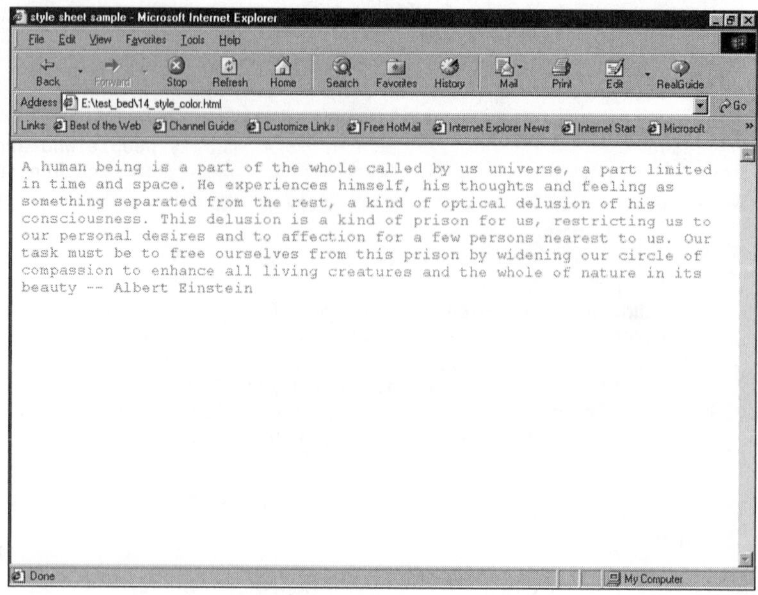

Figure 14.4
In this instance, I've added gray to a typeface using style.

In Listing 14.2, I use another color, type selection, and type size within the STYLE element.

LISTING 14.2 EMBEDDED STYLE WITH FACE, SIZE, AND COLOR

```
<HTML>
<HEAD>

<TITLE>style sheet sample: embedded</TITLE>
<STYLE>

<!—

P {
font-family: garamond, times, serif;
font-size: 18pt;
color: #CC9966;
}

—>

</STYLE>

</HEAD>

<BODY>
<P>
Brain researchers estimate that your unconscious data base outweighs the
conscious on an order exceeding ten million to one. This data base is the
```

```
source of your hidden, natural genius. In other words, a part of you is much
smarter than you are. The wise people regularly consult that smarter part.
</P>

<P>
Crazy people who are productive are geniuses. Crazy people who are rich are
eccentric. Crazy people who are neither productive nor rich are just plain
crazy. Geniuses and crazy people are both out in the middle of a deep ocean;
geniuses swim, crazy people drown. Most of us are sitting safely on the shore.
Take a chance and get your feet wet.
</P>

<P align="left">
— Michael J. Gelb
</P>
</BODY>
</HTML>
```

Figure 14.5 shows the results.

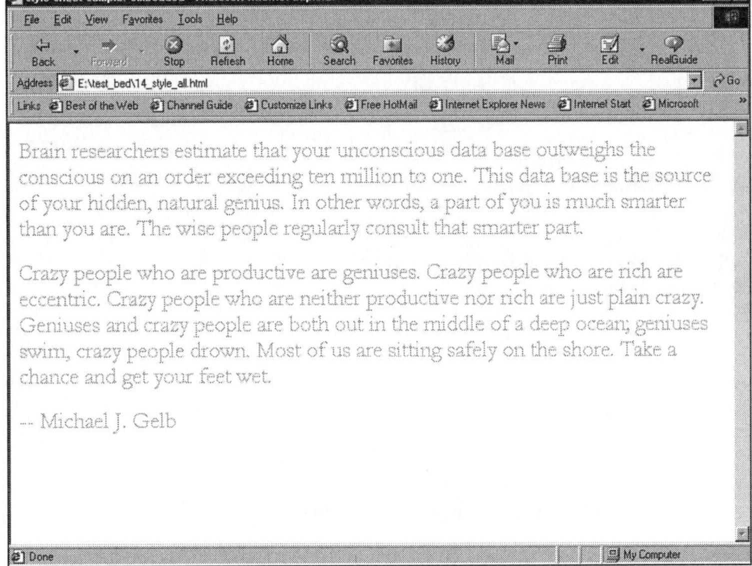

Figure 14.5
The font face is Garamond, the color is sienna (which will show up as gray in the figure but sienna if you test the code in your browser), and a font size of 18 points.

ADDING WEIGHT TO TYPE

Weight is how thick or thin a typeface is. The Arial face, for example, has variations in weight including black (a very heavy face), bold, light, and so forth.

Because typefaces have different variants, unless you are absolutely sure that visitors to your site have a specific typeface, you generally should apply a value that is going to be available to all typefaces you are using in a value. The one near-global value for typefaces is bold.

Having trouble with inline style? See "Come on Inline!," in the Troubleshooting section at the end of this chapter.

The primary purpose, then, for the `font-weight` property is to make a given typeface bold.

Here's an example of weight applied inline:

```
<P style="font-family: arial, helvetica, sans-serif; font-weight: bold;
font-size: 14pt; color=#CCCCCC;">
"I studied the lives of great men and famous women, and I found that the men and
women who got to the top were those who did the jobs they had in hand, with
everything they had of energy and enthusiasm."  -- Harry S. Truman
</P>
```

You can also apply weight to an embedded or linked sheet. In Listing 14.3, I've applied the bold to a header size 1 but have left the paragraph at a standard weight.

LISTING 14.3 USING THE `font-weight` PROPERTY IN A HEADER

```
<HTML>
<HEAD>

<TITLE>style sheet sample: embedded</TITLE>

<STYLE>

<!—

H1 {
font-family: helvetica, arial, sans-serif;
font-weight: bold;
color: #CC9966;
}
P {
font-family: garamond, times, serif;
color: #999999;
}

—>
</STYLE>

</HEAD>

<BODY>
<H1>Quotations from Michael J. Gelb</H1>
<P>
"Brain researchers estimate that your unconscious data base outweighs the
conscious on an order exceeding ten million to one. This data base is the source
of your hidden, natural genius. In other words, a part of you is much smarter
than you are. The wise people regularly consult that smarter part."
</P>

<P>
"Crazy people who are productive are geniuses. Crazy people who are rich are
eccentric. Crazy people who are neither productive nor rich are just plain
crazy. Geniuses and crazy people are both out in the middle of a deep ocean;
geniuses swim, crazy people drown. Most of us are sitting safely on the shore.
Take a chance and get your feet wet."
</P>
```

```
</BODY>
</HTML>
```

Figure 14.6 shows the results.

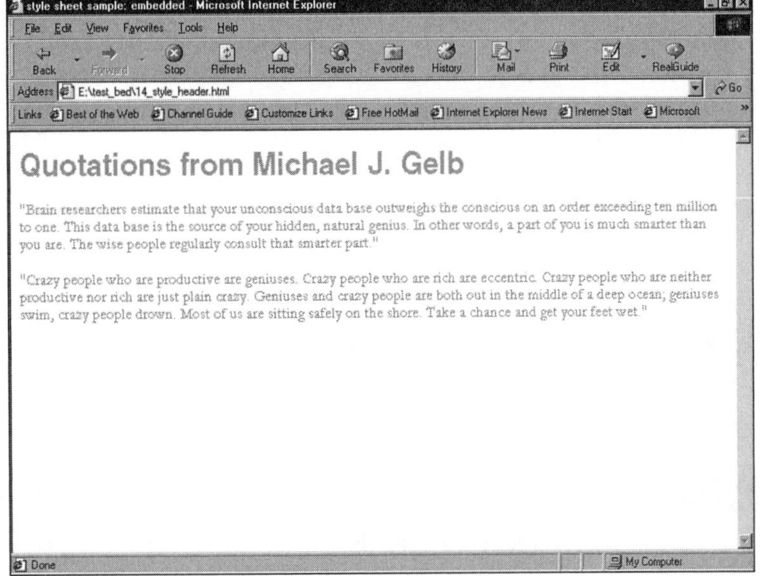

Figure 14.6
The header and paragraph in this example take on different styles as defined by an embedded sheet.

APPLYING FONT STYLE

In this context, *style* refers to the slant of a given typeface. The two styles are italic and oblique. As with weight variations, oblique is a rare option and should be used cautiously. However, italic style is available in most typefaces, so you're pretty safe using it wherever you require italics.

The following is an example of inline font style:

```
<P style="font-family: century schoolbook, times, serif; font-style: italic;
font-size: 14pt; color=#999999;">

"I studied the lives of great men and famous women, and I found that the men and
women who got to the top were those who did the jobs they had in hand, with
everything they had of energy and enthusiasm."  -- Harry S. Truman

</P>
```

Figure 14.7 shows this passage in Century Schoolbook 14-point italics.

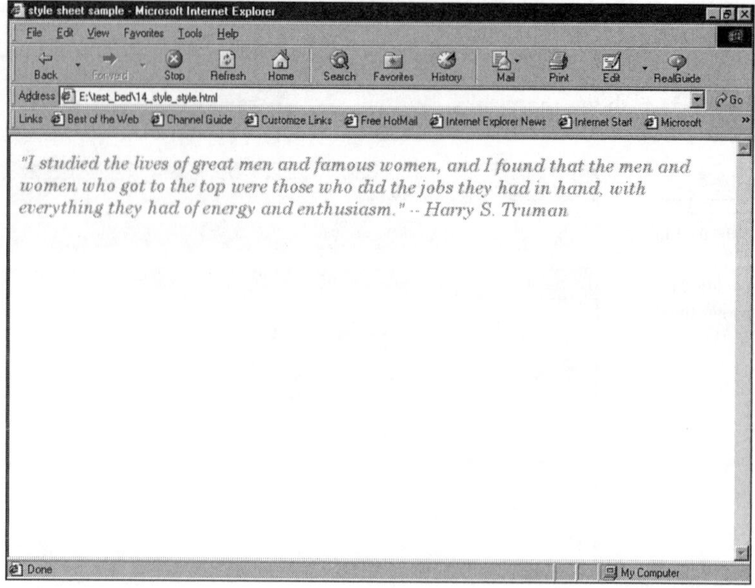

Figure 14.7
Applying italics with the `font-style` property.

Caution

As I've said several times throughout this book, you should use italics and bold sparingly. Their primary function in body type is to emphasize passages of text. Excessive use of bold or italics compromises readability.

SETTING LEADING

Leading is the space between individual lines of text. Normal default leading is usually the same or very near to the point size of the type being used. For example, when you have 12-point type, the leading is going to look very natural at 12 points, too.

To control leading with style sheets, you can use the `line-height` property. Its value is numeric, in whatever measurement you're using. As I've mentioned, I prefer points for a number of reasons.

Listing 14.4 shows normal default line height, followed by a larger value, and in the last paragraph, the line height is a smaller value—making the distance between the lines shorter.

LISTING 14.4 ADDING LINE HEIGHT

```
<HTML>
<HEAD>

<TITLE>A Midsummer Night's Dream</TITLE>

</HEAD>

<BODY>
```

```
<P style="font-family: courier new, courier, monospace; font-size: 12pt; color:
#999999;">
Call you me fair? that fair again unsay.
Demetrius loves your fair: O happy fair!
Your eyes are lode-stars; and your tongue's sweet air
More tuneable, than lark to shepherd's ear,
When wheat is green, when hawthorn buds appear.
</P>

<P style="font-family: courier new, courier, monospace;
font-size: 12pt; line-height: 18pt; color: #999999;">
Sickness is catching: O, were favour so,
Yours would I catch, fair Hermia, ere I go;
My ear should catch your voice, my eye your eye,
My tongue should catch your tongue's sweet melody.
</P>

<P style="font-family: courier new, courier, monospace;
font-size: 12pt; line-height: 9pt; color: #999999;">
Were the world mine, Demetrius being bated,
The rest I'd give to be to you translated.
O, teach me how you look, and with what art
You sway the motion of Demetrius' heart.
</P>

</BODY>
</HTML>
```

Figure 14.8 shows how leading affects each paragraph.

Figure 14.8
Leading, or line height, is applied to this selection of text.

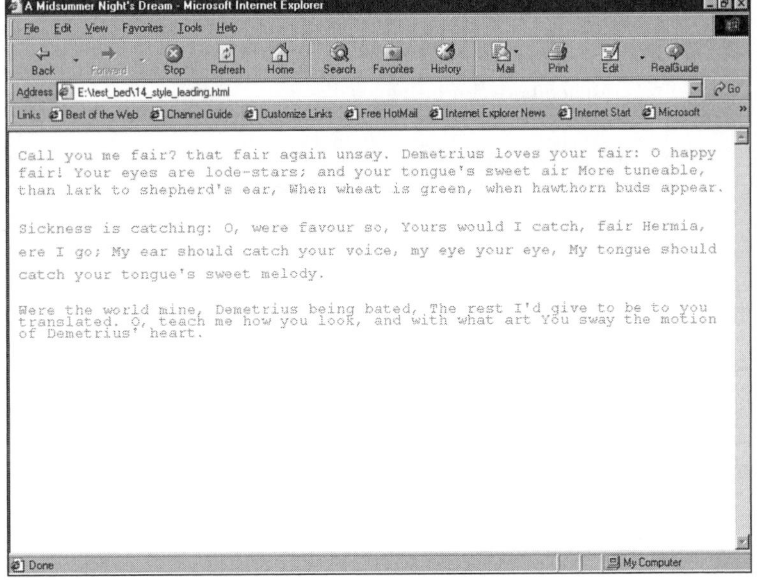

USING TEXT DECORATION AND BACKGROUND

You also should be aware of several other type options, including the following:

- **text-decoration**—This property is extremely useful for turning off link underlining within an anchor. To do so, set `text-decoration` to a value of `none`. The values of `underline`, `italic`, and `line-through` are also supported.
- **background**—If you want to place a color or image behind text, you can do so by using this property. Either use a hexadecimal color or a URL (address) where that address points to a background image tile. Note that you can assign this option not only to the <BODY> tag, but also to any tag or span of text to "highlight" an area on a page.

Listing 14.5 demonstrates a page with the use of text decoration and background.

LISTING 14.5 TEXT DECORATION AND BACKGROUND SETTINGS

```
<HTML>
<HEAD>

<TITLE>A Midsummer Night's Dream</TITLE>

</HEAD>

<BODY>

<P style="font-family: courier new, courier, monospace; font-size: 12pt; color:
#999999;">
Call you me fair? that fair again unsay.
<A href="demetrius.html" style="text-decoration: line-through;">Demetrius</A>
loves your fair: O happy fair!
Your eyes are lode-stars; and your tongue's sweet air
More tuneable, than lark to shepherd's ear,
When wheat is green, when hawthorn buds appear.
Sickness is catching: O, were favour so,
Yours would I catch, fair <A href="hermia.html"
style="text-decoration: none">Hermia</A>, ere I go;
My ear should catch your voice, my eye your eye,
My tongue should catch your tongue's sweet melody.
</P>
<P style="background: #000000; font-family: courier new, courier, monospace; font-
size: 12pt; color: #FFFFFF">
Were the world mine, Demetrius being bated,
The rest I'd give to be to you translated.
O, teach me how you look, and with what art
You sway the motion of Demetrius' heart.
</P>

</BODY>
</HTML>
```

In Figure 14.9, you can see that the first link has been struck through. The second link, however, has no strikethrough. Finally, I've used black to set a background against the final paragraph. This trick can be very handy when you're creating sidebars or offsetting text for emphasis.

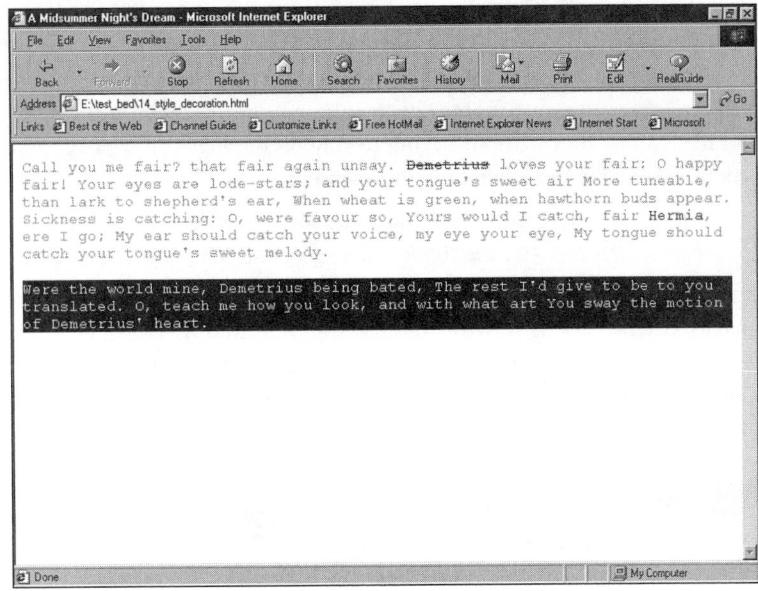

Figure 14.9 The first link in this case has a strikethrough. Notice also the black background achieved behind the bottom paragraph.

→ For information on creating margins and indents, **see** "Cascading Style Sheet Techniques," **p. 264**

→ Positioning and style sheet scripting effects can also be reviewed, **see** "Element Positioning and Style Sheet Scripting," **p. 430**

→ For a comprehensive look at style properties and values, **see** "CSS Reference," **p. 1016**

STYLE SHEET EVOLUTION

Are you having fun yet? I hate to be a spoilsport, but I'm here to let you know that despite the great control style sheets can offer you typographically, you still encounter the problem of cross-browser interoperability.

The ugly truth remains that if you want to appeal to the widest Web audience and keep your designs intact, you need to design across browsers. However, if you combine the FONT element and style sheets, you can create pages that look good for those browsers that support fonts and even better for those visitors who have style-sheet–enabled browsers.

→ For a project exercise in which you create a backward-compatible style sheet, **see** "Cascading Style Sheet Techniques," **p. 277**

Another issue is the ever-chaotic state of affairs at the World Wide Web Consortium (W3C). At this writing, the style sheet recommendation is level CSS2. The additions to the recommendation add a lot of functionality, without changing anything too significant in the basic concepts in CSS1.

However, XSL, which is the style sheet component to XML, is a different story. This style sheet language is also under development, adding more spice to the style soup.

As of May 12, 1998, Cascading Style Sheets version II (CSS2) became the recommendation from the World Wide Web Consortium. Although few properties have been altered, much has been added. These additions include advanced positioning and—most specific to this chapter—downloadable fonts. This feature will most certainly aid you in getting the look and feel you're after without having to rely on the lick-and-a-promise method of stacking typefaces into the style sheet or FONT element.

→ For more information on both CSS1 and CSS2, **see** "CSS Reference," **p. 1016**

→ For details on XML and XSL, **see** "Understanding XHTML, XML, and Emerging Languages," **p. 492**

XSL, or the eXtensible Style Language, has been added to the W3C's working draft of languages. XSL works with XML to modify style within XML pages. The draft specifies that XSL is to be seen as a supportive piece to CSS in that although CSS affects HTML documents, XSL works with XML to create and modify HTML documents, creating a chain of powerful style options.

Note

For more information on both CSS2 and XSL, a visit to the World Wide Web Consortium at `http://w3.org/style/` is in order.

TROUBLESHOOTING

THE ADVANTAGE OF INTRANET DESIGN

I'm creating an intranet design for my company, which uses Microsoft Internet Explorer 4.0 and above exclusively. Can I use style sheets for text design with strict HTML 4.0?

The advantage of designing for closed sites where you have definitive information about the browsers in use, making decisions regarding style sheets and strict HTML 4.0 becomes easy. You immediately see whether or not your users can support them, and after you have that information, you can decide how best to code the pages you create.

→ To learn about intranets, **see** "Designing Corporate Intranets and Extranets," **p. 848**

COME ON INLINE!

I want to set only one letter of a word to a different font size and style, achieving a "drop-cap" effect. How can I do this effectively?

Use inline style with the SPAN element and the styles discussed in this chapter. Avoid using DIV tags as these will force a break.

→ To learn about SPAN and DIV, **see** "Cascading Style Sheet Techniques," **p. 255**

DESIGNING FOR THE REAL WORLD

MAKING COMPLEX STYLE SIMPLE

Last year, I developed a site for the Microsoft Network. One of the interesting challenges was working with the variety of links that we needed in order to accomplish the design. Each link had a different combination of type style, color, and other features. Obviously, we could never do this using conventional HTML, so a complex style sheet was created. Listing 14.6 shows the resulting sheet in detail.

LISTING 14.6 STYLE SHEET FOR LARGE SITE ON MICROSOFT

```
.plumlink{color:#666699;font:9pt arial,helvetica,sans-serif;font-weight:bold;
text-decoration:none;}

A.plumlink:hover{color: #339999;}

.topLinks{color:#003333;font:9pt arial,helvetica,sans-serif;}
A.topLinks:hover{color:#ff9933;}

.LgBodyLinks{color:#669999;font:11pt arial,helvetica,sans-serif;
text-decoration:none;font-weight:bold;}

A.LgBodyLinks:hover{color: #ff9933;}

.BodyLinks{color:#669999;font:9pt arial,helvetica,sans-serif;font-weight:bold;
text-decoration:none;}

A.BodyLinks:hover {color: #ff9933;}

.smBodyLinks{color:"#003333";font:8pt arial,helvetica,sans-serif;
text-decoration:none;}

A.smBodyLinks:hover{color:#ff9933;}

.FeatureLinks{color:#336666;font:14pt arial,helvetica,sans-serif;
font-weight: bold;text-decoration:none;}

A.FeatureLinks:hover {color: #ff9933;}

.ULBodyLinks{color:#669999;font:9pt arial,helvetica,sans-serif;
font-weigh:=bold;}

A.ULBodyLinks:hover {color: #ff9933;}

.ULPlainBodyLinks{color:#669999;font:9pt arial,helvetica,sans-serif;}

A.ULPlainBodyLinks:hover {color: #ff9933;}

.ga{color:#6699CC;font:9pt arial, helvetica, sans-serif;font-weight:bold;
text-decoration:none;}

A.ga:hover {color:#339966;}
```


continues

LISTING 14.6 CONTINUED

```
.navLinkExt{color:#003333;font:9pt arial, helvetica, sans-serif;
font-weight:bold;}

A.navLinkExt:hover {color:#ff9933;}

.navLink{color:#003333;font:11pt arial, helvetica, sans-serif;
text-decoration:none;font-weight:bold;}

A.navLink:hover {color:#ff9933;}

.navLinkActive{color:#666699;font:12pt arial, helvetica, sans-serif
;text-decoration:none;font-weight:bold;}

A.navLinkActive:hover {color:#ff9933;}

.horBar{color:#ffffff;font:9pt arial, helvetica, sans-serif;
text-decoration:none;font-weight:bold;}

A.horBar:hover{color:#ff9933;}

.bl{color: #666666;font:8pt arial, helvetica, sans-serif;}

.bql{color: #666666;font:8pt arial, helvetica, sans-serif;}
```

We then linked to this sheet, and wherever we wanted to apply a given style, we simply added its class to a tag or area within the HTML as follows:

```
<A href="home.html" class="navLink">This link will be bold, no underline,
11 point sans-serif, with the hexadecimal color of #003333.</A>
```

Of course, when you create complex style, you don't have to link to a sheet; you can always use a style to set the typographic elements of selected areas of text within a page (using the `DIV` and `SPAN` elements) or apply a single style sheet to one page only.

→ To learn about hover effects **see** "Element Positioning and Style Sheet Scripting," **p. 430**

CHAPTER 15

Table Fundamentals

In this chapter

THE IMPORTANCE OF TABLES

HTML tables were originally introduced to provide a way to table data. As simple as that might seem, it only took a few weeks for savvy coders to realize that the grid system created by tables could be used as a means of controlling the entire layout of pages.

This realization grew beyond a means and into a convention—soon, the vast majority of sites on the Web came to embrace tables as their underlying structure. The entire infrastructure of most sites uses tables for graphic placement, color arrangement, and text layout control.

The HTML 4.0 standard, in its strict interpretation, recommends that tables as a grid system should be set aside to make way for the ultimate power of Cascading Style Sheets. The absolute positioning available with style sheets steps far beyond the scope of tables, ideally allowing pixel-by-pixel control of objects on a page.

→ For information on using CSS, **see** ""Element Positioning and Style Sheet Scripting," **p. 430**

But, as you by now are aware, the reality of broad-spectrum HTML design with style sheets is limited to those specialty sites where the audience is known to have compliant software. Because so many site visitors are using browsers that are sub-standard, style sheets aren't an option. However, tables still are.

Note

Even if you've been coding tables for some time, I encourage you to work through this fundamental chapter with me. You'll discover tips and insights that might help you troubleshoot problems or refine your current coding style.

Therefore, understanding tables as a layout tool is imperative. Furthermore, as the transition is made from table layout to absolute positioning, a knowledge of how tables work will be extremely helpful to those Webmasters who are required to make those changes.

CREATING A SIMPLE TABLE

The first step in becoming aware of how best to use tables as a fundamental tool in Web design is to understand the basic tags used to create them.

There are really only three absolutely critical tags required to create a table. These include:

- `<TABLE>...</TABLE>`—The main table tag, denoting the beginning and subsequent end of a table.
- `<TR>...</TR>`—The table row tag, and its companion closing tag.
- `<TD>...</TD>`—The table data, or table cell. This tag is used to define individual table cells.

Caution

Many people get confused between the role of table rows and cells. I encourage HTML students to think of table rows as the horizontal axis, and table cells as the vertical, columnar information. Every time you create a row, you're creating a horizontal control. Each new row creates a new horizontal section. Similarly, each time you add a table cell, you're adding a vertical column to the table.

Certainly, there's more to it than these three simple tags, but before we explore the attributes of TABLE tags, you'll want to build a table for practice.

Before you begin, set up a workshop folder on your computer—you will use this to save files that you make for future use. Again, I encourage experienced coders to walk through these steps to learn a highly methodical, clean approach to creating great table layouts.

1. In your favorite HTML editor, set up a basic Web shell, with the <HTML>, <HEAD>, <TITLE>, and <BODY> tags in place:

```
<HTML>
<HEAD><TITLE></TITLE>
</HEAD>
<BODY>


</BODY>
</HTML>
```

2. In between the <TITLE> tags, type the table's title, `Table Exercise I`:

```
<HTML>
<HEAD>
<TITLE>Table Exercise I</TITLE>
</HEAD>
<BODY>


</BODY>
</HTML>
```

3. Now, add the <TABLE> tag below the <BODY> tag. This alerts the HTML browser interpreting your code that a table is beginning. Using the container method, place the closing </TABLE> tag above the </BODY> tag:

```
<HTML>
<HEAD>
<TITLE>Table Exercise I</TITLE>
</HEAD>
<BODY>

<TABLE>



</TABLE>
</BODY>
</HTML>
```

4. Directly underneath the <TABLE> tag, place the <TR> tag. This defines the beginning of your first table row. Directly above the </BODY> tag, place the closing </TR> tag:

```
<HTML>
<HEAD>
<TITLE>Table Exercise I</TITLE>
</HEAD>
<BODY>

<TABLE>
<TR>


</TR>
</TABLE>
</BODY>
</HTML>
```

5. Move down to the next line, and type in the tag to determine the starting point of your first table cell, <TD>. Below this, add a line of text, and then close the cell with the </TD> closing tag:

```
<HTML>
<HEAD>
<TITLE>Table Exercise I</TITLE>
</HEAD>
<BODY>

<TABLE>
<TR>
<TD>
This is my first table cell.
</TD>
</TR>
</TABLE>
</BODY>
</HTML>
```

6. Repeat step 5, adding a second table cell (remember, cells determine columns):

```
<HTML>
<HEAD>
<TITLE>Table Exercise I</TITLE>
</HEAD>
<BODY>

<TABLE>
<TR>
<TD>
This is my first table cell.
</TD>

<TD>
This is my second table cell.
</TD>


</TR>
</TABLE>
</BODY>
</HTML>
```

7. Save this HTML file as `table_exercise_1.html`.
8. Compare the file to Figure 15.1.

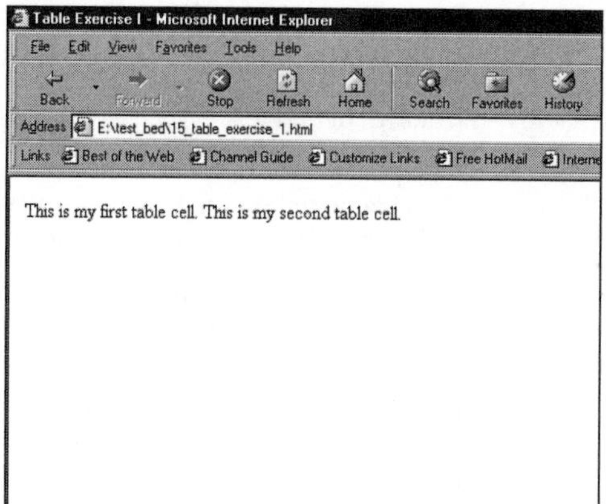

Figure 15.1
The final product is a table with two cells. The data looks as though it is simply placed on a single line, but actually, each sentence is in a different cell.

As every HTML document has a foundational shell, so does a great table layout. This simple exercise can be seen as the table grid shell.

Note

It's important to remember that while I'm focusing on how tables are used for grid layouts, tables can—and do—serve their original function: the tabling of data. You can use the same techniques covered in this chapter to assemble spreadsheet style information as well as understand the grid concepts offered.

UNDERSTANDING TABLE TAG ATTRIBUTES AND VALUES

The <TABLE> tag has a variety of related attributes and values that turn it from a simple tag into the control tower of table layouts.

Following are some of the more common attributes for the `table` tag.

TABLE 15.1 COMMON TABLE ATTRIBUTES

Attribute and Value	Results
`align="x"`	To align tables on a page, you can use this attribute. Options allow `"x"` to equal `left`, `center`, or `right`. Because browsers default alignment to the left, and it's commonplace to center tables by using other tags such as the `DIV` tag. The only really effective use of this attribute is when you specifically want an entire table placed to the far right of the browser field (see Figure 15.2).

continues

TABLE 15.1 CONTINUED

Attribute and Value	Results
`border="x"`	The `"x"` is replaced with a value from 0 on up. This value defines the width of the visual border around the table (see tip directly after this list to show how to turn borders into a handy design tool).
`cellspacing="x"`	Cellspacing defines the amount of space between each individual table cell (in other words, between visual columns and rows). The `"x"` requires a value from 0 on up.
`cellpadding="x"`	This attribute calls for the space around the edges of each cell within the table—its literal "padding."
`width="x%" or width="x"`	To define the width of a table, you can choose to use a number that relates to the percentage of browser space you want to span, or a specific numeral that will be translate into pixel widths.

→ For an overview of how to align text and objects, including tables, **see** "Formatting and Aligning Text," **p. 133**

Caution

While working with tables for page layout, you'll find it extremely helpful to turn on borders by adding a value of `"1"` to the `border` attribute to see the grid you are creating. Then turn them off to see the results without the borders.

Aren't there other table tags? See "Other Table Tags," in the Troubleshooting section at the end of this chapter.

ADDING BORDERS AND WIDTH

Borders and width are primary control attributes and values for a table. Borders are most powerful for grid design when turned completely off, because this is what gives us the invisible control for our layout. However, there are instances in which you might like to have a table border, such as when you are laying out information in a spreadsheet-style fashion.

Caution

When used as design elements, borders around tables cause a site to appear visually constrained, creating a sense of claustrophobia for site visitors. While the instinct to place a border around a table is probably born from a desire to keep things neat and orderly, the results are usually problematic. My recommendation is to only use table borders as a power tool while building the site. Later you'll want to set them to a value of `"0"`. The exception to this is when you're creating data that is meant to be tabled and requires the borders to make sense.

Table width is an important issue—one that bears close examination. The reason is because the width of tables will determine how a table interacts with a browser and the dimension settings of your computer screen.

The maximum viewing space for true crossbrowser, crossplatform, cross-individual computer design is 585 pixels×295 pixels per screen. When coding widths by pixel (referred to as *fixed design* or *fixed-width design)*, this means that anything larger forces a horizontal scrollbar to appear on screens set to a 640×480 resolution. This is a general design problem and should be avoided.

Many developers argue that 800×600 resolution is the most popular screen resolution in use by Web site visitors. I am finding this to be the case with my site. Statistics are showing that the largest percentage of visitors, around 75%, is using 800×600 resolution. The remainder is split between lower and higher resolutions.

I have several reasons why I prefer the conservative rule of 585 pixels wide per screen, but it's important to express that these are *my* reasons and recommendations.

- If you design tables with fixed design for lower screen resolution and the majority of individuals visiting are at higher resolutions, you can still make the site attractive using design-savvy techniques.
- If 100 people are visiting my site per day, and 13 users come in at lower resolution, I want to accommodate them without the horizontal scroll. It's more important to me that a horizontal scroll not appear for fewer users than the other way around.
- Often, people using lower resolutions have vision problems. Low resolution means objects appear larger on the page. I want to accommodate these individuals appropriately.
- Tables using percentages rather than pixels (referred to as *dynamic table designs*) can be employed where and when appropriate to avoid the problem altogether.

Depending on your audience and your preference, you might choose to set your fixed-width designs to higher resolutions.

Note

For the purposes of the examples in this chapter, I'm going to stick to 585 whenever creating a table that will be used as a grid system for the entire screen.

When do you choose to use pixels, and when are percentages a better choice? Pixels give you more control over your page, but you have to be careful and watch your math. This means that every width within a table must add up precisely. You'll see how this realistically unfolds as you work through the stepped exercises in this chapter.

→ For professional tips on how to choose fixed-width, dynamic, or combination tables to accommodate a variety of situations, **see** "Advanced Table Layouts," **p. 336**

Percentages are powerful when you want to create a dynamic table—a table that opens up to the entirety of the available screen space. This sounds like a better option, but because you do lose control and design integrity, the technique should only be used in specific instances. We'll now get a feel for adding the primary attributes of `border` and `width` to the `<TABLE>` tag.

1. Begin by opening the file `table_exercise_1.html` in your HTML editor. Change the title to `Table Exercise 2`. You should see the following:

```
<HTML>
<HEAD>
<TITLE>Table Exercise 2</TITLE>
</HEAD>
<BODY>

<TABLE>
<TR>

<TD>
This is my first table cell.
</TD>

<TD>
This is my second table cell.
</TD>

</TR>
</TABLE>
</BODY>
</HTML>
```

2. The first attribute you're going to add is the border, which you need to set to a numeric value of `"1"`:

```
<HTML>
<HEAD>
<TITLE>Table Exercise 2</TITLE>
</HEAD>
<BODY>

<TABLE border="1">
<TR>

<TD>
This is my first table cell.
</TD>

<TD>
This is my second table cell.
</TD>

</TR>
</TABLE>
</BODY>
</HTML>
```

3. Now add the width in pixels:

```
<HTML>
<HEAD>
<TITLE>Table Exercise 2</TITLE>
</HEAD>
<BODY>

<TABLE border="1" width="585">
```

```
<TR>

<TD>
This is my first table cell.
</TD>

<TD>
This is my second table cell.
</TD>

</TR>
</TABLE>
</BODY>
</HTML>
```

4. Save your file as `table_exercise_2.html` and view it using your browser. It should match Figure 15.2.

Note that in this instance the border is visible, showing you the grid that you've created.

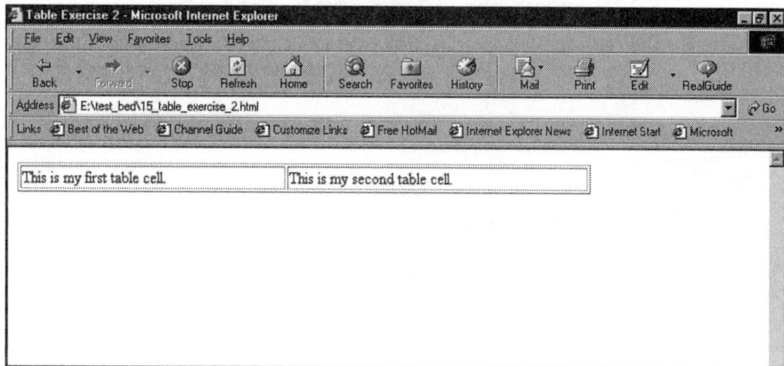

Figure 15.2
The result of this exercise is a table with two visible cells spanning 585 pixels.

CELLPADDING AND CELLSPACING

Cellpadding and spacing are sometimes helpful because they can aid in the addition of whitespace when coding tables without borders. In a desire to gain and maintain control of HTML layouts, however, cellpadding and spacing become problematic.

The following examples show code using these techniques so that you can visualize how they work. Let's begin with cellpadding, demonstrated in Listing 15.1.

LISTING 15.1 CELLPADDING

```
<HTML>
<HEAD>
<TITLE>Cellpadding</TITLE>
</HEAD>
<BODY>

<TABLE border="1" cellpadding="20" width="585">
<TR>
```

continues

LISTING 15.1 CONTINUED

```
<TD>
This is my first table cell.
</TD>

<TD>
This is my second table cell.
</TD>

</TR>
</TABLE>
</BODY>
</HTML>
```

Figure 15.3 shows the results of this table. Note how far apart the border is from the text. This is the result of the padding.

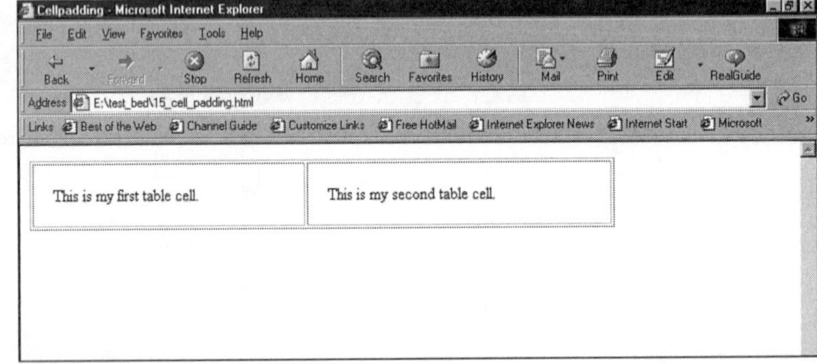

Figure 15.3 Cellpadding within a table adds whitespace between the cell border and its contents so that even when borders are not used, the information on your page won't appear too close to each other giving a cramped feeling on the page.

Listing 15.2 shows you cellspacing only.

LISTING 15.2 CELLSPACING

```
<HTML>
<HEAD>
<TITLE>Cellspacing</TITLE>
</HEAD>
<BODY>

<TABLE border="1" cellspacing="20"  width="585">
<TR>

<TD>
This is my first table cell.
</TD>

<TD>
This is my second table cell.
</TD>
```

```
</TR>
</TABLE>
</BODY>
</HTML>
```

In Figure 15.4, you'll notice that the text is now encased in the cell's border, but there's plenty of space between the cell itself and the edge of the table.

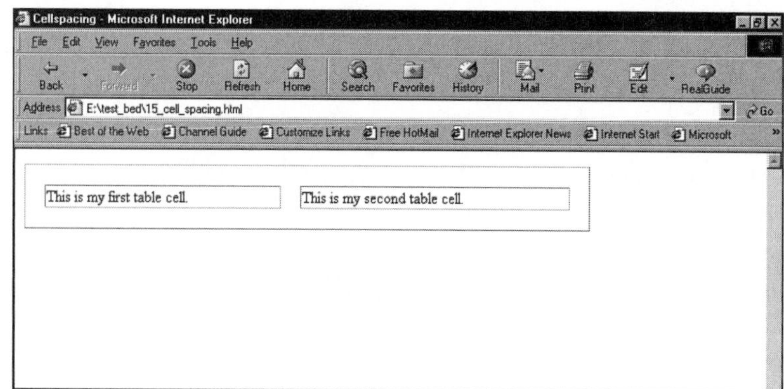

Figure 15.4
In contrast to cell-padding, cellspacing within a table adds space between the cell border and the table border.

Listing 15.3 shows an example with both cellpadding and cellspacing in action at the same time.

Listing 15.3 Cellpadding and Spacing Together

```
<HTML>
<HEAD>
<TITLE>Cellspacing and Cellpadding</TITLE>
</HEAD>
<BODY>

<TABLE border="1" cellspacing="20" cellpadding="20" width="585">
<TR>

<TD>
This is my first table cell.
</TD>

<TD>
This is my second table cell.
</TD>

</TR>
</TABLE>
</BODY>
</HTML>
```

Now there is padding and spacing—giving the text some breathing room within the cell, and some space between the cell's border and the remainder of the table (see Figure 15.5).

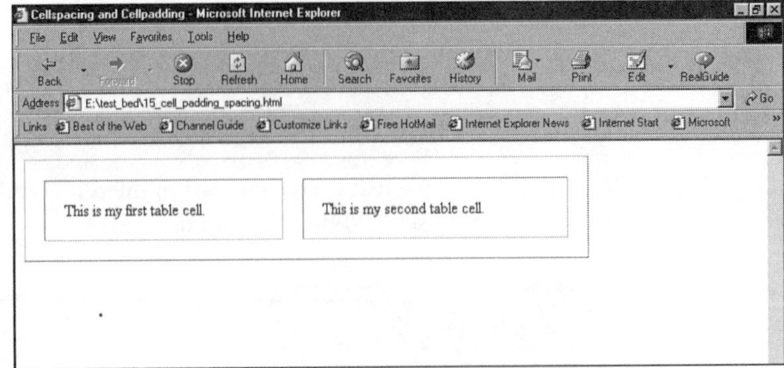

Figure 15.5
Cellpadding and cellspacing work together to help give your page a nice, organized look with plenty of whitespace to aid with readability.

So far, you can't see any problems with the amount of padding and spacing I've added to this example. However, what happens if I added more text, or, as in Listing 15.4, more table cells?

LISTING 15.4 CARELESS MATH FORCES A HORIZONTAL SCROLL AT 640×480

```
<HTML>
<HEAD>
<TITLE>Cellspacing</TITLE>
</HEAD>
<BODY>

<TABLE border="1" cellspacing="20" cellpadding="20" width="585">
<TR>

<TD>
This is my first table cell. This is my first table cell.
</TD>

<TD>
This is my second table cell. This is my second table cell.
</TD>

<TD>
This is my third table cell. This is my third table cell.
</TD>

<TD>
This is my fourth table cell. This is my fourth table cell.
</TD>

<TD>
This is my fifth table cell. This is my fifth table cell.
```

```
</TD>

<TD>
This is my sixth table cell. This is my sixth table cell.
</TD>

<TD>
This is my seventh table cell. This is my seventh table cell.
</TD>
</TR>
</TABLE>
</BODY>
</HTML>
```

The width of the table (585 pixels) cannot accommodate the amount of padding, so a horizontal scrollbar appears (see Figure 15.6). A vertical scrollbar appears as well, but they are considered completely acceptable.

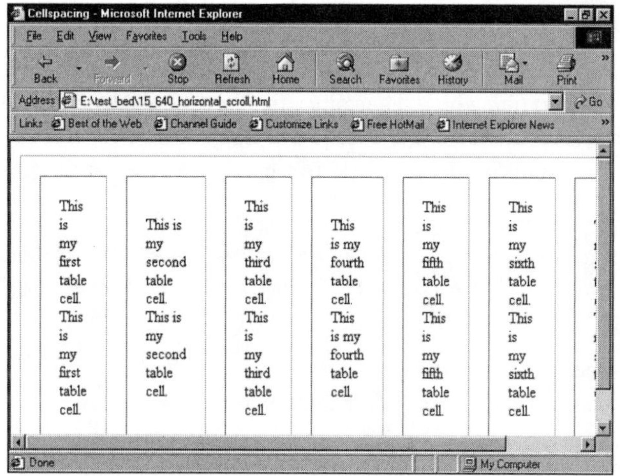

Figure 15.6
The cellpadding and cellspacing values conflict with the table width causing an undesired horizontal scrollbar to appear.

One solution to this problem is to always be sure that you subtract the total amount of the padding and spacing from the maximum pixel width defined. Also, you'll want to fix the widths of each individual cell, as you'll learn later in this chapter when you examine table cell attributes.

However, the best way to avoid disturbing problems with padding and spacing is to *use them sparingly and with forethought* (see Figure 15.7). There are better methods of adding whitespace to tables that allow you to control your design with greater ability, as well.

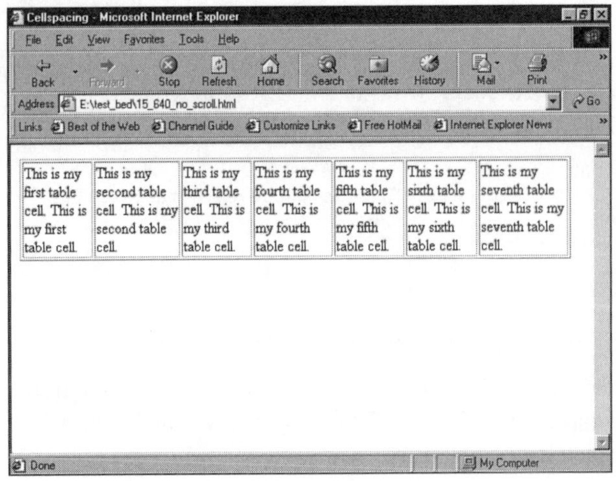

Figure 15.7
The padding and spacing are removed, and all seven cells are accommodated within 585 pixels when the screen is set to full size.

APPLYING ATTRIBUTES TO THE TABLE ROW TAG

The only two attributes ever used within rows include `align`, which controls the row's spatial alignment, and `valign`, which determines the vertical placement of all the data within a row. While these attributes are considered legal, they don't offer the kind of control available in attributes related to the `TABLE` and `TD` elements, so they are rarely used.

> **Note**
>
> To understand table rows best, think of them as the horizontal structure of the grid, whereas table cells will be the columnar, or vertical, structure of that grid.

To show you some of the control issues related to row attributes, take a look at Listing 15.5. The `border` value is set to `"1"` and cellpadding and cellspacing are added, so you can see the rows clearly.

When viewed in my browser (see Figure 15.8), you'll notice how the `valign` attribute used in the first two rows doesn't even apply. Furthermore, while the `align` attribute in the third row does in fact center the text within that row, the fourths row's table cell alignment value *overrides* that of the row.

LISTING 15.5 ROW ATTRIBUTES ARE OFTEN INCONSISTENT

```
<HTML>
<HEAD>
<TITLE>Table Row Attributes and Values</TITLE>
</HEAD>
<BODY>

<TABLE border="1" cellspacing="10" cellpadding="10" width="100%">
<TR valign="top">

<TD>
This is my first table row.
```

```
</TD>

</TR>

<TR valign="bottom">
<TD>
This is my second table row.
</TD>

</TR>

<TR align="middle">
<TD>
This is my third table row, middle alignment.
</TD>
</TR>

<TR align="middle">
<TD align="right">
This is my third table row.
</TD>
</TR>
</TABLE>
</BODY>
</HTML>
```

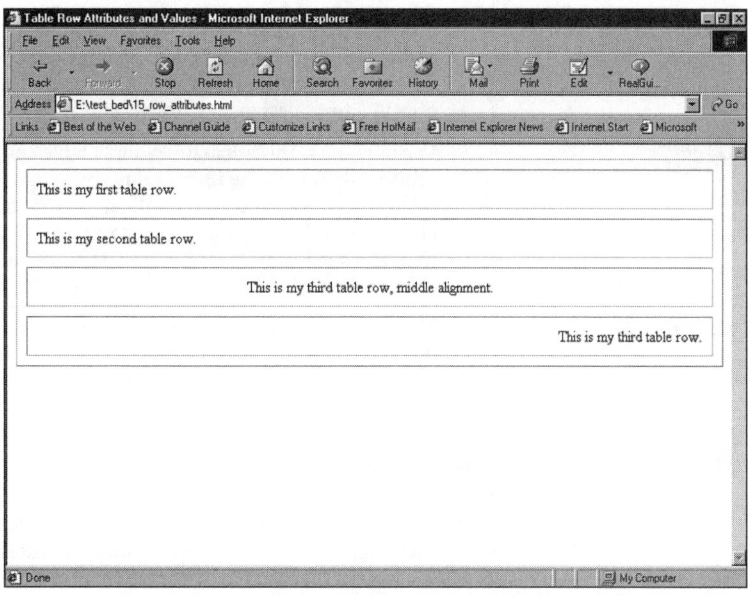

Figure 15.8
Row attributes are inconsistent.

Tip from

It has long been my experience that row attributes do not necessarily lend themselves to strong control over HTML tables. The greatest control comes from the relationship between table tags and attributes and table cell tags.

In the previous example, I've demonstrated an instance where practical wisdom can override the standard to become a convention. It's important to know that you can use attributes within rows, and many coders do. It's perfectly legal, but not always the easiest way to accomplish your table goals.

USING THE TABLE CELL TAG AND ATTRIBUTES

The essence of table design really relies on the table cell, or `TD` tag. This tag has a variety of important attributes that can be applied for maximum table control. The attributes and values are into specific sections, depending upon what type of control they offer.

Primary attributes and values should generally be placed in all table cells. `Column` and `row span` attributes and values are more useful in specific grid designs, and specialty attributes such as `height`, `bgcolor`, and `background` are generally used in more advanced or specialized table design.

PRIMARY ATTRIBUTES

Table 15.2 shows the primary attributes for the table cell tag.

TABLE 15.2 TABLE CELL ATTRIBUTES

Attribute and Value	Results
`width="x%"` or **`width="x"`**	Setting a percentage width with x% will make the cell dynamic within the context of the table. Fixing the cell width to a pixel value fixes that cell within the table. For example, you can have dynamic cells in a fixed design and vice versa.
`align="x"`	When you use this attribute within a table cell, the data inside the cell will align with the literal value you assign to the attribute. In other words, a `<left>` value will left-justify the text or graphic you place within the cell, the `<middle>` value will center the information, and a value of `<right>` will justify the information to the right of the cell.
`valign="x"`	The vertical alignment of a table cell will place the information therein to the `top`, `middle`, or `bottom` of the cell.

Note

I'll mention again that I personally believe primary attributes and related values should be placed in all table cell tags. My rationale for this goes back to the discussion of control offered in Chapter 2. Making sure that the browser is given as much possible information stabilizes the table and creates more realistic crossbrowser, crossplatform HTML design.

Listing 15.6 shows a table with three cells, each cell being completely defined with primary attributes.

LISTING 15.6 DEFINING THE ATTRIBUTES IN EVERY CELL

```
<HTML>
<HEAD>
<TITLE>Table Cell Attributes and Values</TITLE>
</HEAD>
<BODY>

<TABLE border="1" cellspacing="0" cellpadding="0" width="585">
<TR>

<TD width="250" valign="top" align="left">
This is my first table cell. Its width is 250 pixels, the information within it
is vertically aligned to the top of the cell, and is justified to the left of
the cell.
</TD>

<TD width="250" valign="middle" align="right">
This is my second table cell. It, too, has a width of 250 pixels. The
information within this cell is aligned to the middle of the cell, and is
justified to the right.
</TD>

<TD width="90" valign="bottom" align="middle">
This is my third table cell. Its values are completely different than the prior
cells.
</TD>

</TR>
</TABLE>
</BODY>
</HTML>
```

Figure 15.9 shows how the table cell attributes are much more consistent.

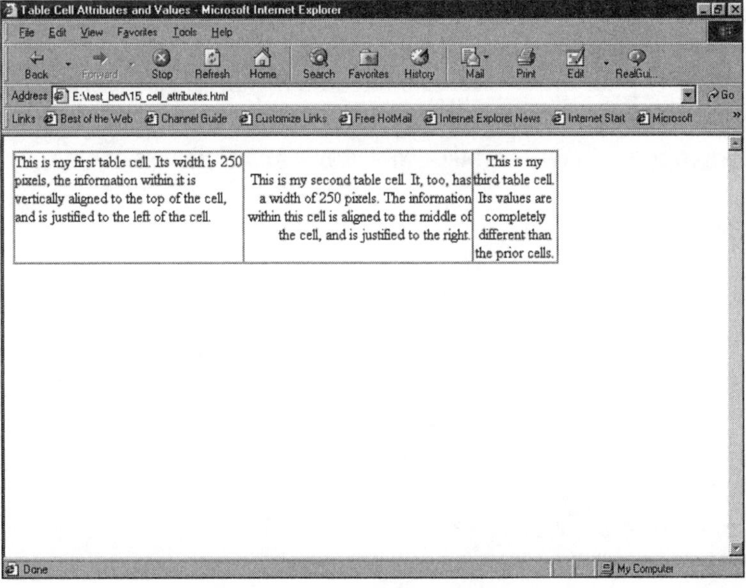

Figure 15.9
These table cells help to clarify just how cells are a critical component of object placement.

In the first cell, the information is vertically aligned to the top of the cell, and justified to the left. The second cell's data is vertically aligned to the middle of the cell and justifies right. Finally, the third cell's content, which is vertically aligned to the bottom of the cell, is also centered. Each cell is fixed to the width called for within the cell and within the table tag itself.

Note

When you don't add attributes to a tag, browsers will seek the default. Table borders default to `0`, cell padding and cellspacing to `1`. Alignment defaults to the left, and width becomes *DYNAMIC*, meaning that the width of a table and the cells within adapt to the combination of browser space and the data you've placed within the cells.

This control relationship between the table cell and the table tag is the most powerful aspect of table coding. Carefully working with this relationship is certain to help you create stable, compatible tables that allow you to firmly secure your data and design.

COLUMN AND ROW SPAN

Spanning columns and rows enables you to create interesting grids and to manage areas of space within a table more completely. The attributes are as follows:

- **`colspan="x"`**—`colspan` refers to the number of columns the cell you are working with will span.
- **`rowspan="x"`**—As with `colspan`, `rowspan` refers to the span of the cell, in this case how many rows the cell stretches.

Column span works by allowing the table to span a set amount of columns (remember, columns are created with cells). If you don't use the `colspan` attribute, the table will try to compensate for any undesignated space.

Consider Listing 15.7, which you'll recognize as a standard table sample with two rows. The top row contains four cells set to a width of 100 pixels each, and the bottom row has two—one with a value of 100 pixels, another with a width of 300 pixels.

LISTING 15.7 STANDARD TABLE WITH ROWS AND COLUMNS

```
<HTML>
<HEAD>
<TITLE>Column Span</TITLE>
</HEAD>
<BODY>

<TABLE border="1" cellspacing="0" cellpadding="0" width="400">
<TR>

<TD width="100" valign="top" align="left">
This is my first table cell in the top row.
</TD>

<TD width="100" valign="top" align="left">
This is my second table cell in the top row.
```

```
</TD>

<TD width="100" valign="top" align="left">
This is my third table cell in the top row.
</TD>

<TD width="100" valign="top" align="left">
This is my fourth table cell in the top row.
</TD>

</TR>

<TR>

<TD width="100" valign="top" align="left">
This is my first table cell in the bottom row.
</TD>

<TD width="300" valign="top" align="left">
This is my second table cell in the bottom row.
</TD>

</TR>

</TABLE>
</BODY>
</HTML>
```

Logically speaking, the browser should know to set the first table cell in the bottom row to 100 pixels and then stretch, or *span*, the remaining cell to reach across the full 300 pixels available. But this doesn't happen. Instead, the browser applies a blank space (see Figure 15.10) to a section of that row.

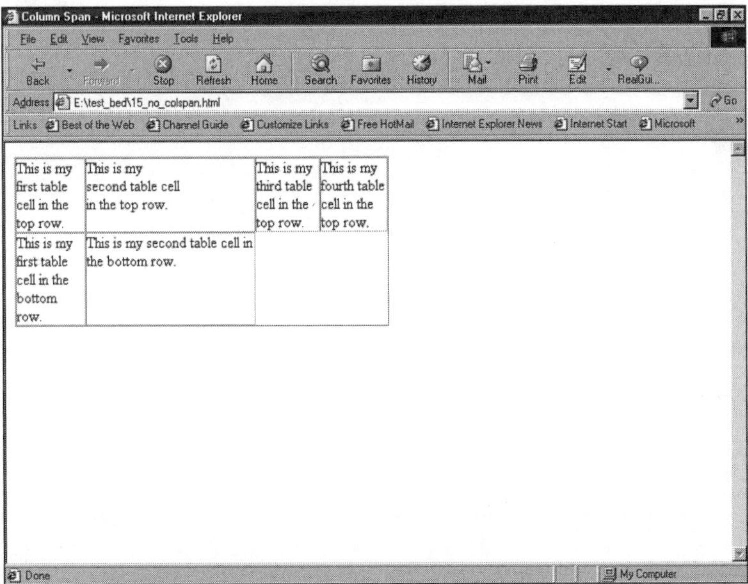

Figure 15.10
Without `colspan`, the browser gets confused!

The `colspan` attribute allows you to tell the browser how to manage that space and avoid this problem.

To do this, you have to subtract the amount of available cells from the *total sum* of possible columns. Because you have a total of four cells, or columns, in the top row, you have to use that as the amount from which to subtract. You have one cell in the bottom row already, so the second cell, which will span the remainder of the row, must take a `colspan` of `"3"`. Subtract the first cell from the total available columns to get this value (see Listing 15.8).

Listing 15.8 Spanning Columns

```
<HTML>
<HEAD>
<TITLE>Column Span</TITLE>
</HEAD>
<BODY>

<TABLE border="1" cellspacing="0" cellpadding="0" width="400">
<TR>

<TD width="100" valign="top" align="left">
This is my first table cell in the top row.
</TD>

<TD width="100" valign="top" align="left">
This is my second table cell in the top row.
</TD>

<TD width="100" valign="top" align="left">
This is my third table cell in the top row.
</TD>

<TD width="100" valign="top" align="left">
This is my fourth table cell in the top row.
</TD>

</TR>

<TR>

<TD width="100" valign="top" align="left">
This is my first table cell in the bottom row.
</TD>

<TD width="300" colspan="3" valign="top" align="left">
This is my second table cell in the bottom row.
</TD>

</TR>

</TABLE>
</BODY>
</HTML>
```

When I add the colspan attribute and value to the second cell, the table knows what to do (see Figure 15.11).

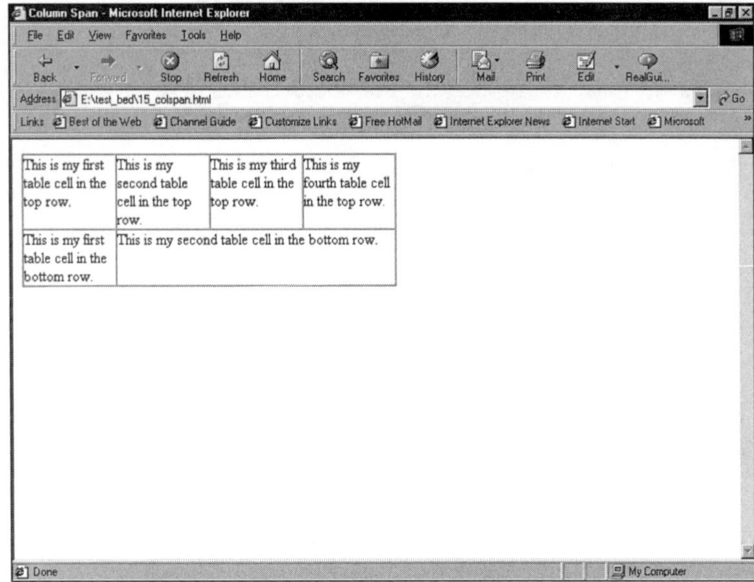

Figure 15.11
The colspan attribute solves the problem.

rowspan, then, works in exactly the same way, but is applied to the rows.

The code in Listing 15.9 shows two rows, each with three cells.

LISTING 15.9 A TABLE WITH ROWS AND CELLS

```
<HTML>
<HEAD>
<TITLE>Row Span</TITLE>
</HEAD>
<BODY>

<TABLE border="1" cellspacing="0" cellpadding="0" width="300">
<TR>

<TD width="100" valign="top" align="left">
This is my first table cell in the top row.
</TD>

<TD width="100" valign="top" align="left">
This is my second table cell in the top row.
</TD>

<TD width="100" valign="top" align="left">
This is my third table cell in the top row.
</TD>
```

continues

LISTING 15.9 CONTINUED

```
</TR>

<TR>

<TD width="100" valign="top" align="left">
This is my first table cell in the bottom row.
</TD>

<TD width="100" valign="top" align="left">
This is my second table cell in the bottom row.
</TD>

<TD width="100" valign="top" align="left">
This is my third table cell in the bottom row.
</TD>

</TR>

</TABLE>
</BODY>
</HTML>
```

Figure 15.12 shows the simple table that this code creates.

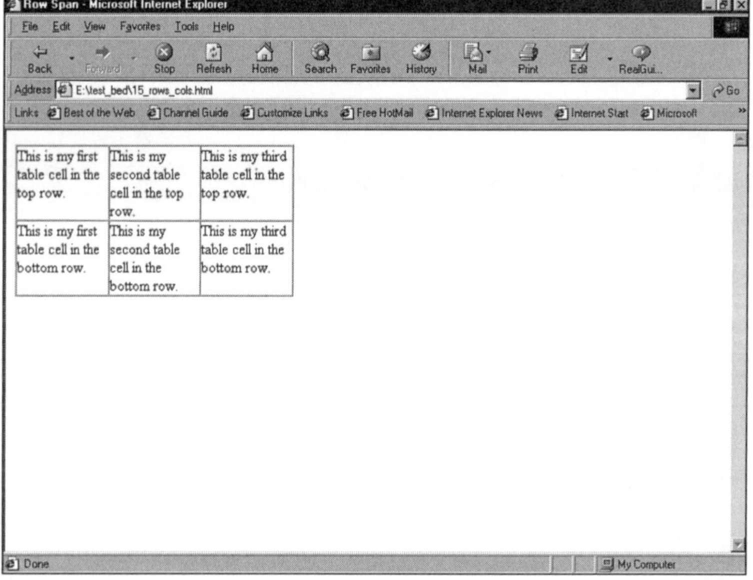

Figure 15.12
The result of Listing 15.9 is a table with two rows and three cells in each row.

Now, let's say you want to have the first cell in the top row, width of 100 pixels, span both rows, creating a vertical column. To do this, you have to first remove a column from the bottom row, because you're going to essentially stretch the first cell across that space. Then, you need to add the `rowspan` attribute and value to the first cell. The way you get `rowspan` value is by simply measuring the amount of rows you want to span—in this case, `"2"`.

Listing 15.10 is resulting code.

LISTING 15.10 SPANNING ROWS

```
<HTML>
<HEAD>
<TITLE>Row Span</TITLE>
</HEAD>
<BODY>

<TABLE border="1" cellspacing="0" cellpadding="0" width="300">
<TR>

<TD width="100" rowspan="2" valign="top" align="left">
This is my first table cell, and it spans two rows.
</TD>

<TD width="100" valign="top" align="left">
This is my second table cell in the top row.
</TD>

<TD width="100" valign="top" align="left">
This is my third table cell in the top row.
</TD>

</TR>

<TR>

<TD width="100" valign="top" align="left">
This is my second table cell in the bottom row.
</TD>

<TD width="100" valign="top" align="left">
This is my third table cell in the bottom row.
</TD>

</TR>

</TABLE>
</BODY>
</HTML>
```

Figure 15.13 shows the table with the first cell now spanning two rows.

Using these attributes can get fairly complex, particularly when you have a table with many rows, and many cells within those rows. The rule of thumb when working with these attributes is to rely on the mathematical formulas described in this chapter.

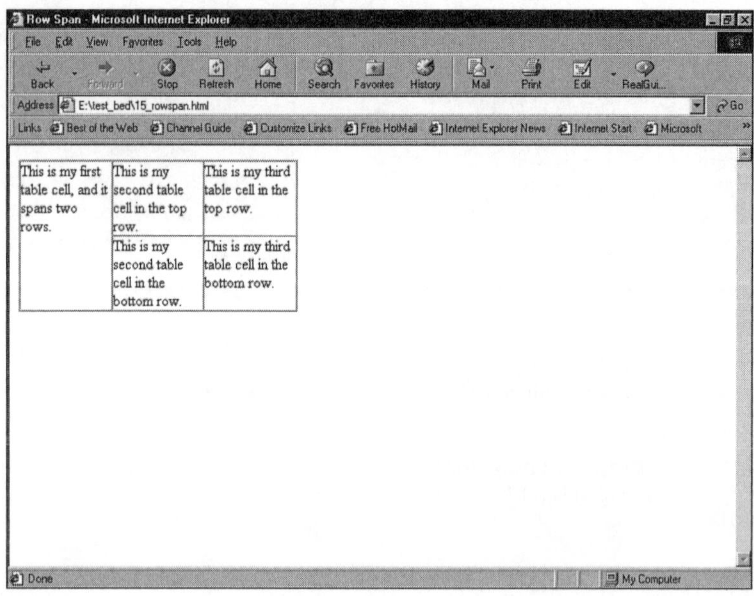

Figure 15.13 Similar to how the `colspan` attribute enables you to span columns within the table, the `rowspan` attribute allows you to span rows.

Caution

Remember that a table data cell creates a column. Because I have four table data cells in this table, I have to account for four individual cells. I'm going to span the second cell, and I want it to stretch from the cell's beginning along the full horizon of the table. Therefore, I will use a value of `"3"` to create the span. This can be very confusing, because it really appears that there are now only three total columns and the logical span for this cell would be `"2"`. The trick is to always count the cell you are working from as being the first part of a span. Then you simply add to that number to reach the total amount of cells, without getting confused by the visual results.

Fix your table width, make sure that your table cells total the appropriate width, and when using `colspan` and `rowspan` attributes, measure how many cells or rows need to be spanned appropriately.

Specialty Table Cell Attributes

There are a number of other table cell tag attributes and values that you can use to empower your table design. They include the following:

Table 15.3 Cell Attributes

Attribute and Value	Result
`bgcolor="x"`	This allows you to add background color to a specific cell.
`background="url"`	Some browsers, including IE 3.0 and higher and Netscape Navigator 4.0 and higher, allow you to place a background graphic in a table cell.
`height="x"`	You can fix the height of a table cell by using this, but this is a browser-dependent measurement.

Background color is especially useful in creating colorful pages that load quickly, because you are getting the color from the browser rather than having to download a graphic to achieve the effects. It's also well supported by browsers that support tables.

→ If you need some help regarding background color, **see** "Using Text and Background Color," **p. 217** (chapter 11)

→ For issues with color in general, **see** "Color Concepts," **p. 528**

ADDING BACKGROUND COLOR TO TABLE CELLS

Let's step through the process of adding different background color to table cells:

1. To add color to cells, you'll use the `bgcolor` attribute and a hexadecimal value to the string within the `<TD>` table cell string. Follow my lead in adding a different color to each cell within the following table:

```
<HTML>
<HEAD>
<TITLE>Table Cell Color</TITLE>
</HEAD>
<BODY>

<TABLE border="1" cellspacing="10" cellpadding="10" width="300">
<TR>

<TD width="100" valign="top" align="left">
This is my first table cell in the top row.
</TD>

<TD width="100" valign="top" align="left">
This is my second table cell in the top row.
</TD>

<TD width="100" valign="top" align="left">
This is my third table cell in the top row.
</TD>

</TR>

<TR>

<TD width="100" valign="top" align="left">
This is my first table cell in the bottom row.
</TD>

<TD width="100" valign="top" align="left">
This is my second table cell in the bottom row.
</TD>

<TD width="100" valign="top" align="left">
This is my third table cell in the bottom row.
</TD>

</TR>

</TABLE>
</BODY>
</HTML>
```

2. Replace the table data information in the first cell of the table with the following:

```
<TD width="100" valign="top" align="left" bgcolor="#CC9999">
This is my first table cell in the top row.
</TD>
```

3. Now replace the table data information in the second table cell of the bottom row with the following:

```
<TD width="100" valign="top" align="left" bgcolor="#FF9966">
This is my second table cell in the bottom row.
</TD>
```

4. Save the file as `cell_color.html` and view it in your browser (see Figure 15.14).

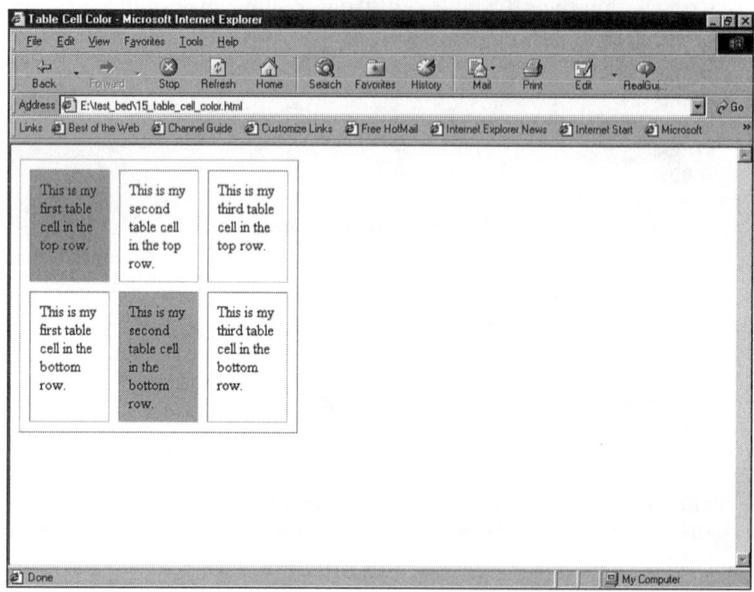

Figure 15.14
Background color in table cells can add areas of color to enhance the visual design without having to use graphics.

Note

I've made a table-based color chart with hexadecimal colors available which you can download at **`http://www.molly.com/molly/webdesign/colorchart.html`**.

PLACING A BACKGROUND GRAPHIC INTO A TABLE CELL

To place a background graphic into table cells, simply add the `background="url"` where *`url`* is the graphic image you want to have tile into the background:

```
<TD width="100" valign="top" align="left" background="yellow_tile.gif">
This is my third table cell in the bottom row.
</TD>
```

Figure 15.15 demonstrates this very powerful way of adding design bits to a site.

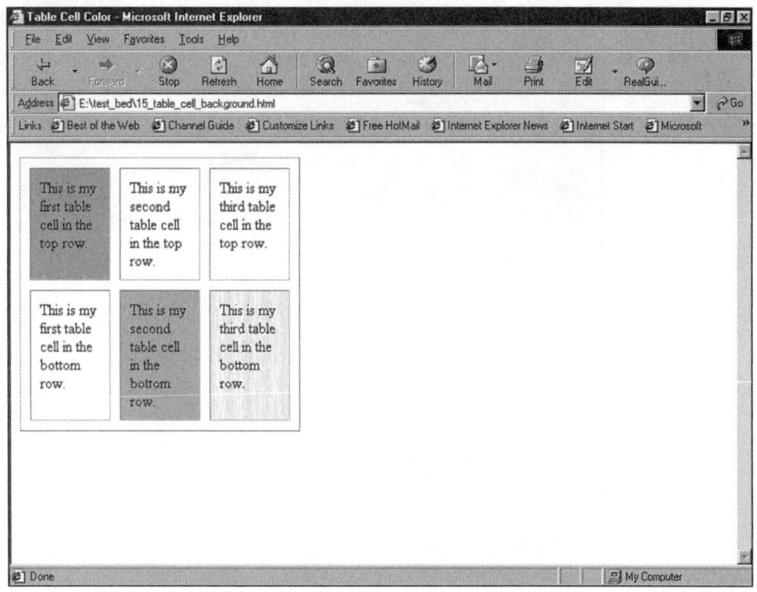

Figure 15.15
A background graphic in table cell. This technique can be used generally to enhance the esthetic appearance of the page, or used specifically to draw the eye to an area of special interest.

While the `background` attribute is not recognized by earlier versions of browsers, particularly Netscape, the good news is that those browsers will simply ignore the tag and attribute—so you won't choke the browser, only lose the background design.

→ For help with designing background graphics, **see** "Creating Professional Web Graphics," **p. 603**

Tip from

To avoid completely losing design integrity when coding backgrounds into table cells, use both the `bgcolor` attribute and the `background` attribute. This way, if the browser can't read the background graphic, it will still load the `bgcolor` that you've requested.

Finally, the `height` attribute can be applied to table cells to gain a bit more control over those cells. Once again, browser support for this is inconsistent, so it's not an extremely reliable method of fixing height. Moreover, if you apply a height to one cell, it will stretch all cells in that row to that height (Figure 15.16).

```
<td width="100" height="200" valign="top" align="left"
background="yellow_tile.gif">
This is my third table cell in the bottom row.
</td>
```

Tip from

Whenever working with tables begins to seem overwhelming, remind yourself that it starts very simply, with three fundamental elements: `TABLE`, `TR`, and `TD`.

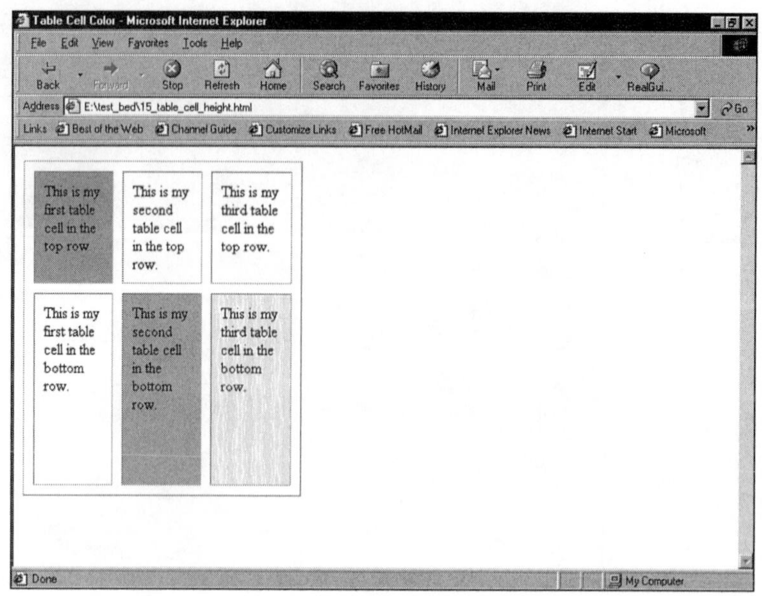

Figure 15.16
Fixed height in the bottom-right table cell forces all cells in that row to adjust to that height.

Table doesn't appear on the page? See "Disappearing Tables," in the Troubleshooting section at the end of this chapter.

TROUBLESHOOTING

OTHER TABLE TAGS

Aren't there any other table tags?

Yes, there are several other tags. Many of them, such as `CAPTION`, can be used to assist in making tables more accessible to special needs audiences. Another is the `TH` element, which stands for Table Header. These are similar to cells but automatically place any text into bold. In table-based grid design, you see these additional tags quite infrequently.

→ For a discussion of table tags specific to access issues, **see** "Accessibility and Internationalization," **p. 474**

DISAPPEARING TABLES

I've built a table, but it isn't appearing on the page. What's wrong?

This is often the result of a missing tag, usually a closing `</td>`, `</tr>`, or `</table>` tag. Check your syntax!

DESIGNING FOR THE REAL WORLD

DESIGN FIRST, THEN PLAN THE TABLE

One of the problems many Web developers face is how to create innovative designs within the constraints of table grids. This is one of the reasons that style sheet positioning is so idealistic and appealing.

When working to create great designs, do the design work first, and then and only then begin to solve the table necessary to lay out the design.

One way to do this is to first sketch your design ideas out on paper. After you have a sketch, you can move to Photoshop to lay out the design. After you're satisfied with the layout, you can then begin to solve the table problem.

I'll teach you more about this in the next chapter, but I want you to start out by creating a design—first by sketching it, then by laying it out in Photoshop (or the imaging software you typically use for graphic layout). I want you to think outside the box—literally! Don't try to force the design into the context of tables. Just let the design flow naturally from you.

No matter your level of experience—this is a great exercise to help you come up with innovative designs. In fact, I'm going to do the exercise with you. Here's what I did:

1. I first took out my sketch pad, and I made several sketches. I chose the one with which I was most satisfied (see Figure 15.17).

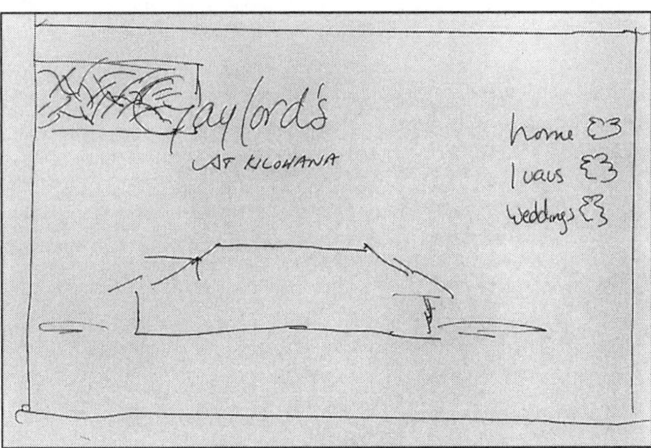

Figure 15.17 I liked this design sketch best.

2. Using the sketch as a guide, I opened up my favorite imaging program, Photoshop. You can use whatever imaging program you are most comfortable with.
3. One by one, I laid out the elements of the design carefully (Figure 15.18), placing the header, background, and navigation on separate layers so I could make adjustments to them at a later time.
4. I saved my file with the layers intact using Photoshop's native format, PSD.

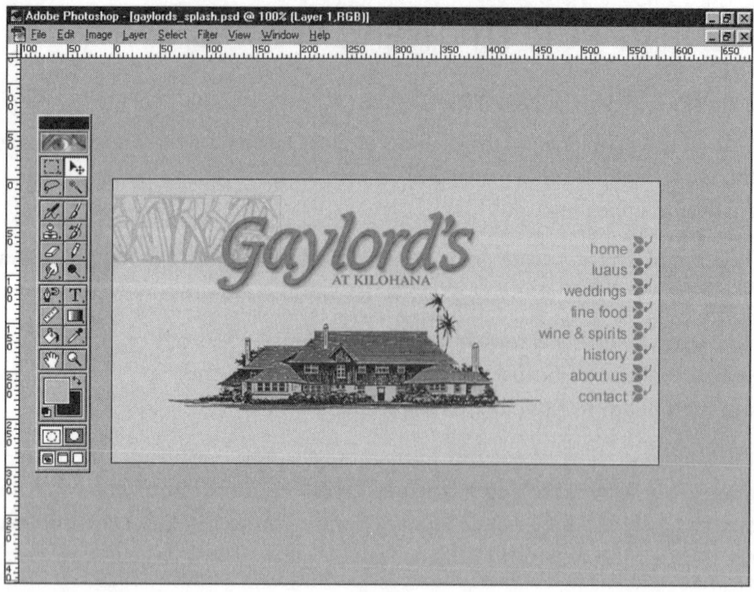

Figure 15.18 Laying out the pieces in Photoshop before creating the table makes it much easier to see what type of table layout is required.

Set aside your file for later. You'll complete the project in Chapter 16, "Advanced Table Layouts."

→ For more information on imaging software, **see** "Web Graphic Formats and Professional Tools," **p. 580** (chapter 27)

CHAPTER 16

Advanced Table Layouts

In this chapter

PLANNING TABLES FOR LAYOUT

In just a few chapters, you're going to read about an aspect of Cascading Style Sheets known as *absolute positioning*. Using this feature within HTML 4.0, you can separate style and layout from the content of an HTML document. The advantage of positioning in this way is that it is, in fact, as absolute as positioning any element on a Web page can get.

As you already are aware, however, what works in the strict interpretation of HTML 4.0 is not necessarily what works in the real world. Or at least, not yet. And, because tables and frames have a longer history than CSS, it's a given that designers will naturally lean toward what works and what is interoperable across platforms and browsers.

Furthermore, although style sheet positioning is preferred for layout within the standard in strict HTML 4.0, HTML has by no means given up on tables as a viable and acceptable method for layout. On the shirttails of this attitude rides some new tags for tables.

UNDERSTANDING TABLE DESIGN

When you're creating page layouts, the idea is to take available Web space and control it. Tables allow you to do that and to do it fairly well. However, the rules are a bit complex. So, in this chapter, I'm going to show you how to take the information you learned in Chapter 15, "Table Fundamentals," and systematically demonstrate how to create powerful page layouts.

Before you jump in, however, let me show you some of the capabilities that are associated with using tables for layout purposes:

- **Placement of graphics**—When you're designing a page with simple HTML, you can left-align, center, or right-align a graphic. You can also control a graphic to some limited degree on the vertical axis. But what you can't do is take graphics and put them at specific, fixed points onto your page. With tables, you can (of course, you can ideally do this even better with CSS).
- **Control of space**—In basic HTML, you can control margins. What you can't do is make elegant columns for text and graphics, or divide a page into specific areas—particularly vertical sections—for use in navigation or textual design. You can, however, control this space using tables.
- **Dynamic Flow**—Creation of pages that flow dynamically to the resolution of the screen, yet maintain a more complex layout than available with basic HTML techniques.

It's undeniable that the use of tables provides some of the most powerful options within the developer's toolkit. But, you need to have a. Without knowing how the pieces will ultimately fit together, you can end up with slipshod, faulty work.

SEEING THE GRID

As I first mentioned in the "Designing for the Real World" section at the end of Chapter 15, many designers begin their designs with a sketch or graphical mockup. Some do both, sketching out some ideas first and then refining them in a layer-based imaging program such as Photoshop. This approach allows you to not only move objects around, but also—most imperative to designing with tables—to *see the grid*. As a result, you can create a design completely free of the logical constraints of HTML. Then, you can look at the design to see how you need to slice it up to create the supporting grid that will position the text and images where you want them.

→ Of course, seeing the grid means relying on your basic knowledge of how tables work. For this reason, **see** "Table Fundamentals," **p. 304** if you're not confident that you understand the basics—rows and columns and how they are created within each.

Figure 16.1 shows a splash page design mockup. To a fairly adept eye, it will be obvious that this design cannot be achieved without the use of either a very large graphic or some combination of graphics and tables.

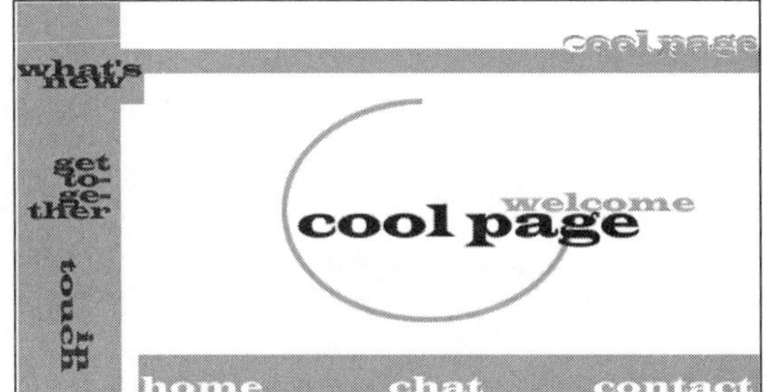

Figure 16.1
Splash page mockup as seen in Photoshop.

Figure 16.2 shows guides in Photoshop that I've denoted as being the grid I want to create. Using guides isn't the only way to create grids, however; you can use other ways, too. As long as you are following syntactical rules, there isn't a right or a wrong per se.

Tip from molly

Always go with the most simple coding solution that provides the kind of control necessary for your design.

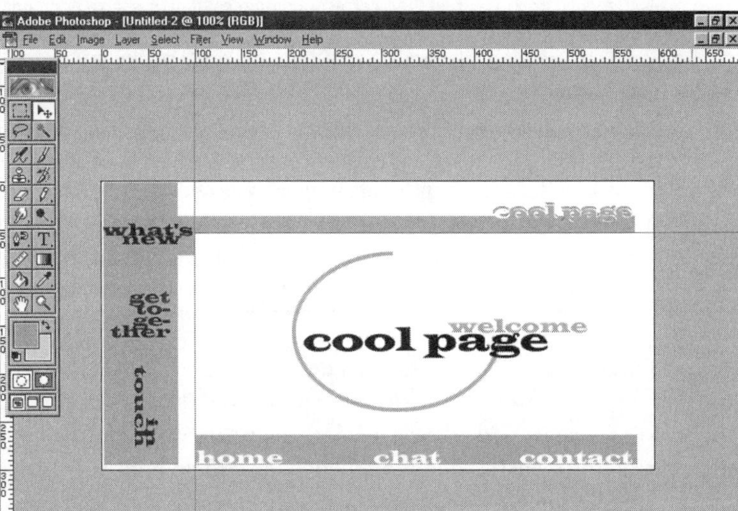

Figure 16.2
Layout with gridlines.

USING FIXED AND DYNAMIC DESIGN

Beyond seeing the grid is the next designer challenge: Deciding whether a design should be *fixed* or *dynamic*.

Note

In this case, *dynamic* refers to the capability of the design to adapt to any variable. In most instances, this variable will be screen resolution.

Fixed designs are created for a specific resolution. *Fixed-width* layouts require very accurate measurement on the designer's part. You must work within the parameters of the resolution—585×295 pixels per screen for the lowest common denominator—and ensure that each section is mathematically fixed within those parameters (see Table 16.1). This is particularly important concerning width, because vertical scrolling is much more acceptable than horizontal scrolling.

TABLE 16.1 SCREEN MEASUREMENTS BY COMMON RESOLUTION (IN PIXELS)

Screen Resolution	Screen Measurement
640×480	585×295
800×600	745×415
1,024×768	969×583
1,280×1,024	1,225×839

Dynamic layouts, however, stretch to meet the resolution of the screen. These layouts rely on percentages or wildcards, essentially saying "put this information here, but this information can take up whatever screen space is available."

The Origin of Fixed Screen Widths

Screen measurements are lower than their corresponding resolution because additional screen space gets eaten up by the browser. Open your favorite Web browser, and you'll see menus on the top, a scrollbar to the right, a status bar along the bottom, and even a thin margin to the left. All of these elements eat away at the available screen space.

There are differences between platforms, too, and the way people use computers! Windows browsing software appears to take up slightly less space, and typically speaking, Windows users open their Windows to the parameters of the available desktop. Macintosh browsing software can eat a little more space on the horizontal–about 10 pixels worth. Mac users tend not to open their browsing windows to the full desktop space.

Because it's impossible to control what users do with their software, the numbers evolve from the desire to offer the best-case scenario for each resolution, avoiding horizontal scrolls wherever possible.

Of fixed and dynamic tables, I use fixed design the most. This tends to be true of people who have some background in visual design, because they are used to having more specific control over elements. However, dynamic design might well be the preferred choice depending on the scenario. You should know how to do both, and how to combine the two for maximum flexibility.

APPLYING A FIXED TABLE DESIGN

In the earlier grid example, I showed you a design that has a left functional margin and an area of body text. One way to approach this design is to use a table. The grid that I drew showed four total columns. The first column manages the left navigation; the second, the whitespace between the navigation and the body text; the third, the body of the document; and the fourth, a precise amount of whitespace.

➔ For more information on working with background designs, **see** "Creating Professional Web Graphics," **p. 603**

To fix this page to a 640×480 resolution (with a 585×295 per screen recommendation), follow these steps:

1. Determine how much space is necessary for each section. (For my page, I want 125 pixels for my navigational margin, 10 pixels of whitespace between the margin and my text, and a right margin of 45.)
2. Add up these sections. (In my example, I get a total of 180 pixels. Subtract that number from 585. I end up with 405 pixels available for my body area.)
3. Fix this information into the table. To do so, create a table with the fixed width of 585 pixels. Then create four cells, each with the appropriate number of fixed pixels for each cell.

Listing 16.1 shows the HTML code necessary to create the grid.

LISTING 16.1 HTML CODE FOR A FIXED, LEFT-MARGIN TABLE

```
<HTML>
<HEAD>
<TITLE>Fixed, left-Margin Table</TITLE>
</HEAD>

<BODY>
<TABLE border="0" width="585" cellpadding="0" cellspacing="0">
<TR>
<TD width="125" align="left" valign="top">

</TD>

<TD width="10" align="left" valign="top">

</TD>
```

continues

LISTING 16.1 CONTINUED

```
<TD width="405" align="left" valign="top">


</TD>


<TD width="45" align="left" valign="top">


</TD>
</TR>
</TABLE>
</BODY>
</HTML>
```

In coding the opening `<TABLE>` tag, note that I included the `border`, `cellpadding`, and `cellspacing` attributes along with the `width`. This approach goes back to the "don't let the browser do the thinking for you" concept.

Along the same lines, every table cell includes the correct width but also the default "left" alignment and top alignment. (You can set these attributes as you ultimately need them to be set; they are the conventions I typically begin with.)

The example in Listing 16.1 isn't the entire picture. Although later generation (4.0 and above) browsers in both the IE and Netscape varieties tend to respect cell widths, you *always* run the risk of a collapsing or drifting table cell unless you fix that cell. One way to do so is to incorporate a graphic into the cell design. My navigation buttons, for example, are all 125 pixels wide, so the cell to the left is going to be sturdy. What about my other cells, however? I either have to do the same thing with a specific graphic, or include a single pixel, transparent GIF (known as a spacer GIF) stretched to the width of the table to ensure that it really *is* fixed.

How to Make a Spacer GIF

In Photoshop or your favorite imaging program, create an image that is 1×1 pixel. Fill the image with a color (I use white). Now, index the color and reduce the bits to the lowest number your imaging program allows. Export the file as a GIF, but before saving, remove all the color and be sure that the image is not interlaced. Save this file as spacer.gif, and place it in your images directory. You can now call upon it at any time.

Listing 16.2 shows the code with the navigation buttons and spacer graphics in place.

LISTING 16.2 FIXED, LEFT-MARGIN DESIGN WITH SPACER GRAPHICS INCLUDED

```
<HTML>
<HEAD>
```

```
<TITLE>Fixed, left-Margin Table</TITLE>

</HEAD>

<BODY background="images/bluebak.gif">

<TABLE border="0" width="585" cellpadding="0" cellspacing="0">

<TR>

<TD width="125" align="left" valign="top">

<P>

<BR>

<BR>

<A href="new.html"><IMG src="images/new.gif" border="0" width="125" height="30"
➥alt="what's new"></A>

<BR>

<A href="about.html"><IMG src="images/about_us.gif" border="0" width="125"
➥height="30" alt="About Us"></A>

<BR>

<A href="products.html"><IMG src="images/products.gif" border="0" width="125"
➥height="30" alt="products"></A>

<BR>

<A href="contact.html"><IMG src="images/contact.gif" border="0" width="125"
➥height="30" alt="contact"></A>

</TD>


<TD width="10" align="left" valign="top">

<IMG src="images/spacer.gif" border="0" width="10" height="1" alt="">

</TD>


<TD width="405" align="left" valign="top">

<IMG src="images/company_header.gif" border="0" width="405" height="50"
➥alt="welcome to the company">

</TD>


<TD width="45" align="left" valign="toptop">

<IMG src="images/spacer.gif" border="0" width="45" height="1" alt="">

</TD>

</TR>

</TABLE>

</BODY>

</HTML>
```

In Figure 16.3, you can see the results. This table will not collapse, because every cell is mathematically accounted for. In Figure 16.4, the table's border is set to 1 so that you can see the grid.

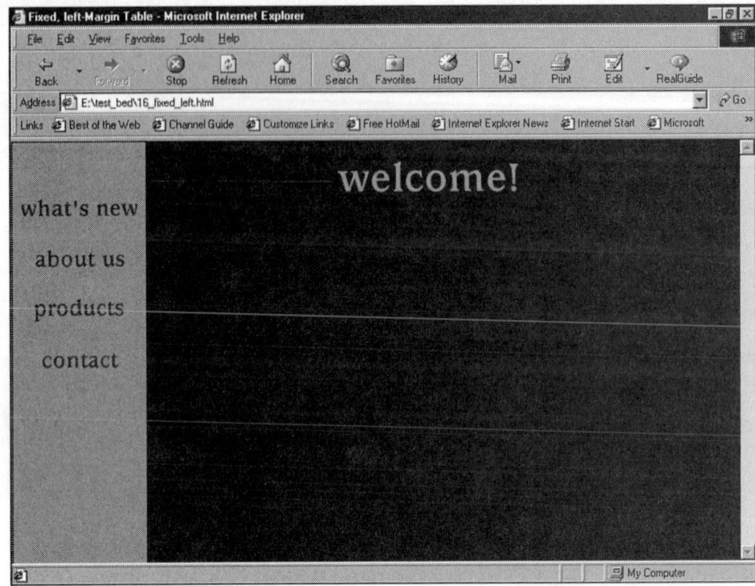

Figure 16.3
Fixed, left-margin table design. This popular design method is used throughout the Web as a method of keeping navigation and content in specific, familiar locations.

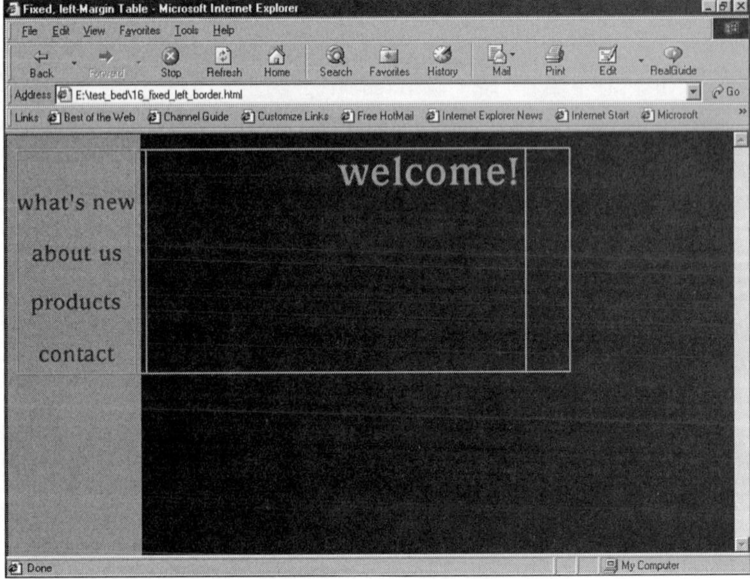

Figure 16.4
This table has a border attribute set to 1 so that you can see the grid—note the cells where the spacer GIFs fill in.

If you want to reverse the process—say you want to fix a table with a right margin—you prepare it exactly the same way. Mark off the exact widths of each section—whether it be whitespace, a navigation area, or a body text area—and do the math.

Of course, one of the problems with designing to the lowest common resolution occurs when someone comes along viewing the page at a higher resolution. In the case of fixed tables, more whitespace is visible at the right and bottom of the page. The design will be set into the left x- and y-axes snugly. Because this design is so prevalent on the Web, most individuals are not distracted by it.

Tip from molly

If you want to balance whitespace around fixed table designs, center the table using the DIV element. It won't be noticeable at low resolution, but at higher resolutions you'll end up with the empty space flowing around the fixed table instead of weighing heavily on one side of the page.

→ To learn more about how to work with the DIV element **see** "Formatting and Aligning Text," **p. 136**

Stick to this process for fixed designs and you'll never force a horizontal scrollbar!

Caution

In fixed design, you must never exceed a cell's parameters. In other words, if you have a cell that is 125 pixels wide, but you put a 200-pixel–wide graphic in it, you will cause the table to render improperly.

WORKING WITH DYNAMIC TABLE DESIGN

To create tables that stretch to accommodate any space, you can make them dynamic by using a percentage for widths instead of a fixed layout. Dynamic tables come in handy when designing tables that contain some graphical information, but are more loosely designed.

Listing 16.3 shows a dynamic table. I've made the entire table dynamic—placing a **100%** value in the <TABLE> tag itself (both height and width) and creating four dynamic columns of 25% each. What's powerful about this table is that it will adjust to the dimensions of the available space, no matter what.

LISTING 16.3 A DYNAMIC TABLE

```
<HTML>
<HEAD>
<TITLE>Dynamic Table</TITLE>
</HEAD>
<BODY>
<TABLE border="1" width="100%" height="100%" cellpadding="1" cellspacing="1">
<TR>
<TD width="25%" align="left" valign="top">
text
</TD>

<TD width="25%" align="left" valign="top">
text
</TD>
```

continues

LISTING 16.3 CONTINUED

```
<TD width="25%" align="left" valign="top">
text

</TD>

<TD width="25%" align="left" valign="top">
text
</TD>
</TR>
</TABLE>
</BODY>
</HTML>
```

In Figure 16.5, you can see the table at full resolution. If I make the browser window smaller (see Figure 16.6), the table automatically adjusts. If I did this with a fixed table, however, I would obscure all the information that fell outside the exact pixel range of my browser window size.

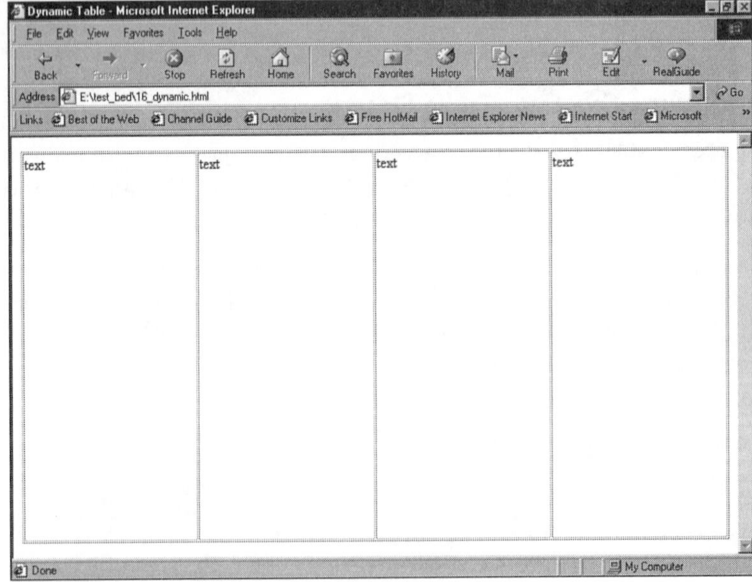

Figure 16.5
A dynamic table at 640×480 resolution.

The greatest challenge with dynamic table design, however, is that you lose the integrity of the fixed grid that allows you to stabilize a precision design within it.

COMBINATION FIXED AND DYNAMIC TABLE DESIGN

One way to reach for the best of both worlds is to combine fixed and dynamic approaches. The wisdom here, however, is to ensure that only one cell is fixed to a percentage width, and that width should be `100%`. This approach helps you maintain the shape of the layout but allows for dynamic positioning of text.

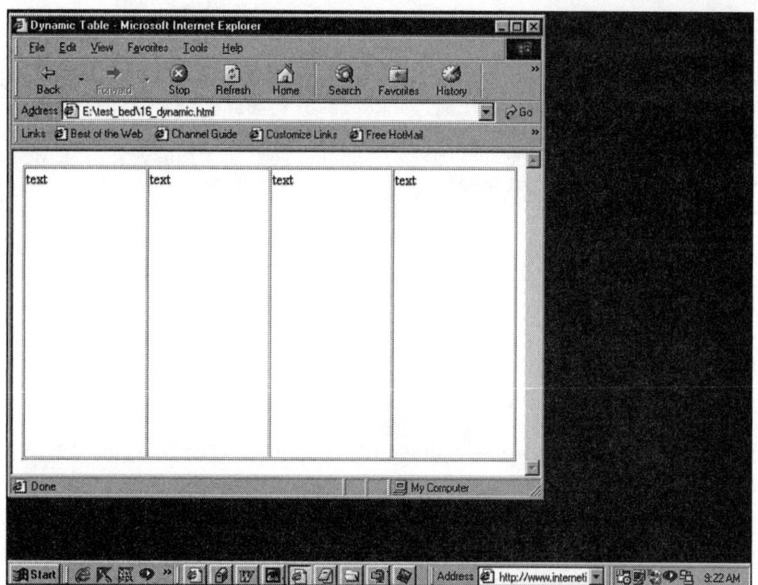

Figure 16.6
Dynamic tables readjusted to browser size fill only the available space.

This approach works well, for example, if I have a left and right margin I want to keep fixed, but I want to keep the center, body area dynamic. I could achieve this effect by fixing the cells to the left and right using both a fixed width cell and spacer GIF set to the dimensions of the cell, but leaving the center cell dynamic. Listing 16.4 shows an example of this effect.

Listing 16.4 Fixed and Dynamic Cells

```
<HTML>
<HEAD>
<TITLE>Fixed and Dynamic Table</TITLE>
</HEAD>
<BODY background="images/decorative.gif" text="#FFFFFF">
<TABLE border="0" width="100%" cellpadding="0" cellspacing="0">
<TR>

<TD width="75" align="left" valign="top">
<IMG src="images/spacer.gif" border="0" width="75" height="1" alt="">
</TD>

<TD width="100%" align="left" valign="top">
<P>A maid servant then brought them water in a beautiful golden ewer and poured it
into a silver basin for them to wash their hands, and she drew a clean table
beside them. An upper servant brought them bread, and offered them many good
things of what there was in the house, the carver fetched them plates of all
manner of meats and set cups of gold by their side, and a man-servant brought them
wine and poured it out for them.
<P>Then the suitors came in and took their places on the benches and seats.
Forthwith men servants poured water over their hands, maids went round with the
bread-baskets, pages filled the mixing-bowls with wine and water, and they laid
their hands upon the good things that were before them.
```

continues

LISTING 16.4 CONTINUED

```
<P>As soon as they had had enough to eat and drink they wanted music and dancing,
which are the crowning embellishments of a banquet, so a servant brought a lyre to
Phemius, whom they compelled perforce to sing to them. As soon as he touched his
lyre and began to sing Telemachus spoke low to Minerva, with his head close to
hers that no man might hear.
</TD>
<TD width="50" align="left" valign="top"><IMG src="images/spacer.gif" border="0"
width="50" height="1" alt="">
</TD>
</TR>
</TABLE>
</BODY>
</HTML>
```

In this case, you have the advantage of being able to fix margins. Here, you can accommodate a left, decorative background and whitespace to the right (see Figure 16.7). You also can allow for the dynamic wrapping of text (see Figure 16.8).

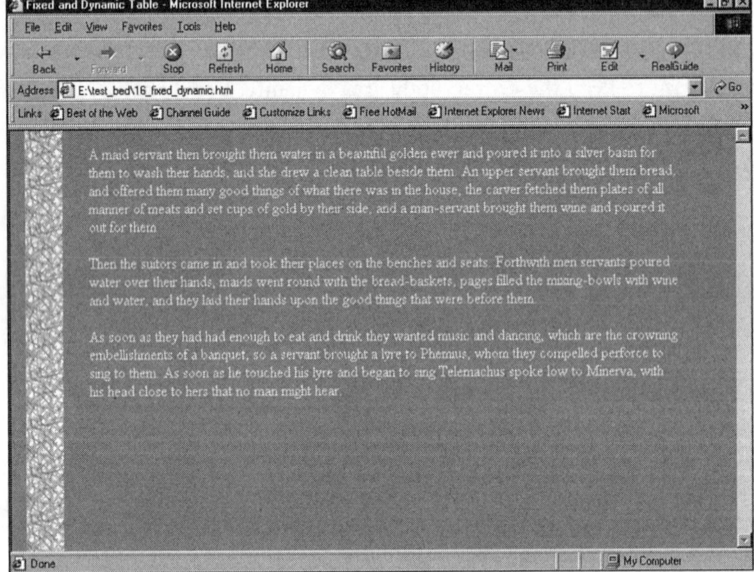

Figure 16.7
Fixed margins over a decorative background allow for better positioning of the text so it does not run into the decorative margin design.

Tip from molly

What happens when you have a fixed table design, but you want it to be available for a variety of resolutions? If you're that committed to providing people with perfection at any resolution, you can create separate designs and route browsers by resolution using JavaScript.

→ To use the JavaScript Route-by-Res script to have site visitors automatically routed to resolution-specific pages, **see** "Using JavaScript," **p. 423**

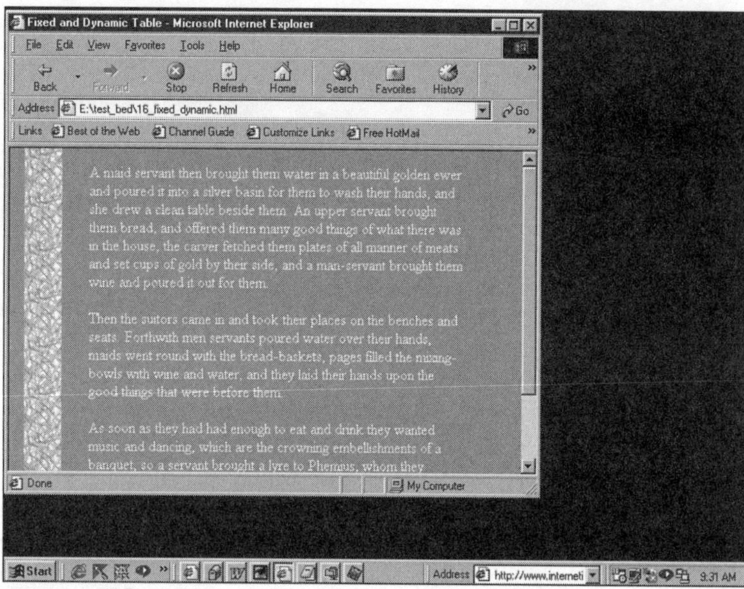

Figure 16.8
The fixed and dynamic combination readjusted. Note how the design adjusts to the screen space, without the appearance of a horizontal scrollbar.

NESTING AND STACKING TABLES

To create complex layouts using tables, you can often employ column and row spanning. Spanning provides options that help designers break from strict column and row design and add some visual diversity.

➔ For information on column and row spanning, **see** "Table Fundamentals," **p. 320**

However, sometimes this technique is limited or cannot provide you with the control you're after. Say you want to create a layout that manages a background margin tile, yet you want to have central sections broken up. And, within those sections, you want to add swatches of background design or color.

One method of enabling complex table design is to nest tables. In this process, you put a table within a table to achieve the layout you require.

Here's the rule: Any table cell within an accurately formed table can accept a complete, new table. Doing so creates a nest:

```
<TD>
     <TABLE>
     <TR>

     <TD>
     </TD>
     </TR>
     </TABLE>
</TD>
```

You can take the nest even further:

```
<TD>
     <TABLE>
```

```
<TR>

<TD>

    <TABLE>
<TR>

<TD>
</TD>
</TR>
</TABLE>

</TD>
</TR>
</TABLE>
</TD>
```

Nesting tables is one of the keys to complex table design. After you've learned the basics, nesting can help you get control over space within space.

Creating great tables, but finding that they take too long to download to the visitor's browser? See "Reducing Fat Table Code" in the Troubleshooting section at the end of this chapter.

Caution

Use nesting creatively, but use it wisely. Nesting anything beyond three levels is a good indicator that you need to go back and examine your grid, looking for a more simple approach to the layout.

In Listing 16.5, I've applied the rule to create a page layout that is both elegant and a bit more complex than you've seen thus far. It employs background graphics in certain cells, as well as column spanning and nested tables.

LISTING 16.5 A COMPLEX TABLE LAYOUT

```
<HTML>
<HEAD>
<TITLE>Nested Table Example</TITLE>
</HEAD>
<BODY background="images/black_strip_bak.gif" text="#FFFFCC">
<TABLE border="0" width="585" cellpadding="0" cellspacing="0">
<TR>
<TD width="70" align="left" valign="top">
<IMG src="images/spacer.gif" width="70" height="1" border="0" alt="">
</TD>

<TD width="500" align="right" valign="top" colspan="3">
<h3><I>An Excerpt from Homer's Odyssey</I></h3>
<TABLE border="0" width="500" cellpadding="0" cellspacing="0">
    <TR>
<TD background="images/flocked.gif" width="350" align="left" valign="top">
<P>A maid servant then brought them water in a beautiful golden ewer and poured it
into a silver basin for them to wash their hands, and she drew a clean table
beside them.
<P>An upper servant brought them bread, and offered them many good things of what
there was in the house, the carver fetched them plates of all manner of meats and
```

```
set cups of gold by their side, and a man-servant brought them wine and poured it
out for them.
<P>Then the suitors came in and took their places on the benches and
seats.Forthwith men servants poured water over their hands, maids went round with
the bread-baskets, pages filled the mixing-bowls with wine and water, and they
laid their hands upon the good things that were before them.
    </TD>
    <TD width="50" align="left" valign="top">
    <IMG src="images/spacer.gif" width="50" height="1" border="0" alt="">
    </TD>
<TD background="images/flocked.gif" width="100" align="left" valign="middle">
<I>So a servant brought a lyre to Phemius, whom they compelled perforce to sing to
them. </I>
    </TD>
    </TR>
    </TABLE>

</TD>
<TD width="20" align="left" valign="top">
<IMG src="images/spacer.gif" width="20" height="1" border="0" alt="">
</TD>
</TR>
</TABLE>
</BODY>
</HTML>
```


In Figure 16.9, I took the liberty of turning the table `border` attributes on, using a value of `1` so that you can see the grid I've created. Figure 16.10 shows the complete results, without the grid.

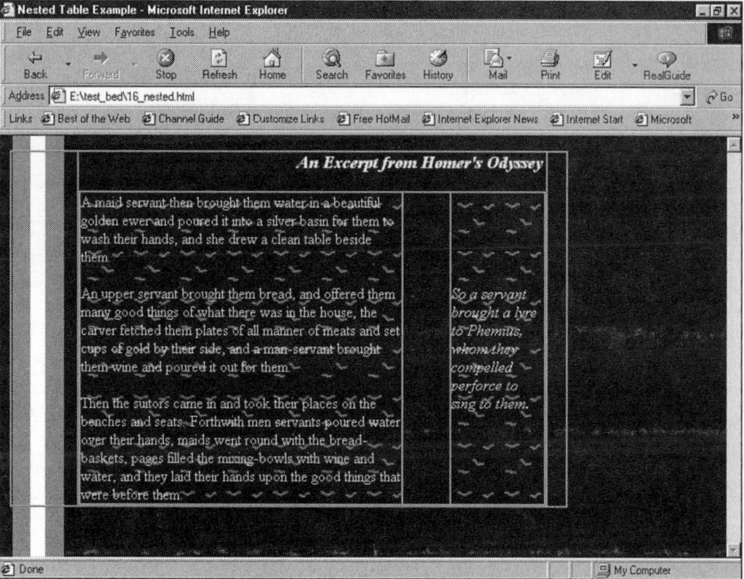

Figure 16.9
Setting the table borders to `1` shows the grid.

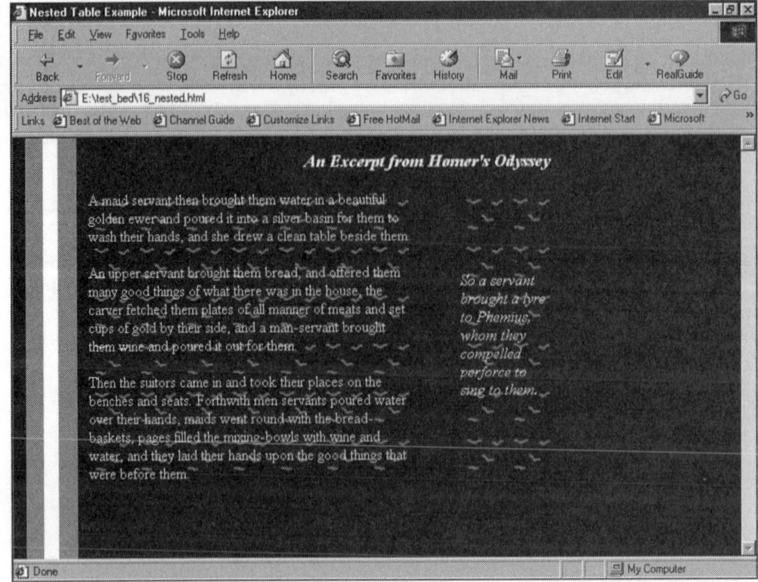

Figure 16.10
Here, I reset the borders to 0 to display the layout.

You can also stack tables. In this process, you take more than one table and place it above another. The advantage of stacking is that you can separate particular sections of a page, revert to standard HTML in between, return to a table, or combine any variety of options to create varied design.

Listing 16.6 demonstrates a set of stacked tables with a numbered list between the two tables.

LISTING 16.6 STACKED TABLES

```
<HTML>
<HEAD>
<TITLE>Stacked Table Example</TITLE>
</HEAD>
<BODY background="images/flocked.gif" text="#FFFFCC">
<TABLE border="0" width="595" cellpadding="0" cellspacing="0">
<TR>
<TD width="100" align="left" valign="top">
<h3>An Excerpt from Homer's Odyssey</h3>
</TD>
<TD width="495" align="left" valign="middle">
A maid servant then brought them water in a beautiful golden ewer and poured it
into a silver basin for them to wash their hands, and she drew a clean table
beside them.
</TD>

</TR>
</TABLE>
<BR>
Then the suitors came in and took their places on the benches and seats:
<BR>
<UL>
```

```
<li>Men servants poured water over their hands
<li>maids went round with the bread-baskets
<li>pages filled the mixing-bowls with wine and water
</UL>
<P>and they laid their hands upon the good things that were before them.
<TABLE border="0" width="595" cellpadding="0" cellspacing="0">
<TR>
<TD width="595" align="left" valign="top">
<IMG SRC="images/lyre.gif" width="100" height="69" border="0" ALT="lyre
image"align="left" hspace="10" Vspace="10">
<P>As soon as they had had enough to eat and drink they wanted music and dancing,
which are the crowning embellishments of a banquet, so a servant brought a lyre to
Phemius, whom they compelled perforce to sing to them.  As soon as he touched his
lyre and began to sing Telemachus spoke low to Minerva, with his head close to
hers that no man might hear.
</TD>
</TR>
</TABLE>
</BODY>
</HTML>
```


Figure 16.11 shows the results.

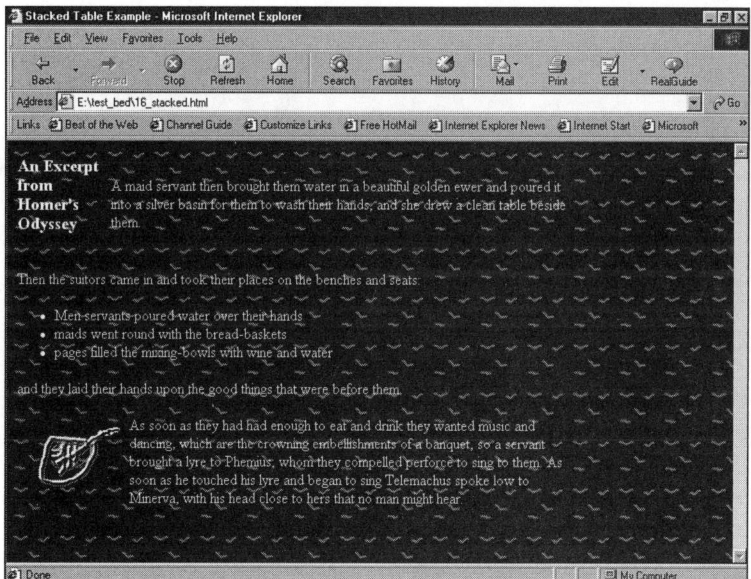

Figure 16.11
Stacked table design.

ALIGNING TABLES

Aligning tables provides you with additional power over the way your table designs are laid out in relation to the screen, as well as in relation to other elements on the page. To align a table horizontally on a page, use the `DIV` element, with a left, center, or right value:

```
<DIV align="right">

<TABLE>
<TR>
<TD>
This table is aligned to the right of the available browser space, but the cell
information will not be right aligned, unless I add an alignment attribute to,
or within, the cell itself.
</TD>
</TR>
</TABLE>
</DIV>
```

Note

Recall that the `align` attribute within table tags typically aligns the information within a table—not the table itself.

You can align tables vertically, too. To do so, use the `height` attribute combined with a middle alignment in a table cell:

```
<TABLE height="100%">
<TR>

<TD valign="middle">
Content goes here
</TD>
</TR>
</TABLE>
```

You also can combine width and height (see Figure 16.12) to combine vertical and horizontal alignment:

```
<TABLE height="100%" width="100%" border="1">
<TR>

<TD valign="middle">
Content goes here
</TD>
</TR>
</TABLE>
```

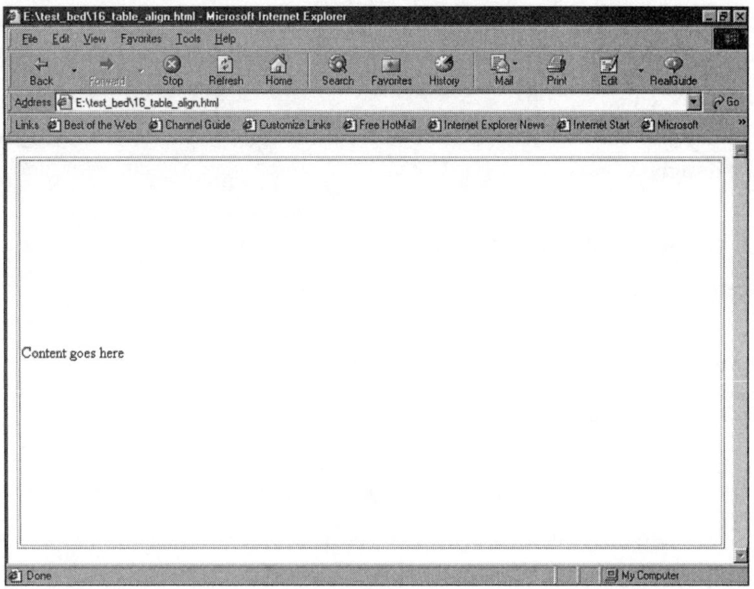

Figure 16.12
A table that is both horizontally and vertically aligned to 100% width and height will take up the entire screen space. Note that with a middle cell alignment, the content appears in the center of the table.

SLICING GRAPHICS FOR PLACEMENT IN A TABLE

One of the more interesting uses of tables is to create a grid system for the placement of graphics. This approach is sensible when you want to animate sections of a larger image or to place images in otherwise difficult-to-reach places on the browser page, such as slightly left of center. Instead of using one really big graphic to accommodate this look, designers slice the graphics, keeping the overall weight down and the load time faster.

→ For more information on working with graphics, **see** "Creating Professional Web Graphics" **p. 598** and "Imagemaps, Animation, and Special Graphic Techniques" **p. 648**

In Figure 16.13, I've captured a Web-based image that is built using numerous pieces. This image has three animated parts: the eye circles around, the mouth opens and closes, and the ear moves, too.

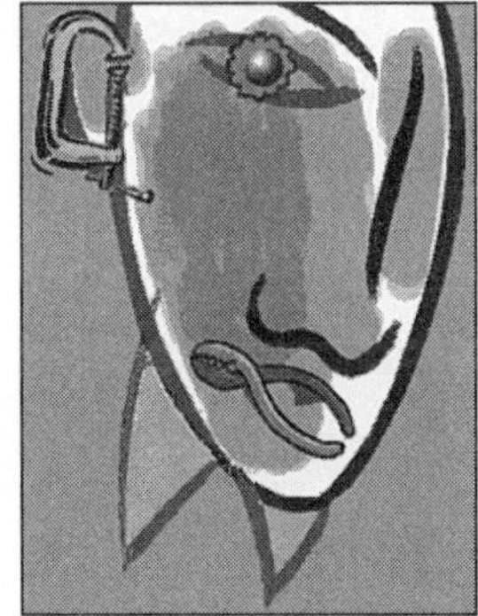

Figure 16.13
An image that is actually made up of several sliced images.

If this image had been created as one graphic, it would have weighed a lot more—to contain all the movement and color information. By slicing the image and placing it within a table, the weight of the image is reduced, and so is the page's load time.

Listing 16.7 shows a section of code for the image. You'll notice some JavaScript included in the design.

LISTING 16.7 SLICING A GRAPHIC

```
<table cellpadding=0 cellspacing=0 border=0>
    <tr>
        <td><a href="../i-methods.html" target="_top"
onMouseOver = "imgOn('img1')" onMouseOut = "imgOff('img1')">
<img src="../graphics/toolhead1.gif" width=71 height=99 border=0
name="img1"></a></td>
        <td><a href="../i-identity.html" target="_top"
onMouseOver = "imgOn('img2')" onMouseOut = "imgOff('img2')">
<img src="../graphics/toolhead2.gif" width=97 height=99 border=0
name="img2"></a></td>
       <td><img src="../graphics/toolhead3.gif" width=51 height=99 border=0></td>
   </tr>
   <tr>
      <td><img src="../graphics/toolhead4.gif" width=71 height=55 border=0></td>
      <td><img src="../graphics/toolhead5.gif" width=97 height=55 border=0></td>
      <td><img src="../graphics/toolhead6.gif" width=51 height=55 border=0></td>
   </tr>
   <tr>
      <td><img src="../graphics/toolhead7.gif" width=71 height=71 border=0></td>
      <td><a href="../i-proof.html" target="_top" onMouseOver = "imgOn('img3')"
onMouseOut = "imgOff('img3')"><img src="../graphics/toolhead8.gif" width=97
height=71 border=0 name="img3"></a></td>
       <td><img src="../graphics/toolhead9.gif" width=51 height=71 border=0></td>
   </tr>
   <tr>
      <td><img src="../graphics/toolhead10.gif" width=71 height=64 border=0></td>
      <td><img src="../graphics/toolhead11.gif" width=97 height=64 border=0></td>
      <td> </td>
   </tr>
</table>
```

Figure 16.14 shows the page before the images load; you can see the outlines that create the grid.

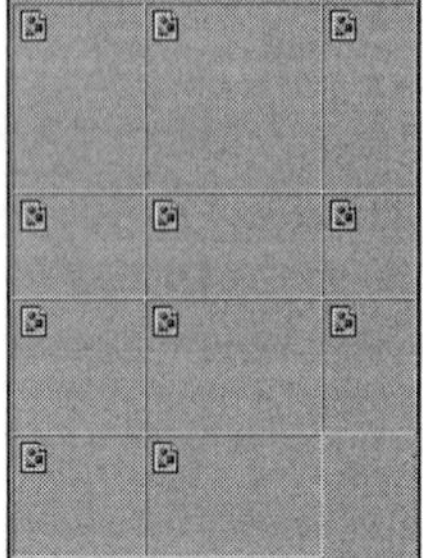

Figure 16.14
The table grid for the sliced images is seen here before the image slices appear.

Tip from molly

When tabling sliced images, you often need to make sure that sequential cells are on the same line of code for the cells to line up properly. Use *no* padding or spacing in the table; otherwise, you cannot line up individual graphics.

More and more tools are becoming available to help with this process. Macromedia Fireworks and Adobe ImageStyler are prime examples. Many designers create grid systems in Photoshop and then slice the larger image into separate images.

→ For more information on Fireworks and other imaging tools, **see** "Web Graphic Formats and Professional Tools," **p. 585**

TROUBLESHOOTING

REDUCING FAT TABLE CODE

How can I keep my tables streamlined so that they load quickly and orderly?

Tables can be notoriously fat—filled with extraneous code that is ultimately unnecessary for the success of that table. Part of this problem emanates from WYSIWYG software, as these applications use tables to lay out every piece of information on a page! Some of this comes from coders who are after precision but might not readily see a more simple approach. Here are some pointers on getting your tables lean and mean:

- Begin with the vertical rather than horizontal arrangement. It's *amazing* how this orientation will change the way your table layouts are designed! Look for how many are absolutely necessary to support the page.
- After you've determined your columns, then *and only then* look at the rows and rigorously work to minimize them. Do you need more than one row? Are you certain? If so, how many do you need to accomplish the layout? Reach for standard HTML elements instead of table elements where you can. Can you use a break tag or two to get the whitespace instead of adding a row? If so, do it!
- Print out a copy of your layout and draw the table grid onto the page. Try a few times to see if you can reduce extraneous code but maintain the table integrity.
- Reduce the number of tables in the layout, if possible. Is there anyway you can reasonably incorporate the contents of the page into only one table?

Less is almost always more in HTML and Web development. This concept is especially true when working with tables.

Note

If an attribute, element, or table technique is absolutely necessary to accomplish a table design, leave it in! Some layouts are going to be complex and weigh more than others. However, following these steps will ensure that you get the slimmest possible code no matter the situation.

DESIGNING FOR THE REAL WORLD

CREATING A TABLE FROM A MOCKUP

Now that you've got some advanced table concepts and pro tips under your belt, it's time to apply what you've learned to the project you began in Chapter 15.

After you have your design mocked up, follow these steps:

1. Print out the mockup. This gives you an opportunity to move away from the screen and think creatively.
2. Draw a table grid directly over your design. Do this several times (see Figure 16.15), trying out different approaches and ideally minimizing the table's complexity (see Figure 16.16).

Figure 16.15
My first attempt at mocking up the table is much more complex than necessary.

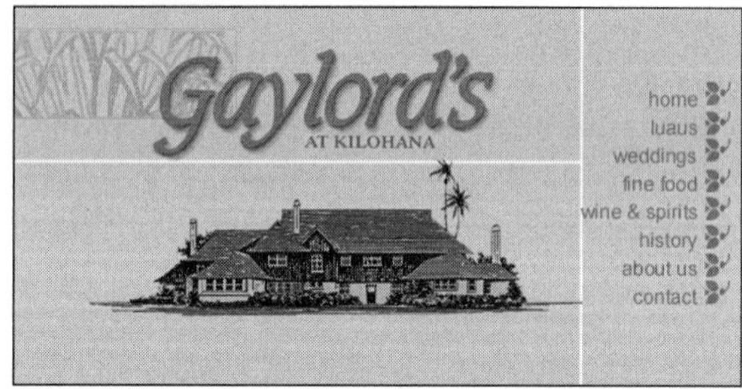

Figure 16.16
A simple, elegant approach to the table design—two columns, two rows. The graphics will be placed on a solid background, and I'll use break tags to gain space where necessary.

3. Move back to your imaging program and set up guides, measuring each table element carefully.

Note

Depending on the style of graphics and background, you can often keep graphics whole without slicing. This is especially true when your graphics contain very few colors, or you don't require movement via GIF animation in a portion of the design.

Now you can generate the graphics and code the table. Ideally, you've worked this process through rigorously enough so that your table is streamlined—achieving what it needs without being too complicated and weighty.

CHAPTER 17

Working with Frames

In this chapter

TO FRAME OR NOT TO FRAME

Frames have been both a source of frustration and empowerment for Web site designers and visitors alike. The frustration comes from a number of concerns. First, frames divide the available browser space, which is preciously restricted to begin with. Frames, particularly in their bordered manifestation, literally take what is a small, contained space and break that space up into smaller, even more contained spaces (see Figure 17.1).

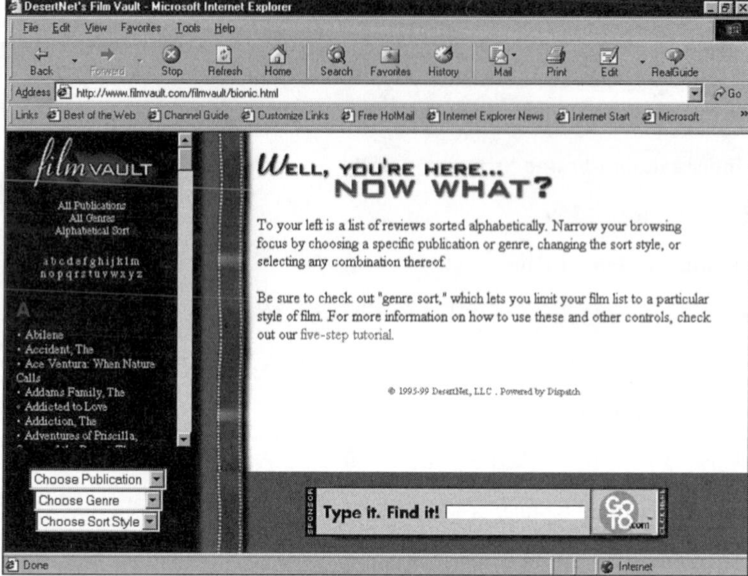

Figure 17.1
Bordered frames break up the screen's visible space.

→ For information about available screen space, **see** "Resolution, Gamma, and the Visual Environment," **p. 555**

Using frames requires an understanding of accessibility options for the site to be made useful to blind and disabled site visitors. This makes frames an unfortunate choice for specific audiences unless the coder knows what he or she is doing. Finally, frames force the designer to write more code, because they require more actual pages of code per visible page.

Because of these difficulties, only the most technologically adept, design-literate of coders can use frames as part of a design well, and even then at the risk of upsetting visitors to the pages they built.

But frames are also empowering. One aspect of this empowerment is that coders can keep sections of a page static while other parts of the page can be used to display other pages. Particularly handy for fixed navigation, this is a common approach to the development of menu bars and other, specialty areas that are to remain in place.

Note

> The significance of frames as a serious option for Web developers is reflected through HTML 4.0's Frameset interpretation. That an entire subset of the language exists demonstrates how important a role frames play within the formal language.

→ For HTML 4.0's interpretations, **see** "Understanding HTML 4.0," **p. 15**

The most juicy bit of news is that frames, particularly of the border*less* variety, give designers another method to create a grid system upon which to base their design (see Figure 17.2).

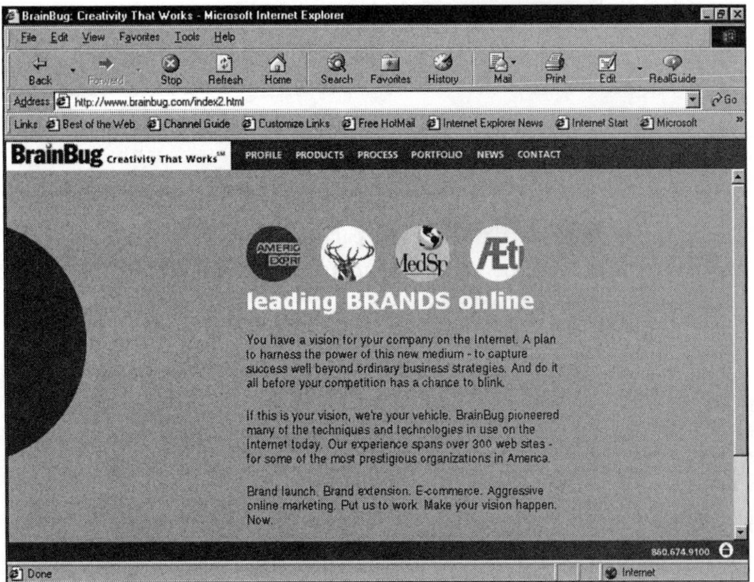

Figure 17.2
Borderless frames create a design system similar to what is available when using tables, however with other capabilities such as keeping sections of the design static.

→ To see if tables are a better option for your particular design needs, **see** "Table Fundamentals," **p. 304**

This system expands frames from their original role as an organizational tool to include page format and design control. With borderless frames, as with borderless tables, individual sections of a page can be defined and controlled.

But where tables can only be used on a page-by-page basis, frame technology introduces the static concept, discussed previously, and the aspect of *targets* allowing a variety of powerful controls.

Webmasters and site designers can now make better choices about how to employ frames. Whether the choice is to use dimensional borders for an attractive interface or to create pages with frames as the silent and strong foundation beneath a complex and multifaceted design, the Web designer is ultimately empowered by having these choices.

No matter how you feel about frames, it's a good idea to know the ropes in terms of coding them. This way, you always have the option to use them if you like or to set them aside if you feel their use is problematic for your audience.

Concerned with issues related to linking to other Web sites from within your frames page? See " Using Frames to Contain Other Sites," in the Troubleshooting section at the end of this chapter.

UNDERSTANDING FRAME STRUCTURE

Before I introduce the practical aspects of how to design a framed page, I want to demonstrate a fundamental aspect of frame design. Much like tables, frames are built by thinking in columns and rows. Tables, as described in Chapter 15, "Table Fundamentals," get a bit complex with the ways columns and rows are spanned, creating a technological blur between horizontal and vertical reference points. Frames approach the issue in a much clearer way. A column is always a vertical control, a row a horizontal one.

Moreover, the syntax is clear. Rows are created using the `rows` attribute, columns use the `cols` attribute. Both columns and rows can be set to a value by using pixels *or* percentages. For example, `cols="240, *"` calls for a left column with a *width* of 240 pixels, and the right column, denoted by the asterisk, will be the *dynamic remainder* of the available viewing space.

To add more columns, simply define each one in turn. For example, if I wanted to create four columns of equal percent, the syntax would read `cols="25%,25%,25%,25%"`. The results of this sequence are shown in Figure 17.3.

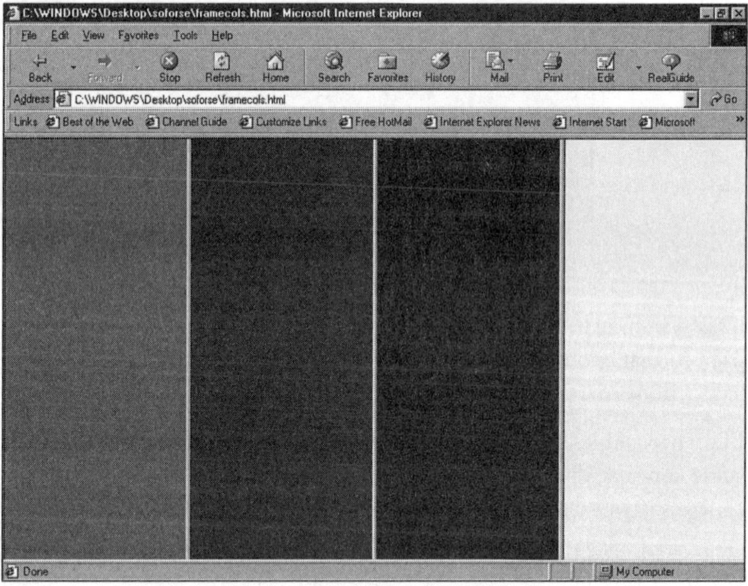

Figure 17.3
Here the frame columns have been designed in equal sizes using percentages.

Similarly, if I wanted to create rows rather than columns, I would simply change the syntax to `rows="240, *"`, and the results would be a top row with a *height* of 240 pixels. To create four individual rows of equal percent, I would call for `rows="25%,25%,25%,25%"`, as demonstrated in Figure 17.4.

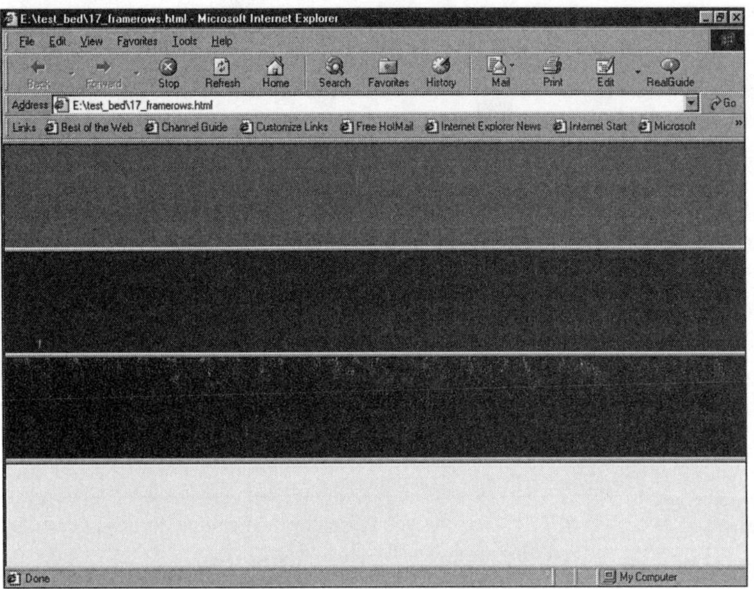

Figure 17.4
The frame rows seen here add up to a total sum of 240 pixels.

Note

To create combinations of columns and rows, the values are simply stacked into the appropriate tags and pages of the framed site.

THE FRAMESET

As with tables, there are only three elements absolutely necessary to build a framed page. Yes, frames can get a bit complicated, depending on the ways you want to employ them, but at the most basic level, all framed sites begin with the factors introduced here.

Note

A well laid-out frame-based site offering up-to-date HTML information, including beginning to advanced level frames data is *Sizzling HTML Jalfrezi*. Point your browser to `http://vzone.virgin.net/sizzling.jalfrezi/iniframe.htm` for a fine HTML and frames tutorial.

Any framed page requires a controlling HTML document that gives the instructions on how the framed page is to be set up. This control is called the *frameset*. Then, an HTML page is required for each individual frame. So how many basic elements does it take to make a framed page? The answer is simple: one HTML page *plus* the total number of frames.

Tip from molly

Remember your sums! A framed page requires one HTML page per each individually defined areas *plus* one HTML page for the control, or *frameset*, page.

The frameset is the control page of your framed site. In it, you'll argue primarily for the rows or columns you want to create and the HTML pages that will fill those rows or columns. This is done using two major tags:

- **<FRAMESET>**—This tag is for the frame, and its basic arguments define rows and columns. The frameset information is closed with a corresponding `</FRAMESET>` tag.
- **<FRAME>**—The `FRAME` tag argues individual frames within the frameset. This includes the location of the HTML document required to fill the frame, using the `src="x"` (where *x* assigns the relative or absolute URL to the location of the HTML page). A variety of other `<FRAME>` tag attributes will be covered later in the chapter.

It's important to remember that the `<FRAMESET>` tag is a conceptual replacement for the `<BODY>` tag in the frameset HTML page. Therefore, in a simple frameset, *no `BODY` tags* should appear.

Note

HTML 4.0 requires you to identify the frameset document by including the version information. This means you'll need to insert

```
<!DOCTYPE HTML PUBLIC "-//W3C//DTD HTML 4.0 Frameset//EN"
"http://www.w3.org/TR/REC-html40/frameset.dtd">
```

into any frameset conforming to transitional or strict HTML 4.0 interpretations. Note that I've left it out of these examples for the purposes of brevity. Depending upon your desire to comply with the standard, you'll want to consider putting it in your final code.

BUILDING A FRAMED PAGE

In this case, we're going to build a two-column page, with the left column serving as a simple menu that could eventually be used to guide a visitor through the site.

First, you'll create the HTML page for the left, or menu, column.

1. In your HTML editor, type the following:

```
<HTML>
<HEAD>
<TITLE>Menu</TITLE>
</HEAD>
<BODY>

<P><A href="about.html">About the Company</A>

<P><A href="clients.html">Company Clients</A>

<P><A href="contact.html">Contact Company</A>

</BODY>
</HEAD>
```

2. Save the file as `menu.html`.
3. View the file in your browser to see how it looks before you apply the frameset to it.
4. Now create the main page of HTML:

```
<HTML>
<HEAD>
<TITLE>Main Page</TITLE>
</HEAD>
<BODY>
<P>
<BR>
<BR>

Welcome to The Company! We specialize in a variety of high quality services.
Our clients encompass just about everyone who is anyone.

</BODY>
</HTML>
```

5. Save the file as `main.html`.
6. View the file in your Web browser to see what it looks like before adding the frameset command file.

Now you'll create the frameset.

1. Open your HTML editor and begin a new page. Type the following container:

```
<HTML>
<HEAD>
<TITLE>Frame Control</TITLE>
</HEAD>
<FRAMESET>

</FRAMESET>

</HTML>
```

2. Now you'll want to add the columns or rows. In this instance, I'm using columns:

```
<HTML>
<HEAD>
<TITLE>Frame Control</TITLE>
</HEAD>

<FRAMESET cols="240, *">
</FRAMESET>

</HTML>
```

3. The individual frames with their corresponding HTML pages are added by using the `FRAME` tag:

```
<HTML>
<HEAD>
<TITLE>Frame Control</TITLE>
</HEAD>
```

```
<FRAMESET cols="240, *">

<FRAME src="menu.html">
<FRAME src="main.html">

</FRAMESET>
</HTML>
```

4. Save the document as `index.html`.
5. Load the frameset page into your browser and view the results. Does it match Figure 17.5? If it does, congratulations!

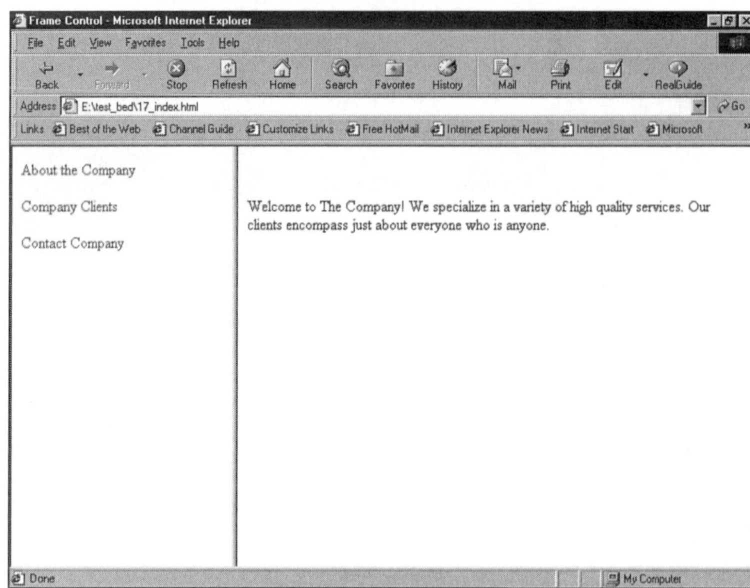

Figure 17.5
This figure displays a simple, framed page.

Note

You may have noticed that the `<FRAME>` tag is an exception to the open/close rule, as there is no counterpart `</FRAME>` tag. All the information for individual frames is placed within the tag and it is considered closed when the right-angle bracket ">" is reached.

Tip from

Pages not matching the examples? Look over your syntax carefully. It's amazing how tiny mistakes can create total HTML havoc.

SETTING FRAMESET AND FRAME TAG ATTRIBUTES

There are several powerful attributes available to the `<FRAMESET>` and `<FRAME>` tags.

The following list covers those used for the `<FRAMESET>`.

- `cols="x"`—As covered earlier, this attribute creates columns. An `"x"` value is given for each column in the framed page, and will be either a pixel value, a percentage value, or a combination of one of those plus the `"*"`, which creates a *dynamic* or *relative size* frame—the remainder of the framed space.
- `rows="x"`—This attribute is used to create rows in the same fashion that the column attribute is used.
- `border="x"`—The `border` attribute is used by Netscape Navigator 3.0, 4.0, and later to control border width. Value is set in pixel width.
- `frameborder="x"`—`frameborder` is used by the Internet Explorer browser to control border width in pixels. Netscape Navigator 3.0, 4.0, and later uses the attribute with a `yes` or `no` value.
- `framespacing="x"`—Used originally by Internet Explorer, this attribute controls border width.

Use the following tag attributes with the `<FRAME>` tag:

- `frameborder="x"`—Use this attribute to control frameborders around individual frames. Netscape Navigator requires a `yes` or `no` value, whereas Internet Explorer will look for a numeric pixel width value.
- `marginheight="x"`—Argue a value in pixels to control the height of the frame's margin.
- `marginwidth="x"`—This attribute argues for a frame's margin width in pixels.
- `name="x"`—This critical attribute allows the designer to name an individual frame. Naming frames permits *targeting* by links within other HTML pages. Names must begin with a standard letter or numeral.
- `noresize`—Simply place this attribute in your string if you want to allow re-sizing of a frame. This fixes the frame into the position and disallows a visitor to alter the size of a frame. You'll note that this is an interesting attribute in that it takes no value.
- `scrolling="x"`—By arguing `"yes"`, `"no"`, or `"auto"`, you can control the appearance of a scrollbar. A `"yes"` value automatically places a scrollbar in the frame, a `"no"` value ensures that no scrollbar ever appears. The `"auto"` argument turns the power over to the browser, which will automatically place a scrollbar in a frame should it be required.
- `src="x"`—The `"x"` value is replaced with the relative or absolute URL of the HTML page you want to place within the frame at hand.

So many choices—ultimately lending to a lot of control with frame-based design.

Exploring a Frame with Margin, Resize, and Scroll Controls

Listing 17.1 shows the code for a framed page with `marginheight`, `marginwidth`, `resize`, and `scrolling` attributes.

Listing 17.1 Frameset with marginheight, width, resize, and scrolling Attributes

```
<HTML>
<HEAD>
<TITLE>Frame With Numerous Controls</TITLE>
</HEAD>

<FRAMESET cols="240, *">
<FRAME src="menu.html" marginheight="5" marginwidth="5" noresize scrolling="auto">
<FRAME src="main.html" marginheight="15" marginwidth="15" noresize
scrolling="auto">

</FRAMESET>
</HTML>
```

The first issue to be aware of is that this is a frameset, therefore no `BODY` tag is used. Instead, the `FRAMESET` tag, and its companion closing tag, are placed around the internal information.

Within the `FRAMESET` tag, I've coded for a left margin of 240 pixels, and I've used the "*" value to allow for the right frame to be dynamic.

Following this information are the two strings of syntax for each of the corresponding frames. The left frame information is placed first, and then the right frame information is coded underneath.

In the first frame instance, I've named the source, and I've added margin information of height and width at 5 pixels each. This gives me a bit of whitespace around any of the information appearing within that frame. I've chosen the `noresize` option, and set `scrolling` to `auto` so that at lower resolutions individuals will see a scrollbar should it become necessary.

I'm of the opinion that a `"yes"` value for scrolling rarely looks good, but is extremely useful when the frame in question contains a long document. A `"no"` value is most valuable for fixed-column frames used for menus.

If you do your math and are absolutely certain that you have allowed for enough viewing area to contain the HTML information, use the `"no"` value. Setting scrolling on `"auto"` is usually the favorable choice, because it allows the browser to make the decision. An `"auto"` value is especially favorable wherever you've argued for *dynamic* or *relative size* (a `"*"` value) rows and columns.

Resizing is similar in concept. Although offering it can foul up your attractive, well-thought out framed pages, resizing can be valuable when you want to give your visitor ultimate control. In this case, I've decided to not allow my visitor that control.

The second frame is coded exactly the same way, with the one distinction of more whitespace allotted to the area via the margin controls.

Targeting Windows

To effectively use frames, a designer must decide where link options will load. For example, in the frame page you've developed so far in this chapter, I've guided you to create a menu on the left, and a larger frame field on the right. This is a natural start for effective design using frames.

There are two basic ways to link, or *target*, HTML pages to specific windows:

- Combine `target` and `name` attributes to specifically target windows.
- Use a magic target name.

`target` and `name` attributes allow you to add more HTML pages to your framed site and to target a specific window by naming that window and targeting the link.

Note A *magic target* name is a special name reserved by browsers to perform a distinct function.

Creating a Frame Using `target` and `name` Attributes

Naming the target is the best place to start. Using the same frameset code in Listing 17.1 shown previously, I've added a name to the right, or "main," frame:

```
<HTML>
<HEAD>
<TITLE>Frames with Targets and Names</TITLE>
</HEAD>

<FRAMESET cols="240, *">

<FRAME src="menu.html" marginheight="5" marginwidth="5" noresize scrolling="auto">
<FRAME src="main.html" name="right" marginheight="15" marginwidth="15" noresize
scrolling="auto">

</FRAMESET>
</HTML>
```

After the target window has a name, the target must be added to the link. In the menu file, I'm going to specify the target, as follows:

```
<HTML>
<HEAD>
<TITLE>Menu</TITLE>
</HEAD>
<BODY>

<A href="about.html" target="right">About the Company</A>
<P>

<A href="clients.html" target="right">Company Clients</A>
<P>

<A href="contact.html" target="right">Contact Company</A>
<P>

</BODY>
</HTML>
```

As long as I've created each of the pages referred to in the links, each click of the link on this menu will load the appropriate page into the right frame (see Figure 17.6).

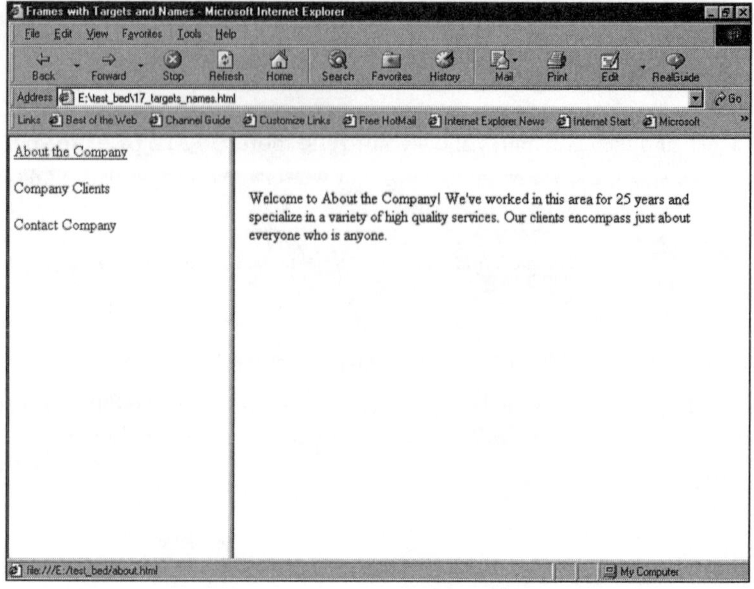

Figure 17.6
Targeting the right frame causes the pages referred to in the links to appear in that frame.

Tip from molly

Want all of a site's pages to load into the same window? Follow the `name` and `target` convention. Within each document you want to load into that window, use the `<BASE>` tag. To load all pages within the framed site you are building would be to place this syntax within the `<HEAD>` of *every* page to be loaded in that window: `<base target="right">`.

Caution

When using the `<BASE>` tag, remember that you are creating a default. This means that if you have any other targets, they will override the default.

MAGIC TARGET NAMES

There are several predefined target names that will cause certain actions to occur when a target link is created.

- **`target="_blank"`**—The `"_blank"` argument causes the targeted document to open in a completely new browser window.
- **`target="_self"`**—The targeted document will load in the same window where the originating link exists.
- **`target="_parent"`**—This will load the targeted document into the link's parent frameset.
- **`target="_top"`**—Use this attribute to load the link into the full window, over-riding any existing frames.

You'll notice that magic target names always begin with an underscore, and to avoid problems, you should always put the quotes around the target value.

The following are issues to bear in mind when using magic target names:

- You should avoid naming standard targets with anything other than an accepted alphanumeric character. An underscore, or any other symbol, will be ignored.
- The magic target name `"_blank"` always forces a new browser window to open. Be careful to use this only when a new window is absolutely necessary, otherwise you run the risk of angering Web site visitors, who will end up with numerous, resource-draining browser windows on the desktop.
- The `target="_top"` attribute and value is usually the right choice when a link takes the visitor out of your framed site into a new site. Some coders like the idea of keeping external sites inside their own site by targeting the remote site into a local frame, allowing the native site's menu or advertisement to remain live while surfing elsewhere. This is not only considered an annoyance—but may get you into legal trouble. Avoid this at all costs.

You can now put your magic to use and try out a magic target name exercise:

1. Begin by opening your HTML editor. You'll need to create two more pages to target. Copy the following into one instance of a blank editing page:

```
<HTML>
<HEAD>
<TITLE>Magic Targets: About</TITLE>
</HEAD>
<BODY>

<H2>About the Company</H2>

<P>This page has information about the company.


</BODY>
</HTML>
```

2. Save the file as `about.html`.
3. Open another blank editing page and enter the following:

```
<HTML>
<HEAD>
<TITLE> Magic Targets: Clients</TITLE>
</HEAD>
<BODY>

<H2>Clients</H2>

<P>This page has information about the clients.


</BODY>
</HTML>
```

4. Save this file as `clients.html`.
5. Now create another:

```
<HTML>
<HEAD>
<TITLE>Magic Targets: Contact</TITLE>
</HEAD>
<BODY>

<H2>Contact</H2>

<P>This page will be set up with a contact form.

</BODY>
</HTML>
```

6. Save this page as `contact.html`.
7. Open the `menu.htm` file you made earlier. This is the file where the *links* to the pages that will be targeted appear. You should see the following:

```
<HTML>
<HEAD>
<TITLE>Menu</TITLE>
</HEAD>
<BODY>

<P><A href="about.html">About the Company</A>


<P><A href="clients.html">Company Clients</A>


<P><A href="contact.html">Contact Company</A>


</BODY>
</HTML>
```

8. You're going to add the syntax first for the "about" page, which we'll make target over the menu frame. The syntax is as follows:

```
<A href="about.html" target="_self">About the Company</A>
```

   Save the file, open the frameset page, and in the menu frame you will notice that `About` is now hot. Click that link and watch how about.html loads into the menu frame.
9. Return to your HTML editor and add the following syntax to the clients reference:

```
<A href="clients.html" target="_blank">Company Clients</A>
```

10. Save the file, and open the frameset page in your browser. `Clients` is now hot. When you click this choice, you'll note how clients.html is loaded into an entirely *new* browser window (see Figure 17.7).
11. Finally, add a link to the contact page itself:

```
<HTML>
<HEAD>
<TITLE>Magic Targets: Contact</TITLE>
</HEAD>
```

```
<BODY>

<H2>Contact</H2>

<P>This page will be set up with a contact form.


<P><A href="menu.html" target="_top">Reload the Menu Only</A>


</BODY>
</HTML>
```

12. Click the link, which loads the menu page over the contact form.

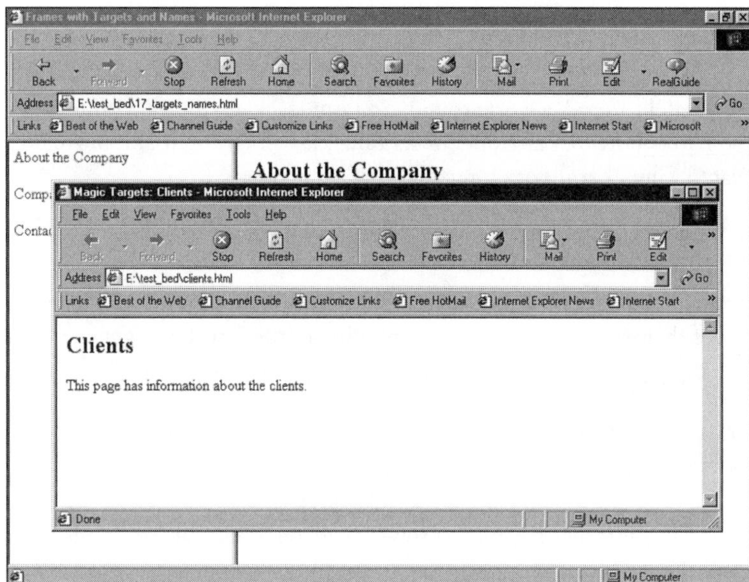

Figure 17.7 Targeting a `"_blank"` magic name.

You've now tackled some of the most difficult aspects of coding for frames. I encourage you to try a few variations using targets and attributes of your own selection. You'll learn a lot from experimentation, and have fun in the process.

Caution

Target names can be sensitive—particularly *case* sensitive. In other words, in some browsers, `"_BlanK"` is going to be different from `"_blaNK"`. One way to avoid running into danger is to always code in the same case. I like to use lowercase, but you might prefer uppercase. It's a style call. The most *be* consistent!

WORKING WITH BORDERLESS FRAMES

Choosing to use borderless frames is a critical issue because using, or not using, borders, is the point where the designer makes decisions about how to use frame technology as a format tool. Removing borders makes formatting a page seamless, and this is a powerful as well as a currently popular method of designing pages.

The first rule in cross-browser design is to know which browsers you are attempting to reach. With borderless frames, that rule is clarified by the fact that only certain browsers, and certain browser versions, interpret borderless frames in the correct manner.

The first thing to remember is that borderless frames are not supported in the Netscape and Microsoft browsers earlier than the 3.0 version.

The challenge of borderless frames doesn't lie in the coding per se, but in the differences in the way popular browsers interpret the code, or require the code to read.

Fortunately, there's a workaround: You can stack attributes within tags, and if a browser doesn't support that attribute or its value, it will ignore it and move on to the attribute and related value that it does interpret.

In HTML 4.0, coding borderless frames are easy. You simply add the attribute and value `frameborder="0"` within the `<FRAME>` tag.

However, browsers without strict HTML 4.0 support, which includes most popular browsers before their 4.0 and later versions, require a little jostling to get the borderless effect.

The Netscape browser (3.0+) allows for borderless frames when

- The `border` attribute is set, in pixels, to a numeric value of `"0"`.
- The `framespacing` attribute is assigned a `"no"` value.

Microsoft's Internet Explorer, browser version 3.0, produces borderless frames if

- The `frameborder` attribute is set, in pixels, to a numeric value of `"0"`.
- The `framespacing` attribute is assigned a width, in pixels, to a numeric value of `"0"`.

If it seems like there's a conflict, well, there really isn't, because each browser either requires a different attribute to control width, or a different value to control spacing. It looks confusing, but if you stack attributes, you can easily create borderless frames that will be read by both browsers without difficulty.

This technique results in two legal syntax options:

```
<FRAMESET frameborder="0" framespacing="0" border="0">
```

or

```
<FRAMESET frameborder="no" framespacing="0" border="0">
```

Either one is correct, and it's just a matter of personal preference as to which you'll use. Remember to add your columns and rows to the string to create a full range of frameset arguments.

Because you already have a fully operational framed page, you can simply add the appropriate syntax to the frameset string to achieve a borderless effect (see Listing 17.2).

LISTING 17.2 CODING BORDERLESS FRAMES

```
<HTML>
<HEAD>
<TITLE>Borderless Frames</TITLE>
</HEAD>

<FRAMESET frameborder="0" framespacing="0" border="0" cols="240, *">
<FRAME src="menu.html" marginheight="5" marginwidth="5" noresize scrolling=
"auto">
<FRAME src="main.html" marginheight="15" marginwidth="15" noresize scrolling
="auto">

</FRAMESET>
</HTML>
```


View the results in both Netscape Navigator 3.0 or later or Internet Explorer 3.0 or later. Your results should match Figure 17.8.

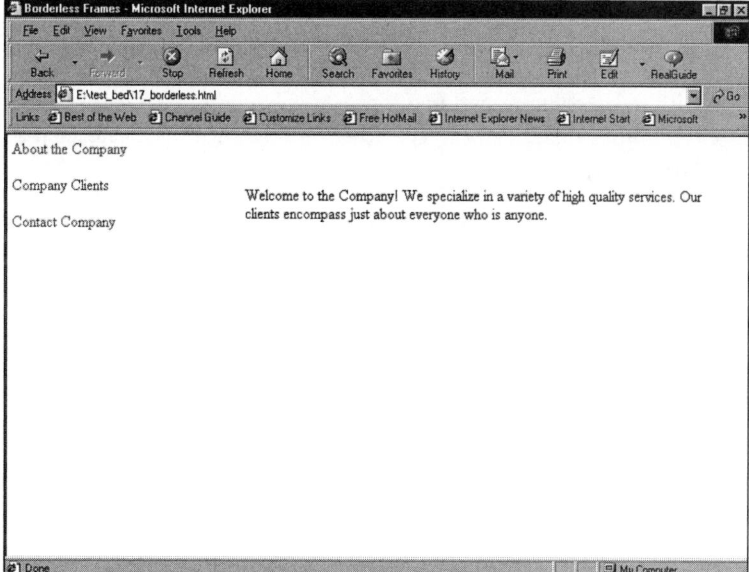

Figure 17.8 A borderless frame gives a cleaner and more professional look to your pages.

ADVANCED FRAME CONCEPTS

Frames are problematic; there's no denying that. For one thing, they require extra work from you, the designer. For each framed page, you have to code, design, and manage more than one page.

Next, frames upset people. As discussed earlier in the chapter, part of the reason is that frames break up space. So, unless you're using borderless frames, the visual clutter they add to a page is detrimental.

Another headache is that they are more difficult to search for, prepare for searches, and print out.

So how do you design a sophisticated, advanced frame-based page? The absolutely, positively, most imperative place to begin is to determine whether your site really needs frames at all. If you can create the same layout with basic HTML or tables, then do it that way.

There's only one really, really good reason to use frames in a page's design, and that is to create an interface that has both static and active parts. In other words, say you want your company logo to dominate the user experience, and you have a standard navigation bar that you want to always be present. Put them in frames. This approach makes sense because the user's experience becomes enhanced rather than problematic.

I also recommend that you use borderless frames. They reinforce the fact that you're using the frames not to constrain design, but to create perpetual information.

You can also use frames for design, such as when creating bleeding or blurred edges. These techniques can't be achieved without frames unless you use background graphics, which limit your options. However, you should never use more frames than absolutely necessary to achieve your goal—especially in the primary body section of your layout. Can you create a page with seven columns and five rows? Absolutely! Unless you can tell me why that's important other than as an exercise to understand how to create such a page, I don't think you should do it.

Finally, the use of tables within the framed pages—especially the content pages—can give you maximum design power when you're laying out complex sites.

Listing 17.3 shows the frameset for a frame design. The top frame handles the logo, and the left frame handles the navigation. A middle frame handles the drop shadow that appears mid-section. Note that the `<NOFRAME>` tag is also employed.

LISTING 17.3 SOPHISTICATED FRAMESET DESIGN

```
<HTML>

<!-- frames -->
<FRAMESET frameborder="0" framespacing="0" border="0" rows="52,7,*">

<FRAME name="internal_hed" src="internal_hed.html" marginwidth="0"
marginheight="0" scrolling="no" noresize>

<FRAME name="middle_soft" src="middle_soft.html" marginwidth="0"
marginheight="0" scrolling="no" noresize>

<FRAMESET frameborder="0" framespacing="0" border="0" cols="220,*">

<FRAME name="left_nav" src="left_nav.html" marginwidth="0" marginheight="0"
scrolling="no" noresize>
```

```
<FRAME name="right" src="results_right.html" marginwidth="0" marginheight="0"
scrolling="yes">

</FRAMESET>
</FRAMESET>

<NOFRAME>
<BODY bgcolor="#FFFFFF" text="#000000" link="#669999" vlink="#FF9900"
alink="#000000">

This Web site requires a browser that supports frames.  You can find updated
browser software by visiting:
<P>

<A href="http://www.microsoft.com/ie/">Microsoft's Internet Explorer Page</A>
<P>

<A href-"http://home.netscape.com/">Netscape's Home Page</A>
<P>

Thank you!
</BODY>
</NOFRAME>
</HTML>
```


Now, look at the final page, shown in Figure 17.9.

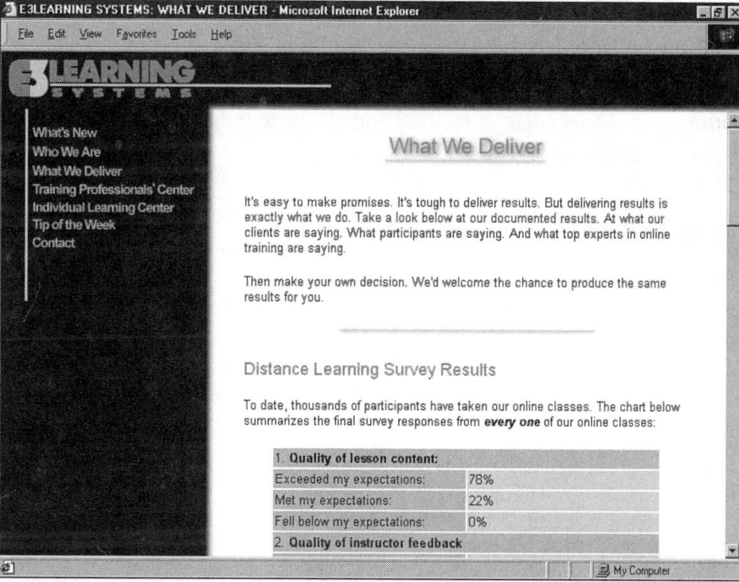

Figure 17.9
This is an example of a sophisticated frame layout using advanced frame features such as having a table within a frame.

This example not only demonstrates a complex layout, but how to mix rows and columns. You'll see that to do this, I have to nest the framesets:

```
<FRAMESET frameborder="0" framespacing="0" border="0" rows="52,7,*">

<FRAME name="internal_hed" src="internal_hed.html" marginwidth="0"
```

```
marginheight="0" scrolling="no" noresize>

<FRAME name="middle_soft" src="middle_soft.html" marginwidth="0"
marginheight="0" scrolling="no" noresize>

        <FRAMESET frameborder="0" framespacing="0" border="0" cols="220,*">

        <FRAME name="left_nav" src="left_nav.html" marginwidth="0"
marginheight="0"
        scrolling="no" noresize>

        <FRAME name="right" src="results_right.html" marginwidth="0"
marginheight="0"
        scrolling="yes">

        </FRAMESET>
</FRAMESET>
```

The more combinations you have, the more careful you have to be in terms of how you set up the order and location of your framesets.

If you have a site that provides a lot of information that site visitors would typically print and are afraid that switching to frames will cause problems for your visitors, see "Printing Frames," in the Troubleshooting section at the end of this chapter.

Designing Fixed and Dynamic Frames

If you want to control how your frames are displayed in terms of browser and screen space, you'll want to make some decisions regarding fixed and dynamic tables. The key to these controls lies in the frameset document. Math is an imperative here.

Listing 17.4 shows the syntax for a framed page with a fixed left frame of 200 pixels and a fixed right frame of 395 pixels.

Listing 17.4 A Fixed Frame Design

```
<HTML>

<FRAMESET cols="400,195">

<FRAME src="yellow.html" noresize scrolling="no">
<FRAME src="red.html" noresize scrolling="no">

</FRAMESET>

</HTML>
```

Figure 17.10 shows the results. Notice that the fixing of pixels occurs within the `col` attribute (or `row` if you're creating rows).

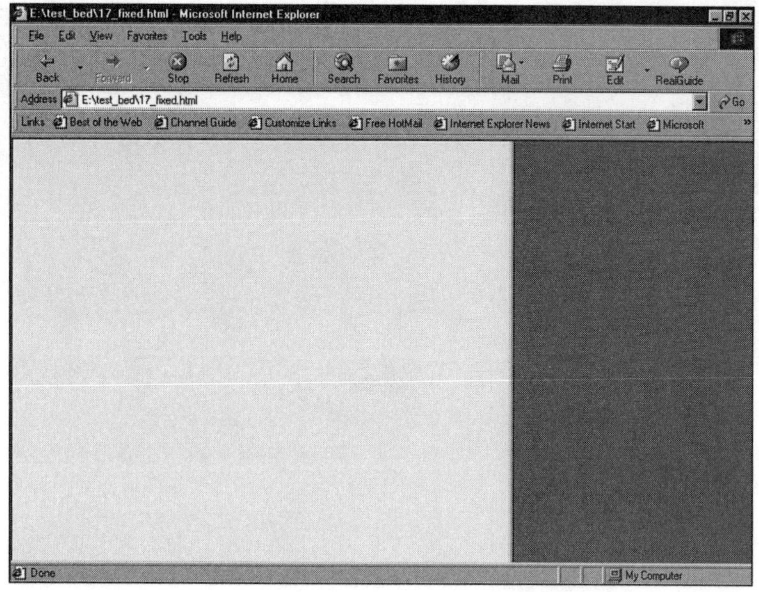

Figure 17.10
Remember that fixing frame widths becomes more important as you add more than two frame columns or rows. Fixing the frames helps secure each frame in place.

Frames, as with tables, can stretch dynamically to fit a specific resolution or screen size. Similarly, you can combine the techniques to achieve a combination of fixed and dynamic frame design.

To make frames dynamic, use percentages rather than numeric values when you're creating your rows or columns:

```
<FRAMESET rows="50%,25%,25%">
<FRAME src="red.html" noresize scrolling="no">
<FRAME src="black.html" noresize scrolling="no">
<FRAME src="yellow.html" noresize scrolling="no">
</FRAMESET>
```

Note that I've split the browser area into three sections (see Figure 17.11). You can split the area into as many sections as you like, actually; however, the concern is to always add up to 100 percent. This way, when you resize the browser (see Figure 17.12), the frames will dynamically adjust.

To make a portion of a frame fixed and another dynamic, you use the * (asterisk symbol) in place of a numeric value or percentage. This symbol simply means that the browser should evaluate what space is available and flex to accommodate that space:

```
<FRAMESET rows="150,*">
<FRAME src="red.html" noresize scrolling="no">
<FRAME src="text.html" noresize scrolling="no">
</FRAMESET>
```

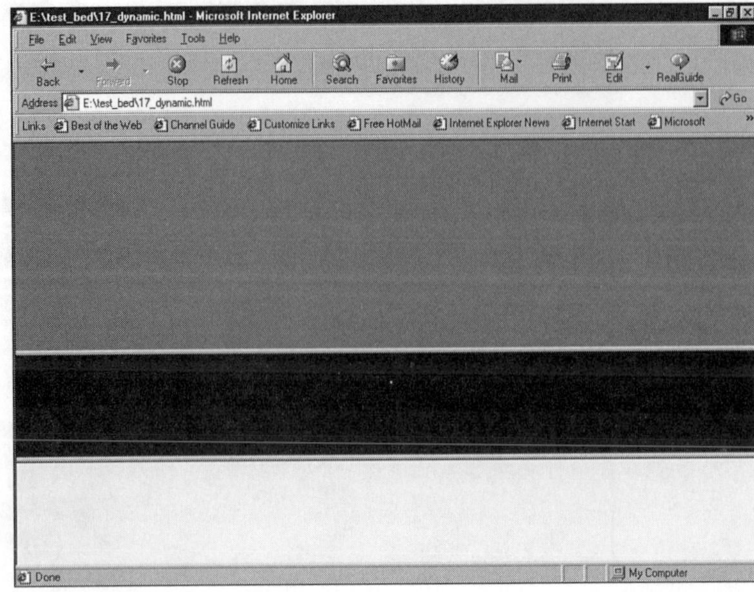

Figure 17.11 Dynamic frames adjust to the available screen space of the browser, making the design more compatible across a variety of environments.

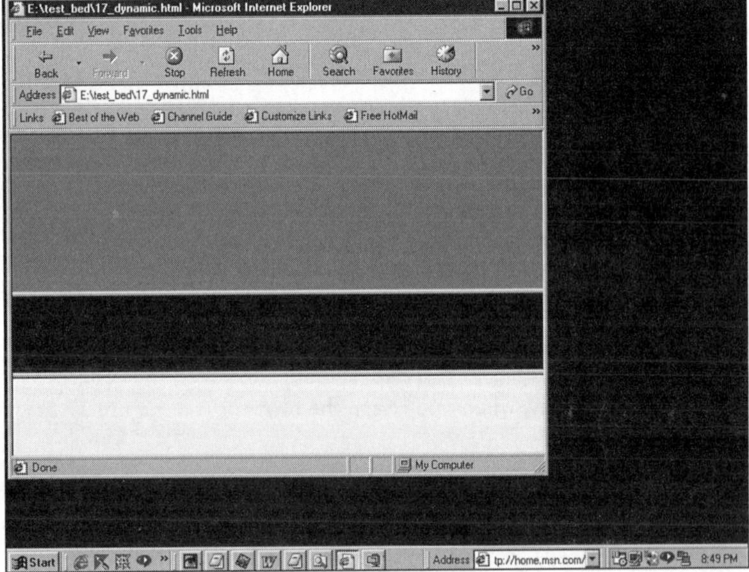

Figure 17.12 Dynamic frames adjusted to the browser or resolution size.

Figure 17.13 shows the results full-frame. In 17.14, I've once again collapsed the browser. Note that the top row stays fixed at 250 pixels, but the bottom row is dynamic.

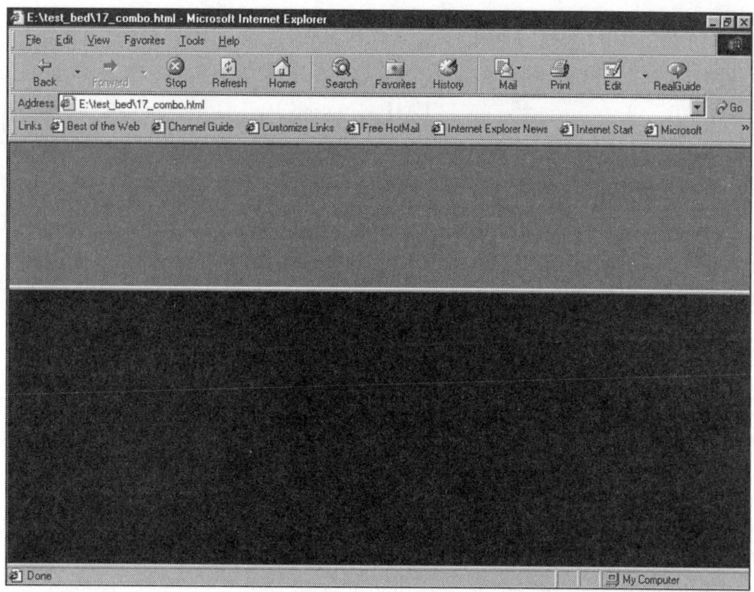

Figure 17.13
Combination of fixed and dynamic frames. The top row is fixed at 150, the bottom is dynamic.

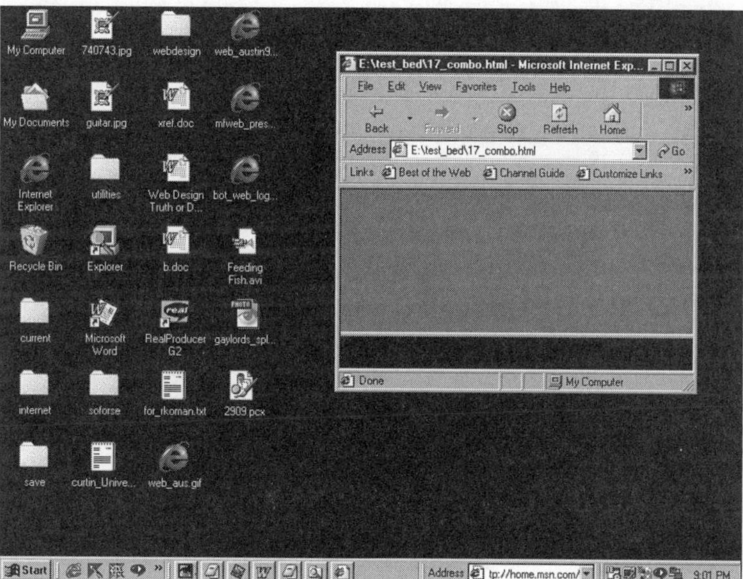

Figure 17.14
After I resized the browser, the dynamic portion collapsed but the top, fixed row remained intact.

Part III
Ch 17

Tip from molly

Frame design is most elegant when borders are turned off and the use of graphics and layout within the framed pages is maximized. More important, however, frame design should never be frivolous. You should always use frames for a good reason, such as when you want static navigation, banner, or branding areas, or you are using borderless frames for fixed layout.

WORKING WITH INLINE FRAMES (I-FRAMES)

Originally introduced by Internet Explorer 3.0, I-Frames—*inline*, or *floating* frames—have been officially adopted as an HTML 4.0 standard. This is good news because they're very effective when put to appropriate use. The bad news, however, is that they aren't supported by Netscape 4.61. Whether 5.0 will support them is anybody's guess at this writing.

I-Frames work a bit differently than standard frames do. First, you don't create a separate frameset for the frame. You place the I-Frame information directly inline any standard HTML page.

Here's a snippet of I-Frame syntax:

```
<IFRAME width=""350" height="200" src="text.html">
<FRAME width=""350" height="200" src="text.html">
</IFRAME>
```

This syntax looks a bit like an `IMAGE` or `OBJECT` tag in action, and in fact, it works in a similar way, too, with the width and height defined in the tags. The oddity, as you've probably noticed, is that in order for the inline frame to work within all browsers that do support it, the inline frame information is coded in both the `<IFRAME>` opening tag and `<FRAME>` tag. In order to be properly parsed, the browser needs the `FRAME` tag to understand that it is actually a frame. The `IFRAME` tags work to denote the location of the frame and specify that the frame floats inline. It's likely that at some point this somewhat confusing method will be refined.

As with standard frames, you can add scrolling and border attributes:

```
<IFRAME width=""350" height="200" src="text.html" scrolling="no"
frameborder="0">

<FRAME width=""350" height="200" src="text.html" scrolling="no"
frameborder="0">
</IFRAME>
```

You can align and space inline frames just as you would an image:

```
<IFRAME width=""350" height="200" src="text.html" scrolling="no"
frameborder="0" align="right" hspace="10" vspace="10">

<FRAME width=""350" height="200" src="text.html" scrolling="no"
frameborder="0" align="right" hspace="10" vspace="10">
</IFRAME>
```

Note

Inline frames support the `name` attribute, as well as magic target names.

Figure 17.15 shows a page using an I-Frame.

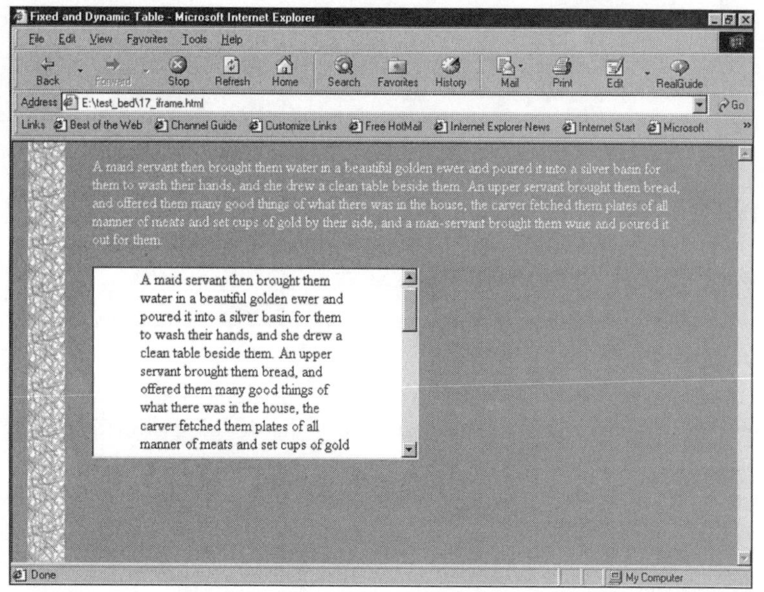

Figure 17.15
Inline frames can be placed anywhere on a page. Unlike standard frames, they do not require a frameset, but as with standard frames, I-Frames do require an additional HTML page in order to work.

THE NOFRAMES TAG AND ACCESSIBILITY

One of the most important considerations when designing with frames is, as mentioned earlier, ensuring that individuals who cannot use frames, such as the blind or mobility impaired, can still have access to important information on a Web site.

The Internet, with its vast wealth of information and communications opportunities, has been empowering for a wide variety of individuals with different needs and circumstances world-over.

Sadly, the graphically rich environment of the Web is at best cumbersome and at worst inaccessible to people who use screen readers, special access tools, or who are accessing sites at slower speeds than those to which we are accustomed.

Note

It's important to point out that tables are also problematic in terms of accessibility, but slightly less so. Tables can be read fairly well by line-based browsers assuming they are coded properly. Graphical browsers used with screen readers often do not perceive table columns as separate entities and therefore will read right across columns. However, Frames, without the NOFRAMES element in use, are inaccessible in either case.

→ For more information on creating accessible pages with HTML 4.0, **see** "Accessibility and Internationalization" **p. 474**

Keeping to the current trends *and* incorporating no-frame and text access addresses cross-browser issues by enabling not only those who *require* text access, but those who prefer it as well.

One of the ways to achieve this in a framed site is by employing the logical <NOFRAMES> tag. This is placed in the *frameset*. Critical information can then be provided at the same URL as the frameset page, and an entirely accessible site can be formed by using the same pages as the framed site.

Troubleshooting

Using Frames to Contain Other Sites

What if I want to keep part of my site available at all times? Can you just link the external site into one of my own frames?

Can you? Technically speaking, yes. Legally speaking? Questionable. People have argued over this very issue and the general sense is that if doing this isn't exactly illegal, it is a complete lack of etiquette. What's more, it doesn't make experienced Web visitors very happy—when I get to a site I want to experience *that* site, not a hybrid. Newcomers to the Web might be completely confused by this action as well. I recommend you never do this.

Printing Frames

How can I make my framed pages easily printable?

Provide a link to a printable format or a downloadable text, HTML, or even PDF (PostScript Document) file available so that individuals who want to print out portions of your site can do so with ease.

Designing for the Real World

Building Accessible Framed Pages

You'll do this using the <NOFRAMES> tag, as described earlier in the chapter. To do so, follow these steps:

1. Create a frameset in your HTML editor:

```
<HTML>
<HEAD>
<TITLE>Frame with NOFRAMES Element</TITLE>
</HEAD>

<FRAMESET frameborder="0" framespacing="0" border="0" cols="240, *">

<FRAME src="menu.html" marginheight="5" marginwidth="5" noresize scrolling=
"auto">
<FRAME src="main.html" name="right" marginheight="15" marginwidth="15"
noresize scrolling="auto">

</FRAMESET>

</HTML>
```

2. Add the <NOFRAMES> tag and its companion </NOFRAMES> in the following fashion:

```
<HTML>
<HEAD>
<TITLE>Frames with NOFRAMES Element</TITLE>
</HEAD>

<FRAMESET frameborder="0" framespacing="0" border="0" cols="240, *">

<FRAME src="menu.html" marginheight="5" marginwidth="5" noresize scrolling=
"auto">
<FRAME src="main.html" name="right" marginheight="15" marginwidth="15"
noresize scrolling="auto">

</FRAMESET>

<NOFRAMES>

</NOFRAMES>
</HTML>
```

3. Now add all the HTML syntax necessary to create a fully functional page within the <NOFRAMES> tag:

```
<HTML>
<HEAD>
<TITLE>Frames with NOFRAMES Element</TITLE>
</HEAD>

<FRAMESET frameborder="0" framespacing="0" border="0" cols="240, *">

<FRAME src="menu.html" marginheight="5" marginwidth="5" noresize scrolling=
"auto">
<FRAME src="main.html" name="right" marginheight="15" marginwidth="15"
noresize scrolling="auto">

</FRAMESET>

<NOFRAMES>
<BODY>

Welcome. We're happy to provide this non-frames access to our Web site. If you
prefer to view our site using frames, please upgrade your browser to a recent
one that fully supports frames. Otherwise, please visit our <A
href="index_noframes.html">non-framed</A> version of this site.
</BODY>
</NOFRAMES>
</HTML>
```

4. Save the page. You've now made the page completely accessible to non-frame browsers.

Figure 17.16 shows how this tag operates when a text-only browser encounters it.

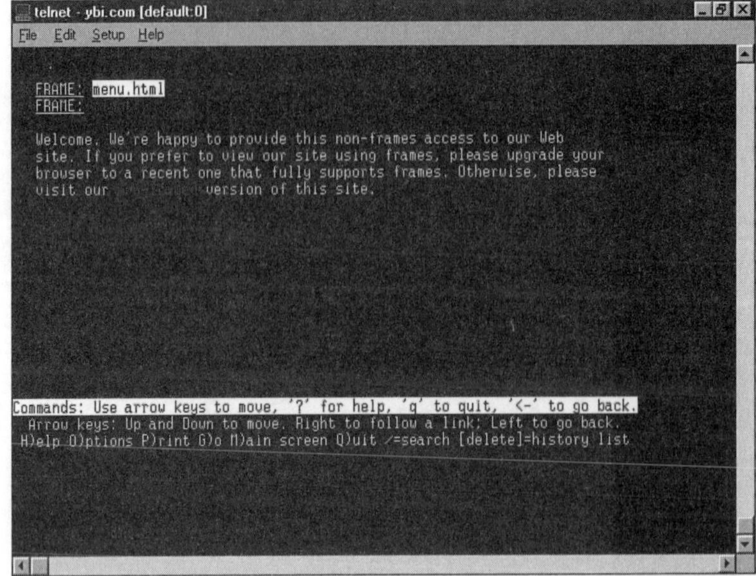

Figure 17.16
The results of this exercise make a framed site accessible to Lynx, a text browser.

Tip from molly

Because you can format an entire HTML document within the NOFRAMES element, consider using the index page as the Welcome page to your site. From there, link to internal pages that are external to the frame design.

→ To find out more about these issues as they relate to HMTL 4.0, **see** "Accessibility and Internationalization" **p. 474**

CHAPTER 18

Building Forms

In this chapter

THE IMPORTANCE OF FORMS

Forms are the oldest and most flexible method of allowing your site visitors to interact with your site, and ultimately, you. Whether you're providing a method of collecting feedback for the site's improvement, collecting demographic information, or receiving orders for products on your site, forms are the interface through which you are most likely to interact with your audience.

Unlike more static HTML methods, forms depend upon a relationship between the site visitor and the page you create *as well as* scripts residing on the Web server.

Typically, this relationship is helped along by a process known as CGI, or the *Common Gateway Interface*. CGI acts as the conduit through which the information passes, and hands off the information server-side to a program—usually written in Perl—for processing.

➔ For help with understanding CGI and Perl, **see** "CGI and Pre-Processing Fundamentals," **p.736**

Forms can encompass a wide range of functions, including the simple gathering of a user's name, address, and contact information which is then sent to an email address (often referred to as a *mailto* form), to the creation of games based on user input.

Note

Server technologies differ, and CGI isn't the only method by which forms are processed. Because of the various methods of processing forms, you will have to work with your ISP (Internet service provider) or systems administrator to find out some information about your server and how it will process the feedback forms.

See the "Designing for the Real World" section at the end of this chapter for an example of how feedback forms are processed on my site.

In this chapter, I'm going to focus specifically on how to create a mailto form interface—how to prepare it for processing, create input fields, and control the behavior of various form elements. Combine your learning from this chapter with the information gathered from your ISP, and you will be able to put this as well as a variety of other forms to work.

USING PROPER FORM SYNTAX

Forms employ tags and special elements to enable diverse input options to be displayed and made functional by the form. The special elements are known as *controls* and I'll be showing you how to make the most out of setting up and using your form controls.

FORM ELEMENTS AND ATTRIBUTES

There are two key form elements and associated attributes that you'll need to know to create forms.

➔ Additional elements that enhance the form's display for accessibility are also covered in this book, **see** "Accessibility and Internationalization," **p. 475**

- **<FORM>...</FORM>**—The foundational element of all forms, the close and end tags are required. Form accepts a variety of attributes. The two most critical are `action`, which combines with a URL to the form processor, and `method`, which takes the value of `get` or `post` depending upon the way the form technology is set up.
- **<INPUT>**—The input element is responsible for managing the input controls that will be placed within the tag, which only has an opening with no associated closing tag. Commonly used attributes for the `<INPUT>` tag are as follows:

  type="x"—This specifies the type of control being called upon. See the "Controls" section for details.

  name="x"—The `name` attribute names the control.

  value="x"—Value describes the input control. This is optional with all controls except for `radio`.

  size="x"—The width of the input control in pixels. Sometimes the number of characters determines the size of the control, as is the case with the `text` and `password` controls.

  maxlength="x"—The maximum numbers of input characters allowed in an input control.

  checked="x"—This option pre-selects a given radio button or checkbox within a form.

  src="x"—Allows you to determine the location of an image to be used for graphical button elements within the form.
- **<TEXTAREA>...</TEXTAREA>**—This element creates a text input area. It's the same in concept as a control, but it is managed using an element instead of an attribute. The attributes it accepts are `name` (see above), `rows="x"` where *x* defines the numbers of lines in the box, and `cols="x"`, where columns specifies the width of the box.
- **<SELECT>...</SELECT>**—The `SELECT` element creates a menu. It can be a drop-down menu or a text list menu, depending upon the way you define the attributes of the element. You can add the `multiple` attribute if you'd like to have a site visitor be able to choose more than one option in the list menu.
- **<OPTION>...</OPTION>**—This element defines each individual list item within a menu. Both the opening and closing tags are required. Note that the end tag is *optional* with the `OPTION` element!

Note

Rows and columns in a text area do not constrain the amount of data allowed. For example, if I have a text area that is 40 columns wide and 20 rows high, I can type into that box continuously. Scrollbars will become available to help me work within the box most effectively.

Controls

Controls define the kind of input option that will appear onscreen. Controls are syntactically an HTML *value* and are placed in the value position of the `type` attribute within an `<INPUT>` tag statement.

The controls available include:

- **`text`** Creates an input text box that consists of a single line. Width of the box is controlled by the `size` attribute.
- **`password`** Exactly like text, except the characters input by the site visitor will reflect back as asterisks.
- **`checkbox`** Creates a box that can be checked. You can have multiple checkboxes in a selection, and all of them may be checked if applicable.
- **`radio`** This creates a radio button. You can have as many as you want in a given subject area, but only one may be selected.
- **`submit`** This control creates the familiar "Submit" button, which appears as a raised button with a push-button look. The word on the control can be customized using the `value` attribute.
- **`reset`** The same in appearance and customization features as `submit`, this control will clear the form so the site visitor can re-enter his or her answers.
- **`file`** This creates a file selection control. The site visitor can then select a file for download.
- **`hidden`** Hidden controls are those that don't render in the browser. They are used to insert information for the recipient of the form data.
- **`image`** Allows for the insertion of a custom image. This gives the designer the ability to use a graphic for submit and reset instead of the default option.
- **`button`** Creates a push button. These must be associated with a script in order to work, since there is no built-in action for them.

> **Note**
>
> There is also a `button` element, which can be used to create graphical options for Submit or Reset with a slightly different interpretation. It creates a visible button and allows for the insertion of an image and descriptive content. This approach is used less than the standard `<INPUT>` tag plus the `button` control.
>
> → For more information, **see** "Customizing Submit and Reset with Images" later in this chapter.

Building a Form

The exercises in the following sections will each focus on the design of a form. I'll first review the foundational elements of the form. Each subsequent section will then examine how a specific control can be used to enhance or customize the form to your design needs.

A form can begin anywhere on a standard HTML page. You'll use the <FORM> tag and its companion closing tag </FORM>, within the body of the HTML page.

1. Open a standard HTML shell or an existing HTML page where you'd like to introduce a form.
2. Add the FORM tag and its companion closing tag. Make sure to leave several spaces in between so you can effectively add form elements to come:
```
<FORM>

</FORM>
```
3. To set up the way in which your form sends information to the server, you'll need to add the method attribute and an appropriate value. Values are get and post:
```
<FORM method="post">

</FORM>
```

Note

To get, or to post, that is the question! The get and post values help determine the way in which data is sent to the server. The difference is that get appends the form's data to the URL specified in the action. On the other hand, post sends the information separately.

4. Naturally, you'll want to ensure that the data you send goes to the correct place for processing. To do this, you'll use the action attribute, combined with the path to the script on the server that will help perform the action:
```
<FORM  method="post" action"http:://www.myserver.com/apps/cgi-bin/mailscript">

</FORM>
```

Tip from molly

Check with your ISP for both the method of preference (get or post) and the location and name of the script available. This will help you properly fill out your method and action attributes.

This bare-bones form can be considered a form shell. Just as this book describes how to power-code from an HTML shell and table shell, you can use this code as the foundation for all of your forms.

ADDING A TEXT FIELD

At this point, you'll want to begin adding areas where people can input data in to the form. One of the most common input areas is known as a *Text Field* (also referred to as a *Text Box*). You will use text fields for information that is entered on a single line, such as a name, address, phone number, and email address.

You'll set up the text field by using the <INPUT> tag and the type attribute. Fields are defined by the type attribute's value. There are also a number of additional attributes and values you'll want to add to your text field, including name, size, and the maximum amount of characters the box will allow.

1. Within the form, add the `INPUT` tag, `type` attribute, and `text` value:

```
<FORM  method="post" action"/cgi-bin/mailscript">

<INPUT type="text">

</FORM>
```

2. Add the descriptive text that will appear on the page, and give the field a name:

```
<FORM  method="post" action"/cgi-bin/mailscript">

First Name: <INPUT type="text" name="firstname">

</FORM>
```

Note

The name is necessary so that when the form comes back, the recipient will understand the information related to it. For example, if you name this field "firstname," the processed form results will look something like firstname: Janey.

3. You can set the size (width) of the text field by using the `size` attribute and a numeric value:

```
<FORM method="post" action"/cgi-bin/mailscript">

First Name: <INPUT type="text" name="firstname" size="25">

</FORM>
```

Note

The size value will stretch the text field to the size of *visible* characters it will hold. Size in this case is not measured in pixels.

4. Text fields can receive more characters than their visual size. For example, if I set the size of the field to be 25, I can still allow the page visitor to input 100 characters if I so choose:

```
<FORM method="post" action"/cgi-bin/mailscript">

First Name: <INPUT type="text" name="firstname" size="25" maxlength="100">


</FORM>
```

5. Continue adding as many text fields as your form requires, modifying the attributes to your needs and tastes:

```
<FORM  method="post" action"/cgi-bin/mailscript">

First Name: <INPUT type="text" name="firstname" size="25" maxlength="100">
<BR>
```

```
Last Name: <INPUT type="text" name="lastname" size="25" maxlength="100">
<BR>

Email: <INPUT type="text" name="email" size="25" maxlength="100">

</FORM>
```

Note

In this case, I've added line breaks between the lines, formatting the form's input areas using HTML as I go.

Tip from

If you'd like to use the text fields for passwords and have the "*" character echoed rather than the actual characters, use "password" in place of "text" for the `type` attribute.

Check your work against Figure 18.1, which displays the information you've added to the form so far.

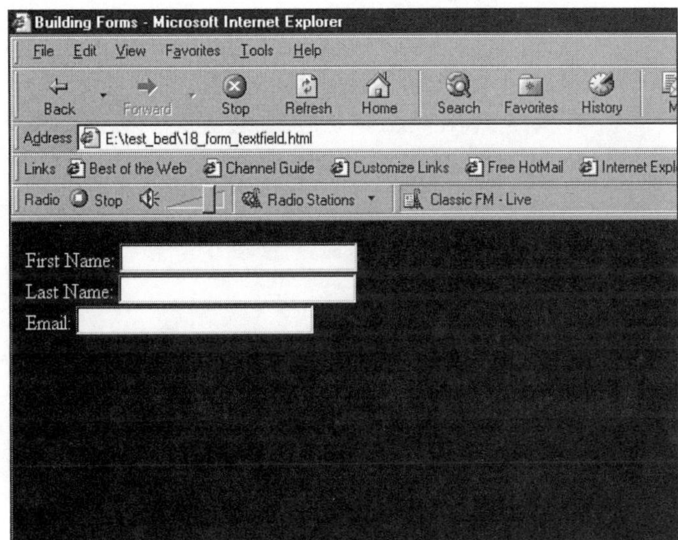

Figure 18.1
This unfinished form contains three text fields, complete with name and maxlength attributes.

MAKING A CHECKBOX

Text fields are powerful, but sometimes you'll want to offer a group of choices to your site visitor to make. Checkboxes will help you set up these choices and then take the user's selection to the server for processing. You'll use the `<INPUT>` tag as before, but this time your `type` value will be `checkbox`.

1. Add the first choice, in this case an age range:

```
<FORM  method="post" action"/cgi-bin/mailscript">

First Name: <INPUT type="text" name="firstname" size="25" maxlength="100">
<BR>

Last Name: <INPUT type="text" name="lastname" size="25" maxlength="100">
<BR>

Email: <INPUT type="text" name="email" size="25" maxlength="100">

<P>Age:
<BR>

25 - 35

</FORM>
```

2. Type in the INPUT tag and the proper attributes:

```
<FORM  method="post" action"/cgi-bin/mailscript">

First Name: <INPUT type="text" name="firstname" size="25" maxlength="100">
<BR>

Last Name: <INPUT type="text" name="lastname" size="25" maxlength="100">
<BR>

Email: <INPUT type="text" name="email" size="25" maxlength="100">

<P>Age:
<BR>

25 - 35 <INPUT type="checkbox" name="25-35">

</FORM>
```

3. Continue to add checkboxes as necessary. You can even pre-select a checkbox for your site visitor by using the solitary checked attribute:

```
<FORM  method="post" action"/cgi-bin/mailscript">

First Name: <INPUT type="text" name="firstname" size="25" maxlength="100">
<BR>

Last Name: <INPUT type="text" name="lastname" size="25" maxlength="100">
<BR>

Email: <INPUT type="text" name="email" size="25" maxlength="100">

<P>Age:
<BR>

25 - 35 <INPUT type="checkbox" name="25-35">
<BR>

36 - 40 <INPUT type="checkbox" name="36-40" checked>

</FORM>
```

Note

Checkboxes also allow you to set up choices where an individual can check more than one box. For example, if you were setting up a selection of choices of films seen in the past six months, you'd want your site visitors to check as many as apply to them.

In Figure 18.2, I've taken a screen shot of the form as it is so far, with text boxes and checkboxes.

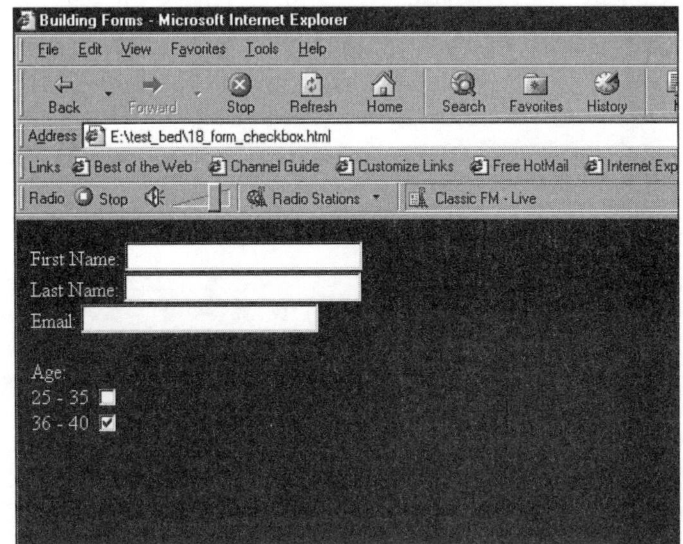

Figure 18.2
The form now contains checkboxes. When completed and activated, site visitors will be able to click the checkbox most appropriate to them.

ADDING A RADIO BUTTON

As with checkboxes, radio buttons allow you to make a selection. However, radio buttons will automatically move to the point of selection. They do not allow more than one choice.

1. Add the selection options required in your form. I'm using gender in my example:

```
<FORM  method="post" action"/cgi-bin/mailscript">

First Name: <INPUT type="text" name="firstname" size="25" maxlength="100">
<BR>

Last Name: <INPUT type="text" name="lastname" size="25" maxlength="100">
<BR>

Email: <INPUT type="text" name="email" size="25" maxlength="100">

<P>Age:
<BR>
25 - 35 <INPUT type="checkbox" name="25-35">
<BR>

36 - 40 <INPUT type="checkbox" name="36-40" checked>
```

```
<P>Gender:
<BR>
Male
<BR>
Female
<BR>
Prefer not to say

</FORM>
```

2. Using the INPUT tag, add the type attribute, radio value, and attributes of your choice:

```
<FORM  method="post" action"/cgi-bin/mailscript">

First Name: <INPUT type="text" name="firstname" size="25" maxlength="100">
<BR>

Last Name: <INPUT type="text" name="lastname" size="25" maxlength="100">
<BR>

Email: <INPUT type="text" name="email" size="25" maxlength="100">
<P>Age:
<BR>
25 - 35 <INPUT type="checkbox" name="25-35">
<BR>

36 - 40 <INPUT type="checkbox" name="36-40" checked>

<P>Gender:
<BR>
<INPUT type="radio" name="button" value="male"> Male
<INPUT type="radio" name="button" value="female" checked>Female
<INPUT type="radio" name="button" value="prefer not to say">Prefer not to say
</FORM>
```

Caution

Radio buttons must each have the same `name` value in a set, or they will not work properly. Differentiate a radio button's identity using the `value` attribute.

Note

Radio buttons can also contain the "checked" attribute. Once the user clicks on another radio button, the checked button will disappear and the user's choice will appear.

The form now contains both radio and checkbox options (see Figure 18.3).

MAKING A MENU LIST

Another powerful method of offering form selections for your visitors is a menu with options. These are especially helpful when you have numerous items in a list, such as a list of states or countries.

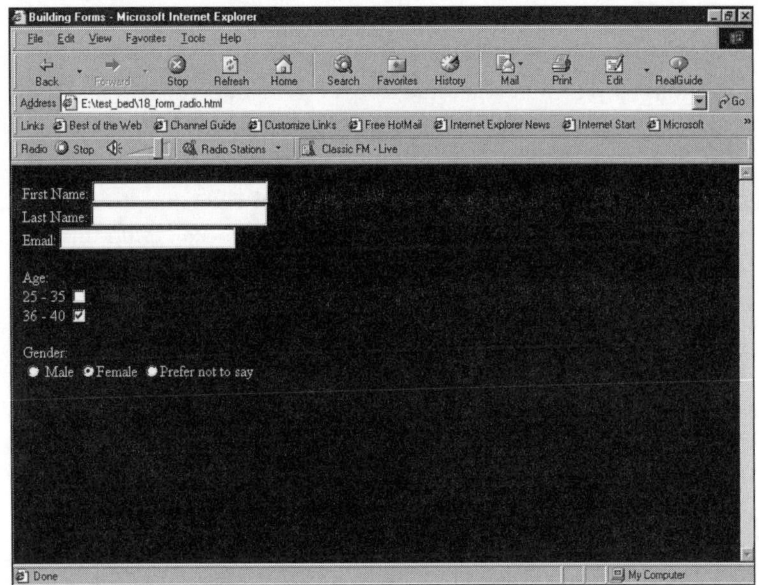

Figure 18.3
With both checkboxes and radio buttons, the form is beginning to become both more technically and visually complex.

Drop-down lists are created by using the `SELECT` element and individual `OPTION` tags. There are several attributes that can modify both, which will be explained as we step through the process.

1. In the area where you'd like to place your drop-down list, input your display text and the opening and closing `SELECT` tags:

```
<FORM  method="post" action"/cgi-bin/mailscript">

State:
<SELECT>


</SELECT>

</FORM>
```

2. If you'd like to set the size by items, you can do so by using the `size` attribute. If you give the numeric value of "4," four items will be shown in the resulting drop-down menu:

```
<FORM  method="post" action"/cgi-bin/mailscript">

State:
<SELECT size="4">


</SELECT>

</FORM>
```

If you have four items and specify a size of four, the menu will be displayed as a list box, with all options fully visible onscreen.

If you specify a numeric value that is less than the total available options, a scrollbar will appear in the menu. Leaving this attribute out is the popular method of choice as it creates the familiar drop-down style menu.

→ To create a drop-down menu for navigation, **see** "Using JavaScript," **p. 403**

3. You can also allow for multiple items to be selected. To do this, add the `multiple` attribute:

```
<FORM  method="post" action"/cgi-bin/mailscript">

State:
<SELECT multiple>


</SELECT>

</FORM>
```

4. Now, add the `OPTION` tag and the first option. Here I've added the name attribute to the option tag. This ensures that the form results will display the selected option:

```
<FORM  method="post" action"/cgi-bin/mailscript">

State:
<SELECT size="4" multiple>
<OPTION name="arizona">Arizona

</SELECT>

</FORM>
```

5. Continue adding options as necessary. You can use the `selected` attribute for the option which you'd like to have set as the default menu selection:

```
<FORM  method="post" action"/cgi-bin/mailscript">

State:
<SELECT>
<OPTION name="arizona">Arizona
<OPTION name="california">California
<OPTION name="nevada" selected>Nevada
</SELECT>

</FORM>
```

Figure 18.4 shows two menu variations. The first is the drop-down menu (you'd need to click on the arrow to see the other options), the second is a list menu (all of the options are visible). The list variation was created by ensuring that the number of list items and the size of the menu are equal.

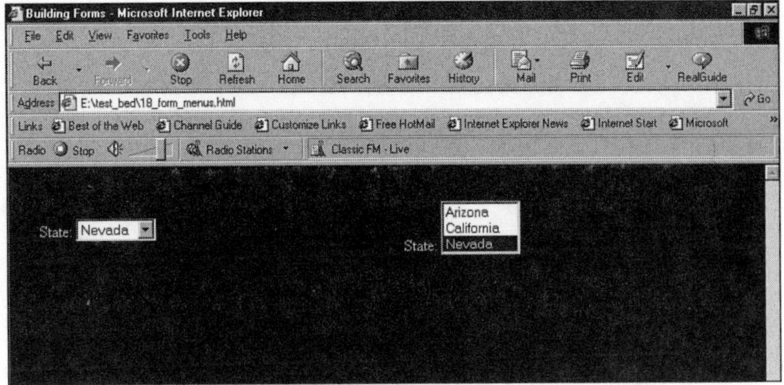

Figure 18.4 Two variations on a menu theme: The left menu is a drop-down menu, and the right menu is a list menu. The code difference is in the attributes used to describe the `SELECT` and `OPTION` elements.

CREATING A TEXT AREA

Text fields are handy for one-line sections of input. However, if you want to give your visitors more room to add their own feedback and thoughts, you can accommodate them by providing them with a TEXTAREA.

Text areas are created using the <TEXTAREA> tag, and its companion closing </TEXTAREA> tag. You'll also add attributes including `rows` and `cols` to determine the amount of rows and columns in your text area, respectively.

1. In the portion of the form where you'd like to add the text area, type in the display text and opening and closing TEXTAREA element tags:

```
<FORM  method="post" action"/cgi-bin/mailscript">

First Name: <INPUT type="text" name="firstname" size="25" maxlength="100">
<BR>

Last Name: <INPUT type="text" name="lastname" size="25" maxlength="100">
<BR>

Email: <INPUT type="text" name="email" size="25" maxlength="100">

<P>Age:
<BR>
25 - 35 <INPUT type="checkbox" name="25-35">
<BR>

36 - 40 <INPUT type="checkbox" name="36-40" checked>

<P>Gender:
<BR>
<INPUT type="radio" name="male"> Male
 <INPUT type="radio" name="male" checked>Female
<INPUT type="radio" name="undisclosed">Prefer not to say

<P>State:
<SELECT>
<OPTION name="arizona">Arizona
<OPTION name="california">California
```

```
<OPTION name="nevada" selected>Nevada
</SELECT>

<P>Do you have additional concerns?

<P><TEXTAREA>



</TEXTAREA>

</FORM>
```

2. To set the rows (how high the text area will be), add the row with a numeric value:

```
<FORM  method="post" action"/cgi-bin/mailscript">

First Name: <INPUT type="text" name="firstname" size="25" maxlength="100">
<BR>

Last Name: <INPUT type="text" name="lastname" size="25" maxlength="100">
<BR>

Email: <INPUT type="text" name="email" size="25" maxlength="100">

<P>Age:
<BR>
25 - 35 <INPUT type="checkbox" name="25-35">
<BR>

36 - 40 <INPUT type="checkbox" name="36-40" checked>

<P>Gender:
<BR>
<INPUT type="radio" name="male"> Male
 <INPUT type="radio" name="male" checked>Female
<INPUT type="radio" name="undisclosed">Prefer not to say

<P>State:
<SELECT>
<OPTION name="arizona">Arizona
<OPTION name="california">California
<OPTION name="nevada" selected>Nevada
</SELECT>

<P>Do you have additional concerns?

<P><TEXTAREA rows="5">


</TEXTAREA>

</FORM>
```

3. To set the width in characters, use the `cols` attribute with a numeric value:

```
<FORM  method="post" action"/cgi-bin/mailscript">

First Name: <INPUT type="text" name="firstname" size="25" maxlength="100">
<BR>
```

```
Last Name: <INPUT type="text" name="lastname" size="25" maxlength="100">
<BR>

Email: <INPUT type="text" name="email" size="25" maxlength="100">

<P>Age:
<BR>
25 - 35 <INPUT type="checkbox" name="25-35">
<BR>

36 - 40 <INPUT type="checkbox" name="36-40" checked>

<P>Gender:
<BR>
<INPUT type="radio" name="male"> Male
 <INPUT type="radio" name="male" checked>Female
<INPUT type="radio" name="undisclosed">Prefer not to say

<P>State:
<SELECT>
<OPTION name="arizona">Arizona
<OPTION name="california">California
<OPTION name="nevada" selected>Nevada
</SELECT>

<P>Do you have additional concerns?

<P><TEXTAREA rows="5" cols="25">


</TEXTAREA>

</FORM>
```


Figure 18.5 shows the form.

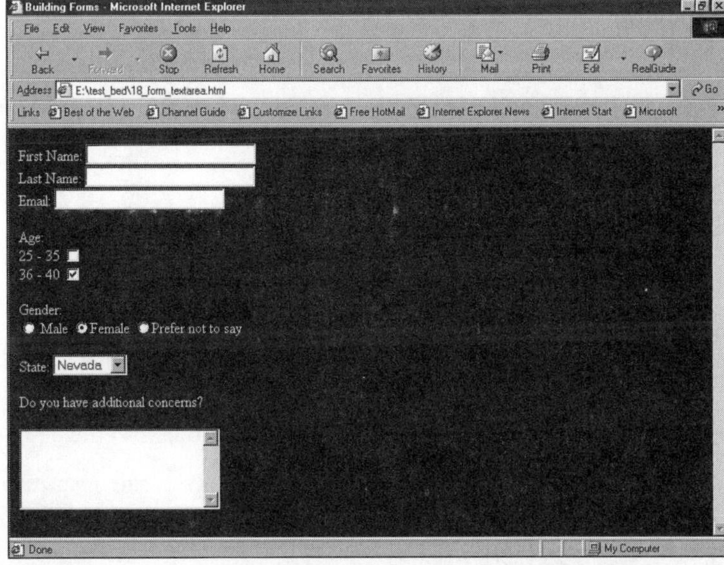

Figure 18.5
The form with the text area displayed. Despite the small size of the text area, the site visitor can input as much information as he or she wants. A scrollbar will appear if necessary.

Wondering if you'll need more than one text area on your form? See, "Multiple Text Areas" in the Troubleshooting section at the end of this chapter for some helpful information.

PROVIDING RESET AND SUBMIT BUTTONS

With the bulk of your form designed, it's time to offer the ability of the page visitor to submit the form, or reset the form data and start over.

1. To add a submit button, use the `INPUT` tag with the `type` attribute. The value "submit" will create the button:

```
<FORM method="post" action"/cgi-bin/mailscript">

<INPUT type="submit">

</FORM>
```

2. You can customize what the submit button says by adding a value:

```
<FORM  method="post" action"/cgi-bin/mailscript">

<INPUT type="submit" value="send it!">

</FORM>
```

3. The reset button works using the same logic. Simply use the `reset` value in the `type attribute` to create a reset button. If you'd like to customize how the button is labeled, use the `value` attribute:

```
<FORM method="post" action"/cgi-bin/mailscript">

<INPUT type="submit" value="send it!">

<INPUT type="reset" value="do it over">

</FORM>
```

Figure 18.6 shows the results of our completed form, which is fully designed but will not function until properly connected with the server-side script.

Tip from

If you want your forms to be very neat and organized, use tables to lay out the form's input controls.

If you'd like to use an image to customize your Submit and Reset buttons, you can do so by first creating the image, and then following one of two options.

→ For more information on creating images, **see** "Creating Professional Web Graphics," **p. 598**

The first option is to insert the image directly into the Submit or Reset control, as follows:

```
<INPUT type="image" src="images/go.gif" width="50" height="25" alt="go"
value="submit">
```

This will result in a seamless look, with the button fitting into the design of the page.

The second option is to use the `BUTTON` element. This sets the image *into* the submit button:

```
<BUTTON name="submit" value="submit" type="submit">
Send <IMG src="images/go.gif" width="50" height="25"  alt="go"></BUTTON>
```

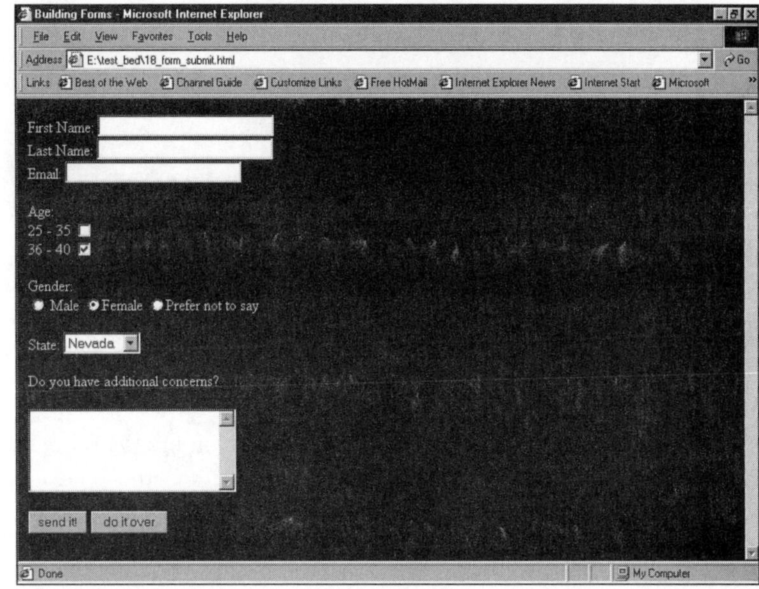

Figure 18.6 Here you see the final form with the Submit and Reset buttons. I've customized the labels to express my own personality and needs.

> **Note**
>
> To set up a Reset button this way, simply change the `value` attribute to `"reset"`. You'll want to make sure you have a corresponding graphic that clearly expresses the reset concept.

As mentioned in the note early on in this chapter, the second option is rarely used. Figure 18.7 shows an example of both styles.

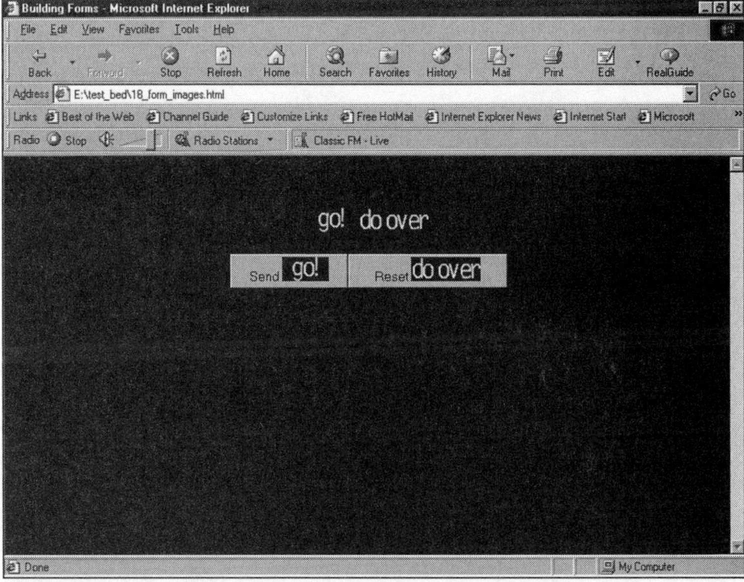

Figure 18.7 Customized Submit and Reset buttons. The first row uses controls, whereas the second uses the `BUTTON` element.

TROUBLESHOOTING

MULTIPLE TEXT AREAS

Can you add more than one text area to a page?

You can use multiple text areas on a page, depending upon your needs. However, determine *before* building your form what elements are necessary. This will result in a more organized, logical form that is easy-to-use for your site visitors.

DESIGNING FOR THE REAL WORLD

METHOD, ACTION, AND HIDDEN FIELDS AT MOLLY.COM

The following syntax is taken from the contact form on my Web site. I want to have you look closely at two issues. First, let's examine the form's method and action attributes.

```
<FORM  method="post" action="http://opus1.com/htbin/mailto">
```

As you can see, `"post"` is the preferred method for my ISP. Also, the action points to a specific script on the server. The first part of the URL is the ISP's address (`opus1.com`), the directory `htbin` is the location of the script, and `mailto` is the name of the script. This simple syntax is what connects my form to the server's script so any information entered into the form can be processed and sent to me via email.

Another real-world issue is the use of *hidden fields*. These are `INPUT` entries that use the `type="hidden"` attribute and value to invisibly include them within the form. The first entry in my form is as follows:

```
<INPUT name="from" type="hidden" value="site visitor">
```

This information will insert the words "site visitor" into the FROM line of any email processed by the form. This next example is similar:

```
<INPUT name="subject" type="hidden" value="Feedback: Molly's Web Site">
```

In this case, the SUBJECT line of email from this form will clearly note that it is in regards to Feedback: Molly's Web Site.

Hidden fields are very powerful. I can use this information to create filters within my email program so all incoming mail from this form goes directly to a specific box. This helps me stay organized, and discriminate between information coming from my personal versus any other Web sites I have.

PART IV

HTML Technologies

CHAPTER 19

Using JavaScript

In this chapter

THE POWER OF SCRIPTING

The power of JavaScript has become extremely significant to Web developers. Used originally to enhance sites with "cool stuff," JavaScript has become a sophisticated method of addressing many previously confounding site development concerns.

JavaScript is a scripting language that was originally derived from Netscape's LiveScript. Sun Microsystems, developer of the Java language, took an interest in this powerful script and, along with Netscape, made some adjustments to re-introduce the script under the new name JavaScript.

Unlike Java, which can be used to develop entirely standalone applications, JavaScript works primarily with Web pages. Furthermore, Java programs for the Web known as *applets* can demand significant resources from an individual's computer and browser. JavaScript, on the other hand, is usually included within the HTML file and interpreted line-by-line by the browser without the need to execute an application.

→ For additional details on Java applets and Active X, **see** "Using Java Applets and ActiveX Components," **p. 704**

JavaScript is used most frequently to:

- Add visual functions such as alert boxes and pop-up windows
- Create animations
- Detect browser, browser version, and platform

Note

JavaScript is also one of the fundamental cornerstones of Dynamic HTML, along with Cascading Style Sheets (CSS). You'll have the opportunity to work with both of those topics.

→ To find out how JavaScript integrates with CSS and DHTML, **see** "JavaScript and Style Sheets," **p. 425** and "Working with Dynamic HTML," **p. 453**

In this chapter, I'll first explain the fundamental elements of JavaScript—objects, operators, statements, and functions. Then, I'll offer a variety of helpful JavaScripts, showing you how to add an alert box, drop-down navigation menu, pop-up window, mouseover animation, and how to detect and route Web browsers for cross-browser design.

UNDERSTANDING JAVASCRIPT

JavaScript isn't HTML, but it works with it. HTML (as you already are aware) is a markup language that is dedicated to describing the *appearance* of elements on a Web page. JavaScript, however, is a general-purpose scripting language.

Some general JavaScript rules to remember include the following:

- JavaScript is case sensitive.

- It's possible that even if someone is using a JavaScript-enabled browser, the JavaScript is turned off—so you need to plan your designs to be non-JavaScript–compliant too.
- JavaScript code should always be commented out so older browsers don't display the code.

Different programming languages vary in syntax and keywords. Syntax is the exact structure of statements in the language, and keywords are the built-in terms that the language is designed to understand. They all have one core concept in common, though: Every programming language works by following a list of instructions.

It's really no different from many of the things you already do in day to day life. When a friend tells you how to get to her house, you follow the directions she gives you—turning left here, driving past a particular store, turning right there, and so forth—until you have completed the list of instructions to travel between your home and hers.

When you go to the grocery, you're following a program too. If you wrote it out step by individual step, it might look something like the following:

1. Leave house
2. Get in car
3. Drive to grocery
4. Park car
5. Get out of car
6. Enter grocery

JavaScript works the same way. You create a list of very specific instructions that will be followed by a Web browser sequentially when it accesses your Web page or when a site visitor takes an action such as a moving or clicking the mouse. When all those instructions are strung together and interpreted in order, a task is performed.

JAVASCRIPT PLACEMENT

JavaScript appears right in the individual HTML file and fits within the `<SCRIPT>` and `</SCRIPT>` tags. The tags are usually placed in the `HEAD` element on your HTML page. You will also often include pieces of JavaScript within HTML tags to control *intrinsic* (inline) events.

Tip from molly

You should also use comment tags around your code so browsers that don't support JavaScript won't try to write the code to the page.

Listing 19.1 shows the structure of a typical HTML document including the JavaScript tags.

LISTING 19.1 AN HTML DOCUMENT WITH JAVASCRIPT TAGS

```
<HTML>
<HEAD>
```

continues

LISTING 19.1 CONTINUED

```
<TITLE>    </TITLE>

<SCRIPT language="JavaScript">
<!— Hide the script from non-JS browsers
javascript code goes here
//—>
</SCRIPT>

</HEAD>
<BODY>
</BODY>
</HTML>
```

Note

You'll see that although the opening portion of the comment tag, `<!--`, looks like any standard comment tag, the closing portion is different from what is used in commenting non-script based HTML (`-->`). The closing portion for comment scripting is `//-->`. This is an important distinction.

You can technically put your *primary* JavaScript anywhere on the page, but there are good and valid reasons to keep it in the `HEAD` element. That way, you can be sure that all your variables and functions will be ready to go *before* anyone visiting your Web site jumps the gun and initiates an action prior to the script's being read and interpreted by the browser.

You also can link HTML pages to a JavaScript file by using the `src` attribute. Many coders like to do this because they don't have to update every individual HTML file when a script needs to be changed; they simply update the linked file.

However, I don't recommend this for a variety of reasons, including that if you're trying to use JavaScript with DHTML, you can run into problems.

→ For further details on how JavaScript works with DHTML, **see** "Working with Dynamic HTML," **p. 450**

OBJECTS AND OPERATORS IN JAVASCRIPT

Objects and operators perform the same roles in JavaScript that nouns and verbs do in human languages. *Objects* are the things (windows, page elements, and so on), while *operators* tell JavaScript what kind of actions should take place.

You can read more about the Document Object Model (DOM—in very simple terms, the main "brain" of the browser) in Chapter 21, "Working with Dynamic HTML (DHTML)," but you should know that the DOM considers each element on every Web page a separate object. The window where you view the page is an object, the title of the page is an object, as is the body. Even things like headings, paragraphs, and images are objects. With the DOM, each object can be accessed and manipulated with JavaScript.

PROPERTIES AND OPERATORS

One of the most important things about objects is that they have *properties*. Properties for a paragraph object, for instance, include such things as font size, font color, and so on. You can use JavaScript to change the values in those properties, so you can change the font color in a paragraph by simply resetting it in a line of program code. Likewise, you can alter the properties of any HTML element in the same way.

Operators are the key to making changes. As the name implies, they are used to perform operations on objects. Those operations include things like adding, subtracting, multiplying, and dividing values. Table 19.1 shows the basic JavaScript arithmetic operators.

TABLE 19.1 COMMONLY USED JAVASCRIPT ARITHMETIC OPERATORS

Operator	Function
+	Addition
-	Subtraction
*	Multiplication
/	Division
++	Increment
—	Decrement

The first four are used in normal math. If you want to add two values, you use `value1 + value2`. If you want to multiply two values, you use `value1 * value2`. It's the same with subtraction and division, except of course for the symbols used.

The increment and decrement operators, though, are unique to programming, and they follow a very special syntax. I'll revisit them shortly. In addition to the basic arithmetic operators, there are others. One of the most common operators is the equals sign (=). You'll be using it a lot. In JavaScript, it's called the *assignment operator* because it's used to assign a value to an object or a *variable*. Variables are names you create to hold values.

Technically, a variable is a value that changes during the course of your program, but you can use a variable to hold an unchanging value (like *pi*) as well. In that case, you have a situation that would give language purists a fit—the variable contains a *constant*. In either case, the syntax is the same.

Before you can use a variable, you have to declare it. Although you simply can declare its existence without assigning any particular value to it, it's a common practice to both declare it and assign it an initial value at the same time. That's called *initializing a variable*. The following are a couple of examples. The first is a simple variable declaration, while the second shows how you initialize a variable.

```
var bananaCost
var orangeCost = 3
```

In both cases, the variable is available for use in your script. You can go right ahead and use them without further ado. But the variable `bananaCost` has no value as yet, so you'll have to include something in your script to take care of that little detail before you can do anything useful with it.

The other variable, `orangeCost`, already contains a value, so you could do things with it like the following:

```
orangeCost + 5
```

Because the variable `orangeCost` contains the value `3`, this would be the same thing as saying `3 + 5`.

There are a bunch of variations on the assignment operator that let you perform commonly used combinations of math and assignment. For example, it's not unusual at all to have an expression like `value = value + 7` or `value = value / 2`.

In the first case, you've got an expression that increases a value by 7 every time it's executed; in the second case, you divide the value by 2 every time you execute that expression. If you want to use a shorthand version of that kind of expression, you can use the *compound assignment operators*. They're specifically designed for the purpose. Table 19.2 shows the basic JavaScript compound assignment operators.

TABLE 19.2 COMMONLY USED JAVASCRIPT COMPOUND ASSIGNMENT OPERATORS

Operator	Function
+=	Addition compound assignment
-=	Subtraction compound assignment
*=	Multiplication compound assignment
/=	Division compound assignment

You use these in place of expressions like the ones in the preceding paragraph. Table 19.3 compares expressions that use compound assignment operators with the equivalent expressions that use both arithmetic operators and the normal assignment operator.

TABLE 19.3 COMPARISON OF COMPOUND ASSIGNMENT OPERATORS AND NORMAL APPROACH

Compound Expression	Normal Expression
value += 7	value = value + 7
value -= 7	value = value - 7
value *= 7	value = value * 7
value /= 7	value = value / 7

Now that you've been introduced to variables and assignments, it's time to take a look at the increment and decrement operators (++ and –). The increment operator adds 1 to a value.

The decrement operator subtracts 1 from a value. They're especially useful when you need to establish a countup or countdown situation.

Of course, you always can use something like `count = count + 1` or even `count += 1`, but its easier to just say `count++` instead. Also, it's readily apparent that you're in a countup or countdown when you see either the increment or the decrement operator.

Now for the special syntax of the increment and decrement operators. You can place them either before or after the variable they apply to (`++count` or `count++`), and it matters very much where you put them. When they're placed before the variable, the increment or decrement operation takes place before the expression that they're a part of is interpreted. When they're placed after, the expression is interpreted first. Take the following two examples:

```
total = ++count
total =  count++
```

Assume the variable count holds the value `4` before these lines are executed. In the first case, the value of `count` will be increased by 1 before its value is assigned to the variable total. In that case, the value in total will be `5` and the value in count will also be `5`. In the second case, the value of count is assigned to the variable total first, and then count is incremented.

The result is that total holds the original value of `4`, but the count now holds a value of `5`. This can make a huge difference in your program. Which one you end up using depends on how you want your program to work, but you need to keep the difference in mind or you'll end up with results other than those you had in mind.

CREATING LOGICAL RELATIONSHIPS

You can write perfectly good programs by using only the assignment and arithmetic operators, but you don't get into the real power until you start using the logical and comparison operators. Logical operators look at the relationship between values, and comparison operators compare values to tell if a comparison is `true` or `false`. This seemingly simple capability is the key to truly sophisticated programs. Tables 19.4 and 19.5 show the JavaScript logical and comparison operators.

TABLE 19.4 COMMONLY USED JAVASCRIPT LOGICAL OPERATORS

Operator	Function
==	Equality
!=	Inequality
>	Greater than
<	Less than
>=	Greater than or equal to
<=	Less than or equal to

TABLE 19.5 JAVASCRIPT COMPARISON OPERATORS

Operator	Function
&&	AND
||	OR
!	NOT

Each of these operators tests for different conditions. If the condition is met, the operator returns a value of `true` (numerically, `1`); if it's not met, the operator returns a value of `false` (numerically, `0`).

The equality operator (==) tests to see if two values are the same. The inequality operator (!=) tests to see if two values are different. Greater than (>) and less than (<) check to see if a value is higher or lower than another one; greater than or equal to (>=) and less than or equal to (<=) do the same thing, but will also return `true` if the value tested is equal.

The comparison operator, AND (&&), checks to see if two conditions are both `true`. If either one of them is `false`, it will return `false`. The OR operator (||), on the other hand, works a bit differently. It checks to see if either one of two conditions are `true`. If either one of them is `true`, it will return `true`. Only if both of them are `false` will it return `false`. The NOT operator (!) simply reverses the truth or falsehood of anything to which it's applied.

Caution

The similarity between the logical equality operator (==) and the assignment operator (=) is one of the most common sources of programming errors. It's not at all unusual for even professional programmers to unconsciously use the assignment operator when testing for equality.

STATEMENTS AND FUNCTIONS IN JAVASCRIPT

Statements are the sentences of JavaScript. They combine objects and operators into instructions to perform actions. A statement is a single action, although it can depend on conditions, and ends in a semicolon (;). The following are some examples of simple statements:

```
petNumber = cats + dogs;
timeLeft = timeHad - timeUsed;
userName = "Elmer Fudd";
```

In addition to the statements you create yourself from scratch, JavaScript has a number of built-in statements you can use in your scripts.

THE if STATEMENT

One of the most widely used is the `if` statement. `if` statements test to see if a condition is `true` and, if it is, they perform some action. If it isn't `true`, nothing happens.

```
if (carPrice < 20000) {buyIt();}
```

The curly braces ({}) are used to contain the statement that gets executed if the condition evaluates as `true`. They act much like the start tags and end tags in HTML, and you always have to have evenly matched pairs of braces. This will become more important later as you get into more complex structures that involve multiple statements.

Caution

Leaving out a brace, either at the beginning or end of a statement, is another common cause of programming errors.

Although a simple `if` statement is often placed on a single line like the previous example, it's not unusual to see it on multiple lines, with each element of it separated for easy reading like the following:

```
if (carPrice < 20000)
    {
    buyIt();
    }
```

This way, the condition the `if` statement is testing is listed first, followed by the action to be performed if it turns out to be `true`.

THE `if...else` STATEMENT

There's also a variant of the `if` statement called the `if...else` statement. Like the `if` statement, it tests to see if a condition is `true`, but it offers an alternative action if the statement is `false`:

```
if (carPrice < 20000)
    {
    buyIt();
    }
else
    {
    forgetIt();
    }
```


LOOPS

Another critical built-in statement type that JavaScript programmers use a lot are known as *loops*. Loops keep the program running in circles, doing little or nothing until some condition is met.

Loops are common to many programming languages. For example, if you're playing a computer game, the program is doing things while in a loop that's waiting for you to move the joystick or press the fire button (or for your plane to fly into a mountain). If you're using a word processor, it sits there waiting in a loop until you use the mouse or the keyboard.

The most common loop is the `for` loop, and it makes heavy use the increment and decrement operators. The `for` loop uses a counter variable that's set to some particular starting value (often 0 or 1). It checks to see if that counter variable has reached a specified limit and then performs a specified action. Next, it increments or decrements the counter variable and starts all over again. The following is what a typical `for` loop looks like:

```
for (counter=1; counter<=10; counter++)
    {
    doSomething();
    }
```

The various parts of this break down into the following steps:

1. Start the counter value at `1`.
2. Test to see if the counter value is less than or equal to `10`.
3. Perform the function named `doSomething()`.
4. Add 1 to the counter value.
5. Go back to step 2. If the counter value is greater than `10`, the loop is finished. Otherwise, steps 3 through 5 are repeated.

The upshot of all this is that you use the `for` loop in this example to perform the same action 10 times in a row. You could just as easily set the counter variable to a value of `10`, say that the action should be repeated as long as the condition `counter>=1` is met, and use the decrement operator (`counter—`) to count down instead of using the increment operator (`counter++`) to count up.

There's another statement that's very similar to the `for` loop, called the `while` loop. They both repeat themselves until some condition is met. The difference between the two is that the `for` loop has a built-in variable and a requirement for that variable to either increase or decrease. The `while` loop, on the other hand, has only the condition itself, with no guarantee that the condition will ever change. The following is a typical `while` loop:

```
while (counter<=10)
    {
    doSomething();
    }
```

As you can see, you need something else in the program to change the condition. Assuming the counter value is less than or equal to `10` when the `while` loop starts, the loop will never end unless that value is changed by the function `doSomething()`. The possibility of an endless loop where no action is taken and the program runs on and on is one of the reasons why most programmers use `while` loops a lot less often than `for` loops.

FUNCTIONS

The actions in the preceding statements look a little different from what you've seen so far. They have those funny parentheses after them. They're actually instructions to perform entire sets of statements, called `functions`. If statements are sentences, `functions` are paragraphs. `functions` are collections of statements. Where a single statement performs a single action, functions combine several statements together to perform a number of actions in a sequence.

You name functions so you can execute the entire sequence of statements at once by just invoking the name of the function. This is known as *calling a* `function`, and you'll come to appreciate its simplicity.

Technically, a `function` can consist of as little as one statement, but they normally include several at a time. The following is a typical `function`:

```
function getSleep()
    {
    turnOffLights = true;
    bed = "yes";
    }
```

You have to start with the keyword function so JavaScript knows what you're defining. As with `if` statements, you need to be sure to place the statements that compose the `function` within curly braces, and you have to make certain that you have an equal number of opening and closing braces flanking the statements. When the `function` is called by your script, both of the statements will be performed one right after the other.

Although the preceding example used a pair of simple assignment statements, `functions` can include much more complex statements as well:

```
function getSleep()
    {
    if (doneWithWork = true)
        {
        turnOffLights = true;
        bed = "yes";
        knockOff();
        }
    else
        {
        turnOffLights = false;
        bed = "not yet";
        keepGoing();
        }
    }
```


This time, the `function` consists of an `if...else` statement that includes conditional testing resulting in the assignment of one or another value to two variables and the possibility of one or another of two different `functions` being called. It's not unusual for one `function` to be called from within another one. The ability to do so enables you to write code that is easily understandable because it can be broken down into several basic functions, each of which is called as needed.

Caution

It's perfectly possible to call a `function` from inside itself as well as from inside another one. This is called *recursion,* and it's a risky thing to do. Recursion can quickly crash a JavaScript program. It can happen even when you don't do it deliberately. If `function` A calls `function` B which, in turn, calls `function` A, `function` A then calls B again, which calls A again, and so on.

JavaScript has a set of built-in `functions`, too, which can make your life a lot easier. In the mock program for going to the grocery that you saw earlier in this chapter, one of the instructions was "Drive to grocery." If that's all you were told to do, you'd know already, without further instructions, that you had to put the key in the ignition, start the car, use the gearshift, the steering wheel, the accelerator pedal, and the brake pedal to perform that task.

That's the way it is with JavaScript's native `functions`, too. All you have to do is tell JavaScript that you want a pop-up window, for instance, and it'll make one for you. You don't have to tell it how to do it, because it already knows how.

JAVASCRIPT APPLICATIONS

Here, you'll look at how to create a simple message box. From there, you'll look at animating graphics and, lastly, you'll take a look at a series of sophisticated browser tests.

> **Note**
>
> The following scripts contain many of the processes described in the language basics sections of this chapter. For example, you may well recognize functions and operators at work. However, I chose to present the code without defining its anatomy. My objective is to familiarize you with JavaScript enough so that you can identify aspects of the language and use scripts freely. To learn more about writing JavaScript on your own, pick up a copy of Joe Burns' *JavaScript Goodies* from Que.

SIMPLE MESSAGE BOX

This JavaScript (see Listing 19.2) allows you to type anything you like into the message box and have it returned to you by using an *alert box*. This is a box that pops up and stays until the visitor clicks OK.

The use of a message box like this isn't particularly functional, but it does demonstrate, in very simple terms, a `function`, a variable, and an alert command. Furthermore, it shows how JavaScript interacts with various aspects of HTML, in this case, a simple form.

LISTING 19.2 SIMPLE MESSAGE BOX

```
<HTML>
<HEAD>

<SCRIPT LANGUAGE="JavaScript">

<!-- Hide JavaScript
function MsgBox (textstring) {
alert (textstring) }
// - End hide JavaScript - -->

</SCRIPT>
</HEAD>
<BODY>
<BR>
```

```
<BR>
<BR>
<BR>

<DIV align="center">
<FORM>
<INPUT NAME="text1" TYPE=Text>
<INPUT NAME="submit" TYPE=Button VALUE="Click Me!"
onClick="MsgBox(form.text1.value)">
</FORM>
</DIV>

</BODY>
</HTML>
```

Figure 19.1 shows me typing into the box, and Figure 19.2 shows the resulting alert button.

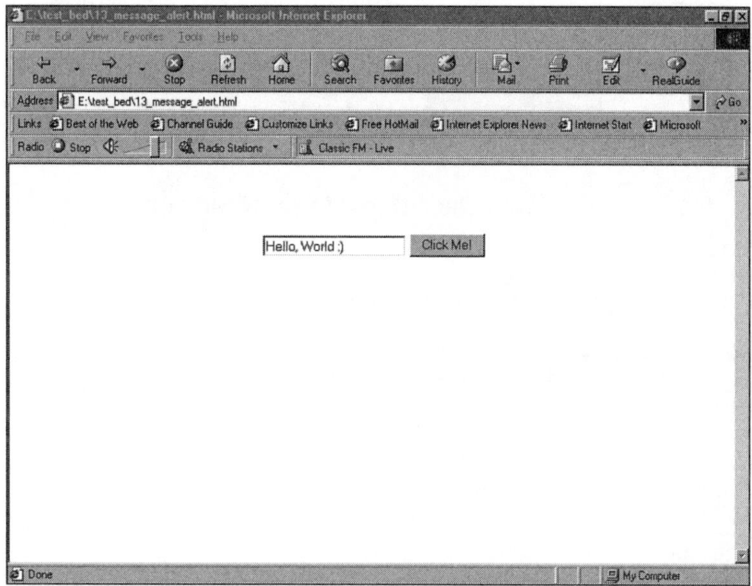

Figure 19.1 I've typed "Hello, World :)" into the text box. No action will take place until I click the Submit button.

Drop-Down Menu Navigation

Using drop-down menus takes the relationship between JavaScript and HTML to a more sophisticated and useful level than the simple message box example. You create the drop-down menu in HTML and control its actions with JavaScript (see Listing 19.3).

I'll use the standard `SELECT` object with `OPTION` tags holding the names of different Web sites for the menu. The value attributes of the option elements will be the URLs of the Web sites.

→ For a description of the `SELECT` and `OPTION` tags, **see** "Building Forms," **p. 383**

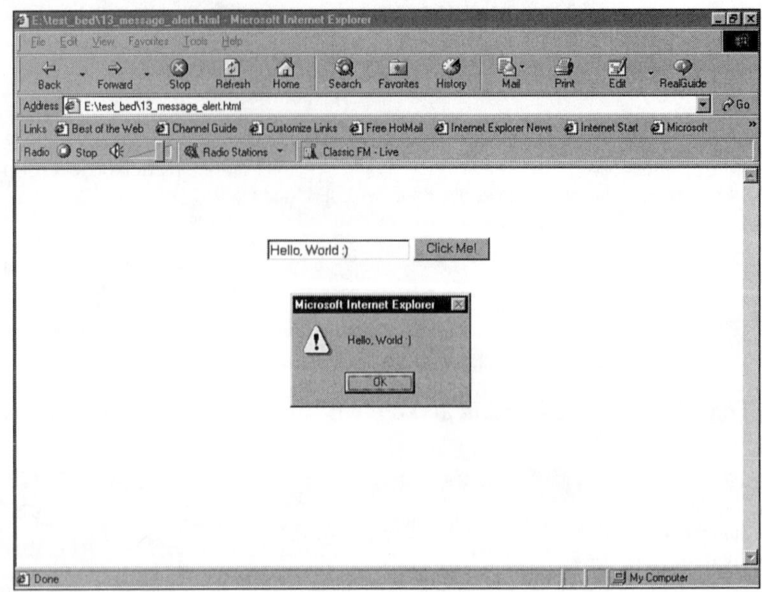

Figure 19.2
The alert button appears after I select Click Me!. The browser has responded to the onClick JavaScript function.

LISTING 19.3 JAVASCRIPT DROP-DOWN MENU NAVIGATION

```
<HTML>
<HEAD>
<TITLE>JavaScript Drop Down Menu</TITLE>

<SCRIPT language="JavaScript">
<!-- Hide the script from non-JS browsers
function goToLink(form)
   {
location.href = form.options[form.selectedIndex].value;
    }
//-->
</SCRIPT>
</HEAD>

<BODY>
<BR>
<BR>
<BR>
<BR>

<DIV align="center">
<FORM name="URLmenu">
<SELECT name="choices">
<OPTION value="http://www.molly.com/">Molly.com
<OPTION value="http://www.builder.com/">Builder.com
<OPTION value="http://www.webtechniques.com/">Web Techniques Magazine
<OPTION value="http://www.mcp.com/">Macmillan Computer Publishing
<OPTION value="13_message_alert.html">Message alert page
</SELECT>
<INPUT type="button" value="Go!" onclick="goToLink(this.form.choices)">
</FORM>
```

```
</DIV>

</BODY>
</HTML>
```

Figure 19.3 shows the drop-down menu. When the user clicks the GO button, he or she will end up at the selected URL.

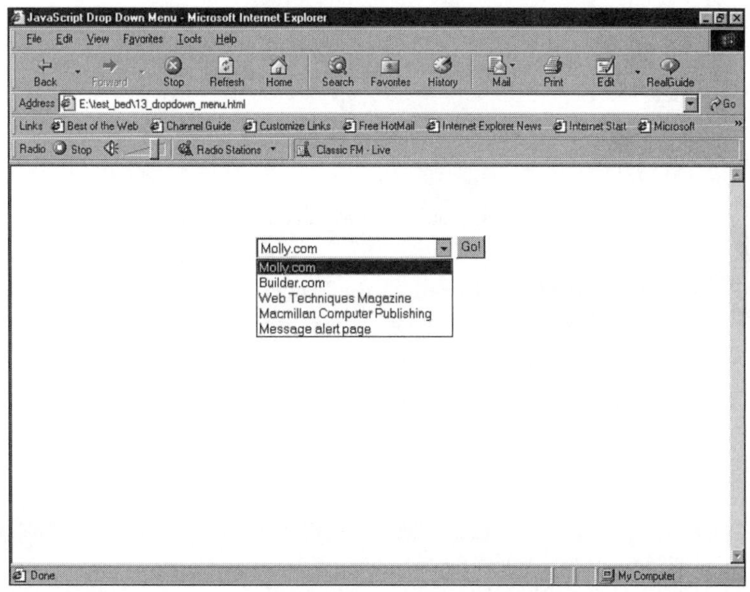

Figure 19.3 Here is an example of a JavaScript drop-down menu navigation. Select your location into the text box and click GO!.

The form included in this menu is a standard piece of HTML. The JavaScript comes in when a user clicks the button. At that point, the `goToLink` function is called. The value in the parentheses (`this.form.choices`) uses a JavaScript shortcut for the name of the form object. `this` refers to the current object.

The `choices` part is the name of the `SELECT` element. When this is passed to the `goToLink` function, it takes a look to see which of the options in that element have been selected, and then takes the value of that option and makes it the current URL of the Web page.

 *JavaScript not working? See "Got Script?" in the Troubleshooting section at the end of this chapter.*

POP-UP WINDOW

The Pop-Up Window is one of the mainstays of JavaScript functionality. It can be used any time you want to have a customized HTML page pop-up to display some element, such as a help menu.

You can control a variety of attributes in this script, such as whether or not there is a toolbar or status bar in the window, by setting them to 1 (or yes) or 0 (or no).

To install this script, follow these simple steps:

1. Type this script into the HEAD of an HTML document where you'd like to have a pop-up window:

```
<script language="JavaScript">
<!--//BEGIN Script

function new_window(url) {

link =
window.open(url,"Link","toolbar=0,location=0,directories=0,status=0,menubar=0,
scrollbars=0,resizable=0,width=200,height=250,left=80,top=180");

}
//END Script-->
</script>
```

2. Create the HTML file you'd like to have load in the pop-up window. Name and save the file.
3. Type this line of JavaScript into the BODY of your original document, where your_popup.html is the name of your pop-up HTML file:

```
<A HREF="javascript:new_window('your_popup.html')">click me</A>
```

4. Save your file and test the page.

Figure 19.4 shows the pop-up in action.

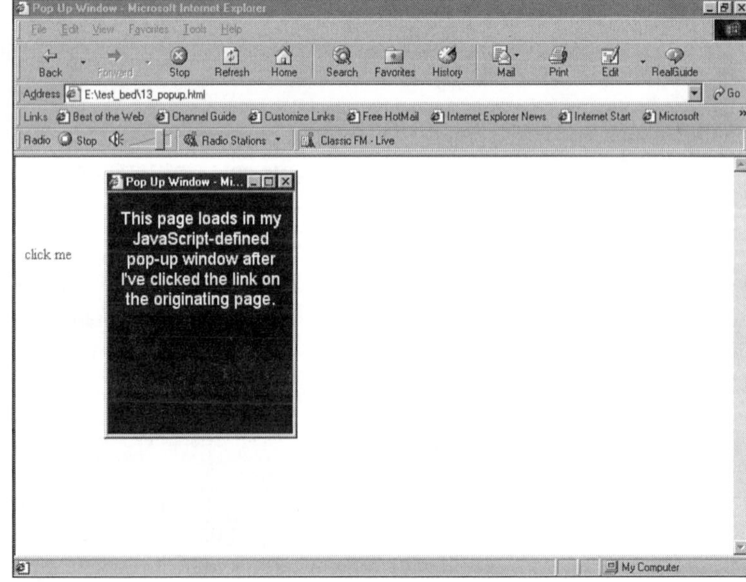

Figure 19.4
This JavaScript pop-up window is handy for adding additional information such as a help page or code sample without having to invoke an entirely new browser window.

Tip from molly

> As helpful as pop-up windows can be, they can also be overused (especially when made automatic and used for advertising). My advice is to use them where they enhance the site: providing help, additional navigation, and code samples. Try to avoid automating pop-ups on page load, and reserving them for user-initiated tasks such as in the example just provided.

JavaScript Mouseovers

An extremely popular use for Web sites, the JavaScript mouseover and pre-load image application is actually quite simple (see Listing 19.4). However, you will need to create graphic buttons to work with this example.

➔ Learn to design mouseover buttons, **see** "Creating Professional Web Graphics," **p. 614**

Listing 19.4 Mouseover Code

```
<HTML>
<HEAD>
    <TITLE>Mouseover</TITLE>
<SCRIPT language="javascript">
<!--
// browser test:
bName = navigator.appName;
bVer = parseInt (navigator.appVersion);
if (bName == "Netscape" && bVer >= 3) version = "n3";
else if (bName == "Netscape" && bVer == 2) version = "n2";
else if (bName == "Microsoft Internet Explorer" && bVer >= 3) version = "n3";
else version = "n2";
// end of browser test

// preload universal images:

// If it is Netscape 3 browser
if (version== "n3") {

b0off = new Image(); b0off.src = "images/new_off.gif";

b0on = new Image(); b0on.src = "images/new_on.gif";

}

function hiLite(imgDocID,imgObjName) {
   if (version == "n3") {
       document.images[imgDocID].src = imgObjName;
       }
   }

function hiLiteOff(imgDocID,imgObjName) {
   if (version == "n3") {
       document.images[imgDocID].src = imgObjName;
       }
   }

//-->
```

continues

Listing 19.4 Continued

```
</SCRIPT>
</HEAD>

<BODY bgcolor="#000000">
<BR>
<BR>
<BR>
<BR>

<DIV align="center">
<A href="new.html" onmouseover="hiLite('b0','images/new_off.gif')"
onmouseout="hiLiteOff('b0','images/new_on.gif')">
<IMG src="images/new_off.gif" name="b0" width="81" height="94" border="0"
alt="what's new"></A>
</DIV>

</BODY>
</HTML>
```

Figure 19.5 shows the mouseover in the normal state, and Figure 19.6 demonstrates the color change as the mouse passes over the graphic.

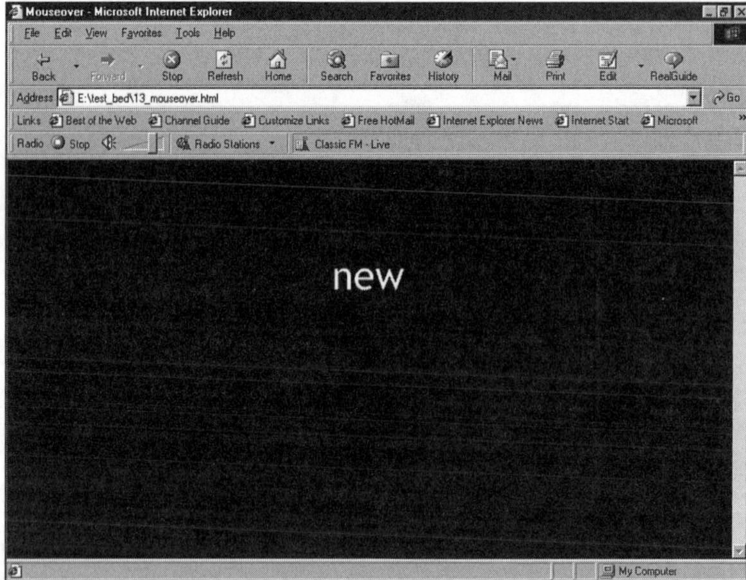

Figure 19.5
In the normal state, the "new" graphic is inert, with no change.

Tip from

Use an imaging program with layers so as to easily create your multiple mouseover images and avoid shifting of text location.

Figure 19.6
As the mouse passes over the graphic, the JavaScript recognized that this event, known as the mouseover state, requires an action. It switches the graphic to one of a different color. In this script, the graphic will return to the original, static one after the mouse passes out of the graphic's range.

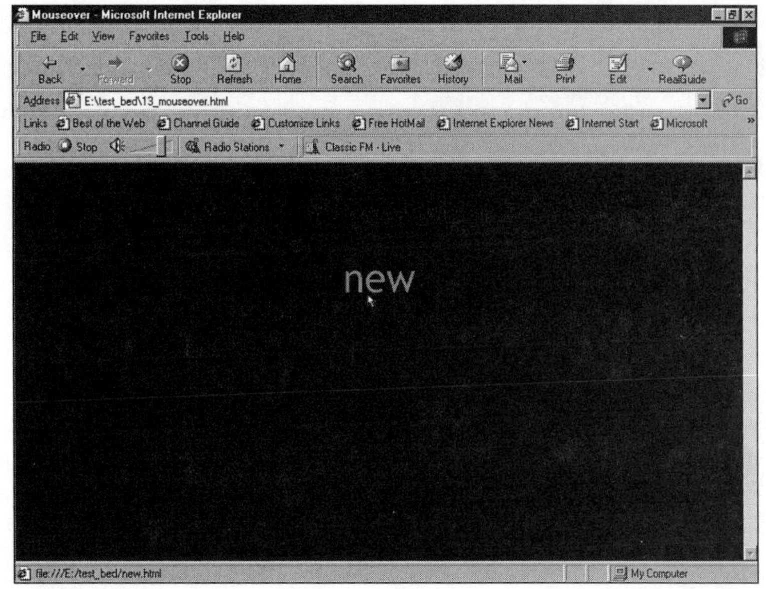

→ For general information on working with imaging programs, **see** "Creating Professional Web Graphics," **p. 598**

→ To learn advanced graphic techniques, **see** "Imagemaps, Animation, and Special Graphic Techniques," **p. 648**

You can add as many images to this code as you like, following these steps.

1. Add the image to the image list in the code:

```
b1off = new Image(); b1off.src = "images/about_off.gif";

b1on = new Image(); b1on.src = "images/about_on.gif";
```

2. Add the HTML referencing the new image:

```
<A href="about.html" onmouseover="hiLite('b1','images/about_off.gif')"
onmouseout="hiLiteOff('b1','images/about_on.gif')">
<IMG src="images/about_off.gif" name="b1" width="81" height="94" border="0"
alt="about us"></A>
```

You can complete this process until you have as many images as you want.

Finding incorrect or missing graphics when testing your script? See "The Wrong Image," in the Troubleshooting section at the end of this chapter.

Browser Testing and Routing

In the mouseover example, you probably noticed code referencing browsers. This is browser testing, also known as *browser sniffing* or *browser detection*:

```
// browser test:
bName = navigator.appName;
bVer = parseInt (navigator.appVersion);
```

```
if (bName == "Netscape" && bVer >= 3) version = "n3";
else if (bName == "Netscape" && bVer == 2) version = "n2";
else if (bName == "Microsoft Internet Explorer" && bVer >= 3) version = "n3";
else version = "n2";
// end of browser test
```

While certainly the visual functions and esthetic applications of JavaScript hold an important role in design, it is the browser detection that has empowered developers greatly. The reason for this is that designers can ensure that the right design goes to the right browser.

Because both Netscape Navigator and Microsoft Internet Explorer have slightly different capabilities, it can be advantageous to determine which one of the major browsers a visitor to your Web site is using.

Tip from molly

> Web designers may wish to please both of their audiences, creating two different versions of their sites, one that exploits the expanded capabilities of Navigator and one that exploits the expanded capabilities of Internet Explorer, and then using browser detection and routing to send the site visitor to the site optimized for their situation.

First you can decipher the browser's header. The following is one way of doing just that:

```
<form name="browserHeader">
<input type="button" name="status" value="View Browser Header Info"
onClick="alert('\nBrowserName: ' + navigator.appName + '\nBrowser Version: ' +
parseInt(navigator.appVersion) + '\n\nUser Agent Info:\n' + navigator.userAgent)">
</form>
```

I put this script right inline in an HTML page. Figure 19.7 shows the results in test one, and Figure 19.8 shows how the test two script figured out I was using Netscape.

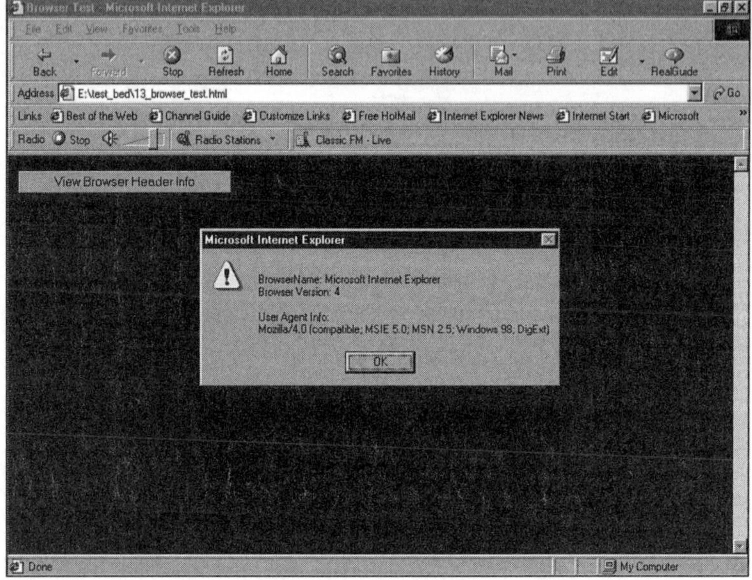

Figure 19.7
The script sees Internet Explorer, which spits back the browser version as 4, although the browser is actually IE 5.0. You can tell this by the compatibility line mentioning IE 5.0.

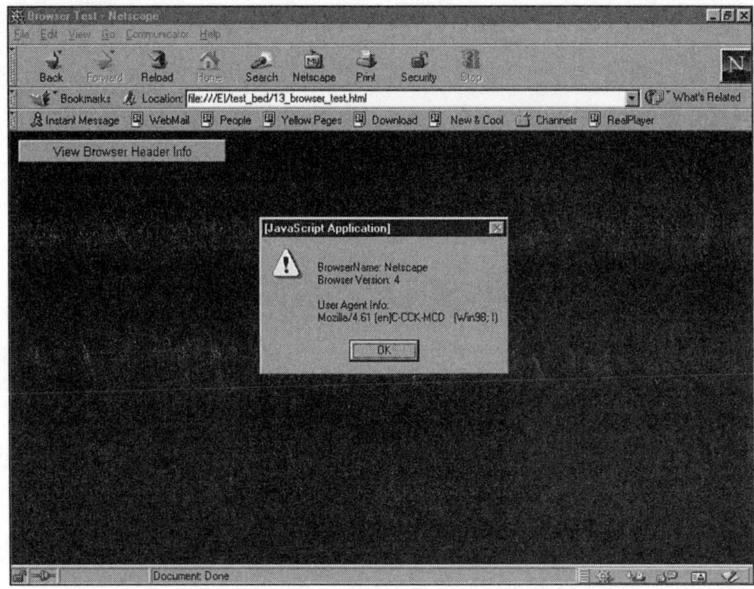

Figure 19.8
Here, the script finds that I'm using Netscape, version 4.0, with the specific release version of 4.61.

You can now put this information together and do some browser detection/routing. The most common need in detection/routing is to send individuals using Netscape one way and Microsoft IE users the other.

This example sends the Internet Explorer 3.0+ people one way, the Netscape 3.0+ people another way, and other browsers, or non-JavaScript-supported browsers a third way.

```
<script language="JavaScript">
function browserRouting() {
  bName = navigator.appName;
  bVer = parseInt(navigator.appVersion);
  if (bName == "Netscape" && bVer >= 3) parent.location='net.html'
    else if (bName == "Microsoft Internet Explorer" && bVer >= 2) parent.location
➥='ie.html'
      else parent.location='other.html';
}
</script>
```

In this case, you'll have to create three corresponding pages, net.html, ie.html, and other.html. The JavaScript then will redirect the visitor to the page for their browser.

Another browser detect and route that is important in today's Web design world is to route by screen resolution. The "Route by Res" script allows you to do just that.

→ For a closer look at screen resolution concerns, **see** "Resolution, Gamma, and the Visual Environment," **p. 546**

You'll need to first create a selection of documents that are designed specifically for a given resolution. I created three files, one for 640×480 resolution (`640.html`), one for 800×600 res (`800.html`), and one for high res (`1024.html`).

Then, you'll add the code in Listing 19.5 to the `HEAD` portion of the default index page.

LISTING 19.5 ROUTE BY RES

```
<SCRIPT LANGUAGE="JavaScript">
<!-- Begin
function redirectPage() {
var url640x480 = "640.html";
var url800x600 = "800.html";
var url1024x768 = "1024.html";
if ((screen.width == 640) && (screen.height == 480))
window.location.href= url640x480;
else if ((screen.width == 800) && (screen.height == 600))
window.location.href= url800x600;
else if ((screen.width == 1024) && (screen.height == 768))
window.location.href= url1024x768;
else window.location.href= url640x480;
}
// End -->
</SCRIPT>
```

In the opening body tag of the HTML document, add the following statement:

```
<body onload="redirectPage()">
```

Save the page as a default or index page, using the appropriate extensions.

Note

The default page should contain content prepared for individuals who do not have JavaScript available or enabled.

Test the script by changing your screen's resolution several times and reloading the page each time. Using this script, you can create designs optimized to the resolution dimensions of your audience (Figure 19.9).

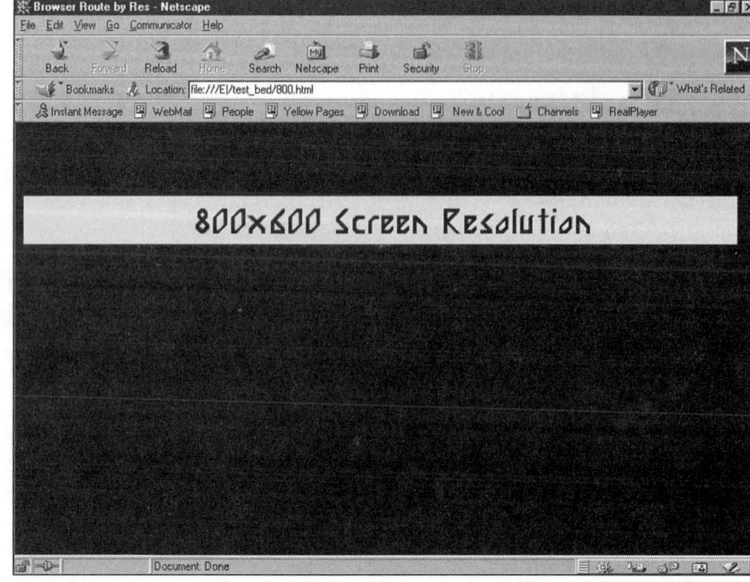

Figure 19.9
I loaded the index page, but my browser quickly read the Route by Res script and seamlessly loaded the 800×600 page to match my current screen resolution.

Note

You don't need to name the files literally in this script. It will automatically load the appropriate HTML page if you've named them according to my lead.

Troubleshooting

Got Script?

The code is correct, but the script isn't working. What's the problem?

If you've checked carefully for syntax errors and are certain that your script is free and clear of any bugs, the problem is probably due to one of two reasons:

- **JavaScript is disabled or unavailable in your browser.** To check to be sure JavaScript is running, look in your browser's preferences and make sure JavaScript is available and enabled.
- **Your browser doesn't support the JavaScript version or syntax in use.** There are differences between browser versions and support for JavaScript versions and syntax. This is most clearly demonstrated in the differences between Netscape and Internet Explorer, but the problems arise between versions as well. Internet Explorer 3.0 simply does not have the JavaScript sophistication found in the 4.0 and later versions, whereas Netscape has almost always been ahead of the game where JavaScript (excluding the use of JavaScript for DHTML and Style Sheets) is concerned.

The Wrong Image

I've used the mouseover script in this section, but the wrong image was loading upon mouseover. Then, I thought I had fixed the code, but no image showed up when I tested the mouseover. What's wrong?

It's very likely that you've named your image files incorrectly either in the `SCRIPT` section of the document, or inline with the image `name` attribute, or both. Look carefully through your code to determine where the misnaming might have occurred.

Designing for the Real World

JavaScript and Style Sheets

JavaScript goes hand-in-hand with Cascading Style Sheets. It can be used to access and act on any CSS attribute. There's a slight difference in the way the names of the attributes are handled in JavaScript, though. Fortunately, the conversion is simple and follows a strict rule.

Where property names in CSS are always in lowercase and the words are separated by hyphens, you drop the hyphens in JavaScript and capitalize the beginning of every word except the first one. For example, the CSS attribute `font-family` would be `fontFamily` in JavaScript. Three word attributes are done the same way; the CSS attribute `page-break-after` would be `pageBreakAfter` in JavaScript.

Let's assume you want to change the font size of a paragraph with JavaScript. Follow these steps:

1. Select an existing HTML page where you'd like to have a link enlarged in type size upon clicking:

```
<HTML>
<HEAD>

<TITLE>JavaScript and Style</TITLE>
</HEAD>

<BODY>

<A href="http://www.molly.com/">Vist Molly's Web page!</A>

</BODY>
</HTML>
```

2. Build a style sheet containing the `A` selector and add type attributes:

```
<HTML>
<HEAD>
<TITLE>JavaScript and Style</TITLE>
<STYLE>
<!--
A    font: 14pt Garamond;
    text-decoration: none
}
-->
</STYLE>
</HEAD>

<BODY>

<A onclick = "this.style.fontSize='24'" href="http://www.molly.com/">Vist
Molly's Web page!</A>

</BODY>
</HTML>
```

3. Add the following JavaScript to any link where you'd like to have the change occur:

```
<A href="http://www.molly.com/">Vist Molly's Web page!</A>
```

4. Save and test your file.

The `font-size` attribute set by the Cascading Style Sheet for this HTML page would be overridden when someone clicked this link. This example uses a single JavaScript statement that's contained within the element it affects. As you might recall from the section on drop-down menus, that's the secret of the shortcut `this`. `this` refers to the current object. CSS attributes can be changed in regular JavaScript functions as well, but you need to use the full name of the affected object to access and change its attributes.

→ For a look into the way JavaScript and CSS work together, **see** "Element Positioning and Style Sheet Scripting," **p. 429**

Note

Due to browser inconsistencies, this example might not work in many browsers, including Netscape 4.6 and below. It will work admirably well in Internet Explorer 4.0 and above, which supports a wider range of mouse-related events.

CHAPTER 20

Element Positioning and Style Sheet Scripting

In this chapter

Working with Style Sheet Positioning

Using Cascading Style Sheet (CSS) properties is generally thought of as a method for controlling the physical appearance of HTML formatting, aspects such as the size of fonts or the background color of a page. One of the most powerful CSS properties, however,is *positioning*. This property gives you total, pixel-level control over the location of every element.

Whether these properties are assigned in a linked style sheet, an embedded style sheet, or via CSS values in the element tags, the results are the same: The kind of power that used to be reserved for high-end desktop publishing programs is finally available to the Web designer.

→ For more information on how CSS can increase this power, **see** "Cascading Style Sheet Techniques," **p. 253**

CSS positioning, however, is not restricted to just creating static Web pages where the elements are carefully positioned. Using JavaScript, you can dynamically alter positions, letting you use mouseovers and other events for animations. With relative simplicity, you can apply just about any technique for interactive position manipulation you can imagine.

→ For more information on JavaScript and DHTML, **see** "Using JavaScript," **p. 404** and "Working with Dynamic HTML (DHTML)," **p. 450**

CSS Positioning Concepts

Cascading Style Sheet positioning works by combining browser technology and HTML, binding the two closely to gain specific positioning power over elements on a page.

Positioning uses the following concepts:

- **Bounding box**—A bounding box is an invisible, rectangular area predetermined by the browser. Style sheets allow you to manipulate this box, setting its position on a page using absolute or relative positioning values.
- **Absolute values**—Also referred to as *absolute positioning*, this feature allows you to position the bounding box in relation to the browser's parameters. Absolute value is determined by the absolute relationship between the bounding box and the browser.
- **Relative values**—In this case, *relative positioning* refers to positioning elements based on the relationship of these elements to other elements on a page. Because elements are not positioned to the browser, the positioning values are considered to be relative (relational).

Positioning relies on the `position` property and an associated value:

```
P {position: absolute}
```

or

```
P {position: relative}
```

You then add any properties that you want to fix the positioning in absolute or relative terms:

```
P {position: absolute; top: 200px; width: 200px; height: 200px;}
```

or

```
P {position: relative; top: 20px; width: 200px; height: 200px;}
```

Note

Don't be disappointed if you can't make this syntax work in the embedded or linked style method. Even CSS-compliant browsers are still catching up to the proper syntax. You can use inline style, shown in the following examples, to achieve positioning.

Using the inline style, Listing 20.1 shows you the bounding box by setting some absolute positioning values using the `DIV` element.

➔ **See** Chapter 7, "Formatting and Aligning Text," for information on using the DIV element.

LISTING 20.1 BOUNDING BOX ABSOLUTELY POSITIONED

```
<HTML>
<HEAD>
<TITLE>Style Sheet Positioning</TITLE>

</HEAD>

<BODY>

<DIV style="position: absolute; top: 150px; width: 200px; height: 200px;
background-color: #000000;">

</DIV>

</BODY>
</HTML>
```

Figure 20.1 shows the bounding box.

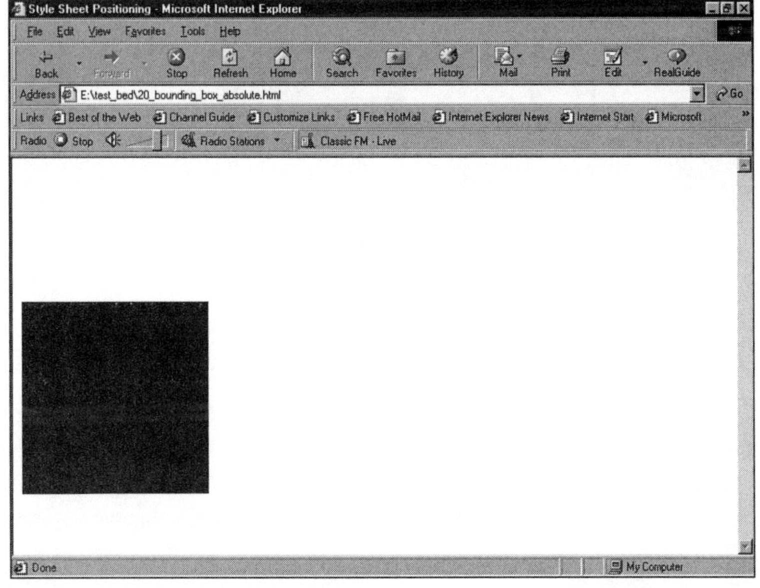

Figure 20.1 You can see in the `DIV` element in Listing 20.1 that the size of the positioned box shown in this figure will be 200×200 pixels.

Listing 20.2 shows the same bounding box, absolutely positioned to another portion of the page.

LISTING 20.2 BOUNDING BOX IN ANOTHER POSITION

```
<HTML>
<HEAD>
<TITLE>Style Sheet Positioning</TITLE>

</HEAD>

<BODY>

<DIV style="position: absolute; top: 10px; left: 200px; width: 200px;
height: 200px; background-color: #000000;">

</DIV>

</BODY>
</HTML>
```

The position of this box is demonstrated in Figure 20.2.

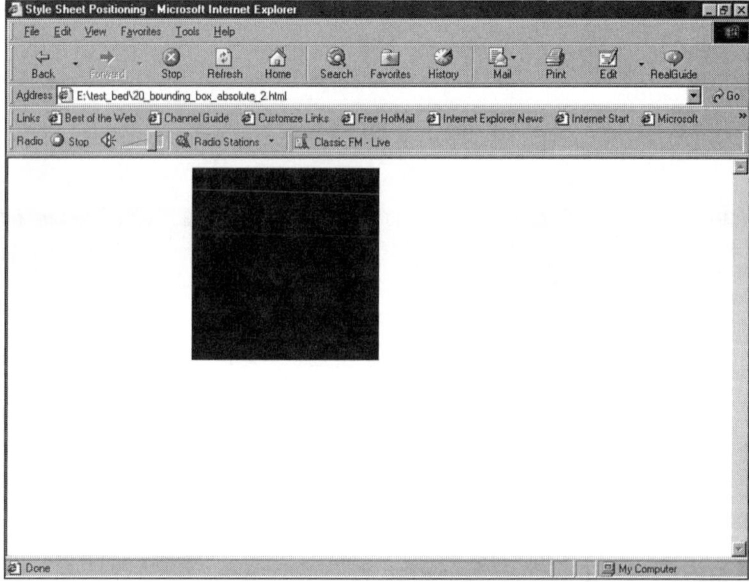

Figure 20.2
The box is now in another position.

Of course, the box is going to be visible or invisible depending on your use. If you want to use the box as a decorative element, just as you would use the background color of a table cell or a background graphic within a table cell, you can do so.

Note

You'll need to use Internet Explorer 4.0 or higher to work with width and height in bounding boxes. Netscape 4.6 and lower does not support this feature if the `DIV` element is empty. If you'd like to experiment for Netscape 4.6 and higher, add an image or other object to the `DIV` element.

➔ For help with using the box as a decorative element, **see** "Advanced Table Layouts," **p. 333**

On the other hand, you can simply use the bounding box as the positioning grid. In Figure 20.3, I've removed the visible box by leaving out the background color and added text. This way, the box becomes invisible. The only visible aspect is now the text.

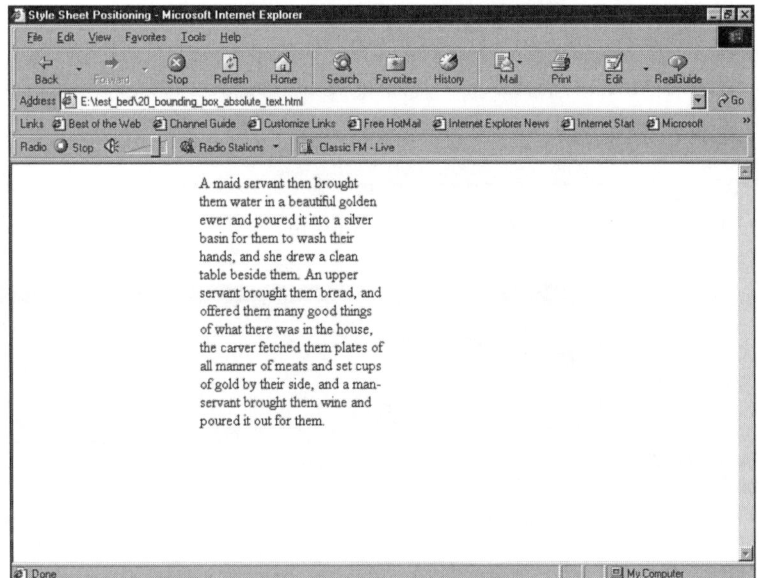

Figure 20.3
Using the box to control the text's position.

The following section looks at relative and absolute positioning in greater depth.

Relative and Absolute Positioning

In the normal document structure of a Web page, one object follows another from top to bottom, displayed in the same order in which they are found in the original HTML code. If you have an `H1` element as the first thing in your HTML document, then a `P` element, and then an `IMG` element, they appear just like that in a Web browser: The heading is placed on the page first, then the paragraph, and then the image.

With absolute positioning, the order of the elements doesn't matter. The third item can show up on top of the Web page, or the first one can be on the bottom. Or the second one can be on the top or bottom. Whatever you decide.

Listing 20.3 shows the code for a standard HTML page.

LISTING 20.3 STANDARD POSITIONING IN HTML

```
<HTML>
<HEAD>

<TITLE>Positioning an Element</TITLE>

</HEAD>

<BODY>

<H1>Sir Isaac Newton</H1>

<P>Newton formulated the theory of universal gravitation.
<BR clear="all">
<BR>

<IMG src="images/newton.gif" width="213" height="222" alt="picture of sir_isaac">

</BODY>
</HTML>
```

In Figure 20.4, the graphic is displayed normally.

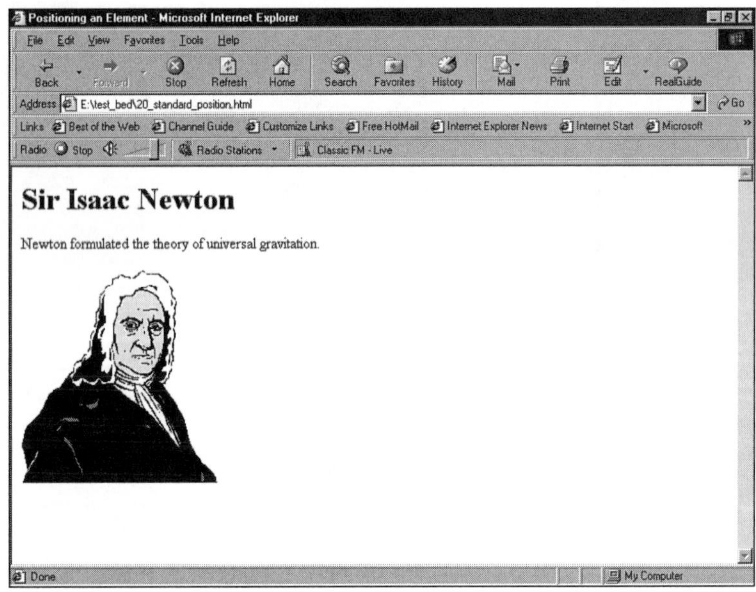

Figure 20.4
Normal HTML positioning. Compare this to Figure 20.5. Looks the same at first glance, but upon closer examination, you'll see that the elements are more precisely controlled when style sheets are used.

You can change that positioning using style sheets. Listing 20.4 shows how to do just that.

LISTING 20.4 USING STYLE SHEETS TO POSITION THE GRAPHIC

```
<HTML>
<HEAD>

<TITLE>Positioning an Element</TITLE>

</HEAD>

<BODY>

<DIV style="position: absolute; top: 10px; left: 10px">
<H1>Sir Isaac Newton</H1>
</DIV>

<DIV style="position: absolute; top: 50px; left: 10px">
<P>Newton formulated the theory of universal gravitation.
</DIV>

<IMG src="images/newton.gif"  style="position: absolute; top: 100px; left: 10px;
width="213" height="222" alt="picture of sir isaac">

</BODY>
</HTML>
```

Figure 20.5 shows that the graphic of Sir Isaac is flush left, as is the header and paragraph. Each are set precisely 10 pixels from the left edge of the browser. Note how, in the code, the header comes *before* the graphic because the positioning is absolute; it's relying on the browser parameters, not other objects on the screen, to determine its position.

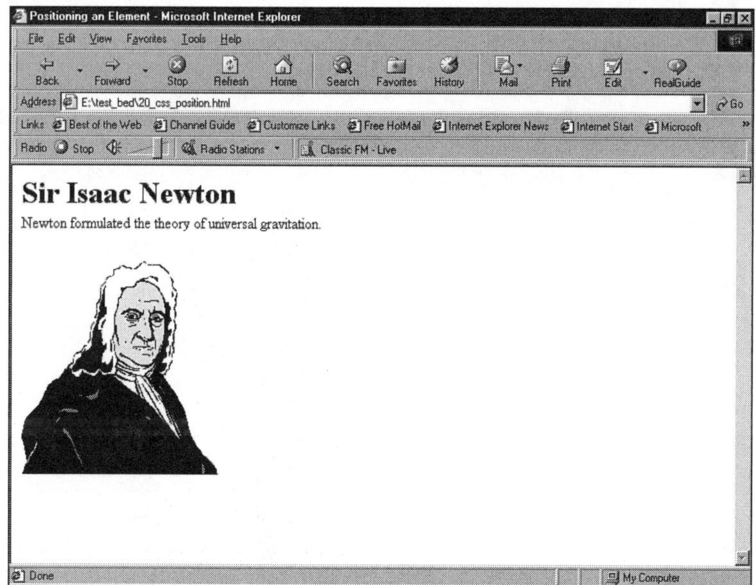

Figure 20.5
Absolute positioning of graphic and text elements. Each element relies on the browser to determine its position.

Now, relative positioning lies somewhere between the HTML approach and the style sheet approach of absolute positioning. The elements are still displayed in the order in which they appear in the HTML code, but the Web browser doesn't decide where to put the elements in relation to one another. That part is up to you.

Listing 20.5 uses a combination of absolute and relative positioning. You need to have an absolute element involved to be able to tell the browser how to position the other elements *in relation*, or relatively, to that element.

LISTING 20.5 RELATIVE POSITIONING

```
<HTML>
<HEAD>
<TITLE>Positioning</TITLE>

</HEAD>

<BODY>

<H1 style="position: absolute; top: 0px; left: 0px;">Sir Isaac Newton</H1>

<P style="position: relative; top: 50px; left: 10px;">Newton formulated the
theory of universal gravitation.

<IMG style="position: relative; top: 0px; left: 5px" SRC="images/newton.gif"
WIDTH="213" HEIGHT="222" alt="picture of sir isaac">

</BODY>
</HTML>
```

Figure 20.6 shows the results.

Tip from

When working with relative positioning, place each element in its expected position. So, when you create your HTML, be sure to place a header first, the paragraph second, and the graphic last if that's the order in which you want them to appear.

Caution

Unfortunately, relative positioning is one area in which style sheets and browsers have yet to mature. So, you might find your relative positioning inaccurate or inconsistent.

Concerned that you may have problems with browser incompatibility when using relative positioning on your pages? See "Addressing Backward Compatibility" in the Troubleshooting section at the end of this chapter.

Extreme Values

If you use a negative number for the position values, the element is moved right off the Web page. How much of it remains visible depends on the size of the element itself. For instance, using a `-50` for the `top` attribute makes the sentence totally disappear. The same value for the `left` attribute simply moves the beginning of the sentence off the side of the screen, but a larger one can make it slide out of sight as well.

Giving an extremely large positive value, however, can also cause unexpected consequences. A `left` value large enough to move the element off the right side of the screen does not cause the same thing as when you give a negative value large enough to move the element off the left side of the screen. What does happen is that the element hits a brick wall. The sentence stops at the right side and wraps around to the next line.

A `top` value large enough to move the element off the bottom of the screen doesn't do either of these things, of course, because there's no such thing as the bottom of a Web page. The element is simply placed where you said to put it, and it can be viewed by anyone who scrolls down far enough to see it.

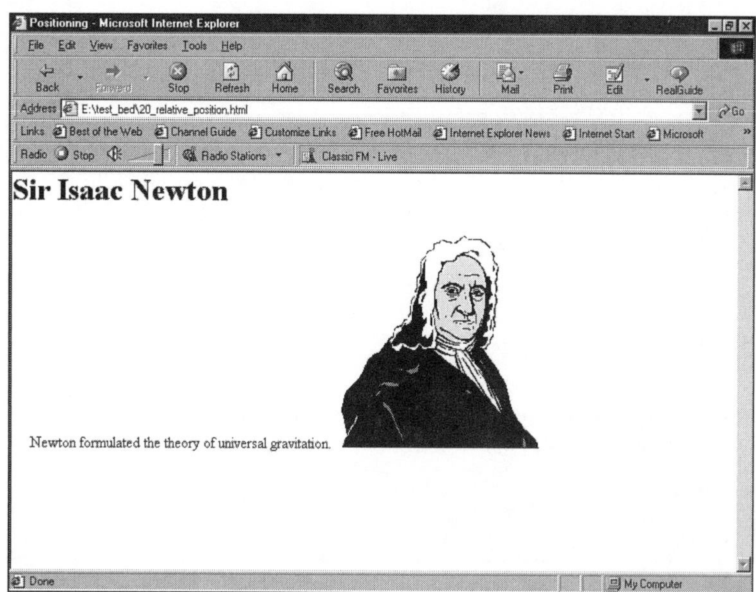

Figure 20.6
Relative positioning—I've changed the layout a little for variety's sake.

Z Order

One of the most compelling aspects of style sheet positioning is that it introduces a third axis. So far, you've worked with the x- and y-axes, or horizontal and vertical. When you use the `z-index` property, as in the following example, the Z Order brings a third dimension, allowing for a dimensional relationship to now exist between elements:

```
P    {
position: absolute;
top: 175px;
left: 330px;
z-index: 1;
}
```

Listing 20.6 shows use of the z-axis with the `z-index` property. In this case, I've used text to demonstrate the effect.

LISTING 20.6 z-index IN ACTION

```
<HTML>
<HEAD>
<TITLE>Z AXIS</TITLE>
<STYLE type="text/css">
<!--
.above     { position: absolute;
    top: 165px;
    left: 320px;
    z-index: 2;

    }

.below     { position: absolute;
    top: 175px;
    left: 330px;
    z-index: 1;

    }
-->
</STYLE>
</HEAD>
<BODY>
<FONT size="5">

<SPAN class="above">Sir Isaac Newton</SPAN>
<SPAN class="below">Sir Isaac Newton</SPAN>

</FONT>
</BODY>
</HTML>
```

Figure 20.7 shows the results.

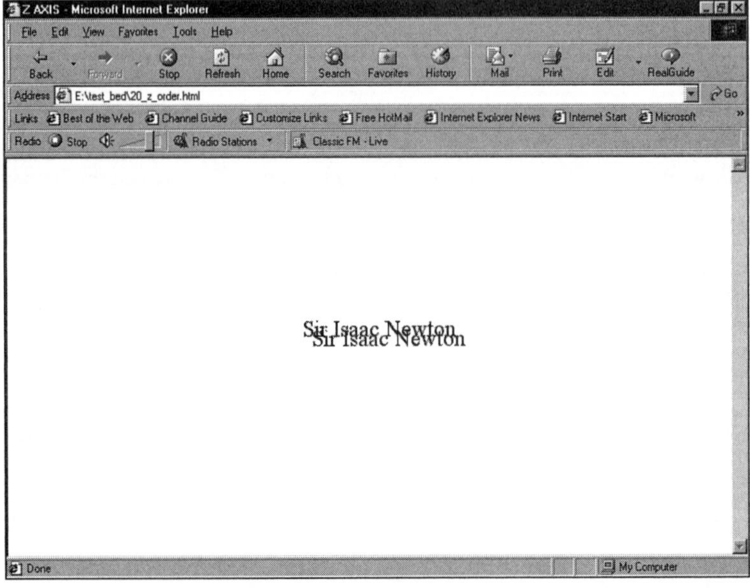

Figure 20.7
Adding a third dimension with z-index. Using z-index gives the designer the opportunity to stack visual objects and text and also create shadows and other effects along the z-axis. This provides visual depth to a page without having to rely on graphic bevels, shadows, and special effects.

You can use `z-index` for images, too. Listing 20.7 demonstrates how.

LISTING 20.7 `z-index` AND IMAGES

```
<HTML>
<HEAD>
<TITLE>Z AXIS</TITLE>
<STYLE type="text/css">
<!--
.above      { position: absolute;
    top: 75px;
    left: 20px;
    z-index: 2;

    }

.below      { position: absolute;
    top: 125px;
    left: 40px;
    z-index: 1;
    }
-->
</STYLE>
</HEAD>
<BODY>

<IMG class="above" src="images/newton.gif" width="213" height="222"
alt="picture of sir isaac">
<IMG class="below" src="images/newton.gif" width="213" height="222"
alt="picture of sir isaac">


</BODY>
</HTML>
```

Figure 20.8 shows Sir Isaac in a three-dimensional view. Something tells me he might have liked that!

Tip from molly

Use z-order to create dimensional effects such as shadows. Place a black text forward on the z-axis, and the same text in gray just behind it, and you'll end up with a shadow that doesn't rely on a graphic.

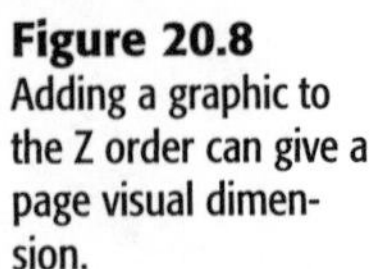

Figure 20.8
Adding a graphic to the Z order can give a page visual dimension.

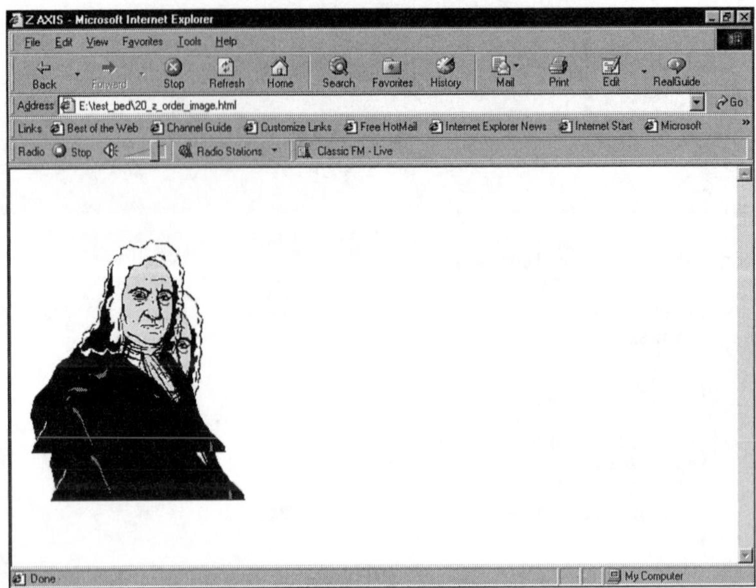

POSITIONING EFFECTS

The following three style sheet positioning effects are important to be familiar with:

- **Clipping**—This positioning effect is the process of allowing objects that are overlapped to be seen.
- **Visibility**—With style sheets, you can choose to make an object visible or invisible. This way, you can use shaped objects to create space and allow for text flow around that invisible shape.
- **Overflow**—This effect allows you to control elements that won't fit into a designated bounding box.

CLIPPING

To clip an object so that another might be seen, you place one object over the other using absolute positioning. Then you clip one object down, using the `clip` property, as shown in Listing 20.8. The other object can then appear.

LISTING 20.8 CLIPPING AN OBJECT

```
<HTML>
<HEAD>
<TITLE>Style Sheet Effects</TITLE>
<STYLE>

<!--
```

```
{

.clip      { position: absolute;
   top: 200px;
   left: 200px;
   width: 150px;
   height: 150px;
   color: yellow;
   background-color: black;
   clip: rect(25px 125px 125px 25px);
   }

-->
</STYLE>
</HEAD>

<BODY>
<DIV class="clip">The text is cut off by the clipping I've performed on the
square.</DIV>

</BODY>
</HTML>
```

The results of clipping are demonstrated in Figure 20.9.

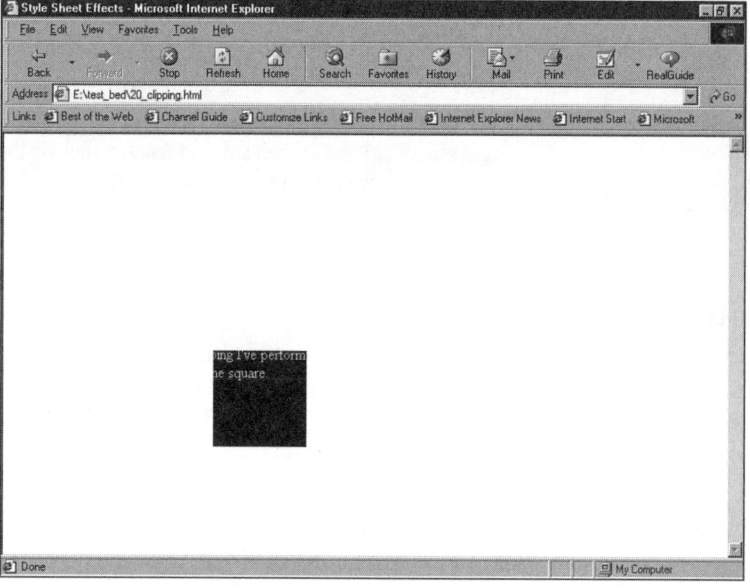

Figure 20.9
Using clipping I was able to obscure the text. If I were to modify the clip values, I could end up with a number of different effects.

Visibility

Using visibility effects is a great way to hide text and objects so that others can appear around them. In this case, I'm going to hide Sir Isaac, as you can see in Listing 20.9. Any text that follows will begin where Sir Isaac ends.

LISTING 20.9 HIDING SIR ISAAC

```
<HTML>
<HEAD>
<TITLE>Style Sheet Effects</TITLE>
<STYLE>

<!--

.hidden  {
        position: relative;
        visibility: hidden

}

-->
</STYLE>
</HEAD>

<BODY>

<IMG class="hidden" src="images/newton.gif" width="213" height="222"
alt="picture of sir isaac">

Sir Isaac Newton formulated the theory of universal gravitation.
</BODY>
</HTML>
```

Sir Isaac is effectively hidden, and the text appears indented (see Figure 20.10).

Tip from

CSS Hiding is especially helpful when you add scripts to unhide the object or text you're hiding. This way, you have control over the appearance and disappearance–the visibility–of any object or text.

OVERFLOW

Overflow is an interesting effect that allows you to control what happens to information within a bounding box. In the example shown in Listing 20.10, I've made the bounding box *smaller* than the image, and I have hidden any overflow. Now the image is forced to fit into the bounding box.

LISTING 20.10 CONTROLLING OVERFLOW

```
<HTML>
<HEAD>
<TITLE>Style Sheet Effects</TITLE>
<STYLE>

<!--

.overflow {
    position: absolute;
```

```
    top: 210px;
    left: 60px;
    width: 175px;
    height: 175px;
    background-color: gray;
    overflow: hidden
}


-->
</STYLE>
</HEAD>

<BODY>


<IMG class="overflow" src="iamges/newton.gif" width="213" height="222"
alt="picture of sir isaac">
<IMG src="images/newton.gif" width="213" height="222"
alt="picture of sir isaac" border=1>


</BODY>
</HTML>
```

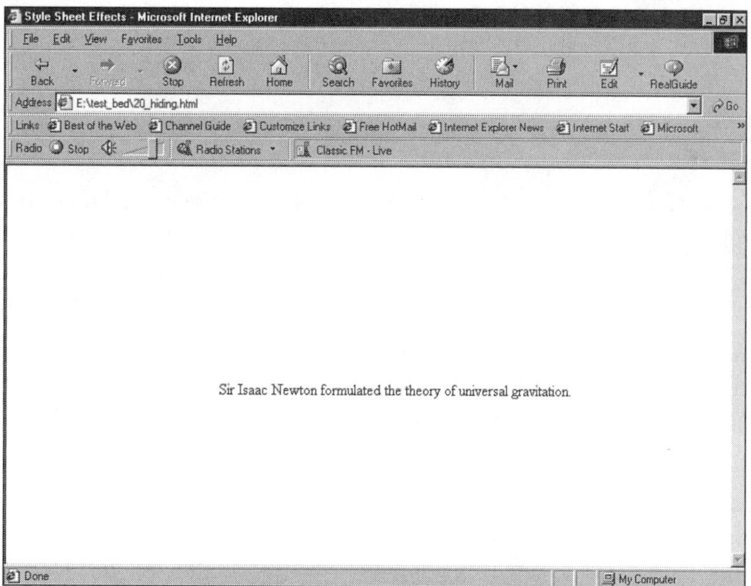

Figure 20.10
It may look as if Sir Isaac isn't included at all on this page, but he's really there, just hidden. It's the image's borders that are actually causing the text to bump over to the right.

In this example, I placed the normal image with a border of 1 above the overflow sample, and I gave the overflow sample a background color so that you can see how the image is affected by this technique (see Figure 20.11).

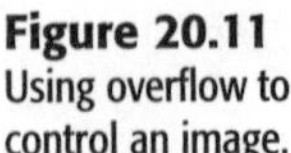

Figure 20.11
Using overflow to control an image.

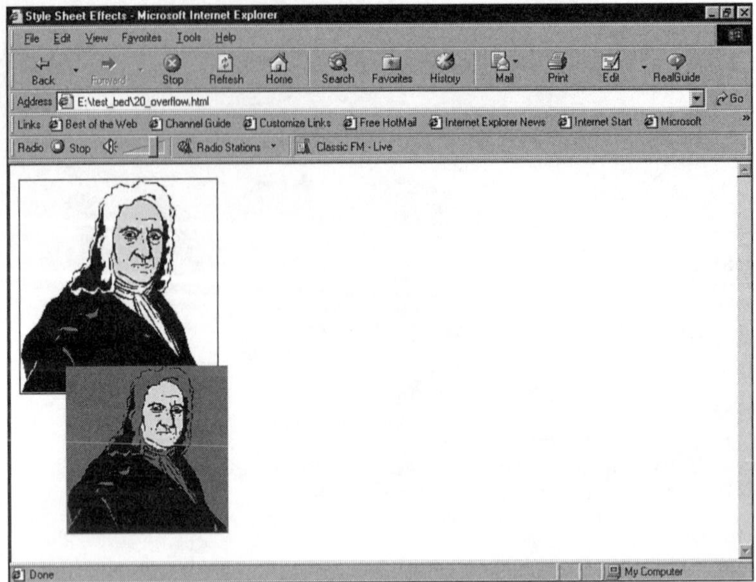

TROUBLESHOOTING

ADDRESSING BACKWARD COMPATIBILITY

CSS and scripting seem so browser dependent. How can a developer be assured that the resulting site will be backward compatible?

Most of the scripting additions to Cascading Style Sheets via DHTML are not currently supported by anything but Microsoft's Internet Explorer version 4 and up. Even users of Internet Explorer can't necessarily count on things working out the way you planned because its implementation of the new CSS/DHTML approach is sometimes a bit spotty.

Although Netscape has implemented some of these features, and Microsoft will doubtless clear up the bugs in future versions of IE, you still must take into consideration the many people who are using earlier browsers.

If you design a Web site that uses absolute positioning, for example, especially if that positioning alters the natural order in which elements appear in the HTML document itself, then users of Web browsers that don't recognize the structure you're assigning will find your pages to be a confusing jumble. Aside from simply not using these technologies, two approaches have been used to handle this sort of problem.

The first is to simply throw up your hands and put a note on the page that it's "enhanced" for a particular brand and version of Web browser. Usually, a link to either Netscape or Microsoft is included along with that note so that people who don't have the necessary software can get it.

Most people, however, faced with the prospect of either moving on and ignoring the page or downloading and installing a new Web browser, will probably just give up on that Web site. The larger and more complex Web browsers get, the less likely people are to put up with the long download and installation times unless they have some really compelling reason.

The other approach is to create different versions of the same Web site, each of which is compatible with different versions and brands of popular Web browsers. Although creating different versions can be a lot of extra work for the Web designer, it's the only real solution that covers all the bases.

→ For more information on using JavaScript to detect browser versions, **see** "Using JavaScript," **p. 403**

DESIGNING FOR THE REAL WORLD

ADDING SCRIPTS TO CSS

One of the major uses for scripts is changing the values of attributes. Any element on the Web page can be controlled in this way, and position is just another attribute, amenable to alteration by your script programs.

→ The addition of scripting to CSS is part of the grouping of technologies known as Dynamic HTML or DHTML. To find more details on DHTML, **see** "Working with Dynamic HTML (DHTML)," **p. 450**

What this means in practical terms is that you can move any element on the page at will. You can even set up elements to move interactively, in response to user input. Of course, this all depends upon whether or not you have a style sheet compliant browser. Internet Explorer 4.0 and above is pretty cooperative, but Netscape 4.6 and below is not.

Let's call in Sir Isaac again for this one. You probably recall the story of how he tumbled onto the idea of gravity, so let's add an apple to the recipe:

1. Create the Web page with two images on it:

```
<HTML>
<HEAD>

<TITLE>Moving an Element</TITLE>

</HEAD>

<BODY>

<IMG style="position: absolute; top: 10px; left: 106px" src="apple.gif"
width="46" height="51" alt="apple">

<IMG style="position: absolute; top: 110px; left: 0px" src="newton.gif"
width="213" height="222" alt="sir isaac">

</BODY>
</HTML>
```

2. Display the Web page in Internet Explorer. The apple is static but poised for action.
3. Add the JavaScript functions and a couple of buttons to control them (see Figure 20.12):

```
<HTML>
<HEAD>

<TITLE>Moving an Element</TITLE>

<SCRIPT language="JavaScript">

var idea;

function launch()
    {
    idea = window.setInterval("dropApple()", 1);
    }

function dropApple()
    {
    if (document.all.fruit.style.pixelTop<=58)
        {
        document.all.fruit.style.pixelTop+=3;
        }
    }

function resetApple()

    {
    document.all.fruit.style.pixelTop=10;
    window.clearInterval(idea);
    }

</SCRIPT>

</HEAD>

<BODY>

<IMG id="fruit" style="position: absolute; top: 10px; left: 106px
" src="apple.gif" width="46" height="51" alt="apple">

<IMG id="scientist" style="position: absolute; top: 110px; left: 0px
" src="newton.gif" width="213" height="222" alt="sir isaac">

<input type="button" value="Drop" onclick="launch()"
style="position: absolute; top:85px; left:250px">

<input type="button" value="Reset" onclick="resetApple()"
style="position: absolute; top:130px; left:250px">

</BODY>
</HTML>
```

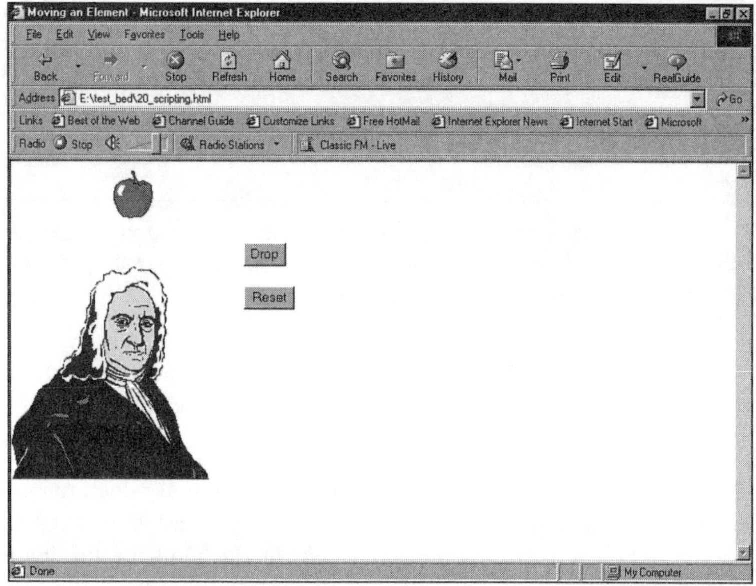

Figure 20.12
Newton and the apple.

4. Display the Web page in Internet Explorer. Click the Drop button to stimulate Sir Isaac's thoughts, as shown in Figure 20.13. Click the Reset button to instantly replace the apple to its original position at the top of the page. You can do so before it reaches Newton if you want to.

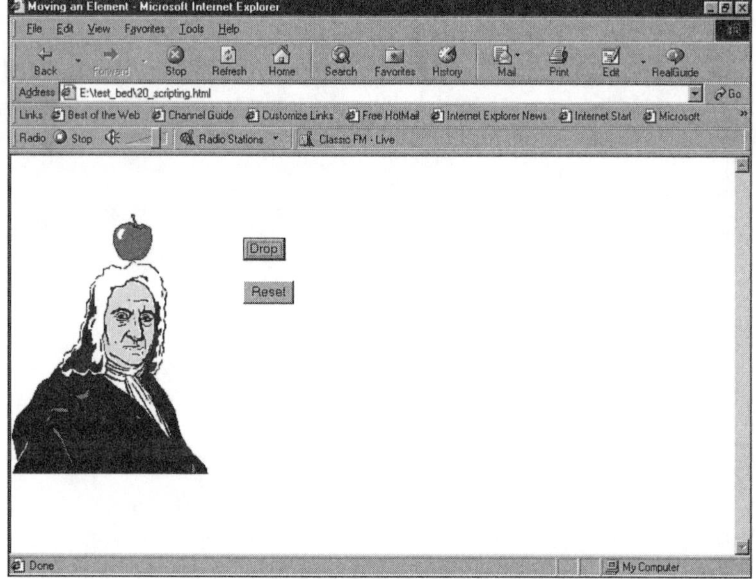

Figure 20.13
Newton meets the apple.

This simple little program contains a lot of information. First, it demonstrates how to use multiple input buttons to set off different actions. The fact that you can click the Reset button to abort the apple drop at any point during its fall not only shows how you don't have to wait for one JavaScript function to finish before launching another one, but it also shows you how to use one JavaScript function to cancel out another one.

Tip from molly

When you're positioning different elements on the screen, take into account the dimension of that element. Considering dimensions is easiest with images, which have defined pixel heights and widths.

The script uses three different functions to perform its actions on the position attribute of the apple. The whole process is set in motion by a click on the Drop button, which calls the `launch` function. That function's a bit unusual, and it's nothing we've ever seen before.

The script uses the window object's `setInterval` method, which causes a function to be evaluated over and over again until it's told to stop by using the `clearInterval` method. The amount of time in between evaluations is set by the number following the name of the function. The `1` used here means a thousandth of a second and is the lowest value possible to apply to `setInterval`.

The actual technique for moving the apple occurs in the `dropApple` function. Thanks to `setInterval`, it repeatedly increases the value in the apple's `pixelTop` property (if it were moving horizontally, you would use the `pixelLeft` property instead). The size of that value is constantly checked by an `if` statement against an absolute value (the point at which the bottom of the apple is resting on the top of Newton's head) that is determined through trial and error.

The apple is returned to its original position by a straight assignment of an absolute value to the `pixelTop` property when a click on the Reset button calls the `resetApple` function. After that function resets the value, it calls the `clearInterval` method to halt the process.

CHAPTER 21

Working with Dynamic HTML (DHTML)

In this chapter

Defining Dynamic

The word *dynamic* is tossed about hourly by Web designers, with some confusion as to what it really means. The best definition I can give, at least in terms of Web design, is to say that dynamic refers to the capability of an element to change or influence change upon another element.

Dynamic HTML, dynamic HTML, DHTML, D-HTML—whatever it's called, whether the "D" is capitalized or not—has been hyped as a new technology that will change the face of the Web. Unlike standard HTML, which creates fixed documents, DHTML can add a variety of changeable enhancements to Web pages. It does this with a complex grouping of methods, some of which are highlighted in this chapter.

Note

DHTML is supported only by Netscape and Internet Explorer browser versions 4.0 and later. The most recent version of a browser is most likely to have the best implementation of DHTML. I used Internet Explorer 5.0 and Netscape 4.61 in this chapter.

To help you gain an understanding of what DHTML really is, how to begin using it, and what important concerns you'll need to watch out for, this chapter shows you both the brightest of DHTML, as well as how to manage its problems in a relatively brief space.

To be effective at this task, the chapter starts with a general, conceptual approach. Then, it shifts gears and shows you some examples of DHTML at its best, which means focusing on browser-specific technology—in this case, Microsoft's Internet Explorer. Finally, the chapter shows you how to approach cross-browser design by giving you the scoop on cross-browser DHTML, showing you what you need to do to design interoperable, dynamic pages using DHTML.

Along the way, you'll see plenty of references and resources so that you can take DHTML into your own hands and decide how you want to use it to add that much-desired dynamism to your pages.

DHTML: Fact and Fiction

DHTML is one of the misunderstood children of Web technologies. There are many things that it is not, and what it is—well, that's really still being hashed out between browser developers.

Table 21.1 shows a short list of what DHTML is and isn't.

Table 21.1 DHTML Is and Is Not

Is	Is Not
A combination of HTML, CSS, and scripting languages	A language unto itself
A client-side operation	A server-side activity

Is	Is Not
A browser-specific application	readily interoperable
An interesting approach to active content	A standard

Officially, DHTML is in a gray area of development. Browsers are often in the position of pushing the envelope when it comes to new and progressive technologies. DHTML is a fine example of just that—it's being developed by browser companies, not standards committees. It's not a specific set of language rules and syntax. Rather, it's a combination of enhancements to static HTML.

Note

Although the W3C doesn't officially manage the standard practices of DHTML, it does work to create standards and recommendations for many of its aspects including HTML, CSS, and the Document Object Model (DOM).

It's important to realize that because of the lack of standards, a great deal of misinformation exists about DHTML. For a while, it was talked about as the coolest new thing in town. Now that the hype has simmered down, it's helpful to look at the real-world components of DHTML.

Tip from

It's helpful to think of the terms *Dynamic HTML* and DHTML as catch-all terms for a combination of Web technologies that work together.

Approaching DHTML

For the sake of ease, I like to think of DHTML as a combination of the following:

- HTML
- The Document Object Model
- Cascading Style Sheets (CSS)
- Scripting Languages

Of course, this doesn't mean that browser developers have *interpreted* these components the same way or that they stay true to this core of components. In fact, DHTML was proposed by Microsoft, so obviously, Microsoft's Internet Explorer has pushed, and continues to push, DHTML the hardest.

But Netscape is no slouch in the game. Although Netscape hasn't been able to cover as much ground with DHTML as Internet Explorer has, it has tried to take the initiative for cross-browser DHTML design.

Note

But what about layers? You might have heard about, or even used the LAYERS tag, as part of Netscape's earliest entries into the world of DHTML. In the fast-changing world of the Web, however, yesterday's news is today's dusty history, and the LAYERS tag is already officially deprecated by the World Wide Web Consortium (W3C).

Unfortunately, cross-browser DHTML is more conceptual than realistic. You have to go through some fairly complicated steps to ensure that your DHTML is going to work effectively across browsers.

If you are unsure as to whether using DHTML is right for your site, take a look at "Dynamically Speaking" in the Troubleshooting section at the end of this chapter.

DHTML AND HTML

The first place to look for an understanding of DHTML is within HTML itself. Dynamic HTML uses the structure of HTML to inject its changeable features. It does this by employing HTML tags to invoke action.

Theoretically, any HTML tag (particularly any tag within the HTML 4.0 standard) is up for DHTML to grab. Of course, you're going to use tags that are logical. Most of these will be formatting elements, such as headers, paragraphs, and, much like style sheets, the `DIV` and `SPAN` elements, which control sections within the `BODY` element of an HTML document.

THE DOCUMENT OBJECT MODEL

The next step is to look to the Document Object Model, known as the DOM. The DOM is one of the primary reasons that browsers are so inconsistent.

The search for control is an effort that binds us together—no matter our platform, no matter our browser patriotism. The bottom line is that we all want to be able to control Web pages because so little control is available! The look and feel, the manipulation of objects—any aspect that we can control, we will collectively try to find a way to do so.

With most of HTML design—as you'll read time and again throughout this book—this control is gained by adding up all the possibilities and then either reducing to the lowest common denominator or finding a workaround for the desired results. In DHTML, however, the heart of control lies within this elusive, yet powerful, concept known as the DOM.

The *Document Object Model* is an API (application programming interface). This is a set of logical rules upon which software applications can be built.

Note

If you're a programmer, or if you just get a kick out of terms like *structural isomorphism*, I encourage you to read more about the DOM:

The World Wide Web Consortium is eye-deep in DOM white papers. Start at **`http://www.w3.org/DOM/`**.

Microsoft has its say, of course! You can begin at **`http://msdn.microsoft.com/workshop/author/om/omdoc.asp`** for a look at the earlier days of the DOM.

Netscape offers a plethora of articles and information on everything DHTML: **`http://developer.netscape.com/tech/dynhtml/index.html`**.

In terms of Web browsers, the DOM tries to provide a standardized method of HTML elements, to recommend standards on how these elements can work harmoniously together, and perhaps most important, to encourage a standard *interface* for getting to the heart of the matter and making those objects do what we want them to do, no matter the browser or platform.

Note

It's important to point out that different browsers have different DOMs. The hope is to stabilize the way browsers interpret DOM information to promote cross-platform compatibility.

How does the DOM do these things? By enabling any HTML tag to be seen as an object. In the Document Object Model, a Web page is seen as a single object, and the elements that compose it are seen as properties of that object. Each of the elements is also an object, although a subordinate one, and the elements have their own properties, in turn.

This process enables you to add scripting to any element, making the actions of the script specific to the actions of that element.

DHTML and Scripting

Now that HTML and the DOM are working together, let's add scripting to the soup. The DOM allows for the application of scripts to have control over every HTML element, so you can take scripts and modify them to enhance HTML elements—which is precisely what browser developers have done.

Of course, herein lies much of the DHTML problem. As you may already be aware, script preferences exist for specific browsers. Microsoft, the initiator of DHTML, has a proprietary relationship with its own VBScript (Visual Basic Script). It also has adapted JavaScript in its own version of JScript to increasingly more stable capacity. On the other hand, JavaScript, developed in part by Netscape, is a very stable, very powerful script that can already be applied to Web pages.

→ To learn more about how JavaScript can be used to help control your Web pages, **see** "Using JavaScript," **p. 404**

Furthermore, scripting for DHTML is an area where Netscape hasn't been particularly aggressive. In fact, and quite ironically—because Netscape is the power behind JavaScript—Internet Explorer has been most aggressive in DHTML scripting. Internet Explorer has added the most powerful and varied aspects of DHTML via scripting, including event handling, behaviors, and filters.

DHTML and Style Sheets

An extension of the relationship between HTML 4.0 and DHTML, is the one that comes to life in the presence of the DOM and style sheets. This relationship has a name: *dynamic style*. Any CSS selector can become dynamic using DHTML.

→ For more information on style sheet selectors, **see** "Cascading Style Sheet Techniques," **p. 263**

If you have a selection of text defined by CSS, for example, you can make that text change appearance by adding events to that selection via DHTML. You can also use DHTML to influence style sheet positioning (Netscape supports this, too) and in related news, font embedding. This is the downloading of parts of typefaces to ensure your typographic decisions are stable and have been included in both Netscape's and IE's interpretation of DHTML.

→ To find information about embedded fonts, **see** "Working with Fonts," **p. 247**

Now its time to move on to look at DHTML at its most comprehensive.

WORKING WITH INTERNET EXPLORER'S DHTML

To help you begin flexing your DHTML muscles, we'll turn to DHTML as it is interpreted by Internet Explorer. This way, you can see the technology in its fullest capacity. However, I won't leave Netscape out of the picture—after a look at IE's interpretation of DHTML, I'll discuss Netscape options and how to manage cross-browser DHTML design.

In this section, you'll look at

- Events
- Event handlers
- Event bubbling
- Adding DHTML to a page
- What's new in Internet Explorer 5.0

Now, think about this. If you click any properly coded link with your mouse, what happens? Easy! You move from that link to the referenced page.

The action of clicking your mouse is an *event*. But some component has to manage that event to pass the event along to the next part of the behind-the-scenes process. This component is known as an *event handler* (it's the equivalent of an usher who leads you to your seat in a theater). After the event handler has the process in hand, it passes along the event and makes the action real—loading the referenced page.

After an event is invoked and properly managed, the action can take place. How that action looks, feels, and behaves can be controlled in a variety of ways.

EVENTS

DHTML draws its information on events directly from scripting. Table 21.2 is a modified list of common, useful events.

TABLE 21.2 COMMONLY USED DHTML EVENTS

Event	Meaning
`onclick`	The mouse button is clicked.
`ondblclick`	The mouse button is double-clicked.

Event	Meaning
`onkeydown`	A key on the keyboard is pressed.
`onkeypress`	A key on the keyboard is pressed and released.
`onkeyup`	A user releases a pressed key on the keyboard.
`onload`	A Web page is loaded into the browser.
`onmousedown`	The mouse button is pressed and held without releasing it.
`onmousemove`	The mouse pointer is moved.
`onmouseout`	The mouse pointer moves off an element.
`onmouseover`	The mouse pointer moves onto an element.
`onmouseup`	A depressed mouse button is released.
`onsubmit`	A Submit button is clicked.

Note

For a complete listing of Internet Explorer DHTML events, visit `http://msdn.microsoft.com/workshop/author/dhtml/reference/events.asp`.

Some of these are so similar in their actions that it would seem they're duplicative, but the slightly differing meaning of events such as `onclick` and `onmousedown` give you a tremendous amount of power when you're programming Web pages. Of course, if all you're going to do is put in one or two possible actions, you can just stick with the `onclick` event and you'll do just fine. But if you're going to get into code where you offer more than one or two actions, you'll find that you really do need to have different actions perform different tasks.

EVENT HANDLERS

Any program you write to respond to an event is called an *event handler*. Two basic approaches exist to writing event handlers. You can write functions that are called when the event takes place, or you can write inline code directly in the affected element's tag.

Which approach is the right one? It depends on how complex the event handler needs to be. If you've got something really simple, such as changing the color of the text in a paragraph, that takes only a little bit of code, so it'll fit neatly into the element itself. If you're going to perform complicated and intricate operations involving multiple statements, conditional loops, and the like, you're probably better off going with a separate function and calling it from the affected element.

No rule exists here. If you want to, you can put a long and complex string of statements in an inline code within an element. Just be sure you remember to separate each statement with a semicolon and to follow proper scripting syntax.

Tip from

Keep in mind that complex scripts often need debugging, and you'll find that your code will be easier to read and the program flow will be easier to trace if you follow other standard scripting procedures too, such as commenting your code.

Listing 21.1 shows the use of inline code for an event handler.

LISTING 21.1 INLINE CODE WITH AN EVENT HANDLER

```
<HTML>
<HEAD>

<TITLE>Using Inline Code</TITLE>

</HEAD>

<BODY>
<P onclick="this.style.fontSize='36';">This paragraph will change its size
when you click on it.
</P>
</BODY>
</HTML>
```

Figure 21.1 shows the page in its original state. Figure 21.2 demonstrates the change in font size after the `onclick` event is triggered.

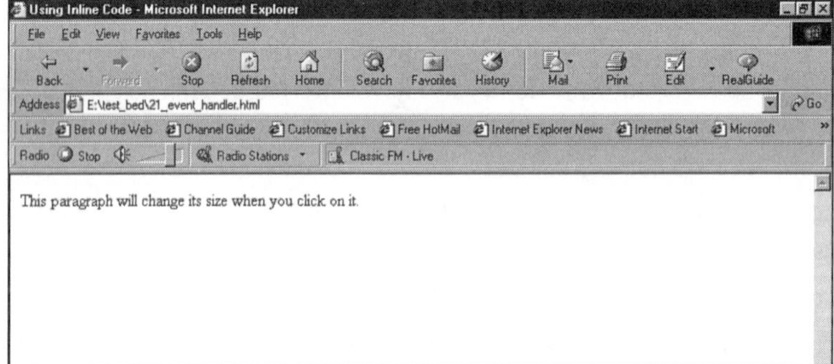

Figure 21.1
The code of this Web page contains an `onclick` event, however it is seen here before the event takes place.

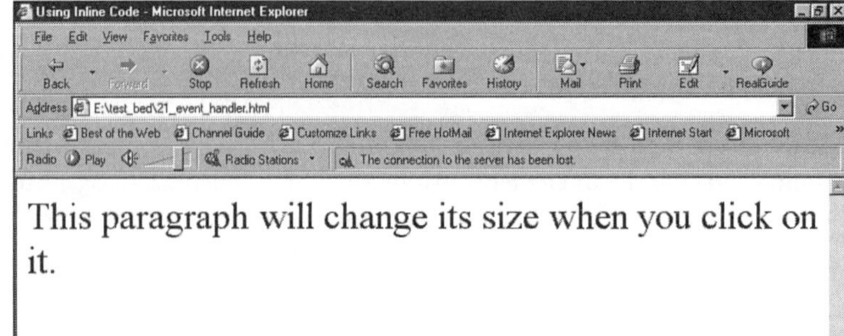

Figure 21.2
The site visitor has now performed the required action–clicking the text–which results in the coded event being performed and displaying the change in the text's appearance.

The identical effect could be achieved with a standard script function approach, as shown in Listing 21.2.

LISTING 21.2 STANDARD SCRIPT VERSION

```
<HTML>
<HEAD>

<TITLE>Standard Script Method</TITLE>

<SCRIPT>

<!—

function changeSize()
    {
    document.all.changeable.style.fontSize='36';
     }

—>

</SCRIPT>

</HEAD>

<BODY>

<P id="changeable" onclick="changeSize()">This paragraph will
change its size when you click on it.
</P>

</BODY>
</HTML>
```

In addition to showing another way to achieve the same effect, this code also introduces a couple of important points. First, the `P` element is given a unique identifier via its `id` attribute.

The `id` attribute is used in referring to the element within the function by using the `document.all` collection. Because that collection contains everything within the document and *`changeable`* is the name of one of the contained elements, the paragraph can be referred to as `document.all.changeable`, using the value of its `id` attribute to identify it.

The actual alteration in font size is done by further extending the DOM's references. Because `style` is a property of the element and `fontSize` is a property of `style`, the entire operation can be done by assigning the desired values to `document.all.changeable.style.fontSize`. The reference doesn't have to be this detailed in the earlier inline code example because the "this" shortcut carries the same meaning in that context as `document.all.changeable` does in this one.

EVENT BUBBLING

It's clear that an element that contains an event handler will respond to that event. But what if an event occurs to an element that doesn't have an event handler? Why, for instance, can you click a DIV or SPAN or IMG element that lacks event handlers and still have the BODY element's event handler respond to it? Because all the visible elements on an HTML page are included within the body, anything that happens to those elements automatically happens to the body, as well.

Although that seems like a fairly obvious thing, it's actually a case of careful and deliberate planning on the part of the people who developed Dynamic HTML. It's a phenomenon called *event bubbling*, and it means that any event that occurs on the Web page either responds to a local event handler (one within the element where the event occurred) or is passed on up the line from an object to its parent object if no event handler is present. This bubbling keeps on occurring until the event bubble reaches a point where it does find an event handler.

Suppose you have a SPAN inside a DIV, which are both inside the BODY element. Only the BODY element has an event handler, but someone clicks the SPAN element. The event can't be handled there, so it *bubbles up* to the DIV, which is the parent for the SPAN element.

Still, no code is there to handle the event, so it goes on up the line to the BODY element, which is the parent to the DIV. The BODY object *does* have an onclick event handler in it, so it takes charge and the event is then handled.

If no event handler is anywhere in the chain of objects, then nothing happens. Of course, even if an event handler exists, it has to be for the specific event that occurred for it to react. An onkeypress event handler, for example, won't do anything for an onclick event, regardless of where it is in the object hierarchy. In that case, it's just as if no event handler at all existed.

Events and event bubbling make up one of most powerful technology sets found in Internet Explorer's DHTML. Some really fun visual effects can be gained using special types of DHTML technology.

SPECIAL EFFECTS

In this section, I'll show you two types of Internet Explorer special effects: visual filters and transitions.

Visual filters use a style sheet property filter and related values to create visual effects. These visual effects are a fairly simple method of adding visual interest to a page.

Transitions can be done in a variety of ways. I'm going to show you an example of transition syntax that resides in the META tag and controls the way a page can be transitioned upon entrance and exit.

VISUAL FILTERS

An important point to note is that visual filters can be added only to HTML elements that are considered *controls*. A control is any element that creates a rectangular space on a Web page.

Some common controls are

BODY

DIV

IMG

```
INPUT

MARQUEE

SPAN

TABLE

TD

TR
```

All filters follow the same basic pattern. The style property `filter` is followed by a colon, then the name of the filter, and then the filter's attributes are listed in parentheses with each parameter separated by commas.

Note

The only difference in coding the various filters is in the number and type of parameters each requires.

Let's look at a few visual filters in action.

The drop-shadow filter gives your text a three-dimensional appearance. Listing 21.3 shows how it's applied.

LISTING 21.3 APPLYING A FILTER

```
<HTML>
<HEAD>

<TITLE>Drop-Shadow Filter</TITLE>

</HEAD>

<BODY>
<P>
<BR>
<BR>
<DIV align="center">

<TABLE border="0" width="500"
style="filter:DropShadow(color=gray,offx=2,offy=2,positive=1)">
<TR>

<TD>

<H1>The drop-shadow filter in action</H1>
</TD>

</TR>
</TABLE>

</DIV>
</BODY>
</HTML>
```

Like any other CSS attribute, filters are added to an element via the style attribute. In this case, I've given the shadow a gray color and an offset value of 2. This means that the shadow will fall 2 pixels to the right and 2 pixels below the text to which the filter is applied.

Tip from

Horizontal offset is controlled with `offx`, and `offy` is the vertical offset. Although they don't have to be the same value, it's usually a better design to have a shadow coded to fall symmetrically on the x- and y-axes.

Figure 21.3 shows the results of the drop-shadow filter.

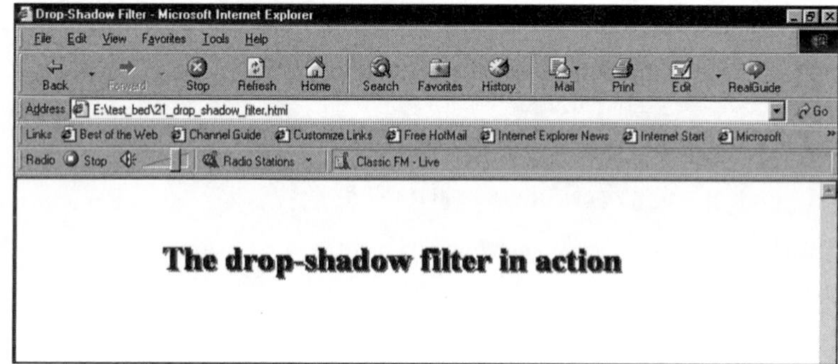

Figure 21.3 The drop-shadow filter is a fun way to add a graphical type of effect to text without having to use an actual image file.

The glow filter is another simple way to make text really stand out on your Web pages. As you might guess from the name, it makes text appear to be surrounded by a glowing aura. Listing 21.4 shows the code used to achieve this effect.

LISTING 21.4 THE GLOW FILTER

```
<HTML>
<HEAD>

<TITLE>Glow Filter</TITLE>

</HEAD>

<BODY>
<P>
<BR>
<BR>

<DIV align="center">

<TABLE BORDER="0" WIDTH="500" STYLE="filter:glow(color=gray,strength=5)">
<TR>

<TD>
<H2>The glow filter gives your text an aura.</H2>
</TD>
```

```
</TR>
</TABLE>

</DIV>
</BODY>
</HTML>
```

As with the drop-shadow filter, the glow was added via the `filter` style property. In this instance, the only parameters I used for the filter affect the color and the size of the glow (see Figure 21.4). The size of the aura is determined by the `strength` attribute; the larger the number value, the wider the glow.

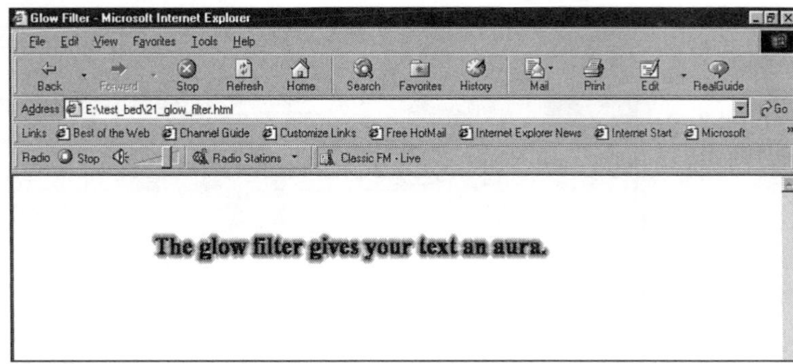

Figure 21.4
The glow filter is another simple way you can use DHTML to enhance your pages.

Another set of fun filters is known as "flip." Two flip filters exist—one for horizontal flipping and one for vertical flipping. Neither one has any parameters; just use the name of the filter. Listing 21.5 demonstrates how to flip horizontally.

Listing 21.5 A Horizontal Flip

```
<HTML>
<HEAD>

<TITLE>Flip</TITLE>

</HEAD>

<BODY>
<P>
<BR>
<BR>

<DIV align="center">

<TABLE border="0" width="300" style="filter:fliph">
<TR>

<TD>
```

continues

LISTING 21.5 CONTINUED

```
<H2>Flip This!</H2>
</TD>

</TR>
</TABLE>

</DIV>
</BODY>
</HTML>
```

Figure 21.5 shows the results.

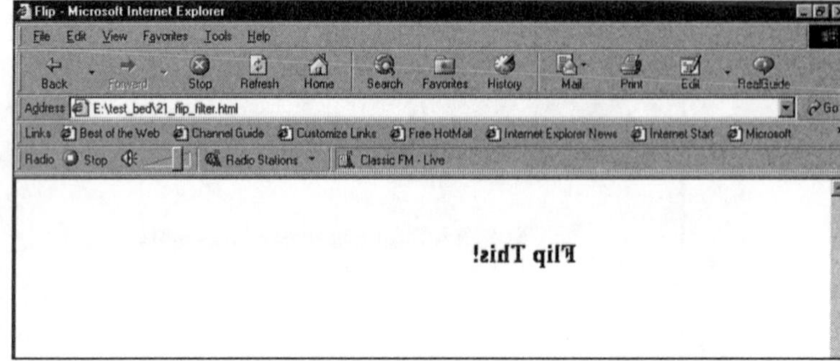

Figure 21.5
The horizontal flip filter causes the text to appear as though you were looking at it in a mirror.

The vertical flip filter is used in DHTML the same way as the horizontal flip filter except that the name is slightly different: flipv. Listing 21.6 shows you how.

LISTING 21.6 THE VERTICAL FLIP FILTER

```
<HTML>
<HEAD>

<TITLE>Flip</TITLE>

</HEAD>

<BODY>
<P>
<BR>
<BR>

<DIV align="center">

<TABLE border="0" width="300" style="filter:flipv">
<TR>

<TD>

<H2>Flip This!</H2>
```

```
</TD>

</TR>
</TABLE>

</DIV>
</BODY>
</HTML>
```

In Figure 21.6, you can see the vertical flip filter in action.

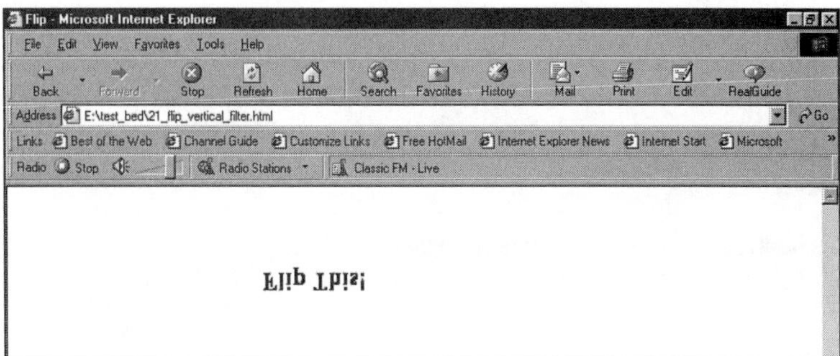

Figure 21.6
The vertical flip filter turns the text upside down. This effect can be useful when creating animations and games.

Filters might seem frivolous (say that 10 times fast!), but if you think about the design options they provide—without the use of graphics, you can begin to get a feel of why DHTML effects can be so useful.

Note

You can find out the latest on CSS filters at **`http://msdn.microsoft.com/workshop/author/filter/filters.asp`**.

TRANSITION SAMPLE

In this example, the transition filter relies on the `META` tag to deliver its action. The reason the `META` tag is involved in this case doesn't have anything to do with DHTML proper—it's because I'm going to be controlling the way a page is entered and exited.

You might recall that you can use `META` tags to refresh documents or to move from one document to another. The addition of DHTML to the `META` tag in this case is, in a sense, an extension of that concept.

→ For a discussion on `META` tags, **see** "Preparing Your Site for Publication," **p. 882**

The type of filter I'm using is called *Reveal*. It literally will reveal a page and do so depending upon the parameters you place within the syntax.

Listing 21.7 shows an HTML page with the Reveal filter in action on both the entrance and exit to the page.

LISTING 21.7 TRANSITION EFFECTS

```
<HTML>
<HEAD>

<TITLE>Transition Filter Example</TITLE>

<META http-equiv="Page-Enter"
CONTENT="RevealTrans(Duration=6.000,Transition=9)">

<META http-equiv="Page-Exit"
CONTENT="RevealTrans(Duration=6.000,Transition=11)">

</HEAD>

<BODY>
<P>
<BR>
<BR>

<H2>A Midsummer Night's Dream</H2>

<P>

<FONT face="arial">
Either to die the death or to abjure <BR>
For ever the society of men. <BR>
Therefore, fair <A href="http://www.shakespeare.com/">Hermia</A>, question your
➥desires <BR>

Know of your youth, examine well your blood, <BR>
Whether, if you yield not to your father's choice, <BR>
You can endure the livery of a nun, <BR>
For aye to be in shady cloister mew'd, <BR>
To live a barren sister all your life, <BR>
Chanting faint hymns to the cold fruitless moon. <BR>
Thrice-blessed they that master so their blood, <BR>
To undergo such maiden <A HREF="http://www.shakespeare.com">pilgrimage</A>; <BR>
But earthlier happy is the rose distill'd, <BR>
Than that which withering on the virgin thorn <BR>
Grows, lives and dies in single blessedness.
</FONT>

</P>

</BODY>
</HTML>
```

In Figure 21.7, you'll see a still shot of the entrance filter at work. Figure 21.8 shows the exit filter, which has a different effect applied.

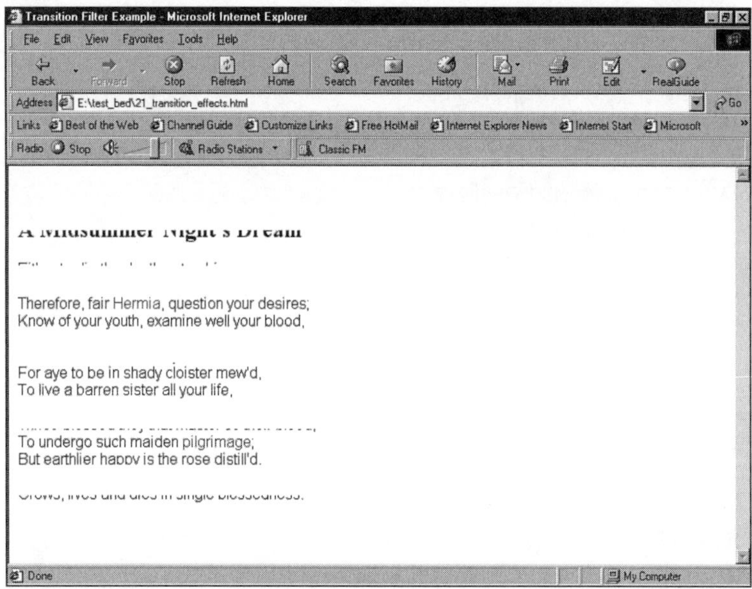

Figure 21.7
Transitioning upon entrance to the page causes the text to appear in stages.

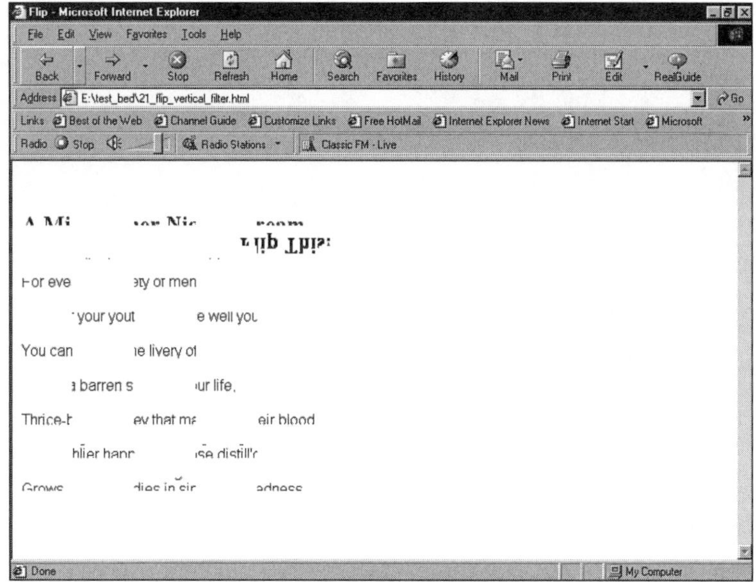

Figure 21.8
The exit transition results in the text breaking up into a checkerboard before the new page is loaded.

In Table 21.3, you'll find the numeric value of a variety of transitions. To see the effect for yourself, replace the numeric value in the `transition="x"` portion of this sample and add it to any HTML page you like that has at least one link on it. When you load the page, you'll see your desired effect, and when you leave the page, you'll see the exit effect.

```
<META http-equiv="Page-Enter"
CONTENT="RevealTrans(Duration=6.000,Transition=9)">

<META http-equiv="Page-Exit"
CONTENT="RevealTrans(Duration=6.000,Transition=11)">
```

TABLE 21.3 TRANSITION EFFECTS

Transition Name	Value
box in	0
box out	1
circle in	2
circle out	3
wipe up	4
wipe down	5
wipe right	6
wipe left	7
vertical blinds	8
horizontal blinds	9
checkerboard across	10
checkerboard down	11
random dissolve	12
split vertical in	13
split vertical out	14
split horizontal in	15
split horizontal out	16
strips left down	17
strips left up	18
strips right down	19
strips right up	20
random bars horizontal	21
random bars vertical	22
random	23

CREATING CROSS-BROWSER DHTML

So how do you create DHTML applications that are cross-browser capable? It's not an easy task, and it involves trying to boil down the common support in each current browser.

Common support theoretically includes

- Cascading Style Sheets Level I (CSS-I)
- Cascading Style Sheet Positioning (CSSP)
- Shared JavaScript support
- Any DOM functions that are common to both browsers
- Events that are common to both browsers

Why do I say theoretically? Well, the reason is that neither Netscape nor Internet Explorer at the 4.0 level had fully implemented any of these. CSS1 and CSSP comes in at the top, with JavaScript compliance next. But the Document Object Model is defined differently in each browser. Finally, events are also managed differently from one to the other.

What a nightmare this makes for the HTML coder who, in his or her desire to work with DHTML, has to resolve problems from information that isn't fully mature at the outset. Furthermore, these differences address only the 4.0 and higher generation of browsers. Earlier browsers have limited, if any, support for DHTML.

So how do you deal with it? Industry experts are taking a variety of approaches, but the most sophisticated seems to be to challenge yourself to write code that not only simultaneously satisfies the needs of the two browsers, but also *degrades* with grace for older browsers.

This gives both Netscape and Internet Explorer 4.0 and later users the opportunity to enjoy the fruits of your hard DHTML labor, and it makes the pages equally accessible to individuals without such sophisticated browsers.

To gain as much control over the situation as possible, it's helpful to begin by specifically defining what *does* work across browsers.

Begin with CSS1

Because the support for CSS1 is moving toward being fairly solid in both Netscape and Internet Explorer 4.0 versions and above, that's a good place to start. This means that you should use CSS1 to define any fixed portions of a page. If you have text that you want to work with, for example, you can set it up with CSS1 and feel fairly certain that it's going to be stable.

The following bit of HTML (see Listing 21.8) will be interpreted equally between Netscape and Internet Explorer 4.0 and later.

Listing 21.8 A Cross-Browser Style Sheet

```
<HTML>
<HEAD>
<TITLE>Fixed CSS1 Example</TITLE>
<STYLE type="text/css">
#mystyle { margin-top:  50px;
         margin-left: 75px;
```

continues

LISTING 21.8 CONTINUED

```
        font: 12pt arial;
        color: #0000FF;
    }
</STYLE>
</HEAD>
<BODY>
<DIV ID="mystyle">
The text within this division will pull the position and color it needs from
the style sheet.
</DIV>
</BODY>
</HTML>
```

Figure 21.9 shows the results in Internet Explorer 5.0. Netscape will display the same results (provided you're using a version that supports DHTML).

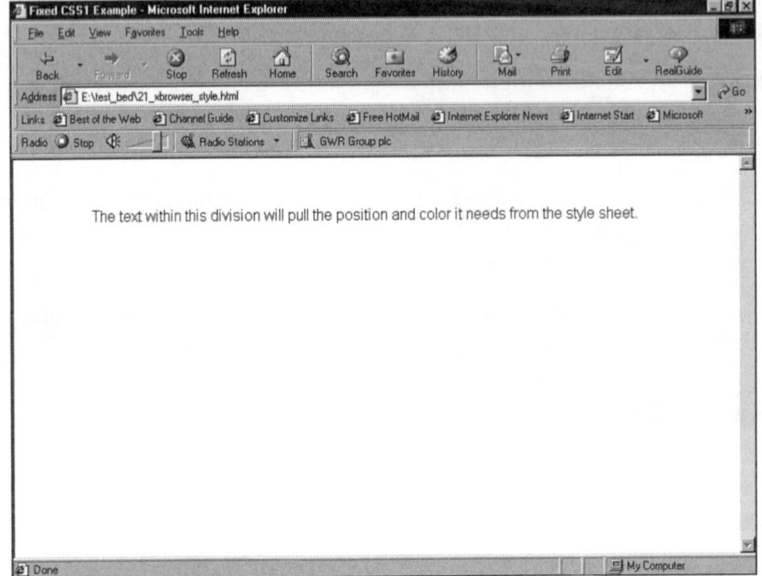

Figure 21.9
Cross-browser style sheet in Internet Explorer. If you look at this in Netscape, you'll see the same results because the technology is available in both browsers.

Now you can add comment tags around the style sheet (see Listing 21.9). This ensures that browsers without style sheet support will *not see* the style information.

LISTING 21.9 HIDING THE STYLE SHEET

```
<HTML>
<HEAD>
<TITLE>Fixed CSS1 Example</TITLE>
<STYLE type="text/css">

<!--
```

```
#mystyle { margin-top:  50px;
         margin-left: 75px;
         font: 12pt arial;
         color: #0000FF;
      }
-->

</STYLE>
</HEAD>
<BODY>
<DIV ID="mystyle">
The text within this division will pull the position and color it needs from the
➥style sheet.

</DIV>
</BODY>
</HTML>
```

Although a page without style is boring, the text information is still displayed. It's also possible to use tables and the FONT element to try to position the information on the page so that it will be similar to the style sheet.

➔ For help with combining the FONT element and style sheets, **see** "Cascading Style Sheet Techniques," **p. 284**

➔ Since many DHTML techniques are visual, they can cause some confusion for the blind. In most instances, text-based DHTML effects will degrade gracefully and express the static text. For more information on how to make your pages more accessible, **see** "Accessibility and Internationalization," **p. 474**

Sniffing Out Browser Type, Version, and Platform Information

In cross-browser, cross-platform, backward-compatible DHTML design, it's helpful for you to "sniff" out some information. By using such a script in an HTML page, your HTML now has information that says, "Hey, I know which browser I'm dealing with, which version, and which platform, so let me be sure to serve up the right code for the resulting profile."

Such a script enables you to allow for your code to work with not only current, but future browser versions.

➔ To read about browser detect and route scripts, **see** "Using JavaScript," **p. 421**

Tip from molly

If you're only looking to create code that works across specific browsers, you won't have to test for this kind of information.

Other Cross-Browser DHTML Tips

Try to always do the following when working with cross-browser DHTML:

- Use JavaScript version 1.2 only. This ensures compatibility for Netscape and IE.
- Put code *inline*. In other words, don't link to an external page holding your JavaScript or style sheet. The code should always be in the document HEAD.

- Create an empty STYLE element in the HEAD with a unique ID:

```
<STYLE ID="mystyle" type="text/css">
</STYLE
```

- Combine scripting techniques for Internet Explorer and Netscape. You'll be using the `.addRule` method, for example, to add style sheet rules within the script to accommodate IE. However, for the same information to appear in Netscape, you'll have to use the DOM as a guideline:

  Internet Explorer:

```
document.styleSheets["mystyle""].addRule("H1", "color: #00FF00");
```

  Netscape:

```
document.tags.H1.color="#00FF00";
```

- Always follow the same order when adding rules.
- Always use `position: absolute` when positioning elements. If you relatively position, you can run into interoperability problems.

DHTML Resources

Use these resources to keep up with the changes in cross-browser DHTML compatibility:

Microsoft Developer Network: DHTML, HTML, and CSS. This workshop will show you all the things you can do when combining these three potent technologies: **`http://microsoft.com/workshop/author/default.asp`**.

Netscape's DevEdge Online Cross-Browser, Cross Platform, Backwardly Compatible JavaScript and Dynamic HTML. If the name made you dizzy, so will sorting out the content, but if you're truly into DHTML, it's worth it: **`http://developer.netscape.com:80/docs/technote/dynhtml/xbdhtml/xbdhtml.html`**.

Web Review's Style Sheet Reference Guide at **`http://style.webreview.com/`** keeps a marvelous listing of Web pages dedicated to the problem of browser compatibility with CSS and DHTML.

TROUBLESHOOTING

DYNAMICALLY SPEAKING

At some point, trying to use dynamic technologies such as DHTML seems really futile because I want pages that are accessible and cross-platform-compatible. How do I remedy this and still keep up with technological trends?

I have three answers to this dilemma.

- Experiment as much as you like on home pages and private pages. Reserve careful cross-browser code for professional, widely accessed public pages.
- Sniff-and-route using JavaScript, or have a subtle note on your page that allows individuals to make a choice based on their browser type.
- Don't use DHTML. Great pages don't have to embrace every available technology! In

fact, I am from the school that says you can create better, more elegant Web sites if you think carefully about what it is you're using and why. If you have a really good reason to use a given technology, then use it! But don't feel you should just because you can.

DESIGNING FOR THE REAL WORLD

DHTML GURU

For a look at DHTML in action, take a look at Jeff Rouyer's stunning site, DHTML Guru. You should check this site out in both IE and Netscape and make a list of the differences between the sites. Look specifically for:

- The page elements that appear in different browsers, and the order in which they appear
- The positioning of elements on the page
- The proximity and spatial relationship of elements
- The look and style of fonts and related issues such as leading (line-height)

You can find Rouyer's site at `http://www.htmlguru.com/`. You'll also find an excellent tutorial there to help you work through designing with DHTML in detail.

CHAPTER 22

Accessibility and Internationalization

In this chapter

ACCESSIBILITY AND HTML 4

One of the most important issues being discussed in terms of present-day and future standards is that of HTML accessibility. Originally designed to be a language that could be easily and readily distributed across platforms and read by anyone, regardless of their software, the browser wars quickly changed that reality. With everyone rushing hither and yon to create the coolest technology on the block, this fundamental aspect of HTML has been disrupted.

In HTML 4, the hope is to bring that accessibility back. By using intelligent options, page authors can add a variety of aids that will help individuals understand and negotiate pages no matter their platform—or their physical abilities.

Many people with low or no vision have tremendous difficulty accessing today's World Wide Web. The reason is largely due to the fact that screen readers who browse the screen and read the content aloud, are significantly more challenged by complex graphical pages. However, with a little forethought, authors can make it much easier. Other individuals with physical limitations are assisted by devices as well—and whether it's a screen reader or special keyboard, the methodologies that HTML 4 proposes to aid access are extremely helpful.

Note

Of course, browser support is an important issue as well. Netscape has lagged far behind Microsoft in this regard. There's some pressure on browser developers to include support for accessibility guidelines, particularly in the United States, where the Americans with Disabilities Act may eventually enforce accessibility guidelines on everyone's part because of the extensive use of the Web in the workplace and commercial enterprise.

ACCESSIBILITY GUIDELINES

The Web Accessibility Initiative of the W3C has an official document involving 14 guidelines that Web developers are encouraged to follow. I've provided a taste of the guidelines here.

- **Provide equivalent alternatives to auditory and visual content**—If you're using sound or graphics, include text descriptions and employ HTML-based aids, such as the `alt` attribute in images, wherever possible.
- **Ensure that text and graphics are understandable when viewed without color**—Many people are color-blind, and many people can't use visual displays with which to see color. Also, contrast is an imperative for all people, even those without vision problems.
- **Use markup and style sheets properly**—This guideline is an important one! It encourages the creation of well-formed documents in accordance with the standards. Of course, you may make decisions that go against the grain, but if you do so, I encourage you to at least do so with *awareness*.
- **Provide clear navigation mechanisms**—Clear and consistent navigation is not only an imperative in accessibility, it's an imperative in user interface design. Links should be clearly identified and organized, and graphical options should have appropriate alternatives available.

→ To read more about the `alt` attribute, **see** "Working with Images," **p. 202**
→ To work with color efficiently, **see** "Color Concepts," **p. 528**
→ To find user interface principles, **see** "Effective Page Design," **p. 506**

Note

Learn all 14 accessibility guidelines and the complex checkpoints required for complete accessibility support at **http://www.w3.org/TR/1999/WAI-WEBCONTENT-19990505/**.

DEVELOPING ACCESSIBLE PAGES

In order to work toward the ideal of creating well-formed documents, the following sections step through a variety of HTML 4.0 exercises that demonstrate how accessibility can be added to your pages.

CREATING AND LINKING TO A TEXT-ONLY PAGE

The `LINK` tag allows you to provide links to alternative pages. This way, if you want to use technology that is not accessible, you can provide accessible pages for your special needs audience.

To use the `LINK` tag to load alternative pages, first you need to create an alternate version of your page. Then, you'll add a `LINK` tag to the original page to redirect capable browsers to the alternate page.

1. Open a complete HTML file in your text or HTML editor and save the file with a new filename, such as `text_pagename.html`.
2. Edit the file to create a text-only version of the page by eliminating extraneous graphics, ensuring that your links are contextual and identifiable as links, and that your content is laid out in an easy-to-follow format.
3. Save this text-only version of the page.
4. Open the original HTML file.
5. In the original HTML file, add a `LINK` tag to the Head of the page that references the text-only page and the media for which it is intended.

```
<HTML>
<HEAD>

<TITLE>Example of Alternate Page Loading</TITLE>

<LINK title="Text-only version" rel="accessible" href="text_page.html"
➥media="aural, Braille, tty">

</HEAD>

</HTML>
```

You'll end up with two pages with the same information, one with a graphical layout and one that is text-only for easy accessibility. Browsers that support the alternative media specified by the LINK tag automatically load the alternative page referenced by the tag.

The media type attribute describes to the visitors what kind of accessibility tools they can use to access this page. Aural refers to speech synthesizers and screen reader software, Braille refers to the fact that the page can be easily printed and read in a special Braille printer, and TTY refers to a teletype terminal.

Tip from

Keep text-only pages free of any scripting or other advanced technologies. Use basic HTML markup such as headers, paragraphs, and lists to format the document. I recommend avoiding FONT tags and style sheets as well.

USING THE LINK TAG FOR ACCESSIBLE NAVIGATION

The LINK tag can also be used in conjunction with navigation. Using the LINK tag to describe the relationship of the page to other pages on a site can enable accessible browsers to make sense of the site's navigation.

1. Open an HTML file in your text or HTML editor. Add the basic Web shell information for a new page:

```
<HTML>
<HEAD>
<TITLE>Your New Puppy</TITLE>
</HEAD>
<BODY>

</BODY>
</HTML>
```

2. Add the LINK tags to the head of the page to provide navigation to other pages within your site (Figure 22.1):

```
<HTML>
<HEAD>
<TITLE>Your New Puppy</TITLE>
<LINK rel="Next" href="training.html">
<LINK rel="Previous" href="feeding.html">
<LINK rel="Home" href="choosing.html">
<LINK rel+"Glossary" href="glossary.html">
</HEAD>
<BODY>

</BODY>
</HTML>
```

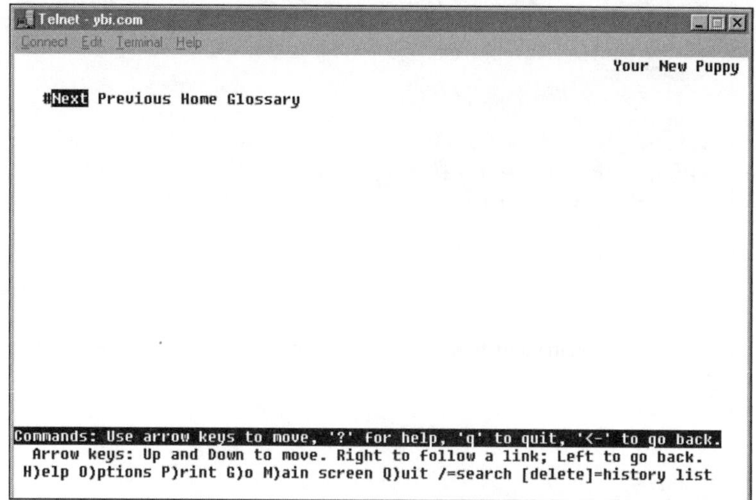

Figure 22.1
The navigation is now available at the top of this text-based page, viewed in the text browser called Lynx.

Note

`LINK` tag navigation guides viewers logically from page to page in your site.

Making Links Understandable with the `title` Attribute

It is important for links to be descriptive, but even contextual links can be confusing when taken out of that context. Trying to fashion each link to be descriptive both in and out of context can make for awkward content, however. The `title` attribute allows you to add extra context to your links without detracting from the flow of your content.

1. Within the BODY of your page, type the following paragraph:

```
<HTML>
<HEAD>
<TITLE>Your New Puppy</TITLE>
</HEAD>
<BODY>
<P>Puppies rely on their owners for food, training, and attention.
</BODY>
</HTML>
```

2. Add links to the words “food”, “training”, and “attention” to contextually link those words to other pages in your site:

```
<HTML>
<HEAD>
<TITLE>Your New Puppy</TITLE>
</HEAD>
<BODY>
<P>Puppies rely on their owners for
<A href="feeding.html">food</A>,
<A href="training.html">training</A>, and
<A href="playing.html">attention</A>.
</BODY>
</HTML>
```

3. Add a `title` attribute to the link to `feeding.html`:

```
<HTML>
<HEAD>
<TITLE>Your New Puppy</TITLE>
</HEAD>
<BODY>
<P>Puppies rely on their owners for
<A href="feeding.html" title="Feeding your puppy">food</A>,
<A href="training.html">training</A>, and
<A href="playing.html">attention</A>.
</BODY>
</HTML>
```

4. Repeat step 3 to add `title` attributes to the other links (see Figure 22.2):

```
<HTML>
<HEAD>
<TITLE>Your New Puppy</TITLE>
</HEAD>
<BODY>
<P>Puppies rely on their owners for
<A href="feeding.html" title="Feeding your puppy">food</A>,
<A href="training.html" title="How to train your puppy">training</A>, and
<A href="playing.html" title="How to play with your puppy">attention</A>.
</BODY>
</HTML>
```

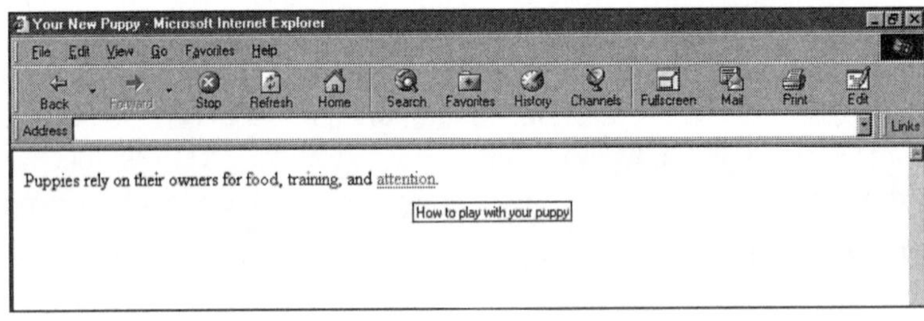

Figure 22.2
As the mouse passes over the link, more information is offered about the link in a ToolTip, which enables the reader to quickly get to the page they are most interested in without having to guess.

> **Note**
> The `title` attribute is not supported yet in Netscape Navigator 4.0 versions. It is fully supported in IE 4.0 and above, however.

ADDING TAB ORDER TO LINKS

You can assign a tab order to your links through use of the `tabindex` attribute. This attribute can be used with the `A`, `AREA`, `BUTTON`, `INPUT`, `OBJECT`, `SELECT`, and `TEXTAREA` elements.

When used on a page, people who are using keyboard navigation will be able to tab first to links with a set tab order. Elements that do not support the `tabindex` attribute are displayed next, in the order in which they appear in your HTML file.

1. Type a paragraph into the BODY of your page:

```
<HTML>
<HEAD>
<TITLE>Your New Puppy</TITLE>
</HEAD>
<BODY>
<P>Puppies rely on their owners for food, training, and attention. The first
step in building a relationship with your puppy is choosing the puppy that's
right for your family.
</BODY>
</HTML>
```

2. Add links to several words to contextually link those words to other pages in your site. (I chose "food", "training", and "attention".):

```
<HTML>
<HEAD>
<TITLE>Your New Puppy</TITLE>
</HEAD>
<BODY>
<P>Puppies rely on their owners for
<A href="feeding.html">food</A>,<A href="training.html">training</A>, and
<A href="playing.html">attention</A>. The first step in building a
relationship with your puppy is
<A href="choosing.html">choosing</A> the puppy that's right for your family.
</BODY>
</HTML>
```

3. Add the tabindex attribute to each of your links:

```
<HTML>
<HEAD>
<TITLE>Your New Puppy</TITLE>
</HEAD>
<BODY>
<P>Puppies rely on their owners for
<A href="feeding.html" tabindex="2">food</A>,
<A href="training.html" tabindex="3">training</A>, and
<A href="playing.html" tabindex="4">attention</A>.
The first step in building a relationship with your puppy is
<A href="choosing.html" tabindex="1">choosing</a> the puppy that's right for
your family.
</BODY>
</HTML>
```

Tip from

The tab index does not necessarily have to correlate to the order in which the links are presented on the page—put them in the order you like. In the previous example, the last link in the paragraph is the first link in the tab order.

Adding Tab Order to Forms

Assigning a tab order is particularly helpful when designing forms. The final links in the tab order should be the Submit and Reset options, with each of the other buttons, check boxes, and text fields presented in a logical order before those options. Because the tab index does not need to be in sequence, you can leave gaps in your tab order numbering, giving you room to add to your form later without having to renumber all the other form elements.

1. Add a form between the BODY tags of the shell:

```
<HTML>
<HEAD>
<TITLE>Puppy Information</TITLE>
</HEAD>
<BODY>
<FORM action="submit" method="post">
<LABEL for="answer-yes-or-no">Do you own a puppy? </LABEL>
<INPUT type="text" name="answer-yes-or-no">
<LABEL for="name-puppy">Name of Puppy: </LABEL>
<INPUT type="text" name="name-puppy">
<INPUT type="submit" name="submit">
</FORM>
</BODY>
</HTML>
```

2. Add the `tabindex` attribute to each of the INPUT elements (see Figure 22.3):

```
<HTML>
<HEAD>
<TITLE>Puppy Information</TITLE>
</HEAD>
<BODY>
<FORM action="submit" method="post">
<LABEL for="answer-yes-or-no">Do you own a puppy? </LABEL>
<INPUT tabindex="1" type="text" name="answer-yes-or-no">
<LABEL for="name-puppy">Name of Puppy: </LABEL>
<INPUT tabindex="2" type="text" name="name-puppy">
<INPUT tabindex="3" type="submit" name="submit">
</FORM>
</BODY>
</HTML>
```

→ For help with building a complete form, **see** "Building Forms," **p. 386**

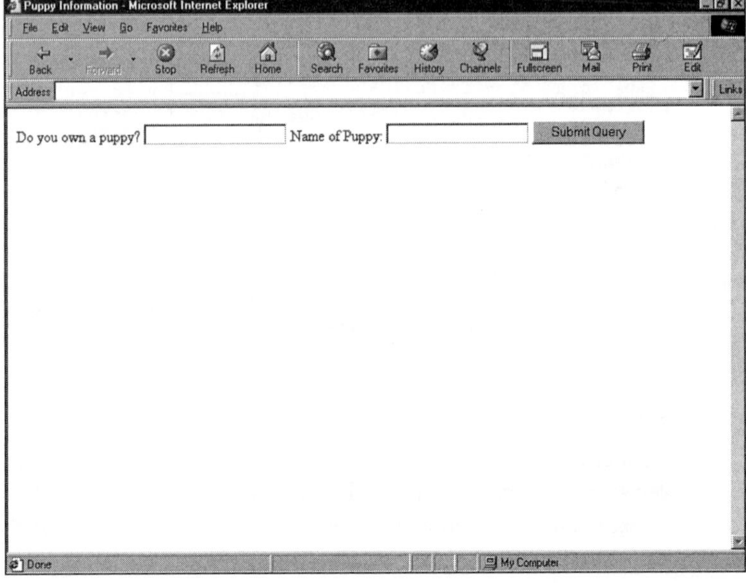

Figure 22.3
The form as it appears within a browser. It looks like a conventional form, but you can tab between the fields in the order specified.

Tip from molly

In a text editor, not only can a form be easily filled out, but the tab indexing takes the user through each tag in order. So, after filling out this form, the user merely tabs to the Submit button, where he or she can press the right-arrow or Return key to submit the form.

USING FIELDSET AND LEGEND IN FORMS

Forms can be very short, with few input areas, or they can be quite lengthy. People with good vision can usually understand the logical grouping of areas of the form. However, for those people with very low vision, or no vision at all—there are no logical cues to group related check boxes or input areas.

The FIELDSET tag is useful for structuring your form controls into logical groups. You must include a LEGEND tag within your FIELDSET to define the group.

Note

LEGEND and FIELDSET are not supported in Netscape 4.61 and below.

1. Create a standard form.
2. Add the FIELDSET element to group the form controls:

```
<HTML>
<HEAD>
<TITLE>Puppy Information</TITLE>
</HEAD>
<BODY>
<FORM action="submit" method="post">
<FIELDSET>
<LABEL for="name-puppy">Name of Puppy: </LABEL>
<INPUT type="text" name="name-puppy">
<LABEL for="age-puppy">Age of Puppy: </LABEL>
<INPUT type="text" name="age-puppy">
<LABEL for="breed-puppy">Breed of Puppy: </LABEL>
<INPUT type="text" name="breed-puppy">
</FIELDSET>

<FIELDSET>
<LABEL for="owner-lastname">Your Last Name: </LABEL>
<INPUT type="text" name="owner-lastname">
<LABEL for="owner-firstname">Your First Name: </LABEL>
<INPUT type="text" name="owner-firstname">
</FIELDSET>
<INPUT type="submit" name="submit">
</FORM>
</BODY>
</HTML>
```

3. Add the LEGEND element to describe each FIELDSET:

```
<HTML>
<HEAD>
<TITLE>Puppy Information</TITLE>
</HEAD>
<BODY>
```

```
<FORM action="submit" method="post">
<FIELDSET>
<LEGEND>Information About Your Puppy</LEGEND>
<LABEL for="name-puppy">Name of Puppy: </LABEL>
<INPUT type="text" name="name-puppy">
<LABEL for="age-puppy">Age of Puppy: </LABEL>
<INPUT type="text" name="age-puppy">
<LABEL for="breed-puppy">Breed of Puppy: </LABEL>
<INPUT type="text" name="breed-puppy">
</FIELDSET>

<FIELDSET>
<LEGEND>Information About You</LEGEND>
<LABEL for="owner-lastname">Your Last Name: </LABEL>
<INPUT type="text" name="owner-lastname">
<LABEL for="owner-firstname">Your First Name: </LABEL>
<INPUT type="text" name="owner-firstname">
</FIELDSET>
<INPUT type="submit" name="submit">
</FORM>
</BODY>
</HTML>
```

Tip from molly

Group `fieldsets` that go together sensibly, clearly identifying which section belongs to what type of questions.

USING OPTGROUP IN FORMS

Being the ideal language that it is, HTML 4.0 also offers a method to organize the options in selection lists within forms. However, this is not yet supported by Internet Explorer 5.0 or below, or Netscape Navigator 4.61 or earlier. You can use `OPTGROUP` now and hope that both browsers will soon encourage compliance.

To group the options on a `SELECT` list within a form, you'll first need to build the form and the options. Then you'll use the `OPTGROUP` element to define the groups of options.

1. Build a basic form, including a `SELECT` element and the options you want defined in the list:

```
<HTML>
<HEAD>
<TITLE>World Tours</TITLE>
</HEAD>
<BODY>
<FORM action="submit" method="post">
<SELECT name="countries" multiple>
<LABEL for="countries">Which Countries Have You Visited? </LABEL>
<OPTION>United States
<OPTION>Canada
<OPTION>Mexico
<OPTION>Spain
<OPTION>United Kingdom
<OPTION>France
```

```
<OPTION>Japan
<OPTION>China
</SELECT>
<INPUT type="submit" name="submit">
</FORM>
</BODY>
</HTML>
```

2. Add the OPTGROUP element:

```
<HTML>
<HEAD>
<TITLE>World Tours</TITLE>
</HEAD>
<BODY>
<FORM action="submit" method="post">
<SELECT name="countries" multiple>
<LABEL for="countries">Which Countries Have You Visited? </LABEL>
<OPTGROUP label="North America">
<OPTION>United States
<OPTION>Canada
<OPTION>Mexico
</OPTGROUP>
<OPTGROUP label="Europe">
<OPTION>Spain
<OPTION>United Kingdom
<OPTION>France
</OPTGROUP>
<OPTGROUP label="Asia">
<OPTION>Japan
<OPTION>China
</OPTGROUP>
</SELECT>
<INPUT type="submit" value="submit">
</FORM>
</BODY>
</HTML>
```

As with other information in this chapter, using accessibility options such as OPTGROUP conforms to the rules set forth by the World Wide Web Consortium's Web Accessibility Initiative (WAI), despite the fact that popular browser support is lacking.

Making Tables Accessible Using a Caption

Tables can be made more accessible by adding captions to them. Fortunately, this technique is well supported. The caption labels the table in a traditional browser, and provides a simple description of the table in an accessible browser. To add a caption to your tables, you simply need to add a CAPTION element beneath your TABLE tag.

1. Add a table to a page, within the BODY of the page:

```
<HTML>
<HEAD>
<TITLE>World Tours</TITLE>
</HEAD>
<BODY>
<TABLE>
<TR>
```

```
<TD>Name</TD>
<TD>Country</TD>
<TD>Days</TD>
</TR>
<TR>
<TD>Jody</TD>
<TD>Japan</TD>
<TD>5</TD>
</TR>
<TR>
<TD>Molly</TD>
<TD>Spain</TD>
<TD>10</TD>
</TR>
</TABLE>
</BODY>
</HTML>
```

2. Add a `CAPTION` element to the table:

```
<HTML>
<HEAD>
<TITLE>World Tours</TITLE>
</HEAD>
<BODY>
<TABLE>
<CAPTION> </CAPTION>
<TR>
<TD>Name</TD>
<TD>Country</TD>
<TD>Days</TD>
</TR>
<TR>
<TD>Jody</TD>
<TD>Japan</TD>
<TD>5</TD>
</TR>
<TR>
<TD>Molly</TD>
<TD>Spain</TD>
<TD>10</TD>
</TR>
</TABLE>
</BODY>
</HTML>
```

3. Write in a descriptive caption (see Figure 22.4):

```
<HTML>
<HEAD>
<TITLE>World Tours</TITLE>
</HEAD>
<BODY>
<TABLE>
<CAPTION>Duration of Trips by Each Traveler</CAPTION>
<TR>
<TD>Name</TD>
```

```
<TD>Country</TD>
<TD>Days</TD>
</TR>
<TR>
<TD>Jody</TD>
<TD>Japan</TD>
<TD>5</TD>
</TR>
<TR>
<TD>Molly</TD>
<TD>Spain</TD>
<TD>10</TD>
</TR>
</TABLE>
</BODY>
</HTML>
```

Making Tables Accessible Using a Summary

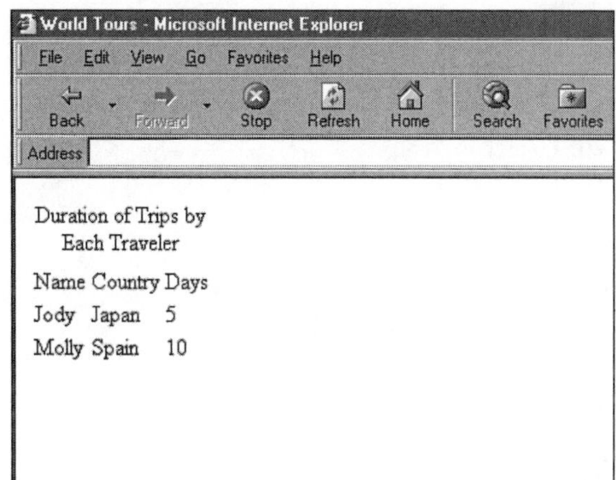

Figure 22.4
The table caption "Duration of Trips by Each Traveler" will be available *before* the table entries to people using a speech synthesizer or other accessible browser. This gives visual context to users in a nonvisual environment.

A SUMMARY element adds a lengthier description of your table. The SUMMARY element enables you to explain the information included in your table, thereby making it easier for people to understand it when using accessibility tools. The SUMMARY appears as a link to this description within most visual browsers.

1. Add a table to the page within the BODY of the file:

```
<HTML>
<HEAD>
<TITLE>World Tours</TITLE>
</HEAD>
<BODY>
<TABLE>
<TR>
<TD>Name</TD>
<TD>Country</TD>
<TD>Days</TD>
```

```
</TR>
<TR>
<TD>Jody</TD>
<TD>Japan</TD>
<TD>5</TD>
</TR>
<TR>
<TD>Molly</TD>
<TD>Spain</TD>
<TD>10</TD>
</TR>
</TABLE>
</BODY>
</HTML>
```

2. Add a summary attribute to the TABLE tag:

```
<HTML>
<HEAD>
<TITLE>World Tours</TITLE>
</HEAD>
<BODY>
<TABLE summary"This table shows the name of each traveler, the country he or
she visited, and the duration of their trip.">
<TR>
<TD>Name</TD>
<TD>Country</TD>
<TD>Days</TD>
</TR>
<TR>
<TD>Jody</TD>
<TD>Japan</TD>
<TD>5</TD>
</TR>
<TR>
<TD>Molly</TD>
<TD>Spain</TD>
<TD>10</TD>
</TR>
</TABLE>
</BODY>
</HTML>
```

Tip from molly

Make summaries concise, but descriptive. The objective is to *summarize*, after all!

CLARIFYING ABBREVIATIONS WITH THE ACRONYM TAG AND THE title ATTRIBUTE

Web writing often needs to be short, sharp, and to the point. Any individual managing content for the Web can use the ACRONYM element to add definition to the acronym without having to place it directly into the text. It is also used to aid screen readers in properly reading an acronym.

This technique ensures that WWW is clearly defined as the Women Writers of Wichita rather than the World Wide Web, if there may be any cause for confusion.

The ACRONYM element is defined using the title attribute.

1. Add a sentence with an acronym to the BODY of the page:

```
<HTML>
<HEAD>
<TITLE>News from the WWW</TITLE>
</HEAD>
<BODY>
<P>Welcome to the WWW!
</BODY>
</HTML>
```

2. Add the ACRONYM tag and title attribute to define "WWW". Figure 22.5 shows the results:

```
<HTML>
<HEAD>
<TITLE>News from the WWW</TITLE>
</HEAD>
<BODY>
<P>Welcome to the <ACRONYM title="Women Writers of Wichita">WWW</ACRONYM>!
</BODY>
</HTML>
```

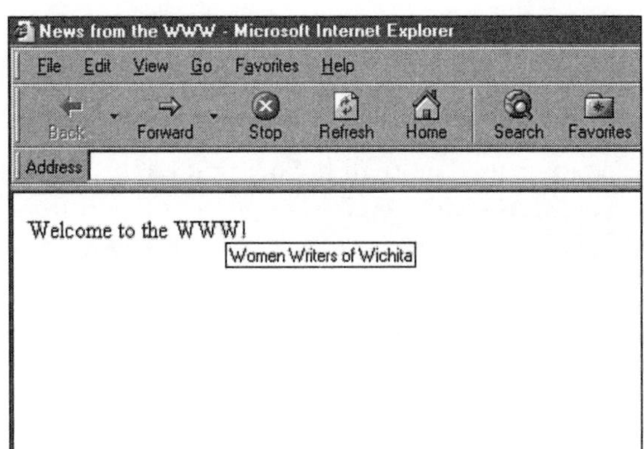

Figure 22.5
In Internet Explorer, the ToolTip shows the acronym for this site spelled out and easy to understand.

Creating Access Through Internationalization

Just as access is important to those with disabilities, it is equally important to ensure that access is worldwide—it is the World Wide Web after all!

To accommodate access for international users, the World Wide Web Consortium is making a concerted effort to define the most needed areas of focus and provide solutions for weak spots.

Current areas of activity include

- Increasing awareness among Web and browser developers regarding international access issues.

- Stressing the importance of Unicode as a mechanism for character encoding.
- Creating study groups within the Consortium to look at details of international concerns.

Note

Internationalization activities can be monitored with a visit to `http://www.w3.org/International/`.

Much of internationalization involves ensuring that characters are available for international languages including Chinese, Japanese, Hebrew, Arabic, and Cyrillic. There are two primary methods by which to do this, although browser support is varied at this time.

→ For a detailed listing of available characters, **see** "Special Characters," **p. 1010**

The first method involves using Unicode characters to accomplish the task. The other method uses the `lang` attribute within any relevant element tag.

A Unicode example would look like this:

```
&#x202B;&#x05F4; &#x05F4;&#x202C;
```

Whereas the `lang` attribute is used as follows:

```
<HTML lang="es">
```

Interestingly, this is the first time many experienced HTML coders will see an attribute placed in the opening `HTML` tag. This code sets up the page to be displayed in Spanish.

Spanish mostly uses characters used in English. So how does the language attribute make a difference in how the HTML is coded? Well, with proper support from browsers, instead of having to use Unicode characters to invoke an N with a tilde above it, all the coder has to do is type in that character with their keyboard, or with a combination of the tilde and N keys. After the appropriate letter is entered, the browser will know how to interpret that code when the language attribute is in place.

The unfortunate reality is that despite the fascinating work being done in the area of internationalization—and despite the fact that many of the proposed elements, attributes, and special characters necessary to support internationalization are considered part of HTML 4.0—the support in browsers is very limited.

Note

Unicode information is available via the Unicode Consortium, `http://www.unicode.org/`.

TROUBLESHOOTING

ACCESSIBILITY AND INTERNATIONALIZATION IN THE REAL WORLD

Why should I take extra measures to learn and incorporate accessibility and internationalization techniques in HTML 4.0 when so many of them aren't supported by most browsers?

Well, as with any technology, a survey of your audiences should be undertaken before you determine what is or is not right for your needs. And, although you may decide to not use specific aspects of these options, it's a darned good idea for serious Web developers to begin gaining an awareness of the concepts and techniques involved. Eventually, browser technology will catch up, and it's a great idea to keep in touch with how things are fairing even if you won't need or want to employ a given technique.

Designing for the Real World

HTML and Access: An Interview with David Oberhart

This case study is included here to impress upon you the importance of accessibility issues in HTML 4.0, and why you as a reader can benefit from understanding the standard and using it appropriately.

David Oberhart is a communications specialist and consultant who started working on UNIX-based computers when at the University of Iowa in the early 1980s. Because David is blind, he has been in a position to experience computer access technology since his first talking computer in 1983. David's years on the Internet have given him a unique perspective when it comes to the Web and how it has grown and changed from a text-based utility to the highly graphical environment it is today.

Currently, David browses the Web using a screen reader known as ASAW combined with a text-to-speech engine that uses his computer's audio to read what's onscreen. He uses Internet Explorer with the images turned off for his browser. I asked David to describe his experience of the Web both in the early years, and today.

MH: David, you got on the Web when it was a text-based environment only. How would you describe that experience?

DO: "Using Lynx on a 14.4 connection was easy for me. Because the Web was text-based, documents were easy to read, links were clearly specified, and navigating those links was fairly simple.

Generally speaking, page content was helpful, interesting, and provided what you wanted quickly. The Web was better organized then than now. Everything has become harder to find."

MH: What is your experience of the Web today?

DO: "I usually use the Web to look for product information, get technical support, and read about computer hardware and software. Most of these sites tend to be easy to use. However, I also want entertainment such as movies, TV, and humor sites. These tend to be very flashy. I can't use the Web for news, because news sites tend to be very flashy also. The columnization of pages is useless.

It seems that sites who have an imperative to provide information *as information* still pay attention to text. For example, it's reasonably easy to find general reference material. Where I run into problems is with very current information. I'm more likely to turn the TV on than use the Web site.

My impression of the people who code pages is that they just don't care. They're going to make their page look as cool as they want it to look, with little or no regard to the way a person navigates. The Web designer determines the look, rarely thinking about what the visitor needs."

HTML 4.0 provides means by which individuals such as David can achieve a better experience of today's Web sites. Even the most active page can offer viable alternatives to users—whether they are blind or have other impairments, are using different hardware and software than what the developer uses, or are visiting a Web site at slow speeds.

Remember: It's World Wide

It is important to remember that the World Wide Web is a *global* phenomenon. On April 30, 1993, CERN's Director made an announcement stating that the World Wide Web would be freely usable by *anyone*, with no fee payable to CERN. No one government, agency, or organization has direct control over the evolution or implementation of the Web. The W3C has as its goal the standardization of the format (HTML) and the various protocols that make the Web a viable, accessible communications medium. It is up to us as HTML authors to determine how to accommodate this goal. Hopefully, we will always balance our progressive and beautiful Web pages to the needs of our audiences.

CHAPTER 23

UNDERSTANDING XHTML, XML, AND EMERGING LANGUAGES

In this chapter

X Marks the Spot

Look closely at the official progress of HTML and related markup languages, and you'll see a lot of X's popping up. This notorious X represents a fundamental concept in the way many Web languages are evolving.

The concept is *extensibility*. Extensible languages are unlimited in terms of their capability to be customized to specific needs yet still understood by the broadest range of user agents as possible. Extensibility allows languages to stretch within the contextual rules of the language and self-define the behavior of a given piece of syntax.

Extensibility is essential to the Web because today's needs to manage data have become much more complex. There's a need for HTML itself to become more flexible in the face of numerous browsers, including specialty browsers being developed for hand-held computers and other devices such as wireless phones and pagers.

Then, there's the desire to customize markup for industry-specific methods. Banking and medicine have different data management needs—extensible languages can be customized to manage that data on the back- and front-end of an intranet or Internet site.

With the push to make the Web more interactive comes a need to go beyond HTML's limitations and find ways to facilitate the management of media via the language rather than browser-dependent applications.

Another important concern is to go back to the grass-roots intelligence of the Web markup point of origin: *Standard Generalized Markup Language*, or *SGML*. SGML rules are quite strict, and as this entire book demonstrates, HTML has become much like a rebellious child in need of some strong discipline to properly behave. Most extensible languages emerging today represent a truer, more proper subset of its mature parent.

Extensibility first gained attention in the public with the appearance of XML, the *Extensible Markup Language*. A flurry of activity and attention surrounded its appearance and at one point XML was thought to be "The HTML Killer." But XML has manifested itself more as a sophisticated method of working on the server-side in step with HTML for the creation and management of specialty data. XML's dominant theme—extensibility—has influenced the progress of HTML and also allowed for numerous other languages to emerge (see Figure 23.1).

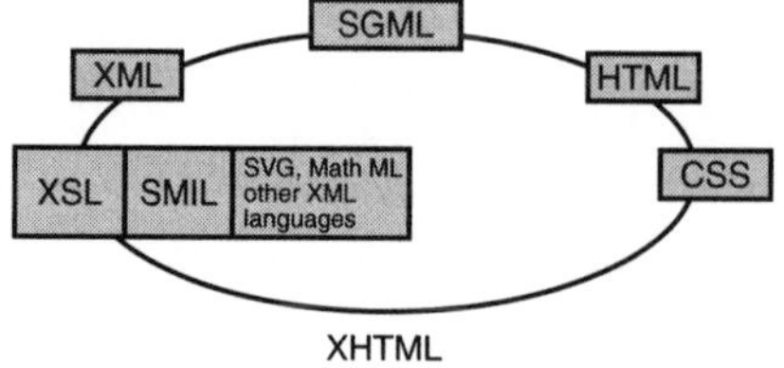

Figure 23.1
This simple markup hierarchy puts emerging Web languages into perspective.

→ For more information on XML, **see** "XML: Fundamental Extensibility," **p. 494**

XHTML: The Present Discussion of HTML's Future Tense

People working primarily with HTML and client-side technologies will want to pay special attention to XHTML, *Extensible Hypertext Markup Language*. XHTML 1.0 is currently a proposal by the World Wide Web Consortium, which reformulates HTML into the extensible concept first brought into view by XML.

The central concern is to ensure that HTML will be readable by upcoming XML-enabled user agents. This allows HTML to extend beyond its current limitations and adopt the flexibility of XML.

XHTML strives to solve many of the problems with HTML that exist today as well as allowing HTML to look toward the future, where the range of browser types will likely be even more diverse than it is today.

Note

The fact that browsers and applications will have to accommodate extensible markup such as XHTML demonstrates that it will take time before the languages can be fully absorbed into the real working world of Web development. As we've seen with HTML 4.0, however, this doesn't mean that XHTML won't be adopted as a recommendation before the support is viable.

Wondering why all the fuss if this technology isn't even supported by current Web browsers? See "Support Me, Please!" in the Troubleshooting section at the end of this chapter for some hints as to why this is important for today's Web programmer/designer.

HTML authors need to focus on the differences in XHTML from their current practices. This will prepare you for conforming to new XHTML rules should XHTML become a formal recommendation, which looks probable. The following concerns should be paid special attention to:

- **The creation of well-formed documents is paramount**—Essentially, this means *no sloppy code*! XHTML documents must be written appropriately—no matter that many browsers are forgiving. A prime example of well-formed code is found in symmetry. No elements can be illegally nested. If you have one section of code in bold and italics, the tags must appear in symmetrical form:

  ```
  <b>Well-formed documents are <i>fundamental</i></b>
  ```

  Asymmetrical code will not be tolerated, so it is incorrect to do this:

  ```
  <b>Well-formed documents are <i>fundamentalto XHTML</b></i>
  ```

- **Element and attribute names must be in lowercase**—I'm tremendously excited about this one, but I know that many coders will be frustrated because they'll have to adjust their style. Because XML is case sensitive, and HTML is not, in order to achieve reformulation effectively, all XHTML elements must be written in lowercase. This way, supporting user agents will be able to differentiate between tags and attributes appropriately.

- **All attributes must be quoted**—Here's another example of XHTML striving for cleaner, better code. Sloppy coders take heed! Every attribute you add to an XHTML document must have quotes around it.
- **End tags will be required in non-empty elements**—HTML has numerous elements that do not require ending tags. A prime example of this is the `P` element, which in HTML 4.0, is perfectly legal when used in open *or* open/close format. In XHTML, however, you must close any element that contains data.
- **Empty elements will require end tags or a start tag with a `/` to indicate a termination**—Empty tags are those tags that do not contain content in and of themselves, such as `<BR>` and `<HR>`. When using these tags in XHTML, you'll need to add a termination, which is indicated by a forward slash *after* the tag markup and before the closing angle bracket, `<br/>` or `<hr/>`.

XHTML obviously places demands on the coder, but of even greater concern will be the demands placed on user agents and applications. Browser developers will be faced with the creation of updated Web browsers that are backward compatible *and* support XML and XHTML. New user agents that are being developed for hand-held devices and cell phones will need to incorporate extensible technology—all to their advantage because the extensibility will allow developers to quickly grow with technology instead of having to wait until the next version of a language is approved.

Application developers must pay attention to these proposed changes. Even best-of-breed HTML editors such as Allaire's Homesite do not currently conform to XHTML's strict coding practices such as ensuring that all attributes are quoted. WYSIWYG software will be especially challenged to revamp, revise, and reissue products that write well-formed code. Although undoubtedly a serious task, the end result is certain to be a much more sophisticated set of development tools.

Note

You can find out more about XHTML and its current status at the World Wide Web Consortium, `http://www.w3.org/`.

XML: FUNDAMENTAL EXTENSIBILITY

As mentioned earlier in this chapter, it was XML that started this entire re-structuring of HTML. XML is a language of fundamental extensibility, giving both client- and server-side developers enormous power over their projects.

Note

XML support on the client-side is currently minimal. Internet Explorer 5.0 was the first XML support built into the browser. Most XML development is taking place on the server-side, although there is strong evidence that browser developers will have to aggressively incorporate XML and XHTML compatibility into their browsers.

XML developers envisioned that the majority of XML documentation would be generated by a computer, processed by software, and even destroyed without the need for humans to enter into the data loop. XML achieves this independence as a general-purpose data representation language by providing a standard approach for describing, capturing, processing, and publishing information.

HTML is a fixed markup language. HTML allows a description of how data should *look*. XML lets you assign what the data *means* and facilitates the preservation of useful information that would be nearly impossible to achieve with HTML. This distinction between HTML and XML is important. XML's approach to the treatment of information shows that it, although certainly a near relation to HTML, is a fundamentally different technology.

XML also enables the incorporation of diverse data types. The level of complexity of the data is not a concern, nor is the amount. Prior to XML, the Web had no mechanism or standard for working with a variety of data types for even nominally complex data.

The goal in creating XML was to provide an easy-to-parse syntax for representing data. Isolating the content portion of the data (what the data says) from the descriptive rendering instructions (how the data should look) is an extension in XML that enables the same data to be used in multiple formats. This capability provides for the separation of content and presentation (in a way, this is like style sheets and HTML—different documents for content and presentation). Each set of details is stored separately. This means that content is always safe and in one piece. This capability also enables you to easily update or change the presentation by simply changing the presentation document.

In XML, data processing and document processing are the same thing. The same cannot be said of HTML. The easy-to-parse syntax of XML that was written to be easily understood by a computer is openly exemplified in simple, flexible, and human-readable code. For example, if I want to mark up a portion of a document as being an invoice, I can simply create a tag called `INVOICE`. This customization is the heart of extensibility, and is not possible within HTML.

> **Note**
>
> The easy-to-understand data in XML becomes an additional benefit by making it easier for search engines to locate and describe a given document.

Another feature of XML is that the author can customize the tags based on this concept of human readability. The following snippet demonstrates how you can customize a tag:

```
<TO> Reader </TO>
<FROM> author </FROM>
<RE> XML READABILITY </RE>

<P>
Think of the flow of an XML document like that of a gift card that already has
the "to" and "from" part in it. All that is left would be to fill in the blanks,
but the flexibility exists to structure the memo part any different way that you
can imagine just by applying a different style sheet. Also you can put any
name(s) in the heading part. This makes for a powerful tool and simplifies mass
```

```
mailing within a corporate database or large data intensive system. The
potential for this document is limited only by the imagination. Your style sheet
will tell the computer how to affect the presentation of your content.
</P>
```

The markup identifies components (called *elements*) of documents in a manner that can be executed by a computer. The start tag `<TO>` marks the beginning of an element. The end tag `</TO>` seals the container.

It is no great stretch of the imagination to consider the cataloging of business documentation such as invoices, inventory lists, profit and loss statements, and so forth. The categories remain constant, but variables change continually. Having a means to update quickly without having to sift through numerous tags is a timesaving advantage:

```
<INVOICE>
<FROM>Supplier</FROM>
<TO>A consumer</TO>
<DATE year = '1998' month = '9' day = '15' />
<AMOUNT currency = 'Dollars'>57.00</AMOUNT>
<TaxRate>07</TaxRate>
<TotalDue currency = 'Dollars'>60.99</TotalDue>
</INVOICE>
```

Compare this code to what it would look like if coded in HTML:

```
<H1>Invoice</H1>
<P>From: Supplier
<P>To: A consumer
<P>Date: 15 September 1998
<P>Amount : $57.00
<P>Tax : 7 %
<P>Total Due : 60.99
```

In the HTML version, the user agents have no indication of what, content-wise, is really there. With the XML version, the user agents use author-designated elements that enable a program to update important information, such as the tax rate per a different state or the day with the computer's internal clock. The data in the first instance (XML) is smart, updateable, and easily altered.

Note

XML has no predefined tags. Any language based on XML displays matching sets of `<ELEMENT>` tags that have been specifically named and performs a designated function within the context of a particular working group or industry. These declared meanings–along with the desired function–are defined by the author who writes the XML code.

The freedom to capture and publish useful information about your data and how it is structured is one of the vital benefits of using XML.

Real content, aptly identified, is more visible to search engines. For a large site or large database, having this content can be a blessing. In HTML, no mechanism can so elegantly define content.

Structured documents share many features in common with databases. XML documents closely resemble traditional relational and object database data in many ways. Generalized markup provides for the expansion of the definition of *document* to include the integration of diverse types of data.

Other, less obvious benefits entail less coding and more precise formatting.

Note

XML is accessibility-friendly and is equally adept at outputting text-to-speech and Braille translations.

→ For more information on accessibility concerns in HTML, **see** "Accessibility and Internationalization" **p. 474**

APPLICATIONS OF XML

Several XML-based languages already exist in industry and are fueling the commercial bloom which is changing the face of the Web with e-commerce. Such XML-based technologies include XSL, SMIL, SVG, and MathML.

EXTENSIBLE STYLE WITH XSL

Just as HTML has its companion-style technology, CSS, so XML has its companion in style, XSL—*Extensible Style Language*. XSL derives from two sources, DSSSL (*Document Style Semantics and Specification Language*) and CSS (*Cascading Style Sheets*). Most of the properties that exist in XSL are derived from CSS, but alone, CSS isn't sufficient to manage the unique needs of XML.

XSL consists of two primary parts:

- A method by which to transform XML documents, which is managed by yet another language known as XSLT, *Extensible Style Language Transformations*. It describes a structure that, although derived from DSSSL and CSS, is unique in its capability to transform XML. Its complexities are natural results of XML's arbitrary nature.
- A set of XML "vocabularies" that is actually still another set of languages which, when used with XSLT, combines to create style sheets for XML.

XSL is intended to be used with both client- and server-side technologies. Browser support is non-existent in today's current popular market, but new tools and extensions are being created regularly.

Note

For more information on the status of XSL, links to related vocabularies, and available tools, visit `http://www.w3.org/Style/XSL/`.

SMIL, YOU'RE ON WEB CAMERA

SMIL, the *Synchronized Multimedia Integration Language*, is an exciting aspect of markup because it defines a user-friendly XML-based language that can be used to create interactive Web content.

The emphasis on user-friendliness is why SMIL is exciting, because unlike the heady XML and complex XSL, SMIL is gaining a lot of attention. Developers such as Real Networks have created an array of tools, and the Consortium is spending time refining the language so that it is easy to use.

The demand for multimedia presentations on the Web is heavy. Commonly used methods, such as downloadable media, Java, Shockwave, and Flash, all come with their unique challenges and problems. SMIL allows designers to combine audio, video, and graphics that can be sent to the browser and quickly rendered (see Figure 23.2).

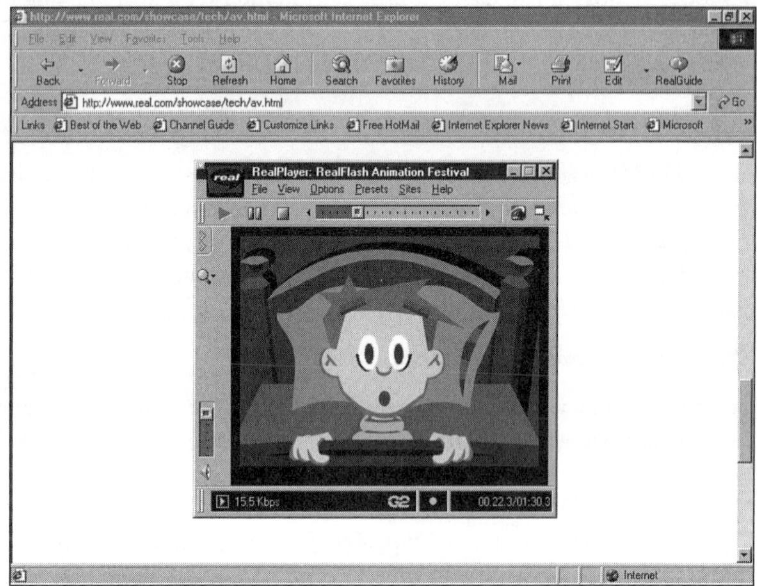

Figure 23.2
A SMIL presentation. Note that although SMIL is alive and thriving, it requires special viewers, in this case RealPlayer G2, to work.

➔ To read more about downloadable media, **see** "Audio, Video, and Streaming Media," **p. 669**
➔ Learn to work with Macromedia Flash, **see** "Working with Shockwave Flash," **p. 690**
➔ For more details on Java, **see** "Using Java Applets and ActiveX Components," **p. 702**

Essentially, SMIL combines a set of tags that help to define various aspects of a given presentation. For example, there are tags to control parallel and sequential viewing of given media. Along with the tag set comes a set of media types. RealVideo, RealAudio, RealPix, and RealText are examples of the media that are incorporated into SMIL presentations.

Note

SMIL does require a player in order to be viewed. RealPlayer G2 enthusiastically supports SMIL and can be downloaded at `http://www.real.com/products/playerplus/index.html`.

SMIL standards can be followed by visiting the World Wide Web Consortium's SMIL site, `http://www.w3.org/AudioVideo/`. The SMIL specification itself is located at `http://www.w3.org/TR/REC-smil/`.

SMIL developer information including tutorials and tools can be found at RealNetwork's Devzone, `http://www.real.com/devzone/index.html`.

Other XML Subsets of Interest

XML has influenced other areas of emerging languages including work on how to deliver graphics and mathematical data to the Web.

SVG, the *Scalable Vector Graphics* standard has evolved from XML as a method to deliver vector graphics to supporting Web browsers that can take advantage of the extensible aspects of XML.

Vector graphics are much more desirable than the currently used bitmapped graphics. The primary reason is that vector graphics are more compact and therefore render less weighty files. Other advantages to vector graphics include the ability to modify their dimensions without loss of quality. Imagine being able to have the browser dynamically scale a graphic to the correct size for a given resolution? That would take care of many a developer headache. Vector graphics also render with crisper, cleaner edges. In other words, no more jagged edges.

Using elements that define shapes, paths, and text, SVG allows developers to write or generate code rather than create heavy bitmaps (see Listing 23.1).

Listing 23.1 SVG Code from a Simple Graphic

```
<?xml version="1.0" standalone="yes"?>
<!DOCTYPE svg SYSTEM "svg-19990730.dtd">
<svg width="588" height="179"
style="text-antialiasing:true; stroke-antialiasing:true">
<desc>Untitled exported by Mayura Draw 3.6</desc>
<rect style="stroke:#000000;stroke-width:1;fill:#cc9966"
transform="matrix(1 0 0 -1 -11 782 )"
x="20.7031" y="612.737" width="569.119" height="160.71"/>
<g transform="matrix(1 0 0 1 -9.526 -573.3 )"
style="fill:#ffff00;
font-family:Arial; font-size:48;
text-align:center"
xml:space="preserve">
<text x="306.737" y="672.505"
>Look, Ma! No Graphics</text>
</g>
</svg>
```

Figure 23.3 shows the visual that results when viewed with an agent that has SVG support.

Figure 23.3
This simple image was created using SGV code. Look, Ma! No graphics.

Look, Ma! No Graphics

Of course, browser support for this intelligent methodology is unavailable, but tools to create and use SVG do exist.

Note SVG information and tools can be found at `http://www.w3.org/Graphics/SVG/`.

How to display scientific and mathematical data on the Web has long been a troublesome concern. XML, in its extensible wisdom, offers some relief in the form of MathML, the *Mathematical Markup Language*.

Currently, developers have had to rely on images to express equations and other scientific information. This means heavy pages that are cumbersome to read and no accessibility for special needs or text-only users.

→ If you want to know more about the special needs of some users, **see** "Accessibility and Internationalization," **p. 474**

MathML will solve the problem of presenting mathematical data by using extensible tags that allow math presentations to be displayed in supporting browsers. Once again, browser support is non-existent in the popular mien, but the W3C's own browser, Amaya, and a range of math tools are available.

Note Tools, language information, and links of interest regarding MathML can be found at `http://www.w3.org/Math/`.

TROUBLESHOOTING

SUPPORT ME, PLEASE!

Okay, this stuff is pretty interesting but it seems completely unusable to me. Why did you include it in a book about real-world HTML?

The information in this chapter is here to help you become more familiar with the role of extensibility in emerging languages, and to familiarize you with languages of specific interest. Although it's absolutely true that emerging languages are not currently supported by browsers and are therefore difficult for developers to use in real-world design, their importance to professional Web developers is critical.

Please visit the Web sites I've included for syntax details, tools, and support tips should you require more familiarity with a specific language.

DESIGNING FOR THE REAL WORLD

ORGANIZING A TOOLKIT FOR THE FUTURE

If you want to begin getting your tools prepared for using and viewing XML, XHTML, and emerging languages, I've made some recommendations that can help you along your way.

- Add XML development tools. Microsoft offers an editor available at **http://msdn.microsoft.com/xml/notepad/intro.asp** and a validator, **http://msdn.microsoft.com/xml/notepad/intro.asp**. Other tools can be found at **http://www.w3.org/XML/#software**.
- Get SMIL players and tools. Begin with RealPlayer G2 and add a variety of SMIL tools to your kit. The Player along with samples, tutorials, and a validator are all available at **http://www.real.com/devzone/library/creating/index.html**.
- SVG tools include Mayura Draw for Windows 95 and 98, which supports .svg export in its 3.6 and higher versions (**http://www.mayura.com/#svg**). For UNIX and UNIX-like systems, try out Sketch, **http://www.online.de/home/sketch/download.html**.
- Math maniacs and anyone interested in emerging languages should check out the Amaya browser, built by the W3C. It has MathML support as well as offering a MathML editor, **http://www.w3.org/Amaya/**.

If you're using an HTML editor or WYSIWYG program that allows you to define the way code is written and want to get your HTML documents closer to XHTML rules, do the following:

1. Set up your program so that all attributes are quoted.
2. Make sure that all your tags and attributes are set to lowercase.
3. Set all non-empty elements to have the closing container. For example, use the closing `</P>` tag if you aren't already doing so. Empty element terminators will have to be added by hand.

PART V

WEB GRAPHIC DESIGN

CHAPTER 24

Effective Page Design

In this chapter

UNDERSTANDING USER INTERFACE DESIGN

Designing a Web page to be effective means understanding a bit about the structure of hypermedia documents, taking the time to plan your page—and how it will interact with other pages on the site—as well as learning at least the principles of User Interface Design (UID).

The structure of hypermedia directly relates to the effectiveness of your page because by understanding the underlying, interactive technology available to you, you can make choices for your site and for your audience—eliminating potential problems on either end. Similarly, planning plays a big role in making sure you know what you want and need *before* you start to work. You spend less time, and in a professional situation, less money by ensuring that your work is well thought out in advance.

User Interface Design has been around a lot longer than the Web. It offers time-honored principles on which site designers can rely to effectively serve up sites that maintain a strongly integrated design. This is invaluable to your end user, as he or she will appreciate the results: always knowing how to get from one point on the site to another; feeling at ease as a large site becomes more complex to navigate; and, perhaps most importantly, maintaining *orientation*—the knowledge that he or she is still on the site you went to visit in the first place.

To design effective sites, it's important to ask yourself a significant question. As simple as it may seem, knowing what a Web site *is* and how it will ultimately serve you, your client, and your visitors, is as natural a place to start as it is overlooked.

So what is a Web site? At first glance, it can be described as a presentation of information that has some intent or purpose. That purpose can include, and sometimes be a combination of, the following:

- To share ideas, as in a personal home page
- To sell products
- To offer customer service
- As a point-of-contact for a non-profit organization
- As a news delivery service
- To offer entertainment and games
- As a news and information service

How this information is submitted can occur in a variety of ways, including the following:

- **Static, or *passive*, presentation**—This is simply information that is posted on the Web that offers fixed, rarely updated, and simplistic options. This kind of presentation is akin to a printed flyer or pamphlet. Although it may serve an individual's needs, it is limited in terms of tapping into the interactive elements that the Web offers.
- **Interactive, or *dynamic*, content**—Web sites that contain dynamic content are considered to be more in step with the Web's interactive structure.

Static, or passive presentations are abundant on the Web. This has more to do with ignorance of the medium than intent, because sites of this nature cannot adequately serve the growing needs of Web users—who are becoming more savvy and demanding by the day.

However, interactive, or *dynamic*, media moves away from the standard media with which most of us are familiar.

UNDERSTANDING INTERACTIVE MEDIA

Media presented in an interactive fashion is classified as *new media* because it takes traditional types of media such as print, graphic presentations, audio, animation, and even video, and places them at our fingertips.

→ Want to learn more about adding audio, video, and animation to your site? **See** "Audio, Video, and Streaming Media," **p. 666**

More importantly, perhaps, is that interactive, new media connects with us individually. Whether it is through community-based interactions, or by the power of choice offered to us via multimedia events, new media should be thought of as *active*. This isn't the TV of our youth. Although entertaining and informative, TV doesn't offer too many interactive events or choices for us.

This isn't to say that TV isn't relevant, but that the Web is *better*. I love television, and I particularly loved it as a child, when, in the quiet of morning with my parents still asleep, I would sneak into the den and turn on my favorite Saturday morning cartoons.

But here's how the Web is different. In my PJs, I would watch those cartoons, laughing at the Road Runner's antics. But while I was involved with the story line and enjoyed the personalities of my favorite cartoon characters, there were limits on this relationship. I could not touch the characters, could not alter their actions, and could not interact with them.

INTERACTING WITH MEDIA

Today's child can visit a Web site or view an interactive media presentation on a CD-ROM and have direct interaction with the characters. He or she can make decisions on where to go, how to follow a certain path of information, and very often, can affect the outcome of the environment by the selections or choices he or she makes within the process.

Not only can Web designers offer this information on a Web site, but interaction with other people via newsgroups, guestbooks, mail programs, and chat rooms can occur—with real people, all over the world.

And we can still do this in our PJs!

So from where does this interactivity come? In terms of the HTML author, the starting point is found within the Web's technical structure. Originally, it was a hypertext environment, delivered through the hypertext transfer protocol (HTTP). The desire that its creators had was to allow for the publication of text-based documents that could be hyperlinked to references and resources within that document.

→ For more understanding of the Hypertext Transfer Protocol (HTTP), **see** "Understanding HTML 4.0," **p. 17**

It didn't take long before hypertext became hypermedia. When graphical interfaces became available and began supporting non-text media such as photographs or art, that media in turn took advantage of the HTTP protocol. This meant that you could set a graphic up as the clickable link into the next document.

Today's many options allow Web developers to tap into this interactive environment.

Forms (see Figure 24.1), interactive games, multimedia events such as virtual reality or live cameras, community bulletin boards (see Figure 24.2), and real-time chat rooms all rely on HTML and the hypertext transfer protocol to enable the end user to interact with a Web site, or with other individuals on the Web.

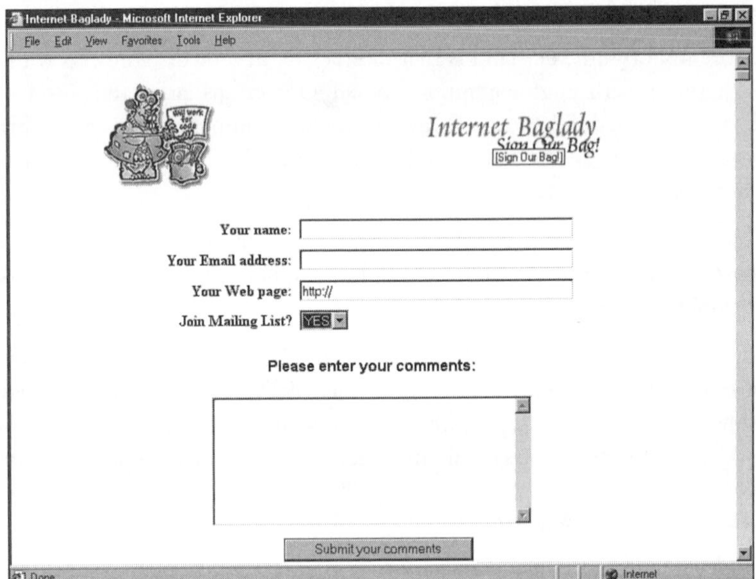

Figure 24.1
This feedback form allows Web site visitors to input information that allows them interaction with the site.

LINEARITY

A compelling aspect of the Web that stems from the hypermedia environment is that the Web's format can be interpreted as being *non-linear*. I believe that putting the Web in this context will help provide you with a frame of reference for a better understanding about how sites are built.

Books are read page-by-page. This is a linear activity. Another familiar, linear act is how most Westerners perceive time. We see it as a logical order of days, one following another in a line. It's interesting to note that in some cultures, time is perceived as a spiral. Linear activities dominate Western civilization, however, and that the Web is such a curiosity—and challenge to its developers—often relates to the fact that it is essentially *unlike* most of our familiar constructs.

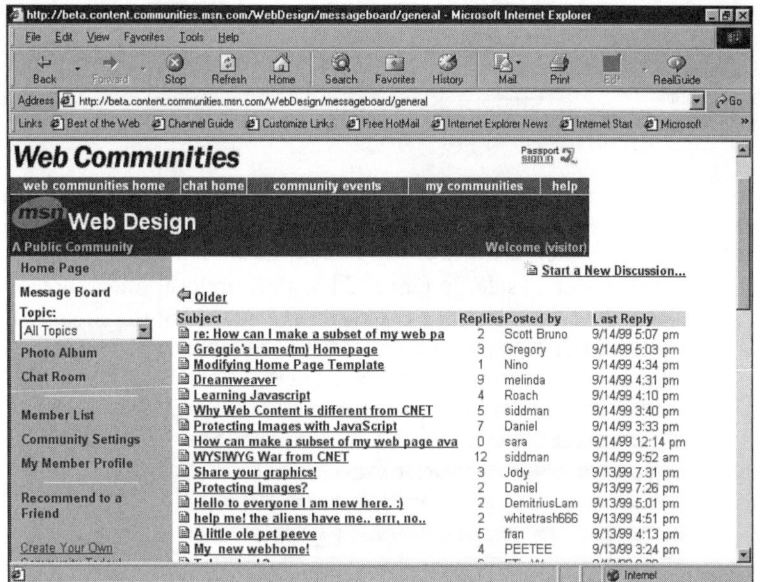

Figure 24.2
This Web design community gets to discuss important issues via the Web.

Web sites, unlike a book, can be constructed to take you from the middle of a sentence or a thought to another, ancillary thought. Or, that link can take you to some data whose relationship to the originating data is not immediately clear.

What happens when a person is interacting with information in this way is that he or she can, and often does, depart from this linear structure into one that allows for a more free-flowing, non-linear event. The popular term, *surfing the Web*, sums up this freedom well—suggesting that moving from Web site to Web site is a fun and fluid journey, rather than a strict, regimented one.

It becomes imperative that the individual designing Web pages understand how this environment offers organizational structures that are both like and unlike those with which we are most familiar—books and flow charts are linear and are perfectly acceptable for certain designs on the Web. But to tap into the non-linear world and make it a relevant experience for the Web site visitor is to enhance his or her experience, and challenge your own capabilities!

SITE STRUCTURE

Because most readers are accustomed to linear structure, and are most familiar with organizing information into such structures, it's very important to give most functional sites enough linearity to be comfortable and navigable.

A linear Web site would be much like a book. Each page is placed to the conceptual "right" of the next, and there's an opportunity to page forward or back. In Figure 24.3, I show a drawing reflecting the forward/back style of navigation.

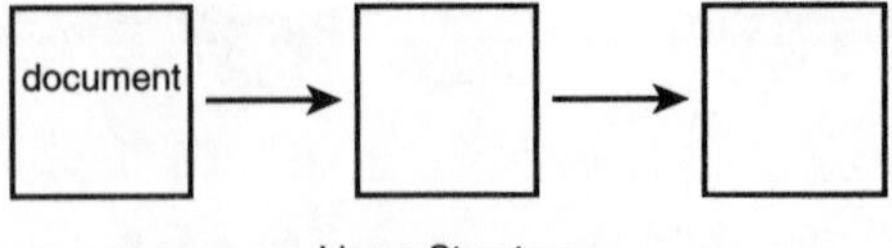

Figure 24.3
Linear structures resemble the forward/back layout of a book's pages.

Another familiar structure in our linear world is the *hierarchical*, or flow-chart method of mapping a Web site. In a case of this nature, I can offer links that move from level to level as well as from side to side. In Figure 24.4, a hierarchical site is shown. As you begin to add links that take you to multiple areas inside and outside of the site (see Figure 24.5), the linearity becomes less evident.

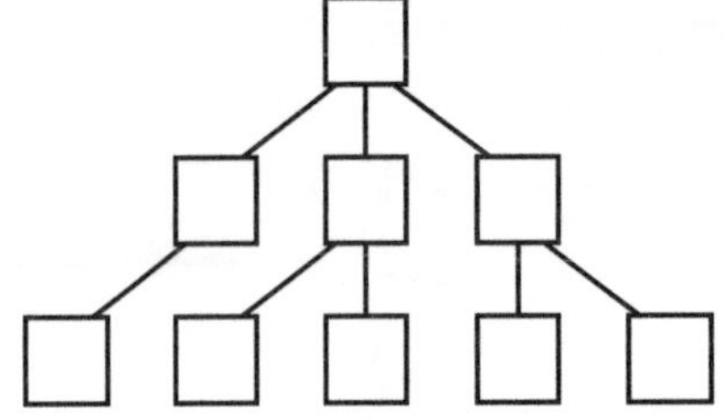

Figure 24.4
Hierarchical structures are more complex linear designs.

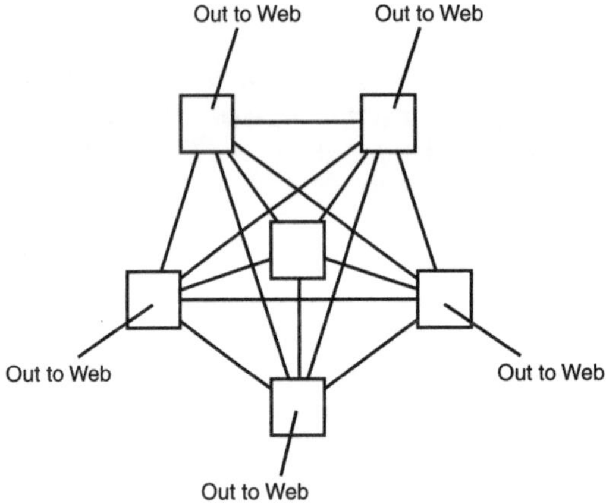

Figure 24.5
Multiple links to and from different documents inside and outside of the site begin to move the site away from a strict linear construct.

So what of a non-linear site? Well, a true non-linear site would have completely random links. What this means is that no matter where I clicked, I wouldn't know where in the Web world I was going to end up (see Figure 24.6).

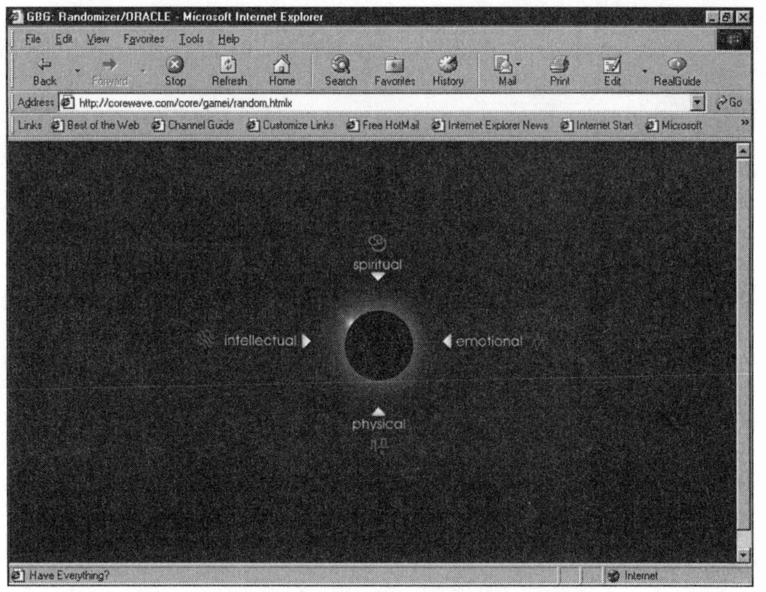

Figure 24.6
CoreWave's A Glass Bead Game I uses randomization so that you never know where you'll end up.

Is there a middle ground? You bet, and it's one that is encouraged because, as I mentioned, in most cases we want to give site visitors enough linearity so they are comfortable within the environment. How do we add some non-linear options to a site?

1. Begin with a linear or hierarchical structure.
2. Add links from any place within that site to another section of that same site.
3. Add links to external sites.

The non-linear experience in the result comes from the allowance for and encouragement of *user choice*. Every person coming to this site can conceivably surf it differently. This, in turn, creates an individual, flowing experience, rather than a highly structured one. However, we've been cautious by beginning with a linear structure to make the site sensible and help people maintain a sense of place.

USER INTERFACE DESIGN

Just as your smile and outward appearance help others identify what is interesting and appealing about you, a user interface is what allows Web visitors to want to stop and enjoy the bounty your site provides.

Interfaces serve to welcome, guide, and provide the functional elements required to assist your visitor in getting to the information or experience he or she is seeking. Considered a critical aspect of multimedia design, a well-built interface is particularly important for the Web. If an individual isn't finding the information required, or isn't having a meaningful adventure on your pages, he or she can simply choose to take a sharp turn off the road and visit another site. One, perhaps, that will be more interesting and informative for the visitor and profitable to your competitor.

One step to avoid creating sites that act as pit-stops or U-turns on the Web's highways and by-ways is to be sure that the sites you build make the visitor feel comfortable and provide that visitor with the goods he or she is after. This is done via a number of methods, including intelligent design as well as an attractive and *useful* site interface.

Several time-honored principles of user interface design should be applied to your Web site plans. These concepts are drawn from other media, such as interactive CD-ROMs, kiosks, and even television. The hypermedia environment of the Web—with its links to here, there, and everywhere in the vast and complex Internet world—is often bereft of these foundational principles. The results are ill-designed interfaces that confuse and frustrate rather than inform and assist the people who visit those Web sites.

The reason for the abundance of problems with user interfaces on the Internet has a lot to do with the fact that Web sites are often being built by computer engineers, high school students—even fine artists—all of whom have much to contribute content-wise to the Web environment, but little or no experience in what it takes to communicate in the unusual, non-linear structure of the Web.

Tip from molly

Ever hear the rather rude acronym, KISS? It stands for *Keep It Simple, Stupid!* User interfaces might be complicated technologically, but they should be easy for any user to understand.

The following principles can assist you in avoiding the potholes that inexperienced Web designers can find themselves driving into. Apply these ideas to the sites you build, and you stand a much better chance of a smooth ride toward your Web success.

METAPHOR

In design, *metaphor* refers to the symbolic representation of the structure you're attempting to build. A metaphor acts as a familiar visual aid around which you build the entryway, interiors, windows, doors, and exits of your environment.

In fact, I used metaphor to write the previous paragraph. I defined a Web site as though it was a building—with a selection of the elements you expect to find in a building. Metaphor helps people feel comfortable because they are familiar with the rules of the setting. A simple example of this can be found on Yahoo!, which uses a series of visual metaphors for its navigation, as you can see in Figure 24.7. Users relate the baby, which represents "new" to the link that has new information, and so forth. Visitors relate easily to the concept and are able to interact with the interface without having to think too much about how to do so.

Tip from molly

Metaphor should use common, everyday concepts that people from any part of the globe who come upon your site will be able to understand immediately.

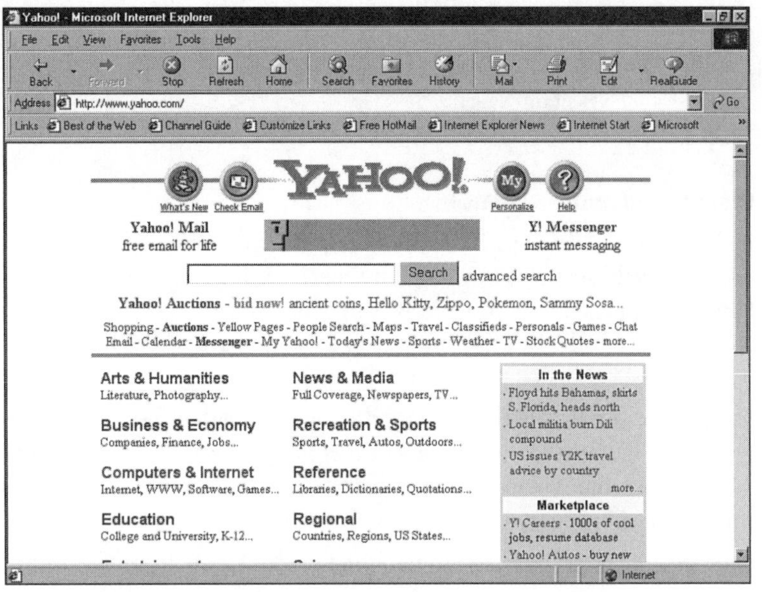

Figure 24.7
Visual metaphor on Yahoo! A Baby represents "What's New," a letter signifies "Check Email," the word My for "Personalize," and a question mark for "Help."

Achieve metaphor, and you're one step closer to helping that person make himself or herself comfortable and visit with you for awhile.

Clarity

To increase a visitor's desire to stay, be sure that he or she understands the elements within your pages. There should be no critical pieces that are abstract or difficult to decipher. This is not to say that abstraction as an art form isn't allowed—a good designer can use abstract art within a very clear Web site. What a good designer cannot do is use abstractions when it comes to those elements necessary to navigate the site, locate information, or return to critical areas within the site.

Elements that fall into this category include any buttons, imagemaps, or links that are necessary for site navigation. A button that leads the visitor to the left shouldn't have an arrow that faces up, a link that offers a mail option shouldn't pull up your newsreader. It's that simple, and that clear. Clarity is a must for precise communication.

Consistency

Consistency is not only one of utmost importance in interface design, it's one of the skeletal necessities of a Web site. All too often I find myself landing on a Web page and thinking "Wow, this looks great!" Then, as I move to the next page, I find myself wondering what happened to the inviting design and promise that first page offered. If I stay long enough to move through the site, backgrounds change, font styles are inconsistent, headers and navigation are completely irregular—in short, I can't tell from one page to the next where the heck in the Web world I am! Being consistent with design elements allows for a cohesive presentation. This keeps your visitors calm instead of tense, confused, and ready to take a hard left—right off of your site.

Tip from

Consistency can be gained by developing a site palette and sticking to the color theme in some regular fashion. Location and order of navigation is also a significant aspect of consistent UID design.

Orientation and Navigation

Following closely along with each of the prior concepts is the idea that a site visitor must know where he or she is at any given time. This is *orientation*. If I'm deep into a site that has hundreds of pages, it helps to know where in that site I am. It's also really good if I have quick access to other areas of the site and can go back where I came from if I find out I'm somewhere I really don't want, or need, to be.

Orientation is achieved by ensuring that each site either has a header that defines that page's purpose, or another, familiar element that instantly tells me where I am. You have probably seen a variety of methods to ensure orientation. As you can tell, navigation is not only connected with orientation, but with every individual user interface premise I've outlined.

One example of orientation can be found on the Wilde Rose Coffee Roastery site at `http://desert.net/wilderose/`. Note that an empty coffee cup helps define my location (see Figure 24.8).

Figure 24.8
The empty coffee cup orients the visitor to the page.

Tip from molly

It's one, two, three clicks away! If you make your visitor click more than three times to get to the information he or she is after, you run the risk of disorienting them. Ideally, no piece of data on your site is more than three clicks away from a related piece of data.

For now, suffice it to say that navigation is an integral part of interface design, and a critical element of any Web site. It's all about getting from way over there to right where you want to be, logically, quickly, and with ease.

Analyzing a Site's Intent

As with any project, one of the most important steps toward achieving effective design is to analyze your goals and contrive to meet them. A good Web site is always better when well-planned. Without planning, the results can be haphazard and confusing.

One place to begin is by examining the relationship between the site's intent, and the audience. The comparison tells you what directions to take in terms of short and long-term planning, what types of technology you need to support the design, and, of course, what kind of interface and site design best meet your needs.

Design Intent

Begin by asking the following questions:

- What is your primary reason for having this Web site?
- What current information and content do you have and consider important to include on the site?
- What are your short- and long-term goals for the site?

Is the site's purpose point-of-sales? Or, perhaps you are interested in providing customer service or product technical support for your company. Other possible intentions for Web sites include entertainment, product advertising and promotions, information and education, news, and special interest communities.

Company brochures, product photos and illustrations, prior advertising campaigns, interesting programs and games, news copy, art, URLs for existing, similar-interest Web sites, and a range of other materials already in your possession will help define the content of your site.

The best way to think about the short and long-term with regard to Web sites is by already knowing what your most immediate goal is. If your site intends to provide customer service for its line of notebook computers and the pressure's on to provide online support to consumers immediately, first determine which notebook models require the most service and support.

Then, look beyond the immediate demand to the long-term vision of the site. This will help determine the structure of the site, and, while you'll begin by providing what your customers need today, you'll also save yourself a lot of headaches by planning for what they're going to want tomorrow.

Audience Intent

Now, define your audience:

- What is your demographic or what demographic are you attempting to attract?
- What experience or information should the audience walk away with?

Are you attempting to sell rare books to collectors? Maybe you want to create a site that raises funds for Multiple Sclerosis. You might want to create a newspaper that caters to educated 30-somethings, or perhaps you want to create an interactive Web site for members of a particular city's gay community. No matter your intent, who you are creating for is going to impact the way your interface is designed.

The answer to the experiential aspect of a site is particularly important. If you have analyzed and planned to meet every other concern, but then fail to provide a specific experience, activity, or resource to your visitor as he or she leaves the site, you've missed your mark. Knowing that you want a visitor to walk away armed with knowledge about family planning options or with a vacation itinerary in hand allows you to design your site to achieve that goal.

SETTING GOALS

After you've successfully answered the questions, consider your goals in the context of the demographic. This is an infinitely important step, because when you sit down to design and code your site, you'll have a very clear idea of what type of interface to design. There will be a much more coordinated effort if your site is well-planned and organized.

Examining the information you've collected, you'll find that you now know several important things. First, you are aware of what your site's intent and long-term goals are. That relates to the practical design of your interface because it tells you what you need to design, and how much you need to design.

You then know what current information is available to you for content, and you know who the audience is, which determines the type of interface you'll use to deliver that information to them. Finally, you know what you want your audience to gain from your Web site. You are now poised to consider the look-and-feel, breadth and scope, and page-by-page content of the project.

→ For a look at methods for gathering demographic statistics, **see** "Using HTML 4.0 in the Real World," **p. 36**

CONCEIVING A DESIGN

With an understanding of what user interface design consists of, what is required of you to analyze the site and audience intent, and an example of a successful interface in hand, you're ready to begin thinking about how to implement a design.

How you actually express the knowledge you've gained in terms of Web technology will depend largely on what skills you have and what human as well as technological resources are available to you. Not everyone reading this chapter is going to have advanced HTML or design skills, but some will.

Another issue is the extent of the material you intend to provide. Some reader might simply want to promote his or her professional services as a massage therapist, but someone else reading this book may be looking for information on how to create interfaces for a daily newspaper with feedback and chat features.

To approach these varying circumstances and provide information to assist you in constructing the design you have in mind, I'm first going to go over some of the site elements with which you'll be working. Then I'll introduce two practical approaches to interface design: a standard level interface that requires basic HTML and graphic skills, and advanced interface design requiring tables for layout.

COMMON PAGES WITHIN A WEB SITE

The following is a list of common pages within a Web site:

- Welcome page
- Content pages
- Feedback page

Other aspects that you might need to accommodate include the following:

- Downloadable media (programs, files, sound, and video)
- Inline media (audio, video, and multimedia presentations that run within the browser's parameters)
- Search functions
- Gateways to chat rooms, bulletin boards, and newsgroups

The challenge now is to incorporate the common elements and special aspects into a single, integrated format. A Welcome page can be very different in look-and-feel than a content-laden page, and those will be different from a page that needs to support inline media such as a surround video presentation of the new car your company is unveiling.

By using the foundations learned earlier in this chapter such as consistency, clarity, orientation, and well-designed navigation, you should have little trouble keeping even the largest of sites conceptually joined from page to page.

WELCOME PAGE: THE FRONT DOOR

The first part of interface design is deciding what the virtual front door of your site is going to look like, and how that front door will integrate with the content pages within the site. Some designers prefer to have a page that is predominantly graphical in nature—much like a traditional magazine cover. Other designers like a functional greeting, or "splash" page, with graphics as well as navigational options available. And there are designers who take the stance that since people want to get to the information fast, a splash page is a waste of time.

I feel that each individual client and site is going to have unique needs. Therefore, it's advisable that you use the research you've conducted concerning goals and audience to determine what is going to work best in a given scenario. Some designers will choose to have a splash page, others will not. Either way, it's critical that you are consistent with your design.

Caution

The glue of a site is integration. This means that if you do have a splash page, and that page looks nothing like your internal pages, you have no interface. Be sure to keep a cohesive look-and-feel for your pages.

A good splash page should convey the site's identity as well as give an introduction to some of the site's design elements including logos, color, shape, typography, and texture (see Figure 24.9).

If you choose not to have a splash page, it's wise to ensure that a visitor is welcomed on your home page. Even if you have a lot of information and detailed navigation on that first page, be sure to let your visitor know who you are and why you are there. It's also handy to tell or suggest to the site visitor what you hope will be experienced or gained from a site's visit.

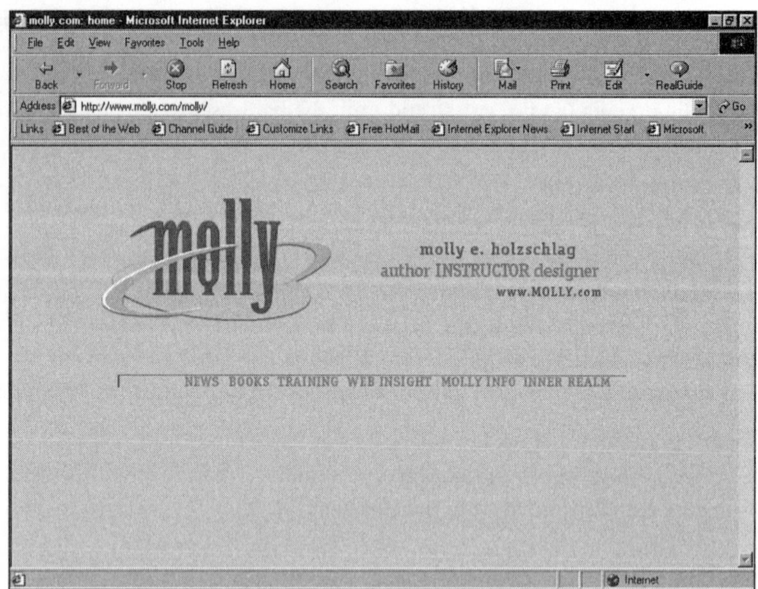

Figure 24.9
My Web site uses my logo, standard colors, shapes, and type styles for identity and branding.

Note

Are there any exceptions to rules such as "always have a welcome" or "identify yourself on a splash page?" Yes, but they will be determined by your audience and intent, and any exceptions will tend to be for entertainment, games, or artistic sites rather than corporate, consumer, or customer service sites.

Remember, your front door is the first opportunity you have to make people feel welcome and interested in the content to come. Think carefully and apply the principles of user interface design to achieve an instant rapport with your visitors.

Content Pages

As a person continues to move through a site, each page should offer a combination of consistent and new features. Consistency can be achieved with such traits as color palettes and fonts, and fresh components can be added by using a variety of layouts, graphics, and other multimedia options.

The objective in terms of interface is to keep each page interesting so that visitors are compelled to see what's coming next—not just in terms of the information you have to impart, but in terms of the visual panorama that unfolds as they move throughout the site (see Figure 24.10).

→ Learn more about working with color, **see** "Color Concepts," **p. 528**

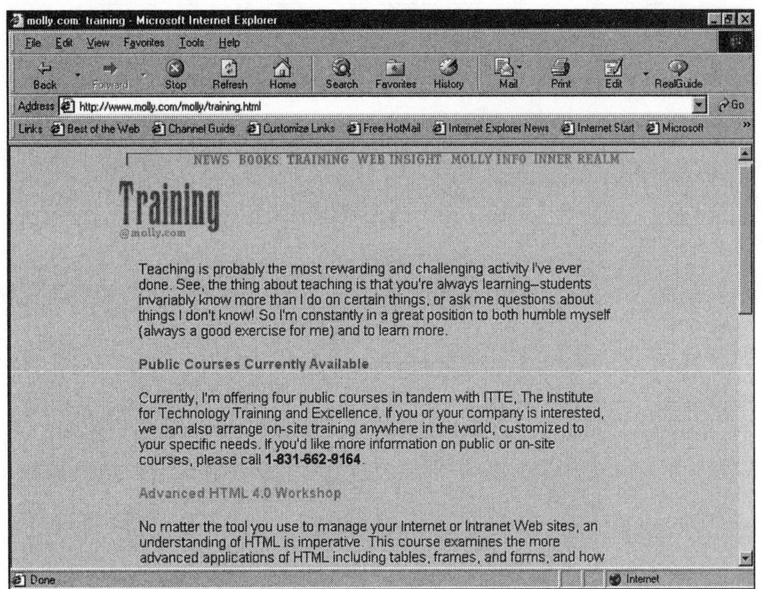

Figure 24.10 Internal content pages should remain consistent with the splash page. Shapes, fonts, and color help maintain this consistency.

FEEDBACK

Feedback forms should be looked at as part of a design. Many good designers keep a consistent look-and-feel in a site and suddenly lose that consistency because they didn't design the form to be neat and attractive, fitting in with the concept of the site.

→ Learn how to design great forms, **see** "Building Forms," **p. 384**

Keep your colors, fonts, and layouts intact when dealing with forms. Wherever possible, align the right end of feedback fields with one another. This creates a neat and tidy appearance, which speaks to the issue of clarity. Web site visitors may not consciously be aware of why your forms are so easy to use, but they will appreciate it and remember your site as one of convenience that they'll use again and even recommend to interested friends.

ADDING MEDIA AND PROGRAMMING

These three elements—welcome page, content pages, and feedback pages—are the most commonly used within all Web sites, even very large ones. However, there is an increasing demand to provide a variety of highly interactive content using advanced scripting, database, multimedia, and Web programming techniques.

Figure 24.11 shows an example of a multimedia exhibit on the Arizona-Sonora Desert Museum Web site, which requires a nice chunk of the page's space. This means that the interface design might have to adjust to accommodate the media. How do you maintain cohesiveness between the design of your interface when so much of the space is being used by an object?

Note

Take a virtual visit to the amazing Arizona-Sonora Desert Museum, `http://www.desertmuseum.org/`.

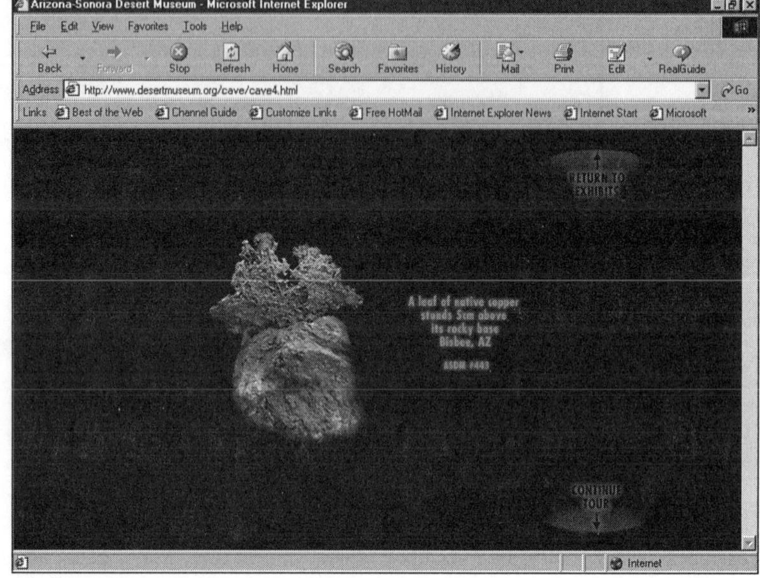

Figure 24.11
This image of native copper ore and the interface features on the Arizona-Sonora Desert Museum site take up significant space which can result in the need to make design adjustments elsewhere in the site.

If you jumped to answer that question and your responses involved consistency, clarity, and maintenance of similar elements from other parts of the site, you're on track to addressing the greatest challenge in interface design.

PAGE LAYOUT TECHNIQUES

Planning and understanding structure provide a strong foundation for the next step: laying out your pages. There are two good ways of doing this.

HAND-DRAWN LAYOUTS

This method is always a great way to get your creative juices flowing. It's also a great starting point for individual page designs.

I personally like to use a sketch board and pencils. I'll simply draw a rectangle representing each screen for the individual pages I require. Then I quickly sketch my ideas. This gives me a preliminary starting point, and from here, I tend to move on to using Photoshop to jump in and lay out my ideas, adding color and style.

USING PHOTOSHOP OR OTHER IMAGING PROGRAM

Some people don't bother with the hand-drawn approach, but I find it a great way to begin. Either way, Photoshop is where I, and most professional designers, do their page mockups. If you use another imaging program, you can still work with the concepts presented here.

→ To decide which imaging tool is best for you, **see** "Web Graphic Formats and Professional Tools," **p. 566**

One of the reasons I find Photoshop to be superior in this application to other graphic tools is due to the layers and history features. Photoshop allows you to put different elements on different layers, and you can then save that file, enabling you to make adjustments in color and style later. And, should you want to go back and make a change, the history palette keeps all your moves in memory.

Furthermore, Photoshop allows you to control the entire grid of your page, pixel by pixel, as shown in Figure 24.12.

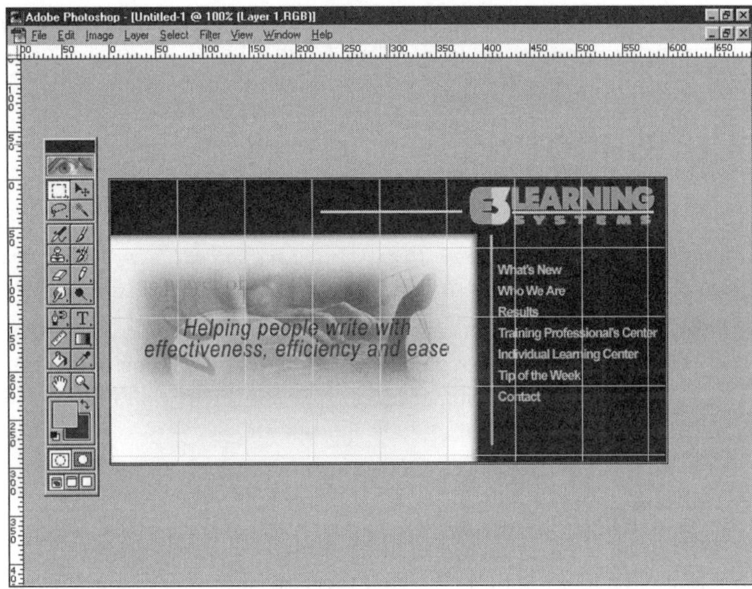

Figure 24.12
Laying out a page in Photoshop. Note the rulers and grid.

The first step is to create a page. To accommodate the varied resolutions on the Web, most Web designers use the 640×480 pixels per screen rule. If you add to that the parts of the browser that eat up Web real estate, you're left with a safe 585×295 pixels per screen working area.

→ For more details about working with the computer screen, **see** "Resolution, Gamma, and the Visual Environment," **p. 546**

Designing to this dimension will create a page with no scrolling on either the horizontal or vertical axes. Although your page length can certainly vary, it's wise to keep to the 585-pixel width to avoid unstable design, or use dynamic layouts.

Note

How long should a Web page be? Most professionals recommend using approximately three screens. That would give you between 295 pixels and about 1,000 pixels per page. Obviously you will need to be flexible with this measurement depending upon your audience and particular needs.

→ To learn more about fixed and dynamic designs using tables, **see** "Advanced Table Layouts," **p. 336**

The concepts and examples in this chapter should set you well on your way to being able to design effective interfaces using HTML.

Remember that understanding the parts of something is important to relating to it as a whole. This is clearly demonstrated when you study user interface design. By thinking carefully about concepts such as metaphor, clarity, and orientation, you become able to strengthen the parts of the interface.

Analyzing audience, intent, and the type of experience you want your site visitors to have give you perspective as to the bigger picture, leading you to a more cohesive, easier to use, and, ultimately, a more professional Web site.

Troubleshooting

Linearity

I want to create a site that moves from page to page without many links within the pages. I understand that this is a linear site. Is it going to upset visitors if I use strict linearity on the Web?

The answer lies in the intent of the site. If you're creating a portal site, a page to page without many links is simply not going to work. However, if you're creating a guided tour where you want to bring your visitor from one piece in an art exhibit to the next in a precise fashion, the linear site will be absolutely appropriate.

Metaphor

Is metaphor necessary to create good sites?

Many sites choose not to use metaphorical images to represent navigation elements. Instead, choosing words for the navigable content, such as New, About Us, and Contact, works perfectly well.

Designing for the Real World

Designing an Effective Page

This project teaches you how to use an imaging program to design an effective page. I'll use Photoshop, but you can use the image tool of your choice—the basic instructions will be the same, except where working with layers comes into play if your software doesn't support layers.

To create a workspace for your page design, follow these steps.

1. Open Photoshop, and choose File, New.
2. In the New dialog box, place your width and height in pixels. Remember that your width should be 585—even if you're going to create a dynamic design. This keeps your page elements to an appropriate size. Your length can vary. In Figure 24.13 I've set up a working area of 585 pixels by 295 pixels for a non-scrolling page.

Figure 24.13

I've set up a work area of 585 pixels by 295 pixels for my non-scrolling splash page.

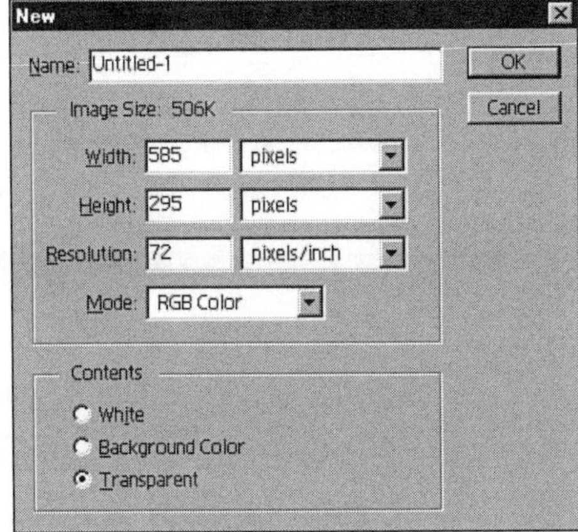

3. Be sure that you're working in RGB (you will optimize individual graphics later), using a transparent page, and that you are set at 72 dpi.

Now you're ready to add color and images.

USING PHOTOSHOP LAYERS

Photoshop layers, as mentioned, are perhaps the most powerful aspect of Photoshop. By using them, you have absolute control over each part of a design.

Remember to create a new layer for each part of your page.

1. With your new image active, choose Layer, New, Layer.
2. Select your background color using the eyedropper tool and color palette. Select Window, Show Color.
3. Fill the layer with the proposed browser-safe color selection you want by choosing Edit, Fill. Make sure you select Foreground and uncheck the Transparency box in the Fill dialog box.
4. Create a new layer, following the directions in step 1.

In this layer, you'll add your background pattern (see Chapter 28, "Creating Professional Web Graphics"). I have mine prepared and saved in native Photoshop format as background.psd.

1. Open your background image file.
2. Choose Select, All.
3. Choose Edit, Select Define Pattern.
4. Move to your new layer on the workspace.
5. Choose Edit, Fill, Pattern, and let your image fill the layer.

Now you can add a text header.

1. Click your workspace to bring up the Text dialog box.
2. Now choose your typeface, size, leading, and spacing. In most cases you'll want to be sure you have the Anti-Aliased check box checked. I've chosen a decorative typeface at 14 points (see Figure 24.14).

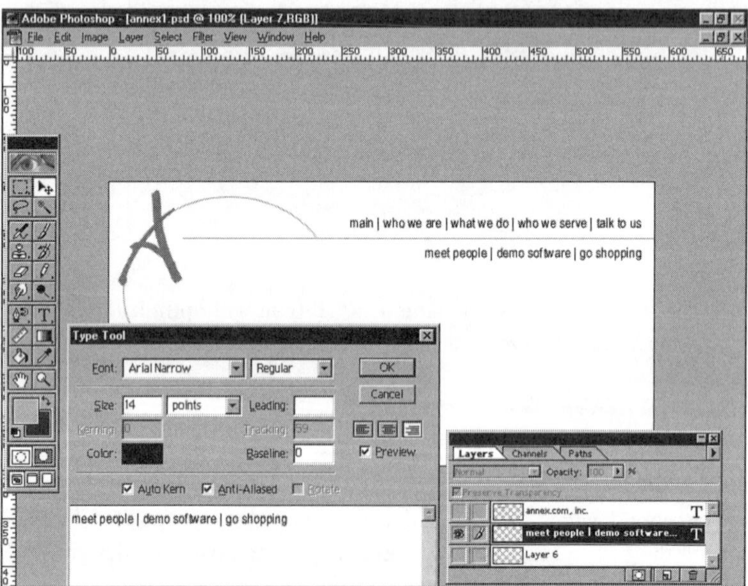

Figure 24.14
Here I've added type to a Photoshop layer that will become part of my overall design.

3. Click OK.
4. Place the text where desired by using the Move tool.

Continue creating layers and adding elements as you want. Remember to create a new layer for each element so that you have optimum control of that element.

Tip from molly

You can anticipate body text by creating individual layers with the paragraphs you'll want to use, but in most cases you'll be relying on HTML to create that text. Default body text is typically around 12-point Times on the PC, and 12-point Geneva on the Macintosh.

After you have a page with which you are satisfied, save the file as a Photoshop file (choose File, Save, PSD). If you're using a different imaging program that has layers, save to that program's native format. I like to do this so that I can keep the layers intact, enabling me to come back later and make any necessary adjustments to the fonts, colors, and positions of my elements.

Caution

Make sure you save the file with the layers intact. Never flatten a file that you want to use for layout. If you do, you'll lose the ability to go in and manipulate the position, size, color, or other attributes of the element on that layer.

You can now use this layout to not only make adjustments to the design, but to actually generate your graphics.

→ To learn how to generate graphics from a layered file, **see** "Creating Professional Web Graphics," **p. 598**

CHAPTER 25

Color Concepts

In this chapter

COLOR THEORY

What color blouse or shirt are you wearing today? I'm wearing white. It's a hot day here in the desert, and white seems to make me feel cooler.

If you think about it carefully, you probably were motivated to pick out the clothing you're wearing right now because of a practical or psychological need. Don't laugh! Okay, so maybe you grabbed the last clean shirt in the pile—but undoubtedly that shirt is from a spectrum of colors in which you feel comfortable.

Color, and how it influences the many facets of our world, is a powerful force. Although HTML is the foundation on which we build our designs, color is a pillar of the design itself—how it impacts the site visitor, the emotional message it sends, and how it blends to create an esthetic Web page.

To understand color, it's important to visit the theory that exists surrounding it. The idea here is to refine your eye and your understanding of how color works so that you can use it in effective ways.

If you have a window nearby, look out. In the natural world, we have a wide range of colors. There's everything from the bright green of a new leaf, to the shocking orange of an Arizona sunset. In between these bold extremes, nature shows its subtle hand—a soft blue sky, a slate gray rock, the light tan patches on my cat's fur.

The computer environment is more limited than nature, and when we take a closer look at the Web environment, these limitations become even more stringent. Yet, an understanding of the colors that exist and how they work gives you an undeniable edge when it comes to using color in Web design that leaves a lasting impression.

SUBTRACTIVE COLOR

Colors in the natural world are made up of pigments. Pigment is a substance that reacts to light. You might have heard it said that without light, there is no color. This is true, and without pigment, there is no *variation* in color.

Subtractive color is the theoretical premise on which color in the natural world is based. It's called subtractive because it absorbs light first, *before* transmitting or reflecting the results that our eyes perceive as color.

Subtractive color theory exists to help both industrialists and artists understand and try to recreate nature's own design. With this premise as a guide, pigments are recreated chemically in paints, dyes, and inks.

Remember the color wheel? A color wheel is the circular representation of subtractive color, with different colors making up pie slices within the wheel. The color wheel begins with what is known as the *primary* colors: red, green, and yellow.

Each of these colors can be mixed together to come up with an entire spectrum of colors.

Digital information, however, is dealt with differently. Computers and computer hardware are quite limited in their capability to deliver color to a screen. You can't compete with nature!

But, we do try. And the way we do this is by using a different color method. Because it's not possible for a computer to first absorb light, it must generate light. Therefore, the type of color we see on our computers is backed by a theory referred to as *additive synthesis*.

Additive Synthesis

In additive synthesis, color is created by the addition of colors. Computers use three colors to do this: red, green, and blue. It's almost as if three individual paint guns are being fired at your screen, combining color and light to create variations.

Red, Green, and Blue color is referred to as "RGB." As we look into how to work with digital color, this will be the technical foundation for the decisions we make. However, it's the subtractive world from which we gain our inspiration. It's important to keep this distinction in mind.

So how come the natural world can make all colors from red, blue, and yellow, but computers cannot? It goes back to the difference between the ability to absorb versus the ability to transmit light, and how light then interacts with what is absorbed or transmitted. If you mix red and green by using paint, you get brown. But guess what happens when a computer mixes those same colors? The resulting color is yellow.

Computer Delivery of Color

Computers rely on three primary pieces of hardware to deliver color information to you, including a computer's CPU, video graphics card, and the computer monitor itself.

It stands to reason then that the quality of color you see at your computer depends on the quality and capability of these components. If any one of these components is incompatible or unequal in its properties, the end results will not be as true and refined as possible.

Furthermore, computer platforms (OSs) have differing capabilities when it comes to color. In terms of the computers and OSs you might be using—the Macintosh is known for its higher-end color; Windows 3.1 is very limited, Windows 95 and later has very good color control, and, if you're using a standard UNIX machine, you're at a disadvantage, with lower color capabilities.

The reason this is important to you is so that you have an understanding of how, and why, you must learn to work with the color limitations and standards that exist. Knowing your own machine, and the capabilities of your viewing audience, will help you do just that.

Add to this the fact that any GUI, such as a browser, affects the management of color, and you've got an important issue in color technology: In Web design, it is the browser that limits its color significantly.

This is the bane of the Web designer's existence when it comes to color, but I promise you, it's not insurmountable. In this chapter I'll show you some techniques to help you manage color effectively.

Note

Does the fact that hardware and software is limited mean that computer color is considered substandard? Not at all. This is especially true of high-end, specialty machines such as SGI (Silicon Graphics Incorporated) machines. SGI is used in film and video because the colors it's capable of are truest to those found in the natural world.

If you come from a graphics background or have worked with Photoshop or other professional graphics programs, you're probably familiar with other color management methods (also referred to as *color spaces*). One of the most familiar is CMYK (Cyan, Magenta, Yellow, Black) output. Other management systems include grayscale, which contains black, white, and gradations of gray; and indexed color, which is a limited palette of specific colors defined by the designer. In Web design, indexed color is extremely important because it provides one method by which to intentionally make graphics smaller in weight and therefore easier to download quickly.

→ To learn how to work with indexed color, **see** "Web Graphic Formats and Professional Tools," **p. 566**

ELEMENTS OF COLOR

As mentioned earlier, there is no color without light. Of course, that could be said for all of life. Plants and animals (including the human variety) require light for their very existence.

Although light is necessary, color is not. In fact, many people cannot perceive color, or they perceive color improperly such as in the common condition known as color blindness. However, for those of us with normal color perception, color is a significant aspect of our emotional and artistic life. In fact, it's so much a part of us that we might not necessarily even know what motivates us to pick out certain colors for our wardrobes—yet we do it.

Artists and designers have been trained to understand and use the elements of color as a method of communication. Web designers, however, often do not come from design backgrounds and don't have a full understanding of what color can do, what it means, and how to harness its power and use it to create sites with maximum communicative potential.

This section will help those individuals who do not have a strong background in design look at a variety of color elements that impact design, including color types, properties, relationships, and special effects. For those of you with an artistic background, revisiting these elements will help you put them into the perspective of the Web.

CATEGORIES OF COLOR

Color is defined by how colors are combined. Although the method of combination is going to differ when we compare the subtractive, natural world to the digital, additive one, the end results are the same in terms of our perception of color.

Colors categories are defined as follows:

- **Primaries**—All colors are the results of some combination of three colors: red, yellow, and blue. These colors are referred to as primary because they are the first colors to technically exist. Without them, no other color is possible.
- **Secondaries**—The next step is to mix pairs of the primaries together. If I mix red and yellow, I come up with orange. Blue and yellow create green, and purple is created by mixing red with blue. Orange, green, and purple are the secondary colors found on the color wheel.
- **Intermediates**—When two primaries are mixed together, the results are referred to as intermediate color. These colors are gradations that lie between the primary and secondary colors.

Along with these categories, you can achieve additional categories by adding white or black. When you add white to a given color, you achieve *tint*. Black added to a color darkens it. This is referred to as *shade*.

Note

Colors that are next to one another on the wheel, such as blue and purple, have a distinct relationship and are considered to be *similar*. Opposing colors, such as orange and blue, are *complementary*. Red and green, which are three colors removed from each other on the wheel, are *contrasting* colors.

PROPERTIES OF COLOR

The past several years have been very exciting in the fashion design world. There's a lot of texture, plenty of style, and a wide host of colorful names for color.

Bordeaux. Banana. Spice. Where do these colors fit into the spectrum? What determines the difference between cobalt and peacock, even if they are both blue?

The way in which differentiation of this nature is made is by defining the *properties* of color. Color properties are determined by the type and amount of color as well as how much light is used in that color, as follows:

- **Hue**—This term is used to differentiate one color from another. For example, red is different than green, and purple is different than brown. Whether a color is primary, secondary, intermediate, or tertiary isn't important with regard to hue, that they are different in terms of actual color is.
- **Value**—Chocolate brown is darker than tan, and sky blue is lighter than navy. A color's value is defined by the amount of light or dark in that color.
- **Saturation**—Also referred to as intensity, you can think of saturation as being the brightness of a color. Peacock blue is very bright, whereas navy is rather dull. Similarly, those popular neon lime greens reminiscent of the 1960s are much more intense than a forest green.

- **Warmth**—Hues found in the yellow-to-red range are considered to be warm. They emit a sense of heat.
- **Coolness**—Cool colors are those ranging from green to blue. Think of ice blue, or the cool sense a deep green forest can inspire.

If you look at these definitions, you can see that a given hue can contain a value and saturation. When you think of all the variations that are potentially held within each of these properties, you can begin to see that color is much more than meets the eye.

Of course, you might notice that black and white are missing from this list. Black can be described as absence of light, and white as *being* light. A more technical way to think about black and white is to refer to the properties of hue and saturation. The fact? Neither black nor white possess hue *or* saturation.

Note

Why then, are there "shades" of gray? The reason is found in value. The amount of light or dark in white or black determines the resulting value of gray.

Color Relationships

"Blue, blue, my world is blue,
blue is my world, since I'm without you.
Red, red, my eyes are red,
crying for you, alone in my bed."

Colors are emotional, and they have emotional relationships with one another. In a compatible relationship, harmony reigns. In a discordant relationship, clashing occurs.

In design, relationships are very important, because both harmonious as well as discordant color schemes can be effective, depending on the circumstances.

If I'm trying to convey a peaceful environment, I'm going to want to use harmonious colors. An example of this would be creating a palette from soft, subtle pastels. The end result is going to be calm and even feminine.

However, if I want to wake people up and jangle them a bit, I might try a discordant relationship. Bright yellow and red with black is going to create discord, but the visual impact is intense. Depending on the audience and the communication issues at hand, the discordant relationship might be a more appropriate choice than the harmonious one.

Special Color Effects

Light, and how it interacts with color, creates special color effects. As a designer, you can learn to use these effects to enhance your designs.

Color effects include the following:

- **Luster**—Luster is the term used to describe a shining quality usually seen in fabrics such as satin or silk. Luster results from the way light is absorbed by certain areas of a texture contrasting with black areas of the background color.
- **Iridescence**—The inside of seashells, pearls, and opals are iridescent. Instead of the light splotches contrasting with black, the background color is usually some shade of gray.
- **Luminosity**—Similar to luster and iridescence, the difference here is the quantity of contrast. When there is very delicate contrast between the lighter areas and background areas, luminosity is created.
- **Transparency**—Think of a piece of tape or colored glass. Light passes through, creating a clear or transparent effect.

You can create all these effects by mimicking what happens in nature.

To demonstrate what these effects look like, I opened up Photoshop and went to work. You can step with me through the process of making examples of special color effects, using any image editor you like that has similar functions.

To create color effects, follow these steps:

1. In Photoshop, select File, New.
2. Create a workspace with the dimensions of 200×200 pixels. Be sure your background is set to Transparent and the mode is RGB. DPI should be 72.
3. On the toolbar, click the color square and fill it with a gray color.
4. Now select Edit, Fill.
5. Fill your workspace with black.
6. Select Layer, Add New Layer from the menu.
7. Select the airbrush from the toolbar.
8. From the brush palette, choose a fairly soft brush (see Figure 25.1).

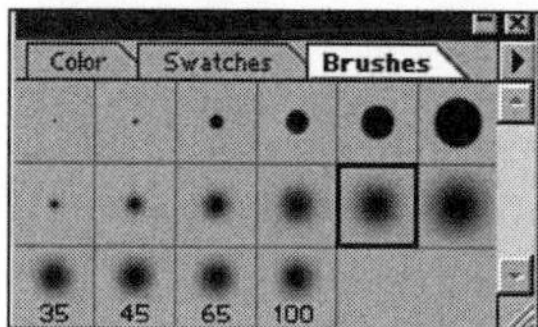

Figure 25.1
Choosing a soft brush from the brushes palette in Photoshop.

9. Now paint a shape on your second layer, allowing some areas to be gray and others showing the first layer's black, as I have done in Figure 25.2.

The results are a lustrous effect. You can save your file as `luster.psd` (in Photoshop format) for an example for later reference and use.

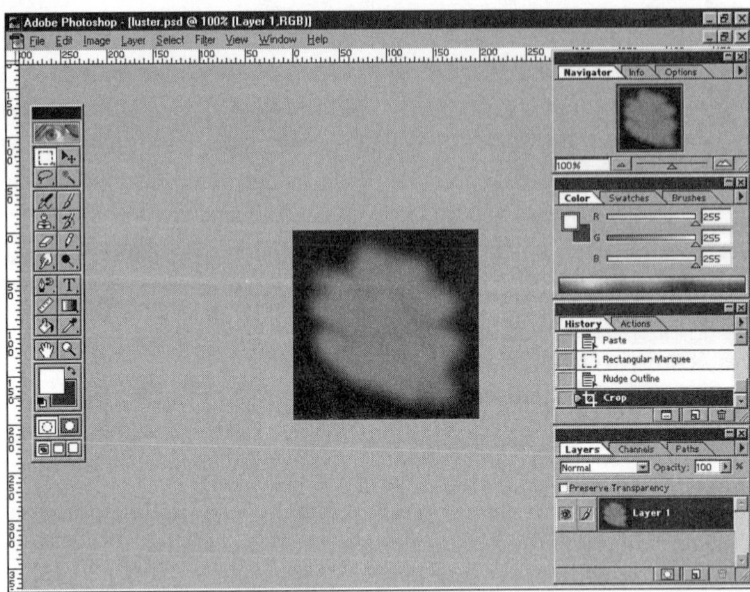

Figure 25.2
Luster is achieved by contrasting color with black.

To create an iridescent look, follow these steps:

1. In Photoshop, open `luster.psd`.
2. Fill the background layer with white.
3. Save your results as `iridescence.psd`, and compare them to Figure 25.3.

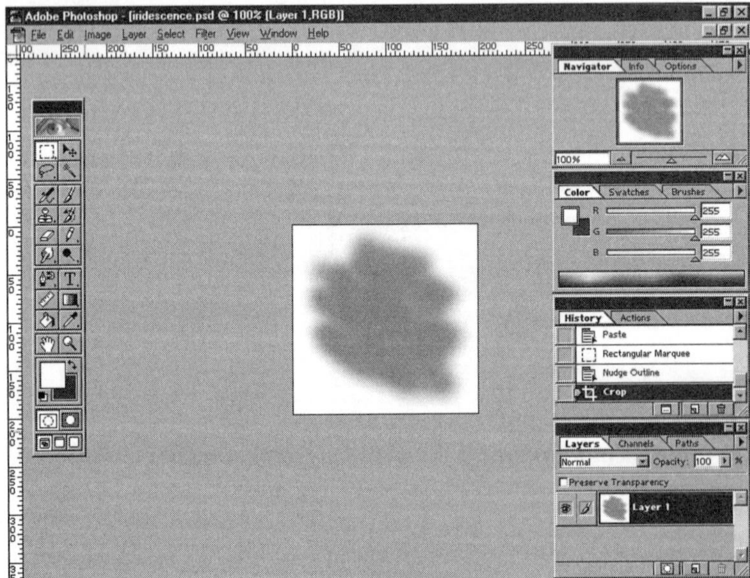

Figure 25.3
Iridescence is the result of mixing light and gray.

Because luminosity is a more delicate approach, I painted a lighter gray around the edges of the form, and then changed the background in `iridescence.psd` to the same gray as in the original luster example. Figure 25.4 shows my results.

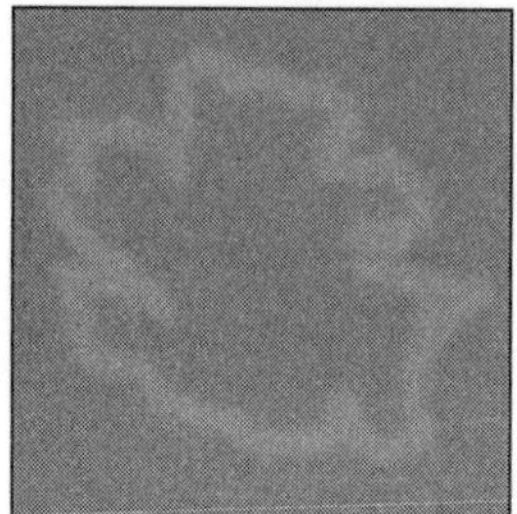

Figure 25.4
Luminescence: delicate, subtle contrast is the name of the luster game.

Transparent effects can be created as follows:

1. In Photoshop, create a new 200×200 pixel area workspace.
2. Select any color from the swatches palette (I selected blue).
3. Create a smaller square within your workspace by using the Marquee tool.
4. Fill that square with the red.
5. From the layers palette, drag the Opacity slider down to 50%.
6. Your color is now transparent (see Figure 25.5).

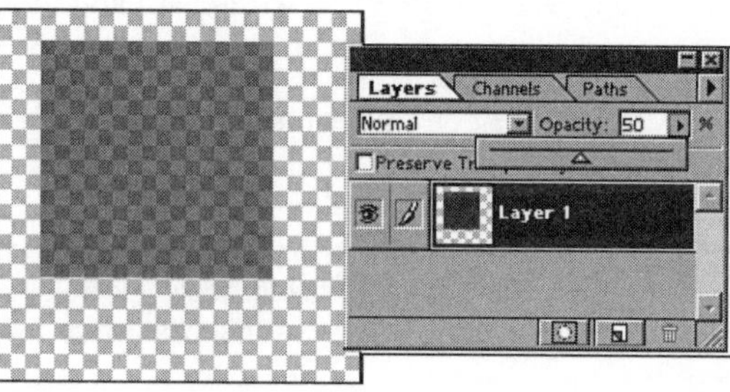

Figure 25.5
Transparent color.

You can save this file as `transparent.psd` for later reference. I went on to add several other sections of transparent color. My results can be seen in Figure 25.6.

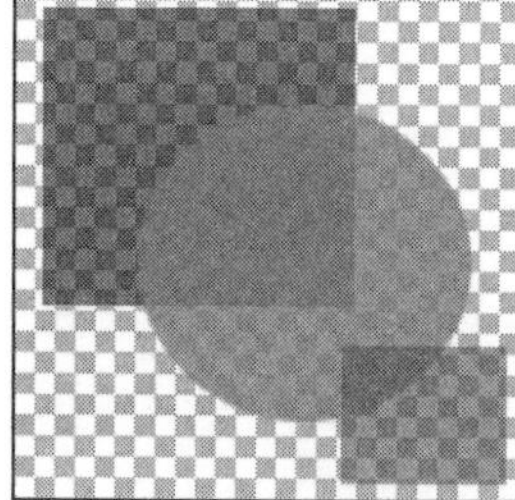

Figure 25.6
In this case, I've layered transparent sections of color on top of one another.

Color Significance

To those of you who are familiar with it, the "Wired" look is memorable. Using neon and discordant colors, the magazine as well as the HotWired Web site (**`http://www.hotwired.com/`**) communicate energy.

My mother hates me in black. She says it makes my skin look lackluster and yellowish. She's right, but I still like to wear black. Why? It soothes me. It neutralizes my sense of my body and calms me.

Ever notice how all-night restaurants are usually very brightly lit? This is thought to help keep people awake.

The more you look for examples of the significance of color, the more you'll find them. Colors are even associated with specific professions, ages, and genders: white and green for doctors and nurses; darker or more neutral colors for older people, pink for girls, and blue for boys.

None of this is accidental. In fact, it's very specific. Color has strong impact on the human psyche. This has been shown to be true in countless studies.

However, the intriguing issue is that color alone doesn't create this impact. Culture has a profound influence in how we perceive color, too.

Recently, there was a trend in some Western countries to marry in black—the bride and her bridesmaids as well as the men used black material in their formal bridal wear. This upset a lot of people, as Westerners tend to associate black with death and mourning.

But in some cultures, the color that we normally associate with purity and brides—white—is the color of death. In East India, for example, white is the color of the death shroud and mourning costumes.

Tip from molly

Since readers of this book come from different backgrounds, it's a great exercise for each of you to determine what specific emotional and cultural responses given colors represent to you.

It's important for you—a Web designer working in a global medium—to have some sense of what colors signify. Although I can't give you a run-down of cultural color significance in one chapter, I can give you some general meanings of color. I do advise that if you're doing work for a client from a different culture, it will be well worth your while to ask a bit about color perception in that individual's culture. This can help you avoid uncomfortable, time-consuming situations.

Here's a bit about color significance in the Western world. Remember, these are generalizations, and other interpretations do exist.

Color	**Significance**
Black	Death, darkness, elegance, sophistication
White	Purity, cleanliness, refinement
Red	Passion, intense energy, anger
Green	Healing, nature, earth
Blue	Dignity, power, stability
Yellow	Happiness, vibrancy, youth
Purple	Royalty, riches, sumptuousness

Note

Color designer and researcher J.L. Morton offers up fascinating information on color at her Web site, Colorcom, at `http://www.colorcom.com/`. Electronic, "Color Voodoo" books can help inspire and guide you when working with color. You can download these (for a fee) from `http://www.colorvoodoo.com/`.

Now that you have familiarity with the types and meanings of color, and have a good foundation in color theory, it's time to apply these ideas to the Web.

WEB COLOR TECHNOLOGY

You've already become familiar with color management methods for the computer screen. The one I emphasized as a starting point for Web-based color is RGB, or "Red, Green, Blue" color management.

To effectively work with color on the Web, however, you have to take RGB a step further and convert it into a system of values that HTML will recognize. This system is known as *hexadecimal*.

Hexadecimal, referred to simply as "hex," is the base 16 number system. Base 16 is an *alphanumeric* system, consisting of both numbers and letters in combinations that in the context of the Web browser translate as color. Hexadecimal uses the numbers 0–9 and the letters A–F. All hexadecimal values should contain a total of six characters for HTML to understand it. The first pair in the series of six equals the amount of red in the color; the second pair equals the amount of green; and the third pair, blue.

Tip from molly

If at any time you get a single character in Hex conversion, such as a single `0` or letter `D`, simply enter a `0` *before* the hex character so that the resulting binary information will be accurate.

Remember your computer science? A single byte is made up of 8 bits of information. Every two characters within a hex value makes up one byte, or 8 bits. This means that each hex value contains 24 bits of color information.

It's no accident that RGB color is also known as *24-bit color*.

How do you find the hex value of RGB colors? A scientific calculator is one way. Another way is to use one of the many converters available right on the Web.

Converting RGB to Hex

To convert an RGB value to hexadecimal by using a scientific calculator, follow these steps:

1. Find the RGB value of your color. You can do this in Photoshop by passing your cursor over the color. The information pop-up (see Figure 25.7) displays the red, green, and blue values. In this case, I chose a medium brown.
2. Write down each of these values. From my chosen color in Figure 25.7, I wrote out the following:

red	86
green	53
blue	13

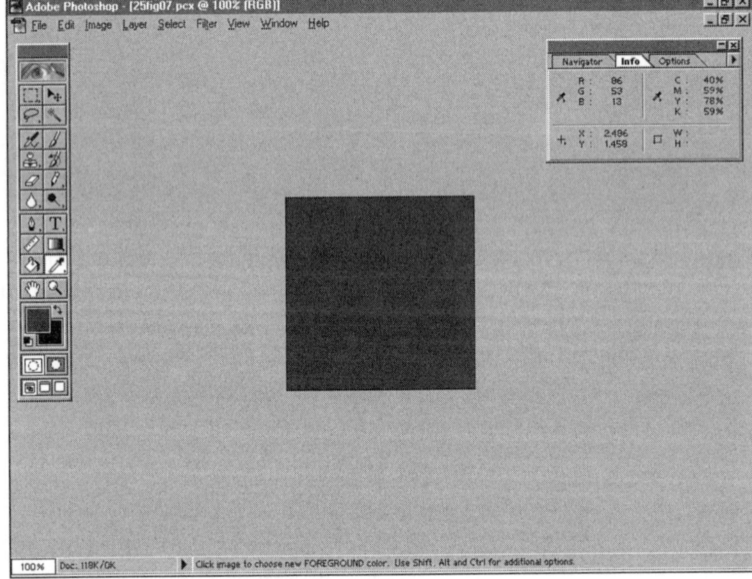

Figure 25.7
RGB color information in Photoshop gives you the information you need to calculate the corresponding hexadecimal value.

3. Enter the first (red) value into a scientific calculator in standard, decimal mode. I'm using the scientific mode of the resident Windows calculator (see Figure 25.8).
4. Switch to hexadecimal mode.

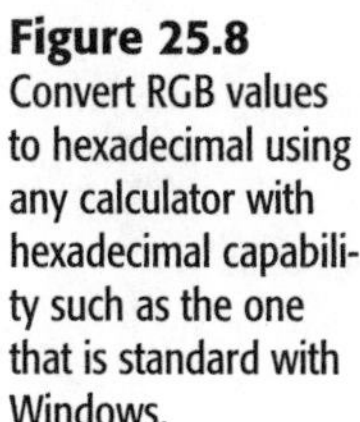

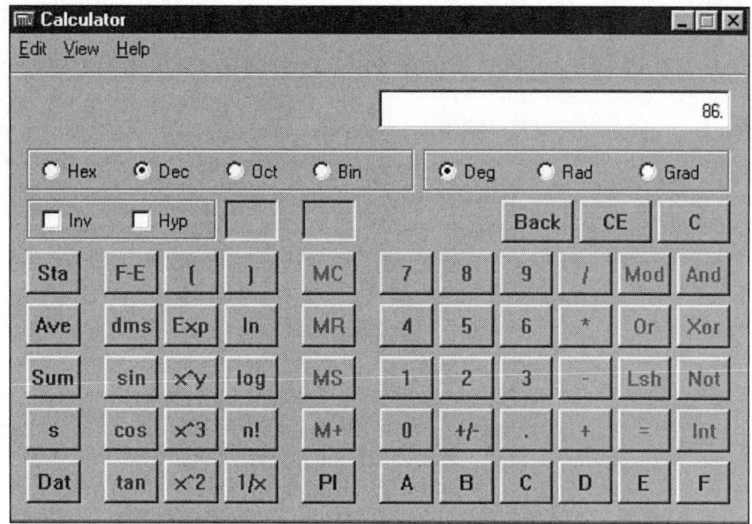

Figure 25.8
Convert RGB values to hexadecimal using any calculator with hexadecimal capability such as the one that is standard with Windows.

A set of two characters is displayed on the screen. This is the hex equivalent of the specific amount of red within the color you've chosen. For 86, I got a hex value of 56.

5. Write this value down.
6. Now switch back to standard decimal mode, and input the green value.
7. Switch again to hexadecimal to get the green alphanumeric set.
8. Repeat this process for the blue (note that you'll end up with a single character here, so enter a `0` before it when writing it down).
9. For the RGB value of 86, 53, 13 you should have a corresponding hex value of `56350D`.

PART V CH 25

Many imaging programs are now providing Hex support. Paint Shop Pro 5.0 is a perfect example.

→ For more information on Paint Shop Pro, **see** "Web Graphic Formats and Professional Tools," **p. 583**

> **Note**
>
> If you want to convert your values over the Internet, visit the following Web sites for RGB-to-Hex converters that you can use:
>
> Russ's RGB to Hex Converter: **`http://www.ecn.bgu.edu/cgi/users/mureg3/tutorial/rgb-hex.scgi`**
>
> Color Center: **`http://www.hidaho.com/colorcenter/cc.html`**

THE SAFE PALETTE

Think of it this way—if you never had to download a graphic, your pages would load really fast. But would you sacrifice speed for visual attraction?

The answer is: probably. But that doesn't mean that you can't use color to create a rich base for the graphics that you will use. What this does is offer the opportunity to have faster loading pages because you're using fewer graphics to achieve visual appeal.

Smoke and mirrors? Hardly! But if you understand how to tap into the colors that are native to your browser, you'll have stable, attractive splashes of color before a graphic is ever downloaded.

To make this happen, you have to understand the *safe palette*. This is a palette of 216 colors that are reserved by browsers on the Macintosh and Windows platforms for immediate access. Instead of having to download information from a remote server, the browser parses the hexadecimal color codes from the page right away.

A safe palette is the palette made up of 216 colors that remain as stable from one browser to another, between platforms, and at as many different monitor color capacities and resolutions as possible.

It's important to use the safe palette in most instances, because it ensures cross-browser, cross-platform stability. If you use colors outside of the safe palette, you can run into serious problems.

→ The safe palette is relevant to fonts, **see** "Working with Fonts," **p. 242**

→ Another important use of safe palette is also relevant in CSS, **see** "Designing Type with Style Sheets," **p. 284**

Picture this: You choose a soft, pale blue color for your background, and a very dark blue for your text. There's enough contrast to be readable, and you're happy with the look—proud of your hard design work done on an upper-end machine capable of full 24-bit color.

You put your page up on the Internet, and along comes a pal to check out your work. He gets to the page and sees you've chosen a bright peacock blue for your background, and a similar color for your text. He can't read the content on your page, and he's confused.

How did this happen? Well, you didn't use safe color. Your friend came along with a more limited set of hardware and software, and his color management system chose to *dither* the colors. This means that his computer grabbed the first blues available because it couldn't identify your unsafe color.

To avoid this, you'll need to choose from the safe palette. I know that it seems like 216 colors is a limited number, and it's true. My only words of solace are to encourage you to be creative. There are enough colors within the safe palette to create beautiful designs—it's done every day on the Web, and I have no doubts that you can do it, too.

Note

If most color systems can display at least 256 colors, how did the safe palette end up with only 216? It's a complicated story that involves Windows 3.1 having reserved colors for the Operating System. Browsers then went on to use just the available colors to avoid the problem, and the end results were a limited palette. The good news is that the 216-color palette is stable and addresses many problems that occur across platforms–something over which Web designers can breathe a sigh of relief.

Many design programs have created special palettes to accommodate Web-safe colors. Photoshop (versions 4.0 and later for Macintoshes and Windows) offers a palette built right into the program.

Note

Safe palette information and tools can be found by visiting the following Web sites:

Victor Engel's Color Cube: **`http://the-light.com/netcol.html`**

Lynda Weinman: **`http://www.lynda.com/hex.html`**

Are you concerned about an image that doesn't contain Web safe colors with which you need to coordinate your overall site design? You may still be able to use it, see "Working with the Safe Palette" in the Troubleshooting section at the end of this chapter.

CONTRAST AND READABILITY

Contrast is a necessary element when designing with color. Simply defined, contrast is two colors that are different enough from one another to provide an obvious separation to the eye. Contrast is necessary to produce readable sites.

Many of you have undoubtedly visited sites where the background and body text have been difficult to read. In most cases, the problem is due to poor contrast. A light blue on a slightly darker blue isn't going to have enough contrast to be readable, as you can *try* to see in Figure 25.9. However, black on white is going to be very readable (see Figure 25.10).

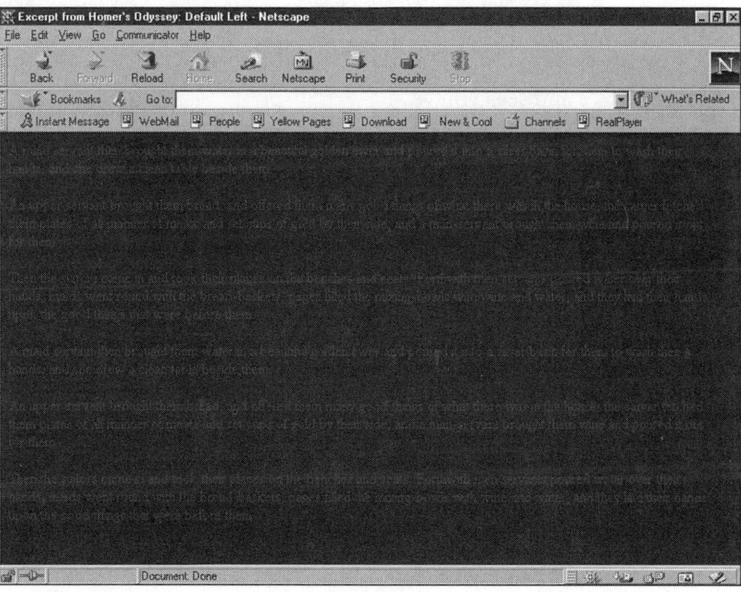

Figure 25.9
Not enough contrast creates readability problems.

Usually, body text should be darker than the background—dark enough so that significant contrast is created, allowing for maximum readability.

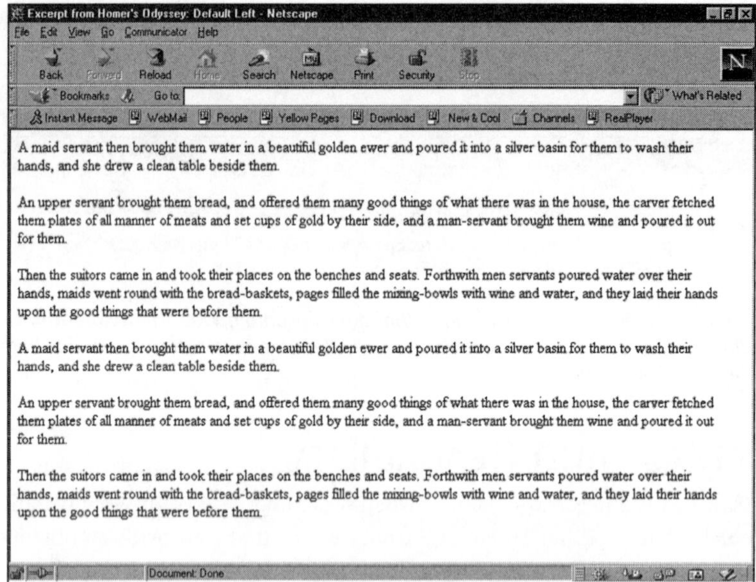

Figure 25.10
Black on white is high contrast, so it's easy to read.

Tip from

Accessibility experts have found that for visually impaired individuals, severe contrasts such as black and white are the best for readability in low vision circumstances. If you know that your audience has a lot of older individuals or visually impaired persons, it's wise to plan ahead and ensure that your contrast colors are as solid as possible: black on white for body text is a sure-fire way to go.

Another approach is to *reverse* this concept, placing light colors on dark colors. This is known as *reverse type* and, if the contrast is good enough, it can be quite effective. Bottom line? Be sure that your content is readable on your background, so people are sure to be able to get to the information you're delivering.

TROUBLESHOOTING

USING UNSAFE COLORS

I want to use the colors found in a professional logo, but when I looked at their RGB and Hex values, I found that they weren't Web safe. Is it okay to use these colors anyway?

Using unsafe color is risky, and I don't recommend it. However, there are times when unsafe color can be used. Here's a helpful set of guidelines:

- You know your audience. And I *mean* know them! One situation where you might know them well would be a corporate intranet.
- If you're less certain about your audience, but still interested in using unsafe color, test the colors for dithering at lower resolutions.

To test colors, drop your monitor down to 256 colors when viewing your page. If the color appears differently from what you originally determined, it's probably a good idea to revert to a safe color. You'll also want to be very thorough, testing your pages on a variety of browsers, platforms, and computer systems.

DESIGNING FOR THE REAL WORLD

WORKING WITH THE SAFE PALETTE

To work effectively with the safe palette, you have to draw from all the information we've covered in this chapter. Beginning with what you know of color, you can think about the look-and-feel, special effects, and emotional expression you want to express on your site.

Let's say I want to create a warm and welcoming personal presence that expresses my personal energy. I would begin by selecting colors that are warm as well as vibrant: orange, red, yellow. Then I would find an appropriate combination of hues—I want the site to be harmonious, not discordant. The harmony of colors helps express the welcoming and personal presence, offering comfort while still conveying energy.

I then turn to my understanding of RGB and Hexadecimal values. Add to that the fact that I know I want to choose my colors from a safe palette, and I've narrowed down my choices to a specific set of colors.

What I like to do at this point is create what I call an *individual* palette. This is a selection of five to seven colors that I choose from the safe palette. In this example, I'll create an individual palette in Photoshop.

1. Create a new file by choosing File, New.
2. Anticipating seven colors, create the file as being 50 pixels wide and 350 pixels long. This creates seven 50×50 pixel spaces along the vertical.
3. From a safe color palette, pick out the first two colors. Although Photoshop has a native safe palette, I prefer opening up a file called nhue.gif (see Figure 25.11). This file, created by Lynda Weinman, not only offers the color itself, but the RGB *and* hexadecimal equivalents of that color. Download nhue.gif from `http://www.lynda.com/hexh.html`.
4. With the Marquee tool, mark off the first 50×50 pixel area at the top of the workspace. Fill it with the first color.
5. Continue filling the rest of each space with the colors you've picked from the safe palette. Usually I reserve the sixth and seventh space for black and white respectively.
6. Then switch to the Type tool, and type in the RGB and Hex color values (see Figure 25.12).
7. Flatten the file by selecting Layer, Flatten Image to combine all the layers into one and save it as a GIF.

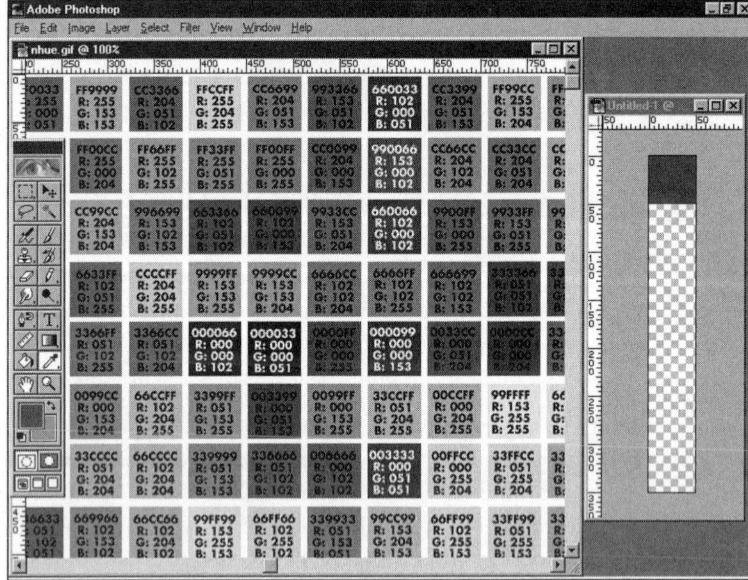

Figure 25.11
Nhue.gif is an extremely useful tool created by author and designer Lynda Weinman.

Figure 25.12
Adding the hex and RGB values to the individual palette gives you all the necessary information to begin creating your site using safe colors.

You now have a custom palette that you can use while working on your site. It is both a reference for the numeric values of the colors and a palette you can leave open in Photoshop as you create the graphics for your site.

CHAPTER 26

RESOLUTION, GAMMA, AND THE VISUAL ENVIRONMENT

In this chapter

UNDERSTANDING THE COMPUTER SCREEN

I spend a lot of time at my computer. I work on it, use it to retrieve news, to communicate with others, and sometimes just to have fun.

I've always been interested in what makes it tick, how it works, and how I can improve both its performance and my experience with it. In fact, ensuring that I'm comfortable using it for long hours is imperative.

One problem I've encountered is with my eyes—having to look at a screen for many hours at a time can take its toll. There are different issues that directly affect what I end up seeing on my screen—the quality and depth of the images, the colors, the space, and the contrast.

As a Web designer, understanding a bit about some of these influences can help you create sites that take the user's experience into consideration—ultimately delivering a higher quality, more effective site to his or her desktop.

SCREEN RESOLUTION

What many Web designers are surely familiar with, but many of their site visitors don't know, is how to manage the *resolution* of their computer monitors.

Resolution refers to how many pixels appear on the horizontal and vertical axes of your computer screen. If my resolution is set to the lowest common denominator of 640×480 pixels, that means that 640 pixels are available in width, and 480 pixels in height, total, for the entire screen.

Most computers ship with 640×480 as a default resolution, and many older computers are only capable of that resolution. For this reason, many Web site visitors are seeing the Web at 640×480, and either cannot change or do not know *how* to change the resolution of their video monitor screens. At 640×480 resolution, the disadvantage is that there is less space to work with (see Figure 26.1), but, for some, the advantage is that everything also appears larger. Similarly, many notebook computers ship at a default of 800×600 resolution. This is a popular resolution, too—perhaps the most popular at this point.

Compare Figure 26.1 to Figure 26.2. In 26.2, you can see what 800×600 looks like. Much more space to maneuver in, but the objects appear smaller. Of course, you can adjust the size of the objects to make things visible while maintaining the extra workspace on many platforms.

Figure 26.1
640×480 screen resolution: the lowest common denominator.

Figure 26.2
800×600: more work-space on my Windows 98 machine.

There are higher resolutions, too. 1,024×768 alters the look of one of my desktops considerably (see Figure 26.3); and I can go even higher on that particular computer—to 1,280×1,024 (see Figure 26.4).

Figure 26.3
At 1,024×768, this desktop is dramatically altered visually.

Figure 26.4
A screen resolution of 1,280×1,024 is reserved for high-resolution work.

Higher resolutions have their advantage when an individual has a large screen for specialty reasons—computer-generated design (where detail matters), or large data management.

The bottom line when it comes to screen resolution is this: Web site visitors are seeing your site at a variety of screen resolutions. This directly affects the way your Web sites will be experienced, and it's up to you to do the best you can to design sites that look good no matter the resolution.

Tip from molly

Professional Web developers should have monitors that support a range of resolutions, so they can test their sites at those various resolutions. I have several Windows machines that allow me to test different resolutions. I also have an iMac, which allows me to test the look of pages from the Mac OS point of view, too.

MANAGING RESOLUTION

"It's bad enough to have to scroll in one (vertical) direction; having to scroll in two directions is intolerable." —Lynch and Horton, Yale C/AIM Web Style Guide

When it comes to Web site design, one of the worst yet easiest mistakes to make is to not design for the audience. If you're a computer buff, like me, you might enjoy working at higher resolutions and don't immediately think of your audience's limitations.

Knowing how serious some of the mishaps that occur when ignoring audience needs are, you're certain to not only know why it's so important to manage screen resolution, but how to do it, too.

One of the first issues you'll need to address is making sure that your pages fit into any screen resolution. This ensures that you'll avoid what Lynch and Horton are referring to: a horizontal scrollbar (see Figure 26.5). To demonstrate the problem, I coded the table in Listing 26.1 to fit a higher rather than lower resolution. I then took the screen shot at a lower resolution and guess what? The horizontal scrollbar appeared.

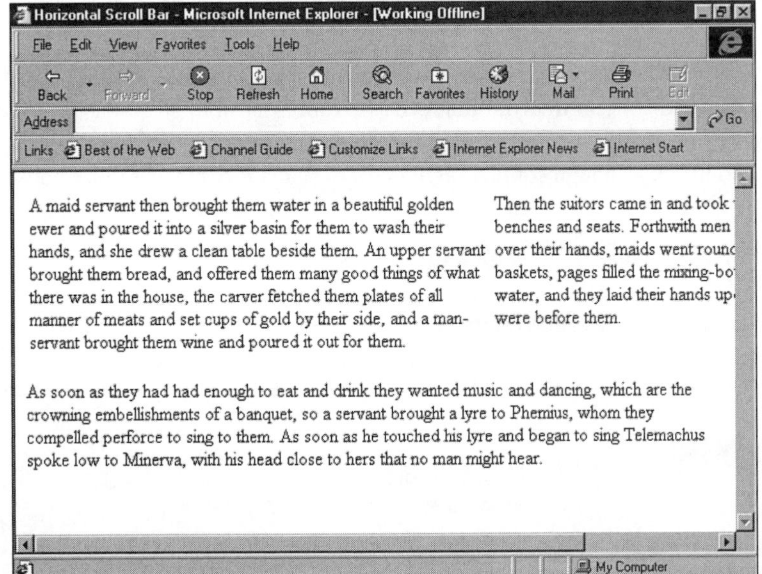

Figure 26.5
A horizontal scrollbar at 640×480 equals unhappy site visitors.

LISTING 26.1 DEMONSTRATING A HORIZONTAL SCROLL

```
<HTML>
<HEAD>
<TITLE>Horizontal Scroll Bar</TITLE>
</HEAD>
<BODY>
<TABLE border="0" width="750">
<TR>
<TD valign="top" width="400">
A maid servant then brought them water in a beautiful golden ewer and poured it
into a silver basin for them to wash their hands, and she drew a clean table
beside them. An upper servant brought them bread, and offered them many good
things of what there was in the house, the carver fetched them plates of all
manner of meats and set cups of gold by their side, and a man-servant brought them
wine and poured it out for them.
</TD>
<TD valign="top" width="350">
Then the suitors came in and took their places on the benches and seats. Forthwith
men servants poured water over their hands, maids went round with the bread-
baskets, pages filled the mixing-bowls with wine and water, and they laid their
hands upon the good things that were before them.
</TD>
</TR>
</TABLE>
<P>As soon as they had had enough to eat and drink they wanted music and dancing,
which are the crowning embellishments of a banquet, so a servant brought a lyre to
Phemius, whom they compelled perforce to sing to them. As soon as he touched his
lyre and began to sing. Telemachus spoke low to Minerva, with his head close to
hers that no man might hear.

</BODY>
</HTML>
```

This bar disappears at higher resolutions. But we do know that *at this time* most people are viewing the Web at either 640×480 resolution, or 800×600 resolution.

Theoretically, this means that anything you create must accommodate the lower 640 pixels wide or less to avoid that evil horizontal scroll in all situations. A lot of arguments occur over this issue, with many developers insisting that it's fine to develop for 800×600 resolution, although some designers (myself included) take a more conservative approach. Whatever you decide, think before you act—and know your audience!

In reality, 640×480 resolution doesn't translate to allowing your fixed designs to measure a full 640 pixels wide. The reason is that significant space is eaten up by the browser itself. Simply open up your Web browser to see what I mean. In the default view (Figure 26.6), the browser will have icons and toolbars along the top, a status bar on the bottom, a thin bar to the left, and a thicker scrollbar to the right. All of this information eats up precious space.

Note

Different browser brands and versions take up different amounts of pixels. The 585×295 recommendation addresses these differences.

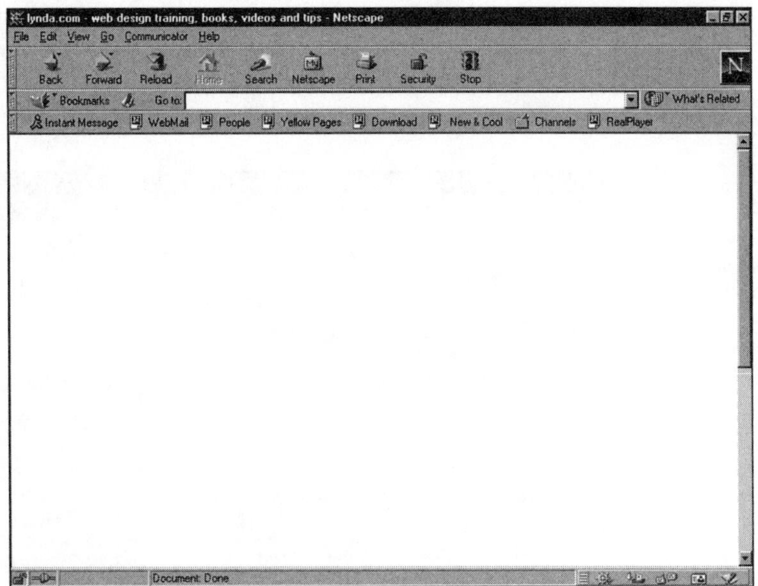

Figure 26.6
The Netscape interface: Note all the real estate the top and bottom bars eat up.

All told, the viewing area is so significantly reduced by the browser's interface that professional Web designers use a new total screen dimension—585 pixels×295 pixels—to avoid problems.

But wait. Before you scream in frustration, let me first explain where this number comes from, and how you can work to best suit your goals and audience. Lynch and Horton recommend 595 pixels to avoid a horizontal scroll when working within the 640 resolution. However, many Mac screens will still have a scroll at this resolution! With the popularity of the iMac, new awareness for Mac users has come into play. Therefore, I recommend 585 pixels for a lowest common-denominator, fixed-width designs. If you decide to design for higher resolutions, do the math and subtract the necessary space from your screen to accommodate the space without causing unwanted scrolling at that resolution.

Let me also reassure you that there are ways to work with this small space to ensure compatibility for higher resolutions, as well as give the illusion that more space exists. What's more—you have dynamic options that allow you to create designs that adjust to the available screen space, and if you're really into covering all your bases—you can use JavaScript to detect and route browsers to the correct resolution for that site visitor.

The following are some screen resolution guidelines that will help you avoid incompatibility problems:

- Design precision layouts to the lowest available resolution. Always design with the 640×480 screen resolution in mind—meaning that you'll need to employ the 585×295 rule.
- For layouts that don't demand precise placement of objects, choose dynamic tables for layout.

- Don't forget that there are people using higher resolutions. Background graphics always tile, so you'll need to control the way those graphics work. Also, when working with tables and frames, be aware that fixed-width tables and frames cause extra space to appear around the fixed design (see Figure 26.7) at higher resolutions (see Figure 26.8).

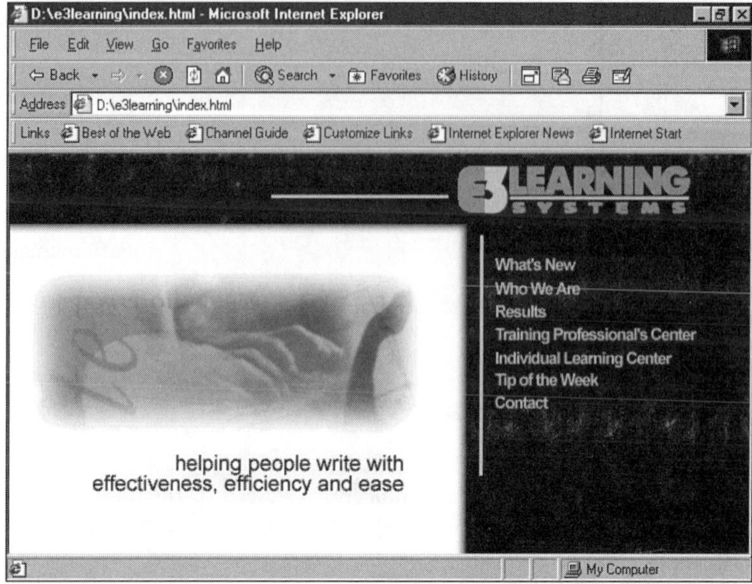

Figure 26.7
Fixed table design at 640×480 presents the navigation information and content to the site visitor in correct proportions to their viewing area.

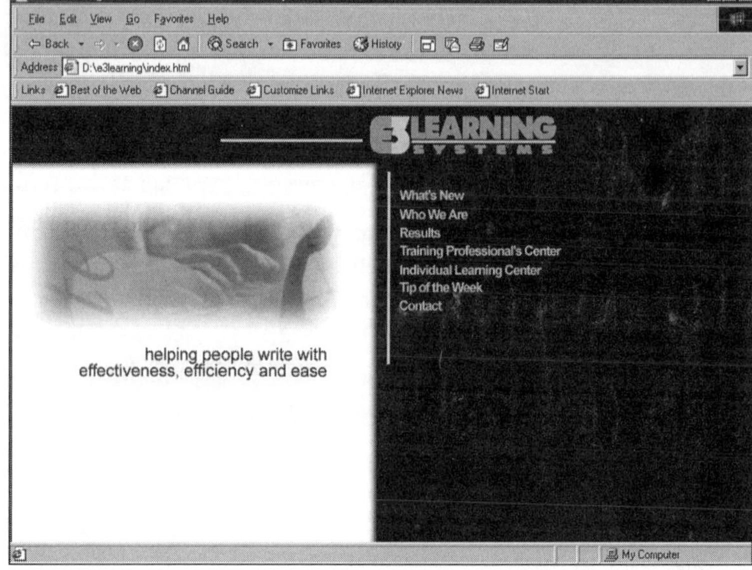

Figure 26.8
The same design at 800×600–more whitespace appears to the right and bottom which looks less appealing to the site visitor.

- Test, test, test! This rule should be firm no matter what the circumstances. Test your pages on different systems, different browsers, and at different resolutions. Now—before your site goes live—is the time to troubleshoot horizontal scrolls or any other troublesome areas.
- Work within the allotted space. In other words, don't pretend you have more space than you really do. You'll need to focus on proportion, dimension, and whitespace, which I'll show you how to do a bit later in this chapter.

→ For more information on creating dynamic tables, **see** "Advanced Table Layouts," **p. 336**

→ You can detect and route visitors based on screen resolution with JavaScript, **see** "Using JavaScript," **p. 421**

These simple guidelines will save you from more trouble than you might imagine. You'll learn how to have greater control over your pages and be able to manage your sites better, providing a much more stable and effective product for your audience.

I can't emphasize how important it is to test your pages—even if you are employing maximum control over your page dimensions. I teach in a computer lab that uses Power PCs set to a resolution of 800×600. Due to security concerns on the part of the administration, I can't have my students change their resolution.

We've run into consistent problems with horizontal scrolls despite employing the general guidelines—it's only in testing that you'll find the smaller, seemingly inconsequential problems with your HTML or graphics.

Tip from molly

If you're just getting started working with resolution issues, set your screen resolution to 640×480 and do all of your graphic design and HTML work at that resolution. This will get you familiar with the way things look at that resolution.

Some designers actually work only in 640×480 resolution and then test at higher resolutions. Whether you choose to do this, or, like me, work at higher resolutions but *test* those pages, doesn't really matter. The bottom line is that you must check and re-check your work in a variety of circumstances to fully troubleshoot any potential problems.

Note

Download a helpful ruler for measuring your Web page from `http://www.wpdfd.com/wpdtame.htm`.

Screen Color and Gamma

Another concern is screen color. Older hardware used on the Web is limited to 256 colors, which in and of itself asks the Web designer to do some pretty fancy tricks.

In general, the "test everything" rule applies with color, because if a visitor is limited to 256 colors and you've been doing your design work in full, 24-bit color, what you see and what your audience sees are going to be different.

→ For more information on working with color, **see** "Color Concepts," **p. 528**

Another important issue related to color that is often overlooked by Web designers is *Gamma*.

Gamma is complex to describe because it involves a lot of math. Put into its most simple terms, Gamma is a system that significantly influences the way that data appears on a computer screen. Gamma must often be manipulated, or *corrected*, to provide the most accurate information to your monitor.

Your hardware determines how Gamma is corrected. One of the reasons Macintoshes have been so popular in the graphic design industry is that a fair amount of Gamma correction is available on the Macintosh. This is especially true with Silicon Graphic machines. It's no wonder that SGIs are the computers of choice for film, animation, and video production.

Because of this correction, Macintoshes and SGIs can display color with greater accuracy. But Windows machines, prevalent on most desktops, are problematic.

Prior to Windows 95 and 98, there was little, if any, Gamma correction available to the Windows platform. Since the release of these more sophisticated GUIs, however, a bit more gamma correction is available, particularly if you've bought top-of-the line hardware. The better and newer your computer, video card, and video monitor are, the better your chances are of having some inherent Gamma correction.

When Gamma is improperly corrected, the video displays images that are problematic. The dominant problem is that images are displayed very dark, so much of the image is obscured. This is especially true in environments such as the World Wide Web.

What a problem for the Web designer who has worked so hard to get high-quality color for his or her site visitors!

Note

To learn more about Gamma, check out the following resources:

"An Explanation of Monitor Gamma," by Robert W. Berger. This excellent article explains monitor problems across platforms, and even provides a visual method of determining your computer's Gamma (**`http://www.vtiscan.com/~rwb/gamma.html`**).

"Frequently Questioned Answers About Gamma," by Charles Poynton. Facts and fallacies about Gamma are examined in great detail at: **`http://www.inforamp.net/~poynton/notes/color/GammaFQA.html`**.

The Gamma Correction Home Page. A comprehensive article and related Gamma resources (**`http://www.cgsd.com/papers/gamma.html`**).

Experts claim that working in high contrast colors is a way around Gamma problems. But of course, this translates into the loss of subtlety in design. Your best defense against Gamma problems is to learn what it is and how it affects your design. As ever, be sure to test your sites with a variety of equipment, gaining a feel for what variations of your design might appear.

WORKING WITH SCREEN SPACE

Here are a few helpful methods to gain maximum control over screen space when designing for the limitations of the Web, beyond those already discussed.

The first place to find control over screen space is to understand that it is a very, very small space that allows little or no opportunity to vary its borders. I call this problem *constraint*. Web space is *constrained space*. When I get home from a long day out and about, the first thing I do is take off my dress shoes. My feet are overjoyed to be free of the constraints. I believe that learning how to manage your sites effectively in constrained space will immediately affect the comfort of your site visitors, making them feel relaxed, at ease, and prepared to enjoy your Web site.

First, look at your computer monitor. It is in and of itself a constrained space with distinctive borders. Externally, the borders physically separate the unit from its environment. Internally, the physical borders create a visual frame around the desktop.

If you revisit the earlier discussion of browsers, you'll remember that the browser then adds its own borders around the available visual screen of the viewing window.

If these two constraints aren't enough, many designers add constraints to their designs. Table borders around tables (see Figure 26.9), borders around images (see Figure 26.10), and large, chunky headers or graphics (see Figure 26.11) all add to the sense that browser space is limited.

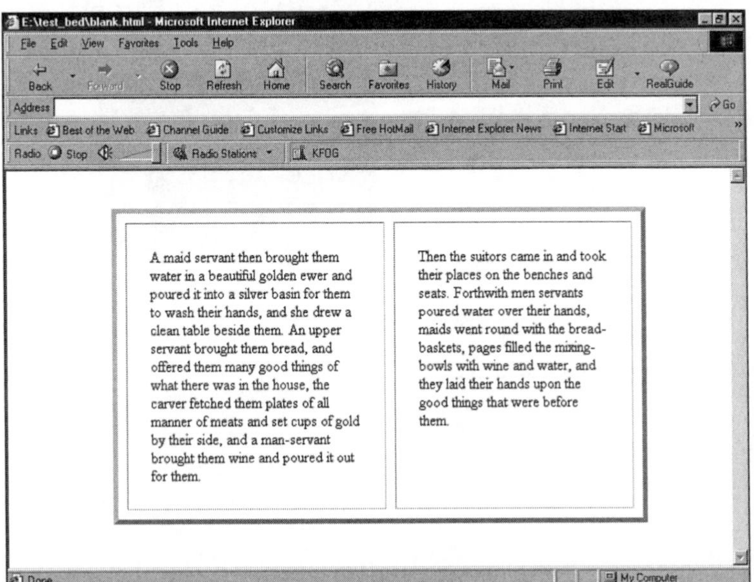

Figure 26.9
Table borders add spatial constraints.

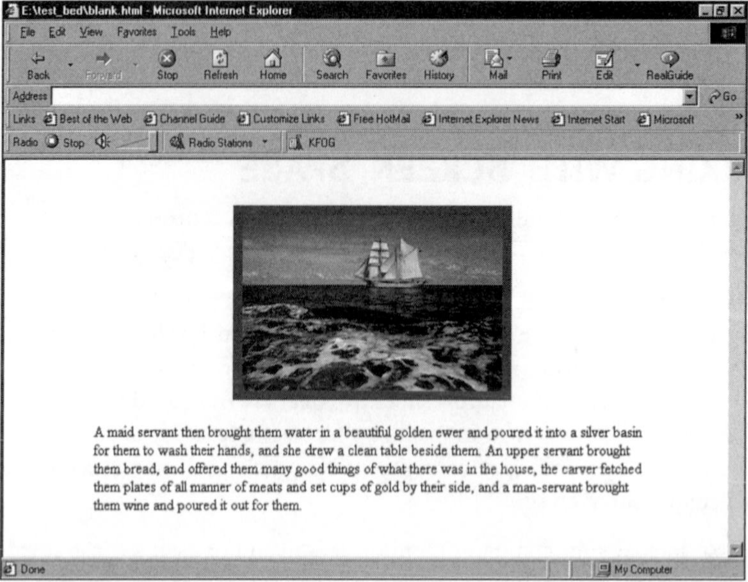

Figure 26.10
Image borders also add to a sense of containment.

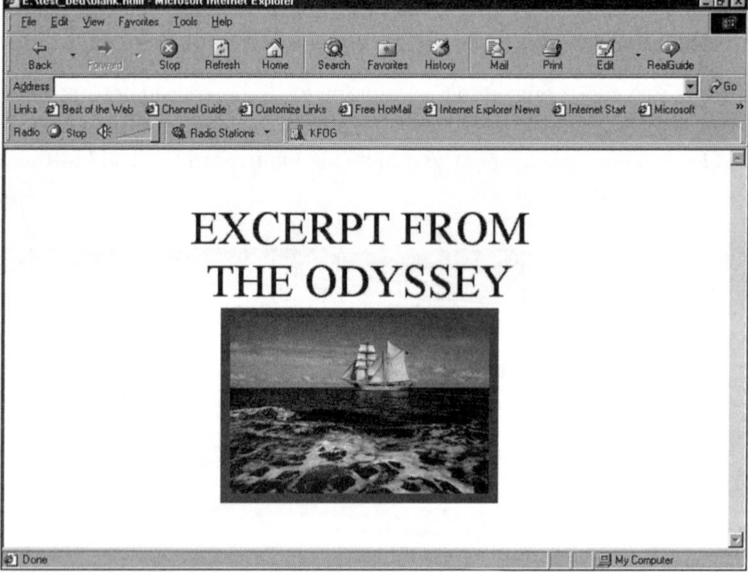

Figure 26.11
Chunky headers and graphics crowd the visually available space.

To make your site visitors more comfortable, you need to divert their attention away from the spatial limitations of the Web.

Note

Why does it seem natural to want to put borders around tables and images? Many designers do it, and they like the results. Matting, or framing, space is a familiar method of handling artwork or design. For example, if I look at the art in my office, it's all been beautifully matted and framed. The frames can be thought of as being similar to the external boundaries of my computer monitor, and the matting around the art similar to a browser's interface. But my walls are tall–about eight feet high–, and they are wide. My monitor is only 17 inches–on the diagonal. Furthermore, I can comfortably rest my eyes on a piece of framed art on a wall, but looking at a framed image on a computer screen will become very uncomfortable after only a few minutes.

The first thing to do is to manage your visual space.

Managing Space

Several design techniques help you create pages that are visually freed from the constraints of the computer and Web environment. They include the following:

- **Use margins**—Add margins wherever you are working with long blocks of text.
- **Think about whitespace**—This is the use of background space (not always white) as a cushion and guide for the eye.
- **Eliminate clutter**—Everything on a page should have a reason for being there.
- **Control dimension and proportion**—Keep the size of your graphic and media elements in balance with not only the size of available space, but with other elements on the page.

Now take a closer look at how to put these methods to work.

Margins

Margins are simply the addition of space, sometimes referred to as *gutters*, along the right and left edge of text. In Figure 26.12, I show a page with no margins, and Figure 26.13 is the same page with margins. You can easily see that margins make sections of text easier to read, and the page looks better, too.

Margins can be achieved in several ways with HTML. The first and most readily available is the <BLOCKQUOTE> element. Although <BLOCKQUOTE> was created specifically to block sections of quoted text, it's used conventionally to add whitespace to a page. If you're an absolute HTML purist, you won't want to choose this method, but it is used frequently to accomplish the goal desired.

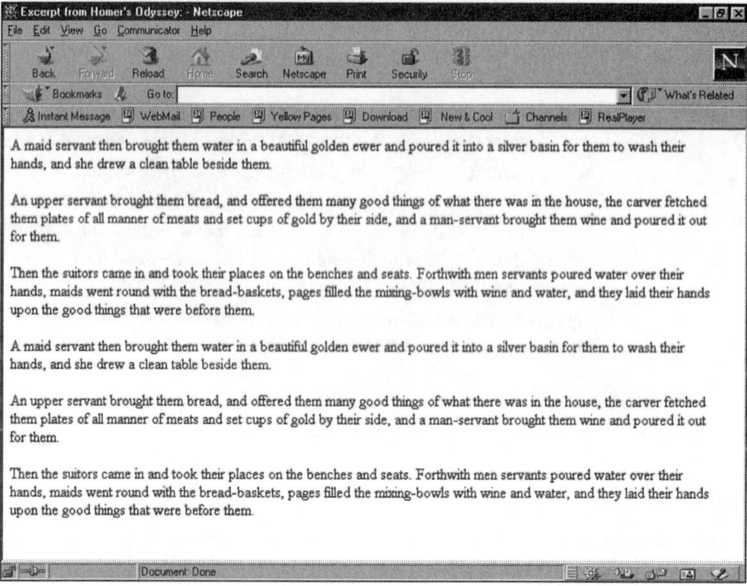

Figure 26.12
An HTML page of text without margins is difficult to read and may cause your site visitor to skip over important content.

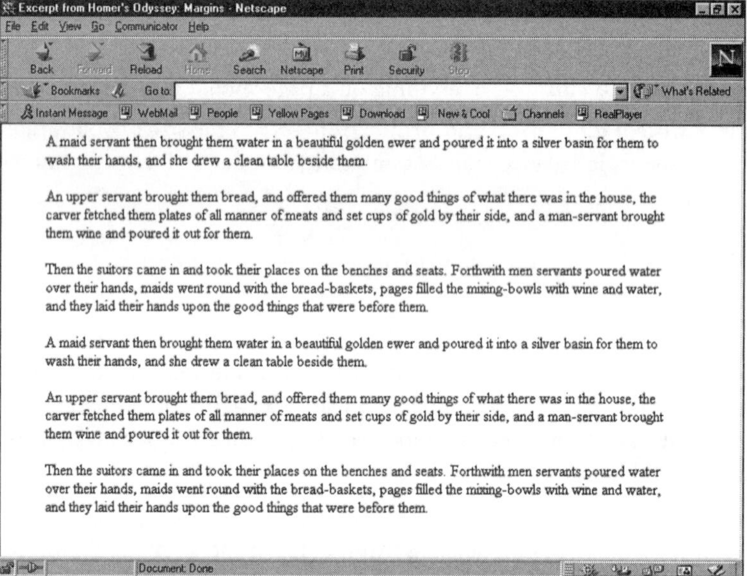

Figure 26.13
Add margins and achieve greater readability as well as esthetic appeal.

Using blockquotes is simple. All you need to do is surround the area to which you want to add margins with the appropriate opening and closing tags (see Listing 26.2).

LISTING 26.2 USING BLOCKQUOTES

```
<HTML>
<HEAD>
<TITLE>Excerpt from Homer's Odyssey</TITLE>
</HEAD>
<BODY>
<BLOCKQUOTE>
<P>A maid servant then brought them water in a beautiful golden ewer and poured it
into a silver basin for them to wash their hands, and she drew a clean table
beside them. An upper servant brought them bread, and offered them many good
things of what there was in the house, the carver fetched them plates of all
manner of meats and set cups of gold by their side, and a man-servant brought them
wine and poured it out for them.

<P>Then the suitors came in and took their places on the benches and seats.
Forthwith men servants poured water over their hands, maids went round with the
bread-baskets, pages filled the mixing-bowls with wine and water, and they laid
their hands upon the good things that were before them.
<P>As soon as they had had enough to eat and drink they wanted music and dancing,
which are the crowning embellishments of a banquet, so a servant brought a lyre to
Phemius, whom they compelled perforce to sing to them. As soon as he touched his
lyre and began to sing. Telemachus spoke low to Minerva, with his head close to
hers that no man might hear.
</BLOCKQUOTE>
</BODY>
</HTML>
```

Another method of adding margins is to employ the `left-margin` and `right-margin` attributes within the opening `BODY` tag:

```
<BODY leftmargin="100" rightmargin="300">
```

However, this method is limited to Internet Explorer, as shown in Figure 26.14.

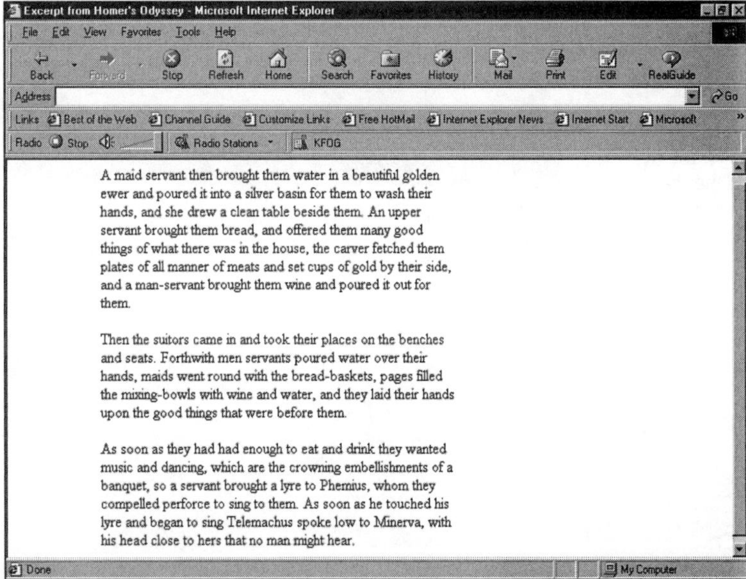

Figure 26.14 Margins with the `left-margin` and `right-margin` attributes look fine, but work only in Internet Explorer.

→ Tables are another way to gain margin control. For more about this technique, **see** "Advanced Table Layouts," **p. 336**

Finally, and most important to the strict HTML 4.0 standard, is the use of style sheets to achieve margin control. For the HTML 4.0 purist, this is the way to go!

→ Check out the use of style sheets for margin control, **see** "Cascading Style Sheet Techniques," **p. 264**

→ For more information and resources on the style sheet method, **see** "Element Positioning and Style Sheet Scripting," **p. 430**

Whitespace

Whitespace is the absence of design, but it is wholly design. What I mean by this axiom is that although we might think of design as being the elements and objects that go into making up a Web page, design is also what *is not* there.

In Figure 26.15 I've blacked out some areas in a layout. I want you to focus only on the white first. If you look carefully, you'll notice that the white area is a shape in and of itself. If I use different shapes, as in Figure 26.16, the whitespace changes, too.

Figure 26.15
Notice the space in between the blacked out elements.

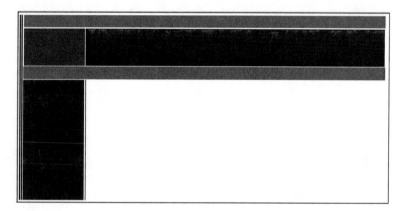

Figure 26.16
Here I've used different shapes for the elements, and the shape of the whitespace changes, too.

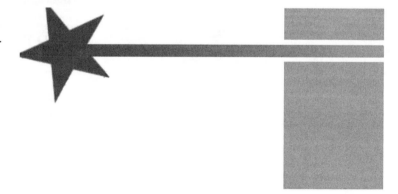

Whitespace adds to design by providing texture and cushioning for page elements. It also can help serve your design by leading and resting the eye.

To work with whitespace, you have to gain a feel not only for what you put on to a page, but what shapes are created between those elements by the space itself.

ELIMINATING CLUTTER

When speaking of space, I always like to tell the story of the New York apartments I remember from my childhood. Often the home of an aunt or other relative, these tiny apartments were crammed full of "chachkes," or knick-knacks. In fact, as small as I might have been at the time, I felt nervous in those apartments—always thinking that I would bump, knock over, or break something.

As designers, eliminating clutter is one of our biggest jobs. I often ask my students how they would decorate a small, dark room without windows to make it look larger. The following are several things that they recommend:

1. Paint the room a light color.
2. Furnish it simply, even sparsely.
3. Make sure the furnishings in the room are not too heavy or ornate.

From these suggestions, you can directly apply some sensible ideas to a heavy Web page (see Figure 26.17). In most cases, you'll want to keep your pages light. Of course, there will be plenty of exceptions to this guideline, but it's a good one to keep in mind. Next, you'll want to ensure that your graphics are carefully chosen and most importantly—each one serves a purpose. Finally, your graphics should not be too heavy or complicated for the page.

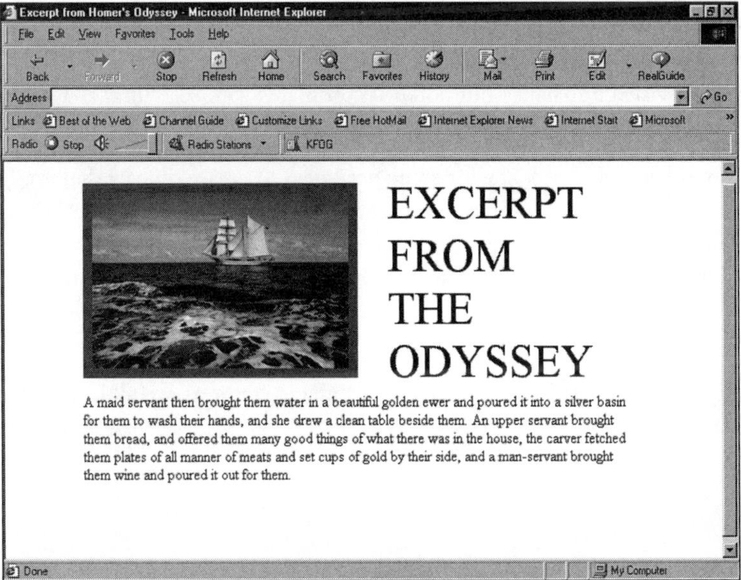

Figure 26.17
A heavy, cluttered page just makes your screen space appear to be smaller.

To sum it up, I believe that less is more when it comes to Web design. Although this is not always going to be practical, especially when dealing with large amounts of data, if you work toward a simpler goal, you can improve your chances of having a more spacious, relaxed page (see Figure 26.18) instead of a cluttered, uptight one.

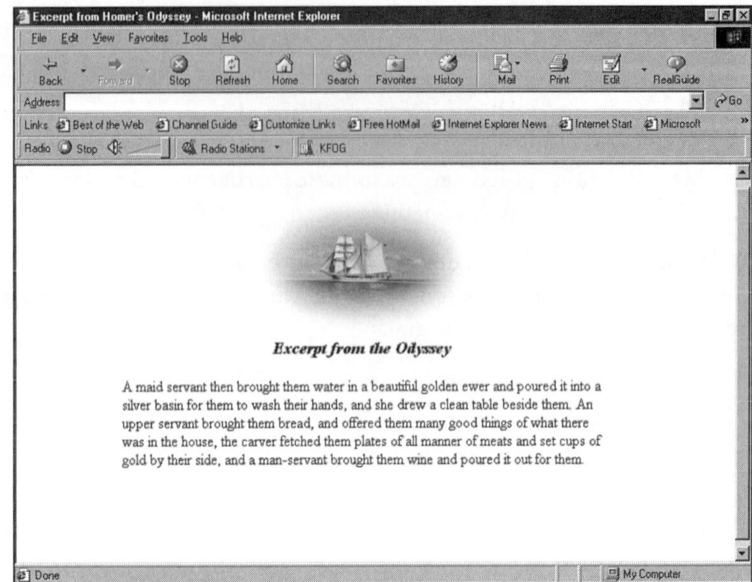

Figure 26.18
A lighter, happier page is more appealing to your site visitor and reduces the feeling of constraint.

DIMENSION AND PROPORTION

Dimension is the size of a given element. Proportion is the relationship of elements to one another.

Dimension is particularly important on a Web page. If a graphic is too large, it causes not only a visual imbalance but potential problems with scrolling, as I mentioned earlier in the chapter.

There's an odd tendency for some designers to create objects that are far too big for a page, as shown in the block layout in Figure 26.19. When this occurs, the page's impact is lost. When sizing images, always keep the 585×295 per screen guidelines in mind. This is sure to help you size your graphics and media elements more appropriately.

The relationship between elements is important. To create visual harmony, you want elements to be the right distance from one another, as well as proportional to one another. In Figure 26.20, the header area, graphic image, and text are all balanced within the page's layout.

Figure 26.19
Viewing the block areas for a layout, you can easily see that an element too large for a page will weigh it down.

Figure 26.20
A more harmonious blocking of elements results invisually interesting whitespace, and a balance of page objects.

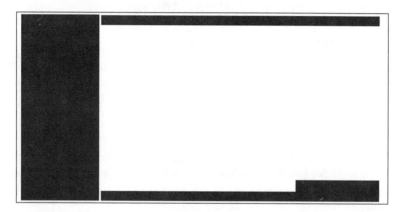

If any one of these elements were too much larger or smaller, the balance of the page would be lost.

TROUBLESHOOTING

RESOLUTION

I've looked at my server statistics, and determined that 80% of my audience is visiting at 800×600 resolution. How can I confidently design my fixed designs for this resolution?

Ultimately, the decision rests with you. However, consider the fact that if you're getting 100 people visiting your site a day, that's 20 people that might see a horizontal scroll. If you have 1,000 people—that's 200 people seeing the unwanted scroll! If you're comfortable with this, go for it. I personally am not comfortable and use the techniques described in Chapter 16, "Advanced Table Layouts," to improve the user experience of my fixed designs. As mentioned, the other option is to use a JavaScript detect and route.

I've noticed that design trends don't always mesh with sensible approaches to working within the visual space of a design. For example, the trend with portal sites has been top-heavy designs. Is it better to follow a trend to keep sites looking contemporary?

There's no reason in my mind that you cannot do both. The top-heavy designs that have been so popular in the portal realm seem to me to be a result of left-margin backlash. What I mean by this is that for several years, left-margin navigation designs dominated the Net. To give sites a fresh look, developers began to move navigation and primary information to the top of the page. However, clutter ensued in many cases. If you stick to your awareness of space and object relationships, you can combine flavor-of-the-moment designs with design intelligence—providing a contemporary look for your site while keeping it clean and attractive.

DESIGNING FOR THE REAL WORLD

CALIBRATING THE MONITOR TO BALANCE COLORS

Because many readers don't have much experience calibrating their monitors, this exercise will help you to do just that. This will improve the way you see color on your screen, work successfully with gamma, and output colors that are as balanced as possible.

Mechanical calibration devices are available. Although they are more accurate, they are also fairly cost–prohibitive for most people, ranging from $600–$1,200. A number of calibration software packages are on the market which are much less expensive, including Pantone's Personal Color Calibrator. Adobe bundles Gamma software with the Adobe Photoshop software package. For the purposes of this exercise, we'll be walking through the Adobe option. However, your software should be quite similar.

Before calibrating the monitor, you should let it warm up for at least 30 minutes. Set the ambient light in the room to the level that you use under normal working conditions. Change the background color on your screen to neutral gray for best results.

The Gamma Wizard walks you through calibration step by step. It explains how to control brightness, contrast, gamma, white point, and black point. To start calibrating your monitor, follow these steps:

1. Start the Gamma Wizard.
2. Click the Load option button.
3. In ICC Profile, select Adobe Monitor. If you already have a previous profile, the name of that profile appears onscreen.
4. Select Next and follow the wizard's instructions.
5. At the final window, you can compare results. After you are satisfied, save the profile.

CHAPTER 27

Web Graphic Formats and Professional Tools

In this chapter

GREAT GRAPHICS AND GREAT TOOLS

Size matters, so they say. On the Web, you want to keep your sizes small without sacrificing quality. Regardless of the media with which you're working—audio, video, animations, or graphics—ensuring that your files are light and your design still bright is a sure way to successful site design.

Understanding the available file formats used in Web graphic design is essential. One of the most daunting aspects of constructing a new Web site from scratch is the need for high-quality, well-designed graphics. The designer's responsibility isn't just limited to creating visual appeal: This is the Web, not clay or canvas, and working in a digital medium brings with it uniquely digital responsibilities.

Web graphic design is rife with myths about what Web graphics are and how they are created. On one hand, the core ideas are incredibly simple; on the other hand, many try their hands at graphics and just can't seem to get the process right.

Whether you're a well-studied and professional designer or are just learning how to create Web graphics, there is no reason why your Web site should be any less visually strong and technically well optimized than any professional site.

File optimization—the act of working with files to achieve both quality appearance and acceptable download times—begins with an understanding of the file formats that are available. I'll begin by describing file formats available on the Web, and which options are available to you within those formats. After you've gained a strong understanding of file formats, you move on to the tools that will help you work with the format and optimization concepts you've learned.

GRAPHIC INTERCHANGE FORMAT (GIF)

GIF is a file format that uses a type of compression known as *lossless*. Compression, as a general rule, is based on complicated, mathematical algorithms that are best saved for those developers interested in working with compression.

For all individuals developing Web pages, you are best served by learning quickly that GIF compression works by figuring out how much of the image uses the same color information. At that point, the compression algorithm saves those sections by using a numeric pattern.

GIF compression is limited to a total of 256 colors so that a numeric pattern is very specific. This is one of the main reasons it's so important to understand more about color theory and restrictions on the Web.

→ For more information about color theory, **see** "Color Concepts," **p. 528**

So, if you have 15 shades of blue within your graphic, that translates to 15 individual patterns. With more than 256 patterns, the algorithm has to decide what to leave out. It does this by limiting those blues to just a few or even just one total blue color.

Because of this process, your neon blue might end up a sky blue, and so forth. This is where experience and a skilled hand comes into play—knowing when and how to deal with color and file types will enable you to gain control over colors within your graphics.

Note

There's a bit of confusion over the pronunciation of GIF. Many people say it with a hard G, because logically, if the "*G*" stands for graphic, it would follow that GIF (as in GIFt) would be the proper pronunciation.

However, many people, including myself, pronounce the *G* like a *J*, or JIF as in JIFFY. Interestingly, when on the phone with Unisys, the owners of the GIF algorithm, they pronounced it just as I do. I figure they're the source, so I've followed suit ever since.

GIFs have been the longest supported graphic file type on the Web, and they are extremely useful for a number of graphic file applications.

There are several important guidelines to determine if you should choose the GIF compression method for a specific graphic:

- **Line-drawn images**—Any graphic that uses few lines, such as a cartoon, is a good choice for GIF compression.
- **Images with few, flat colors**—With only a few colors and no light sources or gradations in that color, there's not going to be a lot of competition for those 256 colors in the compression method.

The image in Figure 27.1 shows a line-drawn cartoon. This image is an excellent choice for GIF compression. Figure 27.2 uses black, white, and two shades of gray—and all the colors are flat, with no light sources or gradations. This makes the image perfect for GIF compression.

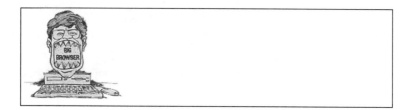

Figure 27.1
A line-drawn cartoon image by cartoonist Joe Forkan is a perfect choice for GIF format.

Figure 27.2
This image, using only black, white, and two shades of flat gray, is also a good choice for the GIF format.

JOINT PHOTOGRAPHIC EXPERTS GROUP (JPEG)

Frustrated with the limitations of GIFs, a group of photographic experts went to work on compression methods that would allow high quality compression while retaining millions of colors. The results are what we know today as *Joint Photographic Experts Group* (JPEG, also written JPG).

Note

The appropriate file extension, or suffix, for JPEG files is .jpg. There's a lot of confusion around this issue, because of the JPEG name. Always follow standard file naming conventions and use the .jpg suffix for all JPEG images.

➔ For more information on naming conventions, **see** "Managing HTML Documents Locally," **p. 62**

The algorithm that makes up the JPEG is, by nature, more complicated than that using the GIF. JPEGs use a *lossy* compression method. The algorithm focuses on removing data that is felt to be unimportant, instead of first mapping out areas of information that should be saved.

The JPEG method does this by dividing the image data into rectangular sections before applying the algorithm. On the one hand, this method gives you a lot of control in terms of how much information you're going to toss away; but, at high compression ratios, you can end up with a blocky, blotchy, blurry result.

These blocky sections are known as *artifacts*. Artifacts occur when you've over-compressed an image. You'll look at this a bit later, when you step through the optimization process. Working with JPEGs, just as with GIFs, requires a bit of skill and a fine hand to achieve the best results.

Because the JPEG format was specifically designed to manage files with a lot of color, there are certain types of images that best lend themselves to JPEG compression. The following list is a helpful guide to use when determining if JPEG is the best format for your image:

- Images with a lot of colors, such as with color photographs
- Graphics using gradient fills (see Figure 27.3)
- Graphics using light sources
- Photographs with much gradation, such as skies, sunsets, and oceans (see Figure 27.4)

Figure 27.3
Gradient fills are appropriate for JPEG format. The reason has to due with JPEGs ability to compress files without reducing the number of colors. If you tried this with a GIF, you'd lose the smooth transitions from one hue to the next.

Figure 27.4
Sunset pictures, particularly when in full color, contain a lot of gradation and will normally be processed by using JPEG format.

GRAPHIC OPTIMIZATION

Optimizing graphics is the technique by which a Web graphic designer reduces the file size of a graphic for acceptable download times, while maintaining the highest quality image he can produce.

The first step in optimization is to determine which file format is appropriate for the file. Using the general guidelines given earlier for GIF and JPEG formats will help you to achieve that crucial first step.

Interestingly, the guidelines discussed within this chapter for GIFs and JPEGs are not always accurate. Take for example a black-and-white photograph, or even a color photograph, with very little color information, light source, and gradients. With this example, it's going to take a little experimentation to determine which file type will help you achieve the smallest file size while retaining the most important information.

There's no cut-and-dry answer to this except through trial-and-error or by using one of the many graphic optimization tools available (see "Optimization Tools" later in this chapter).

After you've determined which file type is most appropriate, work with the available technologies within that graphic file format. To best understand this, follow the step-by-step optimization process by hand, using the professional graphics program Photoshop 4.0.

Note

You can optimize graphics with a wide range of tools. I selected Photoshop because I'm personally most comfortable with its use and find its palette control superior to many of the less professional programs on the market. Later in this chapter, I provide you with an excellent overview of the growing variety of Web-related graphics tools you can use for this process.

Before we begin our step-by-step, I've provided you with a list of helpful terms (see Table 27.1) that are used throughout the remainder of the chapter.

Table 27.1 Terms and Definitions for Web Graphic Optimization

Term	Definition
Color palette	There are several types of color palettes. These are numerically determined sets of colors within the graphic program that enable the designer to make specific choices regarding how an image is processed.
Adaptive palette	This palette allows you to make adaptations to a given image, including controlling color, depth, and dithering.
Indexed color	A software program such as Photoshop will take an image file and count its colors. If there are more than 256 colors in an image, indexing will reduce the image's palette to 256 colors—making it ready for GIF production. At that point, you can use the adaptive palette to further control aspects of the palette.
Exact palette	You'll see this appear when an image already has less than 256 colors—because the colors fit within the indexing limits, the specific number of colors used will appear. You can then determine whether to keep this number, or reduce it further with the adaptive palette.
Bit depth	Also known as *color depth*, this is the amount of total bit data that will be saved with your image. The optimization of images into the GIF format depends upon your ability to control bit depth.
Number of colors	In GIF optimization, there can be as few as 8 colors or as many as 256 colors. Limiting the number of colors is how you reduce the size of a GIF file during the optimization process.
Dithering	This is the process by which the computer and imaging software determine which color to use when reducing a palette. Remember the discussion of the GIF algorithm earlier in this chapter? I mentioned that a neon blue could conceivably show up as a sky blue during reduction. This is *dithering*. Ideally, you don't want your images to dither at all, which speaks to the issue of proper file format selection.
Maximum, High, Medium, Low	These settings are specific to JPEG optimization and refer to how much information is removed during the lossy compression process.

With the terminology defined, we can begin to optimize a graphic.

Optimizing a GIF

With an appropriate file for GIF optimization in hand, you're ready to step through the optimization process. Here's a checklist to be sure you're prepared:

- Your file is obviously ready for GIF optimization if it has flat color, few colors, and is line-drawn.

- You've scanned and sized your file to appropriate Web dimensions.
- The file is in RGB format—either a native Photoshop file, an EPS, or a JPG set to Maximum.

→ For information on scanning and sizing your files, **see** "Creating Professional Web Graphics," **p. 598**

→ To read about details on RGB color **see** "Color Concepts," **p. 529**

In Photoshop:

1. Select Image, Mode.
2. Choose Indexed Color.
3. When the Indexed Color dialog box pops up, select the Adaptive palette, no Dither (see Figure 27.5).

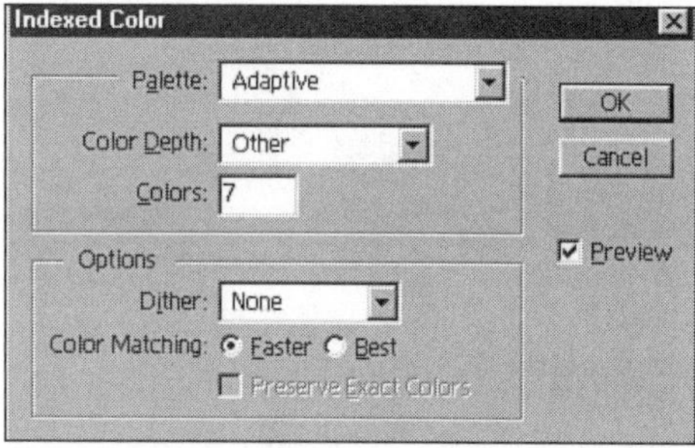

Figure 27.5 Using the Adaptive palette gives the designer specific numeric control over the color (bit) depth of an image. This helps significantly reduce the number of colors in an image without losing necessary visual information.

4. Reduce the Color (Bit) Depth to 7.
5. Save the file using the File, Export, GIF89 feature (see Figure 27.6).
6. Name the file `gif_test_7.gif` (be sure to save your original file as you'll be going back to it) .
7. View your results. You can compare them to mine in Figure 27.7.

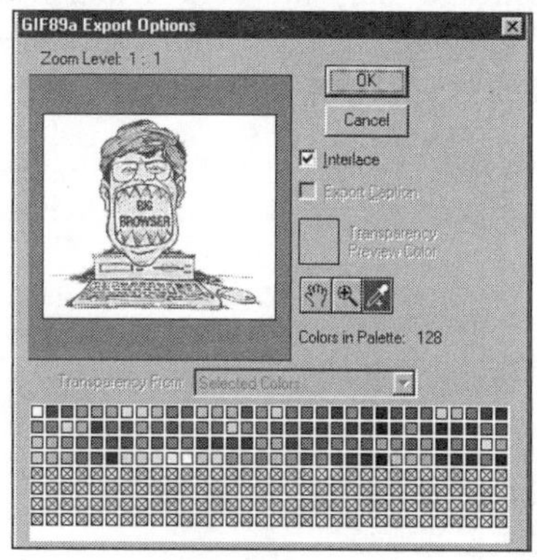

Figure 27.6 Exporting the image with the GIF89 export feature. Using this feature provides you with a dialog box that allows you to control several GIF features including transparency and interlacing.

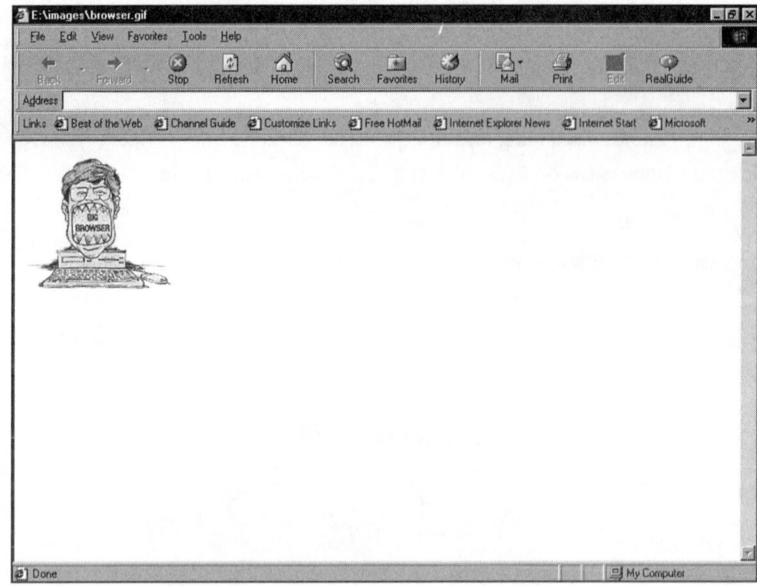

Figure 27.7
My GIF, optimized at 7 bits. The image still contains plenty of detail with no obvious loss of critical visual information.

Now, try reducing the bit depth even more.

1. Open the original file. In my case, it's `gif_optimize.psd`.
2. Select Image, Mode.
3. Once again, select Indexed Color.
4. Choose the Adaptive palette, set to no Dither.
5. Reduce the Bit Depth to 3.
6. Export the file (File, Export, GIF89).
7. Name the file `gif_test_3.gif`.

View your results. Are they acceptable, or did they reduce the colors or line integrity too much? If you liked the first example, but weren't happy with the second at 3 bits, go ahead and try optimizing at a variety of bit depths until you find the right one for your file.

Figure 27.8 shows my results. Note that there's not much visual difference between the two images visually, but the first file, `gif_test_7.gif`, is a total of 9KB, and the second, only 4KB.

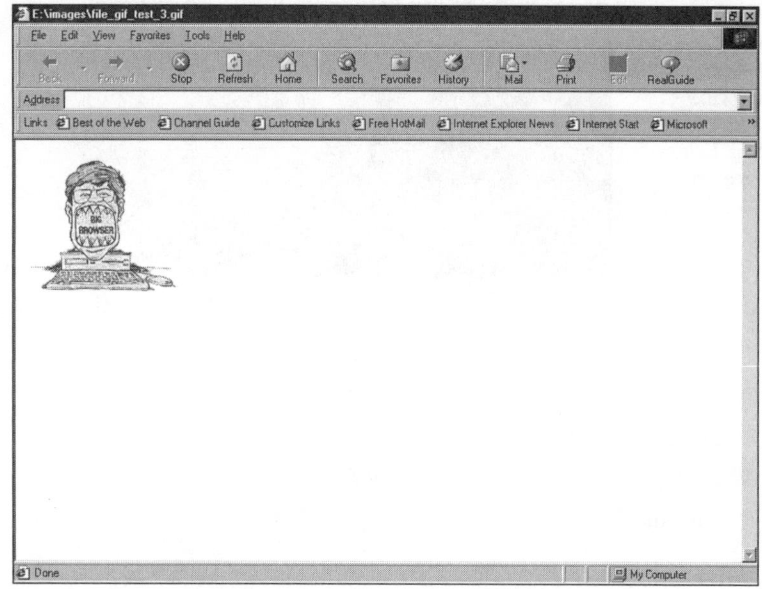

Figure 27.8
My GIF example, this time at a bit depth of 3. This bit depth is quite low, and if you compare it to the results in Figure 27.7, you'll see there's been significant loss of visual information, resulting in speckles rather than a smooth look.

OPTIMIZING A JPEG

Begin with a file appropriate for JPEG optimization. Here's a list of helpful guidelines:

- Images appropriate to optimize as JPEG files should have many colors, light sources, or color gradients.
- Your initial file should be in RGB format, either a native Photoshop file, an EPS, or a maximum set JPEG.
- The file to be optimized should be appropriately sized for Web use.

Now you're ready to optimize the file. In Photoshop:

1. Select File.
2. Choose Save A Copy from the drop-down menu.
3. Select JPG.
4. You now see a dialog box that allows you to make choices regarding your JPEG algorithm. For this exercise, choose High.
5. Save the file as `jpeg_test_high.jpg`.

View your file. It should be very clear and crisp, with no degradation or appearance of artifacts. However, the file size of my graphic (see Figure 27.9) is weighing in at 18KB. I very likely can get this file weight down without reducing the file so much that artifacts appear.

Figure 27.9
With my JPEG optimized at High setting, the quality of the image is very good, although this file can be optimized more without losing clarity.

1. Re-open the original file (mine is called `jpeg_test.psd`).
2. Choose File.
3. Select Save A Copy.
4. In the dialog box, set the JPEG optimization to Low.
5. Save the file as `jpeg_test_low.jpg`.

Looking at my file, I find that the weight has been reduced to 7KB. However, I see artifacts, as shown in Figure 27.10. This isn't to my taste, so I'm going to start at the beginning and try the Medium setting.

Figure 27.10
At Low setting (image magnified to show detail), my JPEG becomes blocky, blotchy, and blurry–filled with artifacts.

In this case, I'm happy with the Medium setting, which weighs 11KB and doesn't have any noticeable artifacts.

Note

High and Medium are often similar in visual quality, but not always similar in terms of weight. You'll find most of your JPEGs are going to be saved at Medium, with some at High, and–if you truly are looking to keep image integrity–very few will be saved at Low. Maximum is a good setting should you have a reason to want full color with absolutely no degradation. This is helpful when using larger files for specialty viewing.

Usually, I tend to let my JPEGs lean toward the higher setting. Given the choice, I'll sacrifice some page weight for image quality. My eye is particular—I can usually see artifacts appear at the Medium setting. This causes what I call the "vaseline effect," a blurry, blotchy result that is disturbing to my eye.

I'm always going to opt for quality when the difference in size is 5KB or so. I'd personally much rather have a slightly larger file size at the cost of download time than poor quality, unprofessional images.

Your JPEG mileage may vary. The more you practice optimization techniques, the more skilled you will become at knowing what type of file format to use, how much or how little to optimize a graphic, and when your specific circumstances allow you leeway for variation in file weight.

ADDITIONAL GRAPHIC TECHNIQUES

There are several graphic techniques involving the GIF and JPEG file formats that are critical to your Web graphic production work. They include progressive rendering, transparency, and animation.

➔ To find detailed information about Animated GIFs, **see** "Imagemaps, Animation, and Special Graphic Techniques," **p. 655**

PROGRESSIVE RENDERING

This technique is used to keep a site visitor's visual attention while graphics are downloading from a server to a Web page. The concept is that the individual will see portions of the graphic until all of its binary data is loaded into the browser.

It's an effective method, and it is better than having images "pop" into a page. The downloading process seems smoother when progressive rendering is in place. However, not all designers agree with me—much less each other. Therefore, you might want to learn progressive rendering techniques and make your own decisions based on personal and professional preferences.

Progressive rendering can be achieved in both the GIF and JPEG format.

INTERLACED GIFS

Interlacing is the term used for GIFs that progressively render.

Photoshop supports interlacing, as do all the popular Web graphic applications.

To create an interlaced GIF in Photoshop, simply be sure that the Interlace box is checked when exporting your GIF file with the GIF89 export utility.

An interlaced GIF will first appear fuzzy, and then slowly clarify as the GIF data downloads to the Web browser.

Progressive JPEGs

It's important to note that you cannot interlace a JPEG. However, a technology has been developed to allow JPEGs to progressively render. This is the *progressive* JPEG format. Photoshop, as well as many contemporary Web imaging programs, allow you to create JPEGS that render progressively.

As mentioned earlier in the chapter, the JPEG algorithm works by reducing rectangular sections of color data within an image. If you conceptually reverse this process and imagine data flowing into the rectangular blocks, you'll be visualizing the way a progressive JPEG renders. An integrated series of blocks create the image that first appears with little graphic data. With each new delivery of information from the server, the JPEG blocks receive more data until the download is complete.

While interlaced GIFs first appear fuzzy and then get clearer, progressive JPEGs first appear blocky and blurry. I'm not a big fan of this, because while the JPEG is loading, it looks, at least to me, like a badly optimized JPEG, complete with those blocky, blurry, blotchy artifacts—the vaseline effect.

Note

When serving progressive JPEGs at high speeds, the vaseline effect is reduced or eliminated, improving the visual experience.

Another consideration when working with progressive JPEGS is that they are not supported by most browsers prior to the 3.0 generation. Therefore, your visitors using older browsers will not see your graphic.

Tip from

Standard GIFs and JPEGS scroll into place rather than render progressively. Some people prefer this look. Still, most usability studies and anecdotal information suggest that progressive rendering helps keep individuals on a page. Therefore, in many cases it's usually wise to progressively render your graphics.

Transparency

Transparency is sometimes described as an effect that places your graphic on a clear piece of tape. This means you can place that tape on a background and the background will show through the tape.

This is particularly effective when you're creating graphics that sit on a background, especially graphics that aren't a standard rectangular shape.

The technique takes a little bit of time, patience, and an excellent hand and eye to learn.

Again, I do my transparencies in Photoshop, but your favorite Web graphics program is likely to have a helpful method by which to make an image transparent.

Note

Only GIFs can be transparent. JPEG technology does not include a transparency option.

Let's say you want to place a text header image over a background texture. The text selection shown here is ornate, with a lot of circular shapes. Follow these steps to create a transparency:

1. Choose File, New.
2. Because you want your header to be 350 pixels wide by 50 pixels high, enter those values into the New Image dialog box.
3. Set the image type to Transparent (note that this only has to do with Photoshop file management, not the creation of GIF transparency—an entirely different mechanism). Mode is set to RGB.
4. Select Edit, Fill.
5. Fill the image with a color that is sufficiently dissimilar to any color you are using.
6. Now choose Layer, New, Layer.
7. Add your text by using the Type Tool.
8. Flatten the image.
9. Optimize the image as described earlier, by using Indexing and the Adaptive palette.
10. Export as a GIF89, and the GIF89 dialog box will appear.
11. Deselect the background color with the color picker.
12. Save your image as `transparency.gif`.

Place the image into your HTML page and view the results. You can see that the image appears to be seamless with the background in Figure 27.11. This is an effective transparency.

→ To learn about how to add images to an HTML document, **see** "Working with Images," **p. 196**

Tip from molly

Don't be disappointed if your image isn't quite correct. You might see white or colored edges or ragged edges around your image. This isn't your fault so much as the limitations of transparency. Keep practicing the technique and selecting from colors that are close enough but far enough from any colors in the image itself. Eventually, you'll master the technique.

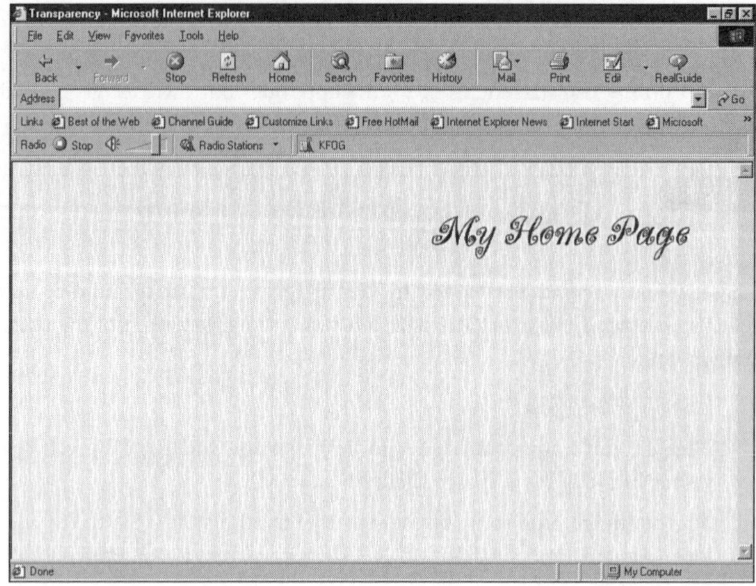

Figure 27.11
A transparent GIF appears seamless over textured backgrounds because the background color has been removed from the images

ADAPTIVE VERSUS WEB PALETTE

In recent editions of Photoshop (4.0 and 5.0), as well as other graphic programs, the inclusion of the Web-safe palette has offered designers a way to save their GIFs specifically to that palette.

→ The Web-safe palette is discussed in detail earlier in this book, **see** "Color Concepts," **p. 539**

There's some dissention over this concept. Doesn't it make perfect sense to just use the Web-safe palette when saving GIFs? There are at least two reasons why you might consider not using this method of saving a file:

1. The 216 color palette is just that—it contains 216 colors. Using the Adaptive palette, you can reduce that number of colors significantly to have greater control over your file weight.
2. Limiting colors by hand gives you much greater control over the palette. The 216-color palette will always dither colors to match that palette, sometimes giving you unacceptable results (see Figure 27.12). Figure 27.13 shows the same file optimized by hand, with profoundly better visual results and only a 4KB increase in file weight.

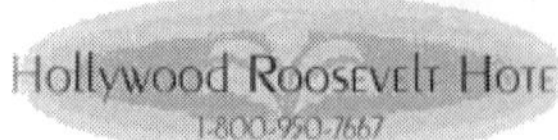

Figure 27.12
The 216 Web-safe palette can sometimes dither graphics unacceptably. The weight is low: 4KB.

Figure 27.13
The same file, optimized with the adaptive palette. The weight is slightly higher: 9KB.

How, then, can Web graphic designers ensure that their graphics don't dither when viewed in unsafe circumstances? You can certainly decide to use the Web-safe palette if you prefer. Here are a few other tips:

- If you're creating graphics from scratch, begin with colors selected from the safe palette.
- If you must use unsafe color, try to be sure that the graphics are enhancements rather than necessary to your site if you are concerned about support. An example of a necessary GIF would be anything that contains text pertinent to the page. If this dithers, it could seriously affect readability.

Note

Remember, unless you create a JPEG yourself or replace every color in that JPEG by hand with a Web-safe color, JPEGs will always be unsafe. The JPEG algorithm doesn't limit the palette and, in fact, supports up to 24 bits of color information–that's a lot of color. Users with browser or monitor limitations will see a poorer-quality graphic in these cases.

PNG and Other Up-and-Coming Graphic Formats

Another file format supported by some Web browsers, including Internet Explorer 4.0 and higher and Netscape Navigator 4.04 and higher is the *Portable Network Graphics* format, or PNG for short. While it's still not widely supported, it is felt that PNG offers even better compression than a GIF.

Caution

Despite the fact that 4.0 generation browsers have chosen to support the PNG format, that support is sometimes buggy. The biggest perpetrator of this is Netscape Navigator. As a result, using PNG for Internet-based Web sites is, at this time, risky at best.

Using the lossless method, the difference between PNG and GIF compression is that PNG isn't limited to a 256-color palette. It can also be interlaced, making it a very attractive option for the future. Photoshop, as well as many other, newer Web graphic imaging programs has PNG support for file development and optimization. For more information on the PNG format, visit the World Wide Web Consortium's specification for PNG at `http://www.w3.org/TR/REC-png-multi.html`.

Because the constant need for better graphic compression is a major concern in Web development, two types of file formats are making the news. First, JPEG 2000 is a new JPEG standard that offers a more sophisticated method of managing color. Its compression algorithm is touted as being artifact free. Second, the SVG, or *Scalable Vector Graphics* takes advantage of the power of vector, rather than raster, graphics, making the end result scalable. Perhaps most interesting, SVG is based on XML and is entirely text-coded. This means that instead of fancy algorithms and compression methods, the way that SVG graphics are generated is using code.

➔ For details about XML and SVG, **see** "Understanding XHTML, XML, and Emerging Languages", **p. 494**

PROFESSIONAL GRAPHICS TOOLS

I've heard many people discuss graphic tools over the years. Some make the argument that only professional graphic design tools will do, others express the well-taken point that it's not the tool but the designer, and ultimately tools don't matter.

For die-hard supporters of tools that are not industry standards, you'll be happy to hear that many of your favorite programs are making a concerted effort to bring you the highest quality output possible. Another exciting issue in the area of Web graphic software is new-and-improved image editing suites from a variety of industry standard vendors.

But the idea that tools don't matter is a very disturbing untruth. While I hardly mean to imply here that shareware or a variety of professional tools are useless for the casual Web designer, I do have a major concern for those of you who are seeking to be employed in the Web design field.

If you're pursuing professional Web design, you must be willing to purchase and learn the sometimes expensive, higher-end tools to compete.

Furthermore, knowing the skills associated with those tools puts you in the driver's seat when it comes to being able to find employment with design firms. They're going to be using industry standards, and you're not going to be as marketable if you don't have the skills.

You are infinitely more attractive as a Web graphic designer with Adobe and Macromedia product skills than you will be with, say, CorelDRAW skills, PHOTO-PAINT skills, or Paint Shop Pro know-how.

On the other hand, if your design needs are more personal, any one of these and other tools will be helpful to you. It's finding the right fit that counts, particularly if you're not interested in pursuing professional level jobs where the pro standards are typically Adobe and Macromedia products.

That said, let's turn and take a look at some of the Web graphic design tools out there.

We'll be looking at a variety of tools here, including imaging and illustration programs, optimization tools, multimedia development tools, plug-in and enhancement programs, and stock art and photography resources.

IMAGING AND ILLUSTRATION PROGRAMS

The following section overviews feature programs that enable you to work with photographs, actually create images with color and type, scan images, add enhancements, and optimize graphics.

ADOBE PHOTOSHOP

This is a key player within professional Web graphic production tools (see Figure 27.14). You'll notice throughout this book that I use it almost exclusively to design and optimize my graphics.

Photoshop's features include the following:

- Photoshop creates raster graphics, which are the suitable type for Web image optimization.
- Photoshop layers are a powerful way to work with images.
- GIF89 Export feature allows for the creation of transparency and interlaced GIFs.
- Versions 4.0 and later contain a Web-safe palette that is useful when optimizing graphics for the Web.
- Full-feature photographic manipulation and filters allow you to improve the quality of photos, as well as alter and arrange them as you please.
- Photoshop 5.0 and higher offer powerful typesetting options and other filter features such as bevel, drop shadow, and light sources.

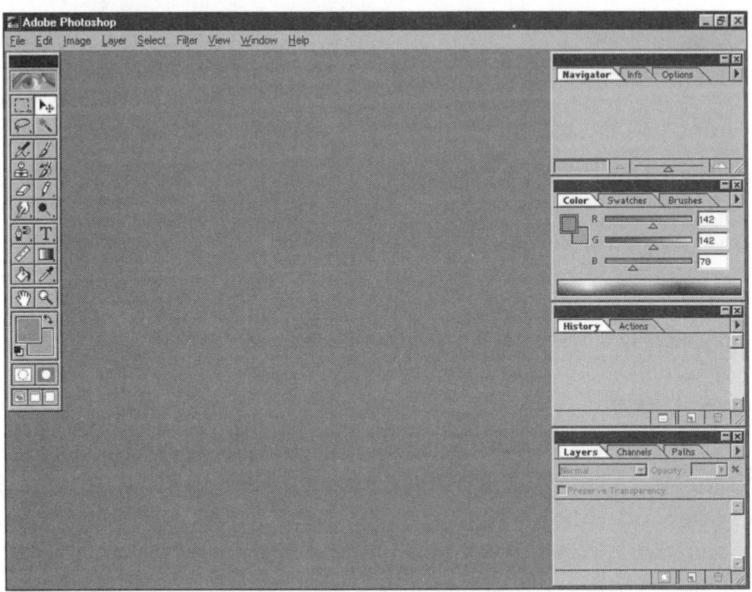

Figure 27.14
The Adobe Photoshop interface. As a design industry standard application, Adobe Photoshop features, support, and third-party solutions are vast.

For product information and costs, go to **`http://www.adobe.com/`**.

Adobe Illustrator

An excellent tool for creating vector-based graphics, Illustrator also offers advanced typesetting options (see Figure 27.15).

Also by Adobe, other features of Illustrator include the ability to link URLs to images.

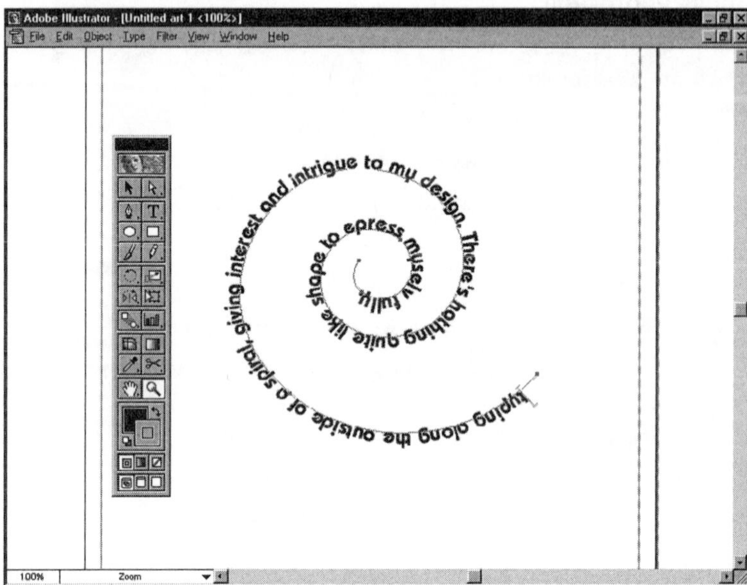

Figure 27.15 Setting type in Illustrator 8.0. Using Illustrator allows you to move, change, and stylize type with advanced tools.

→ Learn more about Adobe Illustrator, **see** "Graphic Type for the Web", **p. 632**

Adobe ImageReady

This exciting product is designed specifically to optimize graphics for Web use. One of its most powerful features is that its interface is similar to Photoshop's (see Figure 27.16), so there is easy adaptability for Photoshop users. In fact, ImageReady is now packaged with Photoshop 5.5, and Photoshop 5.5 has incorporated ImageReady technology into its Save-as-Web optimization feature. As with Photoshop and Illustrator, more information on ImageReady is available at `http://www.adobe.com/`.

CorelDRAW

CorelDRAW holds an esteemed level as a drawing program among certain computer users—usually those involved in business and industry. However, it's still not considered the standard when it comes to professional graphic design. Still, the recent edition of CorelDRAW, version 9.0, includes a number of attractive new features:

- Customizable interface for power users
- Kerning and leading for type
- More sophisticated palette control than in previous versions

- Guidelines for image rotation, nudging, and multiple select
- Interactive tools for Perspective Drop Shadow, Contour, and Mesh Fill

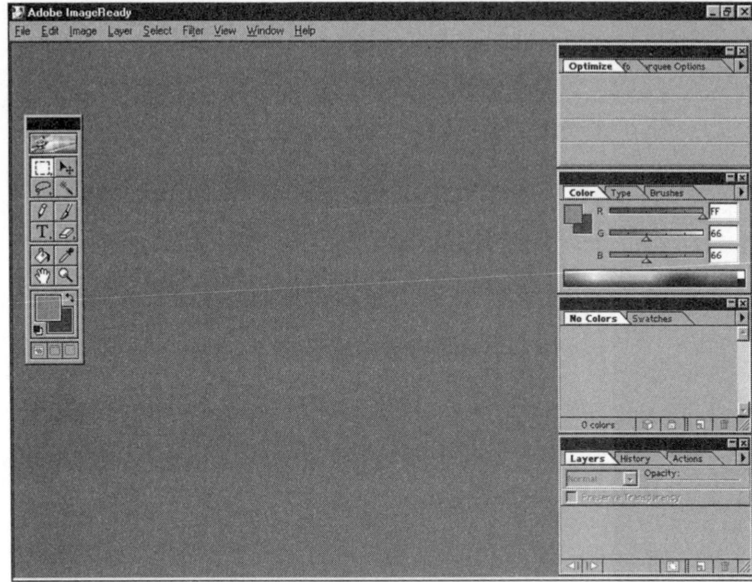

Figure 27.16
The ImageReady interface. ImageReady offers real-time compression and batch processing, as well as tools for animating images.

COREL PHOTO-PAINT

Corel's photographic program allows users to scan and manipulate images. Its features include the following:

- Ability to assign hyperlinks to objects for imagemap creation
- Support for animated GIFs
- Ability to preview JPEGs for optimization determination
- Web-safe palette support

Visit the Corel Web site at **http://www.corel.com/** (see Figure 27.17) for more information on Draw and Photo-Paint.

JASC PAINT SHOP PRO

A favorite among many Web enthusiasts, Paint Shop Pro is gaining features as we speak. Unfortunately, it's only available for the PC platform, making it a tough sell to professional graphic companies using Macs.

In version 5.0, these features allow users to

- Work in layers, as you can in Photoshop
- Create transparencies
- Interlace GIFs
- Make GIF animations with the built-in Animation Shop

Figure 27.17
Corel's Web site uses graphics created by using Corel software.

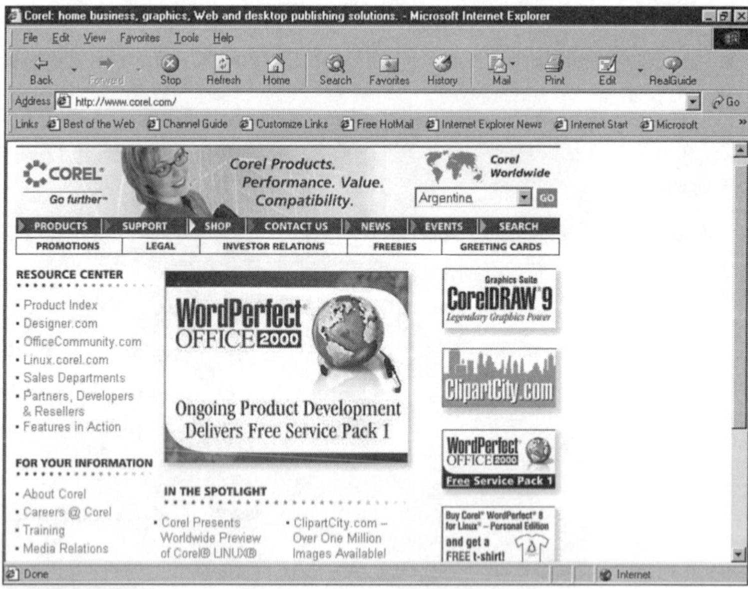

Download a demo of Paint Shop Pro (see figure 27.18) from its parent company, JASC, at `http://www.jasc.com/`. You'll also find support information, extended information about JASC products, and links to related resources.

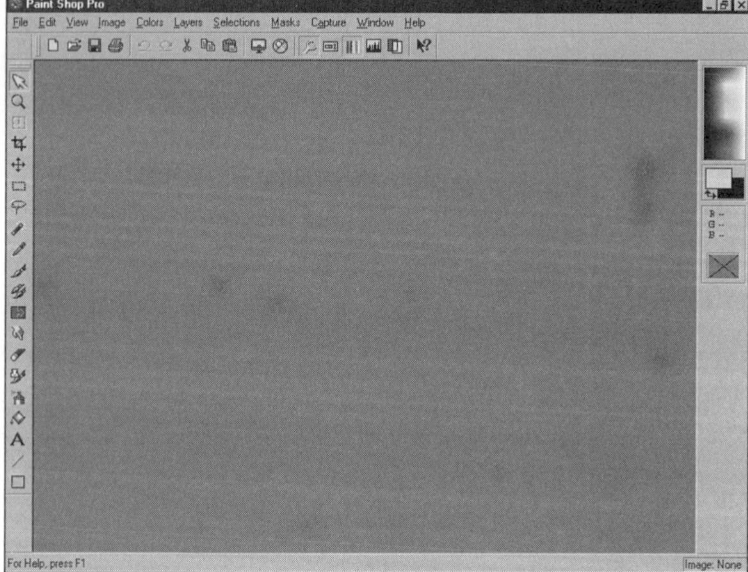

Figure 27.18
The interface for Paint Shop Pro downloaded from JASC.

MACROMEDIA FIREWORKS

This exciting program is from Macromedia. Geared specifically to the creation and management of Web graphics, Fireworks includes the following features:

- Advanced support for imagemapping
- Slicing graphics for table positioning
- HTML generation for graphic positioning
- JavaScript rollovers—Fireworks generates the code for you
- Special effects such as bevels and drop shadows
- Live redraw: no need to undo, simply reset the parameters of an effect and it will automatically redraw
- Comparative, same-screen optimization that allows you to choose between a variety of optimization results before exporting the image

Figure 27.19 demonstrates working on a graphic with Macromedia Fireworks.

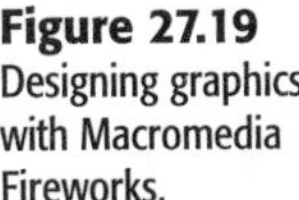

Figure 27.19
Designing graphics with Macromedia Fireworks.

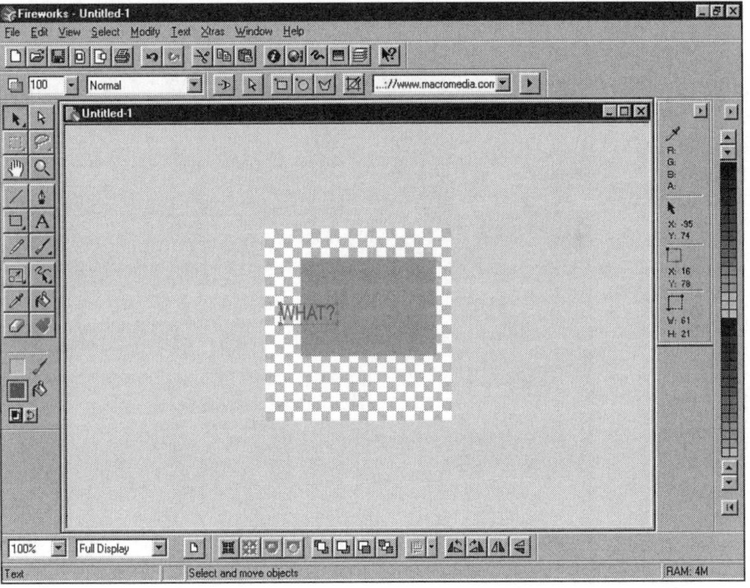

MACROMEDIA FREEHAND

A competitor to Adobe Illustrator, Freehand is a vector graphics design tool with new features added in version 8.0 that make it easier to produce Web-ready image files.

Like Adobe ImageReady, Freehand includes animation capabilities and handy batch processing of graphics.

Macromedia products are available at **http://www.macromedia.com/** (see Figure 27.20). You can download demos, read and join on discussions about Macromedia software, and see Macromedia results in action on their colorful, active Web site.

Ulead PhotoImpact and Web Razor

A very impressive product for a low price: Ulead PhotoImpact and Web Razor are suites designed with the Web in mind. I'm especially impressed with their combined ability to make great specialty graphics, such as background tiles. Note that Web Razor is the effects package that not only works in tangent with PhotoImpact but can be plugged in to both Adobe Photoshop and Paint Shop Pro. Other features include the following:

- Imagemap support
- Button maker
- SmartSaver (a very handy optimization tool)
- Specialty filters

Visit Ulead at **http://www.ulead.com/** for a variety of Web and image-related software applications, clip art, and resources.

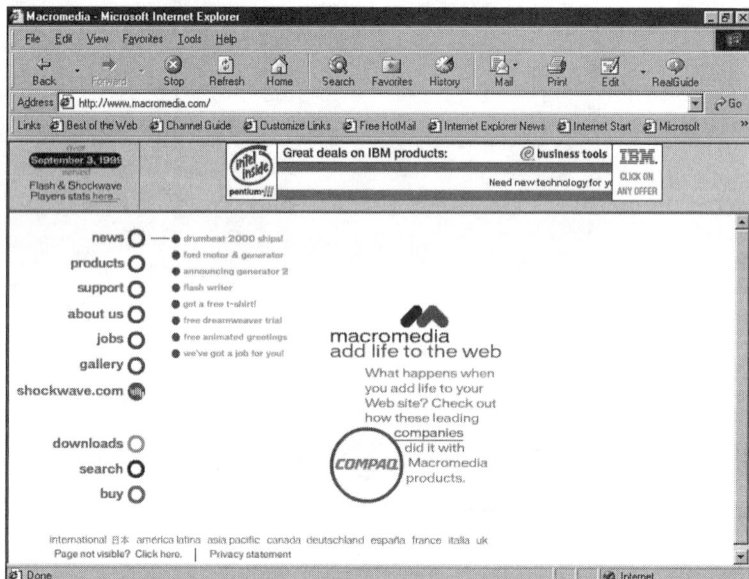

Figure 27.20 Macromedia's exciting Web site makes use of a wide range of Macromedia software.

Microsoft Image Composer

A very nice, compact imaging application (see Figure 27.21), Microsoft Image Composer works in tandem with Microsoft GIF Animator, which gives it maximum impact as a Web imaging program. Image Composer is shipped with FrontPage98 and the standalong version of FrontPage 2000 (Windows versions only). More information on how it works, how to use it, and new and improved enhancements can be found at **http://www.microsoft.com/imagecomposer/**.

The following are some of Image Composer's features:

- Sprites are similar to layers, allowing you control over your images.
- Text and text styles help you create headers, buttons, and typographic images.
- Patterns, fills, and effects give you a lot of power over your images.

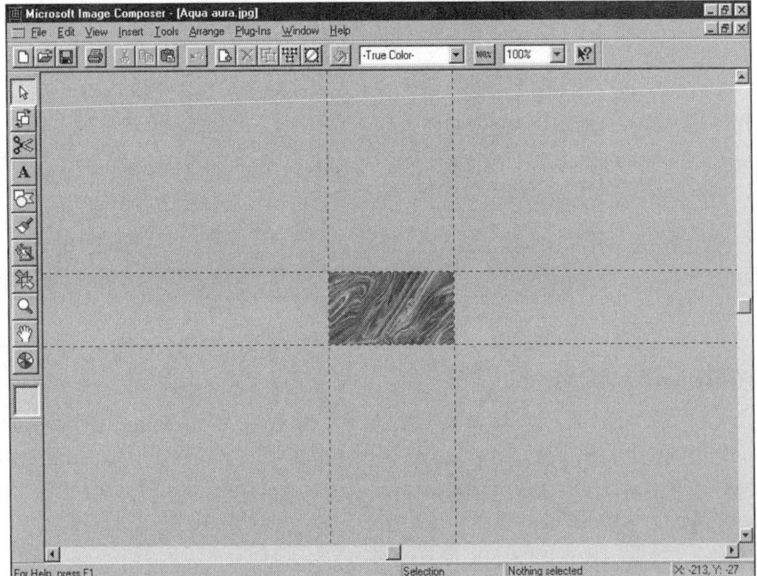

Figure 27.21 In this figure, I'm creating a background graphic using Microsoft's Image Composer.

MICROSOFT PHOTODRAW

With its release of Office 2000, Microsoft introduced a new imaging product, PhotoDraw. This interesting program is intended to work as a user-friendly graphics creation tool for people working in any Office program—whether it is Word, PowerPoint, or FrontPage.

PhotoDraw contains some truly fun predesigned objects and built-in effects, which allow nondesigners to quickly create graphics for a Web site and easily add shadow effects (Figure 27.22). That's the positive side—and I certainly recommend taking a look at the product if even just for fun.

However, sometimes PhotoDraw tries to be too many things to too many programs. Despite its fun features, it fails to optimize graphics with the kind of sophistication you can get from other tools mentioned in this chapter. Moreover, it doesn't allow for precise measurement and manipulation of objects within the interface. So, while it's worth taking a look at, I don't recommend it for your professional Web design needs.

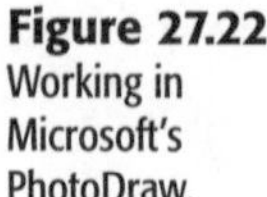

Figure 27.22
Working in Microsoft's PhotoDraw.

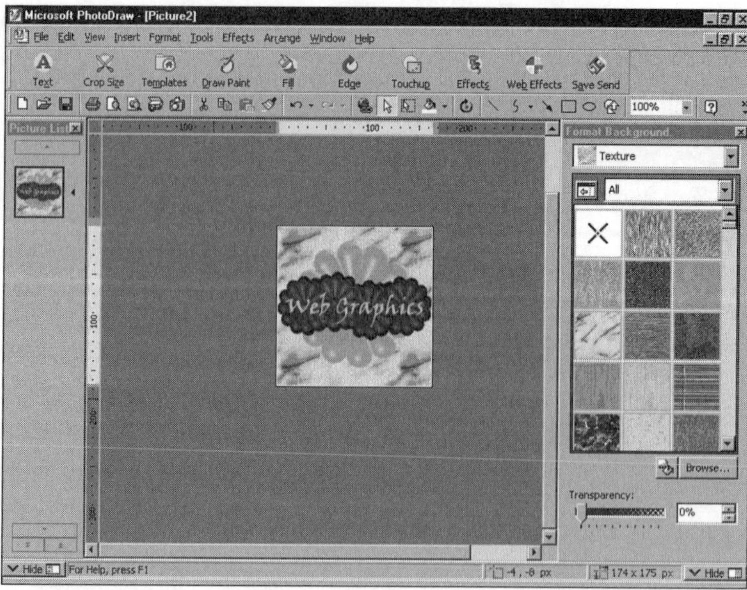

ANIMATED GIF PROGRAMS

One of the easiest ways to add a bit of life to your Web pages is through the use of animated GIF images. The animation is encoded within the image file, meaning that all browsers can read it. Other animation options may cost more money and not be as cross-platform, cross-browser compatible as GIF animations.

Here are some helpful GIF animation programs. As you've already discovered—animation is fast becoming part of the new wave of image production tools, including Photoshop.

GIF CONSTRUCTION SET

A popular shareware tool for constructing animated GIFs on the PC, GIF Construction Set contains a Windows 95-based wizard that walks the creator through the simplified process of creating an animated image. For users more comfortable with the animation process, GIF Construction Set also offers the ability to bypass the wizard and build the images yourself. GIF Construction Set is available at **`http://www.mindworkshop.com/`**.

GIF MOVIE GEAR

The power of this animation tool lies primarily in its palette control and its ability to optimize each individual graphic, removing unnecessary data. GIF Movie Gear is available from Gamani at **`http://www.gamani.com/`** (see Figure 27.23). Alas, it's only for the PC.

ULEAD GIF ANIMATOR

Another great PC utility, I personally love the way you can add special effects to your graphics by using Ulead GIF Animator. Sweeps, fades, fills, and general fun can be had, all with the click of a mouse.

Figure 27.23
Animating in Gamani's GIF Movie Gear. Using the Preview feature, I can see the animation live as I'm building it, and can make adjustments as necessary.

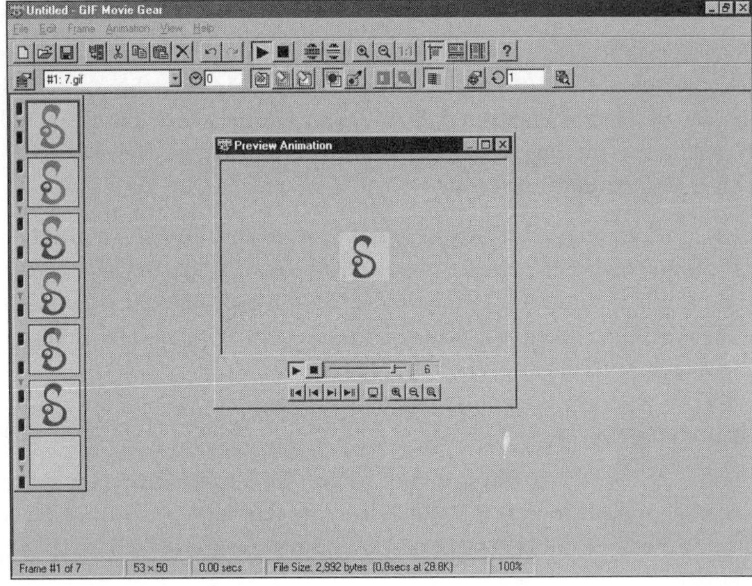

Ulead products are long on productivity and short on expense. A perfect combination for lower budget projects, they can be found at **`http://www.ulead.com/`**.

MICROSOFT GIF ANIMATOR

GIF Animator works with Microsoft's Image Composer. Its features include the following:

- Drag-and-drop images directly from Microsoft Image Composer.
- Special effects such as loop, spin, and fade.
- Customize palettes, or let the application optimize the animation for you.

You can find out more about Microsoft GIF Animator at **`http://www.microsoft.com/imagecomposer/gifanimator/gifanin.htm`**.

GIF BUILDER

Relax, Macintosh fans, here's one for you. GIF Builder allows you to manually build GIF animations or import QuickTime movies. GIF Builder can be found at **`http://iawww.epfl.ch/Staff/Yves.Piguet/clip2gif-home/GifBuilder.html`**.

OPTIMIZATION TOOLS

Optimization tools help get your graphics down to Web-ready size. Here's a look at some of the particularly helpful applications.

DEBABELIZER PRO

You can take tedious guesswork out of optimization with this powerful program that processes and optimizes graphics. While you can do everything that Debabelizer does to a graphic by hand in Photoshop, Debabelizer has the added advantage of batch processing files as well as offering up file type and size comparisons. Debabelizer Pro can be found at `http://www.debabelizer.com/`.

Be wary, however. Debabelizer Pro is a considerable expense. I've only used it when working for design companies requiring large quantities of graphic production. For smaller clients and specific applications, I prefer to use Photoshop and do my optimization by hand or by using one of the other tools listed in this section. You'll need to evaluate your circumstances to come up with the most sensible approach.

ULEAD SMARTSAVER

For the PC user, SmartSaver cannot be beat for a simple interface and great output. What's more, it's a whole lot less expensive than Debabelizer—perfect for smaller Web graphic production facilities and personal use. Ulead SmartSaver can be found at `http://www.ulead.com/`.

GRAPHIC ENHANCEMENT PROGRAMS AND PLUG-INS

The way you present a graphic is as important as the graphic's quality itself. A well-processed image, while strong on its own, is rendered even more classy when enhanced with drop shadows, feathered edges, and geometric edge designs, just to name a few.

These effects, as well as innumerable others, can be achieved through the use of plug-ins to Photoshop or Photoshop-style imaging programs.

ALIEN SKIN SOFTWARE

With 21 filters, Alien Skin's premier plug-in package is Eye Candy. It offers a wide range of powerful standards as well as fun creations such as drop shadows, glows, motion trails, jiggle, weave, and water drop (see Figure 27.24). Find out all about Eye Candy and other Alien Skin products at `http://www.alienskin.com/`.

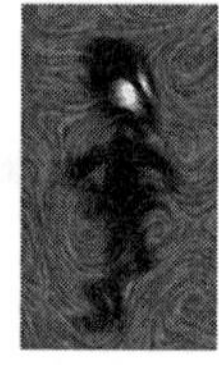

Figure 27.24
Weird and wacky filters from Alien Skin.

AUTO F/X

With such enhancements as photo edges from Photographic Edges (see Figure 27.25), type edging with Typographic Edges, and a powerful image optimizer and color palette controller known as WebVise Totality, Auto F/X makes some mighty plug-ins available on the Macintosh and PC platforms. Visit Auto F/X at **http://www.autofx.com/**.

Figure 27.25
This graphic uses a wavy edge effect from Auto F/X Photographic Edges and a drop-shadow for a professional edge.

KAI'S POWER TOOLS

The king of enhancements, Kai's Power Tools can help you create background tiles, Web buttons, and complex color blends. Kai's Power Tools is available for both the Macintosh and Windows platforms from MetaCreations at **http://www.metacreations.com/kpt/** (see Figure 27.26).

Figure 27.26
Kai's Power Tools from MetaCreations.

GRAPHIC SOURCE MATERIAL

You'll also want to have sources for icons, patterns, stock photos, and fonts. There are numerous sources of freeware or shareware material on the Internet. Higher-quality material can be acquired on CD-ROM and must be used according to the associated license.

For professional projects, it's definitely worth your while to accumulate a solid library of stock photography, clip art, and fonts.

EYEWIRE

Adobe Studios offers an excellent line of quality stock materials. You can get a regular paper catalog delivered via snail mail, or you can browse and purchase stock materials online at **http://www.eyewire.com/**.

PHOTODISC

A visit to Photodisc will provide you with a shopping source for plenty of stock photos, backgrounds, and links to other sites of interest. Free membership entitles you to downloads of comp art and photos at **http://www.photodisc.com/**. You can also order a standard mail catalog.

ARTTODAY

An inexpensive alternative to high-end stock materials such as Adobe Studios and Photodisc, a membership to Art Today (**http://www.arttoday.com/**) gives you unlimited downloads for a very reasonable yearly fee. The quality varies, but you can and will find a variety of useful images and art. I've found this resource to be well worth the price tag of only $29.95 per year.

FUN AND FREE SITES

The Web is filled with sites that offer downloadable clip art, photos, backgrounds, and animations galore. It would be impossible to list them all here, but I've got a few favorites.

- The Internet Baglady—She's a personal friend, and her site is simply fun! The Baglady has searched for and found a wide number of inexpensive and free ways to get art for and information about building a Web site. The Internet Baglady can be found at **http://www.dumpsterdive.com/**.
- Caboodles of Clip Art—A great site for the home page enthusiast or design novice, Caboodles of Clip Art can be found at **http://www.caboodles.com/**.
- Microsoft Images Gallery—high-end selection of images from Microsoft at **http://www.microsoft.com/gallery/images/default.asp**.

TROUBLESHOOTING

STARTING LIKE A PRO

I want to set myself up as a professional Web graphic designer. What tools are absolutely necessary to purchase?

I would buy Photoshop and ImageStyler to start with. Then, I'd think about adding Macromedia Flash to my toolbox. If you're concerned about price and are currently a student, you can get student discounts from resellers. These can often be very significant. Educators can also get impressive discounts on software as well. Try before you buy. Download demos and work with them first—it's better to know you're going to use a program than spend good money for it only to find that it never gets used.

PHOTOSHOP A NECESSITY?

I am an ardent admirer of Jasc's Paint Shop Pro. I get excellent results with my Web graphics and am not interested in spending the money and time on Photoshop. Is this a problem?

I've seen some awesome graphics created with Paint Shop Pro, and I'm convinced that any tool that meets your needs and makes you happy is the tool for you if you have no intention of attempting to look for work as a professional Web designer. If you do, the emphasis is very likely going to be on experience with professional tools from Adobe and Macromedia.

TRAINING

I have Photoshop, Illustrator, and Flash and want to learn how to use them well, but don't know where to go for more information?

There are plenty of good books on the market, but I've found that courses and instructional videos can be a tremendous way to jump over the learning curve of some of these products. Try Ziff-Davis University for low-cost, online courses. Lynda Weinman has produced some great videos.

Note

You can find Ziff-Davis University at `http://www.zdu.com/`. Lynda Weinman's instructional videos can be ordered from `http://store.lynda.com/`.

DESIGNING FOR THE REAL WORLD

CREATING A BACKGROUND GRAPHIC: COMPARE AND CONTRAST

To give you a feel for graphic design tools and how they work, I'm going to ask you to create a Web background graphic using a compare/contrast process with different tools.

If you don't have the tools in question, download demos from the appropriate Web sites and take it from there. Also, feel free to add any design tool of your choice to the compare and contrast exercise.

Then, you do the activity, write down the time it takes to complete each portion of the activity, and then write down your thoughts about what you found to be advantages and disadvantages using these programs.

USING PHOTOSHOP

Begin the exercise by following these steps:

1. Select File, New file. The New dialog appears.
2. Create a file that is 50 pixels wide by 50 pixels high.
3. Fill the file with a color by selecting a color from the Swatches palette, and then choosing Edit, Fill. Choose Foreground Color from the menu and click OK.
4. Select Filter, Noise, Add Noise. You can achieve a recycled paper look by adding a Noise level of 25, Uniform distribution, Monochromatic. Click OK.
5. Optimize and save the file.

You can create a test HTML page including the image, and load the file into your browser to see how it looks.

USING PHOTOIMPACT

PhotoImpact has a terrific tool called Background Designer which you can use to create backgrounds, as follows:

1. Select Web, Background Designer. The Background Designer dialog opens.
2. Click the Generate a new tile option button. Then, put the dimensions of the tile you'd like to create in the Cell-size text boxes. I chose to leave the size at the default 80 pixels by 80 pixels.
3. Choose a Schema from the Schema drop-down menu. I chose Texture 17.
4. Now, select a texture from the texture box. You might like to modify the texture using the Background type choices, the Palette Ramp Editor, and by changing the settings available to you in the dialog box. Each setting you make will be reflected in the preview box at the top right of the Designer's screen (see Figure 27.27).
5. Once you're satisfied with the look of your background, click OK. PhotoImpact will generate the tile.
6. Select File, SmartSaver to optimize the graphic.

→ For more information on creating a variety of background graphics, **see** "Creating Professional Web Graphics", **p. 603**

USING PAINT SHOP PRO

To create a background tile in Paint Shop Pro:

1. Select File, New. The New Image dialog box appears.

2. Enter the width and height in pixels (I used 50×50). Resolution should be set to 72 pixels per inch (ppi). Select the background color of your choice, and the Image type (I used 24-bit color as I can modify this later). Click OK.
3. Using the paintbrush, gently add some light texture to the tile, or select Image, Add Noise and add noise to the tile (Figure 27.28).

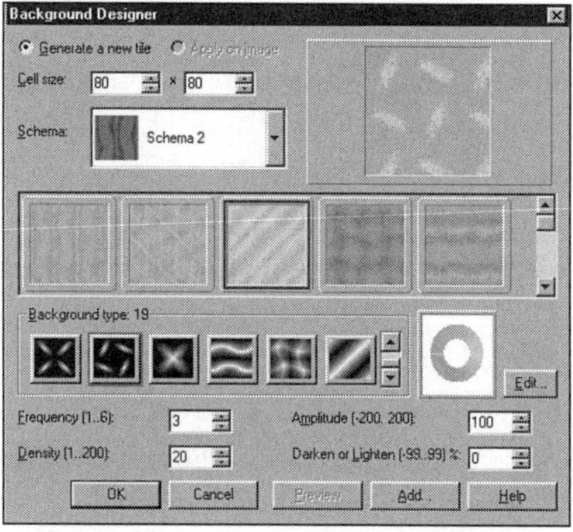

Figure 27.27 PhotoImpact's Background Designer.

Figure 27.28 Monochromatic options were not available when adding noise in Paint Shop Pro.

4. Optimize the file by first selecting Colors, Decrease Color Depth. Select a value that keeps the integrity of the look but allows the lowest number of colors.
5. Select File, Save. Choose GIF format and save your file.

I did the exercises, too. Your results may vary from mine, which is perfectly fine. I just want you to have a chance to actively try the tools and make judgements about how their various features work for you.

Following are some advantages and disadvantages of the process.

PHOTOSHOP

Advantages: I liked the control I had with Photoshop. From being able to choose directly from a color-safe palette to controlling exactly how I would optimize the image, I felt that all decisions were left to me. This enabled me to work quickly and meet my goal with quality results.

Disadvantages: In order to manage Photoshop quickly, users will need to have some experience working with it. It has so many features that it can be confusing to those who aren't familiar with it.

PHOTOIMPACT

Advantages: While the control wasn't the same as with Photoshop, what PhotoImpact offers are options. The Background Designer is so much fun that I could spend a lot of time playing around with it. It is a very creative tool. The interface is also quite easy to maneuver, and SmartSaver helped me to see up front what file formats would work best for optimization. While I already knew what would be the best option in terms of optimization, those designers with less experience are sure to appreciate the features of SmartSaver.

Disadvantages: As with Photoshop, there's a lot of stuff here. Opening up the different applications, which are truly like smaller programs within the parent program, is more time consuming than the pop-up windows in Photoshop and Paint Shop Pro.

PAINT SHOP PRO

Advantages: The easy-to-use interface makes this program especially powerful. There's not a lot you have to think about; you can pretty much jump right in and do what you want to do. And Paint Shop Pro makes the process very simple and straightforward.

Disadvantages: Paint Shop Pro's simplicity is both its power and its problem. I wanted a lot more control over my image production than the program allowed me, and I had to search for workarounds to accommodate my needs.

CHAPTER 28

Creating Professional Web Graphics

In this chapter

Many of the technologies within HTML 4.0 are helping to improve the look and feel of the Web. The inclusion of style sheets into the standard makes a bold statement: people want control over Web style, and they want it now! It's only a matter of time before Web browsers come up to par to enable the kind of style that is technically on the horizon.

Another area of in-depth study and growth is within Web graphic technology. New graphic formats are on the horizon, and a plethora of new and diverse software tools have come to market. There's an increase in the bandwidth available to the desktop, and more sophisticated methods of technically managing documents so that they are processed and loaded with speed and ease, and all have become available within the past two years.

Knowing how to create professional graphics for the Web is important for any serious developer, and for the hobbyist, learning Web graphics skills will most surly assist your pages in being popular and worthy of regular visits.

This chapter will teach you what kind of graphics to use on a page and how to create those graphics. From backgrounds, headers, navigational buttons, bars and rules, to spot art—you'll learn how to use some of the most popular tools, employ professional tricks, and create attractive, appropriate Web graphics.

Using Images on Your Pages

A Web site typically uses graphics to design, to identify, and to navigate.

Some of the images you'll want to consider for your pages include background images, headers, navigation buttons, bars and rules, and spot art.

Background images load into the background of the page. Sometimes referred to as wallpaper, background images set the tone of a page. Headers give an individual page its identity by incorporating the site's logo. Headers can also include the parent site's identity, too, as in Molly's site: What's New. One click of a navigation button and you're on your way to another page within a site. Bars and rules are used to separate text or elements on a page; graphic bars and rules can customize a site's look. Spot art is the term used to describe clip art or photography that will accentuate the textual content on a page.

Within these types of images are a variety of techniques you'll want to employ to ensure professional quality.

➔ For more information on working with background colors, **see** "Working with the BODY Element," **p. 217**

Scanning Techniques and Stock Art

How do you get images? Essentially, three ways exist:

- Scanning and manipulating photographic and organic images (real items)
- Working with stock art and photography
- Designing your own graphics from scratch

Sometimes you'll employ all three methods to create a single image. It all depends on the look and feel you've planned for your site.

→ To learn more about effective site planning, **see** "Effective Page Design," **p. 506**

I like to refer to a famous acronym, GIGO. This means "Garbage In, Garbage Out" and is most appropriate in terms of Web graphics. If you begin with poor images, whether from scan or stock, you'll end up with a poor image.

To avoid that, I'll teach you some basic scanning tricks and then take a look at how to carefully choose quality stock art and photos. To assist you with designing your own graphics, I've set aside an entire section of this chapter to walk you step-by-step through Web graphic creation.

Scanning Images

Scanning is in and of itself an art. The good news is that for the Web, we don't need high resolution scans. This translates into less money spent on hardware, as well as a shorter learning curve for those individuals wishing to get right to the business at hand.

For hardware, a flatbed, color scanner is highly recommended. You can buy very inexpensive scanners that will work well for the Web. The guideline is in resolution—because your final image will be 72 dpi (dots per inch), you need a scanner capable of scanning only at this resolution. Just be sure it supports millions of colors and will work with your computer and imaging software.

→ For a list of the best imaging applications on the market today, **see** "Web Graphic Formats and Professional Tools," **p. 580**

After your scanner is in place, you'll want to choose the item to be scanned. Typically, this will be a photo, hand drawings or prints, or an organic object, such as a pen or bottle (yes, you can scan "stuff!").

Here are some guidelines to follow as you prepare to scan your work:

- Be sure photos are crisp, clean, and free of dust.
- Drawings and prints should be free of smudges and speckles.
- Organic objects should be wiped down and cleaned before they are placed on the scanner screen.
- The scanner screen itself should be clean and free of dust. Follow your manufacturer's guidelines when cleaning your scanner.

Tip from molly

To clean photos and other objects to be scanned, buy a can of air! Compressed air, which you can purchase for a reasonable price at any art supply, office, or computer supply store, is very useful to help in the removal of dust and debris from your input materials. Hold the photo or object an arms length away from you. The canister should be held in your other hand, about a foot away from the object. Aim the nozzle across rather than at the item to be scanned, and clean the item with short shots from the canister. Be careful not to touch any area to be scanned with your fingers after cleaning, as fingerprints can show up on photos and other items.

The next step is to place the item to be scanned on the scanner. Using your favorite software imaging program, you'll import the file from the scanner to the program. I typically use Photoshop to do this, although many popular imaging tools make scanning easy and fast (see Figure 28.1).

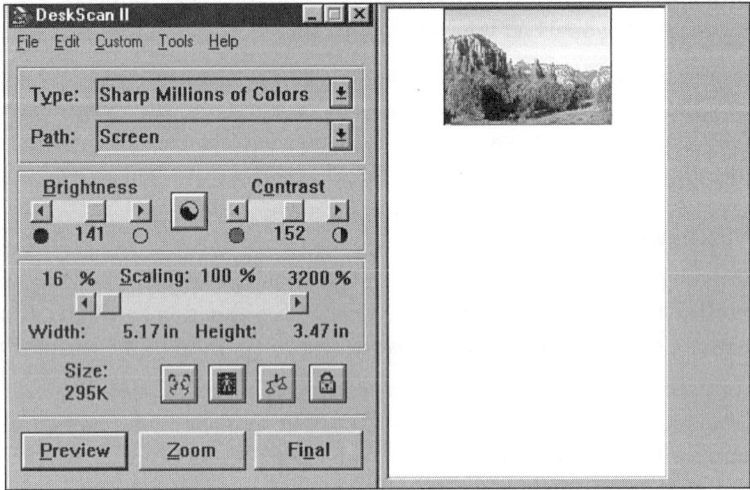

Figure 28.1
Using Photoshop, I initiated my scanner's software, DeskScan, and scanned the photo into the imaging program.

After your item is scanned, you'll want to crop it. At this point, you're probably working larger than any recommended Web graphic—both in terms of dpi and dimension. For now, your crop is a preliminary one to remove any whitespace or extra information that you don't want (see Figure 28.2).

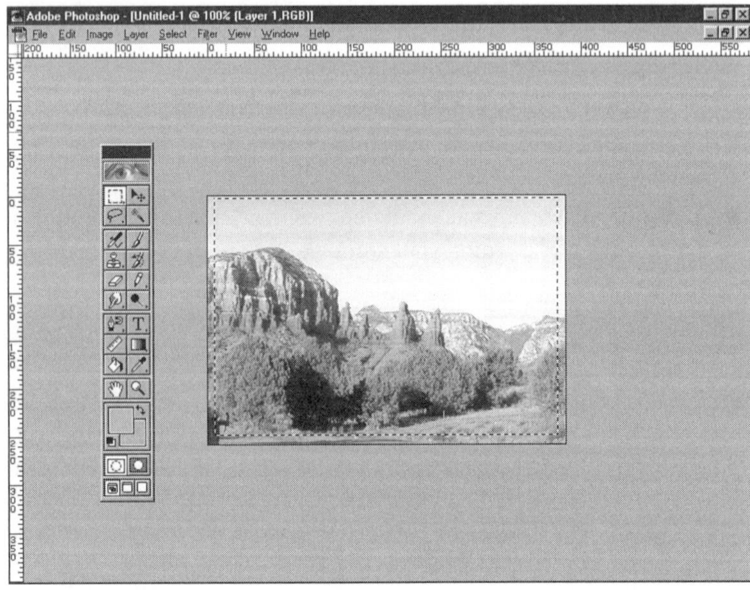

Figure 28.2
Cropping the scan will provide you with just the material you want to work with before you start making color and resolution changes.

You'll want to look for any problems with the scan. Is everything smooth and crisp, or are there smudges and speckles? If the scan isn't acceptable, go back and do it right! It can be time consuming, but it's well worth it.

If you're happy with the scanned results, you'll want to set your dpi to 72. If you scanned in at a higher resolution (check your scanning hardware and software for adjusting this), you will see an automatic reduction in the image's dimension.

If you're at 72 dpi, you're ready to make any adjustments to the scan. Make alterations to the color, blur or sharpen, and generally sweep, dust, and clean the image to your tastes.

When you're satisfied, resize the image to the size you want. Bear in mind that you might be adding a photographic edge effect, such as a drop shadow or a bevel. For this reason, *save your work* at this point—this is your resource file.

Tip from molly

Typically, saving the source file in your imaging program's native format is best, as it will retain the most information possible and not compress the image. Because I'm a Photoshop user, I save the file in native Photoshop format. This helps me maintain all the information so that when I reopen this resource, everything is intact.

I discuss dimensions for each kind of graphic in the individual work exercises found in the "Building Web Graphics" section of this chapter. At this point, it's most important to remember that you're designing for a computer screen.

→ To get up to speed on how color and resolution is to be handled when creating images to be viewed on a monitor screen, **see** "Resolution, Gamma, and the Visual Environment," **p. 546**

Therefore, if you're looking to create a page that is accessible across all platforms and browsers, you're probably working at 640×480 screen resolution or you are anticipating a dynamic design (one that will fit to all screen resolutions no matter the layout). I generally recommend that no matter your resolution goals, no graphic should exceed the width of 585 pixels, with the exception of backgrounds, which I'll explain in just a bit. As for height, some occasions exist where you'll be designing longer graphics, but typically, you want to stick to sizes that fit within the screen.

Note

In some instances, you will want to design for higher resolutions. One example is a c orporate intranet where hardware and software specifications are highly controlled.

→ For information about specialized environments, **see** "Designing Corporate Intranets and Extranets," **p. 848**

You're now ready to make additions or changes to your scanned image or to put it aside for later use.

SELECTING STOCK ART

Stock art is clip art and photography that is commercially available and is ready for production. Stock art is widely available, with professional-level art often commanding a considerable price tag for licensing.

→ For a discussion about stock art, **see** "Web Graphic Formats and Professional Tools," **p. 566**

Some guidelines for choosing stock art:

- Photographic images should be crisp and clear, not blurry.
- Line drawings should have no marks or speckles on them.
- You should be able to choose from the file type. Typically, a JPEG file is acceptable, particularly if it's been saved to maximum capacity. What you want to avoid are optimized GIFs, unless you're going to use that file as is, or make very minimal changes to it.
- Read the licensing agreements *very carefully*. You want to be absolutely certain that you can use the image you're downloading.

In Figure 28.3, I'm browsing through Photodisc. You'll notice that I'm allowed to choose the kind of file I want to purchase—options are available for file type as well as resolution.

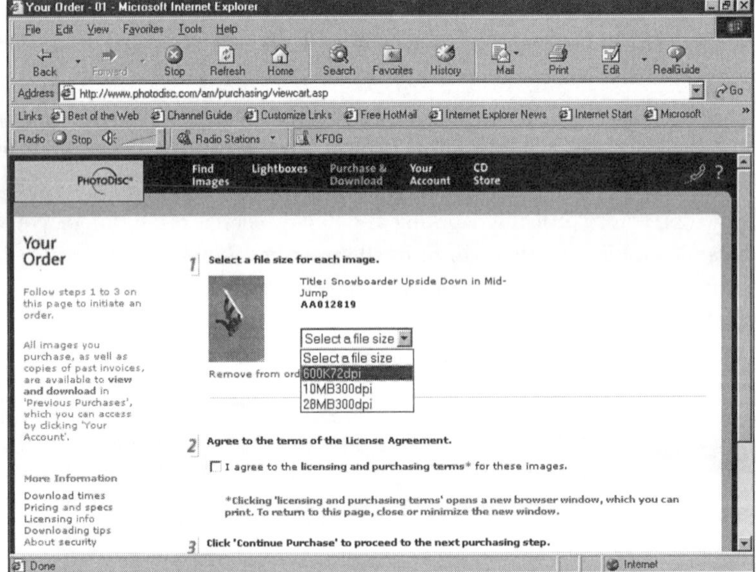

Figure 28.3
Browsing through the stock photos at Photodisc allows you to preview the choices and purchase those images that you want.

ArtToday is a great resource, too. Be a little more selective when choosing images from this site (see Figure 28.4). Many high-quality images are available, but quality consistency is less than that of the more expensive vendors such as Photodisc.

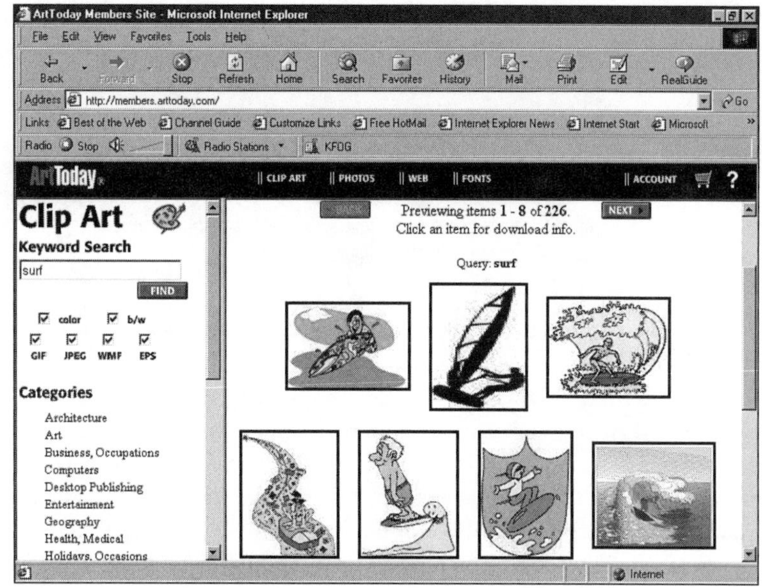

Figure 28.4 Selecting images from ArtToday is a good option, just be careful that you are getting the best quality image for the price.

Free art sites are variable. You can find great stuff, but you need to use the guidelines above to make good decisions when selecting from free clip art and photos.

Note

Visit Photodisc at `http://www.photodisc.com/` and ArtToday at `http://www.arttoday.com/`.

BUILDING WEB GRAPHICS

With a good foundation beneath you, you're ready to create some graphics. I'll step you through a variety of tasks and demonstrate and describe features, pitfalls, and helpful hints that will make your graphics creations as professional as they get.

BACKGROUNDS

Three kinds of background images exist:

- Wallpaper patterns—These are small squares that tile to create a smooth, seamless texture that looks like well-installed wallpaper (no burps, seams, or bungles!).
- Margin tiles—Also referred to as *strips* because they are wide and short, margin tiles can be functional or decorative in nature.
- Watermark style—This is one large background graphic, usually square, that adds an image, logographic material, or color to the background of a page.

One important issue to remember is that *all backgrounds are tiles*. They may not look like a tile, but they will act like a tile whenever the resolution of a screen changes. Wallpaper patterns, which are squares, will tile into the browser one-by-one until the available space is filled.

Note

Tiling will always occur with conventional HTML. If you're using style sheets, you can prevent background tiling from occurring using style sheets. However, the fixing of background tiles will only occur in certain style-sheet compliant browsers, and they will tile in browsers that do not support the style sheet methods.

→ For information on how to fix backgrounds using style sheets, **see** "Element Positioning and Style Sheet Scripting," **p. 430**

Margin tiles fill the browser in the same way—except it might seem as though they don't because of their size and shape. One way to understand this process is to create a strip that isn't as long as it should be and then view it in your browser. You'll see that it does, in fact, tile along both the horizontal and vertical axes (see Figure 28.5). Finally, watermark tiles, which are very large squares, tile in the same way that wallpaper and margin tiles do (see Figure 28.19). Therefore, you have to be careful when creating watermarks.

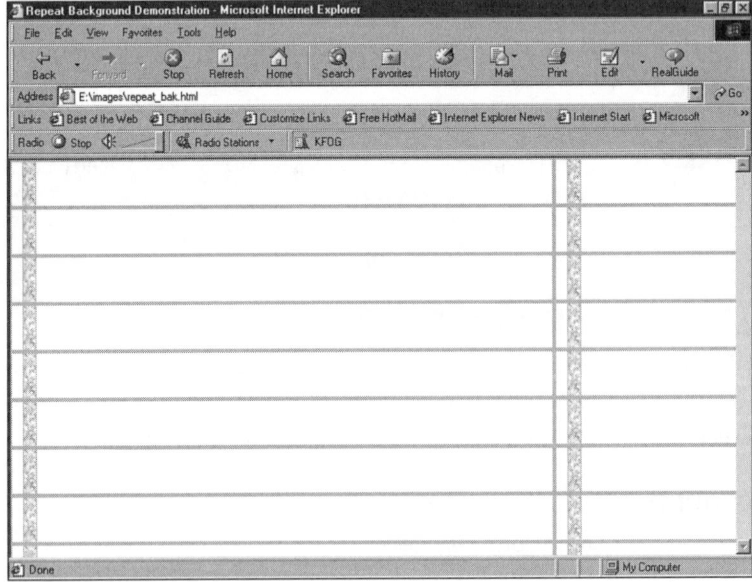

Figure 28.5
I outlined this longer, thin tile so you can see how it flows into the page.

Let's take a closer look at individual types of backgrounds.

WALLPAPER PATTERNS

Wallpaper patterns were the first wave of background graphics. You've probably seen lots of them, in all kinds of styles. They're problematic for a number of reasons, including the fact that if they're too dark or busy, they'll interfere with readability. They're also demanding on the designer—it takes a bit of skill if you're making them completely by hand.

However, if you design them properly, they can create an extremely attractive look for your site.

The following are some general guidelines to use when creating tiles:

- Individual tiles should be at least 50×50 pixels.
- Work hard to ensure that tiles appear seamless.
- Avoid allowing a small tile with a single image to repeat over and over. Imagine one egg in a single square, tiled repeatedly into the browser.
- Always ensure that you do *not* interlace background graphics.

➔ To learn more about interlacing **see** "Web Graphic Formats and Professional Tools," **p. 575**

In this exercise you can create a simple background tile. I'm going to use Paint Shop Pro 5.0, but you can follow along with almost any imaging program.

1. Open the program and create a new file.
2. The New Image dialog box (see Figure 28.6). In this, place the dimensions of your image (I'm making an image 50×50), the resolution, which should be set to 72, the background color of the graphic (I set mine to white), and the amount of colors (set to 256 for GIFs, millions of colors for JPEGs).

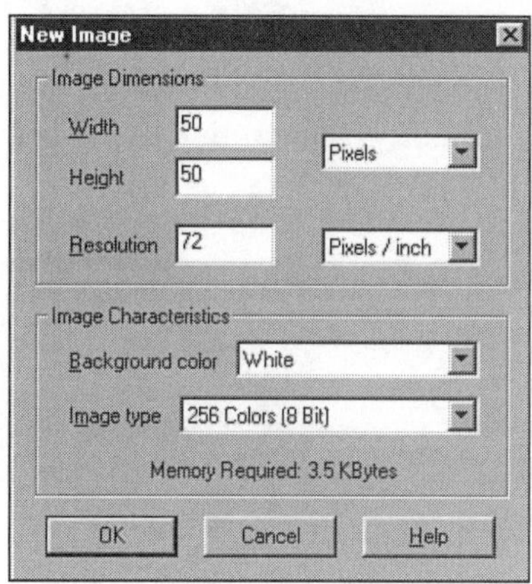

Figure 28.6
The New Image dialog box in Paint Shop Pro enables you to set the size, resolution, and color for the new image before you create it.

3. Now select any one of the drawing tools. You can choose to use a brush, create geometric shapes—whatever you'd like to try. For this example, I chose the brush with a "chalk" setting and set it to round.
4. I chose a light lavender. My goal is to create a floral wallpaper pattern.
5. In the center of my tile, I painted a flower by simply using three brush strokes.
6. Because I anticipated that this image will tile, I put a partial stroke in each corner of the tile, so when the tiles match up, a small flower will be created by the four corners meeting (see Figure 28.7).

7. From the Colors menu, I chose Decrease Color Depth, and then selected 4-bit color.
8. Now choose File, Save As, and save your file.

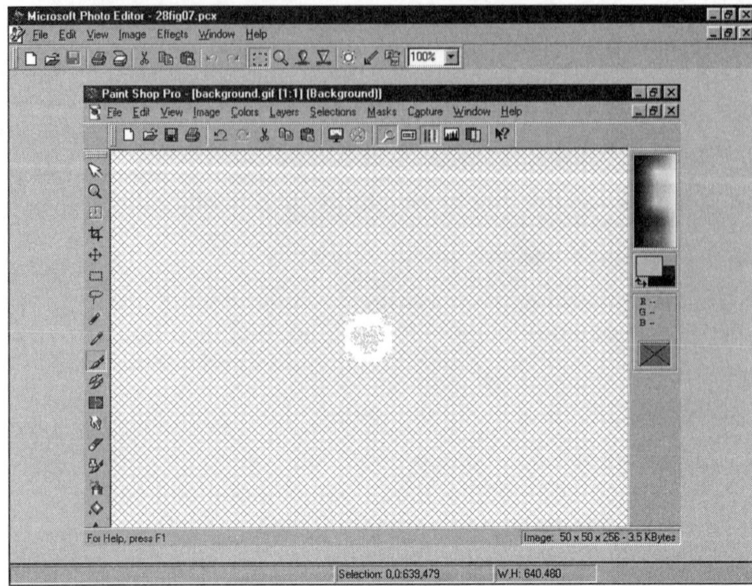

Figure 28.7
Painting the image takes a little practice, but since you only have to create one square and not an entire background, it's easy to experiment.

Now you can load the image as a background graphic within an HTML document. Figure 28.8 shows my flowery results!

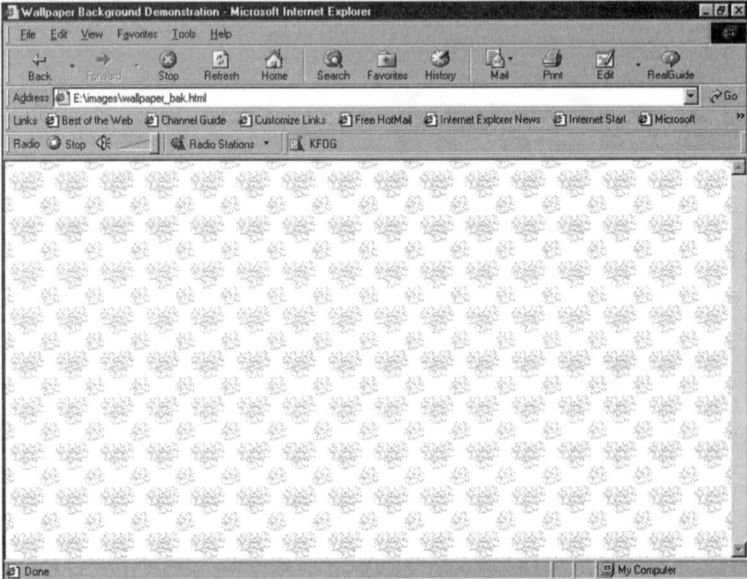

Figure 28.8
Here you can see that, once tiled in the browser, my single flower square has become a flowered, seamless wallpaper.

→ Review how images are dealt with in conventional HTML, **see** "Working with Images," **p. 196**

Tip from molly

> To ensure good contrast, keep background tiles very light or very dark, and the body text the opposite. So, if you have a very light background, black text will help readability because it contrasts well with the background. Similarly, if you have a very dark green background design, a light color such as cream will provide you with good contrast.

MARGIN TILES

Margin tiles are quite prevalent on the Web. Essentially, two types of margin tiles exist:

- Functional—This is a background margin tile that uses the margin space for navigation or other graphic and text information. Because it will be a significant part of your color and design scheme, functional margin design means making sure text, links, and other functional items can be seen and integrated into the margin's space and design (see Figure 28.9).
- Decorative—Decorative margins serve to enhance a design aesthetically. They have no function other than to provide visual interest to a page (see Figure 28.10).

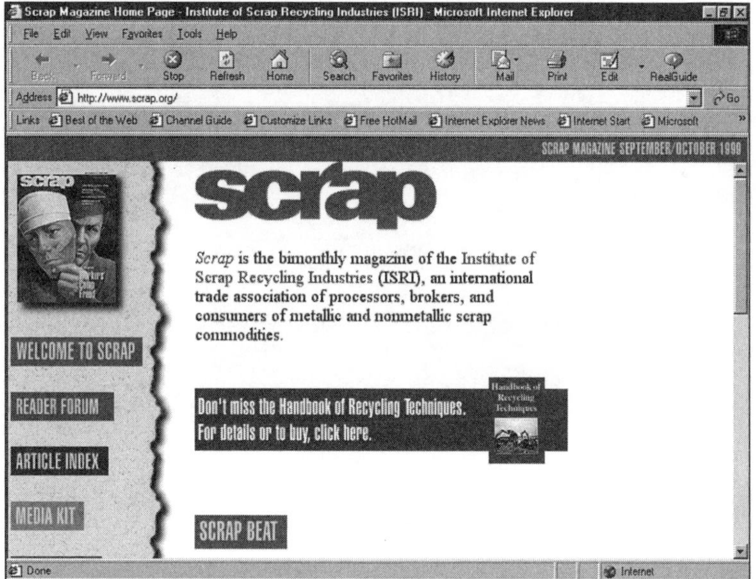

Figure 28.9
This site makes use of a functional margin background by using it to present the navigation for the site.

For effective margin tile design, follow these tips:

- Create long tiles, anticipating various screen resolutions. You'll want your background margin tiles to be at least 1,024 pixels wide. You might even consider making them 1,280 pixels wide, but it's up to you and the awareness of your audience. Choose longer if many of them are using very high resolution monitors; 1,024 is a typical background margin tile width for standard Internet sites. Height will range from around 50 pixels to 250 pixels or so, depending on your design.

- Design using few colors, but be sure to add interest by employing shadow, shape, or texture. Flat margin tiles are very common on the Web. Although they're not unattractive, challenge yourself a bit and create something with a bit more verve.
- Because you have to anticipate a wide range of resolutions, design your image to size. If you're creating a right margin, this means making sure that the design begins within the allotted visual space of 595 pixels. Your image should look good no matter the viewing resolution!

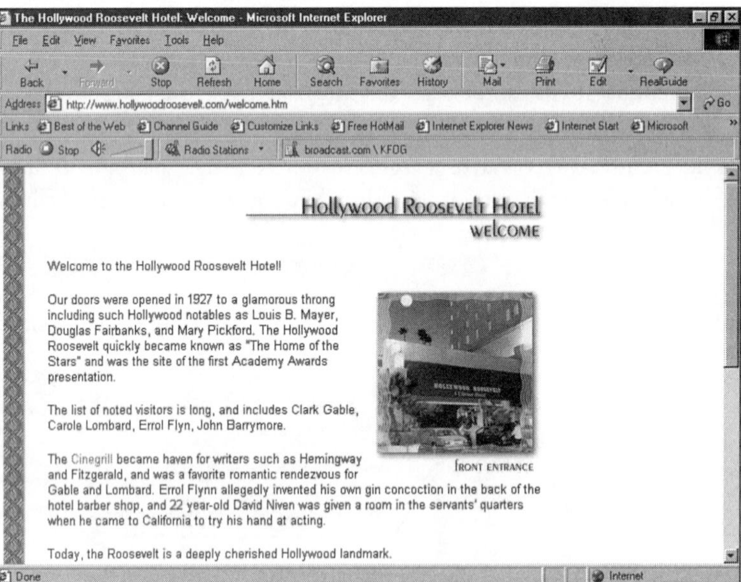

Figure 28.10 This Web site uses a decorative margin background to give an air of sophistication and elegance to the site. The design within the margin portion of the tile can be decorative, as can the body portion. You can use flat areas of color or texture—whatever your imagination and creative influences suggest. However, always lean toward readability!

In this case, I'm going to use Macromedia Fireworks 1.0 to create a functional right-margin image with color and texture.

> **Note**
> This exercise was created using Fireworks 1.0.

1. Open Fireworks and select File, New.
2. In the New Document dialog box (see Figure 28.11), set the width of your image (I set mine at 1,024) and the height (mine is set for 50). Select your background color; I used a Web-safe lilac.

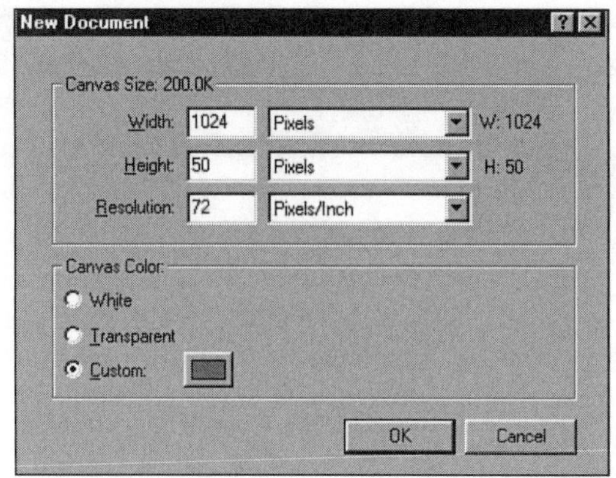

Figure 28.11
The New Document dialog box in Fireworks enables you to set the size, resolution, and canvas color (or transparency) for the new image.

3. Fireworks has some excellent preset texture fills that you can modify. Because I want my margin to be functional, but fun, I'm going to fill it with an interesting texture.
4. Choose the rectangle from the left side of the tools palette.
5. From the Modify menu, select Fill.
6. You can now choose the fill type and intensity you want. My settings are solid, anti-aliased, Fiber (set to 25%).
7. At 450 pixels (remember, we want this to work at 640 resolution), start the rectangle and pull it over to the end of the graphic.
8. Fireworks will fill your graphic with the texture.
9. Go to File, Export.
10. The Export preview will give you a variety of options. I chose to save as a GIF, with the Web Palette, no transparency. I named the file `right_margin.gif`. See Figure 28.12 for the results.

To create a decorative margin graphic, simply place the decorative element as a strip along the left, right, or top margin. Bottom margins might get lost as they won't be immediately seen on longer pages.

Figure 28.13 shows a modification of the functional design I created in the previous exercise, this time designed as a decorative background.

WATERMARKS

Watermarks are especially difficult to create because of the repetitive issue. The idea with watermarks is to keep them simple, with few, flat colors, keeping file sizes low.

I created a watermark using Photoshop. First, I created a very large tile, 1,024×1,200 pixels. This way I know that no matter the resolution, the effect will generally be the same.

I then drew a stylized wave shape onto the tile (see Figure 28.14). I used two colors: white and bright yellow, and optimized the GIF as an 8-bit file. My total file size for this dimensionally large background? 5KB total!

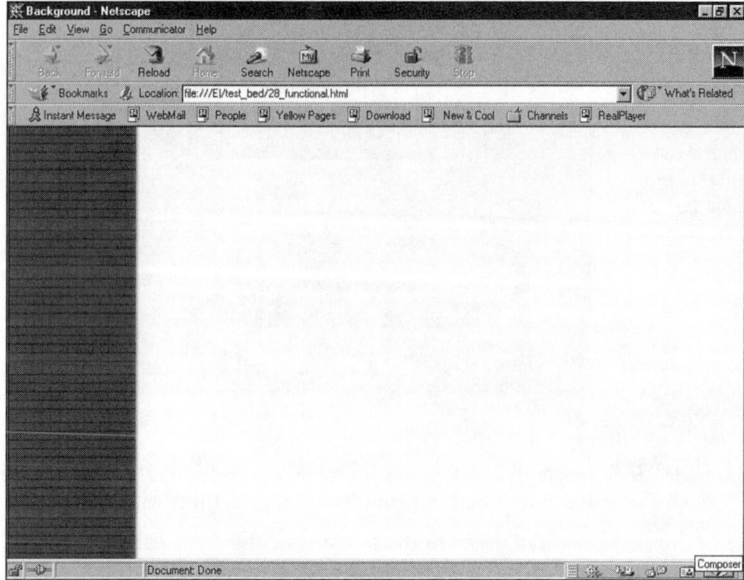

Figure 28.12
A textured, functional margin background.

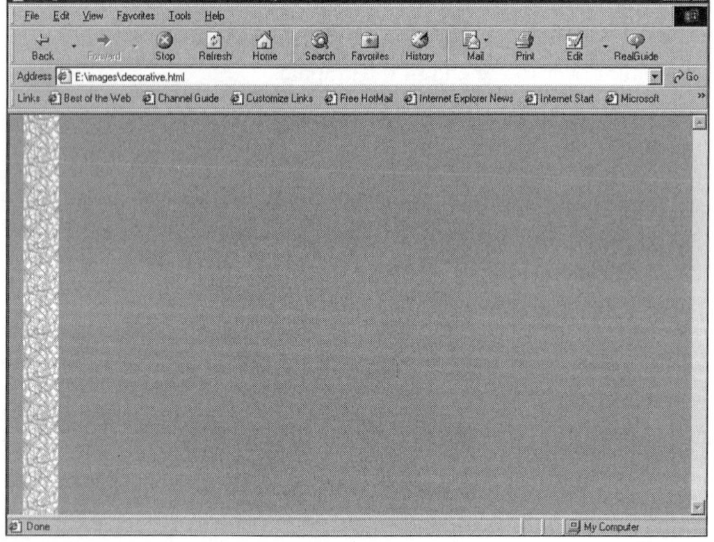

Figure 28.13
A decorative margin helps create a look and feel for a page. Decorative margins are esthetic rather than functional devices.

Now when I add HTML and content to the design, I can use a table to fix the information securely in place. Then, whether the page is viewed at 640×480 resolution or higher, the page is visually attractive.

→ To learn how to fix table designs, **see** "Advanced Table Layouts," **p. 336**

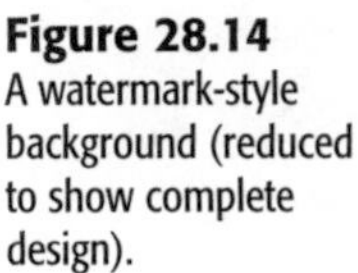

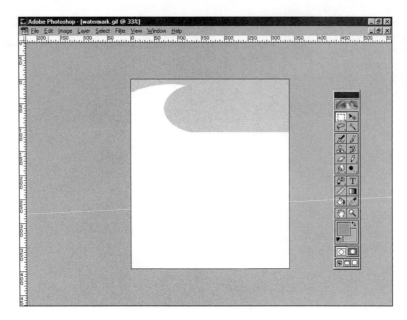

Figure 28.14
A watermark-style background (reduced to show complete design).

Header Graphics

Headers are used to identify a site and a page within a site. One type of header is the *splash* header. This typically fills a larger piece of real estate on the opening page only. It identifies the site with the company logo or brand and sets the visual tone for the rest of the site.

A *page* header is smaller, but still boldly visible along the top and left, middle, or right of an internal page.

Building a Splash Design

In this case, let's create a splash header for the wallpaper background graphic we made in the first exercise.

Because I want to work with interesting type, I'm going to first work in Adobe Illustrator. You can always set type within your favorite imaging program, but Illustrator offers strong typographic options, such as the curving type I'm going to use on this splash.

1. In Illustrator, select File, New.
2. With the Ellipse tool, draw a elliptical path.
3. Select your font, font size, and color, and type along the uppermost curve (see Figure 28.15).
4. Add any other text you'd like.
5. Save the file as an EPS, with font information intact.

→ For details on working with type, **see** "Graphic Type for the Web," **p. 627**

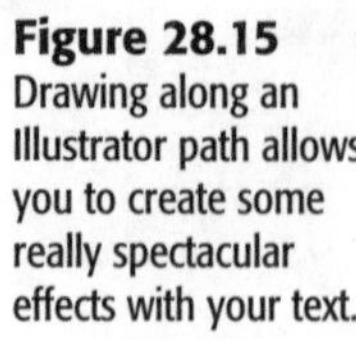

Figure 28.15
Drawing along an Illustrator path allows you to create some really spectacular effects with your text.

Now you'll want to rasterize, crop, and edit the image, which you'll do in Photoshop:

1. Open the EPS file you just created. Be sure to switch from CMYK to RGB color.
2. Crop the file.
3. Add a new layer.
4. Fill the layer with a color suitable for transparency.
5. Send the layer to the back.
6. Flatten the image.
7. From the Image menu, select Mode.
8. Index the colors.
9. Select File, Export.
10. Export the file as a GIF89, processing it as a transparent and interlaced file.
11. Save the file as `splash.gif`.

In Figure 28.16, you can see my splash graphic set over my wallpaper background.

Now, you can create an internal page header using Fireworks (or another imaging software). In this case, I'm going to create a header for the functional background made earlier. My header is a transparent GIF, but depending on your needs, you may choose to use GIF or JPG format.

1. In Fireworks, select File, New.
2. Set up the graphic to be 400×50 pixels.
3. Fill the image with a color suitable for transparency.
4. From the Window menu, make sure Layers is selected.
5. Create a new layer using the drop-down menu.

6. On this layer, set your type, using the Fireworks type tool.
7. When you're satisfied with the look of your graphic, select File, Export.
8. Export as a GIF or JPEG, depending upon your needs.
9. Save the file.
10. Add the file to your HTML and view the results (see Figure 28.17).

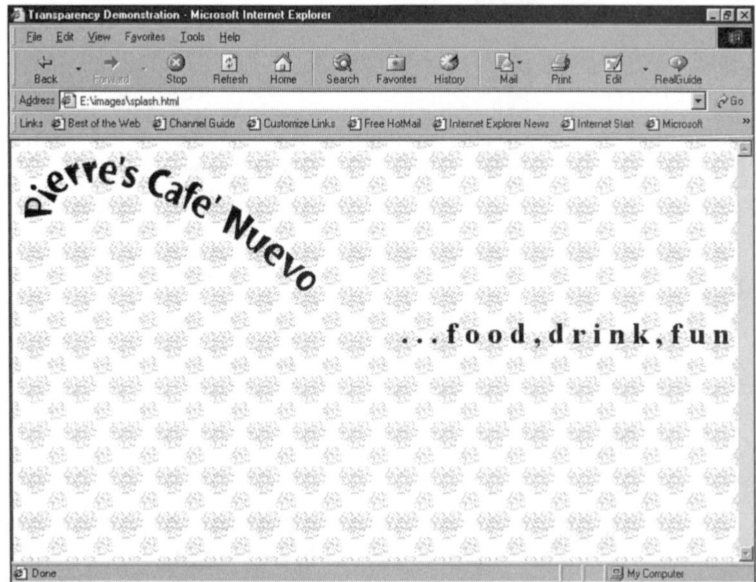

Figure 28.16
The splash graphic in place. The transparency allows the image to flow naturally with the background, creating fluid movement rather than rigid design.

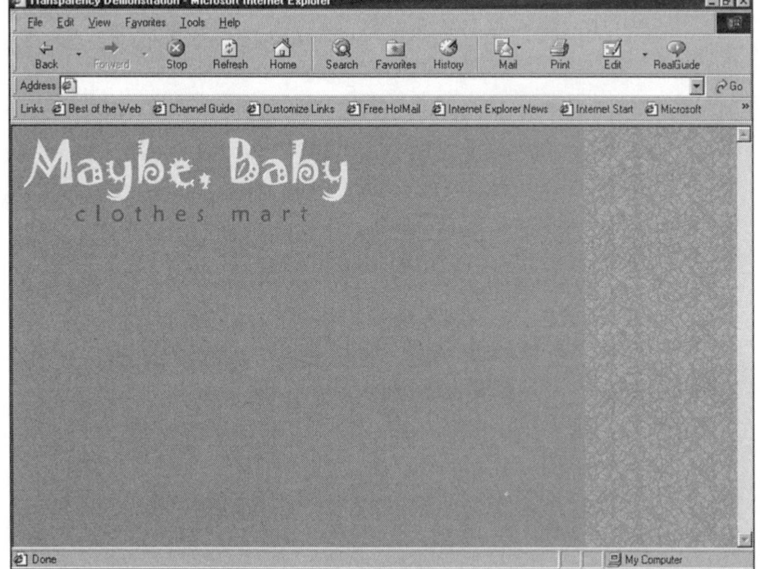

Figure 28.17
An internal page header helps keep a visitor oriented within a site, as well as adding visual interest to the page.

Tip from 

Wherever you have the option to anti-alias type, you should do so when the type is about 11 points or higher. This will smooth out the lines, preventing jagged type. However, at smaller sizes, type sometimes is more clear with anti-aliasing turned off.

BUTTONS

Button, button, who's got the button?

You will, of course, in just a few minutes!

Navigational buttons can be made up of text, images, or a combination of both. You can go simple by using a static navigation button as a link. Or, you may prefer to create visually active buttons, which can be achieved using JavaScript.

→ To learn how to do JavaScript mouseovers, **see** "Using JavaScript," **p. 419**

I'm going to show you two kinds of buttons: a beveled button, and a simple method of doing mouseover text buttons.

Thought your designing was going well until you tested your page in a browser and found that your graphics were ruining your overall design? See, "Bevels, Shadows, and Effects" for some tips on how to make your graphics work well together without overdoing it.

CREATING A BEVELED BUTTON

For this exercise, I'm going to use Photoshop in combination with the Extensis Photo Bevel plug-in. You can use any imaging program; many have bevel effects built right in (as does Photoshop, but I want to give you an example of plug-in use). But if it does not, many of the beveling plug-ins work with a variety of programs, such as Paint Shop Pro.

1. In Photoshop, create a new file that is 100×50 pixels.
2. Fill with the color of your choice (select All, Edit, Fill).
3. Using the text tool, choose your typeface and type size.
4. Set your type with the navigational icon or text.
5. Flatten the image (Layer, Flatten Image).

Now it's time to create the bevel.

1. From the Filter menu, select Extensis PhotoBevel.
2. The Extensis interface will pop up with your image inside (see Figure 28.18).
3. Define the bevel settings until you find a setting you like.
4. Click Apply.
5. Optimize the graphic.
6. Save as `home_button.gif`.

Figure 28.18
The Extensis PhotoBevel plug-in.

Figure 28.19 shows the button in action.

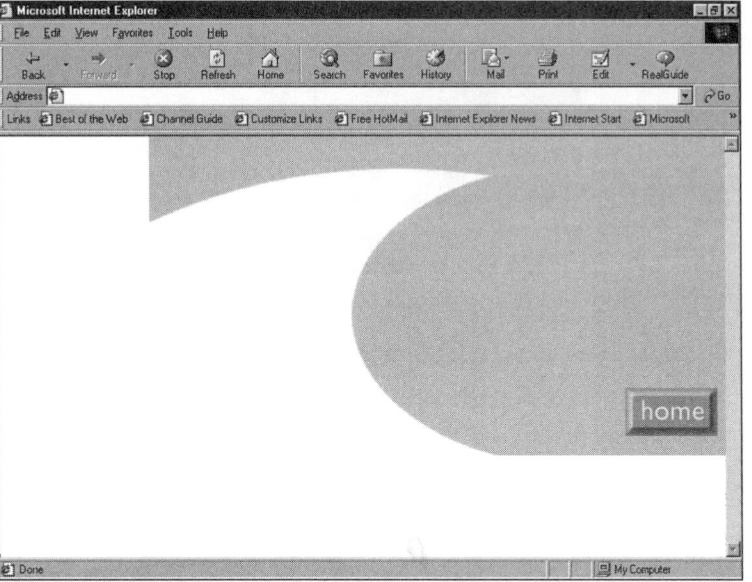

Figure 28.19
A beveled button on a watermarked background.

Note

Download Extensis PhotoBevel from `http://www.extensis.com/`.

CREATING A BUTTON FOR JAVASCRIPT MOUSEOVERS

Use this method with any imaging program that supports layers, including Photoshop, Paint Shop Pro 5.0, ImageReady, and Fireworks. I'm going to do the exercise in Photoshop.

1. Create a new file to the appropriate size and dimension of your button(s). I'm creating a 100×25 pixel file.
2. Fill the background layer with the color appropriate to your design.
3. Now add a new layer; Layer, New, Layer.
4. Select the Type tool and set the type for your standard button (the button people will see onload, or if they don't support JavaScript) on the new layer.
5. Position the type.
6. Make a copy of the type layer.
7. Fill the copy with the mouseover color.

You should now have a three-layer graphic: background color, onload type, and mouseover type (as seen in Figure 28.20).

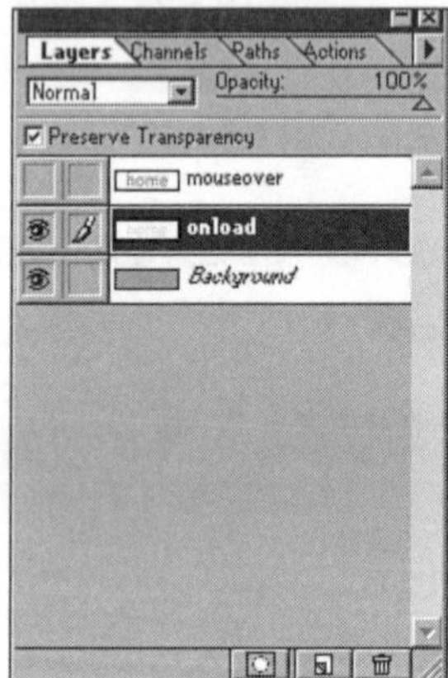

Figure 28.20
The three layers ready for individual export will work together to give the on/off effect on mouseover.

8. Deselect the mouseover layer.
9. Export this combination as a GIF89, File, Export, GIF.
10. Save that file as `home_1.gif`.
11. Now deselect the onload layer, and reselect the mouseover layer.
12. Repeat the Export process and save this file as `home_2.gif`.

You now have the makings of an attractive mouseover. The nice thing about this process is that the text remains in the exact position.

Tip from molly

Creating JavaScript mouseovers using Photoshop Layers helps you to avoid one of the most common problems–slight shifting due to inexact measuring.

BARS AND RULES

At times you might like an effective, decorative bar or rule to demarcate visual sections of a document.

If you're going to create your own bar, I'd recommend the following:

- Don't stretch the bar from margin to margin. Instead, make a bar that is either centered with some whitespace to either side or aligned to the right or left. Cutting off the margins separates space dramatically and could cause disruption in the cohesiveness of both the design and the experience of the content.
- Use a treatment such as a drop shadow, curved or angled lines, something that's hand drawn, or broken lines—anything to give the rule a fresh look.

In this example, I'm going use type to create my horizontal rule. I selected a typeface and then used the tilde symbol to create a wavy look.

Then, I modified the drawing by adding a drop shadow. You can use any number of built-in imaging tools to do this. I did it by creating another layer in Photoshop, filling that duplicate with black, offsetting it 2 pixels to the right, then 2 pixels down, dropping the opacity to 70%, and finally, applying a Guassian blur of 2.5 to the shadow.

Figure 28.21 shows the rule on the wallpaper background created earlier in this chapter.

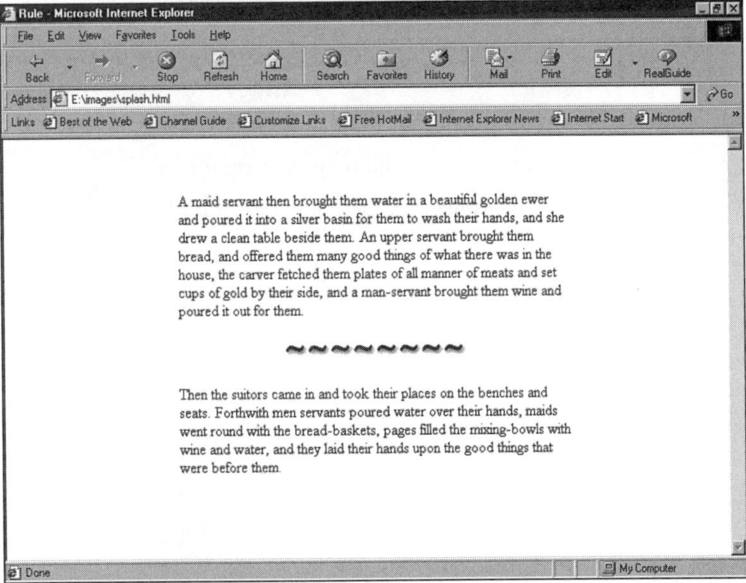

Figure 28.21
A simple but attractive horizontal rule can perk up any Web page.

SPOT ART

Spot art serves to enhance and accentuate text. It can be clip art or photographs.

To make spot art stand out from the norm, it's fun to add edges, shadows, or bevels for effect. However, you do have to be careful with the use of effects because of the additional weight they can add to a page.

Tip from

Effects should be planned so that they are consistent and blend well with the overall design.

Hand-drawn art, cartoons, and clip art can add variety and personality to your sites, too.

Whichever you choose, you should be consistent and creative—not conflicting and cliché—throughout a site. It always surprises me to find that people have created a slick graphic only to mix it with a piece of overused, worn clip art!

Another concern is dimension. Spot art is akin to italic or bold on a page—it's about emphasis, not dominance. You want your spot art to blend well into the overall scheme of your design. Pay close attention not only to the dimension in relation to the screen size, but from one photo to another.

I often like to add edge effects to my photos, and to do this I'm especially fond of the Auto/FX photographic Edge series. In this example I'm going to take a photo and add an edge to it.

Note

Visit `http://www.autofx.com/` for a free trial download of a photographic edge. You can add Auto/FX to Paint Shop Pro or Photoshop.

1. In your imaging program, crop and size the photo to your taste.
2. Choose Filter, Auto F/X, and then your desired filter.
3. The Auto F/X interface will open up (see Figure 28.22).
4. Make your modifications using the sliders and preview pane.
5. Apply the effect.
6. Save the file (usually this will be a JPEG). My file is `photo_1.jpg`.

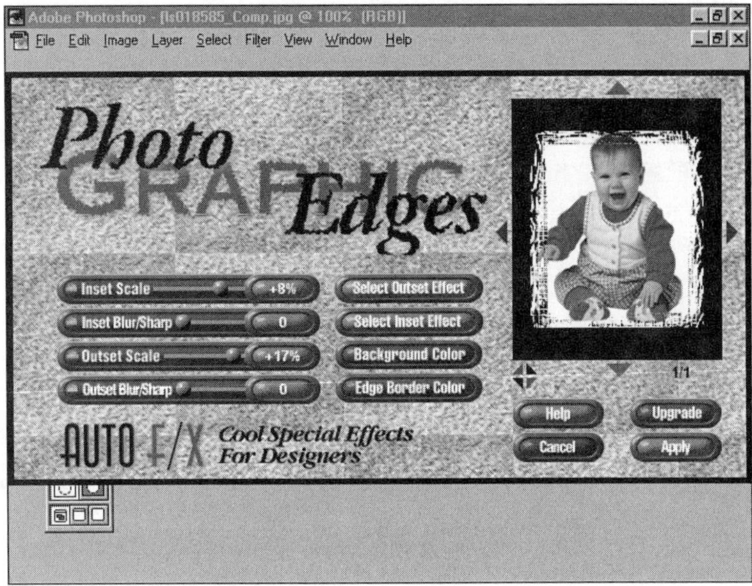

Figure 28.22
The Auto F/X interface is quick and simple to use.

Figure 28.23 shows the edge results.

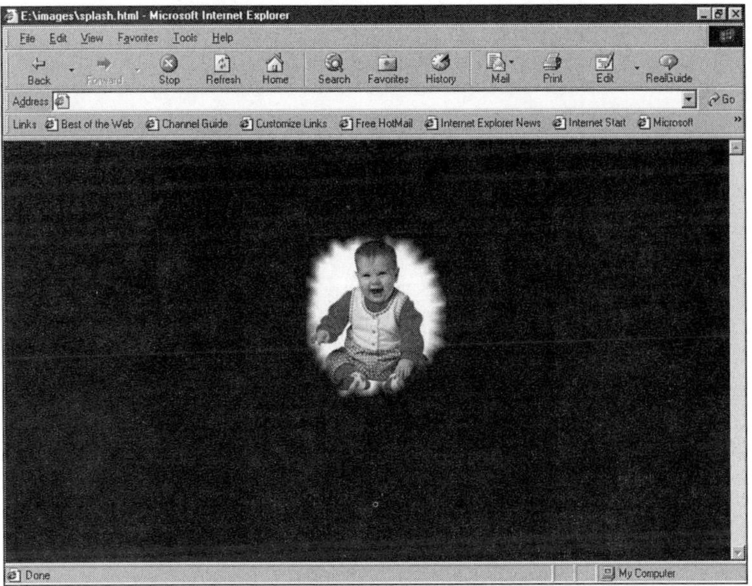

Figure 28.23
A treated photo on a Web page. The result is interesting as it departs from the hard edges so frequently found on the Web.

Backgrounds, headers, rules, and spot art—you're wrapped up and ready to go!

TROUBLESHOOTING

BEVELS, SHADOWS, AND EFFECTS

I wanted to add some panache to to my page, so, I grabbed up all the cool effects and filters I could find and got to work. The designing is going great, but the results are a bit busy—what happened?

I cannot reiterate that effects must be planned and appropriate to the design. Consistency is a big factor, too. You definitely do not want to do something just because you can.

In fact, bevels and shadow effects have been overused (Figure 28.24). They are sometimes exactly what is needed (Figure 28.25), but think carefully before using any effects. And, when you do use them, use them consistently.

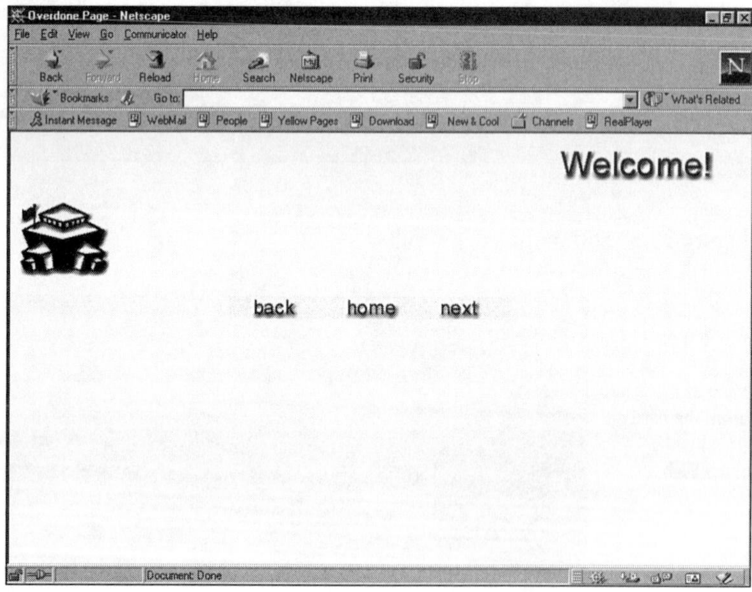

Figure 28.24
I've used bevels on every image on this page. It's too much! Cut down on effects for better results.

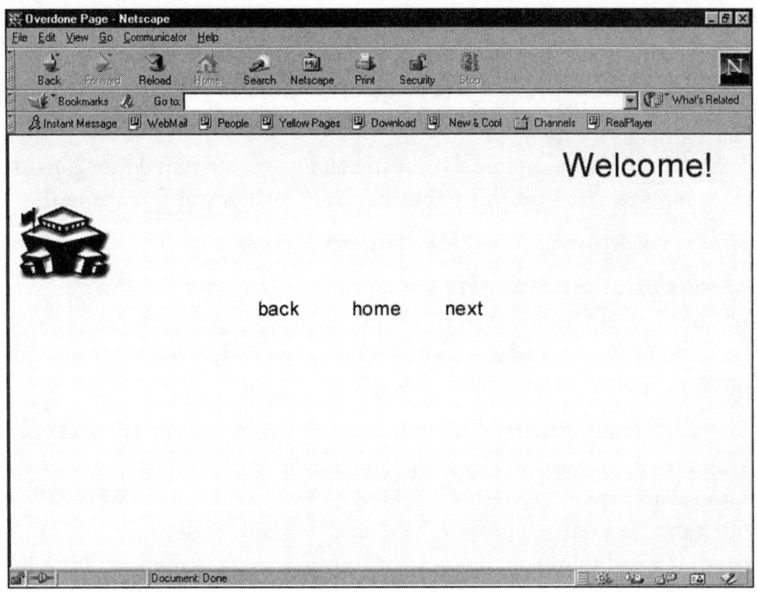

Figure 28.25
In this case, I've used the bevel only on the spot art, and left the header and navigation buttons consistently plain. This effect is more subtle and less overdone.

Designing for the Real World

A Professional's Approach to Designing the Web: Interview with Designer Amy Burnham

Amy Burnham is a professional graphic and Web graphic designer who has created the visual identity for sites such as the Weekly Wire, Tucson Weekly, DesertNet, and Buffalo Exchange.

I interviewed Amy about her work as a Web designer.

Amy, what process do you use when you sit down to determine the look and feel of a site?

I always start with brainstorming on paper—identifying the design problem, working out whatever mood or associated imagery would work for the project, just lists of words really to get me thinking in the right vein. I also clarify what the hierarchy of the site will be by working up a site map or flow chart and determine what the navigation options will be on each page or level of the site.

From there I thumbnail 20-50 sketches and then work up the best 2 or 3 or 4 in Photoshop. Its funny because sometimes the writing part seems unnecessary, especially if I feel I'm really familiar with a project, but anytime I've tried to shortcut that step its backfired on me and I've had to go back to it.

I definitely have to think projects out mentally first. Then free association sketching comes much easier too. I like to work on the thumbnails over a period of days if the timeframe of the job allows, working on it and then putting it away and then coming back to it later.

The best ideas always come when I've had a chance to put something on the back burner and let my subconscious pick at it. That way you make associations with other things around you that might not seem to be related—whether its whatever books or magazines you're reading, movies, elements in nature, dreams, and things in the grocery store!

I also like to have a couple days at the end when the initial mockups are "done". Its the finessing that comes at this point that really makes a difference in the design.

How do you determine the graphic effects you'll use on a site?

I always base the treatments on whatever the look and feel I'm going for is. That sounds obvious but its important to think out what you're trying to accomplish before you start thinking about what effects to use—think about what you want to achieve and then figure out how to do it instead of the other way around.

With that said, I generally try to incorporate mouseovers whenever possible, as long as I can keep the file size down. I like the interactive, tactile feel of it, especially if they're done well. Drop shadows are so overused although there are instances where I'll still use them. But too often they're used as a default, "oh, its a Web site, it needs to be 3D" kind of thing. Not that depth is a bad thing, often you want to imply some depth somehow, but I'd rather explore other ways like relative size and different planes than using the requisite drop shadow. Its not always the best solution.

What are your favorite, most-used Web design software tools? Anything you specifically do NOT like or use?

Photoshop is where I do close to 90% of my work on computer. The other 10% is probably split between ImageReady, which I use for optimizing images and creating GIF animations, and Quark Xpress to quickly lay out text.

The only software I'd say I'd never use is some of the instant 3D software and instant filter effects. They're so overused and obviously computer generated that they're just embarrassing to look at. Design is all about coming up with individual solutions to unique problems and those programs aren't the solution to anything.

Where do you get stock art, fonts, and other materials for your work?

I use a lot of found imagery—string, fabric, leaves, jewelry, stamps, knickknacks, rocks, and so on—in conjunction with my scanner to capture textures or objects to use solo or as part of a larger piece. I also use a Polaroid camera, not a digital camera, to capture images, scanning the photos to use themselves or as templates for illustrations.

For stock photos and illustrations, Photodisc and Artville are very useful and immediate. I also love to use illustrators if the budget allows it.

While all designers will find their own way of working, Amy Burnham's production approaches provide a great example of a professional graphic designer who has moved her method from the print world into that of the Web. The precise method enables her to work faster as well as creating better-looking sites as a result of her brainstorming, planning, and professional techniques.

CHAPTER 29

Graphic Type for the Web

In this chapter

Creating Vector Graphics and Type for the Web

Because most of this book is dedicated to teaching the technology of HTML 4.0 and general design concepts, it's important to bring in some perspective for those individuals who may already have a professional graphics background or desire to learn more about the creation of professional-level Web graphics—particularly, the setting of type.

For this reason, this chapter takes a look at using a professional tool to set type on graphics from the perspective of a graphic designer. In this case, the tool chosen is Illustrator 8.0.

Note

Does this mean that there aren't other ways to create fantastic graphic type? Illustrator may be one of the foremost professional tools, but your skills and favorite imaging tool can be combined to create great graphic type.

→ For a list of other imaging programs, **see** "Web Graphic Formats and Professional Tools," **p. 556**

Illustrator 8.0 comes packed with some interesting Web applications and provides the capability to write HTML code based on imagemapping. You'll get a look at how this is done, and you'll also get a strong background in what Illustrator is and why it differs from most graphic design programs used for the Web. Finally, you'll have the opportunity to walk step-by-step through the development of a Web-ready file.

If you have Illustrator, do the exercise. If not, follow along the visual tour to see how professional typographic effects can enhance the quality of your design.

Having trouble using Illustrator? See "Fumbling Fingers" in the Troubleshooting section at the end of the chapter.

About Vector Graphics and Bezier Curves

Over a decade ago, the introduction of PageMaker (a layout program by Aldus) and PostScript (a printing language by Adobe Systems) transformed the personal computer from the electronic equivalent of an Etch-a-Sketch to a complete professional graphics workstation. Designers could finally output to printers with the assurance of reasonable quality.

No longer did type appear stair-stepped and clunky or curves and shapes have rough, jagged edges. The printing of computer-generated images was transformed due to this new method of mathematically defining the curves.

Vector programs are largely dependent on Bézier (pronounced *bez-ee-ay*) curves (see Figure 29.1) to render lines and shapes and to generate text. Pierre Bézier first introduced the Bézier curve to the European auto industry in the 1960s as a computer-based system of drafting.

Prior to their introduction, designers depended on French curves and laths to render curved shapes and lines by hand. The hand-drawn elements would change slightly from one generation to the next, compromising the form and reflection lines of the chassis. Bézier curves, in addition to being accurate and easy to work with, assured consistency throughout the entire design process.

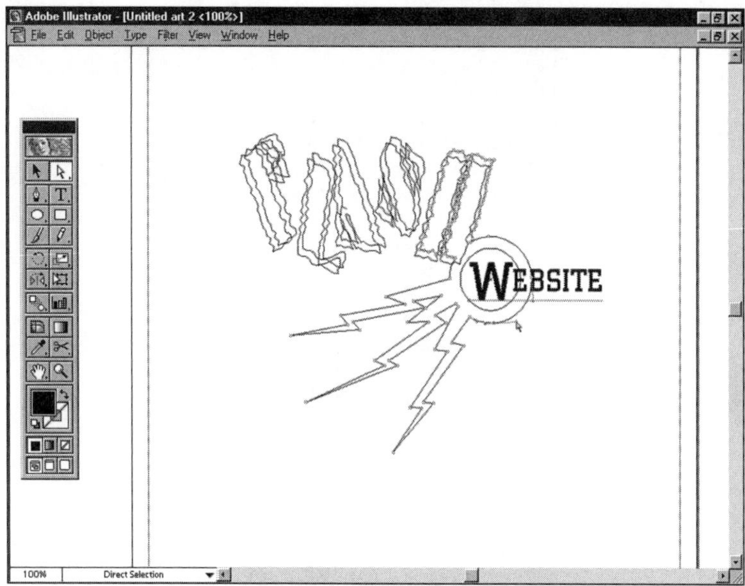

Figure 29.1 Bézier curves allow designers to create accurate and consistent hand-style illustrations.

Vectors are the fundamental graphics engines for illustration programs like Adobe Illustrator, CorelDRAW, and Macromedia Freehand. They are also used to define shapes, lines, and text in layout programs like Quark Xpress and PageMaker. When you draw in a vector-based program, you are invisibly writing PostScript code (see Figure 29.2).

To illustrate the concepts of vector programs in this chapter, I will use the recently released industry standard Adobe Illustrator 8.0 vector-based illustration program.

Note

Quark Xpress 4.0, a layout program, now includes tools to draw Bézier Curves.

DRAWING BÉZIER CURVES

When you draw with Bézier curves or generate type in Adobe Illustrator 8.0 (or any other vector-based illustration or layout program), you create vector objects. This is why illustration and layout programs are sometimes called *object-oriented* software. The edges of these objects contain a finite number of points that define the lines, shape, position, and color of the object. Because these points mathematically articulate smooth curves, they are *resolution independent*, which means that no matter how large you make them, they will appear smooth when printed to a PostScript printer.

Figure 29.2
PostScript code is the vehicle that communicates with a Postscript Printer.

```
%!PS-Adobe-2.0
%%Creator: Adobe Illustrator(TM) 88
%%For: (steve w romaniello) (swr enterprizes)
%%Title: (Godzilla.art)
%%CreationDate: (5/31/98) (2:42 PM)
%%DocumentProcessColors: Magenta Yellow Black
%%DocumentProcSets: Adobe_packedarray 1.0 0
%%DocumentProcSets: Adobe_cmykcolor 1.1 0
%%DocumentProcSets: Adobe_cshow 1.1 0
%%DocumentProcSets: Adobe_customcolor 1.0 0
%%DocumentProcSets: Adobe_pattern 1.9 0
%%DocumentProcSets: Adobe_Illustrator88 1.19 0
%%BoundingBox: 19 -7 381 211
%%ColorUsage: Color
%%DocumentCustomColors: (Gold)
%%CMYKCustomColor: 1 0 0.55 0 (Aqua)
%%+ 1 0.5 0 0 (Blue)
%%+ 0.5 0.4 0.3 0 (Blue Gray)
%%+ 0.8 0.05 0 0 (Blue Sky)
%%+ 0.5 0.85 1 0 (Brown)
%%+ 1 0.9 0.1 0 (Dark Blue)
%%+ 1 0.55 1 0 (Forest Green)
%%+ 0.05 0.2 0.95 0 (Gold)
%%+ 0.75 0.05 1 0 (Grass Green)
%%+ 0 0.45 1 0 (Orange)
%%+ 0.15 1 1 0 (Red)
%%+ 0.45 0.9 0 0 (Violet)
%%TemplateBox: 200 102 200 102
%%TileBox: -112 -129 618 423
%%DocumentPreview: None
%%EndComments
%%EndProlog
%%BeginSetup
Adobe_cmykcolor /initialize get exec
Adobe_cshow /initialize get exec
Adobe_customcolor /initialize get exec
```

This is quite different than *raster* or *bitmap* graphics that depend on a mosaic of colored squares called *pixels* to define lines, shapes, and color. Images generated in Photoshop, PaintShop Pro, or any number of popular imaging programs (a notable exception to this is Macromedia Flash, which is vector-based), for example, can appear pixelated or stair-stepped if they are printed at too low a resolution.

Note

Adobe Photoshop 3.0 and later supports Bézier curves, but they are primarily used for making accurate selections and efficiently saving the selections to the Paths palette. They can be imported as clipping paths to a layout or illustration program to cleanly knock out a portion of the image.

Bézier curves are composed of four elements: anchor points, path segments, direction lines, and direction handles (see Figure 29.3).

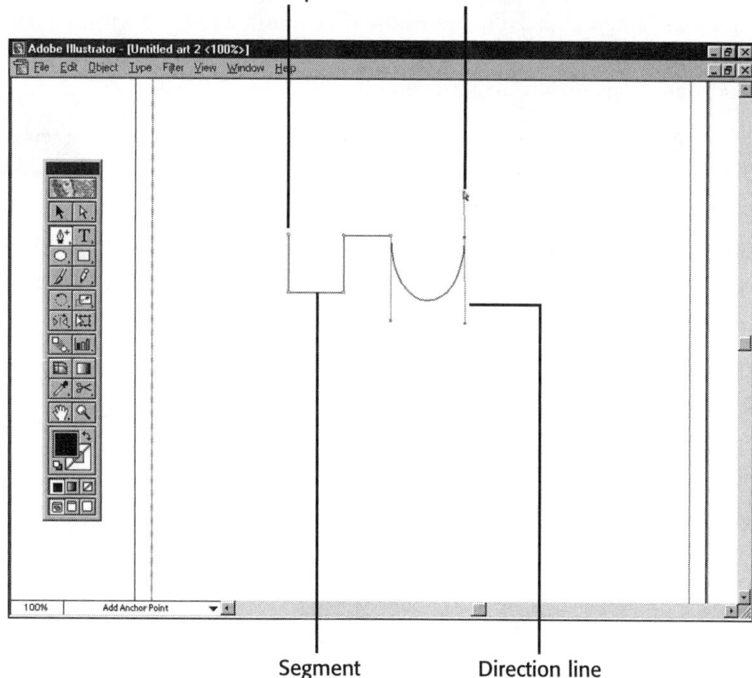

Figure 29.3
Bézier curves and straight path. Note the anchor points, segments, direction lines, and handles.

The basic process for drawing paths in Adobe Illustrator 8.0 is as follows: For a straight path, choose the Pen tool and click the mouse to establish an anchor point. Move the mouse, and click again to establish a second anchor point that is automatically joined to the first by a line segment. Repeat this process to draw a continuous series of straight paths.

To draw a curved path, choose the Pen tool, click the mouse and drag in the direction of the desired curve with the mouse button pressed to establish a direction line. Release the mouse button, move the cursor to a new location, click again and drag another direction line to establish a curved line segment. After two or more segments are drawn, a path can be closed to form a shape by placing the cursor on the beginning anchor point and clicking the mouse to close the path.

After a curved or straight path is drawn, it can be edited by dragging an anchor point, line segment, or direction handle to adjust its shape. A colored fill or stroke can then be assigned to the path. Bear in mind that anchor points, direction lines, and handles do not print, only the filled or stroked segment appear as the final artwork.

All About Digital Type

Type is generated from a series of electronic templates called fonts. There are literally thousands of typefaces available for digital graphics. A *typeface* designates a group of characters with a common set of characteristics, style, and proportions that make it a unique entity. A typeface can be rendered in any material: wood, metal, optically, or digitally.

The term *type family* pertains to groups of typefaces with common characteristics but visual variations. The weight, fill, and width are commonly varied within a family. For example, you may have a text bold or black weight, outline and solid fills, and narrow or extended width variations within the same family.

Traditionally, a *font* consisted of a specific assortment of metal characters, (numbers, letters, and punctuation marks) of the same size. For example, 12-point Baskerville was one font, 14-point Baskerville was another.

→ To read more about HTML-based typography and related concepts, **see** "Working with Fonts," **p. 230**

Digital fonts have changed the definition in that they can be *scalable*—easy to compact or enlarge within the digital environment.

There are a variety of digital fonts, including screen, city-named, scalable, PostScript, True Type, and resident fonts.

Screen Fonts

Also known as bitmapped fonts, screen fonts are actually characters that have been mapped to a grid of pixels on the computer monitor (see Figure 29.4).

Figure 29.4
Pixelated text–the pixel information has been turned on or off depending on what keystroke was sent to the computer. Screen fonts come in fixed sizes.

You can tell what sizes are loaded in your system because they appear in the size list as shown in Figure 29.5. If you use a size that is not loaded, it can appear pixilated on the screen.

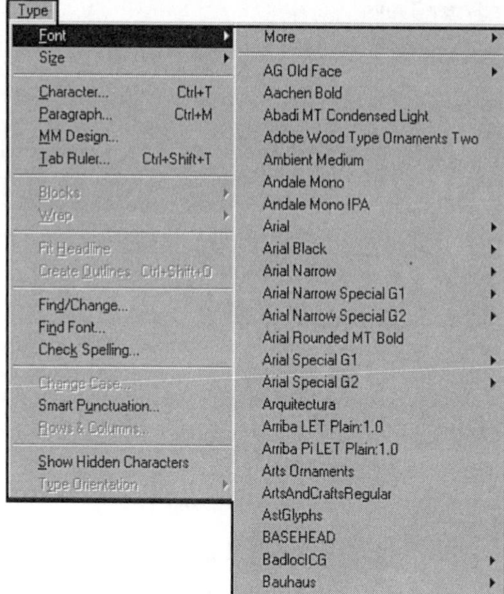

Figure 29.5
Type list as seen on a Macintosh.

Note

If you print a bitmapped font to a non-PostScript printer, it generally prints as you see it on the screen. If you print to a PostScript printer, the type prints smoothly unless it has a city name.

City-Named Fonts

Almost every font with a city name (Chicago, New York, Cairo, Geneva, and so on) is a bitmapped font. Fonts that are not named after a city have an outline, which means they can be scaled. Unless the specific font size is loaded, city-named font characters will print out jagged. The exception to this rule are city-named True Type fonts.

Scalable Fonts

Also known as outline fonts, scalable fonts are stored as mathematical outlines of the character's shape. The printer scales the character to the correct size and fills it with laser dots so that there is no loss of quality. A scalable font can be printed at the maximum resolution of the printer.

If you have Adobe Type Manager (ATM) installed, the scalable font will appear smooth on the monitor. This is similar to *font smoothing* in Windows 95 and 98.

→ For details on font categories and faces **see** "Working with Fonts," **p. 230**

PostScript Fonts

PostScript fonts are broken into types, as show in Table 29.1.

Table 29.1 PostScript Font Types

Font Type	Description
Type 1	This type of font has two separate parts: screen or bitmapped part and an outline part. Both parts must be installed. A printer can't print lines, but it can print tiny laser dots. The PostScript Interpreter takes an outline and rasterizes it, which means that it tells the printer where to fill in the outline with these tiny dots. Type 1 fonts are *resolution independent*. They can be printedin whatever resolution the printer can produce.
Type 2	Actually, no such thing exists. It was proposed as a font technology but was abandoned early in its development.
Type 3	These fonts are usually more ornate with shaded strokes, shadows, and fancy outlines. They have the disadvantage of being slower to print and have a larger file size. Adobe Type Manager cannot rasterize them, so they are generally not in use.

Resident and System Fonts

Resident fonts are outline (printer) fonts that reside in a printer's Read Only Memory (ROM) chips, and system fonts are those that come installed with an operating system. Usually system fonts are the most common typefaces: Arial, Avant Garde, Bookman, Courier, Courier New, Helvetica, New Century Schoolbook, Palatino, Symbol, Times, Zaph Chancelry, and Zaph Dingbats.

System fonts will depend upon your hardware and Operating System. Windows and Mac selections differ.

→ For a list of system fonts, **see** "Working with Fonts," **p. 230**

Downloadable Fonts

PostScript fonts that you purchase and install on your computer's hard drive are automatically downloaded to the printer's memory when you print.

TrueType fonts are scalable fonts whose technology was developed by Apple Computer. As with PostScript, a mathematical outline describes the font. However, the True Type method is not the same as the PostScript outline.

True Type fonts appear smooth on a Macintosh screen and on a Windows 95 or 98 screen with font smoothing installed. They also appear smooth in print at *any* size, even if they are city-named. They only have one part, with screen and printer information all placed in one file. The outline is rasterized to the screen and to the printer.

Editing Type

When type is generated in Adobe Illustrator 8.0, it is anchored to a *type path*. The path can be straight, curved, horizontal, vertical, or contained within a shape. The path is completely editable.

After type is generated, the content of the text can be further edited with advanced word processing features found under Illustrator's Type palette. To modify the weight, size, *leading* (space between lines), *kerning* (space between characters), horizontal and vertical scale, or type characteristics, choose Type, Character to display a comprehensive list.

To visually modify the shape of a character, the font must be converted to a type outline, as shown in Figure 29.6.

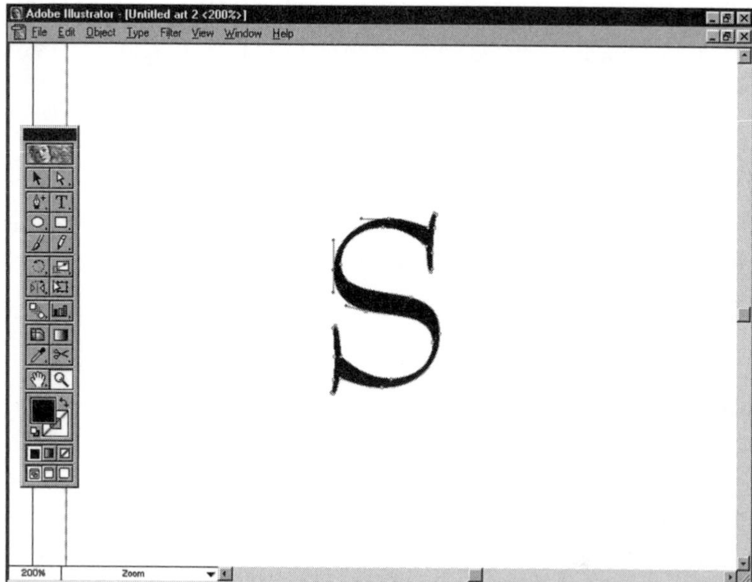

Figure 29.6
Type outline–by converting a type character to type outline, you can make changes directly to the letter using Bézier curves.

To convert type into a type outline, select its path with one of the selection tools and choose Type, Create Outlines. The type characters convert to a series of Bézier curves that can be edited with any of the path editing or transformation tools.

The Vector Look

Photos are almost always raster images because they require subtle blends and gradations of color to portray continuous tone. A photo is usually scanned, manipulated, or color corrected in Photoshop, saved as a TIFF or EPS to be placed in an illustration or layout program, or optimized as a JPEG for the Web.

Vector illustration programs have tools that produce sophisticated blends and gradients, but they are generally applied over larger areas.

The Gradient Mesh tool within Illustrator greatly enhances the application of a gradient to a smaller area, but it cannot ultimately produce the essential quality of raster art. The continuous change of pixel color values over the entire surface of the image produces continuous tonality.

Vector art generally looks harder-edged than raster art. Vector graphics are ideal for the production of maps, graphs, and technical drawings due to the crisp, precise graphics and text and solid color fields that can be created. Vector art also lends itself to cartoons, logos, and illustrations where sharp edges, sumptuous color, and smooth blends are required.

Vector programs are also used to create special type effects. If a photograph is going to be used in conjunction with text and hard-edged graphics, it is likely to be scanned into Photoshop, where it is enhanced, color corrected, or manipulated. It is then saved in an appropriate format and placed within your Web page. The text and graphics are created, and the document is printed with the assurance of crisp detail in the text characters regardless of their point size.

ILLUSTRATOR AND HTML 4.0

You may wonder at this point what *any* of this has to do with the Web and HTML 4.0? After all, images generated from vector programs seem to be primarily designed for print output.

With the exception of Acrobat PDF (Portable Document File) format, Macromedia Flash, and graphics generated with new graphic technologies, Web images are exclusively pixel based.

→ To learn more about Flash, **see** "Working with Shockwave Flash," **p. 689**

→ New vector graphic technologies are also discussed, **see** "Understanding XHTML, XML, and Emerging Languages," **p. 499**

For vector art to appear on the Web, it has to be converted to a Web-ready format, a function that was usually performed in Photoshop. The image was saved as an EPS and imported into Photoshop, which rasterized it. The image was then saved as Gif89a or JPEG format. With the release of Illustrator 7.0, file conversion was built into the program and streamlined. With Illustrator 8.0, new Web-ready features have consolidated and refined. They include the following:

- Direct support for RGB color
- Web Color Swatches palette
- Built-in GIF89a export
- A JPEG Save option
- PNG export capabilities
- The capability to assign a URL to a specific object
- The capability to create imagemaps
- PDF support

The image you create in Illustrator, although drawn with a variety of vector tools, is ultimately sized and saved as raster art to be viewed with a Web browser.

Color

Artwork created for print is usually created by using the ink color model of its final output. A black-and-white image is assigned various tints of black to express tonality, and a full-color image is painted various mixes of cyan, magenta, yellow, and black.

The artist can then be assured that the onscreen image will look as accurate as possible.

The same is true with vector images for the Web. Because the image ultimately is going to be seen in the red, green, and blue phosphors of a color monitor, the working color mode should be RGB. The RGB colors can be assigned directly from the color palette, as shown in Figure 29.7.

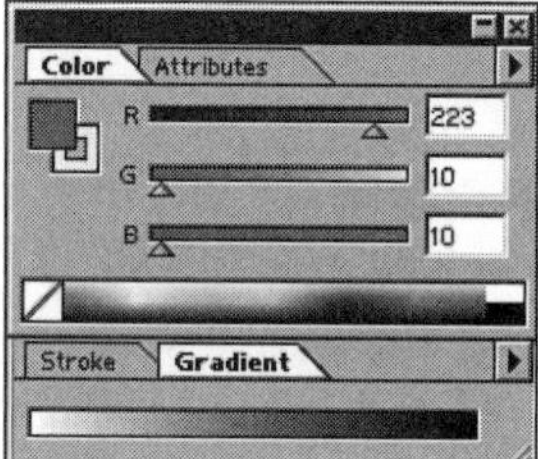

Figure 29.7 Color RGB palette with dynamic sliders. Use these tools to adjust the color to the one you want before optimizing the graphic for use on the Web.

➔ For more on issues with color and the Web, **see** "Color Concepts," **p. 537**

To access the color palette, choose Window, Show Color. Choose the arrow from the upper-right corner of the screen and scroll to RGB from the submenu. The palette offers direct color control in RGB mode.

You can assign an object any of 256 values of color from each of the red, green, or blue dynamic sliders for a total of 16,777,216 different color combinations. The sliders let you place the triangle on the desired color. You can choose to assign colors to a fill (color within an object) or stroke color around the outline of an object by choosing the appropriate icon.

But what if you've already created the file in another color mode, like CMYK (cyan, magenta, yellow, and black) or HSB (hue, saturation, and brightness) for example? It would be labor-intensive to have to adjust all your colors manually.

Fortunately, you can convert the color of your work by applying a filter.

Select the target object or objects. Choose Filter, Colors, Convert to RGB. The color values change to Web-ready RGB values. Because the gamut or range of color varies from one mode to another, some adjustment may be necessary after conversion.

Note

The JPEG export and PDF saving option globally convert colors to RGB.

THE WEB SWATCHES PALETTE

Normally, the colors of a Web-compatible GIF89a image are optimized to decrease file size. To guarantee that the colors of your vector art are completely Web-compatible, you can assign colors to your artwork from the Web swatches palette (see Figure 29.8). Access the swatches palette from Window, Swatch Library, Web to display the 216 cross-platform, Web-compatible colors. Select the object and click a swatch to apply the color.

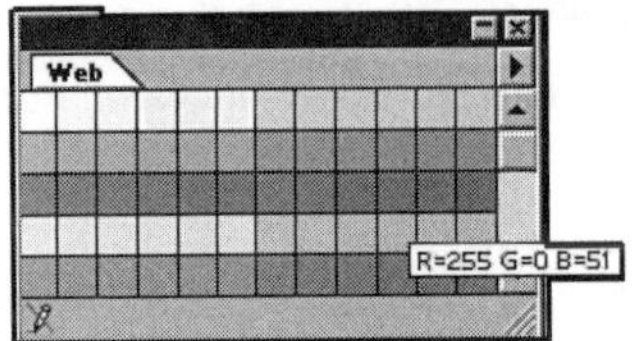

Figure 29.8
Web swatches palette in Illustrator 8.

The swatches are labeled with their RGB values displayed as you drag over them. Knowing their values lets you conveniently match colors in your WYSIWYG or text editor as you compose your Web pages. Exercise caution when using blends, gradients, color filters, or the Pathfinder function because the result may not be what you expect, and you may see dithering in your image. For best Web results, apply solid single colors to your artwork.

MAKING ILLUSTRATOR FILES WEB-READY

As mentioned earlier in the chapter, vector art must be converted into pixels before it can be seen on the Web. Illustrator supports export to four Web-compatible formats; JPEG, GIF89a, PNG, and PDF. These options are all accessed by choosing File, Export, Format.

→ To read about graphic file formats in detail, **see** "Web Graphic Formats and Professional Tools," **p. 566**

Caution

It's important to change the name of the document when you export it so that you don't overwrite the original Illustrator file and make it un-editable.

JPEG

JPEG is an acronym for Joint Photographic Experts Group, the group that originally created this format used to compress files.

To access the JPEG export window (see Figure 29.9) choose File, Export, Format, JPEG. The JPEG Options dialog box allows you to choose between three redundant functions that affect the size and quality of the image. You can enter a value from 1-10, choose Low, Medium, High, or Maximum from the drop-down menu, or move the slider between Smaller File and Larger File.

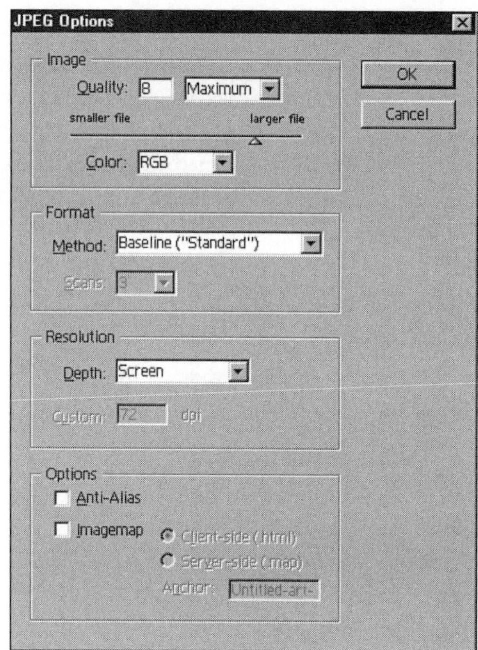

Figure 29.9
The JPEG Options dialog box in Illustrator lets you adjust image options such as the quality and color.

The Color option lets you choose a color mode; RGB, Grayscale, or CMYK.

In the Format area, choose the Method for your baseline function. Choose Baseline Standard for print images, Baseline Optimized for Web images to appear after they have completely loaded, or Baseline Progressive, which causes the image to gradually resolve in the number of scans you specify.

You can determine whether the image is high (300ppi), medium (150ppi), Screen (72ppi), or a custom resolution that you specify by entering a numerical value in the Resolution area. In the Options area, you can also choose the Anti-Alias option or choose the Imagemap option to apply an imagemap, a function that attaches a URL to an object or group of objects. Typically, you will want to choose 72 for Web output. You'll use the Client- and server-side options when making an imagemap (See "Attaching URLs to Objects" below).

PNG Support

The advantage of saving files to this latest format is the ability to keep file sizes small without data loss. PNG supports high-quality 48-bit color. Although no browsers support this format at this time without extra plug-ins, PNG may, in the future, very well replace GIF and JPEG as an efficient Web-ready format. It is supported in other vector drawing programs such as Macromedia Fireworks.

GIF89A

GIF89a is probably the most commonly used Web format for images because of its versatility. GIFs are used to save vector images, raster images, images with transparent backgrounds, and animations (see Figure 29.10). Choose a palette and designate the number of colors. The fewer the number of colors, the smaller the file size. You can choose dithering for halftone screens. In the Options section, choose from a list of specific Web-related characteristics.

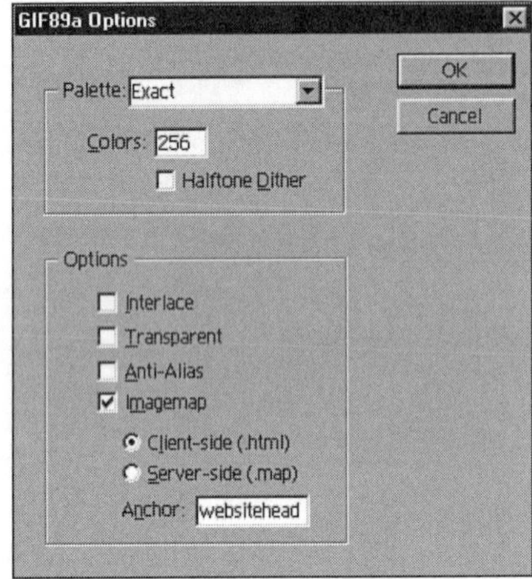

Figure 29.10
The GIF89a window allows you to export to the GIF89a format. This format takes the vector image and makes it a raster image suitable for use on the Web.

PDF

Adobe Systems' Portable Document File is becoming widely used as an across-platform interpreter for text and image files. PDFs are versatile and efficient. The only drawback is that they are not HTML-compatible. You need Acrobat Reader, a shareware program, to read the files.

Note The Acrobat Reader is readily available from Adobe at `http://www.adobe.com/`.

The Illustrator interface is complete and user-friendly, displaying efficient Web-ready options for preparing PDF files (see Figure 29.11).

The Acrobat PDF saving option is located under File, Save As, Formats.

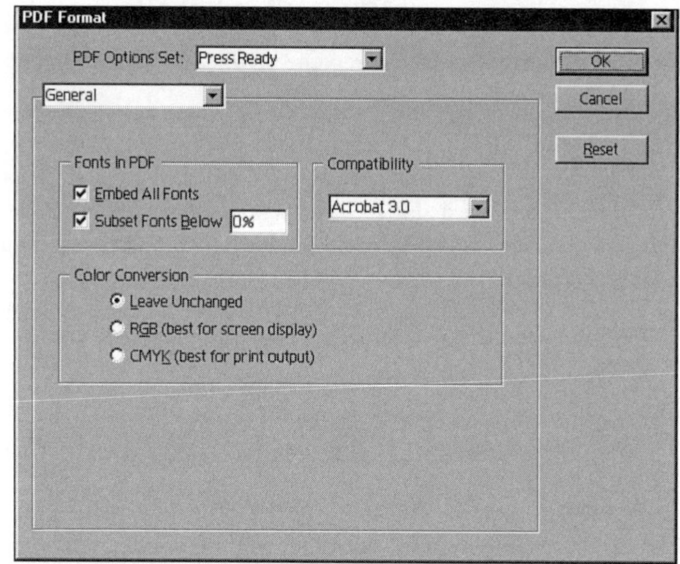

Figure 29.11
The PDF window. PDF files are useful when offering prepared brochures complete with text and graphics for download.

ATTACHING URLS TO OBJECTS

A path or group of objects in Illustrator can be automatically linked to a Uniform Resource Locator (URL) so that you can use the illustration in a Web page as an imagemap. Clicking the image in the browser takes you immediately to the desired URL. To assign a URL to a path or group of objects, do the following:

1. Select the paths or group of objects.
2. Choose Window, Show Attributes (see Figure 29.12).

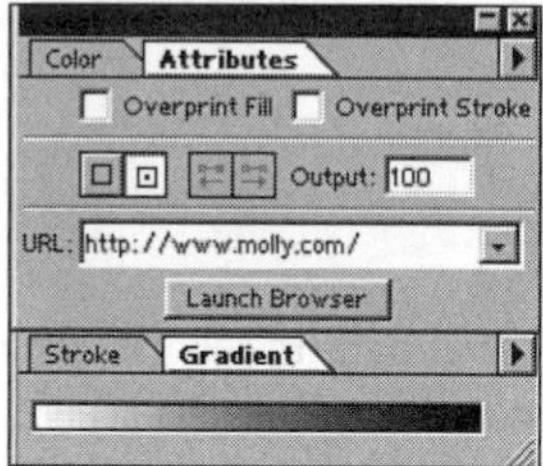

Figure 29.12
The attributes palette allows you to enter the URL to a given object within an Illustrator design.

3. Choose Show All from the Arrow in the upper-right corner to expand the Palette.
4. Type in the complete URL, for example, **`http://www.molly.com/`**.
5. Press the Return or Enter key.

You must now save the imagemap in GIF89a format to be able to access it on the Web:

1. Choose File, Export GIF89a, and rename the file. A .gif ending automatically attaches itself to the document.
2. Choose the Imagemap option in the GIF89a window that appears.
3. Choose Client Side to attach the HTML code to the image, so it can be accessed easily by your browser, or Server Side to attach a script that CGI (see Chapter 30, "Imagemaps, Animation, and Special Graphic Techniques") servers use to designate the rectangular borders of your image.

➔ For other methods of creating image maps, **see** "Imagemaps, Animation, and Special Graphic Techniques" **p.648**

Hands-On Lesson: Adobe Illustrator 8.0 and Type Effects

It is often necessary to employ an object-oriented program like Adobe Illustrator 8.0 to create specialized type effects that would be difficult or impossible to produce in a raster-based imaging or paint program. Illustrator has extraordinary type and distortion capabilities that are unavailable in Photoshop.

Don't have access to Illustrator? There are other programs that you might want to use, see "Other Vector Graphic Programs with Typographic Support," in the Troubleshooting section at the end of this chapter.

The following lesson takes you through a heading composed of headline type on a curved path, a subhead on a separate curved path, and a vector illustration that can be exported as a Web-ready, RGB imagemap. You'll build the vector graphics here, and later—in this section's project page—make the graphics Web ready.

Creating the Text

Begin by creating the text:

1. Open a new document in Illustrator, name it `WebsiteHeading`, and save it as a native Illustrator document (.ai).
2. Choose the Ellipse tool, double-click the pasteboard to display the ellipse options window. Enter a value of `4.5 in` for the Width and `2 in` for the Height (see Figure 29.13).
3. Click the bottom portion of the ellipse with the Direct Selection tool and press (Backspace) [Delete] to remove it (see Figure 29.14).

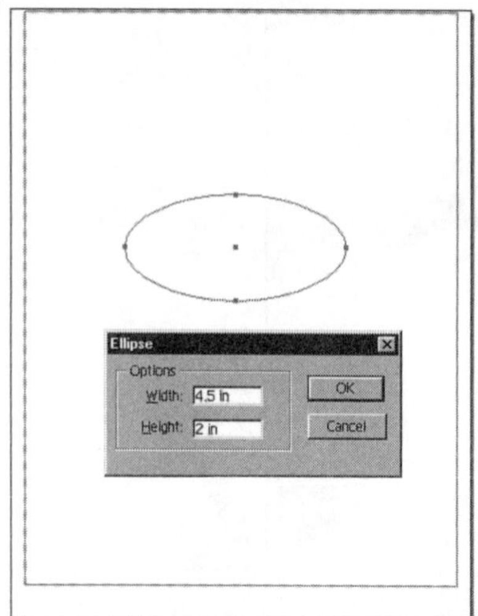

Figure 29.13
Add width and height to the ellipse to prepare it for use.

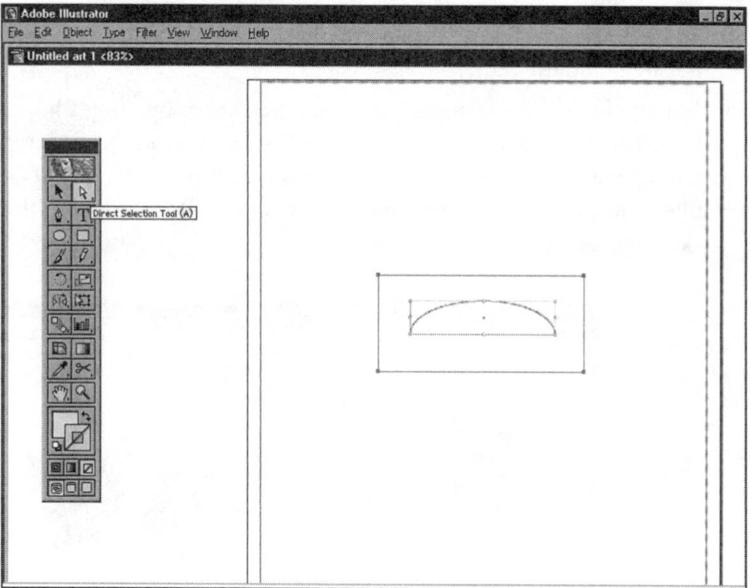

Figure 29.14
Direct Selection tool.

4. Choose the Type Path tool. Choose Type, Character and set the type specifications. (I've chosen 80 point Braggadocio Regular.) Place it on the left of the half ellipse path, click, and enter your text. After you've entered it, you can move the text along the path by clicking a character with the Direct Selection tool. An I-beam appears. Drag the I-beam to center the text on its path as shown in Figure 29.15.

Figure 29.15
Dragging the I-beam allows you to center the text on the path.

5. To modify the character shapes you must first convert them to outlines. Choose Type, Create Outlines.
6. Modify the outline characters to the desired shape by using Illustrator's powerful transformation tools, paint tools, and filters. In this case, I modified, rotated, and sheared the type characters, applied the roughen filter, duplicated the type to a separate layer, and filled and stroked the characters on each layer with colors from the RGB color palette (see Figures 29.16 and 29.17).

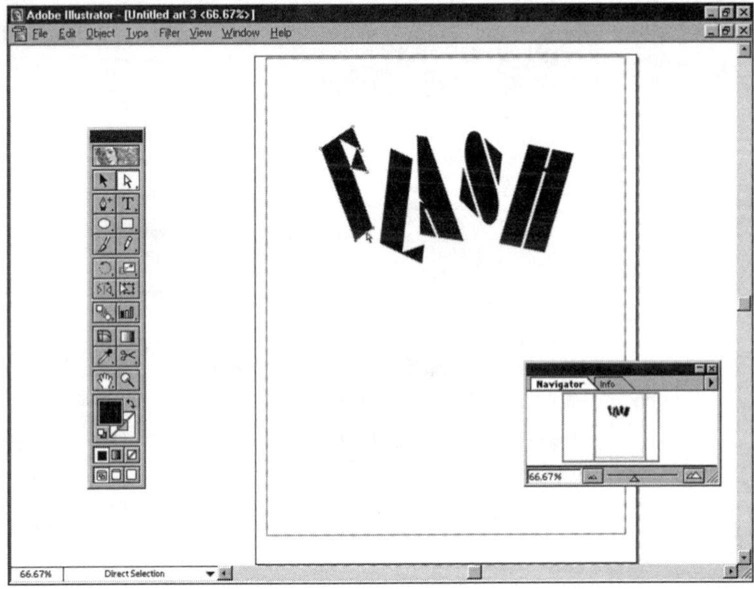

Figure 29.16
Selecting the outline characters allows you to add filters, transform the text, or change the text colors.

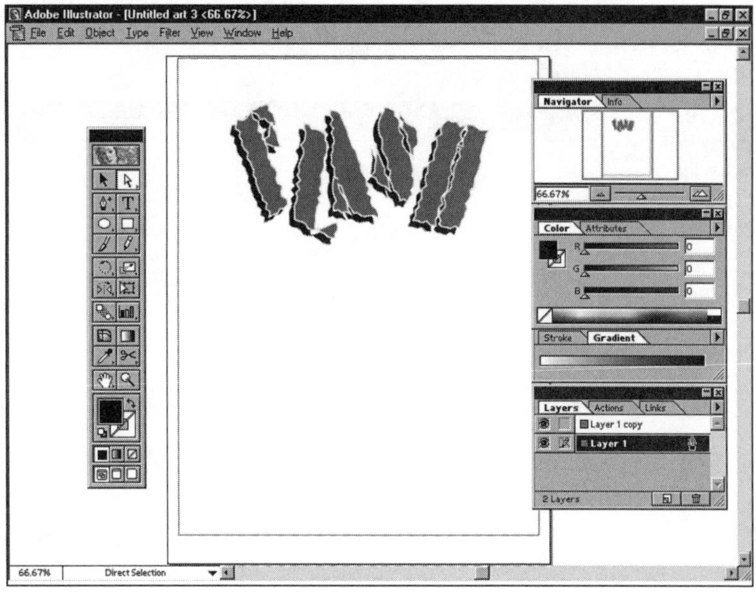

Figure 29.17
This image shows the results of the original text after transformation tools have been applied. The text now has color, shape, and dimension.

CREATING THE GRAPHICS

Now create the graphics for the design:

1. To create the lightning bolt, set anchor points and segments for the shape of the first bolt. Duplicate the object by dragging while pressing (Alt) [Option], as shown in Figure 29.18.

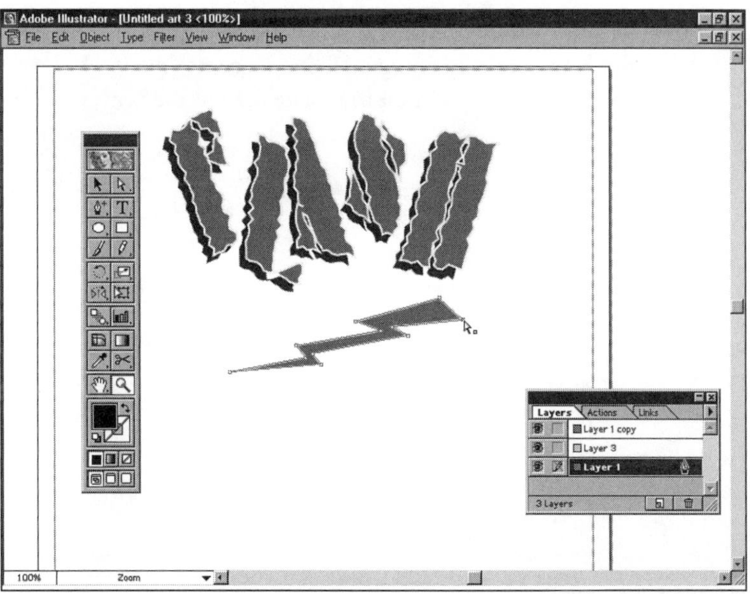

Figure 29.18
Setting anchor points to create the lightning bolt outline.

2. Scale, rotate, or transform the shape of the second and third lightning bolt so that there is variety in each shape (see Figure 29.19).

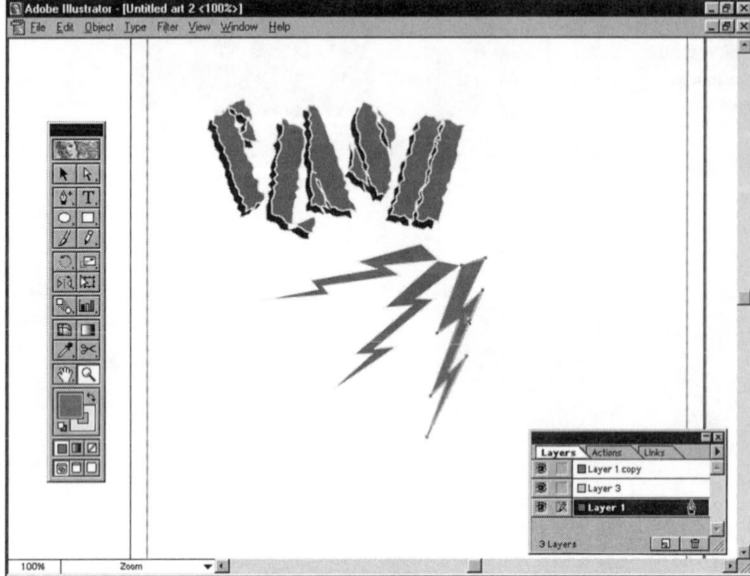

Figure 29.19
Adding variety to the shapes makes the lightning bolt more realistic.

3. Make a circle by dragging the Ellipse tool while pressing the Shift key. Apply the same fill and stroke to the circle and the lightning bolts as the text.
4. Choose the lightning bolts, the H, and the circle by selecting each one in sequence with the Selection tool while pressing the Shift key. Choose Window, Show Pathfinder and click the Unite icon to combine the five shapes into one (see Figure 29.20).
5. Make the inner circle by dragging from the center point while pressing the Shift key to constrain the shape and option to radiate it from the center (see Figure 29.21).

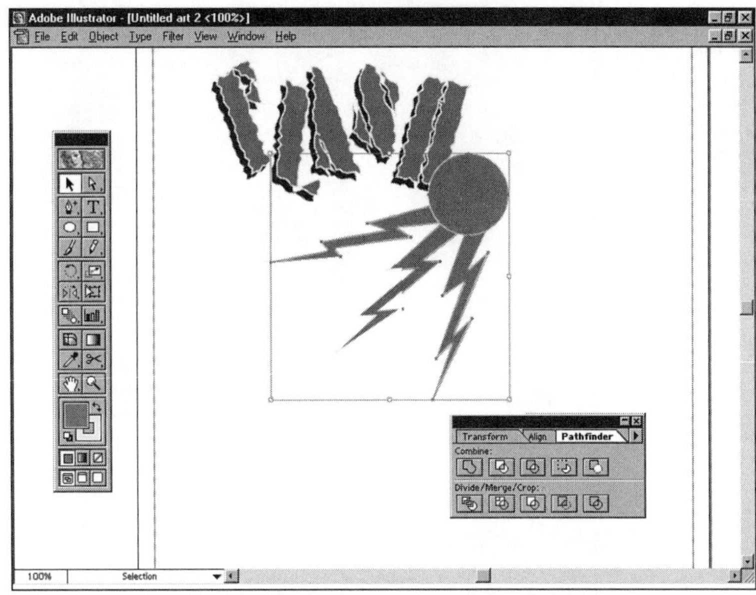

Figure 29.20
Uniting the five shapes into a single shape. The image can now be modified and adjusted as a discrete object rather than several, separate objects.

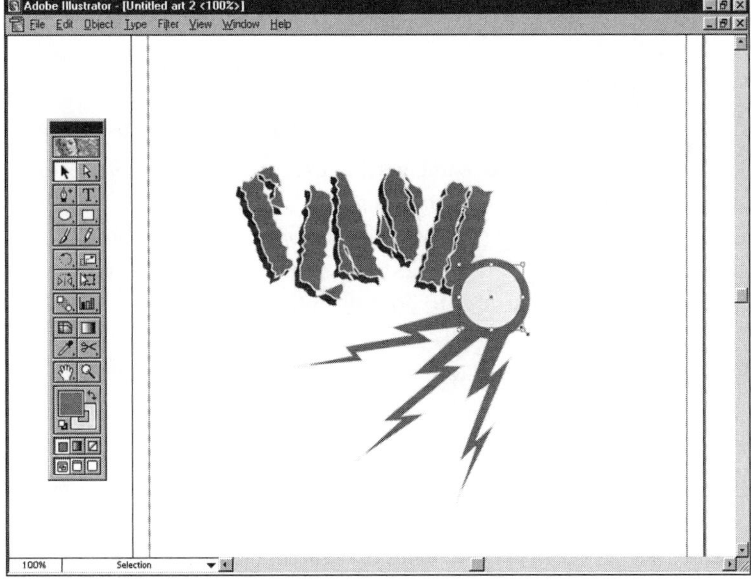

Figure 29.21
In this image, you can see the way the inner circle should appear once you've dragged the center point to the final location.

6. Choose the Type tool and enter the word `Website`. Adjust the character attributes of the type by using the Characters palette (see Figure 29.22).

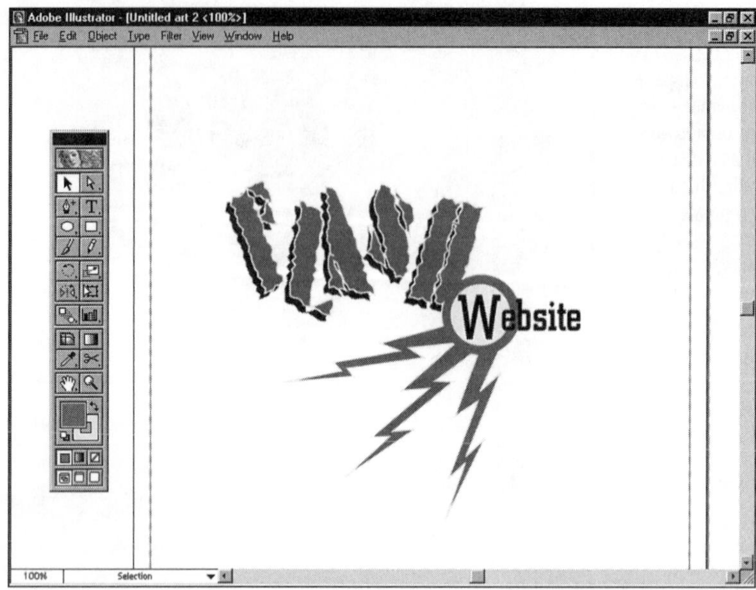

Figure 29.22
Setting the type within the circle finalizes the process. You are now ready to export the image for Web use.

TROUBLESHOOTING

FUMBLING FINGERS

Illustrator seems to be a difficult program to use. Is this my imagination or reality?

Illustrator can indeed take some getting used to. Some readers will have Illustrator experience, but many will not. If you do not, don't let the precision of Illustrator frustrate you. Learning to get things just right does take time. The main objective of the lessons in this chapter is to expose you to methods of creating exceptional type for your pages, whether you choose to use Illustrator to do it or not.

OTHER VECTOR GRAPHIC PROGRAMS WITH TYPOGRAPHIC SUPPORT

Are there other vector programs with the extensive typographic support available in Adobe Illustrator?

If you're a fan of Macromedia products, try Freehand. Another option is CorelDRAW. Both are vector graphic illustration programs. I prefer Adobe Illustrator and consider it the standard. Many professional graphic designers are familiar with Freehand and CorelDRAW as well, and each individual will naturally have a preference. All of these products are available for demo purposes by visiting the respective Web sites of their developers.

DESIGNING FOR THE REAL WORLD

MAKING THE IMAGE WEB-READY

After you've created your graphic, you'll want to make it ready for the Web, naturally! To do so, follow these steps:

1. Select the text and graphics. Choose Window, Show Attributes. Enter the entire URL in the URL box. This anchors the URL to the objects so that when you click the image in your browser, it will launch the URL's Web site (see Figure 29.23).

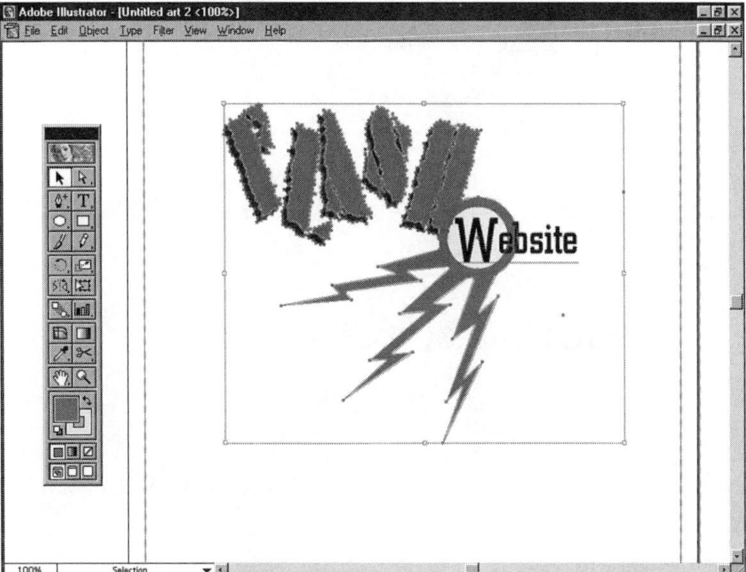

Figure 29.23
In this example, I've selected the text and graphics in order to attach a URL to them.

2. Choose File, Export, GIF89a. Change the name of the document so that you don't overwrite the Illustrator file, and add the .gif extension. Click Save. In the window that appears, choose a palette. Under Options, choose Imagemap. The name of the file should be visible under Anchor. If there is more than one imagemap in the document, choose the one you want (see Figure 29.24).

Illustrator automatically writes an HTML document that can be read in any browser with the graphics you have created. Figure 29.25 shows the "hot" area of the graphic within the browser.

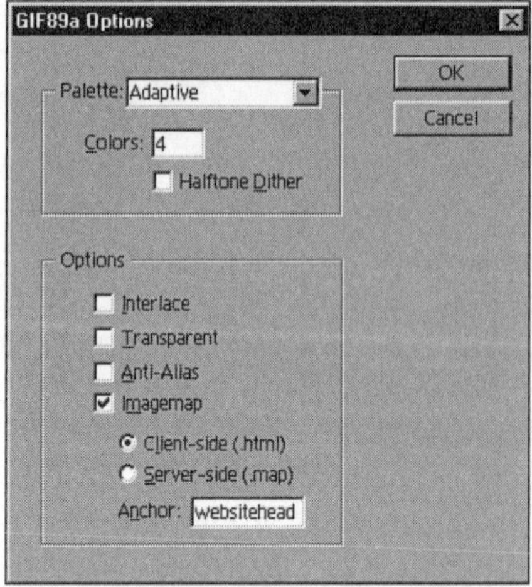

Figure 29.24
Exporting the file as a GIF89a. Be sure you keep an original of the file in Adobe Illustrator's native format (.ai) before exporting the GIF. This way, you can go back and make changes if necessary.

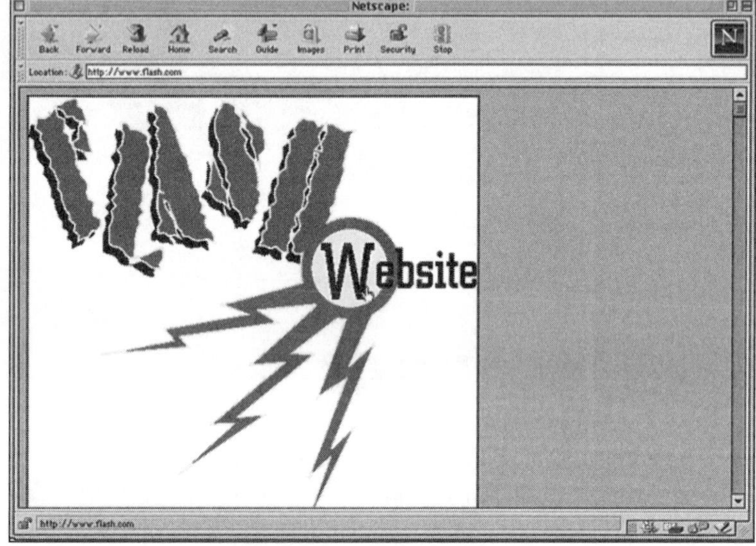

Figure 29.25
This image is now a link—note the URL in the status bar.

CHAPTER 30

Imagemaps, Animation, and Special Graphic Techniques

In this chapter

Exploring Specialty Graphics

There are several types of graphics that I consider to be *specialty* graphics. The reason I separate these from standard Web page graphics is that you won't always want to use them. These graphics are reserved for specific circumstances.

Graphics covered in this chapter are

- Imagemaps—Imagemaps are a single graphic image that can be used for multiple links.
- Animated GIFs—Use animated GIFs to add movement to a page or for advertising purposes.
- Advertising Banners—Gain visibility for your Web site through the use of ad banners.

For some, these image types might be familiar. I'm going to walk you through the creation of a variety of images in order to give newcomers guidelines on how to create specialty images, and for old hats, a refresher course with some tips and techniques that might enable you to work faster and smarter.

Understanding Imagemaps

Imagemaps allow a designer to take a single image and break it down into multiple sections of varying shapes. Each of those sections then can be linked to a different Web page.

While this sounds convenient, and while imagemaps have certainly been a significant part of Web design for some time, the reality is that they are becoming less present on professional sites. Whether this has to do with the fact that more sophisticated and attractive technologies, such as JavaScript mouseovers, are taking precedence over imagemapping, or that mapping is too fixed for today's regularly updated Web sites, is difficult to determine.

→ To learn how to create mouseover effects, **see** "Using JavaScript," **p. 419**

Despite these changes, the technology and tools related to mapping have remained current, and you will certainly want to add the technique to your repertoire of graphic skills.

Client and Server Imagemapping

There are two methods for imagemapping. The old-fashioned method is server-sided mapping, which requires the browser to work with the server to interpret your imagemap.

The newer, more popular method is client-side mapping. This means that the browser can interpret the map data without relying on the server to do so.

Both methods originally required a tedious process of understanding the mapping of coordinates. Fortunately, all of the tools mentioned in the imagemap tools section map coordinates for you, no matter the shape of your defined area.

The client-side mapping technique is preferred, but because some older browsers don't support it, many individuals combine the two techniques, ensuring that no matter the browser, the visitor will be able to use the imagemap.

CLIENT-SIDE MAPPING

Client-side maps are fast and stable because they rely on the browser to do the interpretation for them.

Listing 30.1 is an example of a client-side mapping code. Note that the image, mymap.gif, includes the `#usemap` attribute to work.

LISTING 30.1 CLIENT-SIDE IMAGEMAPPING SYNTAX

```
<HTML>
<HEAD>
<TITLE>Contact Our Company</TITLE>
</HEAD>
<BODY>

<H2>Contact Our Company</H2>

<P>For contact information, please select a city from the map below.

<IMG src="images/arizona_map.gif" width="278" height="328" border="0"
alt="imagemap of arizona" usemap="#arizona_map">
<MAP name="arizona_map">
<AREA shape="rect" alt="contact info for phoenix office" coords="86,173,245,224"
href="phoenix.html">
<AREA shape="rect" alt="click for tucson contact information"
coords="152,245,259,301" href="tucson.html">
<AREA shape="default" nohref>
</MAP>

</BODY>
</HTML>
```

All of the information required to make this map active is now included along with the HTML. This image is active.

Note

The `nohref` attribute means that if an individual clicks outside the defined areas, no action will occur.

Having trouble with links in your imagemap not working properly? See, "Links Won't Work" in the Troubleshooting section at the end of this chapter for some timely tips on how to fix this problem.

SERVER-SIDE MAPPING

To accommodate older browsers, many coders like to use this approach to mapping. To do this, you have to create a map file with the coordinate locations within it, and save it with a .map extension.

This type of imagemapping becomes more complicated because of several factors:

- The .map file will have to reside on the server. Depending on your ISP, this may be a designated spot. Either way, you'll have to find out where your ISP would like you to store this map—it will affect the way you write the HTML output.
- There are two kinds of map files. One is NCSA style, the other is CERN style. Typically, you'll want to use NCSA, but some servers, such as Microsoft's Information Server, require the CERN style. Once again, you'll have to check with your provider before mapping your image to a server.
- Because server-side mapping relies on CGI, you'll be required to find out from your ISP where the mapping utility is and what its name is.

Here's an example of NCSA map code:

```
#contact info for phoenix office
rect phoenix.html 86,173, 245,224
#click for tucson contact information
rect tucson.html 152,245, 259,301
```

Here's the same map in CERN format:

```
rect (86,173) (245,224) phoenix.html
rect (152,245) (259,301) tucson.html
```

Notice that the information is not only ordered differently, but the CERN map leaves out alternate text information shown in the NCSA code.

If you have the information necessary from your ISP, you are now ready to add the map data to your HTML. Server-side imagemaps require an attribute added to the `IMG` tag known as `ismap`.

```
<IMG src="images/arizona_map.gif" width="278" height="328" border="0"
alt="imagemap of arizona" ismap>
```

This lets the server know that this is a mapped image.

To invoke the script that will interpret the imagemap, you'll need to link your image. Listing 30.2 shows the code for an HTML page with an NCSA-style server side imagemap.

LISTING 30.2 SERVER-SIDE IMAGEMAP SYNTAX

```
<HTML>
<HEAD>
<TITLE>Contact Our Company</TITLE>
</HEAD>
<BODY>

<H2>Contact Our Company</H2>

<P>For contact information, please select a city from the map below.

<A href="/cgi-bin/contact.map"><IMG src="images/arizona_map.gif" width="278"
height="328" border="0" alt="imagemap of arizona" ismap></A>

</BODY>
</HTML>
```

If you've uploaded the appropriate .map file to the correct area on your server, and you've linked to the correct area and file on that server within your HTML, this map will now be active.

➔ To review image linking, **see** "Linking Pages," **p. 182**

COMBINATION MAPPING

If you'd like to embrace the power of the client-side map but use the server-side backup just in case, you can combine server- and client-side syntax. What you do in this case is create all of the information required for the client-side map, and then upload it to your server. Then, you add the HTML required to the image. Once that's done, include the coordinates and the HTML server-side within the code that you've just created for the client-side map.

Note

The browser will always interpret the client-side map first. This way, no trip to the server will be taken if not necessary.

Your final HTML page should resemble the code in Listing 30.3.

LISTING 30.3 COMBINATION IMAGEMAPPING SYNTAX

```
<HTML>
<HEAD>
<TITLE>Contact Our Company</TITLE>
</HEAD>
<BODY>

<H2>Contact Our Company</H2>

<P>For contact information, please select a city from the map below.

<P><A href="/cgi-bin/contact.map"><IMG src="images/arizona_map.gif" width="278"
height="328" border="0" alt="imagemap of arizona" usemap="#arizona_map"
ismap></A>

<MAP name="arizona_map">
<AREA shape="rect" alt="contact info for phoenix office" coords="86,173,245,224"
href="phoenix.html">
<AREA shape="rect" alt="click for tucson contact information"
coords="152,245,259,301" href="tucson.html">
<AREA shape="default" nohref>
</MAP>

</BODY>
</HTML>
```

Your client- and server-side bases are now completely covered (see Figure 30.1).

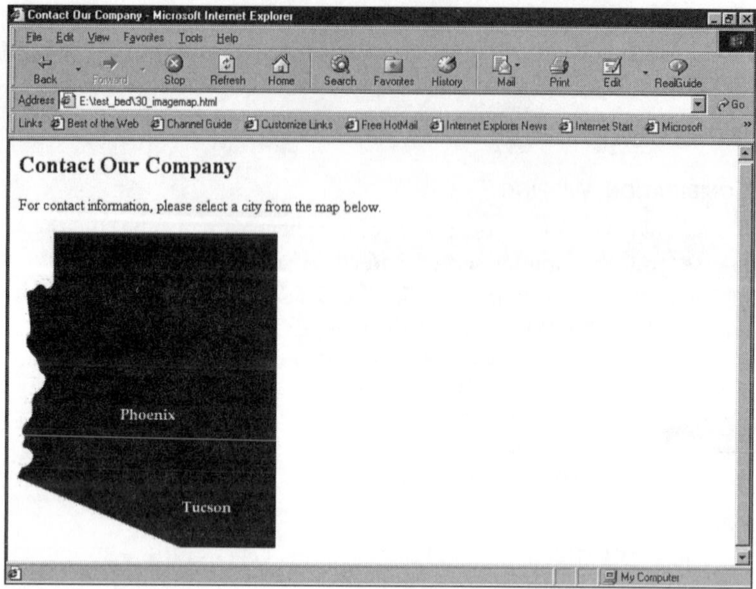

Figure 30.1
An imagemap that is both client- and server-sided ensures that even site visitors with older browsers will be able to use the map.

IMAGEMAPPING TOOLS

There are several kinds of imagemapping tools. They range from those applications packaged with or subsidiary to larger imaging, HTML, or multimedia programs such as ImageReady, Dreamweaver, FrontPage, and even Macromedia Flash.

Standalone mapping tools are also popular. They include the following:

- Mapedit—This popular, inexpensive shareware program is available for download from Boutell at `http://www.boutell.com/mapedit/`. Windows and Macintosh platforms are supported.
- MapMaker—From TwinMoon, MapMaker makes excellent client- and server-side maps. It's only available for the Macintosh at `http://www.kickinit.net/mapmaker/` (see Figure 30.2).
- LiveImage—This is a user-friendly mapping tool. Expanded features include a link checker for your mapped URLs as well as drop-and-drag support. Find Windows platforms only at `http://www.mediatec.com/`.
- Web Hotspots Imagemap Editor—Another popular imagemap editor with HTML, client-side and server-side output at `http://www.1automata.com/hotspots/`.

You can also create client-side imagemaps right online! Use CIMM, the Clickable Image Map Maker. Enter the location of the graphic to be mapped (see Figure 30.3), and follow the online instructions to map your graphic effectively.

Figure 30.2
MapMaker from TwinMoon for the Macintosh makes imagemapping a breeze.

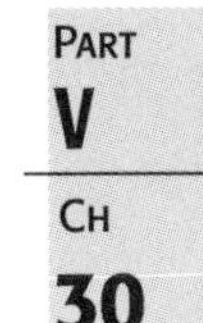

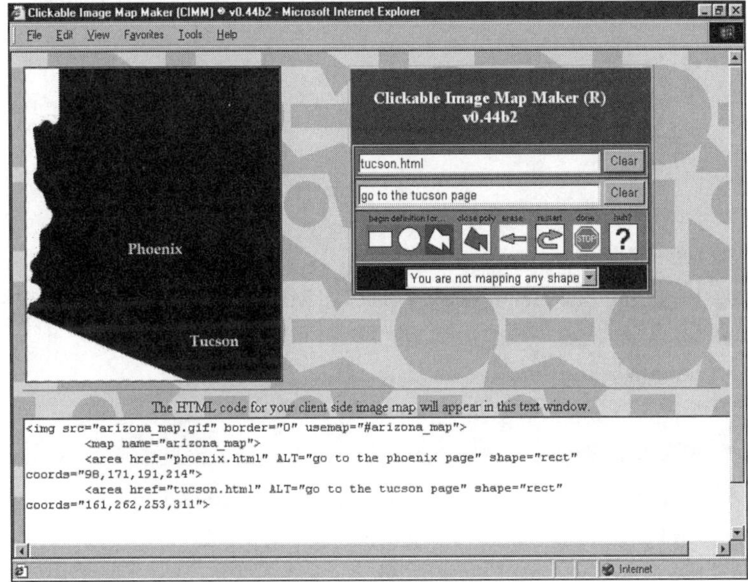

Figure 30.3
Mapping an image right online with CIMM!

Note

Visit **`http://www.linkedresources.com/tools/cimm/-cimm_v0.44b2.html`** to map your graphic right online.

Imagemapping Step-by-Step

In this section, you will find an exercise to take you through the creation of an imagemap.

Note

For this example, I use MapEdit, which is available for both Macintosh and Windows platforms. It also will help you create both client- and server-side imagemaps.

The first step in mapping an image is to select an image appropriate for mapping. This means an image with distinct regions or that logically lends itself to mapping, such as the literal map of Arizona I'm using in this sample.

MapEdit prefers that you code your image into HTML first.

1. Add your image to a standard HTML page:

```
<HTML>
<HEAD>
<TITLE>Contact Our Company</TITLE>
</HEAD>
<BODY>

<H2>Contact Our Company</H2>

<P>For contact information, please select a city from the map below.

<IMG src="images/arizona_map.gif" width="278" height="328" border="0"
alt="image
map of arizona">

</BODY>
</HTML>
```

2. Save the file as `image_map.html`.
3. Open MapEdit.
4. From the File menu, select Open HTML Document. This will cause a dialog box with the images on that page to appear.
5. Highlight the image to be mapped and click OK.
6. MapEdit will now load your image.
7. Now select the shape you'd like to use for the mapped area. I've chosen the rectangle.
8. Hold the mouse down and draw the first area to be mapped.
9. Right-click the mouse, and enter the desired URL and any additional information into the dialog box (see Figure 30.4).
10. Click OK.
11. Repeat steps 7-10 until all of your desired areas are mapped.

Now you'll want to save your file. To save the file as a .map file for server-side mapping, go to the File menu and select Export Old Server Map. Give the map a name, and then select Save. You'll be prompted to save for NCSA or CERN at this point.

To save the file as a client-side imagemap, select Save As from the File menu. You'll then be prompted to save your information to an HTML file. All of the imagemapping coordinates will be placed directly into that file.

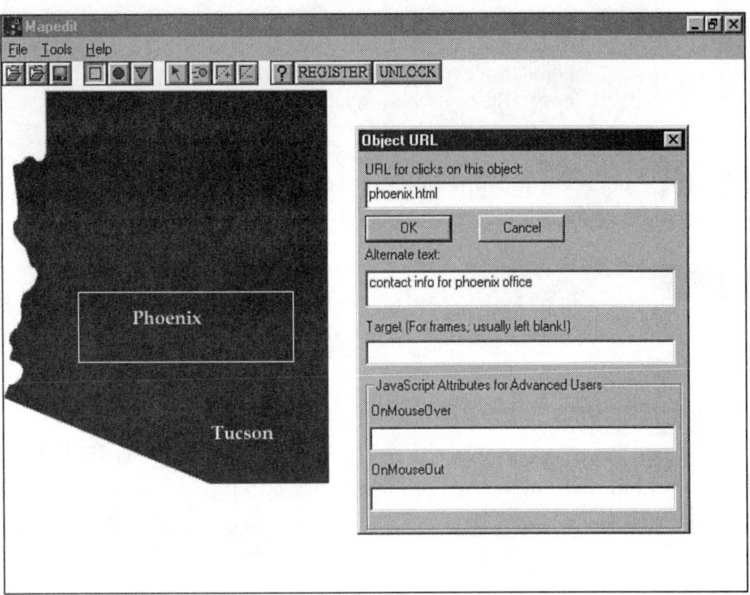

Figure 30.4 Entering a URL and comments into MapEdit. Be sure to type your URLs correctly, or you'll end up with a dead link.

Creating Animated GIFs

Another popular specialty graphic is the Animated GIF. GIF animations exploit a looping process in the GIF89a technology. Compact in size and easy to make, Animated GIFs are a great way to give a page some verve.

→ There are many tools available for making Animated GIFs, **see** "Web Graphic Formats and Professional Tools," **p. 588**

Caution

It's important to keep in mind that animations should enhance, but never detract from, a page's design. Many enthusiastic individuals will place more than one animation on a page. Combine this with mouseovers, audio, and other multimedia, and you will lose your message–and your audience–very quickly. Always use a light hand when adding active media to a page.

I'm going to show you how to make an animated GIF using GIF Construction Set and Photoshop. No matter your preferred imaging and animation tools, the methods are very similar, and my example will serve to get you started making GIF animations right away.

You will first need to create the individual images used within the animation. Known as "cells," imagine each individual image as being a unique action within the animation.

You can use this concept to be as simple or complex as you wish. However, I recommend starting out with something quite simple. You should always think about what you're going to need—any specific graphic images or text—in advance. It's also good to know the dimensions of the animation, so you can create or modify your cells to that size.

Tip from molly

Try to select images that are going to be lightweight, since you always want to keep your individual file weight down. This will help when you combine all the images into the final format. The smaller the input, the less heavy the output.

My plan is to create an animation that reads "I love my cat." However, the words "love" and "cat" will be replaced with a heart and the image of a cat, respectively.

Note

To get the heart and cat, I visited ArtToday at `http://www.arttoday.com/` where I'm a member. I went to the clip art section and did a search for a heart and then a cat.

1. Open an imaging program (in my case, Photoshop).
2. Create the first image in the series. Because the image is 100×100 pixels, select File, New and then input the file dimensions and type (RGB).
3. Because the first word is "I," select the typeface and set the type by using the Type tool.
4. Position the type to the center.
5. Flatten the image.
6. Optimize the image as a GIF.
7. Save the file as `image_1.gif`.

To create the next image

1. Open the existing `image_1.gif` in your imaging program.
2. Size and crop your image to the appropriate dimensions.
3. Index the image and optimize it to the lowest possible number of colors without losing quality.
4. Export as a GIF.
5. Save the file as `image_2.gif`.

Now repeat the steps in the first or second sample, depending on whether you are adding text or a graphic. Name each image with its appropriate numeric value in the sequence.

When I was finished, the following is what I had:

Image_1.gif—A 100×100–pixel GIF of the word, "I"

Image_2.gif—A 100×100–pixel GIF with the image of a heart

Image_3.gif—A 100×100–pixel GIF of the word "my"

Image_4.gif—A 100×100–pixel GIF with the image of a cat

All of these files are now resident on my hard drive (see Figure 30.5).

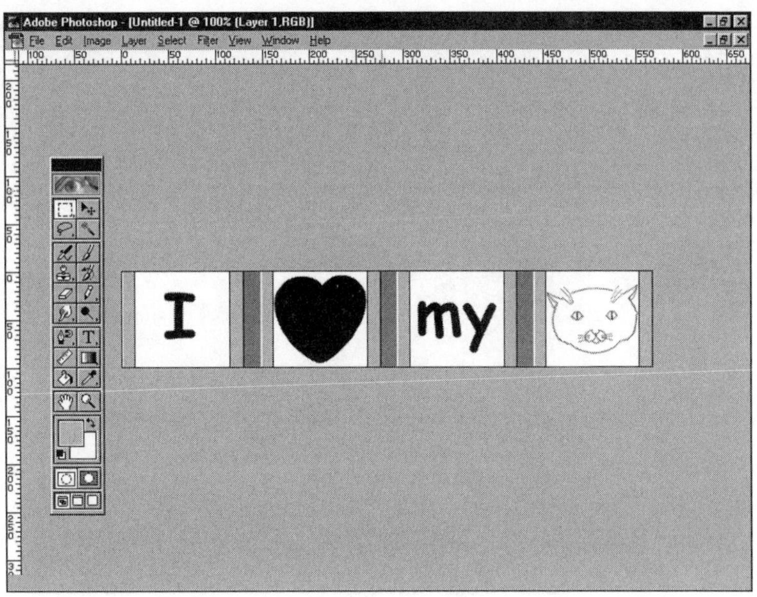

Figure 30.5
My four prepared animation cells as seen in Photoshop.

Follow these steps to animate the graphic with GIF Construction Set:

1. Open the GIF Construction set.
2. From File, select Animation Wizard.
3. Click Next when asked if you are ready to proceed.
4. Select Yes, for Use with a Web Page.
5. Click Next.
6. Select your looping preference. I recommend only once!
7. The next dialog box will offer preferences for types of graphics. Choose the description that best suits your graphic—mine is Drawn (see Figure 30.6).
8. Now you'll set the delay. For demonstration purposes, stick with the default of 100 hundredths, although you can select any delay you prefer in the future—and you can change this setting later.
9. Click Next.
10. Choose Select.
11. Go to the area where your GIFs are stored.
12. Select each image in order of its appearance to be animated.
13. Click Next, Done.
14. When GIF Construction Set is done animating the image, select Save As and save your file. Mine is saved as `animation_1.gif`.
15. Now view your animation by using the View selection.

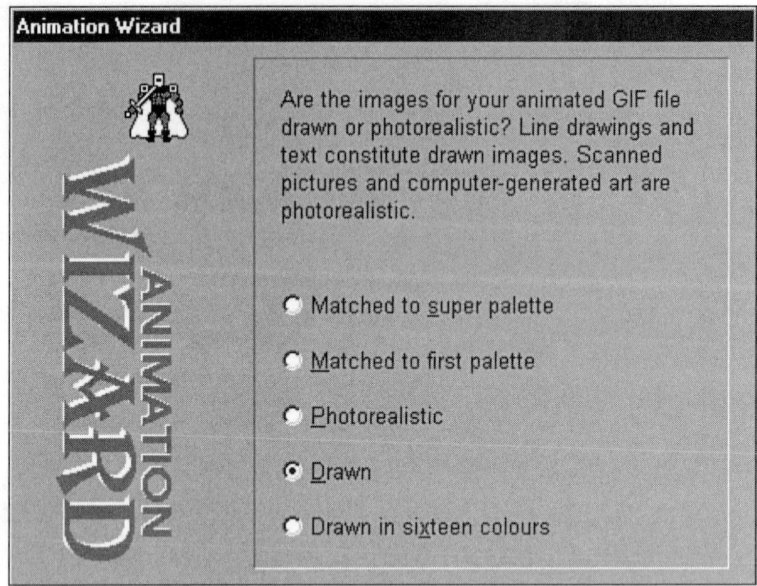

Figure 30.6
Selecting the image type in GIF Construction Set. I've chosen the Drawn radio button because my animation is text and line drawn imagery.

To add your animated image to a Web page, simply use the standard `<IMG>` tag and attributes (see Listing 30.4). Compliant browsers will understand that this is an animated GIF and play it properly.

LISTING 30.4 ADDING AN ANIMATED GIF TO A WEB PAGE

```
<HTML>
<HEAD>
<TITLE>Adding an Animated Image to an HTML Page</TITLE>
</HEAD>
<BODY>
<BR>
<BR>
<BR>
<DIV align="center">
<H2>Tara Made Me Do It!</H2>
<IMG src="images/animation_1.gif" width="100" height="100" border="0" alt="I
love my cat">

</DIV>

</BODY>
</HTML>
```

Figure 30.7 shows the animation within my Web browser. Of course, the animation moves through each of the cells before it stops.

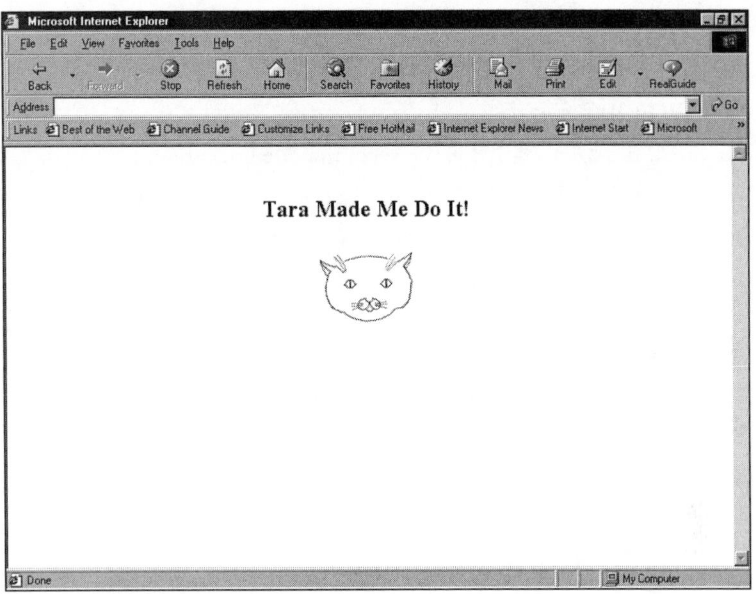

Figure 30.7
My animation within a Web page. When you open your animation in a browser, you can see how the animation changes frames. If it goes too fast or slow, you might want to open it up again in your animation program and adjust the timing.

Caution

You'll notice that I've recommended to loop your animation only once and then stop. Animations that keep looping tend to be annoying. There are some instances in which you'll want to loop continuously, such as if you have a slow moving animation or an advertisement. For accent animations, however, be subtle!

Unsure of whether or not to place multiple animations on your site? See, "Moving Violations" in the Troubleshooting section at the end of this chapter.

Note

For more on GIF animation techniques and technologies, I recommend a visit to Royal E. Frazier's famous GIF Animation site at `http://members.aol.com/royalef/gifanim.htm`.

CREATING ADVERTISING BANNERS

One of the most popular methods of advertising Web sites is getting involved in an advertising banner campaign. Banners improve visibility of a product or Web site and, in some cases, have proven to be a helpful method of gaining product recognition and boosting sales on the Web.

➔ To learn more about marketing your site, **see** "Web Site Marketing and Promotion," **p. 906**

Typically, advertising groups require specific, standardized sizes and guidelines for banner creation. You do have to check with the methods employed by the group you decide to work with, as their guidelines will differ.

The following are some general specifications:

- An average banner size is 468×60 pixels.
- GIF or JPG files.
- Small file sizes—8KB is the recommended maximum.
- Use bright colors—This enhances appearance on the page.
- Animated GIFs are considered very effective. Looping is often acceptable with ad banners, but be sure to check with your ad banner partner for more specific guidelines.

Note

For more information on ad banners, check the popular ad site Doubleclick at `http://www.doubleclick.net/`.

Following the specifications listed earlier, I'm going to walk you through the creation of a static banner.

You'll need

- Your ad material, such as a logo and byline.
- An image editing program such as Photoshop, Paint Shop Pro, or PhotoImpact.

With your materials on hand, do the following:

1. Open the image editor of your choice.
2. Select File, New.
3. Create a file to the specific dimensions of 468×60.
4. Add your graphic logo.
5. Add your text.
6. If using Photoshop or another layering program, flatten the image.
7. For GIFs: index the colors and export as a GIF, saving the file as `ad_sample.gif`.
8. For JPGs: Select Save As and save the file as a JPG High, Medium, or Low setting, depending on your needs. Name this file `ad_sample.jpg`.

Weigh your image. My GIF image (see Figure 30.8) came out to 3KB, very well within the guidelines.

Figure 30.8
An ad banner image. Your advertising banner company will tell you how to add your banners properly to a page. Very often, they have the banners on a rotation. You'll send your banner to them, and they'll send the syntax necessary for your page.

Troubleshooting

Moving Violations

I want to add more than one animation to a page. Should I do it?

The answer lies in audience and context as well as the design of the animation. In most cases, too much movement on a page will distract site visitors and confuse them. This becomes even more true when you've got your own animation *and* an animated banner on the page. I suggest a light hand whenever working with animations and banners.

Links Won't Work

I created an imagemap but one of my areas isn't linking properly. What could be the problem?

Check your URLs first. You may have mistyped or incorrectly coded a link. If everything is fine with the addressing, you'll need to look more closely at the coordinates to be sure they are working properly.

Designing for the Real World

Do Ad Banners Work?

There's no pat answer to this question. Ad banners are set up to provide an extension of a product's branding via a visual billboard-style effect, and also to provide a method by which interested people will click the banner and go directly to the advertiser's site.

The visual effect is known as *impressions* or *views* and refers to how many times an ad banner gets seen. When a banner is clicked on and followed to the next site, this is known as a *click-through*.

In loose polls of adult Web users, very few admit to having ever clicked a banner and followed it. However, people do report noticing them. Stricter polls have taken a look at the Web's most popular sites that use heavy advertising. Let's take a comparison look at the return rate of how much money is spent on a variety of direct marketing ads and how that translates into sales.

Media	Advertising to Sales Ratio
Newspapers	.087
Direct Mail	.096
Magazines	.120
Internet	.143
Radio	.172
Television	.204

Obviously, the Internet is a significant contender, falling happily in the middle (according to this poll) of these most common media. The poll would then suggest that advertising plays a very significant role in improving sales—if you can afford the type of aggressive campaigns as the big companies can. If not, general belief is that you do extend your brand significantly when working with ad banners if only via gaining widespread visibility for your logo, name, product, and service.

Note

The information for this poll was compiled using data found at `http://www.emarketer.com/`.

PART VI

Multimedia and Embedded Objects

CHAPTER 31

AUDIO, VIDEO, AND STREAMING MEDIA

In this chapter

AUDIO, VIDEO, AND THE WEB

Well-managed audio and video can bring your Web pages to life. Poorly managed audio and video can drive your audience away. Who hasn't quickly left a site to escape a droning background sound clip? Who hasn't been excited to see a great video on the Web only to find out that you must commit a good part of an afternoon to downloading it? Audio and video can add a great deal to your site, but it will take some thought and experimentation on your part to make it work for your audience.

If you are interested in venturing into the world of audio and video, there are many factors you must consider. How can you produce high-quality audio and video? How much quality should you sacrifice for efficiency? Should you use downloadable files or streaming technology? Will your audience have the software they need to experience your work? In this chapter, I'll help you make productive decisions and guide you through methodology that will get you up and running with audio and video. First, we'll look at standard audio and video files, and then we'll look more closely at streaming media.

Note

Although downloadable and streaming media are widely used, viable choices in contemporary Web development, professionals are beginning to look toward script-based technologies such as SMIL and HTML+Time.

→ For information on multimedia scripting technologies, **see** "Understanding XHTML, XML, and Emerging Languages," **p. 492**

CREATING AUDIO AND VIDEO FILES

The first step to adding audio and video to your Web site is to create the source files or gather prerecorded source files. It's important to remember that good media content on the Web is the result of good media sampling. If you create a sound clip by taking your tape recorder to a concert and recording your favorite song from the twentieth row, you will have quite a different quality clip than one produced in a studio.

You need a good microphone and good sound editing software if you're recording your own sound sample. For a good video sample, you need a high quality capture device and encoding software.

AUDIO FILES

Most recording devices create analog recordings. To digitize an analog audio source, the signal must be processed through an analog-to-digital (A/D) converter. Most computers now come equipped with the sound cards that have A/D converters. If your computer has a sound input jack, it already has an A/D converter. If your computer has only a sound output jack or an internal speaker, you probably only have digital-to-analog conversion capabilities. Even if you are recording audio from a digital source, such as a digital audio tape (DAT) or compact disc (CD), some kind of A/D conversion is usually involved, because most computers do not come with digital audio inputs yet.

How Audio Is Digitized

An A/D converter uses a *sample and hold* circuit that records the voltage levels of the input signal at a fixed interval. This interval, or rate, at which the signal is sampled is determined by the A/D converter's *sampling rate*. The sampling rate also determines the highest frequency that can be recorded or played back. It is important that the recording be played back at the same sampling rate at which it was recorded. For example, 8KHz is a telephony standard that is emerging as a standard for 8-bit *.au mono files. 48.1KHz is the standard audio CD-ROM sampling rate.

After you create your sound file, you need to edit it with a good sound-editing application. There are many shareware packages that will do the trick for simple projects. It wouldn't hurt to first try some shareware options before deciding to invest in professional software.

Tip from molly

If you decide you need more serious functionality (and you are willing to pay serious money for it), you will want a professional package like Pro Tools by Digidesign (`http://www.digidesign.com/`). A good in-between application, both in terms of price and features, is SoundEdit 16 by Macromedia (`http://www.macromedia.com/`).

The following programs will help get you started with audio editing:

- Cool Edit is a digital sound editor for Windows (see Figure 31.1). With this company you have a variety of software choices from a simple shareware package, Cool Edit 96, to a more sophisticated tool, Cool Edit Pro.

Figure 31.1 Editing audio with Cool Edit. Begin with a simple shareware package, and if you enjoy using it, upgrade to the more sophisticated Cool Edit Pro.

- Sound Forge by Sonic Foundry is professional sound editing software for Windows (see Figure 31.2) that includes an extensive set of audio processes, tools, and effects for manipulating audio. Sound Forge offers full support for the latest streaming technology, including Microsoft Windows NT Server NetShow Services and RealNetworks' RealAudio/RealVideo.

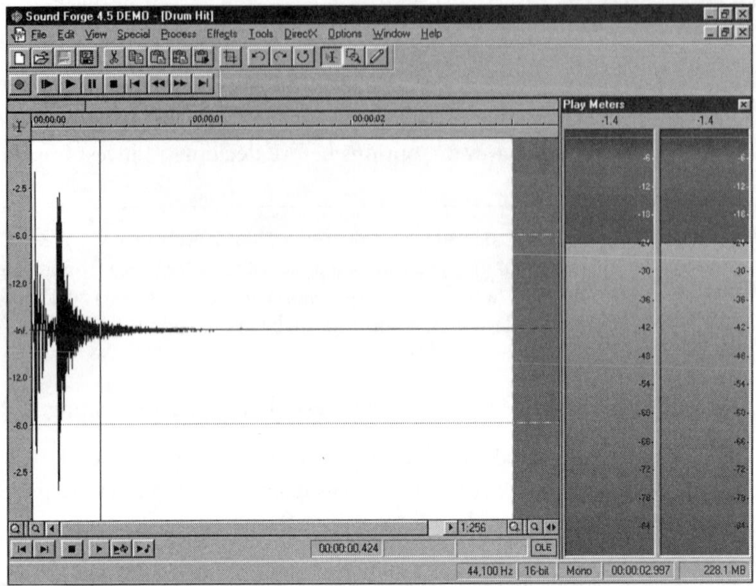

Figure 31.2
Sound Forge has an extensive set of audio editing tools, including MP3 support and streaming audio.

- Waves' AudioTrack is a good audio editor for musicians. It combines audio processors including equalization, compression/expansion, and gating. WaveConvert Pro is a good tool for converting your audio files into another format.

Note

Web sites for the aforementioned products can be found at

Cool Edit by Syntrillium: `http://www.syntrillium.com/`

Sound Forge: `http://www.soundforge.com/`

AudioTrack and WaveConvertPro: `http://www.waves.com/`

Video Files

When considering the possibility of adding video to your Web site, you must look at a hardware investment as well as purchasing software. It was already mentioned that you must have a very high-quality audio source file before you add it to your Web page. That point is even more important when it comes to producing video content. There are two steps in the processes of creating video when you will sacrifice quality if you do not have good tools.

When you encode video, you capture it to your hard drive. The faster the computer, the faster the video because frames are lost if your computer cannot keep up with the video capture. To produce professional quality video, you need a very fast machine and a high-quality video capture card.

You will also sacrifice quality if, during the compression process, you do not choose the best video bitrate, bitrate quality, and frame speed to meet your needs.

Note

To make some of these decisions easier for you, RealNetworks has developed video templates you can follow. You can find a list of these templates at `http://www.real.com/devzone/library/stream/videohints.html`.

DOWNLOADABLE FILE FORMATS

There are two methods for delivering audio and video to your audience—downloading and streaming. Downloadable files are ones that are completely loaded on to the user's hard drive before they are played. Streaming files are delivered to the browser in a somewhat steady stream of information.

With streaming media, the user does not need to wait for the entire file to be received before a player begins to playback the source. Both methods have advantages and disadvantages. This section focuses on downloadable formats, with streaming media discussed after the basics of downloadable audio and video are covered.

Tip from molly

Because downloadable media requires a suitable application, you might consider adding a note to your page about the file type, and a link or selection of links where individuals who do not have suitable software can acquire it.

AUDIO FORMATS

All the following formats require a complete download before starting the sound. This can be a great disadvantage if your sound clip is large, because your audience many not be willing to wait for long.

You must always try to make your audio files as small as possible. One important factor that directly impacts file size is quality. The quality of sound clips varies greatly, and different file formats are better suited for different quality clips.

Higher sampling rates and *resolutions* (the number of bits allocated for each sample) require more storage and throughput. You must decide if you want to sacrifice disk space and bandwidth for high-quality audio files.

A one-minute clip of an 8-bit mono file sampled at 8KHz is approximately 150KB in size. A 16-bit stereo file sampled at 44.1KHz can take up 10MB. Sometimes a lower quality recording will meet the needs of your site's viewers.

The following is a list of the most used audio file formats followed by each one's appropriate MIME type. MIME types allow you to exchange different types of data on the Internet:

- **u-law *.au; audio/basic au snd**—The u-law (pronounced wu-law) format is frequently used on the Internet. Its file size is relatively small, but the quality is considered sub-par because it only supports 8-bit sound. Most people find this format is sufficient for their Web sites, especially because most WWW users are still listening to audio through a monophonic computer speaker.
- **AIFF *.aif; audio/x-aiff aif aiff aifc**—Audio Interchange File Format (AIFF) files can be quite large. AIFF files, used primarily by Macintoshes, are easily converted to other file formats and are often used for high-quality audio applications when storage space is not a concern.
- **AVI *.avi; video/x-msvideo avi** —The Audio/Video Interface is used in Windows operating systems to provide sound and video, with the sound being primary. It may drop frames to keep the sound playing, thereby allowing the format to work on almost any Windows machine, from the least powerful to the most powerful.
- **WAV *.wav; audio/x-wav wav**—A proprietary format sponsored by Microsoft and IBM, it is most commonly used on Windows-based PCs. It is the audio portion of an AVI file.
- **MPEG; *.mp3; audio/x-mpeg mp3**—The International Standard Organization's Moving Picture Expert Group designed this format for both audio and video file compression. The MPEG codecs (compression/decompression methods) have become strong favorites of Internet users. The compression technique yields relatively small files and high-quality files.
- **MIDI *.mid; audio/x-midi mid midi**—Unlike the other formats discussed here, Musical Instrument Digital Interface (MIDI) is not a specification for sampled digital audio. Rather, it contains a bank of digitized sounds and control information for replaying the file—similar to an electronic synthesizer. MIDI files are much smaller than digitized audio files. Unfortunately, Internet Explorer 3.0 and Navigator 3.0's onboard audio players frequently get hung up on MIDI files, Explorer being the worst offender.

Figure 31.3 shows a Web page with a downloadable .midi file. Note that information about the file, such as size and download times, has been included for the site visitor's convenience.

Note

MPEG 3's (MP3s) have taken the Web world by storm in the past year. You can find innumerable audio resources that use this format. In fact, use of this technology has become so widespread that in some cases, bootlegging of this high-quality audio format has become a significant problem for producers of original audio.

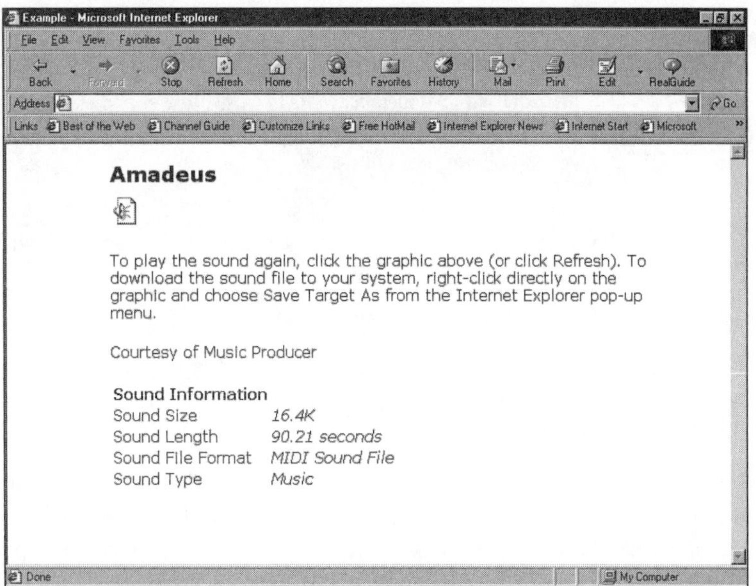

Figure 31.3
This page's authors have taken download times and file sizes into consideration.

Video Formats

The MPEG format is the most standardized video format. It is also a highly efficient format because it has an excellent compression technique. Many developers prefer QuickTime files or AVI files because they are usually smaller and don't require as long to download.

If you want to add video to your Web site, you should experiment with these formats to find what works best for you and your audience. You also must consider that not all video-editing tools support all three formats.

Tip from molly

Selecting a video format will depend on a variety of factors, including platform availability, which tools you like to use for editing, and personal preference. MPEG and QuickTime tend to be a popular choice over AVIs. MPEG is very widely supported platform-wise, and QuickTime tools and plug-ins are popular. AVI tends to be Microsoft-centric, and while it runs inline in the IE browser, support does vary with other browsers.

Adding Audio and Video to a Web Page

There are two ways in which you can place and access Web-based audio and video that will be read successfully across browsers: by using the anchor tag and the <EMBED> tag.

→ For detailed coverage of the anchor tag, **see** "Linking Pages," **p. 174**

Caution

The EMBED tag is not included in HTML 4.0 standard in deference to the OBJECT tag. You can choose to use the OBJECT tag to embed media; however, you won't have the flexibility and interoperability due to cross-browser and platform problems. At this time, it's still recommended that you use EMBED or combine EMBED and OBJECT when working across platforms and browsers

Using the anchor tag (<A>. . .</A>) is the same as placing any link within an HTML document.

```
<a href ="mydogs.mov">see Bowie and Kelsey</a>
```

If you use this method, your users will either save the file to their desktops, launch a plug-in application, or load a new browser page, depending on which browser they're using and how they have set their preferences.

If you want the video to appear on the same page as the rest of the content, you must embed the clip in the page by using the <EMBED> tag. Use of the <EMBED> tag is similar to the use of the <IMG> tag. However, the <EMBED> tag requires users to have the appropriate plug-in installed, or they will not see your work.

The following sample is for a video clip, but the <EMBED> tag also works for audio files, as well as for streaming video and audio.

```
<EMBED src="/home/dogs/rope.mov" height=105 width=100 controller=false autoplay=
true playeveryframe=false pluginspage="getplug.htm" loop=palindrome>
```

<EMBED> tag attributes and values are managed as follows:

- **height="*pixel/percent*"**—Unless you need your movie to scale, set this in pixels according to the dimensions of your movie.
- **width="*pixel/percent*"**—Width is best controlled by pixels, but you can use a percentage to describe how much space within the browser frame you want the embedded object to take up.
- **autoplay="true/false"**—Answer with true, and your movie starts when the page is first accessed. Answer with false, and the user must click the play button on the console for the movie to play.
- **controller="true/false"**—This adds user controls to the movie. If you set this for true, you must find out how many pixels your controller needs for the display and then add that amount to the height of your movie. Otherwise, the movie and the controller will be forced into the space required for the movie.
- **loop="true/false/palindrome"**—If you want the movie to play over and over, set this to true. If you want to play it once and stop, set it to false. Palindrome plays from beginning to end and backwards in a continuous loop.
- **pluginspage="gohere.htm"**—This takes users who don't have the right to a page that tells them where to get it.

Note

Internet Explorer has a specialty tag known as BGSOUND that uses the tag and the source, as follows: `<BGSOUND src="singing.au">`. With this tag, you can load and play a sound clip as the browser loads. Many Web site visitors find this quite annoying, and I don't recommended this approach for professional quality pages. However, Web hobbyists enjoy using this technique.

Tip from molly

If you're loading a sound into the background using EMBED, place the code at the bottom of the page, still within the BODY tag. This allows everything else to load first, with the audio loading last. Your site visitors won't have to wait at a blank page until the audio has loaded.

AUDIO AND VIDEO PLUG-INS

Not too long ago you had to download a special program, or plug-in, to view many audio and video files. Although some file formats still require you to get a special plug-in, many come bundled with operating systems and browsers.

Note

For a list of audio and video plug-ins supported by Netscape, visit `http://www.netscape.com/plugins/audio-video.html`.

Some of the primary and important plug-ins you'll want to have include the following:

- **Apple QuickTime,** `http://www.apple.com/quicktime/`—Apple QuickTime Plug-in allows your audience to view your QuickTime (.mov) video clips as well as many other audio and video formats (see Figure 31.4). It ships with Netscape Navigator 3.0 and higher and works with Navigator 2.0 and as an ActiveX control in Internet Explorer 3.0.
- **Microsoft Media Player,** `http://www.microsoft.com/windows/mediaplayer/`—The new and improved Microsoft Media Player (version 5.2) is being shipped with the later releases of Windows 98 (see Figure 31.5) and is available as a free download for Windows 95 users. This is one-stop shopping for most audio and video formats you will encounter including ASF (a Microsoft format), RealVideo/RealAudio 4.0, MPEG 1, MPEG 2, WAV, AVI, MIDI, MOV, VOD, AU, MP3, and QuickTime files. The Media Player can run as a standalone or can be viewed within Internet Explorer and Netscape.
- **RealPlayer G2 by RealNetworks,** `http://www.real.com/products/player/`—G2 supports all three Real data types: RealAudio, RealVideo, RealFlash, as well as AVI, WAV, MIDI, MPEG, JPEG, VIVO, VRML, and others. RealNetworks is the leader in delivering audio and video over the Web. One of the most promising features of G2 is dynamic bandwidth allocation. This should greatly enhance the overall quality of the content being played.

Figure 31.4
Apple's QuickTime Page. QuickTime supports video, audio, and proprietary virtual reality media as well as having many attractive tools and dedicated developer resources.

Figure 31.5
Microsoft's Media Player in Windows 98. The Media Player that shipped with Windows 95 and the early release of Windows 98 only supports WAV, AVI, and MIDI formats.

When you're deciding on the best format for your audio and video files, you should consider the likelihood that your users will already have the software they need to see your work. Too often, users will not take the time to download a plug-in, so you are better off to provide your files in formats they can already access. Table 31.1 shows an audio file reference, by browser, to assist you when choosing the most applicable sound file for your site.

TABLE 31.1 BROWSER-BASED SUPPORT FOR AUDIO FILES

AIFF	AIF	AIFC	AU	MIDI	SND	WAV
IE 3.0+	x	x	x	x	x	x
NN 4.0+	x			x	x	x

This table demonstrates that if you want to include a downloadable sound file in your site without having to offer a special plug-in, stick with WAV, AIFF, or AU files.

STREAMING MEDIA

An attempt to avoid the eternal bandwidth problem is streaming technology. In 1994, RealAudio introduced a way of delivering Internet audio based on the User Datagram Protocol (UDP) rather than the usual Transmission Control Protocol (TCP). This technology was later used for transferring video files as well.

UDP technology does not require confirmation of the receipt of all the data; instead, it delivers the file as quickly as possible. This means that a user can begin playing the audio or video file even before the whole file is received. The user's wait time is cut dramatically.

The disadvantage of streaming media is that you lose some control over the quality of your data as it travels over the Internet. The quality of the streaming audio and video is dependent on line quality, which varies greatly. However, with the growing proliferation of fast connections such as T1 and ISDN lines, many of these problems are minimized.

STREAMING AUDIO

Adding streaming audio to your Web site is not a decision to be made lightly. You and your client may agree that streaming audio will greatly enhance the site, but you must also weigh the expense in terms of both time and money.

The first steps for creating a streaming audio clip are the same as those for creating a downloadable clip. The next step is to convert the digital recording into the streaming format.

RealNetworks' RealProducer has long been the most popular software for converting files for streaming. The encoding process compresses the files until they are very small. During the compression, some parts of the sound file are left out.

To have the best quality content after compression, you must start with a good source file. If you're creating sound from scratch, you must use professional quality microphones. If you are using content that has already been recorded, you should use CD-ROM or DAT recordings.

Tip from molly

Some excellent hints for creating a good source file can be found at the RealNetworks electronic library at `http://www.real.com/devzone/library/`.

Streaming Video

Creating streaming video content is the same process as creating downloadable video content, but you must convert the file to a streaming format. Once again, RealProducer is a popular tool for making videos ready for streaming technology.

Currently RealProducer supports .AVI and .MOV input files. If your input files are of any other type, you must find another tool to convert that type to .AVI or .MOV files.

Tip from

> To convert a wide range of audio file types to .AVI or .MOVF try CDH's Media Wizard, available for download at `http://www.tiklsoft.com/multimedia/114.html`. Macintosh and Unix/Linux users will want to check out Xing's audio tools for those platforms, `http://www.xing.com/`.

Adding Streaming Media to a Web Page

Adding streaming media to a page often involves the need to set up or have access to streaming hardware. In this section, I'll focus on RealNetworks products, because of the availability of free and inexpensive resources for their use. If you are interested in other methods mentioned earlier in this chapter, please visit their Web sites for more information.

Adding Streaming Audio to a Web Page

To add a streamed audio clip to your page, you will need some special tools and skills.

For my example, I already have a .WAV file that I want to use, which I prepared from a digital sampling by using the techniques discussed earlier in the chapter.

The next step is to convert the .WAV file to a streaming format. To do this, use the RealNetworks product RealProducer. This application allows you to quickly and easily change the .WAV file into the appropriate streaming format.

Note

> The RealProducer is free for download from `http://www.real.com/products/tools/index.html`.

Follow these steps to convert a .WAV file to RealMedia format (my specific choices are provided as an example):

1. When RealProducer starts up, it offers a New Session dialog box. In the Input Source section, click the File option button, click Browse, Find and then select the .WAV file you want to encode. The Output section loads the file location and name under RealMedia file (see Figure 31.6).

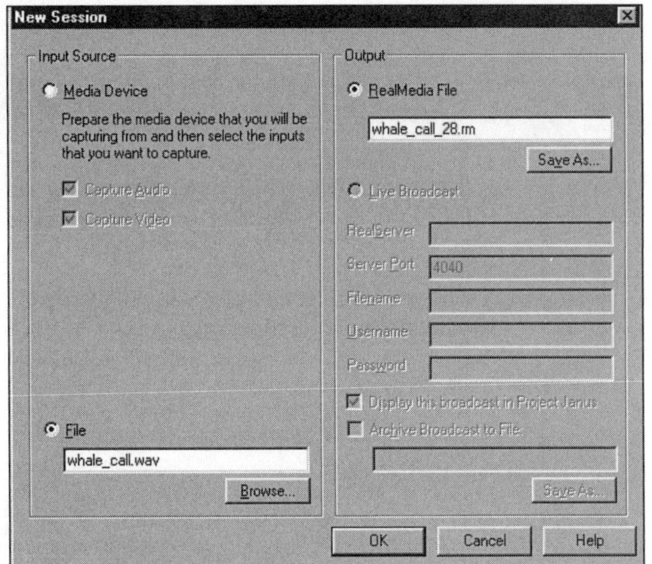

Figure 31.6
Select the input and output files in RealProducer.

2. Then click Save As and type the location and name you want to save the encoded file as (in this case my file is named `whale_call_28.rm`, as shown previously in Figure 31.6).
3. Click Save, and then click OK.
4. In the Clip Information area, add the name of the file, your name, the copyright date, a description, and keywords describing the file.
5. In the Target Audience area there are several check boxes you can use to customize the file to your audience's needs. (I chose the 28K Modem check box, see Figure 31.7, because I want to make sure that I can provide 28.8 access—many of the people coming to the Web site I'm creating are on standard modems.)
6. Under Audio Format, choose the type of audio that is most accurate for your music selection from the drop-down menu (I selected Music) as shown in Figure 31.7.
7. In the File Type area, you must choose between Multi-rate and Single-rate. Choose Multi-rate SureStream if you are not using a Web server.
8. Now click Start under Recording Controls.
9. RealProducer encodes the file with an .rm extension, saving it to the location you identified in step 2.

If you want to provide a higher bandwidth access option, follow these steps again, optimizing the file for T1 access, and then save the file under a new name (mine is saved as `whale_call_t1.rm`).

Note

If you're looking at high-volume video and audio streaming situations such as Web broadcasting or intranet solutions, consider a specialty server for streaming media. More information on servers for Internet and intranet services can be found at **`http://www.real.com/solutions/servers/`**.

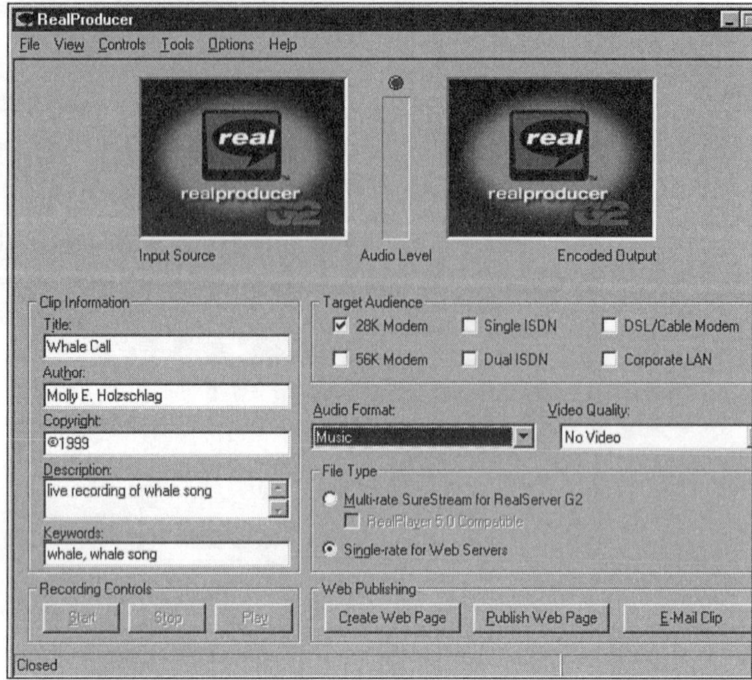

Figure 31.7
Click the appropriate check boxes to determine audience format.

Unsure of the bandwidth issues you might be facing? You'll find additional information on the issue in "Bandwidth Blues" in the Troubleshooting section at the end of this chapter.

Tip from molly

You can create as many bandwidth options as you want by simply working through this process and letting RealProducer process the files with the specific bandwidth preferences you set.

Now that you have the files, you need to create the HTML that will activate the file. This is the simple part—link to the files by using the ANCHOR tag.

Note

RealProducer generates the HTML for you when you click Create Web Page in the Web Publishing section of the application. A wizard is launched that walks you through the process.

In Listing 31.1, I've linked from my page to the files, which reside in a directory on my Web server called audio. You can run files locally, too.

→ For more information on managing and linking your files, **see** "Managing HTML Documents Locally," **p. 62** and "Publishing Sites on the Internet," **p. 906**

Listing 31.1 Embedding Streaming Audio

```
<HTML>
<HEAD>
<TITLE>Whale Call</TITLE>
</HEAD>

<BODY>

My friend, Kelly, enjoyed a trip to Maui last year. She went whale
watching, and recorded this whale call.
<P>

Please select the appropriate file for your bandwidth needs:
<P>

<A href="audio/whale_call_28.rm">Whale Call - 28.8 connection</A>
<P>

<A href="audio/whale_call_t1.rm">Whale Call - t1 connection</A>
<P>

Enjoy the whale's call!
</BODY>
</HTML>
```


Figure 31.8 shows the page, and Figure 31.9 shows the RealMedia player with the file playing after the link has been clicked.

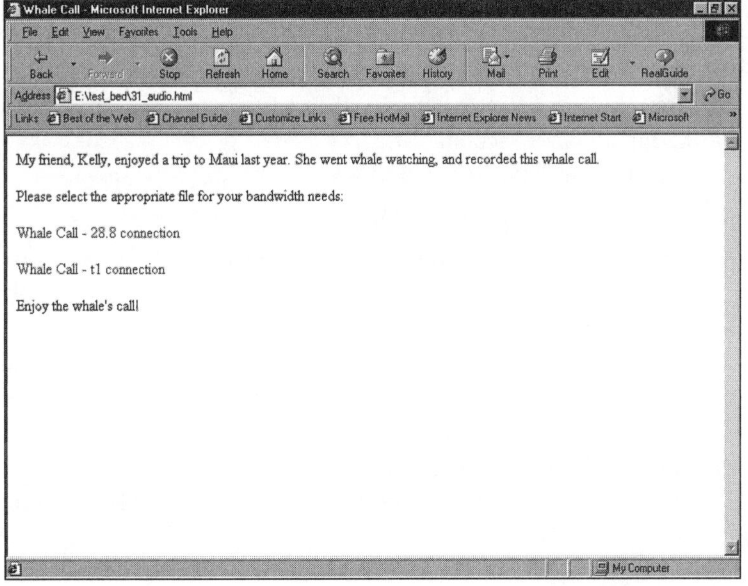

Figure 31.8
My Web page with audio links.

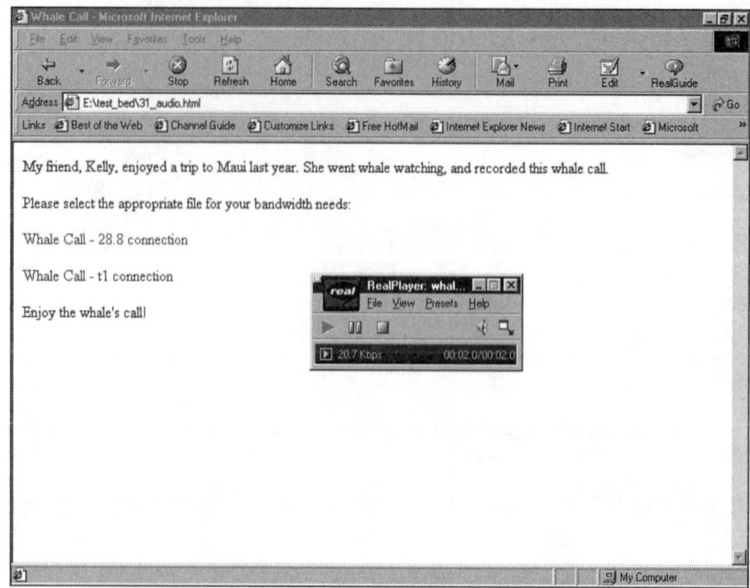

Figure 31.9
RealPlayer provides a control panel that allows the site visitor to control play of the audio file.

WORKING WITH STREAMING VIDEO

Streaming video works similarly to streaming audio. In this case, you begin the process with an .AVI file—I am using one that a friend took while feeding fish on the Great Barrier Reef.

I thought this would be a nice addition to a Web page, so I prepared to encode the file by using the RealProducer as I did for streaming audio. Here's the process to follow with my specific choices in parentheses:

1. From RealProducer New Session dialog box, select the .AVI file you want to encode in the Input Source section.
2. Type the name you want to save the encoded file as(in my case, feeding_fish_28.rm).
3. Click Save As and then click OK.
4. In the RealProducer main screen, locate the area called Clip Information, and give the title to the video, name the author, and provide a copyright date, description, and keywords.
5. Choose one of the several check boxes to determine your target audience. (I chose the 28K Modem check box because I want to make sure that I can provide 28.8 access—many of the people coming to the Web site I'm creating are on 28.8 modems.)
6. Under Audio Format, you can choose to add audio by selecting the audio most appropriate to your .AVI from the drop-down menu (I chose No Audio). Set Video Quality to Normal Motion Video.
7. In the File Type area, choose either Multi-rate or Single-rate; choose Multi-rate SureStream unless you are preparing the file for a Web server.
8. Under Recording Controls, click Start.
9. RealProducer encodes the file with an .rm extension and saves it to the location you identified in step 2.

Now you have a streaming version of the video to place in a Web page. Listing 31.2 is the HTML code demonstrating how this was accomplished.

LISTING 31.2 ADDING STREAMING VIDEO TO HTML

```
<HTML>
<HEAD>
<TITLE>Feeding Fish</TITLE>
</HEAD>
<BODY>
Kelly also went scuba diving along the Great Barrier Reef. In this video,
she can be seen feeding beautifully colored fish.
<P>
Note: this file is optimized for 28.8 connections.
<P>
<A href="video/feeding_fish_28.rm">Kelly Feeding Fish</A>
<P>
It's interesting to note that Kelly is a paraplegic. She is paralyzed from the
mid-chest area down. So if you've been a little concerned about scuba diving,
para-sailing—even extreme sports, Kelly's active life can serve as a great
inspiration.
<P>
<DIV align="center">
No Fear!
</DIV>
</BODY>
</HTML>
```


Figure 31.10 shows the Web page. When a site visitor clicks on the link or Real icon, the RealPlayer will launch. In Figure 31.11, you can see the streaming video in the RealPlayer after the link has been activated.

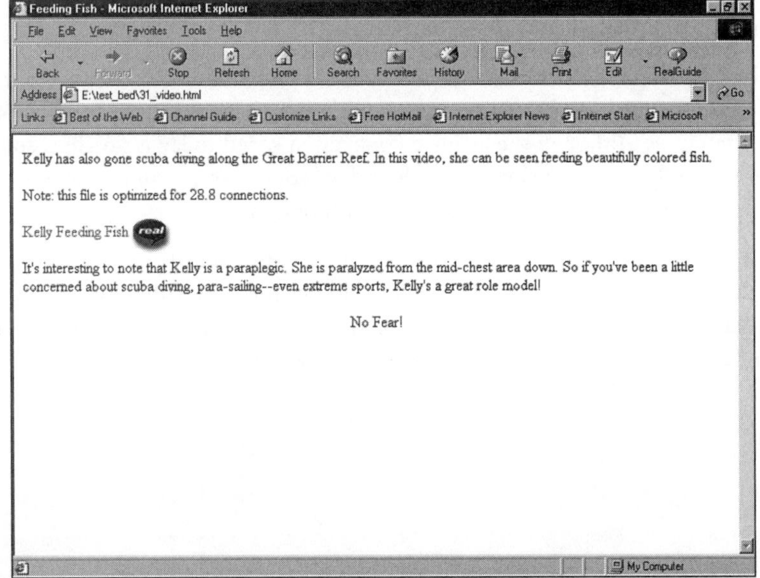

Figure 31.10
A visitor can click on the "Kelly Feeding Fish" link, or the associated "Real" icon and RealPlayer will launch.

Figure 31.11
Click the link and the video is activated within RealPlayer.

Troubleshooting

Bandwidth Blues

Audio and video options are attractive. But how do you deal with the differences in bandwidth?

Obviously, bandwidth is a significant concern with any media files, due to the size of those files and the limitations with streaming technologies. Another concern is accessibility—if a site visitor can't see or hear, the message you are sending with your video or audio can be lost without due consideration.

→ To provide accessible alternatives for your special needs audiences, **see** "Accessibility and Internationalization," **p. 474**

Corporate intranets are especially good candidates for using streaming technology because they most often have high-speed connections and standardized software for viewing the material. Intranets provide an opportunity to develop Web sites for a specific audience.

But, if you are preparing audio and video to be streamed on the Internet to a broad audience, you must remember that not all users have the same hardware and software capabilities. Although the average connection speed today is 56Kbps, some users are still accessing your site at slower speeds and, of course, some connections are much faster. You should consider providing your users with options.

If you are streaming a video, consider offering two speeds for viewing the video, for example, 28.8Kbps and 56Kbps. This will help optimize the video for your user. If you are providing media content that the user might not have the necessary plug-in to view, always offer a link to where the software can be downloaded.

DESIGNING FOR THE REAL WORLD

EXPLORING STREAMING OPTIONS

After you decide to add audio and video to a site, you will find that there is no shortage of companies that want to try to make your job easier. It can make your head spin when you realize how many companies are vying for a piece of the growing online multimedia market.

The following is a tour of some of the leading companies in the audio/video industry and their products. Visit the sites and download any tools and players. Become familiar with both using and working with audio and video online.

- **Microsoft Advanced Streaming Media Format (ASF),** `http://www.microsoft.com/windows/windowsmedia/`—Using proprietary streaming technology referred to as *advanced streaming media*, Microsoft has developed a suite of streaming media products and applications. FM stereo sound can be streamed over modem connections, and the ASF format is considered to offer better compression than MP3.
- **VivoActive,** `http://www.vivo.com/`—Vivo Software (now part of RealNetworks) is a leader in the streaming media market. VideoNow and VideoProducer are easy-to-use and affordable tools that allow you to make synchronized streaming video and audio Web pages by using AVI or WAV files. This technology is great for the Web because the content can be played back on any platform by using the VivoActive Player. The Player works on 486/66 or higher systems running Windows 3.1 or higher and Power Macintosh systems running Mac OS 7.5 or higher.
- **VDOLive,** `http://www.vdonet.com/`—VDONet Corporation has many tools to help you with each step in the streaming video process. The VDOLive Tools package is made up of three programs. VDO Capture is used, along with a video capture card, to convert analog audio and video source material (such as video and audio tapes) into digital format. VDO Clip is used to compress video and audio into VDO format. VDO Producer uses a Windows wizard interface to guide you through all aspects of content creation.
- **Apple QuickTime,** `http://www.apple.com/quicktime/`—Ensures cross-platform and Internet compatibility for your QuickTime Files. Prior to QuickTime 3, a tool called the Internet Movie Tool was sometimes used to prepare movies for Web delivery. Apple recommends that you no longer use this tool for movie preparation because QuickTime and MoviePlayer now prepare the movie for the Internet automatically.
- **RealNetwork's RealProducer/Real Publisher**. `http://www.real.com/g2/developer/`—RealProducer contains all the tools needed to create RealAudio (WAV, AU, MOV, and SND) and RealVideo (AVI and QuickTime format) content, and it's free! RealPublisher is marketed as an upgrade to RealProducer, but auto coding and uploading them to the Web are the only functions exclusive to RealPublisher.
  These products are popular because they are made by the leader in the industry—RealNetworks.

- **Adobe Premiere,** `http://www.adobe.com/prodindex/premiere/`—This is an expensive but powerful tool designed for video professionals. Unlike other tools available to you, this one was not designed specifically for making online video and probably has much more capability than you need. One big benefit of this product is that it can smoothly integrate other Adobe products such as Photoshop and Illustrator.

Adding streaming media is not for every Web designer, nor is it appropriate for every audience. It is important to take a close look at it, however, because it is becoming a more popular option as both the streaming technology gets better and connectivity gets faster.

I have rarely used streaming media in standard Web designs. I have had occasion to create streaming media for specific projects, such as an adventure travel site where video and audio of underwater diving or water skiing can really enhance the site visitor's experience. Other instances where streaming media can make a site more powerful include sites for real estate, music, history, art, and education. In business, streaming media is extremely attractive as a method of communications between distant offices. Of course, the interest in Internet radio and live videocasts have brought a lot of enthusiasm to the medium. Still, as with any media that demands additional software, asks your hardware to work harder, and requires the maximum bandwidth available, careful consideration must be used by the developer before adding it to a given site.

CHAPTER 32

Working with Shockwave Flash

In this chapter

MULTIMEDIA AND THE WEB

Movement, action, interaction. These are components Web developers strive for to keep Web sites vibrant and interesting, and to keep visitors engaged.

Multimedia has been around for a long time and has been used in multitudes of circumstances, including corporate and information-based presentations, educational activities, and recreation in the form of video games.

It's only natural, then, that businesses, educational institutions, and entertainment-based developers are interested in having multimedia options for their Web sites.

As you by now know, a single graphic must be compressed so that it weighs very, very little to load effectively across browser and platform types, and through a variety of bandwidth situations.

That's just one graphic! Multimedia includes graphics—often many graphics—to create animation and movement, input areas, and responses. And, true to its name, the concept is *multiple*—to have more than one media event occurring in the same environment, meaning the addition of audio and video as well as static graphics and special effects.

How to get all this information compressed and delivered to a Web browser has limited developers to a large degree. Bandwidth is the issue, and although we're certainly seeing more affordable bandwidth options become available in certain parts of the United States, there's an entire world out there with a wide range of special circumstances.

Multimedia specialists such as Macromedia, have made some significant advances addressing this concern with their suite of tools; and as the years pass, integration of those tools with one another increases. That concentration and integration has paid off in the form of some impressive options for multimedia design and delivery over the Web.

Furthermore, changes to hardware and software have been made. The PowerPC and higher-level Macintosh systems have long been graphically oriented, so the addition of multiple media isn't a big step. MMX technology has swept the Windows platform market, with Windows 98 offering full support for the technology.

MMX (Multimedia Extensions) is a set of 57 new instructions that Intel added to certain processors to speed up and enhance multimedia. This new technology means improved performance for image processing, video, audio, videoconferencing, and similar functions.

It also suggests that multimedia presentations over the Internet, and intranets, may become more effective and ultimately an essential part of the Internet industry as time goes on.

MACROMEDIA DIRECTOR, SHOCKWAVE, AND FLASH BASICS

High interactivity, lower bandwidth. That's what these programs strive for—and in some cases, truly achieve.

Macromedia has excelled in the procurement and development of multimedia tools, including Director, which is considered one of the premier multimedia development packages. With applications that far exceed Web interests, Director can create interactive, multimedia presentations for kiosks, CD-ROM computers, games, and other interactive media.

The Director Studio package includes many useful tools—including the Aftershock utility. Aftershock generates the HTML that can deliver Director and Flash Shockwave movies and Java applets to all platforms and browsers.

Director is a big package and a serious commitment. The learning curve is high, and therefore it is recommended for only the very serious multimedia developer.

Shockwave is a technology that was created specifically for the Web. Using Director, the Shockwave technology works by streaming information to the Web browser via a plug-in.

Shockwave hit the Web scene with a serious splash. However, because browser technology is still fickle when it comes to integrating advanced support for such a complex program with plug-in style delivery, it has only caught on in certain situations.

Shockwave does, however, have many advantages over most Web-based media programs. It supports audio, animation, and advanced interactive events. Web pages with Shockwave are considered to be "shocked," and they are popular among certain Web enthusiasts.

Note

For a gallery of Director multimedia presentations and Shockwave sites, visit the following:

Director Gallery: `http://www.macromedia.com/software/director/gallery/director/`

ShockWave.Com: `http://www.shockwave.com/`

Figure 32.1 shows the Shockwave site. Stay on the page a few moments, and you can enjoy the action. Figure 32.2 shows a different scene with those rascals from South Park. Definitely a fun experience—taking the days of static pages to a very different level.

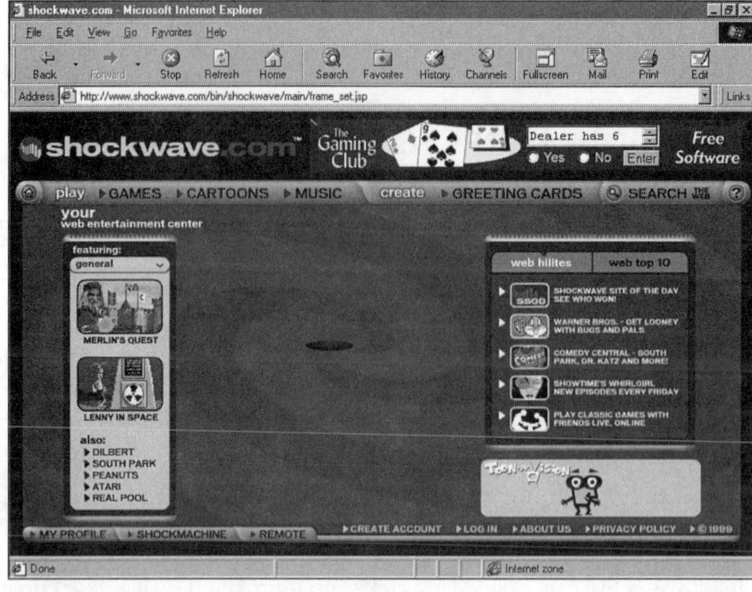

Figure 32.1
The Shockwave site—enjoyable, colorful, and full of promise.

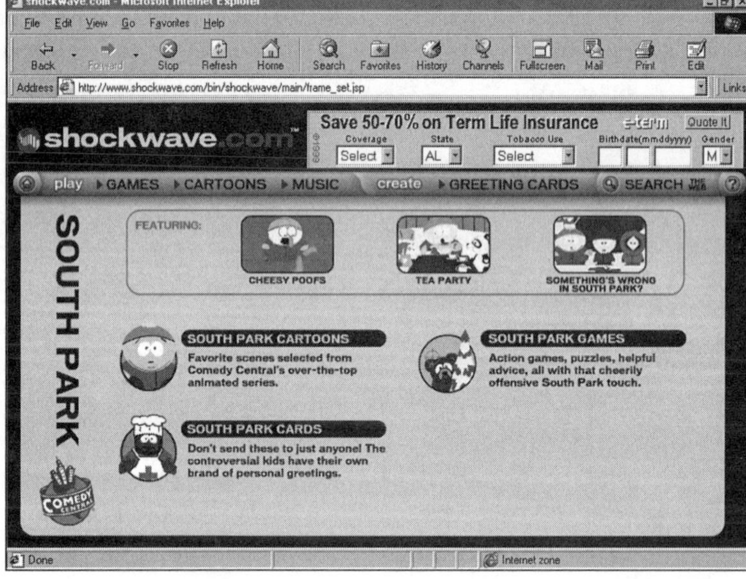

Figure 32.2
Promise fulfilled, especially for South Park fans.

EXPLORING FLASH IN DETAIL

Originally a compact animation tool called FutureSplash and later modified to include sound. With intense support from Microsoft, Macromedia Flash was quickly included as a native part of Internet Explorer. It is now in its 4.0 incarnation, with a lot of interface and publishing improvements.

What's especially interesting about Flash is that it is a vector-based drawing tool, much like Illustrator or Macromedia Freehand, but with the sole purpose of creating Web content.

What this means is that the resulting files are very compact, and can include a wide range of high-quality, low-bandwidth design. Add audio to the mix, and you've got a sophisticated and widely accessible tool.

Another cool aspect of Flash 4.0 is its publishing utilities. Flash 4.0 helps you publish your designs to HTML, making your job much easier. Flash 3.0, despite its lack of these advanced publishing tools, does come with a utility known as Aftershock. This utility is a one-step marvel: It takes what you create in Flash and processes it to work across browsers and across platforms—writing the HTML code, the JavaScript, *and* creating an animated or still GIF for those who can't access the Flash file.

One drawback is that Flash still requires a plug-in for pre-4.0 Netscape support. Flash also lacks a full scripting language, which may limit designers who want to have more control. However, Flash is wise—it offers output not only to its native vector-based formats, but to animated GIFs, which can be used in place of the vector movies in those circumstances where Flash is not supported. Flash hasn't been on every Web developer's list of sensible Web site choices because of these difficulties. But, it is a powerful option and enthusiastically used by many.

Note

Windows 98 users will be happy to know that Flash and Shockwave players are built directly into the operating systems–No plug-ins required.

Still unsure as to whether Flash is the way to go? See "Using Flash in the Real World" in the Troubleshooting section at the end of this chapter for some additional insight.

Flash is affordable, and the learning curve not anywhere near as complex as for Director. Although I've always thought the interface (see Figure 32.3) could be a bit more intuitive, Flash still remains an impressive method of creating enhanced visuals.

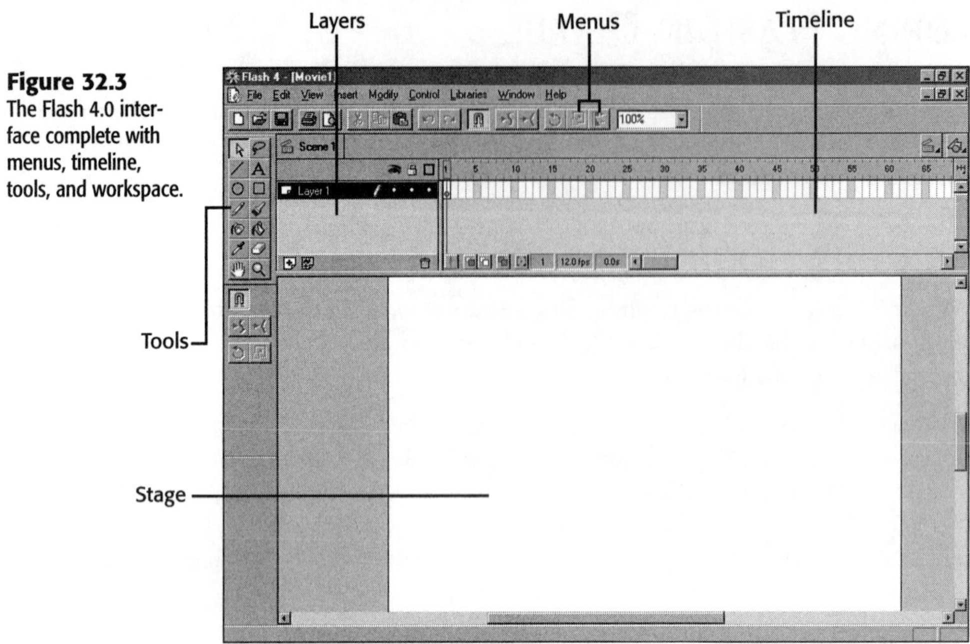

Figure 32.3
The Flash 4.0 interface complete with menus, timeline, tools, and workspace.

WORKING WITH FLASH

A demo version of Flash 4.0 is available for download from Macromedia. You can use the demo to walk through all the exercises in this chapter, and if you get hooked, you can purchase the software at your discretion.

> **Note**
>
> You can download the Flash 4.0 demo from Macromedia, `http://www.macromedia.com/software/flash/trial/`.

CREATING A FLASH ANIMATION

Before diving into the animation, I want to introduce you to two important terms:

- **Key frame**—This is an animator's term used to describe the point in an animation where the action changes. The action is usually simple—a change in movement or color.
- **Tweening**—This is a concept that makes animation easy. If I put an object on a key frame, move it to another key frame down the timeline, and *tween* the object, Flash paces all the movement necessary to get from the first key frame to the second, the in-be*tween* frames are created for you by the program.

First, you'll need to create a Flash animation. Here's a simple animation exercise using text:

1. Open Flash.
2. Choose File, New.
3. From the Modify menu, choose Movie.
4. You'll get a dialog box where you can set some parameters. Focus for now on image size and background color. For example, choose 400×200 pixels, and white as the background color (see Figure 32.4).

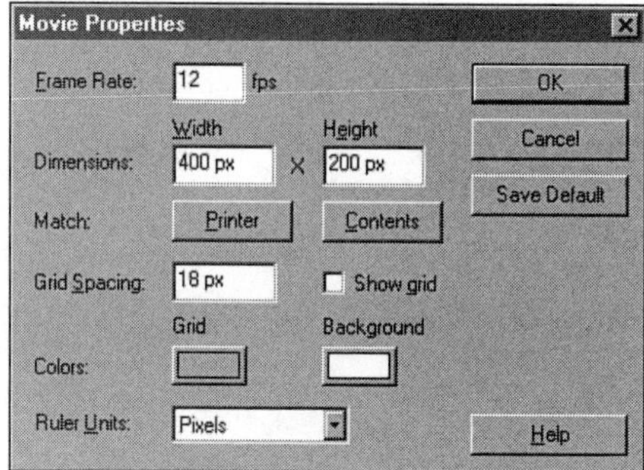

Figure 32.4
Setting the animation's dimensions.

5. Click OK.
6. From the Tools menu, select the Text Tool, represented by an A.
7. Now, select a font, font size, style, and color from the menu that appears.
8. Click the Text Tool cursor on the Stage—the area where you are creating your Flash animation.
9. Now, right-click (Win) or hold your mouse down (Mac) on the circle (which represents the key frame) on the Time Line. Choose Insert Blank Keyframe from the drop-down menu that appears (see Figure 32.5).

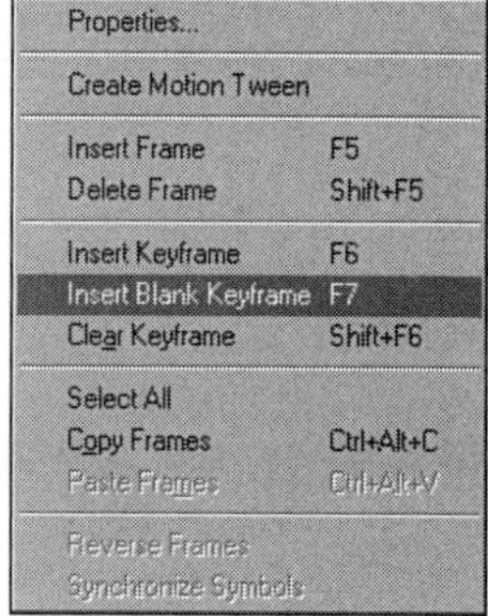

Figure 32.5
The frame shortcut menu enables you to insert a blank keyframe.

10. Move back down to the stage, select the text by highlighting it and move it to the next spot on the stage in which you want it to appear.
11. Deselect the text.
12. On the timeline, drag the dot over until it reaches 10.
13. Stop and right-click (Win) or hold your mouse down (Mac) on the dot for the shortcut menu shown earlier in Figure 32.5.
14. Once again, choose Insert Blank Keyframe.
15. You can check and see your movie at this point by choosing Control, Play.
16. If you like what you see, right-click the dot.
17. Choose Create Motion Tween from the frame shortcut menu (see Figure 32.6). Flash tweens the frames.

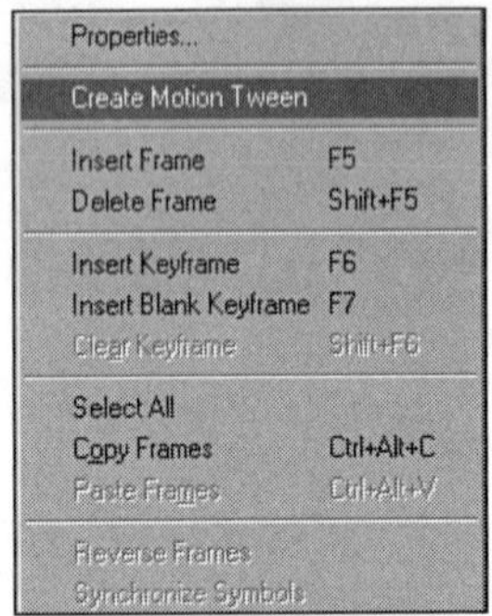

Figure 32.6
Motion tweening automatically creates the in-between frames in the animation.

18. Choose File, Export Movie.
19. Save your file with the .swf (Shockwave Flash) extension (I saved my file as `molly.swf`).

Now you've got your animation. You can either add it to your Web page the old-fashioned way, or use the Publish option to let Flash do it for you.

Note

If you're using Flash 3.0, see the "Publishing with Aftershock" section later in this chapter.

Concerned about Flash file weights? See "Size Matters" in the Troubleshooting section at the end of this chapter for some additional insight.

PUBLISHING WITH FLASH 4

To tap into Flash 4's publishing power, begin by setting up your publishing preferences:

1. Choose File, Publish Settings. The Publish Settings dialog box appears (see Figure 32.7).

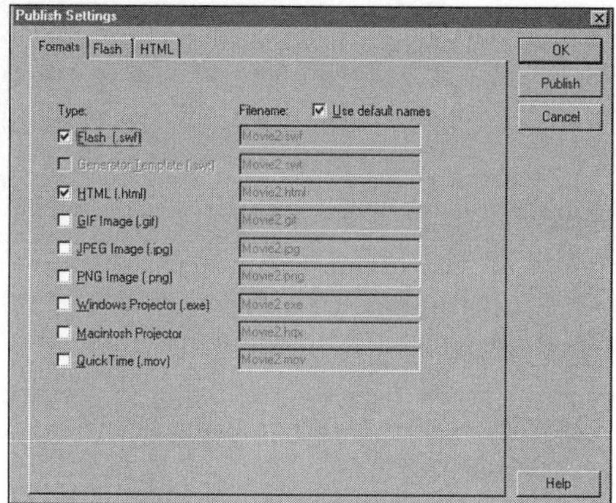

Figure 32.7
The Publish Settings dialog box is Flash's main-brain for the manner in which your Flash designs will be published.

2. The Formats tab is the default view. The two preselected check boxes are Flash and HTML. If you want Flash to generate a wider range of formats, click the corresponding check box.
3. For each check box you click, a new tab appears. You can then make modifications to that format. When you publish, you'll generate all the options you've checked.

To set up the Flash .swf file defaults:

1. Click the Flash tab in the Publish Settings dialog box. The Flash options appear (see Figure 32.8).

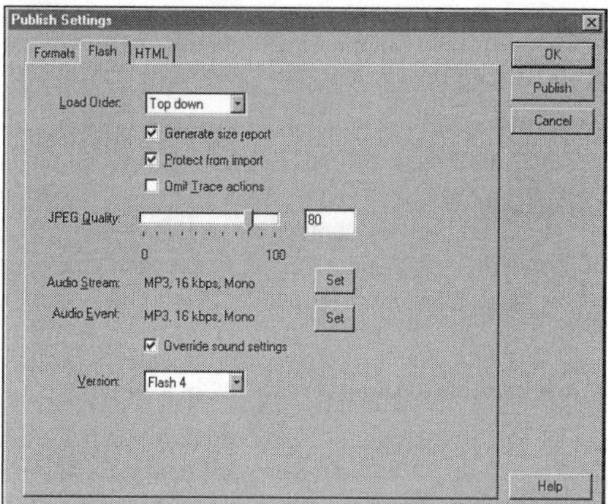

Figure 32.8
Setting up the actual Flash movie options. These options help determine the behavior of the movie.

2. Select a Load Order from the Load Order drop-down menu. Your choices include Bottom up, which loads the movie onto the page from the bottom horizon line to the top; and Top down, which loads the movie from the Top down.

Tip from molly

If you want to satisfy the needs of folks using slower connections, select Top down for the Load Order. This loads the first frame of the Flash animation top-down, allowing the visitor to see the animation appear in logical order.

3. To generate a report that shows the file size of your Flash elements, check the Generate Size Report check box.
4. Your next option is Protect from Import. This handy feature locks your file so that site visitors can't download it and then make their own modifications later on.

Tip from molly

Use the Protect from Import option when you want to provide extra copyright protection for your Flash designs.

5. Omit Trace Actions prompts a window open for certain kinds of actions within a Flash movie. To prevent Trace actions, check this box. Usually, the default—which is unchecked—is fine.
6. Select the JPEG Quality. Note that the higher the quality, the better looking the animation—but the higher the weight of your finished design. I recommend choosing High, but you should always test your animation. If you can use a top-quality JPEG output without compromising download time, do so.
7. If you're using audio along with your animation, you can set the MP3 values here, including Override Sound Settings, which allows you to use more than one size of sound file to best meet your site visitor needs. Check this option when you are offering a choice of sound files.
8. The Version drop-down menu allows for compatibility with other Flash versions. Set this to the version with which you want to provide compatibility.

Caution

Flash 4 contains technology that is not supported in previous versions of Flash. However, without the Flash 4 player, site visitors won't be able to view your Flash 4 designs. Choose the version that best meets the needs of your audience. You can always Publish several different versions and use JavaScript to route browsers to the supported version.

→ For more information about JavaScript, **see** "Using JavaScript," **p. 404**

You'll want to set up the HTML preferences. Flash offers a variety, all available by clicking the HTML tab in the Publish Settings dialog box (see Figure 32.9).

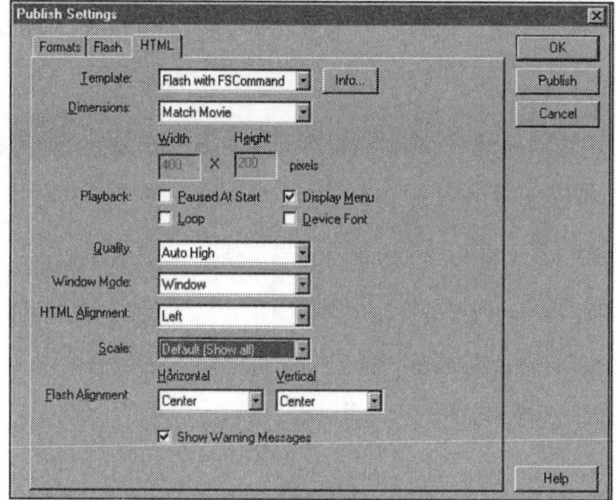

Figure 32.9
To determine how the Flash movie appears in the browser, use the options found in the HTML tab.

After you're in the dialog box, follow these steps to customize the manner in which your HTML page is set up:

1. The Template drop-down menu determines the HTML and scripts that will be generated. Your options are fairly varied. The default is Flash Only. This option sets your Flash file simply into an HTML page using both the `EMBED` and `OBJECT` tags. Flash with FSCommand adds JavaScript to the fundamentals. Image Map allows you to create an Image Map with Flash. The Java Player makes your Flash 4.0 animations readable using a Java Applet. QuickTime exports the movie for QuickTime, using the `EMBED` tag. User Choice generates a JavaScript that sniffs for the Flash 4.0 player. It then routes the incoming browser to an appropriate version of the page.
2. Set the dimensions of the output animation here. Typically, you'll want this to match your Flash animation dimensions, unless you'll be adding additional components to the page.
3. Playback options include Paused At Start, which allows the site visitor to start the animation using a start button. The Loop option allows the animation to repeat continuously. Display Menu ensures that an ancillary Flash menu with shortcuts is available. To disable this menu, uncheck the option. Device Font is a Windows-only option for font substitution. This is usually left unchecked.
4. Quality refers to the level of anti-aliasing that will occur. You can choose from Auto Low (no anti-aliasing), Auto High (adjusts to the frame rate available), High (always uses anti-aliasing), and Best (gives the absolute best quality no matter the speed of the connection or file size).
5. Set Window Mode to Opaque Windowless or Transparent Windowless when working in Internet Explorer-only environments. These modes allow you to tap into positioning and transparency movie options within IE.

6. HTML Alignment aligns the movie. The options are standard to the `IMG` and `OBJECT` tags.
7. Set the Scale to Default (Show all) to show the entire Flash movie. No Border and Exact Fit both are problematic because No Border might result in cropping of the movie, and Exact Fit forces the movie to fit into the area and disregards the original dimensions and aspect ratio of the movie.
8. Flash Alignment is best left to the default Center. Otherwise, unwanted cropping may occur.
9. To show warnings if something goes wrong with the file, leave the Show Warning Messages box checked. If you don't want warnings to show, uncheck the box.
10. Click OK to maintain these settings, or Publish to directly publish the open Flash movie.

➔ To better understand the `EMBED` and `OBJECT` tags, **see** "Audio, Video, and Streaming Media," **p. 672**

➔ For information on anti-aliasing, **see** "Graphic Type for the Web," **p. 634**

➔ For a discussion of image attributes, **see** "Working with Images," **p. 198**

PUBLISHING WITH AFTERSHOCK

If you're using Flash 3.0, you'll want to use Aftershock to achieve cross-browser compatibility:

1. Open Aftershock and choose File, Add, Shockwave.
2. Select your recently saved .swf file.
3. On the right side of the Aftershock interface, you'll see that the *scripting* tab is selected. On this page, you can either stick to the preset defaults or use what you think your audience will best benefit from. For my selections, I chose Shockwave Plug-in/ActiveX Control; Static or Animated GIF; and under Installation, I selected all three options.
4. Click the Page Layout tab. Here, you'll want to make any modifications to the layout that you want. I stuck with the defaults.
5. Under the Shockwave tab, you have many options including background color, playback, and quality. I stuck with the defaults on this one, although I sometimes like to pause the playback at start or use a different background color, depending on my needs.
6. For Alternate Image, I chose Animated GIF and selected my preferences. Doing this lets Aftershock not only create an animated GIF that matches the Flash movie, but also create the code that offers it if the visitor's browser can't support Flash.
7. Finally, you can modify the Java selections. I left these at their defaults.
8. Choose File, Save As.
9. Name your HTML file.
10. Aftershock now processes the HTML, the JavaScript, and any alternate image you've chosen.

Listing 32.1 shows the code that Aftershock generated.

LISTING 32.1 CODE GENERATED BY AFTERSHOCK

```
<HTML>
<HEAD>
<TITLE>Shockwave</TITLE>
</HEAD>
<BODY bgcolor="#000000">

<!-- Aftershock molly.swf 3=400 4=50 6=1 38 45 -->
<SCRIPT LANGUAGE="JavaScript" SRC="http://www.macromedia.com/shockwave/download/
smart/getsw.js">
function getShockwave()
{
window.open( "http://www.macromedia.com/shockwave/download/", "" );
}
</script>
<OBJECT classid="clsid:D27CDB6E-AE6D-11cf-96B8-444553540000"
 codebase="http://active.macromedia.com/flash2/cabs/swflash.cab#version=3,0,0,0"
 ID=molly WIDTH=400 HEIGHT=50>
  <PARAM NAME=movie VALUE="molly.swf">
  <PARAM NAME=quality VALUE=autohigh>
  <PARAM NAME=bgcolor VALUE=#000000>
<SCRIPT LANGUAGE=JavaScript>
<!--
var ShockMode = 0;
var OldVersionOfPlugin = 0;
if (navigator.mimeTypes && navigator.mimeTypes["application/x-shockwave-flash"]
&& navigator.mimeTypes["application/x-shockwave-flash"].enabledPlugin) {
      if (navigator.plugins && navigator.plugins["Shockwave Flash"])
            ShockMode = 1;
      else
            OldVersionOfPlugin = 1;
}
function checkForShockwave()
{
      navigator.plugins.refresh();
      if ( navigator.plugins["Shockwave Flash"] ){
            parent.location.reload();
      } else {
            setTimeout( "checkForShockwave()", 1000 );
      }
}
if (!ShockMode && navigator.appName && navigator.appName.indexOf("Netscape")
!= - 1 && navigator.appVersion.indexOf("4.") != - 1
&& navigator.javaEnabled() && netscape.softupdate.Trigger.UpdateEnabled() &&
document.cookie.indexOf("StartedShockwaveInstall") == -1) {
      var jarPath = new String("");
      if (navigator.platform.indexOf("Win32") >= 0 )
            jarPath = "http://download.macromedia.com/pub/shockwave/jars/
english/silentflash32.jar"
      else if (navigator.platform.indexOf("Win16") >= 0 )
            jarPath = "http://download.macromedia.com/pub/shockwave/jars/
english/silentflash16.jar"
```


continues

LISTING 32.1 CONTINUED

```
      else if (navigator.platform.indexOf("MacPPC") >= 0 )
              jarPath = "http://download.macromedia.com/pub/shockwave/jars/
english/silentflashppc.jar"
      if (jarPath.length) {
              netscape.softupdate.Trigger.StartSoftwareUpdate (jarPath,
netscape.softupdate.Trigger.FORCE_MODE);
              document.cookie='StartedShockwaveInstall;path=/;'
              setTimeout("checkForShockwave()", 1000);
      }
}
if ( ShockMode ) {
      document.write('<EMBED SRC="molly.swf"');
      document.write(' swLiveConnect=FALSE WIDTH=400 HEIGHT=50');
      document.write(' QUALITY=autohigh BGCOLOR=#000000');
      document.write(' TYPE="application/x-shockwave-flash"
PLUGINSPAGE="http://www.macromedia.com/shockwave/download/index.cgi?
P1_Prod_Version=ShockwaveFlash">');
      document.write('</EMBED>');
} else if (!(navigator.appName && navigator.appName.indexOf("Netscape")>=0 &&
navigator.appVersion.indexOf("2.")>=0)){
      document.write('<IMG SRC="molly.gif" WIDTH=400 HEIGHT=50 BORDER=0>');
      if (( navigator.appName.indexOf( "Microsoft" ) != -1 ) &&
( navigator.appVersion.indexOf( "Macintosh" ) != -1 ) &&
( navigator.appVersion.indexOf( "3." ) == 0 ))
      {
              document.write( '<P><A HREF="http://www.macromedia.com/shockwave/
download/">' );
              document.write( '<img src="get_shockwave.gif" WIDTH=88 HEIGHT=31
BORDER=0></A>' );
      } else {
              document.write( '<P><A HREF="#" onClick="getShockwave(' );
              document.write( "'Director 0.0','Flash 2.0'" );
              document.write( ')">' );
              document.write( '<img src="get_shockwave.gif" WIDTH=88 HEIGHT=31
BORDER=0></A>' );
      }
      if ( OldVersionOfPlugin )
              document.write( '<P>This page contains a new format movie that the
current
Shockwave plug-in cannot handle. Please update to the new version.</P>' );
}
//—>
</SCRIPT><NOEMBED><IMG SRC="molly.gif" WIDTH=400 HEIGHT=50 BORDER=0></NOEMBED>
<NOSCRIPT>
<IMG SRC="molly.gif" WIDTH=400 HEIGHT=50 BORDER=0><P><A
HREF="http://www.macromedia.com/shockwave/download/"><IMG SRC="get_shockwave.gif"
WIDTH=88
HEIGHT=31 BORDER=0></A></NOSCRIPT></OBJECT><!— EndAftershock molly.swf —>
</BODY>
</HTML>
```

Despite the complicated code generated by Aftershock, the compatibility that results is quite desirable. Of course, Flash 4.0 offers more elegant solutions in both the way Flash is displayed and the way the HTML code is written.

TROUBLESHOOTING

USING FLASH IN THE REAL WORLD

I want to use Flash, but I'm concerned about reaching a wide audience. How many people actually have Flash support already?

Internet Explorer supports Flash and ships with the technology. This means no plug-in is required. However, Netscape users require a player. Developers using Flash can encourage site visitors to download the plug-in if they have not yet done so.

Macromedia estimates that about 83% of the Web browsing population has support for Flash. However, this isn't for Flash 4.0 specifically—it's Flash support in general. The upshot is that you'll need to make decisions based on your audience.

SIZE MATTERS!

Flash is great! I've used it to create some attractive animations with sound. But the file sizes are larger than recommended. What do I do?

You have several options here. Flash files can be very small—that's part of their appeal. However, if you're creating a major multimedia presentation with audio, your file sizes can grow large. To accommodate everyone, you can create several versions of your site: a text-only version, a non-Flash version, and the Flash version. You can also combine standard HTML and graphics with portions of Flash within a page. Determine which parts of a page should be in static and which can make use of Flash before designing your page instead of trying to do it all with Flash.

DESIGNING FOR THE REAL WORLD

AUSTIN POWERS IS SHOCKING!

In an effort to add even more enjoyable pastimes to the Austin Powers: Spy Who Shagged Me Web site, the developers opted for a shockwave game.

Called Move Your Mojo, you begin by choosing your players. I chose Felicity Shagwell to the tune of funky 60s music and twirling flowers (see Figure 32.10). The goal of the game is to dance with Austin using keys on the keyboard.

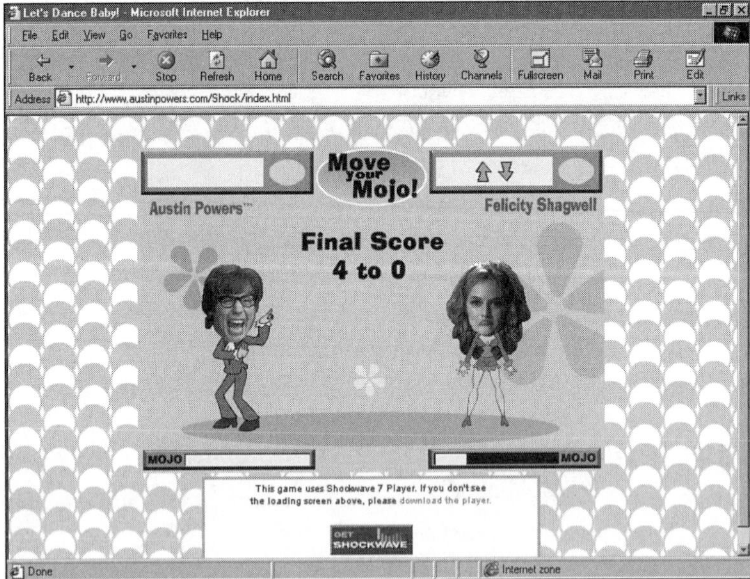

Figure 32.10 Shockwave can be used to create a complex game, such as Move Your Mojo. This game asks the site visitor to use keys on the keyboard that cause the character Felicity Shagwell to perform dance moves. A game of this nature involves the site visitor completely, and can act as a method of bringing people back to the site time and again.

I went four rounds and lost, alas. But I was really having a great time, demonstrating the absorbing aspect of multimedia on the Web. Even if it's not something you'll be using in the majority of your sites, when it is used, it can be a very useful addition to a site.

Note

Play Move Your Mojo, `http://www.austinpowers.com/Shock/index.html`.

CHAPTER 33

Using Java Applets and ActiveX Components

In this chapter

About Java

For the past few years, one Internet-related technology has received more than its fair share of attention and hype. This technology, of course, is Java, Sun's highly touted and highly fought over language.

Since Java emerged on the scene, it has been espoused as everything from a premier application development environment to the operating system platform of the future.

The fact about Java is that it has grown to become less important as a method for delivering scripts to Web pages via applets and more important as a development application for backend, networking, and standalone programs of related interest to the Web.

Those of you with some programming background will quickly see that Java is, at its core, an object-oriented programming language. Unlike C++, which was designed as an object-oriented extension of the immensely popular C language, Java was designed from the ground up as a new language. As such, it is much closer to being a pure object-oriented language than C++ because it doesn't have to support non–object-oriented legacy programs.

It's important to look at Java in the light of object-oriented programming because of the growing relationship of the Web to object models. This is especially clear in Dynamic HTML and with XML.

→ To find DHTML background and tutorials, **see** "Working with Dynamic HTML (DHTML)," **p. 450**

→ To read more about XML, **see** "Understanding XHTML, XML, and Emerging Languages," **p. 494**

Java's real strength is that it's not just a programming language that can be used on the Web; it's a language that can build aspects of Web infrastructure. Despite this distinction, many newcomers to HTML or more advanced HTML students without programming knowledge, don't know what Java really is or how to distinguish it from the script of a similar name, JavaScript.

This chapter helps clarify the difference, shows you how to create a Java applet, and guides you to more advanced resources in the use of Web applets and the actual language itself.

Java History

Java began as a language called Oak in the early 1990s. It was designed by James Gosling of Sun Microsystems (see Figure 33.1), whose other claims to fame include the EMACS editor and the NeWS windowing system. Oak's original application was for use in smart consumer electronics devices, an idea that was probably before its time. A Sun subsidiary named First Person, Inc. was set up to develop the technology.

Figure 33.1
Sun Microsystems: `http://java.sun.com/`. Sun is the point of origin for historical information, code samples, and detailed resources on the Java language.

The smart electronics idea didn't really go anywhere, so the company shifted its focus to set-top boxes (devices that can bring Internet access and PC function to a standard television) when they heard that Time-Warner was looking for bids for an operating system in early 1993. Although First Person lost that bid to SGI, the set-top box focus continued until 1994 when it was decided that there really wasn't a market to be developed. First Person was folded back into Sun in 1994.

About that time, Sun realized the potential of the Oak technology for the growing World Wide Web. Many of the requirements were the same, including platform independence, secure code, and a network-based delivery mechanism, so Sun shifted its focus once again to the Web.

The language was re-christened as Java, the HotJava browser was developed to demonstrate its capabilities, and the program was unveiled to an anxiously waiting Internet development community. In 1996, JavaSoft, a Sun subsidiary, was created to handle the further development and promotion of Java.

The hype surrounding Java, what it will do, and who will be leading the way has been enormous. Microsoft, of course, has sought to capitalize on Java, but because they aren't really interested in the cross-platform capabilities (they see the world through Windows-colored glasses, after all), they have taken some liberties with their development platform.

Microsoft's Java implementation deviates from the Java standard in several ways to optimize the language for Windows and to encourage development of applications specifically for that platform. In an effort to control this issue, which defies an open-platform directive, JavaSoft started the 100% Pure Java initiative, which provides a certification process for Java applications.

Note

It should be noted that Microsoft has been embroiled in ongoing legal issues with Sun. Sun contends that Microsoft has breached their Java license agreement by including Windows-specific functions in the API without labeling them as such, thus making it more difficult to create platform-independent applications. Sun feels that Microsoft is attempting to fragment the Java language and downplay the "Write once-run anywhere" philosophy of Java. Despite the lifting of an injunction against Microsoft by a federal appellate court in August of 1999, analysts predict the feud will continue via appeals and new lawsuits.

Other companies are also hopping onto the Java bandwagon. Apple and IBM undoubtedly see Java's platform independence as a way to break Microsoft's stranglehold as the dominant operating system. Oracle and others have been promoting the Network Computer model, for which Java is an ideal technology.

APPLICATIONS OF JAVA

Java is used mostly in the following instances:

- Java applets
- Full-force development of applications

First, and most relevant to this chapter, is Java applets. Applets are little applications that can be accessed by HTML files and perform activities on a Web page.

A common use for Java technology is to write applets that are included in HTML pages the same way that a file such as an image or a sound is included. When a page with a Java applet is accessed using a Java-compatible browser, the applet's code is transferred to the browser's system and executed there.

Java can also be used to program a wide range of applications. Generally, the biggest differences between Java applications and Java applets revolve around security. Applications are standalone programs that more or less have complete access to the resources of the system on which they're running. The intention of this chapter is to focus on the Web-based applet. However, a section of resources at the end of the chapter will help you learn where to get more information if you are interested.

Applets are usually run in a browser and have limited access to the host system. For instance, applets are not allowed to read or write files or launch programs on the local system, whereas applications can. Applets also tend to be smaller than applications in consideration of the fact that they are downloaded from the server at runtime.

Java and JavaScript: Understanding the Difference

JavaScript is often associated with Java and therefore deserves mention here. JavaScript is a scripting language that is very different from Java. They are not even remotely the same in terms of form and function.

This rather confusing issue came about when Netscape and Sun saw opportunities in a Netscape development language known as LiveScript. By taking LiveScript, adjusting it to look somewhat like Java, and putting the Java name to the script, Java and JavaScript's relationship was forged–more as a marketing device than a true program/script relationship.

Unlike Java, which we've established as being a network-based, downloaded process, JavaScript is an interpreted language that is completely embedded in an HTML page and run on the client side. It is event driven and has the capability to respond to events such as clicking a button or changing a text field. JavaScript is often used to determine browser features and customize the displayed page based on whether certain capabilities are available.

For instance, by using JavaScript, a page could determine whether the browser viewing it supports a more advanced feature such as Java or not, and either use that feature if available or display a message indicating that the user needs a newer browser. JavaScript also cannot draw graphics by itself; it relies on generating HTML to only display existing image files of types that are supported by the browser. Java, on the other hand, has a graphics library and is capable of much more complicated and interactive displays.

→ Use JavaScript to add dynamic elements and a variety of intelligent functions to your pages, **see** "Using JavaScript," **p. 404**

WRITING AN APPLET

This section contains a simple Java applet example. The HTML code needed to launch the application from a Web page is included, so you can try it for yourself.

Note

The applet examples provided in this book can be developed using the Java Developer's Kit 2, (JDK) version 1.2.2. You'll need the JDK to work through these examples. Download the latest JDK from **http://java.sun.com/**. Note that Sun's Java doesn't have a Windows interface. When working with Java on Windows, you must run the compiler from a DOS prompt.

The first program that is traditionally used to demonstrate a new language is the "Hello, World!" program. This shows the absolute minimum functionality that a program needs to support and display a simple message. I'll start with a simple Java application, as shown in Listing 33.1.

LISTING 33.1 THE "HELLO, WORLD!" JAVA APPLICATION

```
class HelloWorld
{
    public static void main (String args[])
    {
        System.out.println("Hello, World!");
}
    }
```

Enter this code into a plain text editor such as Notepad, and save it with the .java extension. Your text editor might want to add the .txt suffix onto the program. In this case, allow it to do so, but then go back and change the name manually.

Note

Java source filenames use the class name with the .java extension, so you would save the Hello World! file as HelloWorld.java. Be aware that Java is case sensitive, so the filename must match the class name.

The next step is to compile the program by using the Java compiler, `javac`. Make sure that the file and the compiler executable are in the same folder, and from the command prompt enter the following command:

```
javac HelloWorld.java
```

When the program successfully compiles, it gives you a file named HelloWorld.class. This file contains the Java information for your program.

To run it, you need to execute the Java interpreter, `java`. Once again, make sure that the file and the compiler are in the same folder, and from the command prompt enter the following command:

```
java HelloWorld
```

You should get Hello, World! printed on your screen in response.

The next step will be to convert the HelloWorld application into an applet that can be executed from a Web page.

Because applets run embedded inside of Web pages, they must provide layout information so that the page knows how much space to give them. Instead of simply being able to print your Hello, World! message, an applet needs to use the Abstract Window Toolkit (AWT) to display the text as a graphical operation. The "Hello, World!" applet code is shown in Listing 33.2.

LISTING 33.2 THE "HELLO, WORLD!" APPLET

```
import java.awt.Graphics;
import java.applet.Applet;

public class HelloWorldApplet extends Applet
{
    public void paint(Graphics g)
    {
        g.drawString("Hello, World!", 5, 30);
    }
}
```

Save this text as HelloWorldApplet.java and compile it the same way as the previous example. If successful, you will end up with the HelloWorldApplet.class file.

Notice these three things about the applet example:

- The `import` lines at the top provide the compiler with the name of any classes referenced by this class. This is somewhat analogous to the `#include` line in C/C++.

- The applet is an extension of the `java.applet.Applet` class. This gives the program basic applet capabilities.
- The `Graphics` class is used to draw the text message.

To include your applet in a Web page, you need to use the `<APPLET>` tag as shown in Listing 33.3:

LISTING 33.3 SIMPLE HTML FILE TO LAUNCH THE "HELLO, WORLD!" APPLET

```
<HTML>
<HEAD>
<TITLE>hello, world example</TITLE>
</HEAD>
<BODY>
My First Java Applet:
<APPLET CODE="HelloWorldApplet.class" WIDTH=150 HEIGHT=30>
</APPLET>
</BODY>
</HTML>
```

To run the applet, you must load the HTML page into a Java-enabled browser. In addition, you can use the applet viewer provided with the JDK.

> **Note**
>
> In HTML 4.0, the `<APPLET>` tag has been deprecated in favor of the `<OBJECT>` tag. However, the issue remains as to whether using the `<OBJECT>` tag affects cross-browser compatibility. This chapter defers to the more stable `<APPLET>` tag in its examples. For more information on HTML 4.0 tag usage, check Appendix A, "HTML 4.0 Element and Tag Reference."

Figure 33.2 shows the Java applet running in Netscape.

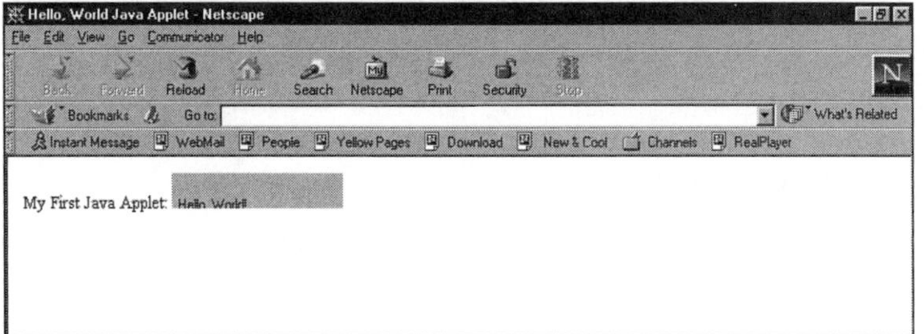

Figure 33.2
The Hello, World! Java Applet example is shown here in the Netscape browser.

Java Resources

Now that you've had a taste of how to program a simple applet in Java, you'll either want to continue learning more about the language or find resources for helpful applets to add to your Web pages. Plenty of online resources are available to get you started on the road to learning about Java. The following are a few of them:

- **The Java Technology Home Page**–Sun Microsystems provides this page as a comprehensive Java information resource, complete with news, articles, Java documentation, and tutorials. It can be found at `http://java.sun.com/`.
- **Developer.com**–Provides information on a wide variety of developer-related topics, including Java. Find Developer.com at `http://www.developer.com/`.
- **Microsoft**–Information on Microsoft's Java products can be found at `http://www.microsoft.com/java/`.
- **Inprise**–Information about the JBuilder IDE and other Inprise products is found at `http://www.inprise.com/`.
- **Symantec**–Information about the Visual Café IDE and other Symantec products can be found at `http://www.symantec.com/`.

To download a variety of applets, visit the following sites:

- Gamelan is a large directory for Java applets and related resources, located at `http://www.gamelan.com/`.
- For Java applets organized by type and rated by independent judges, visit JARS at `http://www.jars.com/`.
- DaveCentral Software Archive is a very comprehensive library of helpful articles, applications, and various downloads. For Java information, check out `http://www.davecentral.com/java.html`.
- JavaSoft has a freebie applet collection with some fun applets, such as a rotating ad banner and quote randomizer. It can be found at `http://www.javasoft.com/openstudio/index.html`.
- Ziff Davis Devhead is my favorite script repository. For Java Applets, visit `http://www.zdnet.com/devhead/resources/scriptlibrary/applets/`.

Note

Learn to add a Java applet to your page in the "Designing for the Real World" section of this chapter.

ACTIVEX CONTROLS

ActiveX controls are executable components that can be embedded into Web pages to give them enhanced capabilities. Over the past few years they have become more and more integrated into the Windows 98 and Internet Explorer software and are therefore less in the limelight. However, interest in this technology still remains high—particularly for individuals and companies using Microsoft FrontPage or Microsoft Visual InterDev for Web development and design.

ActiveX Versus Java

In some respects, ActiveX components and Java applets are very similar. Both are embedded executable components that provide capabilities above and beyond what can be accomplished by using straight HTML and scripting. Both allow for the creation of highly interactive Web pages.

The similarities, however, end there. ActiveX components are platform-specific, natively executing code primarily for the Windows platform. They can be written in almost any language and can take advantage of the full capabilities of the user's system.

Java applets, on the other hand, are platform-independent, compiled bytecode applications, written using the Java language, and dependent on a Virtual Machine to interpret and execute the bytecode.

ActiveX Control Technology

The basis for ActiveX technology is the Component Object Model, or COM. The idea behind COM is to provide a standard interface that software components can use to communicate with each other, either locally or over a network (Distributed COM or DCOM).

An ActiveX control is a specific type of ActiveX object that meets certain interface requirements that allow it to be used as an embedded control. An application that can use ActiveX controls is known as an ActiveX Control Container.

Because ActiveX objects have complete access to the user's machine, some fairly stringent security methods are employed. Microsoft's Authenticode technology allows control authors to digitally sign their controls so that users can choose whether or not to allow a control to have access to their system based on their level of trust of a particular vendor.

The digital signature also serves to ensure that the control hasn't been tampered with.

ActiveX controls work closely with the HTML scripting languages, JavaScript and VBScript. Control methods can be called directly from script code, which in turn can respond to events generated by the controls. This provides a flexible way to integrate a control into your Web page.

Tools for ActiveX Control Development

The most common language for ActiveX control development is currently C++. One of the main reasons C++ is preferred is the wide variety of tools available from various vendors, including Inprise (Borland), Symantec, and Microsoft. All the major C++ compilers include the Microsoft Foundation Classes (MFC) and the Active Template Library (ATL) to make the creation of COM objects easier.

Microsoft Visual C++ includes wizards that you can use to automatically create the basic framework that an ActiveX control needs, which is a good thing because COM objects can be quite complicated.

The Visual C++ AppWizard provides three ways to create ActiveX controls. You can create the control as an MFC (Microsoft Foundation Class) control, an ATL (ActiveX Template Library) control, or both. For our example, we'll create an ATL ActiveX control by using the Visual C++ 5.0 AppWizard to generate the framework. Our example will show a button control that displays text for each of three states: the chosen state, the unchosen state, and the `mouseover` state, where the mouse pointer is over the control.

This example is quite involved, and assumes that you have some familiarity with C++ and Microsoft DevStudio. If you do not, and ActiveX development is important to you, be sure to take a look at the sidebars in this section so that you can get more information to get you started.

Users of FrontPage can add ActiveX components to their pages. However, this doesn't come without certain problems! See, "Adding Components" in the Troubleshooting section at the end of this chapter for details.

EXAMPLE: AN ATL-BASED ACTIVEX CONTROL USING APPWIZARD

The first step in creating an ActiveX control using Visual C++ is to create a project:

1. Choose File, New. Click the Projects tab in the dialog box that appears.
2. In the Location box, enter the path that you want to use for the project.
3. Give it a name in the Project Name box (see Figure 33.3).
4. When you're ready, click the OK button (not shown). The next dialog box lets you choose a server type to use.
5. Select Dynamic Link Library (DLL) and click the Finish button.

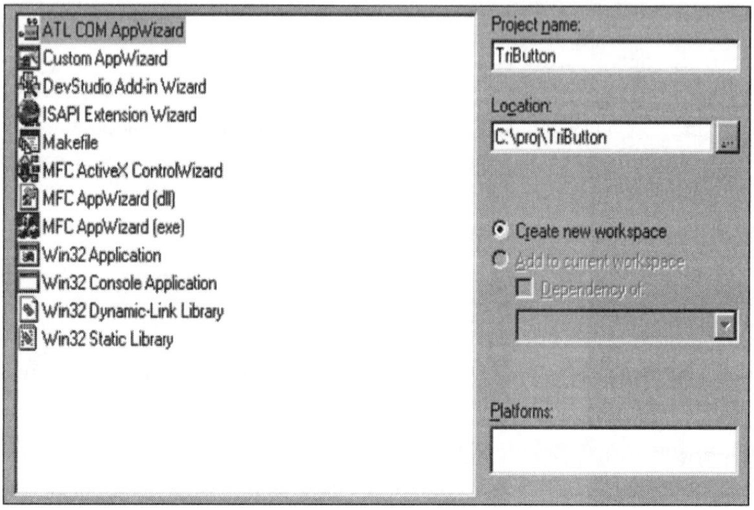

Figure 33.3
Visual C++ is part of Microsoft's Visual Studio suite. Here you see the Visual C++ Project dialog box.

You then see a New Project Information dialog box with a list of files that will be created for the project. Click OK to generate the files.

Table 33.1 shows a description of the files that will be created.

TABLE 33.1 ACTIVEX PROJECT FILES

File	Description
TriButton.dsw and TriButton.dsp	The DevStudio workspace and project files.
TriButton.cpp	This file provides the DLL interface, including the DLLMain function. It will also eventually contain an object map with your project's ATL objects.
TriButton.def	The Windows module definition file for the DLL.
TriButton.idl	The Interface Definition Language file. This file describes the interfaces that your objects provide.
TriButton.rc	The resource file. This initially contains version information.
TriButton.h	The header file that your application loads to get access to resources.
StdAfx.cpp and StdAfx.h	ATL implementation files.

After your project has been created, you can add a control using the ATL Object Wizard:

1. Choose Insert, New ATL Object. This brings up a dialog box that lets you choose the type of object you want to create.
2. Choose Full Control (see Figure 33.4) from the Controls list and click Next.

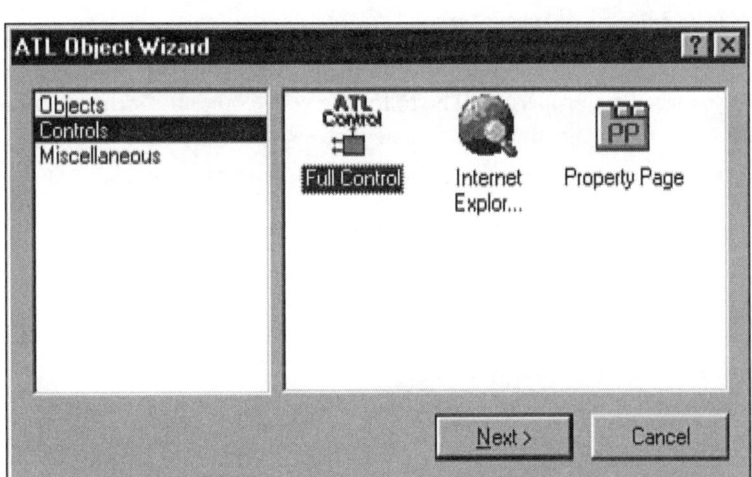

Figure 33.4 The ATL Object Wizard allows you to add ATL controls for your ActiveX component.

3. You now need to enter a name for your control. Enter **TriButtonCtl**.

   The other fields will fill in automatically. Take a look at the other properties you can set so that you get a feel for the various control options.
4. We can use the default settings for our example, so click OK.

Four more files will be created and inserted into the project:

- **TriButtonCtl.cpp and TriButtonCtl.h**—These two files contain most of the implementation details about the `TriButtonCtl` control.
- **TriButtonCtl.rgs**—A Registry script used to register the control.
- **TriButtonCtl.htm**—A simple HTML file with the new control embedded in it for testing in Internet Explorer.

This completes the basic framework of your control. The next step is to add the actual implementation details.

ADDING PROPERTIES TO THE CONTROL

The example control is going to have three parameters sent to it by the HTML file that includes it, so three corresponding properties need to created in the interface.

The properties that the control accepts will be the text for the button for each of its states. Once again, DevStudio automates the task. From the ClassView box, right-click the `ITriButtonCtl` class and choose Add Property.

Enter the first property name, **StaticText**, and choose BSTR as the property type. Because both the `Get` and `Put` methods will be allowed to access this property, leave both boxes checked and click OK. You can now repeat this process for the remaining two properties, `MouseOverText` and `PushedText`.

The wizard creates stub functions in TriButtonCtl.cpp that need to be implemented to get the data for the properties. The following code copies the string data into a local string array for the `Put` methods, and copies it back out for the `Get` methods:

```
STDMETHODIMP CTriButtonCtl::get_StaticText(BSTR * pVal)
{
    *pVal = m_bstrButtonText[0].Copy();
    return S_OK;
}

STDMETHODIMP CTriButtonCtl::put_StaticText(BSTR newVal)
{
    m_bstrButtonText[0] = newVal;
    return S_OK;
}

STDMETHODIMP CTriButtonCtl::get_MouseOverText(BSTR * pVal)
{
    *pVal = m_bstrButtonText[1].Copy();
    return S_OK;
}
```

```
STDMETHODIMP CTriButtonCtl::put_MouseOverText(BSTR newVal)
{
    m_bstrButtonText[1] = newVal;
    return S_OK;
}

STDMETHODIMP CTriButtonCtl::get_PushedText(BSTR * pVal)
{
    *pVal = m_bstrButtonText[2].Copy();
    return S_OK;
}

STDMETHODIMP CTriButtonCtl::put_PushedText(BSTR newVal)
{
    m_bstrButtonText[2] = newVal;
    return S_OK;
}
```

In addition, a declaration must be added for the array of `CComBSTR` objects that are going to be used to hold the strings in TriButtonCtl.h. An index variable also needs to be added so that we can keep track of the current state. These lines go at the bottom of the `CTriButtonCtl` class `definition.private`:

```
    CComBSTR    m_bstrButtonText[3];
    int            m_nIndex;
```

Next, change the `OnDraw` method in TriButtonCtl.cpp to draw the buttons. Let's make it change the background color and the button text depending on the state:

```
HRESULT CTriButtonCtl::OnDraw(ATL_DRAWINFO& di)
{
    USES_CONVERSION;

    RECT& rc = *(RECT*)di.prcBounds;
    SetBkMode(di.hdcDraw, TRANSPARENT);

    HBRUSH hBrush;
    switch (m_nIndex)
    {
        case 0:
            hBrush = CreateSolidBrush(RGB(0,0,0xFF));     //
Unpushed state, make blue
            break;
        case 1:
            hBrush = CreateSolidBrush(RGB(0,0xFF,0));     //
Mouse Over state, make green
            break;
        case 2:
        default:
            hBrush = CreateSolidBrush(RGB(0xFF,0,0));     //
pushed state, make red
            break;
    }

    LPCTSTR lpCTStr = OLE2CT((BSTR)m_bstrButtonText[m_nIndex]);

    SelectObject(di.hdcDraw, hBrush);
```

```
    Rectangle(di.hdcDraw, rc.left, rc.top, rc.right,
rc.bottom);
    DrawText(di.hdcDraw, lpCTStr, -1, &rc, DT_CENTER ¦
DT_VCENTER ¦ DT_SINGLELINE);
    return S_OK;
}
```

ADDING EVENT GENERATORS AND HANDLERS TO THE CONTROL

You can add an OnClick event to the control as well. This will fire an event that we can intercept by using a script in the HTML page. Begin by adding the interface description to the TriButton.idl file:

```
library TRIBUTTONLib
{
    importlib("stdole32.tlb");
    importlib("stdole2.tlb");

  [
        uuid(4CBBC677-507F-11D0-B98B-000000000000),
    helpstring("Event interface for TriButtonCtl")
    ]
  dispinterface _TriBtnEvents
    {
        properties:
        methods:
    [id(1)] void OnClick();
    };

    [
        uuid(46DF060F-304A-11D2-B2D9-006097097C7B),
        helpstring("TriButtonCtl Class")
    ]
    coclass TriButtonCtl
    {
        [default] interface ITriButtonCtl;
    [default, source] dispinterface _TriBtnEvents;
    };
};
```

You now need to rebuild your project so that the type library will be generated. Following a successful rebuild, use the ATL Proxy Generator to generate connection points for the event interface.

Choose Project, Add to Project, and then select Components and Controls. In the Gallery, open the Developer Studio Components folder, select the ATL Proxy Generator and click the Insert button.

When the ATL Proxy Generator dialog box appears, click the "..." button and select the TriButton.tlb file.

Because you are creating a connection point for the OnClick event, highlight the _TriBtnEvents interface and click the > button to move it. Click Insert, and save the resulting file as CPTriButton.h as the Save dialog box recommends.

If you look in the CPTriButton.h file, you will see that an interface class has been generated, `CProxy_TriBtnEvents`, that provides you with a method called `Fire_OnClick()` that you can call from the control whenever you want to send the event to the HTML script.

Next, you need to make some changes to your TriButtonCtl.h file. Include the CPTriButton.h at the top:

```
#include "resource.h"     // main symbols
#include "CPTriButtonCtl.h"
```

Now add the `CProxy_TriBtnEvents` class to the `CTriButtonCtl` class inheritance list in TriButtonCtl.h. You also need to implement `IconnectionPointContainer` by using the ATL supplied interface in the class `IconnectionPointContainerImpl`. To do this, add these two lines to `CTriButtonCtl` class inheritance list.

```
  public CProxy_TriBtnEvents<CTriButtonCtl>,
  public IConnectionPointContainerImpl<CTriButtonCtl>
```

You also need to make the interface `_TriBtnEvents` the default outgoing interface, so change the second parameter of `IprovideClassInfo2Imp`:

```
public IProvideClassInfo2Impl<&CLSID_TriButtonCtl,
&DIID__TriBtnEvents, &LIBID_TRIBUTTONLib>,
```

Now expose the `IConnectionPointContainer` interface by adding it to end of the COM map.

```
COM_INTERFACE_ENTRY_IMPL(IConnectionPointContainer)
```

Add a Connection Point Map to let ATL know about the new connection points.

```
BEGIN_CONNECTION_POINT_MAP(CTriButtonCtl)
  CONNECTION_POINT_ENTRY(DIID__TriBtnEvents)
END_CONNECTION_POINT_MAP()
```


Now that you can fire off an event, you need to add some message handlers so that the control can respond to the mouse. Add the appropriate message handlers to our message map:

```
    MESSAGE_HANDLER(WM_MOUSEMOVE, OnMouseMove)
    MESSAGE_HANDLER(WM_LBUTTONDOWN, OnButtonDown)
```

These will let you handle the `WM_MOUSEMOVE` message, which occurs when the mouse pointer passes over the control, and the `WM_LBUTTONDOWN` message, which occurs when the user clicks the control. The handler functions look like the following:

```
    LRESULT OnButtonDown(UINT, WPARAM wParam, LPARAM lParam,
BOOL& bHandled)
    {
        m_nIndex = 2;
        FireViewChange();
        Fire_OnClick();
        return 0;
    }

    LRESULT OnMouseMove(UINT, WPARAM wParam, LPARAM lParam,
BOOL& bHandled)
    {
        if (m_nIndex == 0)
```

```
        {
            m_nIndex = 1;
            FireViewChange();
        }
        return 0;
    }
```

Notice that the `OnButtonDown` method calls the `Fire_OnClick` event generator that you created earlier. This provides the capability to handle the button click in the HTML code.

One further thing that you should do is provide a timer capability so that if the mouse pointer moves off of the control, it will revert to the static state. To do this you need to add a thread procedure to `CTriButtonCtl`.

The following gives a function to set a timer interval and start a second execution thread that will wait idle until the timer runs out before firing a timer event.

```
    void SetTimerInterval(DWORD dwTimerInterval)
    {
        if (m_bTimerOn && dwTimerInterval == 0)     // Turn timer off
        {
            m_bTimerOn = FALSE;
            AtlWaitWithMessageLoop(m_hThread);
        }
        else
        {
            m_dwTimerInterval = dwTimerInterval;
            if (!m_bTimerOn) // Make sure timer isn't already on.
            {
                m_bTimerOn = TRUE;
                m_dwTimerInterval = dwTimerInterval;
                m_pStream = NULL;

                HRESULT hRes =
CoMarshalInterThreadInterfaceInStream(IID_ITriButtonCtl,
(ITriButtonCtl*)this, &m_pStream);

                // Create thread and pass the thread proc the
this ptr
                DWORD dwThreadID;
                m_hThread = CreateThread(NULL, 0, &_ThreadProc,
(void*)this, 0, &dwThreadID);
            }
        }
    }

    static DWORD WINAPI _ThreadProc(void* pv)
    {
        ((CTriButtonCtl*) pv)->ThreadProc();
        return 0;
    }

    DWORD ThreadProc()
    {
        CoInitialize(NULL);     // Initialilize COM
HRESULT hRes;
```

```
        m_pCP.Release();

        if (m_pStream)
            hRes = CoGetInterfaceAndReleaseStream(m_pStream,
IID_ITriButtonCtl, (void**)&m_pCP);

        // Thread runs until the timer expires
        while(m_bTimerOn)
        {
            Sleep(m_dwTimerInterval);

            // If timer is still on when we wake up, fire the
timer event.
            if (m_bTimerOn)
                m_pCP->_OnTimer();
        }
        m_pCP.Release();

        CoUninitialize();
        return 0;
    }


    BOOL        m_bTimerOn;
    DWORD        m_dwTimerInterval;
    HANDLE        m_hThread;
    LPSTREAM    m_pStream;
    CComPtr<ITriButtonCtl> m_pCP;
```

ADDING THE CONTROL TO AN HTML DOCUMENT

Now that the control is complete, you'll want to employ it in a page. Here is a simple HTML document that embeds a `TriButtonCtl` control. Note that this example is from my hard drive, so you'll want to change the local statement "`c:\proj\tributton\ReleaseMinSize\TriButton.ocx`" to match your own location—whether local or remote.

```
<HTML>
<HEAD>
<TITLE>ATL Tri-state button test</TITLE>
</HEAD>
<BODY>
<SCRIPT language="VBScript">
<!—
Sub CTriButton1_OnClick()
    Window.location.href = "http://www.molly.com"
End Sub
—>
</SCRIPT>

  <OBJECT ID="CTriButton1" WIDTH=100 HEIGHT=50

CODEBASE="c:\proj\tributton\ReleaseMinSize\TriButton.ocx"
  CLASSID="CLSID:46DF060F-304A-11D2-B2D9-006097097C7B">
  <PARAM NAME="StaticText" VALUE="(Unpushed)">
  <PARAM NAME="MouseOverText" VALUE="Mouse Over">
  <PARAM NAME="PushedText" VALUE="Pushed!">
```

```
</BODY>
</HTML>
```

Note

ActiveX controls are embedded into a document by using the <OBJECT> tag.

The OBJECT tag has several fields that provide information about the control. The control is given a name with the ID field; this name is used when referencing the control with a script.

The CODEBASE field tells the browser where to find the control program. In this example, it is looking on the local hard drive for the control, but it could just as easily be an HTTP link over the Internet.

CLASSID sends the GUID string from the IDL file. This is used in registering the control.

The VBScript section of this code shows how to implement an event handler for an ActiveX control. You use the name specified in the ID field, followed by an underscore and the name of the event it should handle. Figure 33.5 shows how clicking the control would send you to a new page.

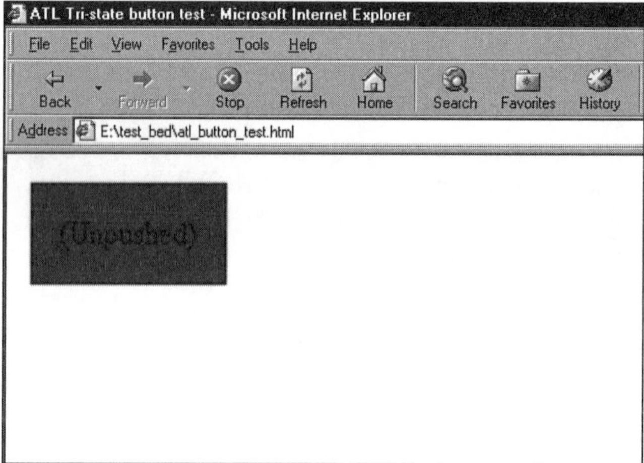

Figure 33.5
ActiveX control at work. The status is "Unpushed."

Whew! That was sure a lot of work just to get a basic ActiveX control working.

This control example doesn't even deal with some very important issues such as security, asynchronous downloading of resources, and the other necessities that need to be added to any truly useful ActiveX control.

If you want to research this further, there are several places on the Internet worth checking out.

Use These Resources for More Information on ActiveX:

Microsoft ActiveX Controls–Microsoft presents plenty of white papers and other information dealing with COM, ActiveX, and other related subjects. It's located at `http://www.microsoft.com/com/activex-f.htm`.

Download.com–C|Net resource filled with ActiveX controls and tools at `http://www.download.com/PC/Activex`.

The (Unofficial) ActiveX Guide–A nice site providing links to ActiveX-rich sites, ActiveX tools, and examples. This site can be found at `http://www.shorrock.u-net.com/index.html`.

TROUBLESHOOTING

ADDING COMPONENTS

I'm using Microsoft FrontPage and want to install a component? Will it work across browsers?

That depends on the component. If it is a Java applet, it will work with all browsers that are Java-enabled. As discussed in this chapter, Java was developed for cross-platform compatibility and portability—that's one of its most attractive strengths. However, if you're adding an ActiveX component, it will not work in a browser other than Internet Explorer.

DESIGNING FOR THE REAL WORLD

ADDING A JAVA APPLET TO A PAGE

Before you can add an Applet to a page, you must write or find the Java applet you want to use.

Note If you're not interested in programming your own Java applets, you can get many free or inexpensive applets online. Visit `http://www.javaboutique.com/` as a good starting place. See the resources sidebar in the Java section of this chapter for more online Java archives.

1. After you've chosen the Java applet you want to use, you need to upload it to a directory on your server. Be sure the file is transferred as binary, and has the appropriate .class extension.
2. The next step is to add the HTML that calls the Java applet to the Web page on which the applet will appear. You'll use the APPLET or OBJECT element. As with EMBED, the APPLET element has been taken out of HTML 4.0 strict standard—but many browsers simply do not support it.

```
<APPLET>

</APPLET>
```

3. Add the code source using the code attribute to point to the .class file.

```
<APPLET code="MyJava.class">

</APPLET>
```

4. Depending on the type of Java applet you're using, you'll need to set up some parameters using the <PARAMETER> tag.

```
<PARAM NAME="text" VALUE="Molly's Web Site">
<PARAM NAME="type" VALUE="wave">
```

5. Continuing adding parameters as required by the applet in question.

```
<PARAM NAME="bgColor" VALUE="#FFFFFF">
<PARAM NAME="fgColor" VALUE="#000000">
```

After the HTML file is uploaded to the server along with the applet, anyone visiting that page with a Java-compliant and enabled browser will enjoy the applet.

CHAPTER 34

Virtual Reality and Specialty Media

In this chapter

SPECIALTY APPLICATIONS

This chapter focuses on specialty applications that can add intrigue to your Web site including Virtual Reality, Push Technology, and Channels. These applications are not for everyone, but learning a bit about them might help you make enhancements to your sites that will appeal to visitors.

Applications covered in this chapter include the following:

- **Virtual Reality**—The term *virtual reality* refers to almost or near real experiences.
- **Push Technology**—Once the source of a lot of hype, Push is essentially information that is delivered to your desktop. It has fallen out of the popular eye, but is still used by certain Web sites.
- **Channel Definition Format (CDF)**—CDF is a file format from Microsoft that allows users to create a channel—a grouping of preselected Web sites. Also a bit out of favor, channels are built in to the Windows 98 operating system and therefore still a relevant technology to be familiar with.

Still not sure that this technology is the right thing for your site? See, "Using Virtually Real Technologies" in the Troubleshooting section at the end of this chapter.

VIRTUAL REALITY

On the Web, the experience of near realistic experiences can be delivered in several ways, including visually through a language called the Virtual Reality Modeling Language (VRML) and seamed graphic formats such as QuickTime Virtual Reality.

VIRTUAL REALITY MODELING LANGUAGE

Don't be fooled. VRML is a four-letter acronym that looks like it might have something in common with HTML, but it's a completely different animal. VRML stands for *Virtual Reality Modeling Language*. HTML, which is a *markup* language, is used mostly for formatting and working with objects (text, images, and so on) that already exist.

When you program in VRML, you create those things, as well as the space they occupy. You can build models of buildings, cities, entire worlds—but to do so, as in Java, you'll need to learn a new language.

Unlike Java, however, VRML is not a programming language in the strictest sense of the concept. You don't use it to create executable applications or objects that perform functions on your computer. Using VRML, you create files which, when viewed through a VRML browser, give the observer the ability to walk through a three-dimensional space and manipulate items in that space.

Note

These three-dimensional spaces are referred to by the term *worlds*. VRML files are easy to identify, as they end in .wrl, for world.

VRML browser applications are available both free-standing and as plug-ins for standard Web browsers like Netscape Communicator and Microsoft Internet Explorer. Such players include Cosmo, FreeWRL, and WorldView. For a complete list of VRML software, see **http://www.web3d.org/vrml/browpi.htm**.

The Web3D Consortium, a group of computer and software companies who collaborate to produce VRML and other 3D standards, sees VRML as more than just a means of enabling 3D images on the Web. "The evolution of the Net from command-line to 2D graphical to emergent 3D interfaces reflects ongoing, fundamental progress toward human-centered interface design—that is, toward a more immersive and responsive computer-mediated experience," says the Consortium's Web site.

Note Visit the Web3D Consortium, **http://www.vrml.org/**.

PROGRAMMING IN VRML

VRML commands (or *nodes*) allow the VRML author to specify the shape, depth, color, surface texture, lighting, and other aspects of the scene under construction. VRML works by visualizing a scene based on its component polygons (circles and squares, for example) and polyhedra (spheres and boxes).

Other 3D graphical objects, such as letters of the alphabet, can be viewed in VRML worlds; however, the beginning VRML programmer will find it simpler to construct VRML worlds out of polygons and polyhedra (see Listing 34.1).

LISTING 34.1 VRML CODE FOR POLYGONS AND POLYHEDRA

```
#VRML V2.0 utf8
#Floppy's VRML 2.0 Tutorial Example File

WorldInfo {
        title "3D Floppyworld"
        info "James's own VRML thingy"
        }

Shape {
        appearance Appearance {
                material Material {
                        diffuseColor 0 0.5 0
                        emissiveColor 0 0.8 0
                        transparency 0.5
                }
        }
        geometry Box {
        }
}

Transform {
        scale 2 0.5 2
```

continues

LISTING 34.1 CONTINUED

```
        rotation 0 1 0 0.78
        translation 0 -1.5 0
        children [
                Shape {
                        appearance Appearance {
                                texture ImageTexture {
                                        url "brick.jpg"
                                        repeatS TRUE
                                        repeatT TRUE
                                }
                        }
                        geometry Box {
                        }
                }
        ]
}
```

You can see the VRML results of this code in Figure 34.1.

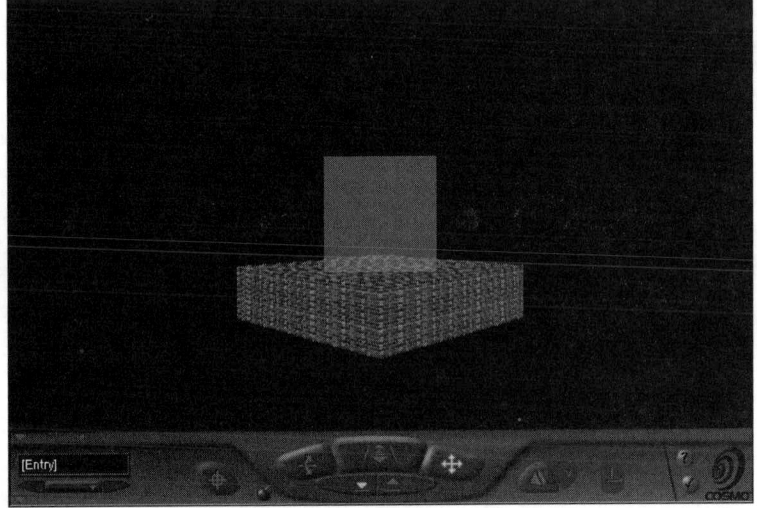

Figure 34.1
VRML polyhedra and polygons. Note the VRML viewing console along the bottom of figure.

Numerous tutorials are available online that walk the beginner VRML programmer through an introduction to the coding language and the theory behind building worlds.

VRML Tutorials Abound

Check out the following sites for help with creating VRML worlds of your own:

James Smith's user-friendly tutorial for writing your own VRML 2.0 code at `http://www.ee.surrey.ac.uk/Personal/ee41rs/vrmlguide/tutorial/`.

A site on using VRML authoring tools to produce worlds is maintained by Johnnie Rose and found at `http://www.hal-pc.org/~johnnie2/vrml/Building.html`.

A tutorial is available from the University of Moncton, Canada, at `http://eve.info.umoncton.ca:8080/VRML/VRML20Tut/toc.htm`.

A tutorial is also available from CERN in Switzerland at `http://www-venus.cern.ch/vrmltut/`.

To view VRML through your Web browser, download one of these plug-in VRML browsers:

- Cosmo Player, the most popular VRML browser, originally an SGI product: `http://cosmosoftware.com/download/index_player.html`.
- Community Place, a Sony-produced browser: `http://www.sonypic.com/vs`.
- Live Picture Viewer, a browser that supports multiple media formats: `http://www.livepicture.com/download/lpviewer_content.html`.
- WorldView, a browser that has been optimized to include support for Microsoft system enhancements such as DirectX: `http://www.intervista.com/worldview/`.

To produce your own VRML worlds or to automate the complicated coding of advanced VRML features, try one of the following VRML authoring tools:

- Cosmo Worlds, a tool that shares its origins with Cosmo Player: `http://cosmosoftware.com/products/worlds/brief.html`.
- Macromedia Extreme3D, from the makers of Director: `http://www.macromedia.com/software/extreme3d/`.
- DesignSpace, a tool made for engineers that automatically generates VRML code: `http://www.designspace.com/`.
- Virtual Studio, a product designed for Web developers looking to include VRML in Internet sites: `http://www.avilon.com/products/vs97/ns40.htm`.

SEAMED VIRTUAL REALITY

Another way of achieving virtual experiences on the Web is through the use of seamed technologies. The most popular of these is Apple's QuickTime Virtual Reality (see Figure 34.2), or QTVR for short. It's available for both Windows and Macintosh platforms.

QTVR allows you to plan out a virtual tour. Then, by using a special camera, you take positioned photographs along that tour. Using QTVR technology, you then seam these photographs together to create the appearance of actual movement through that dimension.

QTVR is a nice feature in certain instances. Let's say you're a manufacturer of RVs or airplanes, and you want your audience to have examples of what it's like to walk through the inside of the RVs or planes. You can simulate this effect with QTVR (see Figure 34.3).

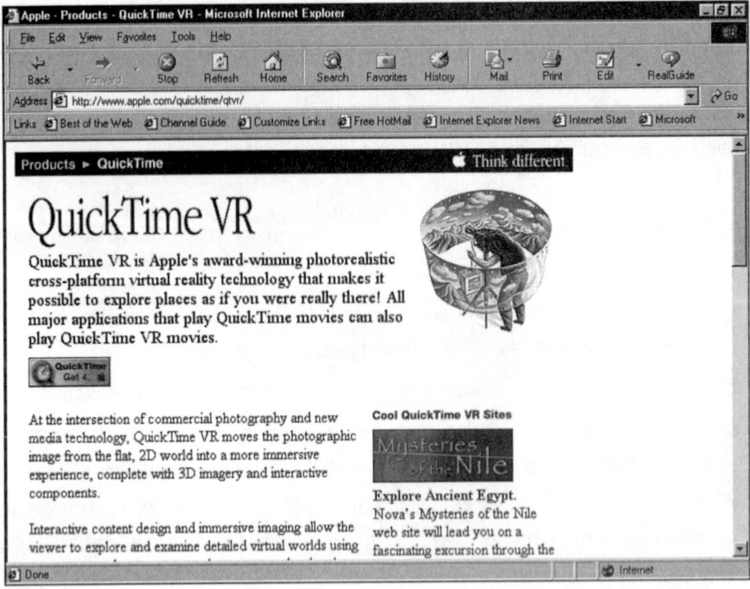

Figure 34.2 Apple's QTVR home page offers you background information on QTVR as well as a download of the software.

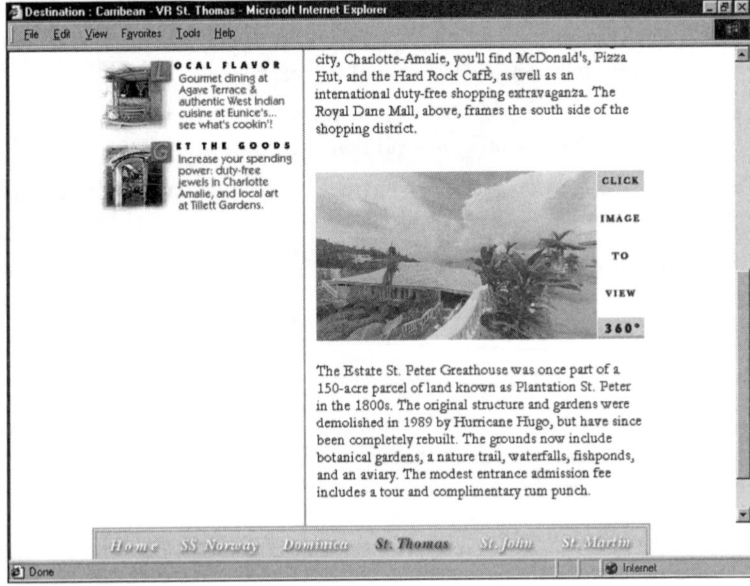

Figure 34.3 A QTVR example. The palm trees, house, and ocean are a panoramic vista. Using my mouse, the shift key, and the control key, I can navigate the picture to see a complete 360-degree view.

Another seamed technology is Virtual Tours by Bamboo.com (see Figure 34.4). The concept is similar to QTVR, using photographs or 3D program output to create a virtual experience.

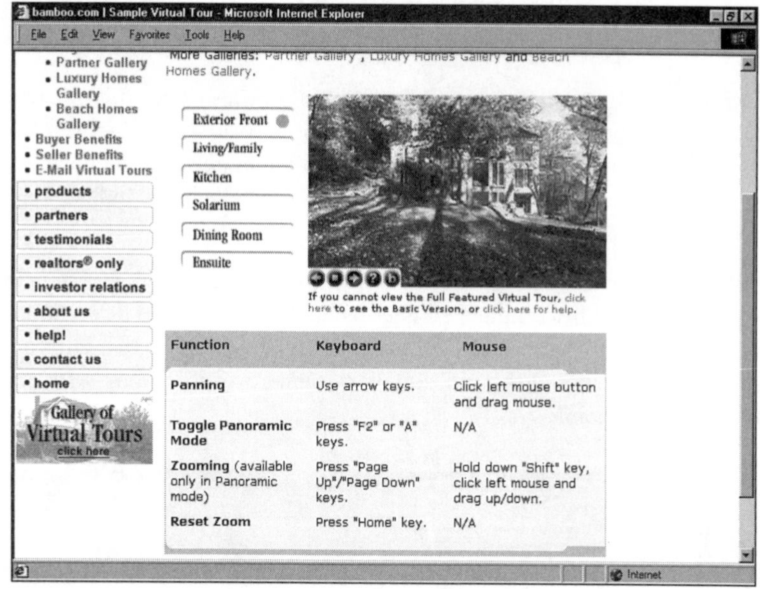

Figure 34.4
Touring a home using Virtual Tours. The scene automatically scrolls panoramically once loaded. I can also use the controls listed on the page to pan and zoom at will.

Note

For more information on Apple QuickTime Virtuality and QuickTime products, visit `http://quicktime.apple.com/`. Visit Bamboo.com at `http://www.bamboo.com/`.

Push Technology

Push Technology, also termed *Webcasting*, is a method of delivering information from a server to a client on a preset schedule.

When you visit a specific Web page, you are requesting information to be sent from a server to your machine. This is referred to as *pull*. Push, then, is a server deciding when and where to send material without a specific query being made.

In 1996, Push technology was all the rage among Internet soothsayers. The ability to tell a service your interests and have it instantly—and constantly—deliver relevant information to your computer seemed to be the greatest thing since email. PointCast immediately became the most popular push service on the Internet as thousands and thousands of users flocked to its site to download its popular news-based screen saver.

Businesses, in which corporate networks were connected to the Internet through controlled gateways called firewalls, were less than thrilled. Zealous employees who signed up for push services quickly filled those networks to capacity with stock quotes, sports scores, news updates, and other miscellany that executives deemed noncritical to the business.

But connection to the Internet doesn't come for free, and companies soon grew tired of push clients' insatiable, ever-increasing demand for expensive bandwidth. In late 1996,

Hewlett-Packard banned PointCast outright from company desktops; other companies followed in its footsteps soon after.

Consumer usage of clients like PointCast was not nearly as widespread, given the fact that most regular people didn't have the luxury of permanent, high-speed Internet connections. After it became clear that businesses wouldn't tolerate such an unprofessional waste of bandwidth, membership in services like PointCast dwindled, and industry analysts trumpeted the death of an industry fad.

Still, push is not dead. PointCast was bought in May of 1999 by Launchpad Technologies which combined it with their eWallet technology and added direct shopping (see Figure 34.5). The new product is known as *entrypoint*. The hope is that entrypoint will work more successfully because of the addition of shopping over the Web—with extra security being the marketing point.

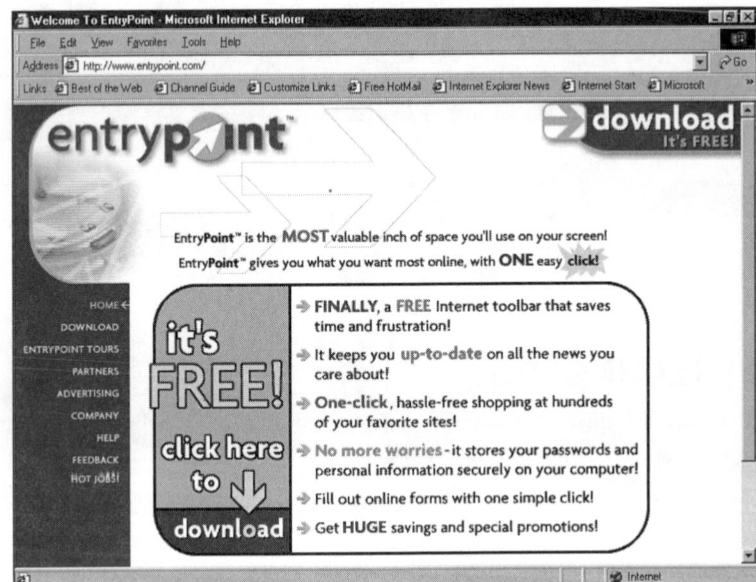

Figure 34.5
entrypoint's Web site: **`http://www.entrypoint.com/`**. Custom news, weather, sports, entertainment—and shopping—delivered live to your desktop.

CHANNELS

In a way, channels are a passive form of push. Conceptually, they still are push, but a lot of the decisions are left up to the site visitor, including what information is to be delivered.

As with subscription channels on TV, a user can order specific information from channels that exist on the Web.

As a developer, you can create channels. Channels are nothing more than Web sites, but, because a user is subscribing to the channel, a lot more activity and updates are incorporated into channels.

Say, for example, I wanted to make my Web site a channel. This would allow site visitors to voluntarily subscribe to my site. Once subscribed, they will receive regular updates and information is sent to their desktop whenever they log on to the Web. This is an attractive concept because it pushes your content to subscriber desktops and does not require them to remember to drop by your site to see if you have new information.

Internet Explorer has taken the lead in channels, integrating them with the Active Desktop that shipped with Internet Explorer 4.0 and above and now with Windows 98. Netscape delivers channels via Netcaster, but the process is more complex, relying on JavaScript and APIs, and not as integrated and accessible as the Active Channel technology.

Note

For more information on how to work with Netcaster, check out the Netscape Developer's Guide manual on netcasting at **`http://developer.netscape.com/docs/manuals/netcast/devguide/index.html`**.

Channels are indexed with a file format known as CDF (Channel Definition Format). This is a text file of data that contains information about your channel and also manages how that channel will interact with the user. Channels work with the Extensible Markup Language (XML) to deliver their information.

→ For details on XML, **see** "Understanding XHTML, XML, and Emerging Languages," **p. 494**

TROUBLESHOOTING

USING VIRTUALLY REAL TECHNOLOGIES

Many real estate sites employ QTVR and other seamed technologies. Can these technologies be relied upon to improve product visibility?

Realistically, not everyone visiting a site is going to know how or want to spend the time to go through virtual tours of your product. However, there are many that may well benefit from the experience and actually be inspired to contact you or purchase as a result of the convenience these technologies provide.

Reliable? Not necessarily, but if appropriate to your product or service and within your budget, I recommend going for it! Just be sure to include options such as an image-only tour so that people without the necessary plug-ins or patience can get the gist of what you're trying to do.

An interesting side note: On the very day I wrote this I passed a billboard advertising a realtor's new Web site. The site featured Virtual Reality and the realtor has created an advertising campaign "Virtual Realty" based on this entire concept!

DESIGNING FOR THE REAL WORLD

BUILDING A CHANNEL

You can build a channel using Microsoft's CDF Generator. Begin by downloading the software from the Microsoft Developer's Network. You may be required to register before you can download the software.

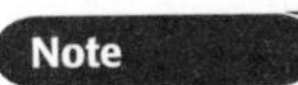

Download the CDF Generator from **`http://premium.microsoft.com/msdnmembers/downloads/tools/423.asp`**.

After you have the software installed, you can begin working with it (see Figure 34.6). The Generator works on the familiar wizard concept and walks you through the process step-by-step.

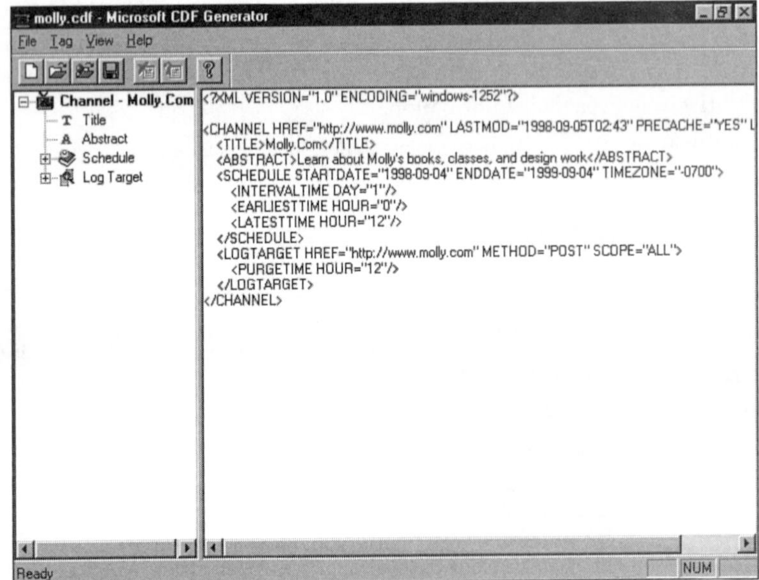

Figure 34.6
CDF Generator from Microsoft makes it simple to create a channel.

Listing 34.2 shows a .cdf file I created with the Generator.

LISTING 34.2 CHANNEL DEFINITION CODE CREATED WITH CDF GENERATOR

```
<?XML VERSION="1.0" ENCODING="windows-1252"?>

<CHANNEL HREF="http://www.molly.com" LASTMOD="1998-09-05T02:43" PRECACHE="YES"
LEVEL="0">
```

```
    <TITLE>Molly.Com</TITLE>
      <ABSTRACT>Learn about Molly's books, classes, and design work</ABSTRACT>
    <SCHEDULE STARTDATE="1998-09-04" ENDDATE="1999-09-04" TIMEZONE="-0700">
        <INTERVALTIME DAY="1"/>
        <EARLIESTTIME HOUR="0"/>
        <LATESTTIME HOUR="12"/>
    </SCHEDULE>
    <LOGTARGET HREF="http://www.molly.com" METHOD="POST" SCOPE="ALL">
        <PURGETIME HOUR="12"/>
    </LOGTARGET>
</CHANNEL>
```

The next step is to place a link to the channel on an HTML page. To do this, you must link to the .cdf file from that page, as I have done in Listing 34.3.

Caution

Because CDF is a server-side technology that relies on Internet Explorer 4.0 and higher, you'll have to upload your files to a server before testing the results with an Internet Explorer 4.0 or higher browser. You can't test CDF files locally.

LISTING 34.3 HTML PAGE WITH A CDF LINK

```
<HTML>
<HEAD>
<TITLE>Adding an Active Channel</TITLE>
</HEAD>

<BODY>
<p>
<br>
<br>

<DIV align="center">
<H2>Molly's Active Channel</H2>


<A href="molly.cdf">
<IMG src="images/active_channel.gif" width="200" height="30" border="0"
alt="molly.com active channel button"></A>

</DIV>

</BODY>
</HTML>
```

When I click the linked image, I will have the opportunity to set my own parameters as to how I, as a visitor, want to manage the information updates from the page. I can use the recommended update schedule, or select one of my own, based on a daily, weekly, or monthly update.

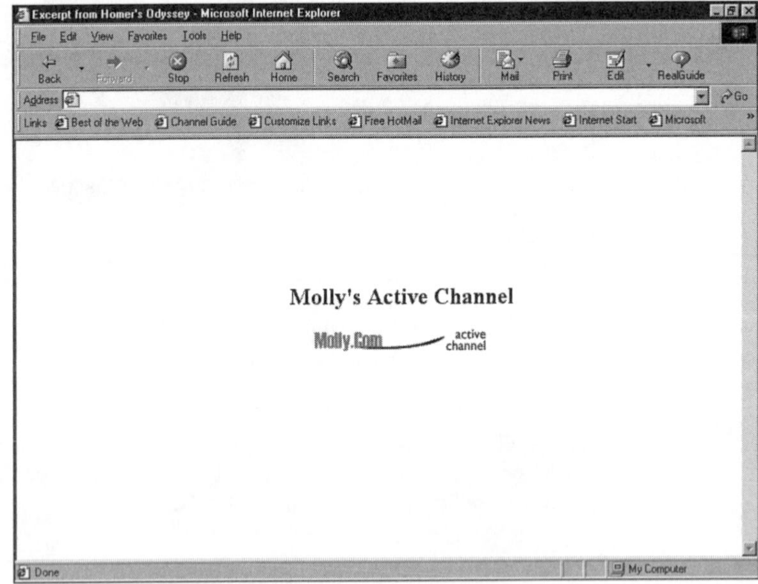

Figure 34.7
The HTML page on my site with the CDF link in place.

Note

You can learn more about how to create channels by following along with the tutorials available on Microsoft Developer Network, **`http://msdn.microsoft.com/workshop/delivery/default.asp`**.

Server-Side and Backend Applications

CHAPTER 35

CGI and Pre-Processing Fundamentals

In this chapter

THE COMMON GATEWAY INTERFACE

Static HTML pages are a useful way to provide information on demand to a lot of people. However, the true power of Web pages lies not in the static nature of HTML, but rather in their interactive capability.

One of the earliest and still widely used methods for making Web pages dynamic and interactive is the use of CGI scripting. The *Common Gateway Interface*, or CGI, provided the first mechanism for integrating applications into your Web site. By using CGI, developers can write applications that can provide some interactive element (such as accepting feedback from the end user) or a dynamic element (such as Web pages generated on demand). The power of CGI allows developers to easily integrate these applications into their Web sites, regardless of the Web server software being used.

Over the past several years, many alternatives to CGI have been introduced. On the Web browser side, much functionality that previously was only possible through CGI is now being performed by JavaScript or some other client-side scripting language. On the server-side, some traditional CGI functionality is now being performed through server-side scripting. However, CGI is still a viable means for creating desired functionality on your Web site.

A common misconception is that CGI programming and scripting refers to using a specific language for creating custom Web applications. This is not the case. It is a set of standards that define how communication takes place between your Web server and your server-side applications. These standards provide the gateway through which data can pass between the Web server and your CGI application.

CGI programs run as separate applications. They are not part of the Web server application, which means they do not have direct access to the information available to the Web server. This information includes data such as the user's Web browser name and version, or more importantly, any form data the user is submitting. Typically, the whole point of creating your CGI application will be to work with this data. Therefore, your script or program must have access to it.

At a basic level, the CGI specification defines how Web servers will make information available to CGI applications and how CGI applications will return data to the Web server. So when you think of the terms CGI programming or CGI scripting, you should think of them as a methodology of programming and scripting, not as a specific language.

The flow of data between your Web server and your CGI application is the core of CGI programming (see Figure 35.1). After you know how to do this, you are ready to begin developing your own CGI applications. How to do this is discussed in the "Understanding How the CGI Works" section later in this chapter. Before you actually start developing CGI applications, though, you do need to choose a programming or scripting language with which to write your CGI applications.

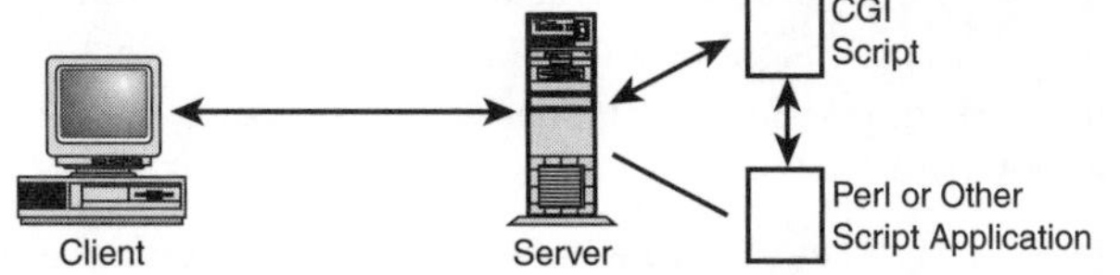

Figure 35.1
The client-server relationship. Site visitors enter information into a form or access a page with a CGI script, which then sends a request to the server. The CGI then processes the information and returns the results back to the client.

Choosing CGI Languages

Because the Common Gateway Interface does not refer to a specific programming language for coding applications for Web sites, you will need to choose one. Fortunately, you can use almost any programming or scripting language that will run on your Web server's machine. However, there are some points you should take into consideration when choosing a language.

When choosing the language to use for creating your CGI applications, you should first consider the languages with which you are familiar. Although some of the languages you might know, such as BASIC, might not be the best choice, most likely you also know a language that will be a good one. By using that language, you have saved yourself the time and effort of learning a new programming language to code CGI applications.

Another consideration when choosing a CGI language is to choose one that is commonly used by other CGI developers. The most common languages used for CGI applications are Perl, C, C++, TCL, UNIX shells, Java, Visual Basic, and AppleScript. One reason for choosing one of these languages is the support you can get from other developers. As you might have already experienced, the Internet contains a wealth of resources in the people that are online. When you have a coding problem, there are numerous bulletin boards, Web sites, listservs, and chat rooms where you can post questions to people who can answer them. However, if you are working in an obscure language that few people are using, you might have more difficulty obtaining help when you need it.

Note

If you're concerned about cost, it's helpful to know that Perl is free, whereas other languages may have costs attached to them. On the other hand, Perl can be complicated for the inexperienced, and it must be set up properly to avoid security risks.

You also should use one of these common languages to save yourself some coding time. There are many Web sites containing free source code for CGI applications that you can download and use on your Web site. Many of these will run with little or no changes by you. And if you need the application to work slightly differently, you can modify it to suit your needs. There also are CGI libraries available that have functions you can call from your own application. These functions are common tasks you have to perform in CGI applications, such as creating valid headers, decoding user data, and returning results to the Web server.

Want to know more about Perl? See "The Power of Perl" in the Troubleshooting section at the end of this chapter.

Typically, the only requirement for using these code samples is that you retain some copyright information in the source code of the script or give the author credit on your Web site. These CGI application archives are great starting points for enhancing your Web site. Keep in mind, though, that these archives will contain examples written in the common languages mentioned previously.

→ Looking for scripts? **See** "HTML and Design Resources," **p. 1050**

Searches and sorts are two of the most processor-intensive tasks you can code in an application. If you will be performing processor-intensive actions, such as searching and sorting on millions of records, you should use a compiled programming language such as C or C++, which will give you much better performance than an interpreted scripting language such as Perl. However, if performance is negligible for the application you are coding, a scripting language such as Perl can greatly reduce your development time because most programmers can write similar code in Perl much faster than in C.

Tip from

Make sure the language you choose can yield the necessary level of performance for the task you need accomplished.

Compiled Languages

After writing your source code, which consists of simple ASCII text, most high level programming languages make use of a process called compiling to transform the statements you entered—such as conditional statements, loops, and variable assignments—into actual machine language executable code. After the program has been compiled, you can then run that program on the platform for which it has been designed without any other programs. A compiled program no longer is a simple text file. It is referred to as a binary file, and opening the file in a text editor will reveal strange characters rather than discernable statements.

Compiled programs have some advantages. First, because the source code is changed into machine-dependant executable code, it will execute much faster than an interpreted program. Because the compiled program does not have to worry about running on other platforms, the compiler can optimize the binary code specifically for that platform.

Another advantage of compiled programs is that you can distribute them without compromising the integrity of your source code. Although the technology exists to disassemble executables back into source code, they do not always work well. Also, the majority of people using your programs will not have the skill or software necessary to disassemble your program. For the most part, you can be assured that your source code is safe.

Along with the advantages of compiled programs come some disadvantages. For example, the process of compiling a program can take some time, depending on the speed of your machine. A simple change to your program can result in a lot of time coding and compiling before you can even test it.

Perhaps the largest disadvantage is the cross platform compatibility problems. In general, code you write for one platform will often not work correctly on other platforms, such as code written for a PC versus a Macintosh.

INTERPRETED LANGUAGES

Scripts are similar to programs in that they both use similar statement structures, depending on the languages being used. Instead of compiling scripts, however, they are run through a command interpreter, which interprets the commands at runtime.

The process of coding a script starts in a similar fashion as coding a program. You write the statements for your code and save them into a text file. After you have completed your source code, however, your script is finished. There is no compilation step.

To run a script, you must have a command interpreter process your source code file. A command interpreter is a compiled program. Like all compiled programs, it is specific to the platform for which it was compiled.

For example, with Perl, which is a common scripting language, you must have a Perl command interpreter on your machine to run Perl scripts. If you have a Windows machine, you must have a version of the Perl command interpreter for Windows platforms. This would be a different version of the Perl interpreter than someone who has a UNIX version of Perl. The key point, though, is that the single script you wrote on your Windows platform will usually run without a problem on the UNIX platform also.

Caution

Cross-platform compatibility of scripts occurs because the commands are stored in a simple text file. If you code your script with statements that are only supported on a single platform, you will get errors when you run it on other platforms.

The natural advantage to scripts over programs is the capability to write and distribute a single code base across many platforms. Scripts typically will need only minor changes to run correctly on various machines.

One of the biggest advantages of scripts is their ease of maintenance. Creating and maintaining a script is as easy as editing a text file. In fact, many people who write scripts use simple text editors such as vi or emacs on UNIX platforms and Notepad on Windows. When you make a change to your script, it is ready to be run as soon as you save the file. You do not have to compile first. This enables you to quickly add a few lines of code and test your script.

In general, because of the capability to make quick changes to scripts and test out the results, you can code a script much faster than you can code a program.

However, there are some disadvantages to scripts. The biggest disadvantage is the speed at which scripts run. Scripts are run by processing the lines of code through a command interpreter at runtime. The command interpreter recognizes statements and then executes the proper machine language code for that statement.

Sound familiar? Although not a direct translation of statements to machine-level code, the act of interpreting a script is not unlike compiling a program. The big difference is that the translation is done at runtime. The end user must endure the wait of this process every time the program is run. With modern computers and with simple programs, this time difference between running a script versus a program can be almost negligible to the user. However, when you start performing computationally intensive actions such as searches and sorts on large blocks of data, you will notice a difference.

The other common disadvantage of scripts over programs is the integrity of your source code. A script is just the source code file. There is nothing else that you can distribute. Everyone who has an executable version of your script also has your source code. Depending on how important this code is to you, this might not be a viable option.

UNDERSTANDING HOW THE CGI WORKS

As you begin to develop CGI applications, you will soon realize that to integrate an application into your Web site two things must happen. First, your application must be able to receive data from the Web browser and Web server. This is imperative to properly perform most functions. In addition, your application must be able to send results back to the user's Web browser after it has finished executing.

CGI defines how to do both of these actions. As for receiving data from the Web browser and Web server, your CGI application does not have to do anything to ensure that this data is made available. The Web server will automatically send this information to your CGI application when it gets started. As for sending data back to the Web browser, that is equally easy. All you must do is create a valid header as defined in the CGI specification and output the results.

Tip from

If you're using an ISP, you'll want to contact them via their Web site or other method and find out where their CGI scripts are located (usually in a directory called `cgi-bin`). Your ISP can also provide you with information on how to work properly within the context of their server. Not all ISPs support CGI or allow you to use their scripts.

HTTP CONNECTIONS AND HEADERS

To fully understand the CGI process, you need to have some idea of how HTTP connections work. An HTTP connection is the communication channel between the Web browser and the Web server. Most HTTP connections begin on the client side, with the Web browser sending an HTTP request to a Web server for a document.

At the beginning of the request is a section referred to as the request header. The request header contains information about the request and about the Web browser requesting the information. A few examples of request header fields are shown in Table 35.1.

Table 35.1 Select HTTP Request Headers

Request Header Field	Meaning
`authorization`	`authorization` is the authentication information sent by the Web browser to identify itself to the Web server.
`pragma`	The `pragma` header contains any special instructions for the Web server. For example, the no-cache `pragma` directive instructs Web servers not to send cached versions of the requested document.
`referrer`	The `referrer` is the URL of the previous document on which the user clicked a link to navigate to the current document.
`user_agent`	The `user_agent` is the name and version of the Web browser making the request. For example, `Mozilla/4.01 (Win95; I)` is the `user_agent` for Netscape 4.0 on Windows 95.

After the Web server receives an HTTP request from a Web browser, it evaluates the request—returning the requested document if it exists—and then shuts down the HTTP connection. Immediately preceding the document, the Web server sends an HTTP response header to the Web browser. The Web browser parses the response header for information about displaying the document being returned by the Web server. A few HTTP response header fields are described in Table 35.2.

Table 35.2 Select HTTP Response Headers

Response Header Field	Meaning
`content-type`	Specifies to the Web browser the MIME type of the data being returned.
`date`	Contains the date the returning document was created.
`link`	Contains information, such as the URL, of the document being returned.
`title`	Specifies the title of the returning document.
`url`	Contains the URL of the returning document.

When a Web browser sends an HTTP request for a CGI application from a Web server, the Web server starts the CGI program or script and then passes on most of the HTTP request information to the CGI application. Most of this information is placed in environment variables. Some of the information can be accessible via standard input to the program or script, depending on the request method used. Accessing the HTTP request information will be discussed in more detail in the next section, "Sending Data to Your CGI Application."

When a CGI application has completed its task, it needs to send output back to the Web server. The Web server then takes the output, forms an HTTP response header, and sends the HTTP response back to the user's Web browser. You do have the option of forming the HTTP response header in your CGI application and sending the data back to the Web browser directly, but sending through the Web server is the most common method.

SENDING DATA TO YOUR CGI APPLICATION

When started by the Web server, CGI programs and scripts run as separate applications on the Web server machine. They are not integrated within the Web server environment. Because of this, your CGI application does not have native access to the data sent from the Web browser in the HTTP request. This includes the HTTP request headers and any user-supplied data, such as HTML form data.

To work with this data from the Web browser, your CGI application needs to have access to it. Fortunately, there is nothing you need to do on the Web server or in your CGI application to make sure this data is available for your CGI application. The Web server will make this available to you automatically.

Remember that the CGI specification defines how information passes between your Web server and your CGI applications. Part of this definition is how the Web server will make available the data coming from the user. All of this data, including both the HTTP request headers and user-supplied data, is sent to your CGI application through either environment variables or standard input. The actual location of these two will vary depending on the request method used. All that is left for your CGI application to do is retrieve the data from one of these two locations.

Note

Standard input is the default location defined by your application from which it will receive data. For example, for most computer applications, such as word processors, standard input is the keyboard.

THE `get` AND `post` REQUEST METHODS

You might already be familiar with the `get` and `post` request methods. These are the same request methods you specify in the `method` attribute of the `<FORM>` tag. These are the two ways a request can be sent to the Web server.

→ To learn how to set up a form for your Web page, **see** "Building Forms," **p. 386**

A `get` request is the most common request method. It is used to specify a request for a document from the Web server. The `post` method, on the other hand, is used when form data is being sent from the user's Web browser to the Web server. Form data is typically sent with the post method. However, you can append additional data to the end of a URL with the get method.

Appending Information to URLs

There are two types of additional information that can be appended to a URL with the get method. The first type is additional path information. Path information is usually the path to a resource on the server machine and is typically used only with CGI applications. For example, with server-side imagemaps, the URL sent by the browser is in the following form:

```
http://www.somedomain.com/cgi-bin/imagemap/maps/groups.map?201,118
```

The URL to the CGI application is only

```
http://www.somedomain.com/cgi-bin/imagemap
```

The remaining part of the URL is the additional information being discussed. The first part of this additional information is

```
/maps/groups.map
```

This is some extra path information being sent to the CGI script. In this example, this specifies the path to the map file on the server machine.

The second part of the additional information is

```
?201,118
```

The question mark in any URL designates the beginning of the second type of additional information appended to a URL. This second form is referred to as a *query string*, and it is typically used only with CGI applications. It is used to supply additional data that the application might need. For this example, the query string contains x and y coordinates of the user's mouse click the imagemap.

The post Method and Standard Input

Earlier in this section, you learned that Web servers send data to your CGI applications through either environment variables or standard input. The only time standard input is used is when the request method used by the Web browser is the post method. The post method is used only when the user is submitting form data. Although the user data is supplied to the CGI application through standard input, the Web server sends the rest of the available information via environment variables.

Caution

The get method also can be used with the method attribute in the <FORM> tag, but it is better to use the post method. Some browsers limit the amount of characters that will be sent by using the get method, which could result in truncated data being sent to your CGI application. Because this limit varies from browser to browser, it is best to use just the post method.

Environment Variables

No matter which method is used to request your CGI application, the Web server will set some environment variables for your application. These environment variables contain useful information about the HTTP request, the Web browser, and the Web server. Unless the post method was used to send data to the Web server, the environment variables will be the only source of information available to your CGI application. Table 35.3 contains all the CGI environment variables that are set by the Web server.

TABLE 35.3 CGI ENVIRONMENT VARIABLES

Environment Variable	Meaning
auth_type	Specifies the authentication method, such as username/password, used by the Web browser, if any.
content_length	Contains the length, in characters, of the user-supplied data, if any.
content_type	Specifies the MIME type of the user-supplied data.
gateway_interface	Designates the version of the CGI specification being used. The current version is 1.1.
path_info	Contains any additional path information appended to the requesting URL.
path_translated	Contains the Web server's translation of the virtual path information, appended to the URL, to the actual path on the server machine.
query_string	Contains any information appended the URL with a question mark.
remote_addr	Contains the IP address of the client machine.
remote_host	Contains the domain name, if available, of the client machine.
remote_ident	Contains the user's login name, if one was used for authentication with the Web server.
remote_user	Contains the remote username, as supplied to the Web server.
request_method	Specifies the request method used by the browser—get or post.
script_name	Contains the virtual path and filename of the CGI script.
server_name	Contains either the domain name or IP address of the Web server machine.
server_port	Contains the port being used by the Web server.
server_protocol	Specifies the protocol being used between the Web server and Web browser, typically HTTP.
server_software	Contains the name and version of the Web server software.

In addition to the CGI environment variables, the Web server also sets environment variables for all the HTTP request headers. The actual environment variable set by the Web server is the prefix HTTP followed by the name of the HTTP request header field. For example, the HTTP environment variable for the REFERER header is HTTP_REFERER.

Getting error messages while testing your scripts? See "Terrors of CGI Errors" in the Troubleshooting section at the end of this chapter.

NAME/VALUE PAIRS

Whether sending form data via the get or post method, the Web browser will always perform two actions on the data before it is sent. The first action is placing the data from each form element into a name/value pair. On the server side, these name/value pairs are used to identify which data came from which form element. The second action performed by the Web browser is a process called URL encoding, which is discussed in the next section.

The name portion of a name/value pair is taken from the name attribute of the form element. When you create form elements with <INPUT>,. <SELECT>, and <TEXTAREA> tags, you supply the name attribute, giving the element a name. When the form is submitted, the Web browser takes the name, appends an equal sign and the data entered by the user if any. The data entered by the user is the value portion of the name/value pair.

```
<INPUT type="checkbox" name="age" value="30-40">
```

Not all form elements have unique names. When you use the multiple attribute with the <SELECT> tag, a user can choose multiple options from the list. Each option the user selects is associated with the same name. For example, using the following <SELECT> tag

```
<SELECT NAME="language" multiple>
<OPTION>English
<OPTION>French
<OPTION>German
<OPTION>Spanish
</SELECT>
```

When the user selects the options English, French, and German and submits the form, the Web browser will create three name/value pairs

```
language=English
language=French
language=German
```

The Web browser sends all the name/value pairs in a single long string. Each name/value pair is separated by an ampersand (&). At the start of your CGI application, you will want to break apart the name/value pairs so you can work with the individual values.

URL ENCODING

The other process performed by the Web browser on all user-supplied form data before sending it to the Web server is URL encoding. URL encoding is the act of changing all spaces in the name/value pairs string to plus signs (+) and changing other reserved characters into their hexadecimal equivalents.

The primary purpose for URL encoding is to remove any characters with which the Web server or CGI application will have a problem. Specifically, this means removing all spaces.

Naturally, spaces are important to the data being sent, and you do not want to permanently remove them. So spaces are replaced with the plus signs, which act as placeholders for where the spaces belong.

This introduces a new problem, though. Suppose the user enters a plus sign in the data being sent to the Web server. How will your CGI application distinguish between that plus sign and the plus signs used as space placeholders?

Additionally, other characters, such as the equal and ampersand signs are used to separate names and values in the name/value pairs. Your CGI application will need some way to distinguish the difference between these characters and ones entered by the user as part of the form data.

Caution

The term *special characters* is used here to distinguish important characters used in CGI from standard characters. The term in this context should not be confused with the term *special characters* referring to HTML encoding methods.

To address these issues, certain special characters, including the three previously described, are converted to their hexadecimal equivalent value. Only special characters entered by the user in the form data are converted. The plus, ampersand, and equal signs inserted by the Web browser as placeholders and separators are not converted.

Because hexadecimal values consist of numbers and letters between A and F, your CGI application also needs a way to designate which values are hexadecimal values and which are simply normal characters. To designate the beginning of a hexadecimal value rather than a normal character, the Web browser inserts a percent sign (`%`).

Note

Before working with form data in your CGI applications, you need to decode any URL encoding. This consists of changing all hexadecimal values back into their equivalent signs and swapping spaces for plus signs.

Tip from molly

When decoding form data, you should first split name/value pairs, change plus signs to spaces, and return hexadecimal values to their respective signs. If you do not do the hexadecimal conversion last, you can make splitting name/value pairs or replacing spaces more difficult. Remember that the user could have included ampersands or plus signs in the form data. After you decode the hexadecimal values, you will have no easy way to distinguish which ampersands and plus signs are being used as placeholders and which are part of the form data.

RETURNING DATA FROM YOUR CGI APPLICATION

After your CGI application is finished executing, it needs to return a result to the user's Web browser. This result will typically be HTML-formatted text. Most of the time, the result from the CGI application is sent through the Web server. Regardless of whether the result returns through the Web server, your CGI application must return a valid header before returning any other data.

Whether returning the header or returning other data, CGI applications typically return results by sending data to *standard output*. Standard output is the counterpart of standard input. Standard output is the default location output from a program. For example, most Windows applications use the monitor as standard output.

The CGI specification is that the Web server listens for results from a CGI application via the applications standard output. When the Web server receives results from a CGI application, it checks for a partial HTTP response header with server directives. The Web server parses the header and forms a complete HTTP response header before sending the results back to the browser.

Creating the Response Header

There are two types of response headers your CGI application can return: parsed and non-parsed. A parsed header is a partial HTTP response header. With parsed headers, the Web server must parse the response from the CGI application and form a complete HTTP response header, before sending the data on to the Web browser. Non-parsed headers, on the other hand, are valid HTTP response headers that do not require any action by the Web server.

Parsed headers can contain any of the HTTP response headers and always must be followed by a blank line. As part of your parsed header, you must include at least one server directive. Server directives are commands that are interpreted by the Web server when it parses the header, which give special instructions to the Web server. The currently defined server directives are shown in Table 35.4.

Table 35.4 Web Server Directives

Directive	Meaning
`content-type`	Designates the MIME type of the data being returned.
`location`	Designates the virtual or absolute URL to which the Web browser is to be redirected.
`status`	Contains an HTTP status code, such as 404 Not Found.

Content-type is the most commonly used server directive. It instructs the Web server that the application is returning data of the specified MIME type. The Web server uses this directive to form the Content-type HTTP response header. The Location directive specifies to the Web server to redirect the Web browser to a different URL. This new URL is then loaded in the user's Web browser. The Status directive is used to specify a status code to the Web server, such as the 404 status code—Not Found. The Status directive is the least used of these three.

When the Web server parses the header returned from a CGI application, it looks for server directives and then performs the associated action. All other HTTP response headers fields a CGI application returns as part of a parsed header become part of the HTTP response header the Web server forms and sends to the Web browser. The following parsed header is the most common one for CGI applications to return:

```
Content-type: text/html
```

Caution

Don't forget to include a blank line after your parsed and non-parsed response headers. If you don't, you will receive error messages.

CALLING CGI APPLICATIONS

After you have developed a CGI application, you are ready to call it from one of your HTML documents. There are a variety of ways in which you can call your application. The method you use will depend on the task your CGI application is designed to perform.

The most common way CGI applications are called is from the `action` attribute in the `<FORM>` tag. These CGI applications are referred to as form handlers and will be called when the form is submitted by the user. When a form is submitted, the form data will be sent to your CGI application via the `query string` environment variable or standard input, depending on whether the request method is `get` or `post`.

➔ To learn how to design forms, **see** "Building Forms," **p. 384**

CGI applications also can be called directly in `<A>`, `<IMG>`, and Server-Side Include tags. When a CGI application is set to the `href` attribute of an `<A>` tag, it will be requested whenever the user clicks the related link in the Web browser. CGI applications referenced in `<IMG>` and Server-Side Includes, on the other hand, are executed automatically by the Web server when the user requests the Web page in which these links are embedded.

For example, you could use the image tag

```
<IMG SRC="/cgi-bin/image">
```

and the Web server would execute the image CGI application and display the results as an image in the Web browser. To use this form of referencing your CGI application, you need to be sure the CGI application returns the binary data for an image.

Server-Side Includes are similar in that they are automatically executed by the Web server when the Web page is requested. Server-Side Includes have the following general syntax:

```
<!--#command tag1="value1" tag2="value2" -->
```

For CGI applications, you must use the `#exec` command to have the Web server execute your CGI application. You then specify the name of the CGI application using the `cgi` attribute. For example, the following Server-Side Include

```
<!--#exec cgi="/cgi-bin/run_me.pl" -->
```

causes the Web server to run the CGI script `run_me.pl`, embedding the results returned from the CGI script in the HTML document where the Server-Side Include was placed.

One final way you can call your CGI applications is from client-side scripts.

Client-side scripts can request any document that has a URL. Having a client-side script request a CGI application is similar to using the <A> tag in that the Web browser will send a simple HTTP request for the CGI application, causing the Web server to execute the application. However, the advantage of using a client-side script over a simple anchor is that your client-side script controls when the CGI application gets requested. With the <A> tag, you have to wait for the user to click the link.

Tip from molly

For most standard, form-style CGI functions, you'll rely on the Web server to execute the application. Reserve calling a CGI from a client-side script for larger processes such as delivery of dynamic pages within personalized sites.

USING POPULAR SCRIPTS AND APPLICATIONS

After reading through the preceding sections, you should have a basic idea of how CGI works. When a CGI application is requested, the Web server passes information to the CGI application through environment variables and sometimes through standard input as well. After the CGI application has completed its processing, the results can be sent back to the Web browser through the Web server.

To better illustrate how this communication interface works, this section will walk you through two examples of commonly used CGI applications. The first example covers the use of a feedback form on your Web site. The second demonstrates how to use a CGI script to maintain a guestbook on your Web site.

HANDLING FORM INPUT

Handling form input is one of the most common uses of CGI applications. This is in large part due to the numerous uses for forms. A form is simply a group of HTML tags that generate such elements as input fields, list boxes, check boxes, radio buttons, and push buttons. Forms allow the user viewing your Web page to interact with you or your Web site by supplying information or making a selection.

SETTING UP THE FEEDBACK FORM

In this section, you will develop a feedback form for your Web site. The first step in creating any form handler CGI scripts or programs is to create the HTML form itself. By doing so, you can identify all the form elements that will be sent to your CGI application and what types of data are to be expected.

For your feedback form, the most common fields to include are single line text input fields for the user's name and email address and a text area field for the user's comments. After stepping through this example, you could easily add additional fields, such as the user's address, phone number, or fax number, depending on your individual needs. The HTML for this feedback.html file is shown in Listing 35.1 and the resulting HTML page is shown in Figure 35.2.

LISTING 35.1 THE FEEDBACK.HTML FILE

```
<HTML>
<HEAD>
<TITLE>Feedback Form</TITLE>
</HEAD>
<BODY bgcolor="#FFFFFF">
<DIV align="center">
<TABLE border="0" width="75%">
<TR>
<TD>
<P align="center"><FONT face="Arial, Helvetica, sans-serif"><B>Feedback
Form</B></FONT><BR><BR>
<FONT face="Arial, Helvetica, sans-serif" size="-1">Please use the
form below to send us your feedback.</FONT></p>
<DIV align="center"><FORM method="post" action="/cgi-bin/feedback.pl">
<TABLE border="0" width="75%">
<TR>
<TD width="43%"><FONT face="Arial, Helvetica, sans-serif" size="-
1"><B>Name:</B></FONT></TD>
<TD width="57%">
<INPUT type="text" name="name" size="30">
</TD>
</TR>
<TR>
<TD width="43%"><FONT face="Arial, Helvetica, sans-serif" size="-1"><B>Email
Address:</B></FONT></TD>
<TD width="57%">
<INPUT type="text" name="email" size="30">
</TD>
</TR>
<TR>
<TD colspan="2"><FONT size="-1" face="Arial, Helvetica, sans-
serif"><B>Comments:</B></FONT><BR>
<TEXTAREA name="comments" cols="40" rows="5"></TEXTAREA>
</TD>
</TR>
<TR>
<TD colspan="2"><BR>
<INPUT type="submit" name="submit" value="Send">
<INPUT type="reset" name="submit2" value="Reset">
</TD>
</TR>
</TABLE>
</FORM>
</DIV>
</TD>
</TR>
</TABLE>
</DIV>
</BODY>
</HTML>
```

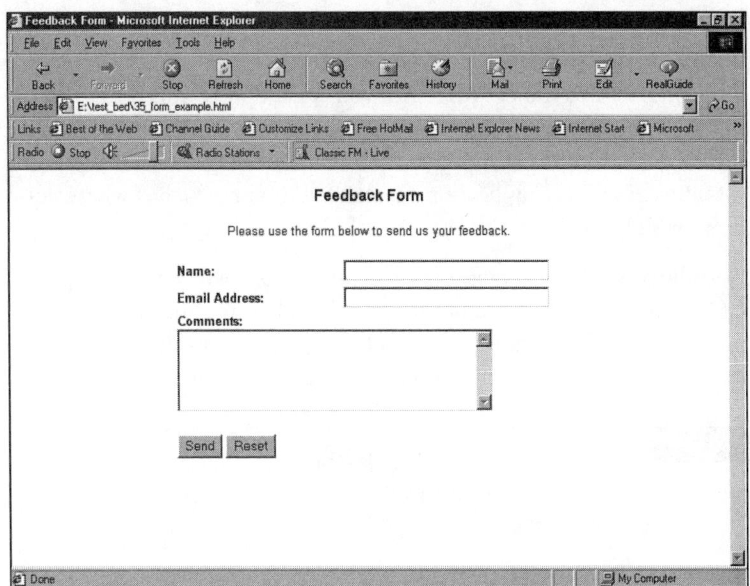

Figure 35.2 The feedback.html file as seen in Internet Explorer.

➔ For details on the various parts of a form beyond what you've seen here, **see** "Building Forms," **p. 384**

PROCESSING FORM INPUT

Now that the HTML for the feedback form is completed, you are ready to start coding the feedback.pl CGI script that will receive the data sent by the user through the form in the Web browser. The tasks your CGI script has to perform are to decode the data sent by the user, forward the data on to someone within your organization, and return a response (see Figure 35.3).

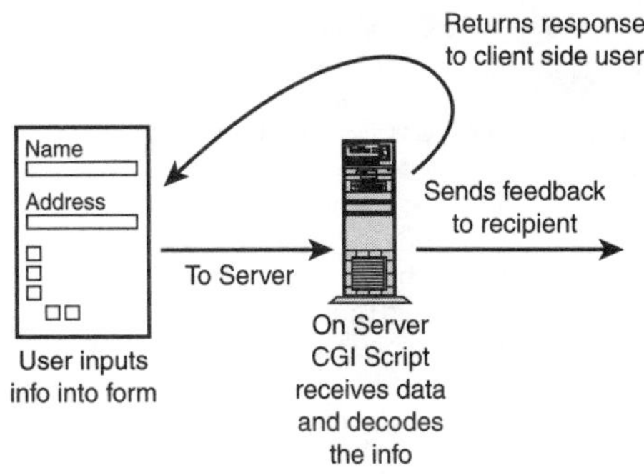

Figure 35.3 Once the CGI script receives the request from the client, it is responsible for managing the information—ensuring that any additional scripts needed run, decoding the data, forwarding the data, and returning a response to the client.

DECODING USER DATA

To decode the user data, you first need to know where the Web server has placed it. Referring back to the HTML form you created in Listing 35.1, you can see you instructed the Web browser to use the post method. In the "The post Method and Standard Input" section earlier in this chapter, you learned that when the post method is used, the user's data is sent to your CGI application via standard input, which is where you will access the user's data for this example.

Decoding user form data is a fairly common task, which you will perform in many of your CGI applications. Because of this, you should write a generic subroutine that will decode user data. You can then reuse this subroutine in any of the other CGI application that need it. Listing 35.2 contains the Perl code for a subroutine that will decode form data.

Note

The # symbol in CGI code is similar to a comment <!-- --> in HTML. It is ignored by the application running the code.

LISTING 35.2 A DECODING SUBROUTINE

```
sub User_Data {
  local (%user_data, $user_string, $name_value_pair,
         @name_value_pairs, $name, $value);

  # If the data was sent via POST, then it is available
  # from standard input. Otherwise, the data is in the
  # QUERY_STRING environment variable.
  if ($ENV{'REQUEST_METHOD'} eq "POST") {
    read(STDIN,$user_string,$ENV{'CONTENT_LENGTH'});
  } else {
    $user_string = $ENV{'QUERY_STRING'};
  }

  # This line changes the + signs to spaces.
  $user_string =~ s/\+/ /g;

  # This line places each name/value pair as a separate
  # element in the name_value_pairs array.
  @name_value_pairs = split(/&/, $user_string);

  # This code loops over each element in the name_value_pairs
  # array, splits it on the = sign, and places the value
  # into the user_data associative array with the name as the
  # key.
  foreach $name_value_pair (@name_value_pairs) {
    ($name, $value) = split(/=/, $name_value_pair);

    # These two lines decode the values from any URL
    # hexadecimal encoding. The first section searches for a
    # hexadecimal number and the second part converts the
   # hex number to decimal and returns the character
    # equivalent.
    $name =~
```

```
      s/%([a-fA-F0-9][a-fA-F0-9])/pack("C",hex($1))/ge;
    $value =~
      s/%([a-fA-F0-9][a-fA-F0-9])/pack("C",hex($1))/ge;

    # If the name/value pair has already been given a value,
    # as in the case of multiple items being selected, then
    # separate the items with a ":".
    if (defined($user_data{$name})) {
      $user_data{$name} .= ":" . $value;
    } else {
      $user_data{$name} = $value;
    }
  }
  return %user_data;
}
```

You use this subroutine by calling it with a line similar to the following:

```
%data_received = &User_Data;
```

which calls the `User_Data` subroutine and places the returned data into the `%data_received` associative array.

In the `User_Data` subroutine, the first block of code is the lines

```
if ($ENV{'REQUEST_METHOD'} eq "POST") {
  read(STDIN,$user_string,$ENV{'CONTENT_LENGTH'});
} else {
  $user_string = $ENV{'QUERY_STRING'};
}
```

These Perl statements read in the user form data from either standard input or from the `query string` environment variable, and place it in the `$user_string` variable. For this example, you know the form data will be coming from standard input. However, because this subroutine is meant to be a generic one that you can use with other CGI applications, you should handle both cases.

With the form data now in the `$user_string` variable, the `User_Data` subroutine begins to decode the data. The first step is to change all plus signs into spaces. This is easily accomplished with the following Perl statement:

```
$user_string =~ s/\+/ /g;
```

Next, all name/value pairs should be separated. Recall from earlier in this chapter that each name/value pair is separated by the ampersand. So, the following Perl statement

```
@name_value_pairs = split(/&/, $user_string);
```

splits up the `$user_string` string into separate name/value pairs. Each pair is placed as a separate element in the `@name_value_pairs` array.

The next block of code in Listing 35.2 is the following `foreach` loop, which performs several actions at the same time.

```
foreach $name_value_pair (@name_value_pairs) {
  ($name, $value) = split(/=/, $name_value_pair);

  $name =~
```

```
    s/%([a-fA-F0-9][a-fA-F0-9])/pack("C",hex($1))/ge;
  $value =~
     s/%([a-fA-F0-9][a-fA-F0-9])/pack("C",hex($1))/ge;

  if (defined($user_data{$name})) {
    $user_data{$name} .= ":" . $value;
  } else {
    $user_data{$name} = $value;
  }
}
```

This `foreach` loop will execute the statements in the body of the loop for each element in the `@name_value_pairs`. The current element, on any loop iteration, is stored in the `$name_value_pair` variable.

After inside the `foreach` loop, the name and value are separated and placed into separate variables. Then, both variables are checked for any hexadecimal values. If they contain any, the hexadecimal value is converted to its character equivalent.

At the end of the loop is an `if` statement that checks to see if there is already a name/value pair having the same name. Select statements and check boxes can return multiple name/value pairs with the same name. If there was a previous name/value pair with the same name, a colon and the new value are appended to the existing entry. Otherwise, a new associative array element is created with the name as the index and the value as the contents of that new array element.

The following is the final line in the `User_Data` subroutine:

```
return %user_data;
```

This line returns the `%user_data` associative array constructed in the previously described `foreach` loop.

EMAILING THE FEEDBACK

After the user form data has been decoded, the data is ready to be worked with. For the purposes of this example, the form data will be sent via email to the Webmaster of your site. To have your CGI script send data via email requires an SMTP mail server to send the email message. SMTP stands for Simple Mail Transfer Protocol. The way you interface with the SMTP mail server varies depending on the Web server machine you are using. Because UNIX is still the predominate Web server platform, this example will demonstrate how to do this on most UNIX machines.

From where you left off in the previous section, your feedback.pl script has the user data in an associative array named `%data_received`. If you just output this array to your email message, the data would be one long string containing all the information. To make that data easier to read, you can break it up into separate lines by using the following code.

```
foreach $key (sort keys(%data_received)) {
  $mail .= "$key:\n";
  foreach (split(" : ", $data_received{$key})) {
    $mail .= "$_\n\n";
  }
}
```

This code contains two loops. The outer one loops over each array element. An associative array is indexed by elements known as keys. So, to loop over the entire array, you have to loop over all the keys. You do this by using the Perl `keys()` function, which returns all the keys for the associative array argument between the parentheses. Each key is then assigned to the `$key` variable.

After inside the outer loop, the key value gets added the `$mail` string along with the `\n` character, which is the new line character. The inner loop then checks the value of each array element for the " : " (space colon space) characters. Recall from the `User_Data` subroutine that these characters are used to separate multiple values assigned to a single name. In this example, you are not using any form elements that would produce multiple values for a single named element. However, writing this code to handle this case allows you to add in these types of elements without changing your code. Finally, the line

```
$mail .= "$_\n\n";
```

puts the values of the name/value pairs into the string that will be sent via email.

Now that you have the message formatted for email, you can send it. For the purposes of this example, the `sendmail` SMTP server will be used. `sendmail` allows you to send the user data in an output stream, so all you have to do is open the output stream, print the email header necessary for `sendmail`, print the message string, and close the output stream. This is accomplished with the following subroutine.

```
sub Unix_Email {
  local ($message) = @_;

  open(MAIL, "¦/usr/sbin/sendmail -t") ¦¦ die "Content-type: text/text\n\nCan't
open /usr/sbin/sendmail!\n";
  print MAIL "To: webmaster\@yourdomain.com\n";
  print MAIL "From: $data_received{'email'}\n";
  print MAIL "Subject: From you Feedback Form\n";
  print MAIL "$message\n\n";

  return close(MAIL);
}
```

The line containing the `open` statement opens a new stream, which in this case is an output stream to the `sendmail` program. The path /usr/sbin/sendmail is the path to the `sendmail` program on many UNIX machines, but your path might be different. The rest of the line causes the CGI script to exit if a stream to `sendmail` cannot be opened. The four print statements all send their output to the `MAIL` stream that you just opened.

The first three print lines output the header that `sendmail` needs to properly address the email message. The final print statement outputs the `$message` variable, which contains the string that you formatted earlier. This string will be the body of the message.

RETURNING A REPLY

After the information has been received and processed, your CGI script should send some response to the user's browser to indicate that the action has been completed. For the feedback.pl example, the simplest response would be to send your home page back to the user's browser. Because this HTML page already exists, you can just send the location of the file rather than sending all the HTML tags and text. The following is the line of Perl code that returns the home page to the user's browser.

```
print "Location: http://www.yourdomain.com\n\n";
```

Now all the pieces of the feedback form are completed. Listing 35.3 contains the complete Perl code for the feedback.pl CGI script.

LISTING 35.3 THE FEEDBACK.PL SCRIPT

```
#!/usr/local/bin/perl

# Decode the user data an place it in the
# data_received associative array.
%data_received = &User_Data();

foreach $key (sort keys(%data_received)) {
  $mail .= "$key:\n";
  foreach (split(" : ", $data_received{$key})) {
    $mail .= "$_\n\n";
  }
}

&Unix_Email($mail);

print "Location: http://www.yourdomain.com\n\n";

sub Unix_Email {
  local ($message) = @_;

  open(MAIL, "¦/usr/sbin/sendmail -t") ¦¦ die "Content-type: text/text\n\nCan't
➥open /usr/sbin/sendmail!\n";
  print MAIL "To: webmaster\@yourdomain.com\n";
  print MAIL "From: $data_received{'email'}\n";
  print MAIL "Subject: From you Feedback Form\n";
  print MAIL "$message\n\n";

  return close(MAIL);
}

sub User_Data {
  local (%user_data, $user_string, $name_value_pair,
         @name_value_pairs, $name, $value);

  # If the data was sent via POST, then it is available
  # from standard input. Otherwise, the data is in the
  # QUERY_STRING environment variable.
  if ($ENV{'REQUEST_METHOD'} eq "POST") {
    read(STDIN,$user_string,$ENV{'CONTENT_LENGTH'});
  } else {
    $user_string = $ENV{'QUERY_STRING'};
  }

  # This line changes the + signs to spaces.
  $user_string =~ s/\+/ /g;
```

```
    # This line places each name/value pair as a separate
    # element in the name_value_pairs array.
    @name_value_pairs = split(/&/, $user_string);

    # This code loops over each element in the name_value_pairs
    # array, splits it on the = sign, and places the value
    # into the user_data associative array with the name as the
    # key.
    foreach $name_value_pair (@name_value_pairs) {
      ($name, $value) = split(/=/, $name_value_pair);

      # These two lines decode the values from any URL
      # hexadecimal encoding. The first section searches for a
      # hexadecimal number and the second part converts the
      # hex number to decimal and returns the character
      # equivalent.
      $name =~
        s/%([a-fA-F0-9][a-fA-F0-9])/pack("C",hex($1))/ge;
      $value =~
         s/%([a-fA-F0-9][a-fA-F0-9])/pack("C",hex($1))/ge;

      # If the name/value pair has already been given a value,
      # as in the case of multiple items being selected, then
      # separate the items with a " : ".
      if (defined($user_data{$name})) {
        $user_data{$name} .= " : " . $value;
      } else {
        $user_data{$name} = $value;
      }
    }
    return %user_data;
}
```

CREATING GUESTBOOKS

In the previous section, you learned the basics about handling form input and created a simple CGI script for handling a feedback form. This section extends the uses of form handler CGIs by demonstrating how you can use a CGI script and HTML forms to maintain a guestbook on your Web site.

A Web site guestbook is the online equivalent of guestbooks you might have seen at art galleries, museums, bed and breakfasts, or retail stores. In these establishments, a guestbook is a blank book in which guests can enter their names and addresses. If you flipped back through the book, you would see information about the people who had visited that location.

For your online guestbook, you want the user to be able to view previous entries. You also want that user to be able to enter his or her own information to the top of the list. You can accomplish all these requirements with a single CGI script. Your guestbook script will display the information of previous visitors and process the form submissions of current visitors. When your script receives a new entry to the guestbook, it will add the entry to the top of your guestbook list and display the current list to the user.

Setting Up the Sign-In Form

As with the feedback form example in the previous section, you will first need to set up the sign-in form that the user will fill out to add his or her entry to your guestbook. To do this, you must decide what information to request from the user. For this guestbook example, you will ask for the user's name, email address, home page URL, city, state, and country. You can capture all these items by using the single-line text input element. You also will include a text area in which the user can add any comments. The HTML for this guestbook.html file is shown in Listing 35.4 and the resulting HTML page is shown in Figure 35.4.

Listing 35.4 The guestbook.html File

```
<HTML>
<HEAD>
<TITLE>Guest Book Sign In</TITLE>
</HEAD>
<BODY bgcolor="#FFFFFF">
<DIV align="center">
<TABLE border="0" width="75%">
<TR>
<TD>
<FONT face="arial, Helvetica, sans-serif"><B>Guest Book
Sign In</B></FONT>
<br>
<FONT face="arial, Helvetica, sans-serif" size="-1">To sign our guest book,
Please fill out the fields below.</FONT>
<DIV align="center">
<FORM method="post" action="/cgi-Bin/guestBook.Pl" name="">
<TABLE border="0" width="75%">
<TR>
<TD width="43%"><FONT face="arial, Helvetica, sans-serif" size="-
1"><B>Name:</B></FONT></TD>
<TD width="57%">
<INPUT TYPE="text" name="name" size="30">
</TD>
</TR>
<TR>
<TD width="43%"><FONT face="arial, Helvetica, sans-serif" size="-1"><B>Email
Address:</B></FONT></TD>
<TD width="57%">
<INPUT TYPE="text" name="email" size="30">
</TD>
</TR>
<TR>
<TD width="43%"><FONT size="-1" face="arial, Helvetica, sans-serif"><B>Home
Page URL:</B></FONT></TD>
<TD width="57%">
<INPUT TYPE="text" name="url" size="30">
</TD>
</TR>
<TR>
<TD width="43%"><B><FONT size="-1" face="arial, Helvetica, sans-
serif">City:</FONT></B></TD>
<TD width="57%">
<INPUT TYPE="text" name="city" size="30">
```

```
</TD>
</TR>
<TR>
<TD width="43%"><FONT size="-1" face="arial, Helvetica, sans-
serif"><B>State:</B></FONT></TD>
<TD width="57%">
<INPUT TYPE="text" name="state" size="4">
</TD>
</TR>
<TR>
<TD width="43%"><B><FONT size="-1" face="arial, Helvetica, sans-
serif">Country:</FONT></B></TD>
<TD width="57%">
<INPUT type="text" name="country" size="30">
</TD>
</TR>
<TR>
<TD colspan="2"><FONT size="-1" face="arial, Helvetica, sans-
serif"><B>Comments:</B></FONT><BR>
<textarea name="comments" cols="40" rows="3"></textarea>
</TD>
</TR>
<TR>
<TD colspan="2"><BR>
<INPUT type="submit" name="submit" value="Sign In">
<INPUT type="reset" name="submit2" value="Reset">
</TD>
</TR>
</TABLE>
</FORM>
</DIV>
</TD>
</TR>
</TABLE>
</DIV>
</BODY>
</HTML>
```

HANDLING THE INPUT FROM THE SIGN-IN FORM

With the sign-in form complete, you can start working on the CGI script for handling the guestbook. The first thing to do is to receive the input from the sign-in form, process it, and then write it to your guestbook file. The guestbook file is a text file that holds all user entries. When you receive an entry, you will place the new information at the top of the guestbook file.

As in the feedback form example in the previous section, you first need to receive the data from the user's browser and decode it. To do so, you can use the same `User_Data` subroutine you developed in the previous section.

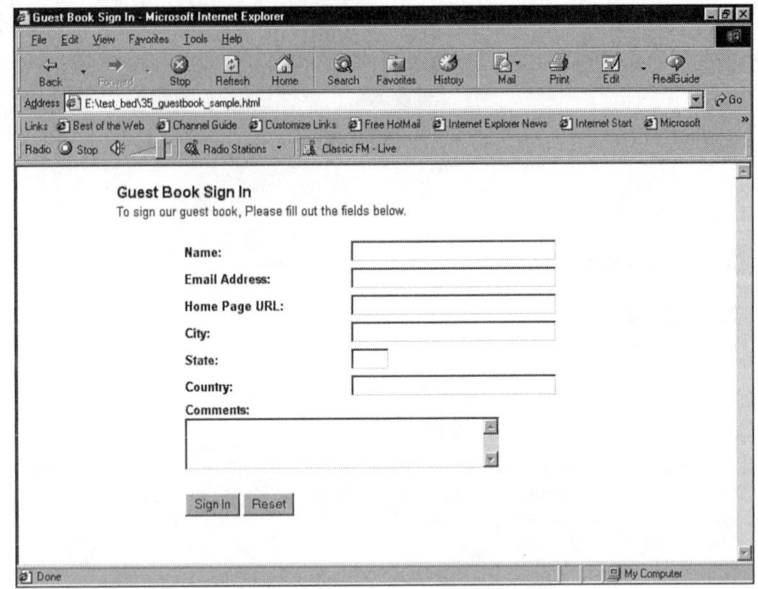

Figure 35.4
The guestbook.html file. The site visitor will fill in the form fields and submit the guestbook comment.

```
# Decode the user data and place it in the
# data_received associative array.
%data_received = &User_Data();
```

In this example, unlike the feedback form in the previous section, you will write this information to a file, later displaying the contents of this file as part of an HTML page. Because of this, you should parse the user's input for any Server-Side Include directives that the user might have entered and remove any you find. You can do this by creating a new subroutine called `noise`.

```
sub noise {
  local (*data) = @_;

  foreach $key (sort keys(%data)) {
    $data{$key} =~ s/<!—(.¦\n)*—>//g;
  }
}
```

This subroutine receives one parameter; the associative array that contains the user's input data. It then loops over each element in the array checking for Server-Side Include directives. The following line

```
$data{$key} =~ s/<!—(.¦\n)*—>//g;
```

is what actually does the work. It is a Perl regular expression that performs the search and substitution. The leading `s` tells the Perl interpreter to replace everything between the first and second slashes with the material between the second and third slashes. In this case, the pattern `<!—(.¦\n)*—>` will match any properly formatted Server-Side Include, which will be replaced with nothing (in other words, will be deleted) because there is nothing between the second and third slashes. The `g` at the end of the line tells the Perl interpreter to change all occurrences instead of only the first one it finds.

You now have the user's data properly decoded and any Server-Side Includes removed. The next thing to do is to enter the information into your guestbook file. You do this by placing all the elements of the user's information into a single string with HTML tags for formatting. This string is then added to the first line of the guestbook file.

When you set up the guestbook form, you told users they had to enter their names. That was the only mandatory field. To make sure this field has a value, you will place an `if` statement around the code to enter the entry into the guestbook file. This if statement checks whether the user's name has been entered. (Actually, it only checks whether the string is not blank. The user could enter any valid string.) If there is a value, the user's information is placed in the `$new_guest` string and that string is added to the beginning of the guestbook file. If the user did not enter a valid string for the name field, he or she is prompted to do so.

```
if ($data_received{"name"} ne "") {
    $new_guest = "<B>Name:</B> $data_received{\"name\"}<BR>\n";
    $new_guest .= "<B>Date:</B> $date<BR>\n";

    $new_guest .= "<B>E-Mail:</B> <A
HREF=\"mailto:$data_received{\"email\"}\">$data_received{\"email\"}</A><BR>\
n" if $data_received{"email"} ne "";
    $new_guest .= "<B>Home Page URL:</B> <A
HREF=\"$data_received{\"url\"}\">$data_received{\"url\"}</A><BR>\n" if
$data_received{"url"} ne "";
    $new_guest .= "$data_received{\"city\"}, " if $data_received{"city"} ne "";
    $new_guest .= "$data_received{\"state\"} " if $data_received{"state"} ne "";
    $new_guest .= "$data_received{\"country\"}<BR>\n" if $data_received{
"country"} ne "";
    $new_guest .= "<B>Comments:</B> $data_received{\"comments\"}\n" if
$data_received{"comments"} ne "";

    $new_guest .= "<P><HR><P>\n";

    open(GUESTBOOK,"$guestbookfile") || die "Content-type: text/text\n\nCannot
➥open $guestbookfile";
    @guestbook = <GUESTBOOK>;
    close(GUESTBOOK);

    unshift(@guestbook, $new_guest);

    open(GUESTBOOK,">$guestbookfile") || die "Content-type: text/text\n\nCannot
➥open $guestbookfile";

    # Lock the guestbook file now.
    flock(GUESTBOOK, 2);

    print GUESTBOOK @guestbook;

    # Unlock the guestbook file now.
    flock(GUESTBOOK, 8);

    close(GUESTBOOK);

    &Display_Book($guestbookfile);
```

```
} else {
  print "Content-type: text/html\n\n";
  print "<H1>Sign-In Unsuccessful</H1>\n";
  print "You must enter your name to be added to the guest book.";
}
```

Notice how each of the first lines within the `if` statement are in the form

```
$new_guest .= "some string" if $data_received{"some element"} ne "";
```

By adding the fields in this manner, you only add the specified element if the user entered a value for it. For example, the line that adds the user's city is

```
$new_guest .= "$data_received{\"city\"}, " if $data_received{"city"} ne "";
```

This line appends the name of the city, `$data_received{"city"}`, to the string `$new_guest` if the user entered a string in the city field of the guestbook form.

After all the user's information and HTML tags have been appended to the variable `$new_guest`, the guestbook file is opened, the contents of the file are placed within the array `@guestbook`, and the file is closed. The name of the guestbook file is stored in the `$guestbookfile` string. The code for placing the path and filename of the guestbook file within the `$guestbookfile` string is shown in Listing 35.5 at the end of this section. The line

```
unshift(@guestbook, $new_guest);
```

makes the string `$new_guest` the first element of the `@guestbook` array, moving all other contents over one index in the array. The guestbook file is then opened again and the contents of the `@guestbook` array are printed to the file, overwriting any previous contents. You might notice the use of the `flock()` Perl function before and after the contents of the `@guestbook` array are printed to the file.

This function, depending on the second parameter used, will place or remove a file lock on the specified file stream. A file lock prevents other programs, or other instances of your CGI script, from writing to the file at the same time. Because many users could be posting to your guestbook at the same time, you should lock the file to ensure only one script instance is modifying the file at a time.

If the user did not enter a valid string for the name field of the guestbook form, the `else` portion of the `if...else` statement is executed. The code in this section prints a response to the user's Web browser stating that he or she needs to enter a value for the name field.

When the user does enter a correct value for the name field and all the code under the `if` block is executed, the user data is added to the guestbook file. At this point, a logical action would be to display the contents of the guestbook to the user. Because you have to have the code for displaying the guestbook in another part of your guestbook script (for when the user just wants to display the guestbook without adding an entry first), the best way to do this is to call a subroutine that displays the guestbook, which is done with the following line:

```
&Display_Book($guestbookfile);
```

Displaying the Contents of the Guestbook

As mentioned, you still need a subroutine that displays the contents of the guestbook file. Because you already placed all relevant HTML tags with the guestbook entries, you just need to print the contents of the file, preceded with and followed by the appropriate HTML header and footer. You do this with the following code:

```
sub Display_Book {
  local ($guestbookfile) = @_;
  local (@guestbook);

  open(GUESTBOOK,"$guestbookfile") || die "Content-type: text/text\n\nCannot open
➥$guestbookfile";
  @guestbook = <GUESTBOOK>;
  close(GUESTBOOK);

  print "Content-type: text/html\n\n";
  print "<HTML><HEAD><TITLE>My Guest Book</TITLE></HEAD><BODY
bgcolor=\"#FFFFFF\"><DIV align=\"center\"><TABLE border=\"0\"
width=\"75%\"><TR><TD>";
  print "<P align=\"center\"><FONT face=\"Arial, Helvetica, sans-serif\"><B>My
➥Guest Book</b></FONT><BR><BR></P><HR width=\"75%\"><BR><BR>";
  print @guestbook;
  print " </TD></TR></TABLE></DIV></BODY></HTML> ";
}
```

This subroutine opens the guestbook file, places all the contents in the array `@guestbook`, prints the parsed header and preceding HTML tags, prints the contents of the `@guestbook` array (which is the contents of the guestbook file), and prints the ending HTML tags.

Putting It All Together

Now you have all the pieces of the guestbook script. All you need to do is to put them together. At the beginning of this section you learned that you can do the entire guestbook with one script. You can accomplish this by checking which request method is used for the CGI script. If it is `post`, the user is trying to sign the guestbook. If it is `get`, the user is trying to view the guestbook.

To make your guestbook script more readable, you can place the code for adding the user data to the guestbook in a subroutine called `Add_Guest` and use the following line to call the appropriate subroutine.

```
$ENV{"REQUEST_METHOD"} eq "POST" ?  &Add_Guest($file) : &Display_Book($file);
```

This statement checks the conditional—everything before the question mark. If the conditional is `true`, it executes the expression between the question mark and colon. If the conditional is `false`, it executes the expression after the colon.

Listing 35.5 contains the Perl code for the completed guestbook script, and Figure 35.5 shows how this guestbook, with a few sample entries, would appear in Netscape.

LISTING 35.5 THE GUESTBOOK.PL FILE

```
#!/usr/local/bin/perl

$file = "/users/robertm/guestbook.dat";
$date = localtime(time);

$ENV{"REQUEST_METHOD"} eq "POST" ?  &Add_Guest($file) : &Display_Book($file);

sub Add_Guest {
  local ($guestbookfile) = @_;
  local (%data_received, $new_guest, @guestbook);

  # Decode the user data and place it in the
  # data_received associative array.
  %data_received = &User_Data();

  &No_SSI(*data_received);

  if ($data_received{"name"} ne "") {
    $new_guest = "<B>Name:</B> $data_received{\"name\"}<BR>\n";
    $new_guest .= "<B>Date:</B> $date<BR>\n";

    $new_guest .= "<B>E-Mail:</B> <A
HREF=\"mailto:$data_received{\"email\"}\">$data_received{\"email\"}</A><BR>\
n" if $data_received{"email"} ne "";
    $new_guest .= "<B>Home Page URL:</B> <A
HREF=\"$data_received{\"url\"}\">$data_received{\"url\"}</A><BR>\n" if
$data_received{"url"} ne "";
    $new_guest .= "$data_received{\"city\"}, " if $data_received{"city"} ne "";
    $new_guest .= "$data_received{\"state\"} " if $data_received{"state"} ne "";
    $new_guest .= "$data_received{\"country\"}<BR>\n" if $data_received{
"country"} ne "";
    $new_guest .= "<B>Comments:</B> $data_received{\"comments\"}\n" if
➥$data_received{"comments"} ne "";

    $new_guest .= "<P><HR><P>\n";

    open(GUESTBOOK,"$guestbookfile") || die "Content-type: text/text\n\nCannot
➥open $guestbookfile";
    @guestbook = <GUESTBOOK>;
    close(GUESTBOOK);

    unshift(@guestbook, $new_guest);

open(GUESTBOOK,">$guestbookfile") || die "Content-type: text/text\n\nCannot open
➥$guestbookfile";

    # Lock the guestbook file now.
    flock(GUESTBOOK, 2);

    print GUESTBOOK @guestbook;

    # Unlock the guestbook file now.
    flock(GUESTBOOK, 8);

    close(GUESTBOOK);
```

```
    &Display_Book($guestbookfile);

  } else {
    print "Content-type: text/html\n\n";
    print "<H1>Sign-In Unsuccessful</H1>\n";
    print "You must enter your name to be added to the guest book.";
  }
}

sub Display_Book {
  local ($guestbookfile) = @_;
  local (@guestbook);

  open(GUESTBOOK,"$guestbookfile") || die "Content-type: text/text\n\nCannot
open $guestbookfile";
  @guestbook = <GUESTBOOK>;
  close(GUESTBOOK);

print "Content-type: text/html\n\n";
  print "<HTML><HEAD><TITLE>My Guest Book</TITLE></HEAD><BODY
bgcolor=\"#FFFFFF\"><DIV align=\"center\"><TABLE border=\"0\"
width=\"75%\"><TR><TD>";
  print "<P align=\"center\"><FONT face=\"Arial, Helvetica, sans-serif\"><B>My
➥Guest Book</B></FONT><BR><BR></p><hr width=\"75%\"><BR><BR>";
  print @guestbook;
  print " </TD></TR></TABLE></DIV></BODY></HTML> ";
}

sub No_SSI {
  local (*data) = @_;

  foreach $key (sort keys(%data)) {
    $data{$key} =~ s/<!—(.|\n)*—>//g;
  }

}

sub User_Data {
  local (%user_data, $user_string, $name_value_pair,
         @name_value_pairs, $name, $value);

  # If the data was sent via POST, then it is available
  # from standard input. Otherwise, the data is in the
  # QUERY_STRING environment variable.
  if ($ENV{"REQUEST_METHOD"} eq "POST") {
    read(STDIN,$user_string,$ENV{"CONTENT_LENGTH"});
  } else {
    $user_string = $ENV{"QUERY_STRING"};
  }

  # This line changes the + signs to spaces.
  $user_string =~ s/\+/ /g;

  # This line places each name/value pair as a separate
  # element in the name_value_pairs array.
  @name_value_pairs = split(/&/, $user_string);
```


continues

LISTING 35.5 CONTINUED

```
  # This code loops over each element in the name_value_pairs
  # array, splits it on the = sign, and places the value
  # into the user_data associative array with the name as the
  # key.
  foreach $name_value_pair (@name_value_pairs) {
    ($name, $value) = split(/=/, $name_value_pair);

    # These two lines decode the values from any URL
    # hexadecimal encoding. The first section searches for a
    # hexadecimal number and the second part converts the
    # hex number to decimal and returns the character
    # equivalent.
    $name =~
      s/%([a-fA-F0-9][a-fA-F0-9])/pack("C",hex($1))/ge;
    $value =~
       s/%([a-fA-F0-9][a-fA-F0-9])/pack("C",hex($1))/ge;

    # If the name/value pair has already been given a value,
    # as in the case of multiple items being selected, then
    # separate the items with a " : ".
    if (defined($user_data{$name})) {
      $user_data{$name} .= " : " . $value;
    } else {
      $user_data{$name} = $value;
    }
  }
  return %user_data;
}
```

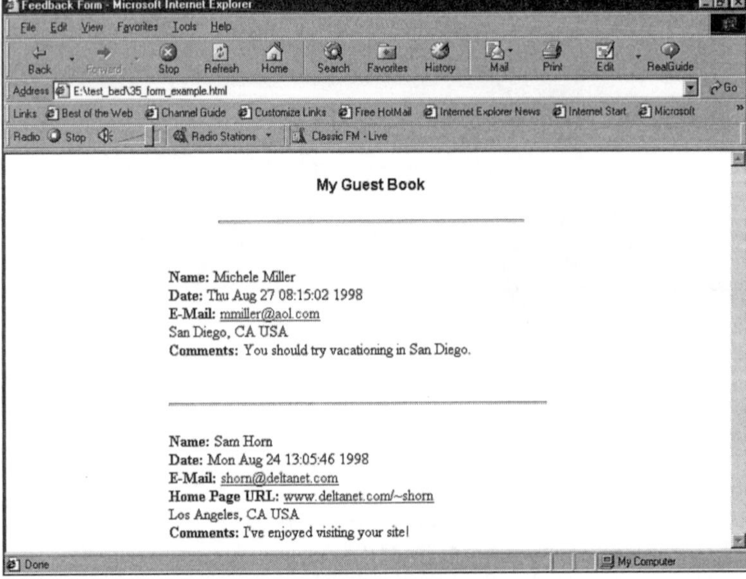

Figure 35.5
Sample contents of the guestbook as the site visitor would see them.

PRE-PROCESSING TECHNIQUES WITH SERVER-SIDE INCLUDES (SSIs)

Pre-Processing is the term applied to having the Web server perform some parsing of your HTML files prior to returning the contents of the file to the user's Web browser. The purpose for having a file pre-processed is to have the Web server add in some dynamic data to the document, such as the current date and time. Currently, there are many ways you can add pre-processing techniques to your Web pages. However, only Server-Side Includes make use of the CGI.

Server-Side Includes are actually an HTML feature that allow you to embed other items in an HTML file. The syntax for a Server-Side Include is

```
<!--#command name="value1" name2="value2" ...-->
```

The feature of Server-Side Includes that is most interesting to our discussion is their capability to include a call to a CGI program. The syntax for a Server-Side Include that calls a CGI program makes use of the exec command and looks like

```
<!--#exec cgi="/cgi-bin/cgi-script.pl"-->
```

Server-Side Includes work through a process known as server parsing. For normal Web pages, the Web server receives the request and then returns the requested Web page, without looking through the contents of the file. With server parsing, the Web Server will skim through the contents of your HTML file looking for server-based commands, such as Server-Side Includes. When it finds one, it performs the requested action, and places the results of the action in the place of the Server-Side Include statement.

Note

With Server-Side Includes, you could have the CGI program provide part of the contents of the Web page. A common application of this is to call a CGI script that inserts a page counter, displaying the number of times that Web page has been requested.

TROUBLESHOOTING

THE POWER OF PERL

Perl seems to be the server-side scripting language of choice for so many people. Why does this continue to hold true despite the influx of other server-side technologies?

Perl is a very powerful language that also is available on just about every platform imaginable, so you can use it whether your server is of the Unix or Windows variety—as long as the systems administrator has it installed and enabled.

With an amazing and dedicated (if not downright fanatic) fan base, Perl resources abound. Perl is an open-source language, meaning that it is completely free. This, combined with its power and flexibility, make it an extremely attractive choice for server-side scripting.

Note

Learn more about Perl with a visit to `http://www.perl.com/`.

TERRORS OF CGI ERRORS

I've been getting a lot of errors when working with CGI scripts. What's going on?

Because CGI is working with a number of variables including `httpd` methods and servers, the form variables, and a script, there's a lot of potential debugging to do. When in doubt, simplify what you're trying to do and build back up, testing as you go along. Also, keep information about your server handy—server documentation will often have lists of errors and their causes, helping you to find the cause of your errors and easily fix them.

DESIGNING FOR THE REAL WORLD

CREATING A PLAIN TEXT ACCESS COUNTER

Access counters are used to display the number of times your page has been requested and can be displayed by using graphical numbers or simple text numbers. Because a text counter uses plain text, it is much easier to implement than a graphical counter.

Before starting your CGI script, you should spend a moment thinking about what it must do. The script needs access to the current value of the access counter. For this information to be available, you must store it in a text file. Every time your text access counter script is called, it opens the counter file in which the current access count is stored, increments the access count, and saves the new number in the counter file. After the counter value has been incremented, the number is included in the Web page.

Your text access counter first needs to read in the current access count, which is stored in the counter file. For this example, the text file containing the access count will be named count.dat. You can read in the value stored in `count.dat` simply by opening the file and reading the first line into the variable `$count`, as in the following lines of Perl code:

```
open(COUNT, "$file") || die "Content-type: text/html\n\nCannot open counter
file!";
$count = <COUNT>;
close(COUNT);
```

The first line opens the file whose name is stored in the variable `$file`. You set this variable to the path and filename of the `count.dat` file on your system. This will be shown in the completed script later in this section.

Now that you have the code to get the current value of the access counter, you need to increment the value and write the new value to the counter file. You can easily increment the value by using the ++ operator. If you append this operator to a variable name, the integer value stored in the variable is increased by 1. For example, if the current value of the access counter were 2, the following Perl code

```
$count++;
```

would change the value to 3.

After the access count has been incremented, you need to store the new value in the counter file for the next time the script is called. The following lines of Perl code open the counter file and write the new access count to the file:

```
open(COUNT, ">$file") || die "Content-type: text/html\n\nCannot open counter
file!";
flock(COUNT, 2);
print COUNT $count;
flock(COUNT, 8);
close(COUNT);
```

Notice the use of the `flock()` Perl function again. Because you are writing to a file and multiple instances of your CGI script might be running at the same time, you should ensure that only one instance will be writing to the file at a time.

For easy readability of your script, you should place this code to increment the counter into a subroutine. For this example, you can name the subroutine `Increment`.

Now that the script can increment the counter, all that remains is to return the value of the counter for display in the Web page. You can do this by using the following three lines of Perl:

```
$access_number = &Increment;
print "Content-type: text/html\n\n";
print $access_number;
```

The first line calls the `Increment` subroutine and assigns the return value to the variable `$access_number`. The next line prints the required parsed header. The last line prints the value of the access counter. The completed access.pl script is shown in Listing 35.6.

Listing 35.6 The access.pl File

```
#!/usr/local/bin/perl

# All users need to change the value of this
# variable to the path for their machine.
$file = "/users/robertm/count.dat";

$access_number = &Increment;
print "Content-type: text/html\n\n";
print $access_number;

sub Increment {
  local ($count);

  # Get the current value of the access counter.
  open(COUNT, "$file") || die "Content-type: text/html\n\nCannot open counter
file!";
  $count = <COUNT>;
  close(COUNT);

  # Increment the access counter
;
  $count++;
```

continues

LISTING 35.6 CONTINUED

```
  # Store the value of the counter in the counter1 file.
  open(COUNT, ">$file") || die "Content-type: text/html\n\nCannot open counter
file!";
  flock(COUNT, 2);
  print COUNT $count;
  flock(COUNT, 8);
  close(COUNT);

  return $count;
}
```

Before using the access counter, you'll want to supply the file count.dat with the initial count value. This is called *seeding the counter*. Normally, you can simply create a text file with the number 0 on the first line. This will start your counter at zero.

To add your counter to your HTML file by using Server-Side Includes, simply choose which Web page you want to display your counter and add some surrounding text and the following Server-Side Include:

```
<!--#exec cgi="/cgi-bin/access.pl" -->
```

When the HTML page you add this line to is requested, the Web server will parse this line before sending the file to the user's Web browser. The CGI script access.pl will be executed and the output from the script is substituted for the preceding line in the HTML.

For example, the HTML code in Listing 35.7 demonstrates how to add the Server-Side Include statement to your existing HTML page with the resulting Web page shown in Figure 35.6

LISTING 35.7 AN HTML PAGE WITH AN ACCESS COUNTER

```
<HTML>
<HEAD>
<TITLE>My Home Page</TITLE>
</HEAD>
<BODY bgcolor="#FFFFFF">
<DIV align="center">
<TABLE border="0" width="75%">
<TR>
<TD height="76">
<P align="center"><FONT face="Arial, Helvetica, sans-serif"><B>My Home
Page </B></FONT><BR>
<BR>
<FONT face="Arial, Helvetica, sans-serif" size="-1">Thank you for visiting
my home page.</FONT></p>
<P align="center"><FONT face="Arial, Helvetica, sans-serif" size="-1">This
page has been accessed
<!—#exec cgi="/cgi-bin/access.pl" —>
times.</FONT></p>
</TD>
</TR>
```

```
</TABLE>
</DIV>
</BODY>
</HTML>
```

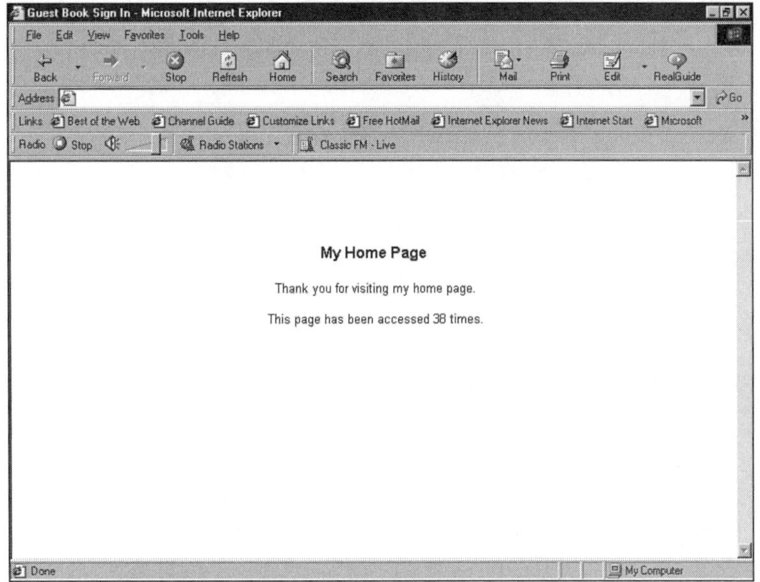

Figure 35.6
The Server-Side Include access counter.

CHAPTER 36

Active Server Pages (ASP) and Related Tools

In this chapter

GETTING STARTED USING ASP

Active Server Pages (ASP) is proving to be one of the major technologies used in Web and intranet applications development today. If you need to access a database, ASP provides an easy and flexible way to do so. An Active Server Page resides, as the name implies, on the server(s). ASPs are simple in concept—files that are executed on the server that contains both HTML and scripting code. ASP is flexible; it supports VBScript, Java, and JavaScript. An Active Server Page can be called from any HTML page as well as from other ASP pages. Active Server Pages use the extension .asp.

Note

ASP technology was developed for use on Windows NT servers running Microsoft IIS, but has proved so powerful that many companies are now offering ASP technology for other environments as well. Chilisoft, a leader in ASP technology for third parties, offers ASP for many UNIX environments and alternative Web servers.

Simple to learn, yet very powerful in its capability, ASP allows for dynamic forms and content, access to databases, updating of content, and customization on a per-user basis. ASP is not a language or an application, rather, it's more like a technology for designing interactive Web pages.

To use ASP, you need a supported environment. There are no special tools or editors required, just server-side ASP support, which is native on Windows NT and optional on many other systems.

The simplest method of creating ASP pages is to simply create an HTML page and then change the file extension to .asp; this permits you to use any editor to make an Active Server Page.

Many tools are available to automate and integrate the ASP and scripting process. These tools are discussed later in the chapter. An ASP can be a simple little bit of code or a complex and sophisticated piece of logic.

Note

ASP and Dynamic HTML sound similar in terms of being able to create active, or dynamic, pages. In fact, they perform much in the same manner. However, ASP code is interpreted and then converted to HTML on the server before sending the results back to the browser. Dynamic HTML is interpreted by the client. ASP is a server-side technology and Dynamic HTML is client-side technology.

→ For more information on using DHTML, **see** "Working with Dynamic HTML (DHTML)," **p. 451**

USING CLIENT-SIDE VERSUS SERVER-SIDE SCRIPTING

Scripting adds life to your Web page or intranet application. It can make a static page an interactive user- and data-aware page. Scripting generally occurs either on the client or the server. Client-side scripting is embedded in an HTML page, and server-side scripting is most often found in an ASP.

CLIENT-SIDE SCRIPTING

Client-side scripting has many uses. For your database-driven Web applications discussions, one of the most useful applications of client-side scripting is for data entry validation. A client-side script is the ideal tool to check ranges and dates, and to incorporate logic into the data entry process or into a form. Client-side scripting is also used for providing animation and validating users.

Note

Client-side scripting is becoming a popular alternative to CGI scripts for validation and other tasks. The benefit is that no network traffic is generated with most client-side scripting.

➔ Another good example of server-side scripting with similar applications to ASP is CGI, **see** "CGI and Pre-Processing Fundamentals," **p. 736**

SERVER-SIDE SCRIPTING

Server-side scripting is often embedded in Active Server Pages. This is where data access and heavy-duty processing can be performed, optimizing performance of the server and improving response time to the user.

ASP code is used in conjunction with HTML to create dynamic pages. In fact, ASP can actually create HTML code.

Listing 36.1 shows a sample client-side script. This script is used to calculate a simple average on a page. Compare this to Listing 36.2, which is a server-side script using ASP. The server-side script is part of a complex ASP page.

LISTING 36.1 CLIENT-SIDE SCRIPT

```
<SCRIPT LANGUAGE = "VBScript">

<! —
Function DoAverage(visit,days)
Dim Total
Total = (visit*days)/2
DoAverage = Total
End Function
!— >
</SCRIPT>
```

LISTING 36.2 SERVER-SIDE SCRIPT (ASP)

```
Set Cn1 = CreateObject( "ADODB.Connection.1.5" )
Cn1.ConnectionString = "DRIVER={Microsoft ODBC for
Oracle};SERVER=MME;UID=mme;PWD=mme;"
Cn1.Open
```

continues

LISTING 36.2 CONTINUED

```
Source = "SELECT * FROM MME.PATIENT WHERE PATIENT.ID = MEDORDER.PATIENT AND
((PATIENT.NEXTDOSE Is Not Null AND (MEDORDER.DISCONTINUETIME>TO_DATE('"&
CurrentTime &"','MM-DD-YYYY HH24:MI:SS')))"
Set Rs1 = CreateObject( "ADODB.Recordset.1.5" )
Rs1.Open Source, Cn1, adOpenForwardOnly
```

As you can see, there are differences in the way the code is presented. On the client-side, the code is managed within the `SCRIPT` element and written in Visual Basic Script. The second code sample is more customized to the complex requirements of the server.

REVIEWING ASP VARIABLES AND OBJECTS

ASP uses an object model similar to that found in Visual Basic.

The following are the basic objects used in ASP:

TABLE 36.1 BASIC OBJECTS USED IN ASP

Object	Description
Request	This object is used to retrieve information entered on a form or to identify a user.
Response	Several properties and methods are available to the Response object. They all are used to make cookies perform their job. You can redirect users, format the value of a cookie, terminate ASP processing, write output to HTTP as a string, and more.
Session	The Session object generates a session id that is stored as a session cookie to keep track of each user session. It controls timeouts and other information about a user session.
Application	Although a Session object is user specific, the Application object spans all users of an ASP-based application.
Server	The Server object is the interface to Active Server Components. These are OLE Automation Components. Active Server Components include critical items such as data access, file access, content linking, and browser capabilities.

UNDERSTANDING ACTIVE SERVER TECHNIQUES AND COMPONENTS

Both VBScript and JavaScript are scripting language choices that have gained prominence within ASP. Although they share many capabilities, some differences exist. It is the differences that often determine the choice of a scripting language. You should note that it is not an all or none choice, you can mix scripting languages in the same application if needed. That is why all scripting is preceded with a `<LANGUAGE>` tag.

Tip from molly

JavaScript is supported by almost every browser, VBScript is only supported on Microsoft browsers. If cross-browser support is necessary, JavaScript is the natural choice.

The tight integration of VBScript with Internet Explorer and Microsoft Operating Systems provides VBScript with enhanced capabilities. You can interact with the OS with VBScript and ActiveX controls. JavaScript is not designed to interact with the OS. Your specific application will determine the choice of scripting language.

Listing 36.3 shows an ASP containing complex VBScript and logic that also calls another ASP from within this page. This example includes different kinds of logic, loops, and other constructs.

LISTING 36.3 COMPLEX VBSCRIPT

```
<%@ LANGUAGE=VBScript%>
<%Option Explicit%>
<!—#include File="adovbs.inc"—>
<HTML>
<META http-Equiv="Refresh" Content="180">
<TITLE>Emar</TITLE>
<BODY>
<%
Dim Source, Connect, Rs1, Cn1, Rs2
dim x, CurrentTime, count, Color
CurrentTime = Month(now()) & "-" & Day(now()) & "-" & year(now()) & " " &
hour(now()) & ":" & minute(now()) & ":" & second(now())

Set Cn1 = CreateObject( "ADODB.Connection.1.5" )Cn1.Connection
String = "DRIVER={Microsoft ODBC for Oracle};SERVER=Emar;UID=mme;PWD=mmee;"
Cn1.Open

Source = "SELECT PATIENT.ID, PATIENT.FIRSTNAME, PATIENT.LASTNAME, PATIENT.
NEXTDOSE, PATIENT.ROOM, PATIENT.BED FROM MMS.MEDORDER MEDORDER, MMS.PATIENT
PATIENT WHERE PATIENT.ID = MEDORDER.PATIENT AND ((PATIENT.
NEXTDOSE Is Not Null) AND (MEDORDER.NEXTDOSE Is Null) AND
(MEDORDER.DISCONTINUETIME Is Null) OR (MEDORDER.DISCONTINUETIME>TO_DATE('"&
CurrentTime &"','MM-DD-YYYY HH24:MI:SS')))"
Set Rs1 = CreateObject( "ADODB.Recordset.1.5" )
Rs1.Open Source, Cn1, adOpenForwardOnly

'Set Rs2 = CreateObject( "ADODB.Recordset.1.5" )

If Rs1.BOF AND Rs1.EOF then
      Response.Write "There Are No Patients to show"
else
%>
      <SCRIPT language=VBScript>
      Sub Test(IDNUMBER)
            document.location = "information.asp?ID=" & IDNUMBER
      end sub
      </SCRIPT>
      <TABLE border=1 bgcolor=gray bordercolor=gray bordercolorlight=white
```

continues

LISTING 36.3 CONTINUED

```
bordercolordark=black align=center cellpadding=0 cellspacing=0 maxlength=20>
      <TR>
   <%
      for x = 1 to 5
            do until Rs1.EOF or count = 7

                  Source = "SELECT * FROM MEDORDER WHERE PATIENT='" & Rs1("ID")
& "'"' AND discontinuetime > TO_DATE('" & CurrentTime & "', 'MM-DD-YYYY
H24:MI:SS')
AND nextdose IS NOT NULL"
'                 Rs2.Open Source, Cn1, adOpenForwardOnly
'                 if not (Rs2.BOF and Rs2.EOF) then
                        count = count + 1
                        Color = "Gray"
                        %>
                        <TD bgcolor='<%Response.Write Color%>' width=200
align=center height=100 onClick="test('<%response.write Rs1("ID")%>')">
                        <FONT Name=Arial SIZE=4 Color=Blue>
                        <%Response.write Rs1("LastName")%><BR>
                        <%Response.write Rs1("FirstName")%><BR></FONT>
                        <FONT Name = Arial SIZE=2 Color=blue>RM:
                        <%Response.write Rs1("Room")%>
                         Bed:
                        <%Response.write Rs1("Bed")%><BR>
                              <BR>
                        <%Response.write Rs1("NEXTDOSE")
'                 end if
'                 Rs2.close
                  Rs1.MoveNext
            loop
            count = 0
            %>
    </FONT>
            <TR>
   <%
      next
      Rs1.Close
      Cn1.Close
      Set Cn1 = Nothing
      Set Rs1 = Nothing
'     set Rs2 = nothing
      %>
      </TR>
      </TABLE>
      </BODY>
      </html>
<%
end if
%>
```

INTEGRATING DATABASES AND ASP

Active Data Objects (ADO) has become the key to Microsoft's data access strategy. It is the first universal data access method that supports multiple database technologies and programming environments. You can use ADO in a straight VB, Java, C++ or other application, as well as in an ASP. ADO is comfortable in almost any environment.

There are other data access technologies with which you may be familiar. The first is Data Access Objects (DAO). This was Microsoft's standard for VB, Access, and other Jet-based environments. DAO is still in wide use today. It is ill suited for the Web and performs best in traditional client-server applications using JET.

Getting lost in the face of all of the options available to you? See, "Server-Side Technologies: Which to Choose?" in the Troubleshooting section at the end of this chapter.

Remote Data Objects (RDO) was the precursor to ADO and is still in wide use today. RDO is mature and supports many different Relational Database Management Systems (RDBMS) through Open Database Connectivity (ODBC). RDO also includes several tools for creating and accessing queries.

ADO improves on the RDO foundation and includes specific features for Web-based applications. ADO made the programming process simpler and more powerful than DAO and RDO by streamlining the hierarchy.

ADO is the ideal choice for data access with Microsoft's Internet Information Server (IIS). ADO is language independent and, when used with Remote Data Service (RDS), ADO exposes data to any client via server-side scripting.

Data access methods such as ADO require a data provider. Data providers can take several forms; ODBC is one of them. A better performer is Object Linking and Embedding Database (OLEdb). OLEdb is COM based, providing easy access to a wide variety of data sources. Any OLEdb provider can expose data to ADO.

One of the compelling qualities of ADO is that it is much flatter than RDO or DAO so you do not have to build a hierarchy. Listing 36.4 is a data connection code example. If you're a database manager, you'll want to compare this code to DAO or RDO.

LISTING 36.4 DATA CONNECTION CODE EXAMPLE

```
Set Cn1 = CreateObject( "ADODB.Connection.1.5" )
Cn1.ConnectionString = "DRIVER={Microsoft ODBC for
Oracle};SERVER=Emar;UID=mme;PWD=mmee;"
Cn1.Open
Source = "SELECT * FROM MMS.PATIENT"
 Set Rs1 = CreateObject( "ADODB.Recordset.1.5" )
Rs1.Open Source, Cn1, adOpenForwardOnly
```

ADO Objects include the `Connection` object, which controls the connection to the database:

```
Set Cn1 = CreateObject( "ADODB.Connection.1.5" )
Cn1.ConnectionString = "DRIVER={Microsoft ODBC for
Oracle};SERVER=Emar;UID=mme;PWD=mmee;"
```

The `Command` object is used to execute a specific command on a database. You do not have to build a hierarchy of objects to carry out a command:

```
Set Cmd1 = New ADODB.Command
Set Cmd1.ActiveConnection = Conn1
Cmd1.CommandText = "SELECT * FROM Authors WHERE AU_ID < ?"
```

```
Set Param1 = Cmd1.CreateParameter(, adInteger, adParamInput, 10)
Param1.Value = 10
Cmd1.Parameters.Append Param1
Set Param1 = Nothing

Set Rs1 = Cmd1.Execute()
```

The `Recordset` object is used to manipulate rows in the database. A `Recordset` can contain the results of a query. The cursor type is also part of the `Recordset` object:

```
Source = "SELECT * FROM MMS.PATIENT"
 Set Rs1 = CreateObject( "ADODB.Recordset.1.5" )
Rs1.Open Source, Cn1, adOpenForwardOnly
```

The `Fields` object references a particular column in a recordset. Use this object to change the contents of a field:

```
Dim F as variant

  F = Rs1.Fields.Item("Au_ID").Value
  F = Rs1.Fields.Item(0).Value
  F = Rs1.Fields("Au_ID").Value
  F = Rs1.Fields(0).Value
  F = Rs1("Au_ID").Value
  F = Rs1(0).Value
  F = Rs1!Au_ID
```

The `Property` object is used to determine what specific properties are supported by the OLEdb provider. One of these might include support for advanced functions such as transactions.

The `Parameter` object is the vehicle for passing parameters. These can be passed to a stored procedure, a query, or to the database (see Listing 36.5).

LISTING 36.5 EXAMPLE OF THE `Parameter` OBJECT

```
Sub ParameterX()
Dim dbsNorthwind As Database
Dim qdfReport As QueryDef
Dim prmBegin As Parameter
Dim prmEnd As Parameter
Set dbsNorthwind = OpenDatabase("Northwind.mdb") ' Create temporary QueryDef
object with two ' parameters.
Set qdfReport = dbsNorthwind.CreateQueryDef("", _ "PARAMETERS dteBegin DateTime,
dteEnd DateTime; " & _ "SELECT EmployeeID, COUNT(OrderID) AS NumOrders " & _
"FROM Orders WHERE ShippedDate BETWEEN " & _ "[dteBegin] AND [dteEnd] GROUP BY
EmployeeID " & _ "ORDER BY EmployeeID") Set prmBegin =
qdfReport.Parameters!dteBegin
Set prmEnd = qdfReport.Parameters!dteEnd
  ' Print report using specified parameter values.
ParametersChange qdfReport, prmBegin, #1/1/95#, _ prmEnd, #6/30/95#
ParametersChange qdfReport, prmBegin, #7/1/95#, _ prmEnd, #12/31/95#
dbsNorthwind.CloseEnd Sub
```

Finally, the `Error` object provides a method of collecting error information when attempting to perform a database function. Errors are captured within this object:

```
<HTML>
<HEAD>
  <SCRIPT LANGUAGE="VBScript">
<!–
Sub Procedure1()
  on error resume next

  badcommand

  if len(err.description) > 1 then
   msgbox "error is: " & err.description
  end if
```

The integration of databases and ASP provides some of the most powerful backend functionality available to Web developers today. Whether used as a method to deliver e-commerce, or as a means by which to create complex intranet management systems, ASP and database integration has gained a strong foothold as a viable solution for complex site management.

Using ASP Tools

Many tools have become available to assist in creating Active Server Pages. Some are integrated into the development environment, such as Visual InterDev (see Figure 36.1), and others are available as standalone products such as ASP Table Wizard.

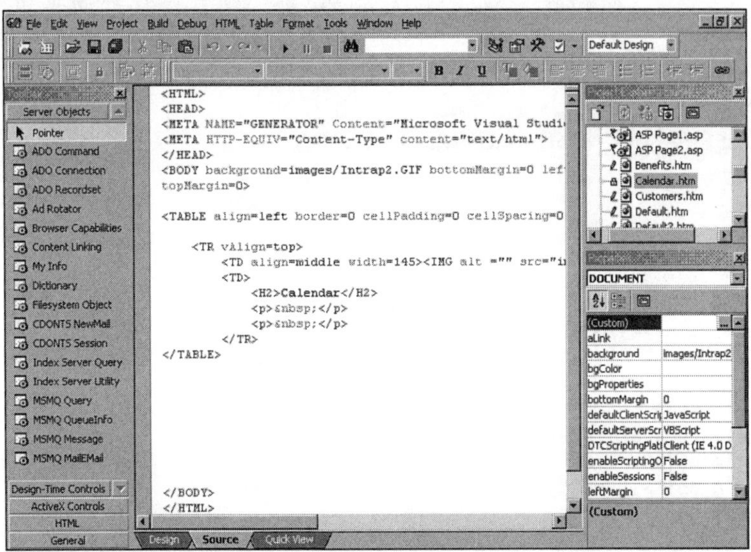

Figure 36.1 Visual InterDev exposes all the objects for ADO in an easy-to-reference manner, just drag and drop. These are used in the construction of an ASP or HTML page.

The ASP Table Wizard (see Figure 36.2) is one of many standalone ASP generators.

Figure 36.2
This product uses a series of VB-like wizards that prompts you through every step of making an Active Server Page.

Listing 36.6 is the output of the wizard.

Note

An evaluation copy of the ASP Table Wizard is available at **http://www.paulsimmons.com/**. Other ASP development products are available from **http://www.infomentum.com/** and **http://www.dameware.com/**.

LISTING 36.6 ASP TABLE WIZARD OUTPUT

```
<%

Option Explicit

'------------------------.
'-- Generated by the ASP Table Wizard --
'-- http://www.paulsimmons.com --
'------------------------.

Dim iCount
Dim sRowColor
Dim objDB
Dim objRS
Dim sDBName

'TODO: Verify database path...
sDBName = "driver={Microsoft Access Driver
(*.mdb)};dbq=d:\50199\50199\db\Northwind.mdb"
```

```
Set objDB = Server.CreateObject("ADODB.Connection")
objDB.Open sDBName

'TODO: Modify the next line to only return the records you want...
Set objRS = objDB.Execute("select * from Products")

Response.Write("<HTML>")
Response.Write("<HEAD>")
Response.Write("<TITLE>Paul Simmons Dot Com</title>")
Response.Write("</HEAD>")
Response.Write("<BODY bgcolor=white>")

Response.Write("<h3>ASP Table Wizard</h3>")
Response.Write("<A href=codebrws.asp?source=tablewiz.asp><div class=tiny>Steal
this code</div></A><P>")

If objRS.EOF Then
Response.Write("<B>No matching records found.</B>")
objRS.Close
objDB.Close
Set objRS = Nothing
Set objDB = Nothing
Response.End
End If

Response.Write("<TABLE border=0 cellpadding=2 cellspacing=2>")
Response.Write("<TR bgcolor=silver>")

'COOL TIP: the <FILTER> tag is used by Excel 97
'if your users save this file from the browser and open it in XL 97, XL will
'parse all the table cells into XL ranges and turn on filtering...

Response.Write("<TH filter=ALL>Productid</TH>")
Response.Write("<TH filter=ALL>Productname</TH>")
Response.Write("<TH filter=ALL>Supplierid</TH>")
Response.Write("<TH filter=ALL>Categoryid</TH>")
Response.Write("<TH filter=ALL>Quantityperunit</TH>")
Response.Write("</TR>")

Do While Not objRS.EOF
'this code alternates the color of the table rows...
iCount = iCount + 1
If iCount Mod 2 = 0 Then
sRowColor = "skyblue"
Else
sRowColor = "#C4CEE5"
End If

Response.Write("<TR bgcolor=" & sRowColor & ">")
Response.Write("<TD align=right>" & objRS("Productid") & "</TD>")
Response.Write("<TD>" & objRS("Productname") & "</TD>")
Response.Write("<TD align=right>" & objRS("Supplierid") & "</TD>")
Response.Write("<TD align=right>" & objRS("Categoryid") & "</TD>")
Response.Write("<TD>" & objRS("Quantityperunit") & "</TD>")
Response.Write("</TR>")
```

continues

LISTING 36.6 CONTINUED

```
objRS.MoveNext
Loop

Response.Write("</TABLE>")
Response.Write("</BODY>")
Response.Write("</HTML>")

objRS.Close
objDB.Close
Set objRS = Nothing
Set objDB = Nothing

%>
```

Tip from molly

As with HTML and any other coding technique, whether you write ASP code by hand or using an application, it's always beneficial to ensure that the code output is readable and correct.

KNOWING ASP CONCERNS

Several considerations to be aware of when using ASP include security, optimization of performance, browsers, debugging, and selection of the right data management techniques.

SECURITY

Security is an important issue today. Proper security procedures must be observed on every layer of the application environment.

Be sure to observe manufacturer's recommendations for securing your Web server, Web application server, database, and operating system. Keep all your Web components in separate directories so that you can control the rights to each type of component. For example, placing ASP pages in a read/write environment permits a user to see the contents of the ASP (such as the connection string to the database).

Use SSL (Secure Sockets Layer) where appropriate. This is the standard for many e-commerce applications. There are also other encrypting techniques available.

Note

SET has gained a lot of momentum. Many companies are now supporting the SET framework.

Internet Explorer also supports code signing or certificates. These are other ways to ensure the origin of any component downloaded by the browser.

Performance Optimizing

One of the best performance enhancing tools available for database drive applications is RAM. Adding RAM is the single greatest hardware improvement you can make in most environments. Also observe manufacturer recommendations for database tuning.

The following are some other performance improvement technique choices:

- Use OLEdb instead of ODBC.
- Scope all variables.
- Use client-side scripting for validation of data.
- Use server-side includes.
- Declare with the `<OBJECT>` tag.
- Use Design Time Controls with Visual InterDev.
- Use ADO for data access.
- Use transactions where possible.
- Use connection pooling.
- Use a Web application sever that includes load balancing and transaction monitoring.

Choosing the Right Database

There has been much discussion and much written about which database is best. There is no correct answer. Your goal should be to arrive at choices that are the best fit for your application.

➔ To learn more about databases and the Web, **see** "Database Basics," **p. 790**

As a rule, small databases with limited numbers of users on a single server work fine with file server–type databases such as Access or Filemaker Pro.

e-Commerce applications—large databases supporting many users—require a RDBMS such as Oracle, Sybase, SQL Server, Informix, or one of the other competitive products. There are a lot of database choices, and often manufacturers offer tools to help scale from a file server–type database to a full RDBMS. Avoid this step if you can and do it right the first time and you'll save time and money.

Almost all manufacturers offer demo or trial versions of their products. If you are engaging a large project, get the trials and perform some tests. Test drive all the tools you will use together, and then make your final choices.

Choosing the Appropriate Data Access Method

Not long ago this was a subject of some debate. In recent months, however, it has become clear that ADO is the data access method of choice for many environments.

If you are not using any Microsoft products and want a pure Java solution, the only viable answer is JDBC, a cousin to ODBC. JDBC, Corba, and EJB are technologies that are just coming into wide use in most non-Microsoft environments.

Every RDBMS vendor supports both environments. Also, be sure to coordinate the capabilities of your front-end development tools with your server technologies.

BROWSER SUPPORT

The browser situation has evolved into two camps. Internet Explorer and everyone else. Internet Explorer has over 50% of the marketplace. The real issue comes to the support of VBScript and ActiveX technology in the browser.

With the large number of developers who know VB and use ActiveX technology, this is something that needs consideration. There are many environments, such as most intranet applications, that need the added functionality of VB and ActiveX. In a controlled environment, the browser selection is easier to manage.

If you need real browser independence, stick to Java for your scripting. Remember that you can use Java in ASP and can call Java servlets from an ASP.

ADDITIONAL RESOURCES

Many free resources on the Web are full of tutorials and sample projects. Download a few and go through them in detail. This exercise alone will save you a lot of resources and accelerate your learning curve.

Note

Start your ASP Web research at these great sites:

Microsoft Developer's Network–Full of great information, tutorials and samples at `http://msdn.microsoft.com/`.

CNET Builder.com–A great resource for all Web technologies at `http://www.builder.com/`.

HTML Station–Chock full of good stuff at `http://www.december.com/`.

Ziff-Davis University–Offers a lot of free information as well as many low cost interactive training classes at `http://www.zdu.com/`.

TROUBLESHOOTING

SERVER-SIDE TECHNOLOGIES: WHICH TO CHOOSE?

CGI, ASP—Server technologies are taking the Web world by storm, particularly in commerce and security situations. How does a developer know how to make the best choice?

Much of that depends on what you have now. If you're starting from scratch, a survey of your current and future needs will help you match the best server type and associated technologies. For example, if you want aggressive support for Microsoft technologies, using Microsoft servers and server-side applications such as ASP will be the best choice. However, if you want more flexibility and greater freedom outside of proprietary server technologies, taking a look at UNIX and Linux servers may well be your best bet.

Of course, if you already have a specific server type at hand, you'll want to consider which technologies are most effective in that server environment.

Designing for the Real World

Understanding Debugging

Debugging is a process by which problems in code are found and eradicated. ASP code requires debugging, and many coders who have been working with ASP for a short while are often challenged by the debugging aspects of the process.

The following do's and don'ts of debugging will help aspiring ASP coders working toward better code.

10 Debugging Do's and Don'ts

1. Learn the basics of database design and practice them.
2. Use a modeler or a database design tool for your application.
3. Use ADO or JDBC for data access.
4. Avoid proprietary systems that do not support multiple databases or scripting languages.
5. Use DHTML or design time controls in your applications.
6. Avoid CGI and server-side data validation where possible.
7. Test your application in the target browser(s) often.
8. Don't underestimate the database technology required to do the job or the amount of hardware needed to perform tests.
9. Remember the user; your site has to flow and be easy and intuitive. Perform usability tests.
10. Don't get caught up in every latest turn of technology. Web technologies move fast. Pick tools that work and use them. Case studies and references are an important part of any successful project.

CHAPTER 37

Database Basics

In this chapter

About Database Systems

A database is a program designed for the storing of data in a centralized, easy to access form. Database technologies exist in several types. The two most common are

- **File server databases**—These databases include most of the familiar, personal computer-style databases such as Microsoft Access, FoxPro, dBASE, Clarion, Paradox, Filemaker Pro, and others. This type of database simply provides a shared file and access method to retrieve the data.
- **Relational databases**—The full, and I'll refer to these sophisticated database environments as RDBMSs throughout the rest of this chapter. RDMBSs tend to be much more powerful and flexible than file server systems. RDBMSs such as Oracle, Informix, Sybase, or Microsoft SQL Server, consist of a set of programs that function independently.

Although file server databases rely on shared integration and file access, the RDBMS stands alone, answers requests for data, and supports many different types of applications. Many of the RDBMS products scale from PC class machines up through the largest mainframes. RDBMS products are the workhorses of industry and power virtually every business application, such as stock trading, airline reservations, manufacturing, and distribution.

All databases use a common structure and terminology. The actual database consists of one or more files that make up a main data storage area. Within the database are *tables*.

A database table contains specific information, such as customer demographics contained in a Customer table or specifics about an order contained in an Orders table. Each table is composed of columns. A column defines a specific data element such as a customer ID, customer name, or order number. Columns have definable attributes such as length and data type (text, date, number, and so on). One or more columns must be used to establish uniqueness in a table. This unique element is a key. The key for a customer table is often the customer ID number.

Most file server type databases provide indexing to speed data access and the definition of relationships. A relationship is defined between columns of different tables to relate to each other. A common example of this is an Order table and an Order Detail table. The Order header information is unique, with one record (row) per order. The Detail items for the order may contain several items for that order (see Figure 37.1).

Comparison of File Server Databases and RDBMS

These handy comparison lists will help you make better choices when choosing your database application.

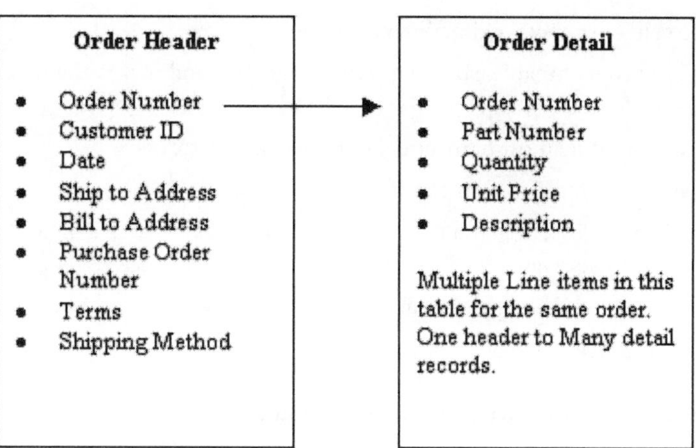

Figure 37.1
The relationship seen here is between the order header and detail items. The order number is the constant between the two tables which creates the relationship.

File server database advantages:

- Easy to use and set up
- Low cost
- Available on most desktop platforms
- Often integrated with other products (Microsoft Access is a part of Microsoft Office Suite and integrated with Word, Excel, and so on)
- Small footprint (they do not require large systems or disk space to run)
- Capable for most small- and many mid-sized applications
- Widely supported

File server database disadvantages:

- Cannot handle very large amounts of data
- Not suited for high availability environments
- Cannot handle large transactional volumes
- No intelligence in the database; they store data, but are not programmable (limited or no support for stored procedures or triggers)
- Lack of enterprise management or maintenance tools
- Limited gateway or replication functions
- High network traffic

Relational Database Management Systems advantages:

- Very scalable, most support Windows NT/Intel systems and scale up to mainframes
- Supports high volume of users and transactions

- Excellent support and maintenance tools
- Very programmable, speeds development time and makes the database less platform dependent
- Supported by most hardware and tools manufacturers
- Greatly reduces network traffic
- Supports clustering and advanced replication technologies (24×7 operations, and support options available)
- Support for Web application servers and transaction processing applications
- Excellent security

Relational Database Management Systems disadvantages:

- Higher cost
- Requires training to set up and program
- Requires more powerful hardware configurations
- May require full-time database administrator

EXPLORING VARIOUS DATABASE PRODUCTS

In this section, you'll see an overview of many of the commonly used database products available in the market today. This information is by no means inclusive but is intended as a starting point for your review and evaluations.

FILE SERVER DATABASES

Some of the popular file server products include Microsoft Access 2000 and Sybase Adaptive Server Anywhere.

MICROSOFT ACCESS 2000

One of the most attractive aspects of Microsoft Access 2000 is that it contains wizards to walk you through complex procedures. The Query Wizard sorts through database information, including data from multiple tables, and then determines how to bring it all together to answer your questions.

With Access 2000, you can save to HTML. This feature permits users to share static views of their data on the Web. Access outputs table, query, and form datasheets as well as completely formatted reports, directly to HTML.

Using other Microsoft products, you can integrate Access with the functionality native to Microsoft Internet Information Server and Personal Web Server. Direct publication features to the Web Wizard allow users to publish any object in their database either statically or dynamically.

This integration makes Access an excellent choice for individuals requiring the advantages of a file server product that works well with Web-based services.

Note For more information on Microsoft Access, visit `http://www.microsoft.com/access/`.

Sybase Adaptive Server Anywhere

Sybase's File Server Anywhere application features simple installation and administration. It also includes transaction processing—an attractive option for many people delivering goods and services via the Web.

Much like high-end RDBMS products, Sybase's Adaptive Server Anywhere allows programmers to put Java code directly into the database. A server-side JDBC driver lets Java objects access SQL data within the database environment, making this entry into the file server–style database list an extremely good choice for Web-based productivity.

Note You can get more information at Sybase's Web at `http://www.sybase.com/`.

RDBMS

Relational Database Management Systems discussed in this section include systems from Oracle, Informix, IBM, and Sybase:

- **Oracle8i**—This relational database system from Oracle (see Figure 37.2) offers some sophisticated features including high-performance data access, a database assistant that helps you create databases, a Web publishing assistant that allows you to output data to the Web with no coding on your part, and that ever-attractive transaction processing. For more about this, and other Oracle products, visit `http://www.oracle.com/`.
- **Informix**—With 64-bit support and large memory addressability, Informix is also Java-enabled. Other features include secure auditing and enterprise gateway support. More information is available at `http://www.informix.com/`.
- **IBM DB2**—IBM's Database2 lets you control resource use of individual users and applications and has excellent backup, recovery, and replication facilities. Find out more about it at `http://www.ibm.com/`.
- **Sybase Adaptive Server Enterprise**—Another selection from Sybase, this database features sort, index creation, and high security standards with online transaction processing capabilities. More information can be found at `http://www.sybase.com/`.

Concerned that with all these options, you might not choose the best one for your site? You can get some additional insight on making this decision by taking a look at "Choosing the Best Database" found in the Troubleshooting section at the end of this chapter.

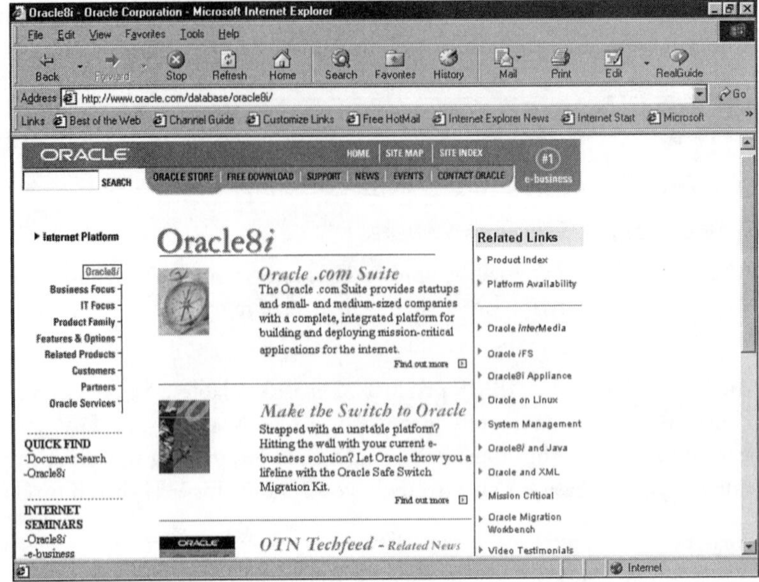

Figure 37.2
Oracle8i's home page. Powerful back-end technologies drive search, personalization, customer tracking, and inventory features.

CHOOSING DATABASE DEVELOPMENT TOOLS

One of the most important things you can do to help ensure the success of a project is to model the database. Modeling has become much more than a mental exercise. Tools now exist that generate code and databases from models. This investment in time provides a significant payback in time for completion. Besides generating code, modeling clearly defines business processing and data elements. Having a clear understanding of the project in advance will save you time and money.

Several tools exist to assist in this endeavor. Take a look at the process and a few choices. These examples are just a small representation of the tools available. Try several and choose the ones that fit your budget and needs.

UNIVERSAL MODELING LANGUAGE

Universal Modeling Language (UML) was developed by engineers at Rational Software Corp. Their UML product Rational Rose is one of many UML products available today. This modeling language has quickly overtaken the industry and has become the standard. Microsoft's Visual Modeler is a light version of Rational Rose and is, itself, an excellent tool.

UML permits a developer to mirror the way application development really occurs. You can create a quick model, implement it, test it, refine it, and repeat the cycle until the desired results have been achieved. The benefit to this process is that no work is lost and nothing is rewritten. UML provides a standard vehicle for round trip engineering, addressing all phases of product development. Most modeling tools do not require a programmer to operate. This is the first time that an environment exists for the programmer and business analyst to collaborate in a manner useful to both parties.

MICROSOFT VISUAL MODELER

Although Microsoft Visual Modeler is tightly integrated into Visual Studio, other products offer more choices. Oracle Designer, for example, generates many database formats and creates client-side code in DHTML, Java, C++, or Visual Basic. Do the design and then pick the target deployment language.

In this example, you look at Microsoft Visual Modeler (MVM). MVM integrates tightly with Visual Studio, and it provides a component-based programming environment. Component-based applications have a longer life and are easier to maintain and modify. Components can also be used in other applications.

You can also use MVM to reverse engineer an existing application and then improve, modify, or add to it.

Note that in Figure 37.3, three tiers exist. These are logical tiers and are not related to any physical hardware server configuration.

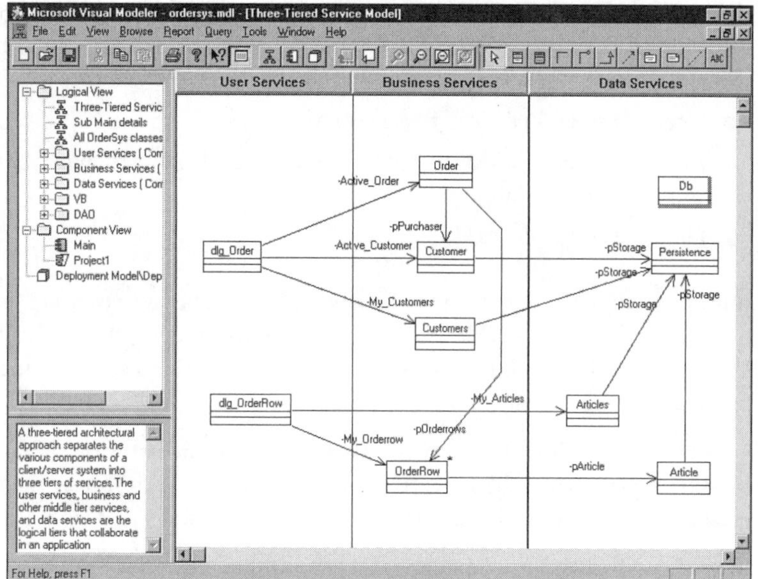

Figure 37.3
Logical tiers in Microsoft Visual Modeler.

USER SERVICES

The User Services tier provides the visual interface for presenting information and gathering data. It also obtains the business services needed to deliver the required application functionality and integrate the user with the application to perform a business process.

BUSINESS SERVICES

Business Services are the bridge between user and data services. They respond to requests from the user (or other business services) to execute a business task. They accomplish this by applying formal procedures and business rules to the relevant data.

When the needed data resides on a database server, Business Services secure the data services needed to accomplish the business task or apply the business rule. This protocol insulates the user from direct interaction with the database. Because business rules tend to change more frequently than the specific business tasks they support, they are ideal candidates for encapsulation in components that are physically separate from the application logic itself.

DATA SERVICES

Data services maintain, access, and update data. They also manage and satisfy requests to manipulate data that is initiated by Business Services. Separating Data Services allows the data structure and access mechanisms to be maintained, modified, or, if necessary, even re-architected without affecting Business or User Services.

WORKING WITH DATABASE APPLICATIONS

In the MVM example you looked at User, Business, and Data Services. This method of partitioning an application is often referred to as N-Tier architecture. A typical toolset for building an N-Tier architecture might look like the following:

- **User Services**—HTML/Java/DHTML.
- **Business Services**—Web application server and transaction server for ASP, data access, and load distribution.
- **Data Services**—RDBMS.

It is important to discuss the terms client and server, because they are used in so many situations today. In a Web-enabled, browser-based environment, there is a single client—the Web browser. The Web browser (such as Internet Explorer or Netscape Navigator) is the first true universal client.

Servers are often described in two flavors, hardware and software. We will be discussing the software type. It seems like everything is a server now; Web server, Web application server, database server, transaction server, commerce server, and so on.

In all these discussions, you must realize that there is not necessarily a one-to-one relationship between hardware and software servers. Software servers are programs, and we all know that more than one program can run on a single computer system. A small site can have a Web server and database server running on a single computer. Conversely, in large environments, software servers can span multiple hardware servers.

Although all this may appear a little confusing at first glance, it provides the developer with a tremendous amount of flexibility and scalability. N-Tier is the vehicle to take advantage of this flexibility by making the design, development, and maintenance processes easier.

EXPLORING N-TIER ARCHITECTURE

One of the greatest advantages to an N-Tier environment is that the User Services reside on a server, not on every user's machine. This is the standard presentation for an Internet Web application—Internet-based shopping or travel reservations systems are a good example of this. Before browser technology, you needed a copy of the software on your machine. The process of creating and distributing updates to every user is expensive in terms of hard costs and labor.

Note

FedEx used to distribute thousands of floppy disks with a proprietary software tracking application to customers who dialed into a FedEx computer to check shipments. This system has been replaced by a browser-based system. When the switch was made, usage grew dramatically, largely because of ease-of-use, familiar interface (the Web browser) and no need to install additional software. This switch to browser-based applications applies not only to the Internet environment but equally to intranet applications. Corporate IS departments spend a significant amount of time and money maintaining and distributing client applications software where browser-based applications are less cumbersome and therefore more effective.

NORMALIZATION OF DATA

An important consideration in designing a database is normalization. To "normalize" a database, in simplest terms, means to be sure that data is stored only once. This prevents duplicate data elements from getting out of sync or you having to write code to keep them in sync. Additionally, this takes up less space. An example of a normalized database is a customer demographics table (see Figure 37.4).

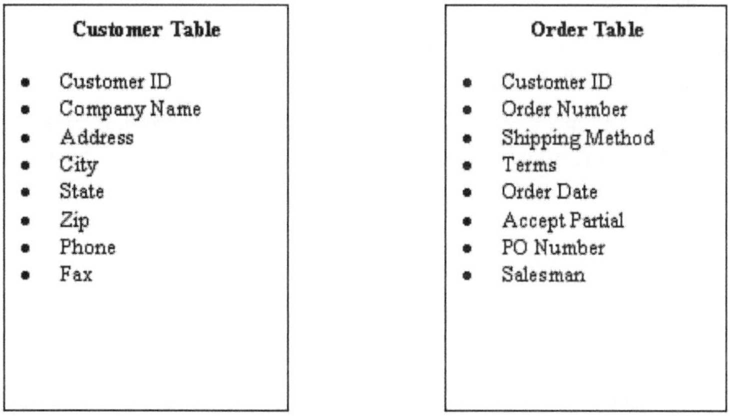

Figure 37.4
As you can see in this example of a normalized table structure, all that is required for the Order table is the customer ID. If you know the customer ID, you also know all the data associated with the customer ID, such as the company name and address.

Customer Table

- Customer ID
- Company Name
- Address
- City
- State
- Zip
- Phone
- Fax

Order Table

- Customer ID
- Order Number
- Shipping Method
- Terms
- Order Date
- Accept Partial
- PO Number
- Salesman

In a denormalized structure, there would be duplicate information. The customer name, address, and so on would exist in both tables. This can create many problems. What if the customer moves before the order is shipped? Which address is correct, the one in the

Customer table or the Order table, and who knows all the places to change to the new address. What if there were 100 orders in the system for this customer?

With proper design, the data is changed once in the Customer table and then referenced in that single place whenever it is needed.

There are times when one would purposely denormalize a database. This often occurs in decision support or data warehouse situations. Denormalization can improve reporting performance and ease query design in some situations. In most cases, strive to normalize the data.

Note

Like most aspects of database design, there is more to this topic than can be covered here. There are entire books on normalization. Learn the basics and practice them. Try *Teach Yourself Database Design in 24 Hours* from Sams for a good starting point.

Understanding Database Relationships

As the name implies, Relational Database Management Systems use relationships as a core technology in data management and design. It is this process of relating data that makes a RDBMS so powerful. The terms *joins* and *foreign keys* also can be used to describe specific relationships. The previous Customer table/Order table example demonstrates a relationship by joining the customer ID column in both tables.

Relationships fall into several categories:

- **One-to-One**—This involves two or more tables where there is literally a one-to-one relationship between the data elements. An example of this might be the Customer table and a table that has corporate headquarters information—one Corp. H.Q. per customer.
- **One-to-Many**—This is the most common situation. One single customer to many orders is a classic example of this.
- **Many-to-One**—Also a common occurrence. An example might be a Salesman table and a Product table—many salesmen selling the same product.

These relationships are the tools that a normalized database uses to retrieve data.

Using Constraints

A constraint is a type of business rule that is a useful technology found in all database systems. Constraints are used to check input, ensure a date is entered correctly, see that a value falls in a specific range, and so on.

Typical constraints for the sample Order table might look like the following:

```
Order Date => Current Date
Shipping Method = Not Null
Salesman = Not Null
```

USING DATABASES

To use databases, you need to understand the concept of *schemas* and *database schemas*.

A database schema is a way of describing all the components of a database. Schemas are also referred to as the DDL or *Database Description Language*.

A schema describes all the basic components of a database:

- **Tablespaces**—A tablespace is the most basic component. Tablespaces hold tables and other database objects. Often there are separate tablespaces on separate disk drives for data, indexes, archive logs, and rollback segments.
- **Indexes**—Databases support many different index technologies. Indexes are used to locate a specific row or record quickly. Often they work just like a book index, rather than flipping a page at a time through a 500-page book, the index is 3 pages and your entry reads "Go to page 387."
- **Tables**—The basic building block of a database. Columns or data elements (also referred to as fields) are grouped together in tables. One table can contain customer data, for example, and another table can contain orders.
- **Columns**—A column is a specific data element. A customer ID number is a column, and a customer name is another. Related columns are grouped together in tables.
- **Triggers**—A trigger is a block of code that is executed in accordance with a specific business rule. Triggers are assigned to a specific table and execute at specified times, such as Before Insert or After Update. Triggers are transactional in nature.
- **Stored Procedures**—Stored procedures are blocks of code that are embedded in a database and called. They execute within the database and take no client resources.
- **Sequences**—A sequence is a feature that automatically increments a value. Sequences are useful and therefore, are used often. For example, you may want system assigned order numbers. The Order Number column in the table would have a sequence assigned to it that started at value X and incremented by 1.
- **Rollback Segments**—The concept of rollback is important. Advanced RDBMS do not just change data. They use a submit/commit/rollback model. A transaction is submitted for processing. If successful, it is committed to the database. A commit makes the transaction permanent. If the transaction fails (for example, a value is missing) the transaction is rolled back or reversed. The transaction is stored in the rollback segment until it is committed.

The following selected code examples in Listings 37.1 and 37.2 show the are created.

LISTING 37.1 TABLESPACE CREATION

```
CREATE TABLESPACE INDEXES
DATAFILE 'E:\Data\Indexes\IndxRMS.Dbf' SIZE 500M REUSE
DEFAULT
```

continues

LISTING 37.1 CONTINUED

```
 STORAGE(
 INITIAL 10240
 NEXT 10240
 PCTINCREASE 50
 MINEXTENTS 1
 MAXEXTENTS 121);

CREATE TABLESPACE DATA
DATAFILE 'D:\Data\RMS\DataRMS.dbf' SIZE 800M REUSE
DEFAULT
 STORAGE(
 INITIAL 10240
 NEXT 10240
 PCTINCREASE 50
 MINEXTENTS 1
 MAXEXTENTS 121);
```

LISTING 37.2 ANATOMY OF A TABLE

```
CREATE TABLE PATIENT - Column definitions first
 (ID VARCHAR2(16) NOT NULL - this is the key
 ,ALTERNATEID VARCHAR2(16)
 ,ACCOUNTNUMBER VARCHAR2(16)
 ,SSN VARCHAR2(16)
 ,FIRSTNAME VARCHAR2(30)
 ,MIDDLEINITIAL CHAR(1)
 ,LASTNAME VARCHAR2(30)
 ,NAMESUFFIX VARCHAR2(3)
 ,ALIASNAME VARCHAR2(30)
 ,ISALIAS CHAR(1) DEFAULT 'N' NOT NULL - set a default value and add a
 ,ISACTIVE CHAR(1) DEFAULT 'Y' NOT NULL        "not null" constraint
 ,BIRTHDATE DATE
 ,SEX CHAR(1)
 ,RACE CHAR(1)
 ,ETHNICGROUP CHAR(1)
 ,LANGUAGE VARCHAR2(30)
 ,MARITALSTATUS CHAR(1)
 ,RELIGION VARCHAR2(3)
 ,WEIGHT NUMBER(7,2)
 ,WEIGHTUOM VARCHAR2(3)
 ,HEIGHT NUMBER(7,2)
 ,HEIGHTUOM VARCHAR2(3)
 ,SURFACE NUMBER(5,0)
 ,SURFACEUOM VARCHAR2(3)
 ,WARD VARCHAR2(6)
 ,ROOM VARCHAR2(5)
 ,BED VARCHAR2(2)
 ,CART NUMBER(3,0)
 ,ALLERGIES VARCHAR2(2000)
 ,NOTES VARCHAR2(2000)
 ,NEXTDOSE DATE
 ,NEXTCRITICAL DATE
 ,WITHIN CHAR(1)
 ,CRITICALITY NUMBER(3,0)
```

```
,NEXTOUTCOME DATE
,NUMCHARTINGREQ NUMBER(4,0) DEFAULT 0 NOT NULL
,LASTADMIN DATE DEFAULT SysDate NOT NULL
,NUMADMIN NUMBER(7,0) DEFAULT 0 NOT NULL
,LASTMODIFIED DATE DEFAULT SysDate NOT NULL
,REVIEWWITHIN NUMBER(3,0) DEFAULT 0 NOT NULL
,NEXTHUMANREVIEW DATE
,LASTHUMANREVIEW DATE
,NUMUNVERIFIED NUMBER(3,0) DEFAULT 0
,NUMSTAT NUMBER(3,0) DEFAULT 0
,CHANGEDBY VARCHAR2(2) DEFAULT 'M' NOT NULL
)
PCTUSED 40 - define table parameters such as size and growth
PCTFREE 10
INITRANS 1
MAXTRANS 255
TABLESPACE DATA
STORAGE(
INITIAL 10240
NEXT 10240
PCTINCREASE 50
MINEXTENTS 1
MAXEXTENTS 121);
```


In Listing 37.3, I've provided a sample trigger from a healthcare application. This trigger runs before any delete action on the table EMAR. (An EMAR is an electronic medication administration record.) This trigger checks the status of medication records and updates the master patient record.

Listing 37.3 Sample Trigger

```
CREATE OR REPLACE TRIGGER EMARDELETE BEFORE DELETE
 ON EMAR
 REFERENCING OLD AS OLD NEW AS NEW FOR EACH ROW
BEGIN
  /* Check the status of the EMAR and update the Patient table */
  IF ( :old.Status = 1) THEN
   /* Decrement NumChartingReq on the Patient table */
   UPDATE Patient SET NumChartingReq = NumChartingReq - 1 WHERE Patient.Id =
:old.Patient;
  END IF;
  EXCEPTION
   WHEN OTHERS THEN
     NULL;
  END;
/
```

Listing 37.2 set up the table data. The code in 37.3 is a status checker, looking at the information within the data before modifying it in any way.

Stored Procedures and Triggers

One of the most useful features of RDBMSs are stored procedures and triggers. A stored procedure is a module of code embedded in the database that is called, much like a procedure in Visual Basic. Procedures are reusable and, most importantly, they execute internally in the database, so there is no need for any network traffic or client-side processing. This design optimizes database performance as the stored procedure uses the existing database cache, indexes, and so on.

A trigger is similar to a stored procedure in that it is a block of code that is stored in the database. The difference, however, is that you can specify default execution plans for triggers. Triggers are assigned to specific tables and will execute automatically. Triggers can be specified to execute Before Insert, After Update, After Insert, and at other times. Remember, triggers are table specific and execute automatically based on a rule.

PERFORMANCE TUNING DO'S AND DON'TS

Both file server and RDBMS-type databases have internal structures that help to find data faster than sequentially reading every record in a table. An index is the most common structure. Advanced databases have many types of index schemes, each optimized for certain types of data or retrieval methods.

Over-indexing hurts performance, but a few basic guidelines apply. Keys to a table are automatically indexed. Generally, you should have an index on any column that is in a `where` clause of a query or is a foreign key or part of a join.

Advanced databases support many indexing schemes such as clustered or star-type indexes and hashtables. Large projects often benefit from these technologies.

Most advanced RDBMSs make use of sophisticated caching schemes. Besides caching data, many systems also cache stored procedures and triggers as well as other reusable components. These caches must be configured properly and can have a substantial influence on performance.

Splitting parts of the database onto separate drives is a feature of most advanced databases. This permits a database to span many drives or spindles to improve performance. Advanced databases have separate objects for data, indexes, rollback segments, and other key components. These can be spread out on many drives, reducing problems associated with overload on one drive.

Many books and courses are available on performance tuning your database. Besides intelligent use of indexes, file server databases are limited in their performance tuning options. A RDBMS will offer a suite of tuning tools.

ADDRESSING DATABASE CONCERNS

Several special concerns exist when working with databases. Three of the most important are how to minimize network traffic, how to configure hardware, and how to use replication.

MINIMIZING NETWORK TRAFFIC

Reducing network traffic is important in both intranet and Internet applications.

You can do several things to minimize traffic:

- Make use of stored procedures and triggers. Any processing that can be performed internal to the database reduces traffic.
- Use DHTML to data bind controls.
- Use native data access methods wherever possible.
- Use application servers to improve performance and reduce traffic.
- Call stored procedures through ASP.

The ASP sample in Listing 37.4 contains SQL to generate a report of all the patients living within the ZIP area 54123. Note that the zip field is a Text field of length 1.

LISTING 37.4 ASP SAMPLE

```
' First create command and recordset objects
Set Cm = Server.CreateObject("ADODB.Command")
Set Rs = Server.CreateObject("ADODB.RecordSet")

' Set the ActiveConnection property of command object to the
' ODBC source you will use
Cm.ActiveConnection = "Your_ODBC_Source"

' Now, create the SQL statement
sSQL = "SELECT * FROM tbl_patient WHERE zip='54123' "

' The CommandText property of Command object should contain
' this SQL statement
Cm.CommandText = sSQL

' Since we are using a SQL Statement in Command object, the
CommandType
' Property should be adCmdText which has a value of 1
Cm.CommandType = 1

' Execute the command, and set the recordset object to the result
' of this execution. We obtain the resulting records in Rs object
Set Rs = Cm.Execute
```

HARDWARE CONFIGURATIONS

The primary concern with configuring hardware is the use of `RAID` and parallel query processing.

`RAID` (redundant array of independent [or inexpensive] disks) arrays provide flexible, low-cost, and highly reliable storage by saving data on more than one disk simultaneously. At its simplest, a `RAID-1` array consists of two drives that store identical information. If one drive goes down, the other continues to work.

However, this is an expensive solution. To save disk drives and space, `RAID-3`, `-4`, and `-5` *stripe* data and parity information across multiple drives (`RAID-3` and `-4` store all parity data on a single drive). If a single disk fails, the parity information can be used to rebuild the lost data. There are performance tradeoffs depending on the RAID type used, and a RAID will be slower than a single drive at either reading or writing data. RAID systems are available in many different sizes and configurations.

Advanced RDBMS systems use *parallelism* to great advantage. Parallelism divides tasks across multiple CPUs or multiple systems. This means that the databases are designed to operate on one or more multi-CPU systems.

REPLICATION

Replication refers to setting up the database to distribute data throughout a network on two or more servers. One typical use of replication prevents a single database from becoming overloaded with demands. By replicating all or any subset of the databases without interrupting operations, no one server or WAN is unduly taxed. Another purpose of replication can be to update existing databases on a less frequent basis such as every Friday night.

Many businesses today are instituting data warehouses and using replication to make critical data available from one or more sources.

TROUBLESHOOTING

CHOOSING THE BEST DATABASE

Most of HTML and design is front-end. Backend technologies are unfamiliar terrain. How on earth can I make the best decisions when choosing the best database solutions for my needs?

If you're not a programmer or database specialist, server and database technologies can indeed seem overwhelming. I know they do to me! They are areas of specialization in Web design that require specific expertise.

The best bet is to do research and consult with your ISP or systems administrator. Seek out knowledge and either educate yourself or work with people who are more familiar with database technologies. Listservs and newsgroups are often wonderful resources. Depending on the applications you are using, you'll find that a variety of support is available on the application Web sites. For example, if you are using Microsoft products, check with the Microsoft Developer Network, **`http://msdn.microsoft.com/`** for additional resources.

DESIGNING FOR THE REAL WORLD

CDNOW.COM

I remember CDnow in its first incarnation as a text-based service! Founded in 1994, CDnow offers an enormous selection of music CDs, tapes, and related gifts. CDnow is an example of a business that was far ahead of its time. The rapid growth of the Web could have caused failure as the business rushed hither and yon to meet the growing technological and service demands of customers. But CDnow remains one of the most successful stories of e-commerce.

With nearly half a million products in their catalog, and close to a million customers, CDnow has been challenged to give their site visitors the best services with the most ease.

Considerations that face CDnow every day include

- Customizing and personalizing the interface to welcome and retain visitors.
- Manage enormous inventory and make it easy for customers to find the products they want.
- Log transactions and track statistics to gain a better understanding of how to serve CDnow customer needs.

The only solution available for these kinds of demands is database management via the backend. CDnow.com chose Oracle8 as its business tool, and successfully manages its vast and growing inventory and clientele. If you, too, are challenged by a project that demands tracking, commerce, and statistics, researching appropriate database solutions is going to be a necessary step in creating a successful, usable site.

Note

For a look at the database-driven personalization and search features of CDnow, visit `http://www.cdnow.com/`.

Putting Your Skills to Work

CHAPTER 38

Home Page Concepts

In this chapter

You and the Rest of the World

Do you have a message you want to share with the world?

Since its early days, the Web has been about people and the exchange of ideas. Long before commerce found its way online, there were personal pages. And even with the explosion of commercial sites and portals, personal pages still have a large majority presence.

By designing a Web page, you can add your own voice to the Internet. The Web offers a tremendous opportunity for self-expression and self-promotion. In the past, self-publishing cost thousands of dollars and reached only a limited audience. Only a small percentage of the population is ever given a lucrative contract to perform their music, create their art, or write their stories—to reach a wide audience and achieve commercial success. The Web is changing all that by allowing people to put their talents online without commercial backing at an affordable rate.

New Web technologies are helping people with diverse talents to share their work. MP3 allows musical groups to distribute their music online in hopes of building an audience and attracting a recording contract. The various streaming video technologies (QuickTime, MPEG, RealMedia) facilitate the distribution of such visual demonstrations as acting abilities or woodworking skills.

→ To gain more insight on including audio and visual content on your site, **see** "Audio, Video, and Streaming Media," **p. 666**

New journalists and writers are gaining fame based on the content they write for their Web sites. Just look at the success of Matt Drudge, writer of the Drudge Report. He broke the news about President Clinton and Monica Lewinsky on his Web site, and is now commanding a multi-million-dollar salary and has his own television news show!

Using Common Sense

Building a Web page is an act of courage. You are daring the world to take a closer look at you—or at least a part of you—and make what judgments they may. While the relative anonymity of the Internet might make you bold, there are still a few guidelines which will make your entry into the online world more successful.

- Never put anything on your home page that you wouldn't tell your mother.
- Never put anything on your home page that you wouldn't talk about in the workplace.
- Never put anything on your home page that will deny you the privacy you might want to maintain offline.
- Never put anything on your home page that could be considered slander or libel.
- Never put anything on your home page that infringes on other people's rights to material they own. Copyright issues are an important concern when dealing with Web page content.

For the most part, the Net remains a unique, incredible, free, creative space (especially in the Western world) where you're allowed to say or do literally anything you'd like—stream video of yourself having a baby, for example, or do a live broadcast of your piano recital—without fear of retribution, regulation, or recrimination of any sort. Just keep in mind that visitors will form a value judgment of *you*, as the creator of the Web site and its content, as much as they will form a judgment of the content itself.

Caution

While the First Amendment protects freedom of speech for Americans, other countries may have limitations on their expression. Historically, however, the Web has been relatively free of inhibitive regulation. Of course, the right to express oneself is always best when coupled with common sense and a sense of responsibility. A wide variety of people of different ages and cultures will visit your site. It's important, therefore, to think carefully about your Web content.

If you express your opinions and share your creativity in a productive manner, your personal page is sure to be a winner!

PLANNING YOUR PAGE

The eventual success of your Web site relies on the content and design of the site. There are many steps between coming up with a basic concept and launching your home page, however. Taking the extra time to plan and organize your effort will definitely reflect in the final product.

FINDING A HOME FOR YOUR PAGE

The first thing you'll need to do is arrange for a place to put your home page. If you've already got access to the Internet, you might already have Web space as part of your account. If you subscribe to one of the few services that does not offer Web space—or if you are already using this space for other purposes—there are several sites that offer free Web space (see Figure 38.1).

Note

The following Web sites offer Web space for home pages:

Yahoo! GeoCities: `http://geocities.yahoo.com/home/`

Tripod: `http://www.tripod.com/`

Angelfire: `http://www.angelfire.com/`

Xoom: `http://www.xoom.com/home/`

Be sure to also check out various Web directories such as `http://www.whowhere.lycos.com/`, `http://people.yahoo.com/`, and `http://www.switchboard.com/`. Many of these sites allow you to customize your entry in their directory.

Figure 38.1
Yahoo! GeoCities, the Web's largest virtual community, gives you access too 11 megabytes of disk space for free. The catch? You've got to use it for a personal home page. No businesses allowed!

Note

Looking for a good ISP? CMP.net, a major Internet publishing and rating service, offers a good ISP search service at `http://www.isps.com/`.

Another site, Mecklermedia's `http://thelist.internet.com/`, indexes nearly 5,000 ISPs from which to choose.

Considerations for Choosing Your Provider

When choosing an ISP, you'll want to compare several criteria including budget, speed, reliability, quality of service, and available space.

Cost

You'll want an ISP that charges a flat monthly fee. Per-minute or hourly charges add up quickly, especially when you start maintaining your site and responding to email, so avoid any ISP that tries to charge them. *Rule of thumb:* In most U.S. areas, you should not pay more than $20 a month.

Connectivity

Can you dial up to your ISP whenever you want to, or are they impossible to access during peak traffic time? A bargain monthly fee isn't much of a bargain if all you can access is a busy signal. When you do get through, do you connect at a speed close to the speed of your modem? No use paying for an expensive modem if it's underutilized by your ISP. *Rule of thumb:* You should never get more than one busy signal in one evening. Ideally, you never get a busy signal!

RELIABILITY

Is their Web server always accessible? Sometimes ISPs have to reboot or perform maintenance on their servers; during that time, your page isn't publicly accessible. *Rule of thumb:* The server where you store your home page should be publicly accessible at least 95% of the time. Furthermore, an ISP that places notices of downtimes on its site or sends out an email if they expect to perform a major maintenance job is going the extra mile—a sign of professional and considerate service.

SERVICE

Especially if you're new to the Internet, you'll want an ISP that provides excellent customer service. Good ISPs have a portion of their company Web site dedicated to answering service-related questions, which can sometimes help you avoid a phone call. Any ISP worth its monthly fee also should have a toll-free technical support number you can call if you're having trouble. *Rule of thumb*: You should never have to wait on hold more than 15 minutes to talk to tech support.

SERVER SPACE

You want enough Web space to put up the home page of your dreams. Some ISPs count the server space your email uses against the space available for your pages, so ask about the policy of any potential ISP. The rates for additional space should be reasonable, so you can add space as your site grows. *Rule of thumb:* You want a minimum of 4MB for a start-up site, but keep in mind that you might eventually need more.

CHOOSING SOFTWARE TO BUILD YOUR HOME PAGE

If you've come this far in this book, chances are you want to learn how to develop your own home pages from scratch. I would be remiss, however, if I didn't mention here the various WYSIWYG packages that are available.

Software such as Microsoft FrontPage, Adobe GoLive, and Macromedia Dreamweaver make it easier for you to build a home page quickly by writing the code for you and helping you upload your pages onto the Web. Some packages even provide templates to take the design decisions out of your hands. Sites such as Yahoo! GeoCities, which provide free Web space, offer home page creation tools, basically a form that allows you to enter your content and then processes your input into an HTML template.

➔ For more information about these packages, **see** "HTML Tools," **p. 40**

In some instances, these packages can be useful. Complicated HTML code, such as nested tables, is more easy to generate using a WYSIWYG HTML application than by hand-coding. You might be making sacrifices in the code quality, though. But for basic Web pages, it can take you as little time to hand-code your home page as it would to learn to use the WYSIWYG software.

Tip from

> If Web-design software is offered to you for free as part of your Internet access package or other bundled software, play with it to see if it can help you or make any interesting design suggestions. Don't head out to the store to invest in an expensive package, however, unless you have a long-term, professional application in mind.

Ultimately, trust in your own ability to compose in HTML, and write the code yourself. You'll definitely be prouder and more in control of the final product.

Composing and Transferring Files

The best environment for creating your Web pages is using a simple text editor, such as SimpleText on the Macintosh or Notepad in Windows. Microsoft Word offers an HTML option, but the code produced by Word is inefficient.

After you have your HTML files completed on your computer and ready to go online, you encounter the issue of how to get them onto the Web server. The answer is an old Internet standard called *File Transfer Protocol*, or FTP.

→ To learn more about FTP, **see** "Publishing Sites on the Internet," **p. 893**

You can obtain both command-line and graphical-interface FTP programs online (see Figure 38.2), many for free.

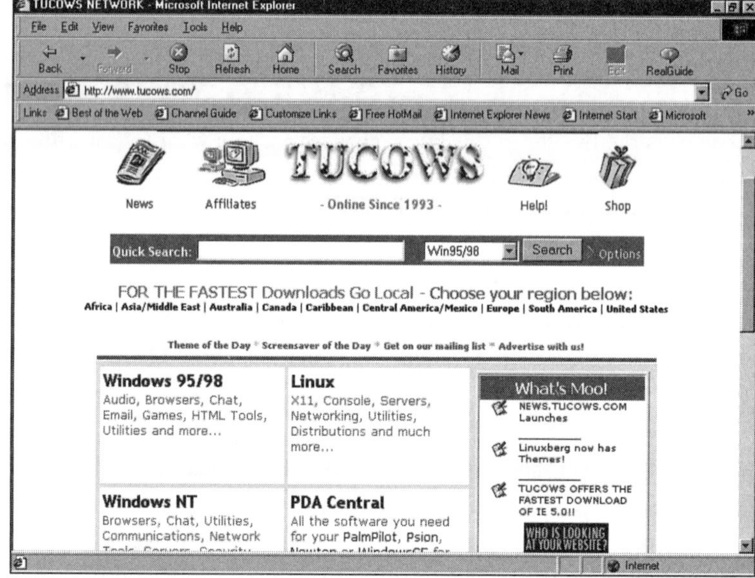

Figure 38.2 Sites like The Ultimate Collection Of Winsock Software (TUCOWS) offer access to numerous shareware and free-ware FTP programs.

Note

Check out the FTP software offerings at:

C|NET: **`http://www.download.com/`**

Stroud's Consummate Winsock Apps: **`http://cws.internet.com/`**

The Ultimate Collection Of Winsock Software: **`http://www.tucows.com/`**

Caution

Note that you're looking for FTP client software, not server software.

Your browser or Web server also might have upload capabilities. Netscape Navigator has an Upload option that allows you to transfer files. Yahoo! GeoCities has an Uploads Page that enables you to browse your hard drive, select files locally, and then click a button to upload them to your Web directory on the GeoCities server. A dedicated FTP package provides extra functionality that makes it more efficient than these options, such as the ability to transfer entire directory structures.

Note

Windows 98 and above, and Windows NT 4.0 and above contain built-in FTP abilities. Simply type the FTP address directly into the Address bar in Windows Explorer while connected to your ISP.

CHOOSING CONTENT

So what should you put on your home page? A quick glance around the Web reveals a range of both exceptionally gorgeous and appallingly dull personal sites. Your goal at the get-go is, quite simply, not to be appallingly dull. Don't be discouraged if the first home page you create isn't a prizewinner, however. Your page will change and grow along with your interests and personality: It doesn't have to be a great work of art to express what you want it to express. Don't be put off or feel outclassed by online phenomena. Remember the Internet is a place where *anyone* can be published. As your site evolves, it is sure to get the attention—read, hits—it rightfully deserves.

At the beginning of this chapter, I said you should not put anything on your home page that puts your privacy at risk. Remember, after your home page is live on the Internet, *anyone* can see it. While 99% of Internet users might be perfectly innocent in their intent, you need to use caution against that remaining 1%.

What can you do to express yourself but stay safe? Here are a few tips:

- Take care when publishing pictures of yourself. Be aware that someone can download your picture and alter it in any way they want. If you are leery of this possibility, you might want to avoid putting photos of yourself and your family online. If the subject of your site *is* your family, proceed with caution. Be sure everyone is clothed and posed appropriately in your photos for your site's potential audience.

- Some less-than-noble marketers search through home pages looking for email addresses. After they find yours, they add it to a giant mailing list that they then sell to various direct marketers. This results in more unwanted email than you probably care to deal with. There are a couple ways to eliminate this problem:
    - You might prefer not to print your email address on your home page. If you'd like people to be able to send you email, add a guestbook page or a form. (More on those later.)
    - Similarly, create a mailto link that's hyperlinked to something (an image or text) other than your address:

```
E-mail <a href="mailto:molly@molly.com">Molly</a>!
```

Are you wondering about legal issues for the content you're planning for your site? See, "Using Licensed Images" in the Troubleshooting section at the end of this chapter for some help with this issue.

Making Your Mark

Of the hundreds of thousands of personal home pages on the Web, you want your site to stand out as a true expression of you and your interests. Think about the message you want to send to the world. What hobbies, views, talents, or interests do you have to share from a unique perspective? Even if there are already hundreds of pages devoted to your favorite topic, what can you add to the mix that will make your pages stand out? Maybe you have a differing opinion or analysis that will make people want to see what you have to say.

Think, too, about what type of design will complement your content. If your site is devoted to your love poems, lots of flashing animated GIFs are going to detract from your message. If your site is about your passion for the Beastie Boys, you might want to rethink that pink, flowered background.

Consider, too, the type of content you plan to put on your home page. Entire novels are difficult to read online because of the amount of scrolling and eyestrain involved. Instead, consider publishing an excerpt of your novel or writing a short story for your home page. Similarly, you don't want to publish all your photographs or every page of your graphic novel. Rather, provide a sample of your very best work. If the complete work is available in another format, you can provide a link to an order form or `mailto` to make it easier for people to obtain your work.

What "Works" Online

The Web is a medium of its own, just like television and radio, and shouldn't be mistaken for a book or newspaper. Here are a few parameters to keep in mind when selecting content for your home page:

- The first page a viewer sees—your index page—will be most effective if it doesn't require scrolling. In some cases, scrolling is unavoidable, such as when you're using both a graphical navigation system and a text-based system. Try to make your index page as short as possible, however, and be sure the page loads quickly.

- Your index page should give the viewer an immediate overview of the content of your page. You *can* have content on your index page, but that space might be best used for a clear navigation path and teasers for the rest of the site.
- Your pages should load quickly. As a guideline, pages should be around 45KB or less, and none of your pages should exceed 65KB. If your pages are getting heavy—exceeding 65KB—consider breaking them up into smaller pages. You can always use links to Back and Next at the bottom of each page to maintain a flow.
- If you use enhancements to your home page that require extra software or plug-ins on your visitor's computer, (such as streaming audio/video or Flash), provide links to that software to make it easy for visitors to obtain. Also make sure the page is still accessible for people whose computers cannot view the bells and whistles.
- Your image files should each be less than 45KB and ideally much smaller than that in weight. If you want to provide high-quality images on your site that will exceed this size guideline, use smaller, lower-quality versions of the images (thumbnails), and link them to the larger images. Visitors can then opt to click the thumbnails and see the larger image if they choose to do so.

→ For more information about making your site accessible, **see** "Accessibility and Internationalization," **p. 473**

→ For help with graphics for your site, **see** "Creating Professional Web Graphics," **p. 597**

Creating a Theme

A theme for your home page is more than just a way of being visually impressive. A theme is an effective means of magnifying the impact of your content and making the page reflect who you are even more clearly. Like Disney World and the Hard Rock Café, association with a common theme throughout will give your home page both stylistic and personal authenticity—and just like the castle at Disney World or the car awning at Hard Rock Café, the theme of your home page will render each individual feature of it distinctive to you.

Because the Web is, above all, a visual place, your theme should boast a set of predominantly visual motifs: A common color scheme and trademark font are a good place to start.

→ For more information on using fonts to add distinction to your site, **see** "Working with Fonts," **p. 229**

You might want a clean, neat format with a solid-color background, understated sidebar, matching images, and an unobtrusive font. You might decide on a vivid splashy theme with intense bright colors and exciting images. Just remember that your page still needs to be readable without hurting someone's eyes.

You also might want to develop a "trademark" image for use throughout your pages, as I have on my home page (see Figure 38.3). A small GIF image—a map of the world, your favorite cartoon character, a baseball and bat, a particular animal or flower—can serve as the basis for your personal logo, and incorporating that logo into your theme will personalize your pages that much more.

Figure 38.3
An example of a trademark image. The idea is to have people always associate the image with my personal brand. My "Molly" logo is established on my splash page and carried through the site. The SM stands for "service mark" and is a special registration format for specific types of formal trademarks.

Show Your True Colors (All 216 of Them)

There are up to seven different color specifications (not counting style sheets) to consider when creating your theme:

- Background color
- Font color
- Link color
- Active link color
- Visited link color
- Sidebar/decorative color
- Background color for table cells

→ For a discussion of the Web-safe color palette, **see** "Web Graphic Formats and Professional Tools," **p. 578**

Ideally, you should choose from the 216 Web-safe colors. As you become more experienced at graphic design and want to get more adventuresome with your home page, you can pick out colors through an image program like Photoshop, noting their red-green-blue (RGB) components, and translating those numerical components into Web-ready hexadecimals by using one of the many utilities available online or by working the numeric values out by using a scientific calculator. For maximum compatibility, however, stick with the Web-safe palette.

→ To find out more about using hexadecimal colors, **see** "Color Concepts," **p. 537**

Fontology

The Web, because it must appeal to common denominators, is still coming to terms with how to handle fonts. In the past, browsers could only recognize whether a font was fixed-width (such as Courier, where each letter is the same width) or proportional (such as Times

New Roman, where letters such as i and l take up less space than m or w). New HTML standards have allowed browsers to become more sophisticated in their font display. There's the common <FONT> tag and its attributes, and HTML 4.0 allows for the font to be controlled by using style sheets.

→ To learn more about fonts, **see** "Working with Fonts," **p. 230**

→ For more information on style sheets, **see** "Cascading Style Sheets Techniques," **p. 254**

Using fonts allows you to specify the typeface in which you'd like your home page to appear—an important part of your theme. Keep in mind, however, that if you use a unique font, visitors to your site will only be able to view that font if it is already installed on their local computer.

Site Mapping

After you've picked the content for your page and settled on a common theme, the next step in building your home page is to plan how it all fits together. You'll want a navigation system that's easy to understand and build on, both for you and your visitors. Here are a few key points to consider when constructing your navigation system:

- **Filenames**—It might be tempting to number your files to keep track of them. This gets very confusing as your site grows, however. It's a much better idea to name your files descriptively. If you have a home page covering a wide variety of interests, how are you going to remember that 1234.html is about books and 1235.html is about music? If you name the files books.html and music.html, you're sure to keep things straight.

→ To learn more about file naming, **see** "Managing HTML Documents Locally," **p. 62**

- **Directories and nesting**—Another way to keep track of your files is to organize them in directories. You can put all your images in one directory, sound files in another, and content in a third. As your site grows, you can nest directories, such as dividing your content directory into one for books and one for music.
- **Links**—The key to navigation on any page is the structure of its links. Can you get to any page from any other page at any time? Are certain pages only accessible if you link to them from certain others? You can group pages into categories for easier navigation, which I'll cover in this next section.

→ For complete details on linking, **see** "Linking Pages," **p. 174**

However you choose to organize your site, make sure that you always know how to get to the page you're looking for—and that others can too. Otherwise, pages can fall through the cracks and fill up valuable disk space. You'll be amazed, a year after you've brought your page online, how many defunct pages a housecleaning will turn up. While you might not be concerned from a server space issue if you have a lot of space, it can be confusing for your visitors. If someone bookmarks a specific page within your site, they might be missing dozens of new pages as you add to the site unless you provide a clear-cut way to get back to your index page or otherwise navigate the entire site.

Hotlists Versus Navigation Bars

So what's the most efficient way to catalog your links? There's a tradeoff here between flexibility and conciseness. If you've organized your site logically, you can probably come up with a fairly constant list of topics to link to. In that case, you can build a navigation bar, or *navbar*—a graphical image or series of images that are hyperlinked to the main areas of your home page. This navbar gives your viewer a quick, concise overview of the contents of your page.

→ For a discussion of graphical navbars, **see** "Imagemaps, Animation, and Special Graphic Techniques," **p. 648**

What about all those links you see on Web sites that link site visitors to other sites of interest? It might not always be good Web etiquette to do so, see "Permission to Link" in the Troubleshooting section at the end of this chapter.

There's a danger in creating a navbar too soon, though, especially if the organization of your page hasn't been finalized or is quickly evolving (see Figure 38.4).

When your site is in its early stages, you might choose to manage your navigation through a hotlist—a straightforward list of text links. This is a rather unromantic way of doing things, but it's highly flexible and functional for the rapidly growing home page. You can trade up to a navbar at any time, too.

Note

Even if you decide to use a navbar in the future, you can still use a hotlist as a site map. Not only will this give visitors an overview of your entire site at a glance, but it can help you during testing and redesigns. You can use the hotlist as a checklist to be sure you test each and every page of your site.

Navigation for Everyone

The majority of surfers who visit your page will be using standard browser software produced by Netscape or Microsoft. The prevalence of Netscape Navigator and Microsoft Internet Explorer has had the effect of allowing many Web designers to grow a bit lazy. Why create a whole text-only version of your site when pretty much everyone can see your images?

There's some truth to the fact that browsers have evolved tremendously, and with them the ability of the average Web surfer to fully profit from a visually stunning page design. Still, a percentage of the visitors to your site might have graphics turned off, or have special needs that are an impediment to them experiencing images at all. For those people, there are a few features you can add that will make your page more accessible without costing you tremendous amounts of time.

→ For more information on creating a text browser accessible site, **see** "Accessibility and Internationalization," **p. 475**

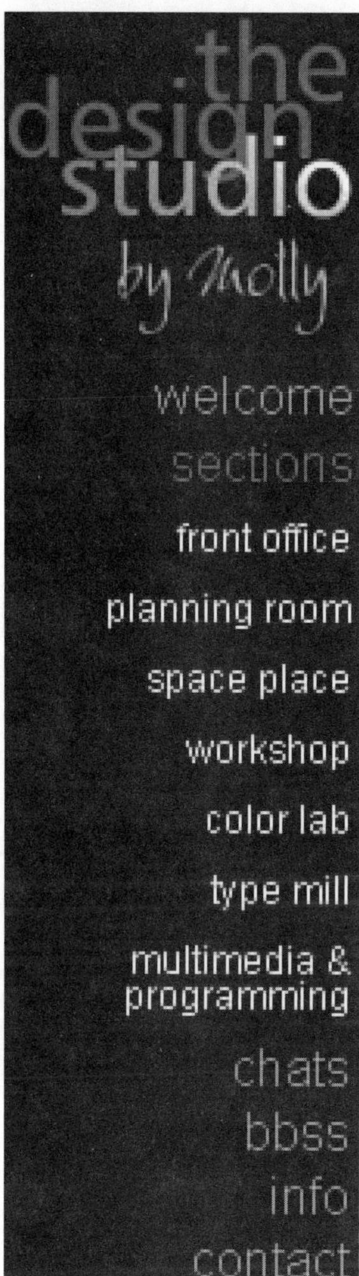

Figure 38.4
This navigation is a complicated system to maintain, because every new link requires a complete remodeling of the navigation image.

First of all, remember the ALT attribute in your image tags. Users of text-based browsers like Lynx are incessantly annoyed by lazy Web designers who forget to label their images. This is most important if you're using a graphical navbar to manage navigation among the areas of your home page. The Lynx user won't be able to navigate at all unless you label the buttons or hotlinked areas on your navbar. Along with using the ALT attribute, you also should provide a text-based navigation system on your page, usually at the bottom of the page. Keeping people on your page is always worth the extra bit of effort.

Secondly, not everyone has a rapid-fire Internet connection. Some people with older modems or slower connections might find themselves waiting and waiting for your images to appear on their screens. A small, unobtrusive text version of your navbar tucked down at the bottom of your index page can solve the problem. People can simply go straight to the area of your page that interests them without waiting for a large navigational image to download.

Finally, be considerate of users who don't have lots of plug-ins configured for their browser. This doesn't mean that you should leave all the exciting extras out of your page, but make sure you also have enough other content to balance things out.

Tip from molly

Try looking at your page with a slow, text-only or barebones graphical browser. Think of ways you could optimize your content for that type of browser without having to reinvent your page. Your audience will be 100% appreciative that you took the time.

Creating a Splash with Images

The easiest way to spice up your home page is with well-placed, visually appealing images. You can find free stock photographs and clip art all over the Web. These are good to play with as you develop your page. Try modifying them in a graphic image software package, and enjoy the results.

If you are looking for a good graphic image package, there are two ways to go. The best commercial package on the market is Adobe Photoshop. This feature-rich package is pricey, however, and might be out of your range if you are only using it for a small personal home page.

The most popular shareware package is JASC Paint Shop Pro, which is available at most shareware download sites. This package has many of the same features as Photoshop.

→ For more information about alternative Web graphic programs, **see** "Web Graphic Formats and Professional Tools," **p. 575**

You also can use your own photos and images. Pick out a few photos you want for your home page and scan them into your computer. From there, you can add backgrounds, crop the picture to hone in on one aspect of the photo, and optimize the file for the Web.

Tip from molly

If you don't own a scanner and don't want to make the investment, you can have your photos scanned at a copy shop for very reasonable rates.

Be sure to save your files in either JPG (for photos) or GIF (for line drawings) format. Also optimize the images using the compression features of your graphic image software to get the files to the smallest possible size without unduly sacrificing quality.

→ For more information about Web graphics, **see** "Creating Professional Web Graphics," **p. 598**

As you get more creative, you might want to animate some of your images. An animated GIF is actually a series of GIFs packed into one GIF file using an animated GIF utility. You embed an animated GIF into your HTML code the same way you do with any other image; the animation is handled by the file itself without requiring any extra coding on your part.

→ To read about animating images, **see** "Imagemaps, Animation, and Special Graphic Techniques," **p. 655**

FUN WITH IMAGEMAPS

If you've graduated to a graphical navbar and want it to appear somehow other than a simple series of buttons, an imagemap might well be the way to go. An imagemap begins with the image of your choice. You then select certain areas of this image to be hyperlinked to files of your choice. As was mentioned earlier, don't forget to provide an alternative (text) means of navigation for people surfing without graphics.

Note

Older browsers can only recognize GIF-based imagemaps, while the current versions of both Internet Explorer and Netscape Navigator can interpret JPG imagemaps as well.

Imagemaps are one instance where middleware is a great help. A shareware program called MapEdit, available at `http://www.boutell.com/`, is one of the best applications available to generate imagemap code. (You also can write it yourself, but it tends to be time consuming.) A wide range of other imagemapping software exists, too, or is built-in to larger programs such as Macromedia Fireworks, Adobe Illustrator, and Adobe ImageStyler.

→ To learn more about creating imagemaps, **see** "Imagemaps, Animation, and Special Graphic Techniques," **p. 648**

MapEdit allows you to select areas of an image by clicking and dragging; after you've created the polygon of your choice around the specified area of your image, the software will then prompt you to enter the URL to which it should be hyperlinked. Code is saved in the file you specify—no need to cut and paste.

Note that it's far more efficient to use a client-side imagemap than a server-side one. In a server-side imagemap, only the computer where the file is stored knows to where the hyperlinks lead. All the viewer sees is a set of coordinates. Client-side imagemaps tell the viewer's computer to where the hyperlinks lead; positioning your mouse over a client-side imagemap will show you the name of the file at the other end of that hyperlink.

GAINING FEEDBACK

One of the most exciting parts of having a home page on the Internet is the feedback you'll get from it. People will experience it and enjoy or dislike it, comment on it, offer suggestions for improvement, sometimes even offer to link to it from their own home pages. To be assured that you receive all this feedback, then, it makes sense to establish on your home page a means of communicating with you.

Remember the caveats relating to problem individuals who might visit your site, though. You don't want to wave your email address too much around your home page if you're trying to avoid email from strangers. By the same token, though, if your page is free from the types of innuendoes that would attract unsavory characters, and you're in the mood for a little adventure, adding a mail link can provide you with interesting feedback, new contacts, and a greater sense of your place on the Internet.

→ To learn how to add a mail link to your page, **see** "Linking Pages," **p. 188**

THE MAILTO: FUNCTION

The simplest way to enable Web surfers to email you is to add a direct `mailto:` link onto your home page. The HTML for this is simple:

```
Email me at <A HREF="mailto:molly@molly.com">molly@molly.com</a>!
```

The `mailto:` command launches the mail program associated with the browser your viewer is using. This might not always be that person's mail program of choice. In case your viewer hasn't configured their browser-based mail program, spelling out your email address elsewhere on your page will enable viewers to copy it into the mail programs they do use.

GUESTBOOKS

A guestbook is another solution to the non-configured mail-program problem. Viewers click your guestbook link and are taken to a page on which you've created an HTML form. Ask any questions you like in this form. You might be surprised at some of the answers you get.

You can have the form return its results to you in raw text form by specifying a `mailto:` link to your address as the "action" of the form. A sample of the code to activate a CGI script can be found in the following code example. Your ISP or Web-hosting service provider might also offer their own form parsing agent.

```
<FORM action="http://www.molly.com/users/lore/cgi-bin/gfm" method="get">
<INPUT type="hidden" name="sendto" value="molly@molly.com">
```

→ For an introduction to CGI scripting and a blank guestbook script for those who can add their own CGI scripts to a Web server, **see** "CGI and Pre-Processing Fundamentals," **p. 749**

A guestbook is also a safe way of ensuring your page against spam and unwanted attention; people who *want* to communicate with you about your page *can*, while people who are collecting email addresses for profit won't bother filling out your guestbook form.

All of these tips and ideas just scratch the surface of what you can do with your home page. As your skills grow, you can add streaming audio and video, message boards, and all manner of other bells and whistles. Follow the advice within this chapter, and there's no doubt your home page will be up and running well in no time!

Troubleshooting

Using Licensed Images

Can I use images from The Simpsons on my site?

This becomes a question of copyright law versus fair use. If you are using one image from *The Simpsons* to illustrate a point you are making in your content—and if you are not making a profit from your discussion of *The Simpsons*—your use of the image *might* fall under fair use. If your site is merely a re-hashing of jokes and images from the show, this is copyright infringement, even if your site is not for-profit. The best bet in every case is to get permission.

Permission to Link

Can I link to any site I choose?

To be a good Internet citizen, you should always ask for permission before linking to someone else's site. Nine times out of ten, the designer of the other site will be honored to be asked. Others might request that you not link to them, however, because their hits are metered or for other legitimate reasons. Don't take a refusal personally; just find another site to which to link.

Designing for the Real World

A Personal Home Page Tour

Lisa and Jim Berglin breed and raise Airedale Terriers. As with most Airedale owners, their interest in the breed also led them to start collecting Airedale antiques and memorabilia. When they created their home page, it was a natural for them to show others their beautiful dogs and treasures, as well as offer a peek into the life of the Berglin family.

The resulting Imprimis Airedales site is a home page delight. The photographs of the Berglin's Airedales are professionally done, and the use of a script font and textured background create an elegant theme. While the pages scroll vertically, visitors are not overwhelmed by the content.

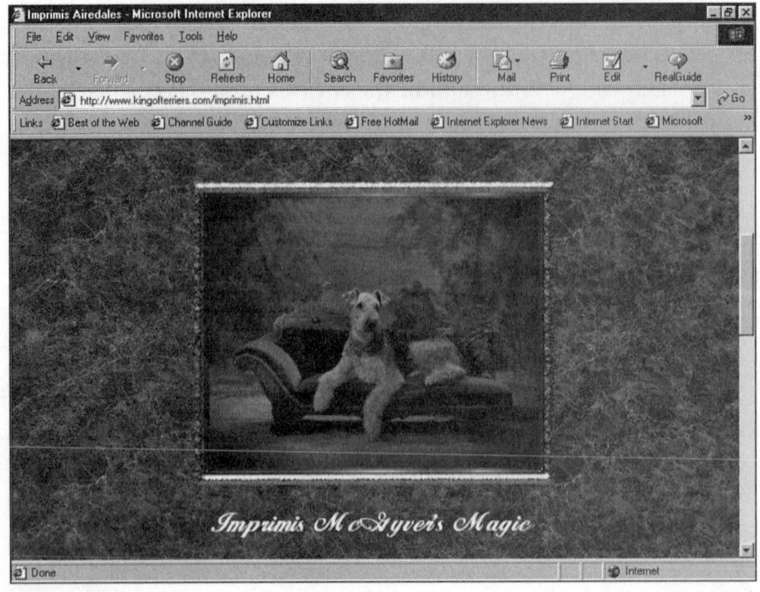

Figure 38.5
The Imprimis Airedales site is a perfect example of how hobbyists can turn a home page into a rich experience for site visitors.

Like many home pages, the Imprimis site contains a list of links, a guestbook, and an email link. The site also is linked to a Web ring, a group of sites that have linked together with a common interest—in this case, Airedale Terriers.

The site makes use of two types of navigation. On the index page are a series of buttons linking to various areas on the site. Each button is tagged with an `ALT` attribute.

Inner pages use an imagemap navbar. While these pages do not offer alternate means of navigation, there is a text link back to the index page, from which visitors can navigate to new areas of the site.

When you put all the pieces of this site together, you come away with a great visitor experience.

Note

The Berglin's Imprimis Airedales site can be found at **`http://www.kingofterriers.com/imprimis.html`**.

CHAPTER 39

Building Business and e-Commerce Sites

In this chapter

Doing Business Online

Perhaps you're the owner of a small hardware store on Main Street and you want some advertising exposure. Maybe you're a skeleton-crew telecom startup who wants to get its distribution channels in order. Maybe you're a fledgling professional Web designer who's looking to build your own business. No matter what your trade, a site on the World Wide Web will give your business a marketing boost that no other medium can.

The advent of the World Wide Web and the increasingly common distribution of personal computers with modems helped the Internet evolve into the marketplace it is today. Commercial Internet service providers like Prodigy and America Online, who had risen to prominence by offering original proprietary content, began aggressively recruiting new customers with access to Internet mail, news, and Web services. Suddenly millions of people were on the Internet looking around for things to do. Business was an obvious answer.

Web design, then, became a marketable and profitable profession. Many large companies hired firms or created entire online departments devoted to planning, constructing, and maintaining corporate Web sites. Newer versions of HTML allowed for greater freedom of design. Companies specifically aimed at increasing the potential of the medium produced better browsers, multimedia browser plug-ins, and various programming tools that permitted greater exchange of information over the Internet. Finally, enhanced encryption technologies allowed for the secure relay of personal financial data and e-commerce (electronic commerce) was born.

e-Commerce is taking the online world by storm. But, the majority of business Web sites still exist as primarily informative or marketing tools. When creating a business site, it's always important to take into account the goals of the site; whether it's going to be a means of communicating with customers, or actually provide them with your product. And yes, it can be both at the same time. Or, if you prefer, it can start out as your salesman and end up as your distributor. The Web is equipped to provide any kind of business service you want it to—how you plan to use it to grow is up to you.

Planning Your Online Business

Often, you'll be building a Web site for a business that has existed for several years. In such a case, you (or they, if they're your client) should have a solid idea of the markets the business competes in, the products it produces or distributes, and who its major competitors are. These will all be key points when producing the business Web site—they'll act as a basis for your site design plan as well as provide ideas for content.

If the site you're constructing is for a new company that isn't yet in business or is just starting up, you've got a little research to do. What is the company going to provide—a product, a service, other people's products? Who else already does the same thing, and how can you present your message differently from them? And if nobody's doing the same thing, how can you make sure that all your customers know this—how can it be obvious in the way you market that company?

Large companies have the luxury of extensive capital available to build Web sites that market individual products. Small businesses tend to be somewhat shorter on resources; the small business Internet site will have a much bigger marketing responsibility than that of the large corporate site.

In one site you'll have to relay everything you want people to know about the company as a whole—corporate culture and values, vision and mission, and more practical concerns like job postings and contact information—as well as each individual product the company produces or service it provides. Fortunately this is simpler than it seems.

RESEARCH THE MARKET: WHAT ARE COMPETITORS DOING?

Basic market research is a *must* when setting up any new business Web site. This may sound like a daunting task, but you've already got on hand the most valuable tool you'll need: the Internet itself.

Go online and search for companies similar to yours. You can do this through any search engine; pick out the keywords that best match your industry and see what kind of sites you return. Even easier, you can browse through the Business and Economy area on Yahoo!, which has already created a thorough system of categorization (see Figure 39.1).

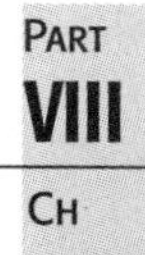

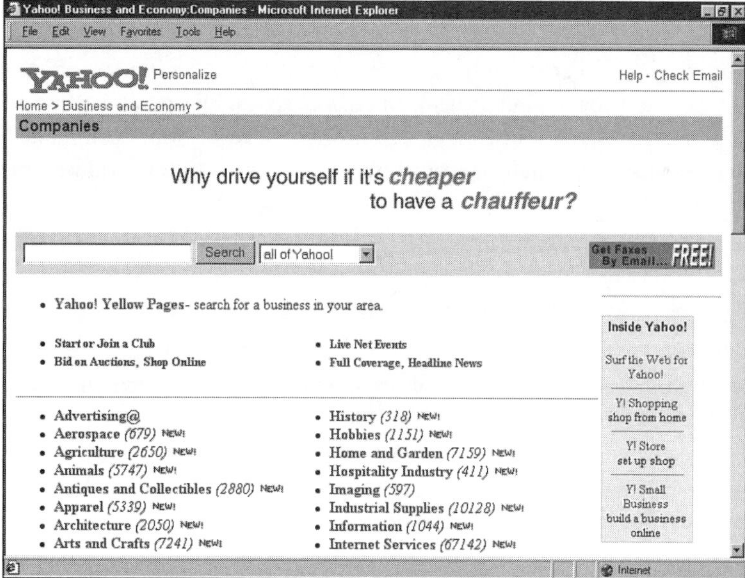

Figure 39.1
Categorize your company! Yahoo! lists top-level categories of businesses with Internet presence.

You may already know who your competition is; In that case it's simple to look up the names of their companies on Yahoo!, Infoseek, Excite, or any other search engine. See what their Web sites look like. What kind of content are they offering? What do you see that you like? What will you do differently to set your site apart from theirs? Do they have a strong visual identity for the company, or is their site mostly text-driven? How do they showcase products? Do they provide any online ordering or distribution services? What are they doing to attract new customers? How do they keep people returning to their site? These questions are mission-critical to setting your small business site success in stone.

KNOW YOURSELF AND YOUR CLIENT

Your business' Web site is going to be all about what your business is: what you do, who you do it for, and how you stay competitive. If you've already written a business plan, you probably have a good solid grasp of the answers to all these questions. If you haven't yet reached the point of business planning, it's a good place to start making marketing decisions—decisions which will affect the design of your business Web site.

Basic Business Plan Considerations

What products or services do we provide now?

What products or services do we want to provide eventually?

How will we sell our products/services? What will they cost?

Who will be our competitors?

How will we be different from our competitors?

What will we do to grow our business and be profitable?

Ideally, your Web business plan should grow out of your basic business plan. You'll decide how much of a marketing investment you need to make to properly promote your business, how to build your brand to be distinct from that of your competitors, what kinds of products or services you'll be selling, and how you'll reach your customers. From the answers to those questions, the path your Internet site needs to take will become much clearer.

Web Site Business Plan Considerations

What kind of image do we want to give our business?

Should our Internet site be designed primarily to recruit new customers?

Is our Internet site going to be a source more for product or corporate information?

Where do we draw the line between informing prospective customers about our business and keeping information out of the hands of competitors?

What percentage of our marketing/advertising budget should be invested in our Internet site?

How should we arrange for our Internet site to grow along with our business? Should we contract with a firm to maintain it or train one of our employees?

DEFINING SITE GOALS

As with any marketing or promotional effort, you don't want to invest a lot of time or money in the development of your company Web site without a clear idea of what you expect it to deliver for you after its completion. You'll need to look at it in terms of both short-term and long-term goals. Again, you'll profit most from the undertaking if these goals match your goals for the development of your business.

Short Term Goals

Setting short-term goals is simple; Whether you realize it or not, you do it daily. A short-term goal is anything you want to see accomplished within a month to six months. Do you want to land your first big customer? Move your business from the garage into an office suite? The short-term goal-setting process for your Internet site follows similar lines.

Why Build a Web Site?

What's the number one reason why your company needs a site on the Internet?

The answer will be different for every company. Maybe it's the most cost-effective way for you to relay company or product information to customers on the opposite coast or in other countries. Maybe your product is specifically technological or Internet-related, and your company needs a presence on the Internet to give it credibility in the industry. Or, maybe you're going to be the first hardware store in Springfield to enter the digital age. Whatever your answer, this is the first goal of your site: to live up to the reason why it was created.

Flesh out your answer a bit to create some auxiliary goals. Maybe there's a *specific* large account in Seattle that you want to land from Atlanta, and you know exactly what they're looking for. A goal of your business site can be to portray your product line in a light that you know will appeal to that particular customer.

Or if you know that there's a Home Depot moving into Springfield soon and you want to make sure that all your loyal longtime customers know you're up for the challenge, maybe your Internet site will be a place to offer special services like Web-only coupons or free carpentry classes to everyone who registers online. See where this is heading? You don't necessarily need a Web site just to *have* one; there's a lot it can do for your business if you plan correctly.

Immediate Needs

The second your business' Internet site goes live, what do you expect it to accomplish? Is it part of a larger marketing scheme including print advertisement and other promotions, or is it a standalone activity that will be publicized with great flourish in all your company literature? After you clear the first hurdle of any new Web site, that of getting people to look at it (or building traffic, in Internet terms), it's time for the site to start accomplishing those short-term goals you set.

Concerned about how the Web may affect your business? See "Solutions for Small Business" in the Troubleshooting section at the end of this chapter for answers to your concerns.

Tip from

It is perfectly appropriate to put out a press release on BusinessWire or PRNewswire announcing the launch of a new Internet site. This is also a great opportunity to get the word out about your business in the appropriate trade media and shouldn't run you more than $500. Check out `http://www.businesswire.com/` or `http://www.prnewswire.com/` for more information about setting up a corporate account.

Maybe you took a different approach. Maybe the Internet site you've mounted is temporary, a small-scale site that fits your budget and is adequate until your business can earn enough to afford a full-scale Internet presence. Its goals, in that case, are simple: to present your business' brand identity in as straightforward a fashion as possible, while still giving the impression that there is more to come.

This is not at all uncommon among startup sites on the Internet; not every small business can afford the man-hours or consulting fees necessary to establish a full-scale Web site. Granted, you should be careful of growing complacent and deciding that your temporary site is enough; still, to seed your brand, a small, introductory site can hold you for several months before the need for more overcomes its usefulness.

Short-term, introductory site startups with limited budgets, provide the opportunity to move into new Internet homes slowly. A minimalist site sets the future tone as well as branding and focusing on the logo and slogan but only invests enough design energy in it to give it a sense of style.

LONG TERM GOALS

Long term goals come from the tactical and strategic portions of your business plan. If you want to launch a new product in three years, how will your Internet site be equipped to incorporate the new product? Or if you eventually intend to consult on the implementation of the software you're currently manufacturing, how will the site need to change in order to accommodate that new offering?

KEEPING CURRENT

Imagine that your business site went live last month. You landed that client in Seattle. Your first Web-only sale was a success. Now what? You didn't invest all that time and money in the development of a Web site for it to outmode itself within a year. You're going to want to build on the concept, watch it grow, help it evolve, and, most of all, keep pace with the development of your business.

One unfortunate truth is that your site, as it currently exists, will *de facto* be inadequate in five years. There's no way a site, in the ever-evolving matrix of the Internet, can stay static for years while the rest of the business world—and the online world—have moved light-years ahead. This doesn't mean that you've wasted the effort in setting up a site however; far from it.

You've laid the groundwork for a part of your business that will grow with you as much as is needed. But that growth is something for which you'll need to plan.

ROOM TO GROW

Here's one basic rule: Your site should be structured in such a way that introducing new content will not disrupt its design. Launching a new product, opening a new branch office, or suddenly needing to double your headcount shouldn't call for a total overhaul of your business Internet site.

There are several checkpoints for implementing this rule. The first of these is the site's navigation. In assembling the infrastructure of your business site, group its content into flexible umbrella categories that will not need to change even if the content does. Products and Services, Corporate Background, Job Opportunities, and Customer Service are good examples of top-level categories. Your umbrella categories should all be accessible from the site's index page—the first page on your site that a customer sees.

After firming up your internal categorization and navigation scheme, turn your attention to the branding of the site. You may find that, as your business grows, this site will evolve into more of a corporate information source than a product-driven marketing tool.

Early on, it's important that your business site have a strong corporate feel as well as provide product information. If you build the site now with a long-term brand in mind, that brand will survive any number of subdirectory reconstructions and other tweaking that the site will necessarily undergo as it develops.

An example of a site focused on company identity rather than product, the United Water corporate Web site contains information for investors and history buffs as well as water utility customers (see Figure 39.2).

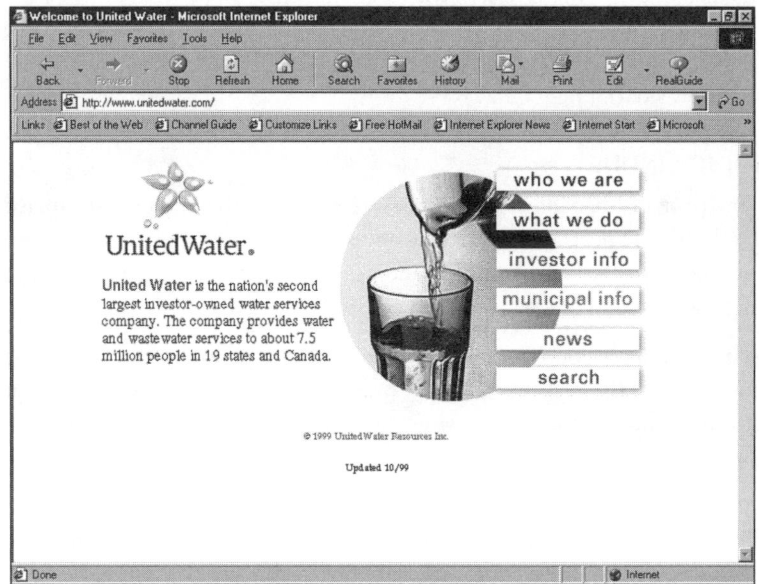

Figure 39.2
United Water has incorporated long-term plans by focusing on company identity.

BRANDING AND IDENTITY

Almost everyone in business worldwide is familiar with Federal Express (FedEx for short). In fact, you've probably already conjured up a variety of images, benefits, and services simply with my writing out their name. The familiar packaging, colors, and visual imagery of the company relates directly with your sense of what they are and what they do. This is because FedEx has a powerful brand identity. Branding is a critical issue for commercial Web site success.

New York University marketing professor Henry Assael defines a brand as more than just a product name or associated imagery. Rather, to be a brand, a name or image must have associated with it a set of product benefits, a visual package, and a set of support services such as a warranty or good technical support. Applying Assael's definition of branding to a business yields the following checklist of needs:

- Strong, identifiable company name/slogan
- Visually meaningful, illustrative logo
- Positive features of company (high-quality products, focused corporate mission, upbeat investor outlook, and so on)
- Positive package (activism in the community, good treatment of employees, and so on)
- Reputation for high-quality support services

Apply this checklist to your business to determine the strength of your brand. Does the name of your company conjure a positive image? Does your slogan, if you use one, cut to the chase as to what business you're in and why you're good at it? How strong is your logo in conveying the meaning you want your brand to bear? Have you succeeded in spreading the message of all your company's good points? These are all jobs where your business Internet site can help out.

Branding Online

The principal benefit of a business Internet site—the one goal it can accomplish most effectively—is the portrayal of your business' brand. This can be either a corporate identity or a product. Most other forms of branding—print advertising, radio or television, and packaging—are limited in what they can convey.

Think about it: you've got a four-inch square, or a 30-second spot, in which to relay to your customer all the reasons why your product is better. For a similar amount of money, you can create an Internet site that says as much about your brand as you want without limitations on time or space.

Tip from molly

Obviously you want to use the Web to represent your brand in its best light. You can add a lot more detail than in traditional media, but do so using the Web's unique interactive qualities. Simply providing a laundry list of all the things that are great about your company or your product will quickly bore Web surfers.

Unlimited ability to plug your brand doesn't mean a license to ramble. You'll want your message to be just as sharp and targeted as it would be in an ad or TV commercial and composed in a visually appealing manner that will provoke surfers to follow your links.

Note

Want to learn about branding from the most effective branding company in history? Check out Landor Associates at `http://www.landor.com/`.

Fortunately, the majority of a brand's components are visual or psychological rather than textual. The visual emphasis of your name, slogan, and logo is an excellent way to create and enforce branding.

Portraying the intangible features of your company is as challenging on the Internet as in any medium. As previously mentioned, the limiting factor when creating content for your corporate Web site is the attention span of your viewers. You won't want to bury them under a headache-load of images or a glut of cheerleading prose.

Simply relaying your business' chosen look-and-feel with well-placed promotional plugs will go a long way toward building your online brand.

Working with a Company Logo

A unique company logo is key to a strong visual identity. Picture Coca-Cola, Ford, Federal Express, and Nike. Each name conjures an image; the image, in turn, conjures a full brand with all the positives and negatives and all the features and benefits associated with using that company rather than Pepsi, Toyota, DHL, or Reebok. This association is cultivated through exposure. To build the connection between a meaningful logo and the meaning you want it to attribute to your business, you need people to see both and equate them. Your business Internet site is an excellent staging ground for building logo recognition.

Consistency of Style

One of the most important aspects of branding is the creation of a logo. A logo must be consistent and pervasive. Logos lose impact when their color changes, their main images are distorted, or any of the visual characteristics are altered from what has been determined as the standard.

Rather than adjusting your corporate logo to fit the desired design of the site, you'll be far better off taking your existing logo into account when developing your site's look-and-feel.

Color Concerns

Choose a color scheme for your site that matches your logo. This doesn't necessarily mean that your entire site has to be done in shades of blue just because your company has a blue logo. Simply think about what is pleasing to the eye. There are many colors and textures your business site can include without clashing with your logo. In fact, designing the entire color scheme of your business site based on the color of your logo will make for a visually uninteresting experience.

Remember that the point is not only to constantly remind people what your logo looks like; they need to know what it stands for, too. An interesting, symbolically meaningful logo won't be detracted from by an equally interesting, subtle visual theme. Ideally your color scheme will blend nicely into the background while drawing attention to your company logo.

→ For more on color choices, **see** "Color Concepts," **p. 528**

IMAGE ISSUES

Your logo should also lose nothing in the translation from paper to digital image. Scan it several times so that you have a large version, several medium-sized versions, and a thumbnail version. High-quality image manipulation programs like Adobe Photoshop allow you to scale images of your company's logo without losing visual quality. The same cannot be said for most browsers, so you're better off scaling your logo image by hand rather than expecting the browser to correctly handle the scale.

Make sure you have both GIF and JPEG images of your logo available. Keep in mind that you'll want to use whichever results in a smaller file size while preserving the maximum integrity of your logo. If you have a two-color logo and find that saving it in JPG format creates a fuzzy, freckled effect, saving it as a GIF should solve that problem.

Tip from molly

If your multicolored logo loses some of its dimension when reduced to GIF-standard 256 colors, JPG format may well be your solution.

→ For more information on image formats and imaging software, **see** "Web Graphic Formats and Professional Tools," **p. 566**

COMPANY LOOK-AND-FEEL

Believe it or not, *look-and-feel* is a technical term. Fortunately, it's one of the few technical terms that actually means what a layman thinks it should. The look-and-feel of your business Internet site is the whole visual effect it creates: the composite of color scheme, font, layout, navigation, and overall organization that comes together to create a sense of identity.

Choose a look-and-feel for your Web site that best fits with the qualities you want to emphasize in your corporate brand. Do you want to portray your business as a young, dynamic, on-the-move company for the new millennium? Or would you better serve your target market by branding your company as mature, established, and authoritative?

The decisions you make when planning how you'll brand your business will serve you in good stead when choosing the look-and-feel for your corporate site. Remember, because a brand is principally visual, look-and-feel is key to establishing a connection with your viewer.

ADDING INTERACTIVE COMPONENTS

Another advantage of the Internet over traditional media is that, in the course of promoting your business, you can proactively interact with prospective customers. Interactivity on the Internet is a far more basic function than you might think.

Your site is already, strictly speaking, interactive. Customers can arrive at your site, follow the links they choose, and take away from the experience any content that interests them while avoiding items they find irrelevant. If it were just a TV commercial, customers wouldn't have that choice.

In addition to your navigational structure, you can add several other components to your business Web site to enhance its interactivity. Depending on your needs, you may add games, audio, video, streaming media, and Flash. Think of each of these enhancements as providing your viewer with a greater level of choice and control over the information you're providing on your site.

→ To read more about providing audio and video files on your site, **see** "Audio, Video, and Streaming Media," **p. 666**

→ For more information on Flash and multimedia, **see** "Working with Shockwave Flash," **p. 687**

MAKING YOUR PRESENCE KNOWN

Your business' Internet presence is by no means limited to your Web site. You must also consider its relation to the rest of the Internet. How will you draw visitors to your site? Your listing in search engines is an important tool; it will help you a great deal if a prospective customer can find your site when searching for a product you sell.

ADVERTISING ONLINE

You probably pulled up a banner ad along with your search. Banner ads are long, narrow rectangular graphics that usually appear across the top of a Web page. Various Internet sites charge advertisers for the privilege of having their particular banner ad appear on that site.

For the less well-heeled, there are several free exchanges to which you can submit your banner. In return for adding the code for a link-exchange window to your own site, you are guaranteed that your banner will eventually show up in a participant's link-exchange window somewhere. It's a gamble, but a worthwhile one because trying it costs you nothing.

Several search engines exist that employ keyword technology to target your banner ad. Say you're a telecom startup. You could arrange with a search engine such as AltaVista at **`http://www.altavista.com/`** or Excite (**`http://www.excite.com/`**) to paste your banner ad only across pages that result from surfers searching for computer telephony, call processing, or ADSL, just to name a few choices.

This sort of targeted advertising is usually cheaper than a front-page banner visible to all surfers who use the engine, and it has the added benefit of being aimed directly at the people who are most likely to be interested in your business.

You can begin advertising this way even before your business site goes live. Most banner ads are hyperlinked to the Web sites they represent; however, not all are, and this is an excellent way of getting your business' name—and brand—out on the Internet while your site is still being developed.

Design your prelaunch banner ads to match your site's look-and-feel; this gives viewers a sense of familiarity with your brand, which translates into an increased comfort level when your site is finally launched.

→ For more information on marketing your site, **see** "Web Site Marketing and Promotion," **p. 906**

GET THAT FEEDBACK!

Interactivity on your business Web site should work just as hard for you as any salesman. After you draw viewers to your site through advertising and search placement, it's a good idea to have a mechanism in place for them to contact your business for further information about your products.

Needless to say, this issue is most obviously resolved by publishing your business' physical street address and phone number (toll free if possible). Many Web site visitors who have come to rely on the Internet to provide them with results for any research they pursue are still skittish when it comes to actually transmitting their own personal information across what might be perceived as insecure digital channels. You overcome that barrier by providing your viewer with a sense of where to find your business and how to contact you.

If you are a business marketing products to other businesses rather than to consumers, it is most definitely a good idea to include a feedback form in the design of your site. This form can be as detailed and probing or as removed and impersonal as you want. There are several good CGI-based form parsing agents available online. The one rule to guide your design should be the simpler, the better. Don't ask for more information than you need (see Figure 39.3).

Figure 39.3

Keeping forms short and sweet helps your site visitors to quickly provide you with feedback.

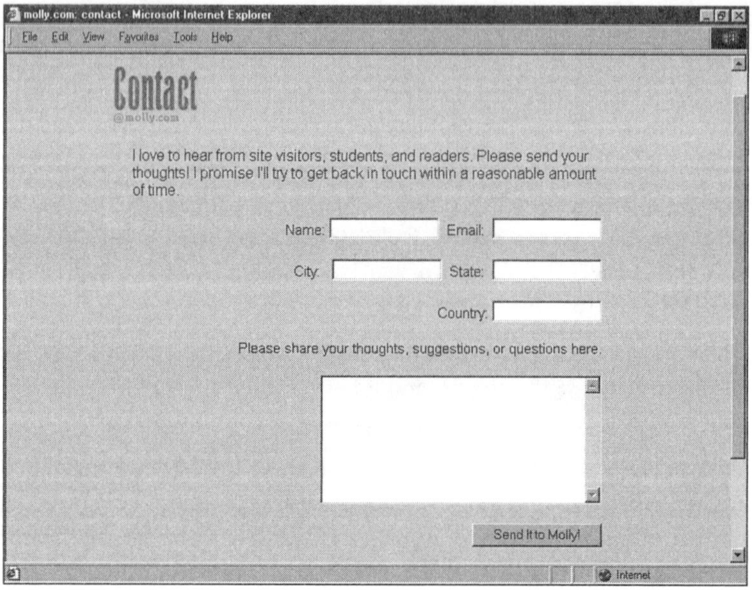

→ For details on creating a form for your site, **see** "Building Forms," **p. 386**

Another key area in which you'll profit from soliciting feedback is the overall design and functionality of your site. Every good site includes a `mailto` link or other means of contacting the site's Webmaster. People can use this link to send you email relating to your actual business, or they may choose to communicate with you in your Webmaster capacity, commenting on technical issues such as how the site didn't load right when using a certain browser.

Keep in mind, as you design and implement your business' Internet site, that you don't want the information to flow one way only. It's every bit as important that you learn about your customers as that they learn about your business.

SELLING ONLINE

You've probably heard a lot about e-commerce, online selling, and the success of startup businesses such as Amazon.com that built a customer base through Web-based sales. Depending on what side of the story you've heard, you're either familiar with the instant rise to fame and fortune of the CEOs of such businesses or of their inability to turn a profit even after mammoth infusions of venture capital.

Both aspects of the situation are true. There is a lot of money to be had in online selling, especially if you've got a strong concept going for your business. There are also, however, plenty of pitfalls associated with the process of implementing a purely Web-based sales paradigm.

How can you convince a prospective customer to enter personal information like a credit card number into the same Web browser they use to download the daily news? Although many more people are growing amenable to the concept of e-commerce, significant concern still remains that security be a foremost issue in the Web developer's mind.

You'll need a secure enough system to be able to encrypt, relay, and decrypt sensitive data without worrying about hackers grabbing it. Fortunately this technology exists; Internetscape's Secure Socket Layer (SSL) encryption system offers a level of encoding adequate for day-to-day use with the RSA standard 56-bit encryption, and Verisign (**`http://digitalid.verisign.com/server/index.html`**) offers 128-bit encryption, the most advanced encoding available today.

The main issue to overcome in offering online sales is not the quality of the technology, but rather the negative public image of e-commerce as being prone to highway robbery.

Setting up an electronic sales system is also a significant incremental expense on top of the basic design and implementation costs for a standard Internet site. If you don't anticipate doing a large percentage of your business over your Web site, it may not be worth the investment.

By the same token, if the vision behind your business entails a Web-based selling paradigm, go for it full throttle. Again, look back to your business plan for the answer to whether or not e-commerce is right for your business.

Note

One of the technologies that lends itself fully to security issues and e-commerce facilitation is XML (eXtensible Markup Language).

→ To find out how your site might benefit from XML, **see** "Understanding XHTML, XML, and Emerging Languages," **p. 494**

Sidebar: Online Storefronts

A variety of electronic commerce server software suites and contracted e-commerce services exist. They vary in price and functionality. Each offers out-of-the box security and online shopping services.

iCat Web Store is a start-to-finish online product that helps you build, manage, and host your business site. Pay by the month for a reasonable price, `http://www.icat.com/services/store/`.

iCat Commerce Cart allows you to add e-commerce to your existing site, also for a low monthly price, `http://www.icat.com/services/cart/`.

Running your own servers? You might be interested in taking a look at IBMs WebSphere Application Server, `http://www-4.ibm.com/software/webservers/appserv/download.html`.

Microsoft offers server-based e-commerce solutions, naturally. Microsoft Site Server is best used in conjunction with other Microsoft technologies or recommended third-party solutions. Get the details at `http://www.microsoft.com/siteserver/commerce/default.htm`.

Intershop Enfinity offers great flexibility and scalability for managing catalogs, merchandise, and transactions. See `http://www.intershop.com/products/index.htm`.

WebSite 2.3 Pro is a highly respected and venerable Web server available for a variety of platforms. It's also reasonably priced as far as server technologies go, `http://website.ora.com/`.

Managing Site Updates

A Web site is a constantly changing thing—or should be. If your business Internet site isn't changing and growing, there's a good chance that your business isn't either. The continuing development of your site should keep pace with the continuing development of your business. Got a new product? Time to put it online. Filled that vacancy? Pull that job posting down off your site. Having a sale this week? Put it online, and make sure to take it down next week after the sale is over.

This means, quite simply, that someone in your business has to take responsibility for the maintenance and ongoing development of your site. If you operate a Web design business of your own, you can offer maintenance services on an ongoing-fee basis to clients whose sites you've built.

Similarly, as a small business, you may find it more cost-effective to outsource the maintenance of your site to the consultant who originally implemented it.

Tip from molly

A good rule of thumb is that an Internet site needs to change some aspect of its content *at least* every 90 days or else it's too static. If this seems like a tall order, think about everything that could happen to your business in the course of three months. When you're small and growing, it's especially important for your Internet site to keep up.

It probably will be most cost-effective to train one of your employees to manage the site—providing he or she has the design as well as technical skills necessary to do so. Webmastery for a small business has the potential to become a full-time job, but this is seldom the case during the early phases of site development.

Traditionally, as a marketing function, site maintenance responsibility will logically fit into your Marketing or Publicity departments. Don't fall into the common trap of believing your Internet site to be an IT function—although it involves computer-based information technology, it serves a completely different strategic function in the development of your business.

Should you choose in-source site maintenance, be sure that your Webmaster is up to the task, with a solid skill set and a good grip of what the duties of Webmaster are.

Note

Webmaster is a soft job title at best; exactly how much you expect from your Webmaster depends a lot on your business, the structure of your company, the number of other people who will be involved with the ongoing maintenance of the site, and the frequency and intensity of changes that it will be undergoing.

If your business launches a new product once a year or only issues a press release every three or four months, the Webmaster's job need not be terribly demanding. By the same token, however, a site that changes on a weekly basis, based on what you're trying to move off the shelf each week, is going to keep your Webmaster busy indeed.

A top-gun small business Webmaster needs, above all, a deep and involved understanding of the nature of the business (another reason why it's a good idea to have an employee serve as your Webmaster). The best Webmasters can contribute ideas and design suggestions for new content as well as implement them.

Ideally, your Webmaster will have a background in or working knowledge of communication and marketing principles, so his or her suggestions will carry real weight. And, obviously, the appropriate level of technical background is invaluable.

Qualities That Make a Good Webmaster

- Extensive familiarity with your business
- Comprehensive knowledge of HTML–familiarity with other Web technologies also beneficial
- Working knowledge of file-transfer procedures
- High comfort level in dealing with your ISP or design consultants

continues

continued

- Expertise in image manipulation software
- Graphic design skills
- Basic knowledge/experience with marketing principles
- Creativity, flexibility, and vision
- Understanding of popular and traditional media

If the Webmaster requirements discussed here seem like a tall order for anyone on your staff, don't worry. There are plenty of training resources available.

TROUBLESHOOTING

SOLUTIONS FOR SMALL BUSINESS

Will I have to hire a full staff to meet my needs? I'm a small business! I want to do this myself.

If you are willing to handle the extra work and are prepared for growth should it happen (and when it does, it does so quickly), then there is no reason you can't run a small business online. Just be sure to set your budget and goals. Don't think that just because you are a smaller interest that you can gloss over the planning stages. It's to your advantage to work out these issues before jumping into the e-commerce fray.

DESIGNING FOR THE REAL WORLD

THE HOLLYWOOD ROOSEVELT HOTEL

Let's take a look at a real-life small business site. We'll examine various aspects of issues discussed in this chapter, including knowing the business, setting goals, and creating identity and look-and-feel.

KNOWING THE BUSINESS AND SETTING GOALS

When the historic Hollywood Roosevelt Hotel (see Figure 39.4) decided that it wanted its own Internet presence, it hired a professional Web design firm to manage the site's creation and implementation. The design team quickly realized that creating a site for the Roosevelt required not only a sense of the hospitality industry but also of the Roosevelt's unique place in the history of Hollywood.

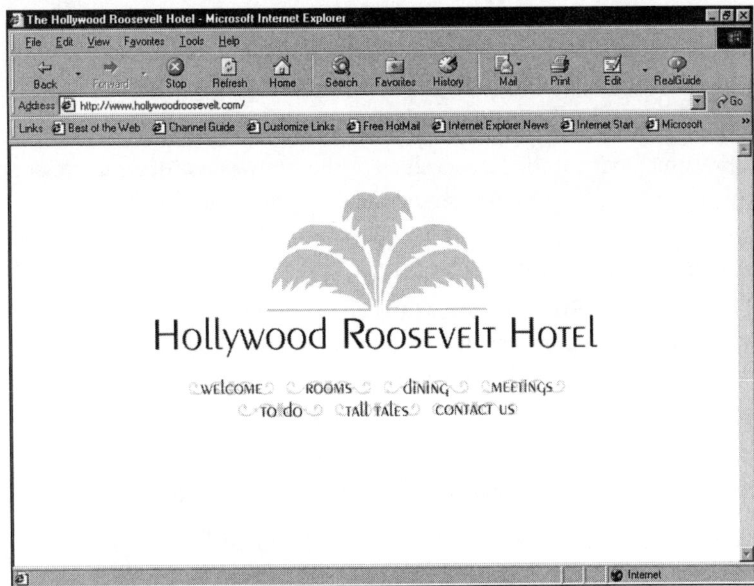

Figure 39.4
The historic Hollywood Roosevelt Hotel.

The Roosevelt had been the site of the first Academy Awards ceremony and, given its prime location directly across from the famed Mann's Chinese Theater, often has premiere-attending celebrities among its guests.

The design team worked closely with the Roosevelt staff to highlight the historical life of the hotel; this resulted, among other things, in a page of Tall Tales (see Figure 39.5) produced entirely by Roosevelt employees.

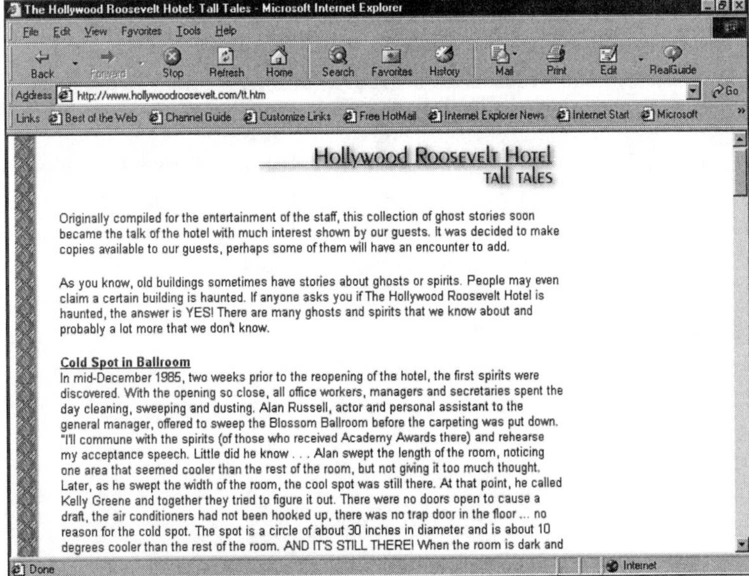

Figure 39.5
Tall Tales page on the Hollywood Roosevelt Hotel site.

The site's main goal was purely a marketing function: educating viewers about the romantic history of the Roosevelt as well as subtly enticing them to visit the hotel and enjoy its current array of features, both in terms of accommodations and environs.

Although the online contact page provides a means for viewers to email, phone, or write various members of the Roosevelt staff, the site was not designed to support extensive e-commerce (such as online reservations or conference bookings).

IDENTITY FEATURES: LOOK-AND-FEEL

The Hollywood Roosevelt knew it needed a Web site and, in anticipation of the site, registered the hollywoodroosevelt.com domain name. A temporary page resided there until the actual site was ready to be launched.

The Roosevelt's logo, a stylized pale-pink palm frond, serves as a subtle basis for the look-and-feel of the site as a whole; the navigation buttons, present on every page, consist of text superimposed over a palm-like curlicue in the same shade of pink.

The hotel itself had previously maintained a marketable brand based on its California-style identity. The responsibility for extending that brand to the Web fell to the designers, who created a visual theme from actual elements within the old-world aspects of the hotel.

The color scheme is based on eggshell white and soft pinks—evoking the feel of California in the early part of this century. Images are framed with a translucent wavy border, and each individual page is bordered with a braided pink-and-peach sidebar that takes its pattern from the carpet of the hotel.

INTERACTIVITY AND UPDATES

The site is designed primarily as an online brochure rather than a promotional vehicle or actual sales tool. The Rooms and Rates page, which offers complete descriptions of all rooms available in the hotel, refrains from quoting actual rates in dollars.

This precaution gives the site a degree of future-proofing—the site won't necessitate updating each time the hotel changes its room rates.

The Contact Us page is informative rather than interactive. Phone numbers and an email address are provided in lieu of a form or online order processing capability, although the design of the site is flexible enough that the hotel could eventually add that option if it chooses to without requiring a redesign. The look-and-feel carries through this page with even the roadmap giving directions to the hotel crafted using the same visual themes as the rest of the site (see Figure 39.6).

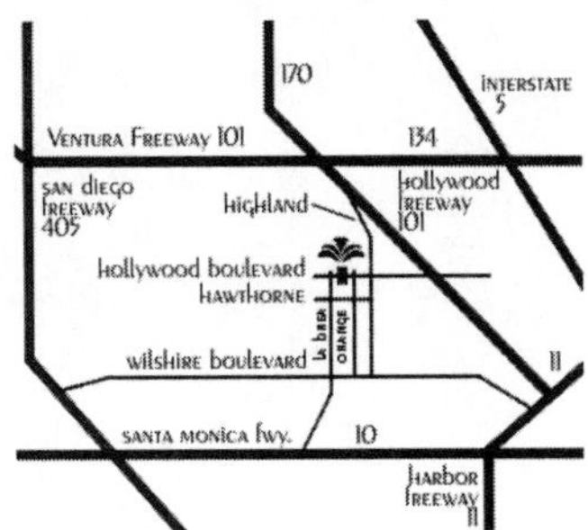

Figure 39.6
Even the map maintains the site's look-and-feel.

Other Features

The Hollywood Roosevelt, unlike the average hotel, has a wealth of history—and urban legends—at its disposal as marketing tools. A page of Tall Tales entices viewers to learn the hotel's lore, while a To Do page (see Figure 39.7) offers suggestions of ways to pass the time in the landmark-filled neighborhood surrounding the hotel.

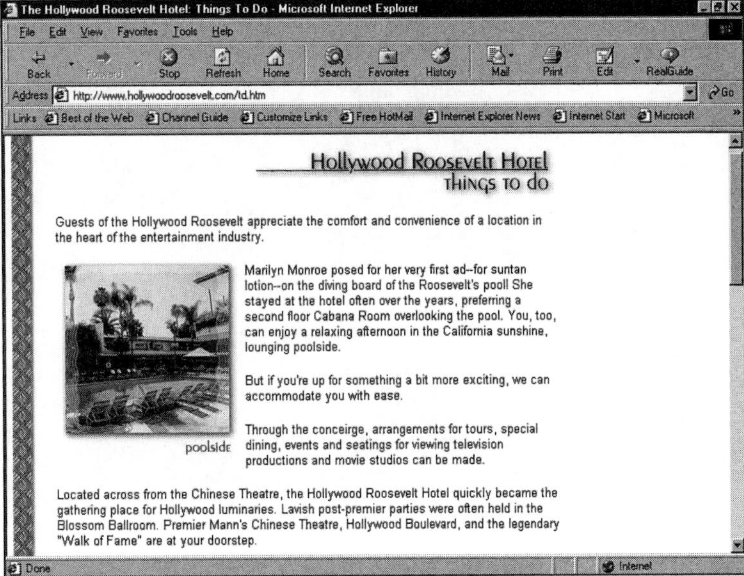

Figure 39.7
Things to do when visiting the Hollywood Roosevelt Hotel.

Any business can find interesting, unique characteristics about itself to publish on the Internet. Viewers will be drawn to a site by influences different from the ones that convince them to stay. The Roosevelt site is an excellent example of solid design and well-chosen content coming together into a top-quality package.

CHAPTER 40

Designing Corporate Intranets and Extranets

In this chapter

Private Networks

The corporate intranet has quickly become the technology of choice for delivering timely business data within corporations and some smaller businesses. Just the other day, I was in the wireless store for a large phone utility. I noticed that they tracked purchases and accounts via their intranet, using Netscape as the interface. I asked the saleswoman about the intranet, and she told me that it was the only software in use—billing, inventory, service issues, orders—all the day-to-day operations of the company are handled in this fashion.

The importance and power of private networks is sometimes overlooked in the rush to create public sites. However, intranet (and the related extranet) technology makes up an enormous chunk of what Web developers do in their daily jobs.

Although many intermediate and advanced readers will already be familiar with the attributes of private networks, I would like to review their qualities here. Many Web developers have only worked on the public side of the firewall, so for these readers, I want to be sure that the subtleties and more overt demands of designing for these types of networks are clear.

Note

A heads up for freelance Web designers: Although exceptions exist, the content and design of local sites are generally created by employees. Few departments outsource this work.

Intranets: Privacy and Power

An intranet is a private network used in a particular company or organization. It includes the following features:

- An intranet is private and proprietary in its information.
- Intranets are typically concerned with security and secured data.
- Access is controlled.
- Intranets are usually built on a single platform, which enables designers to freely use technologies specific to that platform, create platform-dependent dynamic Web applications, and determine both software and hardware parameters.
- Designers can use browser-specific tags and attributes because of predetermined software use.

On an operations level, local or departmental publishing empowers individuals to share resources, increasing collaboration and productivity through more connected and involved employees. On a strategic level, dynamic Web applications deliver up-to-date, accurate data with which to improve decision making and planning.

Note

The following sites provide general intranet information, including discussion forums and white papers:

`http://www.innergy.com/`

`http://www.intranetjournal.com/`

Thinking about starting a private network, but just aren't sure that your needs fall under that option? See "Determining When to Develop Private Networks" in the Troubleshooting section at the end of this chapter for some additional suggestions.

EXTRANETS: SELECTIVE INTERACTION

Extranets are extensions of intranets. They incorporate the privacy issues of intranets, but add areas that are accessible to other associated companies and organizations.

- An extranet is private and proprietary but allows certain access to corporate interests outside the main infrastructure.
- Security is an escalated concern in order to ensure that the entrances to the central core of information are well secured, and that proprietary issues are kept from the view of the external organizations.
- Access is highly controlled.
- Intranets may be built on a specific platform, but there may be a loss of control in terms of browser access from the external organizations. For example, the intranet itself might have Internet Explorer technology in use, while external organizations might be using other browsers or browser versions. Some effort is usually made to streamline platforms for best compatibility practices.
- Designers can use browser-specific tags and attributes because of predetermined software use, but must take into account any external concerns.

Note

To read more about extranet standards, visit Netscape's helpful resource, `http://sitesearch.netscape.com/products/whitepaper/extranetstds.html`. Kerstin Forsberg keeps an updated page on extranet issues with case studies at `http://www.netg.se/~kerfor/extranet.htm`.

DYNAMIC WEB APPLICATIONS

Dynamic Web applications are powerful tools that can leverage and unify company data and legacy systems for specific and timely information not possible on those systems alone. Using the same open standards, protocols, and technologies as found on the Web, advanced applications are developed for intranets—not only tapping into existing databases and applications, but also extending the use of that information beyond static views and linear dimensions to include intuitive and graphical data available throughout the enterprise.

Dynamic Web applications typically combine a variety of available Web technologies, both on the server- and client-side. Typically, intranets tend to make heavy use of server applications due to the database tracking and control necessary to manage business concerns. Which database and server-side technologies are chosen to manage a given intranet will depend heavily upon platform and what technology is already in use.

General Web technologies and languages in use will vary as well, and often depend upon the platform as well as browser or browsers in use. If an intranet is being built on Microsoft technology with standardized Internet Explorer browser versions, intranet application developers will freely use ActiveX, ASP, and HTML tags unique to the IE browser. Similarly, those on alternative platforms or using Netscape will likely make more use of Java, JavaScript, and HTML tags and methods best supported by the Netscape environment.

→ **See** Chapter 37, "Database Basics" for more information on choosing databases,. Chapter 33, Using Java Applets and ActiveX Components will provide information on those technologies. **See** Chapter 36, "Active Server Pages (ASP) and Related Tools" to learn more about ASP. JavaScript is covered in Chapter 19, "Using JavaScript".

TECHNOLOGY ISSUES

Web technology has grown in popularity for several practical reasons. The Web browser is a simple application that employees are familiar with through their experiences with the Internet. The intuitive nature of the Web-based medium is easily understood and appealing, resulting in fewer questions and more user confidence, which saves hours in training and support costs.

Note

In an era in which the end user is bombarded with more and more complex applications, the importance of user appeal should not be underestimated.

Hardware and software start-up costs for the intranet are usually relatively low. In most cases, existing hardware such as PCs, servers, hubs, and network connections can be used, and browser and Web server software are virtually free. An intranet Web server can be run on one PC, for which performance requirements depend on the number of calls for files or "hits" from the browser. In most cases, depending on the size of the company, this is usually minimal in early deployment.

User hardware varies radically from company to company. PCs must sometimes be upgraded or purchased to accommodate graphical interfaces or better publishing tools that integrate with office applications, such as the Microsoft Office Suite and FrontPage 2000. This can be expensive. Corporations commonly squeeze out what they can for a select group first, with the realistic expectation that after the intranet's value is proven, financial support will follow.

Dynamic Web applications can be developed very quickly, offsetting the costs associated with the development of other user applications. Current tools, new development environments, and integrated technologies all contribute to faster programming and easier server administration than ever before.

Note

In the Information Systems field, such quick development is referred to as Rapid Application Development, or RAD.

Initial commitment to some technical resources, usually from within the Information Systems (IS) department, is necessary. For static sites, resources should at least include general guidelines for site planning, design, tools, security, and some initial training. For more powerful Web applications, programming and development tools are required, which vary according to application and are exemplified in this study.

Tip from molly

Although it is ideal to work with a team from several disciplines, intranet professionals usually add project managers, trainers, and visual designers after the intranet's budget and administrative structure is established.

The bottom line is that to expose the real value of the corporate intranet, a new technology must be launched. The upside of this is that with some know-how, minimal expense, and user support, this technology can go a long way, producing data quite unlike any other.

Note

The successful Web application that clearly aligns with business needs often spearheads support for further training and development of the intranet and newer technologies in general.

DESIGN CONSIDERATIONS

It's interesting to note that the design of the Web pages within an intranet is sometimes considered a back-burner issue. Unlike many carefully preplanned Internet retail sites, the look and feel within an intranet site usually evolves later.

To obtain accurate, usable data is what anyone in the corporation will tell you is the main reason to use any technology. The intranet is not excluded from this focus, whether the site is a local, static site or a dynamic application. A local publisher may have to get information online right away and worry about looks later. Also, applications that involve users require usability tests, which have an impact on page design.

Because feedback for a Web application usually comes after deployment, page design is sometimes altered later, as well. Fortunately, unlike some user interfaces, HTML is relatively easy to change.

Note

Highly dependent on usability, page design for dynamic applications usually evolves after feedback and testing.

Page design is only one of many parts of application design, which includes technologies, tools, and teamwork strategies. Page design in this context is commonly referred to as *user interface design*.

Note

Ideally, the intranet application is developed with a team of programmers, designers, and project managers, unlike the static site constructed solely by the typical Internet Web designer.

APPLICATION DEVELOPMENT: A CLOSER LOOK

When a given intranet is platform- and browser-dependent, the focus can be on technologies specific to the platform and browser. This doesn't make the developer's work easier, but it does refine the choices available. However, if there is diversity among the technology in use, the developer must be aware of cross-platform, cross-browser approaches.

Application development in intranets typically follows corporate development techniques and can work very smoothly if properly managed. It's interesting to point out that this smooth management doesn't often translate to what is going on in public Web site development—there has yet to be a major effort to bring defined development into the commercial Web development realm. This may be due to the fact that the development of intranets is an extension of existing corporate development rather than something perceived as a new venture, as is the case with many Web sites.

Software developers will be familiar with RAD methodology. The technique or methods derived from it are often put into place during the production and deployment of intranets. That an intranet is more frequently treated as a software product than another entity is interesting in and of itself, and the methods employed can serve the Web developer—whether he or she is working in the private or public environment.

Application development generally follows these principles:

- Case studies and focus groups are organized and queried. In intranet development, employees of a given company can be formed into groups and asked to provide feedback about their management and organization needs. These groups can be reconvened throughout the process to check on the intranet's efficacy.
- In the early stages of development, the intranet will be tested by the individuals who will be actually using it. This provides feedback that allows the developers to make adjustments during rather than after the development of the intranet. Undeniably, adjustments will be made as time goes on, but this helps deploy the intranet with more relevant features in a timely fashion.
- Existing technology should be reused wherever sensible and possible.
- Scheduling is an imperative for application development. Adherence to schedule is critical to deploy a quality intranet in step with the evolution of the company.

- Development is done by a team managed by a project manager. The project manager must be well versed in a variety of issues, because the team will consist of designers as well as programmers, security experts, and database engineers.

Tip from molly

Project managers can use a variety of collective management and tracking software products to oversee their work. Referred to as *groupware*, they include such products as Microsoft Exchange (`http://www.microsoft.com/exchange`) and Lotus Notes (`http://www.lotusnotes.com/`).

Following a standardized application development process is extremely powerful. It stands to reason that better organization and communication will lead a project to its best potential. By incorporating the basic principles of project management, scheduling, using case studies and focus groups, and quality testing, intranets can be brought to fruition in a timely fashion.

I personally hope that the development standards used in many intranet projects inspire commercial Web design companies to use a combination of traditional production techniques along with application development methodology. Ideally, this will produce better Web sites for public as well as private environments.

TROUBLESHOOTING

DETERMINING WHEN TO DEVELOP PRIVATE NETWORKS

The private network idea is appealing to me, as I have a growing company that must track inventory and keep communications open. We've used a variety of software in the past for billing and so forth. But how do I know it's the right time to begin developing?

Intranet development should be part of the business plan. If it's not currently part of the plan, yet your instincts and business sense are suggesting it may well be time to begin such a project, it may be in your best interests to review your business plan. Then, run a focus group of employees. Listen carefully to their feedback. Almost always, people on the front lines of any company will have insights as well as strong ideas about how they can work more efficiently.

DESIGNING FOR THE REAL WORLD

CASE STUDY: THE TUCSON MEDICAL CENTER INTRANET

Tucson Medical Center's (see Figure 40.1) intranet was chosen as a case study to illustrate the major topics in building an intranet.

Serving the greater Tucson area since the mid-1940s, Tucson Medical Center (TMC) is a major medical facility with about 720 beds and 3,500 employees. TMC's intranet emerged as a direct result of a management need.

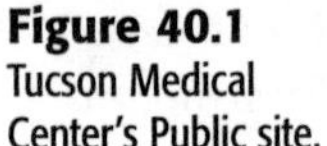

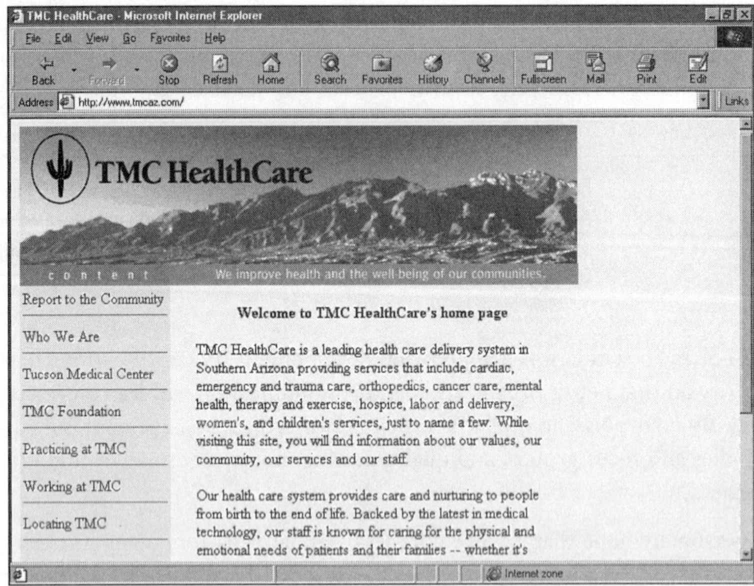

Figure 40.1
Tucson Medical Center's Public site.

TMC was chosen as a corporate case study for several reasons. Not only do the intranet applications demonstrate the dynamic application in action, but they were also sparked by and developed for a universal business need, a key ingredient in the support for transition to Web technology. In addition, the project exemplifies team effort and the importance of a feedback system—both significant to its success.

Also, TMC's size, type of service, and technical resources fall in the middle of the corporate spectrum, offering insight to a broad range of managers, developers, and designers who may be just starting up or beefing up existing intranets. TMC's use of technology is definitely one step ahead of many smaller organizations, yet is still evolving and is not as sophisticated as, perhaps, a more technologically driven Fortune 500 company.

The TMC intranet was not installed intentionally. It came about through a need to find ways to lower costs and improve quality.

A small committee of department leaders at TMC gathered to discuss how to obtain better key indicators for decision support. They wanted a tool that would provide accurate, timely data that could be available at their fingertips so they could, in their words, "steer the ship." At the time, a new technology was not even a topic of discussion.

Clinical leaders and managers in a hospital setting depend on census data to make staffing and patient care decisions. Up to this point, administrators and their secretaries would go through an elaborate process to retrieve, analyze, and disseminate static data about once a week.

First, they would locate and print reports generated by the mainframe, and in many cases they would have to add it by hand to their own local tracking system, usually a spreadsheet or a local database. After combining and re-querying data for their statistical purposes, they would then email or deliver the findings to appropriate staffers.

Obviously, this process was time consuming, and most importantly, reports were only marginally useful because they became outdated very quickly. Clearly, a need existed for retrieving more useful key indicators.

After a couple of weeks of discussion, one of the committee members brought up the idea of a Web site. If Web technology could deliver custom news and stock data via the Internet, he asked, why couldn't they obtain custom data through a Web site? After discussion with IS developers, it was determined that, indeed, Web technology could probably deliver what they needed.

The committee decided to implement a pilot project to test the workability of such a solution. The committee, after some assessment, decided to select a pilot test group, to purchase some new workstations for them to insure optimum results, and to establish team leaders and developers in IS for support and development.

Next steps included

- Determining budget and fiscal concerns.
- Defining of platform, browser, and technology concerns.
- Creating a prototype.
- Growing the project via input from employees testing the site.
- Re-evaluating the site at regular intervals to make adjustments and corrections where necessary.

Note

TMC's intranet applications have grown so popular that users say they can't live without them. Even the IS developers were surprised at the outpouring of support, as these applications were fairly simple in comparison to other kinds of applications rolled out in the past with more complex functionality. The difference appears to be that people actually like using the applications.

Visionary leaders at TMC and throughout corporate America continue to imagine and implement dynamic Web applications that provide solutions to their needs, extending the use of the intranet beyond a data repository.

Because costs are high to support the end user in a myriad of desktop applications, some industry leaders even predict that the use of a browser in combination with several distributed Web applications will become the desktop of the future, reducing end-user training and multiple software installations.

As the business engine drives the need for more complete internal data, the need to reduce support costs, and the need to increase staff productivity, the term *dynamic* truly describes the standard intranet workhorse Web site of the future.

CHAPTER 41

Creating an Online Community

In this chapter

WHAT IS VIRTUAL COMMUNITY?

In this high-tech age, friendships can be formed, pictures exchanged, and the highs and lows of life celebrated and commiserated—all without ever physically meeting the people with whom you are sharing your innermost thoughts. Online communities have crossed cultural boundaries, bringing together people with similar interests from around the globe. The anonymity of the computer has also breached stereotypes such as age, physical appearance, and disability.

Everyone—from the big business site designer to the personal home page developer—is racing to add community components to their arsenal of features. Because these components are still in their infancy, there are few standards and an ever-increasing number of choices. Each offers a different type of visitor experience, so it's important to make your community component choices with your particular audience in mind.

In a nutshell, a virtual or online community is a group of people who use the Internet to communicate. The community can grow in email, chat, forums, or a guestbook. The community can even grow as content on a site through a series of visitor-submitted articles or comments.

Sites such as Amazon.com have grown a community by allowing visitors to provide reviews of the books, music, and videos sold at the site. These reviews allow participants to express their thoughts on the product with other potential purchasers. As new reviews are added, visitors will agree and disagree with others' comments. Thus, a community of sorts is formed.

Note

To look at Amazon.com's online community, visit `http://www.amazon.com/` and do a search on a favorite book title (try this book!). You'll see feedback and discussion about the title.

The largest foundation for online community is email. Families form self-contained "communities" by keeping in touch with each other online. A group of friends might invite other friends into a group, thereby promoting new friendships and community.

There are thousands of mailing lists on the Internet. A mailing list allows members to send one email to an address that automatically forwards the message to everyone else on the list.

Mailing lists offer additional features, such as the capability to receive all the group emails in a digest to avoid cluttering up an email queue. Most mailing lists also allow members to set a "no-mail" option, which allows them to suppress receiving group mail for a period (such as when you're on vacation or going through a busy time at work), without having to ask each member of the group to remember to remove the email address from their list.

Some services have built their entire business model around facilitating email communities. OneList is a service devoted to mailing lists. Anyone can set up a mailing list on any topic they desire, for free.

Mailing lists on OneList can be public or private, moderated or un-moderated. A moderated mailing list requires a moderator (usually the person who established the mailing list) to approve messages before they are forwarded to the group. Public mailing lists are added to a master directory at the OneList site. Visitors can search the list of public mailing lists and join any that match their interests, thereby becoming a member of that email community.

Note

To check out the OneList site, go to `http://www.onelist.com/`.

DEVELOPING COMMUNITY CONTENT

Typically, a community consists of the following infrastructure: Web content, newsgroups or forums, chats, and ancillary content such as photo galleries. Each of these components has so many options, however, that this explanation is really just scratching the surface.

There are many ways to develop community components for your Web site.

Before you start thinking of forums and chats, you need to build a compelling Web site. A well-organized, visually appealing site with intriguing content will establish your Web presence. That presence will draw people to your site, whereupon they can be lured into the community components (see Figure 41.1).

Figure 41.1
The About.com Web sites combine content and community well.

As your site grows, it can be tempting—and often necessary due to time constraints—to let your content slide in favor of devoting time to chats and forums. Don't make this mistake! Content will continue to bring new visitors to your site. Your content can also be designed to introduce new topics of discussion for your community members.

Tip from

If you find that managing your community is taking you away from writing fresh content, ask your members for submissions. Nothing sparks debate better than an opinion piece written by a member with a unique point of view.

When considering your Web site design, give consideration to how the community components will mesh with your theme. If you are using external clients for community, such as newsgroups and IRC chat, this is not an issue. But if you are planning to integrate an in-frame forum into your site, be sure your buttons, logo, and color scheme will be able to be customized into the forum templates.

Using External Technology

The debate over whether a community should be embedded within a Web site or use separate clients is heated, with valid points on either side.

External clients are separate software applications that perform a specific function, such as accessing Internet newsgroups. Microsoft Outlook Express (included with MS Internet Explorer), Netscape Messenger (included with Netscape Communicator), and Free Agent are among the most popular newsreader applications. There are also clients used to access IRC (Internet Relay Chats), such as mIRC and Ircle.

These applications generally have an abundance of features and work on a wide range of computer systems. There are also several different applications available, making it easier for visitors to find the program that works best for them. Many Web surfers do not like to use Java clients, which also makes IRC chat and newsgroups potentially attractive.

The downside of external clients is loss of consistency and control. If a visitor to your site wants to participate in your newsgroups and your IRC channel, they will need three clients—a browser, a newsreader, and an IRC client. This can be intimidating to a new user, as well as create a support nightmare for you, the community manager.

Using external clients can also prevent visitors from associating your Web site with the community components. The member experience is very disjointed, as they associate more with the individual community components and clients than with the site that introduced those features. After a member adds your newsgroup to their newsreader or bookmarks your chat room, they no longer have to return to your site to access those areas. Therefore, it is even more important that you provide compelling content to keep those members returning to the actual site.

Note

Try the following Web sites for more information and downloads for popular chat clients:

mIRC: `http://www.mirc.com/`

Ircle: `http://www.ircle.com/`

Pirch: `http://www.pirch.com/`

Free Agent: `http://www.forteinc.com/agent/freagent.htm`

WORKING WITH INLINE TECHNOLOGY

Inline clients use technologies such as Java, CGI, and ActiveX to embed inline forums and chats into your Web site. There are dozens of prepackaged forums and chats available on the Web. In most cases, these clients can be customized to match your color scheme and use your own buttons. You can also choose between a forum with threaded messaging—where members reply to individual messages and can initiate sub-discussions off the main topic—or linear messaging—where each message is added to the end of the list of messages on that topic.

→ To read more about Java and ActiveX, **see** "Using Java Applets and ActiveX Components," **p. 702**

→ For details on CGI, **see** "CGI and Pre-Processing Fundamentals," **p. 736**

The advantage of an inline client is that you can customize the scripts and applications to suit your specific needs. Of course, to do this, you need to know how to code in Perl or Java. This level of control, however, potentially allows you to create a unique member experience that is not available at any other site on the Web.

The disadvantages of using an in-frame client are cost and maintenance. Although there are several free forum and chat scripts available on the Web, the most full-featured and popular applications come with a price tag.

Note

You may also have to pay extra fees to your ISP before they will enable CGI on your server. Scripts introduce new security issues to your server, so many ISPs are leery of allowing ready access to such services.

On the maintenance front, if the community component resides on your server, you are responsible for supporting it. If you introduce a bug into your code while making modifications, your forum is going to be out of commission until you fix it.

Finally, there is the member aspect of in-frame community. Because the community components are imbedded into your site, members will certainly associate your site with those features. But will members take time away from their email and newsgroups to specifically visit your forum? The answer to that is still changing as these components become more popular and add new features.

You also risk alienating some of your members by using Java applets. Older computers using outdated browsers cannot access Java applets, so those people would not be able to join your chats. Other visitors will not have Java enabled because of security concerns. Consider your audience before choosing an inline client.

Note

To find a great selection of CGI scripts, visit `http://www.cgi-resources.com/`.

CHOOSING THIRD-PARTY WEB COMMUNITIES

An alternative that falls midway between using an external client and using an embedded client is linking to a third-party Web site for your community components. Services like Delphi allow you to establish a Web site, complete with forum and chat. Many Delphi users opt to keep their Delphi pages simple in favor of creating their "real" Web presence on another site. They then link directly to the chat and forum features from their site.

LiveUniverse (see Figure 41.2) is another community provider. Rather than establishing an entire Web site with LiveUniverse, they offer individual components to which you can link from your site. Although your chat or forum resides on the LiveUniverse servers, you are able to customize the surrounding HTML to some extent with your own color scheme and images.

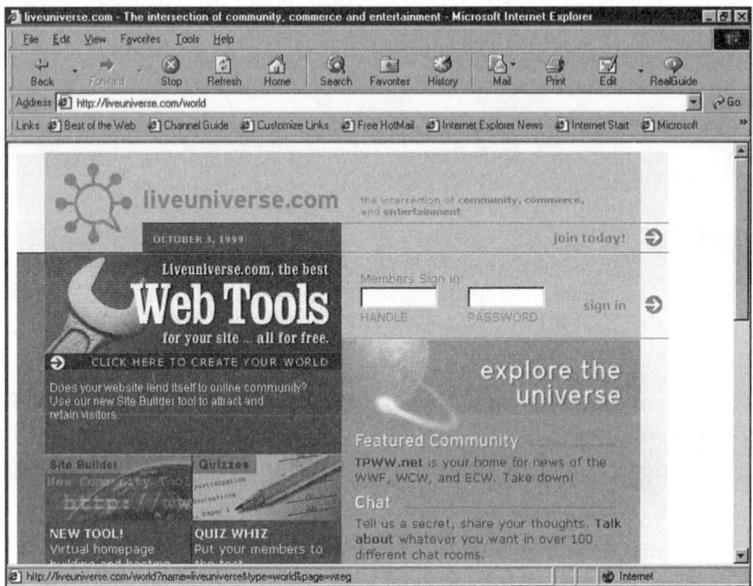

Figure 41.2
LiveUniverse offers several community components to enhance your Web site.

Using Delphi or LiveUniverse takes the maintenance burden off your shoulders. It also provides your members with a virtually seamless integration of your site's content and the community components. These tools are only as reliable as the servers on which they reside, however, so be prepared for unscheduled outages (and the resulting outraged members).

You also have no control over the software itself; if the host site decides to suddenly start using a different package, your only choices are to live with the changes or move your community elsewhere. Because the features of these services can change so frequently, be prepared for member frustration as they have to re-learn the tools.

Note

Experience online communities for yourself with a visit to these community services:

Delphi: `http://www.Delphi.com/`

LiveUniverse: `http://www.liveuniverse.com/`

Yahoo! Clubs: `http://clubs.yahoo.com/`

INTRODUCING PROPRIETARY COMMUNITY SOLUTIONS

There is now a new player on the community market—proprietary community software. These are full-featured solutions, such as Ecobuilder (see Figure 41.3), which include chat, forums, photo galleries, and other components within one package. The software runs on your own server or that of your ISP. Best suited for sites that are seriously interested in aggressively embracing online community, the cost of these packages is much higher than commercial scripts for individual components. This generally puts them out of the range of most home page designers, but are reasonable for a larger, income-bearing site.

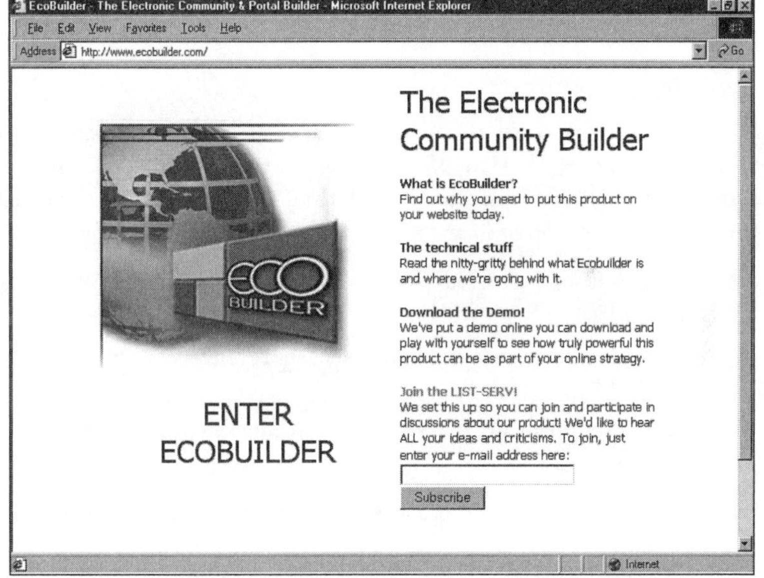

Figure 41.3 EcoBuilder offers everything your site needs in one package, including inline chats, message boards, and Web pages.

The biggest advantage of proprietary community software is consistency. Your chat, forums, photo galleries, and content all have the same look and feel, and are well-integrated. The disadvantage is that you may like the functionality of one or two components and not the others. Because this software comes as a package, it's an all-or-nothing deal.

Note

Build a community site with help from the following tools:

Ecobuilder: `http://www.ecobuilder.com/`

Web Crossing: `http://www.webcrossing.com/`

INSTALLING COMMUNITY COMPONENTS

After you have chosen your community tools, the next step is to install the components and make them accessible via your site. The procedures for creating the necessary components vary widely. Making these tools accessible to your visitors generally entails simply adding a link to the component. The components covered include:

- Newsgroups
- Web-based forums
- Inline chats
- Internet Relay Chat (IRC) clients

NEWSGROUPS

If you have chosen to use newsgroups for your messaging component, you first need to have the newsgroup created. Many ISPs serving the professional Webmaster community are happy to create newsgroups running on NNTP (Network News Transfer Protocol). Talk to your provider for more information about how to get a newsgroup established.

After the newsgroup is created, you can add links to it on your Web pages. The way to do this is with an `<A> . . . </A>` link to a news protocol.

```
<A href="news://news.annexcafe.com/annexcafe.internet.newbies">Internet Newbies
➥Newsgroup</A>
```

This link will automatically open your newsreader client to the designated newsgroup, as you can see in Figure 41.4.

Both the Netscape and Internet Explorer browsers support the news protocol, as long as you have the full versions of these packages installed. IE invokes Outlook Express as the newsreader, while Netscape opens Netscape Messenger.

Caution

If a visitor is using Free Agent to read newsgroups and tries to access your newsgroups via your link, Free Agent will *not* open. Instead, the newsreader associated with the visitor's browser will open. If a Free Agent user wants to access your newsgroups, the user has to configure the news server and newsgroups manually in Free Agent.

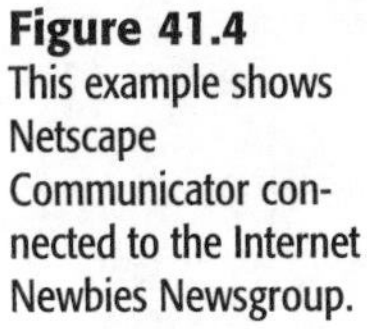

Figure 41.4
This example shows Netscape Communicator connected to the Internet Newbies Newsgroup.

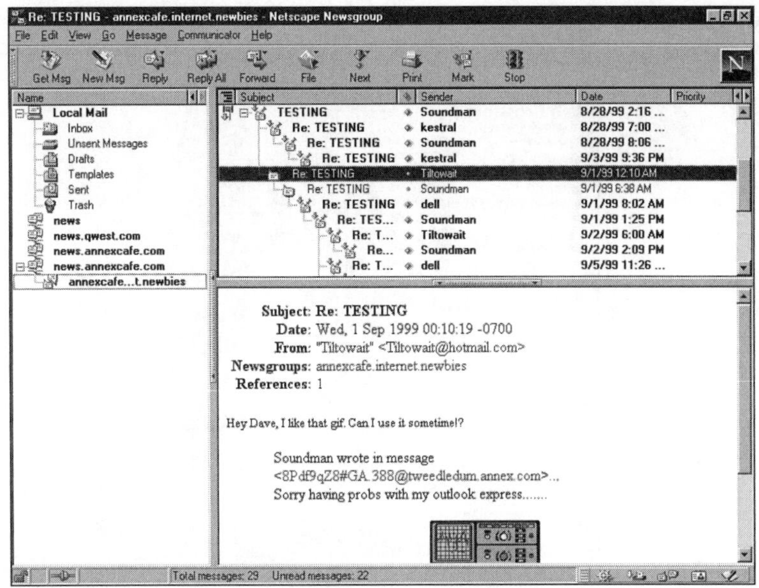

WEB-BASED FORUMS

Web-based message boards, also called forums, can be built using a variety of technologies. The easiest to obtain are CGI programs. Some ISPs offer their own forum solutions. Others, such as Ultimate Bulletin Board and WWWThreads, are easy to find, and there are new forums coming out on a steady basis.

After you've chosen your forum scripts, you'll need to install them on your server. To do that, copy the script into your text editor and save it. Then upload the script to your cgi-bin directory (the directory where CGI scripts are kept) or another directory as instructed by your ISP.

You're hosting a successful forum on your own server, but now are having trouble with your server space allotment? See "Forum Server Space" in the Troubleshooting section at the end of this chapter.

Caution

Be sure you upload your CGI files as ASCII, *not* binary! Otherwise, they won't work properly.

→ To learn more about CGI **see** "CGI and Pre-Processing Fundamentals," **p. 736**

After the script is uploaded, you'll have to change the permissions to make it executable by visitors to your site. This is called changing mode. You can change mode (CHMOD) using most FTP software. For example, WS_FTP for Windows allows you to do this by right-clicking the filename and changing the settings in a pop-up window (see Figure 41.5).

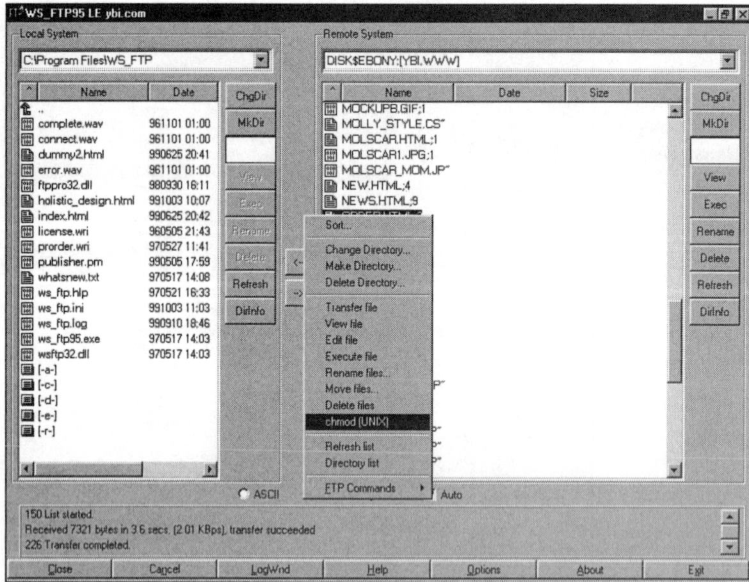

Figure 41.5
Changing mode using WS_FTP for Windows.

If you have Telnet access to your server, you can change mode by typing in the appropriate command at the prompt (see Figure 41.6).

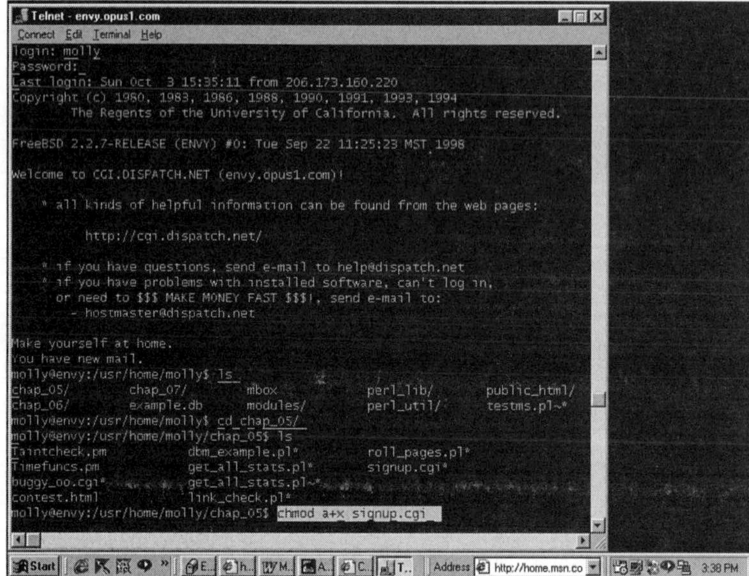

Figure 41.6
Changing mode using Telnet.

After you have made the scripts accessible, you have to create a link from your Web page to the script.

```
<A href="cgi-bin/forumscript.cgi">Join our forum!</A>
```

Note

Find helpful Bulletin Board software for your community at the following Web sites:

Ultimate Bulletin Board: **http://www.ultimatebb.com/**

WWWThreads: **http://www.wwwthreads.org/**

CHAT

Chats are added to Web sites in much the same way as forums and newsgroups, with a few important twists. The important difference between forums and newsgroups and chats is that forums and newsgroups are asynchronous forms of communication, meaning they are not in real-time. Chats, on the other hand, involve people talking together in real-time.

IRC PROTOCOL

Unlike newsgroups, chat gateways are browser specific. Although Internet Explorer comes bundled with a chat client, MS Chat, Netscape does not currently offer such a tool, so Netscape users must install another software client and access the chat manually. In both cases, users may want to use software such as mIRC, Ircle, or Pirch, as these packages are very feature-rich.

To create a chat channel, you must find an IRC server that is willing to host your channel. Some ISPs have their own servers, and there are many public servers that take channel requests.

After your channel is established, link to it from your HTML page using the anchor tag and the chat:// addressing convention.

```
<A  href="chat://chat.annex.com/#designchat">Join our design chats!</A>
```

If you click this link using Internet Explorer, MS Chat opens up to the #designchat room you designated; however, this doesn't work in Netscape.

INLINE CHAT CLIENTS

Inline chats are becoming more and more popular, and are supported by both Internet Explorer and Netscape using a Java applet.

→ For more about Java applets, **see** "Using Java Applets and ActiveX Components," **p. 704**

To add a Java chat applet, use the `<APPLET>` tag. Although the `<OBJECT>` tag is now in favor by the HTML 4.0 standard, most browsers do not yet support this tag. Therefore, using the `<APPLET>` tag ensures cross-browser compatibility.

```
<APPLET code="EmbryoClient.class"
codebase="http://www.spin.de/classes/">
```

```
<PARAM NAME="channel" VALUE="welcome!">
<PARAM NAME="bgcolor" VALUE="CC9966">
<PARAM NAME="fgcolor" VALUE="000000">
<PARAM NAME="fontsize" VALUE="12">
</APPLET>
```

Caution

The parameters of your Java chat client may differ from those shown previously. Be sure to read the instructions that come with your particular Java applet.

You can define the height and width of your chat window within the `<APPLET>` tag.

```
<APPLET code="EmbryoClient.class"
codebase="http://www.spin.de/classes/" width="400" height="300">
<PARAM NAME="channel" VALUE="welcome!">
<PARAM NAME="bgcolor" VALUE="CC9966">
<PARAM NAME="fgcolor" VALUE="000000">
<PARAM NAME="fontsize" VALUE="12">
</APPLET>
```

If you test your Java chat in a Java-compliant, enabled browser, you should see that the chat appears inline on the Web page.

MANAGING AN ONLINE COMMUNITY

Now that you've added community components to your site, you will need to manage them on an ongoing basis to ensure their success. Whether you choose to rule with an iron fist or a velvet glove, your people skills will certainly be put to the test.

As a community manager, you should make it your business to know exactly what is happening in your forums and chats. If you have standards regarding personal attacks or obscenities, then you need to make it your business to read every message in your forums to delete violations. You will also need to interact with your members about such violations.

Be prepared to be inundated with email from your community members. You can expect everything from questions about how to use the forums and chats to members sharing their personal problems with you. As a leader of your community, you are taking on the role of Internet bartender. Be prepared to listen. Be careful to respond in a way that does not alienate your customer, even if you are telling him/her to go back to the forum and leave you alone personally.

SETTING POLICIES AND GUIDELINES

The most important rule for managing an online community is to be consistent. The best way to establish consistency is through carefully composed policies and guidelines.

If your members know the rules in advance, it will minimize (but never totally eliminate) the number of infractions. If you've put thought into the guidelines you want observed on your site, they will help you be more consistent when those guidelines are overlooked.

Some issues to consider when developing your policies and guidelines are

- **Personal Attacks**—Remind your visitors to attack the ideas being discussed, not the person raising the issues.
- **Private Information**—Better to be safe than sorry. Remind your members to only share private information such as addresses and phone numbers through email rather than posting it to the forum or chat at large.
- **Language**—If you don't want cursing or crude language in your community, say so up-front. Each community will have its own standards depending on the subject matter and demographics of the members.
- **Copyrights**—It's always a good idea to remind your members of the importance of copyright laws.
- **Policy Violations**—Decide in advance what the penalties will be for violating your community's policies, and let your members know what they are.

Have you set up well-defined policies and guidelines for your site, but are still having trouble with some members causing problems? See "Three Strike Rule" in the Troubleshooting section at the end of this chapter.

Hiring Staff

As your community becomes more successful, chances are that you will not be able to handle all the traffic yourself. Reading every message on a forum can become tiresome and time-consuming, as can hosting a chat room several hours a day.

When hiring a staff, take your time to find the right people. While you're sure to get plenty of volunteers, you'll thank yourself later if you interview all the candidates to find those with the best people skills and technical knowledge.

Troubleshooting

Forum Server Space

My forum is really taking off, which is great, but it's also causing me to exceed my server space allotment. What should I do?

First of all, pat yourself on the back for building a successful community. Then you need to make some decisions. If your community can handle a change of venue, consider moving your forum to Delphi or another forum service to free up your server space for other content; you can link to the new forum from your site to maintain continuity.

Keep in mind, however, that you are apt to lose a small (or even large) percentage of your visitors by changing tools at this point in the game. A better option would be to increase your server space to handle your current and anticipated future traffic. If money is an issue, it might be time to explore the possibility of offering advertising space on your site to help cover your expenses.

THREE STRIKE RULE

Some of the visitors to my forum keep coming back and causing trouble even after repeated warnings. How do I regain control?

A good rule of thumb is the "three strike rule." After a first offense, send the user a warning. After the second offense, send a warning and a notice that if the behavior doesn't change, they'll be removed from the forum. After the third offense, follow through and lock the person out of your forum, either permanently or temporarily. Most forum packages have tools to track IP addresses and allow for banning of members.

DESIGNING FOR THE REAL WORLD

FAN SITES: THE BEST AND WORST OF ONLINE COMMUNITIES

The fan site is one of the best examples of an online community and they are springing up all over the Web for the celebrity of the moment. These sites bring together a diverse group of people from all walks of life with a common interest in a particular celebrity, film, or television program.

Fan sites exemplify both the best and the worst of online community. With ready access to pictures of the object of the site's affection, these sites are often chock full of images. Links to news articles complement the usual biography, list of credits, story lines, and commentary that comprise the content of the site.

Technically, some fan sites can compete with much larger commercial sites in terms of community components. Affordable forum and chat components, such as WWWThreads and LiveUniverse, are making this competition easier by the day.

The spirit of banding together to support their favored celebrity or show demonstrates just how strong an online community can become. Friendships are formed as discussions turn from the star to personal issues. Members share pictures and information freely with others in the community. In many cases, members negotiate offline exchanges of video tapes, concert tickets, and other memorabilia.

As I said, however, these sites can also represent the worst aspects of a community from a management standpoint. Celebrities come and go, so the life expectancy of a fan site is tied to the life expectancy of the star's fame. So, too, are the emotions of the community members. If their celebrity or show of choice is doing well and getting a lot of press, the members are happy and traffic is high. When the members feel their celebrity is being mistreated or is taking too long to provide new fuel for the discussion fires, however, flame wars may soon follow.

Deciding to create a fan site also has many legal ramifications. Those images that make a site so popular usually come from copyrighted sources, making it illegal to re-purpose them on a Web site. There have been several successful cases where the original source of this material has taken legal action to protect its trademarks and copyrights. Star Trek has made several attempts to put fan sites out of business in favor of building community on its own official site.

Fan sites can also be fraught with defamatory or libelous messages against both the celebrity in question and against members of the community.

As with all types of online communities, it is important to keep your community components under constant and consistent control.

PART IX

Publishing, Maintaining, and Promoting Web Sites

CHAPTER 42

Preparing Your Site for Publication

In this chapter

WHERE YOUR WEB SITE GOES

You've spent hours planning, designing, and implementing your Web site. You've optimized graphics, written content, and you have HTML tags coming out of your ears. At last, the site is complete. Now all you've got to do is make it available to the world.

You have several options when it comes to where your Web site will "sit" on the Web. Every Web site in the world is on a computer somewhere. When you use your Web browser to request a document, you are actually putting in a request to the server on which that site sits. That server then sends the data back to your computer. Deciding what kind of server your Web site sits on is an important decision.

PERSONAL HOME PAGES

To put up a personal Web site, you have quite a few options that cost little or no money. You should first consider how much disk space you'll need to run your site. An extensive home page doesn't normally run more than 6–8KB, less extensive sites won't run more than 5KB.

There are many places on the Internet where you can go for free server space. You will most likely have to put up with some advertising being run on your site in the form of banner ads or "pop-ups" (ads that run in a second window that pops up when a users goes to your URL).

Note

The following are some favorite "free" Web page sites:

`http://www.geocities.yahoo.com/`

`http://www.tripod.com/`

`http://www.angelfire.com/`

`http://xoom.com/home/`

With these services you can get 4–10MB of space, and some provide special services like guestbooks and hit counters. Most have restrictions when it comes to business use and charge fees to sites that are not personal. Each of these services has Terms of Service guidelines that may limit the content of your site or claim rights to use your content in promoting their service. Read the Terms of Service carefully to determine if they are acceptable to you before putting your site on any particular service.

If you use an ISP to connect to the Internet, you might already have Web space available to you. Most ISPs include a small amount of Web space with their monthly packages. If you are unsure, visit your ISP's Web page or review your package contract. If you don't currently have Web space included in your package, you should be able to get it added for a small charge.

Your ISP will then inform you of its policies on running scripts (CGI, Java, Perl) from their server and will give you instructions on how to upload to their server. Your URL then becomes an extension of theirs. If your ISP's URL is `http://www.funISP.com/` and you chose your extension to be your name, the URL for your Web site would then be `http://www.funISP.com/~yourname/`. If you have a registered domain name, your ISP should also be able to arrange domain name service for you.

Business Pages

The choice that many companies make is to have their sites hosted by another company. Internet service providers (ISPs) provide servers and connections for other companies' Web sites. You'll find that most commercial Internet service providers offer everything from simple Web hosting to consultation and Web design services.

Most hosting services have, at minimum, a T1 connection to the Internet and many have multiple T3 lines. This ensures that your Web site has a fast and constant connection to the Internet. Hosting services should also have made a serious investment into the security of their servers. They should be able to provide you with secure servers for databases and e-commerce.

Tip from molly

> Security issues vary from service to service. This is an important issue to investigate. Be sure that your Web hosting service is as concerned about security as you are–this will help you feel confident about passing that confidence along to your Web site visitors.

Almost every commercial ISP will offer you the capability to use JAVA, Perl, and CGI, but availability varies with each service.

ISPs should also be able to give you statistic reports that let you know the effectiveness of your site. Any service worth its salt will give you page impressions, which let you know which pages of your site are being viewed.

→ For more on how to track site performance, **see** "Web Site Marketing and Promotion," **p. 921**

If you are representing a large company, or you have strong Internet/intranet needs, you may want to consider hosting the Web site within your offices.

To do this you'll need the following:

- A server PC that has a large hard disk with at least 32MB of RAM
- A full-time connection to the Internet
- A router (to keep traffic off of your LAN)
- A firewall (to secure your system)
- Power back up
- Human resources (to manage system operation and maintenance issues)

Be prepared to spend approximately $10,000 on startup hardware, plus ISP charges. Depending on the traffic to your site, you may need a T1 line, which can cost

$1,000–$1,500 per month. If your site grows considerably, you may also need to purchase additional server computers to prevent server overload. You also have to have someone in your organization to manage all of this, which is a full-time job all on its own.

Many types of servers and server software are available. Among them are the following:

- Microsoft Internet Information Server 3.0 (IIS), for use on Windows NT and Windows 2000 server
- iPlanet Web Server 4.0 from Netscape and Sun Microsystems, for use across platforms
- Netscape Enterprise Server for Novell NetWare 4.0 and 5.0

Server administration is an engrossing task and should not be considered lightly. It is important to fully investigate all options before investing time or money into on- or offsite administration.

REGISTERING DOMAINS

Understanding domains and domain names requires that you have a little understanding of how the Internet works. The Internet is, essentially, a network of computers that exchange information. When you enter a URL into your Web browser, it sends a message out to another computer on the network, which finds the computer that has the data you requested and then that data is returned to your computer.

This all happens in a matter of seconds. Each computer, host, and server on the network has an Internet Protocol number (IP Address). Internet Protocol (IP) numbers are part of a global, standardized scheme for identifying machines that are connected to the Internet.

Technically speaking, IP numbers are 32-bit addresses that consist of four octets, and they are expressed as four numbers between 0 and 255, separated by periods, for example: 198.41.0.52. The actual IP address is binary, but the 0-255 is expressed as decimal. Domain names are easy-to-remember, alphanumeric addresses that are converted to the numerical addresses that the network uses.

Five top-level domains are currently in use on the Internet:

- **.com**—Initially intended for "commercial" use. It is available to anyone who registers.
- **.edu**—Designated for four-year, degree-giving colleges and universities.
- **.gov**—Designated for agencies and branches of the United States Federal Government.
- **.net**—Initially intended for computers that represent the infrastructure of the Internet, today it is more loosely used for commercial, networked, and organizational sites.
- **.org**—A domain that is used for miscellaneous entities that do not fit under any of the other four domains. Commonly used for not-for-profit organizations.

Secondary domains are commonly referred to as domain names. In `www.networksolutions.com`, networksolutions is the secondary domain.

DO YOU NEED A DOMAIN?

You must first evaluate your needs before jumping into domain registration. Ask yourself the following questions:

- What is the intention of this Web site?
- Does it require brand recognition?
- Will the URL be printed in advertising?

If you intend to use the site to promote yourself or your products, it's a good idea to register a memorable domain name. It is also a good idea if you or your company already has name or brand recognition in your industry or area.

Your domain name becomes your identity on the Internet, so choose it wisely. If the site is a personal page or a small business that doesn't require brand recognition, it isn't necessary to register a domain name.

A lot of helpful information on domain names can be found on the Network Solutions Web site at **`http://www.network solutions.com/`** (see Figure 42.1).

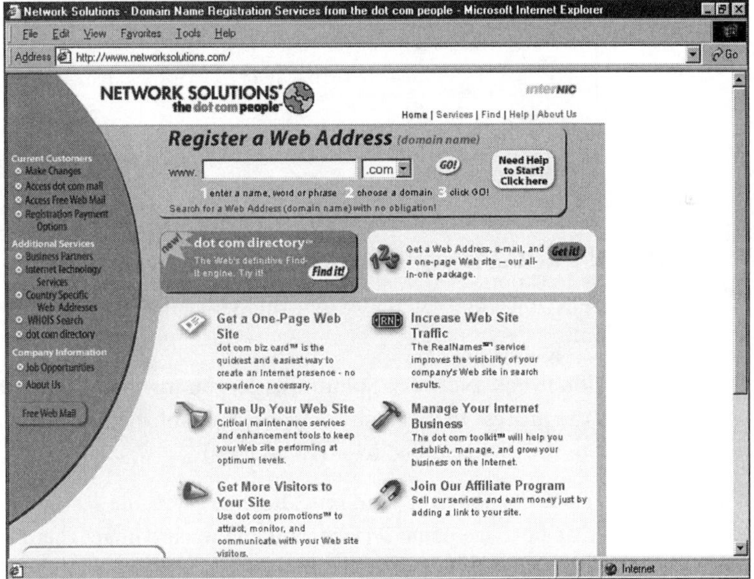

Figure 42.1
The Network Solutions Web site is where you'll find domain registration information as well as other helpful pages and links.

WHOIS DATABASE

After you have decided to register a domain name, you must first determine if the domain name you want is already in use. You can do this by using Network Solutions' WHOIS database.

The WHOIS database contains the records of every domain name that has been registered with Network Solutions. Visit Network Solutions and enter the domain name you're interested in into the WHOIS search service.

WHOIS returns the status of that domain (see Figure 42.2) and, if there is a match, you'll have to select a new domain name.

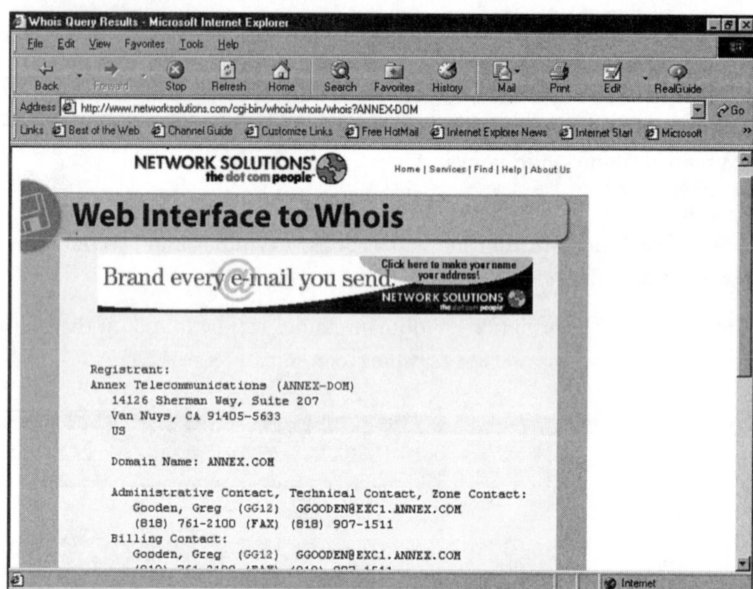

Figure 42.2
Results from a WHOIS search.

THE REGISTRATION PROCESS

After you have selected a domain name that isn't currently in use, you can then proceed with registration.

On its registration forms, Network Solutions asks you for the address of your domain name service. This is the process that actually converts the alphabetical address of a computer (domain name) to the numerical address (IP address).

This process is called "resolution" and must be done by name servers. Your ISP will most likely maintain one or more name servers, and you must contact them to arrange domain name service. Your ISP may even handle domain name registration for you.

→ For detailed information on domain name concerns, **see** "Publishing Sites on the Internet," **p. 903**

Caution

Without a domain name service, Network Solutions will not process your application unless you choose to have Network Solutions reserve the name, which is a bit more expensive, but convenient.

After you have secured domain name service, you can commence with the registration form. You can retrieve a text version of the form via the Web or FTP, fill it out, and then email it to **hostmaster@networksolutions.net**, or you can fill out the online form.

The online form validates the information and guides you through any errors before it is sent along.

Information You'll Need for Domain Registration

Organization name
Organization address
City, State, and Zip (Postal) code
Country
Administrative contact
Technical contact
Billing contact
Primary server hostname (if you are registering the domain rather than having Network Solutions reserve it)
Primary server NetAddress (if you are registering the domain rather than having Network Solutions reserve it)
Secondary server hostname (if you are registering the domain rather than having Network Solutions reserve it)
Secondary server NetAddress (if you are registering the domain rather than having Network Solutions reserve it)

You are able to use the same contact name/address for more than one position (for example, billing and administrative). Choose your contacts carefully; your technical contact should be able to answer questions about your domain name service (primary and secondary servers), and your billing contact will be the person who receives your bill for domain name registration.

Caution

It is extremely important that you fill out this form completely and honestly. Incomplete or incorrect forms can cause problems. If you provide an incomplete billing address, you may not receive notice of your domain name renewal and, in turn, your domain name could be deactivated or deleted.

After Network Solutions receives your request, they assign a tracking number to your request, which they will email to you. Record this number in a secure place because it is required in all correspondence with Network Solutions.

Your request is then checked for errors. If there are no errors, it is sent on to the next step in the registration process. If there are errors and they match common error codes, the request is sent back to you with an explanation of the errors, and you will need to resubmit your request.

If the errors do not match common error codes, your request is put in the queue for staff review. A Network Solutions staff member manually reviews your submission and tries to resolve the error(s). If the errors cannot be easily resolved, he or she contacts you to correct the problem. You then have to resubmit your request.

An error-free request continues through the automated processing system, and you will be notified when the process is complete. The process can be completed in as little as 10 minutes, but generally takes 24 hours.

Your information is then added to the WHOIS database, and you are invoiced for the registration service.

DOMAIN REGISTRATION FEES

As of April 1, 1998 the cost of domain name registration became $70 U.S. (you can pay by check, credit card, or by account; account payment must be arranged in advance). The fee has not changed since. This fee covers the registration process and secures your domain name for a period of two years. Network Solutions invoices your billing contact via email and postal mail within seven days of registration.

Sixty days before the two-year anniversary of your registration, your billing contact will receive an invoice for re-registration (domain name renewal). If Network Solutions does not receive your payment by 12:00 p.m. (Eastern Standard Time) on the due date, they will send your administrative, technical, and billing contact a 15-day deactivation notice via electronic mail.

A 15-day deactivation notice will be physically generated and mailed via the U.S. Postal service to the person you listed as the registrant. If you do not pay within 15 days of the date of the deactivation notice, your domain will be deactivated.

If you still have not paid 60 days after deactivation, your name will be removed from the domain name system and returned to the pool of available names for someone else to register.

META TAGS

One of the things you'll want to be sure of when your site goes live is that it is ready and capable of being indexed. This means getting yourself onto the many search engines and listing services that exist.

→ For help with getting visitors to your site, **see** "Web Site Marketing and Promotion," **p. 908**

One way to prepare your site is by adding `META` tags to keyword and describe the site.

`META` tags may seem daunting, but they are actually just misunderstood common HTML tags. They can identify the creator of the page, give keywords and a description of the page, refresh the page, or load another page. These are just a few of the more common uses for `META` tags.

`META` tags come in two varieties: `http-equiv` and tags with a `name` attribute.

When you request a Web document by using your Web browser, HTTP headers tell your browser things about the document. `http-equiv` `META` tags are designed to act the exact same way. `META` tags with `name` attributes are used for `META` tags that don't correspond to HTTP headers.

USING META TAGS

Implementing META tags is as simple as writing them into the HEAD section of your Web page. Listing 42.1 shows a page with META tags of both the http-equiv and name attributes.

LISTING 42.1 USING META TAGS TO IDENTIFY AND KEYWORD A SITE

```
<HEAD>

<TITLE>Web Design Community: Information</TITLE>

<META http-equiv="Content-Type" content="text/html; charset=iso-8859-1">

<META http-equiv="PICS-Label" content='(PICS-1.1 "http://www.rsac.org/
ratingsv01.html" l comment "RSACi North America Server" r (n 0 s 0 v 0 l 0))'>

<META name="description" content="Web design information, chats, newsgroups,
software and community for web designers, newcomers to web design, and anyone
interested in the Web. Meet new people, learn new web skills, html, graphics,
and design.">

<META name="keywords" content="web, web design, web graphics, web programming,
web programs, webmaster, web designer, community, web design community, code,
coder, html, html author, author, java, javascript, vbscript, web reviews,
molly, holzschlag, molly holzschlag, home, home page, homepage, page, web page,
web pages, webdesign, graphics, graphic, web graphic, GIF, gif, JPG, jpg, JPEG,
software, web site, web site, web site critique, web critiques, critiques, webs,
webhead, computers, computing, computer, microsoft, microsoft network, microsoft
community, network, msn">

</HEAD>
```

Note

You see that a META tag is a single, contained tag, not an element with open and closing tag components. Note also that you stack the tags to accommodate different attributes, rather than stacking attributes within the tag.

Now let's take a more in-depth look at the meaning of these, and other, META tag types and attributes.

KEYWORD AND DESCRIPTION

Using the keywords and description META attributes is extremely important if you plan to submit your site to any search engine. These tags are how most search engines index your page, and what they use to determine its weight and ranking within the search engine.

When someone goes to a search engine and types in Golden Retrievers, that phrase is the keyword and the search engine then searches its database for pages that have that keyword. If you have included Golden Retrievers in your keyword META tag, your page will be one of the pages returned to the user.

```
<META name="keywords" content="dogs, breeding, Golden Retreivers, Golden
Retrievers, puppies, goldens, friendly dogs">
```

Tip from molly

Because retriever is commonly misspelled, both spellings were included to increase the chances of being found by the search engine.

To create a clear description of your page for search engines and indexes, use the `description` within the `META` tag. Then, write out the description, keeping it to one line and including several of your keywords in the description.

```
<META name="description" content="You will find information on breeding Golden
Retrievers, known as friendly dogs, on this page.">
```

It is important to include this description because it is what many search engines will return to a user as a description of your site.

If you work hard to get a high ranking within the search engine but the description of your page is vague or misleading, the user might never click the link to visit you.

EXPIRES AND PRAGMA VALUES

These values are used to prevent people who frequent your site from seeing old versions of your pages that have been cached in their browser as they request a new version of your page from the server.

The expires value works by setting a time after which that page is considered expired. If the browser accesses the page after its "expires" date, it requests a new version. If you set an expires date of `0`, the browser interprets that as expired immediately. Times must always be expressed in GMT format.

```
<META http-equiv="expires" content="Mon, 24 July 1998 08:00:00 GMT">
```

`pragma` prevents the browser from caching the page in the first place.

```
<META http-equiv="pragma" content="no-cache">
```

PICS LABEL

W3C (the World Wide Web Consortium) has developed a standard for labeling Web content. The standard is the Platform for Internet Content Selection, commonly referred to as PICS.

Anything on the Web can be labeled in two ways. A third party service can label the site, and the information is stored on the server of the labeling service. Alternatively, the creator of a site can contact a ratings service, fill out their forms, and have the HTML `META` tag information given to them to place on their pages.

Website Garage provides a free `META` tag generator service at **`http://websitegarage.netscape.com/turbocharge/metatag/`**.

Note

META Info Page: **`http://www.stack.nl/~galactus/html/meta.html`**

Web Developer META Resource Page: **`http://www.Webdeveloper.com/categories/html/html_metatag_res.html`**

REFRESH

The `refresh` value is used to instruct the browser on how many seconds to wait before reloading the document. Because you can specify a different URL for the browser to open, this `META` tag can be used to provide a splashy opening page that automatically reloads to your index page.

```
<META HTTP-EQUIV="refresh" content="0;URL=http://www.url.com">
```

WINDOW-TARGET

The `window-target` value can be used to prevent your page from being viewed inside someone else's framed page. It specifies the named window of the current page and forces the Web browser to put this page at the top of the frameset.

```
<META HTTP-EQUIV="window-target" content="_top">
```

Robots

Some Web developers want to control whether their sites are indexed by a search engine or not. If you are in the same situation, you would then use the `ROBOTS META` tag. This tag instructs the robot (or "spider") what to do with the files on your page.

```
<META name="robots" content="all">
```

allows all files to be indexed. `all` is the default for this tag's content attribute.

```
<META name="robots" content="none">
```

tells the spider not to index any of your files.

```
<META name="robots" content="index">
<META name="robots" content="noindex">
```

`index` instructs the spider that it can index your pages and look for other links, unless you tell it differently. If you use `noindex`, the engine won't index the page, even though it *will* follow links on that page unless you give specific instructions for it not to do so.

```
<META name="robots" content="follow">
<META name="robots" content="nofollow">
```

`follow` allows the spider to follow all links on your page (to index those pages); `nofollow` instructs the spider not to follow any links on that page.

```
<META name="robots" content="index, nofollow">
```

This tag allows the page to be indexed, but instructs the spider not to continue further.

Testing Your Pages Offline

When your Web site is complete on your hard drive, your next step is to test its functionality. Of course all your pages look great, you've been working on them for days or weeks. But your site can look drastically different depending on the platform or system on which they are viewed.

You must view your site by using as many different systems and browsers as possible; that way you can address any functionality or design issues that arise.

You should test your site on PC, Macintosh, and UNIX platforms and, on each system, test how your site looks when viewed with the browsers available for that system. You should also test a variety of resolutions. How does the site look at 640×480, 800×600, and 1,024×768?

➔ For more information on how to prepare for varying screen resolutions, **see** "Resolution, Gamma, and the Visual Environment," **p. 546**

The most popular browsers are Netscape Navigator and Internet Explorer, and they have some big differences in their HTML conventions. It can't be stressed enough how important it is to test your site with both browsers.

They aren'tthe only browsers available, however. Lynx, a text-only browser, is still used today. How does your site look without graphics? If you haven't planned for text-only visitors, it could look pretty awful. Another browser growing in popularity is the one used with WebTV. There are also several up-and-comers hoping to compete with IE and Netscape, including Opera, which has features for older computers and special-needs users.

➔ For more information about designing sites for users with special circumstances, **see** "Accessibility and Internationalization," **p. 475**

It isn't reasonable to expect that you have access to every system and every browser, so poll your friends and colleagues. Ask them what system and browser they use. If they have access to something you don't, ask them to view your page for you. Have them look at the following things:

- Fonts
- Color scheme
- Tables and frames
- Scrolling (Is there any horizontal scroll?)
- Backgrounds (Do they tile correctly at different resolutions?)

It is also *extremely* important to test all your links to be sure they work correctly and that you have no broken images.

COPY AND CODE EDITING

What is visible right away on a site? Your content! You can spend weeks planning a well-designed site. You paid for the best graphics and have a great sense of style. Wouldn't it be terrible if the first thing someone notices on your site is your glaring spelling errors? No one is going to spend $20,000 to hire you as an Internet consultant if you offer them "sulutions" to their Internet needs.

The following is a helpful checklist to use when copyediting your pages:

- **Correct spelling**—You must ensure that every word is spelled correctly and is the correct word (spell checkers will miss correctly spelled words that are used incorrectly such as angel and angle).
- **Contractions**—You should also check that you use contractions correctly. Your/you're and its/it's are two contractions that are commonly misused, and they make the writer look uneducated.
- **Punctuation**—Check your punctuation! I once read a book where the author constantly used short, choppy sentences. "He drove to the store. The neighborhood store. Late at night." It drove me nuts! I kept praying she would throw in a comma somewhere so I could forget about the punctuation and concentrate on the story. Incorrect punctuation can greatly affect the reader's enjoyment of your text. Because it can also affect the meaning of your text, it is imperative that you aren't missing any punctuation. Remember, unless you're writing ad copy, a sentence should contain both a noun and a verb.
- **Typos**—Typographical errors (typos) happen to even the most conscientious writer, and you might not even notice them while proofreading. You should always have someone proofread your pages for you; they will be able to catch the things that you missed. They will also be able to point out any grammatical errors that you wouldn't have noticed.

Copy editing is of utmost importance when you consider the personalities of most Internet users. They typically are well educated with a short attention span. They will not spend any time at a site with poor spelling or grammar, because a few clicks away they can find the same information with no errors.

Even one spelling error can make your site look unprofessional, no matter how much effort you put into it.

During the testing stage, you'll also come to appreciate the importance of good code editing. A missed quotation mark could cause a broken link, or a missed image `alt` attribute could cause confusion.

You can get away with sloppy code, but it could cause problems in the long run. If you work on a team, and your code isn't organized, the next person to work on that code will have a hard time understanding your work. Sloppy code can also result in broken links, broken images, and slow return time to the browser as it tries to interpret your code.

The following are some common mistakes made in sloppy code:

- Not including `alt` attributes within your `IMG` tag. If you don't include an `alt` attribute, any viewer with his or her browser's images option turned off will not know what your image is. This is especially important when you use an image as text or as a hyperlink. The `alt` attribute is included within the `<IMG>` tag and should be descriptive but not overly long: `<IMG src="email.gif" width="50" height="65" alt="Mailbox Image. Click Here to email us!">`.

- `width` and `height` attributes are also regularly left out of the `<IMG>` tag. It is important to include these attributes because if `width` and `height` are included, the image spreads out to those dimensions even before the image is downloaded. This ensures that your layout will not be affected by slow download times.
- Leaving tags "open." Although most of the newer versions of browsers "close" tags for you, it is always better to close every tag that requires closing. Working with the container method can help you get accustomed to properly closing your tags.

→ For a reminder on using the container method when creating your pages, **see** "Building HTML Documents," **p. 96**

Your code is not visible to your visitors right away, but anyone can view it by clicking View Source. Do you really want potential customers to see unorganized, messy code?

Check with your HTML editor or WYSIWYG application for code checking—many software programs come with such a tool. If you don't have a utility, try HTML Validator (see Figure 42.3), a five-star program for validating HTML.

→ For a discussion on a variety of validation programs, **see** "HTML Tools," **p. 44**

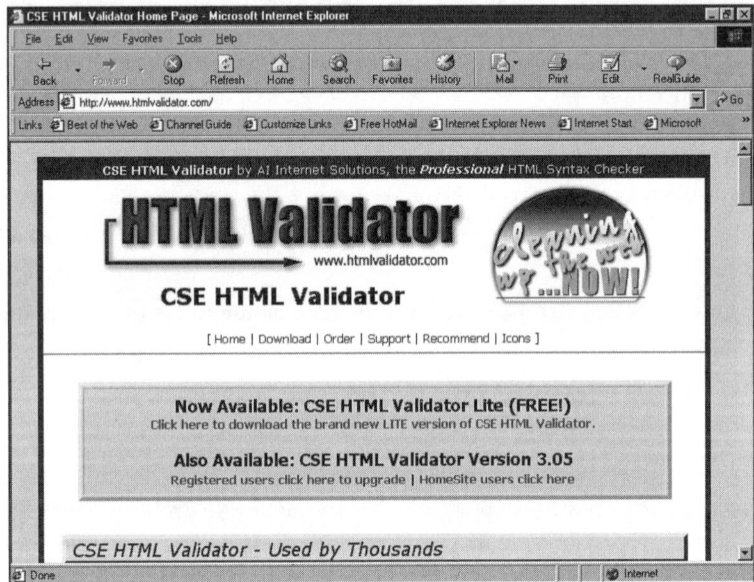

Figure 42.3
HTML Validator is a helpful HTML code validation utility. HTML Validator can be found at `http://www.htmlvalidator.com/`.

There are also online code validating services.

> **Note**
>
> The World Wide Web Consortium's HTML Validation Service: Check with standards compliance at `http://validator.w3.org/`.
>
> Bobby checks your site, not only for HTML syntax, but to see whether you'll stand up to accessibility concerns at `http://www.cast.org/bobby/`.

Note

Doctor HTML 4.0 is a highly recommended syntax checker that is available at `http://www2.imagiware.com/RxHTML/`.

WWWeblint used to be free, but it's now a reasonably priced subscription service that validates your HTML pages online. Check them out at `http://www.unipress.com/cgi-bin/WWWeblint/`.

TROUBLESHOOTING

RESERVING DOMAIN NAMES

I've decided on a domain name, but I'm still searching for a Web hosting service. I'm worried that the chosen domain name will no longer be available when the site is ready to be launched.

Network Solutions allows you to reserve a domain name. There is a fee for this service (currently $119 for two years), but you do not need to provide any technical information, such as an IP address, to reserve the domain name. After you have found an ISP to host your site, you can update your domain information at Network Solutions.

ALL SITE VALIDATORS ARE NOT CREATED EQUAL

I have followed all the HTML syntax instructions in the book, and my site looks fine when I test it on various platforms and browsers. But when I run the site through an HTML validator, I get plenty of errors.

Some validators are pickier than others, particularly in pointing out potential problems in cross-platform or cross-browser situations. Look at the errors generated by your code and use your own knowledge of HTML syntax to decide if those errors are worth correcting in your final code.

DESIGNING FOR THE REAL WORLD

MAKING THE JUMP TO YOUR OWN DOMAIN

It's fortunate when working on the Web that decisions are rarely final. You might think your site is going to have a limited audience, certainly not worth the expense of registering a domain name. Surprise! You suddenly find yourself one of the Internet's hot spots. You start thinking about the advertising revenue possibilities. And if you're going to get paid by the eyeball, you want to ensure that you have *lots* of eyeballs. Suddenly, you find yourself in need of an easily memorized domain name, after all.

Or say you were only planning a simple site with a few pages. A couple months down the road, you decide to add a message board to your site. The problem is that your ISP does not allow CGI or PERL. Guess what, it's time to move to a new Web host. And while you're at it, you decide you might as well register your own domain name to ensure you take your regular visitors with you the next time you switch providers.

Web sites are constantly in a state of evolution. This includes domain names. Take Fontopolis as an example. Fontopolis is a terrific font resource, with new fonts uploaded on a regular basis. Fonts are listed both alphabetically and by style, and the fonts are presented well. In the past six months alone, Fontopolis has gone through three URL changes. Originally found at **http://ourworld.compuserve.com/homepages/fontopolis/**, Fontopolis moved to **http://fontopolis.simplenet.com/** as its popularity grew. The site has recently moved again to an even simpler domain name: **http://www.fontopolis.net/**.

There are a couple of important points to remember when you change the URL for your site. First of all, be sure to use a redirect for the first several weeks or even months. It can take several months for your entries to be updated in all the search engines, and you don't want to lose any visitors. Your redirect should automatically send visitors to your new URL after a short wait and should also include a link to the URL for those using older browsers.

Second, be sure to let everyone know about the URL change. If your site is accessible from another site, be sure to let the Webmaster know so that the links can be updated. Update your search engine listings. Add the new URL to your signature files when you send email or post on newsgroups.

Finally, check your own work. Examine each page of your Web site for references to your old URL. Also consider adding a message to your default page reminding those visitors who got there by way of the redirect to bookmark your new URL.

CHAPTER 43

Publishing Sites on the Internet

In this chapter

What Makes a Site Live?

You've developed your Web site. You've come up with a consistent design, spell-checked your content, and tested all your pages for broken links and collapsed tables. It's time for the accolades to come. But nobody's going to see your site if you don't publish it somewhere.

If your site is intended for your corporate intranet, you may need to follow company procedures to publish your pages. Most developers, however, are designing sites for the Internet to get the largest audience possible, and that's what you'll be learning about in this chapter.

A "live" site is one that is accessible to people browsing the Internet. Sounds simple, and it really is not at all difficult to publish your pages and make your site live. In most cases, your files are accessible within seconds of uploading them to a Web server. But before you upload that first file, you have some choices to make.

To make pages accessible on the Internet, you need to put the files on a Web server. Unless you want to go to the expense of buying a dedicated Web server and a reliable T-1 connection to your house or office (unreasonable unless you are managing a large, active site), you'll want to find a Web-hosting service to host your site.

→ To be sure your site is ready for publication, **see** "Preparing Your Site for Publication," **p. 885**

Most Internet service providers include some amount of Web space along with their access accounts. If you are developing a small home page, this amount of space should be more than adequate. Larger sites, or those with a corporate purpose, require much more server space and might necessitate a unique URL that will bring name recognition to your site.

→ Need help with how to promote your site? **see** "Web Site Marketing and Promotion," **p. 907**

Note

Hundreds of Web-hosting services are available, and the rates vary greatly. One of the best resources for finding a Web-hosting service is The List, which can be found at `http://www.thelist.com/`. This site offers information about thousands of ISPs and Web-hosting services.

Keep in mind that you do not necessarily have to choose a local Web-hosting service. Many national ISPs offer commercial Web hosting, with the added benefit of local access numbers all over the country, so you can access the Internet and maintain your Web site even if you're on the road.

Even if you have a local ISP, you may still choose a Web-hosting service that is more distant if they offer competitive rates. You would use the same local ISP to access the Internet, but your Web site would then be hosted elsewhere.

Prices for Web hosting vary widely depending on the type of service and the amount of space you require. You can generally find an adequate amount of space and bandwidth (amount of usage your site is allocated per month before additional charges accrue) for a medium business site for under $75 per month.

Larger sites—and especially those requiring specialty services such as secure transactions—cost upwards of $100 per month for hosting. If you choose to operate your site under a "vanity" URL, it costs you an additional $70 to register your domain name. This cost covers the initial registration and the first two years of service. You'll be billed an additional $35 per year after the first two years to maintain your own domain name.

TRANSFERRING FILES USING FTP

Uploading your Web site files to the Internet requires the use of File Transfer Protocol (FTP). You use FTP to transfer all the files relating to your Web site—including your HTML files, image files, and any audio/video files—to the remote Web server.

Many FTP packages are available today, including the following:

- **Dedicated packages**—Standalone software products that help you manage your FTP needs.
- **Operating system tools**—Windows 98 allows you to open a window and connect directly to an FTP server. Simply type `FTP://` plus the name of your server. If you're not connected to the Net, you'll be prompted to do so. Simply use drag-and-drop to transfer your files.
- **Built-ins**—Many WYSIWYG HTML software packages and browsers, such as Netscape Navigator, have FTP services built into the application.

→ For more on built-in FTP applications, **see** "HTML Tools," **p. 43**

Dedicated FTP packages offer capabilities that built-in components do not offer, such as the ability to delete old Web pages and rename files on the server.

FTP SOFTWARE AVAILABLE ON THE WEB

The most popular FTP programs are WS_FTP and CuteFTP for the PC, and Fetch for the Macintosh. Each of these programs is available as shareware on the Web. As with all shareware, you are expected to register the software if you use it beyond a reasonable trial period. Currently, the price for each of these programs is under $40.

The method for transferring your files to a Web server is similar for each of these programs. First, you configure the software to locate the remote server and log in with your user ID and password. You locate the directory to which you're transferring your files and identify the files you wish to transfer. Then you let the software do its work.

WS_FTP

WS_FTP, made by Ipswitch, is a powerful program that allows you to customize file types (helpful when you're using lesser-known extensions) and views.

WS_FTP is available for all Windows platforms, including Windows 95 (see Figure 43.1) and Windows 98 (see Figure 43.2).

Note

WS_FTP is available for download at the Ipswitch Web site at `http://www.ipswitch.com/`.

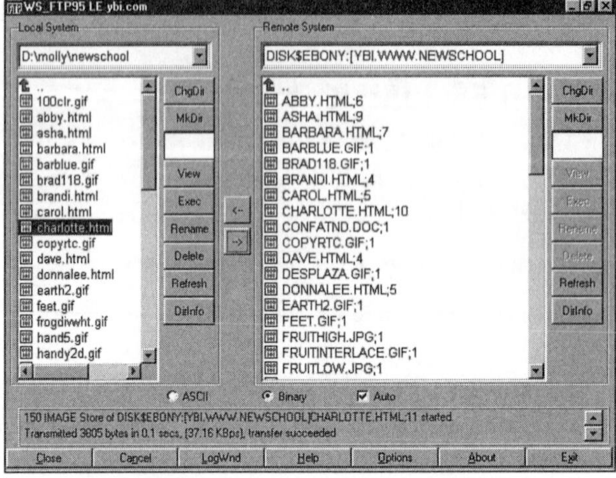

Figure 43.1
WS_FTP Windows 95 version offers a simple interface that allows you to view both your local drives as well as the remote site.

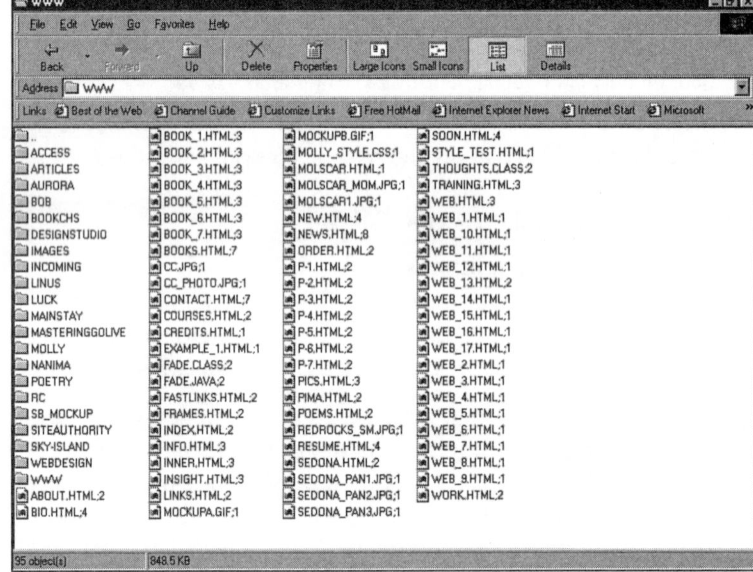

Figure 43.2
For Windows 98, an integrated Web-style version of WS_FTP is available.

Perform the following steps to transfer files using WS_FTP for Windows 95:

1. Click Connect, New to create a new profile.
2. Enter the URL of your Web server in the Host Name field. This URL is usually `ftp.domain-name.com`, where domain-name is the domain of your Web server.

3. Enter your username and password in the User ID and Password fields. This information may be different from the login info for your ISP account, especially if you are using a different Web-hosting service. Click OK.
4. In the upper-right, check the directory to be sure you're uploading to the right place. Navigate through the directory structure on the right, if necessary, to find the appropriate directory.
5. On the left, select the files you want to upload.
6. Click the right-arrow button to upload your files.

Your files now transfer to the Web server.

CUTEFTP

CuteFTP (see Figure 43.3), made by GlobalSCAPE, Inc., is geared more toward beginners than WS_FTP, with more intuitive menus. CuteFTP also allows you to set up categories of configuration profiles, which can be helpful if you're working on multiple sites or want to separate your Web site work from any FTP download sites you access with the same software package.

Note

Download CuteFTP from `http://www.cuteftp.com/`.

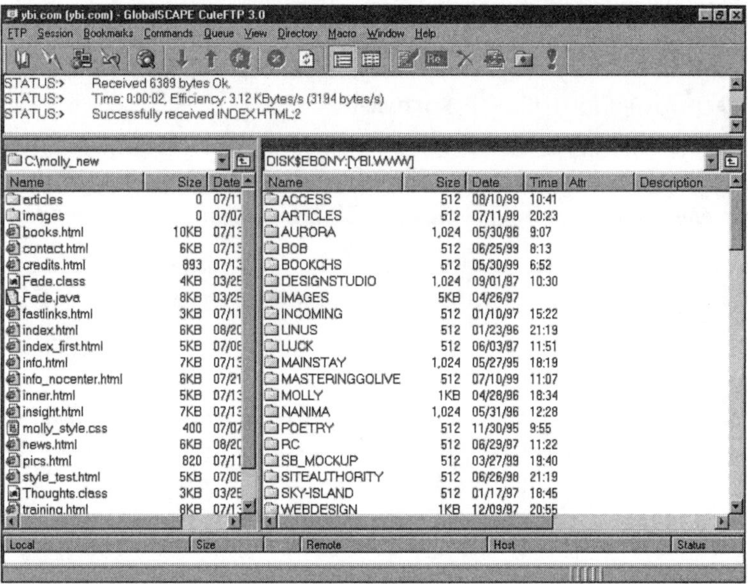

Figure 43.3
Transferring files with CuteFTP. CuteFTP's popularity is a result of its easy interface and international versions.

Although CuteFTP is only available for Windows operating systems, it is available in Spanish (see Figure 43.4) and Japanese.

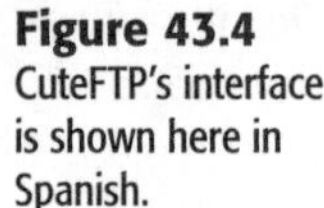

Figure 43.4
CuteFTP's interface is shown here in Spanish.

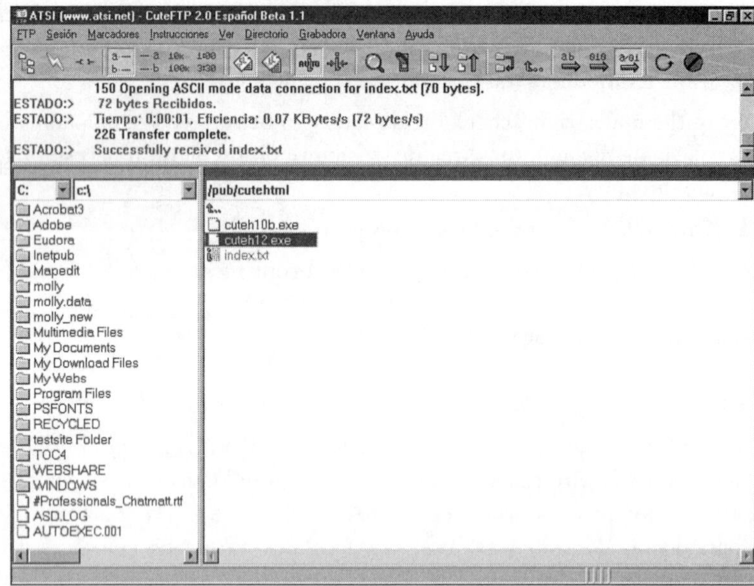

Another nice feature of CuteFTP is the capability to resume uploads if you get disconnected during transfer.

Are you still having difficulty getting connected? Its possible that you haven't configured some of your connection settings correctly, see "Can't Configure FTP Software" in the Troubleshooting section at the end of this chapter.

MACINTOSH AND UNIX FTP SOFTWARE

Fetch is a Macintosh-based FTP program developed by Dartmouth University. It's the most convenient and popular of the Macintosh-based FTP programs. The Fetch interface is extremely user friendly, making the FTP process simple for those new to the game.

Most UNIX systems come with preinstalled FTP packages. For more options, visit your favorite shareware and software sites for a wide range of choices of FTP applications for all platforms.

Note

Download Fetch from `http://www.dartmouth.edu/pages/softdev/fetch.html`. You can also search for FTP tools at `http://www.shareware.com/`, or Macmillan Computer Publishing's Tucows mirror site at `http://tucows.mcp.com/`.

FTP SOFTWARE IN WYSIWYG HTML EDITORS

Many of the WYSIWYG editors, such as Microsoft FrontPage, Adobe GoLive, and Macromedia Dreamweaver, have FTP capabilities built right into the software. As with all aspects of these types of editors, the focus is on ease of use.

FrontPage keeps track of which pages have changed on your site. Both FrontPage and Adobe GoLive upload your pages at the touch of a button after you have configured the software to access your Web server.

Tip from molly

If your site is nested several directories deep on your remote Web server, pay close attention to how you configure FrontPage's Web Publishing Wizard.

I recommend you try uploading one sample page to test your configuration before attempting to FTP your entire site. This can save you a lot of time—and embarrassment with your Web-hosting service—in case the wizard needs to be tweaked a bit to find the right directory.

Dreamweaver (see Figure 43.5) allows you to keep a connection with your Web server open as you edit your files. This allows you to easily transfer files back and forth between your local computer and the Web server as you work.

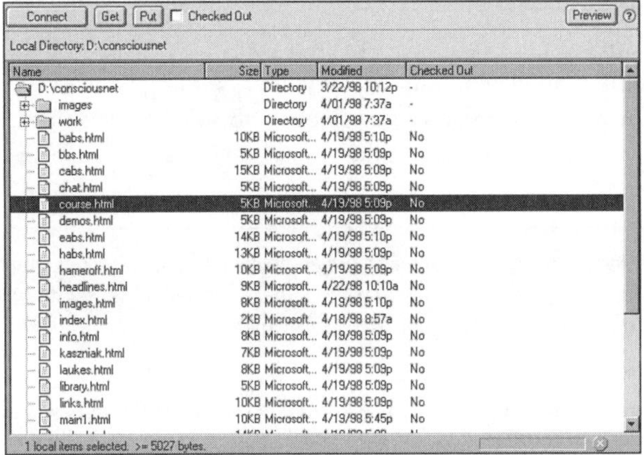

Figure 43.5 Dreamweaver supports FTP, too. Having FTP directly in an editing program reduces the need to switch back and forth between different software programs in order to get the job done.

Dreamweaver automatically recreates the same file structure on the remote server, including subdirectories, which you have on your local machine. This ensures that any relative links you create remain accurate on the remote server.

TESTING FILES LIVE

After you've uploaded your files to your remote Web server, it's time to begin the testing process all over again. No matter how good everything looked on your local machine, it's a good idea to visit every page again and click every link. Did you forget to upload an image file? Did you create an absolute link where you intended to create a relative link? All these little problems can be easily fixed in this testing phase.

When testing your site, look for the following:

- **Does it look good at lower resolutions?**—Many computers these days can handle 800×600 and above, but there are still people out there viewing your pages at 640×480. Even if you're designing for a higher optimal resolution, you want your pages to be legible at this lower resolution.
- **Can you navigate your site without graphics turned on?**—Unless you have a specific audience in mind that can definitely handle a graphics-intensive site, make sure that any graphic navigation also has a text counterpart.
- **How does it look in 256-color?**—Again, more and more Web surfers have video cards that can handle higher color modes, but 256-color is still the standard. Even if you stuck with the Web-safe color palette, it's a good idea to view all your pages in 256-color to make sure there aren't any horrifying surprises.
- **How does it look in different browsers?**—Internet Explorer and Netscape Navigator can make the same page look very different, particularly if you're using table background colors and other design tricks. It may be impossible to have your pages look exactly the same in each browser, but you want the site to still look good in each.
- **How long does it take to load?**—Even if you've kept page weight (the total size of a page, including graphics) in mind when you're building your site, you'll still want to download the pages after you've put them on the Web server to see how everything is loading and check the download time.

Tip from molly

Want to make sure your sites are accessible? Turn off all script, graphics, and media. Test the site using a line browser. Does it make conceptual sense? If not, you may need to look more closely at Web page accessibility methods.

Uploaded your site but friends and clients are unable to access it? Perhaps you've not set up your permissions correctly, see "Permissions" in the Troubleshooting section at the end of this chapter.

→ Learn to code accessible sites, **see** "Accessibility and Internationalization," **p. 475**

→ Check your color compatibility by ensuring your designs follow the correct methodology, **see** "Color Concepts," **p. 528**

→ For information on browser issues, **see** "Resolution, Gamma, and the Visual Environment," **p. 549**

Follow these guidelines, and you'll improved your chances of having a very stable site.

Managing Links

Every time you add or revise a page on your Web site, test your links on the live server. As your site grows, it's easy to move a page from one directory to another and forget to update the link reference on another page.

If you have links to other Internet sites on your pages, you'll also want to check those links on a regular basis. The Web is a moving target with sites coming and going on a daily basis. You might link to a wonderful related site today only to find that it has moved to another URL or disappeared completely by next week.

The topic of a site may change over time, too. Don't let your members be surprised by clicking to an erotic poetry site when they (and you) think they're clicking to a discussion of Shakespeare's sonnets.

Even large, commercial sites can be redesigned in such a way that they're either no longer appropriate for your site or might be a better resource for your viewers if you link to a specific page.

Manual Management

The best and quickest way to manage links on a small site is to maintain a list of all your links. You can do this on a sheet of paper or a database such as Access and manually type them in each time you do a check. Another convenient method is to create a simple HTML file for yourself with hot links to every site and page referenced from your Web site. Perhaps the easiest way to check your links is to bookmark each linked site using your browser. You can then navigate from link to link directly from that list.

Once a week or so, run through your list, calling up each of those sites in your browser. If a site is being redirected, it's best to change your link to the actual URL of the site. Be sure to scan the site briefly to make sure the material hasn't changed to something objectionable to your audience. And, of course, remove any links to sites that have disappeared.

Link Management Programs

As your site grows, manually checking all the links on every page will become cumbersome. That's where a good link management program can come in handy.

A link management program automatically checks every link on a page or site, including both intra-page and inter-site links, and indicates which links are invalid. Dozens of link management programs are available, ranging from freeware applications that check a limited number of links to commercial packages that can check hundreds of links at once. Some packages also generate a site map of your entire Web site. Several packages are mentioned later, under the section "Validating Code."

➔ For more on intra-page linking **see** "Linking Pages," **p. 183**

There are also Web services that provide link checks on a page. Web Site Garage checks one page of a site free of charge (see Figure 43.6). If you want to check your entire site and do regular link checks, you can pay an annual fee that entitles you to automatic monthly updates with results emailed to you.

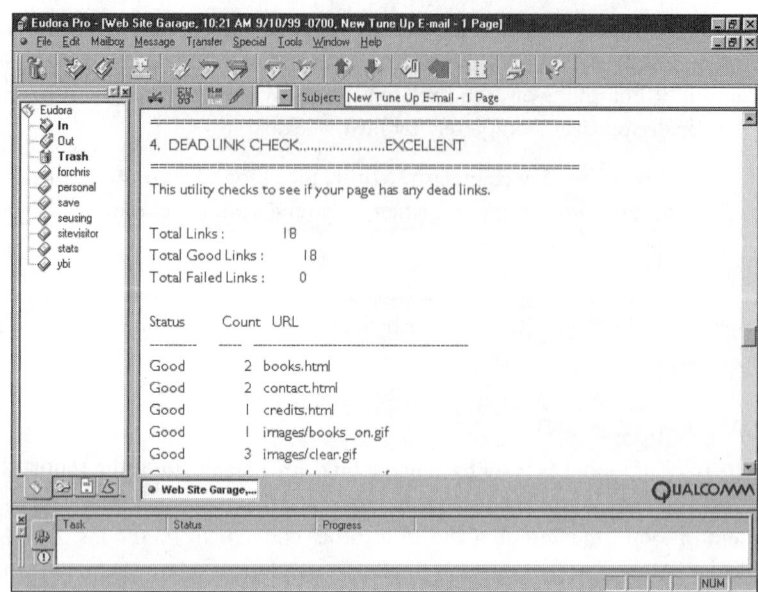

Figure 43.6
Web Site Garage apparently liked my error-free linking!

Another favorite is Doctor HTML gives you feedback on your HTML code.

Note

Visit Web Site Garage at **`http://www.Websitegarage.com/`**, and Doctor HTML at **`http://www2.imagiware.com/RxHTML/`**.

Validating Code

It's important to validate your HTML code to catch any mistakes you may have made. Web browsers try to parse HTML code even if it has errors, so your pages may look right in your browser but contain errors that display incorrectly in other browsers.

If your site makes extensive use of tables, for example, it's easy to unknowingly throw in a few extra tags that aren't picked up by your browser. Internet Explorer, especially, is good at parsing "bad" code. Although this may sound like a feature, it can promulgate bad code unless you're careful about validating your work.

Code Validation Software

If you're using an HTML editor such as Allaire's HomeSite, Microsoft FrontPage, or Macromedia Dreamweaver to develop your site, you can use the HTML validation component of those packages. If you're coding by hand in an ASCII editor such as Notepad or SimpleText, or want to try a standalone option, you'll want to explore other applications.

Note

Check out the HTML Validator. It began as a school project and, in fact, takes its name from the very course where it began. This powerful HTML shareware program does a thorough job of testing your code, and can be found at `http://www.htmlvalidator.com/`.

The Bobby site analyzes your site for accessibility issues for those with special needs. You can find it at `http://www.cast.org/bobby/`.

VALIDATING CODE ON THE WEB

Many HTML validation sites are on the Web, many of which will validate your site at no charge. My favorite is the W3C HTML Validation Services. This site gives immediate results and offers explanations of the problems it encounters with your code.

Another good choice is NetMechanic. This service gives you a choice of running an immediate report or working in the background and sending the report through email.

One caution when using HTML validators: each one can give slightly different results, as some validators will test for strict HTML 4.0 rather than transitional, or be more sensitive to browser-specific tags and attributes.

If you want to be really cautious, run the same page through two or three validators. And, of course, nothing takes the place of double-checking your work yourself.

Note

Hard core coders will appreciate the W3C's validation service at `http://validator.w3.org/`.

NetMechanic can be found at `http://netmechanic.com/`.

COPYRIGHT GUIDELINES

Plagiarism may be the sincerest form of flattery, but it is also illegal. Copyright law is just as applicable on the Internet as offline, no matter what you might see on other sites or read about on Usenet. Any work that is published in a book, magazine, newspaper, or even elsewhere on the Internet is most likely copyrighted.

Graphic images, songs, and video clips are also normally copyrighted. Be very careful about "borrowing" copyrighted material for your Web site. Not only do you risk your reputation, but you also risk serious legal repercussions.

This doesn't necessarily mean that you cannot use copyrighted work, however. If you are quoting a few lines from an article, for example, and cite the original copyright of the author and publisher, you are making "fair use" of the material, which is permitted under law. The trick is in using just enough material to get your point across without re-purposing entire passages of the work.

You can also obtain written permission to use excerpts from a copyrighted work. You do this by contacting the author, publisher, agent, or license-holder of the material. If you want to use a passage from a book or newspaper, the best place to start is with the publisher. If you want to use an audio file, you should contact ASCAP (American Society of Composers, Authors, and Publishers, (**http://www.ascap.com/**) or BMI (Broadcast Music, Inc., **http://www.bmi.com**). Whether or not you obtain the permission you seek is up to the copyright holder, and they may require a fee before they'll grant permission.

Stock photography and music sites are another source of high-quality, copyrighted material. One such site is Photodisc (**http://www.photodisc.com/**). Photodisc allows you to browse thousands of stock photos at their site, and lets you download complimentary ("comp") images to use as you're building your site.

If you want to use the images on a live site, you can purchase a license at a small price. The price per image runs about $20. If you find you are using several images from the same group, you can purchase a license for an entire CD-ROM of images.

Another popular source of stock images is ArtToday (**http://www.arttoday.com/**). Unlike Photodisc, which charges per image, ArtToday charges an annual fee (currently $29.95 per year) to access their site. The quality and depth of the images is generally not as high as Photodisc, but they offer fonts, clip art, Web buttons, and icons in addition to stock photography.

If you are developing a personal home page, it is probably not worth paying a steep fee to license background music or pay for stock graphic images. For commercial sites, however, licensed material can improve the image of the site and may be worth the investment.

As you can see, although the technical aspects of turning your Web site live are quite easy, there are many other considerations and resources to bear in mind first. Choose the level of complexity that is appropriate for your site, your time constraints, and your technical competence, and you'll do fine.

TROUBLESHOOTING

CAN'T CONFIGURE FTP SOFTWARE

I keep getting a log-in error when I try to connect to the server via FTP. I know that my username and password are correct. Why can't I log in?

Some ISPs assign different passwords to access your server space than that assigned for your general account access. Look through your ISP instructions to see if such is the case with your account.

PERMISSIONS

I've FTP'd my pages onto my host's servers, but friends and co-workers cannot access the new site. What is keeping site visitors out?

The permissions on your domain may be set incorrectly. Permission settings differ depending on the type of server. In some cases, you can change the permissions yourself.

Depending on the security limits placed by your Web host, however, you may need to contact the server administrator to set the permissions properly.

DESIGNING FOR THE REAL WORLD

Because copyright, trademark, and the issue of domain names are all of a complex nature, I took an opportunity to speak with Jodi Sax, an entertainment attorney and Internet legal consultant. She was able to clarify a number of issues that are of serious importance to people working on the Web.

Here's what Jodi had to say about copyright:

"A common issue is that people don't realize that everything that is created under U.S. law has a copyright interest. It doesn't mean that someone has to register, or put a copyright notice on their materials."

The good news, then, is that whatever *original* information you create immediately and without registration or notice, is considered copyrighted. On the other hand, this means that original work belonging to *others* is protected as well—meaning that just because it's out on the 'Net with or without a copyright notice or registration, does *not* mean it's free for you to use.

"...it doesn't matter whether you credit your source or not—if you copy something and you don't have permission, you're committing copyright infringement."

This made me think of what is referred to as "fair use." As a writer, I often run into a situation where I want to use some section of material in an article or chapter. But fair use is apparently a more complicated issue than what others, and I, might think:

"Fair use is hard to quantify—this is the subject of litigation all the time. Someone might ask: Isn't it true that I can use 50 words without getting in trouble? There's no existing standard as to what constitutes fair use. It's a combination of factors, determined on a case-by-case basis."

Another question I've heard designers ask is whether their HTML source code is copyrighted. Sax describes this as an issue up for discussion these days.

"There are instances of people trying to claim rights to source code. To a certain extent, people can claim a right in that it's creative. But you can't claim an interest in something that is pure, factual information, such as an `<a href>`*."*

What about music on the Net?

"The problem is that everything is so unknown that it really depends upon bargaining power. Music on the Net is a big mess right now. For people that are building a basic home page, remember that anything you put on there has a copyright interest. If you want copyrighted music, you should go to ASCAP or BMI to purchase the license to use that music on your site. In a legitimate business, get a lawyer to help you learn what kinds of licenses you need."

Any final words of wisdom regarding copyright?

"I always tell people it's much better to be safe than sorry. Only copy something if you have permission, otherwise don't do it."

What about domain names?

"The big issue right now is trademark holder rights versus domain name holder rights. Legislation is pending. Conceivably, somebody could have gone to Network Solutions years ago and registered Coca-Cola.com. This action is referred to as "cybersquatting". The trademark holders get upset as they've put a lot of money into marketing their brand, and they want their domain names."

"Network Solutions has a policy whereby if you have a registered trademark you can have the domain frozen. It goes into a limbo of sorts, where no one gets to use it until the litigation is worked out."

"I will say that courts don't like cybersquatters. Typically, they will lose. Before registering a domain, check for trademark. You can do this for free at the USPTO site."

Note

For helpful information on copyright and trademark concerns, visit these sites:

Fair use issues are defined at **`http://fairuse.stanford.edu/`**.

Learn about copyright and find forms for registration at **`http://www.loc.gov/copyright/`**.

Search trademarks for free! Visit **`http://www.uspto.gov/`**.

If you want to license music for use on your site, check with ASCAP, **`http://www.ascap.com/`** and BMI, **`http://www.bmi.com/`**.

Visit Jodi Sax at her Web site, **`http://www.lawgirl.com/`**.

CHAPTER 44

Web Site Marketing and Promotion

In this chapter

THE WEB AS A COMMERCIAL VENUE

As the Internet continues to grow in popularity, more and more companies are feeling the need to get online. Additionally, there are many companies that are emerging solely on the Web, with no offline counterpart.

With so much commercialism on the Web, it didn't take long for the advertising and marketing firms to step into the act—first to use a Web site as an advertising medium, and now recognizing that many Web sites are not simply the means to a product but the product itself.

Whether you intend to use your Web site as an addition to your offline business, to provide products or services, or as a forum for your expression, you have to put some effort into marketing it. With the millions of Web pages available today, your content could be lost and, as fabulous as it is, it might never get seen.

Every good Web designer knows how important it is to know your target audience. You wouldn't use elegant fonts and understated colors to appeal to the audience of a dance music site, you would use funky fonts and bright vibrant colors.

The same can be said about marketing your site. You wouldn't waste your time marketing your dance music site to members of a quilting club. Sure, there could be some dance music fans there, but the probability is slim.

You have to know your audience before you can effectively market to it. You need to know the following information about your target audience:

- Age
- Gender
- Marital status
- Financial status
- Locale

You should also include categories that specifically apply to your Web site.

After you have determined your primary audience, you should also consider secondary markets. Although your main target audience for a quilting Web site is affluent women over 45, you should also include young teen girls just learning to quilt.

If you are unfamiliar with demographic research and want to be aggressive in your online marketing techniques, it might be a good idea to investigate the type of information you can get from a professional marketing firm or advertising agency. As the composition of the Internet community begins to more closely mirror that of society at large, however, you should also make yourself aware of demographics in general.

Tip from molly

If you want to learn more about demographic research, you can visit the American Demographics Web site at `http://www.demographics.com`. The site offers archives of their magazine from the last several years. Many of these issues include demographic information about Internet usage for various markets.

After you have a good understanding of your audience, you can then market your site directly to them. You could place ads on the search engines they are most likely to use and on the Web sites they frequent. You can also take your advertising offline and target the magazines and newspapers they read or the radio station they tune to.

Marketing your site blindly, without consideration of your target, is counter-productive. An audience that isn't interested will view your ads, and your target audience may never know your site exists.

Considering selling space on your site for advertising but not sure where to start? Check out "Selling Banner Advertising" in the Troubleshooting section at the end of this chapter for helpful ideas on where to begin.

SEARCH ENGINES AND DIRECTORIES AS MARKETING TOOLS

Search engines and directories can be powerful online marketing tools, but you must first understand how they work and how to best use them. Search engines "spider" the Web finding Web pages to add to their database of listings. Directories allow you to submit URLs to categorized listings.

With search engines, users access the database by entering a keyword or phrase that interests them. The search engine then returns a list of Web pages from within their database that matches the query of the user. The results are ranked from most to least relevant, and there are often hundreds of thousands of listings returned with a single query. Directories allow users to submit URLs—usually via a feedback form—and then the information is processed.

There are hundreds of search engines and directories, some appealing to very specific audiences. The most popular search engines appeal to a broad audience and have an easy-to-use interface (see Figure 44.1).

Note

Here's a selection of popular search engines:

Yahoo!: `http://www.yahoo.com/`

AltaVista: `http://www.altavista.com/`

Excite: `http://www.excite.com/`

Lycos: `http://www.lycos.com/`

HotBot: `http://www.hotbot.com/`

Infoseek: `http://www.infoseek.com/`

Dogpile: `http://www.dogpile.com/`

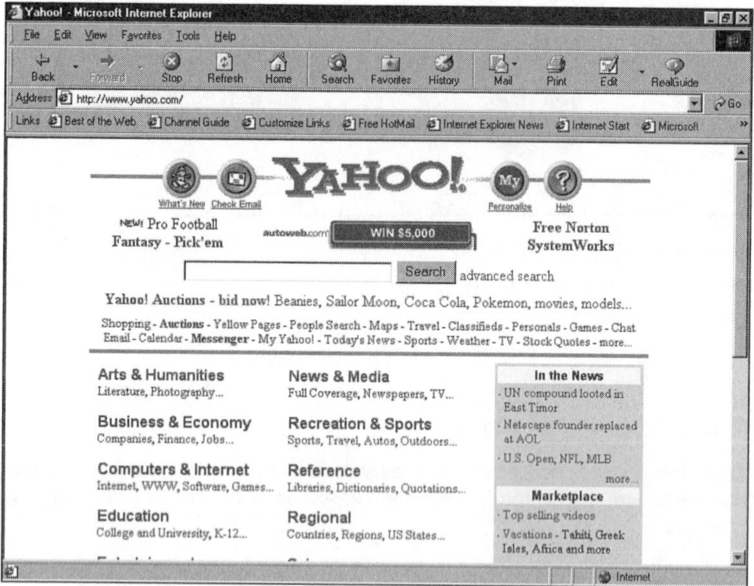

Figure 44.1
Yahoo! has broad appeal and an easy-to-use interface.

How to Get Listed

There are three ways you can get your site listed with a search engine or directory:

- Wait for search engines to find their way to your site.
- Submit your site to the search engines and directories with which you want to be listed.
- Use a listing service, usually for a fee.

Although your first choice is by far the easiest, it is also extremely ineffective. It's like an aspiring actress sitting in a Hollywood restaurant waiting to be discovered. It could happen, but it might take a long, long time, or it might never happen at all.

Submitting your site to be included in a search engine or directory database is remarkably easy. You simply go to the engine you are interested in and look for the "Submit URL" or "Add URL" button or link.

After filling in a few lines of information on a form, your site is submitted, and all that's left to do is wait for your site to appear in the listing.

If you find this process time-consuming, you can subscribe to the services offered at listing services such as `http://www.submit-it.com/` or `http://www.register-it.netscape.com/`.

These services claim to submit your site to many search engines and directories, often charging different amounts for the type or number of search engines to which they submit your site.

Listing services tend to focus on the number of sites to which they will submit your site. "Submit your site to 100 search engines for $29.95!!!" They don't focus on the quality of the search engines. Your money won't be very well spent if your site doesn't get submitted to Yahoo!, Excite, or AltaVista.

Listing services also don't tailor each submission to specific search engine's requirements, perhaps leaving out pertinent information or sending too many pages in a single submission.

Caution

> These services do have their place, but investigate them carefully and know exactly what you are getting for your money.

In most cases, you will be better off submitting your site to a handful of the most popular search engines, and you can certainly do that by yourself.

PREPARING YOUR SITE FOR SUBMISSION

Before submitting your site, make sure it is complete. With some engines taking weeks to list sites after submission, it is tempting to submit your site before it is finished. This may work in some cases, but many engines verify that your site is valid on the day of submission, and if they don't find your index or home page, your submission could be deleted.

Most engines only require that you submit your home page, because they will seek out links on that page and go down two or three levels to find other pages to include in their database. It doesn't hurt to submit a few of your most important pages in addition to your home page. It is not advisable to submit every single page within your site, however. Many engines are taking a stand against people they feel are abusing their service. Some monitor the number of pages a person submits and often limit the number of pages you can submit in one day.

Although submitting your site is easy, it is not enough to make search engines an effective marketing tool. Unless your site is returned within the first 2 or 3 pages of listings, it may never be seen. The challenge when submitting your site is to improve your ranking.

USING META TAGS TO IMPROVE YOUR RANKING

Engines use two methods to rank Web pages: the text of the page and META tags. META tags are specific HTML codes that briefly describe the page and give keywords for the search engine to use.

→ Be sure you're prepared! Read more about META tags in "Preparing Your Site for Publication," **p. 882**

Investing some time in the use and placement of keywords within the text of your document and in your META tags can improve your chances of a high ranking.

Consider your keywords carefully, try to imagine the experience the user has when trying to find your product or service. For example, a user will undoubtedly come up with thousands of results if he or she enters "restaurants". But if a user was looking for a restaurant in Las Vegas, he or she would instinctively type "Las Vegas restaurants".

As a Las Vegas restaurateur, you would be wise to include "Las Vegas restaurants" in your keywords and leave out the vague "restaurants." It is also wise to include common misspellings in your keywords and international spellings of words like color (colour).

Include keywords within the text of your pages, and be aware of their placement. Prominent keywords are weighted higher than words or phrases that occur near the bottom of the page, and some engines only read the first 200 words of a Web pages.

Many search engines take the number of keywords being searched and divide it by the number of words within a document. A short document with frequently repeating phrases or keywords can increase its relevancy and, in turn, its rank. However, what is good for the rank of your page isn't always good for the design and layout of your page.

A common way to circumvent this is to create doorway pages that draw a user into your site through the search engine and then point the user to your home page. If you sold subscriptions to political magazines, you could have doorway pages for each of your magazine titles, and they could have keywords tailored specifically for them.

When users look up "Republicans Unite," they will find your doorway page with a short paragraph and a link saying, "Click Here for more information on Republicans Unite." Because you have only a short paragraph, the keywords and phrases only need to be mentioned a few times to be given more significance.

Because these secondary pages will only be used as an entrance for search engines, there is no need to link to them from your home page, so you won't affect the design of your site and users won't find them accidentally.

Keep keywords in mind when naming your HTML documents and titling your pages. If a user is searching for information on Roses, **`http://www.yourpage.com/roses.html`** will get a higher rank than **`http://www.yourpage.com/redros1.html`**. Giving your pages an appropriate title not only makes good design sense, but the title is also used by search engines and can increase the rank of your page if it includes the keywords.

Finding the right combination of keywords is not a science. It is impossible to predict exactly what someone will type into a search engine when looking for information on your product or service. You can do some research into the habits of searches by doing a few simple things. Ask your friends and colleagues what they would type in while searching for your product or service. You could even sit them down at a computer and write down the words and phrases they use when they are actively searching.

Another helpful device is Metaspy. This page (see Figure 44.2) shows you exactly what keywords and phrases people are using when using the MetaCrawler search engine. The page automatically refreshes every 15 seconds and gives you a new perspective on how people search.

Note

Metaspy is located at **`http://www.metaspy.com/`**.

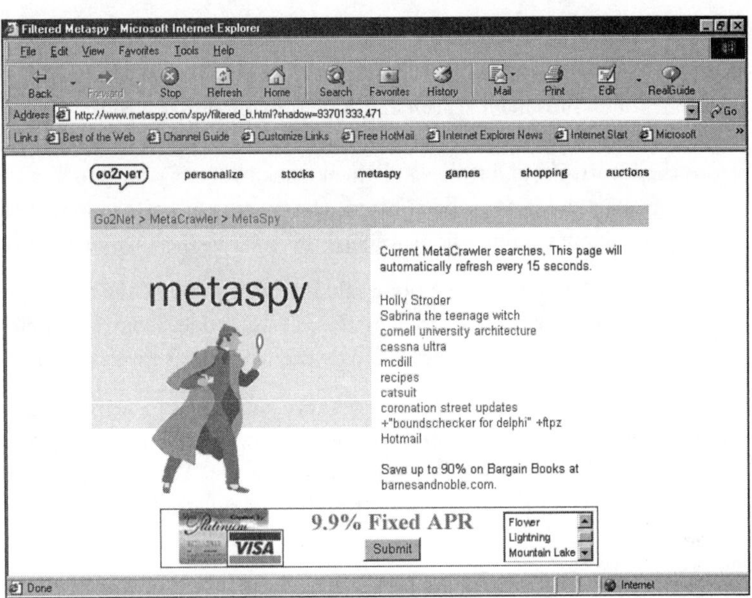

Figure 44.2
Metaspy lets you take a look at how people type in search terms.

AVOIDING KEYWORD SPAM

As important as the preceding steps are to achieving a high ranking, there are some equally important things that you shouldn't do when preparing your pages for submission.

Avoid excessive repetition of keywords. Unscrupulous personalities have sometimes intentionally overused keywords to gain the attention of sites. This is a form of spamming and should be avoided at all costs! If you repeat a keyword more than six or seven times, a red flag goes up at many search engines, and your page could be disqualified from the listing. It is also not a good idea to include popular keywords that don't have any relevance to your site.

Caution

Many search engines have become extremely strict about how you list your pages. Overuse of keywords, inappropriate keywords for your site, and multiple attempts to submit the page are not only frowned on; they may render you disqualified from listing.

"Sex" and "freeware" are popular keywords. But if you have a Home Renovations site, attracting people with those keywords isn't a good idea. After they see that the content of your page is not what they are looking for, they probably won't stay long enough to see your graphics download.

You should also be wary of using trademarked names in your keywords. Playboy successfully sued the owner of an adult entertainment site that used the Playboy name in its `META` tags to attract users to his site. Although the Internet has always had an aura of freedom, big business is catching up and cracking down on trademark infringement.

SUBMISSION FOLLOW-UP

After you have submitted your pages to the search engines you have selected, you have to plan your follow-up. Each search engine has its own turn-around time. Some take only a few hours to list your page, although others can take up to six weeks. It is important to record these turn-around times and check back to see if your site was accepted and, if so, its ranking. If your site has not been listed, you must resubmit it. Some search engines require that you email any resubmissions; record this next to the turn-around time.

If your site was listed but had a poor ranking, visit some of the sites that made the highest ranking and use your browser to view the HTML code. Compare their code to the code from your page and try to determine why their page was given a higher ranking.

Hundreds, if not thousands, of new pages are submitted to search engines daily. Even if you get a high ranking, you could get moved down in the relevancy by new pages that are submitted. This is why follow-up is so important. You should monitor your rank on a regular basis, evaluating and resubmitting if your rank falls.

BANNER ADVERTISING

Banner ads are the most common form of advertising on the Internet to date. It is rare to find a site that doesn't include some form of banner ad somewhere within its pages. They offer a unique approach to advertising not found in print or offline marketing. How often in offline advertising can the reader be at your store within seconds of viewing the ad? With banner advertising, potential customers are virtually one mouse click from your product.

This type of advertising also offers concrete results that you can analyze to better refine your advertising strategy.

To better understand this popular form of online advertising, it is important to be familiar with some industry buzzwords.

- **Banner ad**—This is a graphical advertisement, usually a GIF image and often animated. Standard industry size is 468×60 pixels, with weight between 5–10KB.
- **Click-through**—The number of people who click a banner ad and get to the advertiser's Web site.
- **Page impressions or page views**—These terms refer to the number of visitors who view a page.
- **CPM/Cost-Per-Thousand**—When paying for advertising through CPM, you are paying for how many times your ad is displayed each month. This is the most common type of payment structure, and many larger sites require that you purchase a minimum amount of impressions.
- **Flat fee**—This is where a site owner charges you a flat fee per month for advertising on their site. This price structure is rare and is usually found on smaller sites.

Banner Advertising Costs

Banner advertising can cost anywhere from free to thousands of dollars by using a banner exchange. There are a variety of price structures when dealing with paid advertising. The two most common include:

- Impressions—this is how many times the banner ad is actually seen onscreen.

  For example, Yahoo!, the most popular search engine, has a 500,000 impressions minimum. This is a very high number of impressions per ad, making the impression rate structure very expensive.

  In terms of click-through rates, some sites charge you for how many people click your ad, not how many people see the ad. This payment structure is also quite rare. Click-through rates can range from a few cents to $1 per instance.
- Banner exchange—This is a good way to experiment with banner advertising without involving the large cost of paid advertising. The concept behind an exchange is simple, you allow other members of the exchange to post their banners on your site, and, in return, your banner gets posted on the sites of other members.

  The drawback is, of course, having a banner on your page that can pull a user away before he or she has seen your site. There are, however, many advantages to using a banner exchange. Some exchanges let you target specific sites; this is important in effective banner advertising. Some also offer a high ratio of exchange—you get two views for every one you display—and many will give you hundreds of "free" views for signing up.

  Many exchanges also give you extensive performance statistics, including page impressions and click-throughs. It might be a good idea to use a banner exchange to get a feel for their effectiveness before moving on to paid advertising. Most exchanges don't permit adult entertainment sites to become part of the exchange, but be sure to check into their policies carefully before signing up.

Note

Some popular Banner Exchange programs are

Link Exchange, which offers a 2:1 display ratio on 400×40 7KB ads at `http://www.linkexchange.com/`.

Link Buddies, which offers a 2:1 display ratio on 468×60 10KB ads at `http://www.linkbuddies.com/`.

Have you been advertising your site, but are unsure if the effort you are putting forth is having the desired result? See, "Measuring Success," in the Troubleshooting section at the end of this chapter.

Common Design Guidelines

The industry size standard for an ad banner is 468×60 pixels, with a maximum weight of 10KB (see Figure 44.3). The most effective banners include some sort of animation to attract the eye.

Bad Code. Very Bad Code.

Figure 44.3
Here's the first cell of an animated GIF used in a campaign to advertise Molly.Com training. The banner measures the official size of 468×60 pixels.

Some sites require that your banners be smaller, with sizes ranging from 234×60 pixels to 400×40 pixels. Anything smaller than that wouldn't be considered banner advertising.

If you intend to design your banner yourself, you've got to be part graphic designer and part psychologist. But it's not that difficult if you follow a few simple rules.

Animation is important—it is said to increase click-through ratio by 25%—but don't over-animate. Simple, concise animation that doesn't distract from your message is best. It should catch the eye and then allow the user to read the ad.

Include the words "Click Here." As rudimentary as this may seem, new users won't realize that they are reading a hyper-linked ad and won't know how to get to the site that is being advertised. Including the words Click Here tells the user how to find your site and is said to increase the click-through ratio by 15%.

Be clear in what you are advertising. Don't try to trick people into coming to your site. You may get lots of click-throughs, but if the user feels tricked, he or she is less likely to buy your products or services. However, if you offer something free to customers on your Web site, a banner ad is the perfect place to advertise that.

→ For a step-by-step design example of an ad banner, **see** "Imagemaps, Animation, and Special Graphic Techniques," **p. 659**

You can use any graphics program to design your banner, just be sure that the output is of the quality you desire. This 468×60 banner will be representing your entire site, so it has to be of extremely high quality. There are also many GIF animation programs you can use to animate your banner. If you feel this is too daunting a task, there are many professional banner designers on the Web that will do it for you for a fee.

BANNER PLACEMENT

The placement of your banner is of utmost importance if you want effective marketing. Putting a banner for your Home Renovations site on a Teddy Bear Collectors Web site will not be effective in drawing the customers you want. Put that same ad on a Lumber Store Web site and you will increase the effectiveness of your advertising by targeting the people who are most likely to want or need your service.

The most popular spot for banner advertising is on the top 10 search engines. Yahoo! alone reported $540,000,000 in banner ad revenues last year. One of the most effective forms of advertising within the search engines is purchasing a word or phrase. Using the Home Renovations site example, you could purchase the phrases "Home Repair" and "Home Renovation."

When a user types those phrases into the search engine, your banner ad will appear at the top of the page of results returned. This type of targeting is not inexpensive however, it can cost upwards of $10,000!

It is also important to note the placement of your ad within the page itself. Top-of-the-page placement is most popular, but most users will scroll past the top of the page before they are ready to leave a site. Banners placed 1/3 of the way down the page have a 77% higher click-through rate than ads placed at the top.

Does Banner Advertising Really Work?

Banner ads are an industry standard, you see them everywhere. But how often do you click one? As it stands today, they are effective, but as Web users become more accustomed to them, they will begin to tune them out.

The industry average click-through rate is 2–2.5%, which certainly isn't spectacular. To get any effectiveness out of banner advertising, you must have a great ad that is specifically targeted to your audience. Without that, you are be better off not using banner ads at all.

Other Online Marketing Techniques

A number of other online marketing techniques will help you boost traffic to your site. They include email, newsgroups, and offline marketing.

Email Marketing

Email is the number one reason people connect to the Internet. An email address is becoming almost as important as a phone number as a method of communication. As its popularity grows, so does the opportunity to use it as a marketing tool.

One of the most common ways email is used as a marketing tool is by bulk emailing. This is similar to sending out flyers in "snail mail" (regular post-mail). This is an extremely ineffective marketing strategy. The online community has a name for such unsolicited email: Spam.

Spamming has such a negative reputation on the Internet that there are Web sites devoted to getting rid of it, such as Netizens Against Gratuitous Spamming (NAGS) (`http://www.nags.org/`). Email users take great offense to receiving unsolicited advertising email, much more so than to receiving flyers with their local newspaper. If you were to send out bulk email, the response would be overwhelmingly negative and would not portray your business as trustworthy.

This shouldn't dissuade you from using email as a marketing tool; there are some excellent and appropriate ways you can use this medium.

Encourage users of your Web site to sign up to receive product or services announcements. You can do this by including the option on a form or guestbook section of your site. You then have the permission of the recipient, and your advertisement would not be considered unsolicited Spam. Always include an easy way for people to unsubscribe to your notices.

Similarly, you can write a newsletter relating to the content on your site that can be sent to people who sign up on your Web site. If you had a site devoted to underground poetry, you could send a weekly newsletter giving some insight into the poets featured on your site in the upcoming week—include a sample of the poetry and then point them to your site for more.

This encourages people who have already visited your site to come back again and again. As with your product or services announcements, it is important to give the subscribers to your newsletter a clear and easy way to unsubscribe.

Another easy way to garner more exposure for your site through email is widely underused, and that is including a "Signature file" with all your email correspondence. For example:

> Joe Smith
>
> `http://www.homerepair.com/`
>
> Quality Home Repair, Free Consultations!

Most email programs let you automate a signature that is placed at the bottom of every email you send out. If your email program doesn't have this feature, you should get in the habit of typing your URL and slogan (if you have one) at the bottom of every email.

NEWSGROUPS

Newsgroups are popular discussion groups. Similar to a Bulletin Board concept, users post messages that other users read and can then post responses or messages of their own. They are different from chat groups because the messages do not have to be read and responded to immediately. One user can post a message at 8 p.m. one day, and another user can read it hours, or even days, later.

There are thousands of newsgroups on every imaginable topic, and they easily make up the largest discussion group in the world.

Newsgroup users develop strong community ties with the other users of the group and are frequently more experienced Web users.

If you intend to use a particular newsgroup for marketing purposes, it is extremely important for you to become an active user of that newsgroup. If you just post an advertisement out of the blue, it will be written off as Spam, and you'll get a negative response.

Using the Underground Poetry Web site example, you could subscribe to the **`alt.arts.poetry.comments`** newsgroup and start contributing. It's always a good idea to observe a newsgroup for a few days before jumping in with a post.

Different newsgroups have widely different unspoken rules that the users follow. It's just a case of understanding the feel of the group and respecting their community. After you start posting thoughtful or helpful messages, you will become part of the community. Then if you post a message informing the other users that you are having a special chat with a poet, it won't be viewed as Spam. It's also a good idea to include your email Signature file on your newsgroup posts because it can provide a quick and easy link to your site for other newsgroup members.

LINKS

The beauty of the World Wide Web is its interconnectivity; you can start out on a home page about the *X-Files*, and a few hyperlinks later you are reading about antique grandfather clocks. The whole concept of the Web is these connections that take you to different places within a Web site and out onto the Web itself.

➔ For more information on linking, **see** "Linking Pages," **p. 174**

Getting links to your site on other Web sites is an excellent way to get exposure. Just think about how many times you've discovered a new and wonderful site through a link on a site you've visited.

Do some searching and find sites that you feel would appeal to your audience and contact the owners of those sites to ask for a link. Some site managers might ask for a fee, but many will do it simply for a reciprocal link. Negotiating links on other Web sites is a fantastic way to broaden your audience and your exposure.

AWARDS

Web site "awards" proliferate on the Internet; there are literally thousands of awards that are handed out every week (see Figure 44.4). There are Cool Site awards, Wacky Site of The Week awards, and Rodney Dangerfield even has his Respect award. Some Web site owners display the awards they have been given as a badge of honor.

Figure 44.4
A collection of Web awards can be as impressive to your site visitors as an actress with an Emmy is to a television viewer.

Most awards require that a Web site owner submit his or her site for review and, if deemed worthy, it gets the award. To display the award, the Web site owner must link the award back to the award-giving site. You give the award-giving site a free link by displaying any awards you receive.

Developing an award of your own can be a good way to increase exposure to your Web site. If you had a site that sold specialty cigars, you could develop the Humidor Award and hand it out to the people who devote their home pages to cigar appreciation. This would put a link to your Web site on the sites of your target audience.

Be careful to set a relatively high standard for the sites you award; your award loses its respectability if it's on every site a user visits.

WEB RINGS

Similar to awards, a Web ring (see Figure 44.5) is a grouping of sites that provide links to one another. Each member of the Web ring includes a graphic somewhere on their site stating their membership in the ring and providing a link to the next site in the ring.

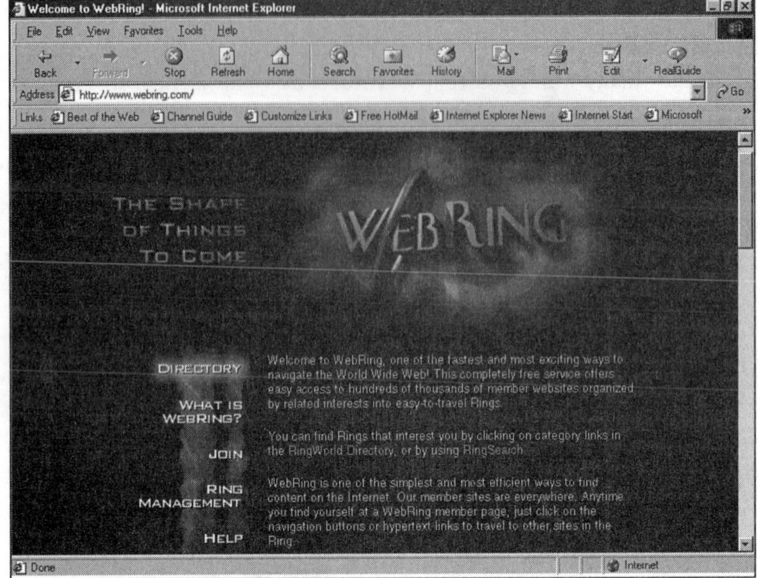

Figure 44.5
Web rings can be helpful in bringing awareness to your site too. Visit the Web Ring site to help get you started.

Caution

Web rings can be effective in drawing new users to your site, but they could also pull members away from your site to the next site in the ring.

WebRing at **`http://www.Webring.org/`** has listings of the thousands of operating Web rings. If there isn't one that appeals to you or is appropriate for your site, they also have instructions for managing your own ring.

Careful! You don't want to join numerous rings because the resulting number of graphics and notices can look cluttered and unprofessional. It is also wise to carefully investigate the policies of the Web ring you are joining and the other member sites; you don't want to unknowingly provide a link to an inappropriate Web site.

OFFLINE MARKETING STRATEGIES

Marketing your site does not end with your online strategies. You must also market your site offline to attract new and regular users.

Watch a television ad for any upcoming movie, and you will notice the Web address for the movie's Web site at the bottom of the screen. Although these sites are basically an addition to the ad campaign surrounding the movie, the same concept can be used for advertising a site that has more business content.

Even talk show staples Sally Jessy Raphael and Oprah have jumped onto the Web-site bandwagon. Sally never ends a show without announcing: "Join me on my Web site at `Sallyjr.com`." Oprah has quite the Web site, too (Figure 44.6). Sitcoms and dramas have joined the online party as well.

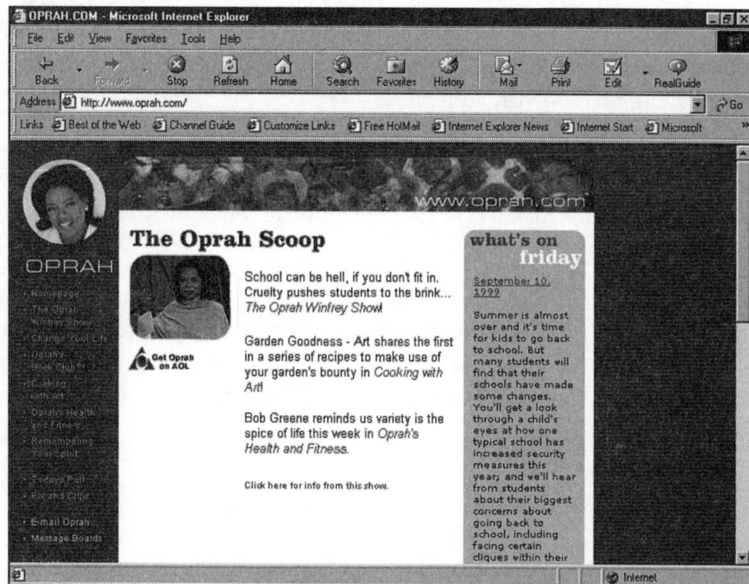

Figure 44.6
Oprah's Web site is easy to find: `http://www.oprah.com/`.

It won't be long before every aspect of the entertainment and business world has a corresponding Web site.

When launching Melanie Doane's album *Adam's Rib*, Sony Canada made online music history by focusing its full marketing campaign on a Web site. The only print ads in the campaign were full-color pictures of Melanie with her Web site URL written underneath; no other text appeared in the ads.

It was the first time that the Web site address was the focus of the ad and not simply an addendum.

Although Sony realized the power of the Internet as an advertising venue, they knew they would have to initially draw people to the Web site. By using the provocative ads focusing on the Web address and not simply adding it to the bottom of a traditional ad, they drew press attention they might not have received otherwise.

Although you might not have the resources to launch a national print ad campaign, there are many things you can include in your offline marketing strategy to increase exposure to your Web site.

If you intend to do a lot of radio, print, and television marketing, it's a good idea to register a domain name. This in itself is a form of marketing; it becomes your brand. Without a registered domain name, your URL can become long and clunky.

If WebGuys hosted your Antique Teddy Bears Web site, your URL could end up something like **`http://www.WebGuys.com/~abc/teddybear.html`**. That certainly becomes harder to advertise and less recognizable than if you had registered the domain name "teddybears.com."

If your Web site is a new addition to your business, announce it to all your current customers. Print up a special announcement and send it out to customers on your mailing list, encouraging them to visit your site.

Let them know if you provide any services on the site that you don't provide offline, such as special online contests, newsletters, or a catalog of products that are only available to online customers. Have your URL printed on all your company literature and letterhead and add it to all your employees' business cards.

Include your URL in all your print advertisements. Encourage people to visit your Web site for more information on your products and services. If you have an intuitive URL, consider placing ads just using the URL. This type of campaign would work for **`http://www.HomeRepair.com/`** but would not be effective for **`http://www.townhall.com/~repair.html`**.

→ For more information to help you with domain registration techniques, **see** "Preparing Your Site for Publication," **p. 878**

This same strategy applies to any radio or television ads you use in your advertising campaign—always mention your URL and even integrate your Web site activities into those of your business and current marketing strategies.

Tip from molly

At this stage in the awareness of the Internet, it is not necessary to state your full URL in radio or television ads. It becomes long and laborious to hear someone spell out h-t-t-p-colon-backslash-backslash-w-w-w-dot-teddybears-dot-com. You can simply say, "Visit us at teddybears-dot-com."

If your company regularly participates in trade shows, this is a terrific opportunity to promote your Web site. Bring along a laptop computer, have your Web site up and running in the browser, and encourage people to see what you've got. This is often an effective way to get right to your audience, showing them what you've got, and how it will benefit them.

TROUBLESHOOTING

SELLING BANNER ADVERTISING

I have been marketing my site for several months and would like to try to generate revenue by selling advertising space. Where's the best place to start?

There are several ways to sell advertising on your site. You can prepare a rate card for your site and hope that people will come to you wanting to advertise. This plan only works if your site attracts those with the interest and money to advertise.

If your site is popular, particularly within a specific demographic, you can sign up as an affiliate with an online advertising brokerage. They will help you set a reasonable CPM rate and will sell your available ad space on your behalf. One such service is Flycast Network, which can be found at **`http://www.flycast.com/`**. Advertising brokerages charge you a percentage of your advertising revenue.

Unless you have designed the next Yahoo!, chances are that you won't be able to retire on the income generated by your advertising space. In many cases, however, you can make enough money to pay for your server space and the latest upgrade to Adobe Photoshop.

Another benefit to selling ad space is getting listed as an affiliate on the ad brokerage sites. Although this will not bring in aimless Web surfers, it will make other businesses aware of your site. If you are developing content that is of interest to a more popular site, this can lead to them linking to your site or even licensing some of your content.

MEASURING SUCCESS

How do I know if my search engine rankings, newsletters, banner advertising, and newsgroup posts are successfully bringing people to my site?

Tracking site usage statistics can be as simple as putting a hit counter on your default page. There are literally hundreds of simple hit counters available on the Internet.

One of the easiest counters to install is FastCounter from Link Exchange, the banner exchange people. You can find FastCounter at **`http://www.fastcounter.com/index.html`**. You can even develop your own hit counter using the instructions at **`http://members.aol.com/htmlguru/access_counts.html`**.

There's a lot more to Web statistics than simply counting page hits, however. If you really want to analyze the usage on your site, you'll want to add a log analysis program to your site. The best-known log analysis tool is NetTracker, available at **`http://www.sane.com/products/NetTracker/`**. NetTracker and Sawmill, another Web statistical tool (found at **`http://www.flowerfire.com/sawmill4/`**) will not only tell you how many people have hit your site, but where they came from, which pages they looked at, how many pages they visited in each session, and where they went when they left your site. This kind of detail costs money, about $200–500, but for a professional site, it might be worth it.

DESIGNING FOR THE REAL WORLD

PARENTSPLACE.COM—FROM COTTAGE TO KINGDOM

The successful parenting site, ParentsPlace.com (**`http://www.parentsplace.com`**), all started four years ago with the birth of a baby. When David and Jackie expanded their family by one, they decided to make it a priority for both of them to stay home and raise their son, Noah. At the same time, they also found that babies didn't come with instruction books.

ParentsPlace.com was created with the intent of combining Jackie and David's need for an income with most parents' needs for information. The information part was easy—put any group of parents together in a (chat) room, and they're going to discuss their kids and how their approaches vary. But to meet their income objectives, Jackie and David needed their site to stand out from the rest.

What followed was a carefully planned marketing strategy. A vast schedule of daily chats and hundreds of message board topics formed the cornerstone of the community. E-commerce provided members with one-stop-shopping for their parenting needs, as well as providing income for Jackie and David.

Not content with just providing a sounding board for parents, ParentsPlace.com sought out advice and information from experts in the areas of obstetrics, pediatrics, and child development. Each day brought new features, thereby bringing loyal visitors back to the site again and again. Jackie and David then marketed this gathering of expertise to both the online and offline press. As a result, ParentsPlace.com was rated as an outstanding resource by the American Academy of Pediatrics, *Sesame Street Magazine*, and leading consumer report magazines. The site also received coverage in the *Wall Street Journal*, *Good Housekeeping*, and *The New York Times*.

It is no wonder that such success soon caught the eye of one of the new mega-sites for women, iVillage, Inc. (**`http://www.ivillage.com`**). ParentsPlace.com merged with iVillage in 1996, giving the site more advertising and promotional resources, as well as a steady income for Jackie and David, while still retaining its family feel.

PART X

APPENDIXES

APPENDIX 

HTML 4.0 Element and Tag Reference

In this Appendix

HTML 4.0 VERSIONS AND SPECIFICATIONS

This appendix is based primarily on the information provided in the *HTML 4.0 Specification W3C Recommendation*, revised on April 24, 1998. The latest version of this document can be found at **http://www.w3.org/TR/REC-html40/**.

> **Note**
>
> There are in fact three versions of HTML 4: Strict (pure HTML 4), Transitional (elements within the Strict Document Type Definition (DTD) plus additional elements held over from HTML 3.2; also called Loose), and Frameset (Transitional plus Frameset). Each one relies upon a document type definition to specify which elements and attributes are to be used.

The majority of this reference is devoted to a detailed alphabetical HTML 4.0 element reference. Following this, the common attributes, intrinsic events, and data types are summarized.

> **Note**
>
> Several elements and attributes have been *deprecated*, which means they have been outdated by the current HTML version, and you should avoid using them. The same or similar functionality is provided using new or different methods.

ALPHABETICAL HTML 4.0 ELEMENT LISTING

All the elements in the HTML 4.0 Recommendation are listed alphabetically in this appendix, and the following information is presented:

- **Element**—The heading shows at a glance:

  The general notation of the element. For example, <TABLE>...</TABLE>.

  Whether start and end tags are

  Required—Tags are present, such as <UL>...</UL>.

  Optional—Tag is in *italics*, such as <P>...*</P>*.

  Not allowed—End tag not present, such as <IMG>.

  The HTML 4.0 DTD the element is associated with:

  Strict—Identified by an S icon.

  Transitional—Identified by a T icon.

  Frameset—Identified by an F icon.

  If the element is deprecated, it is identified by a D icon.
- **Usage**—A general description of the element.
- **Syntax**—The syntax of the element is given, showing where the attributes and content are placed. *Italicized* information (such as *attributes)* is not part of the element but indicates you should replace that with the values described further in the element reference.

- **Start/End Tag**—Indicates whether these tags are required, optional, or illegal.
- **Must be empty?**—Indicates whether the element must be empty.
- **Attributes**—Lists the attributes of the element, the actual values allowed or a value data type, and a short description of their effect. Some attributes have the actual values given, such as `shape="`**`rect`**` | circle | poly | default"`, with the default value in **bold**. Others have *italicized* data types, such as `charset="`*`character-set`*`"`. You should refer to the "Data Types" section at the end of this appendix for an explanation of the different data types allowed. Deprecated and Transitional DTD attributes are annotated with an icon. Strict DTD attributes have no icon and are present in the Transitional and Frameset DTDs. No attempt has been made in this reference to identify browser support for a given attribute.
- **Content**—Shows the possible content allowed inside an element, ranging from document data to a variety of other elements.
- **Formalized**—States the W3C HTML Recommendation in which the element gained official approval.
- **Browsers**—Shows if the element is supported in the top two current browsers (Microsoft Internet Explorer and Netscape Navigator) and the earliest version of the browser supporting the element.
- **Notes**—Relates any special considerations when using the element.

PART X

APP A

<! —... —> COMMENTS S

Usage:	An SGML construct used to insert information that is not to be displayed by the browser.
Syntax:	`<!-- content -->`
Must be empty?	No
Attributes:	None
Content:	User text
Formalized:	HTML 2.0
Notes:	Comments are not restricted to one line and can be any length. The comment close delimiter ("--") and the markup declaration close delimiter (">") are not required to be on the same line as the markup declaration open delimiter ("<!") and the comment open delimiter ("--"). Placing double hyphens inside a comment technically ends the comment and any text after this may not be treated as a comment.
Browser:	MSIE 1; NNav 1

<!DOCTYPE...> S

Usage: Version information appears on the first line of an HTML document in the form of a Standard Generalized Markup Language (SGML) declaration.

Syntax:

```
<!DOCTYPE  top-element availability
"registration//organization//type    label//language"
"URI">
```

Identifiers:

Top element—Top-level element type declared in the DTD. For HTML documents, this value is `HTML`.

Availability—Notes the availability. HTML documents are publicly accessible objects; therefore this value is `PUBLIC`.

Registration—Indicates whether (+) or not (-) the following organization is registered by the ISO. The W3C is not a registered ISO organization.

Organization—The organization responsible for the creation and maintenance of the DTD. The `W3C` is responsible for all official HTML DTDs.

Type—The type of object being referenced. In the case of HTML, this is the HTML `DTD`.

Label—Describes or names the item being referenced. For HTML 4.0 this refers to the HTML DTD (Strict, Transitional, or Frameset) being called upon, `HTML 4.0`, `HTML 4.0 Transitional`, or `HTML 4.0 Frameset` respectively.

Language—The language of the object. For HTML, this is `EN`, meaning English.

URI—Provides the location of the DTD and any entity sets for user agents to download. HTML 4.0 supports the following URIs:

```
"http://www.w3.org/TR/REC-html40/strict.dtd"
"http://www.w3.org/TR/REC-html40/loose.dtd"
"http://www.w3.org/TR/REC-html40/frameset.dtd"
"http://www.w3.org/TR/REC-html40/HTMLlat1.ent"
"http://www.w3.org/TR/REC-html40/HTMLsymbol.ent"
"http://www.w3.org/TR/REC-html40/HTMLspecial.ent"
```

Formalized: HTML 2.0

Notes: Mandatory for document to be valid.

Browser: None appear to process this information.

<A>...</A> S

Usage: Defines anchors that may be the source of one link and/or the destination of multiple links.

Syntax: `<A attributes>content</A>`

Start/End Tag: Required/Required

Must be empty? No

Attributes:

`core`—See "Common Attributes" section.

`i18n`—See "Common Attributes" section.

`events`—See "Intrinsic Events" section.

`charset="character-set"`—Specifies the character encoding of the linked resource. Values (such as `ISO-8859-1` or `US-ASCII`) must be strings approved and registered by IANA, The Internet Assigned Numbers Authority.

`type="content-type"`—Specifies the content or media (MIME) type (such as `text/html`) of the linked resource.

`name="data"`—Names the current anchor so that it can be the destination of other links.

`href="URI"`—Specifies the location of the linked resource or anchor. Anchor URIs are identified by a pound sign # before the `name` value.

`hreflang="language-code"`—Identifies the language of the linked resource. This attribute may only be used in conjunction with the `href` attribute.

T `target="user-defined ¦ _blank ¦ _self ¦ _parent ¦ _top"`—Identifies the frame in which the linked resource will be opened:

`user-defined`—Document opens in the frame designated by the `user-defined` name that is set by the `name` attribute of the frame. The `name` must begin with an alphabetic character.

`_blank`—Document opens in a new, unnamed window.

`_self`—Document opens in same frame as the originating link.

`_parent`—Document opens in the immediate `FRAMESET` parent of the current frame, or itself if the current frame has no parent.

`_top`—Document opens in the full, original window, or itself if the frame has no parent.

`rel="link-type"`—Defines the relationship between the document and that specified by the `href` attribute.

`rev="`*`link-type`*`"`—Defines the relationship between the resource specified by the `href` attribute and the current document.

`accesskey="`*`character`*`"`—Assigns an access key (or shortcut key) to the element. When the key is pressed, the element receives focus and is activated.

`shape="`**`rect`**` ¦ circle ¦ poly ¦ default"`—Defines a region by its shape:

`rect`—Defines a rectangular region.

`circle`—Defines a circular region.

`poly`—Defines a polygonal region.

`default`—Specifies the entire region.

`coords="`*`coordinates`*`"`—Defines the position of a shape displayed on screen. All values are of the length data type and separated by commas. The number and order of the coordinates depends on the value of the `shape` attribute:

`rect`—left-x, top-y, right-x, bottom-y

`circle`—center-x, center-y, radius

`poly`—x1, y1, x2, y2, …, xn, yn

`tabindex="`*`number`*`"`—Defines the tabbing order between elements. This is the order (from lowest first to highest last) in which they receive focus when the user navigates through them using the Tab key.

`onfocus="`*`script`*`"`—Triggered when the element receives focus by either a pointing device (such as a mouse) or tabbed navigation.

`onblur="`*`script`*`"`—Triggered when the element loses focus by either a pointing device (such as a mouse) or tabbed navigation.

Content: Zero or more inline elements, to include the following:

Document text and entities

Fontstyle elements (`TT ¦ I ¦ B ¦ U ¦ S ¦ STRIKE ¦ BIG ¦ SMALL`)

Phrase elements (`EM ¦ STRONG ¦ DFN ¦ CODE ¦ SAMP ¦ KBD ¦ VAR ¦ CITE ¦ ABBR ¦ ACRONYM`)

Special elements (`IMG ¦ APPLET ¦ OBJECT ¦ FONT ¦ BASEFONT ¦ BR ¦ SCRIPT ¦ MAP ¦ Q ¦ SUB ¦ SUP ¦ SPAN ¦ BDO ¦ IFRAME`)

Form Control elements (`INPUT ¦ SELECT ¦ TEXTAREA ¦ LABEL ¦ BUTTON`)

Formalized: HTML 2.0

Notes: Cannot be nested. Anchor names must be unique.

Browser: MSIE 1; NNav 1

<ABBR>...</ABBR> S

Usage: Indicates an abbreviated form.

Syntax: `<ABBR attributes>content</ABBR>`

Start/End Tag: Required/Required

Must be empty? No

Attributes: `core`—See "Common Attributes" section.

`i18n`—See "Common Attributes" section.

`events`—See "Intrinsic Events" section.

Content: Zero or more inline elements, to include the following:

Document text and entities

Fontstyle elements (TT ¦ I ¦ B ¦ U ¦ S ¦ STRIKE ¦ BIG ¦ SMALL)

Phrase elements (EM ¦ STRONG ¦ DFN ¦ CODE ¦ SAMP ¦ KBD ¦ VAR ¦ CITE ¦ ABBR ¦ ACRONYM)

Special elements (A ¦ IMG ¦ APPLET ¦ OBJECT ¦ FONT ¦ BASEFONT ¦ BR ¦ SCRIPT ¦ MAP ¦ Q ¦ SUB ¦ SUP ¦ SPAN ¦ BDO ¦ IFRAME)

Form Control elements (INPUT ¦ SELECT ¦ TEXTAREA ¦ LABEL ¦ BUTTON)

Formalized: HTML 4.0

Notes: The content of the element contains the abbreviated form, which is expanded by using the `title` attribute.

Browser: None at this time.

<ACRONYM>...</ACRONYM> S

Usage: Indicates an acronym.

Syntax: `<ACRONYM attributes>content</ACRONYM>`

Start/End Tag: Required/Required

Must be empty? No

Attributes: core—See "Common Attributes" section.

`i18n`—See "Common Attributes" section.

`events`—See "Intrinsic Events" section.

Content: Zero or more inline elements, to include the following:

Document text and entities

Fontstyle elements (TT ¦ I ¦ B ¦ U ¦ S ¦ STRIKE ¦ BIG ¦ SMALL)

Phrase elements (EM ¦ STRONG ¦ DFN ¦ CODE ¦ SAMP ¦ KBD ¦ VAR ¦ CITE ¦ ABBR ¦ ACRONYM)

Special elements (A ¦ IMG ¦ APPLET ¦ OBJECT ¦ FONT ¦ BASEFONT ¦ BR ¦ SCRIPT ¦ MAP ¦ Q ¦ SUB ¦ SUP ¦ SPAN ¦ BDO ¦ IFRAME)

Form Control elements (INPUT ¦ SELECT ¦ TEXTAREA ¦ LABEL ¦ BUTTON)

Formalized: HTML 4.0

Notes: The content of the element contains the acronym, which is expanded by using the `title` attribute.

Browser: MSIE 5 will display TITLE in a tool tip.

<ADDRESS>...</ADDRESS>

Usage: Provides a special format for author or contact information.

Syntax: `<ADDRESS attributes>content</ADDRESS>`

Start/End Tag: Required/Required

Must be empty? No

Attributes: core—See "Common Attributes" section.

i18n—See "Common Attributes" section.

events—See "Intrinsic Events" section.

Content: Zero or more inline elements, to include the following:

Document text and entities

Fontstyle elements (TT ¦ I ¦ B ¦ U ¦ S ¦ STRIKE ¦ BIG ¦ SMALL)

Phrase elements (EM ¦ STRONG ¦ DFN ¦ CODE ¦ SAMP ¦ KBD ¦ VAR ¦ CITE ¦ ABBR ¦ ACRONYM)

Special elements (A ¦ IMG ¦ APPLET ¦ OBJECT ¦ FONT ¦ BASEFONT ¦ BR ¦ SCRIPT ¦ MAP ¦ Q ¦ SUB ¦ SUP ¦ SPAN ¦ BDO ¦ IFRAME)

Form Control elements (INPUT ¦ SELECT ¦ TEXTAREA ¦ LABEL ¦ BUTTON)

Formalized: HTML 2.0

Notes: The transitional DTD specifies that the P element may also be included in ADDRESS.

Browser: MSIE 1; NNav 1

<APPLET>...</APPLET>

Usage: Includes a Java applet.

Syntax: `<APPLET attributes>content</APPLET>`

Start/End Tag: Required/Required

Must be empty? No

Attributes: core—See "Common Attributes" section.

`codebase="URI"`—Sets the base URI for the applet. If not specified, the default value is the base URI of the current document.

`archive="URI-list"`—List URIs (separated by commas) for archives containing classes and other resources that will be preloaded. This can significantly speed up applet performance.

`code="data"`—Identifies the compiled `.class` file of the applet, to include the path if necessary.

`object="data"`—Names a resource containing a serialized representation of an applet's state.

`alt="text"`—Alternate text to be displayed if the user agent cannot render the element.

`name="data"`—Specifies a name for the applet's instance.

`width="length"`—Sets the initial width of the applet's display area.

`height="length"`—Sets the initial height of the applet's display area.

`align="top | middle |` **`bottom`** `| left | right"`—Aligns the object with respect to context.

`top`—Vertically align the top of the object with the top of the current text line.

`middle`—Vertically align the center of the object with the current baseline.

`bottom`—Vertically align the bottom of the object with the current baseline.

`left`—Float object to the left margin.

`right`—Float object to the right margin.

T D `hspace="pixels"`—Sets the amount of space to be inserted to the left and right of the element.

T D `vspace="pixels"`—Sets the amount of space to be inserted to the top and bottom of the element.

Content: One or more `PARAM` elements.

Zero or more block elements, to include the following:

`P | DL | DIV | CENTER | NOSCRIPT | NOFRAMES | BLOCKQUOTE | FORM | ISINDEX | HR | TABLE | FIELDSET | ADDRESS`

Heading elements (`H1 | H2 | H3 | H4 | H5 | H6`)

List elements (UL ¦ OL ¦ DIR ¦ MENU)

Preformatted elements (PRE)

Zero or more inline elements, to include the following:

Document text and entities

Fontstyle elements (TT ¦ I ¦ B ¦ U ¦ S ¦ STRIKE ¦ BIG ¦ SMALL)

Phrase elements (EM ¦ STRONG ¦ DFN ¦ CODE ¦ SAMP ¦ KBD ¦ VAR ¦ CITE ¦ ABBR ¦ ACRONYM)

Special elements (A ¦ IMG ¦ APPLET ¦ OBJECT ¦ FONT ¦ BASEFONT ¦ BR ¦ SCRIPT ¦ MAP ¦ Q ¦ SUB ¦ SUP ¦ SPAN ¦ BDO ¦ IFRAME)

Form Control elements (INPUT ¦ SELECT ¦ TEXTAREA ¦ LABEL ¦ BUTTON)

Formalized: HTML 3.2

Notes: Either code or codebase attributes must be identified. If both are used, the class files must match.

The content of the element is normally given to provide alternate content for user agents not configured to support Java Applets.

The PARAM element (which resides in the APPLET element content) should come before any other content.

Deprecated in favor of the OBJECT element.

Browser: MSIE 3; NNav 2

<AREA> S

Usage: Specifies the geometric regions of a client-side imagemap and the associated link.

Syntax: <AREA *attributes*>

Start/End Tag: Required/Forbidden

Must be empty? Yes

Attributes: core—See "Common Attributes" section.

i18n—See "Common Attributes" section.

events—See "Intrinsic Events" section.

shape="**rect** ¦ circle ¦ poly ¦ default"—Defines a region by its shape:

rect—Defines a rectangular region.

circle—Defines a circular region.

poly—Defines a polygonal region.

default—Specifies the entire region.

`coords="coordinates"`—Defines the position of a shape displayed onscreen. All values are of the length data type and separated by commas. The number and order of the coordinates depends on the value of the `shape` attribute:

`rect`—left-x, top-y, right-x, bottom-y

`circle`—center-x, center-y, radius

`poly`—x1, y1, x2, y2, ..., xn, yn

`href="URI"`—Specifies the location of the linked resource or anchor.

T `target="user-defined | _blank | _self | _parent | _top"`—Identifies the frame in which the linked resource will be opened:

user-defined—Document opens in the frame designated by the *user-defined* name, which is set by the `name` attribute of the frame. The `name` must begin with an alphabetic character.

`_blank`—Document opens in a new, unnamed window.

`_self`—Document opens in same frame as the originating link.

`_parent`—Document opens in the immediate `FRAMESET` parent of the current frame, or itself if the current frame has no parent.

`_top`—Document opens in the full, original window, or itself if the frame has no parent.

`nohref`—Specifies that the region has no associated link.

`alt="text"`—Alternate text to be displayed if the user agent cannot render the element.

`tabindex="number"`—Defines the tabbing order between elements. This is the order (from lowest first to highest last) in which they receive focus when the user navigates through them using the Tab key.

`accesskey="character"`—Assigns an access key (or shortcut key) to the element. When the key is pressed, the element receives focus and is activated.

`onfocus="script"`—Triggered when the element receives focus either by pointing device (such as a mouse) or by tabbed navigation.

`onblur="script"`—Triggered when the element loses focus either by pointing device (such as a mouse) or by tabbed navigation.

Content: Empty

Formalized: HTML 3.2

Notes: Because the AREA element has no content to be displayed, an imagemap consisting of one or more AREAs should have alternate text for each AREA.

Browser: MSIE 1; NNav 2

<B>...</B> S

Usage: Displays text with a boldface font style.

Syntax: `<B attributes>content</B>`

Start/End Tag: Required/Required

Must be empty? No

Attributes: core—See "Common Attributes" section.

i18n—See "Common Attributes" section.

events—See "Intrinsic Events" section.

Content: Zero or more inline elements, to include the following:

Document text and entities

Fontstyle elements (TT ¦ I ¦ B ¦ U ¦ S ¦ STRIKE ¦ BIG ¦ SMALL)

Phrase elements (EM ¦ STRONG ¦ DFN ¦ CODE ¦ SAMP ¦ KBD ¦ VAR ¦ CITE ¦ ABBR ¦ ACRONYM)

Special elements (A ¦ IMG ¦ APPLET ¦ OBJECT ¦ FONT ¦ BASEFONT ¦ BR ¦ SCRIPT ¦ MAP ¦ Q ¦ SUB ¦ SUP ¦ SPAN ¦ BDO ¦ IFRAME)

Form Control elements (INPUT ¦ SELECT ¦ TEXTAREA ¦ LABEL ¦ BUTTON)

Formalized: HTML 2.0

Notes: Although not deprecated, the W3C recommends using style sheets in place of this element.

Browser: MSIE 1; NNav 1

<BASE> S

Usage: Sets the base URI for the document.

Syntax: `<BASE attributes>`

Start/End Tag: Required/Forbidden

Must be empty? Yes

Attributes: href="*URI*"—Sets the absolute URI against which all other URIs are resolved.

T target="*user-defined* ¦ _blank ¦ _self ¦ _parent ¦ _top"—Identifies the frame in which the linked resource will be opened:

`user-defined`—Document opens in the frame designated by the *`user-defined`* name that is set by the `name` attribute of the frame. The `name` must begin with an alphabetic character.

`_blank`—Document opens in a new, unnamed window.

`_self`—Document opens in same frame as the originating link.

`_parent`—Document opens in the immediate `FRAMESET` parent of the current frame, or itself if the current frame has no parent.

`_top`—Document opens in the full, original window, or itself if the frame has no parent.

Content: Empty

Formalized: HTML 2.0

Notes: The `BASE` element must appear in the `HEAD` element of the document, before any references to an external source.

Browser: MSIE 1; NNav 1

<BASEFONT>

Usage: Sets the base font size.

Syntax: `<BASEFONT attributes>`

Start/End Tag: Required/Forbidden

Must be empty? Yes

Attributes: `id="id"`—A global identifier.

`size="data"`—Sets the font size in absolute terms (`1` through `7`) or as a relative increase or decrease along that scale (for example `+3`).

`color="color"`—Sets the font color. Colors identified by standard RGB in hexadecimal format (`#RRGGBB`) or by predefined color name.

`face="data"`—Identifies the font face for display (if possible). Multiple entries are listed in order of search preference and separated by commas.

Content: Empty

Formalized: HTML 3.2

Notes: Deprecated in favor of style sheets.

Changes to fonts through the `FONT` element are resolved against the values specified in the `BASEFONT` element when present.

There are conflicting implementations across browsers, and contents of tables appear not to be effected by `BASEFONT` values.

Browser: MSIE 1; NNav 1

<BDO>...</BDO> S

Usage: The bidirectional algorithm override element selectively turns off the default text direction.

Syntax: `<BDO attributes>content</BDO>`

Start/End Tag: Required/Required

Must be empty? No

Attributes: core—See "Common Attributes" section.

lang="*language-code*"—Identifies the human (not computer) language of the text content or an element's attribute values.

dir="LTR ¦ RTL"—Specifies the text direction (left-to-right, right-to-left) of element content, overriding inherent directionality. This is a mandatory attribute of the BDO element.

Content: Zero or more inline elements, to include the following:

- Document text and entities
- Fontstyle elements (TT ¦ I ¦ B ¦ U ¦ S ¦ STRIKE ¦ BIG ¦ SMALL)
- Phrase elements (EM ¦ STRONG ¦ DFN ¦ CODE ¦ SAMP ¦ KBD ¦ VAR ¦ CITE ¦ ABBR ¦ ACRONYM)
- Special elements (A ¦ IMG ¦ APPLET ¦ OBJECT ¦ FONT ¦ BASEFONT ¦ BR ¦ SCRIPT ¦ MAP ¦ Q ¦ SUB ¦ SUP ¦ SPAN ¦ BDO ¦ IFRAME)
- Form Control elements (INPUT ¦ SELECT ¦ TEXTAREA ¦ LABEL ¦ BUTTON)

Formalized: HTML 4.0

Notes: Care should be taken when using the BDO element in conjunction with special Unicode characters that also override the bidirectional algorithm.

The BDO element should only be used when absolute control over character sequencing is required.

Browser: MSIE 5

<BIG>...</BIG> S

Usage: Displays text in a larger font size.

Syntax: `<BIG attributes>content</BIG>`

Start/End Tag: Required/Required

Must be empty? No

Attributes: core—See "Common Attributes" section.

i18n—See "Common Attributes" section.

events—See "Intrinsic Events" section.

Content: Zero or more inline elements, to include the following:

Document text and entities

Fontstyle elements (TT ¦ I ¦ B ¦ U ¦ S ¦ STRIKE ¦ BIG ¦ SMALL)

Phrase elements (EM ¦ STRONG ¦ DFN ¦ CODE ¦ SAMP ¦ KBD ¦ VAR ¦ CITE ¦ ABBR ¦ ACRONYM)

Special elements (A ¦ IMG ¦ APPLET ¦ OBJECT ¦ FONT ¦ BASEFONT ¦ BR ¦ SCRIPT ¦ MAP ¦ Q ¦ SUB ¦ SUP ¦ SPAN ¦ BDO ¦ IFRAME)

Form Control elements (INPUT ¦ SELECT ¦ TEXTAREA ¦ LABEL ¦ BUTTON)

Formalized: HTML 3.2

Notes: Although not deprecated, the W3C recommends using style sheets in place of this element.

Browser: MSIE 3; NNav 1.1

<BLOCKQUOTE>...</BLOCKQUOTE> S

Usage: Designates text as a quotation.

Syntax: `<BLOCKQUOTE attributes>content</BLOCKQUOTE>`

Start/End Tag: Required/Required

Must be empty? No

Attributes: core—See "Common Attributes" section.

i18n—See "Common Attributes" section.

events—See "Intrinsic Events" section.

cite="*URI*"—The URI designating the source document or message.

Content: Zero or more inline elements, to include the following:

Document text and entities

Fontstyle elements (TT ¦ I ¦ B ¦ U ¦ S ¦ STRIKE ¦ BIG ¦ SMALL)

Phrase elements (EM ¦ STRONG ¦ DFN ¦ CODE ¦ SAMP ¦ KBD ¦ VAR ¦ CITE ¦ ABBR ¦ ACRONYM)

Special elements (A ¦ IMG ¦ APPLET ¦ OBJECT ¦ FONT ¦ BASEFONT ¦ BR ¦ SCRIPT ¦ MAP ¦ Q ¦ SUB ¦ SUP ¦ SPAN ¦ BDO ¦ IFRAME)

Form Control elements (INPUT ¦ SELECT ¦ TEXTAREA ¦ LABEL ¦ BUTTON)

Formalized: HTML 2.0

Notes: When compared with the Q element, the BLOCKQUOTE element is used for longer quotations and is treated as block-level content.

Quotation marks, if desired, should be added with style sheets. Normally rendered as an indented block of text.

Browser: MSIE 1; NNav 1

<BODY>...</BODY> S

Usage: Contains the content of the document.

Syntax: `content` or

`<BODY attributes>content</BODY>`

Start/End Tag: Optional/Optional

Must be empty? No

Attributes: core—See "Common Attributes" section.

`i18n`—See "Common Attributes" section.

`events`—See "Intrinsic Events" section.

`onload="script"`—Intrinsic event triggered when the document loads.

`onunload="script"`—Intrinsic event triggered when document unloads.

T D `background="URI"`—Location of a background image to be displayed.

T D `bgcolor="color"`—Sets the document background color. Colors identified by standard RGB in hexadecimal format (*#RRGGBB*) or by predefined color name.

T D `text="color"`—Sets the document text color. Colors identified by standard RGB in hexadecimal format (*#RRGGBB*) or by predefined color name.

T D `link="color"`—Sets the link color. Colors identified by standard RGB in hexadecimal format (*#RRGGBB*) or by predefined color name.

T D `vlink="color"`—Sets the visited link color. Colors identified by standard RGB in hexadecimal format (*#RRGGBB*) or by predefined color name.

T D `alink="color"`—Sets the active link color. Colors identified by standard RGB in hexadecimal format (*#RRGGBB*) or by predefined color name.

Content: Zero or more block elements, to include the following:

`P ¦ DL ¦ DIV ¦ CENTER ¦ NOSCRIPT ¦ NOFRAMES ¦ BLOCKQUOTE ¦ FORM ¦ ISINDEX ¦ HR ¦ TABLE ¦ FIELDSET ¦ ADDRESS`

Heading elements (`H1 ¦ H2 ¦ H3 ¦ H4 ¦ H5 ¦ H6`)

List elements (UL ¦ OL ¦ DIR ¦ MENU)

Preformatted elements (PRE)

Zero or more inline elements, to include the following:

Document text and entities

Fontstyle elements (TT ¦ I ¦ B ¦ U ¦ S ¦ STRIKE ¦ BIG ¦ SMALL)

Phrase elements (EM ¦ STRONG ¦ DFN ¦ CODE ¦ SAMP ¦ KBD ¦ VAR ¦ CITE ¦ ABBR ¦ ACRONYM)

Special elements (A ¦ IMG ¦ APPLET ¦ OBJECT ¦ FONT ¦ BASEFONT ¦ BR ¦ SCRIPT ¦ MAP ¦ Q ¦ SUB ¦ SUP ¦ SPAN ¦ BDO ¦ IFRAME)

Form Control elements (INPUT ¦ SELECT ¦ TEXTAREA ¦ LABEL ¦ BUTTON)

Zero or more block/inline elements to include (INS ¦ DEL)

Formalized: HTML 2.0

Notes: Style sheets are the preferred method of controlling the presentational aspects of the BODY.

Browser: MSIE 1; NNav 1

 S

Usage: Forces a line break.

Syntax: `<BR attributes>`

Start/End Tag: Required/Forbidden

Must be empty? Yes

Attributes: core—See "Common Attributes" section.

T D `clear="left ¦ all ¦ right ¦ none"`—Sets the location where next line begins after the line break. This attribute is deprecated in favor of style sheets:

`left`—The next line begins at the nearest line on the left margin following any floating objects.

`all`—The next line begins at the nearest line at either margin following any floating objects.

`right`—The next line begins at the nearest line on the right margin following any floating objects.

`none`—Next line begins normally.

Content: Empty

Formalized: HTML 2.0

Notes: The `clear` attribute is deprecated in favor of style sheets.

Browser: MSIE 1; NNav 1

<BUTTON>...</BUTTON> S

Usage: Creates a button.

Syntax: `<BUTTON attributes>content</BUTTON>`

Start/End Tag: Required/Required

Must be empty? No

Attributes:

core—See "Common Attributes" section.

i18n—See "Common Attributes" section.

events—See "Intrinsic Events" section.

name="*data*"—Defines a control name.

value="*data*"—Assigns an initial value to the button.

type="button ¦ **submit** ¦ reset"—Defines the type of button to be created:

button—Creates a push button.

submit—Creates a submit button.

reset—Creates a reset button.

disabled—Identifies that the button is unavailable in the current context.

tabindex="*number*"—Defines the tabbing order between elements. This is the order (from lowest first to highest last) in which they receive focus when the user navigates through them using the Tab key.

accesskey="*character*"—Assigns an access key (or shortcut key) to the element. When the key is pressed, the element receives focus and is activated.

onfocus="*script*"—Triggered when the element receives focus by either a pointing device (such as a mouse) or tabbed navigation.

onblur="*script*"—Triggered when the element loses focus by either a pointing device (such as a mouse) or tabbed navigation.

Content: Zero or more block elements, to include the following:

P ¦ DL ¦ DIV ¦ CENTER ¦ NOSCRIPT ¦ NOFRAMES ¦ BLOCKQUOTE ¦ HR ¦ TABLE ¦ ADDRESS

Heading elements (H1 ¦ H2 ¦ H3 ¦ H4 ¦ H5 ¦ H6)

List elements (UL ¦ OL ¦ DIR ¦ MENU)

Preformatted elements (PRE)

Zero or more inline elements, to include the following:

Document text and entities

Fontstyle elements (TT ¦ I ¦ B ¦ U ¦ S ¦ STRIKE ¦ BIG ¦ SMALL)

Phrase elements (EM ¦ STRONG ¦ DFN ¦ CODE ¦ SAMP ¦ KBD ¦ VAR ¦ CITE ¦ ABBR ¦ ACRONYM)

Special elements (IMG ¦ APPLET ¦ OBJECT ¦ FONT ¦ BASEFONT ¦ BR ¦ SCRIPT ¦ MAP ¦ Q ¦ SUB ¦ SUP ¦ SPAN ¦ BDO)

Formalized: HTML 4.0

Notes: An important distinction between buttons created with the BUTTON element and those created by the INPUT element is that the former allows content to be associated with the control.

Browser: MSIE 4

<CAPTION>...</CAPTION> S

Usage: Displays a table caption.

Syntax: `<CAPTION attributes>content</CAPTION>`

Start/End Tag: Required/Required

Must be empty? No

Attributes: core—See “Common Attributes” section.

i18n—See “Common Attributes” section.

events—See “Intrinsic Events” section.

T D align="**top** ¦ bottom ¦ left ¦ right"—Positions the CAPTION relative to the TABLE:

top—Places the caption at the top of the table.

bottom—Places the caption at the bottom of the table.

left—Places the caption at the left side of the table.

right—Places the caption at the right side of the table.

Content: Zero or more inline elements, to include the following:

Document text and entities

Fontstyle elements (TT ¦ I ¦ B ¦ U ¦ S ¦ STRIKE ¦ BIG ¦ SMALL)

Phrase elements (EM ¦ STRONG ¦ DFN ¦ CODE ¦ SAMP ¦ KBD ¦ VAR ¦ CITE ¦ ABBR ¦ ACRONYM)

Special elements (A ¦ IMG ¦ APPLET ¦ OBJECT ¦ FONT ¦ BASEFONT ¦ BR ¦ SCRIPT ¦ MAP ¦ Q ¦ SUB ¦ SUP ¦ SPAN ¦ BDO ¦ IFRAME)

Form Control elements (INPUT ¦ SELECT ¦ TEXTAREA ¦ LABEL ¦ BUTTON)

Formalized: HTML 3.2

Notes: The CAPTION may only be placed immediately following the opening TABLE tag, and only one CAPTION per table is allowed.

Browser: MSIE 2; NNav 1.1

<CENTER>...</CENTER>

Usage: Centers content on the page.

Syntax: `<CENTER attributes>content</CENTER>`

Start/End Tag: Required/Required

Must be empty? No

Attributes: core—See "Common Attributes" section.

i18n—See "Common Attributes" section.

events—See "Intrinsic Events" section.

Content: Zero or more block elements, to include the following:

P ¦ DL ¦ DIV ¦ CENTER ¦ NOSCRIPT ¦ NOFRAMES ¦ BLOCKQUOTE ¦ FORM ¦ ISINDEX ¦ HR ¦ TABLE ¦ FIELDSET ¦ ADDRESS

Heading elements (H1 ¦ H2 ¦ H3 ¦ H4 ¦ H5 ¦ H6)

List elements (UL ¦ OL ¦ DIR ¦ MENU)

Preformatted elements (PRE)

Zero or more inline elements, to include the following:

Document text and entities

Fontstyle elements (TT ¦ I ¦ B ¦ U ¦ S ¦ STRIKE ¦ BIG ¦ SMALL)

Phrase elements (EM ¦ STRONG ¦ DFN ¦ CODE ¦ SAMP ¦ KBD ¦ VAR ¦ CITE ¦ ABBR ¦ ACRONYM)

Special elements (A ¦ IMG ¦ APPLET ¦ OBJECT ¦ FONT ¦ BASEFONT ¦ BR ¦ SCRIPT ¦ MAP ¦ Q ¦ SUB ¦ SUP ¦ SPAN ¦ BDO ¦ IFRAME)

Form Control elements (INPUT ¦ SELECT ¦ TEXTAREA ¦ LABEL ¦ BUTTON)

Formalized: HTML 3.2

Notes: Deprecated in favor of style sheets.

Using the CENTER element is the equivalent of `<DIV align="center">`, although this method is also deprecated in favor of style sheets.

Browser: MSIE 1; NNav 1

<CITE>...</CITE> S

Usage: Identifies a citation or a reference.

Syntax: `<CITE attributes>content</CITE>`

Start/End Tag: Required/Required

Must be empty? No

Attributes: core—See "Common Attributes" section.

i18n—See "Common Attributes" section.

events—See "Intrinsic Events" section.

Content: Zero or more inline elements, to include the following:

- Document text and entities
- Fontstyle elements (TT ¦ I ¦ B ¦ U ¦ S ¦ STRIKE ¦ BIG ¦ SMALL)
- Phrase elements (EM ¦ STRONG ¦ DFN ¦ CODE ¦ SAMP ¦ KBD ¦ VAR ¦ CITE ¦ ABBR ¦ ACRONYM)
- Special elements (A ¦ IMG ¦ APPLET ¦ OBJECT ¦ FONT ¦ BASEFONT ¦ BR ¦ SCRIPT ¦ MAP ¦ Q ¦ SUB ¦ SUP ¦ SPAN ¦ BDO ¦ IFRAME)
- Form Control elements (INPUT ¦ SELECT ¦ TEXTAREA ¦ LABEL ¦ BUTTON)

Formalized: HTML 2.0

Notes: Usually rendered as italicized text.

Browser: MSIE 1; NNav 1

<CODE>...</CODE> S

Usage: Identifies a fragment of computer code.

Syntax: `<CODE attributes>content</CODE>`

Start/End Tag: Required/Required

Must be empty? No

Attributes: core—See "Common Attributes" section.

i18n—See "Common Attributes" section.

events—See "Intrinsic Events" section.

Content: Zero or more inline elements, to include the following:

- Document text and entities
- Fontstyle elements (TT ¦ I ¦ B ¦ U ¦ S ¦ STRIKE ¦ BIG ¦ SMALL)
- Phrase elements (EM ¦ STRONG ¦ DFN ¦ CODE ¦ SAMP ¦ KBD ¦ VAR ¦ CITE ¦ ABBR ¦ ACRONYM)
- Special elements (A ¦ IMG ¦ APPLET ¦ OBJECT ¦ FONT ¦ BASEFONT ¦ BR ¦ SCRIPT ¦ MAP ¦ Q ¦ SUB ¦ SUP ¦ SPAN ¦ BDO ¦ IFRAME)

Form Control elements (INPUT ¦ SELECT ¦ TEXTAREA ¦ LABEL ¦ BUTTON)

Formalized: HTML 2.0

Notes: Usually rendered in monospaced font.

Browser: MSIE 1; NNav 1

<COL> S

Usage: Groups columns within column groups to share attribute values.

Syntax: `<COL attributes>`

Start/End Tag: Required/Forbidden

Must be empty? Yes

Attributes: core—See "Common Attributes" section.

i18n—See "Common Attributes" section.

events—See "Intrinsic Events" section.

span="*number*"—Sets the number of columns the COL element spans (1 is the default). Each column spanned in this manner inherits its attributes from that COL element.

width="*multi-length*"—Sets the default width of each column spanned by the COL element.

align="left ¦ center ¦ right ¦ justify ¦ char"—Horizontally aligns the contents of cells:

left—Data and text aligned left. This is the default for table data.

center—Data and text centered. This is the default for table headers.

right—Data and text aligned right.

justify—Data and text aligned flush with left and right margins.

char—Aligns text around a specific character.

char="*character*"—Sets a character on which the column aligns (such as ":"). The default value is the decimal point of the current language.

charoff="*length*"—Offset to the first alignment character on a line. Specified in number of pixels or a percentage of available length.

valign="top ¦ **middle** ¦ bottom ¦ baseline"—Vertically aligns the contents of a cell:

top—Cell data flush with top of cell.

middle—Cell data centered in cell.

bottom—Cell data flush with bottom of cell.

baseline—Aligns all cells in a row with this attribute set. Textual data aligned along a common baseline.

Content: Empty

Formalized: HTML 4.0

Notes: The COL element groups columns only to share attribute values, not group them structurally, which is the role of the COLGROUP element.

Browser: MSIE 3

<COLGROUP>...</COLGROUP> S

Usage: Defines a column group.

Syntax: <COLGROUP *attributes*>*content*

or

<COLGROUP *attributes*>*content*</COLGROUP>

Start/End Tag: Required/Optional

Must be empty? No

Attributes: core—See "Common Attributes" section.

i18n—See "Common Attributes" section.

events—See "Intrinsic Events" section.

span="*number*"—Sets the number of columns in a COLGROUP (1 is the default). Each column spanned in this manner inherits its attributes from that COLGROUP element.

width="*multi-length*"—Sets the default width of each column spanned by the COLGROUP element. An additional value is "0*" (zero asterisk), which means that the width of the each column in the group should be the minimum width necessary to hold the column's contents.

align="left ¦ center ¦ right ¦ justify ¦ char"—Horizontally aligns the contents of cells:

left—Data and text aligned left. This is the default for table data.

center—Data and text centered. This is the default for table headers.

right—Data and text aligned right.

justify—Data and text aligned flush with left and right margins.

`char`—Aligns text around a specific character.

`char="`*`character`*`"`—Sets a character on which the column aligns (such as `":"`). The default value is the decimal point of the current language.

`charoff="`*`length`*`"`—Offset to the first alignment character on a line. Specified in number of pixels or a percentage of available length.

`valign="top ¦` **`middle`** `¦ bottom ¦ baseline"`—Vertically aligns the contents of a cell:

`top`—Cell data flush with top of cell.

`middle`—Cell data centered in cell.

`bottom`—Cell data flush with bottom of cell.

`baseline`—Aligns all cells in a row with this attribute set. Textual data aligned along a common baseline.

Content: Zero or more `COL` elements.

Formalized: HTML 4.0

Notes: The purpose of the `COLGROUP` element is to provide structure to table columns.

Browser: MSIE 3

<DD>...</DD>

Usage: Contains the definition description used in a `DL` (definition list) element.

Syntax: `<DD` *`attributes`*`>`*`content`* or

`<DD` *`attributes`*`>`*`content`*`</DD>`

Start/End Tag: Required/Optional

Must be empty? No

Attributes: core—See “Common Attributes” section.

`i18n`—See “Common Attributes” section.

`events`—See “Intrinsic Events” section.

`compact`—Tells the browser to attempt to display the list more compactly.

Content: Zero or more block elements, to include the following:

`P ¦ DL ¦ DIV ¦ CENTER ¦ NOSCRIPT ¦ NOFRAMES ¦ BLOCKQUOTE ¦ FORM ¦ ISINDEX ¦ HR ¦ TABLE ¦ FIELDSET ¦ ADDRESS`

Heading elements (`H1 ¦ H2 ¦ H3 ¦ H4 ¦ H5 ¦ H6`)

List elements (`UL ¦ OL ¦ DIR ¦ MENU`)

Preformatted elements (PRE)

Zero or more inline elements, to include the following:

Document text and entities

Fontstyle elements (TT ¦ I ¦ B ¦ U ¦ S ¦ STRIKE ¦ BIG ¦ SMALL)

Phrase elements (EM ¦ STRONG ¦ DFN ¦ CODE ¦ SAMP ¦ KBD ¦ VAR ¦ CITE ¦ ABBR ¦ ACRONYM)

Special elements (A ¦ IMG ¦ APPLET ¦ OBJECT ¦ FONT ¦ BASEFONT ¦ BR ¦ SCRIPT ¦ MAP ¦ Q ¦ SUB ¦ SUP ¦ SPAN ¦ BDO ¦ IFRAME)

Form Control elements (INPUT ¦ SELECT ¦ TEXTAREA ¦ LABEL ¦ BUTTON)

Formalized: HTML 2.0

Notes: The DD element may contain block-level or inline content.

Browser: MSIE 1; NNav 1

Usage: Identifies and displays text as having been deleted from the document in relation to a previous version.

Syntax: `<DEL attributes>content</DEL>`

Start/End Tag: Required/Required

Must be empty? No

Attributes: core—See "Common Attributes" section.

i18n—See "Common Attributes" section.

events—See "Intrinsic Events" section.

cite="*URI*"—A URI pointing to a document that should give reason for the change.

datetime="*datetime*"—Sets the date and time of the change.

Content: Zero or more block elements, to include the following:

P ¦ DL ¦ DIV ¦ CENTER ¦ NOSCRIPT ¦ NOFRAMES ¦ BLOCKQUOTE ¦ FORM ¦ ISINDEX ¦ HR ¦ TABLE ¦ FIELDSET ¦ ADDRESS

Heading elements (H1 ¦ H2 ¦ H3 ¦ H4 ¦ H5 ¦ H6)

List elements (UL ¦ OL ¦ DIR ¦ MENU)

Preformatted elements (PRE)

Zero or more inline elements, to include the following:

Document text and entities

Fontstyle elements (TT ¦ I ¦ B ¦ U ¦ S ¦ STRIKE ¦ BIG ¦ SMALL)

Phrase elements (EM ¦ STRONG ¦ DFN ¦ CODE ¦ SAMP ¦ KBD ¦ VAR ¦ CITE ¦ ABBR ¦ ACRONYM)

Special elements (A ¦ IMG ¦ APPLET ¦ OBJECT ¦ FONT ¦ BASEFONT ¦ BR ¦ SCRIPT ¦ MAP ¦ Q ¦ SUB ¦ SUP ¦ SPAN ¦ BDO ¦ IFRAME)

Form Control elements (INPUT ¦ SELECT ¦ TEXTAREA ¦ LABEL ¦ BUTTON)

Formalized: HTML 4.0

Notes: May serve as a block-level or inline element, but not both at the same time. Changes to nested block-level content should be made at the lowest level.

Browser: MSIE 4

<DFN>...</DFN> S

Usage: The defining instance of an enclosed term.

Syntax: `<DFN attributes>content</DFN>`

Start/End Tag: Required/Required

Must be empty? No

Attributes: core—See "Common Attributes" section.

i18n—See "Common Attributes" section.

events—See "Intrinsic Events" section.

Content: Zero or more inline elements, to include the following:

Document text and entities

Fontstyle elements (TT ¦ I ¦ B ¦ U ¦ S ¦ STRIKE ¦ BIG ¦ SMALL)

Phrase elements (EM ¦ STRONG ¦ DFN ¦ CODE ¦ SAMP ¦ KBD ¦ VAR ¦ CITE ¦ ABBR ¦ ACRONYM)

Special elements (A ¦ IMG ¦ APPLET ¦ OBJECT ¦ FONT ¦ BASEFONT ¦ BR ¦ SCRIPT ¦ MAP ¦ Q ¦ SUB ¦ SUP ¦ SPAN ¦ BDO ¦ IFRAME)

Form Control elements (INPUT ¦ SELECT ¦ TEXTAREA ¦ LABEL ¦ BUTTON)

Formalized: HTML 3.2

Notes: Usually rendered in italics.

Browser: MSIE 1

<DIR>...</DIR> T D

Usage: Creates a multicolumn directory list.

Syntax: `<DIR attributes>content</DIR>`

Start/End Tag: Required/Required

Must be empty? No

Attributes: core—See "Common Attributes" section.

i18n—See "Common Attributes" section.

`events`—See "Intrinsic Events" section.

`compact`—Tells the browser to attempt to display the list more compactly.

Content: One or more `LI` element, which may contain the following:

List elements (`UL` ¦ `OL` ¦ `DIR` ¦ `MENU`)

Zero or more inline elements, to include the following:

- Document text and entities
- Fontstyle elements (`TT` ¦ `I` ¦ `B` ¦ `U` ¦ `S` ¦ `STRIKE` ¦ `BIG` ¦ `SMALL`)
- Phrase elements (`EM` ¦ `STRONG` ¦ `DFN` ¦ `CODE` ¦ `SAMP` ¦ `KBD` ¦ `VAR` ¦ `CITE` ¦ `ABBR` ¦ `ACRONYM`)
- Special elements (`A` ¦ `IMG` ¦ `APPLET` ¦ `OBJECT` ¦ `FONT` ¦ `BASEFONT` ¦ `BR` ¦ `SCRIPT` ¦ `MAP` ¦ `Q` ¦ `SUB` ¦ `SUP` ¦ `SPAN` ¦ `BDO` ¦ `IFRAME`)
- Form Control elements (`INPUT` ¦ `SELECT` ¦ `TEXTAREA` ¦ `LABEL` ¦ `BUTTON`)

Formalized: HTML 2.0

Notes: Deprecated in favor of unordered lists (UL).

Browser: MSIE 1; NNav 1

<DIV>...</DIV>

Usage: Creates user-defined block-level structure to the document.

Syntax: `<DIV attributes>content</DIV>`

Start/End Tag: Required/Required

Must be empty? No

Attributes: core—See "Common Attributes" section.

`i18n`—See "Common Attributes" section.

`events`—See "Intrinsic Events" section.

`align="left ¦ center ¦ right ¦ justify"`—Horizontal alignment with respect to context. The default depends on the directionality of the text. For left-to-right it is `left` and for right-to-left it is `right`:

`left`—Text aligned left.

`center`—Text centered.

`right`—Text aligned right.

`justify`—Text aligned flush with left and right margins.

Content: Zero or more block elements, to include the following:

P ¦ DL ¦ DIV ¦ CENTER ¦ NOSCRIPT ¦ NOFRAMES ¦ BLOCKQUOTE ¦ FORM ¦ ISINDEX ¦ HR ¦ TABLE ¦ FIELDSET ¦ ADDRESS

Heading elements (H1 ¦ H2 ¦ H3 ¦ H4 ¦ H5 ¦ H6)

List elements (UL ¦ OL ¦ DIR ¦ MENU)

Preformatted elements (PRE)

Zero or more inline elements, to include the following:

Document text and entities

Fontstyle elements (TT ¦ I ¦ B ¦ U ¦ S ¦ STRIKE ¦ BIG ¦ SMALL)

Phrase elements (EM ¦ STRONG ¦ DFN ¦ CODE ¦ SAMP ¦ KBD ¦ VAR ¦ CITE ¦ ABBR ¦ ACRONYM)

Special elements (A ¦ IMG ¦ APPLET ¦ OBJECT ¦ FONT ¦ BASEFONT ¦ BR ¦ SCRIPT ¦ MAP ¦ Q ¦ SUB ¦ SUP ¦ SPAN ¦ BDO ¦ IFRAME)

Form Control elements (INPUT ¦ SELECT ¦ TEXTAREA ¦ LABEL ¦ BUTTON)

Formalized: HTML 3.2

Notes: Used in conjunction with style sheets this is a powerful device for adding custom block-level structure.

May be nested.

Browser: MSIE 3; NNav 2

<DL>...</DL> S

Usage: Creates a definition list.

Syntax: `<DL attributes>content</DL>`

Start/End Tag: Required/Required

Must be empty? No

Attributes: core—See "Common Attributes" section.

i18n—See "Common Attributes" section.

events—See "Intrinsic Events" section.

T D compact—Tells the browser to attempt to display the list more compactly.

Content: One or more DT or DD elements.

Formalized: HTML 2.0

Notes: This element provides the structure necessary to group definition terms and descriptions into a list. Aside from those elements (DT and DL), no other content is allowed.

Browser: MSIE 1; NNav 1

<DT>...</DT> S

Usage: The definition term (or label) used within a DL (definition list) element.

Syntax: `<DT attributes>content`

or

`<DT attributes>content</DT>`

Start/End Tag: Required/Optional

Must be empty? No

Attributes: core—See "Common Attributes" section.

i18n—See "Common Attributes" section.

events—See "Intrinsic Events" section.

T D compact—Tells the browser to attempt to display the list more compactly.

Content: Zero or more inline elements, to include the following:

Document text and entities

Fontstyle elements (TT ¦ I ¦ B ¦ U ¦ S ¦ STRIKE ¦ BIG ¦ SMALL)

Phrase elements (EM ¦ STRONG ¦ DFN ¦ CODE ¦ SAMP ¦ KBD ¦ VAR ¦ CITE ¦ ABBR ¦ ACRONYM)

Special elements (A ¦ IMG ¦ APPLET ¦ OBJECT ¦ FONT ¦ BASEFONT ¦ BR ¦ SCRIPT ¦ MAP ¦ Q ¦ SUB ¦ SUP ¦ SPAN ¦ BDO ¦ IFRAME)

Form Control elements (INPUT ¦ SELECT ¦ TEXTAREA ¦ LABEL ¦ BUTTON)

Formalized: HTML 2.0

Notes: The DT element may only contain inline content.

Browser: MSIE 1; NNav 1

<EM>...</EM> S

Usage: Displays text with emphasis in relation to normal text.

Syntax: `<EM attributes>content</EM>`

Start/End Tag: Required/Required

Must be empty? No

Attributes: core—See "Common Attributes" section.

i18n—See "Common Attributes" section.

events—See "Intrinsic Events" section.

Content: Zero or more inline elements, to include the following:

Document text and entities

Fontstyle elements (TT ¦ I ¦ B ¦ U ¦ S ¦ STRIKE ¦ BIG ¦ SMALL)

Phrase elements (EM ¦ STRONG ¦ DFN ¦ CODE ¦ SAMP ¦ KBD ¦ VAR ¦ CITE ¦ ABBR ¦ ACRONYM)

Special elements (A ¦ IMG ¦ APPLET ¦ OBJECT ¦ FONT ¦ BASEFONT ¦ BR ¦ SCRIPT ¦ MAP ¦ Q ¦ SUB ¦ SUP ¦ SPAN ¦ BDO ¦ IFRAME)

Form Control elements (INPUT ¦ SELECT ¦ TEXTAREA ¦ LABEL ¦ BUTTON)

Formalized: HTML 2.0

Notes: Usually rendered in italics.

Browser: MSIE 1; NNav 1

<FIELDSET>...</FIELDSET> S

Usage: Groups related controls and labels of a form.

Syntax: `<FIELDSET attributes>content</FIELDSET>`

Start/End Tag: Required/Required

Must be empty? No

Attributes: core—See "Common Attributes" section.

i18n—See "Common Attributes" section.

events—See "Intrinsic Events" section.

Content: One LEGEND element.

Zero or more block elements, to include the following:

P ¦ DL ¦ DIV ¦ CENTER ¦ NOSCRIPT ¦ NOFRAMES ¦ BLOCKQUOTE ¦ FORM ¦ ISINDEX ¦ HR ¦ TABLE ¦ FIELDSET ¦ ADDRESS

Heading elements (H1 ¦ H2 ¦ H3 ¦ H4 ¦ H5 ¦ H6)

List elements (UL ¦ OL ¦ DIR ¦ MENU)

Preformatted elements (PRE)

Zero or more inline elements, to include the following:

Document text and entities

Fontstyle elements (TT ¦ I ¦ B ¦ U ¦ S ¦ STRIKE ¦ BIG ¦ SMALL)

Phrase elements (EM ¦ STRONG ¦ DFN ¦ CODE ¦ SAMP ¦ KBD ¦ VAR ¦ CITE ¦ ABBR ¦ ACRONYM)

Special elements (A ¦ IMG ¦ APPLET ¦ OBJECT ¦ FONT ¦ BASEFONT ¦ BR ¦ SCRIPT ¦ MAP ¦ Q ¦ SUB ¦ SUP ¦ SPAN ¦ BDO ¦ IFRAME)

Form Control elements (INPUT ¦ SELECT ¦ TEXTAREA ¦ LABEL ¦ BUTTON)

Formalized: HTML 4.0

Notes: Proper use of the FIELDSET element facilitates user understanding of the form and eases navigation.

Browser: MSIE 4

<FONT>...</FONT>

Usage: Changes the font size and color.

Syntax: `<FONT attributes>content</FONT>`

Start/End Tag: Required/Required

Must be empty? No

Attributes: core—See "Common Attributes" section.

i18n—See "Common Attributes" section.

size="*data*"—Sets the font size in absolute terms (1 through 7) or as a relative increase or decrease along that scale (for example, +3). If a base font is not specified, the default is 3.

color="*color*"—Sets the font color. Colors are identified by standard RGB in hexadecimal format (*#RRGGBB*) or by predefined color name.

face="*data*"—Identifies the font face for display (if possible). Multiple entries are listed in order of search preference and separated by commas.

Content: Zero or more inline elements, to include the following:

Document text and entities

Fontstyle elements (TT ¦ I ¦ B ¦ U ¦ S ¦ STRIKE ¦ BIG ¦ SMALL)

Phrase elements (EM ¦ STRONG ¦ DFN ¦ CODE ¦ SAMP ¦ KBD ¦ VAR ¦ CITE ¦ ABBR ¦ ACRONYM)

Special elements (A ¦ IMG ¦ APPLET ¦ OBJECT ¦ FONT ¦ BASEFONT ¦ BR ¦ SCRIPT ¦ MAP ¦ Q ¦ SUB ¦ SUP ¦ SPAN ¦ BDO ¦ IFRAME)

Form Control elements (INPUT ¦ SELECT ¦ TEXTAREA ¦ LABEL ¦ BUTTON)

Formalized: HTML 3.2

Notes: Deprecated in favor of style sheets.

Changes to fonts through the `FONT` element are resolved against the values specified in the `BASEFONT` element when present.

Browser: MSIE 1; NNav 1

<FORM>...</FORM> S

Usage: Creates a form that holds controls for user input.

Syntax: `<FORM attributes>content</FORM>`

Start/End Tag: Required/Required

Must be empty? No

Attributes:

`core`—See "Common Attributes" section.

`i18n`—See "Common Attributes" section.

`events`—See "Intrinsic Events" section.

`action="URI"`—Specifies the form processing agent that will process the submitted form.

`method="get ¦ post"`—Specifies the HTTP method used to submit the form data:

`get`—The form data set is appended to the URI specified by the action attribute (with a question mark (`"?"`) as separator), and this new URI is sent to the processing agent.

`post`—The form data set is included in the body of the form and sent to the processing agent.

`enctype="content-type"`—Specifies the content or media (MIME) type used to transmit the form to the server. The default is `"application/x-www-form-urlencoded"`.

`onsubmit="script"`—Triggered when the `FORM` is submitted.

`onreset="script"`—Triggered when the `FORM` is reset.

T `target="user-defined ¦ _blank ¦ _self ¦ _parent ¦ _top"`—Identifies the frame in which the linked resource will be opened:

`user-defined`—Document opens in the frame designated by the *`user-defined`* name, which is set by the `name` attribute of the frame. The `name` must begin with an alphabetic character.

`_blank`—Document opens in a new, unnamed window.

`self`—Document opens in the same frame as the originating link.

`parent`—Document opens in the immediate `FRAMESET` parent of the current frame, or itself if the current frame has no parent.

`_top`—Document opens in the full, original window, or itself if the frame has no parent.

`accept-charset="character-set"`—Specifies the list of character encodings for input data that must be accepted by the server processing this form.

`accept="content-types"`—List of content types.

Content: Zero or more block elements, to include the following:

`P ¦ DL ¦ DIV ¦ CENTER ¦ NOSCRIPT ¦ NOFRAMES ¦ BLOCKQUOTE ¦ ISINDEX ¦ HR ¦ TABLE ¦ FIELDSET ¦ ADDRESS`

Heading elements (`H1 ¦ H2 ¦ H3 ¦ H4 ¦ H5 ¦ H6`)

List elements (`UL ¦ OL ¦ DIR ¦ MENU`)

Preformatted elements (`PRE`)

Zero or more inline elements, to include the following:

Document text and entities

Fontstyle elements (`TT ¦ I ¦ B ¦ U ¦ S ¦ STRIKE ¦ BIG ¦ SMALL`)

Phrase elements (`EM ¦ STRONG ¦ DFN ¦ CODE ¦ SAMP ¦ KBD ¦ VAR ¦ CITE ¦ ABBR ¦ ACRONYM`)

Special elements (`A ¦ IMG ¦ APPLET ¦ OBJECT ¦ FONT ¦ BASEFONT ¦ BR ¦ SCRIPT ¦ MAP ¦ Q ¦ SUB ¦ SUP ¦ SPAN ¦ BDO ¦ IFRAME`)

Form Control elements (`INPUT ¦ SELECT ¦ TEXTAREA ¦ LABEL ¦ BUTTON`)

Formalized: HTML 2.0

Browser: MSIE 1; NNav 1

<FRAME> F

Usage: Defines the contents and appearance of a single frame or subwindow.

Syntax: `<FRAME attributes>`

Start/End Tag: Required/Forbidden

Must be empty? Yes

Attributes: core—See “Common Attributes” section.

`longdesc="URI"`—Links to a resource containing a long description of the frame.

`name="data"`—Names the current frame.

`src="URI"`—Specifies the URI containing the initial contents of the frame.

`frameborder="1 ¦ 0"`—Toggles borders to be drawn around the frame.

`1`—A border is drawn.

`0`—A border is not drawn.

`marginwidth="pixels"`—Sets the margin between the contents of the frame and its left and right borders.

`marginheight="pixels"`—Sets the margin between the contents of the frame and its top and bottom borders.

`noresize`—Prohibits resizing of the frame by the user agent.

`scrolling="auto ¦ yes ¦ no"`—Determines whether the user agent provides scrolling devices for the frame:

`auto`—The user agent provides scrolling devices if necessary.

`yes`—Scrolling devices are provided even if not necessary.

`no`—Scrolling devices are not provided even if necessary.

Content: Empty

Formalized: HTML 4.0

Notes: The contents of a frame must not be in the same document as the frame's definition.

Although found in the transitional DTD, the element is ignored unless the frameset DTD is used.

Browser: MSIE 3; NNav 2

<FRAMESET>...</FRAMESET> F

Usage: Defines the layout of FRAMES within the main window.

Syntax: `<FRAMESET attributes>content</FRAMESET>`

Start/End Tag: Required/Required

Must be empty? No

Attributes: core—See "Common Attributes" section.

`rows="multi-length"`—Defines the horizontal layout, or number of rows, of the FRAMESET.

`cols="multi-length"`—Defines the vertical layout, or number of columns, of the FRAMESET.

`onload="script"`—Intrinsic event triggered when the document loads.

	`onunload="script"`—Intrinsic event triggered when the document unloads.
Content:	One or more FRAMESET or FRAME elements. Zero or one NOFRAMES element
Formalized:	HTML 4.0
Notes:	A frameset document replaces the BODY element with the FRAMESET element. Thus, the frameset document will contain one HTML element containing a HEAD element, which is followed immediately by a FRAMESET. Content between the HEAD and FRAMESET will void the frameset. Although found in the transitional DTD, the element is ignored unless the frameset DTD is used.
Browser:	MSIE 3; NNav 2

<H1>...</H1> Through <H6>...</H6> S

Usage:	The six headings (H1 is the uppermost, or most important) structure information in a hierarchical fashion.
Syntax:	`<Hx attributes>content</Hx>`
Start/End Tag:	Required/Required
Must be empty?	No
Attributes:	core—See "Common Attributes" section. i18n—See "Common Attributes" section. events—See "Intrinsic Events" section. T D `align="left ¦ center ¦ right ¦ justify"`—Horizontal alignment with respect to context. The default depends on the directionality of the text. For left-to-right it is `left`, and for right-to-left it is `right`: `left`—Text aligned left. `center`—Text centered. `right`—Text aligned right. `justify`—Text aligned flush with left and right margins.
Content:	Zero or more inline elements, to include the following: Document text and entities Fontstyle elements (TT ¦ I ¦ B ¦ U ¦ S ¦ STRIKE ¦ BIG ¦ SMALL) Phrase elements (EM ¦ STRONG ¦ DFN ¦ CODE ¦ SAMP ¦ KBD ¦ VAR ¦ CITE ¦ ABBR ¦ ACRONYM)

	Special elements (A ¦ IMG ¦ APPLET ¦ OBJECT ¦ FONT ¦ BASEFONT ¦ BR ¦ SCRIPT ¦ MAP ¦ Q ¦ SUB ¦ SUP ¦ SPAN ¦ BDO ¦ IFRAME)
	Form Control elements (INPUT ¦ SELECT ¦ TEXTAREA ¦ LABEL ¦ BUTTON)
Formalized:	HTML 2.0
Notes:	The headings are rendered from large to small in order of importance (1 to 6).
Browser:	MSIE 1; NNav 1

<HEAD>...</HEAD> S

Usage:	Contains elements that provide information to users and search engines as well as containing other data that is not considered to be document content (for example, style and script information).
Syntax:	*content* or <HEAD *attributes*>*content*</HEAD>
Start/End Tag:	Optional/Optional
Must be empty?	No
Attributes:	i18n—See "Common Attributes" section. profile="*URI*"—Specifies the location of one or more meta data profiles.
Content:	One TITLE element, zero or one ISINDEX, and zero or one BASE elements. Zero or more SCRIPT, STYLE, META, LINK, OBJECT elements.
Formalized:	HTML 2.0
Notes:	Information in the HEAD is not displayed (with the exception of the TITLE, which is displayed in the title bar of the browser). The TITLE element is required.
Browser:	MSIE 1; NNav 1

<HR> S

Usage:	Horizontal rules displayed to separate sections of a document.
Syntax:	<HR *attributes*>
Start/End Tag:	Required/Forbidden
Must be empty?	Yes
Attributes:	core—See "Common Attributes" section. i18n—See "Common Attributes" section (as per the HTML 4.0 Specification Errata, 14 April 1998).

`events`—See "Intrinsic Events" section.

T D `align="left | center | right"`—Alignment of the `HR` with respect to the surrounding context:

`left`—Rule aligned left.

`center`—Rule centered.

`right`—Rule aligned right.

T D `noshade`—Renders the `HR` as a solid color rather than a shaded bump.

T D `size="length"`—Sets the length of the `HR`.

T D `width="length"`—Sets the height of the `HR`.

Content: Empty

Formalized: HTML 2.0

Browser: MSIE 1; NNav 1

<HTML>...</HTML> S

Usage: The topmost container of an `HTML` document.

Syntax: *content*

`<HTML attributes>content</HTML>`

Start/End Tag: Optional/Optional

Must be empty? No

Attributes: `i18n`—See "Common Attributes" section.

T D `version="data"`—Specifies the HTML DTD that governs the current document.

Content: One `HEAD` element and one `BODY` element if using the Strict or Transitional DTD.

One `HEAD` element and one `FRAMESET` element if using the Frameset DTD.

Formalized: HTML 2.0

Notes: `Version` has been deprecated because of its redundancy with the `<!DOCTYPE>` declaration.

Browser: MSIE 1; NNav 1

<I>...</I> S

Usage: Displays italicized text.

Syntax: `<I attributes>content</I>`

Start/End Tag: Required/Required

Must be empty? No

Attributes: core—See "Common Attributes" section.

i18n—See "Common Attributes" section.

events—See "Intrinsic Events" section.

Content: Zero or more inline elements, to include the following:

Document text and entities

Fontstyle elements (TT ¦ I ¦ B ¦ U ¦ S ¦ STRIKE ¦ BIG ¦ SMALL)

Phrase elements (EM ¦ STRONG ¦ DFN ¦ CODE ¦ SAMP ¦ KBD ¦ VAR ¦ CITE ¦ ABBR ¦ ACRONYM)

Special elements (A ¦ IMG ¦ APPLET ¦ OBJECT ¦ FONT ¦ BASEFONT ¦ BR ¦ SCRIPT ¦ MAP ¦ Q ¦ SUB ¦ SUP ¦ SPAN ¦ BDO ¦ IFRAME)

Form Control elements (INPUT ¦ SELECT ¦ TEXTAREA ¦ LABEL ¦ BUTTON)

Formalized: HTML 2.0

Notes: Although not deprecated, the W3C recommends using style sheets in place of this element.

Browser: MSIE 1; NNav 1

<IFRAME>...</IFRAME>

Usage: Creates an inline frame, or window subdivision, within a document.

Syntax: `<IFRAME attributes>content</IFRAME>`

Start/End Tag: Required/Required

Must be empty? No

Attributes: core—See "Common Attributes" section.

longdesc="*URI*"—Links to a resource containing a long description of the frame.

name="*data*"—Names the current frame.

src="*URI*"—Specifies the URI containing the initial contents of the frame.

frameborder="1 ¦ 0"—Toggles borders to be drawn around the frame:

1—A border is drawn.

0—A border is not drawn.

marginwidth="*pixels*"—Sets the margin between the contents of the frame and its left and right borders.

marginheight="*pixels*"—Sets the margin between the contents of the frame and its top and bottom borders.

`noresize`—Prohibits the user agent from resizing the frame.

`scrolling="`**`auto`**` ¦ yes ¦ no"`—Determines whether the user agent provides scrolling devices for the frame:

`auto`—The user agent provides scrolling devices if necessary.

`yes`—Scrolling devices are provided even if not necessary.

`no`—Scrolling devices are not provided even if necessary.

T D `align="top ¦ middle ¦ `**`bottom`**` ¦ left ¦ right"`—Aligns the object with respect to context:

`top`—Vertically aligns the top of the object with the top of the current text line.

`middle`—Vertically aligns the center of the object with the current baseline.

`bottom`—Vertically aligns the bottom of the object with the current baseline.

`left`—Floats object to the left margin.

`right`—Floats object to the right margin.

`height="`*`length`*`"`—Sets the frame height.

`width="`*`length`*`"`—Sets the frame width.

Content: Zero or more block elements, to include the following:

P ¦ DL ¦ DIV ¦ CENTER ¦ NOSCRIPT ¦ NOFRAMES ¦ BLOCKQUOTE ¦ FORM ¦ ISINDEX ¦ HR ¦ TABLE ¦ FIELDSET ¦ ADDRESS

Heading elements (H1 ¦ H2 ¦ H3 ¦ H4 ¦ H5 ¦ H6)

List elements (UL ¦ OL ¦ DIR ¦ MENU)

Preformatted elements (PRE)

Zero or more inline elements, to include the following:

Document text and entities

Fontstyle elements (TT ¦ I ¦ B ¦ U ¦ S ¦ STRIKE ¦ BIG ¦ SMALL)

Phrase elements (EM ¦ STRONG ¦ DFN ¦ CODE ¦ SAMP ¦ KBD ¦ VAR ¦ CITE ¦ ABBR ¦ ACRONYM)

Special elements (A ¦ IMG ¦ APPLET ¦ OBJECT ¦ FONT ¦ BASEFONT ¦ BR ¦ SCRIPT ¦ MAP ¦ Q ¦ SUB ¦ SUP ¦ SPAN ¦ BDO ¦ IFRAME)

Form Control elements (INPUT ¦ SELECT ¦ TEXTAREA ¦ LABEL ¦ BUTTON)

Formalized: HTML 4.0

Notes: The content to be displayed is specified by the src attribute. The content of the element will only be displayed in user agents that do not support frames.

Browser: MSIE 3

<IMG>

Usage: Includes an image in the document.

Syntax: <IMG *attributes*>

Start/End Tag: Required/Forbidden

Must be empty? Yes

Attributes:

core—See "Common Attributes" section.

i18n—See "Common Attributes" section.

events—See "Intrinsic Events" section.

src="*URI*"—Specifies the location of the image to load into the document.

alt="*text*"—Alternate text to be displayed if the user agent cannot render the element.

longdesc="*URI*"—Links to a resource containing a long description of the resource.

height="*length*"—Sets the display height of the image.

width="*length*"—Sets the display width of the image.

usemap="*URI*"—Associates an imagemap as defined by the MAP element with this image.

ismap—Used to define a server-side imagemap. The IMG element must be included in an A element and the ismap attribute set.

align="top ¦ middle ¦ **bottom** ¦ left ¦ right"—Aligns the object with respect to context:

top—Vertically aligns the top of the object with the top of the current text line.

middle—Vertically aligns the center of the object with the current baseline.

bottom—Vertically aligns the bottom of the object with the current baseline.

left—Floats object to the left margin.

right—Floats object to the right margin.

border="*length*"—Sets the border width of the image.

hspace="*pixels*"—Sets the amount of space to be inserted to the left and right of the element.

vspace="*pixels*"—Sets the amount of space to be inserted to the top and bottom of the element.

Content: Empty

Formalized: HTML 2.0

Notes: Has no content.

Browser: MSIE 1; NNav 1

<INPUT>

Usage: Defines controls used in forms.

Syntax: `<INPUT attributes>`

Start/End Tag: Required/Forbidden

Must be empty? Yes

Attributes: core—See "Common Attributes" section.

i18n—See "Common Attributes" section.

events—See "Intrinsic Events" section.

type="**text** ¦ password ¦ checkbox ¦ radio ¦ submit ¦ reset ¦ file ¦ hidden ¦ image ¦ button"—Defines the type of control to create.

text—Creates a single-line text input control.

password—Creates a single-line text input control that hides the characters from the user.

checkbox—Creates a check box.

radio—Creates a radio button.

submit—Creates a submit button.

reset—Creates a reset button.

file—Creates a file select control.

hidden—Creates a hidden control.

image—Creates a graphical submit button that uses the src attribute to locate the image used to decorate the button.

button—Creates a pushbutton.

name="*data*"—Assigns a control name.

value="*data*"—Sets the initial value of the control.

checked—Sets radio buttons and check boxes to a checked state.

disabled—Disables the control in this context.

`readonly`—Changes to the control (text and password) are prohibited.

`size="`*`data`*`"`—Sets the initial size of the control.

`maxlength="`*`number`*`"`—Sets the maximum number of characters a user may enter into a text or password control.

`src="`*`URI`*`"`—Identifies the location of the image when the control type has been set to `image`.

`alt="`*`data`*`"`—Provides a short description of the control.

`usemap="`*`URI`*`"`—Associates an imagemap as defined by the `MAP` element with this control.

`tabindex="`*`number`*`"`—Defines the tabbing order between elements. This is the order (from lowest first to highest last) in which they receive focus when the user navigates through them using the Tab key.

`accesskey="`*`character`*`"`—Assigns an access key (or shortcut key) to the element. When the key is pressed, the element receives focus and is activated.

`onfocus="`*`script`*`"`—Triggered when the element receives focus by either a pointing device (such as a mouse) or tabbed navigation.

`onblur="`*`script`*`"`—Triggered when the element loses focus by either a pointing device (such as a mouse) or tabbed navigation.

`onselect="`*`script`*`"`—The event that occurs when text is selected in a text field.

`onchange="`*`script`*`"`—The event that occurs when a control loses the input focus and its value has been modified since gaining focus.

`accept="`*`content-type`*`"`—A list of content (MIME) types the server will accept for file upload.

T D `align="top | middle |` **`bottom`** `| left | right"`—Aligns the object with respect to context:

`top`—Vertically aligns the top of the object with the top of the current text line.

`middle`—Vertically aligns the center of the object with the current baseline.

`bottom`—Vertically aligns the bottom of the object with the current baseline.

`left`—Floats object to the left margin.

`right`—Floats object to the right margin.

Content: Empty

Formalized: HTML 2.0

Notes: Has no content.

Browser: MSIE 1; NNav 1

<INS>...</INS> S

Usage: Identifies and displays text as having been inserted in the document in relation to a previous version.

Syntax: `<INS attributes>content</INS>`

Start/End Tag: Required/Required

Must be empty? No

Attributes: core—See "Common Attributes" section.

i18n—See "Common Attributes" section.

events—See "Intrinsic Events" section.

cite="*URI*"—A URI pointing to a document that should give reason for the change.

datetime="*datetime*"—Sets the date and time of the change.

Content: Zero or more block elements, to include the following:

P ¦ DL ¦ DIV ¦ CENTER ¦ NOSCRIPT ¦ NOFRAMES ¦ BLOCKQUOTE ¦ FORM ¦ ISINDEX ¦ HR ¦ TABLE ¦ FIELDSET ¦ ADDRESS

Heading elements (H1 ¦ H2 ¦ H3 ¦ H4 ¦ H5 ¦ H6)

List elements (UL ¦ OL ¦ DIR ¦ MENU)

Preformatted elements (PRE)

Zero or more inline elements, to include the following:

Document text and entities

Fontstyle elements (TT ¦ I ¦ B ¦ U ¦ S ¦ STRIKE ¦ BIG ¦ SMALL)

Phrase elements (EM ¦ STRONG ¦ DFN ¦ CODE ¦ SAMP ¦ KBD ¦ VAR ¦ CITE ¦ ABBR ¦ ACRONYM)

Special elements (A ¦ IMG ¦ APPLET ¦ OBJECT ¦ FONT ¦ BASEFONT ¦ BR ¦ SCRIPT ¦ MAP ¦ Q ¦ SUB ¦ SUP ¦ SPAN ¦ BDO ¦ IFRAME)

Form Control elements (INPUT ¦ SELECT ¦ TEXTAREA ¦ LABEL ¦ BUTTON)

Formalized: HTML 4.0

Notes: May serve as a block-level or inline element, but not both at the same time. Changes to nested block-level content should be made at the lowest level.

Browser: MSIE 4

<ISINDEX> T D

Usage:	Creates a single-line text input control.
Syntax:	`<ISINDEX attributes>`
Start/End Tag:	Required/Forbidden
Must be empty?	Yes
Attributes:	core—See "Common Attributes" section.
	i18n—See "Common Attributes" section.
	prompt="*text*"—Displays a prompt for user input.
Content:	Empty
Formalized:	HTML 2.0
Notes:	Deprecated in favor of using INPUT to create text-input controls.
Browser:	MSIE 1; NNav 1

<KBD>...</KBD> S

Usage:	Identifies and displays text a user would enter from a keyboard.
Syntax:	`<KBD attributes>content</KBD>`
Start/End Tag:	Required/Required
Must be empty?	No
Attributes:	core—See "Common Attributes" section.
	i18n—See "Common Attributes" section.
	events—See "Intrinsic Events" section.
Content:	Zero or more inline elements, to include the following: Document text and entities Fontstyle elements (TT ¦ I ¦ B ¦ U ¦ S ¦ STRIKE ¦ BIG ¦ SMALL) Phrase elements (EM ¦ STRONG ¦ DFN ¦ CODE ¦ SAMP ¦ KBD ¦ VAR ¦ CITE ¦ ABBR ¦ ACRONYM) Special elements (A ¦ IMG ¦ APPLET ¦ OBJECT ¦ FONT ¦ BASEFONT ¦ BR ¦ SCRIPT ¦ MAP ¦ Q ¦ SUB ¦ SUP ¦ SPAN ¦ BDO ¦ IFRAME) Form Control elements (INPUT ¦ SELECT ¦ TEXTAREA ¦ LABEL ¦ BUTTON)
Formalized:	HTML 2.0
Notes:	Usually displayed with monospaced font.
Browser:	MSIE 1; NNav 1

<LABEL>...</LABEL> S

Usage: Labels a form control.

Syntax: `<LABEL attributes>content</LABEL>`

Start/End Tag: Required/Required

Must be empty? No

Attributes: core—See "Common Attributes" section.

i18n—See "Common Attributes" section.

events—See "Intrinsic Events" section.

for="*idref*"—Associates the LABEL with a previously identified control.

accesskey="*character*"—Assigns an access key (or shortcut key) to the element. When the key is pressed, the element receives focus and is activated.

onfocus="*script*"—Triggered when the element receives focus by either a pointing device (such as a mouse) or tabbed navigation.

onblur="*script*"—Triggered when the element loses focus by either a pointing device (such as a mouse) or tabbed navigation.

Content: Zero or more inline elements, to include the following:

Document text and entities

Fontstyle elements (TT ¦ I ¦ B ¦ U ¦ S ¦ STRIKE ¦ BIG ¦ SMALL)

Phrase elements (EM ¦ STRONG ¦ DFN ¦ CODE ¦ SAMP ¦ KBD ¦ VAR ¦ CITE ¦ ABBR ¦ ACRONYM)

Special elements (A ¦ IMG ¦ APPLET ¦ OBJECT ¦ FONT ¦ BASEFONT ¦ BR ¦ SCRIPT ¦ MAP ¦ Q ¦ SUB ¦ SUP ¦ SPAN ¦ BDO ¦ IFRAME)

Form Control elements (INPUT ¦ SELECT ¦ TEXTAREA ¦ BUTTON)

Formalized: HTML 4.0

Notes: More than one LABEL may be associated with a control; however, each LABEL is only associated with one control.

Browser: MSIE 4

<LEGEND>...</LEGEND> S

Usage: Assigns a caption to a FIELDSET element.

Syntax: `<LEGEND attributes>content</LEGEND>`

Start/End Tag: Required/Required

Must be empty? No

Attributes: core—See "Common Attributes" section.

i18n—See "Common Attributes" section.

events—See "Intrinsic Events" section.

accesskey="*character*"—Assigns an access key (or shortcut key) to the element. When the key is pressed, the element receives focus and is activated.

T D align="**top** ¦ bottom ¦ left ¦ right"—Specifies the position of the legend with respect to the FIELDSET:

top—Places the legend at the top of the fieldset.

bottom—Places the legend at the bottom of the fieldset.

left—Places the legend at the left side of the fieldset.

right—Places the legend at the right side of the fieldset.

Content: Zero or more inline elements, to include the following:

Document text and entities

Fontstyle elements (TT ¦ I ¦ B ¦ U ¦ S ¦ STRIKE ¦ BIG ¦ SMALL)

Phrase elements (EM ¦ STRONG ¦ DFN ¦ CODE ¦ SAMP ¦ KBD ¦ VAR ¦ CITE ¦ ABBR ¦ ACRONYM)

Special elements (A ¦ IMG ¦ APPLET ¦ OBJECT ¦ FONT ¦ BASEFONT ¦ BR ¦ SCRIPT ¦ MAP ¦ Q ¦ SUB ¦ SUP ¦ SPAN ¦ BDO ¦ IFRAME)

Form Control elements (INPUT ¦ SELECT ¦ TEXTAREA ¦ LABEL ¦ BUTTON)

Formalized: HTML 4.0

Notes: The use of LEGEND improves accessibility for nonvisual user agents as well as aids general understanding of the form layout.

Browser: MSIE 4

<LI>...</LI> S

Usage: Defines a list item within a list.

Syntax: <LI *attributes*>*content*

or

<LI *attributes*>*content*</LI>

Start/End Tag: Required/Optional

Must be empty? No

Attributes: core—See "Common Attributes" section.

i18n—See "Common Attributes" section.

events—See "Intrinsic Events" section.

type="1 ¦ a ¦ A ¦ i ¦ I ¦ disc ¦ square ¦ circle":

1—Arabic numbers.

a—Lowercase alphabet.

A—Uppercase alphabet.

i—Lowercase Roman numerals.

I—Uppercase Roman numerals.

disc—A solid circle.

square—A square outline.

circle—A circle outline.

value="*number*"—Sets the value of the current list item.

Content: Zero or more block elements, to include the following:

P ¦ DL ¦ DIV ¦ CENTER ¦ NOSCRIPT ¦ NOFRAMES ¦ BLOCKQUOTE ¦ FORM ¦ ISINDEX ¦ HR ¦ TABLE ¦ FIELDSET ¦ ADDRESS

Heading elements (H1 ¦ H2 ¦ H3 ¦ H4 ¦ H5 ¦ H6)

List elements (UL ¦ OL ¦ DIR ¦ MENU)

Preformatted elements (PRE)

Zero or more inline elements, to include the following:

Document text and entities

Fontstyle elements (TT ¦ I ¦ B ¦ U ¦ S ¦ STRIKE ¦ BIG ¦ SMALL)

Phrase elements (EM ¦ STRONG ¦ DFN ¦ CODE ¦ SAMP ¦ KBD ¦ VAR ¦ CITE ¦ ABBR ¦ ACRONYM)

Special elements (A ¦ IMG ¦ APPLET ¦ OBJECT ¦ FONT ¦ BASEFONT ¦ BR ¦ SCRIPT ¦ MAP ¦ Q ¦ SUB ¦ SUP ¦ SPAN ¦ BDO ¦ IFRAME)

Form Control elements (INPUT ¦ SELECT ¦ TEXTAREA ¦ LABEL ¦ BUTTON)

Formalized: HTML 2.0

Notes: Used in ordered (OL), unordered (UL), directory (DIR), and menu (MENU) lists.

Browser: MSIE 1; NNav 1

<LINK> S

Usage: Defines a link.

Syntax: `<LINK attributes>`

Start/End Tag: Required/Forbidden

Must be empty? Yes

Attributes:

core—See "Common Attributes" section.

i18n—See "Common Attributes" section.

events—See "Intrinsic Events" section.

charset="*character-set*"—Specifies the character encoding of the linked resource. Values (such as ISO-8859-1 or US-ASCII) must be strings approved and registered by IANA, The Internet Assigned Numbers Authority.

href="*URI*"—Specifies the location of the linked resource or anchor.

hreflang="*language-code*"—Identifies the language of the linked resource. This attribute may only be used in conjunction with the href attribute.

type="*content-type*"—Specifies the content or media (MIME) type (such as text/html) of the linked resource.

rel="*link-type*"—Defines the relationship between the document and that specified by the href attribute.

rev="*link-type*"—Defines the relationship between the resource specified by the href attribute and the current document.

media="*media-descriptor*"—Identifies the intended destination medium for style information. The default is screen.

T target="*user-defined* ¦ _blank ¦ _self ¦ _parent ¦ _top"—Identifies the frame in which the linked resource will be opened:

user-defined—Document opens in the frame designated by the *user-defined* name, which is set by the name attribute of the frame. The name must begin with an alphabetic character.

_blank—Document opens in a new, unnamed window.

_self—Document opens in same frame as the originating link.

_parent—Document opens in the immediate FRAMESET parent of the current frame, or itself if the current frame has no parent.

_top—Document opens in the full, original window, or itself if the frame has no parent.

Content: Empty

Formalized: HTML 2.0

Notes: May only be used in the HEAD of a document, but any number of LINK elements can be used.

Common uses are linking to external style sheets, scripts, and search engines.

Browser: MSIE 2; NNav 4

<MAP>…</MAP> S

Usage: Specifies a client-side imagemap.

Syntax: `<MAP attributes>content</MAP>`

Start/End Tag: Required/Required

Must be empty? No

Attributes: core—See "Common Attributes" section.

i18n—See "Common Attributes" section.

events—See "Intrinsic Events" section.

name="*data*"—Assigns a name to the imagemap.

Content: Zero or more block elements, to include the following:

P ¦ DL ¦ DIV ¦ CENTER ¦ NOSCRIPT ¦ NOFRAMES ¦ BLOCKQUOTE ¦ FORM ¦ ISINDEX ¦ HR ¦ TABLE ¦ FIELDSET ¦ ADDRESS

Heading elements (H1 ¦ H2 ¦ H3 ¦ H4 ¦ H5 ¦ H6)

List elements (UL ¦ OL ¦ DIR ¦ MENU)

Preformatted elements (PRE)

or

One or more AREA elements

Formalized: HTML 3.2

Notes: Can be associated with IMG, OBJECT, or INPUT elements via each element's usemap attribute.

Browser: MSIE 1; NNav 2

<MENU>…</MENU> T D

Usage: Creates a single-column menu list.

Syntax: `<MENU attributes>content</MENU>`

Start/End Tag: Required/Required

Must be empty? No

Attributes: core—See "Common Attributes" section.

i18n—See "Common Attributes" section.

	`events`—See "Intrinsic Events" section.
	(T) (D) `compact`—Tells the browser to attempt to display the list more compactly.
Content:	One or more `LI` elements, which may contain the following: List elements (`UL` ¦ `OL` ¦ `DIR` ¦ `MENU`) Zero or more inline elements, to include the following: Document text and entities Fontstyle elements (`TT` ¦ `I` ¦ `B` ¦ `U` ¦ `S` ¦ `STRIKE` ¦ `BIG` ¦ `SMALL`) Phrase elements (`EM` ¦ `STRONG` ¦ `DFN` ¦ `CODE` ¦ `SAMP` ¦ `KBD` ¦ `VAR` ¦ `CITE` ¦ `ABBR` ¦ `ACRONYM`) Special elements (`A` ¦ `IMG` ¦ `APPLET` ¦ `OBJECT` ¦ `FONT` ¦ `BASEFONT` ¦ `BR` ¦ `SCRIPT` ¦ `MAP` ¦ `Q` ¦ `SUB` ¦ `SUP` ¦ `SPAN` ¦ `BDO` ¦ `IFRAME`) Form Control elements (`INPUT` ¦ `SELECT` ¦ `TEXTAREA` ¦ `LABEL` ¦ `BUTTON`)
Formalized:	HTML 2.0
Notes:	Deprecated in favor of unordered lists (`UL`).
Browser:	MSIE 1; NNav 1

<META> (S)

Usage:	Provides information about the document.
Syntax:	`<META attributes>`
Start/End Tag:	Required/Forbidden
Must be empty?	Yes
Attributes:	`i18n`—See "Common Attributes" section. `http-equiv="name"`—Identifies a name with the meta-information, which may be used by HTTP servers gathering information. `name="name"`—Identifies a name with the meta-information. `content="data"`—The content of the meta-information. `scheme="data"`—Gives user agents more context for interpreting the information in the `content` attribute.
Content:	Empty
Formalized:	HTML 2.0
Notes:	Each `META` element specifies a property/value pair. The `name` attribute identifies the property, and the `content` attribute specifies the property's value.

There can be any number of META elements within the HEAD element.

Browser: MSIE 2; NNav 1.1

<NOFRAMES>...</NOFRAMES> F

Usage: Specifies alternative content when frames are not supported.

Syntax: `<NOFRAMES attributes>content</NOFRAMES>`

Start/End Tag: Required/Required

Must be empty? No

Attributes: core—See “Common Attributes” section.

i18n—See “Common Attributes” section.

events—See “Intrinsic Events” section.

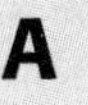

Content: User agents will treat content as in the BODY element (excluding NOFRAMES) if configured to support the NOFRAME element.

Otherwise:

Zero or more block elements, to include the following:

P ¦ DL ¦ DIV ¦ CENTER ¦ NOSCRIPT ¦ NOFRAMES ¦ BLOCKQUOTE ¦ FORM ¦ ISINDEX ¦ HR ¦ TABLE ¦ FIELDSET ¦ ADDRESS

Heading elements (H1 ¦ H2 ¦ H3 ¦ H4 ¦ H5 ¦ H6)

List elements (UL ¦ OL ¦ DIR ¦ MENU)

Preformatted elements (PRE)

Zero or more inline elements, to include the following:

Document text and entities

Fontstyle elements (TT ¦ I ¦ B ¦ U ¦ S ¦ STRIKE ¦ BIG ¦ SMALL)

Phrase elements (EM ¦ STRONG ¦ DFN ¦ CODE ¦ SAMP ¦ KBD ¦ VAR ¦ CITE ¦ ABBR ¦ ACRONYM)

Special elements (A ¦ IMG ¦ APPLET ¦ OBJECT ¦ FONT ¦ BASEFONT ¦ BR ¦ SCRIPT ¦ MAP ¦ Q ¦ SUB ¦ SUP ¦ SPAN ¦ BDO ¦ IFRAME)

Form Control elements (INPUT ¦ SELECT ¦ TEXTAREA ¦ LABEL ¦ BUTTON)

Formalized: HTML 4.0

Notes: The NOFRAMES element can be used within the FRAMESET element.

Browser: MSIE 3; NNav 2

<NOSCRIPT>...</NOSCRIPT> S

Usage: Provides alternative content for browsers unable to execute a script.

Syntax: `<NOSCRIPT attributes>content</NOSCRIPT>`

Start/End Tag: Required/Required

Must be empty? No

Attributes: core—See "Common Attributes" section.

i18n—See "Common Attributes" section.

events—See "Intrinsic Events" section.

Content: Zero or more block elements, to include the following:

P ¦ DL ¦ DIV ¦ CENTER ¦ NOSCRIPT ¦ NOFRAMES ¦ BLOCKQUOTE ¦ FORM ¦ ISINDEX ¦ HR ¦ TABLE ¦ FIELDSET ¦ ADDRESS

Heading elements (H1 ¦ H2 ¦ H3 ¦ H4 ¦ H5 ¦ H6)

List elements (UL ¦ OL ¦ DIR ¦ MENU)

Preformatted elements (PRE)

Zero or more inline elements, to include the following:

Document text and entities

Fontstyle elements (TT ¦ I ¦ B ¦ U ¦ S ¦ STRIKE ¦ BIG ¦ SMALL)

Phrase elements (EM ¦ STRONG ¦ DFN ¦ CODE ¦ SAMP ¦ KBD ¦ VAR ¦ CITE ¦ ABBR ¦ ACRONYM)

Special elements (A ¦ IMG ¦ APPLET ¦ OBJECT ¦ FONT ¦ BASEFONT ¦ BR ¦ SCRIPT ¦ MAP ¦ Q ¦ SUB ¦ SUP ¦ SPAN ¦ BDO ¦ IFRAME)

Form Control elements (INPUT ¦ SELECT ¦ TEXTAREA ¦ LABEL ¦ BUTTON)

Formalized: HTML 4.0

Notes: The content of the element should only be rendered if the user agent does not support scripting.

Browser: MSIE 3; NNav 3

<OBJECT>...</OBJECT> S

Usage: Includes an external object in the document such as an image, a Java applet, or other external application.

Syntax: `<OBJECT attributes>content</OBJECT>`

Start/End Tag: Required/Required

Must be empty? No

Attributes:

core—See "Common Attributes" section.

i18n—See "Common Attributes" section.

events—See "Intrinsic Events" section.

declare—Indicates the object will be declared only and not instantiated.

classid="*URI*"—Used to locate an object's implementation.

codebase="*URI*"—Sets the base URI for the object. If not specified, the default value is the base URI of the current document.

data="*URI*"—Identifies the location of the object's data.

type="*content-type*"—Specifies the content or media (MIME) type (such as application/mpeg) of the object identified by the data attribute.

codetype="*content-type*"—Identifies the content type (MIME) of the data to be downloaded.

archive="*URI*"—List URIs (separated by spaces) for archives containing classes and other resources that will be preloaded. This could significantly speed up object performance.

standby="*text*"—Provides a message to be displayed while the object loads.

height="*length*"—Sets the display height of the object.

width="*length*"—Sets the display width of the object.

usemap="*URI*"—Associates an imagemap as defined by the MAP element with this object.

name="*data*"—Assigns a control name to the object for use as part of a FORM.

tabindex="*number*"—Defines the tabbing order between elements. This is the order (from lowest first to highest last) in which they receive focus when the user navigates through them using the Tab key.

T D align="top ¦ middle ¦ **bottom** ¦ left ¦ right"—Aligns the object with respect to context:

top—Vertically aligns the top of the object with the top of the current text line.

middle—Vertically aligns the center of the object with the current baseline.

bottom—Vertically aligns the bottom of the object with the current baseline.

left—Floats object to the left margin.

right—Floats object to the right margin.

T D border="*pixels*"—Sets the width of the border drawn around the object.

T D hspace="*pixels*"—Sets the amount of space to be inserted to the left and right of the element.

T D vspace="*pixels*"—Sets the amount of space to be inserted to the top and bottom of the element.

Content: One or more PARAM elements.

Zero or more block elements, to include the following:

P ¦ DL ¦ DIV ¦ CENTER ¦ NOSCRIPT ¦ NOFRAMES ¦ BLOCKQUOTE ¦ FORM ¦ ISINDEX ¦ HR ¦ TABLE ¦ FIELDSET ¦ ADDRESS

Heading elements (H1 ¦ H2 ¦ H3 ¦ H4 ¦ H5 ¦ H6)

List elements (UL ¦ OL ¦ DIR ¦ MENU)

Preformatted elements (PRE)

Zero or more inline elements, to include the following:

Document text and entities

Fontstyle elements (TT ¦ I ¦ B ¦ U ¦ S ¦ STRIKE ¦ BIG ¦ SMALL)

Phrase elements (EM ¦ STRONG ¦ DFN ¦ CODE ¦ SAMP ¦ KBD ¦ VAR ¦ CITE ¦ ABBR ¦ ACRONYM)

Special elements (A ¦ IMG ¦ APPLET ¦ OBJECT ¦ FONT ¦ BASEFONT ¦ BR ¦ SCRIPT ¦ MAP ¦ Q ¦ SUB ¦ SUP ¦ SPAN ¦ BDO ¦ IFRAME)

Form Control elements (INPUT ¦ SELECT ¦ TEXTAREA ¦ LABEL ¦ BUTTON)

Formalized: HTML 4.0

Notes: May appear in the HEAD, although it will generally not be rendered. In such cases it is wise to limit OBJECT elements in the HEAD to those with content not requiring visual rendering.

The OBJECT content is meant to be rendered by user agents that do not support the specified type of OBJECT.

OBJECT elements can be nested, allowing the author to provide the same object in various forms in a preferred order.

Browser: MSIE 3

<OL>...</OL> S

Usage: Creates an ordered, or numbered, list.

Syntax: `<OL attributes>content</OL>`

Start/End Tag: Required/Required

Must be empty? No

Attributes:

core—See "Common Attributes" section.

`i18n`—See "Common Attributes" section.

`events`—See "Intrinsic Events" section.

T D `type="1 ¦ a ¦ A ¦ i ¦ I"`:

`1`—Arabic numbers.

`a`—Lowercase alphabet.

`A`—Uppercase alphabet.

`i`—Lowercase Roman numerals.

`I`—Uppercase Roman numerals.

T D `compact`—Tells the browser to attempt to display the list more compactly.

T D `start="number"`—Sets the starting number of the ordered list.

Content: One or more `LI` element

Formalized: HTML 2.0

Notes: When the `start` attribute is a number and the list type is non-numeric, the `start` value refers to that number in the sequence of non-numeric values.

Nested lists are allowed.

Browser: MSIE 1; NNav 1

<OPTGROUP>...</OPTGROUP> S

Usage: Used to group `OPTION` elements within a `SELECT` element.

Syntax: `<OPTGROUP attributes>content</OPTGROUP>`

Start/End Tag: Required/Required

Must be empty? No

Attributes:

core—See "Common Attributes" section.

`i18n`—See "Common Attributes" section.

`events`—See "Intrinsic Events" section.

`disabled`—Disables these controls for user input.

`label="text"`—Labels the option group.

Content: One or more OPTION elements.

Formalized: HTML 4.0

Notes: All OPTGROUP elements must be specified in the SELECT element and cannot be nested.

Browser: None at this time.

<OPTION>...</OPTION> S

Usage: Specifies choices in a SELECT element.

Syntax: `<OPTION attributes>content`

or

`<OPTION attributes>content</OPTION>`

Start/End Tag: Required/Optional

Must be empty? No

Attributes: core—See "Common Attributes" section.

i18n—See "Common Attributes" section.

events—See "Intrinsic Events" section.

selected—Sets the option as being preselected.

disabled—Disables these controls for user input.

label="*text*"—Provides a shorter label for the option than that specified in its content.

value="*data*"—Sets the initial value of the control.

Content: Document text.

Formalized: HTML 2.0

Notes: If the label attribute is not set, user agents will use the contents of the element as the option.

OPTION elements may be grouped in an OPTGROUP element.

Browser: MSIE 1; NNav 1

<P>...</P> S

Usage: Defines a paragraph.

Syntax: `<P attributes>content` or

`<P attributes>content</P>`

Start/End Tag: Required/Optional

Must be empty? No

Attributes: core—See "Common Attributes" section.

i18n—See "Common Attributes" section.

events—See "Intrinsic Events" section.

align="left ¦ center ¦ right ¦ justify"—Horizontal alignment with respect to context. The default depends on the directionality of the text. For left-to-right it is left, and for right-to-left it is right:

left—Text aligned left.

center—Text centered.

right—Text aligned right.

justify—Text aligned flush with left and right margins.

Content: Zero or more inline elements, to include the following:

- Document text and entities
- Fontstyle elements (TT ¦ I ¦ B ¦ U ¦ S ¦ STRIKE ¦ BIG ¦ SMALL)
- Phrase elements (EM ¦ STRONG ¦ DFN ¦ CODE ¦ SAMP ¦ KBD ¦ VAR ¦ CITE ¦ ABBR ¦ ACRONYM)
- Special elements (A ¦ IMG ¦ APPLET ¦ OBJECT ¦ FONT ¦ BASEFONT ¦ BR ¦ SCRIPT ¦ MAP ¦ Q ¦ SUB ¦ SUP ¦ SPAN ¦ BDO ¦ IFRAME)
- Form Control elements (INPUT ¦ SELECT ¦ TEXTAREA ¦ LABEL ¦ BUTTON)

Formalized: HTML 2.0

Notes: Cannot contain block-level elements.

Browser: MSIE 1; NNav 1

<PARAM> S

Usage: Specifies a set of values that may be required by an object at runtime.

Syntax: <PARAM *attributes*>

Start/End Tag: Required/Forbidden

Must be empty? Yes

Attributes: id="*id*"—A unique identification of the element.

name="*data*"—Defines the name of a runtime parameter required by an object (such as width).

value="*data*"—Sets the value required by the runtime parameter previously identified and named.

valuetype="**data** ¦ ref ¦ object"—Identifies the type of runtime parameter being used in the value attribute:

data—Indicates the value will be passed to the OBJECT implementation as a string.

	`ref`—Indicates the `value` is a reference to a URI where run-time values are stored.
	`object`—Indicates that the `value` identifies an `OBJECT` in the same document. The identifier must be the value of the `id` attribute set for the declared `OBJECT`.
	`type="content-type"`—Specifies the content or media (MIME) type (such as `application/mpeg`) of the object when the `valuetype` attribute is set to `ref` (but not `date` or `object`).
Content:	Empty
Formalized:	HTML 4.0
Notes:	Multiple `PARAM` elements are allowed in either the `OBJECT` or `APPLET` elements but must immediately follow the opening tag.
Browser:	MSIE 3; NNav 2

<PRE>...</PRE> S

Usage:	Displays preformatted text, which normally includes extra whitespace and line breaks.
Syntax:	`<PRE attributes>content</PRE>`
Start/End Tag:	Required/Required
Must be empty?	No
Attributes:	core—See "Common Attributes" section.
	`i18n`—See "Common Attributes" section.
	`events`—See "Intrinsic Events" section.
	T D `width="number"`—Identifies the desired width of the preformatted content block.
Content:	Zero or more inline elements, to include the following:
	Document text and entities
	Fontstyle elements (`TT` ¦ `I` ¦ `B` ¦ `U` ¦ `S` ¦ `STRIKE`)
	Phrase elements (`EM` ¦ `STRONG` ¦ `DFN` ¦ `CODE` ¦ `SAMP` ¦ `KBD` ¦ `VAR` ¦ `CITE` ¦ `ABBR` ¦ `ACRONYM`)
	Special elements (`A` ¦ `BR` ¦ `SCRIPT` ¦ `MAP` ¦ `Q` ¦ `SPAN` ¦ `BDO` ¦ `IFRAME`)
	Form Control elements (`INPUT` ¦ `SELECT` ¦ `TEXTAREA` ¦ `LABEL` ¦ `BUTTON`)
Formalized:	HTML 2.0
Notes:	The use of tabs in preformatted text is strongly discouraged because of the possibility of misaligned content.
Browser:	MSIE 1; NNav 1

<Q>...</Q> S

Usage: Designates text as a short quotation.

Syntax: `<Q attributes>content</Q>`

Start/End Tag: Required/Required

Must be empty? No

Attributes: core—See "Common Attributes" section.

i18n—See "Common Attributes" section.

events—See "Intrinsic Events" section.

cite="*URI*"—The URI designating the source document or message.

Content: Zero or more inline elements, to include the following:

- Document text and entities
- Fontstyle elements (TT ¦ I ¦ B ¦ U ¦ S ¦ STRIKE ¦ BIG ¦ SMALL)
- Phrase elements (EM ¦ STRONG ¦ DFN ¦ CODE ¦ SAMP ¦ KBD ¦ VAR ¦ CITE ¦ ABBR ¦ ACRONYM)
- Special elements (A ¦ IMG ¦ APPLET ¦ OBJECT ¦ FONT ¦ BASEFONT ¦ BR ¦ SCRIPT ¦ MAP ¦ Q ¦ SUB ¦ SUP ¦ SPAN ¦ BDO ¦ IFRAME)
- Form Control elements (INPUT ¦ SELECT ¦ TEXTAREA ¦ LABEL ¦ BUTTON)

Formalized: HTML 4.0

Notes: When compared with the BLOCKQUOTE element, the Q element is used for shorter quotations not normally requiring a line break and is treated as inline content.

Quotation marks should be rendered by the browser.

Browser: MSIE 4

<S>...</S> T D

Usage: Displays text as strikethrough.

Syntax: `<S attributes>content</S>`

Start/End Tag: Required/Required

Must be empty? No

Attributes: core—See "Common Attributes" section.

i18n—See "Common Attributes" section.

events—See "Intrinsic Events" section.

Content: Zero or more inline elements, to include the following:

Document text and entities

Fontstyle elements (TT ¦ I ¦ B ¦ U ¦ S ¦ STRIKE ¦ BIG ¦ SMALL)

Phrase elements (EM ¦ STRONG ¦ DFN ¦ CODE ¦ SAMP ¦ KBD ¦ VAR ¦ CITE ¦ ABBR ¦ ACRONYM)

Special elements (A ¦ IMG ¦ APPLET ¦ OBJECT ¦ FONT ¦ BASEFONT ¦ BR ¦ SCRIPT ¦ MAP ¦ Q ¦ SUB ¦ SUP ¦ SPAN ¦ BDO ¦ IFRAME)

Form Control elements (INPUT ¦ SELECT ¦ TEXTAREA ¦ LABEL ¦ BUTTON)

Formalized: HTML 4.0

Notes: Although not deprecated, the W3C recommends using style sheets in place of this element.

Browser: MSIE 1; NNav 3

<SAMP>...</SAMP> S

Usage: Identifies and displays sample output from a computer program, script, and so on.

Syntax: `<SAMP attributes>content</SAMP>`

Start/End Tag: Required/Required

Must be empty? No

Attributes: core—See "Common Attributes" section.

i18n—See "Common Attributes" section.

events—See "Intrinsic Events" section.

Content: Zero or more inline elements, to include the following:

Document text and entities

Fontstyle elements (TT ¦ I ¦ B ¦ U ¦ S ¦ STRIKE ¦ BIG ¦ SMALL)

Phrase elements (EM ¦ STRONG ¦ DFN ¦ CODE ¦ SAMP ¦ KBD ¦ VAR ¦ CITE ¦ ABBR ¦ ACRONYM)

Special elements (A ¦ IMG ¦ APPLET ¦ OBJECT ¦ FONT ¦ BASEFONT ¦ BR ¦ SCRIPT ¦ MAP ¦ Q ¦ SUB ¦ SUP ¦ SPAN ¦ BDO ¦ IFRAME)

Form Control elements (INPUT ¦ SELECT ¦ TEXTAREA ¦ LABEL ¦ BUTTON)

Formalized: HTML 2.0

Notes: Usually displayed with monospaced font.

Browser: MSIE 1; NNav 1

<SCRIPT>...</SCRIPT> S

Usage: Inserts a script into the document.

Syntax: `<SCRIPT attributes>content</SCRIPT>`

Start/End Tag: Required/Required

Must be empty? No

Attributes:

charset="*character-set*"—Specifies the character encoding of the linked resource. Values (such as ISO-8859-1 or US-ASCII) must be strings approved and registered by IANA, The Internet Assigned Numbers Authority.

type="*content-type*"—Specifies the content or media (MIME) type (such as text/javascript) of the script language.

T D language="*data*"—Specifies the scripting language through a predefined name.

src="*URI*"—Identifies the location of an external script.

defer—Indicates to the user agent that no document content will be output by the script and it may continue rendering the page.

Content: Script expression

Formalized: HTML 3.2

Notes: May appear any number of times in the HEAD or BODY of the document.

If the src attribute is present, the user agent loads an external script. Otherwise, the content of the element is treated as the script.

Browser: MSIE 3; NNav 2

<SELECT>...</SELECT> S

Usage: Creates a menu whose choices are represented by OPTION elements, either separately or grouped into OPTGROUP elements.

Syntax: `<SELECT attributes>content</SELECT>`

Start/End Tag: Required/Required

Must be empty? No

Attributes:

core—See "Common Attributes" section.

i18n—See "Common Attributes" section.

events—See "Intrinsic Events" section.

name="*data*"—Assigns a name to the control.

size="*number*"—If represented by a scrolling list box, this sets the number of choices to be displayed at one time.

PART X

APP A

multiple—Allows multiple selections.

disabled—Disables these controls for user input.

tabindex="*number*"—Defines the tabbing order between elements. This is the order (from lowest first to highest last) in which they receive focus when the user navigates through them using the Tab key.

onfocus="*script*"—Triggered when the element receives focus by either a pointing device (such as a mouse) or tabbed navigation.

onblur="*script*"—Triggered when the element loses focus by either a pointing device (such as a mouse) or tabbed navigation.

onchange="*script*"—The event that occurs when a control loses the input focus and its value has been modified since gaining focus.

Content: One or more OPTGROUP or OPTION elements.

Formalized: HTML 2.0

Notes: Must contain at least one OPTION element.

All OPTGROUP elements must be specified in the SELECT element and cannot be nested.

Browser: MSIE 1; NNav 1

<SMALL>...</SMALL> S

Usage: Displays reduced-size or smaller text.

Syntax: <SMALL *attributes*>*content*</SMALL>

Start/End Tag: Required/Required

Must be empty? No

Attributes: core—See "Common Attributes" section.

i18n—See "Common Attributes" section.

events—See "Intrinsic Events" section.

Content: Zero or more inline elements, to include the following:

Document text and entities

Fontstyle elements (TT ¦ I ¦ B ¦ U ¦ S ¦ STRIKE ¦ BIG ¦ SMALL)

Phrase elements (EM ¦ STRONG ¦ DFN ¦ CODE ¦ SAMP ¦ KBD ¦ VAR ¦ CITE ¦ ABBR ¦ ACRONYM)

Special elements (A ¦ IMG ¦ APPLET ¦ OBJECT ¦ FONT ¦ BASEFONT ¦ BR ¦ SCRIPT ¦ MAP ¦ Q ¦ SUB ¦ SUP ¦ SPAN ¦ BDO ¦ IFRAME)

Form Control elements (INPUT ¦ SELECT ¦ TEXTAREA ¦ LABEL ¦ BUTTON)

Formalized: HTML 3.2

Notes: Although not deprecated, the W3C recommends using style sheets in place of this element.

Browser: MSIE 3; NNav 1.1

<SPAN>...</SPAN> (S)

Usage: Creates user-defined inline structure to the document.

Syntax: `<SPAN attributes>content</SPAN>`

Start/End Tag: Required/Required

Must be empty? No

Attributes: core—See "Common Attributes" section.

i18n—See "Common Attributes" section.

events—See "Intrinsic Events" section.

Content: Zero or more inline elements, to include the following:

Document text and entities

Fontstyle elements (TT ¦ I ¦ B ¦ U ¦ S ¦ STRIKE ¦ BIG ¦ SMALL)

Phrase elements (EM ¦ STRONG ¦ DFN ¦ CODE ¦ SAMP ¦ KBD ¦ VAR ¦ CITE ¦ ABBR ¦ ACRONYM)

Special elements (A ¦ IMG ¦ APPLET ¦ OBJECT ¦ FONT ¦ BASEFONT ¦ BR ¦ SCRIPT ¦ MAP ¦ Q ¦ SUB ¦ SUP ¦ SPAN ¦ BDO ¦ IFRAME)

Form Control elements (INPUT ¦ SELECT ¦ TEXTAREA ¦ LABEL ¦ BUTTON)

Formalized: HTML 4.0

Notes: Used in conjunction with style sheets, this is a powerful device for adding custom inline structure.

Browser: MSIE 3; NNav 4

<STRIKE>...</STRIKE> (T) (D)

Usage: Text displayed as strikethrough.

Syntax: `<STRIKE attributes>content</STRIKE>`

Start/End Tag: Required/Required

Must be empty? No

Attributes: core—See "Common Attributes" section.

i18n—See "Common Attributes" section.

events—See "Intrinsic Events" section.

Content: Zero or more inline elements, to include the following:

Document text and entities

Fontstyle elements (TT ¦ I ¦ B ¦ U ¦ S ¦ STRIKE ¦ BIG ¦ SMALL)

Phrase elements (EM ¦ STRONG ¦ DFN ¦ CODE ¦ SAMP ¦ KBD ¦ VAR ¦ CITE ¦ ABBR ¦ ACRONYM)

Special elements (A ¦ IMG ¦ APPLET ¦ OBJECT ¦ FONT ¦ BASEFONT ¦ BR ¦ SCRIPT ¦ MAP ¦ Q ¦ SUB ¦ SUP ¦ SPAN ¦ BDO ¦ IFRAME)

Form Control elements (INPUT ¦ SELECT ¦ TEXTAREA ¦ LABEL ¦ BUTTON)

Formalized: HTML 3.2

Notes: Deprecated in favor of style sheets.

Browser: MSIE 1; NNav 1.1

<STRONG>...</STRONG> S

Usage: Displays text with a stronger emphasis in relation to normal text than that of the EM element.

Syntax: `<STRONG attributes>content</STRONG>`

Start/End Tag: Required/Required

Must be empty? No

Attributes: core—See "Common Attributes" section.

i18n—See "Common Attributes" section.

events—See "Intrinsic Events" section.

Content: Zero or more inline elements, to include the following:

Document text and entities

Fontstyle elements (TT ¦ I ¦ B ¦ U ¦ S ¦ STRIKE ¦ BIG ¦ SMALL)

Phrase elements (EM ¦ STRONG ¦ DFN ¦ CODE ¦ SAMP ¦ KBD ¦ VAR ¦ CITE ¦ ABBR ¦ ACRONYM)

Special elements (A ¦ IMG ¦ APPLET ¦ OBJECT ¦ FONT ¦ BASEFONT ¦ BR ¦ SCRIPT ¦ MAP ¦ Q ¦ SUB ¦ SUP ¦ SPAN ¦ BDO ¦ IFRAME)

Form Control elements (INPUT ¦ SELECT ¦ TEXTAREA ¦ LABEL ¦ BUTTON)

Formalized: HTML 2.0

Notes: Usually rendered in boldface font.

Browser: MSIE 1; NNav 1

<STYLE>...</STYLE> S

Usage: Creates style sheet rules for use in the document.

Syntax: `<STYLE attributes>content</STYLE>`

Start/End Tag: Required/Required

Must be empty? No

Attributes: i18n—See "Common Attributes" section.

type="*content-type*"—Specifies the content or media (MIME) type (such as text/css) of the style language.

media="*media-descriptor*"—Identifies the intended medium (such as screen) of the style information.

title="*text*"—Offers advisory information about the element.

Content: Style sheet rules

Formalized: HTML 3.2

Notes: Any number of STYLE elements may be present, but they must be in the HEAD element only.

User agents that do not support the element should not render its contents.

Browser: MSIE 3; NNav 4

_{...} S

Usage: Displays text as subscript (lower in vertical alignment) in relation to surrounding text.

Syntax: `<SUB attributes>content</SUB>`

Start/End Tag: Required/Required

Must be empty? No

Attributes: core—See "Common Attributes" section.

i18n—See "Common Attributes" section.

events—See "Intrinsic Events" section.

Content: Zero or more inline elements, to include the following:

Document text and entities

Fontstyle elements (TT ¦ I ¦ B ¦ U ¦ S ¦ STRIKE ¦ BIG ¦ SMALL)

Phrase elements (EM ¦ STRONG ¦ DFN ¦ CODE ¦ SAMP ¦ KBD ¦ VAR ¦ CITE ¦ ABBR ¦ ACRONYM)

Special elements (A ¦ IMG ¦ APPLET ¦ OBJECT ¦ FONT ¦ BASEFONT ¦ BR ¦ SCRIPT ¦ MAP ¦ Q ¦ SUB ¦ SUP ¦ SPAN ¦ BDO ¦ IFRAME)

Form Control elements (INPUT ¦ SELECT ¦ TEXTAREA ¦ LABEL ¦ BUTTON)

Formalized: HTML 3.2

Browser: MSIE 3; NNav 1.1

^{...} S

Usage: Displays text as superscript (higher in vertical alignment) in relation to surrounding text.

Syntax: `<SUP attributes>content</SUP>`

Start/End Tag: Required/Required

Must be empty? No

Attributes: core—See “Common Attributes” section.

i18n—See “Common Attributes” section.

events—See “Intrinsic Events” section.

Content: Zero or more inline elements, to include the following:

Document text and entities

Fontstyle elements (TT ¦ I ¦ B ¦ U ¦ S ¦ STRIKE ¦ BIG ¦ SMALL)

Phrase elements (EM ¦ STRONG ¦ DFN ¦ CODE ¦ SAMP ¦ KBD ¦ VAR ¦ CITE ¦ ABBR ¦ ACRONYM)

Special elements (A ¦ IMG ¦ APPLET ¦ OBJECT ¦ FONT ¦ BASEFONT ¦ BR ¦ SCRIPT ¦ MAP ¦ Q ¦ SUB ¦ SUP ¦ SPAN ¦ BDO ¦ IFRAME)

Form Control elements (INPUT ¦ SELECT ¦ TEXTAREA ¦ LABEL ¦ BUTTON)

Formalized: HTML 3.2

Browser: MSIE 3; NNav 1.1

<TABLE>...</TABLE> S

Usage: Creates a table.

Syntax: `<TABLE attributes>content</TABLE>`

Start/End Tag: Required/Required

Must be empty? No

Attributes:

core—See "Common Attributes" section.

i18n—See "Common Attributes" section.

events—See "Intrinsic Events" section.

`summary="`*`text`*`"`—Text explanation of table structure and purpose for nonvisual user agents.

`width="`*`length`*`"`—Sets width of entire table.

`border="`*`pixels`*`"`—Sets the width of a border drawn around the table.

`frame="`**`void`**` | above | below | hsides | lhs | rhs | vsides | box | border"`—Specifies which borders around the table are visible:

void—No sides visible.

above—Top side only.

below—Bottom side only.

hsides—Top and bottom only.

lhs—Left side only.

rhs—Right side only.

vsides—Left and right sides only.

box—Top, bottom, left, and right sides.

border—Top, bottom, left, and right sides.

`rules="`**`none`**` | groups | rows | cols | all"`—Specifies which interior rules of the table are visible:

none—No rules visible.

groups—Rules appear between row groups and column groups only.

rows—Rules between rows only.

cols—Rules between columns only.

all—Rules visible between rows and columns.

`cellspacing="`*`length`*`"`—Determines the spacing between cells.

`cellpadding="`*`length`*`"`—Determines the space between cell content and its borders.

T D `align="`**`left`**` | center | right"`—Aligns the TABLE with respect to the page. Left-to-right is the default inherited directionality, but this can be overridden using the dir attribute:

left—Table aligned left.

center—Table centered.

right—Table aligned right.

	T D bgcolor="*color*"—Sets the background color for cells in the table. Colors identified by standard RGB in hexadecimal format (*#RRGGBB*) or by predefined color name.
Content:	Zero or one CAPTION element
	Zero or more COL or COLGROUP elements
	Zero or one THEAD element
	Zero or one TFOOT element
	One or more TBODY elements
Formalized:	HTML 3.2
Notes:	The TABLE element has no content by itself but relies on other elements to specify content and other formatting attributes.
Browser:	MSIE 2; NNav 1.1

<TBODY>...</TBODY> S

Usage:	Groups table rows into a table body.
Syntax:	*content*
	<TBODY *attributes*>*content*</TBODY>
Start/End Tag:	Optional/Optional
Must be empty?	No
Attributes:	core—See "Common Attributes" section.
	i18n—See "Common Attributes" section.
	events—See "Intrinsic Events" section.
	align="left ¦ center ¦ right ¦ justify ¦ char"—Horizontally aligns the contents of cells:
	left—Data and text aligned left. This is the default for table data.
	center—Data and text centered. This is the default for table headers.
	right—Data and text aligned right.
	justify—Data and text aligned flush with left and right margins.
	char—Aligns text around a specific character.
	char="*character*"—Sets a character on which the column aligns (such as ":"). The default value is the decimal point of the current language.
	charoff="*length*"—Offset to the first alignment character on a line. Specified in number of pixels or a percentage of available length.

valign="top ¦ **middle** ¦ bottom ¦ baseline"—Vertically aligns the contents of a cell:

top—Cell data flush with top of cell.

middle—Cell data centered in cell.

bottom—Cell data flush with bottom of cell.

baseline—Aligns all cells in a row with this attribute set. Textual data aligned along a common baseline.

Content: One or more TR elements.

Formalized: HTML 4.0

Notes: Must contain at least one table row.

The TFOOT and THEAD elements should appear before the TBODY element.

Browser: MSIE 4

<TD>...</TD> S

Usage: Specifies a table cell's data or contents.

Syntax:

```
<TD attributes>content
```

or

```
<TD attributes>content</TD>
```

Start/End Tag: Required/Optional

Must be empty? No

Attributes: core—See "Common Attributes" section.

i18n—See "Common Attributes" section.

events—See "Intrinsic Events" section.

abbr="*text*"—An abbreviated form of the cell's content.

axis="*data*"—Organizes cells into conceptual categories.

headers="*idrefs*"—Associates the content of a cell with a previously identified header.

scope="row ¦ col ¦ rowgroup ¦ colgroup"—Defines the set of data cells for which the header provides header information:

row—Header information provided for the rest of the row.

col—Header information provided for the rest of the column.

rowgroup—Header information provided for the rest of the row group (as defined by a THEAD, TBODY, or TFOOT element) that contains it.

colgroup—Header information provided for the rest of the column group (as defined by a COL or COLGROUP element) that contains it.

rowspan="*number*"—Sets the number of rows spanned by the current cell. The default is 1.

colspan="*number*"—Sets the number of columns spanned by the current cell. The default is 1.

align="**left** ¦ center ¦ right ¦ justify ¦ char"—Horizontally aligns the contents of cells:

left—Data and text aligned left. This is the default for table data.

center—Data and text centered. This is the default for table headers.

right—Data and text aligned right.

justify—Data and text aligned flush with left and right margins.

char—Aligns text around a specific character.

char="*character*"—Sets a character on which the column aligns (such as ":"). The default value is the decimal point of the current language.

charoff="*length*"—Offset to the first alignment character on a line. Specified in number of pixels or a percentage of available length.

valign="top ¦ **middle** ¦ bottom ¦ baseline"—Vertically aligns the contents of a cell:

top—Cell data flush with top of cell.

middle—Cell data centered in cell.

bottom—Cell data flush with bottom of cell.

baseline—Aligns all cells in a row with this attribute set. Textual data aligned along a common baseline.

T D nowrap—Disables automatic text-wrapping for the cell.

T D bgcolor="*color*"—Sets the background color for cell. Colors identified by standard RGB in hexadecimal format (*#RRGGBB*) or by predefined color name.

T D width="*pixels*"—Recommended cell width.

T D height="*pixels*"—Recommended cell height.

Content: Zero or more block elements, to include the following:

P ¦ DL ¦ DIV ¦ CENTER ¦ NOSCRIPT ¦ NOFRAMES ¦ BLOCKQUOTE ¦ FORM ¦ ISINDEX ¦ HR ¦ TABLE ¦ FIELDSET ¦ ADDRESS

Heading elements (H1 ¦ H2 ¦ H3 ¦ H4 ¦ H5 ¦ H6)

List elements (UL ¦ OL ¦ DIR ¦ MENU)

Preformatted elements (PRE)

Zero or more inline elements, to include the following:

Document text and entities

Fontstyle elements (`TT ¦ I ¦ B ¦ U ¦ S ¦ STRIKE ¦ BIG ¦ SMALL`)

Phrase elements (`EM ¦ STRONG ¦ DFN ¦ CODE ¦ SAMP ¦ KBD ¦ VAR ¦ CITE ¦ ABBR ¦ ACRONYM`)

Special elements (`A ¦ IMG ¦ APPLET ¦ OBJECT ¦ FONT ¦ BASEFONT ¦ BR ¦ SCRIPT ¦ MAP ¦ Q ¦ SUB ¦ SUP ¦ SPAN ¦ BDO ¦ IFRAME`)

Form Control elements (`INPUT ¦ SELECT ¦ TEXTAREA ¦ LABEL ¦ BUTTON`)

Formalized: HTML 3.2

Notes: Cells defined by `TD` may be empty.

Browser: MSIE 2; NNav 1.1

Part X App A

<TEXTAREA>...</TEXTAREA> S

Usage: Creates an area for user input with multiple lines.

Syntax: `<TEXTAREA attributes>content</TEXTAREA>`

Start/End Tag: Required/Required

Must be empty? No

Attributes: `core`—See “Common Attributes” section.

`i18n`—See “Common Attributes” section.

`events`—See “Intrinsic Events” section.

`name="data"`—Assigns a name to the control.

`rows="number"`—Sets the number of visible rows or text lines.

`cols="number"`—Sets the number of visible columns measured in average character width.

`disabled`—Disables this control for user input.

`readonly`—Prohibits the user from making changes to the control.

`tabindex="number"`—Defines the tabbing order between elements. This is the order (from lowest first to highest last) in which they receive focus when the user navigates through them using the Tab key.

`accesskey="character"`—Assigns an access key (or shortcut key) to the element. When the key is pressed, the element receives focus and is activated.

onfocus="*script*"—Triggered when the element receives focus by either a pointing device (such as a mouse) or tabbed navigation.

onblur="*script*"—Triggered when the element loses focus by either a pointing device (such as a mouse) or tabbed navigation.

onselect="*script*"—The event that occurs when text is selected in a text field.

onchange="*script*"—The event that occurs when a control loses the input focus and its value has been modified since gaining focus.

Content: Document text.

Formalized: HTML 2.0

Notes: The content of the element serves as the initial value of the control and is displayed by the user agent.

Browser: MSIE 1; NNav 1

<TFOOT>...</TFOOT> S

Usage: Groups a table row or rows into a table footer.

Syntax: `<TFOOT attributes>content`

or

`<TFOOT attributes>content</TFOOT>`

Start/End Tag: Required/Optional

Must be empty? No

Attributes: core—See "Common Attributes" section.

i18n—See "Common Attributes" section.

events—See "Intrinsic Events" section.

align="left | center | right | justify | char"—Horizontally aligns the contents of cells:

left—Data and text aligned left. This is the default for table data.

center—Data and text centered. This is the default for table headers.

right—Data and text aligned right.

justify—Data and text aligned flush with left and right margins.

char—Aligns text around a specific character.

char="*character*"—Sets a character on which the column

aligns (such as ":"). The default value is the decimal point of the current language.

charoff="*length*"—Offset to the first alignment character on a line. Specified in number of pixels or a percentage of available length.

valign="top ¦ **middle** ¦ bottom ¦ baseline"—Vertically aligns the contents of a cell:

top—Cell data flush with top of cell.

middle—Cell data centered in cell.

bottom—Cell data flush with bottom of cell.

baseline—Aligns all cells in a row with this attribute set. Textual data aligned along a common baseline.

Content: One or more TR elements.

Formalized: HTML 4.0

Notes: The table footer contains table data cells that describe the content of the columns above it.

Must contain at least one TR.

Browser: MSIE 3

<TH>...</TH> S

Usage: Specifies a table cell as being an information, or header, cell.

Syntax:

```
<TH attributes>content
```

or

```
<TH attributes>content</TH>
```

Start/End Tag: Required/Optional

Must be empty? No

Attributes: core—See “Common Attributes” section.

i18n—See “Common Attributes” section.

events—See “Intrinsic Events” section.

abbr="*text*"—An abbreviated form of the cell’s content.

axis="*data*"—Organizes cells into conceptual categories.

headers="*idrefs*"—Associates the content of a cell with a previously identified header.

scope="row ¦ col ¦ rowgroup ¦ colgroup"—Defines the set of data cells for which the header provides header information:

row—Header information provided for the rest of the row.

col—Header information provided for the rest of the column.

`rowgroup`—Header information provided for the rest of the row group (as defined by a `THEAD`, `TBODY`, or `TFOOT` element) that contains it.

`colgroup`—Header information provided for the rest of the column group (as defined by a `COL` or `COLGROUP` element) that contains it.

`rowspan="`*`number`*`"`—Sets the number of rows spanned by the current cell. The default is `1`.

`colspan="`*`number`*`"`—Sets the number of columns spanned by the current cell. The default is `1`.

`align="left ¦` **`center`** `¦ right ¦ justify ¦ char"`—Horizontally aligns the contents of cells:

`left`—Data and text aligned left. This is the default for table data.

`center`—Data and text centered. This is the default for table headers.

`right`—Data and text aligned right.

`justify`—Data and text aligned flush with left and right margins.

`char`—Aligns text around a specific character.

`char="`*`character`*`"`—Sets a character on which the column aligns (such as `":"`). The default value is the decimal point of the current language.

`charoff="`*`length`*`"`—Offset to the first alignment character on a line. Specified in number of pixels or a percentage of available length.

`valign="top ¦` **`middle`** `¦ bottom ¦ baseline"`—Vertically aligns the contents of a cell:

`top`—Cell data flush with top of cell.

`middle`—Cell data centered in cell.

`bottom`—Cell data flush with bottom of cell.

`baseline`—Aligns all cells in a row with this attribute set. Textual data aligned along a common baseline.

T D `nowrap`—Disables automatic text-wrapping for the cell.

T D `bgcolor="`*`color`*`"`—Sets the background color for the cell. Colors identified by standard RGB in hexadecimal format (*#RRGGBB*) or by predefined color name.

T D `width="`*`pixels`*`"`—Recommended cell width.

T D `height="`*`pixels`*`"`—Recommended cell height.

Content: Zero or more block elements, to include the following:

P ¦ DL ¦ DIV ¦ CENTER ¦ NOSCRIPT ¦ NOFRAMES ¦ BLOCKQUOTE ¦ FORM ¦ ISINDEX ¦ HR ¦ TABLE ¦ FIELDSET ¦ ADDRESS

Heading elements (H1 ¦ H2 ¦ H3 ¦ H4 ¦ H5 ¦ H6)

List elements (UL ¦ OL ¦ DIR ¦ MENU)

Preformatted elements (PRE)

Zero or more inline elements, to include the following:

Document text and entities

Fontstyle elements (TT ¦ I ¦ B ¦ U ¦ S ¦ STRIKE ¦ BIG ¦ SMALL)

Phrase elements (EM ¦ STRONG ¦ DFN ¦ CODE ¦ SAMP ¦ KBD ¦ VAR ¦ CITE ¦ ABBR ¦ ACRONYM)

Special elements (A ¦ IMG ¦ APPLET ¦ OBJECT ¦ FONT ¦ BASEFONT ¦ BR ¦ SCRIPT ¦ MAP ¦ Q ¦ SUB ¦ SUP ¦ SPAN ¦ BDO ¦ IFRAME)

Form Control elements (INPUT ¦ SELECT ¦ TEXTAREA ¦ LABEL ¦ BUTTON)

Formalized: HTML 3.2

Notes: Header cell usually rendered in boldface font.

Browser: MSIE 2; NNav 1.1

Part X App A

<THEAD>...</THEAD> S

Usage: Groups a table row or rows into a table header.

Syntax: `<THEAD attributes>content`

or

`<THEAD attributes>content</THEAD>`

Start/End Tag: Required/Optional

Must be empty? No

Attributes: core—See "Common Attributes" section.

i18n—See "Common Attributes" section.

events—See "Intrinsic Events" section.

align="left ¦ **center** ¦ right ¦ justify ¦ char"—Horizontally aligns the contents of cells:

left—Data and text aligned left. This is the default for table data.

center—Data and text centered. This is the default for table headers.

right—Data and text aligned right.

	`justify`—Data and text aligned flush with left and right margins.
	`char`—Aligns text around a specific character.
	`char="`*`character`*`"`—Sets a character on which the column aligns (such as `":"`). The default value is the decimal point of the current language.
	`charoff="`*`length`*`"`—Offset to the first alignment character on a line. Specified in number of pixels or a percentage of available length.
	`valign="top ¦ ` **`middle`** ` ¦ bottom ¦ baseline"`—Vertically aligns the contents of a cell:
	`top`—Cell data flush with top of cell.
	`middle`—Cell data centered in cell.
	`bottom`—Cell data flush with bottom of cell.
	`baseline`—Aligns all cells in a row with this attribute set. Textual data aligned along a common baseline.
Content:	One or more `TR` elements.
Formalized:	HTML 4.0
Notes:	The table header contains table data cells that describe the content of the columns below it. Must contain at least one `TR`.
Browser:	MSIE 3

<TITLE>...</TITLE> S

Usage:	Identifies the contents of the document.
Syntax:	`<TITLE `*`attributes`*`>`*`content`*`</TITLE>`
Start/End Tag:	Required/Required
Must be empty?	No
Attributes:	`i18n`—See "Common Attributes" section.
Content:	Document text
Formalized:	HTML 2.0
Notes:	The `TITLE` element is required and is located within the `HEAD` element. The title is displayed in the browser window title bar.
Browser:	MSIE 1; NNav 1

<TR>...</TR> S

Usage:	Defines a row of table cells.

Syntax: `<TR attributes>content` or `<TR attributes>content</TR>`

Start/End Tag: Required/Optional

Must be empty? No

Attributes:

core—See "Common Attributes" section.

i18n—See "Common Attributes" section.

events—See "Intrinsic Events" section.

align="left ¦ center ¦ right ¦ justify ¦ char"—Horizontally aligns the contents of cells:

left—Data and text aligned left. This is the default for table data.

center—Data and text centered. This is the default for table headers.

right—Data and text aligned right.

justify—Data and text aligned flush with left and right margins.

char—Aligns text around a specific character.

char="*character*"—Sets a character on which the column aligns (such as ":"). The default value is the decimal point of the current language.

charoff="*length*"—Offset to the first alignment character on a line. Specified in number of pixels or a percentage of available length.

valign="top ¦ **middle** ¦ bottom ¦ baseline"—Vertically aligns the contents of a cell:

top—Cell data flush with top of cell.

middle—Cell data centered in cell.

bottom—Cell data flush with bottom of cell.

baseline—Aligns all cells in a row with this attribute set. Textual data aligned along a common baseline.

T D bgcolor="*color*"—Sets the background color for a table row. Colors identified by standard RGB in hexadecimal format (*#RRGGBB*) or by predefined color name.

Content: One or more TH or TD elements.

Formalized: HTML 3.2

Notes: No table data is supplied by this element; its sole purpose is to define structural rows of table cells.

Browser: MSIE 2; NNav 1.1

PART X

APP A

<TT>...</TT> S

Usage: Displays text as Teletype or monospaced font.

Syntax: `<TT attributes>content</TT>`

Start/End Tag: Required/Required

Must be empty? No

Attributes: core—See "Common Attributes" section.

i18n—See "Common Attributes" section.

events—See "Intrinsic Events" section.

Content: Zero or more inline elements, to include the following:

Document text and entities

Fontstyle elements (TT ¦ I ¦ B ¦ U ¦ S ¦ STRIKE ¦ BIG ¦ SMALL)

Phrase elements (EM ¦ STRONG ¦ DFN ¦ CODE ¦ SAMP ¦ KBD ¦ VAR ¦ CITE ¦ ABBR ¦ ACRONYM)

Special elements (A ¦ IMG ¦ APPLET ¦ OBJECT ¦ FONT ¦ BASEFONT ¦ BR ¦ SCRIPT ¦ MAP ¦ Q ¦ SUB ¦ SUP ¦ SPAN ¦ BDO ¦ IFRAME)

Form Control elements (INPUT ¦ SELECT ¦ TEXTAREA ¦ LABEL ¦ BUTTON)

Formalized: HTML 2.0

Notes: Although not deprecated, the W3C recommends using style sheets in place of this element.

Browser: MSIE 1; NNav 1

<U>...</U> T D

Usage: Displays underlined text.

Syntax: `<U attributes>content</U>`

Start/End Tag: Required/Required

Must be empty? No

Attributes: core—See "Common Attributes" section.

i18n—See "Common Attributes" section.

events—See "Intrinsic Events" section.

Content: Zero or more inline elements, to include the following:

Document text and entities

Fontstyle elements (TT ¦ I ¦ B ¦ U ¦ S ¦ STRIKE ¦ BIG ¦ SMALL)

Phrase elements (EM ¦ STRONG ¦ DFN ¦ CODE ¦ SAMP ¦ KBD ¦ VAR ¦ CITE ¦ ABBR ¦ ACRONYM)

Special elements (A ¦ IMG ¦ APPLET ¦ OBJECT ¦ FONT ¦ BASEFONT ¦ BR ¦ SCRIPT ¦ MAP ¦ Q ¦ SUB ¦ SUP ¦ SPAN ¦ BDO ¦ IFRAME)

Form Control elements (INPUT ¦ SELECT ¦ TEXTAREA ¦ LABEL ¦ BUTTON)

Formalized: HTML 3.2

Notes: Deprecated in favor of style sheets.

Browser: MSIE 1; NNav 3

<UL>...</UL> S

Usage: Creates an unordered (unnumbered) list.

Syntax: `<UL attributes>content</UL>`

Start/End Tag: Required/Required

Must be empty? No

Attributes: core—See "Common Attributes" section.

i18n—See "Common Attributes" section.

events—See "Intrinsic Events" section.

T D type="disc ¦ square ¦ circle"—Sets the style of bullets in an unordered list:

disc—A solid circle.

square—A square outline.

circle—A circle outline.

T D compact—Tells the browser to attempt to display the list more compactly.

Notes: Nested lists are allowed.

Content: One or more LI elements

Formalized: HTML 2.0

Browser: MSIE 1; NNav 1

<VAR>...</VAR> S

Usage: Identifies and displays a variable or program argument.

Syntax: `<VAR attributes>content</VAR>`

Start/End Tag: Required/Required

Must be empty? No

Attributes: core—See "Common Attributes" section.

i18n—See "Common Attributes" section.

events—See "Intrinsic Events" section.

Content: Zero or more inline elements, to include the following:

- Document text and entities
- Fontstyle elements (TT ¦ I ¦ B ¦ U ¦ S ¦ STRIKE ¦ BIG ¦ SMALL)
- Phrase elements (EM ¦ STRONG ¦ DFN ¦ CODE ¦ SAMP ¦ KBD ¦ VAR ¦ CITE ¦ ABBR ¦ ACRONYM)
- Special elements (A ¦ IMG ¦ APPLET ¦ OBJECT ¦ FONT ¦ BASEFONT ¦ BR ¦ SCRIPT ¦ MAP ¦ Q ¦ SUB ¦ SUP ¦ SPAN ¦ BDO ¦ IFRAME)
- Form Control elements (INPUT ¦ SELECT ¦ TEXTAREA ¦ LABEL ¦ BUTTON)

Formalized: HTML 2.0

Notes: Usually displayed in italics.

Browser: MSIE 1; NNav 1

Common Attributes

Four attributes are abbreviated as `core` in the preceding sections:

- `id="id"`—A global identifier.
- `class="data"`—A list of classes separated by spaces.
- `style="style"`—Style information.
- `title="text"`—Provides more information for a specific element, as opposed to the `TITLE` element, which entitles the entire Web page.

Two attributes for internationalization (`i18n`) are abbreviated as `i18n`:

- `lang="language-code"`—Identifies the human (not computer) language of the text content or an element's attribute values.
- `dir="ltr ¦ rtl"`—Specifies the text direction (left-to-right, right-to-left) of element content, overriding inherent directionality.

Intrinsic Events

The following intrinsic events are abbreviated `events`:

Support for intrinsic events in Netscape Navigator is limited to the 4.0 and above versions, and is only applicable to form elements, links, and images.

- `onclick="script"`—A pointing device (such as a mouse) was single-clicked.
- `ondblclick="script"`—A pointing device (such as a mouse) was double-clicked.

- `onmousedown="`*`script`*`"`—A mouse button was clicked and held down.
- `onmouseup="`*`script`*`"`—A mouse button that was clicked and held down was released.
- `onmouseover="`*`script`*`"`—A mouse moved the cursor over an object.
- `onmousemove="`*`script`*`"`—A mouse was moved within an object.
- `onmouseout="`*`script`*`"`—A mouse moved the cursor off an object.
- `onkeypress="`*`script`*`"`—A key was pressed and released.
- `onkeydown="`*`script`*`"`—A key was pressed and held down.
- `onkeyup="`*`script`*`"`—A key that was pressed has been released.

Data Types

Table A.1 summarizes and explains the data types used in the information in this appendix.

Table A.1 Data Types

Name	Description
character	A single character or character reference from the document character set.
character-set	Specifies the character encoding. Values (such as `ISO-8859-1` or `US-ASCII`) must be strings approved and registered by IANA, The Internet Assigned Numbers Authority.

color	Colors are identified by standard RGB in hexadecimal format (*#RRGGBB*) or by predefined color name (with corresponding hex value) shown here:
	`Black = "#000000"`
	`Silver = "#C0C0C0"`
	`Gray = "#808080"`
	`White = "#FFFFFF"`
	`Maroon = "#800000"`
	`Red = "#FF0000"`
	`Purple = "#800080"`
	`Fuchsia = "#FF00FF"`
	`Green = "#008000"`
	`Lime = "#00FF00"`
	`Olive = "#808000"`
	`Yellow = "#FFFF00"`
	`Navy = "#000080"`
	`Blue = "#0000FF"`

continues

TABLE A.1 CONTINUED

Name	Description
	Teal = "#008080" Aqua = "#00FFFF"
content-type	Content types, also known as MIME types, specify the nature of the resource (such as "text/html" or "image/gif").
data	A sequence of characters or character entities from the document character set.
datetime	Legal datetime strings follow the following format: YYYY-MM-DDThh:mm:ssTZD. YYYY = four-digit year. MM = two-digit month (01 = January, and so on). DD = two-digit day of month (01 through 31). T = beginning of time element. The "T" must appear in uppercase. hh = two digits of hour (00 through 23) (am/pm *not* allowed). mm = two digits of minute (00 through 59). ss = two digits of second (00 through 59). TZD = time zone designator. The time zone designator is one of the following: Z—indicates UTC (Coordinated Universal Time). The "Z" must be uppercase. +hh:mm—indicates that the time is a local time that is hh hours and mm minutes ahead of UTC. -hh:mm—indicates that the time is a local time that is hh hours and mm minutes behind UTC. A valid datetime is 1998-06-13T19:30:02-05:00
id	An identifier token that must begin with a letter (A–Z or a–z) and may be followed by any number of letters, digits (0–9), hyphens (-), underscores (_), colons (:), and periods (.).
idref	A reference to an ID token defined by other attributes.
idrefs	A space-separated reference list to ID tokens defined by other attributes.

Name	Description
language-code	A language code that identifies a natural language spoken, written, or otherwise used for the communication of information among people. Computer languages are explicitly excluded from language codes. Language codes are identified by a primary code (such as `en`) followed by a hyphen and a two-letter subcode (such as `-US`) that identifies the country if necessary. The complete language code is: `en-US` for the U.S. version of English.
length	A value representing either a number of pixels (such as `100`) or a percentage of available space (such as `%50`).
link-type	A space-separated list of link types: `alternate`—Designates substitute versions for the document in which the link occurs. When used together with the `lang` attribute, it implies a translated version of the document. When used together with the `media` attribute, it implies a version designed for a different medium (or media). `appendix`—Refers to a document serving as an appendix in a collection of documents. `bookmark`—Refers to a bookmark. A bookmark is a link to a key entry point within an extended document. `chapter`—Refers to a document serving as a chapter in a collection of documents. `contents`—Refers to a document serving as a table of contents. `copyright`—Refers to a copyright statement for the current document. `glossary`—Refers to a document providing a glossary of terms that pertain to the current document. `help`—Refers to a document offering help. `index`—Refers to a document providing an index for the current document. `next`—Refers to the next document in a linear sequence of documents. `prev`—Refers to the previous document in an ordered series of documents. `section`—Refers to a document serving as a section in a collection of documents. `start`—Refers to the first document in a collection of documents. `stylesheet`—Refers to an external style sheet. This is used together with the link type `alternate` for user-selectable alternate style sheets. `subsection`—Refers to a document serving as a subsection in a collection of documents. *`user-defined`*—Relationship defined by the content author. If used, the `profile` attribute of the `HEAD` element should provide explanatory information.
media-descriptor	A comma-separated list of recognized media descriptors: `all`—Suitable for all devices. `aural`—Intended for speech synthesizers.

continues

Table A.1 Continued

Name	Description
	braille—Intended for Braille tactile feedback devices. handheld—Intended for handheld devices (small screen, monochrome, bitmapped graphics, limited bandwidth). print—Intended for paged, opaque material and for documents viewed onscreen in Print Preview mode. projection—Intended for projectors. screen—Intended for nonpaged computer screens. tty—Intended for media using a fixed-pitch character grid, such as Teletypes, terminals, or portable devices with limited display capabilities. tv—Intended for television-type devices (low resolution, color, limited scrollability).
multi-length	A value representing either a number of pixels (such as 100), a percentage of available space (such as %50), or a relative length designated by an integer followed by an asterisk: "i*". The "i" is a proportional modifier of any remaining space that will be divided among relative length elements. For example, if there are 120 pixels remaining and competing relative lengths of 1*, 2*, and 3*, the space would be allocated as 20, 40, and 60 pixels respectively.
name	An identifier token that must begin with a letter (A–Z or a–z) and may be followed by any number of letters, digits (0–9), hyphens (-), underscores (_), colons (:), and periods (.).
number	A number composed of at least one digit (0–9).
pixels	An integer representing a number of pixels.
script	Script data. This is not evaluated as HTML markup but passed as data to the script engine. Value is determined by scripting language.
style	Style sheet rules. This is not evaluated as HTML markup. Value is determined by style language.
text	Text that is meant to be read and understood by the user.
URI	A Uniform Resource Identifier, which includes Uniform Resource Locators.

APPENDIX

HTML Special Character Set

In this Appendix

SPECIAL CHARACTERS

Special characters are used to create standard or mathematical symbols and letters used in languages other than English.

Note

HTML 4.0 contains a variety of special characters that are not supported by browsers. To learn more about special characters in HTML 4.0 and keep up with changes to the set, visit **`http://www.w3.org/TR/REC-html40/sgml/entities.html`**.

HTML CODE AND ENTITY NAMES

You can use the Code or Entity name. For example, if I want to add an ampersand I can do the following to get Bread & Butter:

```
Bread &#38; Butter
```

or

```
Bread &amp; Butter
```

Tip from

Most people prefer to use entity names, if only for the simple reason that they are more human-friendly.

TABLE B.1 CODE AND ENTITY NAMES FOR SPECIAL CHARACTERS

Description	Code	Entity Name
quotation mark	"	" —> " " —> "
ampersand	&	& —> & & —> &
less-than sign	<	< —> < < —> <;
greater-than sign	>	> —> > > —> >
non-breaking space		—> —>
inverted exclamation	¡	¡ —> ¡ ¡ —> ¡
cent sign	¢	¢ —> ¢ ¢ —> ¢
pound sterling	£	£ —> £ £ —> £
general currency sign	¤	¤ —> ¤ ¤ —> ¤
yen sign	¥	¥ —> ¥ ¥ —> ¥
section sign	§	§ —> § § —> §
copyright	©	© —> © © —> ©
feminine ordinal	ª	ª —> ª ª —> ª
left-angle quote, guillemotleft	«	« —> « « —> «

Description	Code	Entity Name
not sign	¬	¬ —> ¬ ¬ —> ¬
soft hyphen	_	—> _ —> _
registered trademark	®	® —> ® ® —> ®
macron accent	¯	¯ —> ¯ ¯ —> ¯
degree sign	°	° —> ° ° —> °
plus or minus	±	± —> ± ± —> ±
superscript two	_	² —> _ ² —> _
superscript three	_	³ —> _ ³ —> _
acute accent	´	´ —> ´ ´ —> ´
micro sign	µ	µ —> µ µ —> µ
paragraph sign	¶	¶ —> ¶ ¶ —> ¶
middle dot	·	· —> · · —> ·
cedilla	¸	¸ —> ¸ ¸ —> ¸
superscript one	_	¹ —> _ ¹ —> _
masculine ordinal	º	º —> º º —> º
right-angle quote, guillemotright	»	» —> » » —> »
fraction one-fourth	_	¼ —> _ ¼ —> _
fraction one-half	_	½ —> _ ½ —> _
fraction three-fourths	_	¾ —> _ ¾ —> _
inverted question mark	¿	¿ —> ¿ ¿ —> ¿
capital A, grave accent	À	À —> À À —> À
capital A, acute accent	Á	Á —> Á Á —> Á
capital A, circumflex accent	Â	Â —> Â Â —> Â
capital A, tilde	Ã	Ã —> Ã Ã —> Ã
capital A, dieresis or umlaut mark	Ä	Ä —> Ä Ä —> Ä
capital A, ring	Å	Å —> Å Å —> Å
capital AE diphthong (ligature)	Æ	Æ —> Æ Æ —> Æ
capital C, cedilla	Ç	Ç —> Ç Ç —> Ç
capital E, grave accent	È	È —> È È —> È
capital E, acute accent	É	É —> É É —> É
capital E, circumflex accent	Ê	Ê —> Ê Ê —> Ê
capital E, dieresis or umlaut mark	Ë	Ë —> Ë Ë —> Ë

continues

TABLE B.1 CONTINUED

Description	Code	Entity Name
capital I, grave accent	Ì	Ì —> Ì Ì —> Ì
capital I, acute accent	Í	Í —> Í Í —> Í
capital I, circumflex accent	Î	Î —> Î Î —> Î
capital I, dieresis or umlaut mark	Ï	Ï —> Ï Ï —> Ï
capital Eth, Icelandic	_	Ð —> _ Ð —> _
capital N, tilde	Ñ	Ñ —> Ñ Ñ —> Ñ
capital O, grave accent	Ò	Ò —> Ò Ò —> Ò
capital O, acute accent	Ó	Ó —> Ó Ó —> Ó
capital O, circumflex accent	Ô	Ô —> Ô Ô —> Ô
capital O, tilde	Õ	Õ —> Õ Õ —> Õ
capital O, dieresis or umlaut mark	Ö	Ö —> Ö Ö —> Ö
multiply sign	×	× —> × × —> ×
capital O, slash	Ø	Ø —> Ø Ø —> Ø
capital U, grave accent	Ù	Ù —> Ù Ù —> Ù
capital U, acute accent	Ú	Ú —> Ú Ú —> Ú
capital U, circumflex accent	Û	Û —> Û Û —> Û
capital U, dieresis or umlaut mark	Ü	Ü —> Ü Ü —> Ü
capital Y, acute accent	_	Ý —> _ Ý —> _
capital THORN, Icelandic	_	Þ —> _ Þ —> _
small sharp s, German (sz ligature)	ß	ß —> ß ß —> ß
small a, grave accent	à	à —> à à —> à
small a, acute accent	á	á —> á á —> á
small a, circumflex accent	â	â —> â â —> â
small a, tilde	ã	ã —> ã ã —> ã
small a, dieresis or umlaut mark	ä	ä —> ä ä —> ä
small a, ring	å	å —> å å —> å
small ae diphthong (ligature)	æ	æ —> æ æ —> æ
small c, cedilla	ç	ç —> ç ç —> ç
small e, grave accent	è	è —> è è —> è
small e, acute accent	é	é —> é é —> é
small e, circumflex accent	ê	ê —> ê ê —> ê
small e, dieresis or umlaut mark	ë	ë —> ë ë —> ë

Description	Code	Entity Name
small i, grave accent	ì	ì —> ì ì —> ì
small i, acute accent	í	í —> í í —> í
small i, circumflex accent	î	î —> î î —> î
small i, dieresis or umlaut mark	ï	ï —> ï ï —> ï
small eth, Icelandic	_	ð —> _ ð —> _
small n, tilde	ñ	ñ —> ñ ñ —> ñ
small o, grave accent	ò	ò —> ò ò —> ò
small o, acute accent	ó	ó —> ó ó —> ó
small o, circumflex accent	ô	ô —> ô ô —> ô
small o, tilde	õ	õ —> õ õ —> õ
small o, dieresis or umlaut mark	ö	ö —> ö ö —> ö
division sign	÷	÷ —> ÷ ÷ —> ÷
small o, slash	ø	ø —> ø ø —> ø
small u, grave accent	ù	ù —> ù ù —> ù
small u, acute accent	ú	ú —> ú ú —> ú
small u, circumflex accent	û	û —> û û —> û
small u, dieresis or umlaut mark	ü	ü —> ü ü —> ü
small y, acute accent	_	ý —> _ ý —> _
small thorn, Icelandic	_	þ —> _ þ —> _
small y, dieresis or umlaut mark	ÿ	ÿ —> ÿ ÿ —> ÿ

APPENDIX

CSS Reference

In this Appendix

Style Sheets

If you've looked into the details of Cascading Style Sheets–Level 1, much of this appendix will look familiar. However, there are a large number of properties that you won't recognize. Level 2 has taken style sheets to a new level, and this appendix details all the new additions.

Currently, CSS1 is implemented in Netscape Navigator 4+ and Microsoft's Internet Explorer 4+. CSS2 implementation is available to a certain degree in the Internet Explorer 5.0 browser, and expected in Netscape's 5.0 browser as it becomes available. CSS2 is currently in the recommendation stage and can be found at **`http://www.w3.org/TR/REC-CSS2/`**.

Caution

Neither Internet Explorer or Netscape have fully implemented CSS in either the first or second level. For a regularly updated, comprehensive look at style sheet properties and browser support, see Eric Meyer's Safe CSS Properties table in webreview, **`http://webreview.com/wr/pub/guides/style/safegrid.html`**.

The properties in this appendix are grouped into areas according to their function. In many cases, one property affects another and I've tried to present them in a logical order. The property groups include the following:

- Text
- Colors and backgrounds
- Fonts
- Box model
- Visual formatting and positioning
- Generated content and lists
- Tables
- Paged media
- Aural style sheets

Note

All properties that are new to the CSS2 specification are marked with an asterisk right after the property name.

Selectors

Selectors are the tag elements defined at the beginning of a style sheet definition that tell the browser where to apply the style. After the selector, the style definition is included within curly brackets. In this example, `BODY` is the selector.

```
BODY {color: blue)
```

Several selectors can be grouped together if they are separated with commas.

```
H1, H2, H3 {font-family: san-serif}
```

In place of selectors, you can use the `*` wildcard. This example applies a font size style to all tags on the page:

```
* {font-size: 14pt}
```

Another wildcard character is the > sign. This tells the browser to search for child selectors within a certain parent. This example applies the style only to `LI` elements with `OL` lists:

```
OL > LI {list-style-type: decimal}
```

Using class selectors, you can apply different styles to the same tag. A period and a name follow a general selector and the style is applied to the tag whose `class` attribute matches the class name. The following example applies the style to any `H2` tags that have the `class` attribute equal to `"myBlue"`.

```
H2.myBlue {background-color: blue}
<H2 class="myBlue">This header has a blue background.</H2>
```

Selectors can also be identified by the `id` attribute using the `#` character. The following example matches the style to any tags whose ID attribute is `"duckie"`.

```
#duckie {border-color: yellow}
```

PSEUDO CLASSES

To access the control of elements that aren't referred to by normal tags, CSS2 defines several pseudo classes. An example is the first line of a paragraph. HTML has no way of identifying this element, so a pseudo class called `:first-line` is used. All pseudo classes have colons in front of them. They are located after a selector like the following:

```
P:first-line {color: red}
```

The following are identified pseudo classes in CSS2:

- **`:first-child`**—This is the first child element of another element.
- **`:link`**—These are links that have not yet been visited.
- **`:visited`**—These are visited links.
- **`:hover`**—This is an element that the cursor is currently over.
- **`:active`**—This is the currently activated element.
- **`:focus`**—This is the element that has the focus.
- **`:lang`**—This defines the current language.
- **`:first-line`**—This is the first formatted line of a paragraph.
- **`:first-letter`**—This is the first letter of a paragraph.
- **`:before`**—This positions content to come before an element.
- **`:after`**—This positions content to come after an element.

Rules

Rules are used to access files and documents located outside of the current document. There are five rules defined in CSS2, and all of them begin with the `@` character: `@charset`, `@font-face`, `@import`, `@media`, and `@page`.

Properties

Properties are the main descriptors of the style sheet language. They appear within brackets and include the property name and a value separated by a colon. Some properties can include more than one value. These values are typically separated by a single space.

Text

The text properties include aligning properties such as `text-align` and `word-spacing`, as well as style-altering properties such as `text-decoration` and the new `text-shadow` properties.

TEXT-INDENT

Description: Defines the length of the indent applied to the first line of text in a block.

Values: Any valid length—Can include negative values. Default is 0.

Any valid percentage.

`inherit`—Takes the same value as its parent.

Example: `P {text-indent: 40px}`

TEXT-ALIGN

Description: Defines how an inline box of text is aligned.

Values: `left`—Aligns text to the left.

`center`—Aligns text to the center.

`right`—Aligns text to the right.

`justify`—Justifies the text.

Any valid string—Defines a string on which table cells will align.

`inherit`—Takes the same value as its parent.

Example: `P {text-align: right}`

TEXT-DECORATION

Description: Defines decorations added to the text of an element.

Values: `none`—(default) Applies no text decoration.

`underline`—Underlines the text.

`overline`—Puts a line over the text.

`line-through`—Strikes out the text.

`blink`—Causes the text to blink.

`inherit`—Takes the same value as its parent.

Example: `P {text-decoration: underline}`

TEXT-TRANSFORM

Description: Defines capitalization effects to the text of an element.

Values: `none`—(default) Applies no capitalization.

`capitalize`—Capitalizes the first letter of each word.

`uppercase`—Capitalizes all letters.

`lowercase`—Converts all letters to lowercase.

`inherit`—Takes the same value as its parent.

Example: `H3 {text-transform: uppercase}`

TEXT-SHADOW*

Description: Describes values to create a text shadow effect. Several lists of shadow values can be included and must be separated by commas. Each separate shadow effect value list must include offset values and can include a blur radius and color.

Values: `none`—(default) Applies no shadow effect.

`color`—Color of text shadow.

First valid length—Horizontal distance to the right of the text. Negative values are to the left of the text.

Second valid length—Vertical distance below the text. Negative values are above the text.

Third valid length—Text shadow blur radius.

`inherit`—Takes the same value as its parent.

Example: `H1 {text-shadow: blue 5px 5px 3px, yellow -2px -2px 3px}`

LETTER-SPACING

Description: Defines the space between text characters.

Values: `normal`—(default) Applies normal text spacing for the used font.

Any valid length—The length of the space between letters.

`inherit`—Takes the same value as its parent.

Example: `P {letter-spacing: 0.3em}`

WORD-SPACING

Description: Defines the space between words.

Values: `normal`—(default) Applies normal text spacing for the font being used.

Any valid length—The length of the space between letters.

`inherit`—Takes the same value as its parent.

Example: `P {word-spacing—1.3em}`

WHITE-SPACE

Description: Defines how to handle whitespace in an element.

Values: `normal`—(default) Collapses whitespace if necessary to fit boxes. This is the same as how HTML handles whitespace.

`pre`—Treats all whitespace literally as it appears in code.

`nowrap`—Collapses all whitespace.

`inherit`—Takes the same value as its parent.

Example: `P {white-space: pre}`

Colors and Backgrounds

Adding colors and backgrounds to elements creates a visually stimulating Web page. Style sheets include many properties that give your page the zing it needs.

COLOR

Description: Defines the text color.

Values: Any valid color—Colors the text.

`inherit`—Takes the same value as its parent.

Example: `P {color: green}`

`P {color: rgb(0, 255, 0)}`

BACKGROUND-COLOR

Description: Defines the background color of an element.

Values: Any valid color—Colors the text.

`transparent`—(default) Makes the element's background transparent.

`inherit`—Takes the same value as its parent.

Example: `DIV {color: blue}`

`DIV {color: rgb(0, 0, 255)}`

Tip from molly

CSS2 provides access to all the colors used by a viewer's system. All properties that use color can reference the system colors using the following keywords: `ActiveBorder`, `ActiveCaption`, `AppWorkspace`, `Background`, `ButtonFace`, `ButtonHighlight`, `ButtonShadow`, `ButtonText`, `CaptionText`, `GrayText`, `Highlight`, `HighlightText`, `InactiveBorder`, `InactiveCaption`, `InactiveCaptionText`, `InfoBackground`, `InfoText`, `Menu`, `MenuText`, `Scrollbar`, `ThreeDDarkShadow`, `ThreeDFace`, `ThreeDHighlight`, `ThreeDLightShadow`, `ThreeDShadow`, `Window`, `WindowFrame`, and `WindowText`. For example, the `color` property set to `MenuText` would use the same color as the menu text your system uses.

BACKGROUND-IMAGE

Description: Defines the background image of an element.

Values:

`none`—(default) Sets no background image.

Any valid URL—URL of the background image.

`inherit`—Takes the same value as its parent.

Example: `H1 {background-image: url("texture3.gif")}`

BACKGROUND-REPEAT

Description: Defines the direction that the background image is tiled.

Values:

`repeat`—(default) Background image repeats both horizontally and vertically.

`repeat-x`—Background image repeats only horizontally.

`repeat-y`—Background image repeats only vertically.

`no-repeat`—Background image doesn't repeat.

`inherit`—Takes the same value as its parent.

Example: `BLOCKQUOTE {background-repeat: repeat-x}`

BACKGROUND-POSITION

Description: Defines the upper-left corner position of the background image. Single values set the horizontal distance and default the vertical offset to 50%. Several keywords can be combined.

Values:

First valid length—Horizontal distance the background image is placed from the left edge. Accepts negative values.

Second valid length—Vertical distance the background image is placed from the top edge. Accepts negative values.

First valid percentage—Percent of the element box the background image is offset from the left edge. Default is 0% or upper-left corner.

Second valid percentage—Percent of the element box the background image is offset from the top edge.

`top`—Positions the background image along the top edge.

`center`—Positions the background image in the center of the element box.

`bottom`—Positions the background image along the bottom edge.

`left`—Positions the background image along the left edge.

`right`—Positions the background image along the right edge.

`inherit`—Takes the same value as its parent.

Example: `BLOCKQUOTE {background-position: top center}`

BACKGROUND-ATTACHMENT

Description: Defines whether the background image is fixed to the window or scrolls with the document.

Values: `scroll`—(default) Background image scrolls along with the window.

`fixed`—Background image is permanently fixed to its location. Background image repeats only horizontally.

`inherit`—Takes the same value as its parent.

Example: `IMG {background-attachment: fixed}`

BACKGROUND

Description: Shorthand property for defining all background properties at once. If not included, a property is set to its default value.

Values: `background-color`—Background color value.

`background-image`—Background image value.

`background-repeat`—Background repeat value.

`background-attachment`—Background attachment value.

`background-position`—Background position value.

`inherit`—Takes the same value as its parent.

Example:

```
P {background: blue url("texture3.gif") repeat fixed top
right}
```

FONTS

Font control adds style and flair to your Web pages whether you change the family, size, or weight.

FONT-FAMILY

Description: Defines a font to use for the element's text. It can include several font families separated by commas. The list order defines the priority.

Values: Font name—Font to use to render the text. Fonts with more than one word need to be in quotes.

Generic font name—Generic font class to use to render the text. Generic fonts include the following: `serif`, `sans-serif`, `cursive`, `fantasy`, and `monospace`.

`inherit`—Takes the same value as its parent.

Example: `BODY {font-family: "Times Roman", courier, serif}`

FONT-STYLE

Description: Defines a font style, such as italic or oblique.

Values: `normal`—(default) Uses the normal font style.

`italic`—Uses an italic font style.

`oblique`—Uses an oblique or slanted font style.

`inherit`—Takes the same value as its parent.

Example: `SPAN {font-style: italic}`

FONT-VARIANT

Description: Defines whether a font is rendered using small caps.

Values: `normal`—(default) Uses the normal font style.

`small-caps`—Renders the font in small caps.

`inherit`—Takes the same value as its parent.

Example: `H4 {font-variant: small-caps}`

FONT-WEIGHT

Description: Defines how thick text appears.

Values: `normal`—(default) Uses the normal font thickness.

`bold`—Uses a bold font weight.

`bolder`—Uses a bolder font weight.

`lighter`—Uses a lighter font weight.

`100-900`—Number indicates the font thickness. `100` is the lightest (same as `lighter`), `400` is `normal`, `700` is `bold`, and `900` is `bolder`.

`inherit`—Takes the same value as its parent.

Example: `H1 {font-weight: bolder}`

FONT-STRETCH*

Description: Defines the font's width.

Values:

`normal`—(default) Uses the normal font width.

`wider`—Increases the width by one over current setting.

`narrower`—Decreases the width by one over current setting.

`ultra-condensed`—Defines the tightest width setting.

`extra-condensed`—Looser than the preceding value.

`condensed`—Looser than the preceding value.

`semi-condensed`—Looser than the preceding value.

`semi-expanded`—Wider than normal.

`expanded`—Wider than the preceding value.

`extra-expanded`—Wider than the preceding value.

`ultra-expanded`—Defines the widest setting.

`inherit`—Takes the same value as its parent.

Example:

```
BODY {font-stretch: condensed}
```

FONT-SIZE

Description: Defines the size of the font.

Values:

Absolute size—Uses keywords to express font size. Values include `xx-small`, `small`, `medium` (default), `large`, `x-large`, and `xx-large`.

Relative size—Uses relative keywords to express font size. Values include `larger` and `smaller`.

Any valid length—Defines the absolute font size. Negative values are not accepted.

Valid percentage—Defines the percent increase or decrease from the parent font size.

`inherit`—Takes the same value as its parent.

Example:

```
BODY {font-size: 16pt}
```

FONT-SIZE-ADJUST*

Description: Defines an aspect ratio to maintain when sizing fonts. This enables users to adjust for the text height when resizing.

Values:

`none`—(default) Font's aspect ratio ignored.

Any valid number—Number representing the aspect value for the font.

`inherit`—Takes the same value as its parent.

Example:

```
P {font-size-adjust: 0.45}
```

FONT

Description: Shorthand property for defining all font properties at once. If not included, a property is set to its default value.

Values: `font-style`—Font style value.

`font-variant`—Font variant value.

`font-weight`—Font weight value.

`font-size`—Font size value.

`line-height`—Line height value.

`font-family`—Font family value.

`inherit`—Takes the same value as its parent.

Example: `BODY {font: italic bold 16pt 110% impact Garmond san-serif}`

Tip from molly

The `font` property can also use system fonts defined by the system. Valid values include `caption`, `icon`, `menu`, `message-box`, `small-caption`, and `status-bar`. For example, a `font` property set to `menu` would use the same font properties that the menus on your system use.

Box Model

All elements are enveloped in a box made from the actual content, padding, border, and margins. Learning how to control these properties helps as you lay out your pages.

MARGIN-TOP, MARGIN-RIGHT, MARGIN-BOTTOM, MARGIN-LEFT

Description: Defines the margin width for the designated side.

Values: Any valid length—Number representing the width of the margin. Default is `0`.

Any valid percentage—Percentage of window to use for the width of the padding.

`inherit`—Takes the same value as its parent.

Example: `P {margin-top: 20px}`

MARGIN

Description: Shorthand property for defining margins for all sides of an element at once. This property can include one to four values. One value sets only all margins to that value. Two sets the top and bottom to the first and the left and right to the second. Three values set the top to the first, left and right to the second, and the bottom to the third.

Values: `margin-top`—Width of the top margin.

`margin-right`—Width of the right margin.

`margin-bottom`—Width of the bottom margin.

`margin-left`—Width of the left margin.

`inherit`—Takes the same value as its parent.

Example: `BODY {margin: 20px 30px 5px}`

PADDING-TOP, PADDING-RIGHT, PADDING-BOTTOM, PADDING-LEFT

Description: Defines the padding width for the designated side. Padding separates the text from the border.

Values: Any valid length—Number representing the width of the padding. Default is `0`.

Any valid percentage—Percentage of window to use for the width of the padding.

`inherit`—Takes the same value as its parent.

Example: `P {padding-top: 20px}`

PADDING

Description: Shorthand property for defining padding widths for all sides of an element at once. This property can include one to four values. One value sets all padding widths to that value. Two sets the top and bottom to the first and the left and right to the second. Three values set the top to the first, left and right to the second, and the bottom to the third.

Values: `padding-top`—Width of the top padding.

`padding-right`—Width of the right padding.

`padding-bottom`—Width of the bottom padding.

`padding-left`—Width of the left padding.

`inherit`—Takes the same value as its parent.

Example: `BODY {padding: 20px 30px 5px}`

BORDER-TOP-WIDTH, BORDER-RIGHT-WIDTH, BORDER-BOTTOM-WIDTH, BORDER-LEFT-WIDTH

Description: Defines the border width for the designated side. The border comes between the padding and margin.

Values: `thin`—Creates a thin weight border.

`medium`—(default) Creates a medium weight border.

`thick`—Creates a thick weight border.

`inherit`—Takes the same value as its parent.

Example: `P {border-top-width: 10px}`

BORDER-WIDTH

Description: Shorthand property for defining border widths for all sides of an element at once. This property can include one to four values. One value sets all border widths to that value. Two sets the top and bottom to the first and the left and right to the second. Three values set the top to the first, left and right to the second, and the bottom to the third.

Values: `border-top-width`—Width of the top border.

`border-right-width`—Width of the right border.

`border-bottom-width`—Width of the bottom border.

`border-left-width`—Width of the left border.

`inherit`—Takes the same value as its parent.

Example: `BODY {border-width: 20px 30px 5px}`

BORDER-TOP-COLOR, BORDER-RIGHT-COLOR, BORDER-BOTTOM-COLOR, BORDER-LEFT-COLOR

Description: Defines the border color for the designated side. The border comes between the padding and margin.

Values: Any valid color—Specifies the border color.

`inherit`—Takes the same value as its parent.

Example: `P {border-top-color: rgb(255, 0, 255)}`

BORDER-COLOR

Description: Shorthand property for defining border colors for all sides of an element at once. This property can include one to four values. One value sets all border colors to that value. Two sets the top and bottom to the first and the left and right to the second. Three values set the top to the first, left and right to the second, and the bottom to the third.

Values: `border-top-color`—Color of the top border.

`border-right-color`—Color of the right border.

`border-bottom-color`—Color of the bottom border.

`border-left-color`—Color of the left border.

`transparent`—Makes the borders transparent.

`inherit`—Takes the same value as its parent.

Example: `BODY {border-color: blue red pink}`

BORDER-TOP-STYLE, BORDER-RIGHT-STYLE, BORDER-BOTTOM-STYLE, BORDER-LEFT-STYLE

Description: Defines the border style for the designated side. The border comes between the padding and margin.

Values:

`none`—Specifies no border style.

`hidden`—Also specifies no border style, but acts differently for tables.

`dotted`—Creates a series of dots.

`dashed`—Creates a series of dashed lines.

`solid`—Creates a solid, non-breaking line.

`double`—Creates two parallel, solid, non-breaking lines.

`groove`—Creates a 3D carved-style border.

`ridge`—Creates a 3D raised-style border.

`inset`—Creates a 3D inset-style border.

`outset`—Creates a 3D outset-style border.

`inherit`—Takes the same value as its parent.

Example: `P {border-top-style: double}`

BORDER-STYLE

Description: Shorthand property for defining border styles for all sides of an element at once. This property can include one to four values. One value sets all border styles to that value. Two values set the top and bottom to the first and the left and right to the second. Three values set the top to the first, left and right to the second, and the bottom to the third.

Values:

`border-top-style`—Style of the top border.

`border-right-style`—Style of the right border.

`border-bottom-style`—Style of the bottom border.

`border-left-style`—Style of the left border.

`inherit`—Takes the same value as its parent.

Example: `BODY {border-style: double solid}`

BORDER-TOP, BORDER-RIGHT, BORDER-BOTTOM, BORDER-LEFT

Description: Shorthand properties for defining several border properties at once for the designated side. Each separate property applies to its named side. The following definitions use the top.

Values:

`border-top-width`—Width of the top border.

`border-top-style`—Style of the top border.

`border-top-color`—Color of the top border.

`inherit`—Takes the same value as its parent.

Example: `P {border-top: thin double blue}`

BORDER

Description: Shorthand property for defining borders for all sides of an element at once. The values are applied equally to all sides of the element.

Values:
`border-width`—Width of the border.

`border-style`—Style of the border.

`border-color`—Color of the border.

`inherit`—Takes the same value as its parent.

Example: `BODY {border: 4px solid red}`

OUTLINE-WIDTH*

Description: Shorthand property for defining outline widths for all sides of an element at once. This property can include one to four values. One value sets all outline widths to that value. Two values set the top and bottom to the first and the left and right to the second. Three values set the top to the first, left and right to the second, and the bottom to the third.

Values:
`thin`—Creates a thin weight border.

`medium`—(default) Creates a medium weight border.

`thick`—Creates a thick weight border.

`inherit`—Takes the same value as its parent.

Example: `BODY {outline-width: 20px 30px 5px}`

OUTLINE-STYLE*

Description: Shorthand property for defining outline styles for all sides of an element at once. This property can include one to four values. One value sets all outline styles to that value. Two values set the top and bottom to the first and the left and right to the second. Three values set the top to the first, left and right to the second, and the bottom to the third.

Values:
`none`—Specifies no border style.

`dotted`—Creates a series of dots.

`dashed`—Creates a series of dashed lines.

`solid`—Creates a solid, non-breaking line.

`double`—Creates two parallel, solid, non-breaking lines.

`groove`—Creates a 3D carved-style border.

`ridge`—Creates a 3D raised-style border.

`inset`—Creates a 3D inset-style border.

`outset`—Creates a 3D outset-style border.

`inherit`—Takes the same value as its parent.

Example: `BODY {outline-style: double solid}`

OUTLINE-COLOR*

Description: Property for defining outline colors. This property can include one to four values. One value sets all outline colors to that value. Two values set the top and bottom to the first and the left and right to the second. Three values set the top to the first, left and right to the second, and the bottom to the third.

Values: Any valid color—Specifies the border color.

`invert`—(default) Inverts the colors of the outline.

`inherit`—Takes the same value as its parent.

Example: `BODY {outline-color: blue red pink}`

OUTLINE*

Description: Shorthand property for defining outlines. The values are applied equally to all sides of the element.

Values: `outline-width`—Width of the outline.

`outline-style`—Style of the outline.

`outline-color`—Color of the outline.

`inherit`—Takes the same value as its parent.

Example: `BODY {outline: 4px solid red}`

VISUAL FORMATTING AND POSITIONING

The `display` property provides a way to define elements for the style sheet. Once defined, the position properties can place the elements exactly where you want them to go.

DISPLAY

Description: Defines the type of display box the element creates. These different types of boxes interact differently with each other as they are laid out on a page.

Values: `inline`—(default) Creates an inline display box.

`block`—Creates a block display box.

`list-item`—Creates a list-item inline display box.

`marker`—Creates generated content to appear before or after a display box. Only used with the `:before` and `:after` pseudo elements.

`none`—Creates no display box. The element has no effect on the overall layout.

`run-in`—Creates a box like a block display box depending on its location.

`compact`—Creates a box like an inline display box depending on its location.

`table`, `inline-table`, `table-row-group`, `table-column`, `table-column-group`, `table-header-group`, `table-footer-group`, `table-row`, `table-cell`, `table-caption`—Creates a table display box matching the property name.

`inherit`—Takes the same value as its parent.

Example: `P {display: block}`

POSITION

Description: Defines the positioning method to use.

Values:

`static`—(default) Defines a normal box using default HTML layout.

`relative`—Positioned box is offset from its normal layout position.

`absolute`—Positioned box is offset from its containing box's position and they don't effect the layout.

`fixed`—Positioned box is offset like the absolute model, but is fixed in the browser window and doesn't move when the window is scrolled.

`inherit`—Takes the same value as its parent.

Example: `IMG {position: absolute}`

TOP, RIGHT, BOTTOM, LEFT

Description: Defines the offset width from the designated edge.

Values:

`auto`—(default) Enables the browser to select an offset width to position all elements.

Any valid length—Number representing the width from the edge.

Any valid percentage—Percentage of window to offset from the edge.

`inherit`—Takes the same value as its parent.

Example: `UL {top: 20px; right: 40px}`

WIDTH

Description: Defines the width of a display box.

Values:

`auto`—(default) Enables the browser to select a width for the display box.

Any valid length—Number representing the width of the display box.

Any valid percentage—Percentage of window to use for the display box width.

`inherit`—Takes the same value as its parent.

Example: `BLOCKQUOTE {width: 260px}`

MIN-WIDTH*, MAX-WIDTH*

Description: Defines the minimum or maximum widths of a display box.

Values: Any valid length—Number representing the minimum or maximum widths of the display box.

Any valid percentage—Percentage of window to use for the minimum or maximum widths.

`none`—No width limit, applies only to the `max-width` property.

`inherit`—Takes the same value as its parent.

Example: `BLOCKQUOTE {min-width: 100px; max-width: 400px}`

HEIGHT

Description: Defines the height of a display box.

Values: `auto`—(default) Enables the browser to select a height for the display box.

Any valid length—Number representing the height of the display box.

Any valid percentage—Percentage of window to use for the display box height.

`inherit`—Takes the same value as its parent.

Example: `BLOCKQUOTE {height: 260px}`

MIN-HEIGHT*, MAX-HEIGHT*

Description: Defines the minimum or maximum heights of a display box.

Values: Any valid length—Number representing the minimum or maximum heights of the display box.

Any valid percentage—Percentage of window to use for the minimum or maximum heights.

`none`—No height limit, applies only to the `max-height` property.

`inherit`—Takes the same value as its parent.

Example: `BLOCKQUOTE {min-height: 100px; max-height: 400px}`

LINE-HEIGHT

Description: Defines the line spacing for an element box.

Values: `normal`—(default) Enables the browser to set the value to fit all elements on the page.

Any valid length—Number representing the height of the display box.

Any valid percentage—Percentage of window to use for the box height.

Any valid number—Number times the font size height.

`inherit`—Takes the same value as its parent.

Example: `BLOCKQUOTE {line-height: 2.2}`

VERTICAL-ALIGN

Description: Defines the vertical positioning inside a line box.

Values: `baseline`—(default) Aligns the box's baseline to its parent baseline.

`middle`—Aligns the box's middle to its parent's baseline.

`top`—Aligns the box's top with the top of the line box.

`bottom`—Aligns the box's bottom to its parent's baseline.

`sub`—Aligns the box's text to be at subscript level to its parent's baseline.

`super`—Aligns the box's text to be at superscript level of its parent's baseline.

`text-top`—Aligns the box's top to the top of the parent's text.

`text-bottom`—Aligns the box's bottom to the bottom of the parent's baseline.

Any valid length—Defines the distance to raise the box's level. Negative values lower its level.

Any valid percentage—Percentage to raise the box's level. Negative values lower its level.

`inherit`—Takes the same value as its parent.

Example: `BLOCKQUOTE {vertical-align: super}`

FLOAT

Description: Defines whether the display box should float to the left or right.

Values: `none`—(default) The display box doesn't float.

`left`—Causes the display box to float to the left and content flows to the right.

right—Causes the display box to float to the right and content flows to the left.

inherit—Takes the same value as its parent.

Example: `IMG {float: right}`

CLEAR

Description: Defines whether content appears adjacent to the side of float box or not.

Values: none—(default) Content not constrained next to float boxes.

left—Content doesn't appear to the left of a float box.

right—Content doesn't appear to the right of a float box.

both—Content doesn't appear to the left or right of a float box.

inherit—Takes the same value as its parent.

Example: `IMG {clear: both}`

OVERFLOW*

Description: Defines whether a display box is displayed when it overflows the element's box.

Values: visible—(default) The overflowed box is visible and not clipped.

hidden—The overflowed portion is clipped.

scroll—The overflowed portion is clipped and any scrollbars are made visible.

auto—Enables the browser to determine whether overflowed areas are clipped.

inherit—Takes the same value as its parent.

Example: `PRE {overflow: visible}`

CLIP*

Description: Defines the clipping area for overflowed sections.

Values: auto—(default) Causes the clipping region to have the same size and location as the element's box.

rect(top, right, bottom, left)—The clipping area is defined by the offsets from the top, right, bottom, and left length values.

inherit—Takes the same value as its parent.

Example: `BLOCKQUOTE {clip: rect(5px, 4px, 2px, 4px)}`

VISIBILITY

Description: Defines whether an element is visible.

Values: `visible`—Makes the element visible.

`hidden`—Makes the element hidden, but it still effects the layout.

`collapse`—Same as `hidden`, except when used on tables.

`inherit`—(default) Takes the same value as its parent.

Example: `IMG {visibility: visible}`

Z-INDEX

Description: Defines the stacking order for elements.

Values: `auto`—(default) Causes the element box to accept the same stacking order as its parent's box.

Any valid integer—An integer value representing the stacking order. Lower values have a lower stacking order.

`inherit`—Takes the same value as its parent.

Example: `IMG {z-index: 3}`

CURSOR*

Description: Defines how the cursor looks when moved over an element.

Values: `auto`—(default) Cursor determined by the browser.

`crosshair`—Cursor resembles a crosshair.

`default`—Cursor is the default cursor for the user's system.

`pointer`—Cursor resembles a pointer indicating a link.

`move`—Cursor indicates that something is to be moved.

`e-resize`, `ne-resize`, `nw-resize`, `n-resize`, `se-resize`, `sw-resize`, `s-resize`, `w-resize`—Cursor indicates a corner position.

`text`—Cursor text.

`wait`—Cursor indicates the system is busy.

`help`—Cursor indicates a help location.

Any valid URL—URL of a cursor file.

`inherit`—Takes the same value as its parent.

Example: `IMG {cursor: pointer}`

DIRECTION*

Description: Defines the writing direction for text blocks.

Values: `ltr`—(default) Sets writing direction from left to right.

`rtl`—Sets writing direction from right to left.

inherit—Takes the same value as its parent.

Example: `BODY { direction: ltr; unicode-bidi: embed}`

UNICODE-BIDI*

Description: Enables the text writing direction to be changed.

Values: `normal`—(default) Doesn't enable other writing directions.

`embed`—Enables writing direction to be set using the `direction` property.

`bidi-override`—Enables writing direction to be set using the `direction` property. Applies to additional blocks.

`inherit`—Takes the same value as its parent.

Example: `IMG {unicode-bidi: embed}`

GENERATED CONTENT AND LISTS

With these properties, you have control over the style of your list boxes and how the numbers or bullets are presented. They make it easy to have your list count by twos starting from seven.

CONTENT*

Description: Used with the `:before` and `:after` pseudo elements to generate content.

Values: Any valid string—String to appear before or after the element.

Any valid URL—URL to an external file to appear before or after an element.

`counter()`—Defines a counter with a name to insert the value controlled by the `counter-increment` and `counter-reset` properties.

`open-quote`, `close-quote`—Enables quote marks to be included. Used with the `quotes` property.

`no-open-quote`, `no-close-quote`—Inserts no quote marks.

`attr()`—Inserts the value of an attribute for the element.

`inherit`—Takes the same value as its parent.

Example: `PRE:after {content: "thank you and good-night."}`

QUOTES*

Description: Defines the pairs of quotation marks to use for each level of embedded quote marks.

Values: First valid string—Pair of characters to use for the outmost quotation marks.

Second valid string—Pair of characters to use for inner quotation marks.

`none`—No quote marks are created.

`inherit`—Takes the same value as its parent.

Example: `Q {quotes: '"' '"' '<' '>'}`

COUNTER-INCREMENT*

Description: Increases the value of the specified counter.

Values: `none`—(default) Counter is not incremented.

Counter name and valid number—Identifies the counter and accepts an integer value that counter is incremented. Negative values are valid.

`inherit`—Takes the same value as its parent.

Example: `H1 {counter-increment: MyCounter 2}`

COUNTER-RESET*

Description: Resets the value of a specified counter.

Values: `none`—(default) Counter is not reset.

Counter name and valid number—Identifies the counter and accepts an integer value that the counter is reset. Negative values are valid.

`inherit`—Takes the same value as its parent.

Example: `H1 {counter-reset: MyCounter 2}`

MARKER-OFFSET*

Description: Defines the distance between a list marker (such as a bullet) and the text.

Values: `auto`—(default) Enables the browser to determine the spacing.

Any valid length—The space between a marker and the text.

`inherit`—Takes the same value as its parent.

Example: `H1 {marker-offset: 12px}`

LIST-STYLE-TYPE

Description: Defines the list style to be applied to the list markers.

Values: `disc`—(default) Creates a disc-shaped bullet.

`circle`—Creates a circular-shaped bullet.

`square`—Creates a square-shaped bullet.

`decimal`—Numbers lists using decimal numbers, beginning with 1.

`decimal-leading-zero`—Numbers lists using decimal numbers padded with a zero, such as 01, 02, 03, and so on.

`lower-roman`—Numbers lists using lowercase Roman numerals.

`upper-roman`—Numbers lists using uppercase Roman numerals.

`hebrew`—Numbers lists using Hebrew numerals.

`georgian`—Numbers lists using Georgian numerals.

`armenian`—Numbers lists using Armenian numerals.

`cjk-ideographic`—Numbers lists using ideographic numerals.

`lower-latin, lower-alpha`—Uses lowercase ASCII characters.

`upper-latin, upper-alpha`—Uses uppercase ASCII characters.

`lower-greek`—Uses lowercase Greek characters.

`hiragana`—Uses Japanese hiragana characters.

`hiragana-iroha`—Uses Japanese hiragana iroha characters.

`katakana-iroha`—Uses Japanese katakana iroha characters.

Values: `none`—No marker is used.

`inherit`—Takes the same value as its parent.

Example: `OL {list-style: upper-alpha}`

LIST-STYLE-IMAGE

Description: Defines the image of a list marker.

Values: `none`—(default) Sets no marker image.

Any valid URL—URL of the marker image.

`inherit`—Takes the same value as its parent.

Example: `UL {list-style-image: url("bullet3.gif")}`

LIST-STYLE-POSITION

Description: Defines the location of the list box markers.

Values: `inside`—Markers appear within the element box.

`outside`—(default) Markers appear outside the element box.

`inherit`—Takes the same value as its parent.

Example: `H1 {list-style-position: inside}`

LIST-STYLE

Description: Shorthand property for defining all list style properties at once. If not included, a property is set to its default value.

Values: `list-style-type`—Marker type.

`list-style-position`—Marker position.

`list-style-image`—Marker image.

`inherit`—Takes the same value as its parent.

Example: `UL {list-style: circle inside url("bullet4.gif")}`

TABLES

Table control is new to CSS2. These properties enable you to define the style, spacing, and layout of your tables.

CAPTION-SIDE*

Description: Defines the position of a table caption relative to the table.

Values: `top`—(default) Positions the caption at the top of the table.

`right`—Positions the caption to the right of the table.

`bottom`—Positions the caption at the bottom of the table.

`left`—Positions the caption to the left of the table.

`inherit`—Takes the same value as its parent.

Example: `TABLE {caption-side: top}`

TABLE-LAYOUT*

Description: Defines how the table is laid out.

Values: `auto`—(default) Enables the browser to decide how to lay out the table.

`fixed`—Tables are laid out using a fixed method.

`inherit`—Takes the same value as its parent.

Example: `TABLE {table-layout: fixed}`

BORDER-COLLAPSE*

Description: Defines how the table borders are displayed.

Values: `collapse`—(default) Collapses the table cell borders into a common border.

`separate`—Keeps each table cell's border separated.

`inherit`—Takes the same value as its parent.

Example: `TD {border-collapse: separate}`

BORDER-SPACING*

Description: Defines the spacing between table borders. Only one length value applies equally to both horizontal and vertical directions.

Values: First valid length—Defines the horizontal width separating table cell borders.

Second valid length—Defines the vertical width separating table cell borders.

`inherit`—Takes the same value as its parent.

Example: `TABLE {border-spacing: 4px}`

EMPTY-CELLS*

Description: Defines how to render the border of empty cells.

Values: `show`—(default) Enables the borders of empty cells to be seen.

`hide`—Hides the borders of empty cells.

`inherit`—Takes the same value as its parent.

Example: `TABLE {empty-cells: show}`

SPEAK-HEADER*

Description: Enables a screen reader to speak table headers.

Values: `once`—(default) Causes the header to be spoken only once for each column of cells.

`always`—Causes the header to be spoken each time for a column of cells.

`inherit`—Takes the same value as its parent.

Example: `TABLE {speak-header: once}`

COLUMN-SPAN*

Description: Defines the number of columns to span.

Values: Any valid number—The number of columns to span. Default is 1.

`inherit`—Takes the same value as its parent.

Example: `TD {column-span: 3}`

ROW-SPAN*

Description: Defines the number of rows to span.

Values: Any valid number—The number of rows to span. Default is `1`.

`inherit`—Takes the same value as its parent.

Example: `TD {row-span: 3}`

PAGED MEDIA

These properties enable you to split your page content into predefined pages that output correctly to a printer or external device.

SIZE*

Description: Defines the size and orientation of a page.

Values: `auto`—(default) Enables the browser to determine the page size.

First valid length—Sets the page width.

Second valid length—Sets the page height.

`landscape`—Sets the page orientation to landscape.

`portrait`—Sets the page orientation to portrait.

`inherit`—Takes the same value as its parent.

Example: `P {size: 8.5in 11in portrait}`

MARKS*

Description: Enables printed pages to have crop and cross marks.

Values: `none`—(default) No printing marks are included.

`crop`—Displays crop marks.

`cross`—Displays registration marks.

`inherit`—Takes the same value as its parent.

Example: `P {marks: crop cross}`

PAGE-BREAK-BEFORE*

Description: Defines the page breaks for a page.

Values: `auto`—(default) Enables the browser to determine the page breaks.

`always`—Always forces a page break before a box.

`avoid`—Avoids placing a page break before a box.

`left`—Always forces a page break before a box so that the next page is on the left.

`right`—Always forces a page break before a box so that the next page is on the right.

`inherit`—Takes the same value as its parent.

Example: `P {page-break-before: avoid}`

PAGE-BREAK-AFTER*

Description: Defines the page breaks for a page.

Values: `auto`—(default) Enables the browser to determine the page breaks.

`always`—Always forces a page break after a box.

`avoid`—Avoids placing a page break after a box.

`left`—Always forces a page break after a box so that the next page is on the left.

`right`—Always forces a page break after a box so that the next page is on the right.

`inherit`—Takes the same value as its parent.

Example: `P {page-break-after: avoid}`

PAGE-BREAK-INSIDE*

Description: Defines the page breaks for a page.

Values: `auto`—(default) Enables the browser to determine the page breaks.

`avoid`—Avoids placing a page break within a box.

`inherit`—Takes the same value as its parent.

Example: `P {page-break-inside: avoid}`

PAGE*

Description: Identifies a page with a name.

Values: `auto`—(default) Enables the browser to identify pages.

Any valid name—Gives a page a name. The name can be any string.

Example: `P {page: Mypage}`

ORPHANS*

Description: Defines how many sentences can be left at the bottom of a page before starting a new one.

Values: Any valid number—An integer defining the number of sentences that must be left on the bottom of a page. Default is `2`.

`inherit`—Takes the same value as its parent.

Example: `P {orphans: 4}`

WIDOWS*

Description: Defines how many sentences can be left at the top of a new page.

Values: Any valid number—An integer defining the number of sentences that must be left on the top of a page. Default is `2`.

`inherit`—Takes the same value as its parent.

Example: `P {widows: 4}`

AURAL STYLE SHEETS

As a way to define Web pages for individuals with visual handicaps, aural style sheets enable designers to specify how screen readers interpret Web pages.

VOLUME*

Description: Defines the loudness of text read by a screen reader.

Values: Any valid number, 0–100—An integer ranged between 0 and 100 with 0 being minimum and 100 being maximum.

Any valid percentage, 0–100—A percentage increase or decrease from the current value.

`silent`—No sound emitted.

`x-soft`—Quietest level of sound, same as `0`.

`soft`—Quiet level of sound, same as `25`.

`medium`—(default) Normal level of sound, same as `50`.

`loud`—Loud level of sound, same as `75`.

`x-loud`—Loudest level of sound, same as `100`.

`inherit`—Takes the same value as its parent.

Example: `BODY {volume: soft}`

SPEAK*

Description: Defines how the words are spoken.

Values: `normal`—(default) Words are spoken normally.

`none`—Words are not spoken.

`spell-out`—Words are spelled letter by letter.

`inherit`—Takes the same value as its parent.

Example: `SPAN {speak: spell-out}`

PAUSE-BEFORE*

Description: Causes a pause before the element is read.

Values: Any valid time—The amount of time to pause before reading the element.

Any valid percentage—The percent to pause before reading the element.

`inherit`—Takes the same value as its parent.

Example: `SPAN {pause-before: 500ms}`

PAUSE-AFTER*

Description: Causes a pause after the element is read.

Values: Any valid time—The amount of time to pause after reading the element.

Any valid percentage—The percent to pause after reading the element.

	`inherit`—Takes the same value as its parent.
Example:	`SPAN {pause-after: 500ms}`

PAUSE*

Description:	Shorthand property for setting the `pause-before` and `pause-after` the element is read. If only one time or percent value is given, it applies to both before and after.
Values:	First valid time—The amount of time to pause before reading the element.
	Second valid time—The amount of time to pause after reading the element.
	Any valid percentage—The percent to pause before reading the element.
	Any valid percentage—The percent to pause after reading the element.
	`inherit`—Takes the same value as its parent.
Example:	`SPAN {pause: 500ms 300ms}`

CUE-BEFORE*

Description:	Causes a cue before the element is read.
Values:	Any valid URL—URL of an audio file to play before reading the element.
	`none`—No audio is played before the element is read.
	`inherit`—Takes the same value as its parent.
Example:	`SPAN {cue-before: url("bell.wav")}`

CUE-AFTER*

Description:	Causes a cue after the element is read.
Values:	Any valid URL—URL of an audio file to play after reading the element.
	`none`—No audio is played after the element is read.
	`inherit`—Takes the same value as its parent.
Example:	`SPAN {cue-after: url("bell2.wav")}`

CUE*

Description:	Shorthand property that causes a cue before and after the element is read. If only one URL is given, it applies to both before and after.
Values:	First valid URL—URL of an audio file to play before reading the element.

Second valid URL—URL of an audio file to play after reading the element.

`none`—No audio is played before the element is read.

`inherit`—Takes the same value as its parent.

Example: `SPAN {cue: url("ding.wav") url("dong.wav")}`

PLAY-DURING*

Description: Defines an audio file to be played in the background while text is being read.

Values: Any valid URL—URL of an audio file to play in the background while reading the element.

`mix`—Mix the current audio with the parent audio file and play both together.

`repeat`—Repeat the audio until all the text has been read.

`auto`—(default) Enable the parent element's audio to continue to play.

`none`—No background audio is played.

`inherit`—Takes the same value as its parent.

Example: `BODY {play-during: url("chatter.wav") mix}`

AZIMUTH*

Description: Defines the spatial location of an audio file horizontally around the listener's head.

Values: Any valid angle—An angle value between 0 and 360 degrees. Negative values are not allowed.

`left-side`—Sound from the left side of the head, or 270 degrees.

`far-left`—Sound from the distant left of the head, or 300 degrees.

`left`—Sound from the left of the head, or 320 degrees.

`center-left`—Sound from the center left of the head, or 340 degrees.

`center`—Sound from the center of the head, or 0 degrees.

`center-right`—Sound from the center right of the head, or 20 degrees.

`right`—Sound from the right of the head, or 40 degrees.

`far-right`—Sound from the distant right of the head, or 60 degrees.

`left-side`—Sound from the right side of the head, or 270 degrees.

`leftwards`—Sound moved to the left of the current location.

`rightwards`—Sound moved to the right of the current location.

`behind`—Sound moved to behind the head at that location.

`inherit`—Takes the same value as its parent.

Example: `H1 {azimuth: left-side}`

ELEVATION*

Description: Defines the spatial location of an audio file vertically around the listener's head.

Values: Any valid angle—An angle value between 90 and -90 degrees. Negative values are allowed.

`below`—Sound from below the head, or -90 degrees.

`level`—Sound from the front of the head, or 0 degrees.

`above`—Sound from above the head, or 90 degrees.

`higher`—Sound moved up form the current location.

`inherit`—Takes the same value as its parent.

Example: `H1 {elevation: above}`

SPEECH-RATE*

Description: Defines how quickly the element text is read.

Values: Any valid number—The speaking rate in words per minute.

`x-slow`—80 words per minute.

`slow`—120 words per minute.

`medium`—(default) 180–200 words per minute.

`fast`—300 words per minute.

`x-fast`—500 words per minute.

`faster`—Causes the words to be read faster than the current speed, adds 40 words per minute.

`slower`—Causes the words to be read slower than the current speed, subtracts 40 words per minute.

`inherit`—Takes the same value as its parent.

Example: `BODY {speech-rate: fast}`

VOICE-FAMILY*

Description: Defines the voice type to use to read the element's text. It can include several voice families separated by commas. The list order defines the priority.

Values: Voice name—Voice to use to read the text.

Generic voice name—Generic voice class to use to read the text. Generic voices include: `male`, `female`, and `child`.

inherit—Takes the same value as its parent.

Example: `BODY {voice-family: Bob, male}`

PITCH*

Description: Defines the pitch of the element text.

Values: Any valid frequency—The pitch in Hertz (Hz).

x-low—Lowest pitch.

low—Low pitch.

medium—(default) Average pitch.

high—Higher than normal pitch.

x-high—Highest pitch.

inherit—Takes the same value as its parent.

Example: `BODY {pitch: high}`

PITCH-RANGE*

Description: Defines the pitch range of the element text as its read.

Values: Any valid number—A value between 0 and 100 that defines the pitch range. The default, 50, is normal inflection.

inherit—Takes the same value as its parent.

Example: `BODY {pitch-range: 50}`

STRESS*

Description: Defines the stress of the element text as its read.

Values: Any valid number—A value between 0 and 100 that defines the pitch range. The default, 50, is normal.

inherit—Takes the same value as its parent.

Example: `BODY {stress: 50}`

RICHNESS*

Description: Defines the richness of the element text as its read.

Values: Any valid number—A value between 0 and 100 that defines the pitch range. The default, 50, is normal.

inherit—Takes the same value as its parent.

Example: `BODY {richness: 50}`

SPEAK-PUNCTUATION*

Description: Defines how punctuation is spoken.

Values: `code`—Punctuation is spoken literally.

`none`—Punctuation is not spoken.

`inherit`—Takes the same value as its parent.

Example: `BODY {speak-puncuation: code}`

SPEAK-NUMERAL*

Description: Defines how numbers are spoken.

Values: `digits`—Numbers are spoken as individual digits.

`continuous`—Numbers are spoken as a full number.

`inherit`—Takes the same value as its parent.

Example: `BODY {speak-numeral: digits}`

APPENDIX 

HTML and Design Resources

In this Appendix

WEB SITES OF INTEREST

Builder.com

C|NET's entry for Web developers targets information on just about every aspect of Web design. Vast resources, links, and great articles are available.

`http://www.builder.com/`

Devhead

Ziff-Davis offers up this extremely content-rich developer's site. You'll find news, features, and a wonderful script library for Java applets, JavaScript, and Perl/CGI scripts.

`http://www.devhead.com/`

IBM's developerWorks Web Architecture Zone

A new contender among Web development sites, developerWorks offers extensive articles that delve deep into detail. Although there are tips and insights available, the real focus here is coverage on timely development topics with extensive and exhaustive examples for interested developers.

`http://www.ibm.com/developer/`

Hot Source HTML Help

A good source for all HTML help with a good section on DHTML.

`http://www.sbrady.com/hotsource/`

HTML Author's Board

Conversation, brainstorming…ask questions, get answers!

`http://homer.touch.net/~aw/hab/`

The HTML Bad Style Page

I like it for the fact that it shows you what NOT to do with HTML. Sometimes it is nice to see a sample of poor workmanship to avoid it.

`http://www.earth.com/bad-style/`

HTML Goodies

It sure has them! You can find tutorials as well as books and software here.

`http://www.htmlgoodies.com/new.html`

HTML 4.0 Reference and Comparison

Compares HTML 3.0 and HTML 4.0, giving a good description of all the changes made between the two standards.

`http://www.tue.nl/bwk/cheops/via/maker/html4/menu.htm`

Internet Baglady

If you want lots of free and low-cost graphics, guidance, and guff, visit the Internet's very own Baglady.

`http://www.dumpsterdive.com/`

Lynda.Com

Books, color references, and plenty of wisdom from Web graphics expert Lynda Weinman.

`http://www.lynda.com/`

Mark Radcliffe's Advanced HTML

Covering a variety of topics; includes helpful HTML hints.

`http://www.markradcliffe.co.uk/html/advancedhtml.htm`

Meta Content Framework Using XML

Offers a model using XML.

`http://www.textuality.com/mcf/NOTE-MCF-XML.html`

Microsoft Developer Network

An unbelievable variety of information covering Web building and publishing. Lots of community, heavy on Internet Explorer specific information.

`http://msdn.microsoft.com/default.asp`

Molly.com

Books, links, and course information.

`http://www.molly.com/`

Netscape's DevEdge

Rich developer resource with a Netscape bent.

`http://devedge.netscape.com/`

Project Cool Developer Zone

Chock full of tutorials about anything and everything to do with Web design.

`http://www.projectcool.com/developer/`

The Sevloid Guide to Web Design

A collection of over 100 tips, tricks, and techniques on every aspect of Web design. The tips are sorted into the categories of page layout, navigation, content, graphics, and more.

`http://www.sev.com.au/webzone/design.htm`

Waterloo

Tutorials in XML and XSL authoring.

`http://www.csclub.uwaterloo.ca/u/relander/XML_Tutorial/index.html`

Webmonkey's How to Guide for Web Developers

A well done, eye-pleasing page that has a lot of tutorials and a great sense of humor.

`http://www.hotwired.com/webmonkey/`

Web Page Design for Designers

Explore the possibilities of Web design from the standpoint of a designer.

`http://www.wpdfd.com/wpdhome.htm`

Webreference

Vast references, tutorials, and hints about Web design.

`http://www.webreference.com/`

Webreview

A magazine with good articles about Web design.

`http://webreview.com/wr/pub`

Writing HTML

A tutorial for Web page design for beginners and advanced users.

`http://www.mcli.dist.maricopa.edu/tut/`

Yale C/AIM Web Style Guide

An excellent, straightforward overview of interface, site design, graphics, multimedia, and, of course, HTML.

`http://info.med.yale.edu/caim/manual/contents.html`

Books

Dynamic Web Publishing Unleashed

Shelly Powers

This book covers HTML 4, Java, ActiveX, JavaScript, VBScript, CGI, and Dynamic HTML, and explains how to use Cascading Style Sheets.

Sams Teach Yourself Active Server Pages 2.0 in 21 Days

Sanjaya Hettihewa

This book makes it possible for the reader to learn ASP technology in just 21 days.

Lynda Weinman's Web Graphics Resource Library

Lynda Weinman

This three-part resource for Web graphics creation, preparation, and delivery includes Designing Web Graphics.2, Coloring Web Graphics, and the Web Publisher's Graphics Toolkit on CD-ROM, which features a variety of tools, utilities, patterns, backgrounds, color palettes, templates, and more.

Designing Web Graphics 2

Lynda Weinman

A total revision of the best-selling book on preparing graphics for the Web, *Designing Web Graphics 2* includes complete, updated coverage of the latest Web graphics technologies, including file formats, file sizes, file translations, resolution, and browser-specific techniques.

Secrets of Successful Web Sites: Project Management on the World Wide Web

David S. Siegel

Visual case studies show how to manage a Web site effectively. Included are forming an effective designer/client relationship, setting up budgets and schedules, and more.

ORGANIZATIONS

The following organizations are geared toward helping designers inform themselves, organize, and work toward Web design excellence.

World Wide Web Consortium

Standard, standard, who's got the standard? W3C is the first stop for all serious HTML and related technologies students.

`http://www.w3.org/`

Web Design and Developer's Association

A bona-fide trade organization for Web developers.

`http://www.wdda.org/`

The HTML Writers Guild

The world's largest international organization of Web designers. Offers community, classes, events, and an online bookstore.

`http://www.hwg.org/`

Association for Women in Computing

A general organization for women in the computer field.

`http://www.awc-hq.org/`

Her Domain of Austin

A support and networking group for women interested in the World Wide Web—job postings, courses, and resources.

`http://www.herdomain.org/`

Webgrrls

The international networking group for women interested in the Internet. Multiple sites by country and city; start at the home page.

`http://www.webgrrls.com/`

EDUCATION AND CONFERENCES

The following organizations and events offer instruction for Web designers.

Design Workshops of Ojai

Hands-on classes, lectures, training, and seminars organized by Lynda Weinman.

`http://www.lynda.com/classes/index.html`

DigitalThink

A variety of online offerings, with many oriented toward Web design and programming.

`http://www.digitalthink.com/`

Institute for Technical Training and Excellence

Public and on-site training for interested individuals and corporations.

`http://www.itte.org/`

Thunder Lizard Productions

With a focus on the Web, computer graphics, and desktop publishing, Thunder Lizard offers a broad range of high-quality educational events.

`http://www.thunderlizard.com/`

Web Design and Development

Miller Freeman hosts this highly integrated and focused design and development conference. Attendees gain insight into strategy, management, design, usability, content, programming, and other topics of interest to developers.

`http://www.mfiweb.com/`

Ziff-Davis University

A great deal for online, self-paced learning in almost every programming and Web-related topic under the sun—very affordable!

`http://www.zdu.com/`

INDEX

Symbols

A

C

E

G

H

I

J

M

N

Q

S

T

U

V

W

X

Y-Z

WHAT'S ON THE CD-ROM?

The enclosed CD-ROM includes a complete HTML and Web publishing toolkit—for both Windows and Macintosh users—to help you easily design, create, embellish, and maintain professional–quality Web pages and sites.

Note

Unless otherwise noted, all these tools are either demo versions of commercial products that will expire after a fixed period of time, or they are shareware products that require a registration fee if you continue to use the product past a certain period of time. All Windows products listed here are for Windows 95/98 or Windows NT 4.0.

BOOK EXAMPLES

The author has provided many of the files used in the examples found throughout the book as well as sample scripts and templates.

GRAPHICS

We have included 500 selected graphics from one of Macmillan USA's latest products. There are 250 animated graphics and 250 graphic creations to help you make your Web page great. The files are arranged into a convenient interface for viewing.

WEB PAGE AUTHORING TOOLS

- Macromedia Dreamweaver 2.0 (Windows/Macintosh)
- Homesite 4 (Windows)
- HotDog Professional 5.5 (Windows)
- Map Edit 2.6 (Windows)
- PageSpinner (Macintosh)
- WebWeaver (Macintosh)

GRAPHICS TOOLS

- Fireworks 2.0 (Windows/Macintosh)
- GIF Animator 3.0 (Windows)
- Gif-gIf-giF (Windows/Macintosh)

- GIFmation (Windows/Macintosh)
- Illustrator 8 (Windows/Macintosh)
- ImageStyler 1 (Windows/Macintosh)

Plug-Ins and Multimedia

- Flash 4.0 (Windows/Macintosh)
- Eye Candy 3.0 (Windows/Macintosh)
- GIF Movie Gear 2.63 (Windows)
- Xenofex 1.0 (Windows/Macintosh)

Internet Utilities

- Netscape Communicator 4.7 (Windows/Macintosh - Full Version)
- Internet Explorer 5.0 (Windows/Macintosh - Full Version)
- Total Access 2.3.2 (Windows/Macintosh - Sprint's Internet Service)

Programming Tools

- ColdFusion Express 4.0.1 (Windows)
- Drumbeat 2000 (Windows)

Audio Tools

- Cool Edit Pro 1.2 (Windows)

Miscellaneous Utilities

- WS_FTP Pro 6.01 (Windows)
- Transmit (Macintosh)
- CuteFTP (Windows)
- Adobe Acrobat Reader 4.0 (Windows/Macintosh)
- NetFinder (Macintosh)

Licensing Agreement

By opening this package, you are agreeing to be bound by the following agreement:

You may not copy or redistribute the entire CD-ROM as a whole. Copying and redistribution of individual software programs on the CD-ROM is governed by terms set by the licensors or individual copyright holders.

The installer and code from the author(s) are copyrighted by the publisher and the author(s).

This software is sold as-is, without warranty of any kind, either expressed or implied, including but not limited to the implied warranties of merchantability and fitness for a particular purpose. Neither the publisher nor its dealers or distributors assumes any liability for any alleged or actual damages arising from the use of this program. (Some states do not allow for the exclusion of implied warranties, so the exclusion may not apply to you.)

How to Install Products from the CD-ROM

Under Windows NT/98/95, just insert the disc, click Book Examples and follow the directions of the program to create program group for this CD-ROM. From within this program group, you can install the source code. Select Third Party Software to view the list of programs you can install. You may also review documentation, preview files, or install products using Windows Explorer.

Note that if you have AutoPlay disabled on your Windows NT/98/95 computer, the CD-ROM will not automatically start. To start the CD Product Browser manually, go to the Start menu, select Run, and then Browse to find your CD-ROM drive letter. Select the file `Start.exe` from the root directory and follow the instructions above.

Note

This CD-ROM uses long and mixed-case filenames requiring the use of a protected-mode CD-ROM driver. Contact the manufacturer of your CD-ROM driver for information on updating your driver to a protected-mode version if you have problems accessing information on this CD-ROM.